British Army Pensioners Abroad,
1772 - 1899

British
ARMY PENSIONERS ABROAD,
1772–1899

Norman K. Crowder

CLEARFIELD

Copyright © 1995
Norman J. Crowder
All Rights Reserved.
Published by Genealogical Publishing Co., Inc.
Baltimore, Maryland, 1995

Library of Congress Catalogue Card Number 94-73392

Reprinted for Clearfield Company by
Genealogical Publishing Company
Baltimore, Maryland, 2012

ISBN 978-0-8063-1947-6

Made in the United States of America

CONTENTS

Acknowledgements	vi
Introduction	vii
W.O. 120 Volume 35	1
W.O. 120 Volume 69	87
W.O. 120 Volume 70	198
Places of Residence	310
List of Military Units	314
Notes on the Sources	317
Bibliography	320
Index	323

ACKNOWLEDGEMENTS

I wish to express my gratitude to John M. Kitzmiller of the Family History Library in Salt Lake City, Utah for his pioneering work *In Search of the "Forlorn Hope,"* and for taking the time to discuss my plans for the preparation of this book. His advice and suggestions have been unfailingly helpful.

I also wish to thank many others who in various ways advised, assisted, encouraged, or supported me in the completion of this volume, especially:

Angus Baxter, author of *In Search of Your Canadian Roots*

Yvonna E. Brewer, Green Valley, Arizona

Alan Cameron, Canadian War Museum

Timothy Dubé , National Archives of Canada

Norma Gould, National Library of Canada

Peter Lodge, Nepean Public Library

Ivan K. Mitchell, Ottawa, Ontario

Terrence M. Punch, author of *Genealogical Research in Nova Scotia*

Mark Reid, Canadian War Museum

Robert E. Sargeant, Perth, Ontario

Wayne Walker, Ottawa Family History Center

Leon Warmski, Archives of Ontario

INTRODUCTION

This book is intended to serve as an index to the Chelsea regimental pension registers of British veterans who settled abroad with an army pension. They are known as Chelsea pensioners because the Royal Hospital, Chelsea decided on the entitlement and amount of pension to be paid to discharged veterans with disabilities or long service. The hospital in Chelsea was established in 1692 and was generally similar to the earlier military hospital in Kilmainham, Dublin founded in 1679 for soldiers on the Irish establishment.

Registers

The registers are in the custody of the Public Record Office in Kew, England. They are identified as W.O. 120 Volumes 35, 69 and 70. The titles of these volumes refer to pensioners receiving their pensions "in the colonies;" because such places as Rome, Paris and Ostend are clearly not in British colonies, I thought it would be appropriate to describe this work in terms of "pensioners abroad." Even with this modification I still have some difficulty understanding the inclusion of veterans who lived in various places in the British Isles, including Cork, Manchester and Paisley. Among the pensions shown in these three volumes, one was awarded as early as 1772 and another as late as 1899, but the vast majority were granted during the period 1800-1857.

Entries

The entries in this book follow the same sequence as those in the W.O. 120 volumes. They are grouped by military units and within each unit appears a list of men discharged from the unit. At the end of each entry is an index number which is used in a comprehensive every name index at the end of the book. The index number bears no relationship to regimental or serial numbers - I have assigned it strictly for indexing purposes.

Key elements for each entry include the surname and given or personal name of the veteran, date of pension award (shown in the original record as "date admitted"), and, where available, the place of residence and date and place of death. The most significant piece of information for each person is the identity of the unit in which he served at the time of discharge and award of pension.

Discharge Process

When a serviceman was discharged, disability or length of service may have entitled him to a pension. In such cases it was customary to convene a board of officers to review the man's service and compile a summary record, including a medical officer's report. For men being discharged overseas the file was sent to the Royal Hospital, Chelsea for review and determination of entitlement to a pension. Because of the length of time required to transmit papers over great distances, occasionally this resulted in an anomalous situation where the effective date of a pension occurred after the death of a soldier.

Places of Residence

The places of residence shown in the text are those centers where an officer was appointed overseas to pay the quarterly pensions. The veterans did not necessarily live in those cities or towns but resided in the general vicinity, possibly within a forty mile radius. Some who lived in the very remote areas were paid every six months. Most of the places were fairly easy to locate; I have included a section entitled PLACES OF RESIDENCE starting on page 310 which shows the locations of most places. In addition it shows changes of place names, such as Bytown, now Ottawa, and Ceylon, now Sri Lanka.

Canadian place names have been expressed in terms of current jurisdictions, not those that applied in the early days. The changes in the definition of Canada as a political entity can be confusing so I felt that it would be simpler, for example, to refer consistently to Charlottetown, Prince Edward Island, Canada even though Prince Edward Island did not become part of Canada until 1873. I have followed the same approach with Nova Scotia and New Brunswick, which became part of Canada in 1867, and with Newfoundland, which did not join Canada until 1949.

Legibility

The names of the veterans are mostly written in a fine hand and it is rarely difficult to decipher the handwriting. In a few cases the names are partially obliterated by flaws in the documents; on the microfilmed copies some of the names in the lower left hand corner are partly obscured. Although the names are generally legible, the same cannot be said of the information opposite each name. Often the details are written in very tiny writing and are difficult to read even with the aid of a magnifying glass. Consequently there is room for differences of opinion as to the contents of the entries. In difficult cases it may be advisable to obtain photocopies of the original documents from the Public Record Office, Ruskin Avenue, Kew, Richmond, Surrey, England, TW9 4DU. Readers requesting such copies should mention that the page numbers cited are the **handwritten** page numbers and not the imprinted numbers - sometimes they are same but not always. An additional safeguard would be to quote the full name of the person of interest in addition to the page numbers.

The three different volumes have different page numbering systems. In Volume 35 entries extend across two facing sheets and the page number appears at the top left hand corner of the left hand sheet. See pages 318 and 319 for examples. In volume 69 the page number also is placed at the top left hand corner of the left hand sheet but a separate list of names follows on the right hand facing sheet. Volume 70 follows the conventional numbering system with the page number at the top left hand corner of the left hand sheet and the next page number at the top right hand corner of the right hand sheet.

Details

I strongly recommend that readers view the entries themselves, either in the documents at Kew or on microfilm at various institutions. The reference numbers of microfilms at the National Archives of Canada in Ottawa, Canada and the Family History Library in Salt Lake City, Utah appear on page 317 of this book. Not only will readers be able to decide for themselves what the entries contain, they will also find additional details of interest to them. Volume 35 in particular contains information on the place of origin and details of service; in addition, for the Fencible units on pages 76-80 there are some notations identifying specific units. For example, INDEX #2404 Patrick COGLEY was a member of the Newfoundland Fencibles. Volumes 69 and 70 show changes in pension rates and in some cases biographical details including convictions for crimes committed. See pages 318 and 319 for examples. There are notations regarding veterans transferred in 1822 from the Kilmainham rolls to the Chelsea rolls. Often additional details will be found in the Kilmainham records; the original documents are at Kew and microfilm copies may be obtained from the Family History Library.

In-Pensioners

Those veterans who were admitted to residence at Chelsea were known as in-pensioners. They wore a distinctive uniform and followed a semi-military routine, including the mounting of guards and carrying out patrols. While at times they undoubtedly suffered from the mismanagement of funds by officials, on the whole they appear to have been reasonably well treated. For example, their daily rations included 12 ounces of meat or fish along with two loaves of bread, a quarter-pound of cheese and two quarts of beer. The most famous in-pensioner was William Hiseland, a veteran who served for more than eighty years, married when he was 100, and died in 1732, age 112.

Out-Pensioners

The Royal Hospital, Chelsea could accommodate only approximately 500 residents; others had to find accommodation elsewhere. Those who remained in the British Isles often returned to their places of birth and received their pensions from authorized local officials such as excise officers. Some remained in the colonies, usually where they were stationed at time of discharge. A few veterans received special permission to reside in foreign countries and receive their pensions there.

For the history of the hospital, its traditions and customs, and its responsibilities towards both in-pensioners and out-pensioners, see Major-General George Hutt's *Papers Illustrative of the Origin and Early History of the Royal Hospital at Chelsea* and Captain C. G. T. Dean's *The Royal Hospital, Chelsea*.

Terms of Pensions

Pensions were paid to enlisted men or "other ranks," often abbreviated to "ORs" - privates, non-commissioned officers, and warrant officers below the rank of commissioned officers. As a rule the pensions were paid for the lives of the pensioners, although in some instances they were paid for a specified period, especially when a regiment was disbanded. Pensions could be stopped for misconduct or conviction of a crime. Any "violence or outrage" towards the officer paying the quarterly pension could be grounds for taking away the pension - see page xviii. On the death of the pensioner, the pension ceased - there were no benefits for surviving widows or children. Various officials were authorized to pay the amounts quarterly; in Canada officers of the Commissary General were given this responsibility. The daily amount ranged from 5 pence to 3 shillings, with a shilling being a fairly typical amount by the mid-century. A shilling was approximately the wage of a farm labourer in Ontario, Canada in 1851.

Commuted Pensioners

By 1831 the number of Chelea pensioners had increased to more than 84,000 from about 31,200 in 1814. In an effort to stem the drain on Treasury funds, the British

Government offered an inducement to those veterans who would surrender their pensions in exchange for a cash payment and an opportunity to settle in one of the colonies. Typically the lump sum payment would equal the value of payments over up to four years. The cost of transportation would be deducted from the half paid before embarkation. The other half would be paid on arrival in the colony and would enable the man to proceed to the place where he intended to take up residence. For a few months in 1831 a grant of land was offered but this practice was discontinued when colonial officials objected. The scheme was badly handled and resulted in many veterans being reduced to poverty because of misinformation and the lack of information about the conditions abroad. During the period 1831-1839 about 4500 pensioners surrendered their pensions in exchange for a lump sum amount; possibly 2500 went to British North America. By the time the British Treasury finally agreed in 1840 to pay a small charitable allowance of fourpence-halfpenny per day to the destitute commuted pensioners, only 654 surviving men could be located in Canada. For a fuller account of this situation, see *Copies of Despatches and Correspondence Relative to Chelsea Pensioners in Upper and Lower Canada*, J. K. Johnson's "The Chelsea Pensioners in Upper Canada," and Barbara Aitken's "Searching Chelsea Pensioners in Upper Canada and Great Britain." The latter article includes an alphabetized list of the 654 survivors.

Enrolled Pensioners

In 1849 Captain J. D. G. Tulloch was sent to British North America to inspect the conditions in which pensioners lived. His extensive report condemned the deplorable situation in which most of the commuted pensioners found themselves, although he did list a few success stories. Captain Tulloch recommended a new approach - bring to the colonies able-bodied veterans capable of rendering military service, provide them with training for a short period each year, give each man a small plot of Government land on which to settle, and make the men liable to call up for service when needed to supplement the reduced British army forces in the colonies. A similar plan had already been successfully introduced in New Zealand. Tulloch's proposal was adopted for other colonies and was a great improvement over the commuted pensioners scheme. In Canada on several occasions the enrolled pensioners, as those in the new arrangement were called, provided useful service in rendering aid to the civil authorities during riots and disturbances. The men were paid at regular army rates when they were called up for service. Some enrolled pensioners worked as military guards on vessels bringing convicts to Australia and others helped to keep the peace on the gold fields of Australia. For more information see Captain Tulloch's *Report on the Inspection of Pensioners in the North American Provinces*, George K. Raudzens' "A Successful Military Settlement: Earl Grey's Enrolled Pensioners of 1846 in Canada," and Timothy Dubé's 1982 thesis entitled *The Enrolled Pensioner Scheme in Canada West, 1851-1858, With Specific Reference to the Plan at Amherstburg*.

Men Only

It will be noted that all references to veterans are to male soldiers only. For the period under consideration females could not legally enlist in the army. There are, however, two recorded cases of women disguised as men who served in the army and later became out-pensioners: Christina, Christian or Catherine Walsh/Welch/Ross/Davis, who served in Flanders and was cited for her couragous behaviour, received a pension until her death in 1739; and Hannah Snell, who was wounded at Pondicherry, drew a pension until she died in 1792. Both women were buried in Chelsea. I do not believe that any women are listed in Volumes 35, 69 and 70.

Further Biographical Information

In addition to the details in the pension registers, extensive biographical information can usually be found in the soldier's service file which was created when he was discharged with a pension. These documents are arranged by unit in W.O. 97; the service records are then arranged alphabetically by surnames of the pensioners. Typically a man's file will include his enlistment papers showing when and where he joined the army, a summary of his service including transfers, postings and promotions, a medical officer's report on his condition, statements as to the character and conduct of the soldier, certification that he was paid up to date, a description of the man, and in some cases a mention of the place where he intended to reside after discharge. The originals may be seen at the Public Record Office in Kew and microfilm copies may be obtained from the Family History Library in Salt Lake City, Utah. Other institutions may hold the files for selected units; for example the National Archives of Canada in Ottawa has microfilm copies for many of the British units which served in Canada during the 18th and 19th centuries. There are several useful books with more details on the extensive British Army records which may be found in the Public Record Office - John Kitzmiller's *In Search of the "Forlorn Hope,"* Simon Fowler's *Army Records for Family Historians,* and Stella Colwell's *Family Roots: Discovering the Past in the Public Record Office.* For samples of the kinds of documents that may be found in the W.O. 97 files, see pages xii-xvii.

The Family History Library

The Family History Library is located in Salt Lake City, Utah in the United States of America; its postal address is 35 North West Temple, Salt Lake City, UT 84150, U S A. It has a network of several thousand local branches, known as Family History Centers, throughout the world. Microfilm copies of W.O. 97 and W.O. 120 as well as other records may be borrowed through them from the Family History Library for a nominal charge. A list of Family History Centers appears in the supplement to John Kitzmiller's *In Search of the "Forlorn Hope,"* which is available in many libraries, or the addresses of the nearest centers may be obtained by writing to the Family History Library in Salt Lake City.

UNLIMITED SERVICE.
ATTESTATION FOR REGIMENTS.

I Nathaniel Mitchell do make Oath that I am or have been a Weaver and to the best of my knowledge and belief was born in the Parish of Arbow in the County of Tyrone and that I am of the Age of Twenty One Years; that I do not belong to the Militia, or to any other Regiment, or to His Majesty's Navy or Marines, and that I will serve His Majesty, His Heirs and Successors untill I shall be legally discharged.

Witness my Hand,

Sworn before me at Omagh this Twenty fourth day of October One Thousand Eight Hundred and Twenty three

his
Nath.l Mitchell
mark

Signature of the Recruit.

Signature of the Magistrate

Witness present.

County of Omagh to wit.

I _____ One of His Majesty's Justices of the Peace of said County do hereby Certify, that Nath.l Mitchell appearing to be Twenty One Years old, five feet ____ inches high, fair complexion, Brown Eyes, _____ Hair, came before me at _____ on the Twenty fourth day of October One Thousand Eight Hundred and Twenty three and stated himself to be of the Age of Twenty One Years, and that he had no Rupture, and was not troubled with Fits, and was no ways disabled by Lameness, Deafness, or otherwise, but had the perfect use of his Limbs and Hearing, and was not an Apprentice, and acknowledged that he had voluntarily inlisted himself for the Bounty of _____ to serve His Majesty King George the Fourth, His Heirs and Successors, in the Thirty Sixth Regiment of Foot Commanded by _____ untill he should be legally discharged. And I do hereby certify, that in my presence, the Third and Fourth Articles of the Second Section, and the First Article of the Sixth Section, of the Articles of War against Mutiny and Desertion were read over to him, and that he took the Oath of Fidelity mentioned in the said Articles of War, and also the Oath to the effect above set forth; and that he received the Sum of Two Shillings and Six Pence, British, on being attested; and that I have given to the said Nath.l Mitchell a Duplicate of this Certificate signed with my Name.

_____ Signature of the Magistrate.

MEMORANDUM. The above-named Recruit stated that he inlisted himself on the Twenty third Day of October One Thousand Eight Hundred and Twenty three and Received in my Presence the Sum of Two Shillings and Six Pence British, on being Attested

_____ Signature of the Magistrate.

I have examined the above-named Recruit, and find him fit for His Majesty's Service.

_____ Signature of the Surgeon.

N. B. The Magistrate is requested to cause the dates of the Month in each instance to be inserted in Words, not in Figures, and to notice the Particulars contained in the Memorandum.

INTRODUCTION

No. 2005. Private Nath'l Mitchell being asked to what date he has been paid, answered that his Account is balanced up to the latest period required by the Regulations; and being further asked whether he has any claim on the Regiment for Arrears of PAY, ALLOWANCES, or CLOTHING, answered, that he has received all just demands, from his entry into the Service up to the _____ and in confirmation therefore, affixes his signature hereto.

I acknowledge this to be true.

Witness _____

Commanding the Company to which he belongs.

The Board have ascertained that No. 2005, Private Nath'l Mitchell Soldier's Book is correctly balanced, and signed by the Officer Commanding his Company, and they declare, that they have impartially enquired into, and faithfully reported upon all the matters brought before them, in accordance with the Regulations and Instructions issued by Her Majesty's Orders.

_____ President.
_____ } Members.

Detailed Statement of the Services of 2005 Private Nath'l Mitchell

Regiment	Promotions, Reductions, &c.	Rank	Period of Service in each Rank		Amount of Service	
			From	To	Years	Days
36th		Priv.	23 Oct 1823	31 Dec'r 1828	5	70
		"	1 Jan'y 1829	31 March 1842	13	90
59nd	Transferred	"	1 Ap'l 1842	31 Aug't 1844	2	153
74th	Transferred	"	1 Sep't 1844	31 Dec't 1844		122
46th	Transferred	"	1 Jan'y 1845	31 July 1845		212
	Two years service allowed for Volunteering					

For Soldiers Enlisted previous to the 15th March, 1818.

	From	To	Years	Days		
Indies { East					Half period	
West					Half period	

* WATERLOO .... 32 | 272

* Further Service from _____ to the _____ when finally discharged ... | 61
Total Service allowed to reckon to the day of final discharge ... 23 | 333

* To be erased, when not required, by drawing the Pen through the Lines.

The foregoing Report is hereby confirmed by me _____
Commanding 46 Regt. of Foot

Statement of Services from the Soldier's Documents [W.O. 97/607] - Private Nathaniel Mitchell. Crown copyright, used with permission of the Public Record Office, Kew, England.

His Majesty's 104th (or New Brunswick) Regiment, whereof Lieutenant General Martin

THESE are to Certify, that Joseph Swim Sergeant in Captain Rowbric's Company in the aforesaid, born in the Parish of _____ in or near the Town of _____ in the County of _____ hath served in the said Regiment for the space of Thirteen Years and One Hundred Seventy Three days, after the age of eighteen, a Statement.—But the Regiment being Disbanded, is in consequence hereby discharged; having first received all just demands from his entry into the said Regiment to the date of this Discharge, as appears by the receipt on the back hereof.

And to prevent any improper use being made of this Discharge, should it fall into other hands, the following is a description.— Swim He is about Forty Eight years of age, is Six feet One inches in height, Dark Complexion, by trade a Labourer.

STATEMENT OF SERVICE.

[Table of service record]

Given under my Hand and Seal of the Regiment at Montreal the 24th day of May 1817.

Note that this document certifies Sergeant Joseph Swim's service of 13 years and 173 days in the 104th Regiment of Foot and provides a partial description of the man - 48 years old, six feet one inch in height, dark complexion, by trade a labourer.

Statement of Service from the Soldier's Documents [W.O. 97/1071] - Sergeant Joseph Swim. Crown copyright, used with permission of the Public Record Office, Kew, England.

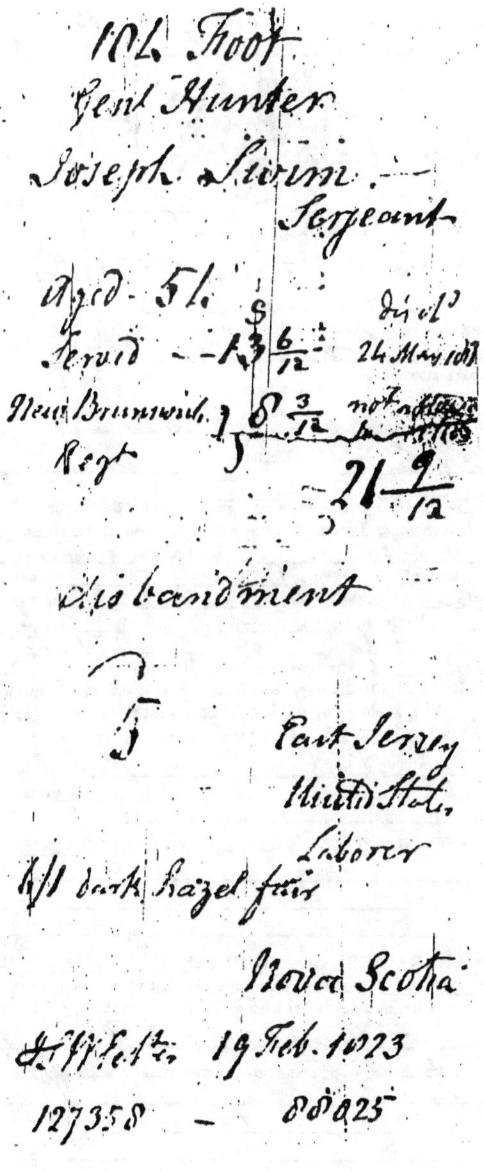

104 Foot
Gen.l Hunter
Joseph Swim
Sergeant
Aged 51
Served 13 6/12 died 24 May 1817
New Brunswick Regt 8 3/12 not allowed
21 9/12
Disbandment
5
East Jersey
United States
Laborer
5/1 dark hazel fair
Nova Scotia
19 Feb. 1823
127358 — 88825

Note that this document from the same file is dated six years later and shows earlier non-pensionable service in the New Brunswick Fencibles. It also shows his place of birth in East Jersey, the easternmost four counties of New Jersey, and adds to his physical description in noting that he had hazel eyes and fair hair.

Discharge certificate from the Soldier's Documents [W.O. 97/1071] - Sergeant Joseph Swim. Crown copyright, used with permission of the Public Record Office, Kew, England.

This man intends residing at Brockville C.W.
23.10.49

HER MAJESTY'S _Royal Canad.__ REGT.
OF _Rifles_
Whereof _____ is Colonel.

[Place and Date] _Niagara C.W. 23 June_ 1849.

PROCEEDINGS OF A REGIMENTAL BOARD, held this day, in conformity to the Articles of War, for the purpose of verifying and recording the Services, Conduct, Character, and cause of Discharge of _Charles Scott No. 90 Private_ of the Regiment above-mentioned.

President.
Captain Harrestone
Capt. Holmes Members. _Lieut Pete_

THE BOARD having examined and compared the Regimental Records, the Soldier's Book, and such other Documents as appeared to them to be necessary, report that _Charles Scott_ by Trade a _Weaver_ was BORN in the Parish of _Midlothian_ in or near the Town of _Midlothian_ in the County of _Midlothian_ and was ATTESTED for the _25th_ Regiment of _Foot_ at _Montrose_ in the County of _Forfar_ on the _21 October 1825_ at the Age of _Nineteen_ that after making every Deduction required by Her Majesty's Regulations, the SERVICE up to this day, which he is entitled to reckon, amounts to _23_ years, _278_ days, as shewn by the detailed Statement on the 2nd page; during which period, he served Abroad _23 7/12_ years, viz.—

at _West Indies_ _12 8/12_ years,
in _North America_ _10 7/12_ years;

and further, that his DISCHARGE is proposed in consequence of _his being_

[In cases of Disability, the Regimental Medical Officer will write his Report on the 3rd page hereof.]

With regard to the CHARACTER and CONDUCT of _Private Charles Scott_ the Board have to report, that upon reference to the Defaulter's Book, and by the Parole testimony that has been given, it appears that _his conduct and character have been very good he is in possession of six good conduct badges with pay_

[Give the particulars required by the Adjutant General's Circular Letter, 29th Sept. 1838.]

> **FINAL DESCRIPTION**
> of _Private Charly Scott_
> of the _Rifle_ Regt. of _Rifles_
> when Discharged the Service at
> _____
> this ____ day of _____
> 184 .
>
> _____
>
> Age _42 9/12_
> Height _5_ Feet _6½_ Inches,
> Hair _Sandy_
> Eyes _Hazel_
> Complexion _Fresh_
> Trade _Weaver_
> Marks, or Scars, whether on the Face,
> or other parts of the Body _None_
>
> 3000.   5—25.   Aug. 1848.

Final Description from the Soldier's Documents [W.O. 97/1193] - Private Charles Scott. Crown copyright, used with permission of the Public Record Office, Kew, England.

BRITISH ARMY PENSIONERS ABROAD

Instructions for the guidance of the Pensioner in drawing his Pension.

PENSIONERS will be paid by the Staff Officers of Pensioners of the Districts in which they may respectively reside, either Quarterly or at such other periods as may hereafter be authorized. Every Pensioner is at liberty to remove to any other District about his lawful business; but he must bear in mind that if he does so without first apprizing his Staff Officer of his intention, and signing his transfer Certificate, no provision can be made for paying him in the District to which he may remove. When a Pensioner resides at the Head Quarters of the District, he should apply in person to the Staff Officer to be transferred, and if at any Out-Station of the said District, to the Staff Officer when he attends to make payments, or in his absence, to the Serjeant of such Out-Station, who will certify his wish to remove to the Staff Officer.

Any Pensioner guilty of violence or outrage towards the Staff Officers, or other Persons employed under them in paying the Pensioners, will be punished by the loss, either of a part or of the whole of his Pension, in addition to any other Punishment which the Law may inflict for such offence.

Any Pensioner convicted of Felony or of an attempt to commit a fraud in the receipt of Pension or Prize Money, will be struck off the Pension List.

Out-Pensioners are not allowed to receive their Pensions in any Foreign Country [not forming part of Her Majesty's Dominions], without special permission from the Secretary at War, or the Commissioners of Chelsea Hospital.

N.B. These Instructions apply equally to the cases of Men residing Abroad, as regards their removal to other Districts, and their conduct towards the Officers by whom their Pensions are paid.

Instructions for the guidance of the Pensioner [W.O. 97/1070] - Private Robert Barr. Crown copyright, used with permission of the Public Record Office, Kew, England.

British Army Pensioners Abroad,
1772 - 1899

WO120 VOLUME 35

2nd Regiment of Dragoon Guards

Ja^s DEIGAN; pension awarded 13 Dec 1826; residence - Montreal, Quebec, Canada. SOURCE: WO120 Volume 35 page 6. INDEX # 1.

3rd Regiment of Dragoon Guards

Jos^h NORMAN; pension awarded 31 Mar 1819; residence - Nova Scotia, Canada. SOURCE: WO120 Volume 35 page 7. INDEX # 2.

4th Regiment of Dragoon Guards

Ja^s BANNON; pension awarded 28 May 1817; residence - Canada. SOURCE: WO120 Volume 35 page 8. INDEX # 3.

6th Regiment of Dragoon Guards

Jno MITCHELL; pension awarded 9 Apr 1834. SOURCE: WO120 Volume 35 page 9. INDEX # 4.

7th Regiment of Dragoon Guards

And^w MOORE; pension awarded 12 Nov 1817; residence - Montreal, Quebec, Canada. SOURCE: WO120 Volume 35 page 10. INDEX # 5.

2nd Regiment of Dragoons

Ge^o CUTHBERTSON; pension awarded 28 Jun 1820; residence - Cape of Good Hope, South Africa. SOURCE: WO120 Volume 35 page 11. INDEX # 6.

3rd Regiment of Dragoons

Jno FOSTER; pension awarded 10 Nov 1819; residence - New South Wales, Australia. SOURCE: WO120 Volume 35 page 12. INDEX # 7.

4th Regiment of Dragoons

Willm BYRNE; pension awarded 5 Aug 1829. SOURCE: WO120 Volume 35 page 13. INDEX # 8.
Hen^y GORDON; pension awarded 5 Aug 1829. SOURCE: WO120 Volume 35 page 13. INDEX # 9.
Alex^r Ja^s ROSE; pension awarded 5 Aug 1829. SOURCE: WO120 Volume 35 page 13. INDEX # 10.
Pat^k PURCELL; pension awarded 8 Jun 1836. SOURCE: WO120 Volume 35 page 13. INDEX # 11.

5th Regiment of Dragoons

Willm PIKE; pension awarded 20 Jul 1772; residence - Canada; died 20 Jan 1822, Canada. SOURCE: WO120 Volume 35 page 14. INDEX # 12.

8th Regiment of Dragoons

Richd LAMBERT; pension awarded 23 Sep 1818; residence - Cape of Good Hope, South Africa. SOURCE: WO120 Volume 35 page 18. INDEX # 13.
Danl HOGAN; pension awarded 23 Sep 1818; residence - Cape of Good Hope, South Africa. SOURCE: WO120 Volume 35 page 18. INDEX # 14.
Willm LUCAS; pension awarded 25 Jul 1821; residence - India. SOURCE: WO120 Volume 35 page 18. INDEX # 15.

BRITISH ARMY PENSIONERS ABROAD

8th Regiment of Dragoons (continued)

Jn⁰ BELL; pension awarded 25 Jul 1821; residence - India; SOURCE: WO120 Volume 35 page 18. INDEX # 16.

Jn⁰ MCQUAY; pension awarded 25 Jul 1821; residence - India; SOURCE: WO120 Volume 35 page 18. INDEX # 17.

Ja⁵ KIRK; pension awarded 25 Jul 1821; residence - India; SOURCE: WO120 Volume 35 page 18. INDEX # 18.

Jn⁰ ROSSE; pension awarded 25 Sep 1822; residence - Bengal, India. SOURCE: WO120 Volume 35 page 18. INDEX # 19.

Edwd MOLLOY; pension awarded 25 Sep 1822; residence - Bengal, India. SOURCE: WO120 Volume 35 page 18. INDEX # 20.

Tho⁵ IRWIN; pension awarded 25 Sep 1822; residence - Bengal, India. SOURCE: WO120 Volume 35 page 18. INDEX # 21.

Jn⁰ MCNIFFE; pension awarded 25 Sep 1822; residence - Bengal, India. SOURCE: WO120 Volume 35 page 18. INDEX # 22.

Peter MURPHY; pension awarded 25 Sep 1822; residence - Bengal, India. SOURCE: WO120 Volume 35 page 18. INDEX # 23.

Cha⁵ WARD; pension awarded 25 Sep 1822; residence - Bengal, India. SOURCE: WO120 Volume 35 page 18. INDEX # 24.

Jn⁰ ASHCROFT; pension awarded 27 Aug 1823; residence - Bengal, India. SOURCE: WO120 Volume 35 page 18. INDEX # 25.

Jn⁰ TRAVERS; pension awarded 27 Aug 1823; residence - Bengal, India. SOURCE: WO120 Volume 35 page 18. INDEX # 26.

11th Regiment of Dragoons

Jn⁰ RYE; pension awarded 24 Nov 1824; residence - Bengal, India. SOURCE: WO120 Volume 35 page 21. INDEX # 27.

Robt ANDREWS; pension awarded 3 Dec 1828; residence - Cawnpore, India. SOURCE: WO120 Volume 35 page 21. INDEX # 28.

Ja⁵ REALE; pension awarded 13 Jan 1830. SOURCE: WO120 Volume 35 page 21. INDEX # 29.

Jn⁰ THOMPSON; pension awarded 13 Jan 1830. SOURCE: WO120 Volume 35 page 21. INDEX # 30.

Law^e BASTLIQUE; pension awarded 10 Mar 1830; residence - Cawnpore, India. SOURCE: WO120 Volume 35 page 21. INDEX # 31.

Hugh TOMASSON; pension awarded 10 Mar 1830. SOURCE: WO120 Volume 35 page 21. INDEX # 32.

Jn⁰ BENNETT; pension awarded 12 Jun 1833; residence - Meerut, India. SOURCE: WO120 Volume 35 page 21. INDEX # 33.

Spalter COUSINS; pension awarded 12 Jun 1833; residence - Cawnpore, India. SOURCE: WO120 Volume 35 page 21. INDEX # 34.

Jn⁰ KEEVES; pension awarded 12 Jun 1833. SOURCE: WO120 Volume 35 page 21. INDEX # 35.

Wm MORRIS; pension awarded 12 Jun 1833. SOURCE: WO120 Volume 35 page 21. INDEX # 36.

Ja⁵ OAKES; pension awarded 12 Jun 1833. SOURCE: WO120 Volume 35 page 21. INDEX # 37.

Silv^r PITCHELLO; pension awarded 12 Jun 1833. SOURCE: WO120 Volume 35 page 21. INDEX # 38.

Tho⁵ SMITH; pension awarded 12 Jun 1833. SOURCE: WO120 Volume 35 page 21. INDEX # 39.

Cha⁵ EARLE; pension awarded 10 Dec 1834. SOURCE: WO120 Volume 35 page 21. INDEX # 40.

Wm BROADHEAD; pension awarded 10 Jun 1835. SOURCE: WO120 Volume 35 page 21. INDEX # 41.

Ge⁰ FARMER; pension awarded 12 Aug 1835. SOURCE: WO120 Volume 35 page 21. INDEX # 42.

John FLYNN; pension awarded 12 Aug 1835. SOURCE: WO120 Volume 35 page 21. INDEX # 43.

John OTTY; pension awarded 12 Aug 1835. SOURCE: WO120 Volume 35 page 21. INDEX # 44.

Wm BARKER; pension awarded 14 Jun 1837; residence - Meerut, India. SOURCE: WO120 Volume 35 page 21. INDEX # 45.

Robt FOSTER; pension awarded 27 Jun 1838. SOURCE: WO120 Volume 35 page 21. INDEX # 46.

Peter BROWN; pension awarded 27 Jun 1838; residence - Cawnpore, India. SOURCE: WO120 Volume 35 page 21. INDEX # 47.

11th Regiment of Dragoons (continued)

Jos^h CHAPMAN; pension awarded 27 Jun 1838; residence - Cawnpore, India. SOURCE: WO120 Volume 35 page 21. INDEX # 48.
Wm DALTON; pension awarded 27 Jun 1838. SOURCE: WO120 Volume 35 page 21. INDEX # 49.
Thos FERGUSON; pension awarded 27 Jun 1838. SOURCE: WO120 Volume 35 page 21. INDEX # 50.
Jno GOODING; pension awarded 27 Jun 1838. SOURCE: WO120 Volume 35 page 22. INDEX # 51.
Benjn HIGH; pension awarded 27 Jun 1838. SOURCE: WO120 Volume 35 page 22. INDEX # 52.
Jno MCKENLEY; pension awarded 27 Jun 1838. SOURCE: WO120 Volume 35 page 22. INDEX # 53.
Ge^o SCALES; pension awarded 27 Jun 1838. SOURCE: WO120 Volume 35 page 22. INDEX # 54.
Ge^o WALKER; pension awarded 27 Jun 1838. SOURCE: WO120 Volume 35 page 22. INDEX # 55.
Richd WILKINS; pension awarded 27 Jun 1838. SOURCE: WO120 Volume 35 page 22. INDEX # 56.
Thos CROSS; pension awarded 22 Aug 1838. SOURCE: WO120 Volume 35 page 22. INDEX # 57.
Wm BALDWIN; pension awarded 22 Aug 1838; residence - Cawnpore, India. SOURCE: WO120 Volume 35 page 22. INDEX # 58.

13th Regiment of Dragoons

Thos HALL; pension awarded 4 Jun 1823; residence - Madras, India. SOURCE: WO120 Volume 35 page 23. INDEX # 59.
Jno MCDONAUGH; pension awarded 3 Mar 1824; residence - Madras, India. SOURCE: WO120 Volume 35 page 23. INDEX # 60.
Willm JONES; pension awarded 4 Aug 1824; residence - Madras, India. SOURCE: WO120 Volume 35 page 23. INDEX # 61.
Edwd MCKEGG; pension awarded 5 Aug 1824; residence - Madras, India. SOURCE: WO120 Volume 35 page 23. INDEX # 62.
Richd THOMPSON; pension awarded 4 Aug 1824; residence - Madras, India. SOURCE: WO120 Volume 35 page 23. INDEX # 63.
Willm GAMMAGE; pension awarded 4 Aug 1824; residence - Madras, India. SOURCE: WO120 Volume 35 page 23. INDEX # 64.
Philip DORNHOFFER; pension awarded 21 Jun 1826; residence - Madras, India. SOURCE: WO120 Volume 35 page 23. INDEX # 65.
Willm LANGLEY; pension awarded 21 Jun 1826; residence - Madras, India. SOURCE: WO120 Volume 35 page 23. INDEX # 66.
Chas RUSSELL; pension awarded 21 Jun 1826; residence - Madras, India. SOURCE: WO120 Volume 35 page 23. INDEX # 67.
Jno DAVIDSON; pension awarded 21 Jun 1826; residence - Madras, India; died 28 Jun 1832. SOURCE: WO120 Volume 35 page 23. INDEX # 68.
Jno PERRY; pension awarded 30 May 1827. SOURCE: WO120 Volume 35 page 23. INDEX # 69.
Ch^r MCLAUGHLIN; pension awarded 30 May 1827. SOURCE: WO120 Volume 35 page 23. INDEX # 70.
Thos MCREA; pension awarded 20 Feb 1828. SOURCE: WO120 Volume 35 page 23. INDEX # 71.
Mic^l BANCE; pension awarded 21 May 1828. SOURCE: WO120 Volume 35 page 23. INDEX # 72.
John HOOPER; pension awarded 21 May 1828. SOURCE: WO120 Volume 35 page 23. INDEX # 73.
Willm BUTLIN; pension awarded 21 May 1828. SOURCE: WO120 Volume 35 page 23. INDEX # 74.
John CHERRINGTON; pension awarded 21 May 1828. SOURCE: WO120 Volume 35 page 23. INDEX # 75.
Chas EVANS; pension awarded 21 May 1828. SOURCE: WO120 Volume 35 page 23. INDEX # 76.
Hen^y JACKSON; pension awarded 21 May 1828. SOURCE: WO120 Volume 35 page 23. INDEX # 77.
Willm LEAR; pension awarded 21 May 1828; died 17 Nov 1832. SOURCE: WO120 Volume 35 page 23. INDEX # 78.
Richd REDROBE; pension awarded 21 May 1828. SOURCE: WO120 Volume 35 page 23. INDEX # 79.
Thos PARKINGTON; pension awarded 21 May 1828. SOURCE: WO120 Volume 35 page 23. INDEX # 80.
John ROGERS; pension awarded 21 May 1828. SOURCE: WO120 Volume 35 page 23. INDEX # 81.
Elea GRIFFITHS; pension awarded 25 Jun 1829. SOURCE: WO120 Volume 35 page 24. INDEX # 82.
Dennis HARRINGTON; pension awarded 25 Jun 1829. SOURCE: WO120 Volume 35 page 24. INDEX # 83.
Chas DICKINS; pension awarded 13 Nov 1833. SOURCE: WO120 Volume 35 page 24. INDEX # 84.

13th Regiment of Dragoons (continued)

Ja^s ARCHBOLD; pension awarded 9 Dec 1835. SOURCE: WO120 Volume 35 page 24. INDEX # 85.
Willm MILLER; pension awarded 10 Aug 1836. SOURCE: WO120 Volume 35 page 24. INDEX # 86.
Saml CROWE; pension awarded 14 Dec 1836. SOURCE: WO120 Volume 35 page 24. INDEX # 87.
Jno PIGG; pension awarded 14 Dec 1836. SOURCE: WO120 Volume 35 page 24. INDEX # 88.
Thos SWINDLES; pension awarded 14 Dec 1836. SOURCE: WO120 Volume 35 page 24. INDEX # 89.
Benjn JOHNSON; pension awarded 9 Aug 1837. SOURCE: WO120 Volume 35 page 24. INDEX # 90.
Jos^h CLARKE; pension awarded 9 Aug 1837. SOURCE: WO120 Volume 35 page 24. INDEX # 91.
Richd EATON; pension awarded 9 Aug 1837. SOURCE: WO120 Volume 35 page 24. INDEX # 92.
Wm LUSCUTT; pension awarded 9 Aug 1837. SOURCE: WO120 Volume 35 page 24. INDEX # 93.
Thos MADDOCK; pension awarded 9 Aug 1837. SOURCE: WO120 Volume 35 page 24. INDEX # 94.
Mich^l SMITH; pension awarded 9 Aug 1837. SOURCE: WO120 Volume 35 page 24. INDEX # 95.
Ja^s GARVEY; pension awarded 23 Oct 1838. SOURCE: WO120 Volume 35 page 24. INDEX # 96.
Wm BEALE; pension awarded 12 Dec 1838. SOURCE: WO120 Volume 35 page 24. INDEX # 97.
Ja^s AXEN; pension awarded 12 Dec 1838. SOURCE: WO120 Volume 35 page 24. INDEX # 98.
Ja^s JONES; pension awarded 12 Dec 1838. SOURCE: WO120 Volume 35 page 24. INDEX # 99.

15th Regiment of Dragoons

Ge^o DEAN; pension awarded 9 May 1832. SOURCE: WO120 Volume 35 page 25. INDEX # 100.

16th Regiment of Dragoons

Thos BROW; pension awarded 28 Mar 1821. SOURCE: WO120 Volume 35 page 26. INDEX # 101.
Jno MCCANN; pension awarded 10 Dec 1834. SOURCE: WO120 Volume 35 page 26. INDEX # 102.
Richd MURRAY; pension awarded 10 Dec 1834. SOURCE: WO120 Volume 35 page 26. INDEX # 103.
Thos RACEY; pension awarded 9 Mar 1836; residence - Cawnpore, India. SOURCE: WO120 Volume 35 page 26. INDEX # 104.
Jos^h WOODS; pension awarded 9 Mar 1836. SOURCE: WO120 Volume 35 page 26. INDEX # 105.
Jno YOUNG; pension awarded 14 Jun 1837. SOURCE: WO120 Volume 35 page 26. INDEX # 106.
Wm DURANT; pension awarded 14 Jun 1837. SOURCE: WO120 Volume 35 page 26. INDEX # 107.
Richd LEECH; pension awarded 14 Jun 1837. SOURCE: WO120 Volume 35 page 26. INDEX # 108.
Jno SHELTON; pension awarded 14 Jun 1837. SOURCE: WO120 Volume 35 page 26. INDEX # 109.
Saml RODGERS; pension awarded 27 Jun 1838; residence - Meerut, India. SOURCE: WO120 Volume 35 page 26. INDEX # 110.
Hugh BROWN; pension awarded 27 Jun 1838. SOURCE: WO120 Volume 35 page 26. INDEX # 111.
Hen^y DIXON; pension awarded 27 Jun 1838. SOURCE: WO120 Volume 35 page 26. INDEX # 112.
Jos^h GRIFFITHS; pension awarded 27 Jun 1838. SOURCE: WO120 Volume 35 page 26. INDEX # 113.
Jno HEYLOTT; pension awarded 27 Jun 1838. SOURCE: WO120 Volume 35 page 26. INDEX # 114.
Jos^h PURCELL; pension awarded 27 Jun 1838. SOURCE: WO120 Volume 35 page 26. INDEX # 115.
Thos SMITH; pension awarded 27 Jun 1838. SOURCE: WO120 Volume 35 page 26. INDEX # 116.
Thos SIMMONDS; pension awarded 27 Jun 1838. SOURCE: WO120 Volume 35 page 26. INDEX # 117.

17th Regiment of Dragoons

Danl OKEEFE; pension awarded 25 Jul 1821. SOURCE: WO120 Volume 35 page 27. INDEX # 118.

18th Regiment of Dragoons

John LARKIN; pension awarded 4 Feb 1822. SOURCE: WO120 Volume 35 page 28. INDEX # 119.

19th Regiment of Dragoons

Jno JEFFREYS; pension awarded 12 May 1824; residence - Canada. SOURCE: WO120 Volume 35 page 29. INDEX # 120.

Benjn HEARD; pension awarded 30 May 1810; residence - Canada. SOURCE: WO120 Volume 35 page 29. INDEX # 121.

Jno COX; pension awarded 12 May 1819. SOURCE: WO120 Volume 35 page 29. INDEX # 122.

And^{w} TIPSON; pension awarded 12 May 1819. SOURCE: WO120 Volume 35 page 29. INDEX # 123.

20th Regiment of Dragoons

Jno THOMPSON; pension awarded 27 Nov 1816; residence - Canada. SOURCE: WO120 Volume 35 page 30. INDEX # 124.

21st Regiment of Dragoons

Jonas BARROWCLOUGH; pension awarded 7 Jan 1818; residence - Cape of Good Hope, South Africa. SOURCE: WO120 Volume 35 page 31. INDEX # 125.

Lionel COLE; pension awarded 7 Jan 1818; residence - Cape of Good Hope, South Africa. SOURCE: WO120 Volume 35 page 31. INDEX # 126.

Ja^{s} CAMPBELL; pension awarded 7 Jan 1818; residence - Cape of Good Hope, South Africa. SOURCE: WO120 Volume 35 page 31. INDEX # 127.

Isaac REED; pension awarded 7 Jan 1818; residence - Cape of Good Hope, South Africa. SOURCE: WO120 Volume 35 page 31. INDEX # 128.

Willm PENNELL; pension awarded 7 Jan 1818; residence - Cape of Good Hope, South Africa. SOURCE: WO120 Volume 35 page 31. INDEX # 129.

Danl JONES; pension awarded 7 Jan 1818; residence - Cape of Good Hope, South Africa. SOURCE: WO120 Volume 35 page 31. INDEX # 130.

Jno ALLEN; pension awarded 7 Jan 1818; residence - Cape of Good Hope, South Africa. SOURCE: WO120 Volume 35 page 31. INDEX # 131.

Robt KEARNS; pension awarded 7 Jan 1818; residence - Cape of Good Hope, South Africa. SOURCE: WO120 Volume 35 page 31. INDEX # 132.

Adam ROSS; pension awarded 7 Jan 1818; residence - Cape of Good Hope, South Africa. SOURCE: WO120 Volume 35 page 31. INDEX # 133.

Ge^{o} BRITTON; pension awarded 23 Sep 1818; residence - Cape of Good Hope, South Africa. SOURCE: WO120 Volume 35 page 31. INDEX # 134.

Willm NEUT; pension awarded 29 Jul 1819; residence - Cape of Good Hope, South Africa. SOURCE: WO120 Volume 35 page 31. INDEX # 135.

Thos BARKER; pension awarded 29 Jul 1819; residence - Cape of Good Hope, South Africa. SOURCE: WO120 Volume 35 page 31. INDEX # 136.

22nd Regiment of Dragoons

Ja^{s} HINSELL; pension awarded 7 Feb 1821; residence - India; died 2 Jan 1825. SOURCE: WO120 Volume 35 page 33. INDEX # 137.

Hen^{y} CARLOS; pension awarded 7 Feb 1821; residence - India. SOURCE: WO120 Volume 35 page 33. INDEX # 138.

Willm LAMB; pension awarded 7 Feb 1821; residence - India. SOURCE: WO120 Volume 35 page 33. INDEX # 139.

Jno Wallis CROKER; pension awarded 24 Oct 1821; residence - India. SOURCE: WO120 Volume 35 page 33. INDEX # 140.

Ja^{s} REED; pension awarded 7 Feb 1821. SOURCE: WO120 Volume 35 page 33. INDEX # 141.

BRITISH ARMY PENSIONERS ABROAD

23rd Regiment of Dragoons

Ja^s SIMPSON; pension awarded 29 Mar 1809; residence - Canada. SOURCE: WO120 Volume 35 page 34. INDEX # 142.

24th Regiment of Dragoons

Peter GILLIS; pension awarded 25 Jul 1821. SOURCE: WO120 Volume 35 page 35. INDEX # 143.
Benjⁿ BLAKE; pension awarded 25 Jul 1821. SOURCE: WO120 Volume 35 page 35. INDEX # 144.
Richd MINES; pension awarded 25 Jul 1821. SOURCE: WO120 Volume 35 page 35. INDEX # 145.
Wi^{llm} STONE; pension awarded 25 Jul 1821. SOURCE: WO120 Volume 35 page 35. INDEX # 146.
Wi^{llm} DOWELL; pension awarded 25 Jul 1821. SOURCE: WO120 Volume 35 page 35. INDEX # 147.
Ja^s TORRING; pension awarded 25 Jul 1821. SOURCE: WO120 Volume 35 page 35. INDEX # 148.

25th Regiment of Dragoons

Wi^{llm} GRIFFEN; pension awarded 17 Mar 1819; residence - Cape of Good Hope, South Africa. SOURCE: WO120 Volume 35 page 37. INDEX # 149.
Thos MURPHY; pension awarded 17 Mar 1819; residence - Cape of Good Hope, South Africa. SOURCE: WO120 Volume 35 page 37. INDEX # 150.
Pat^k TRACEY; pension awarded 17 Mar 1819; residence - Cape of Good Hope, South Africa. SOURCE: WO120 Volume 35 page 37. INDEX # 151.
Ge^o MOORHEAD; pension awarded 17 Mar 1819; residence - Cape of Good Hope, South Africa. SOURCE: WO120 Volume 35 page 37. INDEX # 152.
Lewis OLIVER; pension awarded 17 Mar 1819; residence - Cape of Good Hope, South Africa. SOURCE: WO120 Volume 35 page 37. INDEX # 153.
Danl GREEN; pension awarded 17 Mar 1819; residence - Cape of Good Hope, South Africa. SOURCE: WO120 Volume 35 page 37. INDEX # 154.
Alex^r MCKINNON; pension awarded 17 Mar 1819; residence - Cape of Good Hope, South Africa. SOURCE: WO120 Volume 35 page 37. INDEX # 155.
Ja^s SIMPSON; pension awarded 17 Mar 1819; residence - Cape of Good Hope, South Africa. SOURCE: WO120 Volume 35 page 37. INDEX # 156.
Jno BLACKEY; pension awarded 17 Mar 1819; residence - Cape of Good Hope, South Africa. SOURCE: WO120 Volume 35 page 37. INDEX # 157.
Jno BEDMORE; pension awarded 17 Mar 1819; residence - Cape of Good Hope, South Africa. SOURCE: WO120 Volume 35 page 37. INDEX # 158.
Fra^s HOWSON; pension awarded 17 Mar 1819; residence - Cape of Good Hope, South Africa. SOURCE: WO120 Volume 35 page 37. INDEX # 159.
Richd ROYLE; pension awarded 7 Feb 1821; residence - India. SOURCE: WO120 Volume 35 page 37. INDEX # 160.
Jno BURKE; pension awarded 7 Feb 1821; residence - India. SOURCE: WO120 Volume 35 page 37. INDEX # 161.
Wi^{llm} FEE; pension awarded 7 Feb 1821; residence - India; died 19 Nov 1832. SOURCE: WO120 Volume 35 page 37. INDEX # 162.
Ge^o HARRISON; pension awarded 7 Feb 1821; residence - Poonamalee, India; died 6 Dec 1821. SOURCE: WO120 Volume 35 page 37. INDEX # 163.
Jno HARRISON; pension awarded 7 Feb 1821; residence - Poonamalee, India. SOURCE: WO120 Volume 35 page 37. INDEX # 164.
Ge^o HALL; pension awarded 7 Feb 1821; residence - India. SOURCE: WO120 Volume 35 page 37. INDEX # 165.
Thos JONES; pension awarded 7 Feb 1821; residence - India; died 10 May 1824. SOURCE: WO120 Volume 35 page 37. INDEX # 166.
Hen^y KNABB; pension awarded 7 Feb 1821; residence - India. SOURCE: WO120 Volume 35 page 37. INDEX # 167.

WO120 VOLUME 35

25th Regiment of Dragoons (continued)

Richd MOUNTAIN; pension awarded 7 Feb 1821; residence - India. SOURCE: WO120 Volume 35 page 37. INDEX # 168.

Hen^y MANDRILL; pension awarded 7 Feb 1821; residence - India. SOURCE: WO120 Volume 35 page 37. INDEX # 169.

Willm POPE; pension awarded 7 Feb 1821; residence - India. SOURCE: WO120 Volume 35 page 37. INDEX # 170.

Ja^s PRICE; pension awarded 7 Feb 1821; residence - India. SOURCE: WO120 Volume 35 page 37. INDEX # 171.

Jno RAYMOND; pension awarded 7 Feb 1821; residence - India. SOURCE: WO120 Volume 35 page 37. INDEX # 172.

Richd ROBERTS; pension awarded 7 Feb 1821; residence - India. SOURCE: WO120 Volume 35 page 38. INDEX # 173.

Robt SCOTT; pension awarded 7 Feb 1821; residence - India. SOURCE: WO120 Volume 35 page 38. INDEX # 174.

Jonⁿ STRONG; pension awarded 7 Feb 1821; residence - India. SOURCE: WO120 Volume 35 page 38. INDEX # 175.

Arth^r TURNER; pension awarded 7 Feb 1821; residence - India. SOURCE: WO120 Volume 35 page 38. INDEX # 176.

Neh^{eh} WINDEL; pension awarded 7 Feb 1821; residence - India. SOURCE: WO120 Volume 35 page 38. INDEX # 177.

Thos WILKINS; pension awarded 7 Feb 1821; residence - India. SOURCE: WO120 Volume 35 page 38. INDEX # 178.

Willm WRIGHT; pension awarded 7 Feb 1821; residence - India. SOURCE: WO120 Volume 35 page 38. INDEX # 179.

1st Regiment of Foot

Philip FITZPATRICK; pension awarded 17 Mar 1819; residence - Cape of Good Hope, South Africa. SOURCE: WO120 Volume 35 page 45. INDEX # 180.

Jno DUNCAN; pension awarded 13 Sep 1820. SOURCE: WO120 Volume 35 page 45. INDEX # 181.

Willm HALL; pension awarded 18 Oct 1820. SOURCE: WO120 Volume 35 page 45. INDEX # 182.

Benjⁿ HOLMES; pension awarded 7 Feb 1821; residence - India. SOURCE: WO120 Volume 35 page 45. INDEX # 183.

Thos HALL; pension awarded 7 Feb 1821; residence - India. SOURCE: WO120 Volume 35 page 45. INDEX # 184.

Jno ROWLAND; pension awarded 7 Feb 1821; residence - India. SOURCE: WO120 Volume 35 page 45. INDEX # 185.

Willm BENNETT; pension awarded 7 Feb 1821; residence - India. SOURCE: WO120 Volume 35 page 45. INDEX # 186.

Thos BRENEY; pension awarded 7 Feb 1821; residence - India; died 6 Mar 1821. SOURCE: WO120 Volume 35 page 45. INDEX # 187.

Jno CAMPBELL; pension awarded 7 Feb 1821; residence - India. SOURCE: WO120 Volume 35 page 45. INDEX # 188.

Jno CUNNINGHAM; pension awarded 7 Feb 1821; residence - India. SOURCE: WO120 Volume 35 page 45. INDEX # 189.

Peter DEGOOD; pension awarded 7 Feb 1821; residence - India. SOURCE: WO120 Volume 35 page 45. INDEX # 190.

Mich^l DUFFIE; pension awarded 7 Feb 1821; residence - India. SOURCE: WO120 Volume 35 page 45. INDEX # 191.

Robt GODBY; pension awarded 7 Feb 1821; residence - India. SOURCE: WO120 Volume 35 page 45. INDEX # 192.

Mich^l CARR; pension awarded 7 Feb 1821; residence - India. SOURCE: WO120 Volume 35 page 45. INDEX # 193.

BRITISH ARMY PENSIONERS ABROAD

1st Regiment of Foot (continued)

Pat[k] HOLLAND; pension awarded 7 Feb 1821; residence - India. SOURCE: WO120 Volume 35 page 45. INDEX # 194.

Tho[s] HILL; pension awarded 7 Feb 1821; residence - India. SOURCE: WO120 Volume 35 page 45. INDEX # 195.

Jn[o] HUGHES; pension awarded 7 Feb 1821; residence - India. SOURCE: WO120 Volume 35 page 45. INDEX # 196.

Jn[o] MOORE; pension awarded 7 Feb 1821; residence - India. SOURCE: WO120 Volume 35 page 45. INDEX # 197.

Jn[o] SLATE; pension awarded 7 Feb 1821; residence - India. SOURCE: WO120 Volume 35 page 45. INDEX # 198.

Sipko SIZE; pension awarded 7 Feb 1821. SOURCE: WO120 Volume 35 page 45. INDEX # 199.

Pat[k] TROY; pension awarded 7 Feb 1821; residence - India. SOURCE: WO120 Volume 35 page 45. INDEX # 200.

Fred[k] STOLE; pension awarded 7 Feb 1821; residence - India; died 15 Apr 1827. SOURCE: WO120 Volume 35 page 45. INDEX # 201.

Jn[o] THOMPSON; pension awarded 7 Feb 1821; residence - India. SOURCE: WO120 Volume 35 page 45. INDEX # 202.

Phi[lp] TURNER; pension awarded 7 Feb 1821; residence - India. SOURCE: WO120 Volume 35 page 45. INDEX # 203.

Rich[d] WYBLE; pension awarded 7 Feb 1821; residence - India; died 5 Jul 1826. SOURCE: WO120 Volume 35 page 46. INDEX # 204.

Ed[wd] BARRY; pension awarded 30 Jul 1817; residence - Montreal, Quebec, Canada. SOURCE: WO120 Volume 35 page 46. INDEX # 205.

Jn[o] HALES; pension awarded 15 Mar 1826; residence - Fort St. George, India. SOURCE: WO120 Volume 35 page 46. INDEX # 206.

Jn[o] WIGGINS; pension awarded 15 Mar 1826; residence - Fort St. George, India. SOURCE: WO120 Volume 35 page 46. INDEX # 207.

Tho[s] DORAN; pension awarded 15 Mar 1826; residence - Fort St. George, India. SOURCE: WO120 Volume 35 page 46. INDEX # 208.

Alex[r] THOMPSON; pension awarded 23 Nov 1825; residence - Fort St. George, India. SOURCE: WO120 Volume 35 page 46. INDEX # 209.

Rob[t] BUSSEY; pension awarded 23 Nov 1825; residence - Madras, India. SOURCE: WO120 Volume 35 page 46. INDEX # 210.

Jn[o] BROADHURST; pension awarded 23 Nov 1825. SOURCE: WO120 Volume 35 page 46. INDEX # 211.

Tho[s] PITMAN; pension awarded 23 Nov 1825; residence - Madras, India; died 6 May 1828. SOURCE: WO120 Volume 35 page 46. INDEX # 212.

Jn[o] ROBERTSON; pension awarded 23 Nov 1825; residence - Madras, India. SOURCE: WO120 Volume 35 page 46. INDEX # 213.

Ja[s] DUFFY; pension awarded 21 Jun 1826; residence - Madras, India. SOURCE: WO120 Volume 35 page 46. INDEX # 214.

Ed[wd] PITTMAN; pension awarded 13 Dec 1826; residence - Madras, India. SOURCE: WO120 Volume 35 page 46. INDEX # 215.

Ben[jn] EMMETT; pension awarded 30 May 1827; residence - Madras, India. SOURCE: WO120 Volume 35 page 46. INDEX # 216.

Jer[h] HURLEY; pension awarded 30 May 1827; residence - Madras, India. SOURCE: WO120 Volume 35 page 46. INDEX # 217.

Wil[lm] ACKLEY; pension awarded 30 May 1827; residence - Madras, India. SOURCE: WO120 Volume 35 page 46. INDEX # 218.

Wil[lm] BASTOW; pension awarded 30 May 1827; residence - Madras, India; died 27 Nov 1827. SOURCE: WO120 Volume 35 page 46. INDEX # 219.

Jn[o] COLLINS; pension awarded 31 Oct 1827; residence - Madras, India. SOURCE: WO120 Volume 35 page 46. INDEX # 220.

WO120 VOLUME 35

1st Regiment of Foot (continued)

Hen^y LEIB; pension awarded 12 May 1819. SOURCE: WO120 Volume 35 page 46. INDEX # 221.
Willm HENKELL; pension awarded 12 May 1819. SOURCE: WO120 Volume 35 page 46. INDEX # 222.
Fred^k HAMPE; pension awarded 12 May 1819. SOURCE: WO120 Volume 35 page 46. INDEX # 223.
John CALLAGHAN; pension awarded 21 May 1828. SOURCE: WO120 Volume 35 page 46. INDEX # 224.
Willm PHILLIPS; pension awarded 21 May 1828. SOURCE: WO120 Volume 35 page 46. INDEX # 225.
Thos BRADBURY; pension awarded 21 Oct 1828. SOURCE: WO120 Volume 35 page 46. INDEX # 226.
Robt HOGDEN; pension awarded 21 Oct 1828. SOURCE: WO120 Volume 35 page 46. INDEX # 227.
Step^n TRUEMAN; pension awarded 29 Oct 1828. SOURCE: WO120 Volume 35 page 47. INDEX # 228.
Thos GASCOYNE; pension awarded 7 Jan 1829. SOURCE: WO120 Volume 35 page 47. INDEX # 229.
Thos MCCAMMON; pension awarded 7 Jan 1829. SOURCE: WO120 Volume 35 page 47. INDEX # 230.
Jno FERDINAND; pension awarded 25 Jun 1829. SOURCE: WO120 Volume 35 page 47. INDEX # 231.
Jos^h HENDERSON; pension awarded 25 Jun 1829. SOURCE: WO120 Volume 35 page 47. INDEX # 232.
Ja^s LOANE; pension awarded 25 Jun 1829. SOURCE: WO120 Volume 35 page 47. INDEX # 233.
Thos MCGEE; pension awarded 25 Jun 1829; died 17 Oct 1833. SOURCE: WO120 Volume 35 page 47. INDEX # 234.
Jos^h SMART; pension awarded 25 Jun 1829. SOURCE: WO120 Volume 35 page 47. INDEX # 235.
Ja^s WILLOX; pension awarded 25 Jun 1829. SOURCE: WO120 Volume 35 page 47. INDEX # 236.
Thos KIRBY; pension awarded 11 Nov 1829. SOURCE: WO120 Volume 35 page 47. INDEX # 237.
Dav^d THOMPSON; pension awarded 9 Dec 1829. SOURCE: WO120 Volume 35 page 47. INDEX # 238.
Wm FAIRHURST; pension awarded 12 May 1830. SOURCE: WO120 Volume 35 page 47. INDEX # 239.
Ge^o OLIVER; pension awarded 12 May 1830. SOURCE: WO120 Volume 35 page 47. INDEX # 240.
Willm ROBINSON; pension awarded 12 May 1830; residence - Bangalore, India; died 20 Aug 1832. SOURCE: WO120 Volume 35 page 47. INDEX # 241.
Edwd FOWLES; pension awarded 12 Oct 1831. SOURCE: WO120 Volume 35 page 47. INDEX # 242.
Jno RODGERS; pension awarded 11 Jan 1832; residence - Fort St. George, India. SOURCE: WO120 Volume 35 page 47. INDEX # 243.

3rd Regiment of Foot

Don^d MACGREGOR; pension awarded 30 Aug 1826; residence - New South Wales, Australia. SOURCE: WO120 Volume 35 page 51. INDEX # 244.
Jos^h MEDLEY; pension awarded 30 Aug 1826; residence - New South Wales, Australia. SOURCE: WO120 Volume 35 page 51. INDEX # 245.
Jno COLLINS; pension awarded 30 Aug 1826; residence - New South Wales, Australia. SOURCE: WO120 Volume 35 page 51. INDEX # 246.
Benjn REED; pension awarded 30 Aug 1826; residence - New South Wales, Australia. SOURCE: WO120 Volume 35 page 51. INDEX # 247.
Edwd WHITE; pension awarded 30 Aug 1826; residence - New South Wales, Australia. SOURCE: WO120 Volume 35 page 51. INDEX # 248.
Jno COLLINS; pension awarded 13 Dec 1826; residence - New South Wales, Australia. SOURCE: WO120 Volume 35 page 51. INDEX # 249.
Zach^h BERRY; pension awarded 8 Aug 1827; residence - New South Wales, Australia. SOURCE: WO120 Volume 35 page 51. INDEX # 250.
Pat^k DUFFY; pension awarded 21 May 1828. SOURCE: WO120 Volume 35 page 51. INDEX # 251.
Willm SUTHERLAND; pension awarded 21 May 1828. SOURCE: WO120 Volume 35 page 51. INDEX # 252.
Saml CAVERT; pension awarded 8 Oct 1834. SOURCE: WO120 Volume 35 page 51. INDEX # 253.
Wm BARTHOLOMEW; pension awarded 29 Jun 1838. SOURCE: WO120 Volume 35 page 51. INDEX # 254.

4th Regiment of Foot

Ge^o TUGNETT; pension awarded 14 Aug 1833. SOURCE: WO120 Volume 35 page 52. INDEX # 255.
Job COLEMAN; pension awarded 9 Jul 1834. SOURCE: WO120 Volume 35 page 52. INDEX # 256.
Jos^h COATES; pension awarded 10 Sep 1834. SOURCE: WO120 Volume 35 page 52. INDEX # 257.

BRITISH ARMY PENSIONERS ABROAD

4th Regiment of Foot (continued)

Wm IRWIN; pension awarded 10 Sep 1834. SOURCE: WO120 Volume 35 page 52. INDEX # 258.
J^{no} LAND; pension awarded 10 Sep 1834. SOURCE: WO120 Volume 35 page 52. INDEX # 259.
Thos BYWAY; pension awarded 14 Sep 1836. SOURCE: WO120 Volume 35 page 52. INDEX # 260.
Thos CAVEY; pension awarded 14 Sep 1836. SOURCE: WO120 Volume 35 page 52. INDEX # 261.
J^{no} PROSSER; pension awarded 14 Sep 1836. SOURCE: WO120 Volume 35 page 52. INDEX # 262.
J^{no} MCCROHON; pension awarded 8 Feb 1837. SOURCE: WO120 Volume 35 page 52. INDEX # 263.
Ed^{wd} WILLIAMS; pension awarded 8 Feb 1837. SOURCE: WO120 Volume 35 page 52. INDEX # 264.
Eman^l MARTIN; pension awarded 9 Aug 1837. SOURCE: WO120 Volume 35 page 52. INDEX # 265.
Dav^d COVE; pension awarded 13 Jun 1838. SOURCE: WO120 Volume 35 page 52. INDEX # 266.

5th Regiment of Foot

Simon MANSELL; pension awarded 21 Jun 1826; residence - St. Lucia, West Indies. SOURCE: WO120 Volume 35 page 53. INDEX # 267.
J^{no} LOUGHLIN; pension awarded 20 Feb 1828. SOURCE: WO120 Volume 35 page 53. INDEX # 268.
J^{no} PATTON; pension awarded 20 Feb 1828. SOURCE: WO120 Volume 35 page 53. INDEX # 269.
Ang^s MACKINNON; pension awarded 11 Sep 1833. SOURCE: WO120 Volume 35 page 53. INDEX # 270.
J^{no} MACDONALD; pension awarded 26 Sep 1838. SOURCE: WO120 Volume 35 page 53. INDEX # 271.

6th Regiment of Foot

Ge^o ALGATE; pension awarded 25 Jun 1818; residence - Canada. SOURCE: WO120 Volume 35 page 55. INDEX # 272.
Thos WHITEHEAD; pension awarded 12 May 1819; residence - Canada. SOURCE: WO120 Volume 35 page 55. INDEX # 273.
Willm HEWSON; pension awarded 20 Mar 1822; residence - Nova Scotia, Canada. SOURCE: WO120 Volume 35 page 55. INDEX # 274.
Zach^h KENYON; pension awarded 12 Oct 1825; residence - Cape of Good Hope, South Africa. SOURCE: WO120 Volume 35 page 55. INDEX # 275.

6th Regiment of Foot

Ge^o POLLARD; pension awarded 11 Aug 1830. SOURCE: WO120 Volume 35 page 55. INDEX # 276.
Thos DEANE; pension awarded 12 Mar 1834. SOURCE: WO120 Volume 35 page 55. INDEX # 277.
Wilby GREEN; pension awarded 13 Sep 1837. SOURCE: WO120 Volume 35 page 55. INDEX # 278.
Chas SMITH; pension awarded 22 Aug 1838. SOURCE: WO120 Volume 35 page 55. INDEX # 279.
Saml WARD; pension awarded 22 Aug 1838. SOURCE: WO120 Volume 35 page 55. INDEX # 280.
Hen^y WOODHALL; pension awarded 22 Aug 1838. SOURCE: WO120 Volume 35 page 55. INDEX # 281.

7th Regiment of Foot

Thos FOWLER; pension awarded 23 May 1821; residence - Nova Scotia, Canada. SOURCE: WO120 Volume 35 page 57. INDEX # 282.
Peter MARRS; pension awarded 12 Sep 1821; residence - Nova Scotia, Canada. SOURCE: WO120 Volume 35 page 57. INDEX # 283.
Willm BROOKE; pension awarded 30 Oct 1822. SOURCE: WO120 Volume 35 page 57. INDEX # 284.
Hugh FITZPATRICK; pension awarded 20 Feb 1828. SOURCE: WO120 Volume 35 page 57. INDEX # 285.
Paolo SCISCO; pension awarded 14 Apr 1830. SOURCE: WO120 Volume 35 page 57. INDEX # 286.

8th Regiment of Foot

Chas STEWART; pension awarded 28 Dec 1818; residence - Nova Scotia, Canada. SOURCE: WO120 Volume 35 page 58. INDEX # 287.

WO120 VOLUME 35

8th Regiment of Foot (continued)

Willm SKITT; pension awarded 7 Feb 1822; residence - Canada. SOURCE: WO120 Volume 35 page 58. INDEX # 288.

Willm DARGIE; pension awarded 20 Mar 1822; residence - Nova Scotia, Canada. SOURCE: WO120 Volume 35 page 58. INDEX # 289.

Jno BOYS; pension awarded 31 Jul 1822; residence - Canada. SOURCE: WO120 Volume 35 page 58. INDEX # 290.

Jno BYRNE; pension awarded 12 May 1824; residence - Canada. SOURCE: WO120 Volume 35 page 58. INDEX # 291.

Willm NICHOL; pension awarded 30 Jun 1825; residence - Corfu, Greece. SOURCE: WO120 Volume 35 page 58. INDEX # 292.

Chas COXHEAD; pension awarded 27 Nov 1816; residence - Canada. SOURCE: WO120 Volume 35 page 58. INDEX # 293.

Jno DONAGHOE; pension awarded 26 Mar 1817; residence - Quebec, Canada. SOURCE: WO120 Volume 35 page 58. INDEX # 294.

Hugh MCCLIEVE; pension awarded 29 Sep 1819. SOURCE: WO120 Volume 35 page 58. INDEX # 295.

Wm CONNOR; pension awarded 13 Jan 1836. SOURCE: WO120 Volume 35 page 58. INDEX # 296.

Chas PATTERSON; pension awarded 13 Jan 1836. SOURCE: WO120 Volume 35 page 58. INDEX # 297.

9th Regiment of Foot

Thos STACK; pension awarded 29 Apr 1818. SOURCE: WO120 Volume 35 page 60. INDEX # 298.

Chas ARGENT; pension awarded 13 Apr 1836. SOURCE: WO120 Volume 35 page 60. INDEX # 299.

10th Regiment of Foot

Allen MCDONALD; pension awarded 21 May 1828. SOURCE: WO120 Volume 35 page 61. INDEX # 300.

11th Regiment of Foot

Edwd GILLESPIE; pension awarded 21 Aug 1817; residence - Gibraltar. SOURCE: WO120 Volume 35 page 62. INDEX # 301.

Willm VINEY; pension awarded 21 Aug 1817; residence - Gibraltar. SOURCE: WO120 Volume 35 page 62. INDEX # 302.

Fra^s CAMPBELL; pension awarded 8 Mar 1837. SOURCE: WO120 Volume 35 page 62. INDEX # 303.

Math^w FINIGAN; pension awarded 12 Jul 1837. SOURCE: WO120 Volume 35 page 62. INDEX # 304.

George STEEN; pension awarded 27 Sep 1837. SOURCE: WO120 Volume 35 page 62. INDEX # 305.

12th Regiment of Foot

Saml TODMAN; pension awarded 11 Sep 1833. SOURCE: WO120 Volume 35 page 64. INDEX # 306.

Wm ANDERSON; pension awarded 24 Feb 1818. SOURCE: WO120 Volume 35 page 64. INDEX # 307.

13th Regiment of Foot

Jno MOPSEY; pension awarded 24 Nov 1824; residence - Bengal, India. SOURCE: WO120 Volume 35 page 65. INDEX # 308.

Hen^y CHAPMAN; pension awarded 24 Nov 1824; residence - Bengal, India. SOURCE: WO120 Volume 35 page 65. INDEX # 309.

Jno COOK; pension awarded 24 Nov 1824; residence - Bengal, India. SOURCE: WO120 Volume 35 page 65. INDEX # 310.

Robt REYNOLDS; pension awarded 24 Nov 1824; residence - Bengal, India. SOURCE: WO120 Volume 35 page 65. INDEX # 311.

13th Regiment of Foot (continued)

Robt HERVEY; pension awarded 24 Nov 1824; residence - Bengal, India. SOURCE: WO120 Volume 35 page 65. INDEX # 312.
Ed^{wd} SMITH; pension awarded 24 Nov 1824; residence - Bengal, India. SOURCE: WO120 Volume 35 page 65. INDEX # 313.
Mark CARTER; pension awarded 24 Nov 1824; residence - Bengal, India. SOURCE: WO120 Volume 35 page 65. INDEX # 314.
Arth^r BOXALL; pension awarded 24 Nov 1824; residence - Bengal, India. SOURCE: WO120 Volume 35 page 65. INDEX # 315.
Robt NICHOLS; pension awarded 8 Aug 1827; residence - Bengal, India. SOURCE: WO120 Volume 35 page 65. INDEX # 316.
Ja^s GAWKE; pension awarded 8 Aug 1827; residence - Bengal, India. SOURCE: WO120 Volume 35 page 65. INDEX # 317.

14th Regiment of Foot

Ed^{wd} HARTLETT; pension awarded 25 Jul 1821; residence - India. SOURCE: WO120 Volume 35 page 67. INDEX # 318.
Thos RAYNER; pension awarded 25 Jul 1821; residence - Meerut, India. SOURCE: WO120 Volume 35 page 67. INDEX # 319.
Jno HINE; pension awarded 25 Jul 1821; residence - India. SOURCE: WO120 Volume 35 page 67. INDEX # 320.
Jno MAXWELL; pension awarded 25 Sep 1822; residence - India. SOURCE: WO120 Volume 35 page 67. INDEX # 321.
Jno CUMMINGS; pension awarded 27 Aug 1823; residence - Bengal, India. SOURCE: WO120 Volume 35 page 67. INDEX # 322.
Phil^p NIBLETT; pension awarded 25 Apr 1827; residence - Bengal, India; died 25 May 1827. SOURCE: WO120 Volume 35 page 67. INDEX # 323.
Willm SLATER; pension awarded 25 Apr 1827; residence - Bengal, India. SOURCE: WO120 Volume 35 page 67. INDEX # 324.
Ja^s TUBB; pension awarded 25 Apr 1827; residence - Bengal, India. SOURCE: WO120 Volume 35 page 67. INDEX # 325.
Saml PLOWRIGHT; pension awarded 25 Apr 1827; residence - Bengal, India. SOURCE: WO120 Volume 35 page 67. INDEX # 326.
Saml WARNER; pension awarded 25 Apr 1827; residence - Bengal, India. SOURCE: WO120 Volume 35 page 67. INDEX # 327.
Jno GUEST; pension awarded 30 May 1827; residence - Bengal, India. SOURCE: WO120 Volume 35 page 67. INDEX # 328.
Ja^s GUART; pension awarded 30 May 1827; residence - Bengal, India. SOURCE: WO120 Volume 35 page 67. INDEX # 329.
Jno THOROGOOD; pension awarded 30 May 1827; residence - Bengal, India. SOURCE: WO120 Volume 35 page 67. INDEX # 330.
Thos SMITH; pension awarded 10 Aug 1831; residence - Fort William, India. SOURCE: WO120 Volume 35 page 67. INDEX # 331.
Chas COOK; pension awarded 10 Aug 1831. SOURCE: WO120 Volume 35 page 67. INDEX # 332.
Ja^s THORNHILL; pension awarded 13 Jun 1832. SOURCE: WO120 Volume 35 page 67. INDEX # 333.

15th Regiment of Foot

Dav^d SMITH; pension awarded 4 Jan 1802; residence - Canada; died , . SOURCE: WO120 Volume 35 page 70. INDEX # 334.
Chas POTTAGE; pension awarded 9 Jan 1833. SOURCE: WO120 Volume 35 page 70. INDEX # 335.
Chas SCOTT; pension awarded 9 Jan 1833. SOURCE: WO120 Volume 35 page 70. INDEX # 336.
Jno BROWN; pension awarded 9 Jan 1833. SOURCE: WO120 Volume 35 page 70. INDEX # 337.

15th Regiment of Foot (continued)

Wm HOWERTH; pension awarded 9 Jan 1833. SOURCE: WO120 Volume 35 page 70. INDEX # 338.
Alex^r MURPHY; pension awarded 9 Jan 1833. SOURCE: WO120 Volume 35 page 70. INDEX # 339.
Ja^s BESWICK; pension awarded 11 Nov 1835; residence - Toronto, Ontario, Canada. SOURCE: WO120 Volume 35 page 70. INDEX # 340.
Edwd BOTTERILL; pension awarded 12 Jul 1837. SOURCE: WO120 Volume 35 page 70. INDEX # 341.
Bern^d CARROLL; pension awarded 11 Oct 1837. SOURCE: WO120 Volume 35 page 70. INDEX # 342.
Danl CALLAGHAN; pension awarded 15 Dec 1837; residence - Kingston, Ontario, Canada. SOURCE: WO120 Volume 35 page 70. INDEX # 343.
Wm DAVIDSON; pension awarded 15 Dec 1837. SOURCE: WO120 Volume 35 page 70. INDEX # 344.

16th Regiment of Foot

Ja^s FORD; pension awarded 25 Apr 1827; residence - Bengal, India. SOURCE: WO120 Volume 35 page 71. INDEX # 345.
Thos UNWIN; pension awarded 12 Dec 1827; residence - Ceylon. SOURCE: WO120 Volume 35 page 71. INDEX # 346.
Hen^y MCGUIRE; pension awarded 21 May 1828. SOURCE: WO120 Volume 35 page 71. INDEX # 347.
Jno KIRWIN; pension awarded 8 May 1833. SOURCE: WO120 Volume 35 page 71. INDEX # 348.
Jno PARROTT; pension awarded 8 May 1833; died 21 Oct 1832. SOURCE: WO120 Volume 35 page 71. INDEX # 349.
Ja^s SYKES; pension awarded 12 Jul 1837. SOURCE: WO120 Volume 35 page 71. INDEX # 350.

17th Regiment of Foot

Paul MCPHERSON; pension awarded 20 Jul 1819; residence - Nova Scotia. SOURCE: WO120 Volume 35 page 73. INDEX # 351.
Willm HOBBS; pension awarded 25 Sep 1822; residence - Canada. SOURCE: WO120 Volume 35 page 73. INDEX # 352.
Jos^h TURNER; pension awarded 25 Sep 1822; residence - Canada. SOURCE: WO120 Volume 35 page 73. INDEX # 353.
Jno CHAMPLEY; pension awarded 27 Aug 1823; residence - Bengal, India. SOURCE: WO120 Volume 35 page 73. INDEX # 354.
Robt DYE; pension awarded 27 Aug 1823; residence - Bengal, India. SOURCE: WO120 Volume 35 page 73. INDEX # 355.
Willm GARNHAM; pension awarded 27 Aug 1823; residence - Bengal, India. SOURCE: WO120 Volume 35 page 73. INDEX # 356.
And^w JERUTTA; pension awarded 27 Aug 1823; residence - Bengal, India. SOURCE: WO120 Volume 35 page 73. INDEX # 357.
Abr^m KENT; pension awarded 27 Aug 1823; residence - Bengal, India. SOURCE: WO120 Volume 35 page 73. INDEX # 358.
Jno LOCKETT; pension awarded 27 Aug 1823; residence - Bengal, India. SOURCE: WO120 Volume 35 page 73. INDEX # 359.
Math^w MACK; pension awarded 27 Aug 1823; residence - Bengal, India. SOURCE: WO120 Volume 35 page 73. INDEX # 360.
Jno ROBINSON; pension awarded 27 Aug 1823; residence - Bengal, India. SOURCE: WO120 Volume 35 page 73. INDEX # 361.
Jno TAPLIN; pension awarded 27 Aug 1823; residence - Bengal, India; died 4 Jan 1827 Calcutta, India. SOURCE: WO120 Volume 35 page 73. INDEX # 362.
Peter MCAULEY; pension awarded 10 Apr 1833. SOURCE: WO120 Volume 35 page 73. INDEX # 363.
Jos^h PHILLIPS; pension awarded 12 Jun 1833. SOURCE: WO120 Volume 35 page 73. INDEX # 364.
Wm KEEVERS; pension awarded 10 Sep 1834. SOURCE: WO120 Volume 35 page 73. INDEX # 365.
Jno RAWSON; pension awarded 10 Aug 1836. SOURCE: WO120 Volume 35 page 73. INDEX # 366.
Hugh CRAIG; pension awarded 14 Sep 1836. SOURCE: WO120 Volume 35 page 73. INDEX # 367.

17th Regiment of Foot (continued)

Thos EASTON; pension awarded 14 Sep 1836. SOURCE: WO120 Volume 35 page 73. INDEX # 368.
Jno CHISLETT; pension awarded 8 Feb 1837. SOURCE: WO120 Volume 35 page 73. INDEX # 369.

18th Regiment of Foot

Bernd MAGEE; pension awarded 10 Aug 1831. SOURCE: WO120 Volume 35 page 75. INDEX # 370.
Micl SWEETMAN; pension awarded 8 Feb 1832. SOURCE: WO120 Volume 35 page 75. INDEX # 371.

19th Regiment of Foot

Saml DUNT; pension awarded 11 Nov 1817; residence - Ceylon. SOURCE: WO120 Volume 35 page 77. INDEX # 372.
Abram MILLS; pension awarded 11 Nov 1817; residence - Ceylon. SOURCE: WO120 Volume 35 page 77. INDEX # 373.
Thos BURTON; pension awarded 7 Jan 1818; residence - Ceylon. SOURCE: WO120 Volume 35 page 77. INDEX # 374.
Danl COURTNEY; pension awarded 7 Jan 1818; residence - Ceylon. SOURCE: WO120 Volume 35 page 77. INDEX # 375.
Thos BERRY; pension awarded 7 Jun 1820; residence - Ceylon. SOURCE: WO120 Volume 35 page 77. INDEX # 376.
Peter THOMPSON; pension awarded 7 Jun 1820; residence - Ceylon. SOURCE: WO120 Volume 35 page 77. INDEX # 377.
Evan EDWARDS; pension awarded 7 Jun 1820; residence Ceylon; died 31 May 1832. SOURCE: WO120 Volume 35 page 77. INDEX # 378.
Thos PATTON; pension awarded 7 Jun 1820; residence - Ceylon. SOURCE: WO120 Volume 35 page 77. INDEX # 379.
Jno CASTLES; pension awarded 7 Jun 1820; residence - Ceylon. SOURCE: WO120 Volume 35 page 77. INDEX # 380.
Thos JOYCE; pension awarded 7 Jun 1820; residence - Ceylon. SOURCE: WO120 Volume 35 page 77. INDEX # 381.
Jas OBRIEN; pension awarded 7 Jun 1820; residence - Ceylon. SOURCE: WO120 Volume 35 page 77. INDEX # 382.
Robt HASKINS; pension awarded 7 Jun 1820; residence - Ceylon. SOURCE: WO120 Volume 35 page 77. INDEX # 383.
Saml JONES; pension awarded 7 Jun 1820; residence - Ceylon. SOURCE: WO120 Volume 35 page 77. INDEX # 384.
Willm WILLIAMS; pension awarded 7 Jun 1820; residence - Ceylon. SOURCE: WO120 Volume 35 page 77. INDEX # 385.
Carolus CAMPHOR; pension awarded 7 Jun 1820; residence - Ceylon. SOURCE: WO120 Volume 35 page 77. INDEX # 386.
Thos KELLY; pension awarded 7 Jun 1820; residence - Ceylon. SOURCE: WO120 Volume 35 page 77. INDEX # 387.
Davd REASE; pension awarded 7 Jun 1820; residence - Ceylon. SOURCE: WO120 Volume 35 page 77. INDEX # 388.
Willm FRYER; pension awarded 7 Jun 1820; residence - Ceylon. SOURCE: WO120 Volume 35 page 77. INDEX # 389.
Rowland HARTLEY; pension awarded 7 Jun 1820; residence - Ceylon. SOURCE: WO120 Volume 35 page 77. INDEX # 390.
Jas FRAZER; pension awarded 17 Mar 1819; residence - Cape of Good Hope, South Africa. SOURCE: WO120 Volume 35 page 77. INDEX # 391.
Jno SELLARS; pension awarded 17 Mar 1819; residence - Cape of Good Hope, South Africa. SOURCE: WO120 Volume 35 page 77. INDEX # 392.
Jas PROSSER; pension awarded 17 Mar 1819; residence - Cape of Good Hope, South Africa. SOURCE: WO120 Volume 35 page 77. INDEX # 393.

WO120 VOLUME 35

19th Regiment of Foot (continued)

Willm GEORGE; pension awarded 17 Mar 1819; residence - Cape of Good Hope, South Africa. SOURCE: WO120 Volume 35 page 77. INDEX # 394.
Ja^s RYAN; pension awarded 17 Mar 1819; residence - Cape of Good Hope, South Africa. SOURCE: WO120 Volume 35 page 77. INDEX # 395.
Robt STEVENS; pension awarded 14 Aug 1833. SOURCE: WO120 Volume 35 page 78. INDEX # 396.
Jno BELL; pension awarded 28 Oct 1818. SOURCE: WO120 Volume 35 page 78. INDEX # 397.
Owen HAGGAN; pension awarded 28 Oct 1818. SOURCE: WO120 Volume 35 page 78. INDEX # 398.
Edwd WIXLEY; pension awarded 28 Oct 1818. SOURCE: WO120 Volume 35 page 78. INDEX # 399.
Wm BROWN; pension awarded 28 Oct 1818. SOURCE: WO120 Volume 35 page 78. INDEX # 400.
Benjn TOMBLIN; pension awarded 28 Oct 1818. SOURCE: WO120 Volume 35 page 78. INDEX # 401.
Wm CANNON; pension awarded 28 Oct 1818. SOURCE: WO120 Volume 35 page 78. INDEX # 402.
Step^n HINDLE; pension awarded 28 Oct 1818. SOURCE: WO120 Volume 35 page 78. INDEX # 403.
Tim^y BRODIE; pension awarded 28 Oct 1818. SOURCE: WO120 Volume 35 page 78. INDEX # 404.
Caroley PEORGE; pension awarded 28 Oct 1818. SOURCE: WO120 Volume 35 page 78. INDEX # 405.
Ja^s WRIGHT; pension awarded 28 Oct 1818. SOURCE: WO120 Volume 35 page 78. INDEX # 406.
Richd MUSGROVE; pension awarded 28 Oct 1818. SOURCE: WO120 Volume 35 page 78. INDEX # 407.

20th Regiment of Foot

Jno POTTER; pension awarded 19 Jul 1826; residence - Bombay, India. SOURCE: WO120 Volume 35 page 79. INDEX # 408.
Robt THORNLEY; pension awarded 19 Jul 1826; residence - Bombay, India. SOURCE: WO120 Volume 35 page 79. INDEX # 409.
Jno KEYS; pension awarded 14 Nov 1818; residence - Quebec, Quebec, Canada. SOURCE: WO120 Volume 35 page 79. INDEX # 410.
Ge^o CHATTEN; pension awarded 8 Aug 1827; residence - Bombay, India. SOURCE: WO120 Volume 35 page 79. INDEX # 411.
Don^d MORRISON; pension awarded 8 Aug 1827; residence - Bombay, India. SOURCE: WO120 Volume 35 page 79. INDEX # 412.
Richd BAXTER; pension awarded 8 Aug 1827; residence - Bombay, India. SOURCE: WO120 Volume 35 page 79. INDEX # 413.
Hen^y DOYLE; pension awarded 8 Aug 1827; residence - Bombay, India. SOURCE: WO120 Volume 35 page 79. INDEX # 414.
And^w DUNN; pension awarded 8 Aug 1827; residence - Bombay, India. SOURCE: WO120 Volume 35 page 79. INDEX # 415.
Saml MCCLEMMENS; pension awarded 8 Aug 1827; residence - Bombay, India. SOURCE: WO120 Volume 35 page 79. INDEX # 416.
Fra^s DEDOMINICO; pension awarded 29 Oct 1828. SOURCE: WO120 Volume 35 page 79. INDEX # 417.
Fra^s MCDONALD; pension awarded 29 Oct 1828. SOURCE: WO120 Volume 35 page 79. INDEX # 418.
Thos BROOKS; pension awarded 5 Aug 1829. SOURCE: WO120 Volume 35 page 79. INDEX # 419.
Thos CRANE; pension awarded 5 Aug 1829. SOURCE: WO120 Volume 35 page 79. INDEX # 420.
Willm DRABY; pension awarded 5 Aug 1829. SOURCE: WO120 Volume 35 page 79. INDEX # 421.
Jno WILTSHAN; pension awarded 5 Aug 1829. SOURCE: WO120 Volume 35 page 79. INDEX # 422.
Dav^d YOUNG; pension awarded 5 Aug 1829. SOURCE: WO120 Volume 35 page 79. INDEX # 423.
Hen^y DEER; pension awarded 11 Aug 1830. SOURCE: WO120 Volume 35 page 79. INDEX # 424.
Jno BROWN; pension awarded 11 Aug 1830. SOURCE: WO120 Volume 35 page 79. INDEX # 425.
Ja^s POLLARD; pension awarded 11 Aug 1830. SOURCE: WO120 Volume 35 page 79. INDEX # 426.
Ja^s KOTCHEL; pension awarded 11 Aug 1830. SOURCE: WO120 Volume 35 page 79. INDEX # 427.
Ja^s LARBY; pension awarded 14 Dec 1836. SOURCE: WO120 Volume 35 page 79. INDEX # 428.
Chas WOODWARD; pension awarded 11 Oct 1837. SOURCE: WO120 Volume 35 page 79. INDEX # 429.
Edwd HURD; pension awarded 11 Oct 1837. SOURCE: WO120 Volume 35 page 79. INDEX # 430.
Ja^s QUARTERMAN; pension awarded 11 Oct 1837. SOURCE: WO120 Volume 35 page 79. INDEX # 431.

21st Regiment of Foot

Jos^h SHAW; pension awarded 14 Sep 1836. SOURCE: WO120 Volume 35 page 82. INDEX # 432.
Neil GRIBBON; pension awarded 14 Sep 1836. SOURCE: WO120 Volume 35 page 82. INDEX # 433.
Fra^s THORPE; pension awarded 14 Sep 1836. SOURCE: WO120 Volume 35 page 82. INDEX # 434.
Matt^w WALES; pension awarded 14 Sep 1836. SOURCE: WO120 Volume 35 page 82. INDEX # 435.
Wm A. MACKAY; pension awarded 8 Feb 1837. SOURCE: WO120 Volume 35 page 82. INDEX # 436.
Wm KEEFE; pension awarded 23 Aug 1837. SOURCE: WO120 Volume 35 page 82. INDEX # 437.
Wm BURNS; pension awarded 23 Aug 1837. SOURCE: WO120 Volume 35 page 82. INDEX # 438.

22nd Regiment of Foot

Ja^s MARKEY; pension awarded 17 Mar 1819; residence - Cape of Good Hope, South Africa. SOURCE: WO120 Volume 35 page 84. INDEX # 439.
Ja^s SUTHERLAND; pension awarded 15 Dec 1819. SOURCE: WO120 Volume 35 page 84. INDEX # 440.
Jos^h BIRD; pension awarded 15 Dec 1819. SOURCE: WO120 Volume 35 page 84. INDEX # 441.
Willm CLOVER; pension awarded 15 Dec 1819. SOURCE: WO120 Volume 35 page 84. INDEX # 442.
Richd FORDER; pension awarded 15 Dec 1819. SOURCE: WO120 Volume 35 page 84. INDEX # 443.
Thos LAMPOORT; pension awarded 15 Dec 1819. SOURCE: WO120 Volume 35 page 84. INDEX # 444.
Job BARNARD; pension awarded 15 Dec 1819. SOURCE: WO120 Volume 35 page 84. INDEX # 445.
Wm BLACKBURN; pension awarded 15 Dec 1819. SOURCE: WO120 Volume 35 page 84. INDEX # 446.
Jos^h MONK; pension awarded 15 Dec 1819. SOURCE: WO120 Volume 35 page 84. INDEX # 447.
Wm HOLLAND; pension awarded 15 Dec 1819. SOURCE: WO120 Volume 35 page 84. INDEX # 448.
Isaac WEBB; pension awarded 15 Dec 1819. SOURCE: WO120 Volume 35 page 84. INDEX # 449.
Saml HOBLEY; pension awarded 15 Dec 1819. SOURCE: WO120 Volume 35 page 84. INDEX # 450.
Benjn NICHOLS; pension awarded 15 Dec 1819. SOURCE: WO120 Volume 35 page 84. INDEX # 451.
Richd HIGGINSON; pension awarded 15 Dec 1819. SOURCE: WO120 Volume 35 page 84. INDEX # 452.
Wm KENDRICK; pension awarded 15 Dec 1819. SOURCE: WO120 Volume 35 page 84. INDEX # 453.
Wm CLARKE; pension awarded 15 Dec 1819. SOURCE: WO120 Volume 35 page 84. INDEX # 454.
Ja^s MARTIN; pension awarded 15 Dec 1819. SOURCE: WO120 Volume 35 page 84. INDEX # 455.
Ed^{wd} KENYON; pension awarded 15 Dec 1819. SOURCE: WO120 Volume 35 page 84. INDEX # 456.
Jno SHAW; pension awarded 15 Dec 1819. SOURCE: WO120 Volume 35 page 84. INDEX # 457.
Jno WHITTY; pension awarded 15 Dec 1819. SOURCE: WO120 Volume 35 page 84. INDEX # 458.
And^w MCLEAN; pension awarded 15 Dec 1819. SOURCE: WO120 Volume 35 page 84. INDEX # 459.
Jno BANKS; pension awarded 15 Dec 1819. SOURCE: WO120 Volume 35 page 84. INDEX # 460.
Jno PALMER; pension awarded 15 Dec 1819. SOURCE: WO120 Volume 35 page 84. INDEX # 461.
Ja^s KNIGHT; pension awarded 15 Dec 1819. SOURCE: WO120 Volume 35 page 84. INDEX # 462.
Alex^r TURNER; pension awarded 15 Dec 1819. SOURCE: WO120 Volume 35 page 85. INDEX # 463.
Wm SALISBURY; pension awarded 15 Dec 1819; residence - Port Louis, Mauritius. SOURCE: WO120 Volume 35 page 85. INDEX # 464.
Wm Aug^s MAITLAND; pension awarded 15 Dec 1819. SOURCE: WO120 Volume 35 page 85. INDEX # 465.
Jno MCDONALD; pension awarded 15 Dec 1819. SOURCE: WO120 Volume 35 page 85. INDEX # 466.
Jno WHITMORE; pension awarded 15 Dec 1819. SOURCE: WO120 Volume 35 page 85. INDEX # 467.
Ed^{wd} BOUCHER; pension awarded 15 Dec 1819. SOURCE: WO120 Volume 35 page 85. INDEX # 468.
Ed^{wd} PAWSON; pension awarded 11 Jun 1834; residence - Jamaica. SOURCE: WO120 Volume 35 page 85. INDEX # 469.
Ge^o MEEKLEY; pension awarded 13 Jul 1836. SOURCE: WO120 Volume 35 page 85. INDEX # 470.

23rd Regiment of Foot

Jno CASSADY; pension awarded 5 Aug 1818; residence - New South Wales, Australia. SOURCE: WO120 Volume 35 page 86. INDEX # 471.
Wm WESLEY; pension awarded 11 Sep 1833. SOURCE: WO120 Volume 35 page 86. INDEX # 472.
Jno GOULD; pension awarded 12 Nov 1834. SOURCE: WO120 Volume 35 page 86. INDEX # 473.

WO120 VOLUME 35

23rd Regiment of Foot (continued)

Carey SCOTT; pension awarded 12 Nov 1834. SOURCE: WO120 Volume 35 page 86. INDEX # 474.

24th Regiment of Foot

Geo WARD; pension awarded 12 May 1819. SOURCE: WO120 Volume 35 page 88. INDEX # 475.
Willm LOWE; pension awarded 7 Feb 1822; residence - Cape of Good Hope, South Africa. SOURCE: WO120 Volume 35 page 88. INDEX # 476.
Isaac RUBY; pension awarded 7 Feb 1822; residence - Cape of Good Hope, South Africa. SOURCE: WO120 Volume 35 page 88. INDEX # 477.
Corns NURTON; pension awarded 25 Sep 1822; residence - Canada. SOURCE: WO120 Volume 35 page 88. INDEX # 478.
Jno YORK; pension awarded 27 Aug 1823; residence - Bengal, India. SOURCE: WO120 Volume 35 page 88. INDEX # 479.
Jas TAYLOR; pension awarded 27 Aug 1823; residence - Bengal, India. SOURCE: WO120 Volume 35 page 88. INDEX # 480.
Paul MAURICE; pension awarded 27 Aug 1823; residence - Bengal, India. SOURCE: WO120 Volume 35 page 88. INDEX # 481.
Wm TRACEY; pension awarded 20 Feb 1828. SOURCE: WO120 Volume 35 page 88. INDEX # 482.
Jno PAYLOR; pension awarded 14 Dec 1831. SOURCE: WO120 Volume 35 page 88. INDEX # 483.
Jno WATT; pension awarded 10 Nov 1835. SOURCE: WO120 Volume 35 page 88. INDEX # 484.
Thomas SKYE; pension awarded 12 Oct 1836. SOURCE: WO120 Volume 35 page 88. INDEX # 485.
Jno PEARSON; pension awarded 11 Jan 1837. SOURCE: WO120 Volume 35 page 88. INDEX # 486.
Edmd KEEFFE; pension awarded 11 Jan 1837. SOURCE: WO120 Volume 35 page 88. INDEX # 487.
Thos TURNBULL; pension awarded 10 Jan 1838. SOURCE: WO120 Volume 35 page 88. INDEX # 488.
Jno MONAGHAN; pension awarded 10 Jan 1838. SOURCE: WO120 Volume 35 page 88. INDEX # 489.
Patk DUGGAN; pension awarded 23 Oct 1838. SOURCE: WO120 Volume 35 page 88. INDEX # 490.
Thos MCKEE; pension awarded 26 Dec 1838. SOURCE: WO120 Volume 35 page 88. INDEX # 491.

25th Regiment of Foot

Peter ROBERTSON; pension awarded 13 Jan 1836. SOURCE: WO120 Volume 35 page 90. INDEX # 492.

26th Regiment of Foot

Thos DEACON; pension awarded 25 Jun 1818; residence - Canada. SOURCE: WO120 Volume 35 page 92. INDEX # 493.
Robt DONALDSON; pension awarded 24 Oct 1821; residence - Gibraltar. SOURCE: WO120 Volume 35 page 92. INDEX # 494.
Jno GEORGE; pension awarded 24 Oct 1821; residence - Gibraltar. SOURCE: WO120 Volume 35 page 92. INDEX # 495.
Danl DURHAM; pension awarded 21 Dec 1821; residence - Gibraltar. SOURCE: WO120 Volume 35 page 92. INDEX # 496.
Alexr IMBRIE; pension awarded 21 Dec 1821; residence - Gibraltar. SOURCE: WO120 Volume 35 page 92. INDEX # 497.
Edwd BYRNE; pension awarded 20 Feb 1828. SOURCE: WO120 Volume 35 page 92. INDEX # 498.
Jas WALSH; pension awarded 20 Feb 1828. SOURCE: WO120 Volume 35 page 92. INDEX # 499.
Geo PYKE; pension awarded 23 Aug 1837. SOURCE: WO120 Volume 35 page 92. INDEX # 500.
Wm GRANT; pension awarded 27 Jun 1838. SOURCE: WO120 Volume 35 page 92. INDEX # 501.
Robt PALMER; pension awarded 27 Jun 1838. SOURCE: WO120 Volume 35 page 92. INDEX # 502.
Jno WILKINSON; pension awarded 27 Jun 1838. SOURCE: WO120 Volume 35 page 92. INDEX # 503.

27th Regiment of Foot

Jno CAMPBELL; pension awarded 7 Dec 1820; residence - Canada. SOURCE: WO120 Volume 35 page 94. INDEX # 504.
Jno JOHNSTON; pension awarded 24 Oct 1821; residence - Canada. SOURCE: WO120 Volume 35 page 94. INDEX # 505.
Fras KELLY; pension awarded 7 Feb 1822; residence - Canada. SOURCE: WO120 Volume 35 page 94. INDEX # 506.
Willm OXBOROUGH; pension awarded 1 May 1822; residence - Gibraltar. SOURCE: WO120 Volume 35 page 94. INDEX # 507.
Nichs SMITH; pension awarded 1 May 1822. SOURCE: WO120 Volume 35 page 94. INDEX # 508.
Willm MOUNTAIN; pension awarded 30 Oct 1822; residence - Canada. SOURCE: WO120 Volume 35 page 94. INDEX # 509.
Alexr ACHESON; pension awarded 11 Jun 1817; residence - Canada. SOURCE: WO120 Volume 35 page 94. INDEX # 510.
Wm JORDAN; pension awarded 20 Jun 1817. SOURCE: WO120 Volume 35 page 94. INDEX # 511.
Peter FULLAN; pension awarded 26 Mar 1817; residence - Canada. SOURCE: WO120 Volume 35 page 94. INDEX # 512.
Jno HENDERSON; pension awarded 11 Jun 1817; residence - Quebec, Canada. SOURCE: WO120 Volume 35 page 94. INDEX # 513.
Jno SHAW; pension awarded 30 Jan 1828; residence - Gibraltar. SOURCE: WO120 Volume 35 page 94. INDEX # 514.
Peter FULLAM; pension awarded 19 Jun 1822. SOURCE: WO120 Volume 35 page 94. INDEX # 515.
Jno HENDERSON; pension awarded 19 Jun 1822. SOURCE: WO120 Volume 35 page 94. INDEX # 516.
Wm MCMULLEN; pension awarded 19 Jun 1822. SOURCE: WO120 Volume 35 page 94. INDEX # 517.
Patk KOUGH; pension awarded 9 Feb 1831. SOURCE: WO120 Volume 35 page 94. INDEX # 518.

28th Regiment of Foot

Jas TAYLOR; pension awarded 12 Oct 1825; residence - Corfu, Greece. SOURCE: WO120 Volume 35 page 96. INDEX # 519.
Jno MORGAN; pension awarded 7 Mar 1827. SOURCE: WO120 Volume 35 page 96. INDEX # 520.
Jas KENNEDY; pension awarded 13 Jun 1838. SOURCE: WO120 Volume 35 page 96. INDEX # 521.
Patk WHELAN; pension awarded 13 Jun 1838. SOURCE: WO120 Volume 35 page 96. INDEX # 522.
Jno KEOUGH; pension awarded 8 Aug 1838. SOURCE: WO120 Volume 35 page 96. INDEX # 523.
Jno REGAN; pension awarded 8 Aug 1838. SOURCE: WO120 Volume 35 page 96. INDEX # 524.
Michl HAWKINS; pension awarded 8 Aug 1838. SOURCE: WO120 Volume 35 page 96. INDEX # 525.
Martin HUGHES; pension awarded 8 Aug 1838. SOURCE: WO120 Volume 35 page 96. INDEX # 526.
Jno RAITING; pension awarded 8 Aug 1838. SOURCE: WO120 Volume 35 page 96. INDEX # 527.
Jno KENNEDY; pension awarded 8 Aug 1838. SOURCE: WO120 Volume 35 page 96. INDEX # 528.
Silvester MURPHY; pension awarded 8 Aug 1838. SOURCE: WO120 Volume 35 page 96. INDEX # 529.
Thos NEILL; pension awarded 8 Aug 1838. SOURCE: WO120 Volume 35 page 96. INDEX # 530.

29th Regiment of Foot

Peter ASKINS; pension awarded 14 Sep 1831. SOURCE: WO120 Volume 35 page 98. INDEX # 531.
Alexr GILLON; pension awarded 13 Feb 1833. SOURCE: WO120 Volume 35 page 98. INDEX # 532.
Robt SHERLOCK; pension awarded 13 Aug 1834. SOURCE: WO120 Volume 35 page 98. INDEX # 533.
Geo WYSE; pension awarded 10 May 1837. SOURCE: WO120 Volume 35 page 98. INDEX # 534.
Jas DOUGHERTY; pension awarded 10 May 1837. SOURCE: WO120 Volume 35 page 98. INDEX # 535.
Laughlan THOMPSON; pension awarded 14 Mar 1838. SOURCE: WO120 Volume 35 page 98. INDEX # 536.
Thos MEADOWS; pension awarded 28 Mar 1838. SOURCE: WO120 Volume 35 page 98. INDEX # 537.

WO120 VOLUME 35

30th Regiment of Foot

Willm FLINT; pension awarded 17 Mar 1819; residence - Cape of Good Hope, South Africa. SOURCE: WO120 Volume 35 page 100. INDEX # 538.

Robt BIRD; pension awarded 17 Mar 1819; residence - Cape of Good Hope, South Africa. SOURCE: WO120 Volume 35 page 100. INDEX # 539.

Jno BURKE; pension awarded 29 Sep 1819; residence - Canada. SOURCE: WO120 Volume 35 page 100. INDEX # 540.

Willm CARTHORN; pension awarded 7 Feb 1821; residence - India. SOURCE: WO120 Volume 35 page 100. INDEX # 541.

Willm BESSENT; pension awarded 7 Feb 1821; residence - India; died 5 Dec 1820. SOURCE: WO120 Volume 35 page 100. INDEX # 542.

Robt MURRAY; pension awarded 4 Jun 1823; residence - India; died 15 Dec 1824. SOURCE: WO120 Volume 35 page 100. INDEX # 543.

Thos BIBBEY; pension awarded 23 Nov 1825; residence - India; died 27 Jan 1832. SOURCE: WO120 Volume 35 page 100. INDEX # 544.

Thos BROWN; pension awarded 23 Nov 1825; residence - India. SOURCE: WO120 Volume 35 page 100. INDEX # 545.

Robt HEADY; pension awarded 13 Dec 1826; residence - Madras, India; died 23 Mar 1827. SOURCE: WO120 Volume 35 page 100. INDEX # 546.

Moses WESTWOOD; pension awarded 31 Oct 1827; residence - Madras, India. SOURCE: WO120 Volume 35 page 100. INDEX # 547.

Alex^r MCDONALD; pension awarded 31 Oct 1827; residence - Madras, India. SOURCE: WO120 Volume 35 page 100. INDEX # 548.

Abra^m WRIGHT; pension awarded 31 Oct 1827; residence - Madras, India. SOURCE: WO120 Volume 35 page 100. INDEX # 549.

Jos^h AMERY; pension awarded 31 Oct 1827; residence - Madras, India. SOURCE: WO120 Volume 35 page 100. INDEX # 550.

And^w BLACK; pension awarded 31 Oct 1827; residence - Madras, India. SOURCE: WO120 Volume 35 page 100. INDEX # 551.

Isaac BOWERS; pension awarded 31 Oct 1827; residence - Madras, India. SOURCE: WO120 Volume 35 page 100. INDEX # 552.

Jos^h BELL; pension awarded 31 Oct 1827; residence - Madras, India. SOURCE: WO120 Volume 35 page 100. INDEX # 553.

Wm BROWN; pension awarded 31 Oct 1827; residence - Madras, India. SOURCE: WO120 Volume 35 page 100. INDEX # 554.

Thos BROWN; pension awarded 31 Oct 1827; residence - Madras, India. SOURCE: WO120 Volume 35 page 100. INDEX # 555.

Wm CARTER; pension awarded 31 Oct 1827; residence - Madras, India. SOURCE: WO120 Volume 35 page 100. INDEX # 556.

Step^n COOK; pension awarded 31 Oct 1827; residence - Madras, India. SOURCE: WO120 Volume 35 page 100. INDEX # 557.

Thos CROWE; pension awarded 31 Oct 1827; residence - Madras, India. SOURCE: WO120 Volume 35 page 100. INDEX # 558.

Chas DUPREE; pension awarded 31 Oct 1827; residence - Madras, India. SOURCE: WO120 Volume 35 page 100. INDEX # 559.

Wm FLETCHER; pension awarded 31 Oct 1827; residence - Madras, India. SOURCE: WO120 Volume 35 page 100. INDEX # 560.

Thos GAINER; pension awarded 31 Oct 1827; residence - Madras, India. SOURCE: WO120 Volume 35 page 100. INDEX # 561.

Jos^h HARDING; pension awarded 31 Oct 1827; residence - Madras, India. SOURCE: WO120 Volume 35 page 101. INDEX # 562.

Saml HEATTEY; pension awarded 31 Oct 1827; residence - Madras, India. SOURCE: WO120 Volume 35 page 101. INDEX # 563.

BRITICH ARMY PENSIONERS ABROAD

30th Regiment of Foot (continued)

Wm KIRK; pension awarded 31 Oct 1827; residence - Madras, India. SOURCE: WO120 Volume 35 page 101. INDEX # 564.

J^{no} KERR; pension awarded 31 Oct 1827; residence - Madras, India. SOURCE: WO120 Volume 35 page 101. INDEX # 565.

Thos MEAKIN; pension awarded 31 Oct 1827; residence - Madras, India. SOURCE: WO120 Volume 35 page 101. INDEX # 566.

Wm MITCHELMORE; pension awarded 31 Oct 1827; residence - Madras, India. SOURCE: WO120 Volume 35 page 101. INDEX # 567.

Wm MAPISH; pension awarded 31 Oct 1827; residence - Madras, India. SOURCE: WO120 Volume 35 page 101. INDEX # 568.

Thos MILLETT; pension awarded 31 Oct 1827; residence - Madras, India. SOURCE: WO120 Volume 35 page 101. INDEX # 569.

J^{no} MEASURES; pension awarded 31 Oct 1827; residence - Madras, India; died 18 Feb 1828. SOURCE: WO120 Volume 35 page 101. INDEX # 570.

Ja^s MOULDER; pension awarded 31 Oct 1827; residence - Madras, India. SOURCE: WO120 Volume 35 page 101. INDEX # 571.

Saml MINNY; pension awarded 31 Oct 1827; residence - Madras, India. SOURCE: WO120 Volume 35 page 101. INDEX # 572.

Hen^y PRESTON; pension awarded 31 Oct 1827; residence - Madras, India. SOURCE: WO120 Volume 35 page 101. INDEX # 573.

Robt PANTONY; pension awarded 31 Oct 1827; residence - Madras, India. SOURCE: WO120 Volume 35 page 101. INDEX # 574.

Wm PEPPER; pension awarded 31 Oct 1827; residence - Madras, India. SOURCE: WO120 Volume 35 page 101. INDEX # 575.

Wm ROWE; pension awarded 31 Oct 1827; residence - Madras, India. SOURCE: WO120 Volume 35 page 101. INDEX # 576.

Wm RICHARDSON; pension awarded 31 Oct 1827; residence - Madras, India. SOURCE: WO120 Volume 35 page 101. INDEX # 577.

Wm SMITH; pension awarded 31 Oct 1827; residence - Madras, India. SOURCE: WO120 Volume 35 page 101. INDEX # 578.

Jos^h STENNET; pension awarded 31 Oct 1827; residence - Madras, India. SOURCE: WO120 Volume 35 page 101. INDEX # 579.

Matt^w SEWELL; pension awarded 31 Oct 1827; residence - Madras, India. SOURCE: WO120 Volume 35 page 101. INDEX # 580.

Thos THOMPSON; pension awarded 31 Oct 1827; residence - Madras, India. SOURCE: WO120 Volume 35 page 101. INDEX # 581.

Thos USHER; pension awarded 31 Oct 1827; residence - Madras, India. SOURCE: WO120 Volume 35 page 101. INDEX # 582.

J^{no} VICKERS; pension awarded 31 Oct 1827; residence - Madras, India. SOURCE: WO120 Volume 35 page 101. INDEX # 583.

J^{no} WINDSOR; pension awarded 31 Oct 1827; residence - Madras, India. SOURCE: WO120 Volume 35 page 101. INDEX # 584.

Thos WELLS; pension awarded 31 Oct 1827; residence - Madras, India. SOURCE: WO120 Volume 35 page 101. INDEX # 585.

Jos^h WELLS; pension awarded 31 Oct 1827; residence - Madras, India. SOURCE: WO120 Volume 35 page 102. INDEX # 586.

Thos WILLIAMS; pension awarded 31 Oct 1827; residence - Madras, India. SOURCE: WO120 Volume 35 page 102. INDEX # 587.

Simon WHITE; pension awarded 31 Oct 1827; residence - Madras, India. SOURCE: WO120 Volume 35 page 102. INDEX # 588.

Wm WHITE; pension awarded 31 Oct 1827; residence - Madras, India. SOURCE: WO120 Volume 35 page 102. INDEX # 589.

30th Regiment of Foot (continued)

Thos DUTTON; pension awarded 13 Sep 1820. SOURCE: WO120 Volume 35 page 102. INDEX # 590.
Thos ADCOCK; pension awarded 21 May 1828. SOURCE: WO120 Volume 35 page 102. INDEX # 591.
Timy GITTINGS; pension awarded 21 May 1828. SOURCE: WO120 Volume 35 page 102. INDEX # 592.
James HARRISON; pension awarded 21 May 1828. SOURCE: WO120 Volume 35 page 102. INDEX # 593.
Robt MONK; pension awarded 21 May 1828. SOURCE: WO120 Volume 35 page 102. INDEX # 594.
Richd MALKIN; pension awarded 21 May 1828. SOURCE: WO120 Volume 35 page 102. INDEX # 595.
John MONDIDAN; pension awarded 21 May 1828. SOURCE: WO120 Volume 35 page 102. INDEX # 596.
Wm CHERRY; pension awarded 11 Nov 1829. SOURCE: WO120 Volume 35 page 102. INDEX # 597.
Jno FRANKLIN; pension awarded 11 Nov 1829. SOURCE: WO120 Volume 35 page 102. INDEX # 598.
Wm MARSHALL; pension awarded 11 Nov 1829. SOURCE: WO120 Volume 35 page 102. INDEX # 599.
Jno MASKELL; pension awarded 11 Nov 1829. SOURCE: WO120 Volume 35 page 102. INDEX # 600.
Job SMITH; pension awarded 11 Nov 1829. SOURCE: WO120 Volume 35 page 102. INDEX # 601.
Wm COLEMAN; pension awarded 11 Nov 1829. SOURCE: WO120 Volume 35 page 102. INDEX # 602.
Jas FISHER; pension awarded 11 Nov 1829. SOURCE: WO120 Volume 35 page 102. INDEX # 603.
Jas GILSON; pension awarded 11 Nov 1829. SOURCE: WO120 Volume 35 page 102. INDEX # 604.
Wm HENDRICK; pension awarded 11 Nov 1829. SOURCE: WO120 Volume 35 page 102. INDEX # 605.
Jno KENDALL; pension awarded 11 Nov 1829. SOURCE: WO120 Volume 35 page 102. INDEX # 606.
Jno LAWRENCE; pension awarded 11 Nov 1829. SOURCE: WO120 Volume 35 page 102. INDEX # 607.
Jas LAMBERT; pension awarded 11 Nov 1829. SOURCE: WO120 Volume 35 page 102. INDEX # 608.
Jas ROGERS; pension awarded 11 Nov 1829. SOURCE: WO120 Volume 35 page 102. INDEX # 609.
Giles SEDDON; pension awarded 11 Nov 1829. SOURCE: WO120 Volume 35 page 103. INDEX # 610.
Wm SMITH; pension awarded 11 Nov 1829; residence - Madras, India. SOURCE: WO120 Volume 35 page 103. INDEX # 611.
Chas SNOBER; pension awarded 11 Nov 1829. SOURCE: WO120 Volume 35 page 103. INDEX # 612.
Jas TODD; pension awarded 11 Nov 1829. SOURCE: WO120 Volume 35 page 102. INDEX # 613.
Jno WOODS; pension awarded 11 Nov 1829. SOURCE: WO120 Volume 35 page 103. INDEX # 614.
Wm SMITH; pension awarded 10 Feb 1830. SOURCE: WO120 Volume 35 page 103. INDEX # 615.

32nd Regiment of Foot

Peter BINGHAM; pension awarded 12 Oct 1825; died 16 Feb 1827. SOURCE: WO120 Volume 35 page 104. INDEX # 616.
Jno SMITH; pension awarded 17 Dec 1814; residence - Canada. SOURCE: WO120 Volume 35 page 104. INDEX # 617.
Jno HALL; pension awarded 9 Jan 1833. SOURCE: WO120 Volume 35 page 104. INDEX # 618.
Jno ROGERS; pension awarded 12 Feb 1834. SOURCE: WO120 Volume 35 page 104. INDEX # 619.
Jonn COVE; pension awarded 11 Nov 1835. SOURCE: WO120 Volume 35 page 104. INDEX # 620.
Wm MILLER; pension awarded 11 Nov 1835. SOURCE: WO120 Volume 35 page 104. INDEX # 621.
Robt GRAHAM; pension awarded 14 Dec 1836. SOURCE: WO120 Volume 35 page 104. INDEX # 622.
Michl ROURKE; pension awarded 14 Dec 1836. SOURCE: WO120 Volume 35 page 104. INDEX # 623.
Josh HARRISON; pension awarded 14 Dec 1836. SOURCE: WO120 Volume 35 page 104. INDEX # 624.
Wm ANEAN; pension awarded 23 Oct 1838. SOURCE: WO120 Volume 35 page 104. INDEX # 625.
Wm MCCLEAN; pension awarded 23 Oct 1838. SOURCE: WO120 Volume 35 page 104. INDEX # 626.
Thos HUGHES; pension awarded 23 Oct 1838. SOURCE: WO120 Volume 35 page 104. INDEX # 627.

34th Regiment of Foot

Benjn RICHES; pension awarded 7 Feb 1821; residence - India. SOURCE: WO120 Volume 35 page 108. INDEX # 628.
Thos KELLY; pension awarded 4 Jun 1823; residence - Madras, India. SOURCE: WO120 Volume 35 page 108. INDEX # 629.
Sylvester INCE; pension awarded 4 Jun 1823; residence - Madras, India. SOURCE: WO120 Volume 35 page 108. INDEX # 630.

34th Regiment of Foot (continued)

Fra^s URCY; pension awarded 4 Jun 1823; residence - Madras, India. SOURCE: WO120 Volume 35 page 108. INDEX # 631.

Jno SWEET; pension awarded 4 Jun 1823; residence - Madras, India. SOURCE: WO120 Volume 35 page 108. INDEX # 632.

Alex^r DARBY; pension awarded 4 Jun 1823; residence - Madras, India. SOURCE: WO120 Volume 35 page 108. INDEX # 633.

Matt^w CAVALAN; pension awarded 4 Jun 1823; residence - Madras, India. SOURCE: WO120 Volume 35 page 108. INDEX # 634.

Robt HAMILTON; pension awarded 4 Jun 1823; residence - Madras, India. SOURCE: WO120 Volume 35 page 108. INDEX # 635.

Thos KNIGHT; pension awarded 4 Jun 1823; residence - Madras, India. SOURCE: WO120 Volume 35 page 108. INDEX # 636.

Thos KENT; pension awarded 4 Jun 1823; residence - Madras, India. SOURCE: WO120 Volume 35 page 108. INDEX # 637.

Ja^s GRAVES; pension awarded 4 Jun 1823; residence - Madras, India. SOURCE: WO120 Volume 35 page 108. INDEX # 638.

Thos HALKETT; pension awarded 4 Jun 1823; residence - Madras, India. SOURCE: WO120 Volume 35 page 108. INDEX # 639.

Fred^k FISHER; pension awarded 4 Jun 1823; residence - Madras, India. SOURCE: WO120 Volume 35 page 108. INDEX # 640.

Willm MATTOX; pension awarded 4 Jun 1823; residence - Madras, India. SOURCE: WO120 Volume 35 page 108. INDEX # 641.

Ja^s MCLARE; pension awarded 4 Jun 1823; residence - Madras, India. SOURCE: WO120 Volume 35 page 108. INDEX # 642.

Robt POVER; pension awarded 4 Jun 1823; residence - Madras, India. SOURCE: WO120 Volume 35 page 108. INDEX # 643.

Nathl KEATHLEY; pension awarded 4 Jun 1823; residence - Madras, India; died 19 Feb 1827. SOURCE: WO120 Volume 35 page 108. INDEX # 644.

Jno KENNY; pension awarded 4 Jun 1823; residence - Madras, India. SOURCE: WO120 Volume 35 page 108. INDEX # 645.

Robt LOWRIE; pension awarded 4 Jun 1823; residence - Madras, India. SOURCE: WO120 Volume 35 page 108. INDEX # 646.

Jno SILVESTER; pension awarded 4 Jun 1823; residence - Madras, India. SOURCE: WO120 Volume 35 page 108. INDEX # 647.

Jno CHURCH; pension awarded 4 Jun 1823; residence - Madras, India. SOURCE: WO120 Volume 35 page 108. INDEX # 648.

Jno KING; pension awarded 4 Jun 1823; residence - Madras, India. SOURCE: WO120 Volume 35 page 108. INDEX # 649.

Phil^p MOORE; pension awarded 4 Jun 1823; residence - Madras, India. SOURCE: WO120 Volume 35 page 108. INDEX # 650.

Robt HEIGUE; pension awarded 4 Jun 1823; residence - Madras, India. SOURCE: WO120 Volume 35 page 108. INDEX # 651.

Edw^{dn} MEPHAM; pension awarded 4 Jun 1823; residence - Madras, India. SOURCE: WO120 Volume 35 page 109. INDEX # 652.

Thos CRIMMINS; pension awarded 4 Jun 1823; residence - Madras, India. SOURCE: WO120 Volume 35 page 109. INDEX # 653.

Thos HIGHFIELD; pension awarded 4 Jun 1823; residence - Madras, India. SOURCE: WO120 Volume 35 page 109. INDEX # 654.

Ja^s BROCK; pension awarded 4 Jun 1823; residence - Madras, India. SOURCE: WO120 Volume 35 page 109. INDEX # 655.

Pat^k GILROY; pension awarded 4 Jun 1823; residence - Madras, India. SOURCE: WO120 Volume 35 page 109. INDEX # 656.

34th Regiment of Foot (continued)

Willm WILSON; pension awarded 4 Jun 1823; residence - Madras, India. SOURCE: WO120 Volume 35 page 109. INDEX # 657.

Jno CULLEN; pension awarded 4 Jun 1823; residence - Madras, India. SOURCE: WO120 Volume 35 page 109. INDEX # 658.

Jno DELAHYDE; pension awarded 4 Jun 1823; residence - Madras, India. SOURCE: WO120 Volume 35 page 109. INDEX # 659.

Jno JONES; pension awarded 4 Jun 1823; residence - Madras, India. SOURCE: WO120 Volume 35 page 109. INDEX # 660.

Jos^h MARSHALL; pension awarded 4 Jun 1823; residence - Madras, India. SOURCE: WO120 Volume 35 page 109. INDEX # 661.

Thos MCKEE; pension awarded 4 Jun 1823; residence - Madras, India; died 4 Apr 1827. SOURCE: WO120 Volume 35 page 109. INDEX # 662.

Jno GOULDING; pension awarded 4 Jun 1823; residence - Madras, India. SOURCE: WO120 Volume 35 page 109. INDEX # 663.

Mich^l FORD; pension awarded 4 Jun 1823; residence - Madras, India. SOURCE: WO120 Volume 35 page 109. INDEX # 664.

Mich^l CHRISTIAN; pension awarded 4 Jun 1823; residence - Madras, India. SOURCE: WO120 Volume 35 page 109. INDEX # 665.

Willm COOKE; pension awarded 4 Jun 1823; residence - Madras, India. SOURCE: WO120 Volume 35 page 109. INDEX # 666.

Benjⁿ HARES; pension awarded 4 Jun 1823; residence - Madras, India. SOURCE: WO120 Volume 35 page 109. INDEX # 667.

Jos^h WILTON; pension awarded 4 Jun 1823; residence - Madras, India. SOURCE: WO120 Volume 35 page 109. INDEX # 668.

Thos HANKINS; pension awarded 4 Jun 1823; residence - Madras, India. SOURCE: WO120 Volume 35 page 109. INDEX # 669.

Wm WILLIAMS; pension awarded 12 Sep 1823. SOURCE: WO120 Volume 35 page 109. INDEX # 670.

35th Regiment of Foot

Ja^s NEUBLE; pension awarded 18 Oct 1820; residence - New Brunswick, Canada. SOURCE: WO120 Volume 35 page 111. INDEX # 671.

Wm SHORT; pension awarded 28 Jun 1820; residence - Malta. SOURCE: WO120 Volume 35 page 111. INDEX # 672.

Pat^k CANNON; pension awarded 12 Dec 1838. SOURCE: WO120 Volume 35 page 111. INDEX # 673.

36th Regiment of Foot

Edwd HYNDES; pension awarded 10 Feb 1836. SOURCE: WO120 Volume 35 page 113. INDEX # 674.

37th Regiment of Foot

Pat^k RYAN; pension awarded 28 Nov 1818; residence - Canada. SOURCE: WO120 Volume 35 page 115. INDEX # 675.

Hen^y MCELROY; pension awarded 23 May 1821; residence - Canada. SOURCE: WO120 Volume 35 page 115. INDEX # 676.

Ja^s THOMPSON; pension awarded 25 Sep 1822; residence - Canada. SOURCE: WO120 Volume 35 page 115. INDEX # 677.

Miles KEEGAN; pension awarded 13 Apr 1824; residence - Canada. SOURCE: WO120 Volume 35 page 115. INDEX # 678.

Jno HELFERICK; pension awarded 24 Nov 1824; residence - Canada. SOURCE: WO120 Volume 35 page 115. INDEX # 679.

BRITISH ARMY PENSIONERS ABROAD

37th Regiment of Foot (continued)

Robt EADEY; pension awarded 1 Feb 1826; residence - Canada. SOURCE: WO120 Volume 35 page 115. INDEX # 680.

Peter BRENNEN; pension awarded 7 Mar 1826. SOURCE: WO120 Volume 35 page 115. INDEX # 681.

Thos GUILE; pension awarded 30 May 1827; residence - Quebec, Canada. SOURCE: WO120 Volume 35 page 115. INDEX # 682.

Saml PACK; pension awarded 12 Dec 1827; residence - Canada. SOURCE: WO120 Volume 35 page 115. INDEX # 683.

Ja^s MCNALLY; pension awarded 11 Jul 1832. SOURCE: WO120 Volume 35 page 115. INDEX # 684.

Chas REYNOLDS; pension awarded 12 Sep 1832. SOURCE: WO120 Volume 35 page 115. INDEX # 685.

Mich^l BROPHY; pension awarded 13 Apr 1836. SOURCE: WO120 Volume 35 page 115. INDEX # 686.

Robt BAILEY; pension awarded 12 Oct 1836. SOURCE: WO120 Volume 35 page 115. INDEX # 687.

38th Regiment of Foot

Jno BARNCLIFFE; pension awarded 26 Jul 1820; residence - Cape of Good Hope, South Africa. SOURCE: WO120 Volume 35 page 117. INDEX # 688.

Mich^l LYTH; pension awarded 26 Jul 1820; residence - Cape of Good Hope, South Africa. SOURCE: WO120 Volume 35 page 117. INDEX # 689.

Jno CLOSE; pension awarded 26 Jul 1820; residence - Cape of Good Hope, South Africa. SOURCE: WO120 Volume 35 page 117. INDEX # 690.

Richd SHAW; pension awarded 26 Jul 1820; residence - Cape of Good Hope, South Africa. SOURCE: WO120 Volume 35 page 117. INDEX # 691.

Thos PAGET; pension awarded 7 Feb 1822; residence - Cape of Good Hope, South Africa. SOURCE: WO120 Volume 35 page 117. INDEX # 692.

Richd GOODMAN; pension awarded 31 Jul 1822; residence - Cape of Good Hope, South Africa. SOURCE: WO120 Volume 35 page 117. INDEX # 693.

Fra^s MACLEAN; pension awarded 22 Oct 1823; residence - Cape of Good Hope, South Africa. SOURCE: WO120 Volume 35 page 117. INDEX # 694.

Jos^h BOURNE; pension awarded 3 Mar 1824; residence - Cape of Good Hope, South Africa. SOURCE: WO120 Volume 35 page 117. INDEX # 695.

Willm GROVES; pension awarded 12 May 1824; residence - Cape of Good Hope, South Africa. SOURCE: WO120 Volume 35 page 117. INDEX # 696.

Jno GAZEY; pension awarded 12 May 1824; residence - Cape of Good Hope, South Africa. SOURCE: WO120 Volume 35 page 117. INDEX # 697.

Jno DURAN; pension awarded 15 Mar 1826. SOURCE: WO120 Volume 35 page 117. INDEX # 698.

Alex^r FRAZER; pension awarded 24 Jun 1812; residence - Canada. SOURCE: WO120 Volume 35 page 117. INDEX # 699.

Jos^h PINER; pension awarded 8 Aug 1827; residence - Bengal, India. SOURCE: WO120 Volume 35 page 117. INDEX # 700.

Jos^h WRIGHT; pension awarded 8 Aug 1827; residence - Bengal, India. SOURCE: WO120 Volume 35 page 117. INDEX # 701.

Jno BOLTON; pension awarded 10 Feb 1836. SOURCE: WO120 Volume 35 page 117. INDEX # 702.

Thos MCGUIRE; pension awarded 10 Feb 1836. SOURCE: WO120 Volume 35 page 117. INDEX # 703.

39th Regiment of Foot

Mich^l READE; pension awarded 4 Aug 1824; residence - Canada. SOURCE: WO120 Volume 35 page 119. INDEX # 704.

Wm MANNING; pension awarded 1 May 1822. SOURCE: WO120 Volume 35 page 119. INDEX # 705.

Thos REYNOLDS; pension awarded 1 May 1822. SOURCE: WO120 Volume 35 page 119. INDEX # 706.

Jno ROBINSON; pension awarded 13 Jul 1831; residence - Sydney, New South Wales, Australia. SOURCE: WO120 Volume 35 page 119. INDEX # 707.

Jno WILCOX; pension awarded 13 Feb 1833. SOURCE: WO120 Volume 35 page 119. INDEX # 708.

39th Regiment of Foot (continued)

Estepham PAPPIN; pension awarded 13 Feb 1833. SOURCE: WO120 Volume 35 page 119. INDEX # 709.
Wm AKHURST; pension awarded 13 Feb 1833. SOURCE: WO120 Volume 35 page 119. INDEX # 710.
Jno BUTCHER; pension awarded 13 Feb 1833. SOURCE: WO120 Volume 35 page 119. INDEX # 711.
Ja^s EVANS; pension awarded 13 Feb 1833. SOURCE: WO120 Volume 35 page 119. INDEX # 712.
Chas HUNT; pension awarded 13 Feb 1833. SOURCE: WO120 Volume 35 page 119. INDEX # 713.
Ja^s MARBERTON; pension awarded 13 Feb 1833. SOURCE: WO120 Volume 35 page 119. INDEX # 714.

40th Regiment of Foot

Danl MCGOREY; pension awarded 8 Sep 1830. SOURCE: WO120 Volume 35 page 121. INDEX # 715.
Jos^h RICHENBERG; pension awarded 8 Sep 1830. SOURCE: WO120 Volume 35 page 121. INDEX # 716.
Thos NOAH; pension awarded 8 Sep 1830. SOURCE: WO120 Volume 35 page 121. INDEX # 717.
John REESE; pension awarded 8 Sep 1830. SOURCE: WO120 Volume 35 page 121. INDEX # 718.
Ge^o WEST; pension awarded 20 Aug 1838. SOURCE: WO120 Volume 35 page 121. INDEX # 719.

41st Regiment of Foot

Jno MCGINNIS; pension awarded 25 Jun 1818; residence - Canada. SOURCE: WO120 Volume 35 page 123. INDEX # 720.
Saml SAUNDERS; pension awarded 25 Jun 1818; residence - Canada. SOURCE: WO120 Volume 35 page 123. INDEX # 721.
Den^s NOONAN; pension awarded 5 Aug 1818; residence - Canada. SOURCE: WO120 Volume 35 page 123. INDEX # 722.
Arch^d MCDONALD; pension awarded 25 Nov 1818; residence - Canada. SOURCE: WO120 Volume 35 page 123. INDEX # 723.
Ja^s COLLINS; pension awarded 25 Nov 1818; residence - Canada. SOURCE: WO120 Volume 35 page 123. INDEX # 724.
Jno BELL; pension awarded 28 Dec 1818; residence - Canada. SOURCE: WO120 Volume 35 page 123. INDEX # 725.
Hen^y CLARKE; pension awarded 12 May 1819; residence - Canada. SOURCE: WO120 Volume 35 page 123. INDEX # 726.
Mich^l FLYN; pension awarded 12 May 1819; residence - Canada. SOURCE: WO120 Volume 35 page 123. INDEX # 727.
Thos BELSHAW; pension awarded 12 May 1819; residence - Canada. SOURCE: WO120 Volume 35 page 123. INDEX # 728.
Jno NETTLES; pension awarded 12 May 1819; residence - Canada. SOURCE: WO120 Volume 35 page 123. INDEX # 729.
Jere^h CANNON; pension awarded 12 May 1819; residence - Canada. SOURCE: WO120 Volume 35 page 123. INDEX # 730.
Valent^e HENRY; pension awarded 12 May 1819; residence - Canada. SOURCE: WO120 Volume 35 page 123. INDEX # 731.
Jno MILTON; pension awarded 1 Jul 1819; residence - Canada. SOURCE: WO120 Volume 35 page 123. INDEX # 732.
Matt^w MOUNTAIN; pension awarded 1 Jul 1819; residence - Canada. SOURCE: WO120 Volume 35 page 123. INDEX # 733.
Willm MOLESWORTH; pension awarded 25 Jun 1817; residence - Canada. SOURCE: WO120 Volume 35 page 123. INDEX # 734.
Richd GRIFFITHS; pension awarded 7 Dec 1820; residence - Canada. SOURCE: WO120 Volume 35 page 123. INDEX # 735.
Jno MCAULAY; pension awarded 23 May 1821; residence - Canada. SOURCE: WO120 Volume 35 page 123. INDEX # 736.

BRITISH ARMY PENSIONERS ABROAD

41st Regiment of Foot

Willm SEGAR; pension awarded 12 Sep 1821; residence - Canada. SOURCE: WO120 Volume 35 page 123. INDEX # 737.

Willm TOWERS; pension awarded 5 Mar 1823; residence - Canada. SOURCE: WO120 Volume 35 page 123. INDEX # 738.

Jos^h WILSONCROFT; pension awarded 24 Nov 1824. SOURCE: WO120 Volume 35 page 123. INDEX # 739.

Thos MAHORTER; pension awarded 13 Dec 1826. SOURCE: WO120 Volume 35 page 123. INDEX # 740.

Jno FIELDING; pension awarded 13 Dec 1826. SOURCE: WO120 Volume 35 page 123. INDEX # 741.

Zephaniah DEWETT; pension awarded 7 Dec 1820; residence - New Brunswick, Canada, Canada. SOURCE: WO120 Volume 35 page 123. INDEX # 742.

Ge^o MENCE; pension awarded 7 Dec 1820; residence - New Brunswick, Canada, Canada. SOURCE: WO120 Volume 35 page 123. INDEX # 743.

Jos^h HARVEY; pension awarded 7 Dec 1820; residence - Canada. SOURCE: WO120 Volume 35 page 124. INDEX # 744.

Simon KEMP; pension awarded 12 Sep 1821; residence - Canada. SOURCE: WO120 Volume 35 page 124. INDEX # 745.

Gordon LYON; pension awarded 26 Jun 1816; residence - Canada. SOURCE: WO120 Volume 35 page 124. INDEX # 746.

Ge^o BROOKS; pension awarded 26 Mar 1817; residence - Canada. SOURCE: WO120 Volume 35 page 124. INDEX # 747.

Thos OAKES; pension awarded 29 Apr 1818. SOURCE: WO120 Volume 35 page 124. INDEX # 748.

Wm LLOYD; pension awarded 29 Apr 1818. SOURCE: WO120 Volume 35 page 124. INDEX # 749.

Jno SCOTT; pension awarded 29 Apr 1818. SOURCE: WO120 Volume 35 page 124. INDEX # 750.

Jno WESTON; pension awarded 23 Jul 1828. SOURCE: WO120 Volume 35 page 124. INDEX # 751.

Ge^o AVERS; pension awarded 25 Jun 1829. SOURCE: WO120 Volume 35 page 124. INDEX # 752.

Hen^y FIELD; pension awarded 13 Jan 1836. SOURCE: WO120 Volume 35 page 124. INDEX # 753.

Denis KERRISK; pension awarded 10 Aug 1836. SOURCE: WO120 Volume 35 page 124. INDEX # 754.

Thos MAHON; pension awarded 9 Aug 1837. SOURCE: WO120 Volume 35 page 124. INDEX # 755.

Ja^s WAKEFIELD; pension awarded 9 Aug 1837. SOURCE: WO120 Volume 35 page 124. INDEX # 756.

Edwd ALLEN; pension awarded 23 Oct 1838. SOURCE: WO120 Volume 35 page 124. INDEX # 757.

Fra^s MAYO; pension awarded 23 Oct 1838. SOURCE: WO120 Volume 35 page 124. INDEX # 758.

Saml BAKER; pension awarded 23 Oct 1838. SOURCE: WO120 Volume 35 page 124. INDEX # 759.

Richd GANDY; pension awarded 23 Oct 1838. SOURCE: WO120 Volume 35 page 124. INDEX # 760.

And^w LAUGHLIN; pension awarded 23 Oct 1838. SOURCE: WO120 Volume 35 page 124. INDEX # 761.

Joⁿⁿ RENSHAW; pension awarded 23 Oct 1838. SOURCE: WO120 Volume 35 page 124. INDEX # 762.

Thos SHAW; pension awarded 23 Oct 1838. SOURCE: WO120 Volume 35 page 124. INDEX # 763.

Thos SHAW; pension awarded 23 Oct 1838. SOURCE: WO120 Volume 35 page 124. INDEX # 764.

Jno TUCKER; pension awarded 23 Oct 1838. SOURCE: WO120 Volume 35 page 124. INDEX # 765.

Matt^w WASHINGTON; pension awarded 23 Oct 1838. SOURCE: WO120 Volume 35 page 124. INDEX # 766.

Thos NEIL; pension awarded 12 Dec 1838. SOURCE: WO120 Volume 35 page 124. INDEX # 767.

42nd Regiment of Foot

Don^d MCLEOD; pension awarded 9 May 1823. SOURCE: WO120 Volume 35 page 125. INDEX # 768.

Mich^l CONALLY; pension awarded 29 May 1816; residence - Canada. SOURCE: WO120 Volume 35 page 125. INDEX # 769.

Don^d MCPHERSON; pension awarded 28 Jun 1809; residence - Canada. SOURCE: WO120 Volume 35 page 125. INDEX # 770.

Don^d MCPHERSON; pension awarded 11 May 1831. SOURCE: WO120 Volume 35 page 125. INDEX # 771.

Alex^r ROSS; pension awarded 10 Jul 1833. SOURCE: WO120 Volume 35 page 125. INDEX # 772.

Don^d MCKENZIE; pension awarded 8 Jun 1836. SOURCE: WO120 Volume 35 page 125. INDEX # 773.

43rd Regiment of Foot

Malachy MEALEY; pension awarded 30 Mar 1825; residence - Gibraltar. SOURCE: WO120 Volume 35 page 127. INDEX # 774.
Simon WALLS; pension awarded 30 Mar 1825; residence - Gibraltar. SOURCE: WO120 Volume 35 page 127. INDEX # 775.
Jos^h CATOR; pension awarded 21 Jun 1826; residence - Gibraltar. SOURCE: WO120 Volume 35 page 127. INDEX # 776.
Benjn COURT; pension awarded 21 Jun 1826; residence - Gibraltar. SOURCE: WO120 Volume 35 page 127. INDEX # 777.
Gibeon LIPPETT; pension awarded 21 Jun 1826; residence - Gibraltar. SOURCE: WO120 Volume 35 page 127. INDEX # 778.
Jno CLUER; pension awarded 21 Jun 1826; residence - Gibraltar. SOURCE: WO120 Volume 35 page 127. INDEX # 779.
Jno GANNON; pension awarded 21 Jun 1826; residence - Gibraltar. SOURCE: WO120 Volume 35 page 127. INDEX # 780.
Willm ROBINSON; pension awarded 21 Jun 1826; residence - Gibraltar. SOURCE: WO120 Volume 35 page 127. INDEX # 781.
Ja^s WYNCH; pension awarded 21 Jun 1826; residence - Gibraltar. SOURCE: WO120 Volume 35 page 127. INDEX # 782.
Call MCQUILLIN; pension awarded 12 Dec 1827; residence - Canada. SOURCE: WO120 Volume 35 page 127. INDEX # 783.
Simon TORNEY; pension awarded 12 Dec 1827; residence - Canada; died 14 Jul 1834. SOURCE: WO120 Volume 35 page 127. INDEX # 784.
Robt RAMSOM; pension awarded 9 May 1838. SOURCE: WO120 Volume 35 page 127. INDEX # 785.

44th Regiment of Foot

Mich^l CONALLY; pension awarded 29 May 1816; residence - Canada. SOURCE: WO120 Volume 35 page 129. INDEX # 786.
Ge^o BREADON; pension awarded 4 Jun 1830. SOURCE: WO120 Volume 35 page 129. INDEX # 787.
Thos SMITH; pension awarded 4 Jun 1830. SOURCE: WO120 Volume 35 page 129. INDEX # 788.
Ja^s WOODS; pension awarded 12 Jun 1833. SOURCE: WO120 Volume 35 page 129. INDEX # 789.
Jno LAWRENCE; pension awarded 12 Nov 1834. SOURCE: WO120 Volume 35 page 129. INDEX # 790.
Danl POLSON; pension awarded 27 Jun 1838. SOURCE: WO120 Volume 35 page 129. INDEX # 791.
Eph^m EDMUNDS; pension awarded 27 Jun 1838. SOURCE: WO120 Volume 35 page 129. INDEX # 792.
Saml BALL; pension awarded 27 Jun 1838. SOURCE: WO120 Volume 35 page 129. INDEX # 792.
Ge^o POTTS; pension awarded 27 Jun 1838. SOURCE: WO120 Volume 35 page 129. INDEX # 794.

45th Regiment of Foot

Benjn ROWLAND; pension awarded 11 Nov 1829. SOURCE: WO120 Volume 35 page 131. INDEX # 795.
Jno CAMPBELL; pension awarded 14 Dec 1836. SOURCE: WO120 Volume 35 page 131. INDEX # 796.
Aaron WOOD; pension awarded 9 Aug 1837. SOURCE: WO120 Volume 35 page 131. INDEX # 797.
Ja^s CONLON; pension awarded 13 Jun 1838. SOURCE: WO120 Volume 35 page 131. INDEX # 798.
Wm JACKSON; pension awarded 13 Jun 1838. SOURCE: WO120 Volume 35 page 131. INDEX # 799.
Jno OAKMAN; pension awarded 13 Jun 1838. SOURCE: WO120 Volume 35 page 131. INDEX # 800.
Jno PAIN; pension awarded 13 Jun 1838. SOURCE: WO120 Volume 35 page 131. INDEX # 801.
Thos PAGE; pension awarded 13 Jun 1838. SOURCE: WO120 Volume 35 page 131. INDEX # 802.
Wm WRIGHT; pension awarded 13 Jun 1838. SOURCE: WO120 Volume 35 page 131. INDEX # 803.

46th Regiment of Foot

Ja^s SCOTT; pension awarded 29 Apr 1818; residence - Canada. SOURCE: WO120 Volume 35 page 133. INDEX # 804.

BRITISH ARMY PENSIONERS ABROAD

46th Regiment of Foot (continued)

Jos^h VERTILLS; pension awarded 29 Apr 1818; residence - Canada. SOURCE: WO120 Volume 35 page 133. INDEX # 805.

Thos MCCAFFRY; pension awarded 29 Apr 1818; residence - Canada. SOURCE: WO120 Volume 35 page 133. INDEX # 806.

Hen^y DAVIES; pension awarded 23 Nov 1825; residence - Madras, India. SOURCE: WO120 Volume 35 page 133. INDEX # 807.

Dav^d JOHN; pension awarded 13 Dec 1826; residence - Madras, India. SOURCE: WO120 Volume 35 page 133. INDEX # 808.

Willm HURDLEY; pension awarded 5 Aug 1818; residence - New South Wales, Australia. SOURCE: WO120 Volume 35 page 133.

Willm PITHERS; pension awarded 5 Aug 1818; residence - New South Wales, Australia. SOURCE: WO120 Volume 35 page 133. INDEX # 810.

Thos KEANE; pension awarded 5 Aug 1818; residence - New South Wales, Australia. SOURCE: WO120 Volume 35 page 133. INDEX # 811.

Wm KING; pension awarded 9 Oct 1833. SOURCE: WO120 Volume 35 page 133. INDEX # 812.

47th Regiment of Foot

Ja^s CARTER; pension awarded 4 Aug 1824; residence - Bombay, India. SOURCE: WO120 Volume 35 page 135. INDEX # 813.

Anth^y GAME; pension awarded 4 Aug 1824; residence - Bombay, India; died 10 Jul 1833. SOURCE: WO120 Volume 35 page 135. INDEX # 814.

Thos PLEVINS; pension awarded 4 Aug 1824; residence - Bombay, India. SOURCE: WO120 Volume 35 page 135. INDEX # 815.

Thos TAYLOR; pension awarded 4 Aug 1824. SOURCE: WO120 Volume 35 page 135. INDEX # 816.

48th Regiment of Foot

Willm HAMILTON; pension awarded 15 Dec 1819; residence - New South Wales, Australia. SOURCE: WO120 Volume 35 page 137. INDEX # 817.

Thos RYLEY; pension awarded 15 Dec 1819; residence - New South Wales, Australia. SOURCE: WO120 Volume 35 page 137. INDEX # 818.

Chas WHALAN; pension awarded 28 Mar 1821; residence - New South Wales, Australia. SOURCE: WO120 Volume 35 page 137. INDEX # 819.

Thos POLLIS; pension awarded 28 Mar 1821; residence - New South Wales, Australia. SOURCE: WO120 Volume 35 page 137. INDEX # 820.

Nathl FOWLER; pension awarded 12 Sep 1821; residence - New South Wales, Australia. SOURCE: WO120 Volume 35 page 137. INDEX # 821.

Ge^o LAWSON; pension awarded 12 Sep 1821; residence - New South Wales, Australia. SOURCE: WO120 Volume 35 page 137. INDEX # 822.

Ge^o PLATT; pension awarded 12 Sep 1821; residence - New South Wales, Australia. SOURCE: WO120 Volume 35 page 137. INDEX # 823.

Willm BLIZARD; pension awarded 26 Nov 1823; residence - New South Wales, Australia. SOURCE: WO120 Volume 35 page 137. INDEX # 824.

Thos EVANS; pension awarded 26 Nov 1823; residence - New South Wales, Australia. SOURCE: WO120 Volume 35 page 137. INDEX # 825.

Ja^s TIERNEY; pension awarded 26 Nov 1823; residence - New South Wales, Australia. SOURCE: WO120 Volume 35 page 137. INDEX # 826.

Ge^o MCDONALD; pension awarded 4 Aug 1824; residence - New South Wales, Australia. SOURCE: WO120 Volume 35 page 137. INDEX # 827.

Thos ASHTON; pension awarded 22 Dec 1824; residence - New South Wales, Australia. SOURCE: WO120 Volume 35 page 137. INDEX # 828.

48th Regiment of Foot (continued)

Jn⁰ BOARDMAN; pension awarded 22 Dec 1824; residence - New South Wales, Australia. SOURCE: WO120 Volume 35 page 137. INDEX # 829.
Isiah CRICK; pension awarded 22 Dec 1824; residence - New South Wales, Australia. SOURCE: WO120 Volume 35 page 137. INDEX # 830.
Denˢ CALLAGHAN; pension awarded 22 Dec 1824; residence - New South Wales, Australia. SOURCE: WO120 Volume 35 page 137. INDEX # 831.
Lawᵉ CUMMINGS; pension awarded 22 Dec 1824; residence - New South Wales, Australia. SOURCE: WO120 Volume 35 page 137. INDEX # 832.
Willᵐ DUMMIGAN; pension awarded 22 Dec 1824; residence - New South Wales, Australia. SOURCE: WO120 Volume 35 page 137. INDEX # 833.
Jn⁰ HILTON; pension awarded 22 Dec 1824; residence - New South Wales, Australia. SOURCE: WO120 Volume 35 page 137. INDEX # 834.
Jaˢ MARLAND; pension awarded 22 Dec 1824; residence - New South Wales, Australia. SOURCE: WO120 Volume 35 page 137. INDEX # 835.
Josʰ PILLING; pension awarded 22 Dec 1824; residence - New South Wales, Australia. SOURCE: WO120 Volume 35 page 137. INDEX # 836.
Thoˢ STEEL; pension awarded 22 Dec 1824. SOURCE: WO120 Volume 35 page 137. INDEX # 837.
Robᵗ STEWART; pension awarded 22 Dec 1824; residence - New South Wales, Australia. SOURCE: WO120 Volume 35 page 137. INDEX # 838.
Willᵐ TERNAN; pension awarded 22 Dec 1824; residence - New South Wales, Australia. SOURCE: WO120 Volume 35 page 137. INDEX # 839.
Bishop TOFTS; pension awarded 22 Dec 1824; residence - New South Wales, Australia. SOURCE: WO120 Volume 35 page 137. INDEX # 840.
Benjⁿ WEST; pension awarded 22 Dec 1824; residence - New South Wales, Australia. SOURCE: WO120 Volume 35 page 138. INDEX # 841.
Martin WILSON; pension awarded 22 Dec 1824; residence - New South Wales, Australia. SOURCE: WO120 Volume 35 page 138. INDEX # 842.
Thoˢ WHITTEL; pension awarded 22 Dec 1824; residence - New South Wales, Australia. SOURCE: WO120 Volume 35 page 138. INDEX # 843.
Jaˢ WOOD; pension awarded 22 Dec 1824; residence - New South Wales, Australia. SOURCE: WO120 Volume 35 page 138. INDEX # 844.
Samˡ HILTON; pension awarded 21 May 1828. SOURCE: WO120 Volume 35 page 138. INDEX # 845.
Willᵐ JACKSON; pension awarded 21 May 1828. SOURCE: WO120 Volume 35 page 138. INDEX # 846.
Lawᵉ SKEARNEY; pension awarded 21 May 1828. SOURCE: WO120 Volume 35 page 138. INDEX # 847.
Jonⁿ BIRCH; pension awarded 21 May 1828. SOURCE: WO120 Volume 35 page 138. INDEX # 848.
Jn⁰ HORTON; pension awarded 29 Oct 1828. SOURCE: WO120 Volume 35 page 138. INDEX # 849.
Thoˢ COOPER; pension awarded 29 Oct 1828. SOURCE: WO120 Volume 35 page 138. INDEX # 850.
Wᵐ HAYWOOD; pension awarded 11 Nov 1829; died 31 Aug 1832. SOURCE: WO120 Volume 35 page 138. INDEX # 851.
Lawᵉ CUMMINGS; pension awarded 14 Apr 1830. SOURCE: WO120 Volume 35 page 138. INDEX # 852.
Thoˢ SEARS; pension awarded 10 Jun 1835. SOURCE: WO120 Volume 35 page 138. INDEX # 853.
Wᵐ CHRISTIE; pension awarded 10 Jun 1835. SOURCE: WO120 Volume 35 page 138. INDEX # 854.
Davᵈ GRAHAM; pension awarded 10 Jun 1835. SOURCE: WO120 Volume 35 page 138. INDEX # 855.
Ge⁰ HAMILTON; pension awarded 10 Jun 1835. SOURCE: WO120 Volume 35 page 138. INDEX # 856.
Peter MUNRO; pension awarded 10 Jun 1835. SOURCE: WO120 Volume 35 page 138. INDEX # 857.

49th Regiment of Foot

Jaˢ CARTY; pension awarded 5 Jun 1817; residence - Canada. SOURCE: WO120 Volume 35 page 140. INDEX # 858.
Fredᵏ DILLON; pension awarded 29 Apr 1818; residence - Canada. SOURCE: WO120 Volume 35 page 140. INDEX # 859.

BRITISH ARMY PENSIONERS ABROAD

49th Regiment of Foot (continued)

Zach^a JENNERY; pension awarded 29 Apr 1818; residence - Canada. SOURCE: WO120 Volume 35 page 140. INDEX # 860.

Peter PLUNKETT; pension awarded 29 Apr 1818; residence - Canada. SOURCE: WO120 Volume 35 page 140. INDEX # 861.

Jno JONES; pension awarded 29 Apr 1818; residence - Canada. SOURCE: WO120 Volume 35 page 140. INDEX # 862.

Ge^o BRAITHWAITE; pension awarded 29 Apr 1818; residence - Canada. SOURCE: WO120 Volume 35 page 140. INDEX # 863.

Saml CHAPMAN; pension awarded 29 Apr 1818; residence - Canada. SOURCE: WO120 Volume 35 page 140. INDEX # 864.

Thos COLLINS; pension awarded 29 Apr 1818; residence - Canada. SOURCE: WO120 Volume 35 page 140. INDEX # 865.

Thos DELANY; pension awarded 29 Apr 1818; residence - Canada. SOURCE: WO120 Volume 35 page 140. INDEX # 866.

Bern^d KEELING; pension awarded 29 Apr 1818; residence - Canada. SOURCE: WO120 Volume 35 page 140. INDEX # 867.

Thos KENNEDY; pension awarded 29 Apr 1818; residence - Canada. SOURCE: WO120 Volume 35 page 140. INDEX # 868.

John LAWLESS; pension awarded 29 Apr 1818; residence - Canada. SOURCE: WO120 Volume 35 page 140. INDEX # 869.

Willm MARCH; pension awarded 29 Apr 1818; residence - Canada. SOURCE: WO120 Volume 35 page 140. INDEX # 870.

Ja^s MOORE; pension awarded 29 Apr 1818; residence - Canada. SOURCE: WO120 Volume 35 page 140. INDEX # 871.

Law^e MOORE; pension awarded 29 Apr 1818; residence - Canada. SOURCE: WO120 Volume 35 page 140. INDEX # 872.

Jno WHITAKER; pension awarded 29 Apr 1818; residence - Canada. SOURCE: WO120 Volume 35 page 140. INDEX # 873.

Jno SEXTON; pension awarded 25 Nov 1818; residence - Canada. SOURCE: WO120 Volume 35 page 140. INDEX # 874.

Fra^s MORROW; pension awarded 12 May 1819; residence - Canada. SOURCE: WO120 Volume 35 page 140. INDEX # 875.

Willm PORTER; pension awarded 12 May 1819; residence - Canada. SOURCE: WO120 Volume 35 page 140. INDEX # 876.

Thos ROCHE; pension awarded 12 May 1819; residence - Canada. SOURCE: WO120 Volume 35 page 140. INDEX # 877.

Ge^o EMERSON; pension awarded 12 May 1819; residence - Canada. SOURCE: WO120 Volume 35 page 140. INDEX # 878.

Peter ZAMPHIRE; pension awarded 12 May 1819; residence - Canada. SOURCE: WO120 Volume 35 page 140. INDEX # 879.

Willm HURST; pension awarded 12 May 1819; residence - Canada. SOURCE: WO120 Volume 35 page 140. INDEX # 880.

Robt DAVIS; pension awarded 1 Jul 1819; residence - Canada. SOURCE: WO120 Volume 35 page 140. INDEX # 881.

Robt BISHOP; pension awarded 1 Jul 1819; residence - Canada. SOURCE: WO120 Volume 35 page 141. INDEX # 882.

Jno FRASER; pension awarded 1 Jul 1819; residence - Canada. SOURCE: WO120 Volume 35 page 141. INDEX # 883.

Jos^h MCCRETE; pension awarded 23 May 1821; residence - Canada. SOURCE: WO120 Volume 35 page 141. INDEX # 884.

Jno BOYD; pension awarded 5 Feb 1823; residence - Canada. SOURCE: WO120 Volume 35 page 141. INDEX # 885.

49th Regiment of Foot (continued)

Florence MCCARTHY; pension awarded 24 Nov 1824; residence - Cape of Good Hope, South Africa.
    SOURCE: WO120 Volume 35 page 141. INDEX # 886.
Jn⁰ GALLAGHER; pension awarded 24 Aug 1825; residence - Cape of Good Hope, South Africa.
    SOURCE: WO120 Volume 35 page 141. INDEX # 887.
Tim^y SHELLY; pension awarded 17 May 1826; residence - Cape of Good Hope, South Africa.
    SOURCE: WO120 Volume 35 page 141. INDEX # 888.
Arth^r GILSTAIN; pension awarded 30 Aug 1826; residence - Cape of Good Hope, South Africa.
    SOURCE: WO120 Volume 35 page 141. INDEX # 889.
Jn⁰ MORAN; pension awarded 1 Jul 1819; residence - Canada. SOURCE: WO120 Volume 35 page 141. INDEX # 890.
Jos^h SIMPSON; pension awarded 12 May 1819; residence - Canada. SOURCE: WO120 Volume 35 page 141. INDEX # 891.
Ja^s ONEILL; pension awarded 14 May 1817; residence - Canada. SOURCE: WO120 Volume 35 page 141. INDEX # 892.
Richd SALTER; pension awarded 28 Aug 1806; residence - , Canada; died , . SOURCE: WO120 Volume 35 page 141. INDEX # 893.
Edwd HARFIGH; pension awarded 10 Aug 1836. SOURCE: WO120 Volume 35 page 141. INDEX # 894.

50th Regiment of Foot

Jn⁰ BULLIVANT; pension awarded 13 Apr 1836. SOURCE: WO120 Volume 35 page 143. INDEX # 895.
Jn⁰ HENNESSY; pension awarded 23 Aug 1837. SOURCE: WO120 Volume 35 page 143. INDEX # 896.
Jn⁰ FOX; pension awarded 13 Jun 1838. SOURCE: WO120 Volume 35 page 143. INDEX # 897.
Peter WARD; pension awarded 13 Jun 1838. SOURCE: WO120 Volume 35 page 143. INDEX # 898.
Thos GUNN; pension awarded 13 Jun 1838. SOURCE: WO120 Volume 35 page 143. INDEX # 899.
Wm WOOLDRIDGE; pension awarded 13 Jun 1838. SOURCE: WO120 Volume 35 page 143. INDEX # 900.
Wm TEALE; pension awarded 13 Jun 1838. SOURCE: WO120 Volume 35 page 143. INDEX # 901.
Wm WALKER; pension awarded 8 Aug 1838. SOURCE: WO120 Volume 35 page 143. INDEX # 902.
Den^s GILLESPIE; pension awarded 8 Aug 1838. SOURCE: WO120 Volume 35 page 143. INDEX # 903.
Mic^l BOYLE; pension awarded 8 Aug 1838. SOURCE: WO120 Volume 35 page 143. INDEX # 904.
Hugh GILLIGAN; pension awarded 8 Aug 1838. SOURCE: WO120 Volume 35 page 143. INDEX # 905.
Thos HARROLD; pension awarded 8 Aug 1838. SOURCE: WO120 Volume 35 page 143. INDEX # 906.
Jn⁰ HENSHALL; pension awarded 8 Aug 1838. SOURCE: WO120 Volume 35 page 143. INDEX # 907.
Jn⁰ PARR; pension awarded 8 Aug 1838. SOURCE: WO120 Volume 35 page 143. INDEX # 908.
Ja^s SPITTALE; pension awarded 8 Aug 1838. SOURCE: WO120 Volume 35 page 143. INDEX # 909.
Thos TEEVAN; pension awarded 8 Aug 1838. SOURCE: WO120 Volume 35 page 143. INDEX # 910.

51st Regiment of Foot

Ja^s HARRIS; pension awarded 13 Apr 1831. SOURCE: WO120 Volume 35 page 145. INDEX # 911.
Chas EWENS; pension awarded 8 Feb 1832. SOURCE: WO120 Volume 35 page 145. INDEX # 912.
Wm EVERETT; pension awarded 8 Feb 1832. SOURCE: WO120 Volume 35 page 145. INDEX # 913.
Ja^s PEARSON; pension awarded 13 Jun 1832. SOURCE: WO120 Volume 35 page 145. INDEX # 914.
Hugh GARVIN; pension awarded 12 Sep 1832. SOURCE: WO120 Volume 35 page 145. INDEX # 915.
Edwd RYAN; pension awarded 8 May 1833. SOURCE: WO120 Volume 35 page 145. INDEX # 916.

52nd Regiment of Foot

Willm SMITH; pension awarded 23 Nov 1825; residence - Nova Scotia, Canada. SOURCE: WO120 Volume 35 page 147. INDEX # 917.
Chas MILLER; pension awarded 1 Feb 1826; residence - Nova Scotia, Canada. SOURCE: WO120 Volume 35 page 147. INDEX # 918.
Ja^s BOSSOM; pension awarded 7 Mar 1827. SOURCE: WO120 Volume 35 page 147. INDEX # 919.

# BRITISH ARMY PENSIONERS ABROAD

52nd Regiment of Foot (continued)

Wm DELLICOTE; pension awarded 5 Aug 1829. SOURCE: WO120 Volume 35 page 147. INDEX # 920.
Ge^o CUNNINGHAM; pension awarded 14 Dec 1831. SOURCE: WO120 Volume 35 page 147. INDEX # 921.
Wm ABBOTT; pension awarded 14 Dec 1831. SOURCE: WO120 Volume 35 page 147. INDEX # 922.
Hen^y BOTTS; pension awarded 14 Dec 1831. SOURCE: WO120 Volume 35 page 147. INDEX # 923.
Tarrell COFFELL; pension awarded 14 Dec 1831. SOURCE: WO120 Volume 35 page 147. INDEX # 924.
Pat^k COFFELL; pension awarded 14 Dec 1831. SOURCE: WO120 Volume 35 page 147. INDEX # 925.
Pat^k CURREN; pension awarded 14 Dec 1831. SOURCE: WO120 Volume 35 page 147. INDEX # 926.
Jno DEMPSEY; pension awarded 14 Dec 1831. SOURCE: WO120 Volume 35 page 147. INDEX # 927.
Matt^w HAGUE; pension awarded 14 Dec 1831. SOURCE: WO120 Volume 35 page 147. INDEX # 928.
Carbro HIGGINS; pension awarded 14 Dec 1831. SOURCE: WO120 Volume 35 page 147. INDEX # 929.
And^w HOPEWELL; pension awarded 14 Dec 1831. SOURCE: WO120 Volume 35 page 147. INDEX # 930.
Thos JONES; pension awarded 14 Dec 1838. SOURCE: WO120 Volume 35 page 147. INDEX # 931.
Hen^y JOLLY; pension awarded 14 Dec 1831. SOURCE: WO120 Volume 35 page 147. INDEX # 932.
Jno LANGFORD; pension awarded 14 Dec 1831. SOURCE: WO120 Volume 35 page 147. INDEX # 933.
Jno LEOMAN; pension awarded 14 Dec 1831. SOURCE: WO120 Volume 35 page 147. INDEX # 934.
Thos LOWMAN; pension awarded 14 Dec 1831. SOURCE: WO120 Volume 35 page 147. INDEX # 935.
Ja^s MCFARLANE; pension awarded 14 Dec 1831. SOURCE: WO120 Volume 35 page 147. INDEX # 936.
Pat^k NOONE; pension awarded 14 Dec 1831. SOURCE: WO120 Volume 35 page 147. INDEX # 937.
Wm ONEAL; pension awarded 14 Dec 1831. SOURCE: WO120 Volume 35 page 147. INDEX # 938.
Jno PENCHEON; pension awarded 14 Dec 1831. SOURCE: WO120 Volume 35 page 147. INDEX # 939.
Wm QUILLER; pension awarded 14 Dec 1831. SOURCE: WO120 Volume 35 page 147. INDEX # 940.
Ja^s SHEERIN; pension awarded 14 Dec 1831. SOURCE: WO120 Volume 35 page 148. INDEX # 941.
Jno TASKER; pension awarded 14 Dec 1831. SOURCE: WO120 Volume 35 page 148. INDEX # 942.
Robt WATT; pension awarded 14 Dec 1831. SOURCE: WO120 Volume 35 page 148. INDEX # 943.
Carny WOOD; pension awarded 14 Dec 1831. SOURCE: WO120 Volume 35 page 148. INDEX # 944.
Isaac FOSTER; pension awarded 13 Jun 1838. SOURCE: WO120 Volume 35 page 148. INDEX # 945.
Jno BORSDALE; pension awarded 27 Jun 1838. SOURCE: WO120 Volume 35 pagpage 148. INDEX # 946.

53rd Regiment of Foot

Jno TAYLOR; pension awarded 7 Feb 1821; residence - India. SOURCE: WO120 Volume 35 page 149. INDEX # 947.
Willm WORSLEY; pension awarded 7 Feb 1821; residence - India; died 20 Jul 1824. SOURCE: WO120 Volume 35 page 149. INDEX # 948.
Chas WEBSTER; pension awarded 7 Feb 1821; residence - India; died 12 Jul 1827. SOURCE: WO120 Volume 35 page 149. INDEX # 949.
Peter RATCHFORD; pension awarded 7 Feb 1821; residence - India. SOURCE: WO120 Volume 35 page 149. INDEX # 950.
Jno FINN; pension awarded 7 Feb 1821; residence - India. SOURCE: WO120 Volume 35 page 149. INDEX # 951.
Adam RIDDLE; pension awarded 7 Feb 1821; residence - India. SOURCE: WO120 Volume 35 page 149. INDEX # 952.
Walter GARDNER; pension awarded 7 Feb 1821; residence - India. SOURCE: WO120 Volume 35 page 149. INDEX # 953.
Robt BURGESS; pension awarded 4 Jun 1823; residence - India. SOURCE: WO120 Volume 35 page 149. INDEX # 954.
Chas CURTIS; pension awarded 4 Jun 1823; residence - India. SOURCE: WO120 Volume 35 page 149. INDEX # 955.
Willm GRIMES; pension awarded 4 Jun 1823; residence - India. SOURCE: WO120 Volume 35 page 149. INDEX # 956.
Jno HOLLIDAY; pension awarded 4 Jun 1823; residence - India. SOURCE: WO120 Volume 35 page 149. INDEX # 957.

53rd Regiment of Foot (continued)

Willm LUNN; pension awarded 4 Jun 1823; residence - India. SOURCE: WO120 Volume 35 page 149. INDEX # 958.

Hen^y NORTH; pension awarded 4 Jun 1823; residence - India. SOURCE: WO120 Volume 35 page 149. INDEX # 959.

Ja^s SMITH; pension awarded 4 Jun 1823; residence - India. SOURCE: WO120 Volume 35 page 149. INDEX # 960.

Jos^h TAYLOR; pension awarded 4 Jun 1823; residence - India. SOURCE: WO120 Volume 35 page 149. INDEX # 961.

Richd COTHAM; pension awarded 4 Jun 1823; residence - India. SOURCE: WO120 Volume 35 page 149. INDEX # 962.

Peter CRAMPTON; pension awarded 4 Jun 1823; residence - India. SOURCE: WO120 Volume 35 page 149. INDEX # 963.

Thos CHAPMAN; pension awarded 4 Jun 1823; residence - India. SOURCE: WO120 Volume 35 page 149. INDEX # 964.

Jno CONTADES; pension awarded 4 Jun 1823; residence - India. SOURCE: WO120 Volume 35 page 149. INDEX # 965.

Jos^h BALL; pension awarded 4 Jun 1823; residence - India. SOURCE: WO120 Volume 35 page 149. INDEX # 966.

Willm BARTLETT; pension awarded 4 Jun 1823; residence - India. SOURCE: WO120 Volume 35 page 149. INDEX # 967.

Ja^s BEDDING; pension awarded 4 Jun 1823; residence - India. SOURCE: WO120 Volume 35 page 149. INDEX # 968.

Willm FENTON; pension awarded 4 Jun 1823; residence - India; died 4 Jan 1824. SOURCE: WO120 Volume 35 page 149. INDEX # 969.

Edwd JOHNSON; pension awarded 4 Jun 1823; residence - India; died 29 Mar 1827. SOURCE: WO120 Volume 35 page 149. INDEX # 970.

Danl MORRIS; pension awarded 4 Jun 1823; residence - India; died 1 Apr 1827. SOURCE: WO120 Volume 35 page 150. INDEX # 971.

Willm REYNOLDS; pension awarded 4 Jun 1823; residence - India. SOURCE: WO120 Volume 35 page 150. INDEX # 972.

Thos LLOYD; pension awarded 4 Jun 1823; residence - India. SOURCE: WO120 Volume 35 page 150. INDEX # 973.

Jno DEAN; pension awarded 4 Jun 1823; residence - India. SOURCE: WO120 Volume 35 page 150. INDEX # 974.

John PITT; pension awarded 3 Mar 1824. SOURCE: WO120 Volume 35 page 150. INDEX # 975.

Jos^h SUGDEN; pension awarded 3 Mar 1824. SOURCE: WO120 Volume 35 page 150. INDEX # 976.

John STEWART; pension awarded 3 Mar 1824. SOURCE: WO120 Volume 35 page 150. INDEX # 977.

54th Regiment of Foot

Ja^s CAHILL; pension awarded 7 Feb 1821; residence - Cape of Good Hope, South Africa. SOURCE: WO120 Volume 35 page 152. INDEX # 978.

Peter WHITE; pension awarded 12 Sep 1821; residence - Cape of Good Hope, South Africa. SOURCE: WO120 Volume 35 page 152. INDEX # 979.

Ja^s DOOLAN; pension awarded 7 Feb 1822; residence - Cape of Good Hope, South Africa. SOURCE: WO120 Volume 35 page 152. INDEX # 980.

Matt^w ENRIGHT; pension awarded 20 Mar 1822; residence - Cape of Good Hope, South Africa. SOURCE: WO120 Volume 35 page 152. INDEX # 981.

Jno NORTON; pension awarded 31 Jul 1822; residence - Cape of Good Hope, South Africa. SOURCE: WO120 Volume 35 page 152. INDEX # 982.

Barth^w DONOHUE; pension awarded 31 Jul 1822; residence - Cape of Good Hope, South Africa. SOURCE: WO120 Volume 35 page 152. INDEX # 983.

BRITISH ARMY PENSIONERS ABROAD

54th Regiment of Foot (continued)

Thos MCMAKIN; pension awarded 25 Sep 1822; residence - Cape of Good Hope, South Africa. SOURCE: WO120 Volume 35 page 152. INDEX # 984.

Jno PANCUTT; pension awarded 23 Nov 1825; residence - Cape of Good Hope, South Africa. SOURCE: WO120 Volume 35 page 152. INDEX # 985.

Ge^o WATSON; pension awarded 23 Nov 1825; residence - Cape of Good Hope, South Africa. SOURCE: WO120 Volume 35 page 152. INDEX # 986.

Jno JONES; pension awarded 30 May 1827; residence - Madras, India. SOURCE: WO120 Volume 35 page 152. INDEX # 987.

Jacob LOMBER; pension awarded 8 Aug 1827; residence - Madras, India. SOURCE: WO120 Volume 35 page 152. INDEX # 988.

Ja^s DICKER; pension awarded 7 Jan 1829. SOURCE: WO120 Volume 35 page 152. INDEX # 989.

Edwd MARSH; pension awarded 7 Jan 1829. SOURCE: WO120 Volume 35 page 152. INDEX # 990.

Ge^o THOMAS; pension awarded 7 Jan 1829. SOURCE: WO120 Volume 35 page 152. INDEX # 991.

Jno ARTER; pension awarded 11 Nov 1829. SOURCE: WO120 Volume 35 page 152. INDEX # 992.

Benjn SHELDON; pension awarded 9 Aug 1837. SOURCE: WO120 Volume 35 page 152. INDEX # 993.

Wm MORRISON; pension awarded 11 Aug 1837. SOURCE: WO120 Volume 35 page 152. INDEX # 994.

Jno BRYAN; pension awarded 23 Oct 1838. SOURCE: WO120 Volume 35 page 152. INDEX # 995.

Wm BROWN; pension awarded 23 Oct 1838. SOURCE: WO120 Volume 35 page 152. INDEX # 996.

Thos DANTON; pension awarded 23 Oct 1838. SOURCE: WO120 Volume 35 page 152. INDEX # 997.

Dav^d JOHNSTON; pension awarded 23 Oct 1838. SOURCE: WO120 Volume 35 page 152. INDEX # 998.

Richd LOWNAN; pension awarded 23 Oct 1838. SOURCE: WO120 Volume 35 page 152. INDEX # 999.

Hen^y LAWSON; pension awarded 23 Oct 1838. SOURCE: WO120 Volume 35 page 152. INDEX # 1000.

Robt MARTIN; pension awarded 23 Oct 1838. SOURCE: WO120 Volume 35 page 152. INDEX # 1001.

Robt MOSS; pension awarded 23 Oct 1838. SOURCE: WO120 Volume 35 page 153. INDEX # 1002.

Wm MACE; pension awarded 23 Oct 1838. SOURCE: WO120 Volume 35 page 153. INDEX # 1003.

Jon^n PARKINSON; pension awarded 23 Oct 1838. SOURCE: WO120 Volume 35 page 153. INDEX # 1004.

Ge^o POWELL; pension awarded 23 Oct 1838. SOURCE: WO120 Volume 35 page 153. INDEX # 1005.

55th Regiment of Foot

Jos^h BRUCKSHAW; pension awarded 16 Sep 1829. SOURCE: WO120 Volume 35 page 155. INDEX # 1006.

Jno IRWIN; pension awarded 9 Dec 1836. SOURCE: WO120 Volume 35 page 155. INDEX # 1007.

And^w CLARK; pension awarded 9 Aug 1837. SOURCE: WO120 Volume 35 page 155. INDEX # 1008.

Thos TURNER; pension awarded 9 Aug 1837. SOURCE: WO120 Volume 35 page 155. INDEX # 1009.

Ge^o ARMSTRONG; pension awarded 23 Oct 1838. SOURCE: WO120 Volume 35 page 155. INDEX # 1010.

Jno BRADBURY; pension awarded 23 Oct 1838. SOURCE: WO120 Volume 35 page 155. INDEX # 1011.

Jno CLUFF; pension awarded 23 Oct 1838. SOURCE: WO120 Volume 35 page 155. INDEX # 1012.

Wm DAMARUM; pension awarded 23 Oct 1838. SOURCE: WO120 Volume 35 page 155. INDEX # 1013.

Robt FULLER; pension awarded 23 Oct 1838. SOURCE: WO120 Volume 35 page 155. INDEX # 1014.

Thos FOULSTONE; pension awarded 23 Oct 1838. SOURCE: WO120 Volume 35 page 155. INDEX # 1015.

Peter KENNEDY; pension awarded 23 Oct 1838. SOURCE: WO120 Volume 35 page 155. INDEX # 1016.

Alex^r PEADON; pension awarded 23 Oct 1838. SOURCE: WO120 Volume 35 page 155. INDEX # 1017.

Wm GALVIN; pension awarded 12 Dec 1838. SOURCE: WO120 Volume 35 page 155. INDEX # 1018.

56th Regiment of Foot

Ja^s KING; pension awarded 17 Mar 1819; residence - Cape of Good Hope, South Africa. SOURCE: WO120 Volume 35 page 157. INDEX # 1019.

Bern^d NIBLICK; pension awarded 17 Mar 1819; residence - Cape of Good Hope, South Africa. SOURCE: WO120 Volume 35 page 157. INDEX # 1020.

56th Regiment of Foot

Jn⁰ RYE; pension awarded 17 Mar 1819; residence - Cape of Good Hope, South Africa. SOURCE: WO120 Volume 35 page 157. INDEX # 1021.

Jos^h KENZIE; pension awarded 17 Mar 1819; residence - Cape of Good Hope, South Africa. SOURCE: WO120 Volume 35 page 157. INDEX # 1022.

Thos WOODS; pension awarded 17 Mar 1819; residence - Cape of Good Hope, South Africa. SOURCE: WO120 Volume 35 page 157. INDEX # 1023.

Willm SUTHERWOOD; pension awarded 17 Mar 1819; residence - Cape of Good Hope, ; died , . SOURCE: WO120 Volume 35 page 157. INDEX # 1024.

Thos HUSBAND; pension awarded 17 Mar 1819; residence - Cape of Good Hope, ; died , . SOURCE: WO120 Volume 35 page 157. INDEX # 1025.

Ch^r DATES; pension awarded 17 Mar 1819; residence - Cape of Good Hope, South Africa. SOURCE: WO120 Volume 35 page 157. INDEX # 1026.

Ge⁰ EVANS; pension awarded 17 Mar 1819; residence - Cape of Good Hope, South Africa. SOURCE: WO120 Volume 35 page 157. INDEX # 1027.

Ja^s BECK; pension awarded 15 Dec 1819; residence - Cape of Good Hope, South Africa. SOURCE: WO120 Volume 35 page 157. INDEX # 1028.

Thos BROWN; pension awarded 15 Dec 1819; residence - Cape of Good Hope, South Africa. SOURCE: WO120 Volume 35 page 157. INDEX # 1029.

Dav^d WOODS; pension awarded 15 Dec 1819; residence - Cape of Good Hope, South Africa. SOURCE: WO120 Volume 35 page 157. INDEX # 1030.

Jos^h GREGORY; pension awarded 7 Jun 1820; residence - Mauritius. SOURCE: WO120 Volume 35 page 157. INDEX # 1031.

Jn⁰ ALLEN; pension awarded 7 Jun 1820; residence - Mauritius. SOURCE: WO120 Volume 35 page 157. INDEX # 1032.

Danl DREW; pension awarded 7 Jun 1820; residence - Mauritius. SOURCE: WO120 Volume 35 page 157. INDEX # 1033.

Thos NEWMAN; pension awarded 19 Jul 1826; residence - Mauritius. SOURCE: WO120 Volume 35 page 157. INDEX # 1034.

Willm COFFEY; pension awarded 19 Jul 1826; residence - Mauritius. SOURCE: WO120 Volume 35 page 157. INDEX # 1035.

Hen^y PUNG; pension awarded 19 Jul 1826; residence - Mauritius. SOURCE: WO120 Volume 35 page 157. INDEX # 1036.

Willm GRUBB; pension awarded 19 Jul 1826; residence - Mauritius. SOURCE: WO120 Volume 35 page 157. INDEX # 1037.

Chas CLARKE; pension awarded 19 Jul 1826; residence - Mauritius. SOURCE: WO120 Volume 35 page 157. INDEX # 1038.

Jn⁰ MONTGOMERY; pension awarded 19 Jul 1826; residence - Mauritius. SOURCE: WO120 Volume 35 page 157. INDEX # 1039.

Thos GODFREY; pension awarded 19 Jul 1826; residence - Mauritius. SOURCE: WO120 Volume 35 page 157. INDEX # 1040.

Jn⁰ HALL; pension awarded 19 Jul 1826; residence - Mauritius. SOURCE: WO120 Volume 35 page 157. INDEX # 1041.

Willm KELLY; pension awarded 19 Jul 1826; residence - Mauritius. SOURCE: WO120 Volume 35 page 157. INDEX # 1042.

Ja^s HARRIS; pension awarded 19 Jul 1826; residence - Mauritius. SOURCE: WO120 Volume 35 page 158. INDEX # 1043.

Thos Wm PROBART; pension awarded 20 Feb 1828; residence - Mauritius. SOURCE: WO120 Volume 35 page 158. INDEX # 1044.

Jn⁰ REYNOLDS; pension awarded 14 Jun 1837. SOURCE: WO120 Volume 35 page 158. INDEX # 1045.

57th Regiment of Foot

Thos GUNNING; pension awarded 7 Feb 1821. SOURCE: WO120 Volume 35 page 159. INDEX # 1046.

57th Regiment of Foot (continued)

Wm GREEN; pension awarded 8 Sep 1830. SOURCE: WO120 Volume 35 page 159. INDEX # 1047.
Jas WHITEHEAD; pension awarded 9 Mar 1831. SOURCE: WO120 Volume 35 page 159. INDEX # 1048.
Jno MACRAE; pension awarded 11 Jan 1832. SOURCE: WO120 Volume 35 page 159. INDEX # 1049.
Luke AGNEW; pension awarded 11 Jan 1832. SOURCE: WO120 Volume 35 page 159. INDEX # 1050.
Geo DYER; pension awarded 11 Jan 1832. SOURCE: WO120 Volume 35 page 159. INDEX # 1051.
Jas GIBBONS; pension awarded 11 Jan 1832. SOURCE: WO120 Volume 35 page 159. INDEX # 1052.
Geo GOLDSMITH; pension awarded 11 Jan 1832. SOURCE: WO120 Volume 35 page 159. INDEX # 1053.
Jno HOWELL; pension awarded 11 Jan 1832. SOURCE: WO120 Volume 35 page 159. INDEX # 1054.
Geo NEWBOLT; pension awarded 11 Jan 1832. SOURCE: WO120 Volume 35 page 159. INDEX # 1055.

58th Regiment of Foot

Jno MOORE; pension awarded 25 Jun 1818; residence - Canada. SOURCE: WO120 Volume 35 page 162. INDEX # 1056.
Augustus HORNIBROOK; pension awarded 1 Jul 1819; residence - Canada. SOURCE: WO120 Volume 35 page 162. INDEX # 1057.
Jno HURCHINS; pension awarded 1 Jul 1819; residence - West Indies. SOURCE: WO120 Volume 35 page 162. INDEX # 1058.
Jno DORCEY; pension awarded 29 May 1816; residence - Canada. SOURCE: WO120 Volume 35 page 162. INDEX # 1059.

59th Regiment of Foot

Thos WALLACE; pension awarded 25 Jul 1821; residence - India. SOURCE: WO120 Volume 35 page 164. INDEX # 1060.
Thos WALTON; pension awarded 25 Jul 1821; residence - India. SOURCE: WO120 Volume 35 page 164. INDEX # 1061.
Jno SMITH; pension awarded 25 Sep 1822; residence - Bengal, India. SOURCE: WO120 Volume 35 page 164. INDEX # 1062.
Jas CUNNINGHAM; pension awarded 25 Sep 1822; residence - Bengal, India. SOURCE: WO120 Volume 35 page 164. INDEX # 1063.
Chas TURNER; pension awarded 25 Sep 1822; residence - Bengal, India. SOURCE: WO120 Volume 35 page 164. INDEX # 1064.
Willm WYE; pension awarded 25 Sep 1822; residence - Bengal, India. SOURCE: WO120 Volume 35 page 164. INDEX # 1065.
Anty VAN WILSON; pension awarded 27 Aug 1823; residence - Bengal, India; died 16 Jan 1826 Calcutta, India. SOURCE: WO120 Volume 35 page 164. INDEX # 1066.
Jno CHANDLER; pension awarded 24 Nov 1824; residence - Bengal, India. SOURCE: WO120 Volume 35 page 164. INDEX # 1067.
Jno GILLETT; pension awarded 24 Nov 1824; residence - Bengal, India. SOURCE: WO120 Volume 35 page 164. INDEX # 1068.
Benjn BLAKE; pension awarded 24 Nov 1824; residence - Bengal, India. SOURCE: WO120 Volume 35 page 164. INDEX # 1069.
Jonn COOKE; pension awarded 24 Nov 1824; residence - Bengal, India. SOURCE: WO120 Volume 35 page 164. INDEX # 1070.
Jno GUEST; pension awarded 15 Mar 1826; residence - Bengal, India; died 1 May 1830. SOURCE: WO120 Volume 35 page 164. INDEX # 1071.
Jno HAWKES; pension awarded 15 Mar 1826; residence - Bengal, India. SOURCE: WO120 Volume 35 page 164. INDEX # 1072.
Jno FLAHERTY; pension awarded 25 Apr 1827. SOURCE: WO120 Volume 35 page 164. INDEX # 1073.
Saml STANLEY; pension awarded 30 May 1827; residence - Bengal, India. SOURCE: WO120 Volume 35 page 164. INDEX # 1074.

59th Regiment of Foot (continued)

Arch^d MCLAUGHLAN; pension awarded 30 May 1827. SOURCE: WO120 Volume 35 page 164. INDEX # 1075.

Roger WAITE; pension awarded 30 May 1827; died 2 Apr 1830. SOURCE: WO120 Volume 35 page 164. INDEX # 1076.

Jno SUTHERLAND; pension awarded 30 May 1827. SOURCE: WO120 Volume 35 page 164. INDEX # 1077.

Willm SANSVIE; pension awarded 30 May 1827. SOURCE: WO120 Volume 35 page 164. INDEX # 1078.

Chas GRENWALTZ; pension awarded 30 May 1827. SOURCE: WO120 Volume 35 page 164. INDEX # 1079.

Willm BATTY; pension awarded 30 May 1827. SOURCE: WO120 Volume 35 page 164. INDEX # 1080.

Jno ROBERTSON; pension awarded 7 Feb 1821; residence - Bengal, India. SOURCE: WO120 Volume 35 page 164. INDEX # 1081.

Jno CHECK; pension awarded 3 Dec 1828. SOURCE: WO120 Volume 35 page 164. INDEX # 1082.

Jos^h MOORE; pension awarded 3 Dec 1828. SOURCE: WO120 Volume 35 page 164. INDEX # 1083.

Jno TWEEDALE; pension awarded 13 Jan 1830. SOURCE: WO120 Volume 35 page 165. INDEX # 1084.

Thos BARBER; pension awarded 13 Jan 1830. SOURCE: WO120 Volume 35 page 165. INDEX # 1085.

Willm FINNIGAN; pension awarded 13 Jan 1830. SOURCE: WO120 Volume 35 page 165. INDEX # 1086.

Willm FISHER; pension awarded 13 Jan 1830. SOURCE: WO120 Volume 35 page 165. INDEX # 1087.

Edwd GREEN; pension awarded 13 Jan 1830. SOURCE: WO120 Volume 35 page 165. INDEX # 1088.

Jno HEFFERNON; pension awarded 13 Jan 1830. SOURCE: WO120 Volume 35 page 165. INDEX # 1089.

Fra^s MORROU; pension awarded 13 Jan 1830. SOURCE: WO120 Volume 35 page 165. INDEX # 1090.

Jno MOTLEY; pension awarded 13 Jan 1830. SOURCE: WO120 Volume 35 page 165. INDEX # 1091.

Edwd WISEBY; pension awarded 13 Jan 1830. SOURCE: WO120 Volume 35 page 165. INDEX # 1092.

60th Regiment of Foot

Jno SCHWALLER; pension awarded 23 Sep 1818; residence - Cape of Good Hope, South Africa. SOURCE: WO120 Volume 35 page 168. INDEX # 1093.

Jno ROSENDALL; pension awarded 25 Nov 1818; residence - Canada. SOURCE: WO120 Volume 35 page 168. INDEX # 1094.

Jno LEADER; pension awarded 29 Jul 1819; residence - Cape of Good Hope, South Africa. SOURCE: WO120 Volume 35 page 168. INDEX # 1095.

Ignatius SCHALECK; pension awarded 29 Jul 1819; residence - Cape of Good Hope, South Africa. SOURCE: WO120 Volume 35 page 168. INDEX # 1096.

Thos BELLAMY; pension awarded 26 Aug 1819; residence - Barbados, West Indies. SOURCE: WO120 Volume 35 page 168. INDEX # 1097.

Jos^h BUCHS; pension awarded 7 Dec 1820; residence - Nova Scotia, Canada. SOURCE: WO120 Volume 35 page 168. INDEX # 1098.

Fred^k PRAST; pension awarded 12 Sep 1821; residence - Nova Scotia, Canada. SOURCE: WO120 Volume 35 page 168. INDEX # 1099.

Peter NORDBECK; pension awarded 7 Feb 1822; residence - Nova Scotia, Canada. SOURCE: WO120 Volume 35 page 168. INDEX # 1100.

Fergus MOORE; pension awarded 9 May 1823; residence - Canada. SOURCE: WO120 Volume 35 page 168. INDEX # 1101.

Antoine FREDERICK; pension awarded 9 May 1823; residence - Nova Scotia, Canada. SOURCE: WO120 Volume 35 page 168. INDEX # 1102.

Fred^k BUSHMAN; pension awarded 30 Sep 1823; residence - Nova Scotia, Canada. SOURCE: WO120 Volume 35 page 168. INDEX # 1103.

Ge^o STANKO; pension awarded 30 Sep 1823; residence - Nova Scotia, Canada. SOURCE: WO120 Volume 35 page 168. INDEX # 1104.

Fred^k GAYER; pension awarded 21 Jan 1824; residence - Nova Scotia, Canada. SOURCE: WO120 Volume 35 page 168. INDEX # 1105.

BRITISH ARMY PENSIONERS ABROAD

60th Regiment of Foot (continued)

Peter SCHOUTEN; pension awarded 24 Nov 1824; residence - Canada. SOURCE: WO120 Volume 35 page 168. INDEX # 1106.

Hen^y PETER; pension awarded 24 Nov 1824; residence - Canada. SOURCE: WO120 Volume 35 page 168. INDEX # 1107.

Ge^o KOESTER; pension awarded 24 Nov 1824; residence - Canada. SOURCE: WO120 Volume 35 page 168. INDEX # 1108.

Jacob REITTER; pension awarded 24 Nov 1824; residence - , Canada; died , . SOURCE: WO120 Volume 35 page 168. INDEX # 1109.

Hen^y BOLTE; pension awarded 24 Nov 1824; residence - Canada. SOURCE: WO120 Volume 35 page 168. INDEX # 1110.

Emman^l GEELHOET; pension awarded 24 Nov 1824; residence - Canada. SOURCE: WO120 Volume 35 page 168. INDEX # 1111.

Wortzech JANKOWITZ; pension awarded 24 Nov 1824; residence - Canada. SOURCE: WO120 Volume 35 page 168. INDEX # 1112.

Ant^y GALARDI; pension awarded 24 Nov 1824; residence - Canada. SOURCE: WO120 Volume 35 page 168. INDEX # 1113.

Jno JOYCE; pension awarded 24 Nov 1824; residence - Canada. SOURCE: WO120 Volume 35 page 168. INDEX # 1114.

Phi^lp SHUTTELKOLF; pension awarded 24 Nov 1824; residence - Canada. SOURCE: WO120 Volume 35 page 168. INDEX # 1115.

Fred^k HESSE; pension awarded 24 Nov 1824; residence - Canada. SOURCE: WO120 Volume 35 page 168. INDEX # 1116.

Jos^h SONTAG; pension awarded 24 Nov 1824; residence - Canada. SOURCE: WO120 Volume 35 page 169. INDEX # 1117.

Fred^k BECKER; pension awarded 24 Nov 1824; residence - Canada. SOURCE: WO120 Volume 35 page 169. INDEX # 1118.

Wil^lm GEBHARDT; pension awarded 24 Nov 1824; residence - Canada. SOURCE: WO120 Volume 35 page 169. INDEX # 1119.

Jos^h LEBRE; pension awarded 24 Nov 1824; residence - Canada. SOURCE: WO120 Volume 35 page 169. INDEX # 1120.

Jos^h POSPIESCHEL; pension awarded 24 Nov 1824; residence - Canada. SOURCE: WO120 Volume 35 page 169. INDEX # 1121.

Jno SPERLING; pension awarded 24 Nov 1824; residence - Canada. SOURCE: WO120 Volume 35 page 169. INDEX # 1122.

Peter VANANTWERPEN; pension awarded 24 Nov 1824; residence - Canada. SOURCE: WO120 Volume 35 page 169. INDEX # 1123.

Jno RICKERT; pension awarded 24 Nov 1824; residence - Canada. SOURCE: WO120 Volume 35 page 169. INDEX # 1124.

Fred^k MATTHIAS; pension awarded 22 Dec 1824; residence - New Brunswick, Canada. SOURCE: WO120 Volume 35 page 169. INDEX # 1125.

Matt^w KRIBS; pension awarded 22 Dec 1824; residence - New Brunswick, Canada. SOURCE: WO120 Volume 35 page 169. INDEX # 1126.

Jos^h GODIE; pension awarded 22 Dec 1824; residence - New Brunswick, Canada. SOURCE: WO120 Volume 35 page 169. INDEX # 1127.

Jno RANSCH; pension awarded 22 Dec 1824; residence - New Brunswick, Canada. SOURCE: WO120 Volume 35 page 169. INDEX # 1128.

Leon^d KUPPERSCH; pension awarded 22 Dec 1824; residence - New Brunswick, Canada. SOURCE: WO120 Volume 35 page 169. INDEX # 1129.

Aug^s LIEDER; pension awarded 22 Dec 1824; residence - New Brunswick, Canada; died 30 Jun 1831. SOURCE: WO120 Volume 35 page 169. INDEX # 1130.

Jno VANDERMEY; pension awarded 22 Dec 1824; residence - New Brunswick, Canada. SOURCE: WO120 Volume 35 page 169. INDEX # 1131.

60th Regiment of Foot continued

Jn⁰ HOLTZAPPEL; pension awarded 22 Dec 1824; residence - New Brunswick, Canada. SOURCE: WO120 Volume 35 page 169. INDEX # 1132.

Hen^y HEINECKE; pension awarded 22 Dec 1824; residence - New Brunswick, Canada. SOURCE: WO120 Volume 35 page 169. INDEX # 1133.

Jn⁰ F. CORBIE; pension awarded 22 Dec 1824; residence - New Brunswick, Canada. SOURCE: WO120 Volume 35 page 169. INDEX # 1134.

Christ^n TIEFENBACH; pension awarded 22 Dec 1824; residence - New Brunswick, Canada. SOURCE: WO120 Volume 35 page 169. INDEX # 1135.

Adam SCHOP; pension awarded 1 Feb 1826; residence - Nova Scotia, Canada. SOURCE: WO120 Volume 35 page 169. INDEX # 1136.

Dirk FALANT; pension awarded 15 Mar 1826; residence - Demerara, South America. SOURCE: WO120 Volume 35 page 169. INDEX # 1137.

Jos^h REVEREND; pension awarded 17 May 1826; residence - Berbice, Guyana. SOURCE: WO120 Volume 35 page 169. INDEX # 1138.

Albert SIMONSKY; pension awarded 30 Aug 1826; residence - Canada. SOURCE: WO120 Volume 35 page 169. INDEX # 1139.

Valen^e DELASERAS; pension awarded 12 Sep 1821; residence - Canada. SOURCE: WO120 Volume 35 page 169. INDEX # 1140.

Peter MELANO; pension awarded 12 Sep 1821; residence - Canada. SOURCE: WO120 Volume 35 page 170. INDEX # 1141.

Mich^l BLAIR; pension awarded 12 Sep 1821; residence - Canada. SOURCE: WO120 Volume 35 page 170. INDEX # 1142.

Ignace MARTZIAN; pension awarded 12 Sep 1821; residence - Canada. SOURCE: WO120 Volume 35 page 170. INDEX # 1143.

Gotlieb SCHMIDT; pension awarded 8 Aug 1827; residence - Nova Scotia, Canada. SOURCE: WO120 Volume 35 page 170. INDEX # 1144

And^w HENDRICKSON; pension awarded 23 Jul 1828. SOURCE: WO120 Volume 35 page 170. INDEX # 1145.

Conrad HESSE; pension awarded 24 Nov 1824. SOURCE: WO120 Volume 35 page 170. INDEX # 1146.

Jos^h ZRESSENBACH; pension awarded 12 Mar 1828. SOURCE: WO120 Volume 35 page 170. INDEX # 1147.

Carl GERBER; pension awarded 29 Oct 1828. SOURCE: WO120 Volume 35 page 170. INDEX # 1148.

Chas WILSON; pension awarded 11 Apr 1832. SOURCE: WO120 Volume 35 page 170. INDEX # 1149.

John HOLTZAPPEL; pension awarded 22 Dec 1824. SOURCE: WO120 Volume 35 page 170. INDEX # 1150.

61st Regiment of Foot

Thos WAGER; pension awarded 20 Jul 1825. SOURCE: WO120 Volume 35 page 172. INDEX # 1151.

Jn⁰ LAMBERT; pension awarded 8 Jun 1836. SOURCE: WO120 Volume 35 page 172. INDEX # 1152.

62nd Regiment of Foot

Saml BROWNING; pension awarded 27 Oct 1819; residence - Nova Scotia, Canada. SOURCE: WO120 Volume 35 page 174. INDEX # 1153.

Hen^y MORGAN; pension awarded 23 May 1821; residence - Nova Scotia, Canada. SOURCE: WO120 Volume 35 page 174. INDEX # 1154.

Theoph^s WILSON; pension awarded 25 Sep 1822; residence - Ceylon. SOURCE: WO120 Volume 35 page 174. INDEX # 1155.

Ja^s MCLAUGHLAN; pension awarded 1 Feb 1826; residence - Nova Scotia, Canada. SOURCE: WO120 Volume 35 page 174. INDEX # 1156.

Jn⁰ MCCARNEY; pension awarded 13 Oct 1830. SOURCE: WO120 Volume 35 page 174. INDEX # 1157.

BRITISH ARMY PENSIONERS ABROAD

63rd Regiment of Foot

Saml SMITH; pension awarded 9 Jul 1834. SOURCE: WO120 Volume 35 page 176. INDEX # 1158.
Ja^s SKINE; pension awarded 10 Sep 1834. SOURCE: WO120 Volume 35 page 176. INDEX # 1159.
Wm DAWSON; pension awarded 10 Sep 1834. SOURCE: WO120 Volume 35 page 176. INDEX # 1160.
Ge^o GANT; pension awarded 10 Sep 1834. SOURCE: WO120 Volume 35 page 176. INDEX # 1161.
Isaac MIMMS; pension awarded 10 Sep 1834. SOURCE: WO120 Volume 35 page 176. INDEX # 1162.
Ge^o ARAM; pension awarded 14 Sep 1836. SOURCE: WO120 Volume 35 page 176. INDEX # 1163.
Ed^{wd} LAWRENCE; pension awarded 14 Sep 1836. SOURCE: WO120 Volume 35 page 176. INDEX # 1164.
Jos^h STUCK; pension awarded 14 Sep 1836. SOURCE: WO120 Volume 35 page 176. INDEX # 1165.
Willm ANTINGHAM; pension awarded 14 Sep 1836. SOURCE: WO120 Volume 35 page 176. INDEX # 1166.
Ja^s ONEY; pension awarded 14 Sep 1836. SOURCE: WO120 Volume 35 page 176. INDEX # 1167.
Hen^y STANLEY; pension awarded 23 Oct 1838. SOURCE: WO120 Volume 35 page 176. INDEX # 1168.

64th Regiment of Foot

Ge^o BENNETT; pension awarded 10 Aug 1836. SOURCE: WO120 Volume 35 page 178. INDEX # 1169.

65th Regiment of Foot

Jno BUGGLE; pension awarded 25 Jul 1821; residence - India. SOURCE: WO120 Volume 35 page 180. INDEX # 1170.
Elias MYERS; pension awarded 25 Jul 1821; residence - India. SOURCE: WO120 Volume 35 page 180. INDEX # 1171.
Jno STEIN; pension awarded 25 Jul 1821; residence - India. SOURCE: WO120 Volume 35 page 180. INDEX # 1172.
Thos VALLENSNO; pension awarded 25 Sep 1822; residence - Bombay, India. SOURCE: WO120 Volume 35 page 180. INDEX # 1173.
Hen^y HARLING; pension awarded 25 Sep 1822; residence - Bombay, India. SOURCE: WO120 Volume 35 page 180. INDEX # 1174.
Ja^s IRWIN; pension awarded 5 Mar 1823; residence - Bombay, India. SOURCE: WO120 Volume 35 page 180. INDEX # 1175.
Anth^y LEE; pension awarded 5 Mar 1823; residence - Bombay, India; died 26 May 1824. SOURCE: WO120 Volume 35 page 180. INDEX # 1176.
Jno WARD; pension awarded 5 Mar 1823; residence - Bombay, India. SOURCE: WO120 Volume 35 page 180. INDEX # 1177.
Saml STEWART; pension awarded 5 Mar 1823; residence - Bombay, India; died 29 Aug 1823. SOURCE: WO120 Volume 35 page 180. INDEX # 1178.
Jno VETTERS; pension awarded 5 Mar 1823; residence - Bombay, India. SOURCE: WO120 Volume 35 page 180. INDEX # 1179.
Chas DUFFY; pension awarded 5 Mar 1823; residence - Bombay, India; died 30 May 1824. SOURCE: WO120 Volume 35 page 180. INDEX # 1180.
Robt BULL; pension awarded 5 Mar 1823; residence - Bombay, India; died 1 Jul 1827. SOURCE: WO120 Volume 35 page 180. INDEX # 1181.
Willm CARRICK; pension awarded 5 Mar 1823; residence - Bombay, India; died 11 Jul 1827. SOURCE: WO120 Volume 35 page 180. INDEX # 1182.

66th Regiment of Foot

Ja^s CARMICHAEL; pension awarded 20 Feb 1828. SOURCE: WO120 Volume 35 page 182. INDEX # 1183.
Mau^e EARDLEY; pension awarded 14 Sep 1831. SOURCE: WO120 Volume 35 page 182. INDEX # 1184.
Ja^s ANDERTON; pension awarded 9 Jan 1833. SOURCE: WO120 Volume 35 page 182. INDEX # 1185.
James SMITH; pension awarded 12 Nov 1834. SOURCE: WO120 Volume 35 page 182. INDEX # 1186.

66th Regiment of Foot (continued)

Mich^l BARRY; pension awarded 11 Nov 1835. SOURCE: WO120 Volume 35 page 182. INDEX # 1187.
Ge^o MCDONALD; pension awarded 11 Nov 1835. : WO120 Volume 35 page 182. INDEX # 1188.
Robt GRAHAM; pension awarded 14 Dec 1836. SOURCE: WO120 Volume 35 page 182. INDEX # 1189.
Jno COSTELLO; pension awarded 14 Dec 1836. SOURCE: WO120 Volume 35 page 182. INDEX # 1190.
Robt KIRBY; pension awarded 13 Sep 1837. SOURCE: WO120 Volume 35 page 182. INDEX # 1191.
Chas BARBER; pension awarded 26 Dec 1838. SOURCE: WO120 Volume 35 page 182. INDEX # 1192.

67th Regiment of Foot

Christ^n VERNON; pension awarded 27 Oct 1819; residence - Ceylon. SOURCE: WO120 Volume 35 page 184. INDEX # 1193.
Matt^w KING; pension awarded 4 Aug 1824; residence - Bombay, India. SOURCE: WO120 Volume 35 page 184. INDEX # 1194.
Alex^r DERNING; pension awarded 4 Aug 1824; residence - Bombay, India. SOURCE: WO120 Volume 35 page 184. INDEX # 1195.
Hugh HAMILTON; pension awarded 4 Aug 1824; residence - Bombay, India. SOURCE: WO120 Volume 35 page 184. INDEX # 1196.
Pat^k GIBBONS; pension awarded 2 Jun 1825; residence - Bombay, India. SOURCE: WO120 Volume 35 page 184. INDEX # 1197.
Jno MOORE; pension awarded 19 Jul 1826; residence - Bombay, India. SOURCE: WO120 Volume 35 page 184. INDEX # 1198.
Mich^l GAHAGAN; pension awarded 19 Jul 1826; residence - Bombay, India; died 11 Jun 1827. SOURCE: WO120 Volume 35 page 184. INDEX # 1199.
Jno NEWELL; pension awarded 5 Aug 1824; residence - Bombay, India; died 21 May 1826. SOURCE: WO120 Volume 35 page 184. INDEX # 1200.

68th Regiment of Foot

Jno FOLEY; pension awarded 25 Mar 1818; residence - Canada. SOURCE: WO120 Volume 35 page 186. INDEX # 1201.
Jos^h TAYLOR; pension awarded 9 May 1823; residence - Canada. SOURCE: WO120 Volume 35 page 186. INDEX # 1202.
Jno MCDONALD; pension awarded 30 Mar 1825; residence - Canada. SOURCE: WO120 Volume 35 page 186. INDEX # 1203.
Thos HARTE; pension awarded 30 Mar 1825; residence - Canada. SOURCE: WO120 Volume 35 page 186. INDEX # 1204.
Arth^r BLANEY; pension awarded 30 Mar 1825; residence - Canada. SOURCE: WO120 Volume 35 page 186. INDEX # 1205.
Ja^s COOPER; pension awarded 30 Mar 1825; residence - Canada. SOURCE: WO120 Volume 35 page 186. INDEX # 1206.
Austin JOICE; pension awarded 30 Mar 1825; residence - Canada. SOURCE: WO120 Volume 35 page 186. INDEX # 1207.
Hugh BORLAND; pension awarded 15 Mar 1826; residence - Canada. SOURCE: WO120 Volume 35 page 186. INDEX # 1208.
Abra^m PINCKNEY; pension awarded 7 Mar 1827; residence - Quebec, Canada. SOURCE: WO120 Volume 35 page 186. INDEX # 1209.
Saml CROSS; pension awarded 5 Sep 1827; residence - Canada. SOURCE: WO120 Volume 35 page 186. INDEX # 1210.
Dennis KEELY; pension awarded 29 Sep 1819. SOURCE: WO120 Volume 35 page 186. INDEX # 1211.
Jos^h WHEAT; pension awarded 29 Sep 1819. SOURCE: WO120 Volume 35 page 186. INDEX # 1212.
Ja^s THOROGOOD; pension awarded 29 Oct 1828. SOURCE: WO120 Volume 35 page 186. INDEX # 1213.
Ja^s BARRYMAN; pension awarded 29 Oct 1828. SOURCE: WO120 Volume 35 page 186. INDEX # 1214.

BRITISH ARMY PENSIONERS ABROAD

69th Regiment of Foot

Chas POINT; pension awarded 17 Mar 1819; residence - Cape of Good Hope, South Africa. SOURCE: WO120 Volume 35 page 189. INDEX # 1215.

Herman TILLMAN; pension awarded 17 Mar 1819; residence - Cape of Good Hope, South Africa. SOURCE: WO120 Volume 35 page 189. INDEX # 1216.

Anth^y DOYLE; pension awarded 13 Sep 1820; residence - Cape of Good Hope, South Africa. SOURCE: WO120 Volume 35 page 189. INDEX # 1217.

Thos WELLS; pension awarded 7 Feb 1821; residence - India. SOURCE: WO120 Volume 35 page 189. INDEX # 1218.

Ge^o BAILEY; pension awarded 7 Feb 1821; residence - India. SOURCE: WO120 Volume 35 page 189. INDEX # 1219.

Jno DAY; pension awarded 7 Feb 1821; residence - India. SOURCE: WO120 Volume 35 page 189. INDEX # 1220.

Jno EDWARDS; pension awarded 7 Feb 1821; residence - India. SOURCE: WO120 Volume 35 page 189. INDEX # 1221.

Isaac HENLEY; pension awarded 7 Feb 1821; residence - India. SOURCE: WO120 Volume 35 page 189. INDEX # 1222.

Ja^s GREENFIELD; pension awarded 4 Jun 1823; residence - Madras, India. SOURCE: WO120 Volume 35 page 189. INDEX # 1223.

Thos EGLESTON; pension awarded 4 Jun 1823; residence - Madras, India. SOURCE: WO120 Volume 35 page 189. INDEX # 1224.

Thos COLLESHAW; pension awarded 4 Jun 1823; residence - Madras, India. SOURCE: WO120 Volume 35 page 189. INDEX # 1225.

Danl MCCAMBLY; pension awarded 4 Jun 1823; residence - Madras, India; died 10 Jan 1828. SOURCE: WO120 Volume 35 page 189. INDEX # 1226.

Hugh LOUGHLAN; pension awarded 4 Jun 1823; residence - Madras, India; died 7 Apr 1827. SOURCE: WO120 Volume 35 page 189. INDEX # 1227.

Willm BOWIE; pension awarded 4 Jun 1823; residence - Madras, India. SOURCE: WO120 Volume 35 page 189. INDEX # 1228.

Richd TALBOT; pension awarded 4 Jun 1823; residence - Madras, India. SOURCE: WO120 Volume 35 page 189. INDEX # 1229.

Saml ORMSBY; pension awarded 3 Mar 1824; residence - Madras, India; died 22 May 1827. SOURCE: WO120 Volume 35 page 189. INDEX # 1230.

Jno GUEST; pension awarded 3 Mar 1824; residence - Madras, India. SOURCE: WO120 Volume 35 page 189. INDEX # 1231.

Ja^s POTTER; pension awarded 3 Mar 1824; residence - Madras, India. SOURCE: WO120 Volume 35 page 189. INDEX # 1232.

Willm WALL; pension awarded 3 Mar 1824; residence - Madras, India. SOURCE: WO120 Volume 35 page 189. INDEX # 1233.

Willm PRENTICE; pension awarded 3 Mar 1824; residence - Madras, India. SOURCE: WO120 Volume 35 page 189. INDEX # 1234.

Jno THOMAS; pension awarded 3 Mar 1824; residence - Madras, India. SOURCE: WO120 Volume 35 page 189. INDEX # 1235.

Thos THOMPSON; pension awarded 3 Mar 1824; residence - Madras, India. SOURCE: WO120 Volume 35 page 189. INDEX # 1236.

Ja^s BRENNAN; pension awarded 3 Mar 1824; residence - Madras, India. SOURCE: WO120 Volume 35 page 189. INDEX # 1237.

Hen^y BLADES; pension awarded 3 Mar 1824; residence - Madras, India. SOURCE: WO120 Volume 35 page 189. INDEX # 1238.

Willm BAILEY; pension awarded 3 Mar 1824; residence - Madras, India. SOURCE: WO120 Volume 35 page 190. INDEX # 1239.

Jno CREAKE; pension awarded 3 Mar 1824; residence - Madras, India. SOURCE: WO120 Volume 35 page 190. INDEX # 1240.

69th Regiment of Foot (continued)

Jn⁰ ENDSOR; pension awarded 3 Mar 1824; residence - Madras, India. SOURCE: WO120 Volume 35 page 190. INDEX # 1241.

Jn⁰ FRANCIS; pension awarded 3 Mar 1824; residence - Madras, India. SOURCE: WO120 Volume 35 page 190. INDEX # 1242.

Willm PINDAR; pension awarded 3 Mar 1824; residence - Madras, India. SOURCE: WO120 Volume 35 page 190. INDEX # 1243.

Jn⁰ URSON; pension awarded 3 Mar 1824; residence - Madras, India; died 26 Jul 1833. SOURCE: WO120 Volume 35 page 190. INDEX # 1244.

Jn⁰ WILLIAMS; pension awarded 3 Mar 1824; residence - Madras, India. SOURCE: WO120 Volume 35 page 190. INDEX # 1245.

Jn⁰ HEWINGS; pension awarded 3 Mar 1824; residence - Madras, India. SOURCE: WO120 Volume 35 page 190. INDEX # 1246.

Thos JONES; pension awarded 3 Mar 1824; residence - Madras, India. SOURCE: WO120 Volume 35 page 190. INDEX # 1247.

Fra^s HOLMES; pension awarded 3 Mar 1824; residence - Madras, India. SOURCE: WO120 Volume 35 page 190. INDEX # 1248.

Robt HUSSEY; pension awarded 4 Aug 1824; residence - Madras, India. SOURCE: WO120 Volume 35 page 190. INDEX # 1249.

Jn⁰ CARTTEDGE; pension awarded 4 Aug 1824; residence - Madras, India. SOURCE: WO120 Volume 35 page 190. INDEX # 1250.

Jn⁰ DEVENPORT; pension awarded 4 Aug 1824; residence - Madras, India. SOURCE: WO120 Volume 35 page 190. INDEX # 1251.

Thos GRAY; pension awarded 4 Aug 1824; residence - Madras, India; died 23 Sep 1832. SOURCE: WO120 Volume 35 page 190. INDEX # 1252.

Jos^h BURGESS; pension awarded 4 Aug 1824; residence - Madras, India. SOURCE: WO120 Volume 35 page 190. INDEX # 1253.

Jn⁰ BATTISON; pension awarded 4 Aug 1824; residence - Madras, India. SOURCE: WO120 Volume 35 page 190. INDEX # 1254.

Thos HURST; pension awarded 4 Aug 1824; residence - Madras, India. SOURCE: WO120 Volume 35 page 190. INDEX # 1255.

Elisha ROSIA; pension awarded 4 Aug 1824; residence - Madras, India. SOURCE: WO120 Volume 35 page 190. INDEX # 1256.

Hen^y BOOTH; pension awarded 4 Aug 1824; residence - Madras, India. SOURCE: WO120 Volume 35 page 190. INDEX # 1257.

Jn⁰ JOSEPH; pension awarded 4 Aug 1824; residence - Madras, India. SOURCE: WO120 Volume 35 page 190. INDEX # 1258.

Jabez HARTLEY; pension awarded 4 Aug 1824; residence - Madras, India. SOURCE: WO120 Volume 35 page 190. INDEX # 1259.

Thos BLACKGROVES; pension awarded 4 Aug 1824; residence - Madras, India. SOURCE: WO120 Volume 35 page 190. INDEX # 1260.

Richd HOLDING; pension awarded 4 Aug 1824; residence - Madras, India. SOURCE: WO120 Volume 35 page 190. INDEX # 1261.

Den^s BRANNAN; pension awarded 23 Nov 1825; residence - Madras, India. SOURCE: WO120 Volume 35 page 190. INDEX # 1262.

Jn⁰ EMBLER; pension awarded 23 Nov 1825; residence - Madras, India. SOURCE: WO120 Volume 35 page 191. INDEX # 1263.

Jos^h KING; pension awarded 23 Nov 1825; residence - Madras, India. SOURCE: WO120 Volume 35 page 191. INDEX # 1264.

Thos ROBINSON; pension awarded 23 Nov 1825; residence - Madras, India. SOURCE: WO120 Volume 35 page 191. INDEX # 1265.

Thos MILLINGTON; pension awarded 23 Nov 1825; residence - Madras, India. SOURCE: WO120 Volume 35 page 191. INDEX # 1266.

BRITISH ARMY PENSIONERS ABROAD

69th Regiment of Foot (continued)

Jn⁰ SPOONER; pension awarded 23 Nov 1825; residence - Madras, India. SOURCE: WO120 Volume 35 page 191. INDEX # 1267.

Hen^y GIBBS; pension awarded 15 Mar 1826; residence - Fort St. George, India. SOURCE: WO120 Volume 35 page 191. INDEX # 1268.

Willm ENOCK; pension awarded 15 Mar 1826; residence - Fort St. George, India. SOURCE: WO120 Volume 35 page 191. INDEX # 1269.

Jn⁰ SPENCER; pension awarded 15 Mar 1826; residence - Fort St. George, India. SOURCE: WO120 Volume 35 page 191. INDEX # 1270.

Robt HOLDING; pension awarded 15 Mar 1826; residence - Fort St. George, India. SOURCE: WO120 Volume 35 page 191. INDEX # 1271.

Willm WRIGHT; pension awarded 15 Mar 1826; residence - Fort St. George, India. SOURCE: WO120 Volume 35 page 191. INDEX # 1272.

Willm BREARLEY; pension awarded 15 Mar 1826; residence - Fort St. George, India. SOURCE: WO120 Volume 35 page 191. INDEX # 1273.

Robt IRWIN; pension awarded 15 Mar 1826; residence - Fort St. George, India. SOURCE: WO120 Volume 35 page 191. INDEX # 1274.

Willm BOYD; pension awarded 15 Mar 1826; residence - Fort St. George, India. SOURCE: WO120 Volume 35 page 191. INDEX # 1275.

Willm BOOTH; pension awarded 15 Mar 1826; residence - Fort St. George, India. SOURCE: WO120 Volume 35 page 191. INDEX # 1276.

Jn⁰ NEWBOLD; pension awarded 15 Mar 1826; residence - Fort St. George, India. SOURCE: WO120 Volume 35 page 191. INDEX # 1277.

Willm WARD; pension awarded 15 Mar 1826; residence - Fort St. George, India. SOURCE: WO120 Volume 35 page 191. INDEX # 1278.

Willm ALSOP; pension awarded 15 Mar 1826; residence - Fort St. George, India. SOURCE: WO120 Volume 35 page 191. INDEX # 1279.

Ja^s BRAWN; pension awarded 15 Mar 1826; residence - Fort St. George, India. SOURCE: WO120 Volume 35 page 191. INDEX # 1280.

Robt BAKER; pension awarded 15 Mar 1826; residence - Fort St. George, India. SOURCE: WO120 Volume 35 page 191. INDEX # 1281.

Ja^s BRAILEY; pension awarded 15 Mar 1826; residence - Fort St. George, India. SOURCE: WO120 Volume 35 page 191. INDEX # 1282.

Robt CROSLAND; pension awarded 15 Mar 1826; residence - Fort St. George, India. SOURCE: WO120 Volume 35 page 191. INDEX # 1283.

Dav^d DALTON; pension awarded 15 Mar 1826; residence - Fort St. George, India. SOURCE: WO120 Volume 35 page 191. INDEX # 1284.

Jn⁰ EGLINTON; pension awarded 15 Mar 1826; residence - Fort St. George, India. SOURCE: WO120 Volume 35 page 191. INDEX # 1285.

Richd FARMER; pension awarded 15 Mar 1826; residence - Fort St. George, India; died 14 Dec 1832. SOURCE: WO120 Volume 35 page 191. INDEX # 1286.

Jn⁰ FIELDS; pension awarded 15 Mar 1826; residence - Fort St. George, India. SOURCE: WO120 Volume 35 page 192. INDEX # 1287.

Benjn KUTSBY; pension awarded 15 Mar 1826; residence - Fort St. George, India. SOURCE: WO120 Volume 35 page 192. INDEX # 1288.

Jn⁰ HUBBARD; pension awarded 15 Mar 1826; residence - Fort St. George, India. SOURCE: WO120 Volume 3e 35 page 192. INDEX # 1289.

Ephr^m JOHNSON; pension awarded 15 Mar 1826; residence - Fort St. George, India. SOURCE: WO120 Volume 35 page 192. INDEX # 1290.

Jn⁰ MCCLUSKY; pension awarded 15 Mar 1826; residence - Fort St. George, India. SOURCE: WO120 Volume 35 page 192. INDEX # 1291.

Ja^s NEWTON; pension awarded 15 Mar 1826; residence - Fort St. George, India. SOURCE: WO120 Volume 35 page 192. INDEX # 1292.

69th Regiment of Foot (continued)

Bern^d QUINN; pension awarded 15 Mar 1826; residence - Fort St. George, India. SOURCE: WO120 Volume 35 page 192. INDEX # 1293.
Jos^h RUDGE; pension awarded 15 Mar 1826; residence - Fort St. George, India. SOURCE: WO120 Volume 35 page 192. INDEX # 1294.
Ge^o RICHARDS; pension awarded 15 Mar 1826; residence - Fort St. George, India. SOURCE: WO120 Volume 35 page 192. INDEX # 1295.
Willm SMITH; pension awarded 15 Mar 1826; residence - Fort St. George, India. SOURCE: WO120 Volume 35 page 192. INDEX # 1296.
Anth^y VAUGHAN; pension awarded 15 Mar 1826; residence - Fort St. George, India. SOURCE: WO120 Volume 35 page 192. INDEX # 1297.
Thos WILKINS; pension awarded 15 Mar 1826; residence - Fort St. George, India. SOURCE: WO120 Volume 35 page 192. INDEX # 1298.
Fra^s PEYTON; pension awarded 9 Aug 1837. SOURCE: WO120 Volume 35 page 192. INDEX # 1299.

70th Regiment of Foot

Richd CARROLL; pension awarded 7 Dec 1820; residence - Canada. SOURCE: WO120 Volume 35 page 195. INDEX # 1300.
Bern^d BUCKLEY; pension awarded 12 Sep 1821; residence - Canada. SOURCE: WO120 Volume 35 page 195. INDEX # 1301.
Willm MURDOCK; pension awarded 12 Sep 1821; residence - Canada. SOURCE: WO120 Volume 35 page 195. INDEX # 1302.
Jno REILLY; pension awarded 24 Oct 1821; residence - Canada. SOURCE: WO120 Volume 35 page 195. INDEX # 1303.
Jno KAIN; pension awarded 24 Oct 1821; residence - Canada. SOURCE: WO120 Volume 35 page 195. INDEX # 1304.
Jno RASTON; pension awarded 7 Feb 1822; residence - Canada. SOURCE: WO120 Volume 35 page 195. INDEX # 1305.
Robt HAWKINS; pension awarded 25 Sep 1822; residence - Canada. SOURCE: WO120 Volume 35 page 195. INDEX # 1306.
Thos HUNTER; pension awarded 25 Sep 1822; residence - Canada. SOURCE: WO120 Volume 35 page 195. INDEX # 1307.
Ed^{wd} KAVANAGH; pension awarded 25 Sep 1822; residence - Canada. SOURCE: WO120 Volume 35 page 195. INDEX # 1308.
Thos WARNE; pension awarded 24 Jan 1838. SOURCE: WO120 Volume 35 page 195. INDEX # 1309.
Thos WARREN; pension awarded 24 Jan 1838. SOURCE: WO120 Volume 35 page 195. INDEX # 1310.

71st Regiment of Foot

Willm THOMS; pension awarded 30 Mar 1825. SOURCE: WO120 Volume 35 page 197. INDEX # 1311.
Jno KENNEDY; pension awarded 8 Jun 1831. SOURCE: WO120 Volume 35 page 197. INDEX # 1312.
Hugh MULROGUE; pension awarded 8 Jun 1831. SOURCE: WO120 Volume 35 page 197. INDEX # 1313.
Jno WHELON; pension awarded 8 Jun 1831. SOURCE: WO120 Volume 35 page 197. INDEX # 1314.
Robt ADAMS; pension awarded 13 Jul 1831. SOURCE: WO120 Volume 35 page 197. INDEX # 1315.
Willm BOWIE; pension awarded 13 Jul 1831. SOURCE: WO120 Volume 35 page 197. INDEX # 1316.
Jno COMBS; pension awarded 13 Jul 1831. SOURCE: WO120 Volume 35 page 197. INDEX # 1317.
Alex^r DAVIDSON; pension awarded 13 Jul 1831. SOURCE: WO120 Volume 35 page 197. INDEX # 1318.
Wm GLOVER; pension awarded 13 Jul 1831. SOURCE: WO120 Volume 35 page 197. INDEX # 1319.
Ja^s MCINTYRE; pension awarded 13 Jul 1831. SOURCE: WO120 Volume 35 page 197. INDEX # 1320.
Wm MCLEAN; pension awarded 13 Jul 1831. SOURCE: WO120 Volume 35 page 197. INDEX # 1321.
Wm WILSON; pension awarded 13 Jul 1831. SOURCE: WO120 Volume 35 page 197. INDEX # 1322.
Matt^w CLARKE; pension awarded 13 Jul 1831. SOURCE: WO120 Volume 35 page 197. INDEX # 1323.

BRITISH ARMY PENSIONERS ABROAD

71st Regiment of Foot

Gustavus CLEMENTS; pension awarded 14 Sep 1831. SOURCE: WO120 Volume 35 page 197. INDEX # 1324.
Neil GALLAGHER; pension awarded 14 Dec 1831. SOURCE: WO120 Volume 35 page 197. INDEX # 1325.
Hugh HARVEY; pension awarded 14 Dec 1831. SOURCE: WO120 Volume 35 page 197. INDEX # 1326.
Thos KELLY; pension awarded 14 Dec 1831. SOURCE: WO120 Volume 35 page 197. INDEX # 1327.
Chas MCLEAN; pension awarded 14 Dec 1831. SOURCE: WO120 Volume 35 page 197. INDEX # 1328.
Noble WRIGHT; pension awarded 14 Dec 1831. SOURCE: WO120 Volume 35 page 197. INDEX # 1329.
Geo LESLIE; pension awarded 11 Jul 1832. SOURCE: WO120 Volume 35 page 197. INDEX # 1330.
Jno CULLEN; pension awarded 11 Jul 1832. SOURCE: WO120 Volume 35 page 197. INDEX # 1331.
Dennis MEAGHER; pension awarded 11 Jul 1832. SOURCE: WO120 Volume 35 page 197. INDEX # 1332.
Wm ROBINSON; pension awarded 11 Jul 1832. SOURCE: WO120 Volume 35 page 197. INDEX # 1333.
Jas RUSSELL; pension awarded 11 Jul 1832. SOURCE: WO120 Volume 35 page 197. INDEX # 1334.
Danl MCKAY; pension awarded 12 Sep 1832. SOURCE: WO120 Volume 35 page 198. INDEX # 1335.
Wm CLARKE; pension awarded 9 Jan 1833. SOURCE: WO120 Volume 35 page 198. INDEX # 1336.

72nd Regiment of Foot

Jno MCGOWAN; pension awarded 26 Jul 1820; residence - Nova Scotia, Canada. SOURCE: WO120 Volume 35 page 199. INDEX # 1337.
Thos ALLAN; pension awarded 26 Jul 1820; residence - Nova Scotia, Canada. SOURCE: WO120 Volume 35 page 199. INDEX # 1338.
Jas DIDDLESTON; pension awarded 15 Sep 1820; residence Nova Scotia, Canada. SOURCE: WO120 Volume 35 page 199. INDEX # 1339.
Peter HUNTER; pension awarded 12 Sep 1821; residence - Cape of Good Hope, South Africa. SOURCE: WO120 Volume 35 page 199. INDEX # 1340.
Jno MANN; pension awarded 12 Sep 1821; residence - Cape of Good Hope, South Africa. SOURCE: WO120 Volume 35 page 199. INDEX # 1341.
Thos FERGUSON; pension awarded 7 Feb 1822; residence - Cape of Good Hope, South Africa. SOURCE: WO120 Volume 35 page 199. INDEX # 1342.
Thos COOK; pension awarded 20 Mar 1822; residence - Cape of Good Hope, South Africa. SOURCE: WO120 Volume 35 page 199. INDEX # 1343.
Thos WELSH; pension awarded 20 Mar 1822; residence - Cape of Good Hope, South Africa. SOURCE: WO120 Volume 35 page 199. INDEX # 1344.
Richd MOTT; pension awarded 20 Mar 1822; residence - Cape of Good Hope, South Africa. SOURCE: WO120 Volume 35 page 199. INDEX # 1345.
Wm TAYLOR; pension awarded 20 Mar 1822; residence - Cape of Good Hope, South Africa. SOURCE: WO120 Volume 35 page 199. INDEX # 1346.
Dond ROBERTSON; pension awarded 20 Mar 1822; residence - Cape of Good Hope, South Africa. SOURCE: WO120 Volume 35 page 199. INDEX # 1347.
Clemt RUSSELL; pension awarded 20 Mar 1822; residence - Cape of Good Hope, South Africa. SOURCE: WO120 Volume 35 page 199. INDEX # 1348.
Jno MCKENZIE; pension awarded 20 Mar 1822; residence - Cape of Good Hope, South Africa. SOURCE: WO120 Volume 35 page 199. INDEX # 1349.
Luke GOODWIN; pension awarded 1 May 1822; residence - Cape of Good Hope, South Africa. SOURCE: WO120 Volume 35 page 199. INDEX # 1350.
Jas MIRK; pension awarded 1 May 1822; residence - Cape of Good Hope, South Africa. SOURCE: WO120 Volume 35 page 199. INDEX # 1351.
Andw ROSS; pension awarded 1 May 1822; residence - Cape of Good Hope, South Africa. SOURCE: WO120 Volume 35 page 199. INDEX # 1352.
Jno MCLAREN; pension awarded 1 May 1822; residence - Cape of Good Hope, South Africa. SOURCE: WO120 Volume 35 page 199. INDEX # 1353.
Jas BUCHANNAN; pension awarded 1 May 1822; residence - Cape of Good Hope, South Africa; died 5 Jan 1825. SOURCE: WO120 Volume 35 page 199. INDEX # 1354.

WO120 VOLUME 35

72nd Regiment of Foot (continued)

Jn⁰ SMITH; pension awarded 1 May 1822; residence - Cape of Good Hope, South Africa. SOURCE: WO120 Volume 35 page 199. INDEX # 1355.

Hen⁽ʸ⁾ HUGHES; pension awarded 1 May 1822; residence - Cape of Good Hope, South Africa. SOURCE: WO120 Volume 35 page 199. INDEX # 1356.

Ja⁽ˢ⁾ DENNIS; pension awarded 1 May 1822; residence - Cape of Good Hope, South Africa. SOURCE: WO120 Volume 35 page 199. INDEX # 1357.

Ja⁽ˢ⁾ BROWN; pension awarded 1 May 1822; residence - Cape of Good Hope, South Africa. SOURCE: WO120 Volume 35 page 199. INDEX # 1358.

Rob⁽ᵗ⁾ MORAN; pension awarded 1 May 1822; residence - Cape of Good Hope, South Africa. SOURCE: WO120 Volume 35 page 199. INDEX # 1359.

Rob⁽ᵗ⁾ LINDSAY; pension awarded 1 May 1822; residence - Cape of Good Hope, South Africa. SOURCE: WO120 Volume 35 page 199. INDEX # 1360.

Dun⁽ᶜ⁾ MCPHERSON; pension awarded 1 May 1822; residence - Cape of Good Hope, South Africa. SOURCE: WO120 Volume 35 page 200. INDEX # 1361.

And⁽ʷ⁾ BELL; pension awarded 1 May 1822; residence - Cape of Good Hope, South Africa. SOURCE: WO120 Volume 35 page 200. INDEX # 1362.

Pat⁽ᵏ⁾ GIBLON; pension awarded 1 May 1822; residence - Cape of Good Hope, South Africa. SOURCE: WO120 Volume 35 page 200. INDEX # 1363.

Ja⁽ˢ⁾ DUFF; pension awarded 1 May 1822; residence - Cape of Good Hope, South Africa. SOURCE: WO120 Volume 35 page 200. INDEX # 1364.

Jn⁰ INGRAM; pension awarded 1 May 1822; residence - Cape of Good Hope, South Africa. SOURCE: WO120 Volume 35 page 200. INDEX # 1365.

Ja⁽ˢ⁾ HUGHES; pension awarded 1 May 1822; residence - Cape of Good Hope, South Africa. SOURCE: WO120 Volume 35 page 200. INDEX # 1366.

And⁽ʷ⁾ IRVEN; pension awarded 1 May 1822; residence - Cape of Good Hope, South Africa. SOURCE: WO120 Volume 35 page 200. INDEX # 1367.

Alex⁽ʳ⁾ KIRKWOOD; pension awarded 1 May 1822; residence - Cape of Good Hope, South Africa. SOURCE: WO120 Volume 35 page 200. INDEX # 1368.

Ja⁽ˢ⁾ LEES; pension awarded 1 May 1822; residence - Cape of Good Hope, South Africa. SOURCE: WO120 Volume 35 page 200. INDEX # 1369.

Jn⁰ HILTON; pension awarded 1 May 1822; residence - Cape of Good Hope, South Africa. SOURCE: WO120 Volume 35 page 200. INDEX # 1370.

Will⁽ᵐ⁾ MARKS; pension awarded 1 May 1822; residence - Cape of Good Hope, South Africa. SOURCE: WO120 Volume 35 page 200. INDEX # 1371.

Will⁽ᵐ⁾ HAY; pension awarded 1 May 1822; residence - Cape of Good Hope, South Africa. SOURCE: WO120 Volume 35 page 200. INDEX # 1372.

Rob⁽ᵗ⁾ DENNIS; pension awarded 1 May 1822; residence - Cape of Good Hope, South Africa. SOURCE: WO120 Volume 35 page 200. INDEX # 1373.

Fra⁽ˢ⁾ BROWN; pension awarded 1 May 1822; residence - Cape of Good Hope, South Africa. SOURCE: WO120 Volume 35 page 200. INDEX # 1374.

Will⁽ᵐ⁾ HUNTER; pension awarded 1 May 1822; residence - Cape of Good Hope, South Africa. SOURCE: WO120 Volume 35 page 200. INDEX # 1375.

Jn⁰ FENWICK; pension awarded 1 May 1822; residence - Cape of Good Hope, South Africa. SOURCE: WO120 Volume 35 page 200. INDEX # 1376.

Jn⁰ FOLEY; pension awarded 1 May 1822; residence - Cape of Good Hope, South Africa. SOURCE: WO120 Volume 35 page 200. INDEX # 1377.

Jn⁰ GRANT; pension awarded 19 Jun 1822; residence - Cape of Good Hope, South Africa. SOURCE: WO120 Volume 35 page 200. INDEX # 1378.

Jn⁰ FISON; pension awarded 7 Feb 1822; residence - Cape of Good Hope, South Africa. SOURCE: WO120 Volume 35 page 200. INDEX # 1379.

Arth⁽ʳ⁾ PLUNKETT; pension awarded 7 Feb 1822; residence - Cape of Good Hope, South Africa. SOURCE: WO120 Volume 35 page 200. INDEX # 1380.

72nd Regiment of Foot (continued)

Ja^s HAMILTON; pension awarded 7 Feb 1822; residence - Cape of Good Hope, South Africa. SOURCE: WO120 Volume 35 page 200. INDEX # 1381.

Jno ROBERTSON; pension awarded 7 Feb 1822; residence - Cape of Good Hope, South Africa. SOURCE: WO120 Volume 35 page 200. INDEX # 1382.

Jno BREMNER; pension awarded 7 Feb 1822; residence - Cape of Good Hope, South Africa. SOURCE: WO120 Volume 35 page 200. INDEX # 1383.

Ma^lm MCINTYRE; pension awarded 7 Feb 1822; residence - Cape of Good Hope, South Africa. SOURCE: WO120 Volume 35 page 200. INDEX # 1384.

Alex^r OWENS; pension awarded 7 Feb 1822; residence - Cape of Good Hope, South Africa. SOURCE: WO120 Volume 35 page 201. INDEX # 1385.

Ja^s DANVERS; pension awarded 7 Feb 1822; residence - Cape of Good Hope, South Africa. SOURCE: WO120 Volume 35 page 201. INDEX # 1386.

Jno WATT; pension awarded 7 Feb 1822; residence - Cape of Good Hope, South Africa. SOURCE: WO120 Volume 35 page 201. INDEX # 1387.

Alex^r SMITH; pension awarded 7 Feb 1822; residence - Cape of Good Hope, South Africa. SOURCE: WO120 Volume 35 page 201. INDEX # 1388.

Willm MANSFIELD; pension awarded 7 Feb 1822; residence - Cape of Good Hope, South Africa. SOURCE: WO120 Volume 35 page 201. INDEX # 1389.

And^w HOSIE; pension awarded 7 Feb 1821; residence - Cape of Good Hope, South Africa. SOURCE: WO120 Volume 35 page 201. INDEX # 1390.

Jno GUNN; pension awarded 7 Feb 1821; residence - Cape of Good Hope, South Africa. SOURCE: WO120 Volume 35 page 201. INDEX # 1391.

Jno MCNIEL; pension awarded 7 Feb 1822; residence - Cape of Good Hope, South Africa. SOURCE: WO120 Volume 35 page 201. INDEX # 1392.

Ge^o MACKAY; pension awarded 7 Feb 1822; residence - Cape of Good Hope, South Africa. SOURCE: WO120 Volume 35 page 201. INDEX # 1393.

Robt PIGG; pension awarded 7 Feb 1822; residence - Cape of Good Hope, South Africa. SOURCE: WO120 Volume 35 page 201. INDEX # 1394.

Ge^o FOXCROFT; pension awarded 7 Feb 1822; residence - Cape of Good Hope, South Africa. SOURCE: WO120 Volume 35 page 201. INDEX # 1395.

Alex^r DINGWALL; pension awarded 7 Feb 1822; residence - Cape of Good Hope, South Africa. SOURCE: WO120 Volume 35 page 201. INDEX # 1396.

Thos THOMPSON; pension awarded 7 Feb 1822; residence - Cape of Good Hope, South Africa. SOURCE: WO120 Volume 35 page 201. INDEX # 1397.

Ja^s FERGUSON; pension awarded 7 Feb 1822; residence - Cape of Good Hope, South Africa. SOURCE: WO120 Volume 35 page 201. INDEX # 1398.

Dav^d FITCHET; pension awarded 7 Dec 1823; residence - Cape of Good Hope, South Africa. SOURCE: WO120 Volume 35 page 201. INDEX # 1399.

Ja^s MCDONALD; pension awarded 2 Feb 1801; residence - Cape of Good Hope, South Africa. SOURCE: WO120 Volume 35 page 201. INDEX # 1400.

Ja^s MORRIS; pension awarded 14 Dec 1836. SOURCE: WO120 Volume 35 page 201. INDEX # 1401.

Robt FRASER; pension awarded 13 Sep 1837. SOURCE: WO120 Volume 35 page 201. INDEX # 1402.

Wm HANTON; pension awarded 13 Sep 1837. SOURCE: WO120 Volume 35 page 201. INDEX # 1403.

And^w MCCOULL; pension awarded 8 Nov 1837. SOURCE: WO120 Volume 35 page 201. INDEX # 1404.

Wm MILLER; pension awarded 27 Jun 1838. SOURCE: WO120 Volume 35 page 201. INDEX # 1405.

73rd Regiment of Foot

Willm SPEAR; pension awarded 29 Apr 1818; residence - Canada. SOURCE: WO120 Volume 35 page 203. INDEX # 1406.

Jno BUTCHER; pension awarded 15 Dec 1819; residence - New South Wales, Australia. SOURCE: WO120 Volume 35 page 203. INDEX # 1407.

Jno HARRIS; pension awarded 13 Jul 1831. SOURCE: WO120 Volume 35 page 203. INDEX # 1408.

74th Regiment of Foot

Hugh GORDON; pension awarded 9 May 1823; residence - Nova Scotia, Canada. SOURCE: WO120 Volume 35 page 205. INDEX # 1409.
Geo MERRYMAN; pension awarded 13 Apr 1824; residence - Nova Scotia, Canada. SOURCE: WO120 Volume 35 page 205. INDEX # 1410.
Andw DUNCAN; pension awarded 13 Apr 1824; residence - Nova Scotia, Canada. SOURCE: WO120 Volume 35 page 205. INDEX # 1411.
Hugh MCPHERSON; pension awarded 16 Aug 1825; residence - Nova Scotia, Canada. SOURCE: WO120 Volume 35 page 205. INDEX # 1412.
Jno HUEY; pension awarded 30 Aug 1826; residence - Nova Scotia, Canada. SOURCE: WO120 Volume 35 page 205. INDEX # 1413.
Keans SALTRY; pension awarded 30 Apr 1817; residence - Quebec, Canada. SOURCE: WO120 Volume 35 page 205. INDEX # 1414.

75th Regiment of Foot

Francesco VICENTE; pension awarded 19 Jun 1822; residence - Gibraltar. SOURCE: WO120 Volume 35 page 207. INDEX # 1415.
Keron DEVINE; pension awarded 10 Oct 1832. SOURCE: WO120 Volume 35 page 207. INDEX # 1416.
Jno BROWN; pension awarded 14 Dec 1836. SOURCE: WO120 Volume 35 page 207. INDEX # 1417.
Davd MILLS; pension awarded 14 Dec 1836. SOURCE: WO120 Volume 35 page 207. INDEX # 1418.
Dond MCIVER; pension awarded 8 Mar 1837. SOURCE: WO120 Volume 35 page 207. INDEX # 1419.
Geo MCNAUGHTON; pension awarded 8 Mar 1837. SOURCE: WO120 Volume 35 page 207. INDEX # 1420.
Thos ROSS; pension awarded 25 Oct 1837. SOURCE: WO120 Volume 35 page 207. INDEX # 1421.
Jas SIMPSON; pension awarded 13 Dec 1837. SOURCE: WO120 Volume 35 page 207. INDEX # 1422.

76th Regiment of Foot

Chas VEIT; pension awarded 7 Feb 1822; residence - Cape of Good Hope, South Africa. SOURCE: WO120 Volume 35 page 208. INDEX # 1423.
Wm PAULSON; pension awarded 31 Oct 1827; residence - Canada. SOURCE: WO120 Volume 35 page 208. INDEX # 1424.
Thos FLETCHER; pension awarded 31 Oct 1827; residence - Canada. SOURCE: WO120 Volume 35 page 208. INDEX # 1425.
Jas COWTHORP; pension awarded 7 Dec 1820. SOURCE: WO120 Volume 35 page 208. INDEX # 1426.
Fredk VIET; pension awarded 8 Feb 1832. SOURCE: WO120 Volume 35 page 208. INDEX # 1427.

78th Regiment of Foot

Wm BURROWS; pension awarded 30 Apr 1817; residence - Quebec, Canada. SOURCE: WO120 Volume 35 page 210. INDEX # 1428.
Thos INVERNESS; pension awarded 13 Jul 1831. SOURCE: WO120 Volume 35 page 212. INDEX # 1429.
Anty MARTIN; pension awarded 13 Jul 1831. SOURCE: WO120 Volume 35 page 212. INDEX # 1430.
Wm ASHBOURNE; pension awarded 14 Oct 1835. SOURCE: WO120 Volume 35 page 212. INDEX # 1431.

79th Regiment of Foot

Jno MACDONALD; pension awarded 31 Oct 1827; residence - Canada. SOURCE: WO120 Volume 35 page 214. INDEX # 1432.
Robt MCGILVREY; pension awarded 13 Jul 1831. SOURCE: WO120 Volume 35 page 214. INDEX # 1433.
Geo MCKAY; pension awarded 13 Jul 1831. SOURCE: WO120 Volume 35 page 214. INDEX # 1434.
Thos CAMPBELL; pension awarded 14 Sep 1831. SOURCE: WO120 Volume 35 page 214. INDEX # 1435.

79th Regiment of Foot (continued)

Alex^r SUTHERLAND; pension awarded 14 Sep 1831. SOURCE: WO120 Volume 35 page 214. INDEX # 1436.
Jno BRIMMER; pension awarded 14 Sep 1831. SOURCE: WO120 Volume 35 page 214. INDEX # 1437.
Angus HAMILTON; pension awarded 14 Dec 1831. SOURCE: WO120 Volume 35 page 214. INDEX # 1438.
Jno MCKENZIE; pension awarded 9 Jan 1833. SOURCE: WO120 Volume 35 page 214. INDEX # 1439.
Ge^o MCCANDLISH; pension awarded 9 Jan 1833. SOURCE: WO120 Volume 35 page 214. INDEX # 1440.
Jno MCKINNON; pension awarded 9 Jan 1833. SOURCE: WO120 Volume 35 page 214. INDEX # 1441.
Alex^r PATTERSON; pension awarded 9 Jan 1833. SOURCE: WO120 Volume 35 page 214. INDEX # 1442.
Jno GRANT; pension awarded 13 Nov 1833. SOURCE: WO120 Volume 35 page 214. INDEX # 1443.
Wm NICKLE; pension awarded 13 Nov 1833. SOURCE: WO120 Volume 35 page 214. INDEX # 1444.
Ge^o HENDERSON; pension awarded 11 Dec 1833. SOURCE: WO120 Volume 35 page 214. INDEX # 1445.
Arch^d MCCLELLAND; pension awarded 11 Nov 1835. SOURCE: WO120 Volume 35 page 214. INDEX # 1446.
Robt BEGG; pension awarded 11 Nov 1835. SOURCE: WO120 Volume 35 page 214. INDEX # 1447.
Colin MACDONALD; pension awarded 12 Oct 1836. SOURCE: WO120 Volume 35 page 214. INDEX # 1448.
Ja^s MCPHATERS; pension awarded 14 Dec 1836. SOURCE: WO120 Volume 35 page 214. INDEX # 1449.
Wm MCCREADIE; pension awarded 14 Dec 1836. SOURCE: WO120 Volume 35 page 214. INDEX # 1450.
Peter CAMPBELL; pension awarded 14 Dec 1836. SOURCE: WO120 Volume 35 page 214. INDEX # 1451.
Wm STURROCK; pension awarded 10 May 1837. SOURCE: WO120 Volume 35 page 214. INDEX # 1452.

80th Regiment of Foot

Jacob LUMSDEN; pension awarded 17 May 1826; residence - Berbice, Guyana. SOURCE: WO120 Volume 35 page 216. INDEX # 1453.
Jos^h MEGGISON; pension awarded 8 Aug 1838. SOURCE: WO120 Volume 35 page 216. INDEX # 1454.
Ja^s MCSENNESON; pension awarded 8 Aug 1838. SOURCE: WO120 Volume 35 page 216. INDEX # 1455.

81st Regiment of Foot

Saml MOLYNEUX; pension awarded 16 Jun 1824; residence - Nova Scotia, Canada. SOURCE: WO120 Volume 35 page 218. INDEX # 1456.
Murtagh CORNYN; pension awarded 13 Dec 1826; residence - Nova Scotia, Canada. SOURCE: WO120 Volume 35 page 218. INDEX # 1457.
Jno THOMPSON; pension awarded 13 Dec 1826; residence - Nova Scotia, Canada. SOURCE: WO120 Volume 35 page 218. INDEX # 1458.
Matt^w LEWIS; pension awarded 8 Aug 1827; residence - Nova Scotia, Canada. SOURCE: WO120 Volume 35 page 218. INDEX # 1459.
Ja^s TAYLOR; pension awarded 30 Jan 1828; residence - Nova Scotia, Canada. SOURCE: WO120 Volume 35 page 218. INDEX # 1460.
Windilius BONN; pension awarded 30 Jan 1828. SOURCE: WO120 Volume 35 page 218. INDEX # 1461.
Danl JONES; pension awarded 21 May 1828. SOURCE: WO120 Volume 35 page 218. INDEX # 1462.
Willm COLBOURNE; pension awarded 21 May 1828. SOURCE: WO120 Volume 35 page 218. INDEX # 1463.
Peter BIERY; pension awarded 25 Jun 1829. SOURCE: WO120 Volume 35 page 218. INDEX # 1464.
And^w COLEMAN; pension awarded 9 Dec 1829. SOURCE: WO120 Volume 35 page 218. INDEX # 1465.

82nd Regiment of Foot

Willm CLARK; pension awarded 31 Jul 1822; residence - Canada. SOURCE: WO120 Volume 35 page 220. INDEX # 1466.
Wm BAIRD; pension awarded 11 Jan 1832. SOURCE: WO120 Volume 35 page 220. INDEX # 1467.

82nd Regiment of Foot (continued)

Wm FERGUSON; pension awarded 11 Jan 1832. SOURCE: WO120 Volume 35 page 220. INDEX # 1468.
Jno MARTIN; pension awarded 11 Jan 1832. SOURCE: WO120 Volume 35 page 220. INDEX # 1469.
Pat^k MINTON; pension awarded 11 Jan 1832. SOURCE: WO120 Volume 35 page 220. INDEX # 1470.
Jno GANDY; pension awarded 11 Jan 1832. SOURCE: WO120 Volume 35 page 220. INDEX # 1471.
John JEPSON; pension awarded 11 Jan 1832. SOURCE: WO120 Volume 35 page 220. INDEX # 1472.
Den^s SEXTON; pension awarded 11 Jan 1832. SOURCE: WO120 Volume 35 page 220. INDEX # 1473.
Jno HACK; pension awarded 9 Apr 1834. SOURCE: WO120 Volume 35 page 220. INDEX # 1474.
Ja^s ROSS; pension awarded 9 Apr 1834. SOURCE: WO120 Volume 35 page 220. INDEX # 1475.

83rd Regiment of Foot

Ge^o WRIGHT; pension awarded 23 Sep 1818; residence - Cape of Good Hope, South Africa. SOURCE: WO120 Volume 35 page 222. INDEX # 1476.
Jno GINN; pension awarded 23 Sep 1818; residence - Cape of Good Hope, South Africa. SOURCE: WO120 Volume 35 page 222. INDEX # 1477.
Jno FARRELL; pension awarded 23 Sep 1818; residence - Cape of Good Hope, South Africa. SOURCE: WO120 Volume 35 page 222. INDEX # 1478.
Bry^n KELLY; pension awarded 23 Sep 1818; residence - Cape of Good Hope, South Africa. SOURCE: WO120 Volume 35 page 222. INDEX # 1479.
Richd BURRARD; pension awarded 23 Sep 1818; residence - Cape of Good Hope, South Africa. SOURCE: WO120 Volume 35 page 222. INDEX # 1480.
Thos PARR; pension awarded 25 Nov 1818; residence - Cape of Good Hope, South Africa. SOURCE: WO120 Volume 35 page 222. INDEX # 1481.
Hen^y LENNON; pension awarded 25 Nov 1818; residence - Cape of Good Hope, South Africa. SOURCE: WO120 Volume 35 page 222. INDEX # 1482.
Jno LAYTON; pension awarded 25 Nov 1818; residence - Cape of Good Hope, South Africa. SOURCE: WO120 Volume 35 page 222. INDEX # 1483.
Thos WRIGHT; pension awarded 25 Nov 1818; residence - Cape of Good Hope, South Africa. SOURCE: WO120 Volume 35 page 222. INDEX # 1484.
Thos LITTLER; pension awarded 25 Nov 1818; residence - Cape of Good Hope, South Africa. SOURCE: WO120 Volume 35 page 222. INDEX # 1485.
Jno DONNELLY; pension awarded 25 Nov 1818; residence - Cape of Good Hope, South Africa. SOURCE: WO120 Volume 35 page 222. INDEX # 1486.
Ge^o CHADWICK; pension awarded 25 Nov 1818; residence - Cape of Good Hope, South Africa. SOURCE: WO120 Volume 35 page 222. INDEX # 1487.
Willm TROWBRIDGE; pension awarded 25 Nov 1818; residence - Cape of Good Hope, South Africa. SOURCE: WO120 Volume 35 page 222. INDEX # 1488.
Saml BRIMMER; pension awarded 17 Mar 1819; residence - Cape of Good Hope, South Africa. SOURCE: WO120 Volume 35 page 222. INDEX # 1489.
Jno BURGES; pension awarded 17 Mar 1819; residence - Cape of Good Hope, South Africa. SOURCE: WO120 Volume 35 page 222. INDEX # 1490.
Thos CURRIE; pension awarded 17 Mar 1819; residence - Cape of Good Hope, South Africa. SOURCE: WO120 Volume 35 page 222. INDEX # 1491.
Willm HARDWATER; pension awarded 26 Jul 1820; residence - Cape of Good Hope, South Africa. SOURCE: WO120 Volume 35 page 222. INDEX # 1492.
Willm COOPER; pension awarded 7 Feb 1821; residence - Cape of Good Hope, South Africa. SOURCE: WO120 Volume 35 page 222. INDEX # 1493.
Jno GREEN; pension awarded 7 Feb 1821; residence - Cape of Good Hope, South Africa. SOURCE: WO120 Volume 35 page 222. INDEX # 1494.
Ed^wd JOHNSON; pension awarded 25 Sep 1822; residence - Cape of Good Hope, South Africa. SOURCE: WO120 Volume 35 page 222. INDEX # 1495.
Willm THORP; pension awarded 22 Oct 1823; residence - Cape of Good Hope, South Africa. SOURCE: WO120 Volume 35 page 222. INDEX # 1496.

83rd Regiment of Foot (continued)

Pat^k BROGAN; pension awarded 4 Aug 1824; residence - Cape of Good Hope, South Africa. SOURCE: WO120 Volume 35 page 222. INDEX # 1497.

Robt GALLANT; pension awarded 12 Oct 1825; residence - Ceylon. SOURCE: WO120 Volume 35 page 222. INDEX # 1498.

Jno COMPTON; pension awarded 12 Oct 1825; residence - Ceylon. SOURCE: WO120 Volume 35 page 222. INDEX # 1499.

Thos SULLIVAN; pension awarded 12 Oct 1825; residence - Ceylon. SOURCE: WO120 Volume 35 page 223. INDEX # 1500.

Isaac LUCAS; pension awarded 19 Jul 1826; residence - Ceylon. SOURCE: WO120 Volume 35 page 223. INDEX # 1501.

Mich^l CAHILL; pension awarded 12 Dec 1827; residence - Ceylon; died 8 Jun 1832. SOURCE: WO120 Volume 35 page 223. INDEX # 1502.

Ja^s DICKINSON; pension awarded 12 Dec 1827; residence - Ceylon. SOURCE: WO120 Volume 35 page 223. INDEX # 1503.

Pat^k FOX; pension awarded 12 Dec 1827; residence - Ceylon. SOURCE: WO120 Volume 35 page 223. INDEX # 1504.

Adam STEWART; pension awarded 12 Dec 1827; residence - Ceylon; died 7 May 1832. SOURCE: WO120 Volume 35 page 223. INDEX # 1505.

Ja^s WRIGHT; pension awarded 12 Dec 1827; residence - Ceylon. SOURCE: WO120 Volume 35 page 223. INDEX # 1506.

Ja^s BRITTIAN; pension awarded 20 May 1829. SOURCE: WO120 Volume 35 page 223. INDEX # 1507.

Pat^k MULLERS; pension awarded 20 May 1829. SOURCE: WO120 Volume 35 page 223. INDEX # 1508.

Jno KELLY; pension awarded 5 Aug 1829. SOURCE: WO120 Volume 35 page 223. INDEX # 1509.

Jno BRACKENBURY; pension awarded 5 Aug 1829. SOURCE: WO120 Volume 35 page 223. INDEX # 1510.

Wm CORNWELL; pension awarded 5 Aug 1829. SOURCE: WO120 Volume 35 page 223. INDEX # 1511.

And^w DAVIDSON; pension awarded 5 Aug 1829. SOURCE: WO120 Volume 35 page 223. INDEX # 1512.

Ge^o DAVIS; pension awarded 5 Aug 1829. SOURCE: WO120 Volume 35 page 223. INDEX # 1513.

Ja^s HARRAGE; pension awarded 5 Aug 1829. SOURCE: WO120 Volume 35 page 223. INDEX # 1514.

Ja^s JONES; pension awarded 5 Aug 1829. SOURCE: WO120 Volume 35 page 223. INDEX # 1515.

Jno JONES; pension awarded 5 Aug 1829. SOURCE: WO120 Volume 35 page 223. INDEX # 1516.

Ge^o LEWIS; pension awarded 5 Aug 1829. SOURCE: WO120 Volume 35 page 223. INDEX # 1517.

Chas RICHARDSBY; pension awarded 5 Aug 1829. SOURCE: WO120 Volume 35 page 223. INDEX # 1518.

Mic^l TWYE; pension awarded 5 Aug 1829. SOURCE: WO120 Volume 35 page 223. INDEX # 1519.

Jos^h WAGSTAFF; pension awarded 5 Aug 1829. SOURCE: WO120 Volume 35 page 223. INDEX # 1520.

84th Regiment of Foot

Thos HART; pension awarded 7 Feb 1821; residence - India; died 30 Mar 1824. SOURCE: WO120 Volume 35 page 225. INDEX # 1521.

Ge^o HYLAND; pension awarded 7 Feb 1821; residence - India. SOURCE: WO120 Volume 35 page 225. INDEX # 1522.

Thos HULL; pension awarded 7 Feb 1821; residence - India. SOURCE: WO120 Volume 35 page 225. INDEX # 1523.

Zacchens KAYE; pension awarded 7 Feb 1821; residence - India. SOURCE: WO120 Volume 35 page 225. INDEX # 1524.

Willm NAYLOR; pension awarded 7 Feb 1821; residence - India; died 25 Nov 1824. SOURCE: WO120 Volume 35 page 225. INDEX # 1525.

Ja^s JACKSON; pension awarded 7 Feb 1821; residence - India. SOURCE: WO120 Volume 35 page 225. INDEX # 1526.

Richd HUFFTON; pension awarded 7 Feb 1821; residence - India. SOURCE: WO120 Volume 35 page 225. INDEX # 1527.

84th Regiment of Foot (continued)

Adam ATKINSON; pension awarded 7 Feb 1821; residence - India; died 30 Jan 1824. SOURCE: WO120 Volume 35 page 225. INDEX # 1528.
Quintin CARTWRIGHT; pension awarded 7 Feb 1821; residence - India. SOURCE: WO120 Volume 35 page 225. INDEX # 1529.
Isaac DRACUP; pension awarded 7 Feb 1821; residence - India. SOURCE: WO120 Volume 35 page 225. INDEX # 1530.
Antoni GAST; pension awarded 7 Feb 1821; residence - India. SOURCE: WO120 Volume 35 page 225. INDEX # 1531.
Benjn HARDY; pension awarded 7 Feb 1821; residence - India; died 25 Nov 1824. SOURCE: WO120 Volume 35 page 225. INDEX # 1532.
Willm HOLDING; pension awarded 7 Feb 1821; residence - India; died 14 Mar 1821. SOURCE: WO120 Volume 35 page 225. INDEX # 1533.
Edwd HURST; pension awarded 7 Feb 1821; residence - India. SOURCE: WO120 Volume 35 page 225. INDEX # 1534.
Jno PALLISTER; pension awarded 7 Feb 1821; residence - India; died 10 Jun 1821. SOURCE: WO120 Volume 35 page 225. INDEX # 1535.
Thos PALMER; pension awarded 7 Feb 1821; residence - India; died 25 Nov 1824. SOURCE: WO120 Volume 35 page 225. INDEX # 1536.
Jno COLQUHOUN; pension awarded 12 Sep 1832. SOURCE: WO120 Volume 35 page 225. INDEX # 1537.
Ge^o HARRISON; pension awarded 12 Apr 1837. SOURCE: WO120 Volume 35 page 225. INDEX # 1538.

86th Regiment of Foot

Thos DUGARD; pension awarded 7 Feb 1821; residence - India; died 6 Jul 1821. SOURCE: WO120 Volume 35 page 228. INDEX # 1539.
Thos PERRY; pension awarded 7 Feb 1821; residence - India; died 20 Apr 1827. SOURCE: WO120 Volume 35 page 228. INDEX # 1540.
Ja^s ASHURST; pension awarded 7 Feb 1821; residence - India. SOURCE: WO120 Volume 35 page 228. INDEX # 1541.
Chas MINCHIN; pension awarded 7 Feb 1821; residence - India. SOURCE: WO120 Volume 35 page 228. INDEX # 1542.
Ge^o SUMMERS; pension awarded 7 Feb 1821; residence - India. SOURCE: WO120 Volume 35 page 228. INDEX # 1543.
Jno MILLARD; pension awarded 7 Feb 1821; residence - India. SOURCE: WO120 Volume 35 page 228. INDEX # 1544.
Chas MURRELL; pension awarded 7 Feb 1821; residence - India. SOURCE: WO120 Volume 35 page 228. INDEX # 1545.
Willm EMERY; pension awarded 7 Feb 1821; residence - India. SOURCE: WO120 Volume 35 page 228. INDEX # 1546.
Jno ABEL; pension awarded 7 Feb 1821; residence - India. SOURCE: WO120 Volume 35 page 228. INDEX # 1547.
Trevor BURROWS; pension awarded 7 Feb 1821; residence - India. SOURCE: WO120 Volume 35 page 228. INDEX # 1548.
Edwd BONNINGTON; pension awarded 7 Feb 1821; residence - India. SOURCE: WO120 Volume 35 page 228. INDEX # 1549.
Ja^s BROWN; pension awarded 7 Feb 1821; residence - India. SOURCE: WO120 Volume 35 page 228. INDEX # 1550.
Thos BARNES; pension awarded 7 Feb 1821; residence - India. SOURCE: WO120 Volume 35 page 228. INDEX # 1551.
Jos^h CARR; pension awarded 7 Feb 1821; residence - India. SOURCE: WO120 Volume 35 page 228. INDEX # 1552.
Jno CHRISTIAN; pension awarded 7 Feb 1821; residence - India. SOURCE: WO120 Volume 35 page 228. INDEX # 1553.

86th Regiment of Foot (continued)

Dav^d DAVIS; pension awarded 7 Feb 1821; residence - India. SOURCE: WO120 Volume 35 page 228. INDEX # 1554.

Oliver DICKINSON; pension awarded 7 Feb 1821; residence - India. SOURCE: WO120 Volume 35 page 228. INDEX # 1555.

Richd FRANKLIN; pension awarded 7 Feb 1821; residence - India. SOURCE: WO120 Volume 35 page 228. INDEX # 1556.

Ja^s GREEN; pension awarded 7 Feb 1821; residence - India. SOURCE: WO120 Volume 35 page 228. INDEX # 1557.

Willm HALL; pension awarded 7 Feb 1821; residence - India. SOURCE: WO120 Volume 35 page 228. INDEX # 1558.

And^w HUMPHRIES; pension awarded 7 Feb 1821; residence - India; died 9 Jul 1826. SOURCE: WO120 Volume 35 page 228. INDEX # 1559.

Moses HARVEY; pension awarded 7 Feb 1821; residence - India. SOURCE: WO120 Volume 35 page 228. INDEX # 1560.

Willm JONES; pension awarded 7 Feb 1821; residence - India. SOURCE: WO120 Volume 35 page 228. INDEX # 1561.

Brien KELLY; pension awarded 7 Feb 1821; residence - India. SOURCE: WO120 Volume 35 page 228. INDEX # 1562.

Pat^k KIRK; pension awarded 7 Feb 1821; residence - India. SOURCE: WO120 Volume 35 page 229. INDEX # 1563.

Willm MATHEWS; pension awarded 7 Feb 1821; residence - India. SOURCE: WO120 Volume 35 page 229. INDEX # 1564.

Ed^wd NEAVES; pension awarded 7 Feb 1821; residence - India. SOURCE: WO120 Volume 35 page 229. INDEX # 1565.

Willm PEACHELL; pension awarded 7 Feb 1821; residence - India. SOURCE: WO120 Volume 35 page 229. INDEX # 1566.

Thos PATTERSON; pension awarded 7 Feb 1821; residence - India; died 23 Jun 1821. SOURCE: WO120 Volume 35 page 229. INDEX # 1567.

Matt^w SULLIVAN; pension awarded 7 Feb 1821; residence - India. SOURCE: WO120 Volume 35 page 229. INDEX # 1568.

Willm STEVENS; pension awarded 7 Feb 1821; residence - India. SOURCE: WO120 Volume 35 page 229. INDEX # 1569.

Robt TROTT; pension awarded 7 Feb 1821; residence - India; died 25 Nov 1824. SOURCE: WO120 Volume 35 page 229. INDEX # 1570.

Willm WELLINGS; pension awarded 7 Feb 1821; residence - India. SOURCE: WO120 Volume 35 page 229. INDEX # 1571.

Jno WILLIAMSON; pension awarded 7 Feb 1821; residence - India; died 25 Nov 1824. SOURCE: WO120 Volume 35 page 229. INDEX # 1572.

Richd WHITE; pension awarded 7 Feb 1821; residence - India. SOURCE: WO120 Volume 35 page 229. INDEX # 1573.

Willm YOUNG; pension awarded 7 Feb 1821; residence - India. SOURCE: WO120 Volume 35 page 229. INDEX # 1574.

87th Regiment of Foot

Danl REARDON; pension awarded 25 Jul 1821; residence - India. SOURCE: WO120 Volume 35 page 231. INDEX # 1575.

Jno FITZPATRICK; pension awarded 25 Apr 1827. SOURCE: WO120 Volume 35 page 231. INDEX # 1576.

Mich^l MCDONNELL; pension awarded 20 Feb 1828. SOURCE: WO120 Volume 35 page 231. INDEX # 1577.

Jno KELLY; pension awarded 5 Aug 1829. SOURCE: WO120 Volume 35 page 231. INDEX # 1578.

87th Regiment of Foot (continued)

Ja^s BRACKENBURY; pension awarded 5 Aug 1829. SOURCE: WO120 Volume 35 page 231. INDEX # 1579.
Willm CORNWALL; pension awarded 5 Aug 1829. SOURCE: WO120 Volume 35 page 231. INDEX # 1580.
And^w DAVIDSON; pension awarded 5 Aug 1829. SOURCE: WO120 Volume 35 page 231. INDEX # 1581.
Ge^o DAVIS; pension awarded 5 Aug 1829. SOURCE: WO120 Volume 35 page 231. INDEX # 1582.
Ja^s HARRAGE; pension awarded 5 Aug 1829. SOURCE: WO120 Volume 35 page 231. INDEX # 1583.
Ja^s JONES; pension awarded 5 Aug 1829. SOURCE: WO120 Volume 35 page 231. INDEX # 1584.
Jno JONES; pension awarded 5 Aug 1829. SOURCE: WO120 Volume 35 page 231. INDEX # 1585.
Ge^o LEWIS; pension awarded 5 Aug 1829. SOURCE: WO120 Volume 35 page 231. INDEX # 1586.
Chas RICHARDSBY; pension awarded 5 Aug 1829. SOURCE: WO120 Volume 35 page 231. INDEX # 1587.
Mic^l TWYE; pension awarded 5 Aug 1829. SOURCE: WO120 Volume 35 page 231. INDEX # 1588.
Jos^h WAGSTAFF; pension awarded 5 Aug 1829. SOURCE: WO120 Volume 35 page 231. INDEX # 1589.
Jos^h STATEHAM; pension awarded 8 Sep 1830. SOURCE: WO120 Volume 35 page 231. INDEX # 1590.
Jno SMITH; pension awarded 13 Apr 1836. SOURCE: WO120 Volume 35 page 231. INDEX # 1591.
Saml B BAIRD; pension awarded 13 Jun 1838. SOURCE: WO120 Volume 35 page 231. INDEX # 1592.

88th Regiment of Foot

Hen^y WRIGHT; pension awarded 25 Jun 1818. SOURCE: WO120 Volume 35 page 233. INDEX # 1593.
Willm WARREN; pension awarded 30 May 1827. SOURCE: WO120 Volume 35 page 233. INDEX # 1594.
Saml COOMBES; pension awarded 30 May 1827. SOURCE: WO120 Volume 35 page 233. INDEX # 1595.
Chas COOPER; pension awarded 30 May 1827. SOURCE: WO120 Volume 35 page 233. INDEX # 1596.
Ja^s MORAN; pension awarded 30 May 1827. SOURCE: WO120 Volume 35 page 233. INDEX # 1597.
Willm COUTS; pension awarded 30 May 1827. SOURCE: WO120 Volume 35 page 233. INDEX # 1598.
Willm SMITH; pension awarded 30 May 1827. SOURCE: WO120 Volume 35 page 233. INDEX # 1599.
Willm BANKS; pension awarded 30 May 1827. SOURCE: WO120 Volume 35 page 233. INDEX # 1600.
Ja^s PEARCE; pension awarded 30 May 1827. SOURCE: WO120 Volume 35 page 233. INDEX # 1601.
Jno SMITH; pension awarded 30 May 1827. SOURCE: WO120 Volume 35 page 233. INDEX # 1602.
Barth^w KEARNS; pension awarded 26 Jul 1815; residence - Canada. SOURCE: WO120 Volume 35 page 233. INDEX # 1603.
Robt WILL; pension awarded 8 May 1833. SOURCE: WO120 Volume 35 page 233. INDEX # 1604.

89th Regiment of Foot

Jno JONES; pension awarded 29 Apr 1818; residence - Canada. SOURCE: WO120 Volume 35 page 235. INDEX # 1605.
Thos HOMER; pension awarded 7 Dec 1820; residence - Canada. SOURCE: WO120 Volume 35 page 235. INDEX # 1606.
Willm WILMOT; pension awarded 7 Dec 1820; residence - Canada. SOURCE: WO120 Volume 35 page 235. INDEX # 1607.
Thos HAYES; pension awarded 7 Feb 1821; residence - Madras, India. SOURCE: WO120 Volume 35 page 235. INDEX # 1608.
Pat^k BAXTER; pension awarded 7 Feb 1821; residence - Madras, India. SOURCE: WO120 Volume 35 page 235. INDEX # 1609.
Jno KIERNAN; pension awarded 4 Jun 1823; residence - Madras, India. SOURCE: WO120 Volume 35 page 235. INDEX # 1610.
Ge^o LANG; pension awarded 4 Jun 1823; residence - Madras, India. SOURCE: WO120 Volume 35 page 235. INDEX # 1611.
Pat^k LYTTLE; pension awarded 4 Jun 1823; residence - Madras, India. SOURCE: WO120 Volume 35 page 235. INDEX # 1612.
Thos CROFTS; pension awarded 4 Jun 1823; residence - Madras, India. SOURCE: WO120 Volume 35 page 235. INDEX # 1613.

89th Regiment of Foot (continued)

Pat^k CARROLL; pension awarded 4 Jun 1823; residence - Madras, India. SOURCE: WO120 Volume 35 page 235. INDEX # 1614.

Jos^h BISHOP; pension awarded 3 Mar 1824; residence - Madras, India. SOURCE: WO120 Volume 35 page 235. INDEX # 1615.

John GAVIN; pension awarded 3 Mar 1824; residence - Madras, India. SOURCE: WO120 Volume 35 page 235. INDEX # 1616.

Mich^l DOWNEY; pension awarded 3 Mar 1824; residence - Madras, India. SOURCE: WO120 Volume 35 page 235. INDEX # 1617.

John SLOAN; pension awarded 23 Nov 1825; residence - Madras, India. SOURCE: WO120 Volume 35 page 235. INDEX # 1618.

Jno MCCORMICK; pension awarded 23 Nov 1825; residence - Madras, India. SOURCE: WO120 Volume 35 page 235. INDEX # 1619.

Ge^o WARNER; pension awarded 13 Dec 1826; residence - Madras, India. SOURCE: WO120 Volume 35 page 235. INDEX # 1620.

Ge^o BIGGS; pension awarded 13 Dec 1826; residence - Madras, India. SOURCE: WO120 Volume 35 page 235. INDEX # 1621.

Thos LARKIN; pension awarded 13 Dec 1826; residence - Madras, India. SOURCE: WO120 Volume 35 page 235. INDEX # 1622.

Ja^s DONALDSON; pension awarded 13 Dec 1826; residence - Madras, India. SOURCE: WO120 Volume 35 page 235. INDEX # 1623.

Moses MORGAN; pension awarded 13 Dec 1826; residence - Madras, India. SOURCE: WO120 Volume 35 page 235. INDEX # 1624.

Thos BRADY; pension awarded 13 Dec 1826; residence - Madras, India. SOURCE: WO120 Volume 35 page 235. INDEX # 1625.

Robt ORMSBY; pension awarded 25 Jun 1823. SOURCE: WO120 Volume 35 page 235. INDEX # 1626.

Willm WARREN; pension awarded 30 May 1827; residence - Madras, India; died 23 Apr 1828. SOURCE: WO120 Volume 35 page 235. INDEX # 1627.

Saml COOMBES; pension awarded 30 May 1827; residence - Madras, India. SOURCE: WO120 Volume 35 page 235. INDEX # 1628.

Chas COOPER; pension awarded 30 May 1827; residence - Madras, India. SOURCE: WO120 Volume 35 page 236. INDEX # 1629.

Ja^s MORAN; pension awarded 30 May 1827; residence - Madras, India. SOURCE: WO120 Volume 35 page 236. INDEX # 1630.

Willm COUTS; pension awarded 30 May 1827; residence - Madras, India. SOURCE: WO120 Volume 35 page 236. INDEX # 1631.

Willm SMITH; pension awarded 30 May 1827; residence - Madras, India. SOURCE: WO120 Volume 35 page 236. INDEX # 1632.

Willm BANKS; pension awarded 30 May 1827; residence - Madras, India. SOURCE: WO120 Volume 35 page 236. INDEX # 1633.

Ja^s PEARCE; pension awarded 30 May 1827; residence - Madras, India. SOURCE: WO120 Volume 35 page 236. INDEX # 1634.

Jno SMITH; pension awarded 30 May 1827; residence - Madras, India. SOURCE: WO120 Volume 35 page 236. INDEX # 1635.

Ja^s PRITCHARD; pension awarded 31 Oct 1827; residence - Madras, India. SOURCE: WO120 Volume 35 page 236. INDEX # 1636.

Mich^l CURRAN; pension awarded 31 Oct 1827; residence - Madras, India. SOURCE: WO120 Volume 35 page 236. INDEX # 1637.

Miles BURKE; pension awarded 31 Oct 1827; residence - Madras, India. SOURCE: WO120 Volume 35 page 236. INDEX # 1638.

Jno BURK; pension awarded 31 Oct 1827; residence - Madras, India; died 13 Jan 1828. SOURCE: WO120 Volume 35 page 236. INDEX # 1639.

Jno DONOGHOE; pension awarded 31 Oct 1827; residence - Madras, India. SOURCE: WO120 Volume 35 page 236. INDEX # 1640.

89th Regiment of Foot (continued)

Owen FITZSIMONDS; pension awarded 31 Oct 1827; residence - Madras, India. SOURCE: WO120 Volume 35 page 236. INDEX # 1641.
Jere^h SAUNDERS; pension awarded 31 Oct 1827; residence - Madras, India. SOURCE: WO120 Volume 35 page 236. INDEX # 1642.
Richd THOMPSON; pension awarded 31 Oct 1827; residence - Madras, India. SOURCE: WO120 Volume 35 page 236. INDEX # 1643.
John GEE; pension awarded 21 May 1828. SOURCE: WO120 Volume 35 page 236. INDEX # 1644.
Chas ALDERTON; pension awarded 29 Oct 1828. SOURCE: WO120 Volume 35 page 236. INDEX # 1645.
Ja^s JOBE; pension awarded 29 Oct 1828. SOURCE: WO120 Volume 35 page 236. INDEX # 1646.
Mic^l NORTON; pension awarded 29 Oct 1828. SOURCE: WO120 Volume 35 page 236. INDEX # 1647.
Ge^o COWELL; pension awarded 25 Jun 1829. SOURCE: WO120 Volume 35 page 236. INDEX # 1648.
Ja^s KELLY; pension awarded 11 Nov 1829. SOURCE: WO120 Volume 35 page 236. INDEX # 1649.
Peter BUCKLEY; pension awarded 12 Oct 1831. SOURCE: WO120 Volume 35 page 236. INDEX # 1650.

90th Regiment of Foot

Richd WILLIAMS; pension awarded 13 Apr 1831. SOURCE: WO120 Volume 35 page 238. INDEX # 1651.

91st Regiment of Foot

Allan MCDONALD; pension awarded 10 Nov 1819; residence - Quebec, Canada. SOURCE: WO120 Volume 35 page 240. INDEX # 1652.
Jos^h KERR; pension awarded 13 Jul 1831. SOURCE: WO120 Volume 35 page 240. INDEX # 1653.

93rd Regiment of Foot

Jno MCRAE; pension awarded 26 Jul 1820; residence - Nova Scotia, Canada. SOURCE: WO120 Volume 35 page 244. INDEX # 1654.
Don^d MACINTYRE; pension awarded 30 Apr 1817; residence - British North, America. SOURCE: WO120 Volume 35 page 244. INDEX # 1655.
Mal^m SUTHERLAND; pension awarded 23 Nov 1804; residence - Nova Scotia, Canada. SOURCE: WO120 Volume 35 page 244. INDEX # 1656.
Jno SUTHERLAND; pension awarded 24 Apr 1816; residence - Picton, Ontario, Canada. SOURCE: WO120 Volume 35 page 244. INDEX # 1557.
Jno MORRIS; pension awarded 13 Jun 1832. SOURCE: WO120 Volume 35 page 244. INDEX # 1658.

94th Regiment of Foot

John WHITE; pension awarded 20 May 1829; died 13 Jul 1832. SOURCE: WO120 Volume 35 page 246. INDEX # 1659.

96th Regiment of Foot

Corn^s COLLINS; pension awarded 20 Feb 1828. SOURCE: WO120 Volume 35 page 250. INDEX # 1660.
Ant^y LIEBERT; pension awarded 13 Sep 1820. SOURCE: WO120 Volume 35 page 250. INDEX # 1661.
Jno ARNE; pension awarded 13 Oct 1830. SOURCE: WO120 Volume 35 page 250. INDEX # 1562.
Ja^s PERCY; pension awarded 9 Jul 1834. SOURCE: WO120 Volume 35 page 250. INDEX # 1663.

97th Regiment of Foot

Willm CHARLTON; pension awarded 26 Aug 1819; residence - Canada. SOURCE: WO120 Volume 35 page 252. INDEX # 1664.

97th Regiment of Foot (continued)

Willm MALONE; pension awarded 26 Aug 1819; residence - Canada. SOURCE: WO120 Volume 35 page 252. INDEX # 1665.
Den^s KILEEN; pension awarded 23 Dec 1818; residence - Canada. SOURCE: WO120 Volume 35 page 252. INDEX # 1666.
Pat^k SCALTON; pension awarded 2 Jan 1819; residence - Canada. SOURCE: WO120 Volume 35 page 252. INDEX # 1667.
Pat^k SCALLION; pension awarded 23 Dec 1818; residence - Canada. SOURCE: WO120 Volume 35 page 252. INDEX # 1668.
Laughlin CORCORAN; pension awarded 23 Dec 1818; residence - Canada. SOURCE: WO120 Volume 35 page 252. INDEX # 1669.
Cornelias OBRIEN; pension awarded 30 Dec 1818; residence - Canada. SOURCE: WO120 Volume 35 page 252. INDEX # 1670.
Wm CHARLTON; pension awarded 23 Dec 1818; residence - Canada. SOURCE: WO120 Volume 35 page 252. INDEX # 1671.
Wm MALONE; pension awarded 23 Dec 1818; residence - Canada. SOURCE: WO120 Volume 35 page 252. INDEX # 1672.
Saml CURRELL; pension awarded 23 Dec 1818; residence - Canada. SOURCE: WO120 Volume 35 page 252. INDEX # 1673.
Pat^k JOYCE; pension awarded 23 Dec 1818; residence - Canada. SOURCE: WO120 Volume 35 page 252. INDEX # 1674.
Thos WALSH; pension awarded 23 Dec 1818; residence - Canada. SOURCE: WO120 Volume 35 page 252. INDEX # 1675.
Jno SULLIVAN; pension awarded 23 Dec 1818; residence - Halifax, Nova Scotia, Canada. SOURCE: WO120 Volume 35 page 252. INDEX # 1676.
Ja^s STONE; pension awarded 29 Dec 1819; residence - Halifax, Nova Scotia. Canada. SOURCE: WO120 Volume 35 page 252. INDEX # 1677.
Thos CROZIER; pension awarded 30 Dec 1818; residence - Quebec, Quebec, Canada. SOURCE: WO120 Volume 35 page 252. INDEX # 1678.

98th Regiment of Foot

Ge^o BELL; pension awarded 26 Aug 1819; residence - Nova Scotia, Canada. SOURCE: WO120 Volume 35 page 254. INDEX # 1679.
Anth^y HANNAN; pension awarded 26 Aug 1819; residence - Nova Scotia, Canada. SOURCE: WO120 Volume 35 page 254. INDEX # 1680.
Mich^l COTT; pension awarded 26 Aug 1819; residence - Nova Scotia, Canada. SOURCE: WO120 Volume 35 page 254. INDEX # 1681.
Willm ANDERSON; pension awarded 26 Aug 1819; residence - Nova Scotia, Canada. SOURCE: WO120 Volume 35 page 254. INDEX # 1682.
Willm WILEY; pension awarded 26 Aug 1819; residence - Nova Scotia, Canada. SOURCE: WO120 Volume 35 page 254. INDEX # 1683.
Willm AYRES; pension awarded 26 Aug 1819; residence - Nova Scotia, Canada. SOURCE: WO120 Volume 35 page 254. INDEX # 1684.
Pat^k MOHAN; pension awarded 26 Aug 1819; residence - Nova Scotia, Canada. SOURCE: WO120 Volume 35 page 254. INDEX # 1685.
Mich^l COLLINS; pension awarded 26 Aug 1819; residence - Nova Scotia, Canada. SOURCE: WO120 Volume 35 page 254. INDEX # 1686.
Robt KNOX; pension awarded 26 Aug 1819; residence - Nova Scotia, Canada. SOURCE: WO120 Volume 35 page 254. INDEX # 1687.
Jno MULLEN; pension awarded 26 Aug 1819; residence - Nova Scotia, Canada. SOURCE: WO120 Volume 35 page 254. INDEX # 1688.

98th Regiment of Foot (continued)

Danl BROWN; pension awarded 26 Aug 1819; residence - Nova Scotia, Canada. SOURCE: WO120 Volume 35 page 254. INDEX # 1689.

Ja^s LONG; pension awarded 26 Aug 1819; residence - Nova Scotia, Canada. SOURCE: WO120 Volume 35 page 254. INDEX # 1690.

Danl HALLANAN; pension awarded 26 Aug 1819; residence - Nova Scotia, Canada. SOURCE: WO120 Volume 35 page 254. INDEX # 1691.

Willm ONEAL; pension awarded 26 Aug 1819; residence - Nova Scotia, Canada. SOURCE: WO120 Volume 35 page 254. INDEX # 1692.

Corn^s GARVEY; pension awarded 26 Aug 1819; residence - Nova Scotia, Canada. SOURCE: WO120 Volume 35 page 254. INDEX # 1693.

Jno LARKIN; pension awarded 26 Aug 1819; residence - Nova Scotia, Canada. SOURCE: WO120 Volume 35 page 254. INDEX # 1694.

Pat^k DILLON; pension awarded 26 Aug 1819; residence - Nova Scotia, Canada. SOURCE: WO120 Volume 35 page 254. INDEX # 1695.

Matt^w DYER; pension awarded 26 Aug 1819; residence - Nova Scotia, Canada. SOURCE: WO120 Volume 35 page 254. INDEX # 1696.

Fra^s CODD; pension awarded 26 Aug 1819; residence - Nova Scotia, Canada. SOURCE: WO120 Volume 35 page 254. INDEX # 1697.

Tim^y COLEMAN; pension awarded 26 Aug 1819; residence - Nova Scotia, Canada. SOURCE: WO120 Volume 35 page 254. INDEX # 1698.

Jno BURKE; pension awarded 26 Aug 1819; residence - Nova Scotia, Canada. SOURCE: WO120 Volume 35 page 254. INDEX # 1699.

Willm GRIMES; pension awarded 26 Aug 1819; residence - Nova Scotia, Canada. SOURCE: WO120 Volume 35 page 254. INDEX # 1700.

Willm FANNON; pension awarded 26 Aug 1819; residence - Nova Scotia, Canada. SOURCE: WO120 Volume 35 page 254. INDEX # 1701.

Willm ELLIOTT; pension awarded 26 Aug 1819; residence - Nova Scotia, Canada. SOURCE: WO120 Volume 35 page 254. INDEX # 1702.

Jno OBRINE; pension awarded 26 Aug 1819; residence - Nova Scotia, Canada. SOURCE: WO120 Volume 35 page 255. INDEX # 1703.

Pat^k KEARNEY; pension awarded 26 Aug 1819; residence - Nova Scotia, Canada. SOURCE: WO120 Volume 35 page 255. INDEX # 1704.

Thos ROCHFORD; pension awarded 26 Aug 1819; residence - Nova Scotia, Canada. SOURCE: WO120 Volume 35 page 255. INDEX # 1705.

Jno WHITE; pension awarded 26 Aug 1819; residence - Nova Scotia, Canada. SOURCE: WO120 Volume 35 page 255. INDEX # 1706.

Fra^s TRACEY; pension awarded 26 Aug 1819; residence - Nova Scotia, Canada. SOURCE: WO120 Volume 35 page 255. INDEX # 1707.

Thos MALONEY; pension awarded 26 Aug 1819; residence - Nova Scotia, Canada. SOURCE: WO120 Volume 35 page 255. INDEX # 1708.

Jno FLANAGAN; pension awarded 26 Aug 1819; residence - Nova Scotia, Canada. SOURCE: WO120 Volume 35 page 255. INDEX # 1709.

Pat^k FINEGAN; pension awarded 26 Aug 1819; residence - Nova Scotia, Canada. SOURCE: WO120 Volume 35 page 255. INDEX # 1710.

Thos KELLY; pension awarded 26 Aug 1819; residence - Nova Scotia, Canada. SOURCE: WO120 Volume 35 page 255. INDEX # 1711.

Thos HOMER; pension awarded 7 Dec 1820. SOURCE: WO120 Volume 35 page 255. INDEX # 1712.

Willm WILMOT; pension awarded 7 Dec 1820. SOURCE: WO120 Volume 35 page 255. INDEX # 1713.

Pat^k DONNELLAN; pension awarded 3 May 1820; residence - Canada. SOURCE: WO120 Volume 35 page 255. INDEX # 1714.

Jno BOYLE; pension awarded 5 Jul 1820; residence - Nova Scotia, Canada. SOURCE: WO120 Volume 35 page 255. INDEX # 1715.

98th Regiment of Foot (continued)

Pat^k DARGAN; pension awarded 5 Jul 1820; residence - Nova Scotia, Canada. SOURCE: WO120 Volume 35 page 255. INDEX # 1716.

Ja^s MCCANNA; pension awarded 5 Jul 1820; residence - Nova Scotia, Canada. SOURCE: WO120 Volume 35 page 255. INDEX # 1717.

Pat^k OBRIEN; pension awarded 27 Dec 1815; residence - Nova Scotia, Canada; died 15 Aug 1821. SOURCE: WO120 Volume 35 page 255. INDEX # 1718.

Robt HUMPHRIES; pension awarded 24 Oct 1821; residence - Nova Scotia, Canada. SOURCE: WO120 Volume 35 page 255. INDEX # 1719.

Thos ATKINS; pension awarded 24 Oct 1821; residence - Nova Scotia, Canada. SOURCE: WO120 Volume 35 page 255. INDEX # 1720.

Thos LAWLER; pension awarded 24 Oct 1821; residence - Nova Scotia, Canada. SOURCE: WO120 Volume 35 page 255. INDEX # 1721.

Robt KELLY; pension awarded 24 Oct 1821; residence - Nova Scotia, Canada. SOURCE: WO120 Volume 35 page 255. INDEX # 1722.

Willm AUSTIN; pension awarded 24 Oct 1821; residence - Nova Scotia, Canada. SOURCE: WO120 Volume 35 page 255. INDEX # 1723.

Willm MEARA; pension awarded 24 Oct 1821; residence - Nova Scotia, Canada. SOURCE: WO120 Volume 35 page 255. INDEX # 1724.

Jno BUTLER; pension awarded 24 Oct 1821; residence - Nova Scotia, Canada. SOURCE: WO120 Volume 35 page 255. INDEX # 1725.

Jno MEARA; pension awarded 24 Oct 1821; residence - Nova Scotia, Canada. SOURCE: WO120 Volume 35 page 255. INDEX # 1726.

Pat^k MEARA; pension awarded 24 Oct 1821; residence - Nova Scotia, Canada. SOURCE: WO120 Volume 35 page 256. INDEX # 1727.

Pat^k MURPHY; pension awarded 24 Oct 1821; residence - Nova Scotia, Canada. SOURCE: WO120 Volume 35 page 256. INDEX # 1728.

Jno HAWTHORNE; pension awarded 24 Oct 1821; residence - Nova Scotia, Canada. SOURCE: WO120 Volume 35 page 256. INDEX # 1729.

Richd AUSTIN; pension awarded 24 Oct 1821; residence - Nova Scotia, Canada. SOURCE: WO120 Volume 35 page 256. INDEX # 1730.

Den^s MCCRETE; pension awarded 24 Oct 1821; residence - Nova Scotia, Canada. SOURCE: WO120 Volume 35 page 256. INDEX # 1731.

Wm LONERGAN; pension awarded 24 Oct 1821; residence - Nova Scotia, Canada. SOURCE: WO120 Volume 35 page 256. INDEX # 1733.

Thos QUILTY; pension awarded 24 Oct 1821; residence - Nova Scotia, Canada. SOURCE: WO120 Volume 35 page 256. INDEX # 1733.

Jno OBRIEN; pension awarded 24 Oct 1821; residence - Nova Scotia, Canada. SOURCE: WO120 Volume 35 page 256. INDEX # 1734.

Thos QUADE; pension awarded 24 Oct 1821; residence - Nova Scotia, Canada. SOURCE: WO120 Volume 35 page 256. INDEX # 1735.

Willm QUIRK; pension awarded 24 Oct 1821; residence - Nova Scotia, Canada. SOURCE: WO120 Volume 35 page 256. INDEX # 1736.

Thos HOLMES; pension awarded 24 Oct 1821; residence - Nova Scotia, Canada. SOURCE: WO120 Volume 35 page 256. INDEX # 1737.

Pat^k NOCTON; pension awarded 24 Oct 1821; residence - Nova Scotia, Canada. SOURCE: WO120 Volume 35 page 256. INDEX # 1738.

Jno SCARA; pension awarded 24 Oct 1821; residence - Nova Scotia, Canada. SOURCE: WO120 Volume 35 page 256. INDEX # 1739.

Ja^s OBRIEN; pension awarded 24 Oct 1821; residence - Nova Scotia, Canada. SOURCE: WO120 Volume 35 page 256. INDEX # 1740.

Fred^k MAHONEY; pension awarded 24 Oct 1821; residence - Nova Scotia, Canada. SOURCE: WO120 Volume 35 page 256. INDEX # 1741.

WO120 VOLUME 35   61

98th Regiment of Foot (continued)

Jn⁰ HENNESSEY; pension awarded 24 Oct 1821; residence - Nova Scotia, Canada. SOURCE: WO120 Volume 35 page 256. INDEX # 1742.

Edwd CONNORS; pension awarded 24 Oct 1821; residence - Nova Scotia, Canada. SOURCE: WO120 Volume 35 page 256. INDEX # 1743.

Mich^l HOGAN; pension awarded 24 Oct 1821; residence - Nova Scotia, Canada. SOURCE: WO120 Volume 35 page 256. INDEX # 1744.

Den^s MCCARTHY; pension awarded 24 Oct 1821; residence - Nova Scotia, Canada. SOURCE: WO120 Volume 35 page 256. INDEX # 1745.

Ja^s LANE; pension awarded 24 Oct 1821; residence - Nova Scotia, Canada. SOURCE: WO120 Volume 35 page 256. INDEX # 1746.

Ja^s HUDSON; pension awarded 24 Oct 1821; residence - Nova Scotia, Canada. SOURCE: WO120 Volume 35 page 256. INDEX # 1747.

Mich^l DAWSON; pension awarded 24 Oct 1821; residence - Nova Scotia, Canada. SOURCE: WO120 Volume 35 page 256. INDEX # 1748.

Jn⁰ RYAN; pension awarded 24 Oct 1821; residence - Nova Scotia, Canada. SOURCE: WO120 Volume 35 page 256. INDEX # 1749.

Pat^k RUTH; pension awarded 24 Oct 1821; residence - Nova Scotia, Canada. SOURCE: WO120 Volume 35 page 256. INDEX # 1750.

Willm IRWIN; pension awarded 24 Oct 1821; residence - Nova Scotia, Canada. SOURCE: WO120 Volume 35 page 257. INDEX # 1751.

Jn⁰ DUNN; pension awarded 24 Oct 1821; residence - Nova Scotia, Canada. SOURCE: WO120 Volume 35 page 257. INDEX # 1752.

Alex^r HORNER; pension awarded 24 Oct 1821; residence - Nova Scotia, Canada. SOURCE: WO120 Volume 35 page 257. INDEX # 1753.

Robt STODDART; pension awarded 24 Oct 1821; residence - Nova Scotia, Canada. SOURCE: WO120 Volume 35 page 257. INDEX # 1754.

Ge⁰ TAYLOR; pension awarded 24 Oct 1821; residence - Nova Scotia, Canada. SOURCE: WO120 Volume 35 page 257. INDEX # 1755.

Fra^s COSGROVE; pension awarded 24 Oct 1821; residence - Nova Scotia, Canada. SOURCE: WO120 Volume 35 page 257. INDEX # 1756.

Thos MCGOWAN; pension awarded 24 Oct 1821; residence - Nova Scotia, Canada. SOURCE: WO120 Volume 35 page 257. INDEX # 1757.

Thos BATES; pension awarded 24 Oct 1821; residence - Nova Scotia, Canada. SOURCE: WO120 Volume 35 page 257. INDEX # 1758.

Jn⁰ BURKE; pension awarded 24 Oct 1821; residence - Nova Scotia, Canada. SOURCE: WO120 Volume 35 page 257. INDEX # 1759.

Pat^k CONNELL; pension awarded 24 Oct 1821; residence - Nova Scotia, Canada. SOURCE: WO120 Volume 35 page 257. INDEX # 1760.

Hugh HUTCHINSON; pension awarded 24 Oct 1821; residence - Nova Scotia, Canada. SOURCE: WO120 Volume 35 page 257. INDEX # 1761.

Jn⁰ KELLY; pension awarded 24 Oct 1821; residence - Nova Scotia, Canada. SOURCE: WO120 Volume 35 page 257. INDEX # 1762.

Pat^k KELLY; pension awarded 24 Oct 1821; residence - Nova Scotia, Canada. SOURCE: WO120 Volume 35 page 257. INDEX # 1763.

Mich^l LONERGAN; pension awarded 24 Oct 1821; residence - Nova Scotia, Canada. SOURCE: WO120 Volume 35 page 257. INDEX # 1764.

Willm LONERGAN; pension awarded 24 Oct 1821; residence - Nova Scotia, Canada. SOURCE: WO120 Volume 35 page 257. INDEX # 1765.

Ja^s LYONS; pension awarded 24 Oct 1821; residence - Nova Scotia, Canada. SOURCE: WO120 Volume 35 page 257. INDEX # 1766.

Bern^d MCCONOLLY; pension awarded 24 Oct 1821; residence - Nova Scotia, Canada. SOURCE: WO120 Volume 35 page 257. INDEX # 1767.

98th Regiment of Foot (continued)

Thos MCDONALD; pension awarded 24 Oct 1821; residence - Nova Scotia, Canada. SOURCE: WO120 Volume 35 page 257. INDEX # 1768.

Jno POWER; pension awarded 24 Oct 1821; residence - Nova Scotia, Canada. SOURCE: WO120 Volume 35 page 257. INDEX # 1769.

Jno QUILTY; pension awarded 24 Oct 1821; residence - Nova Scotia, Canada. SOURCE: WO120 Volume 35 page 257. INDEX # 1770.

Caleb REID; pension awarded 24 Oct 1821; residence - Nova Scotia, Canada. SOURCE: WO120 Volume 35 page 257. INDEX # 1771.

Jas RYAN; pension awarded 24 Oct 1821; residence - Nova Scotia, Canada. SOURCE: WO120 Volume 35 page 257. INDEX # 1772.

Fras WALKER; pension awarded 24 Oct 1821; residence - Nova Scotia, Canada. SOURCE: WO120 Volume 35 page 257. INDEX # 1773.

Patk BANNON; pension awarded 7 Feb 1822; residence - Nova Scotia, Canada. SOURCE: WO120 Volume 35 page 257. INDEX # 1774.

Jno NUGENT; pension awarded 1 May 1822; residence - Nova Scotia, Canada. SOURCE: WO120 Volume 35 page 258. INDEX # 1775.

Robt LOWRY; pension awarded 31 Jul 1822; residence - Nova Scotia, Canada. SOURCE: WO120 Volume 35 page 258. INDEX # 1776.

Jno MCCARTHY; pension awarded 9 May 1823; residence - Nova Scotia, Canada. SOURCE: WO120 Volume 35 page 258. INDEX # 1777.

Thos SLATTERY; pension awarded 16 Aug 1825; residence - Nova Scotia, Canada. SOURCE: WO120 Volume 35 page 258. INDEX # 1778.

Thos BARRY; pension awarded 30 Aug 1826; residence - Nova Scotia, Canada. SOURCE: WO120 Volume 35 page 258. INDEX # 1779.

Edwd COSGROVE; pension awarded 30 Aug 1826; residence - Nova Scotia, Canada. SOURCE: WO120 Volume 35 page 258. INDEX # 1780.

Jas HULME; pension awarded 24 Oct 1821; residence - Nova Scotia, Canada. SOURCE: WO120 Volume 35 page 258. INDEX # 1781.

Jno COX; pension awarded 24 Oct 1821; residence - Nova Scotia, Canada. SOURCE: WO120 Volume 35 page 258. INDEX # 1782.

Owen COYLE; pension awarded 24 Oct 1821; residence - Nova Scotia, Canada; SOURCE: WO120 Volume 35 page 258. INDEX # 1783.

Patk MANNION; pension awarded 24 Oct 1821; residence - Nova Scotia, Canada. SOURCE: WO120 Volume 35 page 258. INDEX # 1784.

Geo HARRIS; pension awarded 24 Oct 1821; residence - Nova Scotia, Canada. SOURCE: WO120 Volume 35 page 258. INDEX # 1785.

Thos LELAND; pension awarded 28 Mar 1821; residence - Nova Scotia, Canada. SOURCE: WO120 Volume 35 page 258. INDEX # 1786.

Thos CUMMINGS; pension awarded 28 Mar 1821; residence - Nova Scotia, Canada. SOURCE: WO120 Volume 35 page 258. INDEX # 1787.

Patk HOLMES; pension awarded 23 May 1821; residence - Nova Scotia, Canada. SOURCE: WO120 Volume 35 page 258. INDEX # 1788.

Jno LENNON; pension awarded 23 May 1821; residence - Nova Scotia, Canada. SOURCE: WO120 Volume 35 page 258. INDEX # 1789.

Peter MORAN; pension awarded 23 May 1821; residence - Nova Scotia, Canada. SOURCE: WO120 Volume 35 page 258. INDEX # 1790.

Jno WALSH; pension awarded 23 May 1821; residence - Nova Scotia, Canada. SOURCE: WO120 Volume 35 page 258. INDEX # 1791.

Cornelius LEE; pension awarded 8 Aug 1827; residence - Nova Scotia, Canada. SOURCE: WO120 Volume 35 page 258. INDEX # 1792.

Wm H. PRICE; pension awarded 31 Oct 1827; residence - Cape of Good Hope, South Africa. SOURCE: WO120 Volume 35 page 258. INDEX # 1793.

98th Regiment of Foot (continued)

Ja^s CAVE; pension awarded 20 Feb 1828; residence - Cape of Good Hope, South Africa. SOURCE: WO120 Volume 35 page 258. INDEX # 1794.
James ROBINSON; pension awarded 21 May 1828. SOURCE: WO120 Volume 35 page 258. INDEX # 1795.
Thos NUGENT; pension awarded 19 Jun 1822. SOURCE: WO120 Volume 35 page 258. INDEX # 1796.
John ADAMS; pension awarded 19 Jun 1822. SOURCE: WO120 Volume 35 page 258. INDEX # 1797.
John KAY; pension awarded 11 Oct 1826. SOURCE: WO120 Volume 35 page 258. INDEX # 1798.
John ART; pension awarded 11 Aug 1830. SOURCE: WO120 Volume 35 page 259. INDEX # 1799.
Jno BARCLAY; pension awarded 13 Oct 1830. SOURCE: WO120 Volume 35 page 259. INDEX # 1800.
Phi^p HOLMES; pension awarded 14 Sep 1831. SOURCE: WO120 Volume 35 page 259. INDEX # 1801.
Jno HAYWOOD; pension awarded 12 Dec 1831. SOURCE: WO120 Volume 35 page 259. INDEX # 1802.
Ed^wd TOOLE; pension awarded 9 Nov 1831. SOURCE: WO120 Volume 35 page 259. INDEX # 1803.
Den^s DELAHUNT; pension awarded 9 Nov 1831. SOURCE: WO120 Volume 35 page 259. INDEX # 1804.
Corn^s LEE; pension awarded 9 Nov 1831. SOURCE: WO120 Volume 35 page 259. INDEX # 1805.
Ed^wd JONES; pension awarded 13 Jul 1836. SOURCE: WO120 Volume 35 page 259. INDEX # 1806.
Jno BROWN; pension awarded 10 Aug 1836. SOURCE: WO120 Volume 35 page 259. INDEX # 1807.
Barney FITZPATRICK; pension awarded 23 Aug 1837. SOURCE: WO120 Volume 35 page 259. INDEX # 1808.

99th Regiment of Foot

Jno MORRIS; pension awarded 25 Jun 1818; residence - Canada. SOURCE: WO120 Volume 35 page 264. INDEX # 1809.
Robt MCGILL; pension awarded 15 Dec 1819; residence - Mauritius. SOURCE: WO120 Volume 35 page 264. INDEX # 1810.
Chas KITT; pension awarded 7 Dec 1820; residence - Canada. SOURCE: WO120 Volume 35 page 264. INDEX # 1811.
Willm OSBORNE; pension awarded 12 Sep 1821; residence - Canada. SOURCE: WO120 Volume 35 page 264. INDEX # 1812.
Jno CALLAGHAN; pension awarded 13 Apr 1824; residence - Canada. SOURCE: WO120 Volume 35 page 264. INDEX # 1813.
Dean JUNKIN; pension awarded 12 May 1824; residence - Canada. SOURCE: WO120 Volume 35 page 264. INDEX # 1814.
Willm OWENS; pension awarded 16 Aug 1825; residence - Canada. SOURCE: WO120 Volume 35 page 264. INDEX # 1815.
Thos PHILPOT; pension awarded 12 Oct 1825; residence - Quebec, Canada. SOURCE: WO120 Volume 35 page 264. INDEX # 1816.
Jno COFFEY; pension awarded 1 Feb 1826; residence - Canada. SOURCE: WO120 Volume 35 page 264. INDEX # 1817.
Ed^wd COSGROVE; pension awarded 1 Feb 1826; residence - Canada. SOURCE: WO120 Volume 35 page 264. INDEX # 1818.
Peter CAVANAGH; pension awarded 1 Feb 1826; residence - Canada. SOURCE: WO120 Volume 35 page 264. INDEX # 1819.
Thos RUNCHY; pension awarded 1 Feb 1826; residence - Canada. SOURCE: WO120 Volume 35 page 264. INDEX # 1820.
Ja^s DORRIS; pension awarded 13 Dec 1826; residence - Canada. SOURCE: WO120 Volume 35 page 264. INDEX # 1821.
Chas MCALISTER; pension awarded 7 Mar 1827. SOURCE: WO120 Volume 35 page 264. INDEX # 1822.
And^w SPEARMAN; pension awarded 30 May 1827; residence - Canada. SOURCE: WO120 Volume 35 page 264. INDEX # 1823.
Jno LEE; pension awarded 30 May 1827; residence - Quebec, Canada. SOURCE: WO120 Volume 35 page 264. INDEX # 1824.
Ja^s RYAN; pension awarded 30 May 1827. SOURCE: WO120 Volume 35 page 264. INDEX # 1825.

99th Regiment of Foot (continued)

Wm CONROY; pension awarded 12 May 1819; residence - Canada. SOURCE: WO120 Volume 35 page 264. INDEX # 1826.
Bern^d DUFFY; pension awarded 12 May 1819; residence - Canada. SOURCE: WO120 Volume 35 page 264. INDEX # 1827.
Jno MAXWELL; pension awarded 12 May 1819; residence - Canada. SOURCE: WO120 Volume 35 page 264. INDEX # 1828.
Thos LEARY; pension awarded 12 May 1819; residence - Canada. SOURCE: WO120 Volume 35 page 264. INDEX # 1829.
Robt KERR; pension awarded 12 May 1819; residence - Canada. SOURCE: WO120 Volume 35 page 264. INDEX # 1830.
Wm DALY; pension awarded 12 May 1819; residence - Canada. SOURCE: WO120 Volume 35 page 264. INDEX # 1831.
Bern^d HUGHES; pension awarded 13 Jan 1830. SOURCE: WO120 Volume 35 page 264. INDEX # 1832.
Garrett FITZGERALD; pension awarded 12 Sep 1832. SOURCE: WO120 Volume 35 page 265. INDEX # 1833.
Ja^s FARRELL; pension awarded 5 Jun 1817. SOURCE: WO120 Volume 35 page 265. INDEX # 1834.
Wm BURKE; pension awarded 25 Jun 1818. SOURCE: WO120 Volume 35 page 265. INDEX # 1835.
W^d BADGER; pension awarded 25 Jun 1818. SOURCE: WO120 Volume 35 page 265. INDEX # 1836.
Ge^o EDGE; pension awarded 25 Jun 1818. SOURCE: WO120 Volume 35 page 265. INDEX # 1837.
Sylvest^r DEMPSEY; pension awarded 23 Sep 1818. SOURCE: WO120 Volume 35 page 265. INDEX # 1838.
Ja^s FALLON; pension awarded 23 Sep 1818. SOURCE: WO120 Volume 35 page 265. INDEX # 1839.
Ge^o MCCORMACK; pension awarded 23 SEp 1818. SOURCE: WO120 Volume 35 page 265. INDEX # 1840.
Ja^s PRICE; pension awarded 23 Sep 1818. SOURCE: WO120 Volume 35 page 265. INDEX # 1841.
Hugh GORMLEY; pension awarded 23 Sep 1818. SOURCE: WO120 Volume 35 page 265. INDEX # 1842.
Robt GALES; pension awarded 23 Sep 1818. SOURCE: WO120 Volume 35 page 265. INDEX # 1843.
Thos ELLIOTT; pension awarded 23 Sep 1818. SOURCE: WO120 Volume 35 page 265. INDEX # 1844.
Thos COX; pension awarded 23 Sep 1818. SOURCE: WO120 Volume 35 page 265. INDEX # 1845.
Ja^s BUTLER; pension awarded 23 Sep 1818. SOURCE: WO120 Volume 35 page 265. INDEX # 1846.
Pat^k COX; pension awarded 23 Sep 1818. SOURCE: WO120 Volume 35 page 265. INDEX # 1847.
Thos JONES; pension awarded 23 Sep 1818. SOURCE: WO120 Volume 35 page 265. INDEX # 1848.
Robt QUIN; pension awarded 23 Sep 1818. SOURCE: WO120 Volume 35 page 265. INDEX # 1849.
Jos^h AUSTIN; pension awarded 23 Sep 1818. SOURCE: WO120 Volume 35 page 265. INDEX # 1850.
Danl COUGHLIN; pension awarded 23 Sep 1818. SOURCE: WO120 Volume 35 page 265. INDEX # 1851.
Mich^l COX; pension awarded 23 Sep 1818. SOURCE: WO120 Volume 35 page 265. INDEX # 1852.
Jno FLANNIGAN; pension awarded 23 Sep 1818. SOURCE: WO120 Volume 35 page 265. INDEX # 1853.
Hugh FITZPATRICK; pension awarded 23 Sep 1818. SOURCE: WO120 Volume 35 page 265. INDEX # 1854.
Wm HASKETT; pension awarded 23 Sep 1818. SOURCE: WO120 Volume 35 page 265. INDEX # 1855.
Corn^s HARRINGTON; pension awarded 23 Sep 1818. SOURCE: WO120 Volume 35 page 265. INDEX # 1856.
Den^s MCNAMARA; pension awarded 23 Sep 1818. SOURCE: WO120 Volume 35 page 266. INDEX # 1857.
Jno ONEILL; pension awarded 23 Sep 1818. SOURCE: WO120 Volume 35 page 266. INDEX # 1858.
Wm PATTERSON; pension awarded 23 Sep 1818. SOURCE: WO120 Volume 35 page 266. INDEX # 1859.
Mart^n SMYTH; pension awarded 23 Sep 1818. SOURCE: WO120 Volume 35 page 266. INDEX # 1860.
Jno WETHERS; pension awarded 23 Sep 1818. SOURCE: WO120 Volume 35 page 266. INDEX # 1861.
Richd SHORT; pension awarded 23 Sep 1818. SOURCE: WO120 Volume 35 page 266. INDEX # 1862.
And^w HILL; pension awarded 23 Sep 1818. SOURCE: WO120 Volume 35 page 266. INDEX # 1863.
Wm SHEA; pension awarded 23 Sep 1818. SOURCE: WO120 Volume 35 page 266. INDEX # 1864.
Patt MURPHY; pension awarded 23 Sep 1818. SOURCE: WO120 Volume 35 page 264. INDEX # 1865.
Jos^h BERTH; pension awarded 23 Sep 1818. SOURCE: WO120 Volume 35 page 266. INDEX # 1866.
Wm HUGHES; pension awarded 23 Sep 1818. SOURCE: WO120 Volume 35 page 266. INDEX # 1867.
Patt CAMPBELL; pension awarded 23 Sep 1818. SOURCE: WO120 Volume 35 page 266. INDEX # 1868.
Pat^k COX; pension awarded 23 Sep 1818. SOURCE: WO120 Volume 35 page 266. INDEX # 1869.
Den^s DONAGHOE; pension awarded 23 Sep 1818. SOURCE: WO120 Volume 35 page 266. INDEX # 1870.
Benjn GOODGER; pension awarded 23 Sep 1818. SOURCE: WO120 Volume 35 page 266. INDEX # 1871.
Fra^s MORGAN; pension awarded 23 Sep 1818. SOURCE: WO120 Volume 35 page 266. INDEX # 1872.

WO120 VOLUME 35

99th Regiment of Foot (continued)

Ja^s MCGARRY; pension awarded 23 Sep 1818. SOURCE: WO120 Volume 35 page 266. INDEX # 1873.
Jno MURPHY; pension awarded 23 Sep 1818. SOURCE: WO120 Volume 35 page 266. INDEX # 1874.
Luke DILLON; pension awarded 23 Sep 1818. SOURCE: WO120 Volume 35 page 266. INDEX # 1875.
Fra^s JACKSON; pension awarded 23 Sep 1818. SOURCE: WO120 Volume 35 page 266. INDEX # 1876.
Jno RYAN; pension awarded 23 Sep 1818. SOURCE: WO120 Volume 35 page 266. INDEX # 1877.
Phi^p GRAVES; pension awarded 23 Sep 1818. SOURCE: WO120 Volume 35 page 266. INDEX # 1878.
Ed^{wd} MANNING; pension awarded 23 Sep 1818. SOURCE: WO120 Volume 35 page 266. INDEX # 1879.
Ja^s SHERIDAN; pension awarded 23 Sep 1818. SOURCE: WO120 Volume 35 page 266. INDEX # 1880.
Jno GIBSON; pension awarded 23 Sep 1818. SOURCE: WO120 Volume 35 page 267. INDEX # 1881.
Wm BURNET; pension awarded 23 Sep 1818. SOURCE: WO120 Volume 35 page 267. INDEX # 1882.
Hugh HENRY; pension awarded 23 Sep 1818. SOURCE: WO120 Volume 35 page 267. INDEX # 1883.
Jno HAZELTON; pension awarded 23 Sep 1818. SOURCE: WO120 Volume 35 page 267. INDEX # 1884.
Thos REID; pension awarded 23 Sep 1818. SOURCE: WO120 Volume 35 page 267. INDEX # 1885.
Richd CHAPMAN; pension awarded 23 Sep 1818. SOURCE: WO120 Volume 35 page 267. INDEX # 1886.
Ed^{wd} THORNBURY; pension awarded 23 Sep 1818. SOURCE: WO120 Volume 35 page 267. INDEX # 1887.
Jno BURKE; pension awarded 23 Sep 1818. SOURCE: WO120 Volume 35 page 267. INDEX # 1888.
Jno ANDERSON; pension awarded 23 Sep 1818. SOURCE: WO120 Volume 35 page 267. INDEX # 1889.
Jno MCKEON; pension awarded 23 Sep 1818. SOURCE: WO120 Volume 35 page 267. INDEX # 1890.
Thos HARAGAN; pension awarded 23 Sep 1818. SOURCE: WO120 Volume 35 page 267. INDEX # 1891.
Ed^{wd} MORAN; pension awarded 23 Sep 1818. SOURCE: WO120 Volume 35 page 267. INDEX # 1892.
Wm CARROLL; pension awarded 23 Sep 1818. SOURCE: WO120 Volume 35 page 267. INDEX # 1893.
Jno CROZIER; pension awarded 23 Sep 1818. SOURCE: WO120 Volume 35 page 267. INDEX # 1894.
Mich^l HENDRICK; pension awarded 23 Sep 1818. SOURCE: WO120 Volume 35 page 267. INDEX # 1895.
Jno MCGUIRE; pension awarded 23 Sep 1818. SOURCE: WO120 Volume 35 page 267. INDEX # 1896.
Mich^l COYLE; pension awarded 23 Sep 1818. SOURCE: WO120 Volume 35 page 267. INDEX # 1897.
Robt HARKIN; pension awarded 23 Sep 1818. SOURCE: WO120 Volume 35 page 267. INDEX # 1898.
Ja^s MCGARRY; pension awarded 23 Sep 1818. SOURCE: WO120 Volume 35 page 267. INDEX # 1899.
Cormac KEELAGHER; pension awarded 23 Sep 1818. SOURCE: WO120 Volume 35 page 267. INDEX # 1900.
Fra^s FELLOWS; pension awarded 23 Sep 1818. SOURCE: WO120 Volume 35 page 267. INDEX # 1901.
Ed^{wd} MARCH; pension awarded 23 Sep 1818. SOURCE: WO120 Volume 35 page 267. INDEX # 1902.
Thos MURRAY; pension awarded 23 Sep 1818. SOURCE: WO120 Volume 35 page 267. INDEX # 1903.
Wm VAUGHAN; pension awarded 23 Sep 1818. SOURCE: WO120 Volume 35 page 267. INDEX # 1904.
Pat^k MURPHY; pension awarded 23 Sep 1818. SOURCE: WO120 Volume 35 page 268. INDEX # 1905.
Wm MULDOON; pension awarded 23 Sep 1818. SOURCE: WO120 Volume 35 page 268. INDEX # 1906.
Pat^k MCDONAGH; pension awarded 23 Sep 1818. SOURCE: WO120 Volume 35 page 268. INDEX # 1907.
Jno CRAGEN; pension awarded 23 Sep 1818. SOURCE: WO120 Volume 35 page 268. INDEX # 1908.
Richd ROOKE; pension awarded 23 Sep 1818. SOURCE: WO120 Volume 35 page 268. INDEX # 1909.
Wm NEWTON; pension awarded 23 Sep 1818. SOURCE: WO120 Volume 35 page 268. INDEX # 1910.
Jno DIXON; pension awarded 23 Sep 1818. SOURCE: WO120 Volume 35 page 268. INDEX # 1911.
Pat^k KENNEDY; pension awarded 23 Sep 1818. SOURCE: WO120 Volume 35 page 268. INDEX # 1912.
Wm BRIEN; pension awarded 23 Sep 1818. SOURCE: WO120 Volume 35 page 268. INDEX # 1913.
Hen^y ARNOLD; pension awarded 23 Sep 1818. SOURCE: WO120 Volume 35 page 268. INDEX # 1914.
Wm MURPHY; pension awarded 23 Sep 1818. SOURCE: WO120 Volume 35 page 268. INDEX # 1915.
Jno MURPHY; pension awarded 23 Sep 1818. SOURCE: WO120 Volume 35 page 268. INDEX # 1916.
Ja^s CONNOR; pension awarded 23 Sep 1818. SOURCE: WO120 Volume 35 page 268. INDEX # 1917.
Pat^k REILY; pension awarded 23 Sep 1818. SOURCE: WO120 Volume 35 page 268. INDEX # 1918.
Pat^k FOY; pension awarded 23 Sep 1818. SOURCE: WO120 Volume 35 page 268. INDEX # 1919.
Hen^y BYRNE; pension awarded 23 Sep 1818. SOURCE: WO120 Volume 35 page 268. INDEX # 1920.
Ja^s SIMPSON; pension awarded 23 Sep 1818. SOURCE: WO120 Volume 35 page 268. INDEX # 1921.
Wm CUNNINGHAM; pension awarded 23 Sep 1818. SOURCE: WO120 Volume 35 page 268. INDEX # 1922.
Mau^e CONNOR; pension awarded 23 Sep 1818. SOURCE: WO120 Volume 35 page 268. INDEX # 1923.
Owen DOYLE; pension awarded 23 Sep 1818. SOURCE: WO120 Volume 35 page 268. INDEX # 1924.
Ja^s FINAN; pension awarded 23 Sep 1818. SOURCE: WO120 Volume 35 page 268. INDEX # 1925.

BRITISH ARMY PENSIONERS ABROAD

99th Regiment of Foot (continued)

Hugh WILSON; pension awarded 23 Sep 1818. SOURCE: WO120 Volume 35 page 268. INDEX # 1926.
Thos PHILPOT; pension awarded 23 Sep 1818. SOURCE: WO120 Volume 35 page 268. INDEX # 1927.
Thos RATH; pension awarded 23 Sep 1818. SOURCE: WO120 Volume 35 page 268. INDEX # 1928.
Edwd SLATER; pension awarded 23 Sep 1818. SOURCE: WO120 Volume 35 page 269. INDEX # 1929.
Edwd DOGHERTY; pension awarded 23 Sep 1818. SOURCE: WO120 Volume 35 page 269. INDEX # 1930.
Jas LENNON; pension awarded 23 Sep 1818. SOURCE: WO120 Volume 35 page 269. INDEX # 1931.
Adam FORSYTH; pension awarded 23 Sep 1818. SOURCE: WO120 Volume 35 page 269. INDEX # 1932.
Micl BRADY; pension awarded 23 Sep 1818. SOURCE: WO120 Volume 35 page 269. INDEX # 1933.
Patk CARDELL; pension awarded 23 Sep 1818. SOURCE: WO120 Volume 35 page 269. INDEX # 1934.
Jas MACKILL; pension awarded 23 Sep 1818. SOURCE: WO120 Volume 35 page 269. INDEX # 1935.
Hugh MALLON; pension awarded 23 Sep 1818. SOURCE: WO120 Volume 35 page 269. INDEX # 1936.
Bernd MCBRIDE; pension awarded 23 Sep 1818. SOURCE: WO120 Volume 35 page 269. INDEX # 1937.
Micl OHARA; pension awarded 23 Sep 1818. SOURCE: WO120 Volume 35 page 269. INDEX # 1938.
Jno DUNBAR; pension awarded 23 Sep 1818. SOURCE: WO120 Volume 35 page 269. INDEX # 1939.
Micl MULLEN; pension awarded 23 Sep 1818. SOURCE: WO120 Volume 35 page 269. INDEX # 1940.
Alexr MCCABE; pension awarded 23 Sep 1818. SOURCE: WO120 Volume 35 page 269. INDEX # 1941.
Fras COX; pension awarded 23 Sep 1818. SOURCE: WO120 Volume 35 page 269. INDEX # 1942.
Jno KILTY; pension awarded 23 Sep 1818. SOURCE: WO120 Volume 35 page 269. INDEX # 1943.
Edwd FARRALL; pension awarded 23 Sep 1818. SOURCE: WO120 Volume 35 page 269. INDEX # 1944.
Wm PENDER; pension awarded 23 Sep 1818. SOURCE: WO120 Volume 35 page 269. INDEX # 1945.
Jas STANAGE; pension awarded 23 Sep 1818. SOURCE: WO120 Volume 35 page 269. INDEX # 1946.
Jno CALLAGHAN; pension awarded 23 Sep 1818. SOURCE: WO120 Volume 35 page 269. INDEX # 1947.
Chas JUDGE; pension awarded 23 Sep 1818. SOURCE: WO120 Volume 35 page 269. INDEX # 1948.
Peter DINAN; pension awarded 23 Sep 1818. SOURCE: WO120 Volume 35 page 269. INDEX # 1949.
Patk FLANERY; pension awarded 23 Sep 1818. SOURCE: WO120 Volume 35 page 269. INDEX # 1950.
Mattw CALLAGHAN; pension awarded 23 Sep 1818. SOURCE: WO120 Volume 35 page 269. INDEX # 1951.
Patk TULLY; pension awarded 23 Sep 1818. SOURCE: WO120 Volume 35 page 269. INDEX # 1952.
Patk SHIELDS; pension awarded 23 Sep 1818. SOURCE: WO120 Volume 35 page 270. INDEX # 1953.
Jno GILLON; pension awarded 23 Sep 1818. SOURCE: WO120 Volume 35 page 270. INDEX # 1954.
Nathl BROWNLEE; pension awarded 23 Sep 1818. SOURCE: WO120 Volume 35 page 270. INDEX # 1955.
Wm OWENS; pension awarded 23 Sep 1818. SOURCE: WO120 Volume 35 page 270. INDEX # 1956.
Wm CROMMER; pension awarded 23 Sep 1818. SOURCE: WO120 Volume 35 page 270. INDEX # 1957.
Robt VINCENT; pension awarded 23 Sep 1818. SOURCE: WO120 Volume 35 page 270. INDEX # 1958.
Robt COLE; pension awarded 23 Sep 1818. SOURCE: WO120 Volume 35 page 270. INDEX # 1959.
Jno BRADY; pension awarded 23 Sep 1818. SOURCE: WO120 Volume 35 page 270. INDEX # 1960.
Jno CREEVEY; pension awarded 23 Sep 1818. SOURCE: WO120 Volume 35 page 270. INDEX # 1961.
Davd GRANT; pension awarded 23 Sep 1818. SOURCE: WO120 Volume 35 page 270. INDEX # 1962.
Micl MCLOUGHLIN; pension awarded 23 Sep 1818. SOURCE: WO120 Volume 35 page 270. INDEX # 1963.
Jno MCDERMOTT; pension awarded 23 Sep 1818. SOURCE: WO120 Volume 35 page 270. INDEX # 1964.
Patk MCALEES; pension awarded 23 Sep 1818. SOURCE: WO120 Volume 35 page 270. INDEX # 1965.
Patk KEARNEY; pension awarded 23 Sep 1818. SOURCE: WO120 Volume 35 page 270. INDEX # 1966.
Jas MCALEER; pension awarded 23 Sep 1818. SOURCE: WO120 Volume 35 page 270. INDEX # 1967.
Jno HARKINS; pension awarded 23 Sep 1818. SOURCE: WO120 Volume 35 page 270. INDEX # 1968.
Andw EGAN; pension awarded 23 Sep 1818. SOURCE: WO120 Volume 35 page 270. INDEX # 1969.
Jno SYKES; pension awarded 23 Sep 1818. SOURCE: WO120 Volume 35 page 270. INDEX # 1970.
Simon KERRISON; pension awarded 23 Sep 1818. SOURCE: WO120 Volume 35 page 270. INDEX # 1971.
Fras MCKENA; pension awarded 23 Sep 1818. SOURCE: WO120 Volume 35 page 270. INDEX # 1972.
Jas MCKENNA; pension awarded 23 Sep 1818. SOURCE: WO120 Volume 35 page 270. INDEX # 1973.
Alexr MCCASLIN; pension awarded 23 Sep 1818. SOURCE: WO120 Volume 35 page 270. INDEX # 1974.
Peter FARRELL; pension awarded 23 Sep 1818. SOURCE: WO120 Volume 35 page 270. INDEX # 1975.
Hugh SEMPLE; pension awarded 23 Sep 1818. SOURCE: WO120 Volume 35 page 270. INDEX # 1976.
Edwd DONNELLY; pension awarded 23 Sep 1818. SOURCE: WO120 Volume 35 page 271. INDEX # 1977.
Micl CASSADY; pension awarded 23 Sep 1818. SOURCE: WO120 Volume 35 page 271. INDEX # 1978.

WO120 VOLUME 35

99th Regiment of Foot (continued)

Wm MOORE; pension awarded 23 Sep 1818. SOURCE: WO120 Volume 35 page 271. INDEX # 1979.
Ja^s MCGOREY; pension awarded 23 Sep 1818. SOURCE: WO120 Volume 35 page 271. INDEX # 1980.
Hen^y MCDONELL; pension awarded 23 Sep 1818. SOURCE: WO120 Volume 35 page 271. INDEX # 1981.
Pat^k QUINN; pension awarded 23 Sep 1818. SOURCE: WO120 Volume 35 page 271. INDEX # 1982.
Chas MCALLISTER; pension awarded 23 Sep 1818. SOURCE: WO120 Volume 35 page 271. INDEX # 1983.
Jno DENISON; pension awarded 23 Sep 1818. SOURCE: WO120 Volume 35 page 271. INDEX # 1984.
Ja^s DEVIN; pension awarded 23 Sep 1818. SOURCE: WO120 Volume 35 page 271. INDEX # 1985.
Bern^d HUGHES; pension awarded 23 Sep 1818. SOURCE: WO120 Volume 35 page 271. INDEX # 1986.
Robt LEE; pension awarded 23 Sep 1818. SOURCE: WO120 Volume 35 page 271. INDEX # 1987.
Wm NESBITT; pension awarded 23 Sep 1818. SOURCE: WO120 Volume 35 page 271. INDEX # 1988.
Ch^n ROBINSON; pension awarded 23 Sep 1818. SOURCE: WO120 Volume 35 page 271. INDEX # 1989.
Ja^s ONEILL; pension awarded 23 Sep 1818. SOURCE: WO120 Volume 35 page 271. INDEX # 1990.
Ja^s KEILLY; pension awarded 23 Sep 1818. SOURCE: WO120 Volume 35 page 271. INDEX # 1991.
Felix MCQUINN; pension awarded 23 Sep 1818. SOURCE: WO120 Volume 35 page 271. INDEX # 1992.
Trevor MCKAY; pension awarded 23 Sep 1818. SOURCE: WO120 Volume 35 page 271. INDEX # 1993.
Dean JUNKIN; pension awarded 23 Sep 1818. SOURCE: WO120 Volume 35 page 271. INDEX # 1994.
Ge^o FLEMING; pension awarded 23 Sep 1818. SOURCE: WO120 Volume 35 page 271. INDEX # 1995.
Hugh MCLAUGHLIN; pension awarded 23 Sep 1818. SOURCE: WO120 Volume 35 page 271. INDEX # 1996.
Stafford WALSH; pension awarded 23 Sep 1818. SOURCE: WO120 Volume 35 page 271. INDEX # 1997.
Pat^k MURPHY; pension awarded 23 Sep 1818. SOURCE: WO120 Volume 35 page 271. INDEX # 1998.
Arthur SHARPLEY; pension awarded 23 Sep 1818. SOURCE: WO120 Volume 35 page 271. INDEX # 1999.
Jno GOTT; pension awarded 23 Sep 1818. SOURCE: WO120 Volume 35 page 271. INDEX # 2000.

102nd Regiment of Foot

Chas LANGHAM; pension awarded 23 May 1821; residence - New South Wales, Australia. SOURCE: WO120 Volume 35 page 272. INDEX # 2001.
Thos CHIPP; pension awarded 26 Nov 1823; residence - New South Wales, Australia. SOURCE: WO120 Volume 35 page 272. INDEX # 2002.
Thos TROTTER; pension awarded 15 Mar 1826; residence - New South Wales, Australia. SOURCE: WO120 Volume 35 page 272. INDEX # 2003.

103rd Regiment of Foot

Chas DAVIS; pension awarded 25 Jun 1818; residence - Quebec, Quebec, Canada. SOURCE: WO120 Volume 35 page 274. INDEX # 2004.
Dav^d WILSON; pension awarded 12 May 1819; residence - Canada. SOURCE: WO120 Volume 35 page 274. INDEX # 2005.
Alex^r CAMERON; pension awarded 7 Dec 1820; residence - Canada. SOURCE: WO120 Volume 35 page 274. INDEX # 2006.
Willm WATSON; pension awarded 12 Sep 1821; residence - Canada. SOURCE: WO120 Volume 35 page 274. INDEX # 2007.
Fra^s WILLOCK; pension awarded 9 May 1823; residence - Fort Erie, Ontario, Canada. SOURCE: WO120 Volume 35 page 274. INDEX # 2008.

104th Regiment of Foot

Eber PORTER; pension awarded 31 Jul 1822; residence - Nova Scotia, Canada. SOURCE: WO120 Volume 35 page 276. INDEX # 2009.

104th Regiment of Foot (continued)

Jn⁰ FALING; pension awarded 25 Sep 1822; residence - Nova Scotia, Canada. SOURCE: WO120 Volume 35 page 276. INDEX # 2010.

Jean Baptiste ALLAIRE; pension awarded 4 Aug 1824; residence - Canada. SOURCE: WO120 Volume 35 page 276. INDEX # 2011.

Josʰ SWIM; pension awarded 5 Mar 1823. SOURCE: WO120 Volume 35 page 276. INDEX # 2012.

Jn⁰ MCDONALD; pension awarded 5 Mar 1823; residence - Nova Scotia, Canada. SOURCE: WO120 Volume 35 page 276. INDEX # 2013.

Angus GUNN; pension awarded 30 Jun 1825; residence - Nova Scotia, Canada. SOURCE: WO120 Volume 35 page 276. INDEX # 2014.

Josʰ BOUCHIE; pension awarded 1 Feb 1826; residence - Canada. SOURCE: WO120 Volume 35 page 276. INDEX # 2015.

Robᵗ MOORE; pension awarded 30 Aug 1826; residence - Canada. SOURCE: WO120 Volume 35 page 276. INDEX # 2016.

Alexis LEMERY; pension awarded 13 Dec 1826; residence - Canada. SOURCE: WO120 Volume 35 page 276. INDEX # 2017.

Josʰ LARMONDEAU; pension awarded 28 Mar 1821; residence - Canada. SOURCE: WO120 Volume 35 page 276. INDEX # 2018.

Josʰ WALL; pension awarded 12 Sep 1821; residence - Nova Scotia, Canada. SOURCE: WO120 Volume 35 page 276. INDEX # 2019.

Ge⁰ BAIN; pension awarded 23 May 1821; residence - Nova Scotia, Canada. SOURCE: WO120 Volume 35 page 276. INDEX # 2020.

Henʸ FLEMING; pension awarded 8 Aug 1827; residence - Nova Scotia, Canada. SOURCE: WO120 Volume 35 page 276. INDEX # 2021.

Thoˢ GEE; pension awarded 31 Oct 1827; residence - Nova Scotia, Canada. SOURCE: WO120 Volume 35 page 276. INDEX # 2022.

Wᵐ GRANGER; pension awarded 12 May 1819. SOURCE: WO120 Volume 35 page 276. INDEX # 2023.

Jn⁰ MARLEY; pension awarded 12 May 1819. SOURCE: WO120 Volume 35 page 276. INDEX # 2024.

Charles DESCARROUR; pension awarded 1 Jul 1819. SOURCE: WO120 Volume 35 page 276. INDEX # 2025.

Michˡ RICKETTS; pension awarded 1 Jul 1819. SOURCE: WO120 Volume 35 page 276. INDEX # 2026.

Jn⁰ CUMMINS; pension awarded 2 Feb 1820. SOURCE: WO120 Volume 35 page 276. INDEX # 2027.

Jabish SQUIERS; pension awarded 26 Jul 1820. SOURCE: WO120 Volume 35 276. INDEX # 2028.

Jn⁰ WHITENKNACT; pension awarded 25 Jun 1829. SOURCE: WO120 Volume 35 page 276. INDEX # 2029.

Watt MCFARLANE; pension awarded 5 Jun 1817. SOURCE: WO120 Volume 35 page 276. INDEX # 2030.

Wᵐ HIGGINS; pension awarded 5 Jun 1817. SOURCE: WO120 Volume 35 page 276. INDEX # 2031.

Richᵈ SMITH; pension awarded 5 Jun 1817. SOURCE: WO120 Volume 35 page 276. INDEX # 2032.

Peter KELLER; pension awarded 5 Jun 1817. SOURCE: WO120 Volume 35 page 277. INDEX # 2033.

Peter COTE; pension awarded 5 Jun 1817. SOURCE: WO120 Volume 35 page 277. INDEX # 2034.

Josʰ AVERY; pension awarded 5 Jun 1817. SOURCE: WO120 Volume 35 page 277. INDEX # 2035.

Jn⁰ BADGER; pension awarded 5 Jun 1817. SOURCE: WO120 Volume 35 page 277. INDEX # 2936.

Jaˢ FALKNER; pension awarded 5 Jun 1817. SOURCE: WO120 Volume 35 page 277. INDEX # 2037.

Jn⁰ HARGROVE; pension awarded 5 Jun 1817. SOURCE: WO120 Volume 35 page 277. INDEX # 2038.

Jaˢ WEST; pension awarded 5 Jun 1817. SOURCE: WO120 Volume 35 page 277. INDEX # 2039.

Phiᵖ LONSOR; pension awarded 5 Jun 1817. SOURCE: WO120 Volume 35 page 277. INDEX # 2040.

Christⁿ AURELL; pension awarded 5 Jun 1817. SOURCE: WO120 Volume 35 page 277. INDEX # 2041.

Jn⁰ ROCK; pension awarded 5 Jun 1817. SOURCE: WO120 Volume 35 page 277. INDEX # 2042.

Jn⁰ CAMPBELL; pension awarded 5 Jun 1817. SOURCE: WO120 Volume 35 page 277. INDEX # 2043.

Cato CLARKE; pension awarded 5 Jun 1817. SOURCE: WO120 Volume 35 page 277. INDEX # 2044.

Peter GOMMO; pension awarded 5 Jun 1817. SOURCE: WO120 Volume 35 page 277. INDEX # 2045.

Bernᵈ GEURONE; pension awarded 5 Jun 1817. SOURCE: WO120 Volume 35 page 277. INDEX # 2046.

104th Regiment of Foot (continued)

Duncⁿ HENDERSON; pension awarded 5 Jun 1817. SOURCE: WO120 Volume 35 page 277. INDEX # 2047.
Jno MCLAUCHLAN; pension awarded 5 Jun 1817. SOURCE: WO120 Volume 35 page 277. INDEX # 2048.
Hugh MCDONALD; pension awarded 5 Jun 1817. SOURCE: WO120 Volume 35 page 277. INDEX # 2049.
Edwd REASALL; pension awarded 5 Jun 1817. SOURCE: WO120 Volume 35 page 277. INDEX # 2050.
Jos^h HAYNES; pension awarded 21 Aug 1817. SOURCE: WO120 Volume 35 page 277. INDEX # 2051.
Ab^m EZIAS; pension awarded 21 Aug 1817. SOURCE: WO120 Volume 35 page 277. INDEX # 2052.
Jos^h HURST; pension awarded 21 Aug 1817. SOURCE: WO120 Volume 35 page 277. INDEX # 2053.
Moses HOLMES; pension awarded 21 Aug 1817. SOURCE: WO120 Volume 35 page 277. INDEX # 2054.
Nathl LANG; pension awarded 21 Aug 1817. SOURCE: WO120 Volume 35 page 277. INDEX # 2055.
Dav^d BURIDGE; pension awarded 21 Aug 1817. SOURCE: WO120 Volume 35 page 277. INDEX # 2056.
Edwd CASTER; pension awarded 21 Aug 1817. SOURCE: WO120 Volume 35 page 278. INDEX # 2057.
Jer^h DAILEY; pension awarded 21 Aug 1817. SOURCE: WO120 Volume 35 page 278. INDEX # 2058.
Fred^k DUMPLER; pension awarded 21 Aug 1817. SOURCE: WO120 Volume 35 page 278. INDEX # 2059.
Jer^h HOPKINS; pension awarded 21 Aug 1817. SOURCE: WO120 Volume 35 page 278. INDEX # 2060.
Wm EVANS; pension awarded 21 Aug 1817. SOURCE: WO120 Volume 35 page 278. INDEX # 2061.
Hen^y FLEMMING; pension awarded 21 Aug 1817. SOURCE: WO120 Volume 35 page 278. INDEX # 2062.
Peter TAYETTE; pension awarded 21 Aug 1817. SOURCE: WO120 Volume 35 page 278. INDEX # 2063.
Wm GRAHAM; pension awarded 21 Aug 1817. SOURCE: WO120 Volume 35 page 278. INDEX # 2064.
Richd HARRIS; pension awarded 21 Aug 1817. SOURCE: WO120 Volume 35 page 278. INDEX # 2065.
Thos SHEMINSKIE; pension awarded 21 Aug 1817. SOURCE: WO120 Volume 35 page 278. INDEX # 2066.
Benjⁿ KENNEDY; pension awarded 21 Aug 1817. SOURCE: WO120 Volume 35 page 278. INDEX # 2067.
Jno LIVINGSTONE; pension awarded 21 Agu 1817. SOURCE: WO120 Volume 35 page 278. INDEX # 2068.
Finnon MCDONELL; pension awarded 21 Aug 1817. SOURCE: WO120 Volume 35 page 278. INDEX # 2069.
Arch^d MCLEAN; pension awarded 21 Aug 1817. SOURCE: WO120 Volume 35 page 278. INDEX # 2070.
Wm MCDONALD; pension awarded 21 Aug 1817. SOURCE: WO120 Volume 35 page 278. INDEX # 2071.
Alex^r MURCHESON; pension awarded 21 Aug 1817. SOURCE: WO120 Volume 35 page 278. INDEX # 2072.
Ja^s ROBINSON; pension awarded 21 Aug 1817. SOURCE: WO120 Volume 35 page 278. INDEX # 2073.
Jno WOOD; pension awarded 21 Aug 1817. SOURCE: WO120 Volume 35 page 278. INDEX # 2074.
Ant^y TOLSON; pension awarded 21 Aug 1817. SOURCE: WO120 Volume 35 page 278. INDEX # 2075.
Matt^w THAILE; pension awarded 21 Aug 1817. SOURCE: WO120 Volume 35 page 278. INDEX # 2076.
Owen CRONEN; pension awarded 21 Aug 1817. SOURCE: WO120 Volume 35 page 278. INDEX # 2077.
Wm MCINTOSH; pension awarded 21 Aug 1817. SOURCE: WO120 Volume 35 page 278. INDEX # 2078.
Jno THATCHER; pension awarded 21 Aug 1817. SOURCE: WO120 Volume 35 page 278. INDEX # 2079.
Thos POMPHREY; pension awarded 11 Jul 1838. SOURCE: WO120 Volume 35 page 278. INDEX # 2080.

Rifle Brigade

Thos CUMMING; pension awarded 4 Aug 1824; residence - Cape of Good Hope, South Africa. SOURCE: WO120 Volume 35 page 279. INDEX # 2081.
Jno MORAN; pension awarded 7 Feb 1822. SOURCE: WO120 Volume 35 page 279. INDEX # 2082.
Thos PARSONS; pension awarded 25 Apr 1821. SOURCE: WO120 Volume 35 page 279. INDEX # 2083.
Stewart MULLEN; pension awarded 23 May 1821. SOURCE: WO120 Volume 35 page 279. INDEX # 2084.
Wm BEDWELL; pension awarded 11 Apr 1832. SOURCE: WO120 Volume 35 page 279. INDEX # 2085.
Saml HARDY; pension awarded 12 Sep 1832. SOURCE: WO120 Volume 35 page 279. INDEX # 2086.

BRITISH ARMY PENSIONERS ABROAD

Royal Garrison Company

Edwd GRIFFITHS; pension awarded 7 Jan 1818; residence - Cape of Good Hope, South Africa.
   SOURCE: WO120 Volume 35 page 280. INDEX # 2087.
Terence OBRIEN; pension awarded 7 Jan 1818; residence - Cape of Good Hope, South Africa.
   SOURCE: WO120 Volume 35 page 280. INDEX # 2088.

Cape Cavalry

Jos^h HILL; pension awarded 26 Jul 1820; residence - Nova Scotia, Canada. SOURCE: WO120 Volume 35 page 281. INDEX # 2089.
Ja^s LEE; pension awarded 26 Jul 1820; residence - Nova Scotia, Canada. SOURCE: WO120 Volume 35 page 281. INDEX # 2090.
Thos ALLEN; pension awarded 13 Sep 1820; residence - Cape of Good Hope, South Africa. SOURCE: WO120 Volume 35 page 281. INDEX # 2091.
Dav^d OBRIEN; pension awarded 13 Sep 1820; residence - Cape of Good Hope, South Africa. SOURCE: WO120 Volume 35 page 281. INDEX # 2092.
Wm MATHEWS; pension awarded 7 Feb 1821; residence - Cape of Good Hope, South Africa. SOURCE: WO120 Volume 35 page 281. INDEX # 2093.
Saml LONG; pension awarded 7 Feb 1821; residence - Cape of Good Hope, South Africa. SOURCE: WO120 Volume 35 page 281. INDEX # 2094.
Saml THOMAS; pension awarded 23 May 1821; residence - Cape of Good Hope, South Africa. SOURCE: WO120 Volume 35 page 281. INDEX # 2095.
Willm BOLAND; pension awarded 12 Sep 1821; residence - Cape of Good Hope, South Africa. SOURCE: WO120 Volume 35 page 281. INDEX # 2096.
Christⁿ BEHL; pension awarded 12 Sep 1821; residence - Cape of Good Hope, South Africa. SOURCE: WO120 Volume 35 page 281. INDEX # 2097.
Robt PRICE; pension awarded 12 Sep 1821; residence - Cape of Good Hope, South Africa. SOURCE: WO120 Volume 35 page 281. INDEX # 2098.
Thos GILL; pension awarded 7 Feb 1822; residence - Cape of Good Hope, South Africa. SOURCE: WO120 Volume 35 page 281. INDEX # 2099.
John JOHNSON; pension awarded 9 May 1823; residence - Cape of Good Hope, South Africa. SOURCE: WO120 Volume 35 page 281. INDEX # 2100.
Thos BOWLES; pension awarded 12 Oct 1825; residence - Cape of Good Hope, South Africa. SOURCE: WO120 Volume 35 page 281. INDEX # 2101.
Willm DAY; pension awarded 3 Mar 1824; residence - Cape of Good Hope, South Africa. SOURCE: WO120 Volume 35 page 281. INDEX # 2102.
Wm LUCAS; pension awarded 22 Sep 1824. SOURCE: WO120 Volume 35 page 281. INDEX # 2103.
Hugh DUNN; pension awarded 31 Oct 1827. SOURCE: WO120 Volume 35 page 281. INDEX # 2104.
Ge^o PRICE; pension awarded 21 May 1828. SOURCE: WO120 Volume 35 page 281. INDEX # 2105.
Robt SELF; pension awarded 21 May 1828. SOURCE: WO120 Volume 35 page 281. INDEX # 2106.
Pat^k MCCORMICK; pension awarded 21 May 1828. SOURCE: WO120 Volume 35 page 281. INDEX # 2107.
Dav^d RUDD; pension awarded 21 May 1828. SOURCE: WO120 Volume 35 page 281. INDEX # 2108.
Wil^m REYNOLDS; pension awarded 21 May 1828. SOURCE: WO120 Volume 35 page 281. INDEX # 2109.
Wm FENN; pension awarded 21 May 1828. SOURCE: WO120 Volume 35 page 281. INDEX # 2110.
Wm MAYES; pension awarded 21 May 1828. SOURCE: WO120 Volume 35 page 281. INDEX # 2111.
John BROWN; pension awarded 21 May 1828. SOURCE: WO120 Volume 35 page 281. INDEX # 2112.
John DEMPSEY; pension awarded 21 May 1828. SOURCE: WO120 Volume 35 page 282. INDEX # 2113.
Wm FRIEND; pension awarded 21 May 1828. SOURCE: WO120 Volume 35 page 282. INDEX # 2114.
Robt FEATHERSTONE; pension awarded 9 Jun 1830. SOURCE: WO120 Volume 35 page 282. INDEX # 2115.
Fra^s THORTON; pension awarded 14 Mar 1832. SOURCE: WO120 Volume 35 page 282. INDEX # 2116.

Cape Infantry

Jos^h HILLS; pension awarded 23 Sep 1818; residence - Canada. SOURCE: WO120 Volume 35 page 284. INDEX # 2117.

Hugh FRASER; pension awarded 23 Sep 1818; residence - Canada. SOURCE: WO120 Volume 35 page 284. INDEX # 2118.

Wm FRASER; pension awarded 23 Sep 1818; residence - Canada. SOURCE: WO120 Volume 35 page 284. INDEX # 2119.

Ja^s WARD; pension awarded 23 Sep 1818; residence - Canada. SOURCE: WO120 Volume 35 page 284. INDEX # 2120.

Alex^r MACDONALD; pension awarded 23 May 1821; residence - Cape of Good Hope, South Africa. SOURCE: WO120 Volume 35 page 284. INDEX # 2121.

Wm LOVEDAY; pension awarded 23 May 1821; residence - Cape of Good Hope, South Africa. SOURCE: WO120 Volume 35 page 284. INDEX # 2121.

Jno LORDON; pension awarded 23 May 1821; residence - Cape of Good Hope, South Africa. SOURCE: WO120 Volume 35 page 284. INDEX # 2123.

Thos CANNON; pension awarded 23 May 1821; residence - Cape of Good Hope, South Africa. SOURCE: WO120 Volume 35 page 284. INDEX # 2124.

Robt TORR; pension awarded 23 May 1821; residence - Cape of Good Hope, South Africa. SOURCE: WO120 Volume 35 page 284. INDEX # 2125.

Pat^k GARVEY; pension awarded 23 May 1821; residence - Cape of Good Hope, South Africa. SOURCE: WO120 Volume 35 page 284. INDEX # 2126.

Thos BESTT; pension awarded 23 May 1821; residence - Cape of Good Hope, South Africa. SOURCE: WO120 Volume 35 page 284. INDEX # 2127.

Don^d GUNN; pension awarded 19 Jun 1822; residence - Cape of Good Hope, South Africa. SOURCE: WO120 Volume 35 page 284. INDEX # 2128.

Jos^h LEVEY; pension awarded 21 May 1828. SOURCE: WO120 Volume 35 page 284. INDEX # 2129.

Hen^y MCLOUGHLIN; pension awarded 21 May 1828. SOURCE: WO120 Volume 35 page 284. INDEX # 2130.

Cape Garrison Company

Jno SAMUEL; pension awarded 25 Nov 1818; residence - Cape of Good Hope, South Africa. SOURCE: WO120 Volume 35 page 287. INDEX # 2131.

Bern^d OSTEN; pension awarded 25 Nov 1818; residence - Cape of Good Hope, South Africa. SOURCE: WO120 Volume 35 page 287. INDEX # 2132.

Jno HAYES; pension awarded 25 Nov 1818; residence - Cape of Good Hope, South Africa. SOURCE: WO120 Volume 35 page 287. INDEX # 2133.

Ed^wd ODONNELL; pension awarded 25 Nov 1818; residence - Cape of Good Hope, South Africa. SOURCE: WO120 Volume 35 page 287. INDEX # 2134.

Richd BLACKSHAW; pension awarded 25 Nov 1818; residence - Cape of Good Hope, South Africa. SOURCE: WO120 Volume 35 page 287. INDEX # 2135.

Jno WESTERMAN; pension awarded 25 Nov 1818; residence - Cape of Good Hope, South Africa. SOURCE: WO120 Volume 35 page 287. INDEX # 2136.

Jno ABELL; pension awarded 25 Nov 1818; residence - Cape of Good Hope, South Africa. SOURCE: WO120 Volume 35 page 287. INDEX # 2137.

Jno WINKWORTH; pension awarded 25 Nov 1818; residence - Cape of Good Hope, South Africa. SOURCE: WO120 Volume 35 page 287. INDEX # 2138.

Fra^s GREENSMITH; pension awarded 25 Nov 1818; residence - Cape of Good Hope, South Africa. SOURCE: WO120 Volume 35 page 287. INDEX # 2139.

Benjn BURFORD; pension awarded 25 Nov 1818; residence - Cape of Good Hope, South Africa. SOURCE: WO120 Volume 35 page 287. INDEX # 2140.

Jno CHILVERS; pension awarded 25 Nov 1818; residence - Cape of Good Hope, South Africa. SOURCE: WO120 Volume 35 page 287. INDEX # 2141.

Cape Garrison Company (continued)

Ed^w^d DUKES; pension awarded 25 Nov 1818; residence - Cape of Good Hope, South Africa. SOURCE: WO120 Volume 35 page 287. INDEX # 2142.

Robt FERNE; pension awarded 25 Nov 1818; residence - Cape of Good Hope, South Africa. SOURCE: WO120 Volume 35 page 287. INDEX # 2143.

Wil^lm^ GRENNIER; pension awarded 25 Nov 1818; residence - Cape of Good Hope, South Africa. SOURCE: WO120 Volume 35 page 287. INDEX # 2144.

Jno HARRIS; pension awarded 25 Nov 1818; residence - Cape of Good Hope, South Africa. SOURCE: WO120 Volume 35 page 287. INDEX # 2145.

Jno Hen^y^ HESLER; pension awarded 25 Nov 1818; residence - Cape of Good Hope, South Africa. SOURCE: WO120 Volume 35 page 287. INDEX # 2146.

Luke HENEGAN; pension awarded 25 Nov 1818; residence - Cape of Good Hope, South Africa. SOURCE: WO120 Volume 35 page 287. INDEX # 2147.

Wm KNIGHT; pension awarded 25 Nov 1818; residence - Cape of Good Hope, South Africa. SOURCE: WO120 Volume 35 page 287. INDEX # 2148.

Jos^h^ LILLY; pension awarded 25 Nov 1818; residence - Cape of Good Hope, South Africa. SOURCE: WO120 Volume 35 page 287. INDEX # 2149.

Jos^h^ MARKOSKY; pension awarded 25 Nov 1818; residence - Cape of Good Hope, South Africa. SOURCE: WO120 Volume 35 page 287. INDEX # 2150.

Jno PRESTON; pension awarded 25 Nov 1818; residence - Cape of Good Hope, South Africa. SOURCE: WO120 Volume 35 page 287. INDEX # 2151.

Thos PUGH; pension awarded 25 Nov 1818; residence - Cape of Good Hope, South Africa. SOURCE: WO120 Volume 35 page 287. INDEX # 2152.

Danl RAMM; pension awarded 25 Nov 1818; residence - Cape of Good Hope, South Africa. SOURCE: WO120 Volume 35 page 287. INDEX # 2153.

Ja^s^ SCHOFIELD; pension awarded 25 Nov 1818; residence - Cape of Good Hope, South Africa. SOURCE: WO120 Volume 35 page 287. INDEX # 2154.

Wm SMITH; pension awarded 25 Nov 1818; residence - Cape of Good Hope, South Africa. SOURCE: WO120 Volume 35 page 289. INDEX # 2155.

Jacob MEAD; pension awarded 25 Nov 1818; residence - Cape of Good Hope, South Africa. SOURCE: WO120 Volume 35 page 289. INDEX # 2156.

Jno TILL; pension awarded 29 Jul 1819; residence - Cape of Good Hope, South Africa. SOURCE: WO120 Volume 35 page 289. INDEX # 2157.

Dav^d^ DEASE; pension awarded 29 Jul 1819; residence - Cape of Good Hope, South Africa. SOURCE: WO120 Volume 35 page 289. INDEX # 2158.

West India Regiments

Jno TIMOTHY; pension awarded 21 Aug 1817; residence - Sierra Leone, Africa. SOURCE: WO120 Volume 35 page 291. INDEX # 2159.

Isaac PETER; pension awarded 21 Aug 1817; residence - Sierra Leone, Africa. SOURCE: WO120 Volume 35 page 291. INDEX # 2160.

Thos ROBERTS; pension awarded 21 Aug 1817; residence - Sierra Leone, Africa. SOURCE: WO120 Volume 35 page 291. INDEX # 2161.

Chas LEUBE; pension awarded 24 Oct 1821. SOURCE: WO120 Volume 35 page 291. INDEX # 2162.

Chas REED; pension awarded 24 Oct 1821. SOURCE: WO120 Volume 35 page 291. INDEX # 2163.

Jno MANUEL; pension awarded 24 Oct 1821. SOURCE: WO120 Volume 35 page 291. INDEX # 2164.

Jno PHAIR; pension awarded 24 Oct 1821; died 9 Sep 1838. SOURCE: WO120 Volume 35 page 291. INDEX # 2165.

Jno JOHNSTON; pension awarded 24 Oct 1821. SOURCE: WO120 Volume 35 page 291. INDEX # 2166.

Jno LOWE; pension awarded 24 Oct 1821. SOURCE: WO120 Volume 35 page 291. INDEX # 2167.

Nich^s^ PHILLIPS; pension awarded 24 Oct 1821. SOURCE: WO120 Volume 35 page 291. INDEX # 2168.

Jos^h^ POLLACK; pension awarded 24 Oct 1821. SOURCE: WO120 Volume 35 page 291. INDEX # 2169.

WO120 VOLUME 35

West India Regiments (continued)

Chas FOX; pension awarded 24 Oct 1821. SOURCE: WO120 Volume 35 page 291. INDEX # 2170.
Jno MARIE; pension awarded 24 Oct 1821. SOURCE: WO120 Volume 35 page 291. INDEX # 2171.
Jno CHARLES; pension awarded 24 Oct 1821. SOURCE: WO120 Volume 35 page 291. INDEX # 2172.
Leon CONNETT; pension awarded 24 Oct 1821. SOURCE: WO120 Volume 35 page 291. INDEX # 2173.
Ge^o BADDOW; pension awarded 24 Oct 1821. SOURCE: WO120 Volume 35 page 291. INDEX # 2174.
Pierre ANTOINE; pension awarded 24 Oct 1821. SOURCE: WO120 Volume 35 page 291. INDEX # 2175.
Riquett BELFOUR; pension awarded 24 Oct 1821. SOURCE: WO120 Volume 35 page 291. INDEX # 2176.
Riquett ABDAAM; pension awarded 24 Oct 1821. SOURCE: WO120 Volume 35 page 291. INDEX # 2177.
Reed BOLONGE; pension awarded 24 Oct 1821. SOURCE: WO120 Volume 35 page 291. INDEX # 2178.
Sake COSSAM; pension awarded 24 Oct 1821. SOURCE: WO120 Volume 35 page 291. INDEX # 2179.
Ja^s JARVIS; pension awarded 24 Oct 1821. SOURCE: WO120 Volume 35 page 291. INDEX # 2180.
Jno PETERS; pension awarded 24 Oct 1821; died 1 Oct 1828. SOURCE: WO120 Volume 35 page 291. INDEX # 2181.
Fra^s PIERRE; pension awarded 24 Oct 1821. SOURCE: WO120 Volume 35 page 291. INDEX # 2182.
Wm REED; pension awarded 23 Oct 1821. SOURCE: WO120 Volume 35 page 292. INDEX # 2183.
Domingo FERNANDO; pension awarded 23 Oct 1821. SOURCE: WO120 Volume 35 page 292. INDEX # 2184.
Philip BOOTY; pension awarded 23 Oct 1823. SOURCE: WO120 Volume 35 page 292. INDEX # 2185.
Jos^h FRIANDO; pension awarded 23 Oct 1821. SOURCE: WO120 Volume 35 page 292. INDEX # 2186.
Thos JONES; pension awarded 23 Oct 1821. SOURCE: WO120 Volume 35 page 292. INDEX # 2187.
Jno WESTFORD; pension awarded 23 Oct 1821. SOURCE: WO120 Volume 35 page 292. INDEX # 2188.
Hector MONRO; pension awarded 23 Oct 1821; died 24 Dec 1822, Quebec, Canada. SOURCE: WO120 Volume 35 page 292. INDEX # 2189.
Jno BLACK; pension awarded 23 Oct 1821. SOURCE: WO120 Volume 35 page 292. INDEX # 2191.
Fred^k HEYLIGER; pension awarded 30 Sep 1823. SOURCE: WO120 Volume 35 page 292. INDEX # 2191.
Phil^p BOATERS; pension awarded 22 Dec 1824. SOURCE: WO120 Volume 35 page 292. INDEX # 2192.
Bicente FERRARA; pension awarded 22 Dec 1824; died 27 Apr 1834. SOURCE: WO120 Volume 35 page 292. INDEX # 2193.
Benjn PINTO; pension awarded 2 Jun 1825; residence - West Indies. SOURCE: WO120 Volume 35 page 292. INDEX # 2194.
Jno SERRANT; pension awarded 2 Jun 1825; residence - West Indies. SOURCE: WO120 Volume 35 page 292. INDEX # 2195.
Victor COLE; pension awarded 15 Mar 1826. SOURCE: WO120 Volume 35 page 292. INDEX # 2196.
Jno NIXON; pension awarded 7 Mar 1827. SOURCE: WO120 Volume 35 page 292. INDEX # 2197.
Ant^y JONES; pension awarded 7 Mar 1827. SOURCE: WO120 Volume 35 page 292. INDEX # 2198.
Saml RHODES; pension awarded 7 Mar 1827. SOURCE: WO120 Volume 35 page 292. INDEX # 2199.
Jno COTTER; pension awarded 7 Mar 1827. SOURCE: WO120 Volume 35 page 292. INDEX # 2200.
Willm PERRY; pension awarded 15 Apr 1829. SOURCE: WO120 Volume 35 page 292. INDEX # 2201.
Jno HICKIE; pension awarded 13 Feb 1833. SOURCE: WO120 Volume 35 page 292. INDEX # 2202.
Willm PERKINS; pension awarded 13 Apr 1836. SOURCE: WO120 Volume 35 page 292. INDEX # 2203.

Royal African Corps

Jos^h HALL; pension awarded 11 Nov 1817; residence - Sierra Leone, Africa. SOURCE: WO120 Volume 35 page 295. INDEX # 2204.
Jos^h VERNON; pension awarded 29 Apr 1818; residence - Sierra Leone, Africa. SOURCE: WO120 Volume 35 page 295. INDEX # 2205.
Wm FORBES; pension awarded 25 Nov 1818; residence - Sierra Leone, Africa. SOURCE: WO120 Volume 35 page 295. INDEX # 2206.
Danl FITZMAURICE; pension awarded 28 Dec 1818; residence - Sierra Leone, Africa. SOURCE: WO120 Volume 35 page 295. INDEX # 2207.

BRITISH ARMY PENSIONERS ABROAD

Royal African Corps (continued)

Ge⁰ SIBBALD; pension awarded 19 Jun 1822; residence - Nova Scotia, Canada. SOURCE: WO120 Volume 35 page 295. INDEX # 2208.
Ge⁰ GARRALL; pension awarded 19 Jun 1822; residence - Nova Scotia, Canada. SOURCE: WO120 Volume 35 page 295. INDEX # 2209.
Jn⁰ MCVEIGH; pension awarded 19 Jun 1822; residence - Nova Scotia, Canada. SOURCE: WO120 Volume 35 page 295. INDEX # 2210.
Thoˢ CUMMING; pension awarded 22 Oct 1823. SOURCE: WO120 Volume 35 page 295. INDEX # 2211.

Staff Corps

Ge⁰ Reuben THOMAS; pension awarded 9 Feb 1831. SOURCE: WO120 Volume 35 page 298. INDEX # 2212.
Jaˢ MOUNTSTEPHENS; pension awarded 10 Aug 1831. SOURCE: WO120 Volume 35 page 298. INDEX # 2213.
Richᵈ BIRD; pension awarded 10 Aug 1831. SOURCE: WO120 Volume 35 page 298. INDEX # 2214.
Jaˢ KILBY; pension awarded 11 Apr 1832. SOURCE: WO120 Volume 35 page 298. INDEX # 2215.
Jn⁰ HORNBY; pension awarded 11 Apr 1832. SOURCE: WO120 Volume 35 page 298. INDEX # 2216.
Wᵐ KING; pension awarded 11 Apr 1832. SOURCE: WO120 Volume 35 page 298. INDEX # 2217.
Jaˢ GOODLAND; pension awarded 11 Apr 1832. SOURCE: WO120 Volume 35 page 298. INDEX # 2218.
Jonathan MOSS; pension awarded 11 Apr 1832. SOURCE: WO120 Volume 35 page 298. INDEX # 2219.
Davᵈ REEVES; pension awarded 11 Apr 1832. SOURCE: WO120 Volume 35 page 298. INDEX # 2220.
Jn⁰ SCOTT; pension awarded 11 Apr 1832. SOURCE: WO120 Volume 35 page 298. INDEX # 2221.
Edmᵈ WILLIAMS; pension awarded 11 Apr 1832. SOURCE: WO120 Volume 35 page 298. INDEX # 2222.
Donᵈ CARMACK; pension awarded 8 Aug 1832. SOURCE: WO120 Volume 35 page 298. INDEX # 2223.
Chaˢ HULL; pension awarded 8 Aug 1832. SOURCE: WO120 Volume 35 page 298. INDEX # 2224.
Jaˢ MURRAY; pension awarded 7 Nov 1832. SOURCE: WO120 Volume 35 page 298. INDEX # 2225.
Jn⁰ HILLIARD; pension awarded 7 Nov 1832. SOURCE: WO120 Volume 35 page 298. INDEX # 2226.
Joshˢ BARNFIELD; pension awarded 7 Nov 1832. SOURCE: WO120 Volume 35 page 298. INDEX # 2227.
Jn⁰ BENDALL; pension awarded 7 Nov 1832. SOURCE: WO120 Volume 35 page 298. INDEX # 2228.
Mattʷ FARMSLEY; pension awarded 7 Nov 1832. SOURCE: WO120 Volume 35 page 298. INDEX # 2229.
Jn⁰ KEATLEY; pension awarded 7 Nov 1832. SOURCE: WO120 Volume 35 page 298. INDEX # 2230.
Thoˢ TAYLOR; pension awarded 7 Nov 1832. SOURCE: WO120 Volume 35 page 298. INDEX # 2231.
Jn⁰ HURLEY; pension awarded 12 Dec 1832. SOURCE: WO120 Volume 35 page 298. INDEX # 2232.
Patᵏ RUSSELL; pension awarded 25 Oct 1832. SOURCE: WO120 Volume 35 page 298. INDEX # 2233.
Jaˢ MONTEITH; pension awarded 14 Nov 1838. SOURCE: WO120 Volume 35 page 298. INDEX # 2234.

York Chasseurs

Jn⁰ BROGAN; pension awarded 23 May 1821; residence - Canada. SOURCE: WO120 Volume 35 page 299. INDEX # 2235.
Thoˢ LEONARD; pension awarded 24 Oct 1821; residence - Canada. SOURCE: WO120 Volume 35 page 299. INDEX # 2236.
Jaˢ NASH; pension awarded 1 Feb 1826; residence - Canada. SOURCE: WO120 Volume 35 page 299. INDEX # 2237.

Ceylon Regiment

Edwᵈ WILLIAMS; pension awarded 25 Sep 1822; residence - Ceylon. SOURCE: WO120 Volume 35 page 301. INDEX # 2238.
Jn⁰ WILLIAMS; pension awarded 16 Apr 1823; residence - Ceylon. SOURCE: WO120 Volume 35 page 301. INDEX # 2239.
Peter SHAW; pension awarded 11 Nov 1817; residence - Ceylon. SOURCE: WO120 Volume 35 page 301. INDEX # 2240.

Ceylon Regiment (continued)

Willm HARDY; pension awarded 3 Feb 1819; residence - Ceylon. SOURCE: WO120 Volume 35 page 301. INDEX # 2241.
Hen^y MILLER; pension awarded 12 Dec 1832. SOURCE: WO120 Volume 35 page 301. INDEX # 2242.
Ge^o FOWLER; pension awarded 9 Jan 1833. SOURCE: WO120 Volume 35 page 301. INDEX # 2243.
Ge^o WELLS; pension awarded 9 Mar 1836. SOURCE: WO120 Volume 35 page 301. INDEX # 2244.
Jno CLEMENTS; pension awarded 14 Dec 1836. SOURCE: WO120 Volume 35 page 301. INDEX # 2245.

Duke of Brunswick's Corps

Willm OVERBECK; pension awarded 25 Sep 1822. SOURCE: WO120 Volume 35 page 302. INDEX # 2246.

Royal York Rangers

Ja^s BAILEY; pension awarded 13 Dec 1826; residence - Trinidad. SOURCE: WO120 Volume 35 page 304. INDEX # 2247.

Cambrian Rangers

Silvenus JONES; pension awarded 21 Aug 1817. SOURCE: WO120 Volume 35 page 305. INDEX # 2248.
Angus CAMERON; pension awarded 25 Nov 1818. SOURCE: WO120 Volume 35 page 305. INDEX # 2249.
Jno ADAMSON; pension awarded 25 Nov 1818. SOURCE: WO120 Volume 35 page 305. INDEX # 2250.

Royal Regiment of Malta

Antonio SALAMONE; pension awarded 7 Feb 1821. SOURCE: WO120 Volume 35 page 306. INDEX # 2251.

Glengarry Light Infantry

Thos MCCORD; pension awarded 13 Apr 1824. SOURCE: WO120 Volume 35 page 312. INDEX # 2252.

Military Labourers

Fra^s SCONCE; pension awarded 23 Nov 1825; residence - Barbados. SOURCE: WO120 Volume 35 page 313. INDEX # 2253.
Wm SCOFIELD; pension awarded 30 Aug 1826; residence - Barbados. SOURCE: WO120 Volume 35 page 313. INDEX # 2254.
Jos^h BORDINI; pension awarded 31 Oct 1827. SOURCE: WO120 Volume 35 page 313. INDEX # 2255.
Jno MANCINI; pension awarded 31 Oct 1827. SOURCE: WO120 Volume 35 page 313. INDEX # 2256.
Wm GOODMAN; pension awarded 31 Oct 1827. SOURCE: WO120 Volume 35 page 313. INDEX # 2257.
Willm BARROW; pension awarded 16 Sep 1829. SOURCE: WO120 Volume 35 page 313. INDEX # 2258.
Jasper PETTINARI; pension awarded 10 Mar 1830. SOURCE: WO120 Volume 35 page 313. INDEX # 2259.
Solomon SOOLEY; pension awarded 9 Mar 1834. SOURCE: WO120 Volume 35 page 313. INDEX # 2260.
Danl MCCURDY; pension awarded 13 Jul 1834. SOURCE: WO120 Volume 35 page 313. INDEX # 2261.

De Watteville's Regiment

Chas DIKOW; pension awarded 23 Nov 1825. SOURCE: WO120 Volume 35 page 314. INDEX # 2262.

BRITISH ARMY PENSIONERS ABROAD

New South Wales Veterans

Jn⁰ BRADBURY; pension awarded 25 Nov 1818. SOURCE: WO120 Volume 35 page 315. INDEX # 2263.
Fraˢ HAINSWORTH; pension awarded 25 Nov 1818. SOURCE: WO120 Volume 35 page 315. INDEX # 2264.
Jaˢ PAYNE; pension awarded 25 Nov 1818. SOURCE: WO120 Volume 35 page 315. INDEX # 2265.
Thoˢ MCCONWELL; pension awarded 8 Sep 1830. SOURCE: WO120 Volume 35 page 315. INDEX # 2266.
John GIBZAN; pension awarded 10 Nov 1830. SOURCE: WO120 Volume 35 page 315. INDEX # 2267.
Benjⁿ ABELL; pension awarded 14 Sep 1831. SOURCE: WO120 Volume 35 page 315. INDEX # 2268.
Jn⁰ DUFFY; pension awarded 14 Sep 1831. SOURCE: WO120 Volume 35 page 315. INDEX # 2269.
Wᵐ HEATH; pension awarded 14 Sep 1831. SOURCE: WO120 Volume 35 page 315. INDEX # 2270.
Wᵐ PERKINS; pension awarded 14 Sep 1831. SOURCE: WO120 Volume 35 page 315. INDEX # 2271.
Wᵐ OSBURNE; pension awarded 13 Jun 1832. SOURCE: WO120 Volume 35 page 315. INDEX # 2272.
Alexʳ BARTON; pension awarded 13 Jun 1832. SOURCE: WO120 Volume 35 page 315. INDEX # 2273.
Robᵗ ANDERSON; pension awarded 13 Jun 1832. SOURCE: WO120 Volume 35 page 315. INDEX # 2274.
Thoˢ ASBURY; pension awarded 13 Jun 1832. SOURCE: WO120 Volume 35 page 315. INDEX # 2275.
Wᵐ Joshʰ BAYLIS; pension awarded 13 Jun 1832. SOURCE: WO120 Volume 35 page 315. INDEX # 2276.
Jaˢ BENTON; pension awarded 13 Jun 1832. SOURCE: WO120 Volume 35 page 315. INDEX # 2277.
Thoˢ BOLTON; pension awarded 13 Jun 1832. SOURCE: WO120 Volume 35 page 315. INDEX # 2278.
Jaˢ BRACKENING; pension awarded 13 Jun 1832. SOURCE: WO120 Volume 35 page 315. INDEX # 2279.
Jn⁰ BROWN; pension awarded 13 Jun 1832. SOURCE: WO120 Volume 35 page 315. INDEX # 2280.
Jaˢ BULLOCK; pension awarded 13 Jun 1832. SOURCE: WO120 Volume 35 page 315. INDEX # 2281.
Jn⁰ BIRT; pension awarded 13 Jun 1832. SOURCE: WO120 Volume 35 page 315. INDEX # 2282.
Jn⁰ CARROLL; pension awarded 13 Jun 1832. SOURCE: WO120 Volume 35 page 315. INDEX # 2283.
Wᵐ CHARLTON; pension awarded 13 Jun 1832. SOURCE: WO120 Volume 35 page 315. INDEX # 2284.
Jn⁰ CLARKE; pension awarded 13 Jun 1832. SOURCE: WO120 Volume 35 page 315. INDEX # 2285.
Robᵗ COOPER; pension awarded 13 Jun 1832. SOURCE: WO120 Volume 35 page 315. INDEX # 2286.

Yeomanry

Richᵈ RICHARDS; pension awarded 12 Sep 1821; residence - Perth, Ontario, Canada. SOURCE: WO120 Volume 35 page 316. INDEX # 2287.
Jn⁰ GREENLY; pension awarded 22 May 1819. SOURCE: WO120 Volume 35 page 316. INDEX # 2288.
Jaˢ SAUNDERS; pension awarded 3 Feb 1821; residence - Perth, Ontario, Canada. SOURCE: WO120 Volume 35 page 316. INDEX # 2289.
Richᵈ RICHARDS; pension awarded 13 Sep 1798; residence - Perth, Ontario, Canada. SOURCE: WO120 Volume 35 page 316. INDEX # 2290.

Fencibles

Jaˢ NESBETT; pension awarded 29 Apr 1818. SOURCE: WO120 Volume 35 page 317. INDEX # 2291.
Angˢ CAMERON; pension awarded 25 Nov 1818. SOURCE: WO120 Volume 35 page 317. INDEX # 2292.
Jn⁰ ADAMSON; pension awarded 25 Nov 1818. SOURCE: WO120 Volume 35 page 317. INDEX # 2293.
Wᵐ BORTHICK; pension awarded 17 Feb 1819. SOURCE: WO120 Volume 35 page 317. INDEX # 2294.
Wᵐ NEWMAN; pension awarded 17 Feb 1819. SOURCE: WO120 Volume 35 page 317. INDEX # 2295.
Wᵐ GRIFFIN; pension awarded 17 Feb 1819. SOURCE: WO120 Volume 35 page 317. INDEX # 2296.
Alexʳ MATHESON; pension awarded 12 May 1819. SOURCE: WO120 Volume 35 page 317. INDEX # 2297.
Fraˢ DAWE; pension awarded 12 May 1819. SOURCE: WO120 Volume 35 page 317. INDEX # 2298.
Thoˢ ONEIL; pension awarded 1 Jul 1819. SOURCE: WO120 Volume 35 page 317. INDEX # 2299.
Joshʰ LEARY; pension awarded 1 Jul 1819. SOURCE: WO120 Volume 35 page 317. INDEX # 2300.
Robᵗ DALEY; pension awarded 1 Jul 1819. SOURCE: WO120 Volume 35 page 317. INDEX # 2301.
Jn⁰ CLARKE; pension awarded 29 Sep 1819. SOURCE: WO120 Volume 35 page 317. INDEX # 2302.
Jaˢ BRYANT; pension awarded 3 May 1820. SOURCE: WO120 Volume 35 page 317. INDEX # 2303.

Fencibles (continued)

Jn⁰ RICE; pension awarded 7 Jun 1820. SOURCE: WO120 Volume 35 page 317. INDEX # 2304.
Mich¹ FROOD; pension awarded 7 Jun 1820. SOURCE: WO120 Volume 35 page 317. INDEX # 2305.
Jn⁰ HUNT; pension awarded 5 Jul 1820. SOURCE: WO120 Volume 35 page 317. INDEX # 2306.
Wᵐ LIGHT; pension awarded 5 Jul 1820. SOURCE: WO120 Volume 35 page 317. INDEX # 2307.
Mich¹ SHEA; pension awarded 5 Jul 1820. SOURCE: WO120 Volume 35 page 317. INDEX # 2308.
Ge⁰ PRESTON; pension awarded 5 Jul 1820. SOURCE: WO120 Volume 35 page 317. INDEX # 2309.
Wᵐ LUSH; pension awarded 7 Jun 1820. SOURCE: WO120 Volume 35 page 317. INDEX # 2310.
Wᵐ HASLETT; pension awarded 7 Jun 1820. SOURCE: WO120 Volume 35 page 317. INDEX # 2311.
Richᵈ HARRIS; pension awarded 7 Jun 1820. SOURCE: WO120 Volume 35 page 317. INDEX # 2312.
Richᵈ LANE; pension awarded 7 Jun 1820. SOURCE: WO120 Volume 35 page 317. INDEX # 2313.
Wᵐ PROUT; pension awarded 7 Jun 1820. SOURCE: WO120 Volume 35 page 317. INDEX # 2314.
Jaˢ MARTIN; pension awarded in 1817. SOURCE: WO120 Volume 35 page 317. INDEX # 2315.
Wᵐ WILSON; pension awarded 5 Jul 1820. SOURCE: WO120 Volume 35 page 318. INDEX # 2316.
Wᵐ DRISCOLL; pension awarded 5 Jul 1820. SOURCE: WO120 Volume 35 page 318. INDEX # 2317.
Mattʷ CULLEN; pension awarded 7 Dec 1820. SOURCE: WO120 Volume 35 page 318. INDEX # 2318.
Jaˢ BAKER; pension awarded 7 Dec 1820. SOURCE: WO120 Volume 35 page 318. INDEX # 2319.
Robᵗ BLAIR; pension awarded 7 Dec 1820. SOURCE: WO120 Volume 35 page 318. INDEX # 2320.
Wᵐ KEMBLE; pension awarded 28 Mar 1821. SOURCE: WO120 Volume 35 page 318. INDEX # 2321.
Henʸ OLIVER; pension awarded 28 Mar 1821. SOURCE: WO120 Volume 35 page 318. INDEX # 2322.
Jonas WHITE; pension awarded 28 Mar 1821. SOURCE: WO120 Volume 35 page 318. INDEX # 2323.
Eman¹ MURDEN; pension awarded 28 Mar 1821. SOURCE: WO120 Volume 35 page 318. INDEX # 2324.
Jaˢ BROWN; pension awarded 28 Mar 1821. SOURCE: WO120 Volume 35 page 318. INDEX # 2325.
Jonⁿ MOORE; pension awarded 28 Mar 1821. SOURCE: WO120 Volume 35 page 318. INDEX # 2326.
Edmᵈ DEA; pension awarded 28 Mar 1821. SOURCE: WO120 Volume 35 page 318. INDEX # 2327.
Patᵏ ONEIL; pension awarded 28 Mar 1821; died 31 Mar 1831. SOURCE: WO120 Volume 35 page 318. INDEX # 2328.
Thaddeus LEWIS; pension awarded 23 May 1821. SOURCE: WO120 Volume 35 page 318. INDEX # 2329.
Robᵗ DEA; pension awarded 23 May 1821. SOURCE: WO120 Volume 35 page 318. INDEX # 2330.
Ge⁰ TROWBRIDGE; pension awarded 12 Sep 1821. SOURCE: WO120 Volume 35 page 318. INDEX # 2331.
Peter PATTERSON; pension awarded 12 Sep 1821. SOURCE: WO120 Volume 35 page 318. INDEX # 2332.
Jn⁰ WRIGHT; pension awarded 12 Sep 1821. SOURCE: WO120 Volume 35 page 318. INDEX # 2333.
Jn⁰ HIGGS; pension awarded 12 Sep 1821. SOURCE: WO120 Volume 35 page 318. INDEX # 2334.
Jn⁰ WHITNEY; pension awarded 12 Sep 1821. SOURCE: WO120 Volume 35 page 318. INDEX # 2335.
Henʸ PRESTON; pension awarded 24 Oct 1821. SOURCE: WO120 Volume 35 page 318. INDEX # 2336.
Thoˢ COOKE; pension awarded 24 Oct 1821. SOURCE: WO120 Volume 35 page 318. INDEX # 2337.
Jaˢ MINTY; pension awarded 24 Oct 1821. SOURCE: WO120 Volume 35 page 318. INDEX # 2338.
Edwᵈ POWER; pension awarded 7 Feb 1822. SOURCE: WO120 Volume 35 page 318. INDEX # 2339.
Dan¹ MCDANIEL; pension awarded 7 Feb 1822. SOURCE: WO120 Volume 35 page 319. INDEX # 2340.
Robᵗ HIBBS; pension awarded 25 Sep 1822. SOURCE: WO120 Volume 35 page 319. INDEX # 2341.
Jaˢ BUTLER; pension awarded 20 Mar 1822. SOURCE: WO120 Volume 35 page 319. INDEX # 2342.
Jn⁰ LEWIS; pension awarded 20 Mar 1822. SOURCE: WO120 Volume 35 page 319. INDEX # 2343.
Jn⁰ LEMMING; pension awarded 20 Mar 1822. SOURCE: WO120 Volume 35 page 319. INDEX # 2344.
Jaˢ SWAINFIELD; pension awarded 1 May 1822. SOURCE: WO120 Volume 35 page 319. INDEX # 2345.
Thoˢ PENDEGAST; pension awarded 1 May 1822. SOURCE: WO120 Volume 35 page 319. INDEX # 2346.
Reuben GALTON; pension awarded 1 May 1822. SOURCE: WO120 Volume 35 page 319. INDEX # 2347.
Wᵐ JONES; pension awarded 1 May 1822. SOURCE: WO120 Volume 35 page 319. INDEX # 2348.
Jaˢ NORRIS; pension awarded 1 May 1822. SOURCE: WO120 Volume 35 page 319. INDEX # 2349.
Edwᵈ MAHONEY; pension awarded 19 Jun 1822. SOURCE: WO120 Volume 35 page 319. INDEX # 2350.
Jn⁰ ONEILL; pension awarded 25 Sep 1822. SOURCE: WO120 Volume 35 page 319. INDEX # 2351.
Jn⁰ KARNEY; pension awarded 25 Sep 1822. SOURCE: WO120 Volume 35 page 319. INDEX # 2352.
Thoˢ BURKE; pension awarded 25 Sep 1822. SOURCE: WO120 Volume 35 page 319. INDEX # 2353.

Fencibles (continued)

Jno COREY; pension awarded 25 Sep 1822. SOURCE: WO120 Volume 35 page 319. INDEX # 2354.
Fra^s STEWART; pension awarded 25 Sep 1822. SOURCE: WO120 Volume 35 page 319. INDEX # 2355.
Wm NORRIS; pension awarded 25 Sep 1822. SOURCE: WO120 Volume 35 page 319. INDEX # 2356.
Peter MORAN; pension awarded 25 Sep 1822. SOURCE: WO120 Volume 35 page 319. INDEX # 2357.
Pat^k DRISCOLL; pension awarded 25 Sep 1822. SOURCE: WO120 Volume 35 page 319. INDEX # 2358.
Jno N. REESE; pension awarded 25 Sep 1822. SOURCE: WO120 Volume 35 page 319. INDEX # 2359.
Jos^h GATES; pension awarded 25 Sep 1822. SOURCE: WO120 Volume 35 page 319. INDEX # 2360.
Robt PATTERSON; pension awarded 25 Sep 1822. SOURCE: WO120 Volume 35 page 319. INDEX # 2361.
Ja^s BROPHEY; pension awarded 25 Sep 1822. SOURCE: WO120 Volume 35 page 319. INDEX # 2362.
Ge^o PERRIER; pension awarded 30 Jun 1825. SOURCE: WO120 Volume 35 page 319. INDEX # 2363.
John MURPHY; pension awarded about 1822. SOURCE: WO120 Volume 35 page 319. INDEX # 2364.
Jno CRITCH; pension awarded 25 Sep 1822. SOURCE: WO120 Volume 35 page 320. INDEX # 2365.
Jno BYERS; pension awarded 25 Sep 1822. SOURCE: WO120 Volume 35 page 320. INDEX # 2366.
Jno ODDY; pension awarded 25 Sep 1822. SOURCE: WO120 Volume 35 page 320. INDEX # 2367.
Thos HALY; pension awarded 25 Sep 1822. SOURCE: WO120 Volume 35 page 320. INDEX # 2368.
Jno HILLIER; pension awarded 25 Sep 1822. SOURCE: WO120 Volume 35 page 320. INDEX # 2369.
Lewis BOURNS; pension awarded 5 Mar 1823. SOURCE: WO120 Volume 35 page 320. INDEX # 2370.
Wm WATSON; pension awarded 9 May 1823. SOURCE: WO120 Volume 35 page 320. INDEX # 2371.
Jno SULLIVAN; pension awarded 9 May 1823. SOURCE: WO120 Volume 35 page 320. INDEX # 2372.
Jos^h PENSON; pension awarded 9 May 1823. SOURCE: WO120 Volume 35 page 320. INDEX # 2373.
Jno WALSH; pension awarded 9 May 1823. SOURCE: WO120 Volume 35 page 320. INDEX # 2374.
Jno SHOLES; pension awarded 23 Jul 1823. SOURCE: WO120 Volume 35 page 320. INDEX # 2375.
Danl DONOVAN; pension awarded 23 Jul 1823. SOURCE: WO120 Volume 35 page 320. INDEX # 2376.
Ge^o STENGELL; pension awarded 23 Jul 1823. SOURCE: WO120 Volume 35 page 320. INDEX # 2377.
Pat^k COONEY; pension awarded 23 Jul 1823. SOURCE: WO120 Volume 35 page 320. INDEX # 2378.
Ge^o ELLIOTT; pension awarded 23 Jul 1823. SOURCE: WO120 Volume 35 page 320. INDEX # 2379.
Jacob LOUNDER; pension awarded 23 Jul 1823. SOURCE: WO120 Volume 35 page 320. INDEX # 2380.
Jno MCNEIL; pension awarded 23 Jul 1823. SOURCE: WO120 Volume 35 page 320. INDEX # 2381.
Jno BUCHANAN; pension awarded 23 Jul 1823. SOURCE: WO120 Volume 35 page 320. INDEX # 2382.
Ja^s HUGHES; pension awarded 30 Sep 1823. SOURCE: WO120 Volume 35 page 320. INDEX # 2383.
Ja^s GELLOW; pension awarded 21 Jan 1824. SOURCE: WO120 Volume 35 page 320. INDEX # 2384.
Jno MARTINSON; pension awarded 21 Jan 1824. SOURCE: WO120 Volume 35 page 320. INDEX # 2385.
Edmund FLYNN; pension awarded 21 Jan 1824. SOURCE: WO120 Volume 35 page 320. INDEX # 2386.
Ed^{wd} MEANEY; pension awarded 21 Jan 1824. SOURCE: WO120 Volume 35 page 320. INDEX # 2387.
Isaac BARTLETT; pension awarded 21 Jan 1824. SOURCE: WO120 Volume 35 page 320. INDEX # 2388.
Jos^h LAROUX; pension awarded 13 Apr 1824. SOURCE: WO120 Volume 35 page 321. INDEX # 2389.
Ed^{wd} MANUEL; pension awarded 13 Apr 1824. SOURCE: WO120 Volume 35 page 321. INDEX # 2390.
Lawr^e SOURWINE; pension awarded 12 May 1824. SOURCE: WO120 Volume 35 page 321. INDEX # 2391.
Wm WRIGHT; pension awarded 16 Jun 1824. SOURCE: WO120 Volume 35 page 321. INDEX # 2392.
Melchizideck DAVY; pension awarded 22 Sep 1824. SOURCE: WO120 Volume 35 page 321. INDEX # 2393.
Jno SULLIVAN; pension awarded 24 Nov 1824. SOURCE: WO120 Volume 35 page 321. INDEX # 2394.
Fra^s TOOLE; pension awarded 2 Feb 1825. SOURCE: WO120 Volume 35 page 321. INDEX # 2395.
Jno MITCHELL; pension awarded 30 Jun 1825. SOURCE: WO120 Volume 35 page 321. INDEX # 2396.
Pat^k RILEY; pension awarded 30 Jun 1825. SOURCE: WO120 Volume 35 page 321. INDEX # 2397.
Ge^o PERRIER; pension awarded 30 Jun 1825. SOURCE: WO120 Volume 35 page 321. INDEX # 2398.
Willm CORBIN; pension awarded 30 Jun 1825. SOURCE: WO120 Volume 35 page 321. INDEX # 2399.
Wm MATHESON; pension awarded 23 Nov 1825. SOURCE: WO120 Volume 35 page 321. INDEX # 2400.
Ja^s COCHRAN; pension awarded 1 Feb 1826. SOURCE: WO120 Volume 35 page 321. INDEX # 2401.
Ja^s HENTICOTT; pension awarded 1 Feb 1826. SOURCE: WO120 Volume 35 page 321. INDEX # 2402.
Thos GUEST; pension awarded 1 Feb 1826. SOURCE: WO120 Volume 35 page 321. INDEX # 2403.

WO120 VOLUME 35   79

Fencibles (continued)

Pat^k COGLEY; pension awarded 1 Feb 1826. SOURCE: WO120 Volume 35 page 321. INDEX # 2404.
Errol BOYD; pension awarded 15 Mar 1826. SOURCE: WO120 Volume 35 page 321. INDEX # 2405.
Thos BROWN; pension awarded 15 Mar 1826. SOURCE: WO120 Volume 35 page 321. INDEX # 2406.
Don^d MCINNIS; pension awarded 15 Mar 1826. SOURCE: WO120 Volume 35 page 321. INDEX # 2407.
Jno FOLEY; pension awarded 15 Mar 1826. SOURCE: WO120 Volume 35 page 321. INDEX # 2408.
Gasper TINCLAIR; pension awarded 30 Aug 1826. SOURCE: WO120 Volume 35 page 321. INDEX # 2409.
Den^s BRYAN; pension awarded 30 Aug 1826. SOURCE: WO120 Volume 35 page 321. INDEX # 2410.
Pat^k WALSH; pension awarded 30 Aug 1826. SOURCE: WO120 Volume 35 page 321. INDEX # 2411.
Jno MURPHY; pension awarded 30 Aug 1826. SOURCE: WO120 Volume 35 page 321. INDEX # 2412.
Thos CLEVES; pension awarded 30 Aug 1826. SOURCE: WO120 Volume 35 page 322. INDEX # 2413.
Wm BRIDLE; pension awarded 30 Aug 1826. SOURCE: WO120 Volume 35 page 322. INDEX # 2414.
Jno GRAY; pension awarded 30 Aug 1826. SOURCE: WO120 Volume 35 page 322. INDEX # 2415.
Louis DESCHAMPS; pension awarded 30 Aug 1826. SOURCE: WO120 Volume 35 page 322. INDEX # 2416.
Saml BANCROFT; pension awarded 11 Oct 1826; died 30 Sep 1831. SOURCE: WO120 Volume 35 page 322. INDEX # 2417.
Moses BROWN; pension awarded 11 Oct 1826. SOURCE: WO120 Volume 35 page 322. INDEX # 2418.
Solo^n WILCOX; pension awarded 11 Oct 1826. SOURCE: WO120 Volume 35 page 322. INDEX # 2419.
Ja^s GIFFORD; pension awarded 11 Oct 1826. SOURCE: WO120 Volume 35 page 322. INDEX # 2420.
Willm COOMES; pension awarded 11 Oct 1826. SOURCE: WO120 Volume 35 page 322. INDEX # 2421.
Jno HARMAN; pension awarded 11 Oct 1826. SOURCE: WO120 Volume 35 page 322. INDEX # 2422.
Jno RICE; pension awarded 13 Dec 1826. SOURCE: WO120 Volume 35 page 322. INDEX # 2423.
Jno JONES; pension awarded 13 Dec 1826. SOURCE: WO120 Volume 35 page 322. INDEX # 2424.
Ja^s SECAUR; pension awarded 13 Dec 1826. SOURCE: WO120 Volume 35 page 322. INDEX # 2425.
Jno MCDONALD; pension awarded 16 Jan 1818; residence - Quebec, Canada. SOURCE: WO120 Volume 35 page 322. INDEX # 2426.
Jacob POSSNER; pension awarded 8 Aug 1827; residence - Nova Scotia, Canada. SOURCE: WO120 Volume 35 page 322. INDEX # 2427.
Ja^s ISAAC; pension awarded 8 Aug 1827; residence - Nova Scotia, Canada. SOURCE: WO120 Volume 35 page 322. INDEX # 2428.
Mich^l WALSH; pension awarded 8 Aug 1827. SOURCE: WO120 Volume 35 page 322. INDEX # 2429.
Ed^{wd} MCGWYNN; pension awarded 8 Aug 1827. SOURCE: WO120 Volume 35 page 322. INDEX # 2430.
Jno GRAY; pension awarded 8 Aug 1827. SOURCE: WO120 Volume 35 page 322. INDEX # 2431.
Thos CLORAN; pension awarded 8 Aug 1827. SOURCE: WO120 Volume 35 page 322. INDEX # 2432.
Jno LITCHEN; pension awarded 8 Aug 1827. SOURCE: WO120 Volume 35 page 322. INDEX # 2433.
Ed^{wd} MEANEY; pension awarded 31 Oct 1827; residence - Nova Scotia, Canada. SOURCE: WO120 Volume 35 page 322. INDEX # 2434.
Renoldi CUMMINS; pension awarded 31 Oct 1827; residence - Nova Scotia, Canada. SOURCE: WO120 Volume 35 page 322. INDEX # 2435.
Wm WILKINS; pension awarded 30 Jan 1828; residence - Nova Scotia, Canada. SOURCE: WO120 Volume 35 page 322. INDEX # 2436.
Barney MCGUIRE; pension awarded 5 Jun 1817. SOURCE: WO120 Volume 35 page 323. INDEX # 2437.
Mich^l MEALEY; pension awarded 5 Jun 1817. SOURCE: WO120 Volume 35 page 323. INDEX # 2438.
Jno MCDONALD; pension awarded 16 Jan 1800. SOURCE: WO120 Volume 35 page 323. INDEX # 2439.
Ja^s SMITH; pension awarded 7 Feb 1822. SOURCE: WO120 Volume 35 page 323. INDEX # 2440.
Willm LORRAMER; pension awarded 7 Mar 1827. SOURCE: WO120 Volume 35 page 323. INDEX # 2441.
Wm PARSONS; pension awarded 7 Mar 1827. SOURCE: WO120 Volume 35 page 323. INDEX # 2442.
Isaac BARTLETT; pension awarded 21 May 1828. SOURCE: WO120 Volume 35 page 323. INDEX # 2443.
Thos STACY; pension awarded 29 Oct 1828. SOURCE: WO120 Volume 35 page 323. INDEX # 2444.
Thos HARLEY; pension awarded 25 Jun 1829. SOURCE: WO120 Volume 35 page 323. INDEX # 2445.
Hugh CARMICHAEL; pension awarded 25 Jun 1829. SOURCE: WO120 Volume 35 page 323. INDEX # 2446.

Fencibles (continued)

Moses PIPPY; pension awarded 9 Dec 1829. SOURCE: WO120 Volume 35 page 323. INDEX # 2447.
Ch^n VINER; pension awarded 9 Jun 1830. SOURCE: WO120 Volume 35 page 323. INDEX # 2448.
Ja^s DOWDEN; pension awarded 14 Dec 1836. SOURCE: WO120 Volume 35 page 323. INDEX # 2449.
Wm DWYER; pension awarded 8 Aug 1838. SOURCE: WO120 Volume 35 page 323. INDEX # 2450.
Jer^h CROWLEY; pension awarded 26 Sep 1838. SOURCE: WO120 Volume 35 page 323. INDEX # 2451.

Foreign Veterans Battalion

Hen^y WENNIGSEN; pension awarded 15 Aug 1820. SOURCE: WO120 Volume 35 page 328. INDEX # 2452.
Christian HARTE; pension awarded 15 Aug 1820. SOURCE: WO120 Volume 35 page 328. INDEX # 2453.

4th Veterans Battalion

Saml BRAZIER; pension awarded 5 Jun 1817. SOURCE: WO120 Volume 35 page 332. INDEX # 2454.
Jno BIGNELL; pension awarded 5 Jun 1817. SOURCE: WO120 Volume 35 page 332. INDEX # 2455.
Jno PARKER; pension awarded 5 Jun 1817. SOURCE: WO120 Volume 35 page 332. INDEX # 2456.
Jno ASHBY; pension awarded 5 Jun 1817. SOURCE: WO120 Volume 35 page 332. INDEX # 2457.
Ja^s FRASER; pension awarded 5 Jun 1817. SOURCE: WO120 Volume 35 page 332. INDEX # 2458.
Simon GRAY; pension awarded 5 Jun 1817. SOURCE: WO120 Volume 35 page 332. INDEX # 2459.
Jno OHARA; pension awarded 5 Jun 1817. SOURCE: WO120 Volume 35 page 332. INDEX # 2460.
Fra^s WADE; pension awarded 5 Jun 1817. SOURCE: WO120 Volume 35 page 332. INDEX # 2461.
Ja^s CURRIE; pension awarded 5 Jun 1817. SOURCE: WO120 Volume 35 page 332. INDEX # 2462.
Dav^d BAIRD; pension awarded 5 Jun 1817. SOURCE: WO120 Volume 35 page 332. INDEX # 2463.
Bern^d KELLY; pension awarded 5 Jun 1817. SOURCE: WO120 Volume 35 page 332. INDEX # 2464.
Jos^h JONES; pension awarded 5 Jun 1817. SOURCE: WO120 Volume 35 page 332. INDEX # 2465.
Robt MURRAY; pension awarded 5 Jun 1817. SOURCE: WO120 Volume 35 page 332. INDEX # 2466.
Ja^s WATT; pension awarded 5 Jun 1817. SOURCE: WO120 Volume 35 page 332. INDEX # 2467.
Jno MCKERGOW; pension awarded 5 Jun 1817. SOURCE: WO120 Volume 35 page 332. INDEX # 2468.
Jno LAMB; pension awarded 5 Jun 1817. SOURCE: WO120 Volume 35 page 332. INDEX # 2469.
Thos POWEL; pension awarded 5 Jun 1817. SOURCE: WO120 Volume 35 page 332. INDEX # 2470.
Willm SAXTON; pension awarded 5 Jun 1817. SOURCE: WO120 Volume 35 page 332. INDEX # 2471.
Wm TWIGG; pension awarded 5 Jun 1817. SOURCE: WO120 Volume 35 page 332. INDEX # 2472.
Richd JONES; pension awarded 5 Jun 1817. SOURCE: WO120 Volume 35 page 332. INDEX # 2473.
Ja^s BRIAN; pension awarded 5 Jun 1817. SOURCE: WO120 Volume 35 page 332. INDEX # 2474.
Peter MULLEN; pension awarded 5 Jun 1817. SOURCE: WO120 Volume 35 page 332. INDEX # 2475.
Jno WISTAFF; pension awarded 5 Jun 1817. SOURCE: WO120 Volume 35 page 332. INDEX # 2476.
Wm DANGERFIELD; pension awarded 5 Jun 1817. SOURCE: WO120 Volume 35 page 332. INDEX # 2477.
Jno HUFF; pension awarded 5 Jun 1817. SOURCE: WO120 Volume 35 page 333. INDEX # 2478.
Fra^s CHARRIOTTE; pension awarded 5 Jun 1817. SOURCE: WO120 Volume 35 page 333. INDEX # 2479.
Jno COOTE; pension awarded 5 Jun 1817. SOURCE: WO120 Volume 35 page 333. INDEX # 2480.
Wm CROFT; pension awarded 5 Jun 1817. SOURCE: WO120 Volume 35 page 333. INDEX # 2481.
Jos^h NELSON; pension awarded 5 Jun 1817. SOURCE: WO120 Volume 35 page 333. INDEX # 2482.
Morgan WILLIAMS; pension awarded 5 Jun 1817. SOURCE: WO120 Volume 35 page 333. INDEX # 2483.
Ge^o CARTWRIGHT; pension awarded 5 Jun 1817. SOURCE: WO120 Volume 35 page 333. INDEX # 2484.
Jno DUNBAR; pension awarded 5 Jun 1817. SOURCE: WO120 Volume 35 page 333. INDEX # 2485.
Jno NORRIS; pension awarded 5 Jun 1817. SOURCE: WO120 Volume 35 page 333. INDEX # 2486.
Danl YOUDS; pension awarded 5 Jun 1817. SOURCE: WO120 Volume 35 page 333. INDEX # 2487.
Christ^r HOLLAND; pension awarded 5 Jun 1817. SOURCE: WO120 Volume 35 page 333. INDEX # 2488.
Thos SCOTT; pension awarded 5 Jun 1817. SOURCE: WO120 Volume 35 page 333. INDEX # 2489.

WO120 VOLUME 35

4th Veterans Battalion (continued)

Fras MCDONALD; pension awarded 5 Jun 1817. SOURCE: WO120 Volume 35 page 333. INDEX # 2490.
Jno ADAIR; pension awarded 5 Jun 1817. SOURCE: WO120 Volume 35 page 333. INDEX # 2491.
Heny AYLMER; pension awarded 5 Jun 1817. SOURCE: WO120 Volume 35 page 333. INDEX # 2492.
Thos BURGESS; pension awarded 5 Jun 1817. SOURCE: WO120 Volume 35 page 333. INDEX # 2493.
Jno BURTON; pension awarded 5 Jun 1817. SOURCE: WO120 Volume 35 page 333. INDEX # 2494.
Thos COOK; pension awarded 5 Jun 1817. SOURCE: WO120 Volume 35 page 333. INDEX # 2495.
Thos COUGHLAN; pension awarded 5 Jun 1817. SOURCE: WO120 Volume 35 page 333. INDEX # 2496.
Edwd CONNOLLY; pension awarded 5 Jun 1817. SOURCE: WO120 Volume 35 page 333. INDEX # 2497.
Philip CUSICK; pension awarded 5 Jun 1817. SOURCE: WO120 Volume 35 page 333. INDEX # 2498.
Chas DOBSON; pension awarded 5 Jun 1817. SOURCE: WO120 Volume 35 page 333. INDEX # 2499.
Patk DOWLAN; pension awarded 5 Jun 1817. SOURCE: WO120 Volume 35 page 333. INDEX # 2500.
Jno FINHERTY; pension awarded 5 Jun 1817 SOURCE: WO120 Volume 35 page 333. INDEX # 2501.
Jno GRACE; pension awarded 5 Jun 1817. SOURCE: WO120 Volume 35 page 334. INDEX # 2502.
Josh HEAZLEY; pension awarded 5 Jun 1817. SOURCE: WO120 Volume 35 page 334. INDEX # 2503.
Robt HENRY; pension awarded 5 Jun 1817. SOURCE: WO120 Volume 35 page 334. INDEX # 2504.
Geo HICKS; pension awarded 5 Jun 1817. SOURCE: WO120 Volume 35 page 334. INDEX # 2505.
Christr HILL; pension awarded 5 Jun 1817. SOURCE: WO120 Volume 35 page 334. INDEX # 2506.
Nichs JURE; pension awarded 5 Jun 1817. SOURCE: WO120 Volume 35 page 334. INDEX # 2507.
Richd MACE; pension awarded 5 Jun 1817. SOURCE: WO120 Volume 35 page 334. INDEX # 2508.
Jno MAIR; pension awarded 5 Jun 1817. SOURCE: WO120 Volume 35 page 334. INDEX # 2509.
Nichs MAHON; pension awarded 5 Jun 1817; residence - Canada. SOURCE: WO120 Volume 35 page 334. INDEX # 2510.
Patk MCCARTHY; pension awarded 5 Jun 1817. SOURCE: WO120 Volume 35 page 334. INDEX # 2511.
Patk MCILGREW; pension awarded 5 Jun 1817. SOURCE: WO120 Volume 35 page 334. INDEX # 2512.
Chas PERRY; pension awarded 5 Jun 1817. SOURCE: WO120 Volume 35 page 334. INDEX # 2513.
Davd SMITH; pension awarded 5 Jun 1817. SOURCE: WO120 Volume 35 page 334. INDEX # 2514.
Saml PROSSER; pension awarded 5 Jun 1817. SOURCE: WO120 Volume 35 page 334. INDEX # 2515.
Jno RAY; pension awarded 5 Jun 1817. SOURCE: WO120 Volume 35 page 334. INDEX # 2516.
Wm SIMPSON; pension awarded 5 Jun 1817. SOURCE: WO120 Volume 35 page 334. INDEX # 2517.
Jas SMITHERMAN; pension awarded 5 Jun 1817. SOURCE: WO120 Volume 35 page 334. INDEX # 2518.
Wm THORNTON; pension awarded 5 Jun 1817. SOURCE: WO120 Volume 35 page 334. INDEX # 2519.
Wm WARRINGTON; pension awarded 5 Jun 1817. SOURCE: WO120 Volume 35 page 334. INDEX # 2520.
Chas RUFF; pension awarded 5 Jun 1817. SOURCE: WO120 Volume 35 page 334. INDEX # 2521.
Geo WARD; pension awarded 5 Jun 1817. SOURCE: WO120 Volume 35 page 334. INDEX # 2522.
Peter GEORGE; pension awarded 5 Jun 1817. SOURCE: WO120 Volume 35 page 334. INDEX # 2523.
Jno PEARSON; pension awarded 5 Jun 1817. SOURCE: WO120 Volume 35 page 334. INDEX # 2524.
Lewis STRIPMAN; pension awarded 5 Jun 1817. SOURCE: WO120 Volume 35 page 334. INDEX # 2525.
Jno PETERS; pension awarded 7 Jun 1817. SOURCE: WO120 Volume 35 page 335. INDEX # 2526.
Jno ALLEN; pension awarded 7 Jun 1817. SOURCE: WO120 Volume 35 page 335. INDEX # 2527.
Michl GILLAWAY; pension awarded 7 Jun 1817. SOURCE: WO120 Volume 35 page 335. INDEX # 2528.
Wm CLIFFORD; pension awarded 7 Jun 1817. SOURCE: WO120 Volume 35 page 335. INDEX # 2529.
Jno SUGHRAE; pension awarded 7 Jun 1817. SOURCE: WO120 Volume 35 page 335. INDEX # 2530.
Jno DALL; pension awarded 7 Jun 1817. SOURCE: WO120 Volume 35 page 335. INDEX # 2531.
Hugh HOGG; pension awarded 7 Jun 1817. SOURCE: WO120 Volume 35 page 335. INDEX # 2532.
Jno VANDERDISKIN; pension awarded 7 Jun 1817. SOURCE: WO120 Volume 35 page 335. INDEX # 2533.
Jas HENRY; pension awarded 7 Jun 1817. SOURCE: WO120 Volume 35 page 335. INDEX # 2534.
Richd TOTTON; pension awarded 7 Jun 1817. SOURCE: WO120 Volume 35 page 335. INDEX # 2535.
Richd SLIGHT; pension awarded 7 Jun 1817. SOURCE: WO120 Volume 35 page 335. INDEX # 2536.
Davd GARDNER; pension awarded 7 Jun 1817. SOURCE: WO120 Volume 35 page 335. INDEX # 2537.
Jas BANNAN; pension awarded 7 Jun 1817. SOURCE: WO120 Volume 35 page 335. INDEX # 2538.
Thos MCLEOD; pension awarded 7 Jun 1817. SOURCE: WO120 Volume 35 page 335. INDEX # 2539.
Saml PAYNE; pension awarded 7 Jun 1817. SOURCE: WO120 Volume 35 page 335. INDEX # 2540.

4th Veterans Battalion (continued)

Pat^k CONLAN; pension awarded 7 Jun 1817. SOURCE: WO120 Volume 35 page 335. INDEX # 2541.
Saml GATES; pension awarded 7 Jun 1817. SOURCE: WO120 Volume 35 page 335. INDEX # 2542.
Jno BUCHANAN; pension awarded 7 Jun 1817. SOURCE: WO120 Volume 35 page 335. INDEX # 2543.
Jos^h FARNELL; pension awarded 7 Jun 1817. SOURCE: WO120 Volume 35 page 335. INDEX # 2544.
Thos BACKHOUSE; pension awarded 7 Jun 1817. SOURCE: WO120 Volume 35 page 335. INDEX # 2545.
Jno GORMAN; pension awarded 7 Jun 1817. SOURCE: WO120 Volume 35 page 335. INDEX # 2546.
Jno LILLEY; pension awarded 7 Jun 1817. SOURCE: WO120 Volume 35 page 335. INDEX # 2547.
Allan MCDONALD; pension awarded 7 Jun 1817. SOURCE: WO120 Volume 35 page 335. INDEX # 2548.
Wm MEREDITH; pension awarded 7 Jun 1817. SOURCE: WO120 Volume 35 page 335. INDEX # 2549.
Wm MILLS; pension awarded 5 Jun 1817. SOURCE: WO120 Volume 35 page 336. INDEX # 2550.
Jos^h BEESTON; pension awarded 5 Jun 1817. SOURCE: WO120 Volume 35 page 336. INDEX # 2551.
Wm HILLIARD; pension awarded 5 Jun 1817. SOURCE: WO120 Volume 35 page 336. INDEX # 2552.
Thos BURNS; pension awarded 5 Jun 1817. SOURCE: WO120 Volume 35 page 336. INDEX # 2553.
Peter WELLS; pension awarded 5 Jun 1817. SOURCE: WO120 Volume 35 page 336. INDEX # 2554.
Saml MARMAN; pension awarded 5 Jun 1817. SOURCE: WO120 Volume 35 page 336. INDEX # 2555.
Pat^k LEWIS; pension awarded 5 Jun 1817. SOURCE: WO120 Volume 35 page 336. INDEX # 2556.
Ja^s CUTTS; pension awarded 5 Jun 1817. SOURCE: WO120 Volume 35 page 336. INDEX # 2557.
Terc^e GOLDRICK; pension awarded 5 Jun 1817. SOURCE: WO120 Volume 35 page 336. INDEX # 2558.
Wm FRAYER; pension awarded 5 Jun 1817. SOURCE: WO120 Volume 35 page 336. INDEX # 2559.
Jos^h WINSLOW; pension awarded 5 Jun 1817. SOURCE: WO120 Volume 35 page 336. INDEX # 2560.
Ge^o EDGLEY; pension awarded 5 Jun 1817. SOURCE: WO120 Volume 35 page 336. INDEX # 2561.
Jno MULCAHY; pension awarded 5 Jun 1817. SOURCE: WO120 Volume 35 page 336. INDEX # 2562.
Hen^y SANDERSON; pension awarded 5 Jun 1817. SOURCE: WO120 Volume 35 page 336. INDEX # 2563.
Jno Bern^d KELLY; pension awarded 5 Jun 1817. SOURCE: WO120 Volume 35 page 336. INDEX # 2564.
Miles CONNORS; pension awarded 5 Jun 1817. SOURCE: WO120 Volume 35 page 336. INDEX # 2565.
Jacques BURTON; pension awarded 5 Jun 1817. SOURCE: WO120 Volume 35 page 336. INDEX # 2566.
Saml CHATWIN; pension awarded 5 Jun 1817. SOURCE: WO120 Volume 35 page 336. INDEX # 2567.
Thos DILLON; pension awarded 5 Jun 1817. SOURCE: WO120 Volume 35 page 336. INDEX # 2568.
Ja^s DOUGHERTY; pension awarded 5 Jun 1817. SOURCE: WO120 Volume 35 page 336. INDEX # 2569.
Mich^l FINDLEY; pension awarded 5 Jun 1817. SOURCE: WO120 Volume 35 page 336. INDEX # 2570.
Thos WAUD; pension awarded 5 Jun 1817. SOURCE: WO120 Volume 35 page 336. INDEX # 2571.
Jos^h WEATHERALL; pension awarded 5 Jun 1817. SOURCE: WO120 Volume 35 page 336. INDEX # 2572.
Ja^s STRACHAN; pension awarded 5 Jun 1817. SOURCE: WO120 Volume 35 page 336. INDEX # 2573.
Peter WINRICE; pension awarded 5 Jun 1817. SOURCE: WO120 Volume 35 page 337. INDEX # 2574.
Bern^d DALY; pension awarded 5 Jun 1817. SOURCE: WO120 Volume 35 page 337. INDEX # 2575.
Ja^s ARKIS; pension awarded 5 Jun 1817. SOURCE: WO120 Volume 35 page 337. INDEX # 2576.
Wm BOXER; pension awarded 5 Jun 1817. SOURCE: WO120 Volume 35 page 337. INDEX # 2577.
And^w EVANS; pension awarded 5 Jun 1817. SOURCE: WO120 Volume 35 page 337. INDEX # 2578.
Jno MENTZ; pension awarded 5 Jun 1817. SOURCE: WO120 Volume 35 page 337. INDEX # 2579.
Fred^k MCKAY; pension awarded 5 Jun 1817. SOURCE: WO120 Volume 35 page 337. INDEX # 2580.
Jno HORSALL; pension awarded 5 Jun 1817. SOURCE: WO120 Volume 35 page 337. INDEX # 2581.
Ja^s PRICE; pension awarded 5 Jun 1817. SOURCE: WO120 Volume 35 page 337. INDEX # 2582.
Jno KITSON; pension awarded 5 Jun 1817. SOURCE: WO120 Volume 35 page 337. INDEX # 2583.
Ja^s NOBLE; pension awarded 5 Jun 1817. SOURCE: WO120 Volume 35 page 337. INDEX # 2584.
Danl PORTER; pension awarded 5 Jun 1817. SOURCE: WO120 Volume 35 page 337. INDEX # 2585.
Richd HOLT; pension awarded 5 Jun 1817. SOURCE: WO120 Volume 35 page 337. INDEX # 2586.
Thos SMITH; pension awarded 5 Jun 1817. SOURCE: WO120 Volume 35 page 337. INDEX # 2587.
Wm GOODENOUGH; pension awarded 5 Jun 1817. SOURCE: WO120 Volume 35 page 337. INDEX # 2588.
Wm WELLS; pension awarded 5 Jun 1817. SOURCE: WO120 Volume 35 page 337. INDEX # 2589.
Ja^s HOOK; pension awarded 5 Jun 1817. SOURCE: WO120 Volume 35 page 337. INDEX # 2590.
Jno SAVAGE; pension awarded 5 Jun 1817. SOURCE: WO120 Volume 35 page 337. INDEX # 2591.
Robt DOWELL; pension awarded 5 Jun 1817. SOURCE: WO120 Volume 35 page 337. INDEX # 2592.

4th Veterans Battalion (continued)

Danl FISHER; pension awarded 5 Jun 1817. SOURCE: WO120 Volume 35 page 337. INDEX # 2593.
Ge^o FRANKLAND; pension awarded 5 Jun 1817. SOURCE: WO120 Volume 35 page 337. INDEX # 2594.
Thos GOFF; pension awarded 5 Jun 1817. SOURCE: WO120 Volume 35 page 337. INDEX # 2595.
Ja^s GOUCH; pension awarded 5 Jun 1817. SOURCE: WO120 Volume 35 page 337. INDEX # 2596.
Wm HOLLAND; pension awarded 5 Jun 1817. SOURCE: WO120 Volume 35 page 337. INDEX # 2597.
Ge^o HUNTER; pension awarded 7 Jun 1817. SOURCE: WO120 Volume 35 page 338. INDEX # 2598.
Gilb^t KENNEDY; pension awarded 7 Jun 1817. SOURCE: WO120 Volume 35 page 338. INDEX # 2599.
Wy^{ms} MCCARTER; pension awarded 7 Jun 1817. SOURCE: WO120 Volume 35 page 338. INDEX # 2600.
Ja^s MITCHELL; pension awarded 7 Jun 1817. SOURCE: WO120 Volume 35 page 338. INDEX # 2601.
Pat^k MURPHY; pension awarded 7 Jun 1817. SOURCE: WO120 Volume 35 page 338. INDEX # 2602.
Jno PIERCE; pension awarded 7 Jun 1817. SOURCE: WO120 Volume 35 page 338. INDEX # 2603.
Richd ROBERTS; pension awarded 7 Jun 1817. SOURCE: WO120 Volume 35 page 338. INDEX # 2604.
Hugh ROWE; pension awarded 7 Jun 1817. SOURCE: WO120 Volume 35 page 338. INDEX # 2605.
Ed^{wd} RYAN; pension awarded 7 Jun 1817. SOURCE: WO120 Volume 35 page 338. INDEX # 2606.
Jno SMITH; pension awarded 7 Jun 1817. SOURCE: WO120 Volume 35 page 338. INDEX # 2607.
Thos SHUFFLEBOTTOM; pension awarded 7 Jun 1817. SOURCE: WO120 Volume 35 page 338. INDEX # 2608.
Jno SKUSE; pension awarded 7 Jun 1817. SOURCE: WO120 Volume 35 page 338. INDEX # 2609.
Thos SPECKMAN; pension awarded 7 Jun 1817. SOURCE: WO120 Volume 35 page 338. INDEX # 2610.
Wm STEPHENS; pension awarded 7 Jun 1817. SOURCE: WO120 Volume 35 page 338. INDEX # 2611.
Isaac WALTERS; pension awarded 7 Jun 1817. SOURCE: WO120 Volume 35 page 338. INDEX # 2612.
Thos HEALEY; pension awarded 7 Jun 1817. SOURCE: WO120 Volume 35 page 338. INDEX # 2613.
Ge^o JONES; pension awarded 7 Jun 1817. SOURCE: WO120 Volume 35 page 338. INDEX # 2614.
Thos JONES; pension awarded 7 Jun 1817. SOURCE: WO120 Volume 35 page 338. INDEX # 2615.
Jno MURPHY; pension awarded 7 Jun 1817. SOURCE: WO120 Volume 35 page 338. INDEX # 2616.
Lyman WHITEHEAD; pension awarded 7 Jun 1817. SOURCE: WO120 Volume 35 page 338. INDEX # 2617.
Jos^h GREENWOOD; pension awarded 21 Aug 1817. SOURCE: WO120 Volume 35 page 338. INDEX # 2618.
Richd LANE; pension awarded 21 Aug 1817. SOURCE: WO120 Volume 35 page 338. INDEX # 2619.
Robt HARDY; pension awarded 21 Aug 1817. SOURCE: WO120 Volume 35 page 338. INDEX # 2620.
Fra^s POTTASH; pension awarded 21 Aug 1817. SOURCE: WO120 Volume 35 page 338. INDEX # 2621.
Jno HUTCHESON; pension awarded 12 May 1819. SOURCE: WO120 Volume 35 page 339. INDEX # 2622.
Fred^k MASELAS; pension awarded 1 Jul 1819. SOURCE: WO120 Volume 35 page 339. INDEX # 2623.
Jno HEALEY; pension awarded 28 Mar 1821. SOURCE: WO120 Volume 35 page 339. INDEX # 2624.
Jno COOK; pension awarded 1 Jul 1819. SOURCE: WO120 Volume 35 page 339. INDEX # 2625.

6th Veterans Battalion

Anth^y BEECHAMS; pension awarded 27 Mar 1816; residence - Jamaica. SOURCE: WO120 Volume 35 page 343. INDEX # 2626.
Jno TURNER; pension awarded 12 Jun 1816; residence - New Brunswick, Canada. SOURCE: WO120 Volume 35 page 343. INDEX # 2627.
Alex^r MCQUILLAN; pension awarded 12 Jun 1816; residence - Canada. SOURCE: WO120 Volume 35 page 343. INDEX # 2628.

7th Veterans Battalion

Thos COLCOMB; pension awarded 21 Aug 1817. SOURCE: WO120 Volume 35 page 344. INDEX # 2629.
Wm SMITH; pension awarded 21 Aug 1817. SOURCE: WO120 Volume 35 page 344. INDEX # 2630.

10th Veterans Battalion

Thos MCKIZER; pension awarded 13 Dec 1826. SOURCE: WO120 Volume 35 page 347. INDEX # 2631.

BRITISH ARMY PENSIONERS ABROAD

10th Veterans Battalion (continued)

Allen MCDONALD; pension awarded 21 May 1828. SOURCE: WO120 Volume 35 page 347. INDEX # 2632.

12th Veterans Battalion

Jn⁰ FALLON; pension awarded 17 Jun 1814; residence - Canada. SOURCE: WO120 Volume 35 page 349. INDEX # 2633.

Willᵐ MCLAUGHTIN; pension awarded 17 Jun 1814; residence - Quebec, Canada. SOURCE: WO120 Volume 35 page 349. INDEX # 2634.

Jn⁰ LINTON; pension awarded 25 Jun 1814; residence - Canada. SOURCE: WO120 Volume 35 page 349. INDEX # 2635.

Jn⁰ WILKINSON; pension awarded 17 Jun 1814; residence - Canada. SOURCE: WO120 Volume 35 page 349. INDEX # 2636.

Militia

Jn⁰ HALL; pension awarded 27 Mar 1816; residence - Canada. SOURCE: WO120 Volume 35 page 350. INDEX # 2637.

Jaˢ MILLS; pension awarded 29 Nov 1815; residence - Montreal, Quebec, Canada. SOURCE: WO120 Volume 35 page 350. INDEX # 2638.

Patᵏ GORDON; pension awarded 22 May 1899; residence - Quebec, Canada. SOURCE: WO120 Volume 35 page 350. INDEX # 2639.

Wᵐ MOSS; pension awarded 27 May 1812; residence - Quebec, Canada. SOURCE: WO120 Volume 35 page 350. INDEX # 2640.

Andʷ GIVENS; pension awarded 27 Jun 1810; residence - Quebec, Canada; died , . SOURCE: WO120 Volume 35 page 350. INDEX # 2641.

Hugh JAMES; pension awarded 30 Nov 1814; residence - Quebec, Canada; died , . SOURCE: WO120 Volume 35 page 350. INDEX # 2642.

Michˡ STEDMAN; pension awarded 26 Jul 1815; residence - North America. SOURCE: WO120 Volume 35 page 350. INDEX # 2643.

Wᵐ WILSON; pension awarded 24 Apr 1816; residence - Canada. SOURCE: WO120 Volume 35 page 350. INDEX # 2644.

Wᵐ CLARK; pension awarded 31 Aug 1814; residence - Canada. SOURCE: WO120 Volume 35 page 350. INDEX # 2645.

Michˡ CONNOR; pension awarded 1 Apr 1800; residence - Canada. SOURCE: WO120 Volume 35 page 350. INDEX # 2646.

Robᵗ CAMPBELL; pension awarded 30 Oct 1811; residence - Canada. SOURCE: WO120 Volume 35 page 350. INDEX # 2647.

1st Royal Garrison Battalion

Patᵏ ROURKE; pension awarded 20 Jan 1819. SOURCE: WO120 Volume 35 page 352. INDEX # 2648.

King's German Legion Hussars

Henʸ MEYER; pension awarded 15 Aug 1820. SOURCE: WO120 Volume 35 page 353. INDEX # 2649.

Henʸ COHRS; pension awarded 15 Aug 1820. SOURCE: WO120 Volume 35 page 353. INDEX # 2650.

Christoph ROSE; pension awarded 15 Aug 1820. SOURCE: WO120 Volume 35 page 353. INDEX # 2651.

King's German Legion Infantry

Henʸ REGUA; pension awarded 15 Aug 1820. SOURCE: WO120 Volume 35 page 354. INDEX # 2652.

Christoph DUHRKOP; pension awarded 19 Aug 1820. SOURCE: WO120 Volume 35 page 354. INDEX # 2653.

WO120 VOLUME 35

King's German Legion Infantry (continued)

Lewis PAULMAN; pension awarded 19 Aug 1820. SOURCE: WO120 Volume 35 page 354. INDEX # 2654.
Ernest FEHRENSEN; pension awarded 19 Aug 1820. SOURCE: WO120 Volume 35 page 354. INDEX # 2655.
Fred^k LINDEM; pension awarded 19 Aug 1820. SOURCE: WO120 Volume 35 page 354. INDEX # 2656.
Hen^y BACKHANS; pension awarded 19 Aug 1820. SOURCE: WO120 Volume 35 page 354. INDEX # 2657.
Chas BAHT; pension awarded 19 Aug 1820. SOURCE: WO120 Volume 35 page 354. INDEX # 2658.

31st Regiment of Foot

Mich^l ROCK; pension awarded 11 May 1831. SOURCE: WO120 Volume 35 page 357. INDEX # 2659.
Jno JONES; pension awarded 27 Jun 1838. SOURCE: WO120 Volume 35 page 357. INDEX # 2660.
Pat^k CHAMBERS; pension awarded 27 Jun 1838; residence - Dinapore, India. SOURCE: WO120 Volume 35 page 357. INDEX # 2661.
Jno CURRAN; pension awarded 27 Jun 1838; residence - Dinapore, India. SOURCE: WO120 Volume 35 page 357. INDEX # 2662.
Hugh DOYLE; pension awarded 27 Jun 1838. SOURCE: WO120 Volume 35 page 357. INDEX # 2663.
Ed^{wd} HART; pension awarded 27 Jun 1838. SOURCE: WO120 Volume 35 page 357. INDEX # 2664.
Pat^k MCLOUGHLIN; pension awarded 27 Jun 1838. SOURCE: WO120 Volume 35 page 357. INDEX # 2665.
Tim^y WHITEHEAD; pension awarded 27 Jun 1838. SOURCE: WO120 Volume 35 page 357. INDEX # 2666.
Jno SCOTT; pension awarded 22 Aug 1838. SOURCE: WO120 Volume 35 page 357. INDEX # 2667.

New South Wales Veterans

Jno CUMMINGS; pension awarded 13 Jun 1832. SOURCE: WO120 Volume 35 page 360. INDEX # 2668.
Ge^o CUPITT; pension awarded 13 Jun 1832. SOURCE: WO120 Volume 35 page 360. INDEX # 2669.
Lewis CURRY; pension awarded 13 Jun 1832. SOURCE: WO120 Volume 35 page 360. INDEX # 2670.
Benjn CUSSLEY; pension awarded 13 Jun 1832. SOURCE: WO120 Volume 35 page 360. INDEX # 2671.
Peter DARGIN; pension awarded 13 Jun 1832. SOURCE: WO120 Volume 35 page 360. INDEX # 2672.
Jos^h ELDRIDGE; pension awarded 13 Jun 1832. SOURCE: WO120 Volume 35 page 360. INDEX # 2673.
Saml GIBSON; pension awarded 13 Jun 1832. SOURCE: WO120 Volume 35 page 360. INDEX # 2674.
Giles GOLDING; pension awarded 13 Jun 1832. SOURCE: WO120 Volume 35 page 360. INDEX # 2675.
Mich^l GRIFFIN; pension awarded 13 Jun 1832. SOURCE: WO120 Volume 35 page 360. INDEX # 2676.
Thos GOLLEDGE; pension awarded 13 Jun 1832. SOURCE: WO120 Volume 35 page 360. INDEX # 2677.
Jno HADDICK; pension awarded 13 Jun 1832. SOURCE: WO120 Volume 35 page 360. INDEX # 2678.
Ed^{wd} HARRINGTON; pension awarded 13 Jun 1832. SOURCE: WO120 Volume 35 page 360. INDEX # 2679.
Thos HARRIS; pension awarded 13 Jun 1832. SOURCE: WO120 Volume 35 page 360. INDEX # 2680.
Jno HEFFERON; pension awarded 13 Jun 1832. SOURCE: WO120 Volume 35 page 360. INDEX # 2681.
Jno HOARE; pension awarded 13 Jun 1832. SOURCE: WO120 Volume 35 page 360. INDEX # 2682.
Jno HUGHES; pension awarded 13 Jun 1832. SOURCE: WO120 Volume 35 page 360. INDEX # 2683.
Thos HUMPHREY; pension awarded 13 Jun 1832. SOURCE: WO120 Volume 35 page 360. INDEX # 2684.
Pat^k HUMPHRYS; pension awarded 13 Jun 1832. SOURCE: WO120 Volume 35 page 360. INDEX # 2685.
Jno LEE; pension awarded 13 Jun 1832. SOURCE: WO120 Volume 35 page 360. INDEX # 2686.
Richd LONGFORD; pension awarded 13 Jun 1832. SOURCE: WO120 Volume 35 page 360. INDEX # 2687.
Alex^r MONAGHAN; pension awarded 13 Jun 1832. SOURCE: WO120 Volume 35 page 360. INDEX # 2688.
Richd MORTIMER; pension awarded 13 Jun 1832. SOURCE: WO120 Volume 35 page 360. INDEX # 2689.
Bern^d MCDONALD; pension awarded 13 Jun 1832. SOURCE: WO120 Volume 35 page 360. INDEX # 2690.

New South Wales Veterans (continued)

Doug^l MCKELLAR; pension awarded 13 Jun 1832. SOURCE: WO120 Volume 35 page 360. INDEX # 2691.
Hugh ODONALD; pension awarded 13 Jun 1832. SOURCE: WO120 Volume 35 page 361. INDEX # 2692.
Hugh OWENS; pension awarded 13 Jun 1832. SOURCE: WO120 Volume 35 page 361. INDEX # 2693.
Jno PALMER; pension awarded 13 Jun 1832. SOURCE: WO120 Volume 35 page 361. INDEX # 2694.
Wm PICKSTOCK; pension awarded 13 Jun 1832. SOURCE: WO120 Volume 35 page 361. INDEX # 2695.
Danl POLLARD; pension awarded 13 Jun 1832. SOURCE: WO120 Volume 35 page 361. INDEX # 2696.
Ja^s PRICE; pension awarded 13 Jun 1832. SOURCE: WO120 Volume 35 page 361. INDEX # 2697.
Ge^o RANKIN; pension awarded 13 Jun 1832. SOURCE: WO120 Volume 35 page 361. INDEX # 2698.
Jno ROBERTS; pension awarded 13 Jun 1832. SOURCE: WO120 Volume 35 page 361. INDEX # 2699.
Thos ROWDEN; pension awarded 13 Jun 1832. SOURCE: WO120 Volume 35 page 361. INDEX # 2700.
Richd SALTMARSH; pension awarded 13 Jun 1832. SOURCE: WO120 Volume 35 page 361. INDEX # 2701.
Thos SHERLAND; pension awarded 13 Jun 1832. SOURCE: WO120 Volume 35 page 361. INDEX # 2702.
Jno SMITH; pension awarded 13 Jun 1832. SOURCE: WO120 Volume 35 page 361. INDEX # 2703.
Pat^k SMITH; pension awarded 13 Jun 1832. SOURCE: WO120 Volume 35 page 361. INDEX # 2704.
Hen^y SNELL; pension awarded 13 Jun 1832. SOURCE: WO120 Volume 35 page 361. INDEX # 2705.
Ja^s STRACHAN; pension awarded 13 Jun 1832. SOURCE: WO120 Volume 35 page 361. INDEX # 2706.
Ge^o TILLEY; pension awarded 13 Jun 1832. SOURCE: WO120 Volume 35 page 361. INDEX # 2707.
Mich^l CARROLL; pension awarded 13 Jun 1832. SOURCE: WO120 Volume 35 page 361. INDEX # 2708.
Jno BROWN; pension awarded 10 Oct 1832. SOURCE: WO120 Volume 35 page 361. INDEX # 2709.
Jno BOOKER; pension awarded 10 Oct 1832. SOURCE: WO120 Volume 35 page 361. INDEX # 2710.
Jno DAWSON; pension awarded 9 Jan 1833. SOURCE: WO120 Volume 35 page 361. INDEX # 2711.
Thos MOORE; pension awarded 9 Jan 1833. SOURCE: WO120 Volume 35 page 361. INDEX # 2712.
Thos STACY; pension awarded 29 Oct 1828. SOURCE: WO120 Volume 35 page 361. INDEX # 2713.
Hen^y JAMES; pension awarded 12 Nov 1834. SOURCE: WO120 Volume 35 page 361. INDEX # 2714.

99th Regiment of Foot

Jno OHARA; pension awarded 23 Sep 1818. SOURCE: WO120 Volume 35 page 364. INDEX # 2715.
Jno PHILIPS; pension awarded 23 Sep 1818. SOURCE: WO120 Volume 35 page 364. INDEX # 2716.
Ja^s WEST; pension awarded 23 Sep 1818. SOURCE: WO120 Volume 35 page 364. INDEX # 2717.
Ab^m NICHOLS; pension awarded 23 Sep 1818. SOURCE: WO120 Volume 35 page 364. INDEX # 2718.
Ed^wd DARBY; pension awarded 23 Sep 1818. SOURCE: WO120 Volume 35 page 364. INDEX # 2719.
Jno BURKE; pension awarded 23 Sep 1818. SOURCE: WO120 Volume 35 page 364. INDEX # 2720.
Jno HERLIHY; pension awarded 23 Sep 1818. SOURCE: WO120 Volume 35 page 364. INDEX # 2721.
Jno MALTON; pension awarded 23 Sep 1818. SOURCE: WO120 Volume 35 page 364. INDEX # 2722.
Wm MCGRORY; pension awarded 23 Sep 1818. SOURCE: WO120 Volume 35 page 364. INDEX # 2723.
Hen^y BRERTON; pension awarded 23 Sep 1818. SOURCE: WO120 Volume 35 page 364. INDEX # 2724.
W^m KEY; pension awarded 23 Sep 1818. SOURCE: WO120 Volume 35 page 364. INDEX # 2725.
Thos MCGUIRE; pension awarded 23 Sep 1818. SOURCE: WO120 Volume 35 page 364. INDEX # 2726.
Thos BOYLE; pension awarded 23 Sep 1818. SOURCE: WO120 Volume 35 page 364. INDEX # 2727.
Jno WALSH; pension awarded 23 Sep 1818. SOURCE: WO120 Volume 35 page 364. INDEX # 2728.
Ja^s DOGHERTY; pension awarded 23 Sep 1818. SOURCE: WO120 Volume 35 page 364. INDEX # 2729.
Jno WATERSTONE; pension awarded 13 Apr 1836. SOURCE: WO120 Volume 35 page 364. INDEX # 2730.
Mich^l MURPHY; pension awarded 9 Aug 1837. SOURCE: WO120 Volume 35 page 364. INDEX # 2731.

END OF VOLUME 35

1st Regiment of Life Guards

Anth^y STEELLS; pension awarded 12 May 1824; residence - London, Ontario, Canada; died 15 May 1870. SOURCE: WO120 Volume 69 page 1. INDEX # 2732.

Isaac CARLING; pension awarded 4 Feb 1818; residence - London, Ontario, Canada. SOURCE: WO120 Volume 69 page 1. INDEX # 2733.

Row^d MATHER; pension awarded 19 Jul 1816; residence - Saint Johns, Quebec, Canada. SOURCE: WO120 Volume 69 page 1. INDEX # 2734.

Ja^s BLACK; pension awarded 11 Oct 1818; residence - New South Wales, Australia. SOURCE: WO120 Volume 69 page 1. INDEX # 2735.

Thos SPICER; pension awarded 28 Dec 1818; residence - New South Wales, Australia. SOURCE: WO120 Volume 69 page 1. INDEX # 2736.

Jno WILKINSON; pension awarded 2 Feb 1825; residence - New South Wales, Australia; died 15 May 1855. SOURCE: WO120 Volume 69 page 1. INDEX # 2737.

Jos^h SUTTON; pension awarded 12 Apr 1837; residence - Ostend, Belgium. SOURCE: WO120 Volume 69 page 1. INDEX # 2738.

2nd Regiment of Life Guards

John GILLEY; pension awarded 15 Mar 1826; residence - Toronto, Ontario, Canada; died 13 Sep 1875. SOURCE: WO120 Volume 69 page 3. INDEX # 2739.

Chr^r RUSSELL; pension awarded 4 Dec 1822; residence - Niagara, Ontario, Canada; died 14 May 1872, London, Ontario, Canada. SOURCE: WO120 Volume 69 page 3. INDEX # 2740.

Willm DENTON; pension awarded 7 Feb 1816; residence - Cape of Good Hope, South Africa; died 21 Oct 1873, Cape Town, South Africa. SOURCE: WO120 Volume 69 page 3. INDEX # 2741.

Thos PLAYFORD; pension awarded 16 May 1834; residence - South Australia, Australia; died 18 Sep 1873, Adelaide, Australia. SOURCE: WO120 Volume 69 page 3. INDEX # 2742.

Royal Horse Guards

Thomas NUNNICK; pension awarded 16 Aug 1814; residence - Gore, Canada; died 4 Jan 1849. SOURCE: WO120 Volume 69 page 4. INDEX # 2743.

1st Regiment of Dragoon Guards

Willm BROTHERHOOD; pension awarded 28 Sep 1814; residence - South Australia, Australia. SOURCE: WO120 Volume 69 page 5. INDEX # 2744.

Willm NICHOLSON; pension awarded 27 Sep 1842; residence - Niagara, Ontario, Canada; died 16 Jan 1865, Toronto, Ontario, Canada. SOURCE: WO120 Volume 69 page 5. INDEX # 2745.

John ELLIOTT; pension awarded 14 Oct 1840; residence - Saint Johns, Quebec, Canada; died 24 May 1873, Canterbury. SOURCE: WO120 Volume 69 page 5. INDEX # 2746.

Willm MURRAY; pension awarded 26 Sep 1843; residence - Chambly, Quebec, Canada. SOURCE: WO120 Volume 69 page 5. INDEX # 2747.

John HALL; pension awarded 27 Sep 1842; residence - Toronto, Ontario, Canada; died 14 Dec 1874. SOURCE: WO120 Volume 69 page 5. INDEX # 2748.

Peter HASLEM; pension awarded 27 Sep 1842; residence - Chambly, Quebec, Canada; died in 1846. SOURCE: WO120 Volume 69 page 5. INDEX # 2749.

John HUGHES; pension awarded 27 Sep 1842; residence - Toronto, Ontario, Canada; died 6 Jul 1876. SOURCE: WO120 Volume 69 page 5. INDEX # 2750.

Willm PARKER; pension awarded 27 Sep 1842; residence - Niagara, Ontario, Canada; died 27 Dec 1873, Hamilton, Ontario, Canada. SOURCE: WO120 Volume 69 page 5. INDEX # 2751.

John SMITH; pension awarded 10 Jan 1843; residence - Montreal, Quebec, Canada. SOURCE: WO120 Volume 69 page 5. INDEX # 2752.

1st Regiment of Dragoon Guards (continued)

Robt GRIPTON; pension awarded 22 Jul 1823; residence - London, Ontario, Canada. SOURCE: WO120 Volume 69 page 5. INDEX # 2753.

John LOWRIE; pension awarded 17 Feb 1823; residence - London, Ontario, Canada; died 15 Oct 1850. SOURCE: WO120 Volume 69 page 5. INDEX # 2754.

Thos B. TREACY; pension awarded 25 Jun 1844; residence - Chambly, Quebec, Canada. SOURCE: WO120 Volume 69 page 5. INDEX # 2755.

Richd HERDSMAN; pension awarded 10 Jan 1843; residence - Toronto, Ontario, Canada. SOURCE: WO120 Volume 69 page 5. INDEX # 2756.

2nd Regiment of Dragoon Guards

Willm WINTER; pension awarded 12 Oct 1825; residence - Montreal, Quebec, Canada. SOURCE: WO120 Volume 69 page 8. INDEX # 2757.

John PARNELL; pension awarded 6 May 1799; residence - Chambly, Quebec, Canada. SOURCE: WO120 Volume 69 page 8. INDEX # 2758.

3rd Regiment of Dragoon Guards

John BARBER; pension awarded 21 Aug 1822; residence - Perth, Ontario, Canada. SOURCE: WO120 Volume 69 page 11. INDEX # 2759.

John ALLEN; pension awarded 12 Aug 1821; residence - Toronto, Ontario, Canada. SOURCE: WO120 Volume 69 page 11. INDEX # 2760.

Jos^h NORMAN; pension awarded 13 Sep 1820; residence - Halifax, Nova Scotia, Canada. SOURCE: WO120 Volume 69 page 11. INDEX # 2761.

Thos KIFFORD; pension awarded 13 Jan 1841; residence - Montreal, Quebec, Canada. SOURCE: WO120 Volume 69 page 11. INDEX # 2762.

Chr^r QUINN; pension awarded 19 Jul 1816; residence - Toronto, Ontario, Canada; died 16 Sep 1860, Toronto, Ontario, Canada. SOURCE: WO120 Volume 69 page 11. INDEX # 2763.

Dav^d DOBSON; pension awarded 13 Jan 1841; residence - Bytown, Ontario, Canada; died 29 Mar 1858. SOURCE: WO120 Volume 69 page 11. INDEX # 2764.

4th Regiment of Dragoon Guards

Edwd HOLBURN; pension awarded 26 Oct 1821; residence - Halifax, Nova Scotia, Canada; died 19 Apr 1874, Halifax, Nova Scotia, Canada. SOURCE: WO120 Volume 69 page 13. INDEX # 2765.

Jos^h CHAPMAN; pension awarded 20 Jan 1819; residence - Toronto, Ontario, Canada; died in 1850. SOURCE: WO120 Volume 69 page 13. INDEX # 2766.

Tim^y OBRIEN; pension awarded 10 May 1842; residence - Jamaica; died 26 Dec 1846. SOURCE: WO120 Volume 69 page 13. INDEX # 2767.

5th Regiment of Dragoon Guards

Thos SIMPSON; pension awarded 12 Feb 1817; residence - Toronto, Ontario, Canada; died 6 May 1862, Hamilton, Ontario, Canada. SOURCE: WO120 Volume 69 page 15. INDEX # 2768.

Willm CASSIN; pension awarded 28 Jul 1828; residence - Kingston, Ontario, Canada; died 7 Jun 1880. SOURCE: WO120 Volume 69 page 15. INDEX # 2769.

Danl WINTERS; pension awarded 8 Nov 1826; residence - Kingston, Ontario, Canada; died 8 Aug 1870, Toronto, Ontario, Canada. SOURCE: WO120 Volume 69 page 15. INDEX # 2770.

Robt MCLEAN; pension awarded 7 Feb 1814; residence - Penetanguishene, Ontario, Canada. SOURCE: WO120 Volume 69 page 15. INDEX # 2771.

Saml BAXTER; pension awarded 29 May 1822; residence - Penetanguishene, Ontario, Canada. SOURCE: WO120 Volume 69 page 15. INDEX # 2772.

5th Regiment of Dragoon Guards

Pat^k RYAN; pension awarded 21 Nov 1821; residence - Toronto, Ontario, Canada; died 21 Jul 1847. SOURCE: WO120 Volume 69 page 15. INDEX # 2773.

6th Regiment of Dragoon Guards

Jno WHITEMAN; pension awarded Jul 1811; residence - Belleville, Ontario, Canada; died 13 Jun 1859, Kingston, Ontario, Canada. SOURCE: WO120 Volume 69 page 17. INDEX # 2774.

Thos SAUNDERSON; pension awarded 20 Jan 1819; residence - Toronto, Ontario, Canada; died 2 Mar 1861, London, Ontario, Canada. SOURCE: WO120 Volume 69 page 17. INDEX # 2775.

Robt VERTUE; pension awarded 31 Aug 1814; residence - Toronto, Ontario, Canada; died 10 Sep 1861, Toronto, Ontario, Canada. SOURCE: WO120 Volume 69 page 17. INDEX # 2776.

Luke FOX; pension awarded 9 Jun 1841; residence - Sydney; died 28 Nov 1846. SOURCE: WO120 Volume 69 page 17. INDEX # 2777.

Willm GARNETT; pension awarded 31 Oct 1814; residence - Toronto, Ontario, Canada; died 14 Nov 1844. SOURCE: WO120 Volume 69 page 17. INDEX # 2778.

Adam RUTHERFORD; pension awarded 4 Aug 1824; residence - Toronto, Ontario, Canada; died 22 Jan 1873, Toronto, Ontario, Canada. SOURCE: WO120 Volume 69 page 17. INDEX # 2779.

Thos MOONEY; pension awarded 25 Jul 1843; residence - Adelaide. SOURCE: WO120 Volume 69 page 17. INDEX # 2780.

7th Regiment of Dragoon Guards

Mich^l CORRIGAN; pension awarded 2 Feb 1820; residence - Charlottetown, Prince Edward Island, Canada; died 10 Jul 1874, Halifax, Nova Scotia, Canada. SOURCE: WO120 Volume 69 page 20. INDEX # 2781.

Willm SMITH; pension awarded 22 Sep 1825; residence - Hobart Town, Australia. SOURCE: WO120 Volume 69 page 20. INDEX # 2782.

Edwd LANDERS; pension awarded 12 May 1824; residence - Prescott, Ontario, Canada; died 18 Mar 1873, London, Ontario, Canada. SOURCE: WO120 Volume 69 page 20. INDEX # 2783.

Mich^l HEALEY; pension awarded 12 Nov 1817; residence - Toronto, Ontario, Canada; died 26 Dec 1873, Toronto, Ontario, Canada. SOURCE: WO120 Volume 69 page 20. INDEX # 2784.

Pat^k MEAGHER; pension awarded 24 Oct 1821; residence - Hobart Town, Australia. SOURCE: WO120 Volume 69 page 20. INDEX # 2785.

Willm ANDERSON; pension awarded 3 Feb 1819; residence - Halifax, Nova Scotia, Canada. SOURCE: WO120 Volume 69 page 20. INDEX # 2786.

And^w MOORE; pension awarded 19 Jun 1822; residence - Bytown, Ontario, Canada; died in 1847. SOURCE: WO120 Volume 69 page 20. INDEX # 2787.

Richd WHEELER; pension awarded 12 Aug 1840; residence - Ostend, Belgium; died 27 Mar 1851. SOURCE: WO120 Volume 69 page 20. INDEX # 2788.

Jno DOWNHAM; pension awarded 14 Jul 1846; residence - Cape of Good Hope, South Africa; died 2 Sep 1848. SOURCE: WO120 Volume 69 page 20. INDEX # 2789.

Jno MAGILL; pension awarded 14 Jul 1846; residence - Cape of Good Hope, South Africa; died 31 Dec 1873, Belfast, Ireland. SOURCE: WO120 Volume 69 page 20. INDEX # 2790.

Saml MOFFATT; pension awarded 14 Sep 1847; residence - Cape of Good Hope, South Africa. SOURCE: WO120 Volume 69 page 20. INDEX # 2791.

Jno NETTLETON; pension awarded 14 Sep 1847; residence - Cape of Good Hope, South Africa. SOURCE: WO120 Volume 69 page 20. INDEX # 2792.

Chas MATTHEWS; pension awarded 28 Mar 1848; residence - Cape of Good Hope, South Africa; died in 1854. SOURCE: WO120 Volume 69 page 23. INDEX # 2793.

1st Regiment of Dragoons

Willm COLVIN; pension awarded 30 Sep 1826; residence - Melbourne, Australia. SOURCE: WO120 Volume 69 page 23. INDEX # 2794.

David PARKINSON; pension awarded 13 Sep 1837; residence - Toronto, Ontario, Canada. SOURCE: WO120 Volume 69 page 23. INDEX # 2795.

Job CLARKE; pension awarded 26 Jun 1839; residence - Sydney. SOURCE: WO120 Volume 69 page 23. INDEX # 2796.

2nd Regiment of Dragoons

John KEY; pension awarded 24 Oct 1821; residence - Toronto, Ontario, Canada; died in 1878. SOURCE: WO120 Volume 69 page 26. INDEX # 2797.

3rd Regiment of Dragoons

David BAIN; pension awarded 11 Jun 1844; residence - Kurnool, India. SOURCE: WO120 Volume 69 page 29. INDEX # 2798.

Thos JOHNSON; pension awarded 11 Oct 1842; residence - Bengal, India. SOURCE: WO120 Volume 69 page 29. INDEX # 2799.

Ja^s BIRCHAM; pension awarded 25 Jun 1844; residence - Kurnool, India; died 10 Sep 1846. SOURCE: WO120 Volume 69 page 29. INDEX # 2800.

Amb^re RODERICK; pension awarded 28 Apr 1841; residence - Bengal, India. SOURCE: WO120 Volume 69 page 29. INDEX # 2801.

Ja^s TAYLOR; pension awarded 28 Apr 1841; residence - Bengal, India. SOURCE: WO120 Volume 69 page 29. INDEX # 2802.

Robt LARKE; pension awarded 27 Sep 1842; residence - Bengal, India. SOURCE: WO120 Volume 69 page 29. INDEX # 2803.

Ja^s DEEGAN; pension awarded 9 Jun 1841; residence - Jamaica. SOURCE: WO120 Volume 69 page 29. INDEX # 2804.

Mich^l MURPHY; pension awarded 11 Mar 1845; residence - Umballa, India. SOURCE: WO120 Volume 69 page 29. INDEX # 2805.

Adam HAYFIELD; pension awarded 9 May 1843; residence - Bengal, India. SOURCE: WO120 Volume 69 page 29. INDEX # 2806.

Thos OBRIEN; pension awarded 12 Sep 1821; residence - Ostend, Belgium; died in 1854. SOURCE: WO120 Volume 69 page 29. INDEX # 2807.

Thos WILGOS; pension awarded 19 May 1818; residence - Palermo, Italy. SOURCE: WO120 Volume 69 page 29. INDEX # 2808.

Saml OSBORNE; pension awarded 13 Jan 1846; residence - Meerut, India. SOURCE: WO120 Volume 69 page 29. INDEX # 2809.

Percival BUTLER; pension awarded 11 Jan 1848; residence - Umballa, India. SOURCE: WO120 Volume 69 page 29. INDEX # 2810.

Wm MITCHELL; pension awarded 25 Jan 1848; residence - Umballa, India. SOURCE: WO120 Volume 69 page 29. INDEX # 2811.

Ed^wd LINFIELD; pension awarded 25 Jan 1848; residence - Umballa, India. SOURCE: WO120 Volume 69 page 29. INDEX # 2812.

Chas J. SWAN; pension awarded 28 Mar 1848; residence - Agra, India; died 9 Mar 1877, E. London. SOURCE: WO120 Volume 69 page 29. INDEX # 2813.

Ambrose BOLT; pension awarded 28 Mar 1848; died 2 Jul 1856. SOURCE: WO120 Volume 69 page 29. INDEX # 2814.

Jno HAWKSWORTH; pension awarded 13 Feb 1849; residence - Landour, India. SOURCE: WO120 Volume 69 page 29. INDEX # 2815.

Wm CLARKE; pension awarded 8 Jan 1850; residence - Umballa, India. SOURCE: WO120 Volume 69 page 29. INDEX # 2816.

WO120 VOLUME 69

3rd Regiment of Dragoons (continued)

Ja^s WEST; pension awarded 8 Jan 1850. SOURCE: WO120 Volume 69 page 29. INDEX # 2817.

Randle STONELEY; pension awarded 8 Jan 1850; residence - Umballa, India. SOURCE: WO120 Volume 69 page 30. INDEX # 2818.

Jno WHITTAKER; pension awarded 14 Jan 1851; residence - Umballa, India. SOURCE: WO120 Volume 69 page 30. INDEX # 2819.

4th Regiment of Dragoons

Ed^{wd} HEALY; pension awarded 20 Jul 1825; residence - Saint John, New Brunswick, Canada; died 19 Apr 1871, Halifax, Nova Scotia, Canada. SOURCE: WO120 Volume 69 page 34. INDEX # 2820.

Willm EDMED; pension awarded 4 Aug 1824; residence - Niagara, Ontario, Canada. SOURCE: WO120 Volume 69 page 34. INDEX # 2821.

Robt COLOLOUGH; pension awarded 23 Jul 1828; residence - Kingston, Ontario, Canada; died 9 Nov 1862, Toronto, Ontario, Canada. SOURCE: WO120 Volume 69 page 34. INDEX # 2822.

Willm MOORE; pension awarded 28 Jul 1841; residence - Sydney. SOURCE: WO120 Volume 69 page 34. INDEX # 2823.

Chas HUCKSTEPP; pension awarded 10 May 1842; residence - Bombay, India; died 17 Aug 1849. SOURCE: WO120 Volume 69 page 34. INDEX # 2824.

Alex^r Ja^s ROSE; pension awarded 5 Aug 1819; residence - Bombay, India; died 19 May 1860. SOURCE: WO120 Volume 69 page 34. INDEX # 2825.

Pat^k PURCELL; pension awarded 8 Jun 1816; residence - Bombay, India; died 29 Dec 1847. SOURCE: WO120 Volume 69 page 34. INDEX # 2826.

Wm LAWSON; pension awarded 25 Aug 1841; residence - Bombay, India. SOURCE: WO120 Volume 69 page 34. INDEX # 2827.

5th Regiment of Dragoons

Ja^s BYRNES; pension awarded 7 Jun 1802; residence - Sydney. SOURCE: WO120 Volume 69 page 36. INDEX # 2828.

6th Regiment of Dragoons

H^y PAYNE; pension awarded 7 Sep 1814; residence - Kingston, Ontario, Canada; died 12 May 1857. SOURCE: WO120 Volume 69 page 37. INDEX # 2829.

Ja^s FOSTER; pension awarded 5 Jun 1817; residence - Montreal, Quebec, Canada; died in 1846. SOURCE: WO120 Volume 69 page 37. INDEX # 2830.

Wm FIDDES; pension awarded 10 Feb 1841; residence - Montreal, Quebec, Canada; died 27 May 1845. SOURCE: WO120 Volume 69 page 37. INDEX # 2831.

Robt GLASS; pension awarded 8 Aug 1843; residence - Jamaica. SOURCE: WO120 Volume 69 page 37. INDEX # 2832.

Alex^r MEESSON; pension awarded 5 Jun 1817; residence - Saint Johns, Quebec, Canada. SOURCE: WO120 Volume 69 page 37. INDEX # 2833.

Dav^d LOWRY; pension awarded 16 Dec 1840; residence - Quebec, Quebec, Canada. SOURCE: WO120 Volume 69 page 37. INDEX # 2834.

Alex^r LANG; pension awarded 10 Sep 1844; residence - Woolford. SOURCE: WO120 Volume 69 page 37. INDEX # 2835.

Ed^w MEARE; pension awarded 22 Nov 1842; residence - Montreal, Quebec, Canada; died 2 Jun 1874, Toronto, Ontario, Canada. SOURCE: WO120 Volume 69 page 37. INDEX # 2836.

BRITISH ARMY PENSIONERS ABROAD

7th Regiment of Dragoons

Jos^h OSBORNE; pension awarded 9 Sep 1840; residence - Montreal, Quebec, Canada. SOURCE: WO120 Volume 69 page 38. INDEX # 2837.

Willm CLOSE; pension awarded 26 Nov 1817; residence - New South Wales, Australia. SOURCE: WO120 Volume 69 page 38. INDEX # 2838.

Robt FRITH; pension awarded 29 Aug 1821; residence - New South Wales, Australia. SOURCE: WO120 Volume 69 page 38. INDEX # 2839.

Robt HOGG; pension awarded 22 Dec 1824; residence - New South Wales, Australia; died 6 Mar 1854. SOURCE: WO120 Volume 69 page 38. INDEX # 2840.

Thos GRINDLEY; pension awarded 11 Jul 1843; residence - Toronto, Ontario, Canada. SOURCE: WO120 Volume 69 page 38. INDEX # 2841.

Ge^o BOXALL; pension awarded 9 Sep 1840; residence - Montreal, Quebec, Canada. SOURCE: WO120 Volume 69 page 38. INDEX # 2842.

Thos GORDON; pension awarded 8 Sep 1841; residence - Montreal, Quebec, Canada; died 6 Jul 1849. SOURCE: WO120 Volume 69 page 38. INDEX # 2843.

Ja^s GARRETY; pension awarded 27 Sep 1842; residence - Montreal, Quebec, Canada. SOURCE: WO120 Volume 69 page 38. INDEX # 2844.

Saml HOLLOWAY; pension awarded 13 Dec 1837; residence - Montreal, Quebec, Canada; died 7 Jun 1849. SOURCE: WO120 Volume 69 page 38. INDEX # 2845.

Jno JACKSON; pension awarded 27 Sep 1842; residence - Toronto, Ontario, Canada. SOURCE: WO120 Volume 69 page 38. INDEX # 2846.

Thos LEGGATT; pension awarded 12 Sep 1838; residence - Sydney; died 30 Apr 1846. SOURCE: WO120 Volume 69 page 38. INDEX # 2847.

Henry DRAKE; pension awarded 13 Dec 1837; residence - Calais, France. SOURCE: WO120 Volume 69 page 38. INDEX # 2848.

8th Regiment of Dragoons

Robt HICKS; pension awarded 13 Oct 1825; residence - Quebec, Quebec, Canada. SOURCE: WO120 Volume 69 page 39. INDEX # 2849.

Robt ACRES; pension awarded 10 Nov 1841; residence - Hobart Town, Australia; died 24 Oct 1846. SOURCE: WO120 Volume 69 page 39. INDEX # 2850.

Ja^s WALL; pension awarded 4 Aug 1806; residence - Smiths Falls, Ontario, Canada; died in 1846. SOURCE: WO120 Volume 69 page 39. INDEX # 2851.

Hugh ROSS; pension awarded 25 Nov 1823; residence - New South Wales, Australia. SOURCE: WO120 Volume 69 page 39. INDEX # 2852.

Jno MCNIFFE; pension awarded 25 Sep 1822; residence - Bengal, India; died 5 Oct 1849. SOURCE: WO120 Volume 69 page 39. INDEX # 2853.

Ja^s ANDERSON; pension awarded 1 Jul 1819; residence - Prescott, Ontario, Canada. SOURCE: WO120 Volume 69 page 39. INDEX # 2854.

Richd LAMBERT; pension awarded 23 Sep 1813; residence - Cape of Good Hope, South Africa; died in 1849. SOURCE: WO120 Volume 69 page 39. INDEX # 2855.

Jon^n WILD; pension awarded 25 Nov 1840; residence Jamaica. SOURCE: Volume 69 page 39. INDEX # 2856.

Saml LESLIE; pension awarded 12 May 1820; residence - Toronto, Ontario, Canada. SOURCE: WO120 Volume 69 page 39. INDEX # 2857.

9th Regiment of Dragoons

Ja^s DARBY; pension awarded 24 Oct 1821; residence - Montreal, Quebec, Canada. SOURCE: WO120 Volume 69 page 40. INDEX # 2858.

Saml COAKES; pension awarded 13 Jul 1831; residence - Toronto, Ontario, Canada; died 26 Jul 1853. SOURCE: WO120 Volume 69 page 40. INDEX # 2859.

9th Regiment of Dragoons (continued)

Alexr MCGEE; pension awarded 3 Feb 1819; residence - Bytown, Ontario, Canada; died in 1848. SOURCE: WO120 Volume 69 page 40. INDEX # 2860.

Robt FITZSIMMONS; pension awarded 7 Feb 1811; residence - Perth, Ontario, Canada. SOURCE: WO120 Volume 69 page 40. INDEX # 2861.

John BRADY; pension awarded 28 Jun 1815; residence - Montreal, Quebec, Canada. SOURCE: WO120 Volume 69 page 40. INDEX # 2862.

John LEVICK; pension awarded 11 Nov 1838; residence - Barbados; died 24 Jan 1871. SOURCE: WO120 Volume 69 page 40. INDEX # 2863.

Andw ROARKE; pension awarded 14 Sep 1809; residence - Montreal, Quebec, Canada; died 31 Jul 1856. SOURCE: WO120 Volume 69 page 40. INDEX # 2864.

Chas de GURK; pension awarded 12 Sep 1821; residence - Paris, France. SOURCE: WO120 Volume 69 page 40. INDEX # 2865.

Geo WALKER; pension awarded 9 May 1854; residence - Umballa, India. SOURCE: WO120 Volume 69 page 40. INDEX # 2866.

Richd HAYES; pension awarded 11 Mar 1856. SOURCE: WO120 Volume 69 page 40. INDEX # 2867.

Thos LETT; pension awarded 18 Mar 1856. SOURCE: WO120 Volume 69 page 40. INDEX # 2868.

10th Regiment of Dragoons

Geo JACKSON; pension awarded 15 Dec 1819; residence - St. Johns; died in Aug 1849. SOURCE: WO120 Volume 69 page 45. INDEX # 2869.

11th Regiment of Dragoons

Willm DODD; pension awarded 26 Aug 1825; residence - Montreal, Quebec, Canada. SOURCE: WO120 Volume 69 page 46. INDEX # 2870.

Edwd GRIMES; pension awarded 19 Jul 1826; residence - Sydney; died 12 May 1854. SOURCE: WO120 Volume 69 page 46. INDEX # 2871.

John RYE; pension awarded 26 Nov 1824; residence - Bengal, India; died 8 Nov 1847. SOURCE: WO120 Volume 69 page 46. INDEX # 2872.

Willm BROADHEAD; pension awarded 10 Jun 1835; residence - Bengal, India; died 2 Aug 1856. SOURCE: WO120 Volume 69 page 46. INDEX # 2873.

Hutley BROWN; pension awarded 11 Aug 1830; residence - Charlottetown, Prince Edward Island, Canada. SOURCE: WO120 Volume 69 page 46. INDEX # 2874.

Richd WILKINS; pension awarded 27 Jun 1838; residence - Bengal, India; died 11 Aug 1856. SOURCE: WO120 Volume 69 page 46. INDEX # 2875.

Chas EARLE; pension awarded 10 Dec 1834; residence - Bengal, India. SOURCE: WO120 Volume 69 page 46. INDEX # 2876.

John GOODING; pension awarded 27 Jun 1838; residence - Bengal, India. SOURCE: WO120 Volume 69 page 46. INDEX # 2877.

Josh CHAPMAN; pension awarded 27 Jun 1838; residence - Bengal, India. SOURCE: WO120 Volume 69 page 46. INDEX # 2878.

Spatter COUSINS; pension awarded 12 Jan 1833; residence - Bengal, India; died 27 Jan 1846. SOURCE: WO120 Volume 69 page 46. INDEX # 2879.

Willm BALDWIN; pension awarded 8 Aug 1838; residence - Bengal, India. SOURCE: WO120 Volume 69 page 46. INDEX # 2880.

Silvr PITCHELLO; pension awarded 12 Jun 1833; residence - Bengal, India; died 20 Feb 1849. SOURCE: WO120 Volume 69 page 46. INDEX # 2881.

Benjn HIGH; pension awarded 27 Jun 1838; residence - Bengal, India. SOURCE: WO120 Volume 69 page 46. INDEX # 2882.

Danl MATTHEWS; pension awarded 4 Aug 1824; residence - Montreal, Quebec, Canada. SOURCE: WO120 Volume 69 page 46. INDEX # 2883.

11th Regiment of Dragoons (continued)

Thos FERGUSON; pension awarded 27 Jun 1838; residence - Bengal, India; died 26 Feb 1846. SOURCE: WO120 Volume 69 page 46. INDEX # 2884.

John MCKINLEY; pension awarded 27 Jun 1838; residence - Bengal, India. SOURCE: WO120 Volume 69 page 46. INDEX # 2885.

Robt FOSTER; pension awarded 27 Jun 1838; residence - Bengal, India. SOURCE: WO120 Volume 69 page 46. INDEX # 2886.

Wm BARKER; pension awarded 14 Jun 1837; residence - Bengal, India. SOURCE: WO120 Volume 69 page 46. INDEX # 2887.

Larva BASLLIQUE; pension awarded 13 Jan 1830; residence - Bengal, India. SOURCE: WO120 Volume 69 page 46. INDEX # 2888.

12th Regiment of Dragoons

Robt KEELER; pension awarded 15 Dec 1819; residence - Quebec, Quebec, Canada. SOURCE: WO120 Volume 69 page 47. INDEX # 2889.

Thos LODGE; pension awarded 29 Aug 1821; residence - Newfoundland, Canada. SOURCE: WO120 Volume 69 page 47. INDEX # 2890.

Geo ARMSTRONG; pension awarded 7 Sep 1814; residence - Niagara, Ontario, Canada; died 7 Apr 1859. SOURCE: WO120 Volume 69 page 47. INDEX # 2891.

Ephram HARPER; pension awarded 23 Sep 1818; residence - Perth, Ontario, Canada. SOURCE: WO120 Volume 69 page 47. INDEX # 2892.

John WAGSTAFF; pension awarded 27 Sep 1856. SOURCE: WO120 Volume 69 page 47. INDEX # 2893.

13th Regiment of Dragoons

Hy ROONEY; pension awarded 13 Oct 1814; residence - Penetanguishene, Ontario, Canada; died 10 Apr 1866, Hamilton, Ontario, Canada. SOURCE: WO120 Volume 69 page 48. INDEX # 2894.

John HANAN; pension awarded 5 Jun 1817; residence - New South Wales, Australia. SOURCE: WO120 Volume 69 page 48. INDEX # 2895.

John CORBETT; pension awarded 26 Aug 1840; residence - Jamaica. SOURCE: WO120 Volume 69 page 48. INDEX # 2896.

Thos HARLEY; pension awarded 25 Apr 1817; residence - New South Wales, Australia. SOURCE: WO120 Volume 69 page 48. INDEX # 2897.

Thos SKIPPON; pension awarded 25 Mar 1819; residence - London; died 5 Jan 1857. SOURCE: WO120 Volume 69 page 48. INDEX # 2898.

John HEPWOOD; pension awarded 23 Sep 1840; residence - Madras, India. SOURCE: WO120 Volume 69 page 48. INDEX # 2899.

Thos HALL; pension awarded 6 Jun 1823; residence - Madras, India. SOURCE: WO120 Volume 69 page 48. INDEX # 2900.

Richd THOMPSON; pension awarded 4 Aug 1824; residence - Madras, India; died 19 Dec 1852. SOURCE: WO120 Volume 69 page 48. INDEX # 2901.

Thos PARKINGTON; pension awarded 21 May 1828; residence - Madras, India; died 12 Dec 1847. SOURCE: WO120 Volume 69 page 48. INDEX # 2902.

John HOOPER; pension awarded 21 May 1828; residence - Madras, India. SOURCE: WO120 Volume 69 page 48. INDEX # 2903.

Willm LUSCUTT; pension awarded 9 Aug 1837; residence - Madras, India. SOURCE: WO120 Volume 69 page 48. INDEX # 2904.

Robt GREENWOOD; pension awarded 27 Sep 1840; residence - Madras, India; died 26 May 1878. SOURCE: WO120 Volume 69 page 48. INDEX # 2905.

Isaac PEARCE; pension awarded 27 Sep 1840; residence - Madras, India; died 3 Feb 1853. SOURCE: WO120 Volume 69 page 48. INDEX # 2906.

13th Regiment of Dragoons

John HORAN; pension awarded 27 Sep 1840; residence - Madras, India; died 28 Oct 1855. SOURCE: WO120 Volume 69 page 48. INDEX # 2907.

H^y WOODS; pension awarded 27 Sep 1840; residence - Madras, India. SOURCE: WO120 Volume 69 page 48. INDEX # 2908.

John CHERRINGTON; pension awarded 21 May 1828; residence - Madras, India; died 18 May 1855. SOURCE: WO120 Volume 69 page 48. INDEX # 2909.

Philip DORNHOFFER; pension awarded 21 Jun 1826; residence - Madras, India; died 17 Oct 1850. SOURCE: WO120 Volume 69 page 48. INDEX # 2910.

Thos EVANS; pension awarded 20 Nov 1839; residence - Madras, India. SOURCE: WO120 Volume 69 page 48. INDEX # 2911.

Robt GUTTERSON; pension awarded 20 Nov 1839; residence - Madras, India. SOURCE: WO120 Volume 69 page 48. INDEX # 2912.

Ja^s REYNOLDS; pension awarded 23 Sep 1840; residence - Madras, India. SOURCE: WO120 Volume 69 page 48. INDEX # 2913.

Thos MCCRACKEN; pension awarded 23 Sep 1840; residence - Madras, India; died 28 Apr 1849. SOURCE: WO120 Volume 69 page 49. INDEX # 2914.

Willm BEALE; pension awarded 12 Dec 1838; residence - Madras, India; died 30 Aug 1850. SOURCE: WO120 Volume 69 page 49. INDEX # 2915.

Abr^m WARD; pension awarded 20 Nov 1839; residence - Madras, India. SOURCE: WO120 Volume 69 page 49. INDEX # 2916.

Saml ASHFIELD; pension awarded 23 Sep 1840; residence - Madras, India; died 24 Jul 1853. SOURCE: WO120 Volume 69 page 49. INDEX # 2917.

Richd FLETCHER; pension awarded 23 Sep 1840; residence - Madras, India; died 18 May 1855. SOURCE: WO120 Volume 69 page 49. INDEX # 2918.

Willm ADIE; pension awarded 23 Sep 1840; residence - Madras, India; died 2 Dec 1848. SOURCE: WO120 Volume 69 page 49. INDEX # 2919.

Richd CRIPPEN; pension awarded 23 Sep 1840; residence - Madras, India; died 23 Jan 1864, Madras, India. SOURCE: WO120 Volume 69 page 49. INDEX # 2920.

Ja^s CARROLL; pension awarded 20 Nov 1839; residence - Madras, India; died 2 Jun 1864. SOURCE: WO120 Volume 69 page 49. INDEX # 2921.

Thos WATSON; pension awarded 20 Nov 1839; residence - Madras, India; died 29 Oct 1846. SOURCE: WO120 Volume 69 page 49. INDEX # 2922.

Maur^e KEATINGE; pension awarded 23 Sep 1840; residence - Madras, India. SOURCE: WO120 Volume 69 page 49. INDEX # 2923.

John BURROWS; pension awarded 23 Sep 1840; residence - Madras, India; died 7 Jun 1853. SOURCE: WO120 Volume 69 page 49. INDEX # 2924.

Job HAYWOOD; pension awarded 23 Sep 1840; residence - Madras, India. SOURCE: WO120 Volume 69 page 49. INDEX # 2925.

Ja^s GARVEY; pension awarded 23 Oct 1838; residence - Madras, India; died 5 Jun 1855. SOURCE: WO120 Volume 69 page 49. INDEX # 2926.

John PIGG; pension awarded 16 Dec 1836; residence - Madras, India; died 11 Jul 1855. SOURCE: WO120 Volume 69 page 49. INDEX # 2927.

Willm MILLER; pension awarded 10 Aug 1836; residence - Madras, India. SOURCE: WO120 Volume 69 page 49. INDEX # 2928.

Thos BODELL; pension awarded 23 Sep 1840; residence - Madras, India; died 20 Dec 1853. SOURCE: WO120 Volume 69 page 49. INDEX # 2929.

John ROBERTS; pension awarded 23 Sep 1840; residence - Madras, India. SOURCE: WO120 Volume 69 page 49. INDEX # 2930.

Evan PROBERT; pension awarded 23 Sep 1840; residence - Madras, India; died 15 Feb 1855. SOURCE: WO120 Volume 69 page 49. INDEX # 2931.

Richd JOHNSON; pension awarded 23 Sep 1840; residence - Madras, India; died 4 Sep 1876. SOURCE: WO120 Volume 69 page 49. INDEX # 2932.

BRITISH ARMY PENSIONERS ABROAD

13th Regiment of Dragoons (continued)

John PRICE; pension awarded 23 Sep 1840; residence - Madras, India. SOURCE: WO120 Volume 69 page 49. INDEX # 2933.

John COLE; pension awarded 23 Sep 1840; residence - Madras, India; died 2 Oct 1849. SOURCE: WO120 Volume 69 page 49. INDEX # 2934.

Saml CROWE; pension awarded 16 Dec 1836; residence - Madras, India. SOURCE: WO120 Volume 69 page 49. INDEX # 2935.

Ja^s JONES; pension awarded 12 Dec 1838; residence - Madras, India; died 14 Feb 1848. SOURCE: WO120 Volume 69 page 49. INDEX # 2936.

Dav^d WATERS; pension awarded 20 Nov 1839; residence - Madras, India. SOURCE: WO120 Volume 69 page 49. INDEX # 2937.

Edwd HAGAN; pension awarded 23 Sep 1840; residence - Madras, India. SOURCE: WO120 Volume 69 page 49. INDEX # 2938.

Alex^r MCDONALD; pension awarded 5 Jul 1814; residence - Toronto, Ontario, Canada. SOURCE: WO120 Volume 69 page 49. INDEX # 2939.

Jos^h CLARKE; pension awarded 9 Aug 1837; residence - Madras, India. SOURCE: WO120 Volume 69 page 49. INDEX # 2940.

Charles POWELL; pension awarded 20 Nov 1839; residence - Madras, India; died 28 Apr 1849. SOURCE: WO120 Volume 69 page 49. INDEX # 2941.

Willm WATSON; pension awarded 20 Nov 1839; residence - Madras, India; died 20 Dec 1852. SOURCE: WO120 Volume 69 page 49. INDEX # 2942.

Robt MURDOCK; pension awarded 23 Sep 1840; residence - Madras, India. SOURCE: WO120 Volume 69 page 49. INDEX # 2943.

Benjn JOHNSON; pension awarded 9 Aug 1837; residence - Madras, India; died 12 Apr 1856, Oxford, Staff. SOURCE: WO120 Volume 69 page 49. INDEX # 2944.

Marshall FISHER; pension awarded 20 Nov 1839; residence - Madras, India. SOURCE: WO120 Volume 69 page 49. INDEX # 2945.

Willm KILLMAIN; pension awarded 23 Sep 1840; residence - Madras, India; died 15 Nov 1870. SOURCE: WO120 Volume 69 page 49. INDEX # 2946.

John WHITE; pension awarded 23 Sep 1840; residence - Madras, India. SOURCE: WO120 Volume 69 page 49. INDEX # 2947.

Charles DICKINS; pension awarded 13 Nov 1833; residence - Madras, India. SOURCE: WO120 Volume 69 page 49. INDEX # 2948.

John PARTRIDGE; pension awarded 23 Sep 1840; residence - Madras, India; died 23 Aug 1870. SOURCE: WO120 Volume 69 page 49. INDEX # 2949.

John CUNNINGTON; pension awarded 23 Sep 1840; residence - Madras, India. SOURCE: WO120 Volume 69 page 49. INDEX # 2950.

Ja^s TAYLOR; pension awarded 23 Sep 1840; residence - Madras, India; died 9 Feb 1855. SOURCE: WO120 Volume 69 page 49. INDEX # 2951.

Guiseppe CANDILLO; pension awarded 23 Sep 1840; residence - Palermo, Italy. SOURCE: WO120 Volume 69 page 49. INDEX # 2952.

14th Regiment of Dragoons

Robt FORSTER; pension awarded 20 Mar 1795; residence - Toronto, Ontario, Canada; died 25 Aug 1853. SOURCE: WO120 Volume 69 page 51. INDEX # 2953.

Ja^s GRIFFIN; pension awarded 3 Jun 1802; residence - Charlottetown, Prince Edward Island, Canada; died 5 Jan 1851. SOURCE: WO120 Volume 69 page 51. INDEX # 2954.

Chas MENDS; pension awarded 8 Feb 1835; residence - South Australia, Australia. SOURCE: WO120 Volume 69 page 51. INDEX # 2955.

Benjn LEE; pension awarded 4 Dec 1822; residence - New South Wales, Australia. SOURCE: WO120 Volume 69 page 51. INDEX # 2956.

Wm WAINSBOROUGH; pension awarded 13 Oct 1814; residence - Toronto, Ontario, Canada; died 21 Aug 1857. SOURCE: WO120 Volume 69 page 51. INDEX # 2957.

14th Regiment of Dragoons (continued)

Wm ELLIOTT; pension awarded 28 Apr 1846; residence - Kirkie, India; died 8 Jan 1861. SOURCE: WO120 Volume 69 page 51. INDEX # 2958.

Mich^l MCCLUSKY; pension awarded 10 Feb 1852. SOURCE: WO120 Volume 69 page 51. INDEX # 2959.

John MARKOE; pension awarded 22 Mar 1853; residence - Meerut, India. SOURCE: WO120 Volume 69 page 51. INDEX # 2960.

Ja^s CARROLL; pension awarded 9 May 1854; residence - Meerut, India. SOURCE: WO120 Volume 69 page 51. INDEX # 2961.

Robert BRIGHAM; pension awarded 8 May 1855; residence - Meerut, India. SOURCE: WO120 Volume 69 page 51. INDEX # 2962.

James TOOLE; pension awarded 8 May 1855. SOURCE: WO120 Volume 69 page 51. INDEX # 2963.

Law WILSON; pension awarded 18 Mar 1856. SOURCE: WO120 Volume 69 page 51. INDEX # 2964.

15th Regiment of Dragoons

John ROSE; pension awarded 21 Nov 1821; residence - Van Diemen's Land, Australia; died 4 Oct 1850. SOURCE: WO120 Volume 69 page 52. INDEX # 2965.

Wm EDWARDS; pension awarded 8 Jul 1845; residence - Bangalore, India; died 5 Jan 1870. SOURCE: WO120 Volume 69 page 52. INDEX # 2966.

Law^e BRIDE; pension awarded 24 Oct 1843; residence - Madras, India; died 31 Aug 1876. SOURCE: WO120 Volume 69 page 52. INDEX # 2967.

Geo^e SALMON; pension awarded 24 Oct 1843; residence - Madras, India; died 16 Aug 1855. SOURCE: WO120 Volume 69 page 52. INDEX # 2968.

Wm BAKER; pension awarded 25 May 1847; residence - Bangalore, India; died 13 Jul 1877. SOURCE: WO120 Volume 69 page 52. INDEX # 2969.

Jeremiah RYAN; pension awarded 25 May 1847; residence - Bangalore, India. SOURCE: WO120 Volume 69 page 52. INDEX # 2970.

Ja^s FERGUSON; pension awarded 25 Apr 1848; residence - Bangalore, India ; died 11 Jan 1849. SOURCE: WO120 Volume 69 page 52. INDEX # 2971.

Ja^s JOHNSON; pension awarded 24 Apr 1849; residence - Bangalore, India. SOURCE: WO120 Volume 69 page 52. INDEX # 2972.

Walter BURROUGHS; pension awarded 24 Apr 1849; residence - Bangalore, India; died 7 Feb 1882, Madras, India. SOURCE: WO120 Volume 69 page 52. INDEX # 2973.

Wm TWYMAN; pension awarded 12 Mar 1850; residence - Bangalore, India. SOURCE: WO120 Volume 69 page 52. INDEX # 2974.

Hen^y Arth^r TAYLOR; pension awarded 8 Apr 1851; residence - Bangalore, India; died 12 Sep 1875. SOURCE: WO120 Volume 69 page 52. INDEX # 2975.

Pat^k FLATTERY; pension awarded 8 Apr 1851; residence - Bangalore, India. SOURCE: WO120 Volume 69 page 52. INDEX # 2976.

Pat^k HEANY; pension awarded 8 Apr 1851; residence - Madras, India; died 7 Jan 1857. SOURCE: WO120 Volume 69 page 52. INDEX # 2977.

Ja^s MUIR; pension awarded 8 Apr 1851; residence - Bangalore, India; died 21 May 1863. SOURCE: WO120 Volume 69 page 52. INDEX # 2978.

John SAMWAYS; pension awarded 8 Apr 1851; residence - Madras, India. SOURCE: WO120 Volume 69 page 52. INDEX # 2979.

John DENEHY; pension awarded 9 Mar 1852. SOURCE: WO120 Volume 69 page 52. INDEX # 2980.

Thos LEONARD; pension awarded 9 Mar 1852; died 6 Aug 1871. SOURCE: WO120 Volume 69 page 52. INDEX # 2981.

John REILLY; pension awarded 9 Mar 1852; residence - Fort St. George, Madras, India; died 17 Mar 1855. SOURCE: WO120 Volume 69 page 52. INDEX # 2982.

Jos^h DAVIS; pension awarded 9 Mar 1852; residence - Bangalore, India. SOURCE: WO120 Volume 69 page 52. INDEX # 2983.

And^w EALEY; pension awarded 9 Mar 1852; residence - Bangalore, India; died 10 Feb 1872, Madras, India. SOURCE: WO120 Volume 69 page 52. INDEX # 2984.

15th Regiment of Dragoons (continued)

John GUY; pension awarded 9 Mar 1852; residence - Bangalore, India. SOURCE: WO120 Volume 69 page 52. INDEX # 2985.

Wm HAMILTON; pension awarded 9 Mar 1852; residence - Bangalore, India. SOURCE: WO120 Volume 69 page 52. INDEX # 2986.

Thos SCANLAN; pension awarded 9 Mar 1852; residence - Bangalore, India. SOURCE: WO120 Volume 69 page 52. INDEX # 2987.

John LILLYWHITE; pension awarded 8 Feb 1853; died 10 Jan 1871. SOURCE: WO120 Volume 69 page 52. INDEX # 2988.

Mathew CLAPHAM; pension awarded 8 Feb 1853; residence - Bangalore, India; died 16 May 1879, Madras, India. SOURCE: WO120 Volume 69 page 52. INDEX # 2989.

Thos COLE; pension awarded 8 Feb 1853; residence - Bangalore, India; died 8 Sep 1877. SOURCE: WO120 Volume 69 page 52. INDEX # 2990.

Wm COREY; pension awarded 8 Feb 1853; residence - Bangalore, India; died 17 Jan 1881, Bombay, India. SOURCE: WO120 Volume 69 page 52. INDEX # 2991.

Moses HARDY; pension awarded 8 Feb 1853; residence - Bangalore, India. SOURCE: WO120 Volume 69 page 52. INDEX # 2992.

John THEAKSTON; pension awarded 8 Feb 1853; residence - Bangalore, India. SOURCE: WO120 Volume 69 page 52. INDEX # 2993.

Ja^s WICKSON; pension awarded 8 Feb 1853; residence - Madras, India; died 22 May 1854. SOURCE: WO120 Volume 69 page 52. INDEX # 2994.

Robt WYNN; pension awarded 8 Feb 1853; residence - Bangalore, India. SOURCE: WO120 Volume 69 page 52. INDEX # 2995.

Mich^l DILLON; pension awarded 8 Mar 1853; residence - Bangalore, India; died 11 Mar 1874, Madras, India. SOURCE: WO120 Volume 69 page 52. INDEX # 2996.

John BRAILSFORD; pension awarded 11 Apr 1854; residence - Bangalore, India. SOURCE: WO120 Volume 69 page 52. INDEX # 2997.

Wm REDFORD; pension awarded 11 Apr 1854; residence - Bangalore, India; died 17 Aug 1873, Madras, India. SOURCE: WO120 Volume 69 page 52. INDEX # 2998.

16th Regiment of Dragoons

Ja^s RAINEY; pension awarded 12 May 1841; residence - Bengal, India; died 11 Jan 1848. SOURCE: WO120 Volume 69 page 53. INDEX # 2999.

David WADSWORTH; pension awarded 11 Oct 1842; residence - Meerut, India; died 24 May 1850. SOURCE: WO120 Volume 69 page 53. INDEX # 3000.

Pat^k CUNNINGHAM; pension awarded 26 Aug 1825; residence - Launceston, Australia. SOURCE: WO120 Volume 69 page 53. INDEX # 3001.

Jos^h BARBER; pension awarded 8 Nov 1826; residence - Toronto, Ontario, Canada. SOURCE: WO120 Volume 69 page 53. INDEX # 3002.

Wm CHAPMAN; pension awarded 25 Jun 1846; residence - Meerut, India. SOURCE: WO120 Volume 69 page 53. INDEX # 3003.

Thos SMITH; pension awarded 27 Jun 1838; residence - Bengal, India. SOURCE: WO120 Volume 69 page 53. INDEX # 3004.

Erwin ARMSTRONG; pension awarded 18 Jun 1828; residence - Montreal, Quebec, Canada; died 18 Jul 1853. SOURCE: WO120 Volume 69 page 53. INDEX # 3005.

Hugh BROWN; pension awarded 27 Jun 1838; residence - Bengal, India; died 24 Aug 1852. SOURCE: WO120 Volume 69 page 53. INDEX # 3006.

Richd LEECH; pension awarded 15 Jun 1837; residence - Bengal, India. SOURCE: WO120 Volume 69 page 53. INDEX # 3007.

Thos RACEY; pension awarded 9 Mar 1836; residence - Bengal, India. SOURCE: WO120 Volume 69 page 53. INDEX # 3008.

Richd MURRAY; pension awarded 10 Dec 1836; residence - Bengal, India; died 11 Jan 1872, Dublin. SOURCE: WO120 Volume 69 page 53. INDEX # 3009.

WO120 VOLUME 69

16th Regiment of Dragoons (continued)

John HEYLOTT; pension awarded 27 Jun 1838; residence - Bengal, India. SOURCE: WO120 Volume 69 page 53. INDEX # 3010.
Thos DIXON; pension awarded 23 Aug 1837; residence - Toronto, Ontario, Canada ; died 5 Oct 1856. SOURCE: WO120 Volume 69 page 53. INDEX # 3011.
Jos^h GRIFFITHS; pension awarded 27 Jun 1838; residence - Bengal, India. SOURCE: WO120 Volume 69 page 53. INDEX # 3012.
Saml RODGERS; pension awarded 27 Jun 1838; residence - Bengal, India; died 12 Aug 1853. SOURCE: WO120 Volume 69 page 53. INDEX # 3013.
Thos HOPWOOD; pension awarded 16 Aug 1837; residence - Bengal, India; died 24 Dec 1854. SOURCE: WO120 Volume 69 page 53. INDEX # 3014.
John YOUNG; pension awarded 16 Jan 1837; residence - Bengal, India; died 17 Feb 1851. SOURCE: WO120 Volume 69 page 53. INDEX # 3015.
Robt HALL; pension awarded 11 Apr 1843; residence - Meerut, India. SOURCE: WO120 Volume 69 page 53. INDEX # 3016.
Willm DAILEY; pension awarded 12 Feb 1817; residence - Ostend, Belgium. SOURCE: WO120 Volume 69 page 53. INDEX # 3017.
Robt DURANT; pension awarded 23 Jun 1846; residence - Camp Meerut, India. SOURCE: WO120 Volume 69 page 53. INDEX # 3018.
H^y WILSON; pension awarded 27 Jan 1846; residence - Meerut, India; died 9 Oct 1847. SOURCE: WO120 Volume 69 page 54. INDEX # 3019.

17th Regiment of Dragoons

Matt^w COLLINS; pension awarded 7 Mar 1803; residence - Canada; died 13 Aug 1856. SOURCE: WO120 Volume 69 page 55. INDEX # 3020.
Thos MALLON; pension awarded 17 Dec 1823; residence - Montreal, Quebec, Canada. SOURCE: WO120 Volume 69 page 55. INDEX # 3021.

18th Regiment of Dragoons

Pat^k MAGUIRE; pension awarded 12 Sep 1821; residence - Bytown, Ontario, Canada. SOURCE: WO120 Volume 69 page 56. INDEX # 3022.
Robt LAING; pension awarded 27 Sep 1814; residence - Toronto, Ontario, Canada; died 9 May 1870. SOURCE: WO120 Volume 69 page 56. INDEX # 3023.
Maurice MCCARTHY; pension awarded 30 Oct 1816; residence - Sydney; died in 1847. SOURCE: WO120 Volume 69 page 56. INDEX # 3024.
Henry VINCENT; pension awarded 19 Sep 1821; died 6 May 1869. SOURCE: WO120 Volume 69 page 56. INDEX # 3025.

19th Regiment of Dragoons

John HIGGINS; pension awarded 11 May 1836; residence - Quebec, Canada. SOURCE: WO120 Volume 69 page 57. INDEX # 3026.
Ja^s OHAGAN; pension awarded 10 Dec 1817; residence - St. Johns. SOURCE: WO120 Volume 69 page 57. INDEX # 3027.
Robt ROBERTS; pension awarded 13 Sep 1820; residence - Toronto, Ontario, Canada; died 4 May 1856, Hamilton, Ontario, Canada. SOURCE: WO120 Volume 69 page 57. INDEX # 3028.
Wm ROBSON; pension awarded 10 Dec 1817; residence - Toronto, Ontario, Canada; died 18 Dec 1847. SOURCE: WO120 Volume 69 page 57. INDEX # 3029.
Wm MORRISON; pension awarded 29 Nov 1814; residence - London. SOURCE: WO120 Volume 69 page 57. INDEX # 3030.
John COX; pension awarded 12 May 1819; residence - Perth, Ontario, Canada; died 29 May 1853. SOURCE: WO120 Volume 69 page 57. INDEX # 3031.

21st Regiment of Dragoons

Geo^e BRITTON; pension awarded 23 Sep 1818; residence - Cape of Good Hope, South Africa. SOURCE: WO120 Volume 69 page 59. INDEX # 3032.

Wm TURLEY; pension awarded 7 Jun 1820; residence - New South Wales, Australia; died in Sep 1852. SOURCE: WO120 Volume 69 page 59. INDEX # 3033.

22nd Regiment of Dragoons

John LEECH; pension awarded 26 Aug 1819; residence - Madras, India. SOURCE: WO120 Volume 69 page 60. INDEX # 3034.

23rd Regiment of Dragoons

Willm HALL; pension awarded 5 Jun 1817; residence - New South Wales, Australia; died in Jun 1850. SOURCE: WO120 Volume 69 page 61. INDEX # 3035.

Ja^s SIMPSON; pension awarded 29 Sep 1819; residence - Bytown, Ontario, Canada; died in 1848. SOURCE: WO120 Volume 69 page 61. INDEX # 3036.

24th Regiment of Dragoons

Ja^s HOLMAN; pension awarded 11 Nov 1817; residence - London; died 16 Feb 1871. SOURCE: WO120 Volume 69 page 62. INDEX # 3037.

John SHIPP; pension awarded 11 Nov 1817; residence - Toronto, Ontario, Canada; died 18 Apr 1864. SOURCE: WO120 Volume 69 page 62. INDEX # 3038.

Thos WRIGHT; pension awarded 15 Dec 1819; residence - New South Wales, Australia. SOURCE: WO120 Volume 69 page 62. INDEX # 3039.

25th Regiment of Dragoons

H^y BEAUMONT; pension awarded 19 Oct 1813; residence - South Australia, Australia. SOURCE: WO120 Volume 69 page 63. INDEX # 3040.

John HOWE; pension awarded 20 Oct 1814; residence - Saint John, New Brunswick, Canada. SOURCE: WO120 Volume 69 page 63. INDEX # 3041.

Geo^e HALL; pension awarded 7 Feb 1821; residence - Madras, India. SOURCE: WO120 Volume 69 page 63. INDEX # 3042.

John BURKE; pension awarded 7 Feb 1821; residence - Madras, India; died 13 Dec 1849. SOURCE: WO120 Volume 69 page 63. INDEX # 3043.

Willm POPE; pension awarded 7 Feb 1821; residence - Madras, India; died 3 Dec 1852. SOURCE: WO120 Volume 69 page 63. INDEX # 3044.

Provisional Cavalry

Jacob DALMAGE; pension awarded 23 Mar 1852; residence - London, Ontario, Canada; died 29 Dec 1879 London, Ontario, Canada. SOURCE: WO120 Volume 69 page 63. INDEX # 3045.

Cape Cavalry

Jos^h HILL; pension awarded 26 Jul 1820; residence - Cape of Good Hope, South Africa; died 22 Oct 1849. SOURCE: WO120 Volume 69 page 64. INDEX # 3046.

John BROWN; pension awarded 21 May 1828; residence - Cape of Good Hope, South Africa. SOURCE: WO120 Volume 69 page 64. INDEX # 3047.

David RUDD; pension awarded 21 May 1820; residence - Cape of Good Hope, South Africa. SOURCE: WO120 Volume 69 page 64. INDEX # 3048.

Cape Cavalry (continued)

Pat^k MCCORMICK; pension awarded 21 May 1820; residence - Cape of Good Hope, South Africa. SOURCE: WO120 Volume 69 page 64. INDEX # 3049.

Willm REYNOLDS; pension awarded 21 May 1820; residence - Cape of Good Hope, South Africa. SOURCE: WO120 Volume 69 page 64. INDEX # 3050.

Willm MAYES; pension awarded 21 May 1820; residence - Cape of Good Hope, South Africa. SOURCE: WO120 Volume 69 page 64. INDEX # 3051.

John DEMPSEY; pension awarded 21 May 1820; residence - Cape of Good Hope, South Africa. SOURCE: WO120 Volume 69 page 64. INDEX # 3052.

Cape Mounted Rifles

H^y WOODLAND; pension awarded 16 Jan 1845; residence - Cape of Good Hope, South Africa. SOURCE: WO120 Volume 69 page 65. INDEX # 3053.

John RAKEN; pension awarded 25 Nov 1840; residence - Cape of Good Hope, South Africa. SOURCE: WO120 Volume 69 page 65. INDEX # 3054.

Willm PRESTON; pension awarded 27 Feb 1844; residence - Cape of Good Hope, South Africa. SOURCE: WO120 Volume 69 page 65. INDEX # 3055.

John GUNN; pension awarded 13 Feb 1837; residence - Cape of Good Hope, South Africa; died 18 Oct 1848. SOURCE: WO120 Volume 69 page 65. INDEX # 3056.

Wm LANDS; pension awarded 9 Jan 1839; residence - Cape of Good Hope, South Africa. SOURCE: WO120 Volume 69 page 65. INDEX # 3057.

Thos BROOKS; pension awarded 11 Jan 1848; residence - Cape of Good Hope, South Africa; died 21 Jan 1850. SOURCE: WO120 Volume 69 page 65. INDEX # 3058.

Jos^h WRIGHT; pension awarded 11 Jan 1848; residence - Cape of Good Hope, South Africa; died 13 Aug 1852. SOURCE: WO120 Volume 69 page 65. INDEX # 3059.

David KETTLES; pension awarded 8 May 1849; residence - Cape of Good Hope, South Africa. SOURCE: WO120 Volume 69 page 65. INDEX # 3060.

Bern^d MCCABE; pension awarded 8 May 1849; residence - Cape of Good Hope, South Africa. SOURCE: WO120 Volume 69 page 65. INDEX # 3061.

Robt BELL; pension awarded 10 Jul 1849. SOURCE: WO120 Volume 69 page 65. INDEX # 3062.

Thos LITTLE; pension awarded 10 Jul 1849; died in Jul 1873, Cape of Good Hope, South Africa. SOURCE: WO120 Volume 69 page 65. INDEX # 3063.

Ja^s DAWSON; pension awarded 28 Aug 1849; residence - Cape of Good Hope, South Africa. SOURCE: WO120 Volume 69 page 65. INDEX # 3064.

Wm NEWTH; pension awarded 23 Jul 1850; residence - Cape of Good Hope, South Africa. SOURCE: WO120 Volume 69 page 65. INDEX # 3065.

Wm SLATTERY; pension awarded 23 Jul 1850; residence - Grahams Town, South Africa; died 13 Dec 1851. SOURCE: WO120 Volume 69 page 65. INDEX # 3066.

John KNIGHT; pension awarded 13 Jul 1852; residence - Cape of Good Hope, South Africa. SOURCE: WO120 Volume 69 page 65. INDEX # 3067.

J. BOYLE; pension awarded 13 Jul 1852; residence - Cape of Good Hope, South Africa. SOURCE: WO120 Volume 69 page 65. INDEX # 3068.

Pat^k DOWDELL; pension awarded 13 Jul 1852; residence - Cape of Good Hope, South Africa. SOURCE: WO120 Volume 69 page 65. INDEX # 3069.

Alex^r WILLMORE; pension awarded 13 Sep 1853; residence - Cape of Good Hope, South Africa. SOURCE: WO120 Volume 69 page 65. INDEX # 3070.

Nathl BARRELL; pension awarded 13 Sep 1853; residence - Cape of Good Hope, South Africa; died 3 May 1879 Cape of Good Hope, South Africa. SOURCE: WO120 Volume 69 page 65. INDEX # 3071.

Martin CAHILL; pension awarded 13 Sep 1853; residence - Cape of Good Hope, South Africa. SOURCE: WO120 Volume 69 page 65. INDEX # 3072.

John POLLOCK; pension awarded 13 Sep 1853. SOURCE: WO120 Volume 69 page 65. INDEX # 3073.

Cape Mounted Rifles (continued)

Jas RICHARDSON; pension awarded 13 Sep 1853; residence - Cape of Good Hope, South Africa. SOURCE: WO120 Volume 69 page 65. INDEX # 3074.
Geoe PITT; pension awarded 13 Sep 1853; residence - Cape of Good Hope, South Africa. SOURCE: WO120 Volume 69 page 65. INDEX # 3075.
Thos GALLERY; pension awarded 13 Sep 1853; residence - Cape of Good Hope, South Africa. SOURCE: WO120 Volume 69 page 65. INDEX # 3076.
Andw Todd WILSON; pension awarded 13 Sep 1853; residence - Cape of Good Hope, South Africa. SOURCE: WO120 Volume 69 page 65. INDEX # 3077.
Caleb CHITTY; pension awarded 13 Sep 1853; residence - Cape of Good Hope, South Africa. SOURCE: WO120 Volume 69 page 65. INDEX # 3078.
Willm BROWN; pension awarded 13 Sep 1853; residence - Cape of Good Hope, South Africa. SOURCE: WO120 Volume 69 page 65. INDEX # 3079.
Geoe CAMPBELL; pension awarded 13 Sep 1853; residence - Cape of Good Hope, South Africa. SOURCE: WO120 Volume 69 page 65. INDEX # 3080.
Alfred CLUNEY; pension awarded 13 Sep 1853; residence - Cape of Good Hope, South Africa. SOURCE: WO120 Volume 69 page 65. INDEX # 3081.
Heny COCHRANE; pension awarded 13 Sep 1853; residence - Cape of Good Hope, South Africa. SOURCE: WO120 Volume 69 page 65. INDEX # 3082.
Wm CUSHLEY; pension awarded 13 Sep 1853. SOURCE: WO120 Volume 69 page 65. INDEX # 3083.
Thos DAVIES; pension awarded 13 Sep 1853; residence - Cape of Good Hope, South Africa. SOURCE: WO120 Volume 69 page 65. INDEX # 3084.
John DOVE; pension awarded 13 Sep 1853; residence - Cape of Good Hope, South Africa. SOURCE: WO120 Volume 69 page 65. INDEX # 3085.
Bernd FITZGERALD; pension awarded 13 Sep 1853; residence - Cape of Good Hope, South Africa. SOURCE: WO120 Volume 69 page 65. INDEX # 3086.
Hugh GALLAGHER; pension awarded 13 Sep 1853; residence - Cape of Good Hope, South Africa. SOURCE: WO120 Volume 69 page 65. INDEX # 3087.
Heny JONES; pension awarded 13 Sep 1853. SOURCE: WO120 Volume 69 page 65. INDEX # 3088.
Andw MCQUILLEN; pension awarded 13 Sep 1853; residence - Cape of Good Hope, South Africa. SOURCE: WO120 Volume 69 page 65. INDEX # 3089.
Peter MAIN; pension awarded 13 Sep 1853; residence - Cape of Good Hope, South Africa. SOURCE: WO120 Volume 69 page 65. INDEX # 3090.
Josh MILLER; pension awarded 13 Sep 1853; residence - Cape of Good Hope, South Africa. SOURCE: WO120 Volume 69 page 65. INDEX # 3091.
Wm RUTTER; pension awarded 13 Sep 1853; residence - St. Helena, South Africa. SOURCE: WO120 Volume 69 page 65. INDEX # 3092.

Wagon Train

Josh DENNIS; pension awarded 17 Mar 1819; residence - Ostend, Belgium. SOURCE: WO120 Volume 69 page 66. INDEX # 3093.
Willm LUCAS; pension awarded 23 Aug 1814; residence - Toronto, Ontario, Canada. SOURCE: WO120 Volume 69 page 66. INDEX # 3094.

1st Regiment of Foot Guards

Jas YOUNG; pension awarded 21 Dec 1825; residence - Niagara, Ontario, Canada ; died in Jul 1852. SOURCE: WO120 Volume 69 page 67. INDEX # 3095.
Saml PROCTOR; pension awarded 2 Jul 1816; residence - Adelaide; died 14 Jan 1864, London, Ontario, Canada. SOURCE: WO120 Volume 69 page 67. INDEX # 3096.
John BURKE; pension awarded 16 Apr 1829; residence - Quebec, Canada. SOURCE: WO120 Volume 69 page 67. INDEX # 3097.

WO120 VOLUME 69

1st Regiment of Foot Guards (continued)

Geo^e JOHNSON; pension awarded 11 Nov 1840; residence - Quebec, Canada ; died 13 Sep 1872, Toronto, Ontario, Canada. SOURCE: WO120 Volume 69 page 67. INDEX # 3098.

Pat^k BOND; pension awarded 9 Dec 1840; residence - Kingston, Ontario, Canada ; died 3 Oct 1854. SOURCE: WO120 Volume 69 page 67. INDEX # 3099.

John WALKER; pension awarded 27 Sep 1842; residence - Bytown, Ontario, Canada. SOURCE: WO120 Volume 69 page 67. INDEX # 3100.

Robt BAGGERLEY; pension awarded 22 Nov 1842; residence - Montreal, Quebec, Canada. SOURCE: WO120 Volume 69 page 67. INDEX # 3101.

Jos^h BROOKS; pension awarded 22 Nov 1842; residence - Quebec, Canada. SOURCE: WO120 Volume 69 page 67. INDEX # 3102.

Wm GREEN; pension awarded 22 Nov 1842; residence - Quebec, Canada. SOURCE: WO120 Volume 69 page 67. INDEX # 3103.

Thos IBBETSON; pension awarded 22 Nov 1842; residence - Toronto, Ontario, Canada; died 15 Aug 1878. SOURCE: WO120 Volume 69 page 67. INDEX # 3104.

Thos MASON; pension awarded 22 Nov 1842; residence - Quebec, Canada ; died 18 Aug 1847. SOURCE: WO120 Volume 69 page 67. INDEX # 3105.

Geo^e TURNER; pension awarded 22 Nov 1842; residence - Montreal, Quebec, Canada. SOURCE: WO120 Volume 69 page 67. INDEX # 3106.

Wm WOODS; pension awarded 22 Nov 1842; residence - Quebec, Canada. SOURCE: WO120 Volume 69 page 67. INDEX # 3107.

And^w GARDNER; pension awarded 10 Jan 1843; residence - Montreal, Quebec, Canada; died 20 Jun 1861, Bytown, Canada. SOURCE: WO120 Volume 69 page 67. INDEX # 3108.

Thos HALLIDAY; pension awarded 24 Feb 1815; residence - New South Wales, Australia. SOURCE: WO120 Volume 69 page 67. INDEX # 3109.

Jos^h JACKSON; pension awarded 13 Dec 1842; residence - Quebec, Canada. SOURCE: WO120 Volume 69 page 67. INDEX # 3110.

Geo^e RICHMOND; pension awarded 13 Dec 1842; residence - Wm Henry, Quebec, Canada. SOURCE: WO120 Volume 69 page 67. INDEX # 3111.

John SMITH; pension awarded 9 Dec 1840; residence - Antigua; died 7 Nov 1853. SOURCE: WO120 Volume 69 page 67. INDEX # 3112.

Ja^s DONELEY; pension awarded 13 Dec 1842; residence - Quebec, Canada. SOURCE: WO120 Volume 69 page 67. INDEX # 3113.

Jno THOMPSON; pension awarded 17 May 1825; residence - Launceston, Australia. SOURCE: WO120 Volume 69 page 67. INDEX # 3114.

Matt^w BEBBINGTON; pension awarded 13 Dec 1842; residence - Quebec, Canada. SOURCE: WO120 Volume 69 page 67. INDEX # 3115.

Ja^s GARFORTH; pension awarded 13 Dec 1842; residence - Montreal, Quebec, Canada; died 1 Jan 1851. SOURCE: WO120 Volume 69 page 67. INDEX # 3116.

Jos^h PARKER; pension awarded 13 Dec 1842; residence - Quebec, Canada. SOURCE: WO120 Volume 69 page 67. INDEX # 3117.

Wm WALSH; pension awarded 22 Mar 1820; residence - Charlottetown, Prince Edward Island, Canada; died in Dec 1862, Nova Scotia, Canada. SOURCE: WO120 Volume 69 page 67. INDEX # 3118.

Benjn BUTTERBY; pension awarded 27 Sep 1842; residence - St. Johns, Quebec, Canada; died 21 Apr 1874, Nottingham. SOURCE: WO120 Volume 69 page 67. INDEX # 3119.

John SIDDONS; pension awarded 12 Nov 1834; residence - Toronto, Ontario, Canada. SOURCE: WO120 Volume 69 page 67. INDEX # 3120.

Robt MORGAN; pension awarded 27 Aug 1841; residence - Quebec, Canada. SOURCE: WO120 Volume 69 page 67. INDEX # 3121.

Thos WADSWORTH; pension awarded 9 Jun 1841; residence - Montreal, Quebec, Canada. SOURCE: WO120 Volume 69 page 67. INDEX # 3122.

Walter ELPHICK; pension awarded 1843; residence - Rome, Italy; died 10 Jun 1870. SOURCE: WO120 Volume 69 page 67. INDEX # 3123.

2nd Regiment of Foot Guards

John RICE; pension awarded 12 Sep 1821; residence - Halifax, Nova Scotia, Canada. SOURCE: WO120 Volume 69 page 74. INDEX # 3124.

Don[d] MCDONALD; pension awarded 24 Nov 1824; residence - Sydney. SOURCE: WO120 Volume 69 page 74. INDEX # 3125.

Rob[t] WRIGHT; pension awarded 13 Jan 1841; residence - Quebec, Canada. SOURCE: WO120 Volume 69 page 74. INDEX # 3126.

Ziba FISHER; pension awarded 20 Jul 1813; residence - Toronto, Ontario, Canada; died 24 Aug 1857. SOURCE: WO120 Volume 69 page 74. INDEX # 3127.

H[y] HOWELL; pension awarded 21 Jan 1824; residence - Toronto, Ontario, Canada; died 27 Jun 1857. SOURCE: WO120 Volume 69 page 74. INDEX # 3128.

H[y] SHARP; pension awarded 22 Nov 1842; residence - Montreal, Quebec, Canada. SOURCE: WO120 Volume 69 page 74. INDEX # 3129.

Cha[s] SUTTON; pension awarded 22 Nov 1842; residence - Quebec, Canada; died in Aug 1849. SOURCE: WO120 Volume 69 page 74. INDEX # 3130.

Jos[h] GRAHAM; pension awarded 22 Nov 1842; residence - Quebec, Canada; died 2 Apr 1863, Toronto, Ontario, Canada. SOURCE: WO120 Volume 69 page 74. INDEX # 3131.

Fra[s] KNOTT; pension awarded 22 Nov 1842; residence - Quebec, Canada. SOURCE: WO120 Volume 69 page 74. INDEX # 3132.

Tho[s] WATSON; pension awarded 22 Nov 1842; residence - Quebec, Canada. SOURCE: WO120 Volume 69 page 74. INDEX # 3133.

Benj[n] EGGS; pension awarded 10 Jan 1843; residence - Quebec, Canada. SOURCE: WO120 Volume 69 page 74. INDEX # 3134.

W[m] GREEN; pension awarded 27 Sep 1842; residence - Quebec, Canada; died in 1847. SOURCE: WO120 Volume 69 page 74. INDEX # 3135.

Ja[s] MINGAY; pension awarded 13 Dec 1842; residence - Niagara, Ontario, Canada; died 6 Apr 1846. SOURCE: WO120 Volume 69 page 74. INDEX # 3136.

John CULLINGFORD; pension awarded 27 Sep 1842; residence - Quebec, Canada; died 3 Jul 1886. SOURCE: WO120 Volume 69 page 74. INDEX # 3137.

Tho[s] JACQUES; pension awarded 24 Apr 1842; residence - Quebec, Canada; died 23 Sep 1857. SOURCE: WO120 Volume 69 page 74. INDEX # 3138.

Sam[l] CHURCH; pension awarded 22 Jul 1840; residence - Quebec, Canada. SOURCE: WO120 Volume 69 page 74. INDEX # 3139.

Sam[l] ROOKE; pension awarded 7 Jan 1829; residence - Rio de Janeiro, Brazil. SOURCE: WO120 Volume 69 page 74. INDEX # 3140.

3rd Regiment of Foot Guards

W[m] RANDALL; pension awarded 8 Nov 1837; residence - Kingston, Ontario, Canada. SOURCE: WO120 Volume 69 page 76. INDEX # 3141.

Tho[s] FLEET; pension awarded 4 Aug 1828; residence - Kingston, Ontario, Canada. SOURCE: WO120 Volume 69 page 76. INDEX # 3142.

Ja[s] CAVERS; pension awarded 7 Aug 1811; residence - London, Ontario, Canada; died 4 Feb 1865. SOURCE: WO120 Volume 69 page 76. INDEX # 3143.

Peter MARTIN; pension awarded 28 Oct 1818; residence - Antigua. SOURCE: WO120 Volume 69 page 76. INDEX # 3144.

John WATT; pension awarded 13 Apr 1809; residence - Gibraltar; died 26 Jun 1847. SOURCE: WO120 Volume 69 page 76. INDEX # 3145.

Allison BOWIE; pension awarded 27 Apr 1847; residence - St Helen[s] Isle, Quebec, Canada. SOURCE: WO120 Volume 69 page 76. INDEX # 3146.

WO120 VOLUME 69

1st Regiment of Foot

Robt FINLEY; pension awarded 28 Dec 1818; residence - Montreal, Quebec, Canada. SOURCE: WO120 Volume 69 page 78. INDEX # 3147.

Mich^l PADDLE; pension awarded 19 Jul 1826; residence - Niagara, Ontario, Canada; died in 1849. SOURCE: WO120 Volume 69 page 78. INDEX # 3148.

Dav^d THOMPSON; pension awarded 9 Dec 1829; residence - Niagara, Ontario, Canada; died 7 Jun 1868, Hamilton, Ontario, Canada. SOURCE: WO120 Volume 69 page 78. INDEX # 3149.

Edwd HINDS; pension awarded 9 Dec 1814; residence - Quebec, Canada. SOURCE: WO120 Volume 69 page 78. INDEX # 3150.

Isaac VINCENT; pension awarded 30 Apr 1817; residence - Niagara, Ontario, Canada; died 29 Jun 1861, Hamilton, Ontario, Canada. SOURCE: WO120 Volume 69 page 78. INDEX # 3151.

Jno FRASER; pension awarded 12 Sep 1838; residence - Norfolk Island, Australia. SOURCE: WO120 Volume 69 page 78. INDEX # 3152.

Jno BLACK; pension awarded 16 Sep 1814; residence - Toronto, Ontario, Canada; died 23 Mar 1849. SOURCE: WO120 Volume 69 page 78. INDEX # 3153.

Ja^s BENSON; pension awarded 12 Sep 1821; residence - Halifax, Nova Scotia, Canada. SOURCE: WO120 Volume 69 page 78. INDEX # 3154.

Wm BOYD; pension awarded 4 Oct 1816; residence - Toronto, Ontario, Canada; died 28 May 1878. SOURCE: WO120 Volume 69 page 78. INDEX # 3155.

Jno MCDONALD; pension awarded 7 Oct 1813; residence - Cornwall, Ontario, Canada. SOURCE: WO120 Volume 69 page 78. INDEX # 3156.

Walter FOYAR; pension awarded 2 Nov 1815; residence - New South Wales, Australia. SOURCE: WO120 Volume 69 page 78. INDEX # 3157.

And^w MCDERMOTT; pension awarded 29 Nov 1814; residence - Toronto, Ontario, Canada; died 10 May 1856. SOURCE: WO120 Volume 69 page 78. INDEX # 3158.

Ant^y TOOHEY; pension awarded 20 Jul 1817; residence - New South Wales, Australia. SOURCE: WO120 Volume 69 page 78. INDEX # 3159.

Thos STEVENSON; pension awarded 16 Jun 1825; residence - Toronto, Ontario, Canada. SOURCE: WO120 Volume 69 page 78. INDEX # 3160.

Robt CRAWFORD; pension awarded 27 Aug 1841; residence - Cornwall, Ontario, Canada. SOURCE: WO120 Volume 69 page 78. INDEX # 3161.

John H^y SPEIN; pension awarded 2 Apr 1817; residence - Easthope, Ontario, Canada; died 28 Nov 1871, London, Ontario, Canada. SOURCE: WO120 Volume 69 page 78. INDEX # 3162.

Geo^e HAINES; pension awarded 11 Nov 1840; residence - Toronto, Ontario, Canada. SOURCE: WO120 Volume 69 page 78. INDEX # 3163.

John NIXON; pension awarded 22 Sep 1841; residence - London, Ontario, Canada; died 15 Apr 1857. SOURCE: WO120 Volume 69 page 78. INDEX # 3164.

Chas HALFPENNY; pension awarded 9 Feb 1842; residence - London, Ontario, Canada; died 5 Jul 1849. SOURCE: WO120 Volume 69 page 78. INDEX # 3165.

Alex^r FRASER; pension awarded 25 Oct 1842; residence - London, Ontario, Canada. SOURCE: WO120 Volume 69 page 78. INDEX # 3166.

Willm ROWAN; pension awarded 11 Apr 1843; residence - Montreal, Quebec, Canada. SOURCE: WO120 Volume 69 page 78. INDEX # 3167.

Pat^k PATTON; pension awarded 7 Sep 1814; residence - London, Ontario, Canada; died 29 Jan 1857. SOURCE: WO120 Volume 69 page 78. INDEX # 3168.

Benjn COONEY; pension awarded 6 Mar 1816; residence - Toronto, Ontario, Canada; died 22 Mar 1852. SOURCE: WO120 Volume 69 page 78. INDEX # 3169.

Jno MADDEN; pension awarded 25 Jul 1843; residence - Gibraltar; died 30 Dec 1875. SOURCE: WO120 Volume 69 page 78. INDEX # 3170.

Steph^n TRUEMAN; pension awarded 29 Oct 1828; residence - Madras, India; died 22 Sep 1846. SOURCE: WO120 Volume 69 page 78. INDEX # 3171.

Saml MCGLINN; pension awarded 17 Sep 1828; residence - South Australia, Australia; died 11 Nov 1853. SOURCE: WO120 Volume 69 page 78. INDEX # 3172.

1st Regiment of Foot (continued)

Robt OHARA; pension awarded 11 Oct 1825; residence - Toronto, Ontario, Canada; died 2 Apr 1857. SOURCE: WO120 Volume 69 page 78. INDEX # 3173.

Jno DONNELLY; pension awarded 5 Sep 1843; residence - London, Ontario, Canada; died 16 Jun 1856. SOURCE: WO120 Volume 69 page 78. INDEX # 3174.

Alex^r FRASER; pension awarded 21 Jan 1845; residence - Quebec, Canada; died 14 Sep 1869, London, Ontario, Canada. SOURCE: WO120 Volume 69 page 78. INDEX # 3175.

Mich^l COLLINS; pension awarded 9 Aug 1837; residence - New South Wales, Australia. SOURCE: WO120 Volume 69 page 78. INDEX # 3176.

Ja^s DUFFY; pension awarded 21 Mar 1824; residence - Madras, India; died 13 Jun 1855. SOURCE: WO120 Volume 69 page 78. INDEX # 3177.

Benjⁿ EMMETT; pension awarded 30 May 1827; residence - Madras, India; died 22 Oct 1850. SOURCE: WO120 Volume 69 page 78. INDEX # 3178.

Jno GILMOUR; pension awarded 20 Aug 1825; residence - Bytown, Ontario, Canada. SOURCE: WO120 Volume 69 page 78. INDEX # 3179.

Thos BRADBURY; pension awarded 29 Oct 1828; residence - Madras, India; died 28 Jul 1853. SOURCE: WO120 Volume 69 page 78. INDEX # 3180.

Jno CALLAGHAN; pension awarded 21 May 1828; residence - Madras, India; died 19 Feb 1847. SOURCE: WO120 Volume 69 page 78. INDEX # 3181.

Ja^s WILLEY; pension awarded 25 Jun 1829; residence - Madras, India. SOURCE: WO120 Volume 69 page 78. INDEX # 3182.

Jno COLLINS; pension awarded 31 Oct 1827; residence - Madras, India; died 8 Oct 1850. SOURCE: WO120 Volume 69 page 78. INDEX # 3183.

Wm BENNETT; pension awarded 7 Feb 1821; residence - Madras, India. SOURCE: WO120 Volume 69 page 78. INDEX # 3184.

Robt BUSSEY; pension awarded 23 Nov 1825; residence - Madras, India; died 25 Feb 1864, Madras, India. SOURCE: WO120 Volume 69 page 78. INDEX # 3185.

Sepko SIZE; pension awarded 7 Feb 1821; residence - Madras, India; died 30 Oct 1852. SOURCE: WO120 Volume 69 page 78. INDEX # 3186.

John HALES; pension awarded 15 Mar 1826; residence - Madras, India. SOURCE: WO120 Volume 69 page 79. INDEX # 3187.

Thos CURRY; pension awarded 28 Aug 1839; residence - Montreal, Quebec, Canada. SOURCE: WO120 Volume 69 page 79. INDEX # 3188.

Jno BEATTIE; pension awarded 11 Dec 1839; residence - Toronto, Ontario, Canada. SOURCE: WO120 Volume 69 page 79. INDEX # 3189.

Thos EYRES; pension awarded 28 Jun 1842; residence - Gibraltar. SOURCE: WO120 Volume 69 page 79. INDEX # 3190.

Willm MURPHY; pension awarded 25 Jul 1843; residence - Gibraltar. SOURCE: WO120 Volume 69 page 79. INDEX # 3191.

Thos LEVINS; pension awarded 16 Jan 1844; residence - Gibraltar. SOURCE: WO120 Volume 69 page 79. INDEX # 3192.

Hugh WISE; pension awarded 9 Sep 1845; residence - Montreal, Quebec, Canada. SOURCE: WO120 Volume 69 page 79. INDEX # 3193.

Jno WOODWARD; pension awarded 26 May 1817; residence - Kingston, Ontario, Canada. SOURCE: WO120 Volume 69 page 79. INDEX # 3194.

And^w WALSH; pension awarded 22 Oct 1844; residence - Montreal, Quebec, Canada. SOURCE: WO120 Volume 69 page 79. INDEX # 3195.

John RODGERS; pension awarded 11 Jan 1832; residence - Madras, India. SOURCE: WO120 Volume 69 page 79. INDEX # 3196.

Peter WALSH; pension awarded 23 Jan 1844; residence - Montreal, Quebec, Canada. SOURCE: WO120 Volume 69 page 79. INDEX # 3197.

Mich^l ALFRED; pension awarded 28 Nov 1846; residence - Quebec, Canada. SOURCE: WO120 Volume 69 page 79. INDEX # 3198.

WO120 VOLUME 69   107

1st Regiment of Foot (continued)

Thos BRUNT; pension awarded 25 Sep 1839; residence - Quebec, Canada. SOURCE: WO120 Volume 69 page 79. INDEX # 3199.

Ja^s KELLY; pension awarded 13 Feb 1833; residence - Montreal, Quebec, Canada. SOURCE: WO120 Volume 69 page 79. INDEX # 3200.

Mat^w SHANNAN; pension awarded 28 Nov 1848; residence - St. Andrews, New Brunswick, Canada. SOURCE: WO120 Volume 69 page 79. INDEX # 3201.

Wm CRAWFORD; pension awarded 24 Jul 1849; residence - Fredericton, New Brunswick, Canada. SOURCE: WO120 Volume 69 page 79. INDEX # 3202.

Jno HUGHES; pension awarded 24 Jul 1849; residence - Saint John, New Brunswick, Canada. SOURCE: WO120 Volume 69 page 79. INDEX # 3203.

Martin MULVEY; pension awarded 23 Oct 1849; residence - St. Andrews, New Brunswick, Canada. SOURCE: WO120 Volume 69 page 79. INDEX # 3204.

Jno HUNT; pension awarded 23 Oct 1849; residence - Prince Edward Island, Canada ; died 5 May 1853. SOURCE: WO120 Volume 69 page 79. INDEX # 3205.

Wm HICKLIN; pension awarded 8 Jan 1850; residence - Fredericton, New Brunswick, Canada. SOURCE: WO120 Volume 69 page 79. INDEX # 3206.

Ja^s MCALPINE; pension awarded 11 Jun 1850; residence - Fredericton, New Brunswick, Canada. SOURCE: WO120 Volume 69 page 79. INDEX # 3207.

Alex^r WHITELAW; pension awarded 27 Aug 1850; residence - Fredericton, New Brunswick, Canada; died 15 May 1886, Halifax, Nova Scotia, Canada. SOURCE: WO120 Volume 69 page 79. INDEX # 3208.

Wm SAUNDERS; pension awarded 1 Jul 1851; died 18 Jun 1868, Portsmouth. SOURCE: WO120 Volume 69 page 79. INDEX # 3209.

Laurence CURRAN; pension awarded 1 Jul 1851; residence - Prince Edward Island, Canada. SOURCE: WO120 Volume 69 page 79. INDEX # 3210.

Wm MCCRACKEN; pension awarded 1 Jul 1851; residence - Prince Edward Island, Canada; died 18 Mar 1853. SOURCE: WO120 Volume 69 page 79. INDEX # 3211.

Bryan TIERNAY; pension awarded 1 Jul 1851; residence - St. Andrews, New Brunswick, Canada; died 6 Jan 1882, Nova Scotia, Canada. SOURCE: WO120 Volume 69 page 79. INDEX # 3212.

Hen^y TOOLE; pension awarded 1 Jul 1851; residence - Halifax, Nova Scotia, Canada; died 2 Jan 1876. SOURCE: WO120 Volume 69 page 79. INDEX # 3213.

John WHITE; pension awarded 1 Jul 1851; residence - Halifax, Nova Scotia, Canada; died 15 Feb 1876. SOURCE: WO120 Volume 69 page 79. INDEX # 3214.

John BAILEY; pension awarded 9 Sep 1851; residence - St. Andrews, New Brunswick, Canada. SOURCE: WO120 Volume 69 page 79. INDEX # 3215.

Fra^s CLARKE; pension awarded 9 Sep 1851; residence - Toronto, Ontario, Canada; died 17 May 1880, Toronto, Ontario, Canada. SOURCE: WO120 Volume 69 page 79. INDEX # 3216.

Step^n CORCORAN; pension awarded 9 Sep 1851; residence - Toronto, Ontario, Canada; died 1 Apr 1862, Toronto, Ontario, Canada. SOURCE: WO120 Volume 69 page 79. INDEX # 3217.

Jno DONOVAN; pension awarded 9 Sep 1851; residence - Prince Edward Island, Canada. SOURCE: WO120 Volume 69 page 79. INDEX # 3218.

2nd Regiment of Foot

Hugh BUCKLEY; pension awarded 26 Aug 1825; residence - Penetanguishene, Ontario, Canada. SOURCE: WO120 Volume 69 page 81. INDEX # 3219.

Benjn SHIRE; pension awarded 18 Dec 1822; residence - Hobart Town, Australia; died 27 Jun 1879, Tasmania, Australia. SOURCE: WO120 Volume 69 page 81. INDEX # 3220.

Richd LITTLE; pension awarded 12 May 1819; residence - Montreal, Quebec, Canada. SOURCE: WO120 Volume 69 page 81. INDEX # 3221.

Geo^e SCRAGG; pension awarded 25 Oct 1842; residence - Camp Deesa, India. SOURCE: WO120 Volume 69 page 81. INDEX # 3222.

2nd Regiment of Foot (continued)

Ja^s FERGUSON; pension awarded 21 Nov 1821; residence - Toronto, Ontario, Canada; died 24 Oct 1862, London, Ontario, Canada. SOURCE: WO120 Volume 69 page 81. INDEX # 3223.

Ja^s CAMPBELL; pension awarded 25 Aug 1841; residence - Deesa, India. SOURCE: WO120 Volume 69 page 81. INDEX # 3224.

Thos Day CHISLETE; pension awarded 24 May 1842; residence - Bombay, India. SOURCE: WO120 Volume 69 page 81. INDEX # 3225.

Thos CRONE; pension awarded 13 Jun 1843; residence - Bombay, India. SOURCE: WO120 Volume 69 page 81. INDEX # 3226.

Pat^k GORMAN; pension awarded 11 Jun 1846; residence - Bombay, India. SOURCE: WO120 Volume 69 page 81. INDEX # 3227.

Robt Jno BARRY; pension awarded 11 Jun 1844; residence - Bombay, India; died 4 Apr 1872, New Zealand. SOURCE: WO120 Volume 69 page 81. INDEX # 3228.

Jno MCAFEE; pension awarded 11 Jun 1844; residence - Bombay, India; died 26 Apr 1826. SOURCE: WO120 Volume 69 page 81. INDEX # 3229.

Saml CRANE; pension awarded 21 Nov 1839; residence - Bombay, India; died 8 May 1862. SOURCE: WO120 Volume 69 page 81. INDEX # 3230.

Ja^s WILLIAMSON; pension awarded 20 Nov 1839; residence - Bombay, India. SOURCE: WO120 Volume 69 page 81. INDEX # 3231.

Jno HEALY; pension awarded 13 Jun 1843; residence - Bombay, India. SOURCE: WO120 Volume 69 page 81. INDEX # 3232.

Wm ROWLAND; pension awarded 24 Jul 1837; residence - Ostend, Belgium; died 12 Nov 1864, Dunkirk, France. SOURCE: WO120 Volume 69 page 81. INDEX # 3233.

Ja^s GALVIN; pension awarded 22 Jul 1845; residence - Halifax, Nova Scotia, Canada. SOURCE: WO120 Volume 69 page 81. INDEX # 3234.

Ja^s EAGAN; pension awarded 9 Jun 1841; residence - Quebec, Canada. SOURCE: WO120 Volume 69 page 81. INDEX # 3235.

Bern^d SMITH; pension awarded 30 Aug 1821; residence - Montreal, Quebec, Canada. SOURCE: WO120 Volume 69 page 81. INDEX # 3236.

3rd Regiment of Foot

Peter ANGUS; pension awarded 5 Feb 1823; residence - Montreal, Quebec, Canada; died in 1853. SOURCE: WO120 Volume 69 page 83. INDEX # 3237.

Ja^s BUTLER; pension awarded 9 Jun 1821; residence - Adelaide; died 16 Dec 1877, London, Ontario, Canada. SOURCE: WO120 Volume 69 page 83. INDEX # 3238.

Jno CURRAN; pension awarded 27 Aug 1816; residence - New South Wales, Australia. SOURCE: WO120 Volume 69 page 83. INDEX # 3239.

Const^e KEENAN; pension awarded 16 Nov 1843; residence - Bengal, India; died 21 Dec 1847. SOURCE: WO120 Volume 69 page 83. INDEX # 3240.

Wm SUTHERLAND; pension awarded 21 May 1828; residence - New South Wales, Australia. SOURCE: WO120 Volume 69 page 83. INDEX # 3241.

Thos JOHNSTON; pension awarded 14 Nov 1843; residence - Chinsurah, India. SOURCE: WO120 Volume 69 page 83. INDEX # 3242.

Chas HODDER; pension awarded 11 Mar 1845; residence - Allahabad, India. SOURCE: WO120 Volume 69 page 83. INDEX # 3243.

Benjn REED; pension awarded 30 Aug 1816; residence - New South Wales, Australia; died 27 Feb 1862. SOURCE: WO120 Volume 69 page 83. INDEX # 3244.

Peter MCCORLEY; pension awarded 25 Feb 1845; residence - Allahabad, India. SOURCE: WO120 Volume 69 page 83. INDEX # 3245.

Benjn BILLETT; pension awarded 13 Jun 1843; residence - Calcutta, India. SOURCE: WO120 Volume 69 page 83. INDEX # 3246.

John ALLEN; pension awarded 24 Jun 1840; residence - Bengal, India. SOURCE: WO120 Volume 69 page 83. INDEX # 3247.

3rd Regiment of Foot (continued)

John LEWIE; pension awarded 8 May 1839; residence - Bengal, India; died 4 Mar 1846. SOURCE: WO120 Volume 69 page 83. INDEX # 3248.

Richd EVANS; pension awarded 8 May 1839; residence - Bengal, India. SOURCE: WO120 Volume 69 page 83. INDEX # 3249.

Wm BARTHOLOMEW; pension awarded 27 Jun 1838; residence - Bengal, India. SOURCE: WO120 Volume 69 page 83. INDEX # 3250.

Pat^k DUFFY; pension awarded 21 May 1828; residence - New South Wales, Australia. SOURCE: WO120 Volume 69 page 83. INDEX # 3251.

Geo^e STAFFORD; pension awarded 24 Jun 1845; residence - Calcutta, India. SOURCE: WO120 Volume 69 page 83. INDEX # 3252.

Geo^e MOSS; pension awarded 24 Jun 1840; residence - Bengal, India; died 12 Sep 1863, Berhampore, India. SOURCE: WO120 Volume 69 page 83. INDEX # 3253.

Edwd CLAMP; pension awarded 25 Feb 1845; residence - Allahabad, India. SOURCE: WO120 Volume 69 page 83. INDEX # 3254.

Hen^y BETTS; pension awarded 24 Jun 1845; residence - Calcutta, India; died 11 Sep 1852. SOURCE: WO120 Volume 69 page 83. INDEX # 3255.

Willm HADE; pension awarded 25 Aug 1846; residence - Honduras, West Indies. SOURCE: WO120 Volume 69 page 83. INDEX # 3256.

George TURNER; pension awarded 31 Mar 1819; residence - Bytown, Ontario, Canada. SOURCE: WO120 Volume 69 page 83. INDEX # 3257.

4th Regiment of Foot

Ch^r ECHLIN; pension awarded 24 Aug 1825; residence - New South Wales, Australia. SOURCE: WO120 Volume 69 page 85. INDEX # 3258.

Step^n BEECHING; pension awarded 17 Dec 1823; residence - Saint John, New Brunswick, Canada. SOURCE: WO120 Volume 69 page 85. INDEX # 3259.

Richd DAWES; pension awarded 20 Jan 1819; residence - New South Wales, Australia. SOURCE: WO120 Volume 69 page 85. INDEX # 3260.

John MCGOWAN; pension awarded 26 Jun 1839; residence - Montreal, Quebec, Canada. SOURCE: WO120 Volume 69 page 85. INDEX # 3261.

Mich^l CAMPBELL; pension awarded 14 Oct 1835; residence - St. Johns. SOURCE: WO120 Volume 69 page 85. INDEX # 3262.

Jno PERRYMAN; pension awarded 6 Mar 1816; residence - Adelaide; died 24 Aug 1864, London, Ontario, Canada. SOURCE: WO120 Volume 69 page 85. INDEX # 3263.

Philip MCCAFFRY; pension awarded 25 Jun 1817; residence - Perth, Ontario, Canada. SOURCE: WO120 Volume 69 page 85. INDEX # 3264.

Wm IRWIN; pension awarded 10 Sep 1834; residence - Sydney, New South Wales, Australia. SOURCE: WO120 Volume 69 page 85. INDEX # 3265.

John LAND; pension awarded 10 Sep 1834; residence - New South Wales, Australia. SOURCE: WO120 Volume 69 page 85. INDEX # 3266.

Edwd WILLIAMS; pension awarded 8 Feb 1837; residence - New South Wales, Australia. SOURCE: WO120 Volume 69 page 85. INDEX # 3267.

Em^l MARTIN; pension awarded 9 Aug 1837; residence - New South Wales, Australia. SOURCE: WO120 Volume 69 page 85. INDEX # 3268.

Geo^e TUGNETT; pension awarded 14 Aug 1833; residence - Port Philip, Australia. SOURCE: WO120 Volume 69 page 85. INDEX # 3269.

Jno SIMPSON; pension awarded 2 Nov 1814; residence - Kingston, Ontario, Canada. SOURCE: WO120 Volume 69 page 85. INDEX # 3270.

Wm CHEEK; pension awarded 13 Oct 1841; residence - Madras, India. SOURCE: WO120 Volume 69 page 85. INDEX # 3271.

Thos NEAVES; pension awarded 11 Oct 1842; residence - Madras, India; died 17 Jan 1846. SOURCE: WO120 Volume 69 page 85. INDEX # 3272.

4th Regiment of Foot (continued)

Dav^d THOMAS; pension awarded 11 Oct 1842; residence - Madras, India; died 25 Mar 1877, Liverpool. SOURCE: WO120 Volume 69 page 85. INDEX # 3273.

Thos NICHOLL; pension awarded 24 Oct 1843; residence - Madras, India; died 4 Jan 1848. SOURCE: WO120 Volume 69 page 85. INDEX # 3274.

Wm DEVERELL; pension awarded 23 Jul 1844; residence - Secunderabad, India. SOURCE: WO120 Volume 69 page 85. INDEX # 3275.

Wm DOWNS; pension awarded 14 Oct 1840; residence - New South Wales, Australia. SOURCE: WO120 Volume 69 page 85. INDEX # 3276.

Thos CURTIS; pension awarded 13 Oct 1841; residence - Madras, India; died 17 Sep 1853. SOURCE: WO120 Volume 69 page 85. INDEX # 3277.

George COLEMAN; pension awarded 28 Jul 1841; residence - Cape of Good Hope, South Africa. SOURCE: WO120 Volume 69 page 85. INDEX # 3278.

Saml CHESTER; pension awarded 28 Apr 1846; residence - Secunderabad, India. SOURCE: WO120 Volume 69 page 85. INDEX # 3279.

Ed^wd HALLIBURN; pension awarded 28 Apr 1846; residence - Secunderabad, India; died 17 Sep 1871, Madras, India. SOURCE: WO120 Volume 69 page 85. INDEX # 3280.

Chas MURRELL; pension awarded 25 May 1847. died 16 Aug 1875. SOURCE: WO120 Volume 69 page 85. INDEX # 3281.

Jno STEEL; pension awarded 25 May 1847; residence - Madras, India; died 16 Nov 1854. SOURCE: WO120 Volume 69 page 85. INDEX # 3282.

Hen^y BARRETT; pension awarded 25 May 1847; died 18 Jul 1870. SOURCE: WO120 Volume 69 page 85. INDEX # 3283.

Wm BONE; pension awarded 25 May 1847. SOURCE: WO120 Volume 69 page 85. INDEX # 3284.

Wm COLEMAN; pension awarded 25 May 1847. SOURCE: WO120 Volume 69 page 85. INDEX # 3285.

Chas MOORE; pension awarded 25 May 1847; residence - Madras, India; died 18 Aug 1852. SOURCE: WO120 Volume 69 page 85. INDEX # 3286.

Fra^s SCOTT; pension awarded 25 May 1847; residence - Madras, India; died 5 May 1863. SOURCE: WO120 Volume 69 page 85. INDEX # 3287.

Ja^s WELLS; pension awarded 25 May 1847. SOURCE: WO120 Volume 69 page 85. INDEX # 3288.

Wm THIPTHORPE; pension awarded 25 Apr 1848. SOURCE: WO120 Volume 69 page 85. INDEX # 3289.

Benjn LORD; pension awarded 25 Apr 1848. SOURCE: WO120 Volume 69 page 85. INDEX # 3290.

Chas BOREHAM; pension awarded 25 Apr 1848. SOURCE: WO120 Volume 69 page 85. INDEX # 3291.

Jno BRAY; pension awarded 25 Apr 1848. SOURCE: WO120 Volume 69 page 85. INDEX # 3292.

Jno FOOT; pension awarded 25 Apr 1848; died 1 Aug 1882 Madras, India. SOURCE: WO120 Volume 69 page 85. INDEX # 3293.

Jno KIMPSON; pension awarded 25 Apr 1848; died 28 Feb 1864 Madras, India. SOURCE: WO120 Volume 69 page 85. INDEX # 3294.

Ja^s OPENSHAW; pension awarded 25 Apr 1848; died 9 Sep 1886, Lancaster. SOURCE: WO120 Volume 69 page 85. INDEX # 3295.

Hen^y RALPH; pension awarded 25 Apr 1848. SOURCE: WO120 Volume 69 page 85. INDEX # 3296.

W^m COX; pension awarded 25 Apr 1848. SOURCE: WO120 Volume 69 page 85. INDEX # 3297.

Ed^wd ABBOTT; pension awarded 25 Apr 1848. died 14 Jan 1879 Madras, India. SOURCE: WO120 Volume 69 page 86. INDEX # 3298.

Jno CLARK; pension awarded 25 Apr 1848. SOURCE: WO120 Volume 69 page 86. INDEX # 3299.

And^w CLENDENING; pension awarded 25 Apr 1848; died 10 Mar 1871. SOURCE: WO120 Volume 69 page 86. INDEX # 3300.

Thos COALMAN; pension awarded 25 Apr 1848; residence - Madras, India; died 9 Dec 1853. SOURCE: WO120 Volume 69 page 86. INDEX # 3301.

Mich^l CONLAN; pension awarded 25 Apr 1848. SOURCE: WO120 Volume 69 page 86. INDEX # 3302.

Jno CREANE; pension awarded 25 Apr 1848. SOURCE: WO120 Volume 69 page 86. INDEX # 3303.

Jno ELLIOTT; pension awarded 25 Apr 1848. SOURCE: WO120 Volume 69 page 86. INDEX # 3304.

Jno FAULKNER; pension awarded 25 Apr 1848; residence - Madras, India; died 15 May 1852. SOURCE: WO120 Volume 69 page 86. INDEX # 3305.

4th Regiment of Foot (continued)

Bern^d FITZPATRICK; pension awarded 25 Apr 1848. SOURCE: WO120 Volume 69 page 86. INDEX # 3306.

Jno HIBBERD; pension awarded 25 Apr 1848. SOURCE: WO120 Volume 69 page 86. INDEX # 3307.

Richd Harvey HOLDING; pension awarded 25 Apr 1848; residence - Madras, India; died 4 Oct 1863. SOURCE: WO120 Volume 69 page 86. INDEX # 3308.

Jos^h MASSEY; pension awarded 25 Apr 1848; residence - Madras, India; died 1 Jan 1852. SOURCE: WO120 Volume 69 page 86. INDEX # 3309.

David Edwd MINSON; pension awarded 25 Apr 1848; residence - Madras, India; died 18 Aug 1850. SOURCE: WO120 Volume 69 page 86. INDEX # 3310.

Step^n MORGAN; pension awarded 25 Apr 1848. SOURCE: WO120 Volume 69 page 86. INDEX # 3311.

Wm PARHAM; pension awarded 25 Apr 1848; residence - Madras, India; died 22 Oct 1876. SOURCE: WO120 Volume 69 page 86. INDEX # 3312.

Robt PAVEY; pension awarded 25 Apr 1848; residence - Madras, India; died 5 Jun 1854. SOURCE: WO120 Volume 69 page 86. INDEX # 3313.

Wm REED; pension awarded 25 Apr 1848; died 31 May 1883, Madras, India. SOURCE: WO120 Volume 69 page 86. INDEX # 3314.

Wm Pittman SCOTT; pension awarded 25 Apr 1848; residence - Madras, India; died 7 Mar 1850. SOURCE: WO120 Volume 69 page 86. INDEX # 3315.

Dan^d WARD; pension awarded 25 Apr 1848; residence - Madras, India; died 24 Nov 1853. SOURCE: WO120 Volume 69 page 86. INDEX # 3316.

Wm WARD; pension awarded 6 Jun 1848; died 29 Jul 1875 Birmingham. SOURCE: WO120 Volume 69 page 86. INDEX # 3317.

Wm ANDREWS; pension awarded 6 Jun 1848; died 22 Dec 1873, Madras, India. SOURCE: WO120 Volume 69 page 86. INDEX # 3318.

Jno GIRLING; pension awarded 6 Jun 1848. SOURCE: WO120 Volume 69 page 86. INDEX # 3319.

Wm MASH; pension awarded 6 Jun 1848; residence - Bangalore, India. SOURCE: WO120 Volume 69 page 86. INDEX # 3320.

W^m FRY; pension awarded 6 Jun 1848. SOURCE: WO120 Volume 69 page 86. INDEX # 3321.

And^w FRUISH; pension awarded 6 Jun 1848. SOURCE: WO120 Volume 69 page 86. INDEX # 3322.

And^w HAMON; pension awarded 6 Jun 1848; died 16 Jun 1878, Londonderry. SOURCE: WO120 Volume 69 page 86. INDEX # 3323.

Jno HANDIBO; pension awarded 6 Jun 1848; residence - Madras, India; died 28 Jul 1854. SOURCE: WO120 Volume 69 page 86. INDEX # 3324.

Chas HANDS; pension awarded 6 Jun 1848. SOURCE: WO120 Volume 69 page 86. INDEX # 3325.

Martin IRVINS; pension awarded 6 Jun 1848. SOURCE: WO120 Volume 69 page 86. INDEX # 3326.

Thos KILROY; pension awarded 6 Jun 1848. SOURCE: WO120 Volume 69 page 86. INDEX # 3327.

Jno KING; pension awarded 6 Jun 1848; residence - Madras, India; died 25 Jul 1854. SOURCE: WO120 Volume 69 page 86. INDEX # 3328.

Jos^h RASH; pension awarded 6 Jun 1848; residence - Madras, India; died 3 May 1852. SOURCE: WO120 Volume 69 page 86. INDEX # 3329.

Jno STAPLETON; pension awarded 6 Jun 1848; residence - Madras, India; died 26 Feb 1851. SOURCE: WO120 Volume 69 page 86. INDEX # 3330.

Ja^s SWANN; pension awarded 6 Jun 1848. SOURCE: WO120 Volume 69 page 86. INDEX # 3331.

Richd TASKER; pension awarded 6 Jun 1848; residence - Madras, India; died 28 Jul 1854. SOURCE: WO120 Volume 69 page 86. INDEX # 3332.

5th Regiment of Foot

Saml HERRON; pension awarded 13 Jun 1843; residence - Niagara, Ontario, Canada. SOURCE: WO120 Volume 69 page 95. INDEX # 3333.

Richd HAWKE; pension awarded 9 Mar 1813; residence - Halifax, Nova Scotia, Canada; died 27 Nov 1852. SOURCE: WO120 Volume 69 page 95. INDEX # 3334.

BRITISH ARMY PENSIONERS ABROAD

5th Regiment of Foot (continued)

Simeon MANSELL; pension awarded 21 Jun 1826; residence - Dominica, West Indies. SOURCE: WO120 Volume 69 page 95. INDEX # 3335.

Peter WALSH; pension awarded 11 Oct 1826; residence - Montreal, Quebec, Canada. SOURCE: WO120 Volume 69 page 95. INDEX # 3336.

Thos TYLER; pension awarded 8 Sep 1830; residence - Toronto, Ontario, Canada. SOURCE: WO120 Volume 69 page 95. INDEX # 3337.

John DALTON; pension awarded 27 Jun 1838; residence - Quebec, Canada. SOURCE: WO120 Volume 69 page 95. INDEX # 3338.

Edwd EDWARDS; pension awarded 17 Fen 1819; residence - Paris, France. SOURCE: WO120 Volume 69 page 95. INDEX # 3339.

Robt TOPPING; pension awarded 17 Jan 1827; residence - Paris, France. SOURCE: WO120 Volume 69 page 95. INDEX # 3340.

Thos HARRIS; pension awarded 12 Sep 1821; residence - Ostend, Belgium; died 12 Oct 1849. SOURCE: WO120 Volume 69 page 95. INDEX # 3341.

Leond MIDDENDORF; pension awarded 24 Aug 1825; residence - Rotterdam, Netherlands. SOURCE: WO120 Volume 69 page 95. INDEX # 3342.

Andw MCLAUCHLIN; pension awarded 14 Jun 1853. SOURCE: WO120 Volume 69 page 95. INDEX # 3343.

Court FINNESS; pension awarded 20 Jul 1825; residence - St. Johns. SOURCE: WO120 Volume 69 page 97. INDEX # 3344.

Willm HEWSON; pension awarded 20 Mar 1822; residence - Montreal, Quebec, Canada. SOURCE: WO120 Volume 69 page 97. INDEX # 3345.

6th Regiment of Foot

Zachh KENYON; pension awarded 12 Oct 1825; residence - Cape of Good Hope, South Africa; died 15 Aug 1850. SOURCE: WO120 Volume 69 page 97. INDEX # 3346.

John REILEY; pension awarded 2 Jun 1825; residence - New South Wales, Australia. SOURCE: WO120 Volume 69 page 97. INDEX # 3347.

Richd GRIMLEY; pension awarded 16 Jun 1842; residence - Bombay, India; died 6 Aug 1850. SOURCE: WO120 Volume 69 page 97. INDEX # 3348.

Patk FITZPATRICK; pension awarded 21 Jun 1815; residence - Montreal, Quebec, Canada; died 11 Jan 1853. SOURCE: WO120 Volume 69 page 97. INDEX # 3349.

Josh WOOD; pension awarded 30 Aug 1826; residence - Toronto, Ontario, Canada; died 21 Feb 1860. SOURCE: WO120 Volume 69 page 97. INDEX # 3350.

Jas HAINSWORTH; pension awarded 20 Nov 1839; residence - Bombay, India; died 7 Feb 1850. SOURCE: WO120 Volume 69 page 97. INDEX # 3351.

Jas HOLDING; pension awarded 20 Nov 1839; residence - Bombay, India. SOURCE: WO120 Volume 69 page 97. INDEX # 3352.

Chr SMITH; pension awarded 22 Aug 1838; residence - Bombay, India; died 1 Apr 1857. SOURCE: WO120 Volume 69 page 97. INDEX # 3353.

Thos BENTLEY; pension awarded 13 Oct 1830; residence - Toronto, Ontario, Canada; died 9 Feb 1845. SOURCE: WO120 Volume 69 page 97. INDEX # 3354.

Richd PILKINGTON; pension awarded 13 Aug 1834; residence - Hobart Town, Australia; died 1 Dec 1859. SOURCE: WO120 Volume 69 page 97. INDEX # 3355.

William MARSDEN; pension awarded 12 Jun 1855. SOURCE: WO120 Volume 69 page 97. INDEX # 3356.

Samuel CREIGHTON; pension awarded 27 May 1856. SOURCE: WO120 Volume 69 page 97. INDEX # 3357.

Charles POULTNEY; pension awarded 24 Jun 1856. SOURCE: WO120 Volume 69 page 97. INDEX # 3358.

Robert CAMPBELL; pension awarded 25 May 1857. SOURCE: WO120 Volume 69 page 97. INDEX # 3359.

James BENNETT; pension awarded 25 May 1857. SOURCE: WO120 Volume 69 page 97. INDEX # 3360.

6th Regiment of Foot (continued)

John BRENNAN; pension awarded 25 May 1857. SOURCE: WO120 Volume 69 page 97. INDEX # 3361.
Peter GLAVEY; pension awarded 25 May 1857. SOURCE: WO120 Volume 69 page 97. INDEX # 3362.
Francis MASKELL; pension awarded 25 May 1857. SOURCE: WO120 Volume 69 page 97. INDEX # 3363.
John MOORE; pension awarded 25 May 1857. SOURCE: WO120 Volume 69 page 97. INDEX # 3364.
James SAVAGE; pension awarded 25 May 1857. SOURCE: WO120 Volume 69 page 97. INDEX # 3365.
Robert WARD; pension awarded 25 May 1857. SOURCE: WO120 Volume 69 page 97. INDEX # 3366.

7th Regiment of Foot

Willm BROOKE; pension awarded 30 Oct 1822; residence - Perth, Ontario, Canada. SOURCE: WO120 Volume 69 page 99. INDEX # 3367.
Willm PAYNE; pension awarded 5 Aug 1812; residence - Montreal, Quebec, Canada. SOURCE: WO120 Volume 69 page 99. INDEX # 3368.
Ja^s KINGSBY; pension awarded 16 Mar 1825; residence - New South Wales, Australia. SOURCE: WO120 Volume 69 page 99. INDEX # 3369.
Mich^l KILFOYLE; pension awarded 20 Feb 1828; residence - Halifax, Nova Scotia, Canada. SOURCE: WO120 Volume 69 page 99. INDEX # 3370.
Ja^s CORBETT; pension awarded 16 Aug 1816; residence - Toronto, Ontario, Canada; died 5 May 1874, Hamilton, Ontario, Canada. SOURCE: WO120 Volume 69 page 99. INDEX # 3371.
Richd STRINGER; pension awarded 23 Feb 1845; residence - Gibraltar. SOURCE: WO120 Volume 69 page 99. INDEX # 3372.
Hen^y FARR; pension awarded 8 Sep 1830; residence - Quebec, Canada. SOURCE: WO120 Volume 69 page 99. INDEX # 3373.
George FROMOW; pension awarded 25 Jun 1844; residence - Gibraltar; died 29 Jan 1882, Gibraltar. SOURCE: WO120 Volume 69 page 99. INDEX # 3374.
Paolo SCISCO; pension awarded 14 Apr 1830; residence - Ionian Isls. SOURCE: WO120 Volume 69 page 99. INDEX # 3375.
Jno MCCAFFREY; pension awarded 9 Mar 1830; residence - Gibraltar. SOURCE: WO120 Volume 69 page 99. INDEX # 3376.
Azariah FUDGE; pension awarded 23 Sep 1818; residence - Ostend, Belgium. SOURCE: WO120 Volume 69 page 99. INDEX # 3377.
Ja^s GARDNER; pension awarded 23 Feb 1847; residence - Demerara, British Guiana; died 31 Jan 1851. SOURCE: WO120 Volume 69 page 99. INDEX # 3378.
Pat^k MURPHY; pension awarded 23 Feb 1847. SOURCE: WO120 Volume 69 page 99. INDEX # 3379.
Thos OGDEN; pension awarded 26 Aug 1847; died 20 Dec 1880, Bury. SOURCE: WO120 Volume 69 page 99. INDEX # 3380.
Terence FARRELL; pension awarded 11 Jun 1850. SOURCE: WO120 Volume 69 page 99. INDEX # 3381.
Ja^s WALSH; pension awarded 11 Jun 1850. SOURCE: WO120 Volume 69 page 99. INDEX # 3382.

8th Regiment of Foot

Willm SKITT; pension awarded 7 Feb 1822; residence - Toronto, Ontario, Canada; died 27 May 1855. SOURCE: WO120 Volume 69 page 101. INDEX # 3383.
Willm DANZIE; pension awarded 20 Mar 1822; residence - Halifax, Nova Scotia, Canada. SOURCE: WO120 Volume 69 page 101. INDEX # 3384.
Jno BOYS; pension awarded 31 Jul 1822; residence - Cornwall, Ontario, Canada; died in 1854. SOURCE: WO120 Volume 69 page 101. INDEX # 3385.
Ja^s ACRET; pension awarded 30 Mar 1825; residence - Carrillon, Quebec, Canada. SOURCE: WO120 Volume 69 page 101. INDEX # 3386.

8th Regiment of Foot (continued)

Jn⁰ LEE; pension awarded 18 Apr 1821; residence - Kingston, Ontario, Canada; died 15 May 1863, Toronto, Ontario, Canada. SOURCE: WO120 Volume 69 page 101. INDEX # 3387.

Jn⁰ GULLIVER; pension awarded 23 Jul 1813; residence - Ionian Isls; died 26 Dec 1851. SOURCE: WO120 Volume 69 page 101. INDEX # 3388.

Thos SMITH; pension awarded 19 Sep 1815; residence - Toronto, Ontario, Canada. SOURCE: WO120 Volume 69 page 101. INDEX # 3389.

Jn⁰ THOMPSON; pension awarded 7 Feb 1816; residence - Kingston, Ontario, Canada; died in 1848. SOURCE: WO120 Volume 69 page 101. INDEX # 3390.

Chas STEWART; pension awarded 25 Dec 1818; residence - Fredericton, New Brunswick, Canada. SOURCE: WO120 Volume 69 page 101. INDEX # 3391.

Edwd WATSON; pension awarded 24 Nov 1841; residence - Prescott, Ontario, Canada. SOURCE: WO120 Volume 69 page 101. INDEX # 3392.

Michl CULLEN; pension awarded 7 Feb 1816; residence - Bytown, Ontario, Canada. SOURCE: WO120 Volume 69 page 101. INDEX # 3393.

Davd MCGOWAN; pension awarded 22 Jul 1845; residence - Prince Edward Island, Canada; died 16 Feb 1849. SOURCE: WO120 Volume 69 page 101. INDEX # 3394.

Willm ROBINSON; pension awarded 19 Sep 1815; residence - Perth, Ontario, Canada. SOURCE: WO120 Volume 69 page 101. INDEX # 3395.

Michl MCLAUGHLIN; pension awarded 7 Feb 1816; residence - Montreal, Quebec, Canada; died 1 Nov 1855. SOURCE: WO120 Volume 69 page 101. INDEX # 3396.

George LATIMER; pension awarded 7 Feb 1816; residence - Bytown, Ontario, Canada; died 18 Jun 1858. SOURCE: WO120 Volume 69 page 101. INDEX # 3397.

John DONAGHOE; pension awarded 19 Jun 1822; residence - Bytown, Ontario, Canada; died 29 Mar 1857. SOURCE: WO120 Volume 69 page 101. INDEX # 3398.

Peter REYNOLDS; pension awarded 11 Jun 1832; residence - Montreal, Quebec, Canada; died 18 Jul 1853. SOURCE: WO120 Volume 69 page 101. INDEX # 3399.

Thos SINGLETON; pension awarded 5 Apr 1814; residence - Quebec, Canada; died in 1850. SOURCE: WO120 Volume 69 page 101. INDEX # 3400.

Thos YOUNG; pension awarded 8 Aug 1827; residence - London, Ontario, Canada; died 18 Nov 1855. SOURCE: WO120 Volume 69 page 101. INDEX # 3401.

Chas STONE; pension awarded 9 Mar 1852; died 15 Oct 1853. SOURCE: WO120 Volume 69 page 101. INDEX # 3402.

Robert SMITH; pension awarded 8 May 1855. SOURCE: WO120 Volume 69 page 101. INDEX # 3403.

Ephraim WALKER; pension awarded 8 May 1855. SOURCE: WO120 Volume 69 page 101. INDEX # 3404.

James MCNAB; pension awarded 11 Mar 1856; died 5 Jul 1856, Agra, India. SOURCE: WO120 Volume 69 page 101. INDEX # 3405.

9th Regiment of Foot

Willm BENNETT; pension awarded 3 May 1816; residence - Penitanguishene, Ontario, Canada; died 8 Nov 1852. SOURCE: WO120 Volume 69 page 103. INDEX # 3406.

Chas HARRIS; pension awarded 24 Nov 1824; residence - New Zealand; died in 1870, New Zealand. SOURCE: WO120 Volume 69 page 103. INDEX # 3407.

Chas ARGENT; pension awarded 13 Apr 1836; residence - Mauritius; died 15 Aug 1856. SOURCE: WO120 Volume 69 page 103. INDEX # 3408.

Thos BERGIN; pension awarded 28 Apr 1841; residence - Bengal, India; died 28 Jun 1848. SOURCE: WO120 Volume 69 page 103. INDEX # 3409.

Davd HUNTER; pension awarded 11 Jun 1844; residence - Bengal, India. SOURCE: WO120 Volume 69 page 103. INDEX # 3410.

John BATES; pension awarded 25 Jun 1844; residence - Bengal, India. SOURCE: WO120 Volume 69 page 103. INDEX # 3411.

9th Regiment of Foot (continued)

Jos^h BUCKLEY; pension awarded 12 Jun 1839; residence - Bengal, India. SOURCE: WO120 Volume 69 page 103. INDEX # 3412.

Math^w JAMES; pension awarded 13 May 1840; residence - Bengal, India. SOURCE: WO120 Volume 69 page 103. INDEX # 3413.

Ja^s JENKINS; pension awarded 14 Jul 1841; residence - Bengal, India; died 17 Jan 1850. SOURCE: WO120 Volume 69 page 103. INDEX # 3414.

Ch^r OBRIEN; pension awarded 13 May 1840; residence - Bengal, India; died 24 Oct 1853. SOURCE: WO120 Volume 69 page 103. INDEX # 3415.

Alex^r JENKINS; pension awarded 11 Jun 1844; residence - Bengal, India; died 28 Jan 1850. SOURCE: WO120 Volume 69 page 103. INDEX # 3416.

Jno GRANT; pension awarded 12 May 1815; residence - Toronto, Ontario, Canada; died 9 Oct 1869, London, Ontario, Canada. SOURCE: WO120 Volume 69 page 103. INDEX # 3417.

Ja^s SANKEY; pension awarded 12 Jun 1839; residence - Bengal, India. SOURCE: WO120 Volume 69 page 103. INDEX # 3418.

Jno WHARTON; pension awarded 11 Jun 1844; residence - Bengal, India. SOURCE: WO120 Volume 69 page 103. INDEX # 3419.

Willm GADD; pension awarded 30 Jul 1817; residence - Ostend, Belgium; died in 1849. SOURCE: WO120 Volume 69 page 103. INDEX # 3420.

Willm FULLER; pension awarded 12 Jan 1846; residence - Chinsurah, India. SOURCE: WO120 Volume 69 page 103. INDEX # 3421.

Wm BARNS; pension awarded 22 Jun 1847; residence - Calcutta, India; died 2 May 1854. SOURCE: WO120 Volume 69 page 103. INDEX # 3422.

Andrew DALY; pension awarded 11 Aug 1857. SOURCE: WO120 Volume 69 page 103. INDEX # 3423.

Jeremiah FOREHAM; pension awarded 11 Aug 1857. SOURCE: WO120 Volume 69 page 103. INDEX # 3424.

10th Regiment of Foot

Ja^s BOWDEN; pension awarded 16 Jun 1824; residence - Penetanguishene, Ontario, Canada; died 14 Nov 1874, Hamilton, Ontario, Canada. SOURCE: WO120 Volume 69 page 105. INDEX # 3425.

Tim^y GOODE; pension awarded 16 Mar 1835; residence - St. Johns. SOURCE: WO120 Volume 69 page 105. INDEX # 3426.

Jno HAMMOND; pension awarded 18 Dec 1822; residence - Niagara, Ontario, Canada. SOURCE: WO120 Volume 69 page 105. INDEX # 3427.

Dav^d PEDDIE; pension awarded 8 Jul 1845; residence - Meerut, India. SOURCE: WO120 Volume 69 page 105. INDEX # 3428.

Jno BONE; pension awarded 16 Nov 1814; residence - St. Johns. SOURCE: WO120 Volume 69 page 105. INDEX # 3429.

Jno SMITH; pension awarded 13 Feb 1833; residence - Ionian Isls. SOURCE: WO120 Volume 69 page 105. INDEX # 3430.

Jno STOVEN; pension awarded 2 Aug 1802; residence - Quebec, Canada. SOURCE: WO120 Volume 69 page 105. INDEX # 3431.

Saml JOHNSTON; pension awarded 25 Jun 1823; residence - Hobart Town, Australia; died 18 Mar 1852. SOURCE: WO120 Volume 69 page 105. INDEX # 3432.

John BERNARD; pension awarded 16 Nov 1814; residence - Rotterdam, Netherlands. SOURCE: WO120 Volume 69 page 105. INDEX # 3433.

Wm DOUGLAS; pension awarded 25 Jan 1848; residence - Lahore, Pakistan; died 29 Apr 1849. SOURCE: WO120 Volume 69 page 105. INDEX # 3434.

Peter MULLOWNY; pension awarded 25 Jan 1848; residence - Lahore, Pakistan; died 17 Oct 1848. SOURCE: WO120 Volume 69 page 105. INDEX # 3435.

Mich^l QUIGLEY; pension awarded 23 Jan 1849; residence - Calcutta, India; died in 1849. SOURCE: WO120 Volume 69 page 105. INDEX # 3436.

10th Regiment of Foot (continued)

Benjⁿ FOSTER; pension awarded 8 Jan 1850; residence - Ferozepore, India; died 9 Nov 1852. SOURCE: WO120 Volume 69 page 105. INDEX # 3437.

Ja^s TYGHE; pension awarded 8 Jan 1850; residence - Ferozepore, India. SOURCE: WO120 Volume 69 page 105. INDEX # 3438.

Dennis TORPY; pension awarded 8 Jan 1850; residence - Limerick; died 18 Dec 1851. SOURCE: WO120 Volume 69 page 105. INDEX # 3439.

Ja^s HUNT; pension awarded 12 Mar 1850; residence - Ferozepore, India. SOURCE: WO120 Volume 69 page 105. INDEX # 3440.

11th Regiment of Foot

Ja^s LOVETT; pension awarded 7 Feb 1823; residence - Saint John, New Brunswick, Canada; died Halifax, Nova Scotia, Canada. SOURCE: WO120 Volume 69 page 107. INDEX # 3441.

Jno MCDONALD; pension awarded 2 Apr 1817; residence - Montreal, Quebec, Canada. SOURCE: WO120 Volume 69 page 107. INDEX # 3442.

Jno PHILLIPS; pension awarded 24 Feb 1818; residence - Toronto, Ontario, Canada; died in Jan 1851. SOURCE: WO120 Volume 69 page 107. INDEX # 3443.

Chas CLARKE; pension awarded 27 Mar 1816; residence - Quebec, Canada; died 18 Sep 1846. SOURCE: WO120 Volume 69 page 107. INDEX # 3444.

Ja^s HENDERSON; pension awarded 25 May 1821; residence - Penetanguishene, Ontario, Canada; died 2 May 1858. SOURCE: WO120 Volume 69 page 107. INDEX # 3445.

Dav^d LARMER; pension awarded 7 Dec 1820; residence - Quebec, Canada. SOURCE: WO120 Volume 69 page 107. INDEX # 3446.

Jno REGAN; pension awarded 14 Oct 1840; residence - Cape of Good Hope, South Africa; died 1 Mar 1850. SOURCE: WO120 Volume 69 page 107. INDEX # 3447.

Jno MCCALL; pension awarded 2 Apr 1817; residence - Toronto, Ontario, Canada. SOURCE: WO120 Volume 69 page 107. INDEX # 3448.

Willm ALLEN; pension awarded 18 Apr 1821; residence - Toronto, Ontario, Canada. SOURCE: WO120 Volume 69 page 107. INDEX # 3449.

Ja^s MCMULLEN; pension awarded 29 Sep 1819; residence - Toronto, Ontario, Canada. SOURCE: WO120 Volume 69 page 107. INDEX # 3450.

Willm DALEY; pension awarded 24 Feb 1818; residence - Penetanguishene, Ontario, Canada; died 7 Oct 1874, Hamilton, Ontario, Canada. SOURCE: WO120 Volume 69 page 107. INDEX # 3451.

Willm MOREHEAD; pension awarded 22 Dec 1814; residence - London, Ontario, Canada; died 29 Jan 1857. SOURCE: WO120 Volume 69 page 107. INDEX # 3452.

Willm MCCULLOUGH; pension awarded 29 Feb 1816; residence - Penetanguishene, Ontario, Canada; died 1 Mar 1862, Hamilton, Ontario, Canada. SOURCE: WO120 Volume 69 page 107. INDEX # 3453.

Saml CULLY; pension awarded 14 Oct 1840; residence - Quebec, Canada. SOURCE: WO120 Volume 69 page 107. INDEX # 3454.

Geo^e HAMILTON; pension awarded 29 Feb 1816; residence - Toronto, Ontario, Canada; died 11 Mar 1854. SOURCE: WO120 Volume 69 page 107. INDEX # 3455.

Hugh WHITE; pension awarded 22 Jan 1840; residence - Quebec, Canada. SOURCE: WO120 Volume 69 page 107. INDEX # 3456.

Ja^s UNION; pension awarded 7 Feb 1802; residence - New South Wales, Australia; died in 1850. SOURCE: WO120 Volume 69 page 107. INDEX # 3457.

Fra^s CAMPBELL; pension awarded 8 Mar 1837; residence - Ionian Isls; died 7 Nov 1870. SOURCE: WO120 Volume 69 page 107. INDEX # 3458.

Wm KEELING; pension awarded 8 Mar 1837; residence - South Australia, Australia; died 30 Dec 1857. SOURCE: WO120 Volume 69 page 107. INDEX # 3459.

Jno HALL; pension awarded 11 Oct 1836; residence - Toronto, Ontario, Canada; died 13 Jun 1873. SOURCE: WO120 Volume 69 page 107. INDEX # 3460.

11th Regiment of Foot (continued)

Thos FIELDING; pension awarded 8 Jan 1840; residence - Jamaica. SOURCE: WO120 Volume 69 page 107. INDEX # 3461.

Lawe MORRISON; pension awarded 12 Oct 1813; residence - Toronto, Ontario, Canada; died 3 May 1858. SOURCE: WO120 Volume 69 page 107. INDEX # 3462.

Wm CONNELL; pension awarded 26 Oct 1847. SOURCE: WO120 Volume 69 page 107. INDEX # 3463.

Michl KING; pension awarded 26 Oct 1847. SOURCE: WO120 Volume 69 page 107. INDEX # 3464.

Wm LAVELL; pension awarded 26 Oct 1847. SOURCE: WO120 Volume 69 page 107. INDEX # 3465.

Patk NOWLAN; pension awarded 26 Oct 1847; died 28 Dec 1870 Hobart Town, Australia. SOURCE: WO120 Volume 69 page 107. INDEX # 3466.

Geoe ROYCROFT; pension awarded 26 Oct 1847. SOURCE: WO120 Volume 69 page 107. INDEX # 3467.

Chas ELLIS; pension awarded 27 Jun 1848. SOURCE: WO120 Volume 69 page 107. INDEX # 3468.

Wm BLAVIN; pension awarded 27 Jun 1848; died 15 Jan 1879, Melbourne, Australia. SOURCE: WO120 Volume 69 page 107. INDEX # 3469.

Jas BUTTERWORTH; pension awarded 27 Jun 1848; died 30 Oct 1870. SOURCE: WO120 Volume 69 page 107. INDEX # 3470.

Jno DALTON; pension awarded 27 Jun 1848. SOURCE: WO120 Volume 69 page 107. INDEX # 3471.

Patk MCCARTEN; pension awarded 27 Jun 1848. SOURCE: WO120 Volume 69 page 107. INDEX # 3472.

Jno HOLMES; pension awarded 14 Nov 1848. SOURCE: WO120 Volume 69 page 107. INDEX # 3473.

Patk DUAN; pension awarded 22 May 1849. SOURCE: WO120 Volume 69 page 107. INDEX # 3474.

Wm EDWARDS; pension awarded 22 May 1849. SOURCE: WO120 Volume 69 page 107. INDEX # 3475.

Geoe DINEEN; pension awarded 12 Jun 1849; died 17 Feb 1876. SOURCE: WO120 Volume 69 page 107. INDEX # 3476.

Patk HARRINGTON; pension awarded 12 Jun 1849; residence - Hobart Town, Australia; died 8 Aug 1852. SOURCE: WO120 Volume 69 page 107. INDEX # 3477.

Jno CALLAGHAN; pension awarded 26 Jun 1849. SOURCE: WO120 Volume 69 page 107. INDEX # 3478.

Jno MULLOWNEY; pension awarded 26 Jun 1849. SOURCE: WO120 Volume 69 page 107. INDEX # 3479.

Martin FOX; pension awarded 26 Jun 1849. SOURCE: WO120 Volume 69 page 107. INDEX # 3480.

David BRYAN; pension awarded 26 Jun 1849. SOURCE: WO120 Volume 69 page 108. INDEX # 3481.

Patk GIBBS; pension awarded 26 Jun 1849; died 14 May 1879, Melbourne, Australia. SOURCE: WO120 Volume 69 page 108. INDEX # 3482.

Corns HARRINGTON; pension awarded 26 Jun 1849. SOURCE: WO120 Volume 69 page 108. INDEX # 3483.

Jno WILSON; pension awarded 23 Oct 1849. SOURCE: WO120 Volume 69 page 108. INDEX # 3484.

Heny ELLIS; pension awarded 13 Nov 1849; died 20 Dec 1876, New South Wales, Australia. SOURCE: WO120 Volume 69 page 108. INDEX # 3485.

Robt FREER; pension awarded 13 Nov 1849; died 16 Aug 1874 Sydney, New South Wales, Australia. SOURCE: WO120 Volume 69 page 108. INDEX # 3486.

Martin FEENEY; pension awarded 16 Jul 1850. SOURCE: WO120 Volume 69 page 108. INDEX # 3487.

Gregor MCGREGOR; pension awarded 16 Jul 1850. SOURCE: WO120 Volume 69 page 108. INDEX # 3488.

Jno HALLAGHAN; pension awarded 16 Jul 1850. SOURCE: WO120 Volume 69 page 108. INDEX # 3489.

Wm LANE; pension awarded 16 Jul 1850; died 3 Feb 1860 New South Wales, Australia. SOURCE: WO120 Volume 69 page 108. INDEX # 3490.

Barthw BANNISTER; pension awarded 16 Jul 1850. SOURCE: WO120 Volume 69 page 108. INDEX # 3491.

Bernard BOYLE; pension awarded 16 Jul 1850. SOURCE: WO120 Volume 69 page 108. INDEX # 3492.

Wm CARROLL; pension awarded 16 Jul 1850. SOURCE: WO120 Volume 69 page 108. INDEX # 3493.

Martin CONWAY; pension awarded 16 Jul 1850; died 14 Nov 1872, Ennis. SOURCE: WO120 Volume 69 page 108. INDEX # 3494.

Michl DOYLE; pension awarded 16 Jul 1850; died 30 Nov 1880, New South Wales, Australia. SOURCE: WO120 Volume 69 page 108. INDEX # 3495.

Michl DOUGHANEY; pension awarded 16 Jul 1850. SOURCE: WO120 Volume 69 page 108. INDEX # 3496.

11th Regiment of Foot (continued)

Ja^s GRAVES; pension awarded 16 Jul 1850. SOURCE: WO120 Volume 69 page 108. INDEX # 3497.

Denis LEARY; pension awarded 16 Jul 1850. SOURCE: WO120 Volume 69 page 108. INDEX # 3498.

Jno LOCKETT; pension awarded 16 Jul 1850. SOURCE: WO120 Volume 69 page 108. INDEX # 3499.

Robt MCJANETT; pension awarded 16 Jul 1850. SOURCE: WO120 Volume 69 page 108. INDEX # 3500.

Saml SNEYD; pension awarded 16 Jul 1850; died 1 Jul 1885, Brisbane, Australia. SOURCE: WO120 Volume 69 page 108. INDEX # 3501.

Alex^r THOMPSON; pension awarded 16 Jul 1850; residence - Sydney, New South Wales, Australia. SOURCE: WO120 Volume 69 page 108. INDEX # 3502.

Robt WORSLEY; pension awarded 16 Jul 1850. SOURCE: WO120 Volume 69 page 108. INDEX # 3503.

Edwd Brown BRUCE; pension awarded 27 Aug 1850; died 27 Aug 1880, New South Wales, Australia. SOURCE: WO120 Volume 69 page 108. INDEX # 3504.

Benjn MOORE; pension awarded 27 Aug 1850. SOURCE: WO120 Volume 69 page 108. INDEX # 3505.

Saml CURRY; pension awarded 13 May 1851. SOURCE: WO120 Volume 69 page 108. INDEX # 3506.

Wm HOPLEY; pension awarded 13 May 1851. SOURCE: WO120 Volume 69 page 108. INDEX # 3507.

Jos^h WALSH; pension awarded 13 May 1851. SOURCE: WO120 Volume 69 page 108. INDEX # 3508.

Wm HODGE; pension awarded 13 May 1851; died 14 Apr 1863, New South Wales, Australia. SOURCE: WO120 Volume 69 page 108. INDEX # 3509.

Richd HARRISON; pension awarded 13 May 1851. SOURCE: WO120 Volume 69 page 108. INDEX # 3510.

Pat^k DUFFEY; pension awarded 13 May 1851; died 6 Jan 1881, Melbourne, Australia. SOURCE: WO120 Volume 69 page 108. INDEX # 3511.

Thos HARRINGTON; pension awarded 13 May 1851. SOURCE: WO120 Volume 69 page 108. INDEX # 3512.

Pat^k HELY; pension awarded 13 May 1851. SOURCE: WO120 Volume 69 page 108. INDEX # 3513.

Pat^k MCDONALD; pension awarded 13 May 1851. SOURCE: WO120 Volume 69 page 108. INDEX # 3514.

Hen^y ROSE; pension awarded 13 May 1851. SOURCE: WO120 Volume 69 page 108. INDEX # 3515.

Wm THOMAS; pension awarded 13 May 1851; residence - South Australia, Australia; died in Jun 1857. SOURCE: WO120 Volume 69 page 108. INDEX # 3516.

Thos WHITMILL; pension awarded 13 May 1851. SOURCE: WO120 Volume 69 page 108. INDEX # 3517.

Jno CHANDLER; pension awarded 28 Oct 1851. SOURCE: WO120 Volume 69 page 108. INDEX # 3518.

Mich^l REILLY; pension awarded 28 Oct 1851. SOURCE: WO120 Volume 69 page 108. INDEX # 3519.

Mich^l CLARKE; pension awarded 13 Jul 1852. SOURCE: WO120 Volume 69 page 108. INDEX # 3520.

12th Regiment of Foot

Pat^k FEENEY; pension awarded 28 Aug 1822; residence - Toronto, Ontario, Canada. SOURCE: WO120 Volume 69 page 109. INDEX # 3521.

Jos^h BILSON; pension awarded 27 Jan 1817; residence - Van D^s Land, Australia; died 15 Jun 1872, Hobart Town, Australia. SOURCE: WO120 Volume 69 page 108. INDEX # 3522.

Alex^r TOOLE; pension awarded 9 Mar 1842; residence - Mauritius. SOURCE: WO120 Volume 69 page 109. INDEX # 3523.

Danl FITZPATRICK; pension awarded 4 Aug 1824; residence - New South Wales, Australia; died in 1853. SOURCE: WO120 Volume 69 page 109. INDEX # 3524.

Chas HUTCHINSON; pension awarded 13 Oct 1841; residence - Mauritius. SOURCE: WO120 Volume 69 page 109. INDEX # 3525.

Bryan FAWL; pension awarded 9 Oct 1839; residence - New South Wales, Australia. SOURCE: WO120 Volume 69 page 109. INDEX # 3526.

Jno HARTLEY; pension awarded 25 Oct 1820; residence - Toronto, Ontario, Canada; died 25 Mar 1862. SOURCE: WO120 Volume 69 page 109. INDEX # 3527.

Richd STEVENSON; pension awarded 12 Aug 1845; residence - Montreal, Quebec, Canada; died 26 Mar 1880, Montreal, Quebec, Canada. SOURCE: WO120 Volume 69 page 109. INDEX # 3528.

WO120 VOLUME 69

12th Regiment of Foot (continued)

Martin LOUGHLIN; pension awarded 14 Mar 1848; residence - Mauritius; died 29 Nov 1851. SOURCE: WO120 Volume 69 page 109. INDEX # 3529.

Wm MOTHERSOLE; pension awarded 14 Mar 1848; residence - Mauritius; died 16 Nov 1853. SOURCE: WO120 Volume 69 page 109. INDEX # 3530.

Fra^s RYE; pension awarded 13 Jul 1852; died 10 Jan 1857. SOURCE: WO120 Volume 69 page 109. INDEX # 3531.

Wm KEARNEY; pension awarded 13 Jul 1852; residence - Cape Town, South Africa. SOURCE: WO120 Volume 69 page 109. INDEX # 3532.

Joseph BRINDLEY; pension awarded 12 Jun 1855. SOURCE: WO120 Volume 69 page 109. INDEX # 3533.

Daniel QUINN; pension awarded 12 Jun 1855. SOURCE: WO120 Volume 69 page 109. INDEX # 3534.

Wm BUTWELL; pension awarded 18 Mar 1856. SOURCE: WO120 Volume 69 page 109. INDEX # 3535.

John GREEN; pension awarded 26 Aug 1856. SOURCE: WO120 Volume 69 page 109. INDEX # 3536.

Thomas COLE; pension awarded 31 Mar 1857. SOURCE: WO120 Volume 69 page 109. INDEX # 3537.

Thomas MARTIN; pension awarded 31 Mar 1857. SOURCE: WO120 Volume 69 page 109. INDEX # 3538.

Wm Lowther MORRIS; pension awarded 31 Mar 1857. SOURCE: WO120 Volume 69 page 109. INDEX # 3539.

George SWATMAN; pension awarded 31 Mar 1857. SOURCE: WO120 Volume 69 page 109. INDEX # 3540.

Thomas TODD; pension awarded 23 Jun 1857. SOURCE: WO120 Volume 69 page 109. INDEX # 3541.

Samuel MYERS; pension awarded 15 Sep 1857. SOURCE: WO120 Volume 69 page 109. INDEX # 3542.

13th Regiment of Foot

Ja^s CURRY; pension awarded 5 Aug 1829; residence - Sydney, Australia; died 23 Dec 1848. SOURCE: WO120 Volume 69 page 115. INDEX # 3543.

Mar^n DONAHOE; pension awarded 17 Jan 1827; residence - Montreal, Quebec, Canada. SOURCE: WO120 Volume 69 page 115. INDEX # 3544.

Jno SALTER; pension awarded 9 Mar 1842; residence - Bengal, India; died 30 Jan 1848. SOURCE: WO120 Volume 69 page 115. INDEX # 3545.

Jno BEAGHAN; pension awarded 23 Jul 1823; residence - Kingston, Ontario, Canada; died in Nov 1845. SOURCE: WO120 Volume 69 page 115. INDEX # 3546.

Peter NEYLAND; pension awarded 25 Oct 1842; residence - Bengal, India. SOURCE: WO120 Volume 69 page 115. INDEX # 3547.

Pat^k WYRE; pension awarded 11 Jun 1844; residence - Kussowlie, India; died 11 Nov 1848. SOURCE: WO120 Volume 69 page 115. INDEX # 3548.

John MCCONKEY; pension awarded 8 Aug 1827; residence - St. Johns. SOURCE: WO120 Volume 69 page 115. INDEX # 3549.

Thos LUDLOW; pension awarded 11 Jun 1844; residence - Kussowlie, India; died 1 Mar 1887, W. London. SOURCE: WO120 Volume 69 page 115. INDEX # 3550.

Wm DAVIS; pension awarded 27 Mar 1839; residence - Bengal, India; died 16 Oct 1879, Houghly. SOURCE: WO120 Volume 69 page 115. INDEX # 3551.

Richd JONES; pension awarded 8 May 1839; residence - Bengal, India. SOURCE: WO120 Volume 69 page 115. INDEX # 3552.

Willm SMITH; pension awarded 8 May 1839; residence - Bengal, India. SOURCE: WO120 Volume 69 page 115. INDEX # 3553.

Thos WELLS; pension awarded 27 Sep 1842; residence - Bengal, India. SOURCE: WO120 Volume 69 page 115. INDEX # 3554.

Thos DAILEY; pension awarded 11 Jun 1844; residence - Kussowlie, India. SOURCE: WO120 Volume 69 page 115. INDEX # 3555.

Thos MCGOWAN; pension awarded 9 Mar 1842; residence - Bengal, India. SOURCE: WO120 Volume 69 page 115. INDEX # 3556.

George KNIGHT; pension awarded 27 Mar 1839; residence - Bengal, India. SOURCE: WO120 Volume 69 page 115. INDEX # 3557.

13th Regiment of Foot (continued)

Jer^h SALISBURY; pension awarded 27 Mar 1839; residence - Bengal, India. SOURCE: WO120 Volume 69 page 115. INDEX # 3558.

Fra^s HALLIGAN; pension awarded 11 Jun 1844; residence - Kussowlie, India; died 3 Aug 1851. SOURCE: WO120 Volume 69 page 115. INDEX # 3559.

Jos^h Nelson HASELTINE; pension awarded 25 Feb 1845; residence - Sukkur, India. SOURCE: WO120 Volume 69 page 115. INDEX # 3560.

James MCARDLE; pension awarded 25 May 1857. SOURCE: WO120 Volume 69 page 115. INDEX # 3561.

14th Regiment of Foot

And^w MCCARTHY; pension awarded 27 Sep 1842; residence - Kingston, Ontario, Canada. SOURCE: WO120 Volume 69 page 117. INDEX # 3562.

Ja^s NETHERCOTT; pension awarded 13 Aug 1844; residence - Toronto, Ontario, Canada; died 10 Aug 1847. SOURCE: WO120 Volume 69 page 117. INDEX # 3563.

Saml WARNER; pension awarded 25 Apr 1827; residence - India. SOURCE: WO120 Volume 69 page 117. INDEX # 3564.

Chas COOK; pension awarded 10 Aug 1831; residence - Bengal, India; died 19 Jul 1855. SOURCE: WO120 Volume 69 page 117. INDEX # 3565.

Thos FLETCHER; pension awarded 22 Nov 1842; residence - London, Ontario, Canada; died 3 Nov 1857. SOURCE: WO120 Volume 69 page 117. INDEX # 3566.

Richd EDMONDS; pension awarded 5 Sep 1823; residence - London, Ontario, Canada; died 4 Jun 1854. SOURCE: WO120 Volume 69 page 117. INDEX # 3567.

Wm BIRD; pension awarded 23 Sep 1845; residence - Kingston, Ontario, Canada; died 18 Jul 1874, Toronto, Ontario, Canada. SOURCE: WO120 Volume 69 page 117. INDEX # 3568.

Robt WISHART; pension awarded 26 Sep 1843; residence - London, Ontario, Canada. SOURCE: WO120 Volume 69 page 117. INDEX # 3569.

Thos COURSER; pension awarded 8 Aug 1827; residence - Toronto, Ontario, Canada. SOURCE: WO120 Volume 69 page 117. INDEX # 3570.

Jno MURPHY; pension awarded 21 Aug 1822; residence - Prescott, Ontario, Canada; died 30 Jan 1864, Hamilton, Ontario, Canada. SOURCE: WO120 Volume 69 page 117. INDEX # 3571.

Saml PLOWRIGHT; pension awarded 25 Apr 1827; residence - Bengal, India; died 12 Aug 1845. SOURCE: WO120 Volume 69 page 117. INDEX # 3572.

Wm SLATER; pension awarded 25 Apr 1827; residence - Bengal, India. SOURCE: WO120 Volume 69 page 117. INDEX # 3573.

Pat^k MOFFATT; pension awarded 23 Sep 1845; residence - Montreal, Quebec, Canada. SOURCE: WO120 Volume 69 page 117. INDEX # 3574.

John BLOW; pension awarded 13 Aug 1844; residence - London, Ontario, Canada. SOURCE: WO120 Volume 69 page 117. INDEX # 3575.

Alex^r MILNE; pension awarded 9 Sep 1845; residence - Kingston, Ontario, Canada. SOURCE: WO120 Volume 69 page 117. INDEX # 3576.

Jno GALLAGHER; pension awarded 13 Jan 1846; residence - London, Ontario, Canada; died 26 Sep 1872, London, Ontario, Canada. SOURCE: WO120 Volume 69 page 117. INDEX # 3577.

Ed^w CONNOLLY; pension awarded 22 Sep 1846. SOURCE: WO120 Volume 69 page 117. INDEX # 3578.

Jno HALLS; pension awarded 22 Sep 1846; died 13 Nov 1878, London, Ontario, Canada. SOURCE: WO120 Volume 69 page 117. INDEX # 3579.

Danl BROPHY; pension awarded 22 Sep 1846; residence - Toronto, Ontario, Canada; died 2 Dec 1864. SOURCE: WO120 Volume 69 page 117. INDEX # 3580.

Jno GREEN; pension awarded 22 Sep 1846; residence - Toronto, Ontario, Canada; died 30 Jul 1848. SOURCE: WO120 Volume 69 page 117. INDEX # 3581.

Wm HEARN; pension awarded 22 Sep 1846. SOURCE: WO120 Volume 69 page 117. INDEX # 3582.

Hen^y PEACH; pension awarded 22 Sep 1846; residence - Halifax, Nova Scotia, Canada; died 3 Jul 1851. SOURCE: WO120 Volume 69 page 117. INDEX # 3583.

Edwin HOWARD; pension awarded 22 Sep 1846. SOURCE: WO120 Volume 69 page 117. INDEX # 3584.

WO120 VOLUME 69

14th Regiment of Foot (continued)

Saml RUDDY; pension awarded 14 Sep 1847; residence - Toronto, Ontario, Canada; died 18 Aug 1878. SOURCE: WO120 Volume 69 page 117. INDEX # 3585.

15th Regiment of Foot

Wm ROMNEY; pension awarded 6 Dec 1822; residence - New South Wales, Australia; died in 1845. SOURCE: WO120 Volume 69 page 119. INDEX # 3586.

Wm GODFREY; pension awarded 11 Dec 1839; residence - Montreal, Quebec, Canada; died 16 Nov 1858, Montreal, Quebec, Canada. SOURCE: WO120 Volume 69 page 119. INDEX # 3587.

Tim^y TREACY; pension awarded 22 Jan 1840; residence - Montreal, Quebec, Canada. SOURCE: WO120 Volume 69 page 119. INDEX # 3588.

Pat^k KINSLEY; pension awarded 13 Dec 1820; residence - London, Ontario, Canada. SOURCE: WO120 Volume 69 page 119. INDEX # 3589.

Jno BROWN; pension awarded 9 Jan 1833; residence - Cornwall, Ontario, Canada. SOURCE: WO120 Volume 69 page 119. INDEX # 3590.

Alex^r MURPHY; pension awarded 9 Jan 1833; residence - Montreal, Quebec, Canada. SOURCE: WO120 Volume 69 page 119. INDEX # 3591.

Edw^s BOTTERILL; pension awarded 12 Jul 1837; residence - Kingston, Ontario, Canada. SOURCE: WO120 Volume 69 page 119. INDEX # 3592.

Ja^s DEE; pension awarded 8 Jan 1840; residence - Toronto, Ontario, Canada; died 13 Sep 1872, Toronto, Ontario, Canada. SOURCE: WO120 Volume 69 page 119. INDEX # 3593.

Dav^d SMITH; pension awarded 20 Jan 1819; residence - Prescott, Ontario, Canada; died 3 Apr 1861, Hamilton, Ontario, Canada. SOURCE: WO120 Volume 69 page 119. INDEX # 3594.

Bern^d CARROLL; pension awarded 11 Oct 1837; residence - Saint Johns, Quebec, Canada. SOURCE: WO120 Volume 69 page 119. INDEX # 3595.

Jos^h BILBY; pension awarded 19 Jul 1826; residence - Halifax, Nova Scotia, Canada. SOURCE: WO120 Volume 69 page 119. INDEX # 3596.

Thos BAILEY; pension awarded 9 Sep 1840; residence - Montreal, Quebec, Canada; died 2 Aug 1862, Toronto, Ontario, Canada. SOURCE: WO120 Volume 69 page 119. INDEX # 3597.

Danl CALLAGHAN; pension awarded 27 Dec 1837; residence - Kingston, Ontario, Canada; died 18 Aug 1854. SOURCE: WO120 Volume 69 page 119. INDEX # 3598.

Jno CORNEALSON; pension awarded 20 Mar 1827; residence - Rotterdam, Netherlands; died in Nov 1846. SOURCE: WO120 Volume 69 page 119. INDEX # 3599.

Thos BRENNAM; pension awarded 8 Jan 1840; residence - Montreal, Quebec, Canada; died 18 May 1848. SOURCE: WO120 Volume 69 page 119. INDEX # 3600.

Jno ANDERSON; pension awarded 10 Feb 1846; residence - Ft. Garry. SOURCE: WO120 Volume 69 page 119. INDEX # 3601.

Pat^k KENNY; pension awarded 21 Oct 1845; residence - St. Johns. SOURCE: WO120 Volume 69 page 119. INDEX # 3602.

16th Regiment of Foot

Pat^k MADDEN; pension awarded 8 Sep 1841; residence - Montreal, Quebec, Canada. SOURCE: WO120 Volume 69 page 121. INDEX # 3603.

Ja^s SYKES; pension awarded 12 Jul 1837; residence - Bengal, India. SOURCE: WO120 Volume 69 page 121. INDEX # 3604.

Thos BURTON; pension awarded 9 Jun 1841; residence - Bengal, India; died 15 Oct 1852. SOURCE: WO120 Volume 69 page 121. INDEX # 3605.

Jno SMITH; pension awarded 11 Nov 1818; residence - Sydney. SOURCE: WO120 Volume 69 page 121. INDEX # 3606.

Jno JORDAN; pension awarded 13 May 1840; residence - Bengal, India; died 12 Sep 1845. SOURCE: WO120 Volume 69 page 121. INDEX # 3607.

BRITISH ARMY PENSIONERS ABROAD

16th Regiment of Foot (continued)

Abr^m BELL; pension awarded 29 Jun 1837; residence - Smiths Falls, Ontario, Canada; died 5 Apr 1861, Bytown, Ontario, Canada. SOURCE: WO120 Volume 69 page 121. INDEX # 3608.

Ja^s FORD; pension awarded 25 Apr 1827; residence - Ceylon; died 11 May 1851. SOURCE: WO120 Volume 69 page 121. INDEX # 3609.

Wm HACK; pension awarded 13 May 1840; residence - Bengal, India; died 14 Apr 1852. SOURCE: WO120 Volume 69 page 121. INDEX # 3610.

Ja^s DONAGHUE; pension awarded 14 Jul 1841; residence - Bengal, India; died 15 Mar 1850. SOURCE: WO120 Volume 69 page 121. INDEX # 3611.

Danl HUMM; pension awarded 26 Aug 1840; residence - Sydney, New South Wales, Australia. SOURCE: WO120 Volume 69 page 121. INDEX # 3612.

Ja^s BURKETT; pension awarded 13 May 1840; residence - Bengal, India. SOURCE: WO120 Volume 69 page 121. INDEX # 3613.

Willm HUGGARD; pension awarded 4 Aug 1824; residence - Quebec, Canada; died 11 Jan 1854. SOURCE: WO120 Volume 69 page 121. INDEX # 3614.

Jno WELTON; pension awarded 2 Aug 1845; residence - Gibraltar; died 10 Jul 1847. SOURCE: WO120 Volume 69 page 121. INDEX # 3615.

Patrick DOBBIN; pension awarded 24 Jul 1855. SOURCE: WO120 Volume 69 page 121. INDEX # 3616.

George MCKAY; pension awarded 24 Jul 1855. SOURCE: WO120 Volume 69 page 121. INDEX # 3617.

Thomas MULLONY; pension awarded 24 Jul 1855. SOURCE: WO120 Volume 69 page 121. INDEX # 3618.

Michael DARON; pension awarded 24 Jul 1855. SOURCE: WO120 Volume 69 page 121. INDEX # 3619.

William FOODY; pension awarded 24 Jul 1855. SOURCE: WO120 Volume 69 page 121. INDEX # 3620.

George HANSON; pension awarded 24 Jul 1855. SOURCE: WO120 Volume 69 page 121. INDEX # 3621.

James HETT; pension awarded 24 Jul 1855. SOURCE: WO120 Volume 69 page 121. INDEX # 3622.

Matthew MAHONEY; pension awarded 24 Jul 1855; residence - Montreal, Quebec, Canada; died 2 Mar 1857. SOURCE: WO120 Volume 69 page 121. INDEX # 3623.

Valentine PILMER; pension awarded 24 Jul 1855. SOURCE: WO120 Volume 69 page 121. INDEX # 3624.

Joseph BATES; pension awarded 29 Jul 1856. SOURCE: WO120 Volume 69 page 121. INDEX # 3625.

Samuel BRAY; pension awarded 29 Jul 1856. SOURCE: WO120 Volume 69 page 121. INDEX # 3626.

William BROWN; pension awarded 29 Jul 1856. SOURCE: WO120 Volume 69 page 121. INDEX # 3627.

James DUNN; pension awarded 29 Jul 1856. SOURCE: WO120 Volume 69 page 121. INDEX # 3628.

John GILLIGAN; pension awarded 29 Jul 1856. SOURCE: WO120 Volume 69 page 121. INDEX # 3629.

Alexander HISLOP; pension awarded 29 Jul 1856. SOURCE: WO120 Volume 69 page 121. INDEX # 3630.

Thomas HOWELL; pension awarded 29 Jul 1856. SOURCE: WO120 Volume 69 page 121. INDEX # 3631.

John MATHEWS; pension awarded 29 Jul 1856. SOURCE: WO120 Volume 69 page 121. INDEX # 3632.

Peter RICE; pension awarded 29 Jul 1856. SOURCE: WO120 Volume 69 page 121. INDEX # 3633.

George SAUNDERS; pension awarded 29 Jul 1856. SOURCE: WO120 Volume 69 page 121. INDEX # 3634.

William SAUNDERS; pension awarded 29 Jul 1856. SOURCE: WO120 Volume 69 page 121. INDEX # 3635.

Thomas SCOTT; pension awarded 29 Jul 1856. SOURCE: WO120 Volume 69 page 121. INDEX # 3636.

James SWITZER; pension awarded 29 Jul 1856. SOURCE: WO120 Volume 69 page 121. INDEX # 3637.

Archibald DAVIE; pension awarded 11 Aug 1857. SOURCE: WO120 Volume 69 page 121. INDEX # 3638.

Laurence NOLAN; pension awarded 11 Aug 1857; residence - Kingston, Ontario, Canada; died 23 Nov 1857. SOURCE: WO120 Volume 69 page 121. INDEX # 3639.

Thomas CONNOLLY; pension awarded 11 Aug 1857. SOURCE: WO120 Volume 69 page 121. INDEX # 3640.

Thomas JONES; pension awarded 11 Aug 1857; residence - Toronto, Ontario, Canada; died 16 Jun 1858. SOURCE: WO120 Volume 69 page 121. INDEX # 3641.

John WATERS; pension awarded 11 Aug 1857. SOURCE: WO120 Volume 69 page 121. INDEX # 3642.

16th Regiment of Foot (continued)

George BENTHAM; pension awarded 11 Aug 1857. SOURCE: WO120 Volume 69 page 122. INDEX # 3643.
Edward BOURKE; pension awarded 11 Aug 1857. SOURCE: WO120 Volume 69 page 122. INDEX # 3644.
Joseph COCHRANE; pension awarded 11 Aug 1857. SOURCE: WO120 Volume 69 page 122. INDEX # 3645.
Septimus COCHRANE; pension awarded 11 Aug 1857. SOURCE: WO120 Volume 69 page 122. INDEX # 3646.
Redmond COMMINS; pension awarded 11 Aug 1857. SOURCE: WO120 Volume 69 page 122. INDEX # 3647.
William DAHENNY; pension awarded 11 Aug 1857. SOURCE: WO120 Volume 69 page 122. INDEX # 3648.
Bartholomew GIBNEY; pension awarded 11 Aug 1857. SOURCE: WO120 Volume 69 page 122. INDEX # 3649.
John KELLY; pension awarded 11 Aug 1857. SOURCE: WO120 Volume 69 page 122. INDEX # 3650.
Timothy LANDERS; pension awarded 11 Aug 1857. SOURCE: WO120 Volume 69 page 122. INDEX # 3651.
Richard LLOYD; pension awarded 11 Aug 1857. SOURCE: WO120 Volume 69 page 122. INDEX # 3652.
John MASTERS; pension awarded 11 Aug 1857. SOURCE: WO120 Volume 69 page 122. INDEX # 3653.
Thomas MOORCROFT; pension awarded 11 Aug 1857. SOURCE: WO120 Volume 69 page 122. INDEX # 3654.
Christmas MOORCROFT; pension awarded 11 Aug 1857. SOURCE: WO120 Volume 69 page 122. INDEX # 3655.
Francis MURRAY; pension awarded 11 Aug 1857. SOURCE: WO120 Volume 69 page 122. INDEX # 3656.
Henry PARKER; pension awarded 11 Aug 1857. SOURCE: WO120 Volume 69 page 122. INDEX # 3657.
Thomas READY; pension awarded 11 Aug 1857. SOURCE: WO120 Volume 69 page 122. INDEX # 3658.
James REDDLE; pension awarded 11 Aug 1857. SOURCE: WO120 Volume 69 page 122. INDEX # 3659.
Francis STENSION; pension awarded 11 Aug 1857. SOURCE: WO120 Volume 69 page 122. INDEX # 3660.
Thomas NOICE; pension awarded 11 Aug 1857. SOURCE: WO120 Volume 69 page 122. INDEX # 3661.

17th Regiment of Foot

Ja^s PEGG; pension awarded 23 Jul 1823; residence - New South Wales, Australia. SOURCE: WO120 Volume 69 page 123. INDEX # 3662.
Isaac RIVETT; pension awarded 10 Jun 1840; residence - Bombay, India. SOURCE: WO120 Volume 69 page 123. INDEX # 3663.
Peter MCAULEY; pension awarded 10 Apr 1833; residence - New South Wales, Australia. SOURCE: WO120 Volume 69 page 123. INDEX # 3664.
Jos^h PHILLIPS; pension awarded 12 Jun 1833; residence - New South Wales, Australia; died in 1853. SOURCE: WO120 Volume 69 page 123. INDEX # 3665.
Jno CHISLETT; pension awarded 8 Feb 1837; residence - New South Wales, Australia; died in Sep 1851. SOURCE: WO120 Volume 69 page 123. INDEX # 3666.
Richd APPLETON; pension awarded 24 May 1842; residence - Bombay, India. SOURCE: WO120 Volume 69 page 123. INDEX # 3667.
Edwin RUNDOCK; pension awarded 24 May 1842; residence - Bombay, India. SOURCE: WO120 Volume 69 page 123. INDEX # 3668.
Thos ECHLIN; pension awarded 1 Jun 1844; residence - Bytown, Ontario, Canada; died in Dec 1845. SOURCE: WO120 Volume 69 page 123. INDEX # 3669.
Wm KING; pension awarded 12 May 1841; residence - Bombay, India; died 24 Dec 1846. SOURCE: WO120 Volume 69 page 123. INDEX # 3670.
Abr^m RANSOM; pension awarded 23 Jul 1823; residence - Toronto, Ontario, Canada. SOURCE: WO120 Volume 69 page 123. INDEX # 3671.
Wm KEEVERS; pension awarded 10 Sep 1834; residence - New South Wales, Australia. SOURCE: WO120 Volume 69 page 123. INDEX # 3672.

BRITISH ARMY PENSIONERS ABROAD

17th Regiment of Foot (continued)

Thos STRETTON; pension awarded 23 Jul 1823; residence - New Zealand; died 22 Jan 1857. SOURCE: WO120 Volume 69 page 123. INDEX # 3673.

Saml LEVISTON; pension awarded 11 Jun 1844; residence - Bombay, India; died 24 Jul 1879. SOURCE: WO120 Volume 69 page 123. INDEX # 3674.

Jos^h TURNER; pension awarded 25 Sep 1823; residence - Cape of Good Hope, South Africa; died 3 Apr 1851. SOURCE: WO120 Volume 69 page 123. INDEX # 3675.

Robt DYE; pension awarded 27 Aug 1823; residence - Bengal, India; died 7 Jul 1853. SOURCE: WO120 Volume 69 page 123. INDEX # 3676.

Den^s RYRNES; pension awarded 26 May 1841; residence - Cape of Good Hope, South Africa. SOURCE: WO120 Volume 69 page 123. INDEX # 3677.

Thos BIRD; pension awarded 13 Jun 1843; residence - Bombay, India. SOURCE: WO120 Volume 69 page 123. INDEX # 3678.

Richd NUTTALL; pension awarded 25 Aug 1841; residence - Bombay, India; died 15 Nov 1858. SOURCE: WO120 Volume 69 page 123. INDEX # 3679.

Jno RAWSON; pension awarded 10 Aug 1836; residence - New South Wales, Australia. SOURCE: WO120 Volume 69 page 123. INDEX # 3680.

Jos^h RILEY; pension awarded 11 Jun 1844; residence - Bombay, India. SOURCE: WO120 Volume 69 page 123. INDEX # 3681.

Mich^l WINN; pension awarded 28 Apr 1846; residence - Ahmednuggar, India. SOURCE: WO120 Volume 69 page 123. INDEX # 3682.

Jeremiah SULLIVAN; pension awarded 11 May 1847; died 8 Nov 1877, Bombay, India. SOURCE: WO120 Volume 69 page 123. INDEX # 3683.

Mich^l BYRNE; pension awarded 11 May 1847. SOURCE: WO120 Volume 69 page 123. INDEX # 3684.

Geo^e JOHNSTON; pension awarded 11 May 1847. SOURCE: WO120 Volume 69 page 123. INDEX # 3685.

John FOWLER; pension awarded 11 Aug 1857. SOURCE: WO120 Volume 69 page 123. INDEX # 3686.

Timothy CALLAGHAN; pension awarded 11 Aug 1857. SOURCE: WO120 Volume 69 page 123. INDEX # 3687.

James CANNON; pension awarded 11 Aug 1857. SOURCE: WO120 Volume 69 page 123. INDEX # 3688.

18th Regiment of Foot

Walter MCFARLANE; pension awarded 1 May 1822; residence - Bytown, Ontario, Canada. SOURCE: WO120 Volume 69 page 125. INDEX # 3689.

Willm WATSON; pension awarded 25 Jun 1823; residence - Quebec, Canada. SOURCE: WO120 Volume 69 page 125. INDEX # 3690.

Geo^e CRAWFORD; pension awarded 9 May 1843; residence - Ceylon; died 2 Jul 1880, Armagh. SOURCE: WO120 Volume 69 page 125. INDEX # 3691.

Geo^e MCLERNON; pension awarded 4 Oct 1816; residence - Montreal, Quebec, Canada. SOURCE: WO120 Volume 69 page 125. INDEX # 3692.

Ja^s HASTY; pension awarded 29 Nov 1820; residence - Toronto, Ontario, Canada; died 1 Feb 1856. SOURCE: WO120 Volume 69 page 125. INDEX # 3693.

Ja^s COPELAND; pension awarded 3 Mar 1819; residence - William Henry, Quebec, Canada. SOURCE: WO120 Volume 69 page 125. INDEX # 3694.

Ed^{wd} GODFRAY; pension awarded 24 Oct 1821; residence - Toronto, Ontario, Canada. SOURCE: WO120 Volume 69 page 125. INDEX # 3695.

Pat^k STANTON; pension awarded 3 Mar 1809; residence - Montreal, Quebec, Canada. SOURCE: WO120 Volume 69 page 125. INDEX # 3696.

Wm EKINS; pension awarded 10 Jan 1838; residence - Toronto, Ontario, Canada; died 16 Nov 1844. SOURCE: WO120 Volume 69 page 125. INDEX # 3697.

Wm DALY; pension awarded 27 Aug 1844; residence - Ceylon. SOURCE: WO120 Volume 69 page 125. INDEX # 3698.

Ja^s COLLINS; pension awarded 23 Jun 1845; residence - Hong Kong; died 17 Jun 1849. SOURCE: WO120 Volume 69 page 125. INDEX # 3699.

WO120 VOLUME 69

18th Regiment of Foot (continued)

R^d H^Y FORREST; pension awarded 8 Dec 1846; residence - Ceylon; died 26 Apr 1847. SOURCE: WO120 Volume 69 page 125. INDEX # 3700.

Thos GALLAGHER; pension awarded 9 May 1854; died 20 Dec 1883, Bengal, India. SOURCE: WO120 Volume 69 page 125. INDEX # 3701.

19th Regiment of Foot

Robt HARRISON; pension awarded 17 Sep 1812; residence - Toronto, Ontario, Canada; died in 1847. SOURCE: WO120 Volume 69 page 127. INDEX # 3702.

Wm SKERRER; pension awarded 24 Aug 1825; residence - Hobart Town, Australia; died 20 Oct 1846. SOURCE: WO120 Volume 69 page 127. INDEX # 3703.

Jno CORNER; pension awarded 20 Mar 1822; residence - Montreal, Quebec, Canada. SOURCE: WO120 Volume 69 page 127. INDEX # 3704.

Jno MCCONNELL; pension awarded 27 Sep 1819; residence - Perth, Ontario, Canada. SOURCE: WO120 Volume 69 page 127. INDEX # 3705.

Robt HASKINS; pension awarded 7 Apr 1820; residence - Ceylon; died 13 Jul 1853. SOURCE: WO120 Volume 69 page 127. INDEX # 3706.

Roland HARTLEY; pension awarded 7 Jun 1820; residence - Ceylon. SOURCE: WO120 Volume 69 page 127. INDEX # 3707.

John SELLARS; pension awarded 17 Mar 1819; residence - Cape of Good Hope, South Africa; died 8 Jun 1850. SOURCE: WO120 Volume 69 page 127. INDEX # 3708.

Benjn BLUNDEN; pension awarded 27 May 1822; residence - New South Wales, Australia; died 8 Jul 1848. SOURCE: WO120 Volume 69 page 127. INDEX # 3709.

Jno ELLIOTT; pension awarded 5 Feb 1817; residence - New South Wales, Australia. SOURCE: WO120 Volume 69 page 127. INDEX # 3710.

Benjn TOMBLIN; pension awarded 28 Oct 1818; residence - Ceylon; died 5 Mar 1856. SOURCE: WO120 Volume 69 page 127. INDEX # 3711.

Ja^s ELLIS; pension awarded 19 Oct 1813; residence - Toronto, Ontario, Canada; died 8 Mar 1848. SOURCE: WO120 Volume 69 page 127. INDEX # 3712.

Abr^m MILLS; pension awarded 11 Nov 1817; residence - Ceylon; died 21 Sep 1850. SOURCE: WO120 Volume 69 page 127. INDEX # 3713.

Ed^wd SIMPSON; pension awarded 13 Aug 1846; residence - Hong Kong. SOURCE: WO120 Volume 69 page 127. INDEX # 3714.

Wm MARTIN; pension awarded 24 Oct 1848; residence - Montreal, Quebec, Canada. SOURCE: WO120 Volume 69 page 127. INDEX # 3715.

Pat^k BRENNAN; pension awarded 23 Oct 1849; residence - Montreal, Quebec, Canada. SOURCE: WO120 Volume 69 page 127. INDEX # 3716.

Jno BRIAN; pension awarded 23 Oct 1849; residence - Montreal, Quebec, Canada. SOURCE: WO120 Volume 69 page 127. INDEX # 3717.

Thos BYRON; pension awarded 23 Oct 1849. SOURCE: WO120 Volume 69 page 127. INDEX # 3718.

Fred^k CRAWFORD; pension awarded 23 Oct 1849; died 10 Aug 1879, Toronto, Ontario, Canada. SOURCE: WO120 Volume 69 page 127. INDEX # 3719.

Wm EAGAN; pension awarded 23 Oct 1849; residence - Montreal, Quebec, Canada; died 28 Mar 1857. SOURCE: WO120 Volume 69 page 127. INDEX # 3720.

Pat^k HEFFERAN; pension awarded 23 Oct 1849. SOURCE: WO120 Volume 69 page 127. INDEX # 3721.

Thos KNIGHTON; pension awarded 23 Oct 1849; residence - London, Ontario, Canada; died 25 Sep 1854. SOURCE: WO120 Volume 69 page 127. INDEX # 3722.

Ja^s KENNY; pension awarded 23 Oct 1849; residence - Hamilton, Ontario, Canada; died 14 Dec 1875. SOURCE: WO120 Volume 69 page 127. INDEX # 3723.

Ed^wd MILLER; pension awarded 23 Oct 1849; died 23 Jun 1862, Canada. SOURCE: WO120 Volume 69 page 127. INDEX # 3724.

Saml LINDENBERG; pension awarded 9 Apr 1850; residence - Montreal, Quebec, Canada; died 18 Apr 1880. SOURCE: WO120 Volume 69 page 127. INDEX # 3725.

19th Regiment of Foot (continued)

Art^r CARROLL; pension awarded 1 Oct 1850. SOURCE: WO120 Volume 69 page 127. INDEX # 3726.

Jno CONROY; pension awarded 1 Oct 1850. SOURCE: WO120 Volume 69 page 127. INDEX # 3727.

Martin MOLLOY; pension awarded 1 Oct 1850; died 27 Apr 1876, Galway. SOURCE: WO120 Volume 69 page 127. INDEX # 3728.

Ed^{md} MURPHY; pension awarded 1 Oct 1850; died 14 Mar 1856, Toronto, Ontario, Canada. SOURCE: WO120 Volume 69 page 127. INDEX # 3729.

Corn^s REILLY; pension awarded 1 Oct 1850. SOURCE: WO120 Volume 69 page 127. INDEX # 3730.

Pat^k RYDER; pension awarded 1 Oct 1850. SOURCE: WO120 Volume 69 page 127. INDEX # 3731.

Lambert DEAKERS; pension awarded 5 Aug 1851; residence - London, Ontario, Canada; died 26 Apr 1854. SOURCE: WO120 Volume 69 page 127. INDEX # 3732.

Geo^e HANNA; pension awarded 5 Aug 1851. SOURCE: WO120 Volume 69 page 127. INDEX # 3733.

Ed^{wd} BUXEY; pension awarded 5 Aug 1851. SOURCE: WO120 Volume 69 page 127. INDEX # 3734.

Jno COVELL; pension awarded 5 Aug 1851. SOURCE: WO120 Volume 69 page 127. INDEX # 3735.

Jno CURTIS; pension awarded 5 Aug 1851; residence - Quebec, Canada; died 3 Nov 1852. SOURCE: WO120 Volume 69 page 127. INDEX # 3736.

Thos FITZGERALD; pension awarded 5 Aug 1851; residence - Montreal, Quebec, Canada; died 18 Sep 1877. SOURCE: WO120 Volume 69 page 127. INDEX # 3737.

Jos^h MORLEY; pension awarded 5 Aug 1851; residence - Montreal, Quebec, Canada; died 25 Mar 1857. SOURCE: WO120 Volume 69 page 127. INDEX # 3738.

Isiah SMITH; pension awarded 5 Aug 1851; died 14 Aug 1862, Toronto, Ontario, Canada. SOURCE: WO120 Volume 69 page 127. INDEX # 3739.

Wm SWEENEY; pension awarded 5 Aug 1851. SOURCE: WO120 Volume 69 page 127. INDEX # 3740.

Jno SULLIVAN; pension awarded 5 Aug 1851; residence - Hamilton, Ontario, Canada; died 1 Sep 1867. SOURCE: WO120 Volume 69 page 127. INDEX # 3741.

Wm WATCHORN; pension awarded 5 Aug 1851. SOURCE: WO120 Volume 69 page 128. INDEX # 3742.

20th Regiment of Foot

Gaitino REGAZZO; pension awarded 23 May 1821; residence - Malta; died 15 Mar 1850. SOURCE: WO120 Volume 69 page 130. INDEX # 3743.

Don^d MORRISON; pension awarded 8 Aug 1827; residence - Bombay, India; died 1 Sep 1854. SOURCE: WO120 Volume 69 page 130. INDEX # 3744.

Jno HOLMES; pension awarded 19 Nov 1818; residence - Kingston, Ontario, Canada; died 5 Dec 1870, Toronto, Ontario, Canada. SOURCE: WO120 Volume 69 page 130. INDEX # 3745.

And^w MCKASEY; pension awarded 9 Aug 1837; residence - Halifax, Nova Scotia, Canada; died 15 Sep 1856. SOURCE: WO120 Volume 69 page 130. INDEX # 3746.

John WEST; pension awarded 20 Jul 1825; residence - Halifax, Nova Scotia, Canada. SOURCE: WO120 Volume 69 page 130. INDEX # 3747.

Thos CRYAN; pension awarded 14 Jul 1830; residence - Toronto, Ontario, Canada; died 10 Oct 1867. SOURCE: WO120 Volume 69 page 130. INDEX # 3748.

Malachi HART; pension awarded 13 Oct 1830; residence - Montreal, Quebec, Canada. SOURCE: WO120 Volume 69 page 130. INDEX # 3749.

Jno KEYES; pension awarded 24 Oct 1821; residence - London, Ontario, Canada; died in Oct 1852. SOURCE: WO120 Volume 69 page 130. INDEX # 3750.

Ja^s VICTORY; pension awarded 28 Oct 1818; residence - South Australia, Australia; died 25 Sep 1853. SOURCE: WO120 Volume 69 page 130. INDEX # 3751.

Fra^s D. DOMINICO; pension awarded 29 Sep 1828; residence - Bombay, India; died 3 Apr 1849. SOURCE: WO120 Volume 69 page 130. INDEX # 3752.

Jno SALTRY; pension awarded 29 Jun 1837; residence - Toronto, Ontario, Canada. SOURCE: WO120 Volume 69 page 130. INDEX # 3753.

Ja^s QUARTERMAN; pension awarded 11 Oct 1837; residence - Bombay, India; died 4 Jul 1849. SOURCE: WO120 Volume 69 page 130. INDEX # 3754.

WO120 VOLUME 69

20th Regiment of Foot (continued)

Jn⁰ DOYLE; pension awarded 25 Jul 1821; residence - Hobart Town, Australia. SOURCE: WO120 Volume 69 page 130. INDEX # 3755.

Hen^y DOYLE; pension awarded 8 Aug 1827; residence - Bombay, India; died 2 May 1848. SOURCE: WO120 Volume 69 page 130. INDEX # 3756.

Ed^wd HURD; pension awarded 11 Oct 1837; residence - Bombay, India; died 8 Nov 1849. SOURCE: WO120 Volume 69 page 130. INDEX # 3757.

Geo^e CHATTEN; pension awarded 8 Aug 1827; residence - Bombay, India; died 3 Jul 1857. SOURCE: WO120 Volume 69 page 130. INDEX # 3758.

Jn⁰ BROWN; pension awarded 11 Aug 1830; residence - Bombay, India; died 7 Mar 1846. SOURCE: WO120 Volume 69 page 130. INDEX # 3759.

Fra^s CLARIN; pension awarded 24 Oct 1848; died 14 Jan 1872, London, Ontario, Canada. SOURCE: WO120 Volume 69 page 130. INDEX # 3760.

Jn⁰ CONNELL; pension awarded 24 Oct 1848; died 19 Apr 1879, London, Ontario, Canada. SOURCE: WO120 Volume 69 page 130. INDEX # 3761.

Jn⁰ DOWNING; pension awarded 24 Oct 1848. SOURCE: WO120 Volume 69 page 130. INDEX # 3762.

Jn⁰ MCMAHON; pension awarded 24 Oct 1848; residence - London, Ontario, Canada; died 19 Nov 1854. SOURCE: WO120 Volume 69 page 131. INDEX # 3763.

Barth^w HENNESSY; pension awarded 24 Oct 1848; died 12 Sep 1883, Southampton. SOURCE: WO120 Volume 69 page 131. INDEX # 3764.

Barth^s ROURKE; pension awarded 24 Oct 1848; residence - London, Ontario, Canada. SOURCE: WO120 Volume 69 page 131. INDEX # 3765.

Benjn RUSK; pension awarded 24 Oct 1848. SOURCE: WO120 Volume 69 page 131. INDEX # 3766.

Robt SMITH; pension awarded 24 Oct 1848; died 19 Oct 1883, Toronto, Ontario, Canada. SOURCE: WO120 Volume 69 page 131. INDEX # 3767.

Jn⁰ SULLIVAN; pension awarded 24 Oct 1848; residence - Toronto, Ontario, Canada; died in 1854. SOURCE: WO120 Volume 69 page 131. INDEX # 3768.

Ja^s KENNY; pension awarded 14 Nov 1848. SOURCE: WO120 Volume 69 page 131. INDEX # 3769.

Saml WHAIT; pension awarded 14 Nov 1848; died 4 Jul 1858, London, Ontario, Canada. SOURCE: WO120 Volume 69 page 131. INDEX # 3770.

Jesse UNDERWOOD; pension awarded 28 Nov 1848; died Nova Scotia, Canada. SOURCE: WO120 Volume 69 page 131. INDEX # 3771.

Hen^y MCGEE; pension awarded 26 Dec 1848; died 14 Feb 1882, Canada. SOURCE: WO120 Volume 69 page 131. INDEX # 3772.

Wm HOLLOWELL; pension awarded 27 Mar 1849. SOURCE: WO120 Volume 69 page 131. INDEX # 3773.

Danl MCCARTHY; pension awarded 23 Oct 1849. SOURCE: WO120 Volume 69 page 131. INDEX # 3774.

Pat^k MCDONOUGH; pension awarded 23 Oct 1849. SOURCE: WO120 Volume 69 page 131. INDEX # 3775.

Ja^s READ; pension awarded 23 Oct 1849; residence - Toronto, Ontario, Canada; died 24 Sep 1869. SOURCE: WO120 Volume 69 page 131. INDEX # 3776.

Jn⁰ WHITE; pension awarded 23 Oct 1849; residence - Picton, Ontario, Canada; died in Jul 1852. SOURCE: WO120 Volume 69 page 131. INDEX # 3777.

Wm HICKEY; pension awarded 13 Aug 1850. SOURCE: WO120 Volume 69 page 131. INDEX # 3778.

Thos MCMULLEN; pension awarded 13 Aug 1850; died 23 Jul 1875, London, Ontario, Canada. SOURCE: WO120 Volume 69 page 131. INDEX # 3779.

Wm MCMULLEN; pension awarded 13 Aug 1850. SOURCE: WO120 Volume 69 page 131. INDEX # 3780.

Chas Ed^wd WEST; pension awarded 1 Oct 1850. SOURCE: WO120 Volume 69 page 131. INDEX # 3781.

Nich^s BALDWIN; pension awarded 1 Oct 1850. SOURCE: WO120 Volume 69 page 131. INDEX # 3782.

Mich^l DWYER; pension awarded 1 Oct 1850. SOURCE: WO120 Volume 69 page 131. INDEX # 3783.

Mich^l ONEAL; pension awarded 1 Oct 1850. SOURCE: WO120 Volume 69 page 131. INDEX # 3784.

Jon^n PRESTON; pension awarded 1 Oct 1850; residence - Leicester. SOURCE: WO120 Volume 69 page 131. INDEX # 3785.

Jn⁰ RANKIN; pension awarded 1 Oct 1850. SOURCE: WO120 Volume 69 page 131. INDEX # 3786.

Jn⁰ ROACH; pension awarded 1 Oct 1850. SOURCE: WO120 Volume 69 page 131. INDEX # 3787.

20th Regiment of Foot (continued)

Michl ROBINSON; pension awarded 1 Oct 1850; residence - Kingston, Ontario, Canada; died in 1854. SOURCE: WO120 Volume 69 page 131. INDEX # 3788.

Lawrence WHELAN; pension awarded 1 Oct 1850. SOURCE: WO120 Volume 69 page 131. INDEX # 3789.

Wm WHITE; pension awarded 1 Oct 1850. SOURCE: WO120 Volume 69 page 131. INDEX # 3790.

Jno CRONIN; pension awarded 1 Oct 1850; residence - London, Ontario, Canada; died 15 Apr 1858. SOURCE: WO120 Volume 69 page 131. INDEX # 3791.

Michl MCLOUGHLIN; pension awarded 1 Oct 1850; residence - London, Ontario, Canada; died 6 Sep 1852. SOURCE: WO120 Volume 69 page 131. INDEX # 3792.

Jas CRAY; pension awarded 5 Aug 1851; residence - London, Ontario, Canada; died 6 Apr 1864. SOURCE: WO120 Volume 69 page 131. INDEX # 3793.

Robt CUNNINGHAM; pension awarded 5 Aug 1851. SOURCE: WO120 Volume 69 page 131. INDEX # 3794.

Thos DAWES; pension awarded 5 Aug 1851. SOURCE: WO120 Volume 69 page 131. INDEX # 3795.

Jas FINIGAN; pension awarded 5 Aug 1851. SOURCE: WO120 Volume 69 page 131. INDEX # 3796.

Danl MCALINDAN; pension awarded 5 Aug 1851; died 9 Mar 1878, London, Ontario, Canada. SOURCE: WO120 Volume 69 page 131. INDEX # 3797.

Patk MURPHY; pension awarded 5 Aug 1851. SOURCE: WO120 Volume 69 page 131. INDEX # 3798.

Jno REGAN; pension awarded 5 Aug 1851; residence - Toronto, Ontario, Canada; died 14 Oct 1861. SOURCE: WO120 Volume 69 page 131. INDEX # 3799.

Peter RIELLY; pension awarded 5 Aug 1851. SOURCE: WO120 Volume 69 page 131. INDEX # 3800.

Jno SCARROW; pension awarded 5 Aug 1851; residence - London, Ontario, Canada; died 17 Feb 1856. SOURCE: WO120 Volume 69 page 131. INDEX # 3801.

Jno WARD; pension awarded 5 Aug 1851. SOURCE: WO120 Volume 69 page 131. INDEX # 3802.

Wm PINK; pension awarded 27 Jul 1852. SOURCE: WO120 Volume 69 page 132. INDEX # 3803.

Jas WARDLOW; pension awarded 27 Jul 1852. SOURCE: WO120 Volume 69 page 132. INDEX # 3804.

Jno KEARNS; pension awarded 27 Jul 1852; residence - Montreal, Quebec, Canada; died 2 Feb 1875, London, Ontario, Canada. SOURCE: WO120 Volume 69 page 132. INDEX # 3805.

Thos QUINN; pension awarded 27 Jul 1852; died 14 Apr 1854, Toronto, Ontario, Canada. SOURCE: WO120 Volume 69 page 132. INDEX # 3806.

Thos FRENCH; pension awarded 27 Jul 1852. SOURCE: WO120 Volume 69 page 132. INDEX # 3807.

Heny HUGHES; pension awarded 27 Jul 1852. SOURCE: WO120 Volume 69 page 132. INDEX # 3808.

Jno KAVANAGH; pension awarded 27 Jul 1852; residence - Amherstburg, Ontario, Canada; died 21 Jul 1854. SOURCE: WO120 Volume 69 page 132. INDEX # 3809.

Jas MCCOY; pension awarded 27 Jul 1852. SOURCE: WO120 Volume 69 page 132. INDEX # 3810.

Edwd DAY; pension awarded 19 Jul 1853. SOURCE: WO120 Volume 69 page 132. INDEX # 3811.

Frans MEIGHAN; pension awarded 19 Jul 1853. SOURCE: WO120 Volume 69 page 132. INDEX # 3812.

Jas GUTTERIDGE; pension awarded 19 Jul 1853; residence - London, Ontario, Canada; died 18 Nov 1870. SOURCE: WO120 Volume 69 page 132. INDEX # 3813.

Jas MCFARLAN; pension awarded 19 Jul 1853. SOURCE: WO120 Volume 69 page 132. INDEX # 3814.

Jas TURNEY; pension awarded 19 Jul 1853; residence - Toronto, Ontario, Canada; died 6 May 1856. SOURCE: WO120 Volume 69 page 132. INDEX # 3815.

21st Regiment of Foot

Jas HERTMAN; pension awarded 28 Jul 1841; residence - Western Australia, Australia. SOURCE: WO120 Volume 69 page 133. INDEX # 3816.

Jno HARDIMAN; pension awarded 17 Jul 1829; residence - Quebec, Quebec, Canada. SOURCE: WO120 Volume 69 page 133. INDEX # 3817.

Thos CAMPBELL; pension awarded 28 Dec 1818; residence - Toronto, Ontario, Canada. SOURCE: WO120 Volume 69 page 133. INDEX # 3818.

John PORTER; pension awarded 5 Jul 1820; residence - Chambly, Quebec, Canada. SOURCE: WO120 Volume 69 page 133. INDEX # 3819.

21st Regiment of Foot (continued)

And^w LOW; pension awarded 28 Apr 1813; residence - Kingston, Ontario, Canada. SOURCE: WO120 Volume 69 page 133. INDEX # 3820.

Robt SUTHERLAND; pension awarded 26 Feb 1818; residence - London, Ontario, Canada; died 14 May 1865. SOURCE: WO120 Volume 69 page 133. INDEX # 3821.

John GREEN; pension awarded 8 Jul 1845; residence - Fort St. George, India; died 23 Nov 1849. SOURCE: WO120 Volume 69 page 133. INDEX # 3822.

John JOSEPH; pension awarded 20 Jun 1827; residence - Grenada. SOURCE: WO120 Volume 69 page 133. INDEX # 3823.

Mark HANLON; pension awarded 8 Jul 1845; residence - Fort St. George, India. SOURCE: WO120 Volume 69 page 133. INDEX # 3824.

Fran^s THORPE; pension awarded 14 Sep 1836; residence - Launceston, Australia; died 19 Jun 1869, Hobarton, Tasmania, Australia. SOURCE: WO120 Volume 69 page 133. INDEX # 3825.

Mat^w WALES; pension awarded 14 Sep 1836; residence - Sydney, Australia. SOURCE: WO120 Volume 69 page 133. INDEX # 3826.

Neil GRIBBON; pension awarded 14 Sep 1836; residence - New South Wales, Australia; died in 1845. SOURCE: WO120 Volume 69 page 133. INDEX # 3827.

Mar^n BIRMINGHAM; pension awarded 8 Jul 1845; residence - Fort St. George, India. SOURCE: WO120 Volume 69 page 133. INDEX # 3828.

Jno AUCHIE; pension awarded 24 Apr 1837; residence - Launceston, Australia. SOURCE: WO120 Volume 69 page 133. INDEX # 3829.

Ja^s KYLE; pension awarded 18 Dec 1829; residence - St. Johns. SOURCE: WO120 Volume 69 page 133. INDEX # 3830.

Wm A. MACKAY; pension awarded 8 Feb 1837; residence - Hobart Town, Australia. SOURCE: WO120 Volume 69 page 133. INDEX # 3831.

Jno SMITH; pension awarded 14 Jul 1841; residence - Western Australia, Australia. SOURCE: WO120 Volume 69 page 133. INDEX # 3832.

Aug^s MCLEOD; pension awarded 8 Sep 1830; residence - Hobart Town, Australia; died 12 Feb 1863. SOURCE: WO120 Volume 69 page 133. INDEX # 3833.

Wm BURNS; pension awarded 23 Aug 1837; residence - Hobart Town, Australia; died 4 May 1873. SOURCE: WO120 Volume 69 page 133. INDEX # 3834.

Peter BUCHANAN; pension awarded 28 Aug 1825; residence - Toronto, Ontario, Canada; died 22 Sep 1867. SOURCE: WO120 Volume 69 page 133. INDEX # 3835.

Philip QUIN; pension awarded 6 Mar 1816; residence - St. Jean, Quebec, Canada; died in 1847. SOURCE: WO120 Volume 69 page 133. INDEX # 3836.

John CLIFFORD; pension awarded 23 Feb 1847; residence - Chinsurah, India. SOURCE: WO120 Volume 69 page 133. INDEX # 3837.

22nd Regiment of Foot

Jno HANNAH; pension awarded 8 Apr 1835; residence - Toronto, Ontario, Canada. SOURCE: WO120 Volume 69 page 135. INDEX # 3838.

Ja^s HULL; pension awarded 2 Feb 1820; residence - Mauritius. SOURCE: WO120 Volume 69 page 135. INDEX # 3839.

Jno WHITTY; pension awarded 15 Dec 1819; residence - Mauritius; died 13 Dec 1850. SOURCE: WO120 Volume 69 page 135. INDEX # 3840.

Wm BLACKBURN; pension awarded 15 Dec 1819; residence - Mauritius. SOURCE: WO120 Volume 69 page 135. INDEX # 3841.

Geo^e MECKLY; pension awarded 13 Jul 1836; residence - Jamaica. SOURCE: WO120 Volume 69 page 135. INDEX # 3842.

Thos LAMPORT; pension awarded 15 Dec 1819; residence - Mauritius. SOURCE: WO120 Volume 69 page 135. INDEX # 3843.

22nd Regiment of Foot (continued)

Wm CLOVER; pension awarded 15 Dec 1819; residence - Mauritius; died 16 Mar 1849. SOURCE: WO120 Volume 69 page 135. INDEX # 3844.

Jno MCDONALD; pension awarded 15 Dec 1819; residence - Mauritius; died 20 May 1856. SOURCE: WO120 Volume 69 page 135. INDEX # 3845.

Jacob STANDLEY; pension awarded 18 Aug 1823; residence - Mauritius; died 28 Jun 1856. SOURCE: WO120 Volume 69 page 135. INDEX # 3846.

Jos^h BEESLEY; pension awarded 28 Apr 1846; residence - Camp Poonah, India; died 22 Jan 1854. SOURCE: WO120 Volume 69 page 135. INDEX # 3847.

Edwd GUEST; pension awarded 28 Apr 1846; residence - Camp Poonah, India. SOURCE: WO120 Volume 69 page 135. INDEX # 3848.

Saml INSELL; pension awarded 28 Apr 1846; residence - Camp Poonah, India. SOURCE: WO120 Volume 69 page 135. INDEX # 3849.

Jno FREND; pension awarded 11 Jun 1844; residence - Mauritius; died 17 Nov 1857. SOURCE: WO120 Volume 69 page 135. INDEX # 3850.

Willm BUSH; pension awarded 11 Aug 1846; residence - St. Johns. SOURCE: WO120 Volume 69 page 135. INDEX # 3851.

Jno KNIGHT; pension awarded 11 May 1847; died 29 Nov 1848. SOURCE: WO120 Volume 69 page 135. INDEX # 3852.

Alex^r ONEAL; pension awarded 11 May 1847. SOURCE: WO120 Volume 69 page 135. INDEX # 3853.

Thos CANNON; pension awarded 9 May 1848. SOURCE: WO120 Volume 69 page 135. INDEX # 3854.

Pat^k ROAN; pension awarded 9 May 1848; residence - Poona, India. SOURCE: WO120 Volume 69 page 135. INDEX # 3855.

Wm STANTON; pension awarded 9 May 1848; died 19 Jan 1849. SOURCE: WO120 Volume 69 page 135. INDEX # 3856.

23rd Regiment of Foot

Willm WENNER; pension awarded 7 Jan 1818; residence - Saint John, New Brunswick, Canada. SOURCE: WO120 Volume 69 page 137. INDEX # 3857.

John CASSADY; pension awarded 3 Mar 1800; residence - Hobart Town, Australia. SOURCE: WO120 Volume 69 page 137. INDEX # 3858.

Tobias FIZZALL; pension awarded 25 Oct 1842; residence - Montreal, Quebec, Canada; died 25 Sep 1883, Toronto, Ontario, Canada. SOURCE: WO120 Volume 69 page 137. INDEX # 3859.

Dav^d LEWIS; pension awarded 25 Oct 1842; residence - Toronto, Ontario, Canada. SOURCE: WO120 Volume 69 page 137. INDEX # 3860.

Pat^k NEAL; pension awarded 22 Jul 1845; residence - London, Ontario, Canada. SOURCE: WO120 Volume 69 page 137. INDEX # 3861.

Mich^l ADAMS; pension awarded 27 Sep 1842; residence - Montreal, Quebec, Canada. SOURCE: WO120 Volume 69 page 137. INDEX # 3862.

W^m GAY; pension awarded 27 Aug 1816; residence - Charlottetown, Prince Edward Island, Canada. SOURCE: WO120 Volume 69 page 137. INDEX # 3863.

Robt GOODFELLOW; pension awarded 22 Oct 1844; residence - Kingston, Ontario, Canada; died 27 Jun 1879. SOURCE: WO120 Volume 69 page 137. INDEX # 3864.

Pat^k CONWAY; pension awarded 24 Oct 1843; residence - Bytown, Ontario, Canada; died in Oct 1851. SOURCE: WO120 Volume 69 page 137. INDEX # 3865.

Jno RYAN; pension awarded 16 Oct 1845; residence - Montreal, Quebec, Canada. SOURCE: WO120 Volume 69 page 137. INDEX # 3866.

Ja^s LINCE; pension awarded 8 Nov 1837; residence - Toronto, Ontario, Canada; died 24 Dec 1869. SOURCE: WO120 Volume 69 page 137. INDEX # 3867.

Gabriel WINTER; pension awarded 17 May 1812; residence - Berne, Switzerland. SOURCE: WO120 Volume 69 page 137. INDEX # 3868.

23rd Regiment of Foot (continued)

Thos FLYNN; pension awarded 25 Aug 1846; residence - Kingston, Ontario, Canada; died 21 Sep 1848. SOURCE: WO120 Volume 69 page 137. INDEX # 3869.

Wm QUINLAN; pension awarded 22 Sep 1846; residence - London, Ontario, Canada. SOURCE: WO120 Volume 69 page 137. INDEX # 3870.

Malachi DONAHOE; pension awarded 27 Jun 1843; residence - Sydney. SOURCE: WO120 Volume 69 page 137. INDEX # 3871.

Michl SPELLICY; pension awarded 14 Sep 1847; residence - Halifax, Nova Scotia, Canada; died 12 Sep 1847. SOURCE: WO120 Volume 69 page 137. INDEX # 3872.

Thos MCNERNEY; pension awarded 12 Oct 1847; residence - Kingston, Ontario, Canada; died 14 May 1858. SOURCE: WO120 Volume 69 page 137. INDEX # 3873.

Connor GORMAN; pension awarded 12 Oct 1847; died 19 Jan 1879, London, Ontario, Canada. SOURCE: WO120 Volume 69 page 137. INDEX # 3874.

Loughlin MULVEY; pension awarded 12 Oct 1847; residence - London, Ontario, Canada; died 8 Apr 1857. SOURCE: WO120 Volume 69 page 137. INDEX # 3875.

Jas BROWN; pension awarded 12 Oct 1847; residence - London, Ontario, Canada; died 22 Apr 1871. SOURCE: WO120 Volume 69 page 137. INDEX # 3876.

Sylvester BRYAN; pension awarded 12 Oct 1847. SOURCE: WO120 Volume 69 page 137. INDEX # 3877.

Luke CARTY; pension awarded 12 Oct 1847; died 30 Mar 1867. SOURCE: WO120 Volume 69 page 137. INDEX # 3878.

Alexr DOYLE; pension awarded 12 Oct 1847; residence - London, Ontario, Canada; died 6 Mar 1852. SOURCE: WO120 Volume 69 page 137. INDEX # 3879.

Richd GIBBONS; pension awarded 12 Oct 1847. SOURCE: WO120 Volume 69 page 137. INDEX # 3880.

John HIGGINS; pension awarded 12 Oct 1847; died 30 Apr 1861, London, Ontario, Canada. SOURCE: WO120 Volume 69 page 137. INDEX # 3881.

Luke MCLAUGHLIN; pension awarded 12 Oct 1847; died 31 May 1867. SOURCE: WO120 Volume 69 page 137. INDEX # 3882.

Jno PHILLIPS; pension awarded 12 Oct 1847; residence - London, Ontario, Canada; died 3 May 1849. SOURCE: WO120 Volume 69 page 137. INDEX # 3883.

Michl RYAN; pension awarded 12 Oct 1847. SOURCE: WO120 Volume 69 page 137. INDEX # 3884.

Laure SCANLON; pension awarded 12 Oct 1847; residence - Kingston, Ontario, Canada; died 14 Mar 1849. SOURCE: WO120 Volume 69 page 137. INDEX # 3885.

Jno SULLIVAN; pension awarded 22 Feb 1848. SOURCE: WO120 Volume 69 page 137. INDEX # 3886.

Jno ASHTON; pension awarded 22 Feb 1848; died 5 Mar 1872, London, Ontario, Canada. SOURCE: WO120 Volume 69 page 137. INDEX # 3887.

Corns CARTY; pension awarded 22 Feb 1848; died 27 Sep 1862, Toronto, Ontario, Canada. SOURCE: WO120 Volume 69 page 137. INDEX # 3888.

Thos CHRISTOPHER; pension awarded 22 Feb 1848. SOURCE: WO120 Volume 69 page 137. INDEX # 3889.

Jas TRACY; pension awarded 6 Jun 1848. SOURCE: WO120 Volume 69 page 137. INDEX # 3890.

Fras COOKSON; pension awarded 6 Jun 1848; died 13 Nov 1873, Halifax, Nova Scotia, Canada. SOURCE: WO120 Volume 69 page 137. INDEX # 3891.

Josh TURNER; pension awarded 6 Jun 1848; residence - London, Ontario, Canada; died 23 Dec 1855. SOURCE: WO120 Volume 69 page 137. INDEX # 3892.

Wm TRANTER; pension awarded 6 Jun 1848; residence - Halifax, Nova Scotia, Canada; died 7 Apr 1850. SOURCE: WO120 Volume 69 page 137. INDEX # 3893.

Jno ASPINALL; pension awarded 27 Jun 1848. SOURCE: WO120 Volume 69 page 137. INDEX # 3894.

Wm CONNOR; pension awarded 24 Oct 1848. SOURCE: WO120 Volume 69 page 137. INDEX # 3895.

Jas CONSADINE; pension awarded 24 Oct 1848. SOURCE: WO120 Volume 69 page 137. INDEX # 3896.

Thos HALL; pension awarded 24 Oct 1848; residence - London, Ontario, Canada; died 27 Oct 1850. SOURCE: WO120 Volume 69 page 138. INDEX # 3897.

Thos HOWARTH; pension awarded 24 Oct 1848; residence - London, Ontario, Canada; died 23 Sep 1852. SOURCE: WO120 Volume 69 page 138. INDEX # 3898.

23rd Regiment of Foot (continued)

Thos LEESON; pension awarded 24 Oct 1848; died 20 Jun 1875, Toronto, Ontario, Canada. SOURCE: WO120 Volume 69 page 138. INDEX # 3899.

Jno MCCAFFRY; pension awarded 24 Oct 1848. SOURCE: WO120 Volume 69 page 138. INDEX # 3900.

Jno RIDLER; pension awarded 24 Oct 1848; residence - London, Ontario, Canada; died 20 Jul 1851. SOURCE: WO120 Volume 69 page 138. INDEX # 3901.

Wm SHANLEY; pension awarded 24 Oct 1848. SOURCE: WO120 Volume 69 page 138. INDEX # 3902.

Jno TABBERRAH; pension awarded 24 Oct 1848. SOURCE: WO120 Volume 69 page 138. INDEX # 3903.

Jno WILLIAMS; pension awarded 24 Oct 1848; residence - Toronto, Ontario, Canada; died 15 Jul 1876. SOURCE: WO120 Volume 69 page 138. INDEX # 3904.

Jas MILES; pension awarded 26 Dec 1848; residence - Nova Scotia, Canada; died 3 Aug 1862. SOURCE: WO120 Volume 69 page 138. INDEX # 3905.

Evan EVANS; pension awarded 23 Oct 1849. SOURCE: WO120 Volume 69 page 138. INDEX # 3906.

Jno CHERRY; pension awarded 23 Oct 1849; residence - London, Ontario, Canada; died 7 Jan 1851. SOURCE: WO120 Volume 69 page 138. INDEX # 3907.

Jno HANNEY; pension awarded 23 Oct 1849; died 12 Oct 1872 London, Ontario, Canada. SOURCE: WO120 Volume 69 page 138. INDEX # 3908.

Danl MAHER; pension awarded 23 Oct 1849; residence - Hamilton, Ontario, Canada; died in 1853. SOURCE: WO120 Volume 69 page 138. INDEX # 3909.

Jno MURRAY; pension awarded 23 Oct 1849; residence - London, Ontario, Canada; died 17 May 1855. SOURCE: WO120 Volume 69 page 138. INDEX # 3910.

Simon WHELAN; pension awarded 23 Oct 1849. SOURCE: WO120 Volume 69 page 138. INDEX # 3911.

Philip CONNELLY; pension awarded 1 Oct 1850. SOURCE: WO120 Volume 69 page 138. INDEX # 3912.

Thos KNAPTON; pension awarded 5 Aug 1851; residence - London, Ontario, Canada; died 1 Oct 1876. SOURCE: WO120 Volume 69 page 138. INDEX # 3913.

Robt MOONEY; pension awarded 5 Aug 1851. SOURCE: WO120 Volume 69 page 138. INDEX # 3914.

Geoe WHITE; pension awarded 5 Aug 1851. SOURCE: WO120 Volume 69 page 138. INDEX # 3915.

Thos WILKINSON; pension awarded 27 Jul 1852. SOURCE: WO120 Volume 69 page 138. INDEX # 3916.

Jas VANZANT; pension awarded 27 Jul 1852; residence - Toronto, Ontario, Canada; died 16 Mar 1877. SOURCE: WO120 Volume 69 page 138. INDEX # 3917.

Andw MCKENNA; pension awarded 27 Jul 1852. SOURCE: WO120 Volume 69 page 138. INDEX # 3918.

Arthur CONRE; pension awarded 27 Jul 1852; residence - London, Ontario, Canada; died 9 Jun 1876. SOURCE: WO120 Volume 69 page 138. INDEX # 3919.

Jno CONWAY; pension awarded 27 Jul 1852; residence - London, Ontario, Canada; died 12 Oct 1853. SOURCE: WO120 Volume 69 page 138. INDEX # 3920.

Jas DEAN; pension awarded 27 Jul 1852. SOURCE: WO120 Volume 69 page 138. INDEX # 3921.

Patk FLAHERTY; pension awarded 27 Jul 1852. SOURCE: WO120 Volume 69 page 138. INDEX # 3922.

Robt HANDCOCK; pension awarded 27 Jul 1852. SOURCE: WO120 Volume 69 page 138. INDEX # 3923.

Jno HOGG; pension awarded 27 Jul 1852. SOURCE: WO120 Volume 69 page 138. INDEX # 3924.

Thos KING; pension awarded 27 Jul 1852; residence - London, Ontario, Canada; died 5 Mar 1856. SOURCE: WO120 Volume 69 page 138. INDEX # 3925.

Danl LARKIN; pension awarded 27 Jul 1852; residence - Hamilton, Ontario, Canada; died 20 Jul 1866. SOURCE: WO120 Volume 69 page 138. INDEX # 3926.

Jno MARTELL; pension awarded 27 Jul 1852; died 2 Apr 1883, Wales. SOURCE: WO120 Volume 69 page 138. INDEX # 3927.

Thos WILLIAMS; pension awarded 27 Jul 1852. SOURCE: WO120 Volume 69 page 138. INDEX # 3928.

Jas RAPSEY; pension awarded 19 Jul 1853; died 3 Nov 1866, London, Ontario, Canada. SOURCE: WO120 Volume 69 page 138. INDEX # 3929.

Fredk BAYLISS; pension awarded 19 Jul 1853; died 4 Oct 1877, Worcester. SOURCE: WO120 Volume 69 page 138. INDEX # 3930.

Saml DIGBY; pension awarded 19 Jul 1853. SOURCE: WO120 Volume 69 page 138. INDEX # 3931.

Jas RIORDEN; pension awarded 19 Jul 1853. SOURCE: WO120 Volume 69 page 138. INDEX # 3932.

WO120 VOLUME 69 133

23rd Regiment of Foot (continued)

Saml WREN; pension awarded 19 Jul 1853; residence - London, Ontario, Canada; died 27 Aug 1877. SOURCE: WO120 Volume 69 page 138. INDEX # 3933.

James SIMPSON; pension awarded 18 Sep 1855. SOURCE: WO120 Volume 69 page 138. INDEX # 3934.

24th Regiment of Foot

John LINSTER; pension awarded 23 Sep 1818; residence - Toronto, Ontario, Canada; died 22 Dec 1878, Toronto, Ontario, Canada. SOURCE: WO120 Volume 69 page 140. INDEX # 3935.

H^y DAVIS; pension awarded 9 Nov 1836; residence - Hobart Town, Australia; died 3 Jul 1870, Tasmania, Australia. SOURCE: WO120 Volume 69 page 140. INDEX # 3936.

Edwd MCQUADE; pension awarded 30 Sep 1823; residence - Charlottetown, Prince Edward Island, Canada; died 8 Apr 1853. SOURCE: WO120 Volume 69 page 140. INDEX # 3937.

Jno PAYLOR; pension awarded 14 Feb 1831; residence - Wm Henry, Quebec, Canada; died in 1846. SOURCE: WO120 Volume 69 page 140. INDEX # 3938.

Jno MONAGHAN; pension awarded 10 Jan 1838; residence - Montreal, Quebec, Canada; died in 1847. SOURCE: WO120 Volume 69 page 140. INDEX # 3939.

Ja^s MALONEY; pension awarded 6 May 1802; residence - Quebec, Canada. SOURCE: WO120 Volume 69 page 140. INDEX # 3940.

Thos BRETT; pension awarded 28 Jun 1814; residence - Toronto, Ontario, Canada; died 15 Sep 1864. SOURCE: WO120 Volume 69 page 140. INDEX # 3941.

Paul MAURICE; pension awarded 27 Aug 1823; residence - Bengal, India; died 4 Apr 1852. SOURCE: WO120 Volume 69 page 140. INDEX # 3942.

Ja^s IZZARD; pension awarded 19 Dec 1826; residence - Toronto, Ontario, Canada. SOURCE: WO120 Volume 69 page 140. INDEX # 3943.

Thos MCKEE; pension awarded 26 Dec 1838; residence - Bytown, Ontario, Canada; died in Apr 1851. SOURCE: WO120 Volume 69 page 140. INDEX # 3944.

John WATT; pension awarded 11 Nov 1835; residence - Toronto, Ontario, Canada; died 29 Feb 1868. SOURCE: WO120 Volume 69 page 140. INDEX # 3945.

Pat^k DUGGAN; pension awarded 23 Oct 1838; residence - St. Jean, Quebec, Canada. SOURCE: WO120 Volume 69 page 140. INDEX # 3946.

Thos TURNBULL; pension awarded 10 Jan 1838; residence - Montreal, Quebec, Canada. SOURCE: WO120 Volume 69 page 140. INDEX # 3947.

Jno WALFORD; pension awarded 8 Sep 1841; residence - Montreal, Quebec, Canada; died 29 Sep 1866. SOURCE: WO120 Volume 69 page 140. INDEX # 3948.

Chas ATKINS; pension awarded 25 Jan 1848; residence - Agra, India; died in 1847. SOURCE: WO120 Volume 69 page 140. INDEX # 3949.

John WIGGINS; pension awarded 11 Mar 1856. SOURCE: WO120 Volume 69 page 140. INDEX # 3950.

25th Regiment of Foot

Danl ROBERTSON; pension awarded 14 Dec 1836; residence - St. Johns. SOURCE: WO120 Volume 69 page 142. INDEX # 3951.

Pat^k MCGEE; pension awarded 8 Oct 1836; residence - London, Ontario, Canada; died 29 May 1862, London, Ontario, Canada. SOURCE: WO120 Volume 69 page 142. INDEX # 3952.

Willm TOWNSEND; pension awarded 27 Nov 1839; residence - Madras, India; died 30 Nov 1848. SOURCE: WO120 Volume 69 page 142. INDEX # 3953.

Ter^e MCDERMOTT; pension awarded 10 Mar 1846; residence - Madras, India; died 4 Jul 1853. SOURCE: WO120 Volume 69 page 142. INDEX # 3954.

Jno BANNON; pension awarded 10 Mar 1846; residence - Madras, India. SOURCE: WO120 Volume 69 page 142. INDEX # 3955.

Jno HIGH; pension awarded 10 Mar 1846; residence - Madras, India; died 13 Feb 1874, Bombay, India. SOURCE: WO120 Volume 69 page 142. INDEX # 3956.

BRITISH ARMY PENSIONERS ABROAD

25th Regiment of Foot (continued)

Isaac INGHAM; pension awarded 10 Mar 1846; residence - Madras, India; died 17 Oct 1854. SOURCE: WO120 Volume 69 page 142. INDEX # 3957.

Jn⁰ KILWORTH; pension awarded 10 Mar 1846; residence - Madras, India; died 24 Sep 1854. SOURCE: WO120 Volume 69 page 142. INDEX # 3958.

Nichˢ PALMER; pension awarded 10 Mar 1846; residence - Madras, India; died 31 Aug 1846. SOURCE: WO120 Volume 69 page 142. INDEX # 3959.

Danˡ CARROLL; pension awarded 22 Feb 1848; died 4 Sep 1855. SOURCE: WO120 Volume 69 page 142. INDEX # 3960.

Jn⁰ CARTY; pension awarded 22 Feb 1848. SOURCE: WO120 Volume 69 page 142. INDEX # 3961.

Jn⁰ COZENS; pension awarded 22 Feb 1848; died 26 Jun 1873, Madras, India. SOURCE: WO120 Volume 69 page 142. INDEX # 3962.

Thoˢ DAVIS; pension awarded 22 Feb 1848. SOURCE: WO120 Volume 69 page 142. INDEX # 3963.

Jaˢ DOYLE; pension awarded 22 Feb 1848. SOURCE: WO120 Volume 69 page 142. INDEX # 3964.

Thoˢ HOPWOOD; pension awarded 22 Feb 1848; residence - Madras, India; died 4 Apr 1849. SOURCE: WO120 Volume 69 page 142. INDEX # 3965.

Cormick LOUGHREY; pension awarded 22 Feb 1848; died 21 Dec 1870, Omagh. SOURCE: WO120 Volume 69 page 142. INDEX # 3966.

Patᵏ MCMANUS; pension awarded 22 Feb 1848. SOURCE: WO120 Volume 69 page 142. INDEX # 3967.

Wᵐ NEGUS; pension awarded 22 Feb 1848; residence - Madras, India; died 24 Nov 1853. SOURCE: WO120 Volume 69 page 142. INDEX # 3968.

Jaˢ PORCH; pension awarded 22 Feb 1848; residence - Madras, India; died 15 Feb 1851. SOURCE: WO120 Volume 69 page 142. INDEX # 3969.

Robᵗ TINDALL; pension awarded 22 Feb 1848; died 28 Aug 1885, Madras, India. SOURCE: WO120 Volume 69 page 142. INDEX # 3970.

Geoᵉ WOOLGER; pension awarded 22 Feb 1848. SOURCE: WO120 Volume 69 page 142. INDEX # 3971.

Jonⁿ CARLEY; pension awarded 27 Mar 1849. SOURCE: WO120 Volume 69 page 142. INDEX # 3972.

Absᵐ BARNETT; pension awarded 12 Mar 1850; residence - Fort St. George, India. SOURCE: WO120 Volume 69 page 142. INDEX # 3973.

Robᵗ MEE; pension awarded 12 Mar 1850; died 6 Jan 1871, Madras, India. SOURCE: WO120 Volume 69 page 142. INDEX # 3974.

Richᵈ PHILLIPS; pension awarded 12 Mar 1850. SOURCE: WO120 Volume 69 page 142. INDEX # 3975.

Alexʳ ANDERSON; pension awarded 8 Apr 1851; residence - Baranagar, India; died 19 May 1853. SOURCE: WO120 Volume 69 page 142. INDEX # 3976.

Isaac MASON; pension awarded 8 Apr 1851. SOURCE: WO120 Volume 69 page 142. INDEX # 3977.

Alfred ELDRED; pension awarded 9 Mar 1852; died 10 May 1870. SOURCE: WO120 Volume 69 page 142. INDEX # 3978.

Chaˢ GARNER; pension awarded 9 Mar 1852; died 4 Sep 1869. SOURCE: WO120 Volume 69 page 142. INDEX # 3979.

Wᵐ HALL; pension awarded 9 Mar 1852; residence - Madras, India; died 2 Jan 1854. SOURCE: WO120 Volume 69 page 142. INDEX # 3980.

Wᵐ WATTS; pension awarded 9 Mar 1852. SOURCE: WO120 Volume 69 page 142. INDEX # 3981.

Jaˢ RIDGEWAY; pension awarded 11 Jan 1853. SOURCE: WO120 Volume 69 page 142. INDEX # 3982.

Hugh HANDLON; pension awarded 11 Jan 1853. SOURCE: WO120 Volume 69 page 142. INDEX # 3983.

Wᵐ CLARK; pension awarded 26 Apr 1853; residence - Madras, Canada; died 17 Dec 1854. SOURCE: WO120 Volume 69 page 142. INDEX # 3984.

Jn⁰ MCARTHUR; pension awarded 11 Apr 1854; residence - Fort St. George, India; died 26 May 1855. SOURCE: WO120 Volume 69 page 142. INDEX # 3985.

Jn⁰ SIMPSON; pension awarded 25 Jul 1854. SOURCE: WO120 Volume 69 page 142. INDEX # 3986.

Joshʰ KEAN; pension awarded 25 Jul 1854. SOURCE: WO120 Volume 69 page 142. INDEX # 3987.

Wᵐ LOUGH; pension awarded 25 Jul 1854. SOURCE: WO120 Volume 69 page 142. INDEX # 3988.

Alexʳ MCGOWAN; pension awarded 25 Jul 1854. SOURCE: WO120 Volume 69 page 142. INDEX # 3989.

Wᵐ HALL; pension awarded 25 Jul 1854. SOURCE: WO120 Volume 69 page 142. INDEX # 3990.

WO120 VOLUME 69

25th Regiment of Foot (continued)

Samuel ALEXANDER; pension awarded 13 Mar 1855. SOURCE: WO120 Volume 69 page 143. INDEX # 3991.

James WILTSHIRE; pension awarded 13 Mar 1855. SOURCE: WO120 Volume 69 page 143. INDEX # 3992.

James FURLONG; pension awarded 13 Mar 1855; residence - Madras, India; died 31 Mar 1863. SOURCE: WO120 Volume 69 page 143. INDEX # 3993.

John HARTNETT; pension awarded 13 Mar 1855; residence - Fort St. George, India; died 13 Mar 1855. SOURCE: WO120 Volume 69 page 143. INDEX # 3994.

Frederick PARKER; pension awarded 13 Mar 1855. SOURCE: WO120 Volume 69 page 143. INDEX # 3995.

Martin PARKER; pension awarded 13 Mar 1855. SOURCE: WO120 Volume 69 page 143. INDEX # 3996.

George PHILLIPS; pension awarded 13 Mar 1855. SOURCE: WO120 Volume 69 page 143. INDEX # 3997.

Thomas WEBB; pension awarded 13 Mar 1855. SOURCE: WO120 Volume 69 page 143. INDEX # 3998.

Thomas WOODWARD; pension awarded 13 Mar 1855. SOURCE: WO120 Volume 69 page 143. INDEX # 3999.

26th Regiment of Foot

Jos^h SCOTT; pension awarded 24 Jun 1840; residence - Kingston, Ontario, Canada; died 25 Jul 1866. SOURCE: WO120 Volume 69 page 144. INDEX # 4000.

Richd WILLIS; pension awarded 27 Sep 1842; residence - Prescott, Ontario, Canada. SOURCE: WO120 Volume 69 page 144. INDEX # 4001.

Wm ALLEN; pension awarded 12 Sep 1843; residence - Bengal, India. SOURCE: WO120 Volume 69 page 144. INDEX # 4002.

Thos SAUNDERS; pension awarded 8 May 1839; residence - Bengal, India. SOURCE: WO120 Volume 69 page 144. INDEX # 4003.

Alex^r BOERMELL; pension awarded 13 May 1840; residence - Bengal, India. SOURCE: WO120 Volume 69 page 144. INDEX # 4004.

Mich^l CALLAGHAN; pension awarded 13 May 1840; residence - Bengal, India; died 26 Jan 1846. SOURCE: WO120 Volume 69 page 144. INDEX # 4005.

Noah JONES; pension awarded 10 Oct 1843; residence - Calcutta, India. SOURCE: WO120 Volume 69 page 144. INDEX # 4006.

Isaac SUCKLING; pension awarded 12 Sep 1854. SOURCE: WO120 Volume 69 page 144. INDEX # 4007.

And^w ARMSTRONG; pension awarded 12 Sep 1854. SOURCE: WO120 Volume 69 page 144. INDEX # 4008.

Martin CONNOLLY; pension awarded 12 Sep 1854. SOURCE: WO120 Volume 69 page 144. INDEX # 4009.

27th Regiment of Foot

Wm FRANCIS; pension awarded 8 Sep 1830; residence - Quebec, Canada. SOURCE: WO120 Volume 69 page 146. INDEX # 4010.

Willm QUINN; pension awarded 11 Jun 1817; residence - Fredericton, New Brunswick, Canada; died 10 Mar 1848. SOURCE: WO120 Volume 69 page 146. INDEX # 4011.

Ja^s MCMASTER; pension awarded 28 Jul 1815; residence - Quebec, Quebec, Canada; died in Sep 1853. SOURCE: WO120 Volume 69 page 146. INDEX # 4012.

Jno JOHNSTON; pension awarded 24 Oct 1821; residence - Belleville, Ontario, Canada. SOURCE: WO120 Volume 69 page 146. INDEX # 4013.

Jno HENDERSON; pension awarded 11 Jun 1817; residence - Quebec, Quebec, Canada. SOURCE: WO120 Volume 69 page 146. INDEX # 4014.

Ja^s SCOTT; pension awarded 11 Jun 1817; residence - Fredericton, New Brunswick, Canada. SOURCE: WO120 Volume 69 page 146. INDEX # 4015.

BRITHISH ARMY PENSIONERS ABROAD

27th Regiment of Foot (continued)

Fra^s BAILEY; pension awarded 13 Aug 1811; residence - Quebec, Quebec, Canada; died 9 Nov 1863, Hamilton, Ontario, Canada. SOURCE: WO120 Volume 69 page 146. INDEX # 4016.

Ja^s QUIN; pension awarded 4 Oct 1816; residence - Charlottetown, Prince Edward Island, Canada; died 25 May 1873, Halifax, Nova Scotia, Canada. SOURCE: WO120 Volume 69 page 146. INDEX # 4017.

Peter LENNON; pension awarded 31 Mar 1815; residence - Saint John, New Brunswick, Canada; died 19 Sep 1873, Halifax, Nova Scotia, Canada. SOURCE: WO120 Volume 69 page 146. INDEX # 4018.

Mich^l DALEY; pension awarded 12 Sep 1843; residence - Cape of Good Hope, South Africa. SOURCE: WO120 Volume 69 page 146. INDEX # 4019.

John LACKEY; pension awarded 21 Nov 1821; residence - Belleville, Ontario, Canada; died 15 Sep 1855. SOURCE: WO120 Volume 69 page 146. INDEX # 4020.

Thos HUGHES; pension awarded 11 Jun 1817; residence - Campbellton, New Brunswick, Canada. SOURCE: WO120 Volume 69 page 146. INDEX # 4021.

H^y LIVINGSTONE; pension awarded 11 Jan 1837; residence - Montreal, Quebec, Canada. SOURCE: WO120 Volume 69 page 146. INDEX # 4022.

Ja^s CAMPBELL; pension awarded 7 Dec 1820; residence - Wm Henry, Quebec, Canada. SOURCE: WO120 Volume 69 page 146. INDEX # 4023.

Fra^s KELLY; pension awarded 7 Feb 1822; residence - Wm Henry, Quebec, Canada; died 31 Dec 1848. SOURCE: WO120 Volume 69 page 146. INDEX # 4024.

Thos MCMANUS; pension awarded 23 Aug 1814; residence - St. Jean, Quebec, Canada. SOURCE: WO120 Volume 69 page 146. INDEX # 4025.

Chas BOYLE; pension awarded 18 Aug 1812; residence - Niagara, Ontario, Canada; died 27 Sep 1864, Hamilton, Ontario, Canada. SOURCE: WO120 Volume 69 page 146. INDEX # 4026.

Ja^s MORRISON; pension awarded 27 Mar 1816; residence - Toronto, Ontario, Canada; died 25 Nov 1862. SOURCE: WO120 Volume 69 page 146. INDEX # 4027.

Hugh DONELLY; pension awarded 28 May 1817; residence - St. Jean, Quebec, Canada; died in 1852. SOURCE: WO120 Volume 69 page 146. INDEX # 4028.

Edwd TIERNEY; pension awarded 13 Dec 1826; residence - New South Wales, Australia; died 11 Jan 1858, Calcutta, India. SOURCE: WO120 Volume 69 page 146. INDEX # 4029.

Dav^d MCENANY; pension awarded 28 Nov 1815; residence - Toronto, Ontario, Canada; died 25 Nov 1862. SOURCE: WO120 Volume 69 page 147. INDEX # 4030.

Hen^y WATSON; pension awarded 13 Aug 1813; residence - Bytown, Ontario, Canada. SOURCE: WO120 Volume 69 page 147. INDEX # 4031.

Edwd KELLY; pension awarded 28 May 1817; residence - Kingston, Ontario, Canada; died 27 Jan 1857. SOURCE: WO120 Volume 69 page 147. INDEX # 4032.

Willm OHARA; pension awarded 20 Jun 1817; residence - Prescott, Ontario, Canada; died 4 Jul 1852. SOURCE: WO120 Volume 69 page 147. INDEX # 4033.

Jno FISHER; pension awarded 26 Mar 1817; residence - Montreal, Quebec, Canada; died 12 Sep 1848. SOURCE: WO120 Volume 69 page 147. INDEX # 4034.

Jno GARDNER; pension awarded 26 Mar 1817; residence - Penetanguishene, Ontario, Canada. SOURCE: WO120 Volume 69 page 147. INDEX # 4035.

Ja^s DEVLIN; pension awarded 26 Jun 1816; residence - Toronto, Ontario, Canada; died 5 May 1858, Toronto, Ontario, Canada. SOURCE: WO120 Volume 69 page 147. INDEX # 4036.

Willm MCCOY; pension awarded 30 Oct 1822; residence - Hobart Town, Australia. SOURCE: WO120 Volume 69 page 147. INDEX # 4037.

Jno SUTHERLAND; pension awarded 20 Jun 1817; residence - Halifax, Nova Scotia, Canada. SOURCE: WO120 Volume 69 page 147. INDEX # 4038.

Mich^l NEALIS; pension awarded 11 Jun 1817; residence - Toronto, Ontario, Canada. SOURCE: WO120 Volume 69 page 147. INDEX # 4039.

W^m COX; pension awarded 1 Jun 1813; residence - New South Wales, Australia. SOURCE: WO120 Volume 69 page 147. INDEX # 4040.

WO120 VOLUME 69

27th Regiment of Foot (continued)

Henry CURREN; pension awarded 21 May 1817; residence - Montreal, Quebec, Canada. SOURCE: WO120 Volume 69 page 147. INDEX # 4041.

Jas MCCLURE; pension awarded 20 Jun 1817; residence - Toronto, Ontario, Canada; died 28 Jun 1862. SOURCE: WO120 Volume 69 page 147. INDEX # 4042.

Wm OXBOROUGH; pension awarded 1 May 1822; residence - Gibraltar; died 12 Nov 1849. SOURCE: WO120 Volume 69 page 147. INDEX # 4043.

Nichs SMITH; pension awarded 1 May 1822; residence - Ostend, Belgium. SOURCE: WO120 Volume 69 page 147. INDEX # 4044.

Thos LARNEY; pension awarded 14 Apr 1846; residence - Grahams Town, Cape of Good Hope, South Africa. SOURCE: WO120 Volume 69 page 147. INDEX # 4045.

Jas COURTNEY; pension awarded 8 Aug 1832; residence - Montreal, Quebec, Canada. SOURCE: WO120 Volume 69 page 147. INDEX # 4046.

Thos THOMPSON; pension awarded 31 Dec 1816; residence - Grenada. SOURCE: WO120 Volume 69 page 147. INDEX # 4047.

Bernd MCCABE; pension awarded 12 Jan 1846; residence - Grahams Town, Cape of Good Hope, South Africa; died 13 Apr 1853. SOURCE: WO120 Volume 69 page 147. INDEX # 4048.

Jas SMITH; pension awarded 25 May 1847. SOURCE: WO120 Volume 69 page 147. INDEX # 4049.

Jno PENTLETON; pension awarded 14 Dec 1847; residence - Cape of Good Hope, South Africa; died 27 Sep 1848. SOURCE: WO120 Volume 69 page 147. INDEX # 4050.

Jno ACTON; pension awarded 27 Jun 1848; died 10 May 1859. SOURCE: WO120 Volume 69 page 147. INDEX # 4051.

Josh BROWNE; pension awarded 27 Jun 1848. SOURCE: WO120 Volume 69 page 147. INDEX # 4052.

Thos BILLETT; pension awarded 27 Jun 1848; died 1 Nov 1872 Cape of Good Hope, South Africa. SOURCE: WO120 Volume 69 page 147. INDEX # 4053.

Wm BRIGHT; pension awarded 27 Jun 1848. SOURCE: WO120 Volume 69 page 147. INDEX # 4054.

Wm BUSTARD; pension awarded 27 Jun 1848. SOURCE: WO120 Volume 69 page 147. INDEX # 4055.

Chas DONOHOE; pension awarded 27 Jun 1848; died 29 Nov 1871. SOURCE: WO120 Volume 69 page 147. INDEX # 4056.

Patk DUNN; pension awarded 27 Jun 1848. SOURCE: WO120 Volume 69 page 147. INDEX # 4057.

Michl FEENY; pension awarded 27 Jun 1848. SOURCE: WO120 Volume 69 page 147. INDEX # 4058.

Mathw FLYNN; pension awarded 27 Jun 1848. SOURCE: WO120 Volume 69 page 147. INDEX # 4059.

Jas FITZSIMMONS; pension awarded 27 Jun 1848; residence - Grahams Town, Cape of Good Hope, South Africa; died 3 Jul 1853. SOURCE: WO120 Volume 69 page 147. INDEX # 4060.

Michl GURREN; pension awarded 27 Jun 1848; residence - Cape of Good Hope, South Africa; died 30 Jun 1856. SOURCE: WO120 Volume 69 page 147. INDEX # 4061.

Owen KELLY; pension awarded 27 Jun 1848; died 17 Nov 1875. SOURCE: WO120 Volume 69 page 147. INDEX # 4062.

Jas KIMMETT; pension awarded 27 Jun 1848; residence - Port Louis, Mauritius; died 2 Oct 1857. SOURCE: WO120 Volume 69 page 147. INDEX # 4063.

Jas MCGARR; pension awarded 27 Jun 1848. SOURCE: WO120 Volume 69 page 147. INDEX # 4064.

Chas REYNOLDS; pension awarded 27 Jun 1848. SOURCE: WO120 Volume 69 page 147. INDEX # 4065.

Heny ROCKFORD; pension awarded 27 Jun 1848; died 8 Jun 1875. SOURCE: WO120 Volume 69 page 147. INDEX # 4066.

Jas HUSTON; pension awarded 27 Jun 1848; died 28 Dec 1885, Armagh. SOURCE: WO120 Volume 69 page 147. INDEX # 4067.

28th Regiment of Foot

Traver SMYTH; pension awarded 18 Apr 1821; residence - Penetanguishene, Ontario, Canada; died 17 Dec 1866, Hamilton, Ontario, Canada. SOURCE: WO120 Volume 69 page 149. INDEX # 4068.

Geoe MCCOPPEN; pension awarded 14 Oct 1829; residence - Toronto, Ontario, Canada; died 10 Sep 1876. SOURCE: WO120 Volume 69 page 149. INDEX # 4069.

28th Regiment of Foot (continued)

Bern^d SHANNON; pension awarded 7 Mar 1808; residence - Charlottetown, Prince Edward Island, Canada. SOURCE: WO120 Volume 69 page 149. INDEX # 4070.

Pat^k MCDERMOTT; pension awarded 8 Feb 1832. SOURCE: WO120 Volume 69 page 149. INDEX # 4071.

Mich^l DOGHERTY; pension awarded 22 Sep 1824; residence - Corfu, Greece. SOURCE: WO120 Volume 69 page 149. INDEX # 4072.

Martin DEADY; pension awarded 29 Jul 1819; residence - Toronto, Ontario, Canada; died 15 Apr 1857. SOURCE: WO120 Volume 69 page 149. INDEX # 4073.

Tim^y CROWLEY; pension awarded 25 Aug 1841; residence - New South Wales, Australia. SOURCE: WO120 Volume 69 page 149. INDEX # 4074.

Abr^m CHAPMAN; pension awarded 28 Aug 1839; residence - Norfolk Island, Australia. SOURCE: WO120 Volume 69 page 149. INDEX # 4075.

Mich^l HAWKINS; pension awarded 8 Aug 1838; residence - New South Wales, Australia. SOURCE: WO120 Volume 69 page 149. INDEX # 4076.

Jno FERGUSON; pension awarded 7 Mar 1818; residence - Toronto, Ontario, Canada; died 19 Oct 1850. SOURCE: WO120 Volume 69 page 149. INDEX # 4077.

Martin HUGHES; pension awarded 8 Aug 1838; residence - New South Wales, Australia. SOURCE: WO120 Volume 69 page 149. INDEX # 4078.

John KENNEDY; pension awarded 8 Aug 1838; died 3 Oct 1862, Melbourne, Australia. SOURCE: WO120 Volume 69 page 149. INDEX # 4079.

Pat^k DUNN; pension awarded 25 Aug 1841. SOURCE: WO120 Volume 69 page 149. INDEX # 4080.

Ch^r SCALLEY; pension awarded 25 Aug 1841. SOURCE: WO120 Volume 69 page 149. INDEX # 4081.

Law^e DOOLAN; pension awarded 9 Aug 1842; residence - Sydney, New South Wales, Australia; died in 1854. SOURCE: WO120 Volume 69 page 149. INDEX # 4082.

Ja^s MCLEAN; pension awarded 9 Aug 1842. SOURCE: WO120 Volume 69 page 149. INDEX # 4083.

Wm BURKE; pension awarded 9 Sep 1835; residence - Trinidad. SOURCE: WO120 Volume 69 page 149. INDEX # 4084.

John KEATING; pension awarded 8 Aug 1838; residence - Sydney, New South Wales, Australia. SOURCE: WO120 Volume 69 page 149. INDEX # 4085.

Ja^s MURPHY; pension awarded 22 Sep 1829; residence - New South Wales, Australia. SOURCE: WO120 Volume 69 page 149. INDEX # 4086.

Ja^s FIELDING; pension awarded 9 Jan 1829; residence - New South Wales, Australia. SOURCE: WO120 Volume 69 page 149. INDEX # 4087.

Jos^h HAWKINS; pension awarded 11 Sep 1839; residence - Toronto, Ontario, Canada. SOURCE: WO120 Volume 69 page 149. INDEX # 4088.

Jno MCMULLIN; pension awarded 10 Jun 1845; residence - Poona, India; died 20 Aug 1860, Belgaum, India. SOURCE: WO120 Volume 69 page 149. INDEX # 4089.

Mich^l MALLON; pension awarded 28 Aug 1839; residence - New South Wales, Australia; died 10 May 1848. SOURCE: WO120 Volume 69 page 149. INDEX # 4090.

Jno ONEIL; pension awarded 25 Aug 1841; residence - Sydney, New South Wales, Australia. SOURCE: WO120 Volume 69 page 149. INDEX # 4091.

Fra^s HANRAHAN; pension awarded 14 Oct 1840; residence - New South Wales, Australia. SOURCE: WO120 Volume 69 page 149. INDEX # 4092.

Fra^s HANRAN; pension awarded 14 Oct 1840; residence - New South Wales, Australia. SOURCE: WO120 Volume 69 page 149. INDEX # 4093.

Pat^k WHELAN; pension awarded 13 Jun 1838; residence - New South Wales, Australia. SOURCE: WO120 Volume 69 page 149. INDEX # 4094.

Jno CRABB; pension awarded 28 Jul 1815; residence - Fredericton, New Brunswick, Canada; died 23 Nov 1868. SOURCE: WO120 Volume 69 page 149. INDEX # 4095.

Jno KEOUGH; pension awarded 8 Aug 1838; residence - New South Wales, Australia; died in 1848. SOURCE: WO120 Volume 69 page 149. INDEX # 4096.

Wm MARTIN; pension awarded 28 Aug 1839; residence - New South Wales, Australia. SOURCE: WO120 Volume 69 page 149. INDEX # 4097.

28th Regiment of Foot (continued)

Richd IRWIN; pension awarded 1 Feb 1826; residence - London, Ontario, Canada; died 20 Feb 1871. SOURCE: WO120 Volume 69 page 149. INDEX # 4098.

Jno REGAN; pension awarded 8 Aug 1838; residence - New South Wales, Australia. SOURCE: WO120 Volume 69 page 149. INDEX # 4099.

Hen^y FORSTER; pension awarded 28 Aug 1839; residence - New South Wales, Australia. SOURCE: WO120 Volume 69 page 149. INDEX # 4100.

John COOK; pension awarded 28 Apr 1846; residence - Poona, India; died 22 Jul 1862. SOURCE: WO120 Volume 69 page 149. INDEX # 4101.

Thos MATHERS; pension awarded 28 Apr 1846; died 9 Dec 1883, Poona, India. SOURCE: WO120 Volume 69 page 149. INDEX # 4102.

Pat^k MEEHAN; pension awarded 28 Apr 1846; died 17 Jul 1854. SOURCE: WO120 Volume 69 page 149. INDEX # 4103.

Wm TILLY; pension awarded 28 Apr 1846; died 16 Mar 1858. SOURCE: WO120 Volume 69 page 149. INDEX # 4104.

Ephriam BAILEY; pension awarded 11 May 1847; died 18 Dec 1879, Bombay, India. SOURCE: WO120 Volume 69 page 149. INDEX # 4105.

Stepⁿ KENNY; pension awarded 11 May 1847; died 19 Dec 1847. SOURCE: WO120 Volume 69 page 149. INDEX # 4106.

Saml CLAY; pension awarded 9 May 1848; residence - Bombay, India; died 15 Oct 1850. SOURCE: WO120 Volume 69 page 149. INDEX # 4107.

Jno OWENS; pension awarded 9 May 1848; residence - Bombay, India; died 9 Oct 1850. SOURCE: WO120 Volume 69 page 149. INDEX # 4108.

29th Regiment of Foot

Geo^e BIRNEY; pension awarded 27 Aug 1816; residence - Toronto, Ontario, Canada; died 9 Aug 1861. SOURCE: WO120 Volume 69 page 151. INDEX # 4109.

Thos MARTIN; pension awarded 22 Dec 1824; residence - Toronto, Ontario, Canada. SOURCE: WO120 Volume 69 page 151. INDEX # 4110.

Jno FREEMAN; pension awarded 28 Sep 1818; residence - Constantinople, Turkey. SOURCE: WO120 Volume 69 page 151. INDEX # 4111.

Robt STARS; pension awarded 8 Dec 1830; residence - Bytown, Ontario, Canada. SOURCE: WO120 Volume 69 page 151. INDEX # 4112.

Peter ASKINS; pension awarded 16 Sep 1831; residence - Mauritius; died in Dec 1852. SOURCE: WO120 Volume 69 page 151. INDEX # 4113.

Ja^s DOUGHERTY; pension awarded 10 May 1837; residence - Mauritius; died 3 Jun 1854. SOURCE: WO120 Volume 69 page 151. INDEX # 4114.

Laughlan THOMPSON; pension awarded 14 Mar 1838; residence - Mauritius. SOURCE: WO120 Volume 69 page 151. INDEX # 4115.

Thos MEADOWS; pension awarded 28 Mar 1838; residence - Mauritius. SOURCE: WO120 Volume 69 page 151. INDEX # 4116.

Pat^k JAMESON; pension awarded 10 Aug 1825; residence - Montreal, Quebec, Canada. SOURCE: WO120 Volume 69 page 151. INDEX # 4117.

Alex^r NELSON; pension awarded 14 Dec 1813; residence - St. Johns; died 20 May 1872, Nova Scotia, Canada. SOURCE: WO120 Volume 69 page 151. INDEX # 4118.

Willm WATT; pension awarded 24 Oct 1821; residence - Toronto, Ontario, Canada; died 22 May 1852. SOURCE: WO120 Volume 69 page 151. INDEX # 4119.

Benjⁿ BAY; pension awarded 23 Jul 1828; residence - South Australia, Australia. SOURCE: WO120 Volume 69 page 151. INDEX # 4120.

Ja^s WILSON; pension awarded 13 Dec 1842; residence - Norfolk Island, Australia. SOURCE: WO120 Volume 69 page 151. INDEX # 4121.

Alex^r TROUP; pension awarded 18 Aug 1823; residence - Halifax, Nova Scotia, Canada; died 27 Dec 1856. SOURCE: WO120 Volume 69 page 151. INDEX # 4122.

BRITISH ARMY PENSIONERS ABROAD

29th Regiment of Foot (continued)

Hugh MCLAUGHLIN; pension awarded 10 Feb 1836; residence - Quebec, Canada. SOURCE: WO120 Volume 69 page 151. INDEX # 4123.

Fra^s MCDOWALL; pension awarded 23 Feb 1847; residence - Calcutta, India. SOURCE: WO120 Volume 69 page 151. INDEX # 4124.

Thos DORAN; pension awarded 23 Feb 1847; residence - Calcutta, India. SOURCE: WO120 Volume 69 page 151. INDEX # 4125.

Jos^h KENNEY; pension awarded 23 Feb 1847; residence - Calcutta, India. SOURCE: WO120 Volume 69 page 151. INDEX # 4126.

John MOSES; pension awarded 23 Feb 1847; residence - Meerut, India. SOURCE: WO120 Volume 68 page 151. INDEX # 4127.

Wm NOWLAN; pension awarded 25 Jan 1848; residence - Calcutta, India; died 3 Apr 1849. SOURCE: WO120 Volume 69 page 151. INDEX # 4128.

Arch^d WILSON; pension awarded 13 Feb 1849. SOURCE: WO120 Volume 69 page 152. INDEX # 4129.

Jno DOUBLE; pension awarded 8 Jan 1850; residence - Calcutta, India; died 5 May 1852. SOURCE: WO120 Volume 69 page 152. INDEX # 4130.

Martin MALONE; pension awarded 8 Jan 1850; residence - Bombay, India; died 16 May 1854. SOURCE: WO120 Volume 69 page 152. INDEX # 4131.

Jno MCBRIEN; pension awarded 12 Nov 1850. SOURCE: WO120 Volume 69 page 152. INDEX # 4132.

Thos MOONEY; pension awarded 22 Mar 1853; died 17 Sep 1876, India. SOURCE: WO120 Volume 69 page 152. INDEX # 4133.

30th Regiment of Foot

Jno ALLEN; pension awarded 2 Feb 1813; residence - Montreal, Quebec, Canada. SOURCE: WO120 Volume 69 page 154. INDEX # 4134.

Wm HOLLIDAY; pension awarded 21 May 1817; residence - Van Diemen's Land, Tasmania, Australia; died 13 Jul 1878, Melbourne, Australia. SOURCE: WO120 Volume 69 page 154. INDEX # 4135.

Mich^l SILK; pension awarded 27 Aug 1828; residence - Penetanguishene, Ontario, Canada; died 17 Feb 1855. SOURCE: WO120 Volume 69 page 154. INDEX # 4136.

Ja^s BLOWES; pension awarded 21 May 1817; residence - Sydney; died 21 Jul 1884, Sydney. SOURCE: WO120 Volume 69 page 154. INDEX # 4137.

Jno SMITH; pension awarded 22 Dec 1814; residence - New South Wales, Australia; died 2 Jun 1854. SOURCE: WO120 Volume 69 page 154. INDEX # 4138.

Step^n COOK; pension awarded 30 Oct 1827; residence - Madras, India. SOURCE: WO120 Volume 69 page 154. INDEX # 4139.

Ja^s GILSON; pension awarded 11 Nov 1829; residence - Montreal, Quebec, Canada; died 15 May 1853. SOURCE: WO120 Volume 69 page 154. INDEX # 4140.

Jno KENDALL; pension awarded 11 Nov 1829; residence - Montreal, Quebec, Canada; died 13 May 1855. SOURCE: WO120 Volume 69 page 154. INDEX # 4141.

Thos CROWE; pension awarded 31 Oct 1827; residence - Madras, India. SOURCE: WO120 Volume 69 page 154. INDEX # 4142.

Simon WHITE; pension awarded 31 Oct 1827; residence - Madras, India. SOURCE: WO120 Volume 69 page 154. INDEX # 4143.

Saml HEATLEY; pension awarded 31 Oct 1827; residence - Madras, India. SOURCE: WO120 Volume 69 page 154. INDEX # 4144.

Robt PANTONY; pension awarded 31 Oct 1827; residence - Madras, India; died 1 Jan 1847. SOURCE: WO120 Volume 69 page 154. INDEX # 4145.

Robt MONK; pension awarded 21 May 1828; residence - Madras, India; died 18 Jan 1853. SOURCE: WO120 Volume 69 page 154. INDEX # 4146.

Wm FLETCHER; pension awarded 31 Oct 1827; residence - Madras, India; died 2 Jan 1851. SOURCE: WO120 Volume 69 page 154. INDEX # 4147.

30th Regiment of Foot (continued)

Jos^h HARDING; pension awarded 31 Oct 1827; residence - Madras, India; died 25 Jun 1854. SOURCE: WO120 Volume 69 page 154. INDEX # 4148.

Jno VICKERS; pension awarded 31 Oct 1827; residence - Madras, India; died 6 Jan 1847. SOURCE: WO120 Volume 69 page 154. INDEX # 4149.

Thos WILLIAMS; pension awarded 31 Oct 1827; residence - Madras, India. SOURCE: WO120 Volume 69 page 154. INDEX # 4150.

Matt^w SEWELL; pension awarded 31 Oct 1827; residence - Madras, India; died 8 Mar 1853. SOURCE: WO120 Volume 69 page 154. INDEX # 4151.

Saml MINNY; pension awarded 31 Oct 1827; residence - Madras, India; died 27 Jun 1847. SOURCE: WO120 Volume 69 page 154. INDEX # 4152.

Willm PEPPER; pension awarded 31 Oct 1827; residence - Madras, India; died 23 Oct 1850. SOURCE: WO120 Volume 69 page 154. INDEX # 4153.

Willm COLEMAN; pension awarded 11 Nov 1829; residence - Madras, India; died 10 Aug 1848. SOURCE: WO120 Volume 69 page 155. INDEX # 4154.

Thos THOMPSON; pension awarded 31 Oct 1827; residence - Madras, India; died 1 Jan 1857. SOURCE: WO120 Volume 69 page 155. INDEX # 4155.

Thos WELLS; pension awarded 31 Oct 1827; residence - Madras, India; died 5 Sep 1851. SOURCE: WO120 Volume 69 page 155. INDEX # 4156.

Thos MEAKIN; pension awarded 31 Oct 1827; residence - Madras, India; died 5 Oct 1854. SOURCE: WO120 Volume 69 page 155. INDEX # 4157.

Giles SEDDON; pension awarded 11 Nov 1829; residence - Madras, India; died 22 Feb 1848. SOURCE: WO120 Volume 69 page 155. INDEX # 4158.

Willm SMITH; pension awarded 10 Feb 1830; residence - Madras, India; died 13 May 1870. SOURCE: WO120 Volume 69 page 155. INDEX # 4159.

Tim^y GITTINGS; pension awarded 21 May 1828; residence - Madras, India; died 11 Jan 1855. SOURCE: WO120 Volume 69 page 155. INDEX # 4160.

Ja^s FISHER; pension awarded 11 Nov 1829; residence - Madras, India; died 2 Sep 1854. SOURCE: WO120 Volume 69 page 155. INDEX # 4161.

Ja^s TODD; pension awarded 11 Nov 1829; residence - Madras, India. SOURCE: WO120 Volume 69 page 155. INDEX # 4162.

Abr^m WRIGHT; pension awarded 31 Oct 1827; residence - Madras, India; died 6 Apr 1853. SOURCE: WO120 Volume 69 page 155. INDEX # 4163.

Job SMITH; pension awarded 11 Nov 1829; residence - Madras, India. SOURCE: WO120 Volume 69 page 155. INDEX # 4164.

John MASKELL; pension awarded 11 Nov 1829; residence - Madras, India. SOURCE: WO120 Volume 69 page 155. INDEX # 4165.

John RIELLY; pension awarded 24 Oct 1843; residence - Cape of Good Hope, South Africa. SOURCE: WO120 Volume 69 page 155. INDEX # 4166.

Ja^s WALKER; pension awarded 24 Oct 1843; residence - Saint John, New Brunswick, Canada. SOURCE: WO120 Volume 69 page 155. INDEX # 4167.

31st Regiment of Foot

Mich^l ROCK; pension awarded 11 May 1831; residence - Bytown, Ontario, Canada. SOURCE: WO120 Volume 69 page 157. INDEX # 4168.

Pat^k MURPHY; pension awarded 7 Feb 1821; residence - Penetanguishene, Ontario, Canada; died 3 Jun 1874, Hamilton, Ontario, Canada. SOURCE: WO120 Volume 69 page 157. INDEX # 4169.

Wm WINCKWORTH; pension awarded 4 Aug 1824; residence - Toronto, Ontario, Canada; died 18 Apr 1867, Hamilton, Ontario, Canada. SOURCE: WO120 Volume 69 page 157. INDEX # 4170.

Wm SMALL; pension awarded 10 Jul 1839; residence - Toronto, Ontario, Canada; died 25 Jul 1869. SOURCE: WO120 Volume 69 page 157. INDEX # 4171.

BRITISH ARMY PENSIONERS ABROAD

31st Regiment of Foot (continued)

Jn⁰ MCGHEE; pension awarded 11 Mar 1845; residence - Umballa, India; died 9 Jan 1847.
SOURCE: WO120 Volume 69 page 157. INDEX # 4172.

Pat^k WALSH; pension awarded 11 Mar 1845; residence - Umballa, India; died 26 May 1851.
SOURCE: WO120 Volume 69 page 157. INDEX # 4173.

Ja^s QUINNELL; pension awarded 25 Jun 1844; residence - Umballa, India. SOURCE: WO120 Volume 69 page 157. INDEX # 4174.

Ja^s EDWARDS; pension awarded 11 Jun 1844; residence - Umballa, India. SOURCE: WO120 Volume 69 page 157. INDEX # 4175.

Chas ELLIS; pension awarded 11 Jun 1844; residence - Umballa, India. SOURCE: WO120 Volume 69 page 157. INDEX # 4176.

Thos HUGHES; pension awarded 11 Jun 1844; residence - Umballa, India; died 1 Apr 1847.
SOURCE: WO120 Volume 69 page 157. INDEX # 4177.

Chas ROBERTS; pension awarded 25 Jun 1844; residence - Umballa, India; died 31 Aug 1856.
SOURCE: WO120 Volume 69 page 157. INDEX # 4178.

Martin CROWE; pension awarded 11 Mar 1845; residence - Umballa, India; died in May 1851.
SOURCE: WO120 Volume 69 page 157. INDEX # 4179.

Henry JAMES; pension awarded 11 Mar 1845; residence - Umballa, India; died 18 Jan 1849.
SOURCE: WO120 Volume 69 page 157. INDEX # 4180.

Ja^s LEARY; pension awarded 11 Mar 1845; residence - Umballa, India. SOURCE: WO120 Volume 69 page 157. INDEX # 4181.

Ja^s ROUTE; pension awarded 28 Nov 1821; residence - Toronto, Ontario, Canada; died 14 Nov 1849. SOURCE: WO120 Volume 69 page 157. INDEX # 4182.

Robt HANDCOCK; pension awarded 13 Apr 1809; residence - New South Wales, Australia; died 3 Dec 1849. SOURCE: WO120 Volume 69 page 157. INDEX # 4183.

Edwd BARNS; pension awarded 12 Oct 1831; residence - Toronto, Ontario, Canada. SOURCE: WO120 Volume 69 page 157. INDEX # 4184.

Edwd HART; pension awarded 27 Jun 1838; residence - Bengal, India; died in Oct 1852.
SOURCE: WO120 Volume 69 page 157. INDEX # 4185.

Wm SAUNDERS; pension awarded 23 May 1840; residence - Bengal, India; died 27 Jan 1847.
SOURCE: WO120 Volume 69 page 157. INDEX # 4186.

Jn⁰ KENWORTHY; pension awarded 17 Mar 1819; residence - Hobart Town, Australia; died 30 Jan 1851. SOURCE: WO120 Volume 69 page 157. INDEX # 4187.

John FEELEY; pension awarded 11 Aug 1841; residence - Toronto, Ontario, Canada. SOURCE: WO120 Volume 69 page 157. INDEX # 4188.

Jos^h SHADBOLT; pension awarded 24 Apr 1841; residence - Bengal, India; died 27 May 1853.
SOURCE: WO120 Volume 69 page 157. INDEX # 4189.

Pat^k MCLOUGHLIN; pension awarded 27 Jun 1838; residence - Bengal, India; died 4 Nov 1853. SOURCE: WO120 Volume 69 page 157. INDEX # 4190.

Jn⁰ CURRAN; pension awarded 27 Jun 1838; residence - Bengal, India; died 18 Jun 1851.
SOURCE: WO120 Volume 69 page 157. INDEX # 4191.

Ja^s TOWNSEND; pension awarded 27 Jun 1838; residence - Bengal, India. SOURCE: WO120 Volume 69 page 157. INDEX # 4192.

Ch^r SHIELD; pension awarded 13 Jan 1846; residence - Meerut, India. SOURCE: WO120 Volume 69 page 157. INDEX # 4193.

Isaac COLLINS; pension awarded 13 Oct 1846; residence - Dinapore, India. SOURCE: WO120 Volume 69 page 157. INDEX # 4194.

Ja^s REILLY; pension awarded 24 Nov 1846; residence - Simla, India; died 3 Apr 1857.
SOURCE: WO120 Volume 69 page 157. INDEX # 4195.

Wm BURNS; pension awarded 24 Nov 1846; residence - Bengal, India; died in Sep 1851.
SOURCE: WO120 Volume 69 page 157. INDEX # 4196.

Jn⁰ COUGHLAN; pension awarded 24 Nov 1846; residence - India; died in Feb 1854. SOURCE: WO120 Volume 69 page 157. INDEX # 4197.

31st Regiment of Foot (continued)

William LONG; pension awarded 29 Jul 1819; residence - Toronto, Ontario, Canada. SOURCE: WO120 Volume 69 page 157. INDEX # 4198.

32nd Regiment of Foot

Wm JENKINS; pension awarded 4 Aug 1824; residence - Hobart Town, Australia. SOURCE: WO120 Volume 69 page 159. INDEX # 4199.

Simon CARSON; pension awarded 27 Jan 1817; residence - Hobart Town, Australia. SOURCE: WO120 Volume 69 page 159. INDEX # 4200.

John HALL; pension awarded 9 Jan 1833; residence - Quebec, Canada. SOURCE: WO120 Volume 69 page 159. INDEX # 4201.

Thos REED; pension awarded 8 Jun 1831; residence - Toronto, Ontario, Canada. SOURCE: WO120 Volume 69 page 159. INDEX # 4202.

Wm MILLER; pension awarded 11 Nov 1835; residence - London, Ontario, Canada; died 3 Mar 1870. SOURCE: WO120 Volume 69 page 159. INDEX # 4203.

Robt GRAHAM; pension awarded 14 Dec 1836; residence - Prescott, Ontario, Canada; died 20 May 1857. SOURCE: WO120 Volume 69 page 159. INDEX # 4204.

Wm MCCLEAN; pension awarded 23 Oct 1838; residence - Montreal, Quebec, Canada. SOURCE: WO120 Volume 69 page 159. INDEX # 4205.

John BROWN; pension awarded 11 Dec 1839; residence - London, Ontario, Canada; died 18 Feb 1849. SOURCE: WO120 Volume 69 page 159. INDEX # 4206.

Jos^h DYSON; pension awarded 8 Sep 1841; residence - Toronto, Ontario, Canada; died 26 Apr 1885, Toronto, Ontario, Canada. SOURCE: WO120 Volume 69 page 159. INDEX # 4207.

J^{no} MCCLEAN; pension awarded 8 Sep 1841; residence - London, Ontario, Canada; died 19 Apr 1862, London, Ontario, Canada. SOURCE: WO120 Volume 69 page 159. INDEX # 4208.

Bern^d MURRAY; pension awarded 8 Sep 1841; residence - Toronto, Ontario, Canada. SOURCE: WO120 Volume 69 page 159. INDEX # 4209.

Thos MCDOWALL; pension awarded 23 Jul 1844; residence - Montreal, Quebec, Canada. SOURCE: WO120 Volume 69 page 159. INDEX # 4210.

Thos HUGHES; pension awarded 23 Oct 1838; residence - Montreal, Quebec, Canada. SOURCE: WO120 Volume 69 page 159. INDEX # 4211.

Pat^k MCLARNEY; pension awarded 8 Nov 1826; residence - Toronto, Ontario, Canada; died 25 Jul 1850. SOURCE: WO120 Volume 69 page 159. INDEX # 4212.

Ter^e MCCROCKIN; pension awarded 22 Jan 1840; residence - Montreal, Quebec, Canada. SOURCE: WO120 Volume 69 page 159. INDEX # 4213.

Peter LOVE; pension awarded 8 Sep 1841; residence - Toronto, Ontario, Canada; died in Dec 1845. SOURCE: WO120 Volume 69 page 159. INDEX # 4214.

Ja^s LOVE; pension awarded 8 Sep 1841; residence - Toronto, Ontario, Canada. SOURCE: WO120 Volume 69 page 159. INDEX # 4215.

Wm ANEAR; pension awarded 23 Oct 1838; residence - Montreal, Quebec, Canada; died in Oct 1851. SOURCE: WO120 Volume 69 page 159. INDEX # 4216.

Saml COLERICK; pension awarded 8 Jan 1840; residence - London, Ontario, Canada; died 10 Jun 1864. SOURCE: WO120 Volume 69 page 159. INDEX # 4217.

Jos^h WATTS; pension awarded 22 Jan 1840; residence - Montreal, Quebec, Canada. SOURCE: WO120 Volume 69 page 159. INDEX # 4218.

Fra^s HIGGINS; pension awarded 9 Aug 1842; residence - Toronto, Ontario, Canada. SOURCE: WO120 Volume 69 page 160. INDEX # 4219.

Thos REEKS; pension awarded 22 Sep 1841; residence - London, Ontario, Canada; died 12 Jan 1878, London, Ontario, Canada. SOURCE: WO120 Volume 69 page 160. INDEX # 4220.

Val^e BYRON; pension awarded 11 Apr 1843; residence - London, Ontario, Canada. SOURCE: WO120 Volume 69 page 160. INDEX # 4221.

Thos VALE; pension awarded 10 Dec 1834; residence - Jamaica. SOURCE: WO120 Volume 69 page 160. INDEX # 4222.

BRITISH ARMY PENSIONERS ABROAD

32nd Regiment of Foot (continued)

Geo^e RICHARDSON; pension awarded 18 Jun 1828; residence - Montreal, Quebec, Canada. SOURCE: WO120 Volume 69 page 160. INDEX # 4223.

Ja^s LOVE; pension awarded 8 Sep 1841; residence - Toronto, Ontario, Canada. SOURCE: WO120 Volume 69 page 160. INDEX # 4224.

John SPURRILL; pension awarded 12 May 1846; residence - Toronto, Ontario, Canada. SOURCE: WO120 Volume 69 page 160. INDEX # 4225.

Robt WINTER; pension awarded 12 May 1846; residence - Toronto, Ontario, Canada; died 9 Dec 1864. SOURCE: WO120 Volume 69 page 160. INDEX # 4226.

Pat^k MULCAHY; pension awarded 12 May 1846; residence - Montreal, Quebec, Canada; died in 1849. SOURCE: WO120 Volume 69 page 160. INDEX # 4227.

Thos MCCARTHY; pension awarded 26 Sep 1838. SOURCE: WO120 Volume 69 page 160. INDEX # 4228.

Mich^l CLANCY; pension awarded 26 Jun 1849. SOURCE: WO120 Volume 69 page 160. INDEX # 4229.

Jno MCCARTHY; pension awarded 10 Jul 1849. SOURCE: WO120 Volume 69 page 160. INDEX # 4230.

Mich^l CLANCY; pension awarded 26 Jul 1849. SOURCE: WO120 Volume 69 page 160. INDEX # 4231.

Thos LEECH; pension awarded 8 Jan 1850; residence - Jullundar, India; died 3 Jul 1851. SOURCE: WO120 Volume 69 page 160. INDEX # 4232.

Wm HART; pension awarded 8 Jan 1850. SOURCE: WO120 Volume 69 page 160. INDEX # 4233.

Ja^s MCGINNESS; pension awarded 8 Jan 1850; died 18 Dec 1869, Omagh. SOURCE: WO120 Volume 69 page 160. INDEX # 4234.

Jno SYMS; pension awarded 8 Jan 1850. SOURCE: WO120 Volume 69 page 160. INDEX # 4235.

Ja^s GATES; pension awarded 9 Apr 1850. SOURCE: WO120 Volume 69 page 160. INDEX # 4236.

Pat^k DULLARD; pension awarded 14 Jan 1851. SOURCE: WO120 Volume 69 page 160. INDEX # 4237.

Affleck KIRK; pension awarded 22 Mar 1853. SOURCE: WO120 Volume 69 page 160. INDEX # 4238.

John CROWLY; pension awarded 11 Mar 1856; died 31 Jun 1858, Calcutta, India. SOURCE: WO120 Volume 69 page 160. INDEX # 4239.

Anthony DOREY; pension awarded 5 May 1857. SOURCE: WO120 Volume 69 page 160. INDEX # 4240.

33rd Regiment of Foot

Ja^s HULME; pension awarded 22 Dec 1814; residence - Halifax, Nova Scotia, Canada; died 6 Jan 1848. SOURCE: WO120 Volume 69 page 162. INDEX # 4241.

Bern^d GAFFNEY; pension awarded 25 Jun 1823; residence - Prescott, Ontario, Canada. SOURCE: WO120 Volume 69 page 162. INDEX # 4242.

Thos RODWELL; pension awarded 27 Aug 1816; residence - New South Wales, Australia. SOURCE: WO120 Volume 69 page 162. INDEX # 4243.

Saml ROGERS; pension awarded 16 Apr 1828; residence - London, Ontario, Canada. SOURCE: WO120 Volume 69 page 162. INDEX # 4244.

Jon^n HOPKINSON; pension awarded 23 Dec 1845; residence - Fredericton, New Brunswick, Canada. SOURCE: WO120 Volume 69 page 162. INDEX # 4245.

Jno THOMPSON; pension awarded 26 Feb 1840; residence - Gibraltar. SOURCE: WO120 Volume 69 page 162. INDEX # 4246.

Richd BENNETT; pension awarded 27 Mar 1839; residence - Gibraltar. SOURCE: WO120 Volume 69 page 162. INDEX # 4247.

Martin SHEEHAN; pension awarded 27 Oct 1846; residence - St. Andrews, New Brunswick, Canada. SOURCE: WO120 Volume 69 page 162. INDEX # 4248.

Jos^h WADSWORTH; pension awarded 14 Sep 1847. SOURCE: WO120 Volume 69 page 162. INDEX # 4249.

Edwd MCINTYRE; pension awarded 28 Sep 1847; residence - Saint John, New Brunswick, Canada; died 30 Aug 1851. SOURCE: WO120 Volume 69 page 162. INDEX # 4250.

Jno SHANNON; pension awarded 28 Sep 1847. SOURCE: WO120 Volume 69 page 162. INDEX # 4251.

Peter TETLOW; pension awarded 12 Oct 1847; residence - Halifax, Nova Scotia, Canada. SOURCE: WO120 Volume 69 page 162. INDEX # 4252.

33rd Regiment of Foot (continued)

Robt AITKEN; pension awarded 9 May 1848; died in 1869, Nova Scotia, Canada. SOURCE: WO120 Volume 69 page 162. INDEX # 4253.

David STRATTON; pension awarded 11 Jul 1848. SOURCE: WO120 Volume 69 page 162. INDEX # 4254.

Ed^{wd} CROSSLAND; pension awarded 11 Jul 1848; residence - Nova Scotia, Canada; died 3 Jun 1863. SOURCE: WO120 Volume 69 page 162. INDEX # 4255.

Wm SMITH; pension awarded 11 Jul 1848. SOURCE: WO120 Volume 69 page 162. INDEX # 4256.

Jno MUIR; pension awarded 11 Jul 1848; residence - Paisley; died 31 Jan 1862. SOURCE: WO120 Volume 69 page 162. INDEX # 4257.

Thos BELL; pension awarded 11 Jul 1848; died 30 Sep 1864, New Brunswick, Canada. SOURCE: WO120 Volume 69 page 162. INDEX # 4258.

Robt CLARK; pension awarded 11 Jul 1848. SOURCE: WO120 Volume 69 page 162. INDEX # 4259.

Geo^e DOWNIE; pension awarded 11 Jul 1848. SOURCE: WO120 Volume 69 page 162. INDEX # 4260.

Jno HINDSON; pension awarded 11 Jul 1848; residence - Nova Scotia, Canada; died in Feb 1854. SOURCE: WO120 Volume 69 page 163. INDEX # 4261.

Stepⁿ JACKSON; pension awarded 11 Jul 1848. SOURCE: WO120 Volume 69 page 163. INDEX # 4262.

Wm NEWMAN; pension awarded 11 Jul 1848; died 9 Apr 1882, Nova Scotia, Canada. SOURCE: WO120 Volume 69 page 163. INDEX # 4263.

Arthur MCFARLANE; pension awarded 11 Jul 1848. SOURCE: WO120 Volume 69 page 163. INDEX # 4264.

Wm SUTCLIFFE; pension awarded 11 Jul 1848; residence - New Brunswick, Canada; died in 1850. SOURCE: WO120 Volume 69 page 163. INDEX # 4265.

And^w WHITE; pension awarded 11 Jul 1848. SOURCE: WO120 Volume 69 page 163. INDEX # 4266.

Jos^h DAVIS; pension awarded 22 Aug 1848. SOURCE: WO120 Volume 69 page 163. INDEX # 4267.

Henry SNELLING; pension awarded 6 Oct 1857. SOURCE: WO120 Volume 69 page 163. INDEX # 4268.

James SNELLING; pension awarded 6 Oct 1857. SOURCE: WO120 Volume 69 page 163. INDEX # 4269.

James BROCK; pension awarded 4 Jun 1823; residence - Madras, India. SOURCE: WO120 Volume 69 page 165. INDEX # 4270.

34th Regiment of Foot

Wm WILLIAMS; pension awarded 12 Sep 1832; residence - Fredericton, New Brunswick, Canada. SOURCE: WO120 Volume 69 page 165. INDEX # 4271.

Jno MCGOWAN; pension awarded 28 Jul 1841; residence - Prescott, Ontario, Canada; died 29 Nov 1854. SOURCE: WO120 Volume 69 page 165. INDEX # 4272.

Thos EASTON; pension awarded 2 Nov 1814; residence - Penetanguishene, Ontario, Canada; died 23 Nov 1864, Hamilton, Ontario, Canada. SOURCE: WO120 Volume 69 page 165. INDEX # 4273.

Jno CRAWFORD; pension awarded 22 Mar 1820; residence - Quebec, Quebec, Canada. SOURCE: WO120 Volume 69 page 165. INDEX # 4274.

Thos HIGHFIELD; pension awarded 4 Jun 1823; residence - Madras, India. SOURCE: WO120 Volume 69 page 165. INDEX # 4275.

Ja^s GRAY; pension awarded 4 Aug 1824; residence - Quebec, Quebec, Canada; died in Jul 1849. SOURCE: WO120 Volume 69 page 165. INDEX # 4276.

Benjⁿ RICHES; pension awarded 7 Feb 1821; residence - Madras, India; died 27 Feb 1851. SOURCE: WO120 Volume 69 page 165. INDEX # 4277.

Mich^l FORD; pension awarded 4 Jun 1823; residence - Madras, India; died 24 Mar 1849. SOURCE: WO120 Volume 69 page 165. INDEX # 4278.

Willm WILSON; pension awarded 4 Jun 1823; residence - Madras, India; died 5 Nov 1855. SOURCE: WO120 Volume 69 page 165. INDEX # 4279.

Robt HAMILTON; pension awarded 4 Jun 1823; residence - Madras, India; died 29 Aug 1855. SOURCE: WO120 Volume 69 page 165. INDEX # 4280.

Jos^h MARSHALL; pension awarded 4 Jun 1823; residence - Madras, India; died 3 Oct 1852. SOURCE: WO120 Volume 69 page 165. INDEX # 4281.

34th Regiment of Foot (continued)

Thos KENT; pension awarded 4 Jun 1823; residence - Madras, India; died 24 Feb 1851. SOURCE: WO120 Volume 69 page 165. INDEX # 4282.

Thos HALKETT; pension awarded 4 Jun 1823; residence - Madras, India; died 9 Oct 1847. SOURCE: WO120 Volume 69 page 165. INDEX # 4283.

Jas DONNELLY; pension awarded 25 Sep 1839; residence - Quebec, Quebec, Canada; died 27 Nov 1873, Auckland, New Zealand. SOURCE: WO120 Volume 69 page 165. INDEX # 4284.

Horatio STEWART; pension awarded 25 Apr 1848. SOURCE: WO120 Volume 69 page 165. INDEX # 4285.

35th Regiment of Foot

Willm WALTERS; pension awarded 16 May 1816; residence - Toronto, Ontario, Canada. SOURCE: WO120 Volume 69 page 165. INDEX # 4286.

Geoe DENNISON; pension awarded 28 Dec 1818; residence - Cape of Good Hope, South Africa. SOURCE: WO120 Volume 69 page 167. INDEX # 4287.

Patk CANNON; pension awarded 12 Dec 1838; residence - Mauritius; died 12 Jun 1854. SOURCE: WO120 Volume 69 page 167. INDEX # 4288.

Thos RYAN; pension awarded 13 Dec 1842; residence - Mauritius; died 17 Apr 1848. SOURCE: WO120 Volume 69 page 167. INDEX # 4289.

Michl MCCARROLL; pension awarded 27 Jan 1819; residence - Kingston, Ontario, Canada; died 30 Apr 1854. SOURCE: WO120 Volume 69 page 167. INDEX # 4290.

Wm WEST; pension awarded 13 Dec 1826; residence - Montreal, Quebec, Canada. SOURCE: WO120 Volume 69 page 167. INDEX # 4291.

Geoe GOBLE; pension awarded 13 Dec 1826; residence - Amherstburg, Ontario, Canada; died 18 Sep 1853. SOURCE: WO120 Volume 69 page 167. INDEX # 4292.

Thos KIRBY; pension awarded 28 Dec 1818; residence - Malta. SOURCE: WO120 Volume 69 page 167. INDEX # 4293.

36th Regiment of Foot

Edwd Thos DAY; pension awarded 12 Dec 1825; residence - London, Ontario, Canada; died 5 Nov 1869. SOURCE: WO120 Volume 69 page 169. INDEX # 4294.

Willm PAGE; pension awarded 17 Jan 1827; residence - Hobart Town, Australia; died 21 Apr 1847. SOURCE: WO120 Volume 69 page 169. INDEX # 4295.

Edws KERR; pension awarded 12 Dec 1827; residence - Quebec, Quebec, Canada; died in 1848. SOURCE: WO120 Volume 69 page 169. INDEX # 4296.

Willm FLECK; pension awarded 9 Jun 1819; residence - London, Ontario, Canada; died 1 Jan 1872, London, Ontario, Canada. SOURCE: WO120 Volume 69 page 169. INDEX # 4297.

Willm PETERS; pension awarded 12 Oct 1825; residence - Jamaica; died in 1854. SOURCE: WO120 Volume 69 page 169. INDEX # 4298.

Luke DUNN; pension awarded 13 Nov 1849. SOURCE: WO120 Volume 69 page 169. INDEX # 4299.

John BREEZE; pension awarded 8 Apr 1840; died 13 Nov 1864, Birmingham. SOURCE: WO120 Volume 69 page 169. INDEX # 4300.

37th Regiment of Foot

Robt EADEY; pension awarded 1 Feb 1826; residence - Bytown, Ontario, Canada. SOURCE: WO120 Volume 69 page 171. INDEX # 4301.

Thos GUILE; pension awarded 30 May 1827; residence - Bytown, Ontario, Canada. SOURCE: WO120 Volume 69 page 171. INDEX # 4302.

Jno HELFRICK; pension awarded 24 Nov 1824; residence - Amherstburg, Ontario, Canada; died 1 Feb 1865, London, Ontario, Canada. SOURCE: WO120 Volume 69 page 171. INDEX # 4303.

37th Regiment of Foot (continued)

Pat^k RYAN; pension awarded 25 Nov 1818; residence - Perth, Ontario, Canada; died 8 May 1879, Ottawa, Ontario, Canada. SOURCE: WO120 Volume 69 page 171. INDEX # 4304.

Chas REYNOLDS; pension awarded 12 Sep 1832; residence - Halifax, Nova Scotia, Canada; died 6 Nov 1846. SOURCE: WO120 Volume 69 page 171. INDEX # 4305.

Mich^l SWEENEY; pension awarded 12 Aug 1835; residence - Kingston, Ontario, Canada. SOURCE: WO120 Volume 69 page 171. INDEX # 4306.

Miles KEEGAN; pension awarded 13 Apr 1824; residence - Kingston, Ontario, Canada; died 25 Nov 1867, Toronto, Ontario, Canada. SOURCE: WO120 Volume 69 page 171. INDEX # 4307.

Benjⁿ HUNT; pension awarded 18 Dec 1822; residence - Quebec, Quebec, Canada. SOURCE: WO120 Volume 69 page 171. INDEX # 4308.

Wm MCLEAN; pension awarded 26 May 1841; residence - Halifax, Nova Scotia, Canada. SOURCE: WO120 Volume 69 page 171. INDEX # 4309.

Thos HOCKADAY; pension awarded 29 Jun 1837; residence - Honduras. SOURCE: WO120 Volume 69 page 171. INDEX # 4310.

Jos^h HUNT; pension awarded 17 Sep 1828; residence - Quebec, Quebec, Canada. SOURCE: WO120 Volume 69 page 171. INDEX # 4311.

John SMITH; pension awarded 11 Oct 1842; residence - Montreal, Quebec, Canada; died 8 Aug 1878, Toronto, Ontario, Canada. SOURCE: WO120 Volume 69 page 171. INDEX # 4312.

Willm MOLES; pension awarded 20 Jun 1827; residence - Quebec, Quebec, Canada. SOURCE: WO120 Volume 69 page 171. INDEX # 4313.

Pat^k GOLDING; pension awarded 9 Feb 1847; residence - Halifax, Nova Scotia, Canada. SOURCE: WO120 Volume 69 page 171. INDEX # 4314.

Wm CARR; pension awarded 23 Jan 1855. SOURCE: WO120 Volume 69 page 171. INDEX # 4315.

38th Regiment of Foot

Richd SHAW; pension awarded 11 Jul 1820; residence - Cape of Good Hope, South Africa; died in 1847. SOURCE: WO120 Volume 69 page 173. INDEX # 4316.

Jos^h BOURNE; pension awarded 3 Mar 1824; residence - Cape of Good Hope, South Africa; died in 1845. SOURCE: WO120 Volume 69 page 173. INDEX # 4317.

Phelan COOK; pension awarded 2 Feb 1815; residence - Belleville, Ontario, Canada. SOURCE: WO120 Volume 69 page 173. INDEX # 4318.

Wm KIERNAN; pension awarded 22 Mar 1822; residence - Bytown, Ontario, Canada. SOURCE: WO120 Volume 69 page 173. INDEX # 4319.

Jos^h PINER; pension awarded 8 Aug 1827; residence - Bengal, India; died 12 Mar 1851. SOURCE: WO120 Volume 69 page 173. INDEX # 4320.

Alex^r FRASER; pension awarded 15 Dec 1819; residence - Halifax, Nova Scotia, Canada. SOURCE: WO120 Volume 69 page 173. INDEX # 4321.

Geo^e ARMSTRONG; pension awarded 29 Jun 1808; residence - Bytown, Ontario, Canada. SOURCE: WO120 Volume 69 page 173. INDEX # 4322.

Redm^d JENNINGS; pension awarded 11 Jan 1837; residence - Hobart Town, Australia. SOURCE: WO120 Volume 69 page 173. INDEX # 4323.

Willm YOUNG; pension awarded 1 May 1822; residence - Toronto, Ontario, Canada; died 10 Apr 1856. SOURCE: WO120 Volume 69 page 173. INDEX # 4324.

Thos CORDINGLY; pension awarded 5 Aug 1829; residence - Toronto, Ontario, Canada; died 26 Jan 1860. SOURCE: WO120 Volume 69 page 173. INDEX # 4325.

Wm GROVES; pension awarded 12 May 1824; residence - Cape of Good Hope, South Africa; died 20 Jan 1852. SOURCE: WO120 Volume 69 page 173. INDEX # 4326.

Ja^s FEARIS; pension awarded 25 Nov 1845; residence - Toronto, Ontario, Canada. SOURCE: WO120 Volume 69 page 173. INDEX # 4327.

Pat^k ENRIGHT; pension awarded 14 Oct 1845; residence - Gibraltar; died 3 Jan 1852. SOURCE: WO120 Volume 69 page 173. INDEX # 4328.

BRITISH ARMY PENSIONERS ABROAD

38th Regiment of Foot (continued)

Thos VEITCH; pension awarded 9 Dec 1845; residence - Quebec, Quebec, Canada. SOURCE: WO120 Volume 69 page 173. INDEX # 4329.

Michl FIZETT; pension awarded 26 Sep 1848. SOURCE: WO120 Volume 69 page 173. INDEX # 4330.

Jno SPAIN; pension awarded 24 Oct 1848; died in 1869 Nova Scotia, Canada. SOURCE: WO120 Volume 69 page 173. INDEX # 4331.

Jas ROLSTON; pension awarded 14 Aug 1849. SOURCE: WO120 Volume 69 page 173. INDEX # 4332.

Michl FITZPATRICK; pension awarded 14 Aug 1849. SOURCE: WO120 Volume 69 page 173. INDEX # 4333.

Thos WARHAM; pension awarded 11 Jun 1850. SOURCE: WO120 Volume 69 page 173. INDEX # 4334.

Jas BUTTS; pension awarded 11 Jun 1850; died 15 Nov 1882 Toronto, Ontario, Canada. SOURCE: WO120 Volume 69 page 173. INDEX # 4335.

Jas MARTIN; pension awarded 9 Sep 1851. SOURCE: WO120 Volume 69 page 173. INDEX # 4336.

Patk FARRELL; pension awarded 9 Sep 1851. SOURCE: WO120 Volume 69 page 173. INDEX # 4337.

39th Regiment of Foot

Jas BALLCOTT; pension awarded 3 May 1816; residence - New South Wales, Australia. SOURCE: WO120 Volume 69 page 175. INDEX # 4338.

Jno STOREY; pension awarded 8 Jul 1823; residence - New South Wales, Australia. SOURCE: WO120 Volume 69 page 175. INDEX # 4339.

Michl CHAMBERS; pension awarded 17 May 1825; residence - Quebec, Quebec, Canada; died 7 Oct 1879, Toronto, Ontario, Canada. SOURCE: WO120 Volume 69 page 175. INDEX # 4340.

Jas MCCOURT; pension awarded 21 Jun 1816; residence - Quebec, Quebec, Canada. SOURCE: WO120 Volume 69 page 175. INDEX # 4341.

Josh JAMES; pension awarded 7 Feb 1821; residence - New South Wales, Australia; died in 1852. SOURCE: WO120 Volume 69 page 175. INDEX # 4342.

Thos CHAPMAN; pension awarded 13 Dec 1826; residence - Wm. Henry, Quebec, Canada; died 2 Feb 1882, Montreal, Quebec, Canada. SOURCE: WO120 Volume 69 page 175. INDEX # 4343.

Lawre BYRNE; pension awarded 13 Oct 1841; residence - Cape of Good Hope, South Africa. SOURCE: WO120 Volume 69 page 175. INDEX # 4344.

Willm AKHURST; pension awarded 13 Feb 1833; residence - New Zealand. SOURCE: WO120 Volume 69 page 175. INDEX # 4345.

Chas HUNT; pension awarded 13 Feb 1833; residence - New South Wales, Australia; died in 1846. SOURCE: WO120 Volume 69 page 175. INDEX # 4346.

Jno DOOLITTLE; pension awarded 30 Oct 1827; residence - Penetanguishene, Ontario, Canada; died in 1846. SOURCE: WO120 Volume 69 page 175. INDEX # 4347.

Willm MCQUILLAN; pension awarded 29 Jan 1813; residence - Montreal, Quebec, Canada. SOURCE: WO120 Volume 69 page 175. INDEX # 4348.

Willm NIXON; pension awarded 16 Jun 1825; residence - Amherstburg, Ontario, Canada; died 20 May 1858. SOURCE: WO120 Volume 69 page 175. INDEX # 4349.

Saml BROWNE; pension awarded 25 Feb 1845; residence - Agra, India. SOURCE: WO120 Volume 69 page 175. INDEX # 4350.

Thos PORTER; pension awarded 25 Feb 1845; residence - Agra, India; died 19 Mar 1846. SOURCE: WO120 Volume 69 page 175. INDEX # 4351.

Chas REVILL; pension awarded 25 Feb 1845; residence - Agra, India. SOURCE: WO120 Volume 69 page 175. INDEX # 4352.

Jas GAMBLES; pension awarded 23 Sep 1840; residence - Madras, India; died 12 Oct 1853. SOURCE: WO120 Volume 69 page 175. INDEX # 4353.

Robt DUNLOP; pension awarded 20 Nov 1839; residence - Madras, India. SOURCE: WO120 Volume 69 page 175. INDEX # 4354.

Simon ELLIOTT; pension awarded 16 Aug 1813; residence - New South Wales, Australia; died in 1850. SOURCE: WO120 Volume 69 page 175. INDEX # 4355.

39th Regiment of Foot (continued)

Clay KIRKE; pension awarded 20 Nov 1839; residence - Madras, India; died 26 Mar 1852. SOURCE: WO120 Volume 69 page 175. INDEX # 4356.

John WILCOX; pension awarded 13 Feb 1833; residence - New South Wales, Australia. SOURCE: WO120 Volume 69 page 175. INDEX # 4357.

Thos SMITH; pension awarded 9 Sep 1835; residence - New South Wales, Australia. SOURCE: WO120 Volume 69 page 175. INDEX # 4358.

Danl TURNER; pension awarded 28 Apr 1846; residence - Madras, India; died 16 Mar 1853. SOURCE: WO120 Volume 69 page 175. INDEX # 4359.

Patk TRAYNOR; pension awarded 28 Apr 1846; residence - Bengal, India; died 11 Aug 1848. SOURCE: WO120 Volume 69 page 175. INDEX # 4360.

Jno ASHER; pension awarded 28 Apr 1846. SOURCE: WO120 Volume 69 page 175. INDEX # 4361.

Jas FLYNNE; pension awarded 28 Apr 1846. SOURCE: WO120 Volume 69 page 175. INDEX # 4362.

Denis GRADY; pension awarded 28 Apr 1846; residence - Bengal, India; died 6 Mar 1849. SOURCE: WO120 Volume 69 page 175. INDEX # 4363.

Josh MORGAN; pension awarded 28 Apr 1846. SOURCE: WO120 Volume 69 page 175. INDEX # 4364.

Patk RYAN; pension awarded 28 Apr 1846; residence - Dinapore, India. SOURCE: WO120 Volume 69 page 175. INDEX # 4365.

Willm SULLIVAN; pension awarded 28 Apr 1846; residence - India; died in 1847. SOURCE: WO120 Volume 69 page 175. INDEX # 4366.

Josh SUTTON; pension awarded 28 Apr 1846. SOURCE: WO120 Volume 69 page 175. INDEX # 4367.

Jno MARSH; pension awarded 23 Mar 1847; died 25 Dec 1879, Madras, India. SOURCE: WO120 Volume 69 page 175. INDEX # 4368.

Thos DEE; pension awarded 23 Mar 1847. SOURCE: WO120 Volume 69 page 175. INDEX # 4369.

Michl CALLAGHAN; pension awarded 23 Mar 1847; died 11 Sep 1869. SOURCE: WO120 Volume 69 page 175. INDEX # 4370.

Valentine ALLTIMES; pension awarded 23 Mar 1847. SOURCE: WO120 Volume 69 page 175. INDEX # 4371.

Jno CAHILL; pension awarded 23 Mar 1847; residence - Madras, India; died 15 Aug 1853. SOURCE: WO120 Volume 69 page 175. INDEX # 4372.

Thos DAVENNY; pension awarded 23 Mar 1847; residence - Madras, India; died 22 Oct 1850. SOURCE: WO120 Volume 69 page 175. INDEX # 4373.

Jas Michl GUNN; pension awarded 23 Mar 1847; residence - Madras, India; died 12 Apr 1849. SOURCE: WO120 Volume 69 page 175. INDEX # 4374.

Wm HAMSON; pension awarded 23 Mar 1847. SOURCE: WO120 Volume 69 page 175. INDEX # 4375.

Thos MALONE; pension awarded 23 Mar 1847. SOURCE: WO120 Volume 69 page 175. INDEX # 4376.

Thos MATHER; pension awarded 23 Mar 1847. SOURCE: WO120 Volume 69 page 175. INDEX # 4377.

Denis MCARTIE; pension awarded 23 Mar 1847. SOURCE: WO120 Volume 69 page 176. INDEX # 4378.

Jerh MILLANE; pension awarded 23 Mar 1847; residence - Wt London; died 29 Jul 1852. SOURCE: WO120 Volume 69 page 176. INDEX # 4379.

Abram POLLEY; pension awarded 23 Mar 1847. SOURCE: WO120 Volume 69 page 176. INDEX # 4380.

Robt SHANNON; pension awarded 23 Mar 1847; residence - Bangalore, India; died 13 Aug 1877. SOURCE: WO120 Volume 69 page 176. INDEX # 4381.

Mattw BROOKES; pension awarded 23 Mar 1847; died in Dec 1846. SOURCE: WO120 Volume 69 page 176. INDEX # 4382.

Thos CURTIS; pension awarded 23 Mar 1847; died 10 Mar 1847. SOURCE: WO120 Volume 69 page 176. INDEX # 4383.

Jas ELLIS; pension awarded 23 Mar 1847; residence - Calcutta, India; died 13 Jan 1852. SOURCE: WO120 Volume 69 page 176. INDEX # 4384.

Jno GREGORY; pension awarded 23 Mar 1847; residence - Calcutta, India; died 30 Dec 1847. SOURCE: WO120 Volume 69 page 176. INDEX # 4385.

Thos MILLS; pension awarded 23 Mar 1847; died 7 Apr 1875. SOURCE: WO120 Volume 69 page 176. INDEX # 4386.

39th Regiment of Foot (continued)

Samuel BROWNE; pension awarded 25 Feb 1845; residence - Agra, India; died 14 Sep 1873, Madras, India. SOURCE: WO120 Volume 69 page 176. INDEX # 4387.

Thomas PORTER; pension awarded 25 Feb 1845; residence - Agra, India. SOURCE: WO120 Volume 69 page 176. INDEX # 4388.

Charles REVILL; pension awarded 25 Feb 1845; residence - Agra, India. SOURCE: WO120 Volume 69 page 176. INDEX # 4389.

40th Regiment of Foot

Wm MASKALL; pension awarded 7 Dec 1840; residence - New South Wales, Australia. SOURCE: WO120 Volume 69 page 178. INDEX # 4390.

Jno HAYSTEAD; pension awarded 29 Dec 1813; residence - Toronto, Ontario, Canada. SOURCE: WO120 Volume 69 page 178. INDEX # 4391.

Willm BRYEN; pension awarded 15 May 1817; residence - Kingston, Ontario, Canada; died 31 Dec 1863, Toronto, Ontario, Canada. SOURCE: WO120 Volume 69 page 178. INDEX # 4392.

Jos^h WEEKS; pension awarded 2 Feb 1815; residence - Smiths Falls, Ontario, Canada; died 26 May 1854. SOURCE: WO120 Volume 69 page 178. INDEX # 4393.

Jos^h HALLS; pension awarded 11 Jun 1844; residence - Bombay, India. SOURCE: WO120 Volume 69 page 178. INDEX # 4394.

Danl ONEILL; pension awarded 30 Aug 1826; residence - Launceston, Australia; died in 1867, Hobarton, Tasmania, Australia. SOURCE: WO120 Volume 69 page 178. INDEX # 4395.

Thos NOAH; pension awarded 8 Sep 1830; residence - Hobart Town, Australia. SOURCE: WO120 Volume 69 page 178. INDEX # 4396.

Mich^l BARRETT; pension awarded 14 Oct 1829; residence - Quebec, Quebec, Canada. SOURCE: WO120 Volume 69 page 178. INDEX # 4397.

Geo^e RICKABY; pension awarded 24 May 1842; residence - Bombay, India. SOURCE: WO120 Volume 69 page 178. INDEX # 4398.

Peter KEANE; pension awarded 24 May 1842; residence - Bombay, India. SOURCE: WO120 Volume 69 page 178. INDEX # 4399.

Willm COOK; pension awarded 25 Mar 1819; residence - New South Wales, Australia. SOURCE: WO120 Volume 69 page 178. INDEX # 4400.

Thos SPENCELY; pension awarded 9 Jun 1841; residence - Hobart Town, Australia; died 21 Mar 1865, Leeds. SOURCE: WO120 Volume 69 page 178. INDEX # 4401.

Benjn WICKHAM; pension awarded 25 Aug 1813; residence - South Australia, Australia. SOURCE: WO120 Volume 69 page 178. INDEX # 4402.

Jos^h RICHENBERG; pension awarded 8 Sep 1830; residence - Hobart Town, Australia; died 31 Jan 1851. SOURCE: WO120 Volume 69 page 178. INDEX # 4403.

Jos^h CAHILL; pension awarded 14 Oct 1829; residence - Hobart Town, Australia. SOURCE: WO120 Volume 69 page 178. INDEX # 4404.

Mich^l DYER; pension awarded 8 Sep 1841; residence - Hobart Town, Australia; died 5 Jan 1875, Chester. SOURCE: WO120 Volume 69 page 178. INDEX # 4405.

Jno MARKHAM; pension awarded 8 Jul 1845; residence - Calcutta, India; died 22 Aug 1856, Cork. SOURCE: WO120 Volume 69 page 178. INDEX # 4406.

Willm CARTER; pension awarded 13 Jan 1846; residence - Calcutta, India. SOURCE: WO120 Volume 69 page 178. INDEX # 4407.

Martin WALSH; pension awarded 11 Jul 1854. SOURCE: WO120 Volume 69 page 178. INDEX # 4408.

Ja^s Cooper RIDDETT; pension awarded 11 Jul 1854. SOURCE: WO120 Volume 69 page 178. INDEX # 4409.

John NIELL; pension awarded 3 Jun 1856. SOURCE: WO120 Volume 69 page 179. INDEX # 4410.

Patrick HENRY; pension awarded 3 Jun 1856. SOURCE: WO120 Volume 69 page 179. INDEX # 4411.

William JUNIPER; pension awarded 3 Jun 1856. SOURCE: WO120 Volume 69 page 179. INDEX # 4412.

James ABREY; pension awarded 4 Nov 1856. SOURCE: WO120 Volume 69 page 179. INDEX # 4413.

WO120 VOLUME 69

40th Regiment of Foot (continued)

James RYAN; pension awarded 4 Nov 1856. SOURCE: WO120 Volume 69 page 179. INDEX # 4414.
Edward WALSH; pension awarded 4 Nov 1856. SOURCE: WO120 Volume 69 page 179. INDEX # 4415.
Patrick BUTLER; pension awarded 30 Dec 1856. SOURCE: WO120 Volume 69 page 179. INDEX # 4416.
Edward ODELL; pension awarded 21 Apr 1857. SOURCE: WO120 Volume 69 page 179. INDEX # 4417.
William RYAN; pension awarded 21 Apr 1857. SOURCE: WO120 Volume 69 page 179. INDEX # 4418.
John GOULD; pension awarded 2 Jun 1857. SOURCE: WO120 Volume 69 page 179. INDEX # 4419.
John Jonah CROW; pension awarded 2 Jun 1857. SOURCE: WO120 Volume 69 page 179. INDEX # 4420.
John MCGRATH; pension awarded 2 Jun 1857. SOURCE: WO120 Volume 69 page 179. INDEX # 4421.
Richard WALSH; pension awarded 2 Jun 1857. SOURCE: WO120 Volume 69 page 179. INDEX # 4422.

41st Regiment of Foot

John WESTON; pension awarded 23 Jul 1828; residence - Franktown, Ontario, Canada; died 19 Dec 1846. SOURCE: WO120 Volume 69 page 181. INDEX # 4423.
Hy CLARKE; pension awarded 12 May 1819; residence - Niagara, Ontario, Canada. SOURCE: WO120 Volume 69 page 181. INDEX # 4424.
Jno NETTLES; pension awarded 12 May 1819; residence - Cornwall, Ontario, Canada; died 8 Sep 1855. SOURCE: WO120 Volume 69 page 181. INDEX # 4425.
Jno FIELDING; pension awarded 13 Dec 1826; residence - Madras, India; died 30 Sep 1850. SOURCE: WO120 Volume 69 page 181. INDEX # 4426.
Wm FOX; pension awarded 9 Aug 1842; residence - Toronto, Ontario, Canada; died in 1846. SOURCE: WO120 Volume 69 page 181. INDEX # 4427.
Wm SEGAR; pension awarded 2 Sep 1821; residence - Montreal, Quebec, Canada. SOURCE: WO120 Volume 69 page 181. INDEX # 4428.
Wm VINCENT; pension awarded 25 Oct 1815; residence - Toronto, Ontario, Canada; died 24 Apr 1867. SOURCE: WO120 Volume 69 page 181. INDEX # 4429.
Jno FULLER; pension awarded 27 Nov 1839; residence - Madras, India; died 28 Dec 1872. SOURCE: WO120 Volume 69 page 181. INDEX # 4430.
Jno OWENS; pension awarded 28 Apr 1841; residence - Madras, India; died 29 Nov 1874, Madras, India. SOURCE: WO120 Volume 69 page 181. INDEX # 4431.
Jas BLAKES; pension awarded 26 May 1842; residence - Bombay, India; died in 1849. SOURCE: WO120 Volume 69 page 181. INDEX # 4432.
Geoe CARR; pension awarded 24 May 1842; residence - Madras, India; died 9 Aug 1852. SOURCE: WO120 Volume 69 page 181. INDEX # 4433.
Mark MUTLOW; pension awarded 24 May 1842; residence - Madras, India. SOURCE: WO120 Volume 69 page 181. INDEX # 4434.
Edwin PRIESTLEY; pension awarded 24 May 1842; residence - Madras, India; died 12 May 1852. SOURCE: WO120 Volume 69 page 181. INDEX # 4435.
Timy GORMONLY; pension awarded 13 Jun 1843; residence - Madras, India; died 5 May 1870. SOURCE: WO120 Volume 69 page 181. INDEX # 4436.
Jas WILSON; pension awarded 13 Jun 1843; residence - Bombay, India; died 14 May 1864, Poona, India. SOURCE: WO120 Volume 69 page 181. INDEX # 4437.
Lenox SIMPSON; pension awarded 26 Sep 1843; residence - Gambia, West Africa. SOURCE: WO120 Volume 69 page 181. INDEX # 4438.
Zephr DEWETT; pension awarded 7 Dec 1820; residence - Bytown, Ontario, Canada; died in 1845. SOURCE: WO120 Volume 69 page 181. INDEX # 4439.
Jno IMPETT; pension awarded 24 May 1842; residence - Bombay, India. SOURCE: WO120 Volume 69 page 181. INDEX # 4440.
Jno MCAULEY; pension awarded 23 May 1821; residence - Cornwall, Ontario, Canada; died 15 Jun 1854. SOURCE: WO120 Volume 69 page 181. INDEX # 4441.
Willm HUTTON; pension awarded 16 Sep 1829; residence - Hamilton, Ontario, Canada. SOURCE: WO120 Volume 69 page 181. INDEX # 4442.

41st Regiment of Foot (continued)

Geo^e BROOKS; pension awarded 20 Jan 1819; residence - Bytown, Ontario, Canada; died 5 Oct 1856. SOURCE: WO120 Volume 69 page 181. INDEX # 4443.

Jos^h HARVEY; pension awarded 7 Dec 1820; residence - Belleville, Ontario, Canada; died in 1847. SOURCE: WO120 Volume 69 page 181. INDEX # 4444.

Fra^s MEEHAN; pension awarded 8 Apr 1840; died 4 Sep 1864, Poona, India. SOURCE: WO120 Volume 69 page 181. INDEX # 4445.

Fra^s MAYO; pension awarded 23 Oct 1838; residence - Ceylon; died 1 Dec 1853. SOURCE: WO120 Volume 69 page 181. INDEX # 4446.

Jno SUNSMAN; pension awarded 24 Jun 1840; residence - Madras, India. SOURCE: WO120 Volume 69 page 181. INDEX # 4447.

Wm WATSON; pension awarded 28 Apr 1841; residence - Madras, India; died 13 May 1846. SOURCE: WO120 Volume 69 page 181. INDEX # 4448.

Jno SHANDLY; pension awarded 26 Jun 1840; residence - Madras, India; died 6 Oct 1872. SOURCE: WO120 Volume 69 page 181. INDEX # 4449.

Matt^w WASHINGTON; pension awarded 23 Oct 1838; residence - Madras, India. SOURCE: WO120 Volume 69 page 181. INDEX # 4450.

Saml BAKER; pension awarded 23 Oct 1838; residence - Madras, India; died 28 Oct 1855. SOURCE: WO120 Volume 69 page 181. INDEX # 4451.

Jno TUCKER; pension awarded 23 Oct 1838; residence - Madras, India; died 3 Dec 1848. SOURCE: WO120 Volume 69 page 181. INDEX # 4452.

Thos BROWNE; pension awarded 28 Apr 1841; residence - Madras, India. SOURCE: WO120 Volume 69 page 181. INDEX # 4453.

Wm HARRIS; pension awarded 27 Nov 1839; residence - Madras, India; died 30 Dec 1870. SOURCE: WO120 Volume 69 page 181. INDEX # 4454.

Wm MATHEWS; pension awarded 1 May 1822; residence - Perth, Ontario, Canada; died 24 Jun 1847. SOURCE: WO120 Volume 69 page 181. INDEX # 4455.

Jno PALMER; pension awarded 27 Nov 1839; residence - Madras, India; died 31 Jan 1846. SOURCE: WO120 Volume 69 page 181. INDEX # 4456.

Ja^s PERKINS; pension awarded 27 Nov 1839; residence - Madras, India; died 26 Mar 1846. SOURCE: WO120 Volume 69 page 181. INDEX # 4457.

Chas TREADWELL; pension awarded 27 Nov 1839; residence - Madras, India. SOURCE: WO120 Volume 69 page 181. INDEX # 4458.

And^w LAUGHLIN; pension awarded 23 Oct 1838; residence - Madras, India; died 8 Oct 1848. SOURCE: WO120 Volume 69 page 181. INDEX # 4459.

Wm TAYLOR; pension awarded 20 Nov 1839; residence - Madras, India. SOURCE: WO120 Volume 69 page 181. INDEX # 4460.

Saml COOGHRAN; pension awarded 27 Nov 1839; residence - Madras, India. SOURCE: WO120 Volume 69 page 181. INDEX # 4461.

Ja^s ROWAN; pension awarded 27 Nov 1839; residence - Madras, India. SOURCE: WO120 Volume 69 page 181. INDEX # 4462.

John APPLEGATE; pension awarded 28 Apr 1841; residence - Madras, India. SOURCE: WO120 Volume 69 page 182. INDEX # 4463.

Silas COOPER; pension awarded 28 Apr 1841; residence - Madras, India; died 24 Dec 1871. SOURCE: WO120 Volume 69 page 182. INDEX # 4464.

Ja^s GREENE; pension awarded 28 Apr 1841; residence - Madras, India; died 27 Aug 1851. SOURCE: WO120 Volume 69 page 182. INDEX # 4465.

Robt ANGEL; pension awarded 24 May 1842; residence - Bombay, India. SOURCE: WO120 Volume 69 page 182. INDEX # 4466.

Jon^n RENSHAW; pension awarded 23 Oct 1838; residence - Madras, India; died 11 Dec 1852. SOURCE: WO120 Volume 69 page 182. INDEX # 4467.

Ja^s SINCLAIR; pension awarded 13 Jun 1843; residence - Bombay, India. SOURCE: WO120 Volume 69 page 182. INDEX # 4468.

WO120 VOLUME 69

41st Regiment of Foot (continued)

John SKELLETT; pension awarded 27 Nov 1839; residence - Madras, India; died 17 Jul 1850. SOURCE: WO120 Volume 69 page 182. INDEX # 4469.

Richd GANDY; pension awarded 23 Oct 1838; residence - Madras, India; died 16 Aug 1854. SOURCE: WO120 Volume 69 page 182. INDEX # 4470.

Ja^s BARTLEY; pension awarded 27 Nov 1839; residence - Madras, India. SOURCE: WO120 Volume 69 page 182. INDEX # 4471.

Jos^h EMSLEY; pension awarded 28 Apr 1841; residence - Madras, India. SOURCE: WO120 Volume 69 page 182. INDEX # 4472.

Thos STEPHENSON; pension awarded 27 Nov 1839; residence - Madras, India; died 24 Jul 1849. SOURCE: WO120 Volume 69 page 182. INDEX # 4473.

Ja^s CLAIR; pension awarded 26 Oct 1843; residence - Madras, India. SOURCE: WO120 Volume 69 page 182. INDEX # 4474.

Jno PERRINS; pension awarded 24 May 1842; residence - Bombay, India; died 29 Apr 1860. SOURCE: WO120 Volume 69 page 182. INDEX # 4475.

Jno BELL; pension awarded 28 Dec 1818; residence - Montreal, Quebec, Canada. SOURCE: WO120 Volume 69 page 182. INDEX # 4476.

Ja^s PETTIGREW; pension awarded 24 May 1842; residence - Madras, India; died 5 May 1863. SOURCE: WO120 Volume 69 page 182. INDEX # 4477.

Thos MAHON; pension awarded 9 Aug 1837; residence - Madras, India. SOURCE: WO120 Volume 69 page 182. INDEX # 4478.

Gordon LYON; pension awarded 20 Jan 1819; residence - Chambly, Quebec, Canada; died 10 Jun 1845. SOURCE: WO120 Volume 69 page 182. INDEX # 4479.

Ja^s WAKEFIELD; pension awarded 9 Aug 1837; residence - Madras, India. SOURCE: WO120 Volume 69 page 182. INDEX # 4480.

Connor FEENEY; pension awarded 22 Jul 1845; residence - Cape of Good Hope, South Africa. SOURCE: WO120 Volume 69 page 182. INDEX # 4481.

Denis KERRISH; pension awarded 11 Jan 1837; residence - Canada; died 11 Dec 1857, Toronto, Ontario, Canada. SOURCE: WO120 Volume 69 page 182. INDEX # 4482.

42nd Regiment of Foot

Don^d MCLEOD; pension awarded 9 May 1823; residence - Halifax, Nova Scotia, Canada. SOURCE: WO120 Volume 69 page 184. INDEX # 4483.

Don^d MCPHERSON; pension awarded 20 Jan 1819. SOURCE: WO120 Volume 69 page 184. INDEX # 4484.

Ewen MCPHERSON; pension awarded 19 Jul 1816; residence - Perth. SOURCE: WO120 Volume 69 page 184. INDEX # 4485.

Don^d HOSSACK; pension awarded 11 Nov 1818; residence - Fredericton, New Brunswick, Canada. SOURCE: WO120 Volume 69 page 184. INDEX # 4486.

Ron^d MCDONALD; pension awarded 19 Jul 1816; residence - Toronto, Ontario, Canada. SOURCE: WO120 Volume 69 page 184. INDEX # 4487.

Jno HENDERSON; pension awarded 7 Dec 1809; residence - Perth, Ontario, Canada. SOURCE: WO120 Volume 69 page 184. INDEX # 4488.

Geo^e LENNAN; pension awarded 23 Feb 1820; residence - Prescott, Ontario, Canada; died 20 Nov 1854. SOURCE: WO120 Volume 69 page 184. INDEX # 4489.

Ja^s PANTON; pension awarded 9 Aug 1816; residence - Hobart Town, Australia. SOURCE: WO120 Volume 69 page 184. INDEX # 4490.

Benjⁿ VINT; pension awarded 18 Aug 1823; residence - Penetanguishene, Ontario, Canada; died 21 Aug 1871, Hamilton, Ontario, Canada. SOURCE: WO120 Volume 69 page 184. INDEX # 4491.

John STUART; pension awarded 11 Sep 1833; residence - Van Diemen's Land, Australia. SOURCE: WO120 Volume 69 page 184. INDEX # 4492.

42nd Regiment of Foot (continued)

John LATHAM; pension awarded 8 Jul 1845; residence - Malta; died 1 Apr 1882, Western Australia, Australia. SOURCE: WO120 Volume 69 page 184. INDEX # 4493.

Alexr ROSS; pension awarded 30 Aug 1820; residence - Toronto, Ontario, Canada; died 17 Apr 1864. SOURCE: WO120 Volume 69 page 184. INDEX # 4494.

Willm ROSS; pension awarded 2 Nov 1809; residence - London, Ontario, Canada; died in 1846. SOURCE: WO120 Volume 69 page 184. INDEX # 4495.

Willm LOCKERBIE; pension awarded 11 Mar 1835; residence - Toronto, Ontario, Canada; died 27 Dec 1856. SOURCE: WO120 Volume 69 page 184. INDEX # 4496.

Dun{n} MCPHERSON; pension awarded 9 Jun 1841; residence - Belleville, Ontario, Canada; died 8 Feb 1878 Toronto, Ontario, Canada. SOURCE: WO120 Volume 69 page 184. INDEX # 4497.

John JESSMAN; pension awarded 9 Jun 1841; residence - Toronto, Ontario, Canada; died 27 Dec 1872, Hamilton, Ontario, Canada. SOURCE: WO120 Volume 69 page 184. INDEX # 4498.

Wm GRAY; pension awarded 28 Sep 1815; residence - Huntingdon, Quebec, Canada. SOURCE: WO120 Volume 69 page 184. INDEX # 4499.

Jno MCKAY; pension awarded 12 Oct 1813; residence - Penetanguishene, Ontario, Canada; died 7 May 1876, Hamilton, Ontario, Canada. SOURCE: WO120 Volume 69 page 184. INDEX # 4500.

Alexr ROSS; pension awarded 10 Jul 1833; residence - Gibraltar; died 2 Oct 1876. SOURCE: WO120 Volume 69 page 184. INDEX # 4501.

Geo{e} BAILLIE; pension awarded 10 Aug 1831; residence - Chambly, Quebec, Canada. SOURCE: WO120 Volume 69 page 184. INDEX # 4502.

Don{d} MCKENZIE; pension awarded 8 Jun 1836; residence - Ionian Isles. SOURCE: WO120 Volume 69 page 185. INDEX # 4503.

Dav{d} MCLAREN; pension awarded 13 Dec 1842; residence - Norfolk Island, Australia. SOURCE: WO120 Volume 69 page 185. INDEX # 4504.

Jno GARDINER; pension awarded 16 Jul 1845; residence - Malta; died 13 Nov 1849. SOURCE: WO120 Volume 69 page 185. INDEX # 4505.

Wm SMITH; pension awarded 20 Dec 1848; residence - Bermuda; died 19 Sep 1853. SOURCE: WO120 Volume 69 page 185. INDEX # 4506.

43rd Regiment of Foot

Robt HUTCHINS; pension awarded 13 Apr 1824; residence - Niagara, Ontario, Canada; died 24 Mar 1862, Hamilton, Ontario, Canada. SOURCE: WO120 Volume 69 page 187. INDEX # 4507.

Jno BURGESS; pension awarded 8 Sep 1841; residence - St. Johns. SOURCE: WO120 Volume 69 page 187. INDEX # 4508.

Jno HERRING; pension awarded 27 Sep 1842; residence - Toronto, Ontario, Canada; died in 1852. SOURCE: WO120 Volume 69 page 187. INDEX # 4509.

Jno BROWN; pension awarded 5 Sep 1842; residence - Toronto, Ontario, Canada; died 16 Aug 1867. SOURCE: WO120 Volume 69 page 187. INDEX # 4510.

Willm CLARKE; pension awarded 30 May 1821; residence - Quebec, Quebec, Canada. SOURCE: WO120 Volume 69 page 187. INDEX # 4511.

Chas LAVERY; pension awarded 9 Jan 1833; residence - Amherstburg, Ontario, Canada; died 1 Feb 1862, London, Ontario, Canada. SOURCE: WO120 Volume 69 page 187. INDEX # 4512.

Willm MATTHEWS; pension awarded 22 Dec 1824; residence - New South Wales, Australia; died in 1849. SOURCE: WO120 Volume 69 page 187. INDEX # 4513.

Rees JONES; pension awarded 3 Mar 1824; residence - South Australia, Australia; died 4 Apr 1883, South Australia, Australia. SOURCE: WO120 Volume 69 page 187. INDEX # 4514.

John ADAMS; pension awarded 10 Apr 1833; residence - Hobart Town, Australia. SOURCE: WO120 Volume 69 page 187. INDEX # 4515.

WO120 VOLUME 69   155

43rd Regiment of Foot (continued)

Ja^s MILLER; pension awarded 26 Nov 1846; residence - Montreal, Quebec, Canada; died 28 Sep 1877, Toronto, Ontario, Canada. SOURCE: WO120 Volume 69 page 187. INDEX # 4516.

Mich^l BRADY; pension awarded 11 Dec 1839; residence - Toronto, Ontario, Canada. SOURCE: WO120 Volume 69 page 187. INDEX # 4517.

Thos PETTIT; pension awarded 8 Sep 1841; residence - Montreal, Quebec, Canada. SOURCE: WO120 Volume 69 page 187. INDEX # 4518.

Enoch EVANS; pension awarded 13 Aug 1846; residence - Montreal, Quebec, Canada. SOURCE: WO120 Volume 69 page 187. INDEX # 4519.

Pat^k HAMILL; pension awarded 2 Jun 1825; residence - Montreal, Quebec, Canada. SOURCE: WO120 Volume 69 page 187. INDEX # 4520.

Ed^{wd} H. HIRD; pension awarded 5 Sep 1843; residence - Quebec, Quebec, Canada; died in Dec 1855. SOURCE: WO120 Volume 69 page 187. INDEX # 4521.

Uriah POULTNEY; pension awarded 9 Jan 1839; residence - Fredericton, New Brunswick, Canada; died 8 Apr 1865, Caventry. SOURCE: WO120 Volume 69 page 187. INDEX # 4522.

Jno MCKEON; pension awarded 22 Sep 1841; residence - Montreal, Quebec, Canada; died 28 Dec 1853. SOURCE: WO120 Volume 69 page 187. INDEX # 4523.

Robt COOPER; pension awarded 27 Sep 1842; residence - Quebec, Quebec, Canada. SOURCE: WO120 Volume 69 page 187. INDEX # 4524.

Ja^s WABBY; pension awarded 28 Dec 1818; residence - New South Wales, Australia. SOURCE: WO120 Volume 69 page 187. INDEX # 4525.

Joseph MCDERMOTT; pension awarded 12 Jun 1855. SOURCE: WO120 Volume 69 page 187. INDEX # 4526.

George MAJOR; pension awarded 12 Jun 1855. SOURCE: WO120 Volume 69 page 187. INDEX # 4527.

Patrick MURPHY; pension awarded 12 Jun 1855. SOURCE: WO120 Volume 69 page 187. INDEX # 4528.

Frederick BROWN; pension awarded 11 Mar 1856. SOURCE: WO120 Volume 69 page 187. INDEX # 4529.

Joseph HEWETT; pension awarded 11 Mar 1856. SOURCE: WO120 Volume 69 page 187. INDEX # 4530.

William BACON; pension awarded 10 Feb 1857. SOURCE: WO120 Volume 69 page 187. INDEX # 4531.

Michael KENNEDY; pension awarded 10 Feb 1857. SOURCE: WO120 Volume 69 page 187. INDEX # 4532.

Patrick ALLAN; pension awarded 28 Apr 1857. SOURCE: WO120 Volume 69 page 187. INDEX # 4533.

James NUNN; pension awarded 28 Apr 1857; residence - Madras, India; died 13 Mar 1857. SOURCE: WO120 Volume 69 page 187. INDEX # 4534.

George ASHMAN; pension awarded 28 Apr 1857. SOURCE: WO120 Volume 69 page 187. INDEX # 4535.

Richard GOLDING; pension awarded 28 Apr 1857. SOURCE: WO120 Volume 69 page 187. INDEX # 4536.

44th Regiment of Foot

Alex^r MCGIVENEY; pension awarded 31 Jul 1817; residence - Quebec, Quebec, Canada; died 3 Aug 1857. SOURCE: WO120 Volume 69 page 189. INDEX # 4537.

Jos^h WARD; pension awarded 9 Dec 1812; residence - London, Ontario, Canada; died 18 Sep 1858. SOURCE: WO120 Volume 69 page 189. INDEX # 4538.

Wm CANTRELL; pension awarded 4 Dec 1822; residence - Toronto, Ontario, Canada; died 28 Aug 1862, Hamilton, Ontario, Canada. SOURCE: WO120 Volume 69 page 189. INDEX # 4539.

Ja^s BURNIP; pension awarded 18 Nov 1818; residence - Hobart Town, Australia. SOURCE: WO120 Volume 69 page 189. INDEX # 4540.

Thos MCGLYNN; pension awarded 25 Jun 1844; residence - Fort William, India; died 21 Nov 1849. SOURCE: WO120 Volume 69 page 189. INDEX # 4541.

Jno MORRISON; pension awarded 31 Jul 1822; residence - London, Ontario, Canada; died 17 Dec 1849. SOURCE: WO120 Volume 69 page 189. INDEX # 4542.

44th Regiment of Foot (continued)

Jn⁰ MARSHALL; pension awarded 26 Sep 1843; residence - India; died 15 May 1851. SOURCE: WO120 Volume 69 page 189. INDEX # 4543.

George SMITH; pension awarded 14 Nov 1843; residence - Bengal, India; died 5 Jul 1851. SOURCE: WO120 Volume 69 page 189. INDEX # 4544.

Willm SUMPTER; pension awarded 25 Jun 1844; residence - Fort William, India. SOURCE: WO120 Volume 69 page 189. INDEX # 4545.

Leslie MCGINN; pension awarded 17 Jun 1805; residence - London, Ontario, Canada; died 20 Jan 1855. SOURCE: WO120 Volume 69 page 189. INDEX # 4546.

Thos SMITH; pension awarded 9 Jun 1830; residence - Bengal, India; died 14 Oct 1851. SOURCE: WO120 Volume 69 page 189. INDEX # 4547.

Edwd HILL; pension awarded 28 Apr 1841; residence - Bengal, India; died 7 Oct 1876, New Zealand. SOURCE: WO120 Volume 69 page 189. INDEX # 4548.

Edwd HALES; pension awarded 28 Apr 1841; residence - Bengal, India; died 7 Oct 1876, New Zealand. SOURCE: WO120 Volume 69 page 189. INDEX # 4549.

Robt HAMER; pension awarded 9 Jun 1841; residence - Bengal, India; died 31 Dec 1846. SOURCE: WO120 Volume 69 page 189. INDEX # 4550.

George POTTS; pension awarded 27 Jun 1838; residence - Bengal, India; died 26 May 1849. SOURCE: WO120 Volume 69 page 189. INDEX # 4551.

Ja^s HAMILTON; pension awarded 12 Jun 1839; residence - Bengal, India. SOURCE: WO120 Volume 69 page 189. INDEX # 4552.

Jn⁰ SYMES; pension awarded 24 Oct 1843; residence - Bengal, India; died 26 Dec 1846. SOURCE: WO120 Volume 69 page 189. INDEX # 4553.

Willm STUBBS; pension awarded 28 Apr 1841; residence - Bengal, India; died 5 Jul 1852. SOURCE: WO120 Volume 69 page 189. INDEX # 4554.

Thos PINKNEY; pension awarded 10 Jul 1839; residence - Hobart Town, Australia; died 6 Dec 1849. SOURCE: WO120 Volume 69 page 189. INDEX # 4555.

John GOING; pension awarded 25 Jul 1838; residence - Bengal, India; died 20 Oct 1850. SOURCE: WO120 Volume 69 page 189. INDEX # 4556.

45th Regiment of Foot

John SULLIVAN; pension awarded 13 Sep 1836; residence - Canada. SOURCE: WO120 Volume 69 page 189. INDEX # 4557.

Willm SUGDEN; pension awarded 4 Jun 1823; residence - New South Wales, Australia; died in Jun 1852. SOURCE: WO120 Volume 69 page 191. INDEX # 4558.

Pat^k MCGUIRE; pension awarded 31 Jul 1822; residence - New South Wales, Australia. SOURCE: WO120 Volume 69 page 191. INDEX # 4559.

Ja^s CONLON; pension awarded 13 Jun 1838; residence - Madras, India. SOURCE: WO120 Volume 69 page 191. INDEX # 4560.

Thos PAGE; pension awarded 13 Jun 1838; residence - Madras, India; died 11 Nov 1849. SOURCE: WO120 Volume 69 page 191. INDEX # 4561.

Edwd BOYLE; pension awarded 20 Jan 1841; residence - Quebec, Quebec, Canada; died 2 Oct 1849. SOURCE: WO120 Volume 69 page 191. INDEX # 4562.

Willm JACKSON; pension awarded 13 Jun 1838; residence - Madras, India; died 22 Feb 1875. SOURCE: WO120 Volume 69 page 191. INDEX # 4563.

John PAIN; pension awarded 13 Jun 1838; residence - Madras, India; died 1 May 1853. SOURCE: WO120 Volume 69 page 191. INDEX # 4564.

Willm WRIGHT; pension awarded 13 Jun 1838; residence - Madras, India. SOURCE: WO120 Volume 69 page 191. INDEX # 4565.

Wm ROTHWELL; pension awarded 25 May 1847; died 15 Nov 1873, Cape, of Good Hope, South Africa. SOURCE: WO120 Volume 69 page 191. INDEX # 4566.

Raphael JACOB; pension awarded 6 Jun 1848. SOURCE: WO120 Volume 69 page 191. INDEX # 4567.

WO120 VOLUME 69

45th Regiment of Foot (continued)

Jno MASLIN; pension awarded 13 Feb 1849; residence - Cape of Good Hope, South Africa; died 18 Mar 1852. SOURCE: WO120 Volume 69 page 191. INDEX # 4568.
Wm PETERS; pension awarded 24 Apr 1849. SOURCE: WO120 Volume 69 page 191. INDEX # 4569.
Thos WRIGHT; pension awarded 10 Jul 1849. SOURCE: WO120 Volume 69 page 191. INDEX # 4570.
Thos HORN; pension awarded 26 Mar 1850; died 5 Aug 1871. SOURCE: WO120 Volume 69 page 191. INDEX # 4571.
Geoe KELLY; pension awarded 23 Apr 1850; residence - Cape of Good Hope, South Africa; died 1 Feb 1856. SOURCE: WO120 Volume 69 page 191. INDEX # 4572.
Jno BYERS; pension awarded 23 Jul 1850. SOURCE: WO120 Volume 69 page 191. INDEX # 4573.
Edwd GRIFFITH; pension awarded 12 Aug 1851; died 10 Nov 1886, Manchester. SOURCE: WO120 Volume 69 page 191. INDEX # 4574.
Denis DOYLE; pension awarded 13 Jul 1852. SOURCE: WO120 Volume 69 page 191. INDEX # 4575.
Edwd MCCOOEY; pension awarded 13 Jul 1852. SOURCE: WO120 Volume 69 page 191. INDEX # 4576.
Richd IRVINE; pension awarded 13 Sep 1853. SOURCE: WO120 Volume 69 page 191. INDEX # 4577.
Jno FISHER; pension awarded 13 Sep 1853. SOURCE: WO120 Volume 69 page 191. INDEX # 4578.
Josh HOLGATE; pension awarded 13 Sep 1853. SOURCE: WO120 Volume 69 page 191. INDEX # 4579.
Patk RODGERS; pension awarded 13 Sep 1853; died 28 May 1885, Cape of Good Hope, South Africa. SOURCE: WO120 Volume 69 page 191. INDEX # 4580.
Josh SMITH; pension awarded 13 Sep 1853. SOURCE: WO120 Volume 69 page 191. INDEX # 4581.
Edwd SHAW; pension awarded 13 Sep 1853. SOURCE: WO120 Volume 69 page 191. INDEX # 4582.
Fras TATTLER; pension awarded 13 Sep 1853. SOURCE: WO120 Volume 69 page 191. INDEX # 4583.
Robt WHITAKER; pension awarded 13 Sep 1853. SOURCE: WO120 Volume 69 page 191. INDEX # 4584.
John WHITE; pension awarded 26 Jun 1855. SOURCE: WO120 Volume 69 page 191. INDEX # 4585.
Alexander STEWART; pension awarded 26 Jun 1855. SOURCE: WO120 Volume 69 page 191. INDEX # 4586.
William HINCHLIFF; pension awarded 26 Jun 1855. SOURCE: WO120 Volume 69 page 191. INDEX # 4587.
Patrick HAYES; pension awarded 7 Aug 1855. SOURCE: WO120 Volume 69 page 191. INDEX # 4588.
Francis MURPHY; pension awarded 25 Sep 1855. SOURCE: WO120 Volume 69 page 191. INDEX # 4589.
Robert SPINK; pension awarded 25 Sep 1855; residence - Cape of Good Hope, South Africa; died 1 Jul 1856. SOURCE: WO120 Volume 69 page 191. INDEX # 4590.
Thomas BRANNON; pension awarded 26 Aug 1856. SOURCE: WO120 Volume 69 page 191. INDEX # 4591.
Robert CLARKE; pension awarded 26 Aug 1856. SOURCE: WO120 Volume 69 page 192. INDEX # 4592.
John ELLIOTT; pension awarded 26 Aug 1856. SOURCE: WO120 Volume 69 page 192. INDEX # 4593.
James FARLEY; pension awarded 26 Aug 1856. SOURCE: WO120 Volume 69 page 192. INDEX # 4594.
Francis FERNEY; pension awarded 26 Aug 1856. SOURCE: WO120 Volume 69 page 191. INDEX # 4595.
Jesse SAVEALL; pension awarded 9 Jun 1857. SOURCE: WO120 Volume 69 page 191. INDEX # 4596.
Peter FLYNN; pension awarded 7 Jul 1857. SOURCE: WO120 Volume 69 page 191. INDEX # 4597.
James HIGGINS; pension awarded 7 Jul 1857. SOURCE: WO120 Volume 69 page 192. INDEX # 4598.
James INSKIP; pension awarded 7 Jul 1857. SOURCE: WO120 Volume 69 page 192. INDEX # 4599.
Wm Henry KIRKLAND; pension awarded 7 Jul 1857. SOURCE: WO120 Volume 69 page 192. INDEX # 4600.
Samuel BAKER; pension awarded 18 Aug 1857; died 24 Jul 1863, Cape of Good Hope, South Africa. SOURCE: WO120 Volume 69 page 192. INDEX # 4601.

46th Regiment of Foot

Josh CLARK; pension awarded 3 May 1820; residence - Van Diemen's Land, Australia. SOURCE: WO120 Volume 69 page 193. INDEX # 4602.
Thos MCCAFFRY; pension awarded 29 Apr 1818; residence - New South Wales, Australia. SOURCE: WO120 Volume 69 page 193. INDEX # 4603.
Josh HOLDSWORTH; pension awarded 19 Jul 1816; residence - New South Wales, Australia. SOURCE: WO120 Volume 69 page 193. INDEX # 4604.

46th Regiment of Foot (continued)

Nathl MITCHELL; pension awarded 11 Nov 1845; residence - Prince Edward Island, Canada; died 14 Apr 1854. SOURCE: WO120 Volume 69 page 193. INDEX # 4605.

Jos^h CRADOCK; pension awarded 29 Apr 1818; residence - New South Wales, Australia. SOURCE: WO120 Volume 69 page 193. INDEX # 4606.

Willm PITHERS; pension awarded 5 Aug 1818; residence - New South Wales, Australia. SOURCE: WO120 Volume 69 page 193. INDEX # 4607.

Dav^d MCCLELLAND; pension awarded 22 Nov 1825; residence - Halifax, Nova Scotia, Canada. SOURCE: WO120 Volume 69 page 193. INDEX # 4608.

Jos^h TAYLOR; pension awarded 11 Mar 1830; residence - New South Wales, Australia; died 10 May 1857. SOURCE: WO120 Volume 69 page 193. INDEX # 4609.

Dav^d JOHN; pension awarded 13 Dec 1826; residence - Madras, India. SOURCE: WO120 Volume 69 page 193. INDEX # 4610.

John WALTERS; pension awarded 2 Feb 1820; residence - Toronto, Ontario, Canada; died 3 Mar 1878, Hamilton, Ontario, Canada. SOURCE: WO120 Volume 69 page 193. INDEX # 4611.

John GUEST; pension awarded 16 Dec 1836; residence - New South Wales, Australia; died 9 Sep 1863, Sydney, Australia. SOURCE: WO120 Volume 69 page 193. INDEX # 4612.

John HENBERGH; pension awarded 19 Jul 1826; residence - Quebec, Quebec, Canada. SOURCE: WO120 Volume 69 page 193. INDEX # 4613.

Danl MCSWEENEY; pension awarded 28 Jan 1845; residence - New Brunswick, Canada. SOURCE: WO120 Volume 69 page 193. INDEX # 4614.

Danl COUGHLAN; pension awarded 22 Mar 1820; residence - Montreal, Quebec, Canada; died 16 Jul 1847. SOURCE: WO120 Volume 69 page 193. INDEX # 4615.

Pat^k CARR; pension awarded 22 Sep 1846. SOURCE: WO120 Volume 69 page 193. INDEX # 4616.

Mich^l COFFEE; pension awarded 22 Sep 1846; residence - Toronto, Ontario, Canada; died 13 Jun 1848. SOURCE: WO120 Volume 69 page 193. INDEX # 4617.

Bryan HANLON; pension awarded 22 Sep 1846. SOURCE: WO120 Volume 69 page 193. INDEX # 4618.

Jno FEAGAN; pension awarded 13 Oct 1846. SOURCE: WO120 Volume 69 page 193. INDEX # 4619.

Jno WALSH; pension awarded 9 Mar 1847. SOURCE: WO120 Volume 69 page 193. INDEX # 4620.

Jno THURMAN; pension awarded 14 Sep 1847; died 24 Nov 1884, Toronto, Ontario, Canada. SOURCE: WO120 Volume 69 page 193. INDEX # 4621.

Jno PHELAN; pension awarded 12 Oct 1847. SOURCE: WO120 Volume 69 page 193. INDEX # 4622.

Ja^s GOSLING; pension awarded 12 Oct 1847; died 21 May 1882, Montreal, Quebec, Canada. SOURCE: WO120 Volume 69 page 193. INDEX # 4623.

Jno CAFFREY; pension awarded 12 Oct 1847; died 27 Apr 1873, London, Ontario, Canada. SOURCE: WO120 Volume 69 page 193. INDEX # 4624.

Pat^k MURPHY; pension awarded 12 Oct 1847. SOURCE: WO120 Volume 69 page 193. INDEX # 4625.

Peter MALONEY; pension awarded 14 Oct 1847. SOURCE: WO120 Volume 69 page 193. INDEX # 4626.

Chas BANKS; pension awarded 9 May 1848; died 28 May 1880, Halifax, Nova Scotia, Canada. SOURCE: WO120 Volume 69 page 193. INDEX # 4627.

Nich^s FAHY; pension awarded 9 May 1848. SOURCE: WO120 Volume 69 page 193. INDEX # 4628.

Ja^s GLINN; pension awarded 9 May 1848. SOURCE: WO120 Volume 69 page 193. INDEX # 4629.

Danl MCGUIRE; pension awarded 9 May 1848. SOURCE: WO120 Volume 69 page 193. INDEX # 4630.

Thos SHILLINGTON; pension awarded 9 May 1848; died 16 Mar 1881, Ottawa, Ontario, Canada. SOURCE: WO120 Volume 69 page 193. INDEX # 4631.

47th Regiment of Foot

John FAIR; pension awarded 12 May 1819; residence - London, Ontario, Canada; died 20 Oct 1867. SOURCE: WO120 Volume 69 page 196. INDEX # 4632.

Robt MCMULLEN; pension awarded 7 Dec 1820; residence - Bytown, Ontario, Canada. SOURCE: WO120 Volume 69 page 196. INDEX # 4633.

WO120 VOLUME 69

47th Regiment of Foot (continued)

Alex^r MCGEE; pension awarded 29 Apr 1811; residence - Toronto, Ontario, Canada; died 15 Jun 1847. SOURCE: WO120 Volume 69 page 196. INDEX # 4634.

Jno KELLY; pension awarded 8 Mar 1837; residence - Fredericton, New Brunswick, Canada. SOURCE: WO120 Volume 69 page 196. INDEX # 4635.

Peter TURBETT; pension awarded 5 Sep 1827; residence - St. Johns; died in Apr 1850. SOURCE: WO120 Volume 69 page 196. INDEX # 4636.

John LOWRY; pension awarded 2 Apr 1817; residence - Quebec, Quebec, Canada. SOURCE: WO120 Volume 69 page 196. INDEX # 4637.

Ja^s REED; pension awarded 2 Apr 1814; residence - New South Wales, Australia. SOURCE: WO120 Volume 69 page 196. INDEX # 4638.

Jno CASEY; pension awarded 11 Jan 1832; residence - Toronto, Ontario, Canada; died 24 May 1855. SOURCE: WO120 Volume 69 page 196. INDEX # 4639.

Thos TAYLOR; pension awarded 4 Aug 1824; residence - Bombay, India; died 21 Nov 1855. SOURCE: WO120 Volume 69 page 196. INDEX # 4640.

Thos MAHER; pension awarded 27 Aug 1823; residence - Quebec, Quebec, Canada; died 7 Dec 1873, Longford. SOURCE: WO120 Volume 69 page 196. INDEX # 4641.

Jno DAVIS; pension awarded 7 Jul 1841; residence - Hobart Town, Australia; died in Sep 1850. SOURCE: WO120 Volume 69 page 196. INDEX # 4642.

Ja^s POLLOCK; pension awarded 16 Sep 1831; residence - Toronto, Ontario, Canada; died 12 Jun 1864. SOURCE: WO120 Volume 69 page 196. INDEX # 4643.

Mich^l CARSON; pension awarded 18 Oct 1820; residence - Quebec, Quebec, Canada; died in Oct 1852. SOURCE: WO120 Volume 69 page 196. INDEX # 4644.

Richd NEWTON; pension awarded 7 Dec 1820; residence - Sydney. SOURCE: WO120 Volume 69 page 196. INDEX # 4645.

Thos BODY; pension awarded 17 Jun 1827; residence - Kingston, Ontario, Canada. SOURCE: WO120 Volume 69 page 196. INDEX # 4646.

Arthur GOODWIN; pension awarded 8 Sep 1830; residence - Canada. SOURCE: WO120 Volume 69 page 196. INDEX # 4647.

48th Regiment of Foot

Thos EVANS; pension awarded 26 Nov 1823; residence - New South Wales, Australia. SOURCE: WO120 Volume 69 page 198. INDEX # 4648.

Lawr^e CUMMINGS; pension awarded 16 Apr 1830; residence - Hobart Town, Australia; died 17 Sep 1849. SOURCE: WO120 Volume 69 page 198. INDEX # 4649.

Bishop TOFTS; pension awarded 22 Dec 1824; residence - New South Wales, Australia; died in Jun 1870. SOURCE: WO120 Volume 69 page 198. INDEX # 4650.

Robert CAMPBELL; pension awarded 30 Aug 1816; residence - Toronto, Ontario, Canada; died 20 Dec 1866. SOURCE: WO120 Volume 69 page 198. INDEX # 4651.

Cinnamon WILKINSON; pension awarded 25 Jun 1823; residence - Toronto, Ontario, Canada; died 26 May 1853. SOURCE: WO120 Volume 69 page 198. INDEX # 4652.

Edwd MURDOCK; pension awarded 14 Oct 1835; residence - Kingston, Ontario, Canada; died 16 Jun 1884, Toronto, Ontario, Canada. SOURCE: WO120 Volume 69 page 198. INDEX # 4653.

John MARTIN; pension awarded 16 Sep 1829; residence - Toronto, Ontario, Canada. SOURCE: WO120 Volume 69 page 198. INDEX # 4654.

Geo^e TURNER; pension awarded 19 Jul 1826; residence - New South Wales, Australia; died in Sep 1851. SOURCE: WO120 Volume 69 page 198. INDEX # 4655.

Benjn WEST; pension awarded 22 Dec 1824; residence - New South Wales, Australia. SOURCE: WO120 Volume 69 page 198. INDEX # 4656.

And^w LOWDON; pension awarded 12 May 1815; residence - New South Wales, Australia; died 18 Jul 1848. SOURCE: WO120 Volume 69 page 198. INDEX # 4657.

Jno BOARDMAN; pension awarded 25 May 1825; residence - New South Wales, Australia. SOURCE: WO120 Volume 69 page 198. INDEX # 4658.

BRITISH ARMY PENSIONERS ABROAD

48th Regiment of Foot (continued)

Thos STEEL; pension awarded 22 Dec 1824; residence - New South Wales, Australia. SOURCE: WO120 Volume 69 page 198. INDEX # 4659.

George SEADON; pension awarded 8 Jan 1817; residence - Penetanguishene, Ontario, Canada. SOURCE: WO120 Volume 69 page 198. INDEX # 4660.

Peter TRAYNER; pension awarded 20 Oct 1814; residence - Charlottetown, Prince Edward Island, Canada; died 30 May 1845. SOURCE: WO120 Volume 69 page 198. INDEX # 4661.

Nathl FOWLER; pension awarded 12 Sep 1821; residence - New South Wales, Australia; died in 1852. SOURCE: WO120 Volume 69 page 198. INDEX # 4662.

Willm CRITCHLEY; pension awarded 26 Aug 1825; residence - New South Wales, Australia; died 13 Jun 1848. SOURCE: WO120 Volume 69 page 198. INDEX # 4663.

Willm JEPSON; pension awarded 21 May 1828; residence - Madras, India; died 8 Jul 1849. SOURCE: WO120 Volume 69 page 198. INDEX # 4664.

Thos COOPER; pension awarded 29 Oct 1828; residence - Madras, India; died 30 Mar 1863, Madras, India. SOURCE: WO120 Volume 69 page 198. INDEX # 4665.

Bern^d MCGINN; pension awarded 8 Dec 1841; residence - Gibraltar; died 26 Aug 1860, Liverpool. SOURCE: WO120 Volume 69 page 198. INDEX # 4666.

Thos MACGUIRE; pension awarded 11 Mar 1840; residence - Madras, India; died 23 Dec 1853. SOURCE: WO120 Volume 69 page 198. INDEX # 4667.

W^m HY JONES; pension awarded 11 Mar 1840; residence - New South Wales, Australia; died 14 Dec 1881, New Zealand. SOURCE: WO120 Volume 69 page 198. INDEX # 4668.

Wm MERCER; pension awarded 27 Apr 1847. SOURCE: WO120 Volume 69 page 198. INDEX # 4669.

49th Regiment of Foot

Fred^k DILLON; pension awarded 29 Apr 1818; residence - Niagara, Ontario, Canada; died 21 Feb 1865. SOURCE: WO120 Volume 69 page 200. INDEX # 4670.

Lawr^e MOORE; pension awarded 29 Apr 1818; residence - Drummondsville, Quebec, Canada; died in Jun 1855. SOURCE: WO120 Volume 69 page 200. INDEX # 4671.

Jno FRASER; pension awarded 1 Jul 1819; residence - Wm Henry, Quebec, Canada. SOURCE: WO120 Volume 69 page 200. INDEX # 4672.

Danl SWEENEY; pension awarded 27 Jan 1817; residence - Chambly, Quebec, Canada; died 18 Apr 1847. SOURCE: WO120 Volume 69 page 200. INDEX # 4673.

Danl SULLIVAN; pension awarded 28 Aug 1839; residence - Toronto, Ontario, Canada; died in 1846. SOURCE: WO120 Volume 69 page 200. INDEX # 4674.

Ja^s CARLY; pension awarded 5 Jun 1816; residence - Wm Henry, Quebec, Canada; died 30 Sep 1849. SOURCE: WO120 Volume 69 page 200. INDEX # 4675.

Ge^o EMMERSON; pension awarded 12 May 1819; residence - Wm Henry, Quebec, Canada; died 13 Sep 1849. SOURCE: WO120 Volume 69 page 200. INDEX # 4676.

Willm MARCH; pension awarded 29 Apr 1818; residence - Carillon, Quebec, Canada. SOURCE: WO120 Volume 69 page 200. INDEX # 4677.

Peter PLUNKETT; pension awarded 29 Apr 1818; residence - Wm Henry, Quebec, Canada. SOURCE: WO120 Volume 69 page 200. INDEX # 4678.

Edwd HARFIGH; pension awarded 10 Aug 1836; residence - Bengal, India; died 16 Feb 1847. SOURCE: WO120 Volume 69 page 200. INDEX # 4679.

Ja^s BELL; pension awarded 14 Nov 1843; residence - Bengal, India; died 9 Jan 1856. SOURCE: WO120 Volume 69 page 200. INDEX # 4680.

Hiram PINDAR; pension awarded 15 Mar 1814; residence - Quebec, Quebec, Canada. SOURCE: WO120 Volume 69 page 200. INDEX # 4681.

Richd SALTER; pension awarded 28 Aug 1816; residence - Montreal, Quebec, Canada; died in 1847. SOURCE: WO120 Volume 69 page 200. INDEX # 4682.

Thos BRANDON; pension awarded 14 May 1817; residence - Toronto, Ontario, Canada; died 11 Apr 1866. SOURCE: WO120 Volume 69 page 200. INDEX # 4683.

49th Regiment of Foot (continued)

Alex^r WALES; pension awarded 30 Jun 1816; residence - Quebec, Quebec, Canada; died in 1848. SOURCE: WO120 Volume 69 page 200. INDEX # 4684.

Thos CORRIGAN; pension awarded 13 Feb 1844; residence - Bengal, India. SOURCE: WO120 Volume 69 page 200. INDEX # 4685.

Hugh FARELLY; pension awarded 13 Feb 1844; residence - Bengal, India; died in 1847. SOURCE: WO120 Volume 69 page 200. INDEX # 4686.

Ja^s FITZPATRICK; pension awarded 13 Feb 1844; residence - Bengal, India. SOURCE: WO120 Volume 69 page 200. INDEX # 4687.

Peter FRENCH; pension awarded 13 Feb 1844; residence - Bengal, India; died 11 Jan 1849. SOURCE: WO120 Volume 69 page 200. INDEX # 4688.

Thos ROUNDTREE; pension awarded 13 Feb 1844; residence - Bengal, India; died 27 Feb 1846. SOURCE: WO120 Volume 69 page 200. INDEX # 4689.

Jno SLATTERY; pension awarded 13 Feb 1844; residence - Bengal, India; died 20 Apr 1847. SOURCE: WO120 Volume 69 page 201. INDEX # 4690.

Ja^s TILLIARD; pension awarded 13 Feb 1844; residence - Bengal, India. SOURCE: WO120 Volume 69 page 201. INDEX # 4691.

Mar^n WALSH; pension awarded 13 Feb 1844; residence - Bengal, India. SOURCE: WO120 Volume 69 page 201. INDEX # 4692.

Willm FARLEY; pension awarded 28 Aug 1837; residence - Bengal, India; died in 1849. SOURCE: WO120 Volume 69 page 201. INDEX # 4693.

Ja^s HOLTON; pension awarded 13 Oct 1841; residence - Bengal, India; died 16 Sep 1849. SOURCE: WO120 Volume 69 page 201. INDEX # 4694.

Jos^h HOWE; pension awarded 13 Oct 1841; residence - Bengal, India. SOURCE: WO120 Volume 69 page 201. INDEX # 4695.

Chas LUCAS; pension awarded 13 Oct 1841; residence - Bengal, India. SOURCE: WO120 Volume 69 page 201. INDEX # 4696.

Benjn WRIGHT; pension awarded 14 Nov 1843; residence - Bengal, India; died 17 Apr 1846. SOURCE: WO120 Volume 69 page 201. INDEX # 4697.

Justinian JONES; pension awarded 13 Feb 1844; residence - Bengal, India; died 19 Apr 1849. SOURCE: WO120 Volume 69 page 201. INDEX # 4698.

Den^s SHEA; pension awarded 14 Nov 1843; residence - Bengal, India. SOURCE: WO120 Volume 69 page 201. INDEX # 4699.

Thos BASLEY; pension awarded 14 Nov 1843; residence - Bengal, India. SOURCE: WO120 Volume 69 page 201. INDEX # 4700.

Jessie OSBOURNE; pension awarded 13 Feb 1844; residence - Bengal, India. SOURCE: WO120 Volume 69 page 201. INDEX # 4701.

John BOYD; pension awarded 5 Feb 1823; residence - Quebec, Quebec, Canada. SOURCE: WO120 Volume 69 page 201. INDEX # 4702.

Silas WILLIAMSON; pension awarded 13 Feb 1844; residence - Bengal, India; died 8 May 1879, S. London. SOURCE: WO120 Volume 69 page 201. INDEX # 4703.

Wm TYDD; pension awarded ; residence - Bengal, India. SOURCE: WO120 Volume 69 page 201. INDEX # 4704.

John CLIFFORD; pension awarded 2 Jun 1825; residence - Canada; died 20 Jun 1855. SOURCE: WO120 Volume 69 page 201. INDEX # 4705.

50th Regiment of Foot

Robt LEVISTON; pension awarded 13 Dec 1826; residence - St. Johns. SOURCE: WO120 Volume 69 page 203. INDEX # 4706.

John DUFFY; pension awarded 25 Jun 1817; residence - New South Wales, Australia. SOURCE: WO120 Volume 69 page 203. INDEX # 4707.

Thos TEEVAN; pension awarded 8 Aug 1838; residence - Sydney, New South Wales, Australia. SOURCE: WO120 Volume 69 page 203. INDEX # 4708.

50th Regiment of Foot (continued)

Simon RYAN; pension awarded 8 Apr 1840; residence - New South Wales, Australia. SOURCE: WO120 Volume 69 page 203. INDEX # 4709.

Ja^s HICKEY; pension awarded 27 Jun 1843; residence - New South Wales, Australia. SOURCE: WO120 Volume 69 page 203. INDEX # 4710.

Owen BRIEN; pension awarded 14 Oct 1840. SOURCE: WO120 Volume 69 page 203. INDEX # 4711.

Thos IRWIN; pension awarded 3 Aug 1809; residence - Toronto, Ontario, Canada; died 8 Sep 1859. SOURCE: WO120 Volume 69 page 203. INDEX # 4712.

Chas BENNETT; pension awarded 23 Aug 1814; residence - Launceston, Australia. SOURCE: WO120 Volume 69 page 203. INDEX # 4713.

Ja^s SPITTALS; pension awarded 8 Aug 1838; residence - New South Wales, Australia. SOURCE: WO120 Volume 69 page 203. INDEX # 4714.

Jno REILLY; pension awarded 28 Aug 1839; residence - Hobart Town, Australia. SOURCE: WO120 Volume 69 page 203. INDEX # 4715.

George SMART; pension awarded 4 Jun 1823; residence - Montreal, Quebec, Canada. SOURCE: WO120 Volume 69 page 203. INDEX # 4716.

Jos^h CHAMBERS; pension awarded 25 Aug 1841; residence - New South Wales, Australia. SOURCE: WO120 Volume 69 page 203. INDEX # 4717.

Jno BURROWS; pension awarded 16 Aug 1814; residence - Toronto, Ontario, Canada; died 6 May 1862, Hamilton, Ontario, Canada. SOURCE: WO120 Volume 69 page 203. INDEX # 4718.

Willm TEALE; pension awarded 13 Jun 1838; residence - New South Wales, Australia. SOURCE: WO120 Volume 69 page 203. INDEX # 4719.

Ed^wd MCCORMICK; pension awarded 28 Aug 1839; residence - New South Wales, Australia. SOURCE: WO120 Volume 69 page 203. INDEX # 4720.

Ter^e GUNN; pension awarded 13 Jun 1838; residence - New South Wales, Australia. SOURCE: WO120 Volume 69 page 203. INDEX # 4721.

Willm WOOLDRIDGE; pension awarded 13 Jun 1838; residence - New South Wales, Australia. SOURCE: WO120 Volume 69 page 203. INDEX # 4722.

Thos HARROLD; pension awarded 8 Aug 1838; residence - New South Wales, Australia. SOURCE: WO120 Volume 69 page 203. INDEX # 4723.

Mich^l BOYLE; pension awarded 8 Aug 1838; residence - New South Wales, Australia; died in Jan 1855. SOURCE: WO120 Volume 69 page 203. INDEX # 4724.

Hugh GILLIGAN; pension awarded 8 Aug 1838; residence - New South Wales, Australia; died 15 Aug 1876. SOURCE: WO120 Volume 69 page 203. INDEX # 4725.

Ja^s SEYMOUR; pension awarded 12 Aug 1840. SOURCE: WO120 Volume 69 page 203. INDEX # 4726.

Jno HENSHALL; pension awarded 8 Aug 1838; residence - New South Wales, Australia. SOURCE: WO120 Volume 69 page 203. INDEX # 4727.

Den^s GILLESPIE; pension awarded 8 Aug 1838; residence - New South Wales, Australia; died 27 Mar 1863. SOURCE: WO120 Volume 69 page 203. INDEX # 4728.

Willm MOSLEY; pension awarded 22 May 1839; residence - New South Wales, Australia; died 1 Jul 1863, Melbourne, Australia. SOURCE: WO120 Volume 69 page 203. INDEX # 4729.

John MURRAY; pension awarded 25 Jun 1817; residence - New South Wales, Australia; died in Sep 1857. SOURCE: WO120 Volume 69 page 203. INDEX # 4730.

Wm WALKER; pension awarded 8 Aug 1838; residence - New South Wales, Australia. SOURCE: WO120 Volume 69 page 203. INDEX # 4731.

Jno BULLIVANT; pension awarded 13 Apr 1846; residence - New South Wales, Australia. SOURCE: WO120 Volume 69 page 203. INDEX # 4732.

Thos HICKESSEY; pension awarded 22 Apr 1845; residence - Quebec, Quebec, Canada; died 15 Feb 1875, Hamilton, Ontario, Canada. SOURCE: WO120 Volume 69 page 203. INDEX # 4733.

H^y MCTERNON; pension awarded 27 Aug 1844; residence - Berlin. SOURCE: WO120 Volume 69 page 203. INDEX # 4734.

Jno HENNESSEY; pension awarded 23 Aug 1837; residence - Hobart Town, Australia. SOURCE: WO120 Volume 69 page 203. INDEX # 4735.

50th Regiment of Foot (continued)

Jos^h BARNETT; pension awarded 13 Apr 1847; residence - Calcutta, India; died 7 Mar 1851. SOURCE: WO120 Volume 69 page 203. INDEX # 4736.
Wm HERRITAGE; pension awarded 25 Jan 1848. SOURCE: WO120 Volume 69 page 203. INDEX # 4737.
Robt TAYLOR; pension awarded 25 Jan 1848; residence - Fort William, India; died 19 Nov 1850. SOURCE: WO120 Volume 69 page 203. INDEX # 4738.
Dennis SINNOTT; pension awarded 25 Jan 1848. SOURCE: WO120 Volume 69 page 203. INDEX # 4739.
Jno WYATT; pension awarded 25 Jan 1848. SOURCE: WO120 Volume 69 page 203. INDEX # 4740.
David OWENS; pension awarded 28 Mar 1848; residence - Calcutta, India; died 4 Aug 1848. SOURCE: WO120 Volume 69 page 203. INDEX # 4741.
Thos BESTWICK; pension awarded 24 Oct 1848. SOURCE: WO120 Volume 69 page 203. INDEX # 4742.

51st Regiment of Foot

Ed^{wd} TURNER; pension awarded 27 Sep 1817; residence - Charlottetown, Prince Edward Island, Canada. SOURCE: WO120 Volume 69 page 206. INDEX # 4743.
John HAVERTY; pension awarded 16 Nov 1814; residence - Montreal, Quebec, Canada. SOURCE: WO120 Volume 69 page 206. INDEX # 4744.
Willm BURNS; pension awarded 1 May 1822; residence - Sydney. SOURCE: WO120 Volume 69 page 206. INDEX # 4745.
Ed^{wd} MAHER; pension awarded 12 Aug 1840; residence - Hobart Town, Australia; died in Dec 1850. SOURCE: WO120 Volume 69 page 206. INDEX # 4746.
Stepⁿ HOLT; pension awarded 23 May 1821; residence - Quebec, Quebec, Canada. SOURCE: WO120 Volume 69 page 206. INDEX # 4747.
Chas EWENS; pension awarded 8 Feb 1832; residence - Ionian Isles; died 27 Jul 1848. SOURCE: WO120 Volume 69 page 206. INDEX # 4748.
Ed^{wd} RYAN; pension awarded 8 May 1833; residence - Ionian Isles. SOURCE: WO120 Volume 69 page 206. INDEX # 4749.
Thos ATKINSON; pension awarded 3 Feb 1808; residence - Quebec, Quebec, Canada. SOURCE: WO120 Volume 69 page 206. INDEX # 4750.
Wm HUGHES; pension awarded 8 Jul 1840; residence - Hobart Town, Australia; died 26 Oct 1845. SOURCE: WO120 Volume 69 page 206. INDEX # 4751.
John NORRIS; pension awarded 14 Jul 1841; residence - Hobart Town, Australia; died 23 May 1849. SOURCE: WO120 Volume 69 page 206. INDEX # 4752.
Saml FRAZER; pension awarded 11 Oct 1826; residence - Montreal, Quebec, Canada; died 20 Apr 1857. SOURCE: WO120 Volume 69 page 206. INDEX # 4753.
Jos^h ABBOTT; pension awarded 27 Sep 1842; residence - Hobart Town, Australia; died 22 Apr 1871. SOURCE: WO120 Volume 69 page 206. INDEX # 4754.
Pat^k SHIELS; pension awarded 27 Sep 1842; residence - Hobart Town, Australia; died 26 Mar 1875, Tasmania, Australia. SOURCE: WO120 Volume 69 page 206. INDEX # 4755.
John MCDAVID; pension awarded 27 Sep 1842; residence - Hobart Town, Australia. SOURCE: WO120 Volume 69 page 206. INDEX # 4756.
John EMSWELL; pension awarded 27 Sep 1842; residence - Hobart Town, Australia. SOURCE: WO120 Volume 69 page 206. INDEX # 4757.
Pat^k MURPHY; pension awarded 24 Oct 1843; residence - Hobart Town, Australia; died 17 Apr 1874, Tasmania, Australia. SOURCE: WO120 Volume 69 page 206. INDEX # 4758.
Fra^s DRAKE; pension awarded 23 Jul 1844; residence - Hobart Town, Australia. SOURCE: WO120 Volume 69 page 206. INDEX # 4759.
John GABBETT; pension awarded 23 Jul 1844; residence - Hobart Town, Australia. SOURCE: WO120 Volume 69 page 206. INDEX # 4760.
Roger GALLAGHER; pension awarded 23 Jul 1844; residence - Hobart Town, Australia. SOURCE: WO120 Volume 69 page 206. INDEX # 4761.
John HINES; pension awarded 27 Sep 1842; residence - Hobart Town, Australia; died 17 Jul 1881, Hobart Town, Australia. SOURCE: WO120 Volume 69 page 206. INDEX # 4762.

BRITISH ARMY PENSIONERS ABROAD

51st Regiment of Foot (continued)

Ibodnagh WARN; pension awarded 8 Jul 1840; residence - Hobart Town, Australia. SOURCE: WO120 Volume 69 page 206. INDEX # 4763.

Ja^s SIMMONDS; pension awarded 24 Oct 1843; residence - Hobart Town, Australia. SOURCE: WO120 Volume 69 page 206. INDEX # 4764.

Jos^h FORD; pension awarded 8 Jul 1840; residence - Hobart Town, Australia; died 11 Jul 1871, Tasmania, Australia. SOURCE: WO120 Volume 69 page 206. INDEX # 4765.

John ELLIOTT; pension awarded 8 Jul 1840; residence - Hobart Town, Australia; died 19 Jul 1872, Enniskillen. SOURCE: WO120 Volume 69 page 206. INDEX # 4766.

Willm KELLY; pension awarded 14 Jul 1841; residence - Hobart Town, Australia. SOURCE: WO120 Volume 69 page 206. INDEX # 4767.

Willm GRIFFIN; pension awarded 24 Jan 1843; residence - Hobart Town, Australia; died 1 Oct 1869, S. London. SOURCE: WO120 Volume 69 page 206. INDEX # 4768.

Dav^d KING; pension awarded 24 Oct 1843; residence - Hobart Town, Australia; died 18 Oct 1848. SOURCE: WO120 Volume 69 page 206. INDEX # 4769.

Pat^k PEANE; pension awarded 27 Sep 1842; residence - Launceston, Australia. SOURCE: WO120 Volume 69 page 206. INDEX # 4770.

Thos NORTON; pension awarded 22 Dec 1841; residence - Hobart Town, Australia. SOURCE: WO120 Volume 69 page 206. INDEX # 4771.

Jno MENSFORTH; pension awarded 10 Nov 1841; residence - Launceston, Australia. SOURCE: WO120 Volume 69 page 206. INDEX # 4772.

Thos NEWALL; pension awarded 10 Nov 1841; residence - Hobart Town, Australia; died 2 Nov 1877. SOURCE: WO120 Volume 69 page 206. INDEX # 4773.

Jos^h CONREY; pension awarded 25 Sep 1839; residence - Ionian Isles; died 23 Apr 1848. SOURCE: WO120 Volume 69 page 206. INDEX # 4774.

Ant^y MCEVOY; pension awarded 14 Nov 1838; residence - Montreal, Quebec, Canada. SOURCE: WO120 Volume 69 page 206. INDEX # 4775.

H^y SIMMONDS; pension awarded 27 Sep 1842; residence - Hobart Town, Australia. SOURCE: WO120 Volume 69 page 206. INDEX # 4776.

Philip MAHER; pension awarded 27 Jul 1844; residence - Van Diemen's Land, Australia; died 31 Mar 1847. SOURCE: WO120 Volume 69 page 206. INDEX # 4777.

Thos HILL; pension awarded 14 Apr 1845; residence - Hobart Town, Australia. SOURCE: WO120 Volume 69 page 206. INDEX # 4778.

Pat^k DOYLE; pension awarded 3 Jun 1844; residence - Canada. SOURCE: WO120 Volume 69 page 206. INDEX # 4779.

Edwd KELLY; pension awarded 22 Sep 1846; residence - Auckland, New Zealand. SOURCE: WO120 Volume 69 page 206. INDEX # 4780.

Iain BLOMLY; pension awarded 22 Sep 1846; residence - Van Diemans L^d, Australia; died 15 Jun 1866, Manch^r. SOURCE: WO120 Volume 69 page 206. INDEX # 4781.

Ja^s CUNNINGHAM; pension awarded 24 Aug 1847; died 18 May 1871. SOURCE: WO120 Volume 69 page 206. INDEX # 4782.

Chas HOLT; pension awarded 24 Aug 1847. SOURCE: WO120 Volume 69 page 207. INDEX # 4783.

Saml MOTTRAM; pension awarded 24 Aug 1847. SOURCE: WO120 Volume 69 page 207. INDEX # 4784.

Peter MCGLADE; pension awarded 24 Aug 1847. SOURCE: WO120 Volume 69 page 207. INDEX # 4785.

Thos PRENDAVILLE; pension awarded 24 Aug 1847; residence - Australia; died 17 Aug 1847. SOURCE: WO120 Volume 69 page 207. INDEX # 4786.

Thos SWIFT; pension awarded 24 Aug 1847; residence - Australia; died 13 Aug 1847. SOURCE: WO120 Volume 69 page 207. INDEX # 4787.

Jno WILLIAMS; pension awarded 24 Aug 1847. SOURCE: WO120 Volume 69 page 207. INDEX # 4788.

Saml WYNNE; pension awarded 24 Aug 1847. SOURCE: WO120 Volume 69 page 207. INDEX # 4789.

Joshua WOOD; pension awarded 24 Aug 1847; residence - Perth, Western Australia, Australia; died 6 Apr 1876. SOURCE: WO120 Volume 69 page 207. INDEX # 4790.

Jno BREWER; pension awarded 8 Apr 1851; died 13 Sep 1851. SOURCE: WO120 Volume 69 page 207. INDEX # 4791.

51st Regiment of Foot (continued)

Wm WATSON; pension awarded 23 May 1854; died 17 Jul 1855. SOURCE: WO120 Volume 69 page 207. INDEX # 4792.

52nd Regiment of Foot

Willm MCKENZIE; pension awarded 30 Oct 1816; residence - Fredericton, New Brunswick, Canada. SOURCE: WO120 Volume 69 page 209. INDEX # 4793.

Willm SAGEMAN; pension awarded 28 Nov 1815; residence - Amherstburg, Ontario, Canada; died 3 Sep 1861, London, Ontario, Canada. SOURCE: WO120 Volume 69 page 209. INDEX # 4794.

Pat^k WOODS; pension awarded 29 Jan 1813; residence - Toronto, Ontario, Canada; died 30 Mar 1863. SOURCE: WO120 Volume 69 page 209. INDEX # 4795.

Danl LUNNEY; pension awarded 29 Mar 1823; residence - Quebec, Quebec, Canada; died in 1850. SOURCE: WO120 Volume 69 page 209. INDEX # 4796.

Ja^s MCDONALD; pension awarded 29 Jan 1813; residence - Saint John, New Brunswick, Canada. SOURCE: WO120 Volume 69 page 209. INDEX # 4797.

Simon JOHNSON; pension awarded 12 Dec 1832; residence - Halifax, Nova Scotia, Canada. SOURCE: WO120 Volume 69 page 209. INDEX # 4798.

Dav^d MCGLINN; pension awarded 8 Sep 1830; residence - Halifax, Nova Scotia, Canada; died 13 Sep 1856. SOURCE: WO120 Volume 69 page 209. INDEX # 4799.

Saml ALCORN; pension awarded 8 Sep 1830; residence - Halifax, Nova Scotia, Canada; died in Nov 1862, Nova Scotia, Canada. SOURCE: WO120 Volume 69 page 209. INDEX # 4800.

Ed^{wd} KELK; pension awarded 8 Sep 1830; residence - Toronto, Ontario, Canada; died 10 Dec 1878, Hamilton, Ontario, Canada. SOURCE: WO120 Volume 69 page 209. INDEX # 4801.

Carbro HIGGINS; pension awarded 14 Dec 1831; residence - Halifax, Nova Scotia, Canada. SOURCE: WO120 Volume 69 page 209. INDEX # 4802.

And^w HOPEWELL; pension awarded 14 Dec 1831; residence - Halifax, Nova Scotia, Canada. SOURCE: WO120 Volume 69 page 209. INDEX # 4803.

Ja^s SHEERIN; pension awarded 14 Dec 1831; residence - Halifax, Nova Scotia, Canada. SOURCE: WO120 Volume 69 page 209. INDEX # 4804.

Robt WATT; pension awarded 14 Dec 1831; residence - Halifax, Nova Scotia, Canada; died 7 Jan 1846. SOURCE: WO120 Volume 69 page 209. INDEX # 4805.

Carney WOOD; pension awarded 14 Dec 1831; residence - Halifax, Nova Scotia, Canada. SOURCE: WO120 Volume 69 page 209. INDEX # 4806.

Isaac FOSTER; pension awarded 13 Jun 1838; residence - Ionian Isles. SOURCE: WO120 Volume 69 page 209. INDEX # 4807.

John BORSDALE; pension awarded 27 Jun 1838; residence - Gibraltar. SOURCE: WO120 Volume 69 page 209. INDEX # 4808.

Laughlin ENNIS; pension awarded 5 Sep 1843; residence - Fredericton, New Brunswick, Canada. SOURCE: WO120 Volume 69 page 209. INDEX # 4809.

Jos^h LETT; pension awarded 5 Sep 1843; residence - Fredericton, New Brunswick, Canada. SOURCE: WO120 Volume 69 page 209. INDEX # 4810.

Ja^s GORMAN; pension awarded 23 Sep 1845; residence - Prince Edward Island, Canada; died 24 Jan 1880, Halifax, Nova Scotia, Canada. SOURCE: WO120 Volume 69 page 209. INDEX # 4811.

Thos STIRLEY; pension awarded 9 Feb 1803; residence - Cape of Good Hope, South Africa; died 2 Oct 1848. SOURCE: WO120 Volume 69 page 209. INDEX # 4812.

Jno MCCOY; pension awarded 27 Jun 1817; residence - Montreal, Quebec, Canada; died 13 Dec 1857. SOURCE: WO120 Volume 69 page 209. INDEX # 4813.

H^y GEE; pension awarded 29 May 1822; residence - Adelaide; died 14 Feb 1861, London, Ontario, Canada. SOURCE: WO120 Volume 69 page 209. INDEX # 4814.

Marcus GUNN; pension awarded 19 Apr 1826; residence - London, Ontario, Canada. SOURCE: WO120 Volume 69 page 209. INDEX # 4815.

52nd Regiment of Foot (continued)

And^w KELLY; pension awarded 19 Jul 1842; residence - Halifax, Nova Scotia, Canada. SOURCE: WO120 Volume 69 page 209. INDEX # 4816.

Thos CLEARY; pension awarded 22 Oct 1844; residence - Halifax, Nova Scotia, Canada; died 26 May 1866, Hamilton, Ontario, Canada. SOURCE: WO120 Volume 69 page 209. INDEX # 4817.

John HARE; pension awarded 26 Aug 1845; residence - Canada; died 13 Jul 1863, Toronto, Ontario, Canada. SOURCE: WO120 Volume 69 page 209. INDEX # 4818.

Jer^h SULLIVAN; pension awarded 26 Aug 1845; residence - Prince Edward Island, Canada. SOURCE: WO120 Volume 69 page 209. INDEX # 4819.

Ja^s ORMSBY; pension awarded 8 Sep 1830; residence - Penetanguishene, Ontario, Canada; died 1 Aug 1873, Hamilton, Ontario, Canada. SOURCE: WO120 Volume 69 page 209. INDEX # 4820.

Henry BOTTS; pension awarded 14 Dec 1831; residence - Charlottetown, Prince Edward Island, Canada; died 14 Apr 1851. SOURCE: WO120 Volume 69 page 209. INDEX # 4821.

And^w CURRAN; pension awarded 8 Aug 1832; residence - Bytown, Ontario, Canada; died 18 Feb 1858. SOURCE: WO120 Volume 69 page 209. INDEX # 4822.

Willm SMITH; pension awarded 23 Nov 1825; residence - Saint John, New Brunswick, Canada. SOURCE: WO120 Volume 69 page 209. INDEX # 4823.

Jno MCFADDEN; pension awarded 5 Oct 1807; residence - Toronto, Ontario, Canada; died 2 Mar 1858. SOURCE: WO120 Volume 69 page 209. INDEX # 4824.

Ja^s BOSSOM; pension awarded 7 Mar 1837; residence - Halifax, Nova Scotia, Canada; died 5 Jan 1857. SOURCE: WO120 Volume 69 page 209. INDEX # 4825.

Mich^l DOWD; pension awarded 22 Sep 1846; died 12 Jul 1862, Toronto, Ontario, Canada. SOURCE: WO120 Volume 69 page 209. INDEX # 4826.

Richd FEARMAN; pension awarded 22 Sep 1846. SOURCE: WO120 Volume 69 page 209. INDEX # 4827.

Geo^e HUNT; pension awarded 22 Sep 1846. SOURCE: WO120 Volume 69 page 209. INDEX # 4828.

Ed^{wd} LENAGHAN; pension awarded 22 Sep 1846. SOURCE: WO120 Volume 69 page 209. INDEX # 4829.

Jno ONEIL; pension awarded 22 Sep 1846. SOURCE: WO120 Volume 69 page 209. INDEX # 4830.

Thos REED; pension awarded 22 Sep 1846; residence - London, Ontario, Canada; died 18 Nov 1857. SOURCE: WO120 Volume 69 page 209. INDEX # 4831.

Bern^d REILLEY; pension awarded 22 Sep 1846. SOURCE: WO120 Volume 69 page 209. INDEX # 4832.

Stepⁿ FLYNN; pension awarded 22 Sep 1846. SOURCE: WO120 Volume 69 page 210. INDEX # 4833.

Jno ROLLINS; pension awarded 14 Sep 1847. SOURCE: WO120 Volume 69 page 210. INDEX # 4834.

Pat^k MCVEIGH; pension awarded 12 Oct 1847; died 8 Jan 1867. SOURCE: WO120 Volume 69 page 210. INDEX # 4835.

Wm HATCH; pension awarded 12 Oct 1847; died 12 Dec 1879, Royal Chelsea Hospital, England. SOURCE: WO120 Volume 69 page 210. INDEX # 4836.

Isaac MASDEN; pension awarded 12 Oct 1847; died in Nov 1880, Nova Scotia, Canada. SOURCE: WO120 Volume 69 page 210. INDEX # 4837.

John BACON; pension awarded 30 Oct 1855. SOURCE: WO120 Volume 69 page 210. INDEX # 4838.

53rd Regiment of Foot

John PITT; pension awarded 3 May 1824; residence - Madras, India. SOURCE: WO120 Volume 69 page 212. INDEX # 4839.

Adam RIDDLE; pension awarded 7 Feb 1821; residence - Madras, India. SOURCE: WO120 Volume 69 page 212. INDEX # 4840.

Jno PURDON; pension awarded 26 Aug 1815; residence - Cape of Good Hope, South Africa. SOURCE: WO120 Volume 69 page 212. INDEX # 4841.

Thos BAXTER; pension awarded 12 Jul 1837; residence - Quebec, Quebec, Canada; died 13 Feb 1847. SOURCE: WO120 Volume 69 page 212. INDEX # 4842.

Robt BURGESS; pension awarded 4 Jun 1823; residence - Madras, India. SOURCE: WO120 Volume 69 page 212. INDEX # 4843.

53rd Regiment of Foot (continued)

H^y USHER; pension awarded 22 Nov 1842; residence - South Australia, Australia; died 24 Dec 1851. SOURCE: WO120 Volume 69 page 212. INDEX # 4844.

Corn^s MURPHY; pension awarded 25 May 1847. SOURCE: WO120 Volume 69 page 212. INDEX # 4845.

Jno LITTLE; pension awarded 25 Jan 1848. SOURCE: WO120 Volume 69 page 212. INDEX # 4846.

Hugh MCGIVERN; pension awarded 25 Jan 1848; residence - Poonamalee, India; died 18 Mar 1852. SOURCE: WO120 Volume 69 page 212. INDEX # 4847.

Lawrence DONNELLY; pension awarded 13 Feb 1849; residence - Meerut, India; died 9 Dec 1850. SOURCE: WO120 Volume 69 page 212. INDEX # 4848.

Ja^s HINDS; pension awarded 13 Feb 1849; residence - Calcutta, India; died 10 Jan 1851. SOURCE: WO120 Volume 69 page 212. INDEX # 4849.

Danl MCASHEE; pension awarded 10 Jul 1849; residence - Calcutta, India; died 26 May 1851. SOURCE: WO120 Volume 69 page 212. INDEX # 4850.

Jno OWENS; pension awarded 10 Aug 1852; died 26 Nov 1872, Simla, India. SOURCE: WO120 Volume 69 page 212. INDEX # 4851.

James MUNROTT; pension awarded 5 May 1857. SOURCE: WO120 Volume 69 page 212. INDEX # 4852.

Thomas TROY; pension awarded 5 May 1857. SOURCE: WO120 Volume 69 page 212. INDEX # 4853.

54th Regiment of Foot

Ja^s BARRY; pension awarded 10 Jun 1822; residence - Kingston, Ontario, Canada; died 24 Nov 1876, Toronto, Ontario, Canada. SOURCE: WO120 Volume 69 page 214. INDEX # 4854.

Ed^{wd} SCOLTOR; pension awarded 15 Mar 1826; residence - Cape of Good Hope, South Africa. SOURCE: WO120 Volume 69 page 214. INDEX # 4855.

Ja^s DICKER; pension awarded 7 Jan 1829; residence - Madras, India; died 11 May 1853. SOURCE: WO120 Volume 69 page 214. INDEX # 4856.

Wm PHILLIPS; pension awarded 3 Dec 1804; residence - Toronto, Ontario, Canada. SOURCE: WO120 Volume 69 page 214. INDEX # 4857.

Wm WARMINGHAM; pension awarded 23 Sep 1840; residence - Madras, India; died 29 Dec 1869. SOURCE: WO120 Volume 69 page 214. INDEX # 4858.

Pat^k CHERRY; pension awarded 23 Sep 1840; residence - Madras, India. SOURCE: WO120 Volume 69 page 214. INDEX # 4859.

Willm GOODWIN; pension awarded 23 Sep 1840; residence - Madras, India. SOURCE: WO120 Volume 69 page 214. INDEX # 4860.

Ja^s CRANSTON; pension awarded 24 Jun 1840; residence - Montreal, Quebec, Canada. SOURCE: WO120 Volume 69 page 214. INDEX # 4861.

Willm BROWN; pension awarded 23 Oct 1838; residence - Madras, India; died 11 Sep 1869. SOURCE: WO120 Volume 69 page 214. INDEX # 4862.

Jno HOLSBY; pension awarded 24 Jun 1840; residence - Madras, India; died 14 Feb 1862. SOURCE: WO120 Volume 69 page 214. INDEX # 4863.

Robt MARTIN; pension awarded 23 Oct 1838; residence - Madras, India; died 22 May 1862. SOURCE: WO120 Volume 69 page 214. INDEX # 4864.

Richd WAYNE; pension awarded 23 Sep 1840; residence - Madras, India. SOURCE: WO120 Volume 69 page 214. INDEX # 4865.

Willm DICKENSON; pension awarded 24 Jun 1840; residence - Madras, India; died 27 May 1855. SOURCE: WO120 Volume 69 page 214. INDEX # 4866.

John BRYAN; pension awarded 23 Oct 1838; residence - Madras, India; died 14 Oct 1850. SOURCE: WO120 Volume 69 page 214. INDEX # 4867.

Be^{ld} HILTON; pension awarded 24 Jun 1840; residence - Madras, India; died 7 Apr 1846. SOURCE: WO120 Volume 69 page 214. INDEX # 4868.

John LEE; pension awarded 24 Jun 1840; residence - Madras, India; died 22 Jan 1854. SOURCE: WO120 Volume 69 page 214. INDEX # 4869.

Willm MACE; pension awarded 23 Oct 1838; residence - Madras, India. SOURCE: WO120 Volume 69 page 214. INDEX # 4870.

54th Regiment of Foot (continued)

Arch^d IRWIN; pension awarded 24 Jun 1840; residence - Madras, India; died 9 Jan 1852. SOURCE: WO120 Volume 69 page 214. INDEX # 4871.

Chas MILES; pension awarded 24 Jun 1840; residence - Madras, India. SOURCE: WO120 Volume 69 page 214. INDEX # 4872.

H^y LAWSON; pension awarded 23 Oct 1838; residence - Madras, India; died in 1853. SOURCE: WO120 Volume 69 page 214. INDEX # 4873.

George POWELL; pension awarded 23 Oct 1838; residence - Madras, India; died 7 Nov 1846. SOURCE: WO120 Volume 69 page 215. INDEX # 4874.

Willm WRIGHT; pension awarded 24 Jun 1840; residence - Madras, India; died 25 Apr 1862. SOURCE: WO120 Volume 69 page 215. INDEX # 4875.

Robt MOSS; pension awarded 23 Oct 1838; residence - Madras, India; died 16 Jun 1846. SOURCE: WO120 Volume 69 page 215. INDEX # 4876.

Thos STUBBINS; pension awarded 14 Apr 1841; residence - London, Ontario, Canada. SOURCE: WO120 Volume 69 page 215. INDEX # 4877.

Jno BAVINGTON; pension awarded 24 Jun 1840; residence - Madras, India; died 3 May 1872. SOURCE: WO120 Volume 69 page 215. INDEX # 4878.

Wm MORRISON; pension awarded 9 Aug 1837; residence - Madras, India; died 22 Sep 1849. SOURCE: WO120 Volume 69 page 215. INDEX # 4879.

Henry GRIEF; pension awarded 24 Jun 1840; residence - Madras, India; died 3 Jun 1854. SOURCE: WO120 Volume 69 page 215. INDEX # 4880.

John POOLE; pension awarded ; residence - Madras, India. SOURCE: WO120 Volume 69 page 215. INDEX # 4881.

Ja^s SCHOCH; pension awarded 25 Feb 1819; residence - Berne, Switzerland. SOURCE: WO120 Volume 69 page 215. INDEX # 4882.

Thos REYNOLDS; pension awarded 8 Feb 1848; died 6 Mar 1872, W. London. SOURCE: WO120 Volume 69 page 215. INDEX # 4883.

Fra^s FORD; pension awarded 27 Jul 1852. SOURCE: WO120 Volume 69 page 215. INDEX # 4884.

John HOWLING; pension awarded 27 Jul 1852. SOURCE: WO120 Volume 69 page 215. INDEX # 4885.

Wm MARCHAM; pension awarded 27 Jul 1852. SOURCE: WO120 Volume 69 page 215. INDEX # 4886.

Henry MARCHAM; pension awarded 27 Jul 1852. SOURCE: WO120 Volume 69 page 215. INDEX # 4887.

Thos REYNOLDS; pension awarded 19 Jul 1853. SOURCE: WO120 Volume 69 page 215. INDEX # 4888.

Saml GILMAR; pension awarded 19 Jul 1853. SOURCE: WO120 Volume 69 page 215. INDEX # 4889.

Jno DREW; pension awarded 13 Sep 1853. SOURCE: WO120 Volume 69 page 215. INDEX # 4890.

Thos DWYER; pension awarded 12 Sep 1854; died 8 Jan 1876, Limerick. SOURCE: WO120 Volume 69 page 215. INDEX # 4891.

Ja^s LINTON; pension awarded 12 Sep 1854; residence - London, Ontario, Canada; died 14 Nov 1857. SOURCE: WO120 Volume 69 page 215. INDEX # 4892.

Mich^l MCGARRY; pension awarded 12 Sep 1854; died 10 Feb 1873, London, Ontario, Canada. SOURCE: WO120 Volume 69 page 215. INDEX # 4893.

55th Regiment of Foot

Sol^n BROWN; pension awarded 26 Jul 1820; residence - St. Johns. SOURCE: WO120 Volume 69 page 217. INDEX # 4894.

Ja^s SMITH; pension awarded 25 Feb 1819; residence - St. Johns. SOURCE: WO120 Volume 69 page 217. INDEX # 4895.

Step^n WHITAKER; pension awarded 25 Feb 1819; residence - New South Wales, Australia. SOURCE: WO120 Volume 69 page 217. INDEX # 4896.

Ja^s HURLEY; pension awarded 23 Jul 1844; residence - Madras, India; died 13 May 1864. SOURCE: WO120 Volume 69 page 217. INDEX # 4897.

Thos ELLIOTT; pension awarded 13 Oct 1841; residence - Madras, India. SOURCE: WO120 Volume 69 page 217. INDEX # 4898.

55th Regiment of Foot (continued)

John CARTER; pension awarded 12 Sep 1843; residence - Madras, India. SOURCE: WO120 Volume 69 page 217. INDEX # 4899.

Thos NETTING; pension awarded 12 Sep 1843; residence - Bengal, India; died in Jun 1862. SOURCE: WO120 Volume 69 page 217. INDEX # 4900.

Geoe WELLS; pension awarded 12 Sep 1843; residence - Bengal, India; died 11 Oct 1848. SOURCE: WO120 Volume 69 page 217. INDEX # 4901.

Jno SIMMONDS; pension awarded 14 Nov 1843; residence - Bengal, India. SOURCE: WO120 Volume 69 page 217. INDEX # 4902.

Wm DALLING; pension awarded 14 Nov 1843; residence - Bengal, India. SOURCE: WO120 Volume 69 page 217. INDEX # 4903.

Fras SULLIVAN; pension awarded 14 Nov 1843; residence - Bengal, India; died 17 May 1849. SOURCE: WO120 Volume 69 page 217. INDEX # 4904.

Hy POTTS; pension awarded 14 Nov 1843; residence - Bengal, India; died 21 Jun 1845. SOURCE: WO120 Volume 69 page 217. INDEX # 4905.

Jas BROWN; pension awarded 14 Nov 1843; residence - Bengal, India; died 5 Oct 1847. SOURCE: WO120 Volume 69 page 217. INDEX # 4906.

Josh HODGES; pension awarded 14 Nov 1843; residence - Madras, India; died 7 Jun 1880, Madras, India. SOURCE: WO120 Volume 69 page 217. INDEX # 4907.

Arthr DEVANNEY; pension awarded 14 Nov 1843; residence - Madras, India; died 5 Jul 1863. SOURCE: WO120 Volume 69 page 217. INDEX # 4908.

Jas SULLIVAN; pension awarded 14 Nov 1843; residence - Madras, India; died 23 Mar 1854. SOURCE: WO120 Volume 69 page 217. INDEX # 4909.

Saml ROBINSON; pension awarded 14 Nov 1843; residence - Madras, India. SOURCE: WO120 Volume 69 page 217. INDEX # 4910.

John ARMITAGE; pension awarded 24 Oct 1843; residence - Madras, India. SOURCE: WO120 Volume 69 page 217. INDEX # 4911.

Jno MARLBOROUGH; pension awarded 11 Jun 1844; residence - Chusan, China; died 28 Aug 1852. SOURCE: WO120 Volume 69 page 217. INDEX # 4912.

Josh CARR; pension awarded 23 Jul 1844; residence - Madras, India; died 30 Sep 1851. SOURCE: WO120 Volume 69 page 217. INDEX # 4913.

Thos COOKE; pension awarded 23 Jul 1844; residence - Madras, India; died 10 Sep 1881, Bangalore, India. SOURCE: WO120 Volume 69 page 218. INDEX # 4914.

Jno CONNELLY; pension awarded 23 Jul 1844; residence - Madras, India. SOURCE: WO120 Volume 69 page 218. INDEX # 4915.

Philip WHITBREAD; pension awarded 23 Jul 1844; residence - Madras, India. SOURCE: WO120 Volume 69 page 218. INDEX # 4916.

Robt ONEILL; pension awarded 23 Jul 1844; residence - Madras, India. SOURCE: WO120 Volume 69 page 218. INDEX # 4917.

Geoe BEST; pension awarded 11 Jul 1838; residence - Amherstburg, Ontario, Canada; died 28 Jan 1862, London, Ontario, Canada. SOURCE: WO120 Volume 69 page 218. INDEX # 4918.

Jno CAIRNS; pension awarded 26 Nov 1844; residence - Prince Edward Island, Canada. SOURCE: WO120 Volume 69 page 218. INDEX # 4919.

John LAVERY; pension awarded 14 Nov 1843; residence - Bengal, India; died 10 Oct 1849. SOURCE: WO120 Volume 69 page 218. INDEX # 4920.

Jas HIGGS; pension awarded 26 Jun 1839; residence - Cape of Good Hope, South Africa; died 24 Jun 1874, Cape Town, South Africa. SOURCE: WO120 Volume 69 page 218. INDEX # 4921.

Wm DAMARUM; pension awarded 23 Oct 1838; residence - Madras, India. SOURCE: WO120 Volume 69 page 218. INDEX # 4922.

Chas BUCKLEY; pension awarded 26 Jun 1839; residence - Cape of Good Hope, South Africa; died in 1846. SOURCE: WO120 Volume 69 page 218. INDEX # 4923.

John MOORE; pension awarded 23 Sep 1840; residence - Madras, India; died 21 Dec 1848. SOURCE: WO120 Volume 69 page 218. INDEX # 4924.

55th Regiment of Foot (continued)

Wm PENGILLEY; pension awarded 14 Nov 1843; residence - Bengal, India; died 9 Jul 1849. SOURCE: WO120 Volume 69 page 218. INDEX # 4925.

Fra^s ROSE; pension awarded 22 Nov 1839; residence - Madras, India. SOURCE: WO120 Volume 69 page 218. INDEX # 4926.

Thos KELLY; pension awarded 9 Jul 1844; residence - Cape of Good Hope, South Africa; died 3 Apr 1845. SOURCE: WO120 Volume 69 page 218. INDEX # 4927.

Alex^r PEADON; pension awarded 24 Oct 1838; residence - Madras, India. SOURCE: WO120 Volume 69 page 218. INDEX # 4928.

John GROOM; pension awarded 26 Jun 1839; residence - Cape of Good Hope, South Africa; died in 1846. SOURCE: WO120 Volume 69 page 218. INDEX # 4929.

Saml BALL; pension awarded 28 Apr 1841; residence - Madras, India. SOURCE: WO120 Volume 69 page 218. INDEX # 4930.

Wm DEACON; pension awarded 14 Nov 1843; residence - Bengal, India; died 11 Jan 1847. SOURCE: WO120 Volume 69 page 218. INDEX # 4931.

Thos EAMES; pension awarded 23 Sep 1840; residence - Madras, India; died 9 Feb 1853. SOURCE: WO120 Volume 69 page 218. INDEX # 4932.

Saml BARNES; pension awarded 14 Nov 1843; residence - Madras, India. SOURCE: WO120 Volume 69 page 218. INDEX # 4933.

Richd STONE; pension awarded 14 Nov 1843; residence - Madras, India; died 17 Apr 1852. SOURCE: WO120 Volume 69 page 218. INDEX # 4934.

Wm PRICE; pension awarded 11 Jun 1844; residence - Chusan, China; died 16 Jul 1846. SOURCE: WO120 Volume 69 page 218. INDEX # 4935.

Thos FOULSTONE; pension awarded 23 Oct 1838; residence - Madras, India; died 3 Mar 1849. SOURCE: WO120 Volume 69 page 218. INDEX # 4936.

Willm LAMBERT; pension awarded 26 Jun 1839; residence - Cape of Good Hope, South Africa; died 25 Mar 1854. SOURCE: WO120 Volume 69 page 218. INDEX # 4937.

Thos HOPKINSON; pension awarded 20 Nov 1839; residence - Madras, India; died 25 May 1879, Madras, India. SOURCE: WO120 Volume 69 page 218. INDEX # 4938.

Robt TUCKER; pension awarded 23 Oct 1838; residence - Madras, India; died 13 Jan 1848. SOURCE: WO120 Volume 69 page 218. INDEX # 4939.

Wm DALY; pension awarded 20 Nov 1839; residence - Madras, India; died 28 Jan 1853. SOURCE: WO120 Volume 69 page 218. INDEX # 4940.

Ja^s STAFFORD; pension awarded 20 Nov 1839; residence - Madras, India. SOURCE: WO120 Volume 69 page 218. INDEX # 4941.

Thos HAYLOCK; pension awarded 23 Sep 1840; residence - Madras, India. SOURCE: WO120 Volume 69 page 218. INDEX # 4942.

Geo^e TOWNSEND; pension awarded 14 Nov 1843; residence - Bengal, India. SOURCE: WO120 Volume 69 page 218. INDEX # 4943.

Jos^h TAYLOR; pension awarded 20 Nov 1839; residence - Madras, India; died 21 Aug 1850. SOURCE: WO120 Volume 69 page 218. INDEX # 4944.

Saml WHITT; pension awarded 12 Sep 1843; residence - Madras, India; died 9 Nov 1863. SOURCE: WO120 Volume 69 page 218. INDEX # 4945.

Thos HORTON; pension awarded 12 Sep 1843; residence - Madras, India; died 29 Mar 1863, Madras, India. SOURCE: WO120 Volume 69 page 218. INDEX # 4946.

Pat^k FORD; pension awarded 23 Jul 1844; residence - Madras, India. SOURCE: WO120 Volume 69 page 218. INDEX # 4947.

Ja^s CONNALLY; pension awarded 20 Nov 1839; residence - Madras, India. SOURCE: WO120 Volume 69 page 218. INDEX # 4948.

Ja^s BARTON; pension awarded 23 Sep 1840; residence - Madras, India; died 7 Oct 1862. SOURCE: WO120 Volume 69 page 218. INDEX # 4949.

Geo^e HARVEY; pension awarded 23 Sep 1840; residence - Madras, India; died 8 Aug 1853. SOURCE: WO120 Volume 69 page 218. INDEX # 4950.

55th Regiment of Foot (continued)

Gavin HENDERSON; pension awarded 28 Apr 1841; residence - Madras, India. SOURCE: WO120 Volume 69 page 218. INDEX # 4951.

Peter WHITE; pension awarded 28 Apr 1841; residence - Madras, India; died 11 Feb 1862. SOURCE: WO120 Volume 69 page 218. INDEX # 4952.

Jno ANDERSON; pension awarded 14 Nov 1843; residence - Bengal, India. SOURCE: WO120 Volume 69 page 218. INDEX # 4953.

Jas DAMERUM; pension awarded 14 Nov 1843; residence - Madras, India; died 15 May 1871. SOURCE: WO120 Volume 69 page 219. INDEX # 4954.

Jas FURMAGE; pension awarded 20 Nov 1839; residence - Madras, India. SOURCE: WO120 Volume 69 page 219. INDEX # 4955.

Josh THRUSSELL; pension awarded 20 Nov 1839; residence - Madras, India. SOURCE: WO120 Volume 69 page 219. INDEX # 4956.

Thos DONOUGHEY; pension awarded 14 Nov 1843; residence - Bengal, India; died 18 Jan 1851. SOURCE: WO120 Volume 69 page 219. INDEX # 4957.

Wm LAWRENCE; pension awarded 23 Jul 1844; residence - Madras, India. SOURCE: WO120 Volume 69 page 219. INDEX # 4958.

Lewis SWASBROOK; pension awarded 23 Jul 1844; residence - Madras, India; died 9 Apr 1872. SOURCE: WO120 Volume 69 page 219. INDEX # 4959.

Thos TURNER; pension awarded 9 Aug 1837; residence - Madras, India; died 4 Sep 1872. SOURCE: WO120 Volume 69 page 219. INDEX # 4960.

Richd WELLS; pension awarded 28 Apr 1841; residence - Madras, India. SOURCE: WO120 Volume 69 page 219. INDEX # 4961.

Thos SANDERSON; pension awarded 22 Nov 1842; residence - Toronto, Ontario, Canada; died 16 Feb 1870. SOURCE: WO120 Volume 69 page 218. INDEX # 4962.

John KIRK; pension awarded 14 Nov 1843; residence - Madras, India. SOURCE: WO120 Volume 69 page 219. INDEX # 4963.

Wm RICHARDSON; pension awarded 20 Nov 1839; residence - Madras, India; died 31 Jul 1846. SOURCE: WO120 Volume 69 page 219. INDEX # 4964.

Wm KENNEBY; pension awarded 13 Apr 1840; residence - Cape of Good Hope, South Africa. SOURCE: WO120 Volume 69 page 219. INDEX # 4965.

Wm ONIS; pension awarded 20 Nov 1839; residence - Madras, India. SOURCE: WO120 Volume 69 page 219. INDEX # 4966.

Josh HOWARD; pension awarded 23 Sep 1840; residence - Madras, India; died 5 Aug 1853. SOURCE: WO120 Volume 69 page 219. INDEX # 4967.

Wm TAIT; pension awarded 20 Nov 1839; residence - Madras, India. SOURCE: WO120 Volume 69 page 219. INDEX # 4968.

Peter KENNEDY; pension awarded 23 Oct 1838; residence - Madras, India; died 13 Sep 1845. SOURCE: WO120 Volume 69 page 219. INDEX # 4969.

Wm WAINWRIGHT; pension awarded 20 Nov 1839; residence - Madras, India; died 1 Jul 1844. SOURCE: WO120 Volume 69 page 219. INDEX # 4970.

David WHEATON; pension awarded 10 Jun 1845; residence - Calcutta, India; died 8 May 1849. SOURCE: WO120 Volume 69 page 219. INDEX # 4971.

Stepn WILKS; pension awarded 9 Feb 1847; died 2 Jul 1847. SOURCE: WO120 Volume 69 page 219. INDEX # 4972.

Jas CARTER; pension awarded 22 May 1849. SOURCE: WO120 Volume 69 page 219. INDEX # 4973.

56th Regiment of Foot

John GRIMSTON; pension awarded 20 Jul 1825; residence - New South Wales, Australia; died 18 Nov 1882, Sydney, New South Wales, Australia. SOURCE: WO120 Volume 69 page 222. INDEX # 4974.

Jno ORCHARD; pension awarded 21 Nov 1821; residence - Launceston, Australia. SOURCE: WO120 Volume 69 page 222. INDEX # 4975.

56th Regiment of Foot (continued)

W^m Ed^{wd} GUY; pension awarded 30 May 1827; residence - Cape of Good Hope, South Africa; died 10 Mar 1854. SOURCE: WO120 Volume 69 page 222. INDEX # 4976.

Pat^k DEVEREUX; pension awarded 13 Dec 1842; residence - Wm Henry, Quebec, Canada; died 9 Sep 1847. SOURCE: WO120 Volume 69 page 222. INDEX # 4977.

Geo^e ADAIR; pension awarded 13 Oct 1830; residence - Prescott, Ontario, Canada; died in Dec 1847. SOURCE: WO120 Volume 69 page 222. INDEX # 4978.

Bern^d NIBLICK; pension awarded 17 Mar 1819; residence - Cape of Good Hope, South Africa; died 25 Jan 1854. SOURCE: WO120 Volume 69 page 222. INDEX # 4979.

Pat^k RYAN; pension awarded 13 Dec 1842; residence - Toronto, Ontario, Canada; died 27 Feb 1875. SOURCE: WO120 Volume 69 page 222. INDEX # 4980.

Wm GRUBB; pension awarded 19 Jul 1826; residence - Mauritius; died 10 Sep 1854. SOURCE: WO120 Volume 69 page 222. INDEX # 4981.

Jno HILL; pension awarded 21 Aug 1822; residence - Prescott, Ontario, Canada. SOURCE: WO120 Volume 69 page 222. INDEX # 4982.

Thos GODFREY; pension awarded 19 Jul 1826; residence - Mauritius; died 26 May 1846. SOURCE: WO120 Volume 69 page 222. INDEX # 4983.

Lawr^e CLARKE; pension awarded 27 Sep 1842; residence - Quebec, Quebec, Canada; died 9 Jul 1876, Paisley. SOURCE: WO120 Volume 69 page 222. INDEX # 4984.

Chas CLARKE; pension awarded 19 Jul 1816; residence - Mauritius. SOURCE: WO120 Volume 69 page 222. INDEX # 4985.

Hy PUNG; pension awarded 19 Jul 1826; residence - Mauritius; died 8 Apr 1846. SOURCE: WO120 Volume 69 page 222. INDEX # 4986.

Willm LEE; pension awarded 18 Dec 1822; residence - Hobart Town, Australia. SOURCE: WO120 Volume 69 page 222. INDEX # 4987.

Robt ROGERS; pension awarded 22 Aug 1848. SOURCE: WO120 Volume 69 page 222. INDEX # 4988.

Ja^s POTTER; pension awarded 26 Jun 1849. SOURCE: WO120 Volume 69 page 222. INDEX # 4989.

Wm BLACKMAN; pension awarded 14 Sep 1852; died 10 Apr 1887, Bermuda. SOURCE: WO120 Volume 69 page 222. INDEX # 4990.

Pat^k CUSACK; pension awarded 22 Feb 1853; residence - Bermuda; died 4 Sep 1853. SOURCE: WO120 Volume 69 page 222. INDEX # 4991.

57th Regiment of Foot

Jos^h PHILLIPS; pension awarded 7 Aug 1816; residence - Bytown, Ontario, Canada; died 3 Aug 1857. SOURCE: WO120 Volume 69 page 225. INDEX # 4992.

Mich^l CAVANAGH; pension awarded 23 Sep 1818; residence - Bytown, Ontario, Canada. SOURCE: WO120 Volume 69 page 225. INDEX # 4993.

Stepⁿ PITCHER; pension awarded 22 Dec 1814; residence - New Zealand. SOURCE: WO120 Volume 69 page 225. INDEX # 4994.

Jno THOMPSON; pension awarded 24 Nov 1824; residence - New South Wales, Australia. SOURCE: WO120 Volume 69 page 225. INDEX # 4995.

Willm GREEN; pension awarded 8 Sep 1830; residence - Sydney, New South Wales, Australia. SOURCE: WO120 Volume 69 page 225. INDEX # 4996.

Danl SMITH; pension awarded 17 Sep 1812; residence - Amherstburg, Ontario, Canada; died 23 Jan 1853. SOURCE: WO120 Volume 69 page 225. INDEX # 4997.

Thos SAGE; pension awarded 20 Jan 1819; residence - Toronto, Ontario, Canada; died 10 May 1874, Hamilton, Ontario, Canada. SOURCE: WO120 Volume 69 page 225. INDEX # 4998.

Burket MANSER; pension awarded 11 Mar 1831; residence - Toronto, Ontario, Canada; died 28 Oct 1869, Toronto, Ontario, Canada. SOURCE: WO120 Volume 69 page 225. INDEX # 4999.

George DYER; pension awarded 11 Jan 1832; residence - New South Wales, Australia. SOURCE: WO120 Volume 69 page 225. INDEX # 5000.

Jno HOWELL; pension awarded 11 Jan 1832; residence - New South Wales, Australia. SOURCE: WO120 Volume 69 page 225. INDEX # 5001.

WO120 VOLUME 69

57th Regiment of Foot (continued)

Geo^e NEWBOLT; pension awarded 11 Jan 1832; residence - New South Wales, Australia. SOURCE: WO120 Volume 69 page 225. INDEX # 5002.

Jesse GEAR; pension awarded 23 Dec 1845; residence - India; died 1 Jan 1847. SOURCE: WO120 Volume 69 page 225. INDEX # 5003.

Alex^r MCINNIS; pension awarded 6 Jun 1796; residence - Perth, Ontario, Canada. SOURCE: WO120 Volume 69 page 225. INDEX # 5004.

Jesse WESTMAN; pension awarded 11 Oct 1842; residence - Madras, India; died 9 Jun 1855. SOURCE: WO120 Volume 69 page 225. INDEX # 5005.

Geo^e MIDDLETON; pension awarded 24 Oct 1843; residence - Madras, India; died 18 Jan 1850. SOURCE: WO120 Volume 69 page 225. INDEX # 5006.

Wm RYAN; pension awarded 24 Oct 1843; residence - Madras, India; died 30 Jul 1863. SOURCE: WO120 Volume 69 page 225. INDEX # 5007.

Ja^s WOOD; pension awarded 24 Oct 1843; residence - Madras, India. SOURCE: WO120 Volume 69 page 225. INDEX # 5008.

Ja^s TAPLEY; pension awarded 11 Jun 1844; residence - Madras, India. SOURCE: WO120 Volume 69 page 225. INDEX # 5009.

Ja^s WHITEHEAD; pension awarded 9 Mar 1831; residence - Launceston, Australia; died 23 Jan 1859, Exeter. SOURCE: WO120 Volume 69 page 225. INDEX # 5010.

And^w CHRISTIE; pension awarded 20 Nov 1839; residence - Madras, India; died 14 Aug 1854. SOURCE: WO120 Volume 69 page 225. INDEX # 5011.

Thos BAYLIS; pension awarded 13 Oct 1841; residence - Madras, India; died 18 Apr 1873, Madras, India. SOURCE: WO120 Volume 69 page 226. INDEX # 5012.

Jno HAUGHTON; pension awarded 11 Oct 1842; residence - Madras, India; died 3 Jun 1853. SOURCE: WO120 Volume 69 page 226. INDEX # 5013.

Thos ROBERTS; pension awarded 24 Oct 1843; residence - Madras, India; died 16 Dec 1853. SOURCE: WO120 Volume 69 page 226. INDEX # 5014.

Thos THISTLEWAITE; pension awarded 24 Oct 1843; residence - Madras, India; died 28 Dec 1849. SOURCE: WO120 Volume 69 page 226. INDEX # 5015.

Ja^s LOVELL; pension awarded 9 Jan 1833; residence - Sydney, New South Wales, Australia; died in Oct 1848. SOURCE: WO120 Volume 69 page 226. INDEX # 5016.

Ja^s GIRMAN; pension awarded 11 Apr 1843; residence - Madras, India. SOURCE: WO120 Volume 69 page 226. INDEX # 5017.

Wm SINDON; pension awarded 26 Sep 1838; residence - Bombay, India. SOURCE: WO120 Volume 69 page 226. INDEX # 5018.

Jon^n TIPPING; pension awarded 13 Jun 1843; residence - Madras, India. SOURCE: WO120 Volume 69 page 226. INDEX # 5019.

Jos^h FREEMAN; pension awarded 28 Apr 1846. SOURCE: WO120 Volume 69 page 226. INDEX # 5020.

Jno BELL; pension awarded 28 Apr 1846. SOURCE: WO120 Volume 69 page 226. INDEX # 5021.

Mich^l TOOMEY; pension awarded 28 Apr 1846; residence - Madras, India; died 28 Aug 1850. SOURCE: WO120 Volume 69 page 226. INDEX # 5022.

Wm FLOOD; pension awarded 28 Apr 1846; died 4 Mar 1864, Madras, India. SOURCE: WO120 Volume 69 page 226. INDEX # 5023.

Pat^k GAYNOR; pension awarded 28 Apr 1846. SOURCE: WO120 Volume 69 page 226. INDEX # 5024.

Noah SMITH; pension awarded 28 Apr 1846; died 31 Jan 1875. SOURCE: WO120 Volume 69 page 226. INDEX # 5025.

Fra^s WATSON; pension awarded 28 Apr 1846. SOURCE: WO120 Volume 69 page 226. INDEX # 5026.

John BRENAN; pension awarded 28 Apr 1846; residence - Madras, India; died 3 Dec 1849. SOURCE: WO120 Volume 69 page 226. INDEX # 5027.

Ja^s DANIELS; pension awarded 28 Apr 1846; residence - Madras, India; died 25 Dec 1872. SOURCE: WO120 Volume 69 page 226. INDEX # 5028.

Ja^s EMMETT; pension awarded 28 Apr 1846; residence - Madras, India; died 21 Mar 1863. SOURCE: WO120 Volume 69 page 226. INDEX # 5029.

57th Regiment of Foot (continued)

Saml FEARMAN; pension awarded 28 Apr 1846; died 30 May 1878. SOURCE: WO120 Volume 69 page 226. INDEX # 5030.

Wm GURNEY; pension awarded 28 Apr 1846. SOURCE: WO120 Volume 69 page 226. INDEX # 5031.

Jos^h LAMBKIN; pension awarded 28 Apr 1846. SOURCE: WO120 Volume 69 page 226. INDEX # 5032.

Pat^k MCMANUS; pension awarded 28 Apr 1846; died 29 Mar 1881, Madras, India. SOURCE: WO120 Volume 69 page 226. INDEX # 5033.

Thos MAPLE; pension awarded 28 Apr 1846; residence - Madras, India; died 28 Jul 1849. SOURCE: WO120 Volume 69 page 226. INDEX # 5034.

Alex^r ROSS; pension awarded 28 Apr 1846; residence - Madras, India; died 22 Nov 1849. SOURCE: WO120 Volume 69 page 226. INDEX # 5035.

Ja^s TOMLIN; pension awarded 28 Apr 1846; died 17 Jun 1870. SOURCE: WO120 Volume 69 page 226. INDEX # 5036.

Benjn BATES; pension awarded 23 Jun 1846; residence - Madras, India; died 24 Jan 1848. SOURCE: WO120 Volume 69 page 226. INDEX # 5037.

58th Regiment of Foot

Bern^d FITZPATRICK; pension awarded 16 Nov 1828; residence - Kingston, Ontario, Canada; died 13 Dec 1870, Toronto, Ontario, Canada. SOURCE: WO120 Volume 69 page 229. INDEX # 5038.

Ja^s SIZELAND; pension awarded 17 Feb 1819; residence - Prescott, Ontario, Canada. SOURCE: WO120 Volume 69 page 229. INDEX # 5039.

Jno WINN; pension awarded 3 Mar 1826; residence - London, Ontario, Canada. SOURCE: WO120 Volume 69 page 229. INDEX # 5040.

Geo^e SAYWELL; pension awarded 21 Jan 1824; residence - New Zealand. SOURCE: WO120 Volume 69 page 229. INDEX # 5041.

Mich^l MCNAMARA; pension awarded 28 Jul 1815; residence - Quebec, Quebec, Canada; died in Sep 1849. SOURCE: WO120 Volume 69 page 229. INDEX # 5042.

John BRATT; pension awarded 30 Oct 1816; residence - Bytown, Ontario, Canada. SOURCE: WO120 Volume 69 page 229. INDEX # 5043.

Allan RUTHERFORD; pension awarded 30 Dec 1816; residence - Toronto, Ontario, Canada; died 28 Jul 1865, Hamilton, Ontario, Canada. SOURCE: WO120 Volume 69 page 229. INDEX # 5044.

Wm BUCKLEY; pension awarded 27 Nov 1839; residence - New South Wales, Australia; died 24 Jun 1857, Victoria, New South Wales, Australia. SOURCE: WO120 Volume 69 page 229. INDEX # 5045.

John ARMSTRONG; pension awarded 22 Jul 1840; residence - Mauritius; died 10 Jan 1879, Birr. SOURCE: WO120 Volume 69 page 229. INDEX # 5046.

Geo^e ROSS; pension awarded 4 Dec 1822; residence - Toronto, Ontario, Canada; died 18 May 1862, London, Ontario, Canada. SOURCE: WO120 Volume 69 page 229. INDEX # 5047.

Dennis MOLONEY; pension awarded 19 Jun 1842; residence - Quebec, Quebec, Canada; died 1 Aug 1859, Toronto, Ontario, Canada. SOURCE: WO120 Volume 69 page 229. INDEX # 5048.

John JEFFERYS; pension awarded 23 Feb 1847; residence - New South Wales, Australia. SOURCE: WO120 Volume 69 page 229. INDEX # 5049.

Ja^s CARLAND; pension awarded 23 Feb 1847. SOURCE: WO120 Volume 69 page 229. INDEX # 5050.

Hen^y JUSTIN; pension awarded 23 Feb 1847; died 12 Nov 1877, New Zealand. SOURCE: WO120 Volume 69 page 229. INDEX # 5051.

Ja^s NOAKES; pension awarded 23 Feb 1847. SOURCE: WO120 Volume 69 page 229. INDEX # 5052.

Jno MCGRATH; pension awarded 23 Feb 1847. SOURCE: WO120 Volume 69 page 229. INDEX # 5053.

Jno KEENAN; pension awarded 23 Feb 1847. SOURCE: WO120 Volume 69 page 229. INDEX # 5054.

Jno KENNY; pension awarded 23 Feb 1847. SOURCE: WO120 Volume 69 page 229. INDEX # 5055.

58th Regiment of Foot (continued)

Thos WALTERS; pension awarded 23 Feb 1847; died 15 Dec 1872, New Zealand. SOURCE: WO120 Volume 69 page 229. INDEX # 5056.
Wm RHODES; pension awarded 14 Sep 1847. SOURCE: WO120 Volume 69 page 229. INDEX # 5057.
Pat^k CONNOLLY; pension awarded 14 Sep 1847. SOURCE: WO120 Volume 69 page 229. INDEX # 5058.
Jno NESBITT; pension awarded 14 Sep 1847. SOURCE: WO120 Volume 69 page 230. INDEX # 5059.
Wm MOWLAN; pension awarded 14 Sep 1847. SOURCE: WO120 Volume 69 page 230. INDEX # 5060.
Mich^l MAHER; pension awarded 25 Jan 1848. SOURCE: WO120 Volume 69 page 230. INDEX # 5061.
Pat^k NOWLAN; pension awarded 25 Jan 1848. SOURCE: WO120 Volume 69 page 230. INDEX # 5062.
Jno BERRICREE; pension awarded 25 Jan 1848; died 18 Jan 1880, Melbourne, Australia. SOURCE: WO120 Volume 69 page 230. INDEX # 5063.
Jno POOLE; pension awarded 25 Jan 1848; residence - Parramatta, New South Wales, Australia; died 6 Sep 1849. SOURCE: WO120 Volume 69 page 230. INDEX # 5064.
Richd COSSER; pension awarded 6 Jun 1848. SOURCE: WO120 Volume 69 page 230. INDEX # 5065.
Jos^h CLOUT; pension awarded 6 Jun 1848. SOURCE: WO120 Volume 69 page 230. INDEX # 5066.
Ew^d CORMAC; pension awarded 6 Jun 1848. SOURCE: WO120 Volume 69 page 230. INDEX # 5067.
Edwd HANDS; pension awarded 6 Jun 1848. SOURCE: WO120 Volume 69 page 230. INDEX # 5068.
Saml HAUGHY; pension awarded 6 Jun 1848. SOURCE: WO120 Volume 69 page 230. INDEX # 5069.
Jno MCGILLICUDDY; pension awarded 6 Jun 1848. SOURCE: WO120 Volume 69 page 230. INDEX # 5070.
Mich^l NELIS; pension awarded 6 Jun 1848; died 21 Feb 1876. SOURCE: WO120 Volume 69 page 230. INDEX # 5071.
Thos SCALES; pension awarded 6 Jun 1848. SOURCE: WO120 Volume 69 page 230. INDEX # 5072.
Wm EASTON; pension awarded 26 Dec 1848. SOURCE: WO120 Volume 69 page 230. INDEX # 5073.
Mich^l FIELD; pension awarded 26 Dec 1848; died 21 Feb 1876. SOURCE: WO120 Volume 69 page 230. INDEX # 5074.
Mich^l HARTNELL; pension awarded 26 Dec 1848. SOURCE: WO120 Volume 69 page 230. INDEX # 5075.
Danl MCGINNIS; pension awarded 26 Dec 1848; residence - New South Wales, Australia; died 6 May 1853. SOURCE: WO120 Volume 69 page 230. INDEX # 5076.
Ja^s BRADY; pension awarded 26 Dec 1848. SOURCE: WO120 Volume 69 page 230. INDEX # 5077.
Pat^k BONFIELD; pension awarded 26 Dec 1848; died 8 Oct 1876, New Zealand. SOURCE: WO120 Volume 69 page 230. INDEX # 5078.
Jno FAHEY; pension awarded 26 Dec 1848; died 21 Oct 1863, New Zealand. SOURCE: WO120 Volume 69 page 230. INDEX # 5079.
Peter MCGOVERN; pension awarded 26 Dec 1848. SOURCE: WO120 Volume 69 page 230. INDEX # 5080.
Denis MURPHY; pension awarded 26 Dec 1848. SOURCE: WO120 Volume 69 page 230. INDEX # 5081.
Jno READY; pension awarded 26 Dec 1848. SOURCE: WO120 Volume 69 page 230. INDEX # 5082.
Ja^s ROCHE; pension awarded 26 Dec 1848. SOURCE: WO120 Volume 69 page 230. INDEX # 5083.
Jno SAVAGE; pension awarded 26 Dec 1848. SOURCE: WO120 Volume 69 page 230. INDEX # 5084.
Tim^y LOWRIE; pension awarded 13 Nov 1849; died 7 Jun 1878, New Zealand. SOURCE: WO120 Volume 69 page 230. INDEX # 5085.
Pat^k SULLIVAN; pension awarded 11 Dec 1849. SOURCE: WO120 Volume 69 page 230. INDEX # 5086.
Pat^k COYLE; pension awarded 22 Jan 1850; died 17 Jan 1885, New Zealand. SOURCE: WO120 Volume 69 page 230. INDEX # 5087.
Benjn CLOUT; pension awarded 22 Jan 1850; died 23 Feb 1884, New Zealand. SOURCE: WO120 Volume 69 page 230. INDEX # 5088.
Jno CRUMMY; pension awarded 22 Jan 1850; died 20 Nov 1883, New Zealand. SOURCE: WO120 Volume 69 page 230. INDEX # 5089.
Pat^k FLANDERS; pension awarded 22 Jan 1850. SOURCE: WO120 Volume 69 page 230. INDEX # 5090.
Edmond FLEMMING; pension awarded 22 Jan 1850. SOURCE: WO120 Volume 69 page 230. INDEX # 5091.
Ja^s GOODALL; pension awarded 22 Jan 1850. SOURCE: WO120 Volume 69 page 230. INDEX # 5092.
Ja^s KENNEDY; pension awarded 22 Jan 1850. SOURCE: WO120 Volume 69 page 230. INDEX # 5093.
Bern^d MCDONNELL; pension awarded 22 Jan 1850. SOURCE: WO120 Volume 69 page 230. INDEX # 5094.

58th Regiment of Foot (continued)

Philip OBRIEN; pension awarded 22 Jan 1850; died 20 Mar 1886, New Zealand. SOURCE: WO120 Volume 69 page 230. INDEX # 5095.

Jn⁰ RIELLY; pension awarded 22 Jan 1850; residence - New South Wales, Australia; died in Jan 1852. SOURCE: WO120 Volume 69 page 230. INDEX # 5096.

Jn⁰ SHEAL; pension awarded 22 Jan 1850. SOURCE: WO120 Volume 69 page 230. INDEX # 5097.

Pat^k TRAINOR; pension awarded 22 Jan 1850; died 7 Aug 1871, Omagh. SOURCE: WO120 Volume 69 page 230. INDEX # 5098.

Ja^s TOOLE; pension awarded 22 Jan 1850. SOURCE: WO120 Volume 69 page 231. INDEX # 5099.

Ja^s STAFFORD; pension awarded 26 Feb 1850. SOURCE: WO120 Volume 69 page 231. INDEX # 5100.

Pat^k BROWN; pension awarded 26 Feb 1850. SOURCE: WO120 Volume 69 page 231. INDEX # 5101.

Jn⁰ DUNN; pension awarded 14 Jan 1851; died 21 Jun 1886, New Zealand. SOURCE: WO120 Volume 69 page 231. INDEX # 5102.

Geo^e DODDS; pension awarded 13 May 1851. SOURCE: WO120 Volume 69 page 231. INDEX # 5103.

Wm GRIFFITHS; pension awarded 13 May 1851. SOURCE: WO120 Volume 69 page 231. INDEX # 5104.

Edwd MCKENNA; pension awarded 13 May 1851; died 10 Sep 1872, New Zealand. SOURCE: WO120 Volume 69 page 231. INDEX # 5105.

Lawrence REDMOND; pension awarded 13 May 1851; died 17 Jul 1880, Sydney, Australia. SOURCE: WO120 Volume 69 page 231. INDEX # 5106.

Mich^l DINNIN; pension awarded 25 May 1852; died 11 Dec 1883, New Zealand. SOURCE: WO120 Volume 69 page 231. INDEX # 5107.

Wm BYRNE; pension awarded 25 May 1852; died 26 Aug 1870. SOURCE: WO120 Volume 69 page 231. INDEX # 5108.

Jn⁰ CAVANAGH; pension awarded 25 May 1852. SOURCE: WO120 Volume 69 page 231. INDEX # 5109.

Ferigle GALLAGHER; pension awarded 25 May 1852; died 24 Jan 1883, New Zealand. SOURCE: WO120 Volume 69 page 231. INDEX # 5110.

Ja^s GALLAGHER; pension awarded 25 May 1852. SOURCE: WO120 Volume 69 page 231. INDEX # 5111.

Fran^s GALLAGHER; pension awarded 25 May 1852; died 13 Oct 1878, Londonderry. SOURCE: WO120 Volume 69 page 231. INDEX # 5112.

Wm GIBSON; pension awarded 25 May 1852. SOURCE: WO120 Volume 69 page 231. INDEX # 5113.

And^w JOHNSTONE; pension awarded 25 May 1852. SOURCE: WO120 Volume 69 page 231. INDEX # 5114.

Saml LINDSEY; pension awarded 25 May 1852; residence - New Zealand; died 3 Jun 1852. SOURCE: WO120 Volume 69 page 231. INDEX # 5115.

Ja^s MCILHEANEY; pension awarded 25 May 1852. SOURCE: WO120 Volume 69 page 231. INDEX # 5116.

Jn⁰ MCGINLEY; pension awarded 25 May 1852; died 16 Jun 1880, New Zealand. SOURCE: WO120 Volume 69 page 231. INDEX # 5117.

Robt DOBBIE; pension awarded 19 Jul 1853. SOURCE: WO120 Volume 69 page 231. INDEX # 5118.

Alex^r SMITH; pension awarded 19 Jul 1853; died 26 Oct 1873, Auckland, New Zealand. SOURCE: WO120 Volume 69 page 231. INDEX # 5119.

Ja^s DEVATT; pension awarded 19 Jul 1853; residence - New South Wales, Australia. SOURCE: WO120 Volume 69 page 231. INDEX # 5120.

Jn⁰ MCMAHON; pension awarded 19 Jul 1853. SOURCE: WO120 Volume 69 page 231. INDEX # 5121.

Denis SCULLEN; pension awarded 19 Jul 1853; died 26 Sep 1886, New Zealand. SOURCE: WO120 Volume 69 page 231. INDEX # 5122.

Jn⁰ SMITH; pension awarded 19 Jul 1853. SOURCE: WO120 Volume 69 page 231. INDEX # 5123.

Ge⁰ SELLORS; pension awarded 13 Jun 1854; died 12 Aug 1864, Western Australia, Australia. SOURCE: WO120 Volume 69 page 231. INDEX # 5124.

Pat^k GORMAN; pension awarded 13 Jun 1854. SOURCE: WO120 Volume 69 page 231. INDEX # 5125.

Fra^s MCMAHON; pension awarded 13 Jun 1854; died 27 Dec 1883, New Zealand. SOURCE: WO120 Volume 69 page 231. INDEX # 5126.

Jn⁰ MIDDLETON; pension awarded 13 Jun 1854. SOURCE: WO120 Volume 69 page 231. INDEX # 5127.

Jn⁰ MORTON; pension awarded 13 Jun 1854; died 29 Apr 1887, Belfast. SOURCE: WO120 Volume 69 page 231. INDEX # 5128.

WO120 VOLUME 69

58th Regiment of Foot (continued)

Pat^k MULLIN; pension awarded 13 Jun 1854; died 2 Jun 1885, New Zealand. SOURCE: WO120 Volume 69 page 231. INDEX # 5129.

Benjn SHEPPARD; pension awarded 13 Jun 1854. SOURCE: WO120 Volume 69 page 231. INDEX # 5130.

Jno CAFFRY; pension awarded 13 Jun 1854; died 6 May 1864, New Zealand. SOURCE: WO120 Volume 69 page 231. INDEX # 5131.

Ja^s NAUGHTON; pension awarded 14 Nov 1854; died 18 Mar 1870. SOURCE: WO120 Volume 69 page 231. INDEX # 5132.

Mich^l KETTLE; pension awarded 14 Nov 1854. SOURCE: WO120 Volume 69 page 231. INDEX # 5133.

George GALLAGHER; pension awarded 8 May 1855; died 4 Jun 1879, New Zealand. SOURCE: WO120 Volume 69 page 231. INDEX # 5134.

William MCLOUGHLIN; pension awarded 8 May 1855. SOURCE: WO120 Volume 69 page 231. INDEX # 5135.

Patrick MCMAHON; pension awarded 8 May 1855. SOURCE: WO120 Volume 69 page 231. INDEX # 5136.

Patrick SULLIVAN; pension awarded 8 May 1855. SOURCE: WO120 Volume 69 page 231. INDEX # 5137.

Jeremiah CASEY; pension awarded 1 Jan 1856. SOURCE: WO120 Volume 69 page 231. INDEX # 5138.

William HARRAD; pension awarded 1 Jan 1856. SOURCE: WO120 Volume 69 page 232. INDEX # 5139.

John BELLENGER; pension awarded 16 Dec 1856. SOURCE: WO120 Volume 69 page 232. INDEX # 5140.

59th Regiment of Foot

Ja^s DYKES; pension awarded 30 May 1827; residence - Hobart Town, Australia. SOURCE: WO120 Volume 69 page 233. INDEX # 5141.

Jno LINGARD; pension awarded 7 Sep 1814; residence - New Zealand. SOURCE: WO120 Volume 69 page 233. INDEX # 5142.

Ja^s MELERICK; pension awarded 13 Nov 1839; residence - Montreal, Quebec, Canada. SOURCE: WO120 Volume 69 page 233. INDEX # 5143.

Neil MURRAY; pension awarded 30 May 1810; residence - Toronto, Ontario, Canada; died 11 May 1861. SOURCE: WO120 Volume 69 page 233. INDEX # 5144.

Jno MCKEE; pension awarded 11 Aug 1838; residence - New South Wales, Australia. SOURCE: WO120 Volume 69 page 233. INDEX # 5145.

Ed^{wd} PETTICK; pension awarded 16 Sep 1814; residence - Toronto, Ontario, Canada; died 11 Nov 1853. SOURCE: WO120 Volume 69 page 233. INDEX # 5146.

Ed^{wd} PETTRICK; pension awarded 16 Sep 1814; residence - Toronto, Ontario, Canada; died 11 Nov 1853. SOURCE: WO120 Volume 69 page 233. INDEX # 5147.

Jer^h THOMAS; pension awarded 21 Aug 1817; residence - Charlottetown, Prince Edward Island, Canada; died 21 Feb 1873, Halifax, Nova Scotia, Canada. SOURCE: WO120 Volume 69 page 233. INDEX # 5148.

Chas GREENWALZ; pension awarded 30 May 1827; residence - Bengal, India; died in 1852. SOURCE: WO120 Volume 69 page 233. INDEX # 5149.

John HOSEA; pension awarded ; residence - Montreal, Quebec, Canada; died 25 Nov 1849. SOURCE: WO120 Volume 69 page 233. INDEX # 5150.

George BEATTY; pension awarded 16 Sep 1829; residence - Coteau du Lac, Quebec, Canada; died 30 Aug 1849. SOURCE: WO120 Volume 69 page 233. INDEX # 5151.

Wm FINNIGAN; pension awarded 13 Jan 1830; residence - Bengal, India; died 20 Aug 1849. SOURCE: WO120 Volume 69 page 233. INDEX # 5152.

Jno BURNIE; pension awarded 21 Aug 1817; residence - Toronto, Ontario, Canada; died 10 Jan 1856. SOURCE: WO120 Volume 69 page 233. INDEX # 5153.

Jno BUTCHER; pension awarded 12 Dec 1842; residence - Ionian Isles; died 14 Aug 1888, Southampton. SOURCE: WO120 Volume 69 page 233. INDEX # 5154.

Jno WILLIS; pension awarded 16 Aug 1814; residence - Perth, Ontario, Canada; died 11 Mar 1856. SOURCE: WO120 Volume 69 page 233. INDEX # 5155.

BRITISH ARMY PENSIONERS ABROAD

59th Regiment of Foot (continued)

Jn⁰ TWEEDALE; pension awarded 13 Jan 1830; residence - Calcutta, India. SOURCE: WO120 Volume 69 page 233. INDEX # 5156.

Jn⁰ BYRNE; pension awarded 22 Jul 1842; residence - Demerara. SOURCE: WO120 Volume 69 page 233. INDEX # 5157.

Aug^s BRENNAN; pension awarded 11 Oct 1816; residence - Colombo, Ceylon. SOURCE: WO120 Volume 69 page 233. INDEX # 5158.

Thos FAY; pension awarded 30 May 1827; residence - Canada. SOURCE: WO120 Volume 69 page 233. INDEX # 5159.

60th Regiment of Foot

Gotlieb SCHMIDT; pension awarded 8 Aug 1827; residence - Halifax, Nova Scotia, Canada. SOURCE: WO120 Volume 69 page 236. INDEX # 5160.

Jos^h LEBRE; pension awarded 26 Nov 1824; residence - Quebec, Quebec, Canada. SOURCE: WO120 Volume 69 page 236. INDEX # 5161.

Peter PRETTIG; pension awarded 12 Aug 1840; residence - Bytown, Ontario, Canada. SOURCE: WO120 Volume 69 page 236. INDEX # 5162.

Chas SCHWEITZER; pension awarded 12 Aug 1840; residence - Richmond, Ontario, Canada. SOURCE: WO120 Volume 69 page 236. INDEX # 5163.

Adam SCHOP; pension awarded 11 Feb 1826; residence - Halifax, Nova Scotia, Canada. SOURCE: WO120 Volume 69 page 236. INDEX # 5164.

Val^e DELASERAS; pension awarded 12 Sep 1821; residence - Richmond, Ontario, Canada, died 18 Jul 1856. SOURCE: WO120 Volume 69 page 236. INDEX # 5165.

Chas CRAWFORD; pension awarded 25 Apr 1827; residence - New South Wales, Australia. SOURCE: WO120 Volume 69 page 236. INDEX # 5166.

Ignace MARTZIAN; pension awarded 12 Sep 1821; residence - Sydney. SOURCE: WO120 Volume 69 page 236. INDEX # 5167.

Danl BUSHMAN; pension awarded 15 Dec 1819; residence - Cape of Good Hope, South Africa; died 20 Sep 1855. SOURCE: WO120 Volume 69 page 236. INDEX # 5168.

Peter NORDBECK; pension awarded 7 Feb 1822; residence - Halifax, Nova Scotia, Canada. SOURCE: WO120 Volume 69 page 236. INDEX # 5169.

Ant^y GALARIDI; pension awarded 24 Nov 1824; residence - Quebec, Quebec, Canada. SOURCE: WO120 Volume 69 page 236. INDEX # 5170.

Guisippe MOLINARY; pension awarded 2 Feb 1825; residence - Malta. SOURCE: WO120 Volume 69 page 236. INDEX # 5171.

Ignatius SCHALECK; pension awarded 29 Jul 1819; residence - Cape of Good Hope, South Africa; died 7 Sep 1848. SOURCE: WO120 Volume 69 page 236. INDEX # 5172.

Phi^p SCHUTTLESKOPF; pension awarded 24 Nov 1824; residence - Quebec, Quebec, Canada; died in Feb 1848. SOURCE: WO120 Volume 69 page 236. INDEX # 5173.

Jn⁰ RANSCH; pension awarded 22 Dec 1824; residence - Halifax, Nova Scotia, Canada. SOURCE: WO120 Volume 69 page 236. INDEX # 5174.

And^w HENDRICKSON; pension awarded 23 Jul 1828; residence - Huntingdon, Quebec, Canada. SOURCE: WO120 Volume 69 page 236. INDEX # 5175.

Peter SCHOUTEN; pension awarded 24 Nov 1824; residence - Quebec, Quebec, Canada. SOURCE: WO120 Volume 69 page 236. INDEX # 5176.

John MILLER; pension awarded 11 Aug 1828; residence - Toronto, Ontario, Canada. SOURCE: WO120 Volume 69 page 236. INDEX # 5177.

Jacob JASCOITZ; pension awarded 4 Feb 1818; residence - Jamaica. SOURCE: WO120 Volume 69 page 236. INDEX # 5178.

Fargus MOORE; pension awarded 9 May 1823; residence - Perth, Ontario, Canada; died 4 Apr 1863, Toronto, Ontario, Canada. SOURCE: WO120 Volume 69 page 236. INDEX # 5179.

Peter VANANTWIRPEN; pension awarded 24 Nov 1824; residence - Quebec, Quebec, Canada. SOURCE: WO120 Volume 69 page 237. INDEX # 5180.

WO120 VOLUME 69

60th Regiment of Foot (continued)

Thos COURTNEY; pension awarded 26 Aug 1845; residence - Toronto, Ontario, Canada; died 4 Jun 1857. SOURCE: WO120 Volume 69 page 237. INDEX # 5181.

Lewis FARLARDE; pension awarded 10 Nov 1830; residence - Quebec, Quebec, Canada. SOURCE: WO120 Volume 69 page 236. INDEX # 5182.

Alexis LAPOINTE; pension awarded 9 Aug 1842; residence - St. Jean, Quebec, Canada. SOURCE: WO120 Volume 69 page 237. INDEX # 5183.

Patk MCNESPY; pension awarded 10 Nov 1830; residence - St. Johns. SOURCE: WO120 Volume 69 page 237. INDEX # 5184.

Jno COOGAN; pension awarded 26 Aug 1845; residence - Quebec, Quebec, Canada. SOURCE: WO120 Volume 69 page 237. INDEX # 5185.

Fras HENRION; pension awarded 7 Dec 1820; residence - Halifax, Nova Scotia, Canada; died 21 Jan 1847. SOURCE: WO120 Volume 69 page 237. INDEX # 5186.

Jno COUSINS; pension awarded 21 Aug 1822; residence - Montreal, Quebec, Canada; died 11 Feb 1867. SOURCE: WO120 Volume 69 page 237. INDEX # 5187.

Anty SUNNEVILLE; pension awarded 15 Dec 1802; residence - Quebec, Quebec, Canada. SOURCE: WO120 Volume 69 page 237. INDEX # 5188.

Thos JAMESON; pension awarded 14 Jun 1837; residence - Halifax, Nova Scotia, Canada; died 12 Oct 1873, Halifax, Nova Scotia, Canada. SOURCE: WO120 Volume 69 page 237. INDEX # 5189.

Thos CALDWELL; pension awarded 28 Nov 1815; residence - St. Johns; died 14 May 1856. SOURCE: WO120 Volume 69 page 237. INDEX # 5190.

Derik FALANT; pension awarded 15 Mar 1826; residence - Demerara; died 16 Jan 1853. SOURCE: WO120 Volume 69 page 237. INDEX # 5191.

Thos ENGLISH; pension awarded 22 Sep 1846; residence - Toronto, Ontario, Canada; died in 1847. SOURCE: WO120 Volume 69 page 237. INDEX # 5192.

Heny HASPLINK; pension awarded 22 Sep 1846; residence - St. Jean, Quebec, Canada; died 25 Sep 1847. SOURCE: WO120 Volume 69 page 237. INDEX # 5193.

Geo HAMMILL; pension awarded 22 Dec 1846; died 6 May 1875, London, Ontario, Canada. SOURCE: WO120 Volume 69 page 237. INDEX # 5194.

Isaac PLUMB; pension awarded 8 Jun 1847. SOURCE: WO120 Volume 69 page 237. INDEX # 5195.

Saml WATSON; pension awarded 8 Jun 1847. SOURCE: WO120 Volume 69 page 237. INDEX # 5196.

Michl BOLGER; pension awarded 8 Jun 1847. SOURCE: WO120 Volume 69 page 237. INDEX # 5197.

Wm FEST; pension awarded 8 Jun 1847. SOURCE: WO120 Volume 69 page 237. INDEX # 5198.

Michl FILLACKY; pension awarded 8 Jun 1847. SOURCE: WO120 Volume 69 page 237. INDEX # 5199.

Heny LUCAS; pension awarded 8 Jun 1847; died 7 Dec 1878, New Brunswick, Canada. SOURCE: WO120 Volume 69 page 237. INDEX # 5200.

Richd STEWART; pension awarded 8 Jun 1847; died 26 Apr 1876, Toronto, Ontario, Canada. SOURCE: WO120 Volume 69 page 237. INDEX # 5201.

Robt JACOBS; pension awarded 28 Sep 1847; died 19 Aug 1881, Nova Scotia, Canada. SOURCE: WO120 Volume 69 page 237. INDEX # 5202.

Patk LEAHENY; pension awarded 25 Jan 1848; residence - London, Ontario, Canada; died 23 Nov 1853. SOURCE: WO120 Volume 69 page 237. INDEX # 5203.

Thos TREGEAR; pension awarded 26 Jun 1849; died 18 Jun 1884, Taunton. SOURCE: WO120 Volume 69 page 237. INDEX # 5204.

Patk MCCULLEN; pension awarded 9 Apr 1850. SOURCE: WO120 Volume 69 page 237. INDEX # 5205.

Thos BURNS; pension awarded 14 May 1850. SOURCE: WO120 Volume 69 page 237. INDEX # 5206.

Wm BISSET; pension awarded 13 Sep 1853. SOURCE: WO120 Volume 69 page 237. INDEX # 5207.

Jno RIDGEWAY; pension awarded 13 Sep 1853. SOURCE: WO120 Volume 69 page 237. INDEX # 5208.

Robert BETTISON; pension awarded 11 Mar 1856. SOURCE: WO120 Volume 69 page 237. INDEX # 5209.

Charles WELLER; pension awarded 9 Jun 1857. SOURCE: WO120 Volume 69 page 237. INDEX # 5210.

Alexander LECKIE; pension awarded 18 Aug 1857. SOURCE: WO120 Volume 69 page 237. INDEX # 5211.

61st Regiment of Foot

Jn⁰ ARMSTRONG; pension awarded 10 Aug 1810; residence - Quebec, Quebec, Canada. SOURCE: WO120 Volume 69 page 240. INDEX # 5212.

Jn⁰ GIBBINS; pension awarded 16 Dec 1825; residence - Cape of Good Hope, South Africa. SOURCE: WO120 Volume 69 page 240. INDEX # 5213.

Jn⁰ HOGAN; pension awarded 28 Dec 1814; residence - Montreal, Quebec, Canada. SOURCE: WO120 Volume 69 page 240. INDEX # 5214.

Thos MCGOFF; pension awarded 28 Dec 1814; residence - Toronto, Ontario, Canada. SOURCE: WO120 Volume 69 page 240. INDEX # 5215.

Don^d MCDONALD; pension awarded 22 Apr 1840; residence - Ceylon. SOURCE: WO120 Volume 69 page 240. INDEX # 5216.

Mich^l MCGRATH; pension awarded 13 Feb 1839; residence - Bermuda; died 10 Jul 1870 Cork. SOURCE: WO120 Volume 69 page 240. INDEX # 5217.

Dav^d RUSSELL; pension awarded 6 Aug 1844; residence - Amherstburg, Ontario, Canada. SOURCE: WO120 Volume 69 page 240. INDEX # 5218.

Tim^y OBRIEN; pension awarded 23 Sep 1840; residence - New South Wales, Australia; died 29 Mar 1855. SOURCE: WO120 Volume 69 page 240. INDEX # 5219.

Geo^e WILSON; pension awarded 10 Sep 1834; residence - Cape of Good Hope, South Africa; died 19 Jun 1853. SOURCE: WO120 Volume 69 page 240. INDEX # 5220.

Geo^e WARREN; pension awarded 25 Jan 1848; residence - Meerut, India; died 21 Oct 1857. SOURCE: WO120 Volume 69 page 240. INDEX # 5221.

Mathew TURNER; pension awarded 11 Mar 1856. SOURCE: WO120 Volume 69 page 240. INDEX # 5222.

62nd Regiment of Foot

Jn⁰ MCCARNEY; pension awarded 13 Oct 1830; residence - Halifax, Nova Scotia, Canada; died 18 Feb 1853. SOURCE: WO120 Volume 69 page 243. INDEX # 5223.

Ja^s MCLOUGLAN; pension awarded 1 Feb 1826; residence - Halifax, Nova Scotia, Canada. SOURCE: WO120 Volume 69 page 243. INDEX # 5224.

Philip SIMMONDS; pension awarded 3 Sep 1830; residence - Halifax, Nova Scotia, Canada. SOURCE: WO120 Volume 69 page 243. INDEX # 5225.

Ja^s EMMINGS; pension awarded 23 Sep 1840; residence - Madras, India; died 12 Jul 1852. SOURCE: WO120 Volume 69 page 243. INDEX # 5226.

Jos^h ALLEN; pension awarded 16 Jun 1824; residence - Launceston, Australia. SOURCE: WO120 Volume 69 page 243. INDEX # 5227.

Wm WILLIAMS; pension awarded 26 Jun 1832; residence - Cape of Good Hope, South Africa. SOURCE: WO120 Volume 69 page 243. INDEX # 5228.

Ja^s THOMPSON; pension awarded 20 Nov 1839; residence - Madras, India; died 26 Apr 1847. SOURCE: WO120 Volume 69 page 243. INDEX # 5229.

Ja^s CARTER; pension awarded 20 Nov 1839; residence - Madras, India; died 7 Oct 1848. SOURCE: WO120 Volume 69 page 243. INDEX # 5230.

Jn⁰ CREIGHTON; pension awarded 10 Jul 1839; residence - Montreal, Quebec, Canada. SOURCE: WO120 Volume 69 page 243. INDEX # 5231.

Simon DRING; pension awarded 23 Feb 1847; residence - Poonamalee, India; died 1 Apr 1873, Madras, India. SOURCE: WO120 Volume 69 page 243. INDEX # 5232.

John SLANE; pension awarded 23 Feb 1847; residence - Meerut, India; died 8 Oct 1854. SOURCE: WO120 Volume 69 page 243. INDEX # 5233.

Geo^e THAIN; pension awarded 23 Feb 1847; residence - Poonamalee, India; died 16 Oct 1850. SOURCE: WO120 Volume 69 page 243. INDEX # 5234.

63rd Regiment of Foot

Chas STEWART; pension awarded 19 Sep 1816; residence - Bytown, Ontario, Canada. SOURCE: WO120 Volume 69 page 246. INDEX # 5235.

63rd Regiment of Foot (continued)

Ja^s HALL; pension awarded 5 Aug 1829; residence - Kingston, Ontario, Canada. SOURCE: WO120 Volume 69 page 246. INDEX # 5236.

Willm DAWSON; pension awarded 10 Sep 1834; residence - Van Diemen's Land, Australia. SOURCE: WO120 Volume 69 page 246. INDEX # 5237.

Geo^e GANT; pension awarded 10 Sep 1834; residence - Van Diemen's Land, Australia; died 2 Jan 1855. SOURCE: WO120 Volume 69 page 246. INDEX # 5238.

Jno MITCHELL; pension awarded 26 Jun 1839; residence - Sydney. SOURCE: WO120 Volume 69 page 246. INDEX # 5239.

Ja^s BLACK; pension awarded 23 Jul 1828; residence - Montreal, Quebec, Canada. SOURCE: WO120 Volume 69 page 246. INDEX # 5240.

Den^s BOLAND; pension awarded 20 Nov 1839; residence - Madras, India. SOURCE: WO120 Volume 69 page 246. INDEX # 5241.

Wm ANTINGHAM; pension awarded 14 Sep 1836; residence - Hobart Town, Australia. SOURCE: WO120 Volume 69 page 246. INDEX # 5242.

H^y STANLEY; pension awarded 23 Oct 1838; residence - Madras, India; died 28 Feb 1851. SOURCE: WO120 Volume 69 page 246. INDEX # 5243.

Edwd LAWRENCE; pension awarded 14 Sep 1836; residence - Hobart Town, Australia. SOURCE: WO120 Volume 69 page 246. INDEX # 5244.

Stepⁿ WEST; pension awarded 5 Jul 1820; residence - Amherstburg, Ontario, Canada. SOURCE: WO120 Volume 69 page 246. INDEX # 5245.

Saml SMITH; pension awarded 9 Jan 1834; residence - Van Diemen's Land, Australia. SOURCE: WO120 Volume 69 page 246. INDEX # 5246.

Hugh ALLEN; pension awarded 13 Oct 1841; residence - Madras, India. SOURCE: WO120 Volume 69 page 246. INDEX # 5247.

Rich^d LEE; pension awarded 3 Mar 1806; residence - Quebec, Quebec, Canada. SOURCE: WO120 Volume 69 page 246. INDEX # 5248.

Ja^s SKINE; pension awarded 10 Sep 1834; residence - Hobart Town, Australia; died 2 May 1875. SOURCE: WO120 Volume 69 page 246. INDEX # 5249.

Abr^m HORSHAM; pension awarded 28 Jul 1841; residence - Hobart Town, Australia; died 5 Nov 1850. SOURCE: WO120 Volume 69 page 246. INDEX # 5250.

John LANGFORD; pension awarded 8 Jul 1845; residence - Bellary, India; died 19 Jan 1870, Birmingham. SOURCE: WO120 Volume 69 page 246. INDEX # 5251.

Ja^s FULTON; pension awarded 16 Jun 1835; residence - New London. SOURCE: WO120 Volume 69 page 246. INDEX # 5252.

Jos^h COLLIS; pension awarded 23 Jun 1846; residence - Bellary, India; died 9 Apr 1850. SOURCE: WO120 Volume 69 page 246. INDEX # 5253.

Peter PEGGS; pension awarded ; residence - Hamburgh; died 23 Jul 1857, Ipswich. SOURCE: WO120 Volume 69 page 246. INDEX # 5254.

Moses HAYS; pension awarded 25 May 1847; residence - Madras, India; died 9 Nov 1852. SOURCE: WO120 Volume 69 page 246. INDEX # 5255.

Wm JACKSON; pension awarded 25 May 1847. SOURCE: WO120 Volume 69 page 246. INDEX # 5256.

Jno KEELEY; pension awarded 25 May 1847. SOURCE: WO120 Volume 69 page 246. INDEX # 5257.

Wm PAGE; pension awarded 25 May 1847. SOURCE: WO120 Volume 69 page 246. INDEX # 5258.

Jeremiah QUINTON; pension awarded 25 May 1847; residence - Madras, India; died 24 Apr 1853. SOURCE: WO120 Volume 69 page 246. INDEX # 5259.

64th Regiment of Foot

Robt GAMBLE; pension awarded 14 Jun 1837; residence - Canada. SOURCE: WO120 Volume 69 page 249. INDEX # 5260.

Henry LANG; pension awarded 19 Dec 1816; residence - St. Johns; died in 1847. SOURCE: WO120 Volume 69 page 249. INDEX # 5261.

BRITISH ARMY PENSIONERS ABROAD

64th Regiment of Foot (continued)

Edwd MALONE; pension awarded 8 Aug 1827; residence - Montreal, Quebec, Canada; died 26 Jul 1856. SOURCE: WO120 Volume 69 page 249. INDEX # 5262.

Jno MCKERNON; pension awarded 19 Dec 1826; residence - Toronto, Ontario, Canada; died 9 Mar 1853. SOURCE: WO120 Volume 69 page 249. INDEX # 5263.

Robt CLARKE; pension awarded 25 Sep 1817; residence - Montreal, Quebec, Canada; died 28 Jan 1848. SOURCE: WO120 Volume 69 page 249. INDEX # 5264.

Saml MITCHELL; pension awarded 22 Jul 1845; residence - Prince Edward Island, Canada. SOURCE: WO120 Volume 69 page 249. INDEX # 5265.

Chas GRUBB; pension awarded 27 Jun 1838; residence - Hobart Town, Australia; died 27 Sep 1873, Tasmania, Australia. SOURCE: WO120 Volume 69 page 249. INDEX # 5266.

Geo^e BENNETT; pension awarded 10 Aug 1836; residence - Jamaica. SOURCE: WO120 Volume 69 page 249. INDEX # 5267.

Major BLAKEY; pension awarded 18 Mar 1856; died 3 Nov 1864, Bombay, India. SOURCE: WO120 Volume 69 page 249. INDEX # 5268.

Lawrence MURRY; pension awarded 18 Mar 1856. SOURCE: WO120 Volume 69 page 249. INDEX # 5269.

William GEORGE; pension awarded 24 Mar 1857. SOURCE: WO120 Volume 69 page 249. INDEX # 5270.

65th Regiment of Foot

Geo^e BURROWS; pension awarded 18 Mar 1838; residence - Toronto, Ontario, Canada; died 22 Jul 1862, Toronto, Ontario, Canada. SOURCE: WO120 Volume 69 page 252. INDEX # 5271.

Dav^d MCKEE; pension awarded 28 Nov 1843; residence - Kingston, Ontario, Canada. SOURCE: WO120 Volume 69 page 252. INDEX # 5272.

Mich^l KERNAN; pension awarded 9 Sep 1840; residence - Montreal, Quebec, Canada. SOURCE: WO120 Volume 69 page 252. INDEX # 5273.

Jer^h BOWLES; pension awarded 27 Sep 1837; residence - New South Wales, Australia. SOURCE: WO120 Volume 69 page 252. INDEX # 5274.

Ja^s BRYCE; pension awarded 16 Jul 1828; residence - South Australia, Australia. SOURCE: WO120 Volume 69 page 252. INDEX # 5275.

Temple MCBETH; pension awarded 18 Mar 1818; residence - Toronto, Ontario, Canada; died 3 Aug 1863. SOURCE: WO120 Volume 69 page 252. INDEX # 5276.

Thos VALLENSNE; pension awarded 25 Sep 1822; residence - Bombay, India; died 16 Jul 1851. SOURCE: WO120 Volume 69 page 252. INDEX # 5277.

Jos^h BLORE; pension awarded 2 Feb 1820; residence - Sydney. SOURCE: WO120 Volume 69 page 252. INDEX # 5278.

John CARSON; pension awarded 12 Aug 1845; residence - Canada; died 10 Nov 1883, Halifax, Nova Scotia, Canada. SOURCE: WO120 Volume 69 page 252. INDEX # 5279.

Benjⁿ LEWIS; pension awarded 8 Feb 1848; died 20 Aug 1865, Auckland, New Zealand. SOURCE: WO120 Volume 69 page 252. INDEX # 5280.

Geo^e HARRIS; pension awarded 23 May 1848; died 6 Jul 1880, New Zealand. SOURCE: WO120 Volume 69 page 252. INDEX # 5281.

Hen^y LYNCH; pension awarded 26 Dec 1848. SOURCE: WO120 Volume 69 page 252. INDEX # 5282.

Thos MCDONOUGH; pension awarded 26 Dec 1848. SOURCE: WO120 Volume 69 page 252. INDEX # 5283.

Mich^l ENNIS; pension awarded 26 Dec 1848; died 18 Mar 1877, Dublin. SOURCE: WO120 Volume 69 page 252. INDEX # 5284.

Jno ALLSOP; pension awarded 12 Feb 1850; died 17 May 1859, South London, England. SOURCE: WO120 Volume 69 page 252. INDEX # 5285.

Wm ABBOTT; pension awarded 12 Feb 1850. SOURCE: WO120 Volume 69 page 252. INDEX # 5286.

Fra^s BURNS; pension awarded 12 Feb 1850. SOURCE: WO120 Volume 69 page 252. INDEX # 5287.

Saml DOOLE; pension awarded 12 Feb 1850. SOURCE: WO120 Volume 69 page 252. INDEX # 5288.

Ja^s GILLIGAN; pension awarded 12 Feb 1850; died 10 Oct 1873, Auckland, New Zealand. SOURCE: WO120 Volume 69 page 252. INDEX # 5289.

65th Regiment of Foot (continued)

Harrison GREEN; pension awarded 12 Feb 1850; died New Zealand. SOURCE: WO120 Volume 69 page 252. INDEX # 5290.

Wm SEXTON; pension awarded 12 Feb 1850. SOURCE: WO120 Volume 69 page 253. INDEX # 5291.

Geo^e GRAY; pension awarded 8 Apr 1851; died in Jun 1870. SOURCE: WO120 Volume 69 page 253. INDEX # 5292.

Thos FRANSHAM; pension awarded 13 May 1851. SOURCE: WO120 Volume 69 page 253. INDEX # 5293.

Jno BROWN; pension awarded 13 May 1851. SOURCE: WO120 Volume 69 page 253. INDEX # 5294.

Chas CARTY; pension awarded 2 Sep 1851. SOURCE: WO120 Volume 69 page 253. INDEX # 5295.

Jno PALMER; pension awarded 9 Sep 1851; died 19 Jun 1884, Sydney. SOURCE: WO120 Volume 69 page 253. INDEX # 5296.

Jer^h BURDETT; pension awarded 28 Dec 1852; died 28 Jul 1853. SOURCE: WO120 Volume 69 page 253. INDEX # 5297.

Wm BENNARD; pension awarded 28 Dec 1852; died 9 Jun 1877, New Zealand. SOURCE: WO120 Volume 69 page 253. INDEX # 5298.

Jno DESMOND; pension awarded 28 Dec 1852. SOURCE: WO120 Volume 69 page 253. INDEX # 5299.

Mich^l GREEN; pension awarded 28 Dec 1852; residence - Auckland, New Zealand; died 28 Dec 1852. SOURCE: WO120 Volume 69 page 253. INDEX # 5300.

David HOGAN; pension awarded 28 Dec 1852; died 26 Mar 1873, Auckland, New Zealand. SOURCE: WO120 Volume 69 page 253. INDEX # 5301.

Jno MCNAMARA; pension awarded 28 Dec 1852. SOURCE: WO120 Volume 69 page 253. INDEX # 5302.

Jno BALMER; pension awarded 13 Sep 1853; died 7 Dec 1873, Auckland, New Zealand. SOURCE: WO120 Volume 69 page 253. INDEX # 5303.

Pat^k BRAHANY; pension awarded 13 Sep 1853. SOURCE: WO120 Volume 69 page 253. INDEX # 5304.

Jer^h HURLEY; pension awarded 13 Sep 1853. SOURCE: WO120 Volume 69 page 253. INDEX # 5305.

Hugh MCCRUM; pension awarded 13 Sep 1853. SOURCE: WO120 Volume 69 page 253. INDEX # 5306.

Ja^s FILLIS; pension awarded 11 Jul 1854. SOURCE: WO120 Volume 69 page 253. INDEX # 5307.

Ja^s HAMMILL; pension awarded 11 Jul 1854. SOURCE: WO120 Volume 69 page 253. INDEX # 5308.

Hen^y HUGHES; pension awarded 26 Dec 1854. SOURCE: WO120 Volume 69 page 253. INDEX # 5309.

Jno MEE; pension awarded 26 Dec 1854. SOURCE: WO120 Volume 69 page 253. INDEX # 5310.

Wm Jno PHILLIPS; pension awarded 26 Dec 1854. SOURCE: WO120 Volume 69 page 253. INDEX # 5311.

Edm^d SPENCER; pension awarded 26 Dec 1854; died 9 Jul 1886, New Zealand. SOURCE: WO120 Volume 69 page 253. INDEX # 5312.

Geo^e WILLIS; pension awarded 26 Dec 1854. SOURCE: WO120 Volume 69 page 253. INDEX # 5313.

Charles THOMPSON; pension awarded 9 Oct 1855. SOURCE: WO120 Volume 69 page 253. INDEX # 5314.

Joseph WEIGHT; pension awarded 9 Oct 1855. SOURCE: WO120 Volume 69 page 253. INDEX # 5315.

Andrew TYNAN; pension awarded 31 Mar 1857. SOURCE: WO120 Volume 69 page 253. INDEX # 5316.

66th Regiment of Foot

Const^e RIELLY; pension awarded 9 Nov 1836; residence - Toronto, Ontario, Canada. SOURCE: WO120 Volume 69 page 255. INDEX # 5317.

Robt TACKLE; pension awarded 8 Nov 1810; residence - South Australia, Australia. SOURCE: WO120 Volume 69 page 255. INDEX # 5318.

Ja^s ANDERTON; pension awarded 9 Jan 1833; residence - Kingston, Ontario, Canada; died 18 Dec 1873, Toronto, Ontario, Canada. SOURCE: WO120 Volume 69 page 255. INDEX # 5319.

Mich^l BARRY; pension awarded 11 Nov 1835; residence - Kingston, Ontario, Canada; died 19 Oct 1848. SOURCE: WO120 Volume 69 page 255. INDEX # 5320.

Geo^e MCDONALD; pension awarded 11 Nov 1835; residence - Quebec, Quebec, Canada. SOURCE: WO120 Volume 69 page 255. INDEX # 5321.

Jno COSTELLO; pension awarded 14 Dec 1836; residence - Toronto, Ontario, Canada; died 21 Aug 1855. SOURCE: WO120 Volume 69 page 255. INDEX # 5322.

66th Regiment of Foot (continued)

Chas BARBER; pension awarded 26 Dec 1838; residence - Quebec, Quebec, Canada; died 24 Jul 1849. SOURCE: WO120 Volume 69 page 255. INDEX # 5323.

Ja^s^ MULLAMY; pension awarded 10 Jul 1833; residence - Quebec, Quebec, Canada. SOURCE: WO120 Volume 69 page 255. INDEX # 5324.

Ja^s^ SMITH; pension awarded 12 Nov 1834; residence - Toronto, Ontario, Canada; died in Mar 1850. SOURCE: WO120 Volume 69 page 255. INDEX # 5325.

Mich^l^ HEALY; pension awarded 22 Nov 1827; residence - Toronto, Ontario, Canada; died 3 Oct 1860, Toronto, Ontario, Canada. SOURCE: WO120 Volume 69 page 255. INDEX # 5326.

George HASLETT; pension awarded 8 Jul 1840; residence - Quebec, Quebec, Canada. SOURCE: WO120 Volume 69 page 255. INDEX # 5327.

Pat^k^ LACE; pension awarded 14 Oct 1835; residence - Toronto, Ontario, Canada. SOURCE: WO120 Volume 69 page 255. INDEX # 5328.

John LOVETT; pension awarded 9 Dec 1840; residence - Montreal, Quebec, Canada. SOURCE: WO120 Volume 69 page 255. INDEX # 5329.

Wm CRAWFORD; pension awarded 26 Aug 1819; residence - Niagara, Ontario, Canada; died 18 Jul 1845. SOURCE: WO120 Volume 69 page 255. INDEX # 5330.

Wm HALL; pension awarded 18 Jul 1827; residence - Bytown, Ontario, Canada; died 16 Feb 1858. SOURCE: WO120 Volume 69 page 255. INDEX # 5331.

Pat^k^ C. MULVEY; pension awarded 17 Jan 1827; residence - Saint John, New Brunswick, Canada. SOURCE: WO120 Volume 69 page 255. INDEX # 5332.

Robt KIRBY; pension awarded 13 Sep 1837; residence - Chambly, Quebec, Canada. SOURCE: WO120 Volume 69 page 255. INDEX # 5333.

Mich^l^ WOODS; pension awarded 9 Sep 1840; residence - Quebec, Quebec, Canada. SOURCE: WO120 Volume 69 page 255. INDEX # 5334.

Maur^e^ EARDLEY; pension awarded 14 Sep 1831; residence - Montreal, Quebec, Canada. SOURCE: WO120 Volume 69 page 255. INDEX # 5335.

John GOSS; pension awarded 19 Sep 1816; residence - Toronto, Ontario, Canada; died 30 Jul 1849. SOURCE: WO120 Volume 69 page 255. INDEX # 5336.

H^y^ FRY; pension awarded 7 Jan 1829; residence - Niagara, Ontario, Canada. SOURCE: WO120 Volume 69 page 255. INDEX # 5337.

Thos BROMNLEY; pension awarded 14 Nov 1846; residence - Kingston, Ontario, Canada. SOURCE: WO120 Volume 69 page 255. INDEX # 5338.

Wm JONES; pension awarded 26 Aug 1819; residence - London, Ontario, Canada; died 12 Oct 1868. SOURCE: WO120 Volume 69 page 255. INDEX # 5339.

John GORDAN; pension awarded 12 Dec 1811; residence - Amherstburg, Ontario, Canada; died 2 Jan 1871, London, Ontario, Canada. SOURCE: WO120 Volume 69 page 255. INDEX # 5340.

Jno DUNN; pension awarded 27 Jul 1852. SOURCE: WO120 Volume 69 page 255. INDEX # 5341.

Jos^h^ KING; pension awarded 27 Jul 1852. SOURCE: WO120 Volume 69 page 255. INDEX # 5342.

Henry LAVERY; pension awarded 27 Jul 1852. SOURCE: WO120 Volume 69 page 255. INDEX # 5343.

Peter OMALLEY; pension awarded 27 Jul 1852. SOURCE: WO120 Volume 69 page 255. INDEX # 5344.

Fra^s^ LACE; pension awarded 19 Jul 1853; died 29 Nov 1883, Toronto, Ontario, Canada. SOURCE: WO120 Volume 69 page 255. INDEX # 5345.

Jos^h^ BANKS; pension awarded 19 Jul 1853. SOURCE: WO120 Volume 69 page 255. INDEX # 5346.

Jos^h^ BROOKS; pension awarded 12 Sep 1854. SOURCE: WO120 Volume 69 page 255. INDEX # 5347.

Pat^k^ BRIEN; pension awarded 12 Sep 1854. SOURCE: WO120 Volume 69 page 255. INDEX # 5348.

Geo^e^ CUMMINS; pension awarded 12 Sep 1854. SOURCE: WO120 Volume 69 page 255. INDEX # 5349.

Ja^s^ GOODEY; pension awarded 12 Sep 1854. SOURCE: WO120 Volume 69 page 255. INDEX # 5350.

Fra^s^ HIGGINS; pension awarded 12 Sep 1854. SOURCE: WO120 Volume 69 page 255. INDEX # 5351.

Pat^k^ HEALY; pension awarded 12 Sep 1854. SOURCE: WO120 Volume 69 page 255. INDEX # 5352.

Jno LYALL; pension awarded 12 Sep 1854. SOURCE: WO120 Volume 69 page 255. INDEX # 5353.

Jno MARTIN; pension awarded 12 Sep 1854. SOURCE: WO120 Volume 69 page 255. INDEX # 5354.

Jno TAYLOR; pension awarded 12 Sep 1854. SOURCE: WO120 Volume 69 page 255. INDEX # 5355.

WO120 VOLUME 69

66th Regiment of Foot (continued)

Philip WARD; pension awarded 12 Sep 1854. SOURCE: WO120 Volume 69 page 255. INDEX # 5356.
Pat^k ROCK; pension awarded 26 Dec 1854. SOURCE: WO120 Volume 69 page 256. INDEX # 5357.
Henry BRISTER; pension awarded 29 Jul 1856. SOURCE: WO120 Volume 69 page 256. INDEX # 5358.

67th Regiment of Foot

Peter MAHER; pension awarded 14 May 1807; residence - Montreal, Quebec, Canada. SOURCE: WO120 Volume 69 page 258. INDEX # 5359.
Nich^s HEANY; pension awarded 9 Jun 1819; residence - Toronto, Ontario, Canada; died 16 Jul 1867. SOURCE: WO120 Volume 69 page 258. INDEX # 5360.
Mich^l FEENY; pension awarded 23 May 1821; residence - Charlottetown, Prince Edward Island, Canada. SOURCE: WO120 Volume 69 page 258. INDEX # 5361.
Jno OCONNOR; pension awarded 30 May 1827; residence - Quebec, Quebec, Canada. SOURCE: WO120 Volume 69 page 258. INDEX # 5362.
Danl CONNELL; pension awarded 2 Jun 1825; residence - Kingston, Ontario, Canada. SOURCE: WO120 Volume 69 page 258. INDEX # 5363.
Mich^l SHANNON; pension awarded 18 Oct 1820; residence - Toronto, Ontario, Canada; died 1 May 1851. SOURCE: WO120 Volume 69 page 258. INDEX # 5364.
Hugh HAMILTON; pension awarded 4 Aug 1824; residence - Bombay, India. SOURCE: WO120 Volume 69 page 258. INDEX # 5365.
Pat^k RYAN; pension awarded ; residence - Montreal, Quebec, Canada. SOURCE: WO120 Volume 69 page 258. INDEX # 5366.

68th Regiment of Foot

Willm GODFREY; pension awarded 17 Sep 1828; residence - Toronto, Ontario, Canada; died 31 Oct 1864. SOURCE: WO120 Volume 69 page 261. INDEX # 5367.
Jno ODONNELL; pension awarded 8 Sep 1830; residence - Penetanguishene, Ontario, Canada; died 20 Dec 1863, Hamilton, Ontario, Canada. SOURCE: WO120 Volume 69 page 261. INDEX # 5368.
Jos^h TAYLOR; pension awarded 9 May 1823; residence - Kingston, Ontario, Canada; died 23 Jul 1854. SOURCE: WO120 Volume 69 page 261. INDEX # 5369.
Willm JOHNSTON; pension awarded 20 Oct 1823; residence - Amherstburg, Ontario, Canada; died in 1850. SOURCE: WO120 Volume page . INDEX # 5370.
Ja^s COOPER; pension awarded 30 Mar 1825; residence - Prescott, Ontario, Canada. SOURCE: WO120 Volume 69 page 261. INDEX # 5371.
Henry REED; pension awarded 25 Apr 1827; residence - Toronto, Ontario, Canada. SOURCE: WO120 Volume 69 page 261. INDEX # 5372.
Jno BANNON; pension awarded 12 Dec 1803; residence - Toronto, Ontario, Canada; died 7 Aug 1854. SOURCE: WO120 Volume 69 page 261. INDEX # 5373.
Willm WARDE; pension awarded 13 Oct 1830; residence - Bytown, Ontario, Canada. SOURCE: WO120 Volume 69 page 261. INDEX # 5374.
Ja^s THOROGOOD; pension awarded 29 Oct 1828; residence - Kingston, Ontario, Canada. SOURCE: WO120 Volume 69 page 261. INDEX # 5375.
And^w CRAWFORD; pension awarded 13 Apr 1836; residence - Toronto, Ontario, Canada; died 18 Jul 1868. SOURCE: WO120 Volume 69 page 261. INDEX # 5376.
Thos STRUDGEON; pension awarded 14 Oct 1835; residence - London, Ontario, Canada. SOURCE: WO120 Volume 69 page 261. INDEX # 5377.
Matt^w MCNAMARA; pension awarded 12 Jun 1833; residence - Toronto, Ontario, Canada; died 4 Feb 1853. SOURCE: WO120 Volume 69 page 261. INDEX # 5378.
Jno SWEENEY; pension awarded 12 Jun 1833; residence - Toronto, Ontario, Canada; died in Feb 1848. SOURCE: WO120 Volume 69 page 261. INDEX # 5379.

68th Regiment of Foot (continued)

Geo^e STAUNTON; pension awarded 14 Sep 1831; residence - Montreal, Quebec, Canada. SOURCE: WO120 Volume 62 page 261. INDEX # 5380.

Saml BURFIELD; pension awarded 13 Aug 1844; residence - Toronto, Ontario, Canada; died 14 Aug 1853. SOURCE: WO120 Volume 69 page 261. INDEX # 5381.

Fra^s FOLEY; pension awarded 13 Aug 1844; residence - Toronto, Ontario, Canada; died 17 Jul 1871, Toronto, Ontario, Canada. SOURCE: WO120 Volume 69 page 261. INDEX # 5382.

Abr^m PINCKNEY; pension awarded 7 Mar 1827; residence - Quebec, Quebec, Canada. SOURCE: WO120 Volume 69 page 261. INDEX # 5383.

Ja^s BARRYMAN; pension awarded 29 Oct 1828; residence - Quebec, Quebec, Canada. SOURCE: WO120 Volume 69 page 261. INDEX # 5384.

Robt HUNT; pension awarded 10 Jan 1843; residence - Wm Henry, Quebec, Canada. SOURCE: WO120 Volume 69 page 261. INDEX # 5385.

Jer^h DRISCOLL; pension awarded 26 Sep 1843; residence - Toronto, Ontario, Canada; died 21 Nov 1881, Hamilton, Ontario, Canada. SOURCE: WO120 Volume 69 page 261. INDEX # 5386.

Wm HORNBY; pension awarded 13 Aug 1844; residence - Kingston, Ontario, Canada. SOURCE: WO120 Volume 69 page 261. INDEX # 5387.

Pat^k HEALY; pension awarded 12 Jul 1837; residence - Penetanguishene, Ontario, Canada. SOURCE: WO120 Volume 69 page 261. INDEX # 5388.

Ja^s OBRYAN; pension awarded 27 Sep 1842; residence - Bytown, Ontario, Canada. SOURCE: WO120 Volume 69 page 261. INDEX # 5389.

Mich^l MILES; pension awarded 27 Sep 1842; residence - Montreal, Quebec, Canada; died in Jul 1854. SOURCE: WO120 Volume 69 page 261. INDEX # 5390.

Hy FLEMING; pension awarded 13 Aug 1844; residence - Quebec, Quebec, Canada. SOURCE: WO120 Volume 69 page 261. INDEX # 5391.

Jno DEVINE; pension awarded 27 Sep 1842; residence - Halifax, Nova Scotia, Canada. SOURCE: WO120 Volume 69 page 261. INDEX # 5392.

Robt BROWNE; pension awarded 13 Aug 1844; residence - Wm Henry, Quebec, Canada. SOURCE: WO120 Volume 69 page 261. INDEX # 5393.

John LARNER; pension awarded 13 Aug 1844; residence - Toronto, Ontario, Canada. SOURCE: WO120 Volume 69 page 261. INDEX # 5394.

Den^s KEELEY; pension awarded 29 Sep 1819; residence - Niagara, Ontario, Canada; died 10 Feb 1851. SOURCE: WO120 Volume 69 page 261. INDEX # 5395.

Robt BELL; pension awarded 13 Aug 1844; residence - Toronto, Ontario, Canada; died 8 Aug 1878, Halifax, Nova Scotia, Canada. SOURCE: WO120 Volume 69 page 261. INDEX # 5396.

Jno BRACKIN; pension awarded 11 May 1831; residence - Niagara, Ontario, Canada. SOURCE: WO120 Volume 69 page 261. INDEX # 5397.

Laughlin CURRIE; pension awarded 9 Jul 1834; residence - Niagara, Ontario, Canada; died 25 May 1872, Hamilton, Ontario, Canada. SOURCE: WO120 Volume 69 page 261. INDEX # 5398.

Thos POPE; pension awarded 26 Sep 1843; residence - Wm Henry, Quebec, Canada; died in Aug 1846. SOURCE: WO120 Volume 69 page 261. INDEX # 5399.

Thos KETTLE; pension awarded 9 Jul 1834; residence - Penetanguishene, Ontario, Canada; died 2 Jan 1853. SOURCE: WO120 Volume 69 page 261. INDEX # 5400.

Willm PORTER; pension awarded 25 Apr 1838; residence - Gibraltar. SOURCE: WO120 Volume 69 page 261. INDEX # 5401.

Lawr^e MADDEN; pension awarded 26 Jun 1839; residence - Montreal, Quebec, Canada. SOURCE: WO120 Volume 69 page 261. INDEX # 5402.

John JESSOP; pension awarded 31 Dec 1814; residence - Sydney. SOURCE: WO120 Volume 69 page 261. INDEX # 5403.

69th Regiment of Foot

Jno DENSMORE; pension awarded 23 Jul 1823; residence - Toronto, Ontario, Canada; died 19 Feb 1862, Toronto, Ontario, Canada. SOURCE: WO120 Volume 69 page 264. INDEX # 5404.

69th Regiment of Foot (continued)

Ja^s GILLIS; pension awarded 17 Jun 1838; residence - Jamaica; died 5 Jan 1848. SOURCE: WO120 Volume 69 page 264. INDEX # 5405.

Thos KING; pension awarded 22 Mar 1820; residence - Sydney. SOURCE: WO120 Volume 69 page 264. INDEX # 5406.

Jno JOSEPH; pension awarded 4 Aug 1824; residence - Madras, India. SOURCE: WO120 Volume 69 page 264. INDEX # 5407.

Willm BOOTH; pension awarded 15 Mar 1826; residence - Madras, India; died 31 Oct 1863. SOURCE: WO120 Volume 69 page 264. INDEX # 5408.

John ENOS; pension awarded 18 Aug 1835; residence - Prescott, Ontario, Canada. SOURCE: WO120 Volume 69 page 264. INDEX # 5409.

Elisha ROSID; pension awarded 4 Aug 1824; residence - Madras, India; died 10 Jan 1848. SOURCE: WO120 Volume 69 page 264. INDEX # 5410.

Jno FRANCIS; pension awarded 3 Mar 1824; residence - Madras, India; died 29 Aug 1874. SOURCE: WO120 Volume 69 page 264. INDEX # 5411.

Wm ALSOP; pension awarded 15 Mar 1826; residence - Madras, India. SOURCE: WO120 Volume 69 page 264. INDEX # 5412.

H^y BLADES; pension awarded 3 Mar 1824; residence - Madras, India. SOURCE: WO120 Volume 69 page 264. INDEX # 5413.

Jno THOMAS; pension awarded 3 Mar 1824; residence - Madras, India. SOURCE: WO120 Volume 69 page 264. INDEX # 5414.

Richd HOLDING; pension awarded 4 Aug 1824; residence - Madras, India. SOURCE: WO120 Volume 69 page 264. INDEX # 5415.

Den^s BRANNAN; pension awarded 23 Nov 1825; residence - Madras, India. SOURCE: WO120 Volume 69 page 264. INDEX # 5416.

Willm BAILEY; pension awarded 3 Mar 1824; residence - Madras, India; died 25 Apr 1853. SOURCE: WO120 Volume 69 page 264. INDEX # 5417.

Jos^h RUDGE; pension awarded 15 Mar 1825; residence - Madras, India; died 13 May 1853. SOURCE: WO120 Volume 69 page 264. INDEX # 5418.

Jno SPOONER; pension awarded 23 Nov 1825; residence - Madras, India; died 11 Nov 1853. SOURCE: WO120 Volume 69 page 264. INDEX # 5419.

Willm BOYD; pension awarded 15 Mar 1825; residence - Madras, India; died 23 Mar 1849. SOURCE: WO120 Volume 69 page 264. INDEX # 5420.

Jos^h KING; pension awarded 23 Nov 1825; residence - Madras, India; died 10 Nov 1851. SOURCE: WO120 Volume 69 page 264. INDEX # 5421.

Jno NEWBOLD; pension awarded 15 Mar 1825; residence - Madras, India; died 29 Jul 1848. SOURCE: WO120 Volume 69 page 264. INDEX # 5422.

Willm WARD; pension awarded 15 Mar 1825; residence - Madras, India; died 4 Dec 1849. SOURCE: WO120 Volume 69 page 264. INDEX # 5423.

Ja^s BROWN; pension awarded 15 Mar 1826; residence - Madras, India; died 17 Apr 1853. SOURCE: WO120 Volume 69 page 265. INDEX # 5424.

Ephr^m JOHNSON; pension awarded 15 Mar 1826; residence - Madras, India. SOURCE: WO120 Volume 69 page 265. INDEX # 5425.

Geo^e RICHARDS; pension awarded 15 Mar 1826; residence - Madras, India; died 10 May 1848. SOURCE: WO120 Volume 69 page 265. INDEX # 5426.

Thos WILKINS; pension awarded 15 Mar 1826; residence - Madras, India. SOURCE: WO120 Volume 69 page 265. INDEX # 5427.

Thos HOLLIS; pension awarded 13 Jun 1832; residence - Bengal, India; died 30 Jul 1853. SOURCE: WO120 Volume 69 page 265. INDEX # 5428.

John SPENCER; pension awarded 15 Mar 1826; residence - Madras, India; died 11 Mar 1864. SOURCE: WO120 Volume 69 page 265. INDEX # 5429.

Henry GIBBS; pension awarded 15 Mar 1826; residence - Madras, India. SOURCE: WO120 Volume 69 page 265. INDEX # 5430.

69th Regiment of Foot (continued)

Jn⁰ ARTHURS; pension awarded 9 Oct 1833; residence - London, Ontario, Canada. SOURCE: WO120 Volume 69 page 265. INDEX # 5431.

Danl MCKIVER; pension awarded ; residence - St. Johns. SOURCE: WO120 Volume 69 page 265. INDEX # 5432.

Godfrey BURN; pension awarded 15 Dec 1841; residence - New Brunswick, Canada. SOURCE: WO120 Volume 69 page 265. INDEX # 5433.

Ja^s DORAN; pension awarded 18 Jul 1843; residence - Montreal, Quebec, Canada; died in 1847. SOURCE: WO120 Volume 69 page 265. INDEX # 5434.

Thos BOSWARD; pension awarded 13 Aug 1850. SOURCE: WO120 Volume 69 page 265. INDEX # 5435.

70th Regiment of Foot

Claudius CHRISTIE; pension awarded 9 Dec 1845; residence - London, Ontario, Canada; died 8 Oct 1867. SOURCE: WO120 Volume 69 page 268. INDEX # 5436.

Willm WARREN; pension awarded 26 Nov 1844; residence - Gibraltar. SOURCE: WO120 Volume 69 page 268. INDEX # 5437.

Bern^d LINUS; pension awarded 5 Sep 1843; residence - Montreal, Quebec, Canada. SOURCE: WO120 Volume 69 page 268. INDEX # 5438.

Thos WELSH; pension awarded 5 Sep 1843; residence - Quebec, Quebec, Canada; died 18 Aug 1849. SOURCE: WO120 Volume 69 page 268. INDEX # 5439.

Hugh FERGUSON; pension awarded 28 May 1844; residence - Quebec, Quebec, Canada. SOURCE: WO120 Volume 69 page 268. INDEX # 5440.

Mich^l WHITE; pension awarded 10 Oct 1843; residence - Quebec, Quebec, Canada. SOURCE: WO120 Volume 69 page 268. INDEX # 5441.

Mich^l MURRAY; pension awarded 9 Aug 1837; residence - Gibraltar; died 10 Aug 1854, Woolwich, England. SOURCE: WO120 Volume 69 page 268. INDEX # 5442.

Matt^w GLENN; pension awarded 5 Jul 1820; residence - Toronto, Ontario, Canada. SOURCE: WO120 Volume 69 page 268. INDEX # 5443.

Thos WARNE; pension awarded 24 Jan 1838; residence - Gibraltar; died 18 Aug 1849. SOURCE: WO120 Volume 69 page 268. INDEX # 5444.

Thos WARREN; pension awarded 24 Jan 1838; residence - Gibraltar; died 18 Aug 1849. SOURCE: WO120 Volume 69 page 268. INDEX # 5445.

Jn⁰ WRAY; pension awarded 13 Apr 1836; residence - Quebec, Quebec, Canada; died 4 Oct 1857. SOURCE: WO120 Volume 69 page 268. INDEX # 5446.

Geo^e MATHISON; pension awarded 27 Sep 1842; residence - Quebec, Quebec, Canada. SOURCE: WO120 Volume 69 page 268. INDEX # 5447.

Willm LANDS; pension awarded 26 Sep 1843; residence - Kingston, Ontario, Canada; died 11 Aug 1878, Toronto, Ontario, Canada. SOURCE: WO120 Volume 69 page 268. INDEX # 5448.

Willm ALLEN; pension awarded 27 Sep 1842; residence - Quebec, Quebec, Canada. SOURCE: WO120 Volume 69 page 268. INDEX # 5449.

Jn⁰ TOOLE; pension awarded 26 Jul 1853. SOURCE: WO120 Volume 69 page 268. INDEX # 5450.

Ja^s MOONEY; pension awarded 9 May 1854. SOURCE: WO120 Volume 69 page 268. INDEX # 5451.

John James ROBINSON; pension awarded 5 May 1857. SOURCE: WO120 Volume 69 page 268. INDEX # 5452.

71st Regiment of Foot

Pat^k OBRYAN; pension awarded 13 Oct 1806; residence - St. Johns; died 12 Dec 1846. SOURCE: WO120 Volume 69 page 272. INDEX # 5453.

Willm BULLOCK; pension awarded 5 Aug 1818; residence - Kingston, Ontario, Canada; died 23 Apr 1860. SOURCE: WO120 Volume 69 page 272. INDEX # 5454.

71st Regiment of Foot (continued)

Robt QUAILS; pension awarded 17 Dec 1814; residence - Penetanguishene, Ontario, Canada; died 1 Aug 1886, Toronto, Canada. SOURCE: WO120 Volume 69 page 272. INDEX # 5455.

Benjn BOWERS; pension awarded 9 Sep 1840; residence - Huntingdon, Quebec, Canada. SOURCE: WO120 Volume 69 page 272. INDEX # 5456.

Wm FERGUSON; pension awarded 22 Mar 1820; residence - Montreal, Quebec, Canada. SOURCE: WO120 Volume 69 page 272. INDEX # 5457.

Finlay MCCRAW; pension awarded 6 Dec 1814; residence - Sydney, Nova Scotia, Canada; died 9 Jul 1872, Halifax, Nova Scotia, Canada. SOURCE: WO120 Volume 69 page 272. INDEX # 5458.

Jno HARKINS; pension awarded 7 Sep 1816; residence - Toronto, Ontario, Canada; died 16 Dec 1862. SOURCE: WO120 Volume 69 page 272. INDEX # 5459.

Ja^s URE; pension awarded 8 Sep 1830; residence - Toronto, Ontario, Canada; died 17 Mar 1859. SOURCE: WO120 Volume 69 page 272. INDEX # 5460.

Richd WARDROPE; pension awarded 8 Sep 1830; residence - Toronto, Ontario, Canada; died 12 May 18??, Toronto, Ontario, Canada. SOURCE: WO120 Volume 69 page 272. INDEX # 5461.

Robt ADAMS; pension awarded 13 Jul 1831; residence - Toronto, Ontario, Canada. SOURCE: WO120 Volume 69 page 272. INDEX # 5462.

Alex^r DAVIDSON; pension awarded 13 Jul 1831; residence - Toronto, Ontario, Canada; died 10 Dec 1859. SOURCE: WO120 Volume 69 page 272. INDEX # 5463.

Wm GLOVER; pension awarded 13 Jul 1831; residence - Toronto, Ontario, Canada; died 11 Apr 1867. SOURCE: WO120 Volume 69 page 272. INDEX # 5464.

Wm WILSON; pension awarded 13 Jul 1831; residence - Amherstburg, Ontario, Canada. SOURCE: WO120 Volume 69 page 272. INDEX # 5465.

Matt^w CLARKE; pension awarded 13 Jul 1831; residence - Quebec, Quebec, Canada. SOURCE: WO120 Volume 69 page 272. INDEX # 5466.

Gus^ts CLEMENTS; pension awarded 14 Sep 1831; residence - Bytown, Ontario, Canada; died 26 May 1855. SOURCE: WO120 Volume 69 page 272. INDEX # 5467.

Chas MCLEAN; pension awarded 14 Dec 1831; residence - Niagara, Ontario, Canada. SOURCE: WO120 Volume 69 page 272. INDEX # 5468.

John CULLEN; pension awarded 11 Jul 1832; residence - Toronto, Ontario, Canada. SOURCE: WO120 Volume 69 page 272. INDEX # 5470.

Wm ROBINSON; pension awarded 11 Jul 1832; residence - Toronto, Ontario, Canada. SOURCE: WO120 Volume 69 page 272. INDEX # 5471.

Danl MCKAY; pension awarded 12 Sep 1832; residence - Amherstburg, Ontario, Canada; died 19 Jun 1850. SOURCE: WO120 Volume 69 page 272. INDEX # 5472.

Willm CLARKE; pension awarded 9 Jan 1833; residence - Quebec, Quebec, Canada; died 1 Aug 1849. SOURCE: WO120 Volume 69 page 273. INDEX # 5473.

John MERCES; pension awarded 26 Oct 1843; residence - London, Ontario, Canada. SOURCE: WO120 Volume 69 page 273. INDEX # 5474.

John SHARP; pension awarded 26 Sep 1843; residence - Saint John, New Brunswick, Canada. SOURCE: WO120 Volume 69 page 273. INDEX # 5475.

John CHISHOLME; pension awarded 15 Jun 1812; residence - Saint John, New Brunswick, Canada. SOURCE: WO120 Volume 69 page 273. INDEX # 5476.

Hugh MCMASTER; pension awarded 1 Jun 1813; residence - Cornwall, Ontario, Canada; died in Jul 1847. SOURCE: WO120 Volume 69 page 273. INDEX # 5477.

Arch^d PROVAN; pension awarded 25 Jun 1817; residence - Perth, Ontario, Canada. SOURCE: WO120 Volume 69 page 273. INDEX # 5478.

John FEEHAN; pension awarded 8 Sep 1841; residence - Toronto, Ontario, Canada. SOURCE: WO120 Volume 69 page 273. INDEX # 5479.

Dav^d COLBERT; pension awarded 26 Aug 1845; residence - Montreal, Quebec, Canada. SOURCE: WO120 Volume 69 page 273. INDEX # 5480.

BRITISH ARMY PENSIONERS ABROAD

71st Regiment of Foot (continued)

Alex^r GUNN; pension awarded 11 Mar 1835; residence - Toronto, Ontario, Canada; died 11 Aug 1861. SOURCE: WO120 Volume 69 page 273. INDEX # 5481.

Danl CAMERON; pension awarded 14 Nov 1843; residence - Montreal, Quebec, Canada. SOURCE: WO120 Volume 69 page 273. INDEX # 5482.

Geo^e LESLIE; pension awarded 11 Jul 1832; residence - Amherstburg, Ontario, Canada; died 13 Apr 1853. SOURCE: WO120 Volume 69 page 273. INDEX # 5483.

Ja^s YORK; pension awarded 27 Sep 1842; residence - St. Jean, Quebec, Canada. SOURCE: WO120 Volume 69 page 273. INDEX # 5484.

Thos LITTLE; pension awarded 26 Aug 1845; residence - Canada; died 21 Jan 1848. SOURCE: WO120 Volume 69 page 273. INDEX # 5485.

Angus COOK; pension awarded 8 Feb 1832; residence - Niagara, Ontario, Canada; died 29 Nov 1860, Hamilton, Ontario, Canada. SOURCE: WO120 Volume 69 page 273. INDEX # 5486.

Willm PATON; pension awarded 22 Sep 1846; residence - Montreal, Quebec, Canada; died 18 Sep 1847. SOURCE: WO120 Volume 69 page 273. INDEX # 5487.

Danl MCRAE; pension awarded 22 Sep 1846; residence - Kingston, Ontario, Canada. SOURCE: WO120 Volume 69 page 273. INDEX # 5488.

Ja^s ODAM; pension awarded 22 Sep 1846; residence - Kingston, Ontario, Canada; died 18 Jul 1849. SOURCE: WO120 Volume 69 page 273. INDEX # 5489.

Peter WELLS; pension awarded 22 Sep 1846; residence - Kingston, Ontario, Canada; died 23 Mar 1865, Toronto, Ontario, Canada. SOURCE: WO120 Volume 69 page 273. INDEX # 5490.

Chas GOLDSMITH; pension awarded 12 Oct 1847; residence - Toronto, Ontario, Canada; died 7 Jan 1864. SOURCE: WO120 Volume 69 page 273. INDEX # 5491.

Ja^s VENN; pension awarded 12 Oct 1847; residence - Kingston, Ontario, Canada; died 27 Apr 1857. SOURCE: WO120 Volume 69 page 273. INDEX # 5492.

Jno COCHRANE; pension awarded 12 Oct 1847. SOURCE: WO120 Volume 69 page 273. INDEX # 5493.

Wm BRABY; pension awarded 12 Oct 1847. SOURCE: WO120 Volume 69 page 273. INDEX # 5494.

Ja^s MOORE; pension awarded 12 Oct 1847; died 4 Dec 1879, Toronto, Ontario, Canada. SOURCE: WO120 Volume 69 page 273. INDEX # 5495.

Robt MCKECHNIE; pension awarded 12 Oct 1847. SOURCE: WO120 Volume 69 page 273. INDEX # 5496.

Wm BATES; pension awarded 1 Oct 1850. SOURCE: WO120 Volume 69 page 273. INDEX # 5497.

Thos MIERS; pension awarded 1 Oct 1850. SOURCE: WO120 Volume 69 page 273. INDEX # 5498.

Ja^s MCCANN; pension awarded 5 Aug 1851. SOURCE: WO120 Volume 69 page 273. INDEX # 5499.

Geoffrey HORNBY; pension awarded 5 Aug 1851. SOURCE: WO120 Volume 69 page 273. INDEX # 5500.

Richd PICKETT; pension awarded 5 Aug 1851. SOURCE: WO120 Volume 69 page 273. INDEX # 5501.

Jno MCLOUGHLIN; pension awarded 27 Jul 1852; residence - Toronto, Ontario, Canada; died 5 Jul 1855. SOURCE: WO120 Volume 69 page 273. INDEX # 5502.

Jos^h HEATH; pension awarded 27 Jul 1852. SOURCE: WO120 Volume 69 page 273. INDEX # 5503.

Jno HUGHES; pension awarded 27 Jul 1852. SOURCE: WO120 Volume 69 page 273. INDEX # 5504.

Thos KYLE; pension awarded 19 Jul 1853. SOURCE: WO120 Volume 69 page 273. INDEX # 5505.

Jno STEEL; pension awarded 19 Jul 1853. SOURCE: WO120 Volume 69 page 273. INDEX # 5506.

Alex^r Wm MURDOCK; pension awarded 23 Aug 1853; died 31 Dec 1872, Toronto, Ontario, Canada. SOURCE: WO120 Volume 69 page 273. INDEX # 5507.

Alex^r BISSLAND; pension awarded 12 Sep 1854. SOURCE: WO120 Volume 69 page 273. INDEX # 5508.

Wm BLACK; pension awarded 12 Sep 1854. SOURCE: WO120 Volume 69 page 273. INDEX # 5509.

Robt WINGFIELD; pension awarded 12 Sep 1854; residence - Toronto, Ontario, Canada; died 5 May 1857. SOURCE: WO120 Volume 69 page 273. INDEX # 5510.

Alex^r SUTHERLAND; pension awarded 26 Dec 1854; died 27 Sep 1880, Inverness. SOURCE: WO120 Volume 69 page 273. INDEX # 5511.

Dav^d BEATTIE; pension awarded 26 Dec 1854; died 24 Dec 1883, Toronto, Ontario, Canada. SOURCE: WO120 Volume 69 page 273. INDEX # 5512.

72nd Regiment of Foot

Thos EDWARDS; pension awarded 23 Jan 1844; residence - Grahams Town, South Africa. SOURCE: WO120 Volume 69 page 275. INDEX # 5513.

Jno CAMERON; pension awarded 4 Oct 1816; residence - Charlottetown, Prince Edward Island, Canada. SOURCE: WO120 Volume 69 page 275. INDEX # 5514.

Ja^s DENNIS; pension awarded 1 May 1822; residence - Cape of Good Hope, South Africa. SOURCE: WO120 Volume 69 page 275. INDEX # 5515.

Ja^s MCDONALD; pension awarded 20 Jan 1819; residence - Toronto, Ontario, Canada; died 22 Aug 1855. SOURCE: WO120 Volume 69 page 275. INDEX # 5516.

Jno MCKENZIE; pension awarded 20 Mar 1822; residence - Cape of Good Hope, South Africa. SOURCE: WO120 Volume 69 page 275. INDEX # 5517.

Alex^r SMITH; pension awarded 7 Feb 1822; residence - Cape of Good Hope, South Africa. SOURCE: WO120 Volume 69 page 275. INDEX # 5518.

Ja^s LEVINSTONE; pension awarded 18 Jul 1843; residence - Cape of Good Hope, South Africa; died 12 Oct 1853. SOURCE: WO120 Volume 69 page 275. INDEX # 5519.

And^w MCCOULL; pension awarded 8 Nov 1837; residence - Cape of Good Hope, South Africa. SOURCE: WO120 Volume 69 page 275. INDEX # 5520.

John FOLEY; pension awarded 1 May 1822; residence - Cape of Good Hope, South Africa. SOURCE: WO120 Volume 69 page 275. INDEX # 5521.

Robt MORAN; pension awarded 1 May 1822; residence - Toronto, Ontario, Canada; died 24 Dec 1846. SOURCE: WO120 Volume 69 page 275. INDEX # 5522.

Willm MARKS; pension awarded 1 May 1822; residence - Cape of Good Hope, South Africa. SOURCE: WO120 Volume 69 page 275. INDEX # 5523.

Ja^s DUFF; pension awarded 1 May 1822; residence - Cape of Good Hope, South Africa. SOURCE: WO120 Volume 69 page 275. INDEX # 5524.

Geo^e MACKAY; pension awarded 7 Feb 1822; residence - Cape of Good Hope, South Africa. SOURCE: WO120 Volume 69 page 275. INDEX # 5525.

Wm GIBSON; pension awarded 25 Sep 1822; residence - Toronto, Ontario, Canada; died 2 May 1856. SOURCE: WO120 Volume 69 page 275. INDEX # 5526.

Alex^r DINGWALL; pension awarded 7 Feb 1822; residence - Cape of Good Hope, South Africa. SOURCE: WO120 Volume 69 page 275. INDEX # 5527.

John SMITH; pension awarded 1 May 1822; residence - Cape of Good Hope, South Africa. SOURCE: WO120 Volume 69 page 275. INDEX # 5528.

Willm SHORT; pension awarded 16 May 1823; residence - Hobart Town, Australia; died 19 Jan 1873. SOURCE: WO120 Volume 69 page 275. INDEX # 5529.

Dav^d DOWIE; pension awarded 8 Apr 1840; residence - Cape of Good Hope, South Africa. SOURCE: WO120 Volume 69 page 275. INDEX # 5530.

Willm D. WHEELER; pension awarded 12 Jul 1842; residence - Malta. SOURCE: WO120 Volume 69 page 275. INDEX # 5531.

Robt FRASER; pension awarded 13 Sep 1837; residence - Cape of Good Hope, South Africa; died 15 Mar 1851. SOURCE: WO120 Volume 69 page 275. INDEX # 5532.

Willm BLACK; pension awarded 19 Jun 1822; residence - Toronto, Ontario, Canada. SOURCE: WO120 Volume 69 page 276. INDEX # 5533.

Dav^d FITCHETT; pension awarded 7 Feb 1823; residence - Cape of Good Hope, South Africa. SOURCE: WO120 Volume 69 page 276. INDEX # 5534.

Ja^s MORRIS; pension awarded 14 Dec 1836; residence - Cape of Good Hope, South Africa. SOURCE: WO120 Volume 69 page 276. INDEX # 5535.

Alex^r MCARTHUR; pension awarded 8 Aug 1843; residence - Montreal, Quebec, Canada; died 10 Aug 1846. SOURCE: WO120 Volume 69 page 276. INDEX # 5536.

Alex^r MCCARTER; pension awarded 8 Aug 1843; residence - Montreal, Quebec, Canada; died 10 Aug 1846. SOURCE: WO120 Volume 69 page 276. INDEX # 5537.

And^w HOSIE; pension awarded 7 Feb 1821; residence - Cape of Good Hope, South Africa; died 29 Jul 1864. SOURCE: WO120 Volume 69 page 276. INDEX # 5538.

72nd Regiment of Foot (continued)

Art{r} PLUNKETT; pension awarded 7 Feb 1822; residence - Cape of Good Hope, South Africa. SOURCE: WO120 Volume 69 page 276. INDEX # 5539.

John GRANT; pension awarded 19 Jun 1822; residence - Cape of Good Hope, South Africa. SOURCE: WO120 Volume 69 page 276. INDEX # 5540.

Willm HANTON; pension awarded 13 Sep 1837; residence - Cape of Good Hope, South Africa. SOURCE: WO120 Volume 69 page 276. INDEX # 5541.

Willm MILLER; pension awarded 27 Jun 1838; residence - Cape of Good Hope, South Africa. SOURCE: WO120 Volume 69 page 276. INDEX # 5542.

Jno FOSTER; pension awarded 28 Jul 1846; residence - Gibraltar. SOURCE: WO120 Volume 69 page 276. INDEX # 5543.

David DALLAS; pension awarded 26 Oct 1847; died 12 Sep 1876 Gibraltar. SOURCE: WO120 Volume 69 page 276. INDEX # 5544.

Jno COLLINS; pension awarded 11 Nov 1851; residence - Nova Scotia, Canada; died in 1853. SOURCE: WO120 Volume 69 page 276. INDEX # 5545.

Edwd MCDONALD; pension awarded 13 Jul 1852; residence - Saint John, New Brunswick, Canada; died in Apr 1853. SOURCE: WO120 Volume 69 page 276. INDEX # 5546.

Mich{l} OSHEA; pension awarded 13 Jul 1852. SOURCE: WO120 Volume 69 page 276. INDEX # 5547.

Robt WAYSON; pension awarded 28 Sep 1852. SOURCE: WO120 Volume 69 page 276. INDEX # 5548.

Mich{l} SULLIVAN; pension awarded 26 Apr 1853. SOURCE: WO120 Volume 69 page 276. INDEX # 5549.

Jno ROSE; pension awarded 19 Jul 1853. SOURCE: WO120 Volume 69 page 276. INDEX # 5550.

Wm CLARK; pension awarded 19 Jul 1853; died 19 Feb 1872, Dundee. SOURCE: WO120 Volume 69 page 276. INDEX # 5551.

Sack HANLON; pension awarded 19 Jul 1853. SOURCE: WO120 Volume 69 page 276. INDEX # 5552.

Hugh MCLEAN; pension awarded 19 Jul 1853. SOURCE: WO120 Volume 69 page 276. INDEX # 5553.

Jno BOOTH; pension awarded 11 Oct 1853. SOURCE: WO120 Volume 69 page 276. INDEX # 5554.

Alexr MCKENZIE; pension awarded 22 Aug 1854. SOURCE: WO120 Volume 69 page 276. INDEX # 5555.

Paul BRODIE; pension awarded 14 Nov 1854. SOURCE: WO120 Volume 69 page 276. INDEX # 5556.

Allan MCNICOL; pension awarded 14 Nov 1854. SOURCE: WO120 Volume 69 page 276. INDEX # 5557.

73rd Regiment of Foot

Fra{s} MORRISON; pension awarded 29 Jul 1819; residence - New South Wales, Australia. SOURCE: WO120 Volume 69 page 282. INDEX # 5558.

John LOWREY; pension awarded 5 Feb 1817; residence - Sydney. SOURCE: WO120 Volume 69 page 282. INDEX # 5559.

Jos{h} SLATER; pension awarded 16 Aug 1816; residence - New South Wales, Australia. SOURCE: WO120 Volume 69 page 282. INDEX # 5560.

John COCUS; pension awarded 13 Sep 1820; residence - Hobart Town, Australia. SOURCE: WO120 Volume 69 page 282. INDEX # 5561.

John MORRISON; pension awarded 24 Feb 1818; residence - Toronto, Ontario, Canada; died 7 Jul 1859. SOURCE: WO120 Volume 69 page 282. INDEX # 5562.

John GRIERSON; pension awarded 25 Oct 1815; residence - New South Wales, Australia. SOURCE: WO120 Volume 69 page 282. INDEX # 5563.

John CEACY; pension awarded 22 Jan 1840; residence - Quebec, Quebec, Canada. SOURCE: WO120 Volume 69 page 282. INDEX # 5564.

John CASEY; pension awarded 22 Jan 1840; residence - Quebec, Quebec, Canada. SOURCE: WO120 Volume 69 page 282. INDEX # 5565.

Danl MOLLOY; pension awarded 8 Jan 1840; residence - Toronto, Ontario, Canada; died 15 Jul 1873. SOURCE: WO120 Volume 69 page 282. INDEX # 5566.

John EDNEY; pension awarded 25 Sep 1817; residence - New South Wales, Australia. SOURCE: WO120 Volume 69 page 282. INDEX # 5567.

WO120 VOLUME 69

73rd Regiment of Foot (continued)

John HARRIS; pension awarded 13 Jul 1831; residence - Malta. SOURCE: WO120 Volume 69 page 282. INDEX # 5568.

Robt THOMPSON; pension awarded 22 May 1839; residence - Toronto, Ontario, Canada; died 12 Nov 1855. SOURCE: WO120 Volume 69 page 282. INDEX # 5569.

Willm MOTT; pension awarded 9 Jun 1841; residence - Carillon, Quebec, Canada. SOURCE: WO120 Volume 69 page 282. INDEX # 5570.

Harding OBRIEN; pension awarded 12 Feb 1820; residence - London, Ontario, Canada; died 10 Jan 1856. SOURCE: WO120 Volume 69 page 282. INDEX # 5571.

Jno ROBINSON; pension awarded 25 Sep 1817; residence - New South Wales, Australia; died in 1852. SOURCE: WO120 Volume 69 page 282. INDEX # 5572.

Danl STEP; pension awarded 25 Sep 1817; residence - New South Wales, Australia. SOURCE: WO120 Volume 69 page 282. INDEX # 5573.

Henry HOYLE; pension awarded 9 Aug 1816; residence - New South Wales, Australia; died 12 Aug 1849. SOURCE: WO120 Volume 69 page 282. INDEX # 5574.

Jer^h BRYANT; pension awarded 29 Jul 1819; residence - New South Wales, Australia. SOURCE: WO120 Volume 69 page 282. INDEX # 5575.

Alex^r ALEXANDER; pension awarded 6 May 1816; residence - Perth, Ontario, Canada. SOURCE: WO120 Volume 69 page 282. INDEX # 5576.

John BAXTER; pension awarded 3 Feb 1820; residence - New South Wales, Australia; died 27 Nov 1872, Melbourne, Australia. SOURCE: WO120 Volume 69 page 282. INDEX # 5577.

John RICHARDSON; pension awarded 25 Sep 1817; residence - Hobart Town, Australia. SOURCE: WO120 Volume 69 page 282. INDEX # 5578.

John MATTHEWS; pension awarded 31 Jul 1816; residence - New South Wales, Australia. SOURCE: WO120 Volume 69 page 283. INDEX # 5579.

Don^d MCLEAN; pension awarded 7 Jan 1818; residence - Halifax, Nova Scotia, Canada; died in 1852. SOURCE: WO120 Volume 69 page 283. INDEX # 5580.

John FOLLENUS; pension awarded 14 Oct 1840; residence - Montreal, Quebec, Canada. SOURCE: WO120 Volume 69 page 283. INDEX # 5581.

Benjn URCH; pension awarded 14 Aug 1823; residence - New South Wales, Australia; died 4 Oct 1878, Melbourne, Australia. SOURCE: WO120 Volume 69 page 283. INDEX # 5582.

Wm ASHENDEN; pension awarded 11 Jul 1823; residence - New South Wales, Australia; died 9 Aug 1846. SOURCE: WO120 Volume 69 page 283. INDEX # 5583.

Jno COOPER; pension awarded 11 Mar 1835; residence - New Zealand; died 14 Feb 1852. SOURCE: WO120 Volume 69 page 283. INDEX # 5584.

Roger MORAN; pension awarded 7 Feb 1822; residence - Canada. SOURCE: WO120 Volume 69 page 283. INDEX # 5585.

Wm JARVIS; pension awarded 25 Jul 1821; residence - Sydney. SOURCE: WO120 Volume 69 page 283. INDEX # 5586.

Fran^s RENNIE; pension awarded 13 Jul 1852. SOURCE: WO120 Volume 69 page 283. INDEX # 5587.

Robt SAUNDERS; pension awarded 13 Jul 1852. SOURCE: WO120 Volume 69 page 283. INDEX # 5588.

Jno SHANAHAN; pension awarded 13 Jul 1852. SOURCE: WO120 Volume 69 page 283. INDEX # 5589.

Jno Hen^y VICARS; pension awarded 13 Jul 1852. SOURCE: WO120 Volume 69 page 283. INDEX # 5590.

Jno YOUNG; pension awarded 13 Sep 1853. SOURCE: WO120 Volume 69 page 283. INDEX # 5591.

Saml CARSON; pension awarded 13 Sep 1853; died 25 Feb 1883, Sydney. SOURCE: WO120 Volume 69 page 283. INDEX # 5592.

Hugh GILMORE; pension awarded 13 Sep 1853. SOURCE: WO120 Volume 69 page 283. INDEX # 5593.

Wm Jos^h HENLEY; pension awarded 13 Sep 1853. SOURCE: WO120 Volume 69 page 283. INDEX # 5594.

Thos FOLEY; pension awarded 13 Sep 1853. SOURCE: WO120 Volume 69 page 283. INDEX # 5595.

Ja^s CARROLL; pension awarded 13 Jun 1854. SOURCE: WO120 Volume 69 page 283. INDEX # 5596.

William BROWN; pension awarded 14 Aug 1855. SOURCE: WO120 Volume 69 page 283. INDEX # 5597.

James COURTNEY; pension awarded 18 Aug 1857. SOURCE: WO120 Volume 69 page 283. INDEX # 5598.

Thomas GILL; pension awarded 18 Aug 1857. SOURCE: WO120 Volume 69 page 283. INDEX # 5599.

BRITISH ARMY PENSIONERS ABROAD

73rd Regiment of Foot (continued)

John LITTLE; pension awarded 18 Aug 1857. SOURCE: WO120 Volume 69 page 283. INDEX # 5600.
George SMITH; pension awarded 18 Aug 1857. SOURCE: WO120 Volume 69 page 283. INDEX # 5601.
Samuel TOWERS; pension awarded 18 Aug 1857. SOURCE: WO120 Volume 69 page 283. INDEX # 5602.

74th Regiment of Foot

George LITTLE; pension awarded 23 Nov 1825; residence - Halifax, Nova Scotia, Canada. SOURCE: WO120 Volume 69 page 285. INDEX # 5603.
John MURRAY; pension awarded 29 Mar 1815; residence - New South Wales, Australia; died 15 Jun 1864. SOURCE: WO120 Volume 69 page 285. INDEX # 5604.
Moses LITTLE; pension awarded 1 Feb 1809; residence - Toronto, Ontario, Canada; died 14 Jul 1848. SOURCE: WO120 Volume 69 page 285. INDEX # 5605.
And^w DUNCAN; pension awarded 13 Apr 1824; residence - Charlottetown, Prince Edward Island, Canada. SOURCE: WO120 Volume 69 page 285. INDEX # 5606.
Pat^k HUGHES; pension awarded 28 Feb 1825; residence - Toronto, Ontario, Canada; died 28 Feb 1872, Toronto, Ontario, Canada. SOURCE: WO120 Volume 69 page 285. INDEX # 5607.
Thos PURDY; pension awarded 9 Dec 1829; residence - Toronto, Ontario, Canada; died 1 Jun 1856. SOURCE: WO120 Volume 69 page 285. INDEX # 5608.
Richd BROWN; pension awarded 13 Oct 1830; residence - St. Johns. SOURCE: WO120 Volume 69 page 285. INDEX # 5609.
Jno HUEY; pension awarded 30 Aug 1826; residence - Halifax, Nova Scotia, Canada. SOURCE: WO120 Volume 69 page 285. INDEX # 5610.
Robt BOYD; pension awarded 7 Oct 1813; residence - Toronto, Ontario, Canada; died 4 Dec 1880, Toronto, Ontario, Canada. SOURCE: WO120 Volume 69 page 285. INDEX # 5611.
Jno MONAHAN; pension awarded 5 Sep 1843; residence - St. Jean, Quebec, Canada. SOURCE: WO120 Volume 69 page 285. INDEX # 5612.
Ja^s ELLIOTT; pension awarded 26 Sep 1843; residence - Montreal, Quebec, Canada. SOURCE: WO120 Volume 69 page 285. INDEX # 5613.
Jno DOBSON; pension awarded 12 Aug 1844; residence - Bytown, Ontario, Canada. SOURCE: WO120 Volume 69 page 285. INDEX # 5614.
Ja^s LYNCH; pension awarded 10 Dec 1834; residence - St. Kitts, West Indies. SOURCE: WO120 Volume 69 page 285. INDEX # 5615.
Jno MCKAY; pension awarded 14 Mar 1832; residence - Charlottetown, Prince Edward Island, Canada; died 25 Apr 1853. SOURCE: WO120 Volume 69 page 285. INDEX # 5616.
Ja^s CAIN; pension awarded 16 Apr 1818; residence - Toronto, Ontario, Canada; died 15 Jun 1877, London, Ontario, Canada. SOURCE: WO120 Volume 69 page 285. INDEX # 5617.
Mich^l VAUGHAN; pension awarded 23 Sep 1845; residence - Madras, India; died 4 Jan 1848. SOURCE: WO120 Volume 69 page 285. INDEX # 5618.
Corn^s BROMELL; pension awarded 26 Nov 1844; residence - Montreal, Quebec, Canada. SOURCE: WO120 Volume 69 page 285. INDEX # 5619.
Philip DOWLING; pension awarded 26 Nov 1844; residence - Quebec, Quebec, Canada. SOURCE: WO120 Volume 69 page 285. INDEX # 5620.
Peter PIDGEON; pension awarded 26 Nov 1844; residence - Quebec, Quebec, Canada; died 21 Oct 1883, Montreal, Quebec, Canada. SOURCE: WO120 Volume 69 page 285. INDEX # 5621.
Robt MCKENZIE; pension awarded 14 Feb 1854. SOURCE: WO120 Volume 69 page 285. INDEX # 5622.
Jno MCCABE; pension awarded 28 Mar 1856. SOURCE: WO120 Volume 69 page 285. INDEX # 5623.
Vincent MIST; pension awarded 12 Jun 1855. SOURCE: WO120 Volume 69 page 285. INDEX # 5624.
William CHAPMAN; pension awarded 11 Mar 1856. SOURCE: WO120 Volume 69 page 285. INDEX # 5625.
John EATON; pension awarded 11 Mar 1856. SOURCE: WO120 Volume 69 page 285. INDEX # 5626.
John MURPHY; pension awarded 11 Mar 1856. SOURCE: WO120 Volume 69 page 285. INDEX # 5627.
William PEPWORTH; pension awarded 11 Mar 1856. SOURCE: WO120 Volume 69 page 285. INDEX # 5628.

WO120 VOLUME 69

74th Regiment of Foot (continued)

William WEBSTER; pension awarded 11 Mar 1856. SOURCE: WO120 Volume 69 page 285. INDEX # 5629.
William MAISEY; pension awarded 6 May 1856. SOURCE: WO120 Volume 69 page 285. INDEX # 5630.
James PERRY; pension awarded 28 Apr 1857. SOURCE: WO120 Volume 69 page 285. INDEX # 5631.
George GUMMER; pension awarded 28 Apr 1857. SOURCE: WO120 Volume 69 page 285. INDEX # 5632.
James FURLONG; pension awarded 28 Apr 1857. SOURCE: WO120 Volume 69 page 285. INDEX # 5633.

75th Regiment of Foot

Pat^k KEARNEY; pension awarded 27 Aug 1823; residence - Toronto, Ontario, Canada. SOURCE: WO120 Volume 69 page 289. INDEX # 5634.
John QUINLISH; pension awarded 15 Oct 1842; residence - Bytown, Ontario, Canada; died 8 Jul 1851. SOURCE: WO120 Volume 69 page 289. INDEX # 5635.
Fotheringham FRASER; pension awarded 4 Dec 1822; residence - Sydney. SOURCE: WO120 Volume 69 page 289. INDEX # 5636.
Matt^w WELDING; pension awarded 13 Jun 1839; residence - Cape of Good Hope, South Africa. SOURCE: WO120 Volume 69 page 289. INDEX # 5637.
Don^d MCKAY; pension awarded 5 Jun 1817; residence - Halifax, Nova Scotia, Canada. SOURCE: WO120 Volume 69 page 289. INDEX # 5638.
Thos ROSSBOROUGH; pension awarded 9 Sep 1840; residence - Toronto, Ontario, Canada; died 29 Dec 1849. SOURCE: WO120 Volume 69 page 289. INDEX # 5639.
Bern^d MCKEOWN; pension awarded 13 Dec 1842; residence - Cape of Good Hope, South Africa. SOURCE: WO120 Volume 69 page 289. INDEX # 5640.
Ja^s MILLER; pension awarded 12 Jun 1839; residence - Cape of Good Hope, South Africa. SOURCE: WO120 Volume 69 page 289. INDEX # 5641.
Peter KILGOUR; pension awarded 11 Oct 1842; residence - Cape of Good Hope, South Africa; died 18 Oct 1872, Cape of Good Hope, South Africa. SOURCE: WO120 Volume 69 page 289. INDEX # 5642.
Willm ROSS; pension awarded 12 Jun 1811; residence - Penetanguishene, Ontario, Canada; died in 1853. SOURCE: WO120 Volume 69 page 289. INDEX # 5643.
Dav^d MILLS; pension awarded 14 Dec 1836; residence - Cape of Good Hope, South Africa; died 4 Aug 1853. SOURCE: WO120 Volume 69 page 289. INDEX # 5644.

11th Regiment of Foot

Jno BAGWILL; pension awarded 13 Jul 1852; residence - Sydney, New South Wales, Australia. SOURCE: WO120 Volume 69 page 291. INDEX # 5645.
Mich^l CASSIDY; pension awarded 13 Jul 1852. SOURCE: WO120 Volume 69 page 291. INDEX # 5646.
Saml CROKER; pension awarded 13 Jul 1852. SOURCE: WO120 Volume 69 page 291. INDEX # 5647.
Mat^w CROSHAW; pension awarded 13 Jul 1852. SOURCE: WO120 Volume 69 page 291. INDEX # 5648.
Hen^y GRAHAM; pension awarded 13 Jul 1852. SOURCE: WO120 Volume 69 page 291. INDEX # 5649.
Jno GRICE; pension awarded 13 Jul 1852. SOURCE: WO120 Volume 69 page 291. INDEX # 5650.
Jos^h HEWITT; pension awarded 13 Jul 1852. SOURCE: WO120 Volume 69 page 291. INDEX # 5651.
Jno RIDDLE; pension awarded 13 Jul 1852. SOURCE: WO120 Volume 69 page 291. INDEX # 5652.
Step^n SAUNDERS; pension awarded 13 Jul 1852. SOURCE: WO120 Volume 69 page 291. INDEX # 5653.
Edwd GILES; pension awarded 14 Dec 1852. SOURCE: WO120 Volume 69 page 291. INDEX # 5654.
Wm KERSHAW; pension awarded 14 Dec 1852. SOURCE: WO120 Volume 69 page 291. INDEX # 5655.
Denis FEENEY; pension awarded 11 Jan 1853. SOURCE: WO120 Volume 69 page 291. INDEX # 5656.
Jno HOLMES; pension awarded 11 Jan 1853. SOURCE: WO120 Volume 69 page 291. INDEX # 5657.
Jno WILLINGDALE; pension awarded 11 Jan 1853. SOURCE: WO120 Volume 69 page 291. INDEX # 5658.

11th Regiment of Foot (continued)

Mich^l QUILLINAN; pension awarded 9 Aug 1853; died in Sep 1876. SOURCE: WO120 Volume 69 page 291. INDEX # 5659.

Geo^e GIRLING; pension awarded 9 Aug 1853; died in Mar 1878, Sydney, New South Wales, Australia. SOURCE: WO120 Volume 69 page 291. INDEX # 5660.

Lewis WALSH; pension awarded 9 Aug 1853. SOURCE: WO120 Volume 69 page 291. INDEX # 5661.

Jere^h REARDON; pension awarded 9 Aug 1853. SOURCE: WO120 Volume 69 page 291. INDEX # 5662.

Thos BRESINGTON; pension awarded 9 Aug 1853. SOURCE: WO120 Volume 69 page 291. INDEX # 5663.

Ja^s BUSH; pension awarded 9 Aug 1853. SOURCE: WO120 Volume 69 page 291. INDEX # 5664.

Richd CHILDS; pension awarded 9 Aug 1853; died 22 Jun 1873, New South Wales, Australia. SOURCE: WO120 Volume 69 page 291. INDEX # 5665.

Jos^h DAWES; pension awarded 9 Aug 1853. SOURCE: WO120 Volume 69 page 291. INDEX # 5666.

Jno HEUSE; pension awarded 9 Aug 1853. SOURCE: WO120 Volume 69 page 291. INDEX # 5667.

Jno LYLE; pension awarded 9 Aug 1853; died 18 Jan 1883, South Australia, Australia. SOURCE: WO120 Volume 69 page 291. INDEX # 5668.

Hen^y LOWE; pension awarded 9 Aug 1853; died 21 Mar 1879, Melbourne, Australia. SOURCE: WO120 Volume 69 page 291. INDEX # 5669.

Philip MULLIGAN; pension awarded 9 Aug 1853. SOURCE: WO120 Volume 69 page 291. INDEX # 5670.

Wm PARKER; pension awarded 9 Aug 1853. SOURCE: WO120 Volume 69 page 291. INDEX # 5671.

Hen^y SCAMMELL; pension awarded 9 Aug 1853; died 13 Jan 1878, Sydney, New South Wales, Australia. SOURCE: WO120 Volume 69 page 291. INDEX # 5672.

David THOMAS; pension awarded 22 Nov 1853. SOURCE: WO120 Volume 69 page 291. INDEX # 5673.

Jno OCONNOR; pension awarded 22 Nov 1853. SOURCE: WO120 Volume 69 page 291. INDEX # 5674.

Wm JONES; pension awarded 22 Nov 1853. SOURCE: WO120 Volume 69 page 291. INDEX # 5675.

Wm AREM; pension awarded 25 Jul 1854; residence - Geelong, Australia. SOURCE: WO120 Volume 69 page 291. INDEX # 5676.

Ed^wd NEWMAN; pension awarded 25 Jul 1854. SOURCE: WO120 Volume 69 page 291. INDEX # 5677.

Jno SPRENT; pension awarded 25 Jul 1854. SOURCE: WO120 Volume 69 page 291. INDEX # 5678.

Dav^d ADAMS; pension awarded 25 Jul 1854; residence - Sydney, New South Wales, Australia; died 21 Nov 1876, New South Wales, Australia. SOURCE: WO120 Volume 69 page 291. INDEX # 5679.

Isaiah BARKER; pension awarded 25 Jul 1854. SOURCE: WO120 Volume 69 page 291. INDEX # 5680.

Wm BLOCKSOME; pension awarded 25 Jul 1854; died 21 Jun 1873, Melbourne, Australia. SOURCE: WO120 Volume 69 page 291. INDEX # 5681.

Thos CORMICK; pension awarded 25 Jul 1854. SOURCE: WO120 Volume 69 page 291. INDEX # 5682.

Ja^s DONALDSON; pension awarded 25 Jul 1854; died 13 Jun 1865, Belfast. SOURCE: WO120 Volume 69 page 291. INDEX # 5683.

Wm HEWS; pension awarded 25 Jul 1854. SOURCE: WO120 Volume 69 page 291. INDEX # 5684.

Pat^k JOYER; pension awarded 25 Jul 1854. SOURCE: WO120 Volume 69 page 292. INDEX # 5685.

Pat^k JOYCE; pension awarded 25 Jul 1854. SOURCE: WO120 Volume 69 page 291. INDEX # 5686.

Jno LYONS; pension awarded 25 Jul 1854. SOURCE: WO120 Volume 69 page 292. INDEX # 5687.

Ja^s MARSHALL; pension awarded 25 Jul 1854. SOURCE: WO120 Volume 69 page 292. INDEX # 5688.

Nich^s WATERS; pension awarded 25 Jul 1854. SOURCE: WO120 Volume 69 page 292. INDEX # 5689.

Thomas BAYNES; pension awarded 19 Jun 1855. SOURCE: WO120 Volume 69 page 292. INDEX # 5690.

Thomas COSTIGAN; pension awarded 19 Jun 1855. SOURCE: WO120 Volume 69 page 292. INDEX # 5691.

Isaac BENNETT; pension awarded 19 Jun 1855. SOURCE: WO120 Volume 69 page 292. INDEX # 5692.

Hen^y STEED; pension awarded 19 Jun 1855. SOURCE: WO120 Volume 69 page 292. INDEX # 5693.

John COURTNEY; pension awarded 19 Jun 1855. SOURCE: WO120 Volume 69 page 292. INDEX # 5694.

James DAVIDSON; pension awarded 19 Jun 1855. SOURCE: WO120 Volume 69 page 292. INDEX # 5695.

Darby KELLY; pension awarded 19 Jun 1855. SOURCE: WO120 Volume 69 page 292. INDEX # 5696.

David MURDOCH; pension awarded 19 Jun 1855. SOURCE: WO120 Volume 69 page 292. INDEX # 5697.

John MULLIGAN; pension awarded 12 Aug 1856. SOURCE: WO120 Volume 69 page 292. INDEX # 5698.

11th Regiment of Foot (continued)

William SMITH; pension awarded 12 Aug 1856. SOURCE: WO120 Volume 69 page 292. INDEX # 5699.
William WILLIAMS; pension awarded 12 Aug 1856. SOURCE: WO120 Volume 69 page 292. INDEX # 5700.
John JACKSON; pension awarded 12 Aug 1856. SOURCE: WO120 Volume 69 page 292. INDEX # 5701.
George JONES; pension awarded 12 Aug 1856. SOURCE: WO120 Volume 69 page 292. INDEX # 5702.
James SMITH; pension awarded 12 Aug 1856. SOURCE: WO120 Volume 69 page 292. INDEX # 5703.
Francis OREILLY; pension awarded 8 Sep 1857. SOURCE: WO120 Volume 69 page 292. INDEX # 5704.
Walter KYLE; pension awarded 8 Sep 1857. SOURCE: WO120 Volume 69 page 292. INDEX # 5705.
Garrett OCONNOR; pension awarded 8 Sep 1857. SOURCE: WO120 Volume 69 page 292. INDEX # 5706.

Cape Mounted Rifles

Isaac ISAACS; pension awarded 14 Feb 1854. SOURCE: WO120 Volume 69 page 295. INDEX # 5707.
Martin STEWART; pension awarded 13 Jun 1854. SOURCE: WO120 Volume 69 page 295. INDEX # 5708.
Geo^e Hen^y BROOKS; pension awarded 13 Jun 1854. SOURCE: WO120 Volume 69 page 295. INDEX # 5709.
Otto Fr^k Edwd POHL; pension awarded 13 Jun 1854. SOURCE: WO120 Volume 69 page 295. INDEX # 5710.
Adam ZIEDMAN; pension awarded 13 Jun 1854. SOURCE: WO120 Volume 69 page 295. INDEX # 5711.
Jno SMITH; pension awarded 13 Jun 1854. SOURCE: WO120 Volume 69 page 295. INDEX # 5712.
Felix ONEIL; pension awarded 12 Jun 1855. SOURCE: WO120 Volume 69 page 295. INDEX # 5713.
Robert MCDONALD; pension awarded 28 Aug 1855. SOURCE: WO120 Volume 69 page 295. INDEX # 5714.
George HARRIS; pension awarded 25 Sep 1855. SOURCE: WO120 Volume 69 page 295. INDEX # 5715.
Robert ARNOLD; pension awarded 27 May 1856. SOURCE: WO120 Volume 69 page 295. INDEX # 5716.
William BLAKE; pension awarded 27 May 1856. SOURCE: WO120 Volume 69 page 295. INDEX # 5717.
Richard HOOD; pension awarded 19 May 1857. SOURCE: WO120 Volume 69 page 295. INDEX # 5718.
John LEONARD; pension awarded 19 May 1857. SOURCE: WO120 Volume 69 page 295. INDEX # 5719.
George STEPHENS; pension awarded 9 Jun 1857. SOURCE: WO120 Volume 69 page 295. INDEX # 5720.
Thomas CAMPBELL; pension awarded 18 Aug 1857. SOURCE: WO120 Volume 69 page 295. INDEX # 5721.

END OF VOLUME 69

76th Regiment of Foot

Fred^k .VIET; pension awarded 8 Feb 1832; residence - Montreal, Quebec, Canada; died 14 Jun 1889, Montreal, Quebec, Canada. SOURCE: WO120 Volume 70 page 1. INDEX # 5722.

Charles MURKELL; pension awarded 26 Jun 1811; residence - Amherstburg, Ontario, Canada. SOURCE: WO120 Volume 70 page 1. INDEX # 5723.

James SIMMONS; pension awarded 13 Jul 1831; residence - St. Johns. SOURCE: WO120 Volume 70 page 1. INDEX # 5724.

Jno REDDING; pension awarded 12 Dec 1827; residence - Quebec, Quebec, Canada. SOURCE: WO120 Volume 70 page 1. INDEX # 5725.

Thos FLETCHER; pension awarded 31 Oct 1827; residence - Niagara, Ontario, Canada; died 6 Feb 1847. SOURCE: WO120 Volume 70 page 1. INDEX # 5726.

Ja^s COWLLTHORPE; pension awarded 7 Dec 1827; residence - Prescott, Ontario, Canada; died 5 May 1846. SOURCE: WO120 Volume 70 page 1. INDEX # 5727.

Richd HISCOTT; pension awarded 11 Nov 1830; residence - Niagara, Ontario, Canada; died 26 Mar 1874, Hamilton, Ontario, Canada. SOURCE: WO120 Volume 70 page 1. INDEX # 5728.

Jno SAVAGE; pension awarded 12 Dec 1831; residence - Niagara, Ontario, Canada; died 21 Mar 1870, Hamilton, Ontario, Canada. SOURCE: WO120 Volume 70 page 1. INDEX # 5729.

Wm ROLLINGS; pension awarded 11 May 1831; residence - Toronto, Ontario, Canada; died 26 Aug 1859. SOURCE: WO120 Volume 70 page 1. INDEX # 5730.

WW^m PAULSON; pension awarded 31 Oct 1827; residence - Quebec, Quebec, Canada. SOURCE: WO120 Volume 70 page 1. INDEX # 5731.

Jno DEEGAN; pension awarded 9 Aug 1853. SOURCE: WO120 Volume 70 page 1. INDEX # 5732.

Wm MARTIN; pension awarded 9 Aug 1853; died 17 Sep 1889 Halifax, Nova Scotia, Canada. SOURCE: WO120 Volume 70 page 1. INDEX # 5733.

Ja^s STANELAND; pension awarded 11 Oct 1853. SOURCE: WO120 Volume 70 page 1. INDEX # 5734.

Geo^e ASKEW; pension awarded 14 Nov 1854. SOURCE: WO120 Volume 70 page 1. INDEX # 5735.

Jno DILLON; pension awarded 14 Nov 1854. SOURCE: WO120 Volume 70 page 1. INDEX # 5736.

Ja^s STRAIN; pension awarded 14 Nov 1854. SOURCE: WO120 Volume 70 page 1. INDEX # 5737.

Thos WETHERALL; pension awarded 14 Nov 1854. SOURCE: WO120 Volume 70 page 1. INDEX # 5738.

Thomas SAVAGE; pension awarded 28 Aug 1855. SOURCE: WO120 Volume 70 page 1. INDEX # 5739.

John HALL; pension awarded 28 Aug 1855. SOURCE: WO120 Volume 70 page 1. INDEX # 5740.

Cornelius NEAL; pension awarded 13 Nov 1855. SOURCE: WO120 Volume 70 page 1. INDEX # 5741.

Patrick DOHERTY; pension awarded 6 May 1856. SOURCE: WO120 Volume 70 page 2. INDEX # 5742.

Alexander HARPER; pension awarded 29 Jul 1856. SOURCE: WO120 Volume 70 page 2. INDEX # 5743.

Patrick Healy ODONNELL; pension awarded 17 Mar 1857. SOURCE: WO120 Volume 70 page 2. INDEX # 5744.

Richard HUDSON; pension awarded 20 Oct 1857. SOURCE: WO120 Volume 70 page 2. INDEX # 5745.

Matthew SULLIVAN; pension awarded 20 Oct 1857. SOURCE: WO120 Volume 70 page 2. INDEX # 5746.

John Edward ALEXANDER; pension awarded 20 Oct 1857. SOURCE: WO120 Volume 70 page 2. INDEX # 5747.

George EGLETON; pension awarded 20 Oct 1857. SOURCE: WO120 Volume 70 page 2. INDEX # 5748.

Andrew GILMORE; pension awarded 20 Oct 1857. SOURCE: WO120 Volume 70 page 2. INDEX # 5749.

Henry LOUGHLIN; pension awarded 20 Oct 1857. SOURCE: WO120 Volume 70 page 2. INDEX # 5750.

John MCKAY; pension awarded 20 Oct 1857. SOURCE: WO120 Volume 70 page 2. INDEX # 5751.

Benjamin TAYLOR; pension awarded 20 Oct 1857. SOURCE: WO120 Volume 70 page 2. INDEX # 5752.

Saml CHITTOCK; pension awarded 20 May 1856. SOURCE: WO120 Volume 70 page 2. INDEX # 5753.

77th Regiment of Foot

Thos MADDEN; pension awarded 21 Nov 1818; residence - Toronto, Ontario, Canada; died 13 Dec 1845. SOURCE: WO120 Volume 70 page 7. INDEX # 5754.

Thos FARMER; pension awarded 31 May 1815; residence - D^n Ville. SOURCE: WO120 Volume 70 page 7. INDEX # 5755.

77th Regiment of Foot (continued)

Jn⁰ FINLAYSON; pension awarded 18 Dec 1812; residence - Sydney, Nova Scotia, Canada; died in 1846, Halifax, Nova Scotia, Canada. SOURCE: WO120 Volume 70 page 7. INDEX # 5756.

Isaac CHESTNUT; pension awarded 14 Jun 1837; residence - St. Johns. SOURCE: WO120 Volume 70 page 7. INDEX # 5757.

Chas MASON; pension awarded 14 Dec 1836; residence - New South Wales, Australia. SOURCE: WO120 Volume 70 page 7. INDEX # 5758.

Benjn SERGEANT; pension awarded 14 Sep 1847; died 14 Jan 1859, Toronto, Ontario, Canada. SOURCE: WO120 Volume 70 page 7. INDEX # 5759.

Geoe PALMER; pension awarded 12 Oct 1847; died 24 Jan 1869, Manchester. SOURCE: WO120 Volume 70 page 7. INDEX # 5760.

Michl BURKE; pension awarded 12 Oct 1847. SOURCE: WO120 Volume 70 page 7. INDEX # 5761.

Wm MAXWELL; pension awarded 12 Oct 1847. SOURCE: WO120 Volume 70 page 7. INDEX # 5762.

Heny CREED; pension awarded 12 Oct 1847; residence - Niagara, Ontario, Canada; died 10 Sep 1853. SOURCE: WO120 Volume 70 page 7. INDEX # 5763.

Michl MCGITTRIE; pension awarded 12 Oct 1847; residence - London, Ontario, Canada; died 5 Jul 1863. SOURCE: WO120 Volume 70 page 7. INDEX # 5764.

Jn⁰ WELLS; pension awarded 12 Oct 1847; residence - Toronto, Ontario, Canada; died 16 Apr 1866. SOURCE: WO120 Volume 70 page 7. INDEX # 5765.

Jn⁰ GENTLEMAN; pension awarded 14 Dec 1847; residence - Toronto, Ontario, Canada; died in 1851. SOURCE: WO120 Volume 70 page 7. INDEX # 5766.

Jn⁰ R. BREADING; pension awarded 14 Mar 1848. SOURCE: WO120 Volume 70 page 7. INDEX # 5767.

Josh REID; pension awarded 27 Jun 1848; died 19 Oct 1872, Toronto, Ontario, Canada. SOURCE: WO120 Volume 70 page 7. INDEX # 5768.

Michl CALLAGAHN; pension awarded 27 Jun 1848; residence - Montreal, Quebec, Canada; died in 1849. SOURCE: WO120 Volume 70 page 7. INDEX # 5769.

Chas DIXON; pension awarded 27 Jun 1848; residence - London, Ontario, Canada; died 16 Feb 1850. SOURCE: WO120 Volume 70 page 7. INDEX # 5770.

Angus MCPHIE; pension awarded 27 Jun 1848. SOURCE: WO120 Volume 70 page 7. INDEX # 5771.

Jn⁰ WATT; pension awarded 27 Jun 1848; died 14 Nov 1863. SOURCE: WO120 Volume 70 page 7. INDEX # 5772.

Lot ASHTON; pension awarded 27 Jun 1848; residence - Toronto, Ontario, Canada; died 3 Jul 1852. SOURCE: WO120 Volume 70 page 7. INDEX # 5773.

Thos ATKINS; pension awarded 27 Jun 1848. SOURCE: WO120 Volume 70 page 8. INDEX # 5774.

Thos ATKINSON; pension awarded 27 Jun 1848; residence - Toronto, Ontario, Canada; died 23 Jul 1852. SOURCE: WO120 Volume 70 page 8. INDEX # 5775.

Geoe CAMPBELL; pension awarded 27 Jun 1848; residence - London, Ontario, Canada; died in 1852. SOURCE: WO120 Volume 70 page 8. INDEX # 5776.

Josh CATELLA; pension awarded 27 Jun 1848; died 7 Jan 1883, Toronto, Ontario, Canada. SOURCE: WO120 Volume 70 page 8. INDEX # 5777.

Jn⁰ CONNING; pension awarded 27 Jun 1848. SOURCE: WO120 Volume 70 page 8. INDEX # 5778.

Jas HAMILTON; pension awarded 27 Jun 1848. SOURCE: WO120 Volume 70 page 8. INDEX # 5779.

Patk HUGHES; pension awarded 27 Jun 1848. SOURCE: WO120 Volume 70 page 8. INDEX # 5780.

Michl KENNY; pension awarded 27 Jun 1848; residence - London, Ontario, Canada; died in 1865. SOURCE: WO120 Volume 70 page 8. INDEX # 5781.

Jn⁰ LOCHEAD; pension awarded 27 Jun 1848; residence - London, Ontario, Canada; died in Nov 1848. SOURCE: WO120 Volume 70 page 8. INDEX # 5782.

Geoe LONG; pension awarded 27 Jun 1848; died 18 Dec 1884, Toronto, Ontario, Canada. SOURCE: WO120 Volume 70 page 8. INDEX # 5783.

Jn⁰ MCLAREN; pension awarded 27 Jun 1848; residence - Canada; died 12 May 1854. SOURCE: WO120 Volume 70 page 8. INDEX # 5784.

Jn⁰ ROCHE; pension awarded 27 Jun 1848; residence - Saint John, New Brunswick, Canada; died 30 Jun 1851. SOURCE: WO120 Volume 70 page 8. INDEX # 5785.

BRITISH ARMY PENSIONERS ABROAD

78th Regiment of Foot

Don^d MORRISON; pension awarded 9 Sep 1810; residence - St. Johns; died in 1817. SOURCE: WO120 Volume 70 page 16. INDEX # 5786.

Ja^s MCGILLIVRAY; pension awarded 28 Jun 1814; residence - Quebec, Quebec, Canada. SOURCE: WO120 Volume 70 page 16. INDEX # 5787.

Murd^k MCKAY; pension awarded 19 May 1818; residence - New South Wales, Australia. SOURCE: WO120 Volume 70 page 16. INDEX # 5788.

Ja^s SUTHERLAND; pension awarded 13 Aug 1813; residence - St. Johns. SOURCE: WO120 Volume 70 page 16. INDEX # 5789.

Thos INVERNESS; pension awarded 13 Jul 1831; residence - Ceylon; died 9 Oct 1845. SOURCE: WO120 Volume 70 page 16. INDEX # 5790.

Willm ROSS; pension awarded 9 Jun 1819; residence - London, Ontario, Canada; died 23 Aug 1856. SOURCE: WO120 Volume 70 page 16. INDEX # 5791.

Alex^r ROBERTSON; pension awarded 24 Jan 1816; residence - Talbot, Ontario, Canada; died 22 Aug 1855. SOURCE: WO120 Volume 70 page 16. INDEX # 5792.

John GUNN; pension awarded 10 Jun 1845; residence - Sukkur, India. SOURCE: WO120 Volume 70 page 16. INDEX # 5793.

Wm ASHBURNE; pension awarded 14 Oct 1835; residence - Ceylon; died 28 Feb 1847. SOURCE: WO120 Volume 70 page 16. INDEX # 5794.

Thos FRASER; pension awarded 13 Jun 1838; residence - Jamaica. SOURCE: WO120 Volume 70 page 16. INDEX # 5795.

Wm MCKAY; pension awarded 10 Aug 1831; residence - Charlottetown, Prince Edward Island, Canada. SOURCE: WO120 Volume 70 page 16. INDEX # 5796.

John WILSON; pension awarded 26 May 1841; residence - Cape of Good Hope, South Africa; died 15 May 1847. SOURCE: WO120 Volume 70 page 16. INDEX # 5797.

Evander MCIVER; pension awarded 16 Jun 1824; residence - Drummondville, Quebec, Canada. SOURCE: WO120 Volume 70 page 16. INDEX # 5798.

Jno DALZIEL; pension awarded 9 May 1838; residence - Ceylon; died 23 May 1873, E. London. SOURCE: WO120 Volume 70 page 16. INDEX # 5799.

Wm MCKENZIE; pension awarded 16 Mar 1825; residence - Quebec, Quebec, Canada; died 1 Apr 1873, London, Ontario, Canada. SOURCE: WO120 Volume 70 page 16. INDEX # 5800.

John ELLIS; pension awarded 28 Oct 1845; residence - Jamaica. SOURCE: WO120 Volume 70 page 16. INDEX # 5801.

John MOULDER; pension awarded 11 May 1847; residence - Bombay, India; died 19 Oct 1850. SOURCE: WO120 Volume 70 page 16. INDEX # 5802.

Jno WALLIS; pension awarded 11 May 1847; died 10 Jan 1848. SOURCE: WO120 Volume 70 page 16. INDEX # 5803.

Danl DOOGAN; pension awarded 27 Jun 1848; died 3 Aug 1884, Tasmania, Australia. SOURCE: WO120 Volume 70 page 16. INDEX # 5804.

79th Regiment of Foot

Ja^s MUNRO; pension awarded 10 Aug 1808; residence - Toronto, Ontario, Canada; died 18 Jun 1865. SOURCE: WO120 Volume 70 page 22. INDEX # 5805.

Chas MCKAY; pension awarded 25 Feb 1817; residence - Halifax, Nova Scotia, Canada; died 3 Jan 1872, Nova Scotia, Canada. SOURCE: WO120 Volume 70 page 22. INDEX # 5806.

Ja^s HAMILTON; pension awarded 15 Apr 1819; residence - Toronto, Ontario, Canada; died 1 Sep 1873. SOURCE: WO120 Volume 70 page 22. INDEX # 5807.

Wm NICKLE; pension awarded 13 Nov 1833; residence - London, Ontario, Canada; died 4 Aug 1855. SOURCE: WO120 Volume 70 page 22. INDEX # 5808.

Don^d MCLEOD; pension awarded 25 Feb 1819; residence - Montreal, Quebec, Canada. SOURCE: WO120 Volume 70 page 22. INDEX # 5809.

John GRANT; pension awarded 13 Nov 1833; residence - Toronto, Ontario, Canada; died 1 Dec 1853. SOURCE: WO120 Volume 70 page 22. INDEX # 5810.

79th Regiment of Foot (continued)

John BANNERMAN; pension awarded 29 Mar 1815; residence - Toronto, Ontario, Canada; died 25 Apr 1864. SOURCE: WO120 Volume 70 page 22. INDEX # 5811.

Ja^s SCROGUE; pension awarded 7 Jan 1802; residence - Toronto, Ontario, Canada; died 13 Jan 1854. SOURCE: WO120 Volume 70 page 22. INDEX # 5812.

Angus HAMILTON; pension awarded 14 Dec 1831; residence - Toronto, Ontario, Canada; died 27 Dec 1846. SOURCE: WO120 Volume 70 page 22. INDEX # 5813.

Peter CAMPBELL; pension awarded 14 Dec 1836; residence - Toronto, Ontario, Canada; died in 1846. SOURCE: WO120 Volume 70 page 22. INDEX # 5814.

John LESLIE; pension awarded 23 Aug 1814; residence - Toronto, Ontario, Canada; died 10 Nov 1870, Toronto, Ontario, Canada. SOURCE: WO120 Volume 70 page 22. INDEX # 5815.

Ja^s LAING; pension awarded 20 Mar 1816; residence - Quebec, Quebec, Canada; died in 1849. SOURCE: WO120 Volume 70 page 22. INDEX # 5816.

Ja^s MCLEOD; pension awarded 7 Nov 1811; residence - Halifax, Nova Scotia, Canada. SOURCE: WO120 Volume 70 page 22. INDEX # 5817.

Noble SPROUL; pension awarded 29 Nov 1820; residence - Penetanguishene, Ontario, Canada; died 10 Apr 1867, Hamilton, Ontario, Canada. SOURCE: WO120 Volume 70 page 22. INDEX # 5818.

Ja^s SUTHERLAND; pension awarded 15 Mar 1826; residence - London, Ontario, Canada; died 11 Apr 1873, London, Ontario, Canada. SOURCE: WO120 Volume 70 page 22. INDEX # 5819.

Dug^l CAMERON; pension awarded 7 Jun 1818; residence - New South Wales, Australia. SOURCE: WO120 Volume 70 page 22. INDEX # 5820.

Willm STURROCK; pension awarded 10 May 1837; residence - Quebec, Quebec, Canada. SOURCE: WO120 Volume 70 page 22. INDEX # 5821.

Thos WHEELER; pension awarded 12 Jul 1842; residence - Gibraltar; died 4 Dec 1871. SOURCE: WO120 Volume 70 page 22. INDEX # 5822.

John MURRAY; pension awarded 19 Jul 1816; residence - Toronto, Ontario, Canada; died 28 Apr 1855. SOURCE: WO120 Volume 70 page 22. INDEX # 5823.

Wm MCCREADIE; pension awarded 14 Dec 1836; residence - Toronto, Ontario, Canada; died 6 Sep 1876, Toronto, Ontario, Canada. SOURCE: WO120 Volume 70 page 22. INDEX # 5824.

Ja^s GLEN; pension awarded 26 Feb 1840; residence - Toronto, Ontario, Canada; died 5 Apr 1846. SOURCE: WO120 Volume 70 page 23. INDEX # 5825.

Ja^s MCPHATERS; pension awarded 14 Dec 1836; residence - Toronto, Ontario, Canada. SOURCE: WO120 Volume 70 page 23. INDEX # 5826.

Jno MCKENZIE; pension awarded 9 Jan 1833; residence - Toronto, Ontario, Canada; died 10 Jun 1872, Toronto, Ontario, Canada. SOURCE: WO120 Volume 70 page 23. INDEX # 5827.

Hector ROSS; pension awarded 12 Jun 1833; residence - Halifax, Nova Scotia, Canada. SOURCE: WO120 Volume 70 page 23. INDEX # 5828.

Jno MCINNES; pension awarded 9 Mar 1842; residence - Gibraltar. SOURCE: WO120 Volume 70 page 23. INDEX # 5829.

Geo^e HENDERSON; pension awarded 11 Dec 1833; residence - Toronto, Ontario, Canada; died 2 Nov 1872, Toronto, Ontario, Canada. SOURCE: WO120 Volume 70 page 23. INDEX # 5830.

Colin MCDONALD; pension awarded 12 Oct 1836; residence - Montreal, Quebec, Canada. SOURCE: WO120 Volume 70 page 23. INDEX # 5831.

Wm MCALLISTER; pension awarded 13 Feb 1849; residence - Canada; died 16 Sep 1849. SOURCE: WO120 Volume 70 page 23. INDEX # 5832.

Wm LASKIE; pension awarded 23 Oct 1849. SOURCE: WO120 Volume 70 page 23. INDEX # 5833.

Wm PEAT; pension awarded 23 Oct 1849; residence - Canada; died in 1849. SOURCE: WO120 Volume 70 page 23. INDEX # 5834.

Angus MCDONALD; pension awarded 23 Oct 1849; residence - Toronto, Ontario, Canada; died 3 Nov 1859. SOURCE: WO120 Volume 70 page 23. INDEX # 5835.

Hugh MCKECHNIE; pension awarded 23 Oct 1849; residence - London, Ontario, Canada; died 3 Sep 1855. SOURCE: WO120 Volume 70 page 23. INDEX # 5836.

79th Regiment of Foot (continued)

Geo^e CONNOLLY; pension awarded 1 Oct 1850. SOURCE: WO120 Volume 70 page 23. INDEX # 5837.

Geo^e HENDERSON; pension awarded 1 Oct 1850. SOURCE: WO120 Volume 70 page 23. INDEX # 5838.

Wm HOSTLER; pension awarded 1 Oct 1850. SOURCE: WO120 Volume 70 page 23. INDEX # 5839.

Thos MCQUEEN; pension awarded 1 Oct 1850. SOURCE: WO120 Volume 70 page 23. INDEX # 5840.

Wm YUILLE; pension awarded 1 Oct 1850. SOURCE: WO120 Volume 70 page 23. INDEX # 5841.

Alex^r LEIGHTON; pension awarded 11 Feb 1851; residence - Canada. SOURCE: WO120 Volume 70 page 23. INDEX # 5842.

Thos SCOTT; pension awarded 5 Aug 1851; died 3 Jan 1880, Edinburgh. SOURCE: WO120 Volume 70 page 23. INDEX # 5843.

Jos^h MCLAUCHLAN; pension awarded 5 Aug 1851. SOURCE: WO120 Volume 70 page 23. INDEX # 5844.

Wm Gunn HAMILTON; pension awarded 5 Aug 1851. SOURCE: WO120 Volume 70 page 23. INDEX # 5845.

Alex^r BLACK; pension awarded 5 Aug 1851. SOURCE: WO120 Volume 70 page 24. INDEX # 5846.

Jno BOWIE; pension awarded 5 Aug 1851. SOURCE: WO120 Volume 70 page 24. INDEX # 5847.

Wm CHAMBERS; pension awarded 5 Aug 1851; residence - Toronto, Ontario, Canada; died 13 Oct 1855. SOURCE: WO120 Volume 70 page 24. INDEX # 5848.

Wm CLARK; pension awarded 5 Aug 1851. SOURCE: WO120 Volume 70 page 24. INDEX # 5849.

Jno CLEMENT; pension awarded 5 Aug 1851. SOURCE: WO120 Volume 70 page 24. INDEX # 5850.

Dugald COLQUHOUN; pension awarded 5 Aug 1851. SOURCE: WO120 Volume 70 page 24. INDEX # 5851.

Jno DINNON; pension awarded 5 Aug 1851. SOURCE: WO120 Volume 70 page 24. INDEX # 5852.

Wm GRAHAM; pension awarded 5 Aug 1851. SOURCE: WO120 Volume 70 page 24. INDEX # 5853.

Robt LAING; pension awarded 5 Aug 1851; residence - Toronto, Ontario, Canada; died 23 Jul 1864. SOURCE: WO120 Volume 70 page 24. INDEX # 5854.

Dugald LIVINGSTON; pension awarded 5 Aug 1851. SOURCE: WO120 Volume 70 page 24. INDEX # 5855.

Fran^s MCGRATH; pension awarded 5 Aug 1851. SOURCE: WO120 Volume 70 page 24. INDEX # 5856.

Ja^s MCILREA; pension awarded 5 Aug 1851; died 12 Jan 1862, Toronto, Ontario, Canada. SOURCE: WO120 Volume 70 page 24. INDEX # 5857.

Wm MCKAY; pension awarded 5 Aug 1851. SOURCE: WO120 Volume 70 page 24. INDEX # 5858.

Alex^r MCKENZIE; pension awarded 5 Aug 1851. SOURCE: WO120 Volume 70 page 24. INDEX # 5859.

Chas MILLER; pension awarded 5 Aug 1851. SOURCE: WO120 Volume 70 page 24. INDEX # 5860.

Wm MITCHELL; pension awarded 5 Aug 1851; residence - London, Ontario, Canada; died 3 Jan 1864. SOURCE: WO120 Volume 70 page 24. INDEX # 5861.

Abr^m MOFFAT; pension awarded 5 Aug 1851. SOURCE: WO120 Volume 70 page 24. INDEX # 5862.

Wm MORE; pension awarded 5 Aug 1851. SOURCE: WO120 Volume 70 page 24. INDEX # 5863.

Thos ORR; pension awarded 5 Aug 1851; residence - Hamilton, Ontario, Canada; died in 1853. SOURCE: WO120 Volume 70 page 24. INDEX # 5864.

W^m RAE; pension awarded 5 Aug 1851. SOURCE: WO120 Volume 70 page 25. INDEX # 5865.

Jno ROBERTSON; pension awarded 5 Aug 1851. SOURCE: WO120 Volume 70 page 25. INDEX # 5866.

Jno ROSS; pension awarded 5 Aug 1851. SOURCE: WO120 Volume 70 page 25. INDEX # 5867.

Robt RUSSELL; pension awarded 5 Aug 1851. SOURCE: WO120 Volume 70 page 25. INDEX # 5868.

Jno STALKER; pension awarded 5 Aug 1851; died 6 Sep 1862, Toronto, Ontario, Canada. SOURCE: WO120 Volume 70 page 25. INDEX # 5869.

Jno TELFER; pension awarded 5 Aug 1851. SOURCE: WO120 Volume 70 page 25. INDEX # 5870.

Danl WILKINS; pension awarded 5 Aug 1851. SOURCE: WO120 Volume 70 page 25. INDEX # 5871.

Duncan MCINNES; pension awarded 23 Sep 1851; residence - London, Ontario, Canada; died 21 Jul 1856. SOURCE: WO120 Volume 70 page 25. INDEX # 5872.

80th Regiment of Foot

Willm BALDWIN; pension awarded 10 Nov 1817; residence - Bytown, Ontario, Canada. SOURCE: WO120 Volume 70 page 29. INDEX # 5873.

80th Regiment of Foot (continued)

Thos WILLIAMS; pension awarded 28 Aug 1839; residence - New South Wales, Australia. SOURCE: WO120 Volume 70 page 29. INDEX # 5874.

Jno PEARNS; pension awarded 17 Mar 1819; residence - New South Wales, Australia. SOURCE: WO120 Volume 70 page 29. INDEX # 5875.

Willm MANNING; pension awarded 12 Sep 1821; residence - Kingston, Ontario, Canada; died 15 Nov 1845. SOURCE: WO120 Volume 70 page 29. INDEX # 5876.

John DENN; pension awarded 28 Aug 1839; residence - Sydney, New South Wales, Australia. SOURCE: WO120 Volume 70 page 29. INDEX # 5877.

Mark COLEMAN; pension awarded 14 Oct 1840; residence - New South Wales, Australia; died 15 Jul 1846. SOURCE: WO120 Volume 70 page 29. INDEX # 5878.

Saml EVANS; pension awarded 21 Jan 1843; residence - New South Wales, Australia. SOURCE: WO120 Volume 70 page 29. INDEX # 5879.

Jas DARLING; pension awarded 28 Aug 1839; residence - New South Wales, Australia. SOURCE: WO120 Volume 70 page 29. INDEX # 5880.

Jas TOWELL; pension awarded 25 Aug 1841; residence - New South Wales. SOURCE: WO120 Volume 70 page 29. INDEX # 5881.

Jno HARDY; pension awarded 27 Sep 1842; residence - Sydney, New South Wales, Australia. SOURCE: WO120 Volume 70 page 29. INDEX # 5882.

Thos TAYLOR; pension awarded 8 Aug 1843; residence - New South Wales, Australia. SOURCE: WO120 Volume 70 page 29. INDEX # 5883.

Alexr BOWIE; pension awarded 14 Oct 1840; residence - New South Wales, Australia. SOURCE: WO120 Volume 70 page 29. INDEX # 5884.

Jas SHANNAGHAN; pension awarded 28 Aug 1839; residence - New South Wales, Australia. SOURCE: WO120 Volume 70 page 29. INDEX # 5885.

Geoe SMITH; pension awarded 9 Jan 1839; residence - New South Wales, Australia. SOURCE: WO120 Volume 70 page 29. INDEX # 5886.

Thos INGRAM; pension awarded 14 Oct 1840; residence - New South Wales, Australia. SOURCE: WO120 Volume 70 page 29. INDEX # 5887.

Josh SCOTT; pension awarded 25 Aug 1841. SOURCE: WO120 Volume 70 page 29. INDEX # 5888.

Willm FLOREY; pension awarded 27 Aug 1844; residence - New South Wales, Australia; died in 1846. SOURCE: WO120 Volume 70 page 29. INDEX # 5889.

Jas SANDY; pension awarded 27 Sep 1842; residence - New South Wales, Australia; died 21 Aug 1850. SOURCE: WO120 Volume 70 page 29. INDEX # 5890.

Jno MCJAMMESON; pension awarded 8 Aug 1843; residence - New South Wales, Australia; died 9 Jul 1880, New South Wales, Australia. SOURCE: WO120 Volume 70 page 29. INDEX # 5891.

Lewis MOORE; pension awarded 28 Aug 1839; residence - New South Wales, Australia. SOURCE: WO120 Volume 70 page 29. INDEX # 5892.

John SMITH; pension awarded 27 Sep 1842; residence - New South Wales, Australia. SOURCE: WO120 Volume 70 page 30. INDEX # 5893.

Jas PROUDLOVE; pension awarded 26 Aug 1845; residence - Sydney, New South Wales, Australia. SOURCE: WO120 Volume 70 page 30. INDEX # 5894.

Chas ANDRAOS; pension awarded 16 Oct 1840; residence - New South Wales, Australia; died 10 Mar 1883, Sydney, New South Wales, Australia. SOURCE: WO120 Volume 70 page 30. INDEX # 5895.

Jno FORSTER; pension awarded 8 Aug 1843; residence - New South Wales, Australia. SOURCE: WO120 Volume 70 page 30. INDEX # 5896.

Jno ANDREWS; pension awarded 14 Oct 1840; residence - New South Wales, Australia; died 12 May 1879, Sydney, New South Wales, Australia. SOURCE: WO120 Volume 70 page 30. INDEX # 5897.

Wm HART; pension awarded 27 Dec 1842; residence - New South Wales, Australia. SOURCE: WO120 Volume 70 page 30. INDEX # 5898.

80th Regiment of Foot (continued)

Saml EDGERTON; pension awarded 14 Oct 1840; residence - New South Wales, Australia; died 16 Aug 1878, Sydney, New South Wales, Australia. SOURCE: WO120 Volume 70 page 30. INDEX # 5899.

Abel HARDMAN; pension awarded 27 Sep 1842; residence - New South Wales, Australia. SOURCE: WO120 Volume 70 page 30. INDEX # 5900.

Ja^s HENNESSEY; pension awarded 23 Mar 1847; residence - Calcutta, India. SOURCE: WO120 Volume 70 page 30. INDEX # 5901.

Wm JONES; pension awarded 25 Jan 1848; residence - Chinsurah, India; died 30 Apr 1854. SOURCE: WO120 Volume 70 page 30. INDEX # 5902.

Ja^s BURNS; pension awarded 25 Jan 1848; residence - Meerut, India; died 15 Jul 1849. SOURCE: WO120 Volume 70 page 30. INDEX # 5903.

Wm PRICE; pension awarded 25 Jan 1848. SOURCE: WO120 Volume 70 page 30. INDEX # 5904.

Jno TAYLOR; pension awarded 25 Jan 1848. SOURCE: WO120 Volume 70 page 30. INDEX # 5905.

Jno WATERS; pension awarded 25 Jan 1848; residence - Meerut, India; died 31 Mar 1849. SOURCE: WO120 Volume 70 page 30. INDEX # 5906.

Wm BARNETT; pension awarded 13 Feb 1849; died 30 Oct 1869, Royal Hospital, Chelsea, Engl^d. SOURCE: WO120 Volume 70 page 30. INDEX # 5907.

Mich^l CAHILL; pension awarded 13 Feb 1849; residence - Meerut, India; died 18 Dec 1856. SOURCE: WO120 Volume 70 page 30. INDEX # 5908.

Martin CUDDY; pension awarded 13 Feb 1849; residence - Dinapore, India; died 20 May 1850. SOURCE: WO120 Volume 70 page 30. INDEX # 5909.

Ja^s HAMILTON; pension awarded 13 Feb 1849; residence - Dinapore, India; died 29 Aug 1851. SOURCE: WO120 Volume 70 page 30. INDEX # 5910.

Jno KEARNEY; pension awarded 1 Oct 1850; residence - Dinapore, India; died 17 May 1851. SOURCE: WO120 Volume 70 page 30. INDEX # 5911.

Ja^s BERRY; pension awarded 9 May 1854. SOURCE: WO120 Volume 70 page 30. INDEX # 5912.

81st Regiment of Foot

Ter^e MARTIN; pension awarded 1 Feb 1826; residence - Halifax, Nova Scotia, Canada. SOURCE: WO120 Volume 70 page 39. INDEX # 5913.

Pat^k KELLY; pension awarded 15 Apr 1829; residence - Toronto, Ontario, Canada; died in 1854. SOURCE: WO120 Volume 70 page 39. INDEX # 5914.

Peter BIERY; pension awarded 25 Jun 1827; residence - Halifax, Nova Scotia, Canada; died in 1819, Nova Scotia, Canada. SOURCE: WO120 Volume 70 page 39. INDEX # 5915.

Ja^s ROBINSON; pension awarded 12 May 1815; residence - New South Wales, Australia; died in 1853. SOURCE: WO120 Volume 70 page 39. INDEX # 5916.

Danl CONNOLLY; pension awarded 9 Sep 1845; residence - St. Jean, Quebec, Canada. SOURCE: WO120 Volume 70 page 39. INDEX # 5917.

Tim^y HURLEY; pension awarded 29 Nov 1820; residence - Toronto, Ontario, Canada; died 14 Oct 1857. SOURCE: WO120 Volume 70 page 39. INDEX # 5918.

John BRADY; pension awarded 13 Aug 1844; residence - Chambly, Quebec, Canada. SOURCE: WO120 Volume 70 page 39. INDEX # 5919.

John CONROY; pension awarded 13 Aug 1844; residence - St. Jean, Quebec, Canada. SOURCE: WO120 Volume 70 page 39. INDEX # 5920.

Den^s OBRIEN; pension awarded 13 Aug 1844; residence - Toronto, Ontario, Canada; died 18 Jul 1873. SOURCE: WO120 Volume 70 page 39. INDEX # 5921.

Dav^d PEASLEY; pension awarded 13 Aug 1844; residence - London, Ontario, Canada; died Toronto, Ontario, Canada. SOURCE: WO120 Volume 70 page 39. INDEX # 5922.

H^y IRWIN; pension awarded 26 Nov 1844; residence - Toronto, Ontario, Canada. SOURCE: WO120 Volume 70 page 39. INDEX # 5923.

Ja^s BOYD; pension awarded 26 Aug 1845; residence - Montreal, Quebec, Canada. SOURCE: WO120 Volume 70 page 39. INDEX # 5924.

81st Regiment of Foot (continued)

Jno MCGUINNESS; pension awarded 26 Aug 1845; residence - St. Jean, Quebec, Canada; died 20 Feb 1856. SOURCE: WO120 Volume 70 page 39. INDEX # 5925.

Thos FALLON; pension awarded 13 Jan 1830; residence - Fredericton, New Brunswick, Canada. SOURCE: WO120 Volume 70 page 39. INDEX # 5926.

Edwd THOMAS; pension awarded 10 Oct 1832; residence - St. Johns; died 25 Jun 1847. SOURCE: WO120 Volume 70 page 39. INDEX # 5927.

John MATHIAS; pension awarded 13 Dec 1826; residence - Halifax, Nova Scotia, Canada. SOURCE: WO120 Volume 70 page 39. INDEX # 5928.

Widelius BONN; pension awarded 30 Jun 1825; residence - Halifax, Nova Scotia, Canada; died in Jul 1851. SOURCE: WO120 Volume 70 page 39. INDEX # 5929.

Jas MCEVOY; pension awarded 11 Mar 1840; residence - Gibraltar. SOURCE: WO120 Volume 70 page 39. INDEX # 5930.

Wm ROBERTS; pension awarded 11 Aug 1841; residence - Gibraltar. SOURCE: WO120 Volume 70 page 39. INDEX # 5931.

Danl JONES; pension awarded 21 May 1828; residence - Halifax, Nova Scotia, Canada. SOURCE: WO120 Volume 70 page 39. INDEX # 5932.

Mattw LEWIS; pension awarded 8 Aug 1827; residence - Halifax, Nova Scotia, Canada. SOURCE: WO120 Volume 70 page 40. INDEX # 5933.

Patk ONEILL; pension awarded 13 Aug 1844; residence - Wm Henry, Quebec, Canada; died 7 Oct 1863, Toronto, Ontario, Canada. SOURCE: WO120 Volume 70 page 40. INDEX # 5934.

Andw COLEMAN; pension awarded 9 Dec 1829; residence - St. Johns. SOURCE: WO120 Volume 70 page 40. INDEX # 5935.

Saml MOLQNEANY; pension awarded 16 Jun 1824; residence - Kingston, Ontario, Canada; died 5 Feb 1857. SOURCE: WO120 Volume 70 page 40. INDEX # 5936.

Wm COULBOURNE; pension awarded 21 May 1828; residence - Halifax, Nova Scotia, Canada; died 23 Jul 1854. SOURCE: WO120 Volume 70 page 40. INDEX # 5937.

Richd LANDERS; pension awarded 13 Aug 1844; residence - Prescott, Ontario, Canada; died 28 May 1852. SOURCE: WO120 Volume 70 page 40. INDEX # 5938.

Thos IRWIN; pension awarded 19 Jul 1816; residence - Niagara, Ontario, Canada. SOURCE: WO120 Volume 70 page 40. INDEX # 5939.

Jno BOURNES; pension awarded 16 Apr 1846; residence - Montreal, Quebec, Canada. SOURCE: WO120 Volume 70 page 40. INDEX # 5940.

Jno BURNES; pension awarded 16 Apr 1846; residence - Montreal, Quebec, Canada. SOURCE: WO120 Volume 70 page 40. INDEX # 5941.

Michl WHITE; pension awarded 16 Oct 1845; residence - Quebec, Quebec, Canada; died 23 Aug 1854. SOURCE: WO120 Volume 70 page 40. INDEX # 5942.

Andw CARLISLE; pension awarded 14 Jan 1835; residence - Toronto, Ontario, Canada; died 25 Oct 1850. SOURCE: WO120 Volume 70 page 40. INDEX # 5943.

Jas CARLISLE; pension awarded 25 Oct; residence - Toronto, Ontario, Canada; died in 1851. SOURCE: WO120 Volume 70 page 40. INDEX # 5944.

Jas MASON; pension awarded 14 Sep 1847. SOURCE: WO120 Volume 70 page 40. INDEX # 5945.

82nd Regiment of Foot

Wm HEIGHLAND; pension awarded 26 Dec 1805; residence - Penetanguishene, Ontario, Canada; died 6 Mar 1863, Hamilton, Ontario, Canada. SOURCE: WO120 Volume 70 page 46. INDEX # 5946.

Richd TERCE; pension awarded 13 Apr 1809; residence - New South Wales, Australia. SOURCE: WO120 Volume 70 page 46. INDEX # 5947.

John DAVIS; pension awarded 13 Oct 1814; residence - Toronto, Ontario, Canada; died 1 Apr 1864. SOURCE: WO120 Volume 70 page 46. INDEX # 5948.

Willm FERGUSON; pension awarded 11 Jan 1832; residence - Mauritius; died 10 Jan 1848. SOURCE: WO120 Volume 70 page 46. INDEX # 5949.

BRITISH ARMY PENSIONERS ABROAD
82nd Regiment of Foot (continued)

Ja^s MCCANN; pension awarded 16 Jan 1844; residence - Montreal, Quebec, Canada. SOURCE: WO120 Volume 70 page 46. INDEX # 5950.

Robt QUAIL; pension awarded 13 Aug 1844; residence - Toronto, Ontario, Canada; died 22 Aug 1870, Toronto, Ontario, Canada. SOURCE: WO120 Volume 70 page 46. INDEX # 5951.

Pat^k BRYAN; pension awarded 26 Oct 1843; residence - Montreal, Quebec, Canada; died 13 Jun 1855. SOURCE: WO120 Volume 70 page 46. INDEX # 5952.

Ja^s LITTLEWORTH; pension awarded 26 Jun 1816; residence - Adelaide. SOURCE: WO120 Volume 70 page 46. INDEX # 5953.

Robt ROSS; pension awarded 17 Jan 1829; residence - Quebec, Quebec, Canada. SOURCE: WO120 Volume 70 page 46. INDEX # 5954.

Ja^s PEARSON; pension awarded 16 Jan 1835; residence - St. Johns; died in Apr 1851. SOURCE: WO120 Volume 70 page 46. INDEX # 5955.

Pat^k MINTON; pension awarded 11 Jan 1832; residence - Mauritius; died in 1847. SOURCE: WO120 Volume 70 page 46. INDEX # 5956.

John HACK; pension awarded 9 Apr 1834; residence - Mauritius. SOURCE: WO120 Volume 70 page 46. INDEX # 5957.

Willm ROSE; pension awarded 23 Dec 1845; residence - Toronto, Ontario, Canada; died 26 Feb 1883, Toronto, Ontario, Canada. SOURCE: WO120 Volume 70 page 46. INDEX # 5958.

Saml MOORE; pension awarded 10 Aug 1836; residence - Bermuda; died 27 Jul 1881, Montreal, Quebec, Canada. SOURCE: WO120 Volume 70 page 46. INDEX # 5959.

And^w ELLIOTT; pension awarded 13 Jan 1846; residence - Montreal, Quebec, Canada. SOURCE: WO120 Volume 70 page 46. INDEX # 5960.

Simon BYRNE; pension awarded 22 Sep 1846; residence - Montreal, Quebec, Canada; died 9 Mar 1879, Toronto, Ontario, Canada. SOURCE: WO120 Volume 70 page 46. INDEX # 5961.

Willm GARLAND; pension awarded 22 Sep 1846; residence - Quebec, Quebec, Canada; died 10 Oct 1873, Toronto, Ontario, Canada. SOURCE: WO120 Volume 70 page 46. INDEX # 5962.

John RILEY; pension awarded 22 Sep 1846; residence - Toronto, Ontario, Canada; died 29 Oct 1856. SOURCE: WO120 Volume 70 page 46. INDEX # 5963.

Ed^{wd} WALDRON; pension awarded 22 Sep 1846; residence - Montreal, Quebec, Canada. SOURCE: WO120 Volume 70 page 46. INDEX # 5964.

Paul TURNER; pension awarded 13 Oct 1846; residence - Toronto, Ontario, Canada; died in 1850. SOURCE: WO120 Volume 70 page 46. INDEX # 5965.

Thos BRAND; pension awarded 12 Oct 1847. SOURCE: WO120 Volume 70 page 47. INDEX # 5966.

Jno Robt POTTER; pension awarded 12 Oct 1847; died 11 Feb 1873, London, Ontario, Canada. SOURCE: WO120 Volume 70 page 47. INDEX # 5967.

Jno TWYFORD; pension awarded 12 Oct 1847. SOURCE: WO120 Volume 70 page 47. INDEX # 5968.

Jno BICKNELL; pension awarded 12 Oct 1847; residence - Hamilton, Ontario, Canada; died 19 Aug 1859. SOURCE: WO120 Volume 70 page 47. INDEX # 5969.

Jos^h HARDY; pension awarded 12 Oct 1847; residence - London, Ontario, Canada; died 21 Aug 1851. SOURCE: WO120 Volume 70 page 47. INDEX # 5970.

Mich^l CONROY; pension awarded 12 Oct 1847. SOURCE: WO120 Volume 70 page 47. INDEX # 5971.

Saml FARRAH; pension awarded 12 Oct 1847; died 20 Feb 1867. SOURCE: WO120 Volume 70 page 47. INDEX # 5972.

Chas LINDSAY; pension awarded 12 Oct 1847; residence - London, Ontario, Canada. SOURCE: WO120 Volume 70 page 47. INDEX # 5973.

Robt MCVEY; pension awarded 12 Oct 1847; residence - London, Ontario, Canada; died 21 May 1855. SOURCE: WO120 Volume 70 page 47. INDEX # 5974.

Jno MARSHALL; pension awarded 12 Oct 1847; residence - London, Ontario, Canada; died 8 Aug 1863. SOURCE: WO120 Volume 70 page 47. INDEX # 5975.

Robt ORIORDAN; pension awarded 12 Oct 1847; died 15 Mar 1861. SOURCE: WO120 Volume 70 page 47. INDEX # 5976.

Ja^s RAMPLIN; pension awarded 12 Oct 1847. SOURCE: WO120 Volume 70 page 47. INDEX # 5977.

Tim^y SHEA; pension awarded 12 Oct 1847. SOURCE: WO120 Volume 70 page 47. INDEX # 5978.

WO120 VOLUME 70 207

82nd Regiment of Foot (continued)

Richd SPEIGHT; pension awarded 12 Oct 1847. SOURCE: WO120 Volume 70 page 47. INDEX # 5979.

Thos WINTER; pension awarded 12 Oct 1847; died 14 Sep 1874, London, Ontario, Canada. SOURCE: WO120 Volume 70 page 47. INDEX # 5980.

Ja^s HAY; pension awarded 14 Dec 1847. SOURCE: WO120 Volume 70 page 47. INDEX # 5981.

Wm ROGERS; pension awarded 28 Dec 1847; residence - London, Ontario, Canada; died 8 Nov 1852. SOURCE: WO120 Volume 70 page 47. INDEX # 5982.

Ja^s DARRAGH; pension awarded 9 May 1848. SOURCE: WO120 Volume 70 page 47. INDEX # 5983.

Hugh HANWAY; pension awarded 9 May 1848; residence - Halifax, Nova Scotia, Canada; died 6 Apr 1856. SOURCE: WO120 Volume 70 page 47. INDEX # 5984.

Saml BARTON; pension awarded 9 May 1848. SOURCE: WO120 Volume 70 page 47. INDEX # 5985.

Jno BRIDGE; pension awarded 9 May 1848; died 17 Oct 1864, Toronto, Ontario, Canada. SOURCE: WO120 Volume 70 page 48. INDEX # 5986.

Robt FRANCIS; pension awarded 9 May 1848; residence - London, Ontario, Canada; died 6 Apr 1850. SOURCE: WO120 Volume 70 page 48. INDEX # 5987.

Wm HAZELL; pension awarded 9 May 1848; residence - London, Ontario, Canada; died 21 Jun 1855. SOURCE: WO120 Volume 70 page 48. INDEX # 5988.

Wm SEARGEANT; pension awarded 9 May 1848. SOURCE: WO120 Volume 70 page 48. INDEX # 5989.

Nathan SCOWAN; pension awarded 9 May 1848; residence - London, Ontario, Canada; died 26 Dec 1861. SOURCE: WO120 Volume 70 page 48. INDEX # 5990.

83rd Regiment of Foot

Arth^r WILKINSON; pension awarded 6 May 1799; residence - Penetanguishene, Ontario, Canada; died 12 Mar 1860. SOURCE: WO120 Volume 70 page 57. INDEX # 5991.

Pat^k HAMILTON; pension awarded 31 Dec 1814; residence - Prescott, Ontario, Canada. SOURCE: WO120 Volume 70 page 57. INDEX # 5992.

Jno HAMILTON; pension awarded 27 Dec 1815; residence - Kingston, Ontario, Canada. SOURCE: WO120 Volume 70 page 57. INDEX # 5993.

Danl SULLIVAN; pension awarded 9 Jun 1841; residence - London, Ontario, Canada; died in 1847. SOURCE: WO120 Volume 70 page 57. INDEX # 5994.

Robt COPELAND; pension awarded 5 Sep 1843; residence - Toronto, Ontario, Canada. SOURCE: WO120 Volume 70 page 57. INDEX # 5995.

John LAYTON; pension awarded 25 Nov 1818; residence - Cape of Good Hope, South Africa; died 19 Sep 1850. SOURCE: WO120 Volume 70 page 57. INDEX # 5996.

Ja^s BRINDLEY; pension awarded 19 Sep 1820; residence - Hobart Town, Australia. SOURCE: WO120 Volume 70 page 57. INDEX # 5997.

Jno JONES; pension awarded 5 Aug 1829; residence - Ceylon. SOURCE: WO120 Volume 70 page 57. INDEX # 5998.

And^w DAVIDSON; pension awarded 5 Aug 1829; residence - Ceylon; died 28 Jun 1850. SOURCE: WO120 Volume 70 page 57. INDEX # 5999.

Geo^e DAVIS; pension awarded 5 Aug 1829; residence - Ceylon. SOURCE: WO120 Volume 70 page 57. INDEX # 6000.

Chas RICHARDSBY; pension awarded 5 Aug 1829; residence - Ceylon; died in 1847. SOURCE: WO120 Volume 70 page 57. INDEX # 6001.

Willm MAYO; pension awarded 11 Jun 1844; residence - London, Ontario, Canada; died 15 Dec 1868. SOURCE: WO120 Volume 70 page 57. INDEX # 6002.

Thos PARR; pension awarded 25 Nov 1818; residence - Cape of Good Hope, South Africa. SOURCE: WO120 Volume 70 page 57. INDEX # 6003.

Matt^w NANGLE; pension awarded 8 Nov 1837; residence - Halifax, Nova Scotia, Canada. SOURCE: WO120 Volume 70 page 57. INDEX # 6004.

John KELLY; pension awarded 5 Aug 1829; residence - Ceylon. SOURCE: WO120 Volume 70 page 57. INDEX # 6005.

83rd Regiment of Foot (continued)

Willm COOPER; pension awarded 7 Feb 1821; residence - Cape of Good Hope, South Africa. SOURCE: WO120 Volume 70 page 57. INDEX # 6006.

Jno MCCARTHY; pension awarded 10 Apr 1839; residence - Kingston, Ontario, Canada; died in 1847. SOURCE: WO120 Volume 70 page 57. INDEX # 6007.

Jno SHEA; pension awarded 25 Apr 1827; residence - Canada; died 27 Jan 1877, Toronto, Ontario, Canada. SOURCE: WO120 Volume 70 page 57. INDEX # 6008.

James GRIMES; pension awarded 18 Mar 1856. SOURCE: WO120 Volume 70 page 57. INDEX # 6009.

Patrick MORAN; pension awarded 24 Mar 1857. SOURCE: WO120 Volume 70 page 57. INDEX # 6010.

84th Regiment of Foot

Geo^e EDGE; pension awarded 9 Nov 1813; residence - Bytown, Ontario, Canada. SOURCE: WO120 Volume 70 page 64. INDEX # 6011.

H^y WILDE; pension awarded 7 Jun 1820; residence - Sydney, New South Wales, Australia. SOURCE: WO120 Volume 70 page 64. INDEX # 6012.

Pat^k FARLEY; pension awarded 2 Feb 1815; residence - Toronto, Ontario, Canada; died 8 Sep 1876. SOURCE: WO120 Volume 70 page 64. INDEX # 6013.

Thos HOLLIWELL; pension awarded 3 May 1820; residence - New South Wales, Australia; died 6 Apr 1850. SOURCE: WO120 Volume 70 page 64. INDEX # 6014.

Mich^l BARRY; pension awarded 8 Jul 1845; died 8 Sep 1847. SOURCE: WO120 Volume 70 page 64. INDEX # 6015.

Jos^h SNAPE; pension awarded 7 Feb 1822; residence - New South Wales, Australia. SOURCE: WO120 Volume 70 page 64. INDEX # 6016.

Ed^wd HURST; pension awarded 7 Feb 1822; residence - Madras, India. SOURCE: WO120 Volume 70 page 64. INDEX # 6017.

Jno COLQUHOUN; pension awarded 12 Sep 1832; residence - Toronto, Ontario, Canada. SOURCE: WO120 Volume 70 page 64. INDEX # 6018.

H^y BROWN; pension awarded 10 Jul 1839; residence - Amherstburg, Ontario, Canada; died London, Ontario, Canada. SOURCE: WO120 Volume 70 page 64. INDEX # 6019.

Chas CLARKE; pension awarded 25 May 1847; residence - Madras, India; died 4 Jun 1852. SOURCE: WO120 Volume 70 page 64. INDEX # 6020.

Wm HAMILTON; pension awarded 25 May 1847; residence - Madras, India; died 9 Jan 1849. SOURCE: WO120 Volume 70 page 64. INDEX # 6021.

Hen^y KENNEDY; pension awarded 25 Apr 1848; residence - Madras, India; died 8 Jul 1848. SOURCE: WO120 Volume 70 page 64. INDEX # 6022.

Jno COLLINS; pension awarded 25 Apr 1848. SOURCE: WO120 Volume 70 page 64. INDEX # 6023.

Pat^k CODE; pension awarded 24 Apr 1849; residence - Madras, India; died 31 Mar 1850. SOURCE: WO120 Volume 70 page 64. INDEX # 6024.

Ed^wd HOSSOP; pension awarded 24 Apr 1851; residence - Madras, India; died 15 Jul 1854. SOURCE: WO120 Volume 70 page 64. INDEX # 6025.

Jno KELCHER; pension awarded 9 Mar 1852. SOURCE: WO120 Volume 70 page 64. INDEX # 6026.

Wm BOREBANK; pension awarded 8 Mar 1853. SOURCE: WO120 Volume 70 page 64. INDEX # 6027.

Jno BRYAN; pension awarded 8 Mar 1853. SOURCE: WO120 Volume 70 page 64. INDEX # 6028.

Jno PHILLIPS; pension awarded 8 Mar 1853. SOURCE: WO120 Volume 70 page 64. INDEX # 6029.

Ed^wd CAREY; pension awarded 11 Apr 1856. SOURCE: WO120 Volume 70 page 64. INDEX # 6030.

Edward COOPER; pension awarded 6 May 1856. SOURCE: WO120 Volume 70 page 65. INDEX # 6031.

Thomas BUTLER; pension awarded 6 May 1856; died 29 Mar 1864 Madras, India. SOURCE: WO120 Volume 70 page 65. INDEX # 6032.

Daniel BRENNAN; pension awarded 6 May 1856. SOURCE: WO120 Volume 70 page 65. INDEX # 6033.

William CARROLL; pension awarded 6 May 1856. SOURCE: WO120 Volume 70 page 65. INDEX # 6034.

Henry LEE; pension awarded 6 May 1856. SOURCE: WO120 Volume 70 page 65. INDEX # 6035.

John NEWMAN; pension awarded 6 May 1856. SOURCE: WO120 Volume 70 page 65. INDEX # 6036.

84th Regiment of Foot (continued)

Cornelius OCONNELL; pension awarded 6 May 1856. SOURCE: WO120 Volume 70 page 65. INDEX # 6037.
William DUNNE; pension awarded 28 Apr 1857. SOURCE: WO120 Volume 70 page 65. INDEX # 6038.
Joseph CONLIN; pension awarded 28 Apr 1857. SOURCE: WO120 Volume 70 page 65. INDEX # 6039.
John GREEN; pension awarded 28 Apr 1857. SOURCE: WO120 Volume 70 page 65. INDEX # 6040.
James HARPER; pension awarded 28 Apr 1857. SOURCE: WO120 Volume 70 page 65. INDEX # 6041.
William MOORHEAD; pension awarded 28 Apr 1857. SOURCE: WO120 Volume 70 page 65. INDEX # 6042.
William POWER; pension awarded 28 Apr 1857. SOURCE: WO120 Volume 70 page 65. INDEX # 6043.

85th Regiment of Foot

Geo^e W. PERCIVAL; pension awarded 27 Jun 1821; residence - New South Wales, Australia; died in 1845. SOURCE: WO120 Volume 70 page 70. INDEX # 6044.
Saml MURPHY; pension awarded 7 Sep 1814; residence - New South Wales, Australia. SOURCE: WO120 Volume 70 page 70. INDEX # 6045.
Mich^l PILKINGTON; pension awarded 28 Nov 1818; residence - New Zealand; died 10 Sep 1847. SOURCE: WO120 Volume 70 page 70. INDEX # 6046.
Wm HARBISON; pension awarded 12 Mar 1828; residence - Bytown, Ontario, Canada. SOURCE: WO120 Volume 70 page 70. INDEX # 6047.
Wm SULLIVAN; pension awarded 30 Aug 1826; residence - Van Diemen's Land, Australia; died 27 Jan 1847. SOURCE: WO120 Volume 70 page 70. INDEX # 6048.
Ja^s POUND; pension awarded 7 Feb 1816; residence - Toronto, Ontario, Canada; died 7 Jan 1870, Hamilton, Ontario, Canada. SOURCE: WO120 Volume 70 page 70. INDEX # 6049.
Richd LANDERS; pension awarded 29 Jul 1815; residence - Fermoy, Ireland; died 21 Apr 1857. SOURCE: WO120 Volume 70 page 70. INDEX # 6050.
John DALEY; pension awarded 27 Sep 1842; residence - Montreal, Quebec, Canada; died 11 Jul 1862. SOURCE: WO120 Volume 70 page 70. INDEX # 6051.
John WYLIE; pension awarded 5 Sep 1843; residence - Montreal, Quebec, Canada. SOURCE: WO120 Volume 70 page 70. INDEX # 6052.
Pat^k BURKE; pension awarded 27 Sep 1842; residence - St. Jean, Quebec, Canada. SOURCE: WO120 Volume 70 page 70. INDEX # 6053.
Erwin ARMSTRONG; pension awarded 9 Dec 1840; residence - Toronto, Ontario, Canada. SOURCE: WO120 Volume 70 page 70. INDEX # 6054.
Chas DUFF; pension awarded 9 Dec 1840; residence - Kingston, Ontario, Canada. SOURCE: WO120 Volume 70 page 70. INDEX # 6055.
John CANNELL; pension awarded 8 Sep 1841; residence - Kingston, Ontario, Canada; died in 1846. SOURCE: WO120 Volume 70 page 70. INDEX # 6056.
Thos RUDDY; pension awarded 8 Sep 1841; residence - Montreal, Quebec, Canada. SOURCE: WO120 Volume 70 page 70. INDEX # 6057.
Richd TUAFE; pension awarded 8 Sep 1841; residence - Toronto, Ontario, Canada; died in 1848. SOURCE: WO120 Volume 70 page 70. INDEX # 6058.
Thos MCMAHON; pension awarded 27 Sep 1842; residence - Montreal, Quebec, Canada. SOURCE: WO120 Volume 70 page 70. INDEX # 6059.
John WILSON; pension awarded 27 Sep 1842; residence - Montreal, Quebec, Canada. SOURCE: WO120 Volume 70 page 70. INDEX # 6060.
Willm EVANS; pension awarded 25 Oct 1837; residence - Launceston, Australia; died 13 Sep 1846. SOURCE: WO120 Volume 70 page 70. INDEX # 6061.
Mark BARNES; pension awarded 12 Jan 1842; residence - Montreal, Quebec, Canada; died 18 Nov 1871, Hamilton, Ontario, Canada. SOURCE: WO120 Volume 70 page 70. INDEX # 6062.
Thos KELLY; pension awarded 5 Sep 1843; residence - St. Jean, Quebec, Canada. SOURCE: WO120 Volume 70 page 70. INDEX # 6063.

85th Regiment of Foot (continued)

John ROBERTS; pension awarded 9 Jun 1841; residence - Amherstburg, Ontario, Canada. SOURCE: WO120 Volume 70 page 71. INDEX # 6064.

Garrett FITZGERALD; pension awarded 26 Sep 1843; residence - Montreal, Quebec, Canada; died 16 Feb 1852. SOURCE: WO120 Volume 70 page 71. INDEX # 6065.

Geo^e NICHOLSON; pension awarded 27 Sep 1842; residence - St. Jean, Quebec, Canada; died 4 Jan 1856. SOURCE: WO120 Volume 70 page 71. INDEX # 6066.

Ed^d HILLAN; pension awarded 9 Sep 1840; residence - London, Ontario, Canada; died 12 Oct 1867. SOURCE: WO120 Volume 70 page 71. INDEX # 6067.

John BYRNE; pension awarded 10 Jun 1835; residence - Perth. SOURCE: WO120 Volume 70 page 71. INDEX # 6068.

Geo^e SMITH; pension awarded 8 Jul 1840; residence - Montreal, Quebec, Canada; died 20 Nov 1849. SOURCE: WO120 Volume 70 page 71. INDEX # 6069.

Edwin DAVIS; pension awarded 7 Jul 1857. SOURCE: WO120 Volume 70 page 71. INDEX # 6070.

86th Regiment of Foot

Pat^k COOKLEY; pension awarded 31 Jul 1816; residence - Wm Henry, Quebec, Canada. SOURCE: WO120 Volume 70 page 78. INDEX # 6071.

Ed^d MORRIS; pension awarded 9 Aug 1837; residence - Toronto, Ontario, Canada. SOURCE: WO120 Volume 70 page 78. INDEX # 6072.

Pat^k MORGAN; pension awarded 9 Dec 1816; residence - Niagara, Ontario, Canada; died 26 May 1845. SOURCE: WO120 Volume 70 page 78. INDEX # 6073.

Dav^d MCCALL; pension awarded 30 Oct 1822; residence - London, Ontario, Canada; died 1 Jul 1861, London, Ontario, Canada. SOURCE: WO120 Volume 70 page 78. INDEX # 6074.

Pat^k COLLINS; pension awarded 21 Dec 1821; residence - Saint John, New Brunswick, Canada; died 27 Sep 1878, Saint John, New Brunswick, Canada. SOURCE: WO120 Volume 70 page 78. INDEX # 6075.

Ed^d NEAVES; pension awarded 7 Feb 1821; residence - Madras, India. SOURCE: WO120 Volume 70 page 78. INDEX # 6076.

Richd DINAHAN; pension awarded 13 Aug 1844; residence - Toronto, Ontario, Canada; died 26 Oct 1883, Montreal, Quebec, Canada. SOURCE: WO120 Volume 70 page 78. INDEX # 6077.

Jos^h CARR; pension awarded 7 Feb 1821; residence - Madras, India; died 16 Jan 1857. SOURCE: WO120 Volume 70 page 78. INDEX # 6078.

Geo^e REYNOLDS; pension awarded 21 Dec 1821; residence - Montreal, Quebec, Canada. SOURCE: WO120 Volume 70 page 78. INDEX # 6079.

John DWYER; pension awarded 13 Feb 1841; residence - Quebec, Quebec, Canada. SOURCE: WO120 Volume 70 page 78. INDEX # 6080.

Geo^e LACK; pension awarded 9 May 1848; died 30 Jan 1884 Bombay, India. SOURCE: WO120 Volume 70 page 78. INDEX # 6081.

Roger MCGRATH; pension awarded 9 May 1848; residence - Poona, India; died 18 Nov 1849. SOURCE: WO120 Volume 70 page 78. INDEX # 6082.

Jos^h MCCRACKIN; pension awarded 8 Mar 1853. SOURCE: WO120 Volume 70 page 78. INDEX # 6083.

William BEARD; pension awarded 15 Mar 1856. SOURCE: WO120 Volume 70 page 78. INDEX # 6084.

James SMITHERS; pension awarded 15 Mar 1856. SOURCE: WO120 Volume 70 page 78. INDEX # 6085.

87th Regiment of Foot

John BURROWS; pension awarded 18 Oct 1820; residence - Bytown, Ontario, Canada. SOURCE: WO120 Volume 70 page 84. INDEX # 6086.

Alex^r THOMPSON; pension awarded 2 Feb 1815; residence - Kingston, Ontario, Canada; died 7 Dec 1867, Toronto, Ontario, Canada. SOURCE: WO120 Volume 70 page 84. INDEX # 6087.

WO120 VOLUME 70

87th Regiment of Foot (continued)

Mich^l OBRIEN; pension awarded 27 Dec 1814; residence - Kingston, Ontario, Canada. SOURCE: WO120 Volume 70 page 84. INDEX # 6088.

Wm MCKEE; pension awarded 14 Feb 1843; residence - Mauritius; died 31 Dec 1855. SOURCE: WO120 Volume 70 page 84. INDEX # 6089.

Saml BAIRD; pension awarded 13 Jun 1838; residence - Mauritius; died 5 Jan 1854. SOURCE: WO120 Volume 70 page 84. INDEX # 6090.

Mich^l HANLEY; pension awarded 25 Jun 1817; residence - Montreal, Quebec, Canada. SOURCE: WO120 Volume 70 page 84. INDEX # 6091.

John SMITH; pension awarded 13 Apr 1836; residence - Mauritius; died 4 Jun 1856. SOURCE: WO120 Volume 70 page 84. INDEX # 6092.

Geo^e GRAHAM; pension awarded 21 Dec 1803; residence - Hamilton, Ontario, Canada. SOURCE: WO120 Volume 70 page 84. INDEX # 6093.

John MURNANE; pension awarded 24 Sep 1844; residence - Mauritius. SOURCE: WO120 Volume 70 page 84. INDEX # 6094.

88th Regiment of Foot

Willm CLEARY; pension awarded 18 Apr 1821; residence - Hobart Town, Australia; died 20 Sep 1850. SOURCE: WO120 Volume 70 page 90. INDEX # 6095.

Mich^l MAXWELL; pension awarded 25 Feb 1819; residence - Quebec, Quebec, Canada. SOURCE: WO120 Volume 70 page 90. INDEX # 6096.

Pat^k RILEY; pension awarded 10 Oct 1811; residence - Charlottetown, Prince Edward Island, Canada. SOURCE: WO120 Volume 70 page 90. INDEX # 6097.

H^y WRIGHT; pension awarded 25 Jun 1818; residence - Wm Henry, Quebec, Canada. SOURCE: WO120 Volume 70 page 90. INDEX # 6098.

John KEEFE; pension awarded 26 Jul 1815; residence - Toronto, Ontario, Canada. SOURCE: WO120 Volume 70 page 90. INDEX # 6099.

John MACHESTNEY; pension awarded 31 Apr 1815; residence - Toronto, Ontario, Canada; died 3 Dec 1874, Toronto, Ontario, Canada. SOURCE: WO120 Volume 70 page 90. INDEX # 6100.

Willm PHILLIPS; pension awarded 16 May 1825; residence - Sydney. SOURCE: WO120 Volume 70 page 90. INDEX # 6101.

Thos BRERETON; pension awarded 3 Jul 1839; residence - Jamaica. SOURCE: WO120 Volume 70 page 90. INDEX # 6102.

John CAWLEY; pension awarded 17 Nov 1817; residence - St. Johns. SOURCE: WO120 Volume 70 page 90. INDEX # 6103.

Ja^s YOUNG; pension awarded 31 May 1815; residence - Toronto, Ontario, Canada. SOURCE: WO120 Volume 70 page 90. INDEX # 6104.

Ja^s KELLY; pension awarded 27 Oct 1828; residence - St. Johns. SOURCE: WO120 Volume 70 page 90. INDEX # 6105.

Chas BROOK; pension awarded 12 Apr 1837; residence - London, Ontario, Canada; died 16 Feb 1849. SOURCE: WO120 Volume 70 page 90. INDEX # 6106.

Robt MOORE; pension awarded 19 Jul 1842; residence - Jamaica. SOURCE: WO120 Volume 70 page 90. INDEX # 6107.

Jno TEMPLETON; pension awarded 31 May 1815; residence - Bytown, Ontario, Canada; died 23 Jan 1847. SOURCE: WO120 Volume 70 page 90. INDEX # 6108.

Pat^k MINEHAN; pension awarded 8 Mar 1837; residence - Ionian Isles. SOURCE: WO120 Volume 70 page 90. INDEX # 6109.

Mich^l WALSH; pension awarded ; residence - Paris. SOURCE: WO120 Volume 70 page 90. INDEX # 6110.

Wm PIKE; pension awarded 20 Jun 1827; residence - Ostend, Belgium; died in Jun 1846. SOURCE: WO120 Volume 70 page 90. INDEX # 6111.

88th Regiment of Foot (continued)

Arthur DAVIS; pension awarded 10 Oct 1811; residence - Montreal, Quebec, Canada. SOURCE: WO120 Volume 70 page 90. INDEX # 6112.

Robt MCFADDEN; pension awarded 11 Aug 1846; residence - Malta; died 5 May 1884, Kilmainham, Ireland. SOURCE: WO120 Volume 70 page 90. INDEX # 6113.

Wm BROW; pension awarded 1 Jul 1851; died 20 Jan 1872, Nova Scotia, Canada. SOURCE: WO120 Volume 70 page 90. INDEX # 6114.

Pat^k SULLIVAN; pension awarded 1 Jul 1851. SOURCE: WO120 Volume 70 page 91. INDEX # 6115.

89th Regiment of Foot

Richd THOMPSON; pension awarded 31 Oct 1827; residence - Madras, India; died 26 Apr 1854. SOURCE: WO120 Volume 70 page 96. INDEX # 6116.

Luck SHALLOW; pension awarded 28 Nov 1815; residence - St. Johns. SOURCE: WO120 Volume 70 page 96. INDEX # 6117.

Thos COSGROVE; pension awarded 13 Jan 1830; residence - New South Wales, Australia; died 1 Jun 1864. SOURCE: WO120 Volume 70 page 96. INDEX # 6118.

Ja^s SMITH; pension awarded 17 Aug 1844; residence - Montreal, Quebec, Canada. SOURCE: WO120 Volume 70 page 96. INDEX # 6119.

Ja^s DARCEY; pension awarded 9 Sep 1845; residence - Montreal, Quebec, Canada. SOURCE: WO120 Volume 70 page 96. INDEX # 6120.

Fran^s MCCLURE; pension awarded 13 Aug 1844; residence - Three Rivers, Quebec, Canada; died 7 Jun 1856. SOURCE: WO120 Volume 70 page 96. INDEX # 6121.

Pat^k CURRY; pension awarded 26 Nov 1844; residence - Kingston, Ontario, Canada; died in 1847. SOURCE: WO120 Volume 70 page 96. INDEX # 6122.

Wm HEATH; pension awarded 26 Nov 1844; residence - Montreal, Quebec, Canada. SOURCE: WO120 Volume 70 page 96. INDEX # 6123.

Dav^d SMYTH; pension awarded 26 Aug 1845; residence - Montreal, Quebec, Canada. SOURCE: WO120 Volume 70 page 96. INDEX # 6124.

Arch^d STEWART; pension awarded 26 Aug 1845; residence - Toronto, Ontario, Canada. SOURCE: WO120 Volume 70 page 96. INDEX # 6125.

Chas COOPER; pension awarded 30 May 1827; residence - Bombay, India. SOURCE: WO120 Volume 70 page 96. INDEX # 6126.

Chas MCGURRAN; pension awarded 12 Dec 1836; residence - Kingston, Ontario, Canada; died in 1847. SOURCE: WO120 Volume 70 page 96. INDEX # 6127.

Jos^h BISHOP; pension awarded 4 Mar 1824; residence - Madras, India; died 25 Jul 1855. SOURCE: WO120 Volume 70 page 96. INDEX # 6128.

Jno GAVIN; pension awarded 4 Mar 1824; residence - Madras, India; died 10 Mar 1853. SOURCE: WO120 Volume 70 page 96. INDEX # 6129.

Mich^l NORTON; pension awarded 29 Oct 1828; residence - Bombay, India. SOURCE: WO120 Volume 70 page 96. INDEX # 6130.

Geo^e BIGGS; pension awarded 13 Dec 1826; residence - Madras, India; died 9 Apr 1851. SOURCE: WO120 Volume 70 page 96. INDEX # 6131.

John GEE; pension awarded 21 May 1828; residence - Madras, India. SOURCE: WO120 Volume 70 page 96. INDEX # 6132.

Thos MARA; pension awarded 26 Aug 1845; residence - Toronto, Ontario, Canada. SOURCE: WO120 Volume 70 page 96. INDEX # 6133.

John DONAGHOE; pension awarded 31 Oct 1827; residence - Madras, India; died 23 Jul 1852. SOURCE: WO120 Volume 70 page 96. INDEX # 6134.

Ja^s DONALDSON; pension awarded; died 9 Jun 1845. SOURCE: WO120 Volume 70 page 96. INDEX # 6135.

Miles BURKE; pension awarded 31 Oct 1827; residence - Madras, India. SOURCE: WO120 Volume 70 page 97. INDEX # 6136.

89th Regiment of Foot (continued)

Chas ALDERTON; pension awarded 29 Oct 1828; residence - Madras, India. SOURCE: WO120 Volume 70 page 97. INDEX # 6137.

John BELL; pension awarded 26 Nov 1844; residence - Montreal, Quebec, Canada. SOURCE: WO120 Volume 70 page 97. INDEX # 6138

John HEMPHILL; pension awarded 26 Aug 1845; residence - Quebec, Quebec, Canada; died 3 Oct 1868, London, Ontario, Canada. SOURCE: WO120 Volume 70 page 97. INDEX # 6139.

Geo^e LANG; pension awarded 4 Jun 1823; residence - Madras, India; died 8 Aug 1851. SOURCE: WO120 Volume 70 page 97. INDEX # 6140.

John DUNN; pension awarded 30 Aug 1821; residence - Halifax, Nova Scotia, Canada. SOURCE: WO120 Volume 70 page 97. INDEX # 6141.

Geo^e BIRCH; pension awarded 22 Aug 1845; residence - Montreal, Quebec, Canada. SOURCE: WO120 Volume 70 page 97. INDEX # 6142.

Jno GREADY; pension awarded 16 Jul 1844; residence - Prescott, Ontario, Canada. SOURCE: WO120 Volume 70 page 97. INDEX # 6143.

Jno ATHERSTON; pension awarded 25 Aug 1846. SOURCE: WO120 Volume 70 page 97. INDEX # 6144.

Jno FERGUSON; pension awarded 22 Sep 1846. SOURCE: WO120 Volume 70 page 97. INDEX # 6145.

Mich^l BALF; pension awarded 22 Sep 1846; residence - Montreal, Quebec, Canada. SOURCE: WO120 Volume 70 page 97. INDEX # 6146.

Mich^l BARDEN; pension awarded 22 Sep 1846; died 15 Sep 1886, Toronto, Ontario, Canada. SOURCE: WO120 Volume 70 page 97. INDEX # 6147.

Jno DEALY; pension awarded 22 Sep 1846. SOURCE: WO120 Volume 70 page 97. INDEX # 6148.

Wm FROST; pension awarded 22 Sep 1846. SOURCE: WO120 Volume 70 page 97. INDEX # 6149.

Fra^s KELLY; pension awarded 22 Sep 1846. SOURCE: WO120 Volume 70 page 97. INDEX # 6150.

Jno MCGOWAN; pension awarded 22 Sep 1846. SOURCE: WO120 Volume 70 page 97. INDEX # 6151.

Wm MARTIN; pension awarded 22 Sep 1846. SOURCE: WO120 Volume 70 page 97. INDEX # 6152.

Jno MERRETT; pension awarded 22 Sep 1846; residence - Montreal, Quebec, Canada; died 20 Nov 1855. SOURCE: WO120 Volume 70 page 97. INDEX # 6153.

Robt PATTERSON; pension awarded 22 Sep 1846; died 8 Oct 1883, Toronto, Ontario, Canada. SOURCE: WO120 Volume 70 page 97. INDEX # 6154.

Peter RODGERS; pension awarded 22 Sep 1846. SOURCE: WO120 Volume 70 page 97. INDEX # 6155.

David SEELER; pension awarded 22 Sep 1846. SOURCE: WO120 Volume 70 page 98. INDEX # 6156.

Matt^w SLATTERY; pension awarded 22 Sep 1846; residence - Montreal, Quebec, Canada; died 2 Apr 1848. SOURCE: WO120 Volume 70 page 98. INDEX # 6157.

Danl TEAHAN; pension awarded 22 Sep 1846; residence - Montreal, Quebec, Canada; died 19 Nov 1847. SOURCE: WO120 Volume 70 page 98. INDEX # 6158.

Ed^{wd} PINDAR; pension awarded 22 Sep 1846. SOURCE: WO120 Volume 70 page 98. INDEX # 6159.

Mich^l PHELAN; pension awarded 13 Apr 1847. SOURCE: WO120 Volume 70 page 98. INDEX # 6160.

Geo^e MALCOLM; pension awarded 8 Jun 1847. SOURCE: WO120 Volume 70 page 98. INDEX # 6161.

Robt CULBERT; pension awarded 8 Jun 1847; residence - Montreal, Quebec, Canada; died in Oct 1847. SOURCE: WO120 Volume 70 page 98. INDEX # 6162.

Thos DOWLING; pension awarded 8 Jun 1847; residence - Montreal, Quebec, Canada; died in 1851. SOURCE: WO120 Volume 70 page 98. INDEX # 6163.

Wm GRAHAM; pension awarded 8 Jun 1847; residence - Toronto, Ontario, Canada; died 26 Jun 1851. SOURCE: WO120 Volume 70 page 98. INDEX # 6164.

Mich^l HIGGINS; pension awarded 8 Jun 1847. SOURCE: WO120 Volume 70 page 98. INDEX # 6165.

Pat^k MCGURK; pension awarded 8 Jun 1847. SOURCE: WO120 Volume 70 page 98. INDEX # 6166.

Jno POWER; pension awarded 8 Jun 1847; residence - New London; died 17 May 1848. SOURCE: WO120 Volume 70 page 98. INDEX # 6167.

Jno ROBINSON; pension awarded 8 Jun 1847; residence - Bermuda; died 13 Jan 1857. SOURCE: WO120 Volume 70 page 98. INDEX # 6168.

Jno TAYLOR; pension awarded 8 Jun 1847. SOURCE: WO120 Volume 70 page 98. INDEX # 6169.

Nicholas HERLEY; pension awarded 27 Oct 1857. SOURCE: WO120 Volume 70 page 98. INDEX # 6170.

BRITISH ARMY PENSIONERS ABROAD

89th Regiment of Foot (continued)

James BIRMINGHAM; pension awarded 27 Oct 1857. SOURCE: WO120 Volume 70 page 98. INDEX # 6171.

Francis HOLMES; pension awarded 27 Oct 1857. SOURCE: WO120 Volume 70 page 98. INDEX # 6172.

Jonathan MCILROY; pension awarded 27 Oct 1857. SOURCE: WO120 Volume 70 page 98. INDEX # 6173.

90th Regiment of Foot

Jos^h VARNEY; pension awarded 24 Mar 1841; residence - Ceylon. SOURCE: WO120 Volume 70 page 106. INDEX # 6174.

Alex^r MCDONALD; pension awarded 27 Sep 1842; residence - Ceylon; died 10 May 1874, Ceylon. SOURCE: WO120 Volume 70 page 106. INDEX # 6175.

Jno DONALDSON; pension awarded 12 Dec 1843; residence - Ceylon; died 15 Nov 1852. SOURCE: WO120 Volume 70 page 106. INDEX # 6176.

Richd BULCHOR; pension awarded 17 Dec 1844; residence - Ceylon. SOURCE: WO120 Volume 70 page 106. INDEX # 6177.

Chas SMITH; pension awarded 14 Oct 1845; residence - Kandy, Ceylon; died 14 May 1850. SOURCE: WO120 Volume 70 page 106. INDEX # 6178.

Ja^s RATTRAY; pension awarded 19 Dec 1816; residence - Kingston, Ontario, Canada; died 27 Sep 1859. SOURCE: WO120 Volume 70 page 106. INDEX # 6179.

And^w INGRAM; pension awarded 20 Jun 1827; residence - Toronto, Ontario, Canada; died 7 Jan 1855. SOURCE: WO120 Volume 70 page 106. INDEX # 6180.

Ja^s PATTERSON; pension awarded 21 Oct 1823; residence - Toronto, Ontario, Canada. SOURCE: WO120 Volume 70 page 106. INDEX # 6181.

Ja^s KENNEDY; pension awarded 9 Aug 1842; residence - Hobart Town, Australia. SOURCE: WO120 Volume 70 page 106. INDEX # 6182.

Philip OHARE; pension awarded 10 Dec 1834; residence - Jamaica. SOURCE: WO120 Volume 70 page 106. INDEX # 6183.

Willm STAFFORD; pension awarded 9 Jul 1834; residence - Montreal, Quebec, Canada. SOURCE: WO120 Volume 70 page 106. INDEX # 6184.

Thos COSTELLO; pension awarded 13 Jan 1846; residence - Hong Kong. SOURCE: WO120 Volume 70 page 106. INDEX # 6185.

Ja^s PIPER; pension awarded 13 Oct 1846; residence - Colombo, Ceylon. SOURCE: WO120 Volume 70 page 106. INDEX # 6186.

Willm KNIGHT; pension awarded 12 Jan 1831; residence - Halifax, Nova Scotia, Canada. SOURCE: WO120 Volume 70 page 106. INDEX # 6187.

Chr^r ANSON; pension awarded 27 Jun 1848. SOURCE: WO120 Volume 70 page 106. INDEX # 6188.

Chas JOHNSON; pension awarded 27 Jun 1848; died 11 May 1872, Cape of Good Hope, South Africa. SOURCE: WO120 Volume 70 page 106. INDEX # 6189.

91st Regiment of Foot

Thos LOWRIE; pension awarded 25 Jun 1823; residence - New South Wales, Australia. SOURCE: WO120 Volume 70 page 112. INDEX # 6190.

Jno DIGNEY; pension awarded 3 Feb 1819; residence - Van Diemen's Land, Australia; died 21 Oct 1873, Hobarton, Australia. SOURCE: WO120 Volume 70 page 112. INDEX # 6191.

Jno TANNEHILL; pension awarded 20 Jun 1803; residence - Montreal, Quebec, Canada; died in 1850. SOURCE: WO120 Volume 70 page 112. INDEX # 6192.

Alex^r CRERAR; pension awarded 25 Jun 1817; residence - London, Ontario, Canada. SOURCE: WO120 Volume 70 page 112. INDEX # 6193.

Thos CAITIN; pension awarded 11 Jun 1843; residence - Cape of Good Hope, South Africa. SOURCE: WO120 Volume 70 page 112. INDEX # 6194.

WO120 VOLUME 70

91st Regiment of Foot (continued)

Peter HOWIE; pension awarded 11 Jun 1843; residence - Cape of Good Hope, South Africa. SOURCE: WO120 Volume 70 page 112. INDEX # 6195.

Martin MANNON; pension awarded 7 Jun 1819; residence - Cornwall, Ontario, Canada; died in 1851. SOURCE: WO120 Volume 70 page 112. INDEX # 6196.

Arch^d GRAY; pension awarded 12 Aug 1845; residence - Cape of Good Hope, South Africa; died 23 Oct 1857, Stockport. SOURCE: WO120 Volume 70 page 112. INDEX # 6197.

Alex^r FALCONER; pension awarded 11 Nov 1846; residence - Grahams Town, South Africa; died 7 Jan 1875, Edinburgh. SOURCE: WO120 Volume 70 page 112. INDEX # 6198.

Neil SINCLAIR; pension awarded 20 Jun 1803; residence - London, Ontario, Canada; died 29 Sep 1852. SOURCE: WO120 Volume 70 page 112. INDEX # 6199.

Philip GRANNARY; pension awarded 25 Jul 1843; residence - Cape of Good Hope, South Africa; died 10 Mar 1848. SOURCE: WO120 Volume 70 page 112. INDEX # 6200.

Don^d MCKINNON; pension awarded 28 Aug 1838; residence - Prince Edward Island, Canada; died 26 Sep 1853. SOURCE: WO120 Volume 70 page 112. INDEX # 6201.

Arch^d LIVEWRIGHT; pension awarded 31 May 1816; residence - Montreal, Quebec, Canada. SOURCE: WO120 Volume 70 page 112. INDEX # 6202.

Jno MCINTYRE; pension awarded 25 Jul 1821; residence - London, Ontario, Canada; died 3 Mar 1871. SOURCE: WO120 Volume 70 page 112. INDEX # 6203.

Robt BURNETT; pension awarded 25 Jul 1838; residence - Antigua. SOURCE: WO120 Volume 70 page 112. INDEX # 6204.

Dav^d MCPHERSON; pension awarded 8 Aug 1832; residence - London, Ontario, Canada. SOURCE: WO120 Volume 70 page 112. INDEX # 6205.

John WALKER; pension awarded 25 Jul 1838; residence - London, Ontario, Canada. SOURCE: WO120 Volume 70 page 112. INDEX # 6206.

Robt MCTAVISH; pension awarded 12 Aug 1845; residence - Cape of Good Hope, South Africa; died in Mar 1848. SOURCE: WO120 Volume 70 page 112. INDEX # 6207.

Robt MILLER; pension awarded 28 Apr 1846. SOURCE: WO120 Volume 70 page 112. INDEX # 6208.

Jno LOWRIE; pension awarded 14 Jul 1846; died 16 Jul 1875. SOURCE: WO120 Volume 70 page 112. INDEX # 6209.

Hugh ODONNELL; pension awarded 14 Jul 1846. SOURCE: WO120 Volume 70 page 113. INDEX # 6210.

Lewis COUTTS; pension awarded 28 Jul 1846. SOURCE: WO120 Volume 70 page 113. INDEX # 6211.

Jno HADDIEAN; pension awarded 28 Jul 1846. SOURCE: WO120 Volume 70 page 113. INDEX # 6212.

Jno GORMAN; pension awarded 23 May 1848. SOURCE: WO120 Volume 70 page 113. INDEX # 6213.

Jno MCDONALD; pension awarded 23 May 1848. SOURCE: WO120 Volume 70 page 113. INDEX # 6214.

Ja^s SNODGRASS; pension awarded 23 May 1848. SOURCE: WO120 Volume 70 page 113. INDEX # 6215.

Jno BYRNE; pension awarded 23 May 1848; residence - Ft. Beaufort, Cape of Good Hope, South Africa; died 14 Jan 1850. SOURCE: WO120 Volume 70 page 113. INDEX # 6216.

Jno CASSELS; pension awarded 23 May 1848. SOURCE: WO120 Volume 70 page 113. INDEX # 6217.

Matt^w QUINN; pension awarded 23 May 1848; residence - Auckland, Cape of Good Hope, South Africa; died in 1851. SOURCE: WO120 Volume 70 page 113. INDEX # 6218.

Ja^s WALKER; pension awarded 23 May 1848; residence - Auckland, Cape of Good Hope, South Africa; died in 1851. SOURCE: WO120 Volume 70 page 113. INDEX # 6219.

Peter TRACY; pension awarded 6 Jun 1848; residence - Auckland, Cape of Good Hope, South Africa; died in 1851. SOURCE: WO120 Volume 70 page 113. INDEX # 6220.

Wm WRIGHT; pension awarded 6 Jun 1848; died 12 Nov 1885, Cape of Good Hope, South Africa. SOURCE: WO120 Volume 70 page 113. INDEX # 6221.

Alex^r ROSE; pension awarded 6 Jun 1848; died 18 May 1863, Cape of Good Hope, South Africa. SOURCE: WO120 Volume 70 page 113. INDEX # 6222.

Wm CLARKE; pension awarded 6 Jun 1848; residence - Auckland, Cape of Good Hope, South Africa; died in 1851. SOURCE: WO120 Volume 70 page 113. INDEX # 6223.

Pat^k RYAN; pension awarded 6 Jun 1848. SOURCE: WO120 Volume 70 page 113. INDEX # 6224.

Pat^k YEATES; pension awarded 6 Jun 1848. SOURCE: WO120 Volume 70 page 113. INDEX # 6225.

Wm GRANT; pension awarded 27 Jun 1848. SOURCE: WO120 Volume 70 page 113. INDEX # 6226.

91st Regiment of Foot (continued)

Edmond GRANGE; pension awarded 27 Jun 1848; residence - Auckland, Cape of Good Hope, South Africa; died in 1851. SOURCE: WO120 Volume 70 page 113. INDEX # 6227.

And^w BOGIE; pension awarded 27 Jun 1848; died 4 Oct 1871 Cape of Good Hope, South Africa. SOURCE: WO120 Volume 70 page 113. INDEX # 6228.

And^w JAMIESON; pension awarded 27 Jun 1848. SOURCE: WO120 Volume 70 page 113. INDEX # 6229.

Ja^s MILNE; pension awarded 27 Jun 1848; residence - Auckland, Cape of Good Hope, South Africa; died in 1851. SOURCE: WO120 Volume 70 page 114. INDEX # 6230.

Hen^y NEWMAN; pension awarded 27 Jun 1848; residence - Fort Beaufort, Cape of Good Hope, South Africa; died 19 Apr 1852. SOURCE: WO120 Volume 70 page 114. INDEX # 6231.

Jno ROSS; pension awarded 27 Jun 1848. SOURCE: WO120 Volume 70 page 114. INDEX # 6232.

Chas DONNELL; pension awarded 26 Dec 1848. SOURCE: WO120 Volume 70 page 114. INDEX # 6233.

Isaac SPYRON; pension awarded 26 Dec 1848; residence - Auckland, Cape of Good Hope, South Africa; died in 1849. SOURCE: WO120 Volume 70 page 114. INDEX # 6234.

Don^d MCKAY; pension awarded 13 Feb 1849. SOURCE: WO120 Volume 70 page 114. INDEX # 6235.

Danl TRIBE; pension awarded 13 Feb 1849. SOURCE: WO120 Volume 70 page 114. INDEX # 6236.

Wm CUMMINGS; pension awarded 13 Feb 1849. SOURCE: WO120 Volume 70 page 114. INDEX # 6237.

Jno RENNIE; pension awarded 13 Feb 1849; residence - Auckland, Cape of Good Hope, South Africa; died in 1849. SOURCE: WO120 Volume 70 page 114. INDEX # 6238.

Step^n MCCONOCHIE; pension awarded 13 Feb 1849. SOURCE: WO120 Volume 70 page 114. INDEX # 6239.

Ja^s WOODS; pension awarded 13 Feb 1849. SOURCE: WO120 Volume 70 page 114. INDEX # 6240.

Wm STEVENSON; pension awarded 24 Apr 1849. SOURCE: WO120 Volume 70 page 114. INDEX # 6241.

Malcolm SILLERS; pension awarded 10 Jul 1849. SOURCE: WO120 Volume 70 page 114. INDEX # 6242.

Arch^d MCKENZIE; pension awarded 10 Jul 1849; residence - Cape of Good Hope, South Africa; died 18 Jul 1851. SOURCE: WO120 Volume 70 page 114. INDEX # 6243.

Wm MOFFATT; pension awarded 10 Jul 1849; died 18 Apr 1883, Cape of Good Hope, South Africa. SOURCE: WO120 Volume 70 page 114. INDEX # 6244.

Ja^s ALSTON; pension awarded 14 Aug 1849; residence - Cape of Good Hope, South Africa; died 29 Aug 1850. SOURCE: WO120 Volume 70 page 114. INDEX # 6245.

Robt HOUSTON; pension awarded 23 Jul 1850. SOURCE: WO120 Volume 70 page 114. INDEX # 6246.

Jno BISHOP; pension awarded 13 Jul 1852; died 7 Dec 1878, Dorchester. SOURCE: WO120 Volume 70 page 114. INDEX # 6247.

Jno CARNEY; pension awarded 13 Jul 1852. SOURCE: WO120 Volume 70 page 114. INDEX # 6248.

Ed^{wd} WALKER; pension awarded 13 Jul 1852; died 11 May 1872, Cape of Good Hope, South Africa. SOURCE: WO120 Volume 70 page 114. INDEX # 6249.

Jere^h NUNAN; pension awarded 11 Oct 1853. SOURCE: WO120 Volume 70 page 115. INDEX # 6250.

Thos BOWMAN; pension awarded 13 Jun 1854. SOURCE: WO120 Volume 70 page 115. INDEX # 6251.

Jno BURKE; pension awarded 13 Jun 1854; died 24 Dec 1865, Tembunland. SOURCE: WO120 Volume 70 page 115. INDEX # 6252.

Wm CAMPBELL; pension awarded 13 Jun 1854. SOURCE: WO120 Volume 70 page 115. INDEX # 6253.

Chas CORNES; pension awarded 13 Jun 1854. SOURCE: WO120 Volume 70 page 115. INDEX # 6254.

Hen^y CALLAGHAN; pension awarded 13 Jun 1854. SOURCE: WO120 Volume 70 page 115. INDEX # 6255.

Ed^{wd} FAIR; pension awarded 13 Jun 1854. SOURCE: WO120 Volume 70 page 115. INDEX # 6256.

Hugh GORMAN; pension awarded 13 Jun 1854. SOURCE: WO120 Volume 70 page 115. INDEX # 6257.

Jno IVES; pension awarded 13 Jun 1854. SOURCE: WO120 Volume 70 page 115. INDEX # 6258.

Pat^k ROWE; pension awarded 13 Jun 1854. SOURCE: WO120 Volume 70 page 115. INDEX # 6259.

Ja^s WRIGHT; pension awarded 13 Jun 1854; died 2 Jan 1873, Capetown, South Africa. SOURCE: WO120 Volume 70 page 115. INDEX # 6260.

John GALVIN; pension awarded 12 Jun 1855. SOURCE: WO120 Volume 70 page 115. INDEX # 6261.

Thomas INGRAM; pension awarded 12 Jun 1855. SOURCE: WO120 Volume 70 page 115. INDEX # 6262.

92nd Regiment of Foot

Don^d MCKINNON; pension awarded 27 May 1802; residence - Halifax, Nova Scotia, Canada. SOURCE: WO120 Volume 70 page 121. INDEX # 6263.

And^w MCNEIL; pension awarded 6 Feb 1812; residence - Cornwall, Ontario, Canada; died in 1846. SOURCE: WO120 Volume 70 page 121. INDEX # 6264.

And^w MUNRO; pension awarded 30 Oct 1816; residence - Halifax, Nova Scotia, Canada. SOURCE: WO120 Volume 70 page 121. INDEX # 6265.

Peter MCPHERSON; pension awarded 11 Nov 1829; residence - Toronto, Ontario, Canada; died 21 Mar 1851. SOURCE: WO120 Volume 70 page 121. INDEX # 6266.

Jno ANDERSON; pension awarded 16 Nov 1814. SOURCE: WO120 Volume 70 page 121. INDEX # 6267.

Wm MCLEOD; pension awarded 9 Aug 1816; residence - Charlottetown, Prince Edward Island, Canada; died in Apr 1851. SOURCE: WO120 Volume 70 page 121. INDEX # 6268.

Dav^d ROSS; pension awarded 9 Aug 1816; residence - Toronto, Ontario, Canada; died 12 Jun 1864. SOURCE: WO120 Volume 70 page 121. INDEX # 6269.

Peter LEE; pension awarded 27 Jan 1817; residence - Perth, Ontario, Canada; died in 1854. SOURCE: WO120 Volume 70 page 121. INDEX # 6270.

Jno MCINTYRE; pension awarded 21 Nov 1816; residence - Toronto, Ontario, Canada. SOURCE: WO120 Volume 70 page 121. INDEX # 6271.

Jno MCINTOSH; pension awarded 16 Nov 1814; residence - Toronto, Ontario, Canada; died 25 Jun 1877, London, Ontario, Canada. SOURCE: WO120 Volume 70 page 121. INDEX # 6272.

Mau^re FITZGERALD; pension awarded 25 Apr 1838; residence - Gibraltar; died 3 Dec 1849. SOURCE: WO120 Volume 70 page 121. INDEX # 6273.

Ja^s FRASER; pension awarded 11 Oct 1826; residence - Halifax, Nova Scotia, Canada. SOURCE: WO120 Volume 70 page 121. INDEX # 6274.

93rd Regiment of Foot

Malc^m SUTHERLAND; pension awarded 20 Jan 1819; residence - Halifax, Nova Scotia, Canada; died 15 Aug 1846. SOURCE: WO120 Volume 70 page 127. INDEX # 6275.

Jno CAMPBELL; pension awarded 9 Sep 1845; residence - Canada. SOURCE: WO120 Volume 70 page 127. INDEX # 6276.

Robt MCKAY; pension awarded 24 Apr 1816; residence - Toronto, Ontario, Canada; died 2 Jun 1856. SOURCE: WO120 Volume 70 page 127. INDEX # 6277.

Jno FORBES; pension awarded 11 Nov 1818; residence - Halifax, Nova Scotia, Canada. SOURCE: WO120 Volume 70 page 127. INDEX # 6278.

Willm HENRY; pension awarded 3 Sep 1823; residence - Toronto, Ontario, Canada; died 11 Apr 1846. SOURCE: WO120 Volume 70 page 127. INDEX # 6279.

Don^d GUNN; pension awarded 28 Nov 1815; residence - London, Ontario, Canada; died in 1845. SOURCE: WO120 Volume 70 page 127. INDEX # 6280.

Adam SUTHERLAND; pension awarded 23 Sep 1845; residence - Toronto, Ontario, Canada. SOURCE: WO120 Volume 70 page 127. INDEX # 6281.

Jno SUTHERLAND; pension awarded 25 Sep 1822; residence - Halifax, Nova Scotia, Canada; died 3 Mar 1851. SOURCE: WO120 Volume 70 page 127. INDEX # 6282.

Geo^e ROSS; pension awarded 5 Jul 1820; residence - Bytown, Ontario, Canada. SOURCE: WO120 Volume 70 page 127. INDEX # 6283.

Don^d MURRAY; pension awarded 3 May 1815; residence - Toronto, Ontario, Canada; died 17 Mar 1849. SOURCE: WO120 Volume 70 page 127. INDEX # 6284.

Wm MCKAY; pension awarded 31 Mar 1815; residence - Halifax, Nova Scotia, Canada. SOURCE: WO120 Volume 70 page 127. INDEX # 6285.

Jno MCBEATH; pension awarded 20 Jan 1819; residence - Halifax, Nova Scotia, Canada. SOURCE: WO120 Volume 70 page 127. INDEX # 6286.

Hugh LOGAN; pension awarded 17 Dec 1823; residence - Charlottetown, Prince Edward Island, Canada. SOURCE: WO120 Volume 70 page 127. INDEX # 6287.

93rd Regiment of Foot (continued)

Robt SUTHERLAND; pension awarded 5 Jun 1822; residence - London, Ontario, Canada; died 12 Sep 1855. SOURCE: WO120 Volume 70 page 127. INDEX # 6288.

Stⁿ GORDON; pension awarded 28 Nov 1821; residence - Halifax, Nova Scotia, Canada; died in Aug 1862, Nova Scotia, Canada. SOURCE: WO120 Volume 70 page 127. INDEX # 6289.

Angus MCDONALD; pension awarded 27 Jun 1821; residence - London, Ontario, Canada; died 20 Mar 1850. SOURCE: WO120 Volume 70 page 127. INDEX # 6290.

Ja^s MCKAY; pension awarded 5 Jun 1822; residence - London, Ontario, Canada; died 14 Mar 1855. SOURCE: WO120 Volume 70 page 127. INDEX # 6291.

Willm FERGUSON; pension awarded 22 Sep 1841; residence - Toronto, Ontario, Canada; died 3 Mar 1860. SOURCE: WO120 Volume 70 page 127. INDEX # 6292.

Robt ROSS; pension awarded 2 Nov 1825; residence - Bytown, Ontario, Canada; died 20 Sep 1857. SOURCE: WO120 Volume 70 page 127. INDEX # 6293.

David GRANT; pension awarded 17 Sep 1823; residence - Halifax, Nova Scotia, Canada. SOURCE: WO120 Volume 70 page 127. INDEX # 6294.

Willm MACKAY; pension awarded 18 Aug 1823; residence - London, Ontario, Canada; died 20 Nov 1864. SOURCE: WO120 Volume 70 page 128. INDEX # 6295.

Thos THOMSON; pension awarded 26 Sep 1843; residence - Toronto, Ontario, Canada; died 12 Aug 1867. SOURCE: WO120 Volume 70 page 128. INDEX # 6296.

Jno URQUHART; pension awarded 27 Aug 1844; residence - Kingston, Ontario, Canada; died in 1856. SOURCE: WO120 Volume 70 page 128. INDEX # 6297.

Alex^r SUTHERLAND; pension awarded 26 Nov 1844; residence - Toronto, Ontario, Canada; died 10 Apr 1885, Toronto, Ontario, Canada. SOURCE: WO120 Volume 70 page 128. INDEX # 6298.

Geo^e HENDERSON; pension awarded 25 Aug 1846; died 11 Nov 1884, Toronto, Ontario, Canada. SOURCE: WO120 Volume 70 page 128. INDEX # 6299.

Jno GRIEVE; pension awarded 22 Sep 1846; residence - Toronto, Ontario, Canada; died 15 Jan 1863. SOURCE: WO120 Volume 70 page 128. INDEX # 6300.

Ja^s SUTHERLAND; pension awarded 12 Oct 1847; residence - London, Ontario, Canada; died 23 Jun 1865. SOURCE: WO120 Volume 70 page 128. INDEX # 6301.

Saml MARSHALL; pension awarded 12 Oct 1847. SOURCE: WO120 Volume 70 page 128. INDEX # 6302.

Ja^s ROSS; pension awarded 27 Jun 1848. SOURCE: WO120 Volume 70 page 128. INDEX # 6303.

Peter HUTTON; pension awarded 27 Jun 1848. SOURCE: WO120 Volume 70 page 128. INDEX # 6304.

Jno STEWART; pension awarded 27 Jun 1848. SOURCE: WO120 Volume 70 page 128. INDEX # 6305.

Alex^r BROOK; pension awarded 27 Jun 1848. SOURCE: WO120 Volume 70 page 128. INDEX # 6306.

Jno GAIR; pension awarded 27 Jun 1848. SOURCE: WO120 Volume 70 page 128. INDEX # 6307.

David TEMPLETON; pension awarded 27 Jun 1848. SOURCE: WO120 Volume 70 page 128. INDEX # 6308.

94th Regiment of Foot

Ja^s ROSS; pension awarded 7 Mar 1827; residence - Cornwall, Ontario, Canada; died 13 Oct 1850. SOURCE: WO120 Volume 70 page 137. INDEX # 6309.

Ja^s WAUGH; pension awarded 30 Dec 1818; residence - Montreal, Quebec, Canada; died 2 Dec 1861, London, Ontario, Canada. SOURCE: WO120 Volume 70 page 137. INDEX # 6310.

Tim^y REILLY; pension awarded 16 Sep 1829; residence - Fredericton, New Brunswick, Canada; died in 1853. SOURCE: WO120 Volume 70 page 137. INDEX # 6311.

Robt KING; pension awarded 11 Mar 1845; residence - Madras, India. SOURCE: WO120 Volume 70 page 137. INDEX # 6312.

Willm PARROTT; pension awarded 11 Mar 1845; residence - Madras, India; died 25 Mar 1853. SOURCE: WO120 Volume 70 page 137. INDEX # 6313.

Jno PRITCHARD; pension awarded 12 Jun 1833; residence - Halifax, Nova Scotia, Canada. SOURCE: WO120 Volume 70 page 137. INDEX # 6314.

WO120 VOLUME 70

94th Regiment of Foot (continued)

Jno WATSON; pension awarded 28 Apr 1846; residence - Madras, India; died 17 Jun 1852. SOURCE: WO120 Volume 70 page 137. INDEX # 6315.

Danl BUDD; pension awarded 23 Mar 1847; residence - Madras, India; died 24 Jun 1824. SOURCE: WO120 Volume 70 page 137. INDEX # 6316.

Armour NOBLE; pension awarded 23 Mar 1847; residence - Madras, India; died 1 Sep 1854. SOURCE: WO120 Volume 70 page 137. INDEX # 6317.

Maurice KEANE; pension awarded 23 Mar 1847. SOURCE: WO120 Volume 70 page 137. INDEX # 6318.

Edwd STEWART; pension awarded 23 Mar 1847; residence - Calcutta, India; died 15 Nov 1851. SOURCE: WO120 Volume 70 page 137. INDEX # 6319.

Hen^y THOMPSON; pension awarded 13 Apr 1847. SOURCE: WO120 Volume 70 page 137. INDEX # 6320.

Pat^k DOWNIE; pension awarded 25 Apr 1848; residence - Madras, India; died 23 Dec 1849. SOURCE: WO120 Volume 70 page 137. INDEX # 6321.

Jno FAIR; pension awarded 25 Apr 1848; residence - Madras, India; died 18 May 1852. SOURCE: WO120 Volume 70 page 137. INDEX # 6322.

Mich^l GEERIN; pension awarded 25 Apr 1848. SOURCE: WO120 Volume 70 page 137. INDEX # 6323.

David MARJORAM; pension awarded 25 Apr 1848; died 11 Apr 1848. SOURCE: WO120 Volume 70 page 137. INDEX # 6324.

Jos^h THOMPSON; pension awarded 25 Apr 1848; died 15 Aug 1855. SOURCE: WO120 Volume 70 page 137. INDEX # 6325.

Wm TAYLOR; pension awarded 25 Apr 1848; residence - Madras, India; died 15 Nov 1851. SOURCE: WO120 Volume 70 page 137. INDEX # 6326.

David BLACKLAWS; pension awarded 14 Nov 1848. SOURCE: WO120 Volume 70 page 137. INDEX # 6327.

Jno GILMORE; pension awarded 27 Mar 1849. SOURCE: WO120 Volume 70 page 137. INDEX # 6328.

Goliah SMITH; pension awarded 27 Mar 1849; residence - Cannanore, India; died 12 Mar 1849. SOURCE: WO120 Volume 70 page 138. INDEX # 6329.

Smith UTTON; pension awarded 27 Mar 1849. SOURCE: WO120 Volume 70 page 138. INDEX # 6330.

Geo^e WESTCOMBE; pension awarded 27 Mar 1849. SOURCE: WO120 Volume 70 page 138. INDEX # 6331.

Geo^e PRATT; pension awarded 12 Feb 1850. SOURCE: WO120 Volume 70 page 138. INDEX # 6332.

Abr^m JACKSON; pension awarded 8 Apr 1851; died 4 Aug 1871, Madras, India. SOURCE: WO120 Volume 70 page 138. INDEX # 6333.

Pat^k OBRIEN; pension awarded 8 Apr 1851. SOURCE: WO120 Volume 70 page 138. INDEX # 6334.

Hen^y TURNER; pension awarded 13 Apr 1852. SOURCE: WO120 Volume 70 page 138. INDEX # 6335.

Jno WATSON; pension awarded 13 Apr 1852; died 20 May 1874, Lynn. SOURCE: WO120 Volume 70 page 138. INDEX # 6336.

Ja^s FAULKNER; pension awarded 14 Dec 1852; died 21 May 1854, Madras, India. SOURCE: WO120 Volume 70 page 138. INDEX # 6337.

Peter WATERS; pension awarded 11 Jan 1854. SOURCE: WO120 Volume 70 page 138. INDEX # 6338.

Hen^y HUBBARD; pension awarded 11 Apr 1854. SOURCE: WO120 Volume 70 page 138. INDEX # 6339.

Thos KING; pension awarded 11 Apr 1854. SOURCE: WO120 Volume 70 page 138. INDEX # 6340.

Jno WALKER; pension awarded 9 May 1854. SOURCE: WO120 Volume 70 page 138. INDEX # 6341.

Jno SHIBLY; pension awarded 23 May 1854. SOURCE: WO120 Volume 70 page 138. INDEX # 6342.

95th Regiment of Foot

Wil^m WIGMORE; pension awarded 19 Jul 1826; residence - Toronto, Ontario, Canada; died 14 Jan 1881, Toronto, Ontario, Canada. SOURCE: WO120 Volume 70 page 145. INDEX # 6343.

Jos^h BENNETT; pension awarded 17 Feb 1819; residence - New South Wales, Australia. SOURCE: WO120 Volume 70 page 145. INDEX # 6344.

Wm HAUGHTON; pension awarded 9 Mar 1813; residence - Halifax, Nova Scotia, Canada; died 14 Mar 1872, Waterford. SOURCE: WO120 Volume 70 page 145. INDEX # 6345.

95th Regiment of Foot (continued)

Jno MCCOLLEN; pension awarded 5 Apr 1810; residence - Quebec, Quebec, Canada. SOURCE: WO120 Volume 70 page 145. INDEX # 6346.

Peter MCDERMOTT; pension awarded 16 Sep 1814; residence - Bytown, Ontario, Canada; died 2 Nov 1854. SOURCE: WO120 Volume 70 page 145. INDEX # 6347.

Jas MURRAY; pension awarded 8 Aug 1838; residence - Malta; died 11 Nov 1847. SOURCE: WO120 Volume 70 page 145. INDEX # 6348.

Michl MORRISON; pension awarded 10 Nov 1846; residence - Malta; died 9 Feb 1847. SOURCE: WO120 Volume 70 page 145. INDEX # 6349.

Michl DYER; pension awarded 14 Mar 1848. SOURCE: WO120 Volume 70 page 145. INDEX # 6350.

Jno RYAN; pension awarded 27 Jun 1848; died 17 Mar 1872, Kilkainny. SOURCE: WO120 Volume 70 page 145. INDEX # 6351.

Patk MCMAHON; pension awarded 12 Nov 1850; died 26 Nov 1874, Ennis. SOURCE: WO120 Volume 70 page 145. INDEX # 6352.

96th Regiment of Foot

Patk EARLY; pension awarded 10 Sep 1844; residence - Van Diemen's Land, Australia. SOURCE: WO120 Volume 70 page 152. INDEX # 6353.

Danl FOLEY; pension awarded 10 Sep 1844; residence - Van Diemen's Land, Australia; died 28 Feb 1869, Hobarton, Tasmania, Australia. SOURCE: WO120 Volume 70 page 152. INDEX # 6354.

Jno COURNAN; pension awarded 26 Aug 1845; residence - Van Diemen's Land, Australia; died 15 Mar 1847. SOURCE: WO120 Volume 70 page 152. INDEX # 6355.

Jas DONAHUE; pension awarded 23 Dec 1818; residence - New South Wales, Australia. SOURCE: WO120 Volume 70 page 152. INDEX # 6356.

Michl MCMAHON; pension awarded 26 Aug 1845; residence - Van Diemen's Land, Australia. SOURCE: WO120 Volume 70 page 152. INDEX # 6357.

Archd CAMPBELL; pension awarded 10 Nov 1846; residence - Van Diemen's Land, Australia; died 6 Jun 1878, Tasmania, Australia. SOURCE: WO120 Volume 70 page 152. INDEX # 6358.

Martin FINN; pension awarded 10 Nov 1846; died 7 Mar 1882, Melbourne, Australia. SOURCE: WO120 Volume 70 page 152. INDEX # 6359.

Willm BRYAN; pension awarded 10 Nov 1840; residence - Van Diemen's Land, Australia. SOURCE: WO120 Volume 70 page 152. INDEX # 6360.

Hugh KAIN; pension awarded 10 Nov 1846; residence - Van Diemen's Land, Australia. SOURCE: WO120 Volume 70 page 152. INDEX # 6361.

Jas CONWAY; pension awarded 26 Oct 1847. SOURCE: WO120 Volume 70 page 152. INDEX # 6362.

Jno HILL; pension awarded 26 Oct 1847. SOURCE: WO120 Volume 70 page 152. INDEX # 6363.

Fras COUGHLAN; pension awarded 26 Oct 1847. SOURCE: WO120 Volume 70 page 152. INDEX # 6364.

Wm MCDONALD; pension awarded 26 Oct 1847. SOURCE: WO120 Volume 70 page 152. INDEX # 6365.

Andw WOODS; pension awarded 26 Oct 1847; died 27 Jul 1877, Tasmania, Australia. SOURCE: WO120 Volume 70 page 152. INDEX # 6366.

Jas BEIRNE; pension awarded 11 Mar 1848. SOURCE: WO120 Volume 70 page 152. INDEX # 6367.

Jno LENNON; pension awarded 11 Mar 1848. SOURCE: WO120 Volume 70 page 152. INDEX # 6368.

Jas SPENCER; pension awarded 11 Mar 1848; residence - Van Diemen's Land, Australia; died 19 Apr 1848. SOURCE: WO120 Volume 70 page 152. INDEX # 6369.

Patk HANRAHAN; pension awarded 11 Jul 1848. SOURCE: WO120 Volume 70 page 152. INDEX # 6370.

Mark LEES; pension awarded 11 Jul 1848; residence - Australia; died in Dec 1856. SOURCE: WO120 Volume 70 page 152. INDEX # 6371.

Geoe MARSH; pension awarded 13 Feb 1849; died 28 Jan 1883. SOURCE: WO120 Volume 70 page 152. INDEX # 6372.

Thos PEARCE; pension awarded 13 Feb 1849. SOURCE: WO120 Volume 70 page 153. INDEX # 6373.

96th Regiment of Foot (continued)

Jos^h CLARKE; pension awarded 22 May 1849; died 31 Mar 1883 South Australia, Australia. SOURCE: WO120 Volume 70 page 153. INDEX # 6374.
Jno GREEN; pension awarded 22 May 1849. SOURCE: WO120 Volume 70 page 153. INDEX # 6375.
Jno CARTER; pension awarded 14 Aug 1849. SOURCE: WO120 Volume 70 page 153. INDEX # 6376.
Thos FARRELL; pension awarded 14 Aug 1849; died 6 May 1874, Tasmania, Australia. SOURCE: WO120 Volume 70 page 153. INDEX # 6377.
Edwd Jno HAMPTON; pension awarded 14 Aug 1849; died 20 Jul 1872, Hobarton, Australia. SOURCE: WO120 Volume 70 page 153. INDEX # 6378.
Geo^e MURPHY; pension awarded 14 Aug 1849. SOURCE: WO120 Volume 70 page 153. INDEX # 6379.
Jno HARRIS; pension awarded 14 Aug 1849. SOURCE: WO120 Volume 70 page 153. INDEX # 6380.
Ja^s LEONARD; pension awarded 14 Aug 1849. SOURCE: WO120 Volume 70 page 153. INDEX # 6381.
Thos MERRETT; pension awarded 14 Aug 1849. SOURCE: WO120 Volume 70 page 153. INDEX # 6382.
Jos^h TRINDER; pension awarded 14 Aug 1849. SOURCE: WO120 Volume 70 page 153. INDEX # 6383.
Jno WINDUS; pension awarded 14 Aug 1849; died 24 Jul 1873, Tasmania, Australia. SOURCE: WO120 Volume 70 page 153. INDEX # 6384.
Mich^l FORD; pension awarded 9 Oct 1849. SOURCE: WO120 Volume 70 page 153. INDEX # 6385.
Ja^s DOYLE; pension awarded 9 Aug 1849. SOURCE: WO120 Volume 70 page 153. INDEX # 6386.
Ja^s ROCK; pension awarded 9 Oct 1849. SOURCE: WO120 Volume 70 page 153. INDEX # 6387.
Hen^y WOODS; pension awarded 9 Oct 1849; died 31 Dec 1875. SOURCE: WO120 Volume 70 page 153. INDEX # 6388.
Wm BRUNDLE; pension awarded 13 Nov 1849. SOURCE: WO120 Volume 70 page 153. INDEX # 6389.
Ja^s SHEERAN; pension awarded 13 Nov 1849; died 10 Oct 1870. SOURCE: WO120 Volume 70 page 153. INDEX # 6390.
Thos SMITH; pension awarded 13 Nov 1849. SOURCE: WO120 Volume 70 page 153. INDEX # 6391.
Ja^s ALLEN; pension awarded 13 Nov 1849. SOURCE: WO120 Volume 70 page 153. INDEX # 6392.
Mich^l CAREY; pension awarded 13 Nov 1849. SOURCE: WO120 Volume 70 page 154. INDEX # 6393.
Jno ALLISON; pension awarded 13 Nov 1849; died 14 Nov 1876, East London. SOURCE: WO120 Volume 70 page 154. INDEX # 6394.
Ja^s BEASLEY; pension awarded 13 Nov 1849; died 15 Nov 1884, Tasmania, Australia. SOURCE: WO120 Volume 70 page 154. INDEX # 6395.
Edwd DARCY; pension awarded 13 Nov 1849; died 7 Jul 1872, Hobarton. SOURCE: WO120 Volume 70 page 154. INDEX # 6396.
Geo^e RINGWOOD; pension awarded 13 Nov 1849. SOURCE: WO120 Volume 70 page 154. INDEX # 6397.
Ja^s SPILLARD; pension awarded 13 Nov 1849. SOURCE: WO120 Volume 70 page 154. INDEX # 6398.
Stephen SMITH; pension awarded 13 Nov 1849. SOURCE: WO120 Volume 70 page 154. INDEX # 6399.
Robt YOUNG; pension awarded 13 Nov 1849. SOURCE: WO120 Volume 70 page 154. INDEX # 6400.
Jno HAMMOND; pension awarded 13 Nov 1849. SOURCE: WO120 Volume 70 page 154. INDEX # 6401.
Nathl NEWSTEAD; pension awarded 13 Nov 1849. SOURCE: WO120 Volume 70 page 154. INDEX # 6402.
Robt BULLOCK; pension awarded 13 Nov 1849. SOURCE: WO120 Volume 70 page 154. INDEX # 6403.
Angus MCLACHLAN; pension awarded 13 Nov 1849; residence - Launceston, Australia; died 22 Jun 1850. SOURCE: WO120 Volume 70 page 154. INDEX # 6404.
Geo^e POLLARD; pension awarded 13 Nov 1849; died 7 Jun 1879, New Zealand. SOURCE: WO120 Volume 70 page 154. INDEX # 6405.
Step^n EMERSON; pension awarded 28 May 1850. SOURCE: WO120 Volume 70 page 154. INDEX # 6406.
Hen^y ENGLAND; pension awarded 28 May 1850. SOURCE: WO120 Volume 70 page 154. INDEX # 6407.
Richd FANNING; pension awarded 28 May 1850. SOURCE: WO120 Volume 70 page 154. INDEX # 6408.
Barth^w HOPKINS; pension awarded 16 Jul 1850. SOURCE: WO120 Volume 70 page 154. INDEX # 6409.
Jno HOUSIGO; pension awarded 16 Jul 1850; died 19 Aug 1878, Tasmania, Australia. SOURCE: WO120 Volume 70 page 154. INDEX # 6410.
Ja^s LAPRAIK; pension awarded 16 Jul 1850. SOURCE: WO120 Volume 70 page 154. INDEX # 6411.
Mich^l HORNBY; pension awarded 11 Mar 1851. SOURCE: WO120 Volume 70 page 154. INDEX # 6412.
John AGNEW; pension awarded 8 May 1855. SOURCE: WO120 Volume 70 page 154. INDEX # 6413.

96th Regiment of Foot (continued)

William WALE; pension awarded 8 May 1855. SOURCE: WO120 Volume 70 page 154. INDEX # 6414.

97th Regiment of Foot

Ja^s LALLY; pension awarded 30 Dec 1818; residence - Belleville, Ontario, Canada; died 5 Jul 1873, Toronto, Ontario, Canada. SOURCE: WO120 Volume 70 page 164. INDEX # 6415.

Lough^n CORCORCAN; pension awarded 1 Jul 1819; residence - St. Johns. SOURCE: WO120 Volume 70 page 164. INDEX # 6416.

Wm BARNETT; pension awarded 16 Jan 1844; residence - Ionian Isles; died 11 Feb 1848. SOURCE: WO120 Volume 70 page 164. INDEX # 6417.

Pat^k SCALLON; pension awarded 1 Jul 1819; residence - Quebec, Quebec, Canada. SOURCE: WO120 Volume 70 page 164. INDEX # 6418.

Corn^s OBRIEN; pension awarded 30 Dec 1818; residence - Halifax, Nova Scotia, Canada; died 3 Oct 1851. SOURCE: WO120 Volume 70 page 164. INDEX # 6419.

Den^s KILLEEN; pension awarded 26 Aug 1819; residence - Bytown, Ontario, Canada. SOURCE: WO120 Volume 70 page 164. INDEX # 6420.

Willm HEAPHY; pension awarded 25 Jun 1817; residence - Kingston, Ontario, Canada; died 20 Mar 1873, Athlone. SOURCE: WO120 Volume 70 page 164. INDEX # 6421.

Martin RYAN; pension awarded 11 Jul 1838; residence - Toronto, Ontario, Canada; died 12 Apr 1855. SOURCE: WO120 Volume 70 page 164. INDEX # 6422.

Thos MONTFORD; pension awarded 27 Jul 1847; residence - Malta; died 2 Feb 1851. SOURCE: WO120 Volume 70 page 164. INDEX # 6423.

Wm TIMMINS; pension awarded 27 Jul 1847. SOURCE: WO120 Volume 70 page 164. INDEX # 6424.

Ja^s KELLY; pension awarded 26 Oct 1848; died 19 Mar 1874, Kilmainham, Ireland. SOURCE: WO120 Volume 70 page 164. INDEX # 6425.

Chas NOLAN; pension awarded 10 Jul 1849. SOURCE: WO120 Volume 70 page 164. INDEX # 6426.

Mich^l REDMOND; pension awarded 10 Jul 1849; residence - Montreal, Quebec, Canada; died 9 Feb 1856. SOURCE: WO120 Volume 70 page 164. INDEX # 6427.

Ja^s MURPHY; pension awarded 12 Mar 1850. SOURCE: WO120 Volume 70 page 164. INDEX # 6428.

Jno FITZGERALD; pension awarded 11 Jun 1850. SOURCE: WO120 Volume 70 page 164. INDEX # 6429.

Wm CARR; pension awarded 2 Sep 1851; residence - Halifax, Nova Scotia, Canada; died 29 Apr 1876. SOURCE: WO120 Volume 70 page 164. INDEX # 6430.

Hen^y CURRY; pension awarded 3 Sep 1851. SOURCE: WO120 Volume 70 page 164. INDEX # 6431.

Geo^e GILMORE; pension awarded 3 Sep 1851. SOURCE: WO120 Volume 70 page 164. INDEX # 6432.

Jno GRAHAM; pension awarded 2 Sep 1851. SOURCE: WO120 Volume 70 page 164. INDEX # 6433.

Jno OSHEA; pension awarded 2 Sep 1851. SOURCE: WO120 Volume 70 page 164. INDEX # 6434.

Robt STUART; pension awarded 2 Sep 1851. SOURCE: WO120 Volume 70 page 165. INDEX # 6435.

Pat^k NORMAN; pension awarded 25 Nov 1851. SOURCE: WO120 Volume 70 page 164. INDEX # 6436.

Wm BURNS; pension awarded 25 Nov 1851. SOURCE: WO120 Volume 70 page 164. INDEX # 6437.

Thos THOMPSON; pension awarded 25 Nov 1851. SOURCE: WO120 Volume 70 page 165. INDEX # 6438.

Hen^y ADAMS; pension awarded 22 Jun 1852. SOURCE: WO120 Volume 70 page 165. INDEX # 6439.

Jno COYLE; pension awarded 22 Jun 1852; residence - Nova Scotia, Canada; died 21 Jan 1858. SOURCE: WO120 Volume 70 page 165. INDEX # 6440.

Pat^k DILLON; pension awarded 22 Jun 1852. SOURCE: WO120 Volume 70 page 164. INDEX # 6441.

Peter DONOVAN; pension awarded 22 Jun 1852; died 20 Dec 1873, Halifax, Nova Scotia, Canada. SOURCE: WO120 Volume 70 page 165. INDEX # 6442.

Mich^l DONOVAN; pension awarded 22 Jun 1852. SOURCE: WO120 Volume page . INDEX # 6443.

Jno FARROW; pension awarded 22 Jun 1852. SOURCE: WO120 Volume 70 page 165. INDEX # 6444.

Chas HALL; pension awarded 22 Jun 1852. SOURCE: WO120 Volume 70 page 165. INDEX # 6445.

Wm HARVEY; pension awarded 22 Jun 1852; residence - Halifax, Nova Scotia, Canada; died 3 Jan 1876. SOURCE: WO120 Volume 70 page 165. INDEX # 6446.

Jno WHITE; pension awarded 22 Jun 1852. SOURCE: WO120 Volume 70 page 165. INDEX # 6447.

Jer^h BRENNAN; pension awarded 24 Aug 1852. SOURCE: WO120 Volume 70 page 165. INDEX # 6448.

WO120 VOLUME 70

97th Regiment of Foot (continued)

Jno LAPHAM; pension awarded 24 Aug 1852. SOURCE: WO120 Volume 70 page 165. INDEX # 6449.

Jas MCGUIRE; pension awarded 24 Aug 1852. SOURCE: WO120 Volume 70 page 165. INDEX # 6450.

Fredk BLACK; pension awarded 26 Apr 1853; died 8 Feb 1873, Bristol. SOURCE: WO120 Volume 70 page 165. INDEX # 6451.

Patk ROCHE; pension awarded 26 Apr 1853. SOURCE: WO120 Volume 70 page 165. INDEX # 6452.

Jas STONE; pension awarded 26 Apr 1853. SOURCE: WO120 Volume 70 page 165. INDEX # 6453.

James KELLY; pension awarded 26 Apr 1853. SOURCE: WO120 Volume 70 page 165. INDEX # 6454.

Danl QUILTY; pension awarded 26 Apr 1853; died 15 Feb 1878, Halifax, Nova Scotia, Canada. SOURCE: WO120 Volume 70 page 166. INDEX # 6455.

Murtaugh CALLAGHAN; pension awarded 19 Jul 1853; died 18 Sep 1872, Nova Scotia, Canada. SOURCE: WO120 Volume 70 page 166. INDEX # 6456.

98th Regiment of Foot

Wm ELLIOTT; pension awarded 26 Aug 1819; residence - Fredericton, New Brunswick, Canada. SOURCE: WO120 Volume 70 page 170. INDEX # 6457.

Wm FANNON; pension awarded 26 Aug 1819; residence - Fredericton, New Brunswick, Canada. SOURCE: WO120 Volume 70 page 170. INDEX # 6458.

Patk HOLMES; pension awarded 23 May 1821; residence - Fredericton, New Brunswick, Canada; died 27 Sep 1862, Nova Scotia, Canada. SOURCE: WO120 Volume 70 page 170. INDEX # 6459.

Geoe HARRIS; pension awarded 24 Oct 1821; residence - Halifax, Nova Scotia, Canada. SOURCE: WO120 Volume 70 page 170. INDEX # 6460.

Patk MURPHY; pension awarded 24 Oct 1821; residence - Fredericton, New Brunswick, Canada. SOURCE: WO120 Volume 70 page 170. INDEX # 6461.

Jno MCCARTHY; pension awarded 9 May 1823; residence - Halifax, Nova Scotia, Canada. SOURCE: WO120 Volume 70 page 170. INDEX # 6462.

Edwd TOOLE; pension awarded 9 Nov 1831; residence - Halifax, Nova Scotia, Canada. SOURCE: WO120 Volume 70 page 170. INDEX # 6463.

John WALSH; pension awarded 23 May 1821; residence - Fredericton, New Brunswick, Canada. SOURCE: WO120 Volume 70 page 170. INDEX # 6464.

Patk DILLEN; pension awarded 29 Apr 1818; residence - Halifax, Nova Scotia, Canada. SOURCE: WO120 Volume 70 page 170. INDEX # 6465.

John NUGENT; pension awarded 11 May 1822; residence - Halifax, Nova Scotia, Canada. SOURCE: WO120 Volume 70 page 170. INDEX # 6466.

Michl KEARNS; pension awarded 28 Oct 1818; residence - New South Wales, Australia. SOURCE: WO120 Volume 70 page 170. INDEX # 6467.

Willm REYNOLDS; pension awarded 12 Jan 1842; residence - Toronto, Ontario, Canada. SOURCE: WO120 Volume 70 page 170. INDEX # 6468.

Thos ATKINS; pension awarded 24 Oct 1821; residence - Halifax, Nova Scotia, Canada; died 10 Mar 1847. SOURCE: WO120 Volume 70 page 170. INDEX # 6469.

Richd AUSTIN; pension awarded 24 Oct 1821; residence - St. Johns; died 15 May 1851. SOURCE: WO120 Volume 70 page 170. INDEX # 6470.

Jno BURKE; pension awarded 26 May 1819; residence - Fredericton, New Brunswick, Canada. SOURCE: WO120 Volume 70 page 170. INDEX # 6471.

Jno BOYLE; pension awarded 5 Jul 1820; residence - St. Johns. SOURCE: WO120 Volume 70 page 170. INDEX # 6472.

Jno BUTLER; pension awarded 24 Oct 1821; residence - Halifax, Nova Scotia, Canada. SOURCE: WO120 Volume 70 page 170. INDEX # 6473.

Thos BALES; pension awarded 24 Oct 1821; residence - Halifax, Nova Scotia, Canada; died in May 1854. SOURCE: WO120 Volume 70 page 170. INDEX # 6474.

BRITISH ARMY PENSIONERS ABROAD

98th Regiment of Foot (continued)

Jn⁰ BROWN; pension awarded 10 Aug 1836; residence - Fredericton, New Brunswick, Canada. SOURCE: WO120 Volume 70 page 170. INDEX # 6475.

Fraˢ COSGROVE; pension awarded 24 Oct 1821; residence - Halifax, Nova Scotia, Canada. SOURCE: WO120 Volume 70 page 170. INDEX # 6476.

Patᵏ CONNELL; pension awarded 24 Oct 1821; residence - Halifax, Nova Scotia, Canada; died 17 Jul 1872, Halifax, Nova Scotia, Canada. SOURCE: WO120 Volume 70 page 171. INDEX # 6477.

John COX; pension awarded 24 Oct 1821; residence - Halifax, Nova Scotia, Canada; died in 1848. SOURCE: WO120 Volume 70 page 171. INDEX # 6478.

Patᵏ DILLON; pension awarded 26 Aug 1819. SOURCE: WO120 Volume 70 page 171. INDEX # 6479.

Mattʷ DWYER; pension awarded 26 Aug 1819. SOURCE: WO120 Volume 70 page 171. INDEX # 6480.

Patᵏ DONNELLAN; pension awarded 3 May 1820; residence - Halifax, Nova Scotia, Canada. SOURCE: WO120 Volume 70 page 171. INDEX # 6481.

Michˡ DAWSON; pension awarded 24 Oct 1821. SOURCE: WO120 Volume 70 page 171. INDEX # 6482.

John DUNN; pension awarded 24 Oct 1821; residence - Halifax, Nova Scotia, Canada. SOURCE: WO120 Volume 70 page 171. INDEX # 6483.

Willᵐ GRIMES; pension awarded 26 Aug 1819; residence - Fredericton, New Brunswick, Canada; died 5 May 1851. SOURCE: WO120 Volume 70 page 171. INDEX # 6484.

Jn⁰ HENNESSY; pension awarded 24 Oct 1821; residence - St. Johns. SOURCE: WO120 Volume 70 page 171. INDEX # 6485.

Alexʳ HORNER; pension awarded 24 Oct 1821; residence - Halifax, Nova Scotia, Canada. SOURCE: WO120 Volume 70 page 171. INDEX # 6486.

Hugh HUTCHINSON; pension awarded 24 Oct 1821; residence - Halifax, Nova Scotia, Canada. SOURCE: WO120 Volume 70 page 171. INDEX # 6487.

Robᵗ KNOX; pension awarded 26 Aug 1819; residence - St. Johns; died 6 Mar 1853. SOURCE: WO120 Volume 70 page 171. INDEX # 6488.

Patᵏ KEARNEY; pension awarded 26 Aug 1819; residence - St. Johns. SOURCE: WO120 Volume 70 page 171. INDEX # 6489.

Thoˢ KELLY; pension awarded 24 Oct 1820; residence - St. Johns. SOURCE: WO120 Volume 70 page 171. INDEX # 6490.

Jaˢ LONG; pension awarded 26 Aug 1819; residence - Halifax, Nova Scotia, Canada. SOURCE: WO120 Volume 70 page 171. INDEX # 6491.

Thoˢ LELAND; pension awarded 28 Mar 1821; residence - St. Johns. SOURCE: WO120 Volume 70 page 171. INDEX # 6492.

Jaˢ LYONS; pension awarded 24 Oct 1821; residence - Halifax, Nova Scotia, Canada; died 12 Aug 1847. SOURCE: WO120 Volume 70 page 171. INDEX # 6493.

Willᵐ LONERGAN; pension awarded 24 24 Oct 1821; residence - Halifax, Nova Scotia, Canada. SOURCE: WO120 Volume 70 page 171. INDEX # 6494.

William LONERGAN; pension awarded 24 Oct 1821; residence - Halifax, Nova Scotia, Canada. SOURCE: WO120 Volume 70 page 171. INDEX # 6495.

Robᵗ LOWRY; pension awarded 31 Jul 1822; residence - Halifax, Nova Scotia, Canada. SOURCE: WO120 Volume 70 page 172. INDEX # 6496.

Bernᵈ MCCONNOLLY; pension awarded 24 Oct 1821; residence - Halifax, Nova Scotia, Canada; died 16 Jul 1851. SOURCE: WO120 Volume 70 page 172. INDEX # 6497.

Thoˢ MCDONALD; pension awarded 24 Oct 1821; residence - Halifax, Nova Scotia, Canada; died 13 Jan 1873, Halifax, Nova Scotia, Canada. SOURCE: WO120 Volume 70 page 172. INDEX # 6498.

Thoˢ MALONEY; pension awarded 26 Aug 1819; residence - Fredericton, New Brunswick, Canada; died 13 Sep 1847. SOURCE: WO120 Volume 70 page 172. INDEX # 6499.

Peter MORAN; pension awarded 23 May 1821; residence - Fredericton, New Brunswick, Canada. SOURCE: WO120 Volume 70 page 172. INDEX # 6500.

Fredᵏ MAHONEY; pension awarded 24 Oct 1821; residence - Halifax, Nova Scotia, Canada. SOURCE: WO120 Volume 70 page 172. INDEX # 6501.

98th Regiment of Foot (continued)

Wm ONEAL; pension awarded 26 Aug 1819; residence - St. Johns. SOURCE: WO120 Volume 70 page 172. INDEX # 6502.

Ja^s OBRIEN; pension awarded 24 Oct 1821; residence - Sydney. SOURCE: WO120 Volume 70 page 172. INDEX # 6503.

John QUILTY; pension awarded 24 Oct 1821; residence - Halifax, Nova Scotia, Canada. SOURCE: WO120 Volume 70 page 172. INDEX # 6504.

Thos RICHFORD; pension awarded 24 Aug 1819; residence - Halifax, Nova Scotia, Canada. SOURCE: WO120 Volume 70 page 172. INDEX # 6505.

John RYAN; pension awarded 24 Oct 1821; residence - Halifax, Nova Scotia, Canada. SOURCE: WO120 Volume 70 page 172. INDEX # 6506.

Pat^k RUTH; pension awarded 24 Oct 1821; residence - St. Johns. SOURCE: WO120 Volume 70 page 172. INDEX # 6507.

Robt STODDART; pension awarded 24 Oct 1821; residence - Halifax, Nova Scotia, Canada. SOURCE: WO120 Volume 79 page 172. INDEX # 6508.

Thos SLATTERY; pension awarded 16 Aug 1825; residence - Fredericton, New Brunswick, Canada; died 28 Sep 1851. SOURCE: WO120 Volume 70 page 172. INDEX # 6509.

Geo^e TAYLOR; pension awarded 24 Oct 1821; residence - Halifax, Nova Scotia, Canada. SOURCE: WO120 Volume 70 page 172. INDEX # 6510.

Willm WILEY; pension awarded 26 Aug 1819; residence - Halifax, Nova Scotia, Canada; died in 1846. SOURCE: WO120 Volume 70 page 172. INDEX # 6511.

Art^r GRUBERT; pension awarded 28 Oct 1818; residence - Newfoundland, Canada; died 29 Dec 1856. SOURCE: WO120 Volume 70 page 172. INDEX # 6512.

Fred^k WALKER; pension awarded 24 Oct 1821; residence - Halifax, Nova Scotia, Canada; died in Apr 1851. SOURCE: WO120 Volume 70 page 172. INDEX # 6513.

Pat^k FINNEGAN; pension awarded 26 Aug 1819; residence - Halifax, Nova Scotia, Canada. SOURCE: WO120 Volume 70 page 172. INDEX # 6514.

John SPROWLES; pension awarded 11 Mar 1845; residence - Madras, India; died 3 Oct 1878, Madras, India. SOURCE: WO120 Volume 70 page 172. INDEX # 6515.

George REYNOLDS; pension awarded 13 Aug 1824; residence - Toronto, Ontario, Canada. SOURCE: WO120 Volume 70 page 173. INDEX # 6516.

Jno HAYWOOD; pension awarded 12 Oct 1831; residence - Cape of Good Hope, South Africa. SOURCE: WO120 Volume 70 page 173. INDEX # 6517.

Edwd JONES; pension awarded 13 Jul 1836; residence - Cape of Good Hope, South Africa; died 5 Oct 1849. SOURCE: WO120 Volume 70 page 173. INDEX # 6518.

Robt KIRBY; pension awarded 13 May 1845; residence - Cape of Good Hope, South Africa; died 8 Dec 1848. SOURCE: WO120 Volume 70 page 173. INDEX # 6519.

Chas Wm BLAKENEY; pension awarded 10 Jun 1845; residence - Mauritius; died 10 Jul 1848. SOURCE: WO120 Volume 70 page 173. INDEX # 6520.

Thos COSTELLO; pension awarded 13 Jan 1846; residence - Hong Kong; died 8 Aug 1878, Plymouth. SOURCE: WO120 Volume 70 page 173. INDEX # 6521.

John KINGSLEY; pension awarded 24 Nov 1846; residence - Hong Kong. SOURCE: WO120 Volume 70 page 173. INDEX # 6522.

Geo^e NEWMAN; pension awarded 12 Jan 1847; residence - Hong Kong; died 16 Apr 1859, W. London. SOURCE: WO120 Volume 70 page 173. INDEX # 6523.

Fra^s Hugh MCMAHON; pension awarded 9 Feb 1847; residence - Halifax, Nova Scotia, Canada; died 30 Sep 1875. SOURCE: WO120 Volume 70 page 173. INDEX # 6524.

Richd WATSON; pension awarded 25 Jan 1848; residence - India; died 27 Apr 1854. SOURCE: WO120 Volume 70 page 173. INDEX # 6525.

Pat^k KENNEDY; pension awarded 25 Jan 1848; residence - Madras, India; died 24 May 1854. SOURCE: WO120 Volume 70 page 173. INDEX # 6526.

Wm MURCH; pension awarded 25 Jan 1848. SOURCE: WO120 Volume 70 page 173. INDEX # 6527.

Mich^l SULLIVAN; pension awarded 25 Jan 1848; residence - Dinapore, India; died 10 Oct 1848. SOURCE: WO120 Volume 70 page 173. INDEX # 6528.

BRITISH ARMY PENSIONERS ABROAD

98th Regiment of Foot (continued)

Pat^k MORGAN; pension awarded 25 Jan 1848; residence - Dinapore, India; died 1 Nov 1849. SOURCE: WO120 Volume 70 page 173. INDEX # 6529.

Wm JARDINE; pension awarded 13 Feb 1849; died 30 Sep 1885 Bengal, India. SOURCE: WO120 Volume 70 page 173. INDEX # 6530.

Jno WHITE; pension awarded 13 Feb 1849. SOURCE: WO120 Volume 70 page 173. INDEX # 6531.

99th Regiment of Foot

John BRADY; pension awarded 23 Sep 1818; residence - Bytown, Ontario, Canada. SOURCE: WO120 Volume 70 page 184. INDEX # 6532.

Wm CUNNINGHAM; pension awarded 23 Sep 1818; residence - Bytown, Ontario, Canada. SOURCE: WO120 Volume 70 page 184. INDEX # 6533.

Pat^k CARDELL; pension awarded 23 Sep 1818; residence - Richmond, Ontario, Canada; died in 1847. SOURCE: WO120 Volume 70 page 184. INDEX # 6534.

Jno CALLAGHAN; pension awarded 13 Apr 1824; residence - St. Jean, Quebec, Canada. SOURCE: WO120 Volume 70 page 184. INDEX # 6535.

Jno COFFEY; pension awarded 1 Feb 1826; residence - Bytown, Ontario, Canada. SOURCE: WO120 Volume 70 page 184. INDEX # 6536.

Peter CAVANAUGH; pension awarded 1 Feb 1826; residence - Richmond, Ontario, Canada. SOURCE: WO120 Volume 70 page 184. INDEX # 6537.

Ja^s DEVIN; pension awarded 23 Oct 1818; residence - Bytown, Ontario, Canada; died 26 Dec 1846. SOURCE: WO120 Volume 70 page 184. INDEX # 6538.

Ja^s DORRIS; pension awarded 13 Dec 1826; residence - Bytown, Ontario, Canada; died in 1853. SOURCE: WO120 Volume 70 page 184. INDEX # 6539.

Garrett FITZGERALD; pension awarded 12 Sep 1832; residence - Bytown, Ontario, Canada; died in 1853. SOURCE: WO120 Volume 70 page 184. INDEX # 6540.

Bern^d HUGHES; pension awarded 13 Jan 1830; residence - Bytown, Ontario, Canada. SOURCE: WO120 Volume 70 page 184. INDEX # 6541.

Dean JUNKIN; pension awarded 12 May 1824; residence - Bytown, Ontario, Canada. SOURCE: WO120 Volume 70 page 184. INDEX # 6542.

Ja^s LENNON; pension awarded 23 Sep 1818; residence - Richmond, Ontario, Canada; died 11 Jul 1855. SOURCE: WO120 Volume 70 page 184. INDEX # 6543.

Robt LEE; pension awarded 23 Sep 1818; residence - Bytown, Ontario, Canada. SOURCE: WO120 Volume 70 page 184. INDEX # 6544.

John LEE; pension awarded 30 May 1827; residence - Bytown, Ontario, Canada; died 9 Jul 1851. SOURCE: WO120 Volume 70 page 184. INDEX # 6545.

Bern^d MCBRIDE; pension awarded 23 Sep 1818; residence - Bytown, Ontario, Canada; died 22 Nov 1854. SOURCE: WO120 Volume 70 page 184. INDEX # 6546.

Alex^r MCCASLIN; pension awarded 23 Sep 1818; residence - Bytown, Ontario, Canada; died 1 Aug 1858. SOURCE: WO120 Volume 70 page 184. INDEX # 6547.

Wm MCFADDEN; pension awarded 26 Feb 1840; residence - Bytown, Ontario, Canada; died 22 Sep 1881, Ottawa, Ontario, Canada. SOURCE: WO120 Volume 70 page 184. INDEX # 6548.

Ja^s MULHOLLAND; pension awarded 10 Jul 1839; residence - Richmond, Ontario, Canada. SOURCE: WO120 Volume 70 page 184. INDEX # 6549.

Mich^l OHARA; pension awarded 23 Sep 1818; residence - Bytown, Ontario, Canada. SOURCE: WO120 Volume 70 page 184. INDEX # 6550.

Abr^m NICHOLS; pension awarded 23 Sep 1818; residence - Prescott, Ontario, Canada. SOURCE: WO120 Volume 70 page 184. INDEX # 6551.

Pat^k QUINN; pension awarded 23 Sep 1818; residence - Bytown, Ontario, Canada; died in 1847. SOURCE: WO120 Volume 70 page 185. INDEX # 6552.

Pat^k REILY; pension awarded 23 Sep 1818; residence - Richmond, Ontario, Canada. SOURCE: WO120 Volume 70 page 185. INDEX # 6553.

99th Regiment of Foot (continued)

Thos RATH; pension awarded 23 Sep 1818; residence - Richmond, Ontario, Canada; died in 1853, Bytown, Ontario, Canada. SOURCE: WO120 Volume 70 page 185. INDEX # 6554.

Jno SYKES; pension awarded 23 Sep 1818; residence - Bytown, Ontario, Canada. SOURCE: WO120 Volume 70 page 185. INDEX # 6555.

Andw SPEARMAN; pension awarded 30 May 1827; residence - Bytown, Ontario, Canada. SOURCE: WO120 Volume 70 page 185. INDEX # 6556.

John CAFFRAY; pension awarded 20 Nov 1839; residence - Bytown, Ontario, Canada. SOURCE: WO120 Volume 70 page 185. INDEX # 6557.

John FALIHE; pension awarded 11 Nov 1840; residence - Smithsfalls, Ontario, Canada. SOURCE: WO120 Volume 70 page 185. INDEX # 6558.

John POWELL; pension awarded 14 Apr 1841; residence - Bytown, Ontario, Canada; died 15 Mar 1855. SOURCE: WO120 Volume 70 page 185. INDEX # 6559.

Heny MCDONNELL; pension awarded 23 Oct 1839; residence - Bytown, Ontario, Canada; died 3 Jan 1857. SOURCE: WO120 Volume 70 page 185. INDEX # 6560.

Jas RYAN; pension awarded 30 May 1827; residence - Quebec, Quebec, Canada. SOURCE: WO120 Volume 70 page 185. INDEX # 6561.

Josh AUSTIN; pension awarded 23 Sep 1818; residence - Richmond, Ontario, Canada. SOURCE: WO120 Volume 70 page 185. INDEX # 6562.

Jas BUTLER; pension awarded 23 Sep 1818; residence - Bytown, Ontario, Canada. SOURCE: WO120 Volume 70 page 185. INDEX # 6563.

Patk COX; pension awarded 23 Sep 1818; residence - Montreal, Quebec, Canada. SOURCE: WO120 Volume 70 page 185. INDEX # 6564.

Michl COX; pension awarded 23 Sep 1818; residence - Chambly, Quebec, Canada; died 26 Sep 1881, Montreal, Quebec, Canada. SOURCE: WO120 Volume 70 page 185. INDEX # 6565.

Patk CAMPBELL; pension awarded 23 Sep 1818; residence - Coteau du Lac, Quebec, Canada. SOURCE: WO120 Volume 70 page 185. INDEX # 6566.

John CROZIER; pension awarded 23 Sep 1818; residence - Bytown, Ontario, Canada. SOURCE: WO120 Volume 70 page 185. INDEX # 6567.

Danl COUGHLIN; pension awarded 23 Sep 1818; residence - Prescott, Ontario, Canada. SOURCE: WO120 Volume 70 page 185. INDEX # 6568.

Patk CONROY; pension awarded 10 Dec 1817; residence - Toronto, Ontario, Canada; died 16 Apr 1867. SOURCE: WO120 Volume 70 page 185. INDEX # 6569.

Luke DILLON; pension awarded 23 Sep 1818; residence - Toronto, Ontario, Canada. SOURCE: WO120 Volume 70 page 185. INDEX # 6570.

Jas FARRELL; pension awarded 5 Jun 1817; residence - Montreal, Quebec, Canada. SOURCE: WO120 Volume 70 page 185. INDEX # 6571.

Hugh FITZPATRICK; pension awarded 23 Sep 1818; residence - Kingston, Ontario, Canada. SOURCE: WO120 Volume 70 page 186. INDEX # 6572.

Patk FOY; pension awarded 23 Sep 1818; residence - Bytown, Ontario, Canada. SOURCE: WO120 Volume 70 page 186. INDEX # 6573.

Adam FORSYTH; pension awarded 23 Sep 1818; residence - Bytown, Ontario, Canada; died in Dec 1845. SOURCE: WO120 Volume 70 page 186. INDEX # 6574.

Robt GALES; pension awarded 23 Sep 1818; residence - Smithsfalls, Ontario, Canada. SOURCE: WO120 Volume 70 page 186. INDEX # 6575.

Davd GRANT; pension awarded 23 Sep 1818; residence - Richmond, Ontario, Canada. SOURCE: WO120 Volume 70 page 186. INDEX # 6576.

Corns HARRINGTON; pension awarded 23 Sep 1818; residence - Toronto, Ontario, Canada; died 24 Oct 1857. SOURCE: WO120 Volume 70 page 186. INDEX # 6577.

Hugh HENRY; pension awarded 23 Sep 1818; residence - Montreal, Quebec, Canada; died 17 Jun 1850. SOURCE: WO120 Volume 70 page 186. INDEX # 6578.

Thos HARAGAN; pension awarded 23 Sep 1818; residence - Kingston, Ontario, Canada; died in 1853. SOURCE: WO120 Volume 70 page 186. INDEX # 6579.

99th Regiment of Foot (continued)

Mich^l HENDRICK; pension awarded 23 Sep 1818; residence - Cornwall, Ontario, Canada. SOURCE: WO120 Volume 70 page 186. INDEX # 6580.

Robt KERR; pension awarded 12 May 1819; residence - Kingston, Ontario, Canada. SOURCE: WO120 Volume 70 page 186. INDEX # 6581.

Alex^r MCCABE; pension awarded 23 Sep 1818; residence - Bytown, Ontario, Canada. SOURCE: WO120 Volume 70 page 186. INDEX # 6582.

John MCDERMOTT; pension awarded 23 Sep 1818; residence - St. Jean, Quebec, Canada. SOURCE: WO120 Volume 70 page 186. INDEX # 6583.

John MCGUIRE; pension awarded 23 Sep 1818; residence - Bytown, Ontario, Canada; died in 1846. SOURCE: WO120 Volume 70 page 186. INDEX # 6584.

Trevor MCKAY; pension awarded 23 Sep 1818; residence - Prescott, Ontario, Canada. SOURCE: WO120 Volume 70 page 186. INDEX # 6585.

Hugh MCLAUGHLIN; pension awarded 23 Sep 1818; residence - Toronto, Ontario, Canada; died 6 Nov 1857, Amherstburg, Ontario, Canada. SOURCE: WO120 Volume 70 page 186. INDEX # 6586.

Fra^s MORGAN; pension awarded 23 Sep 1818; residence - Huntingdon, Quebec, Canada. SOURCE: WO120 Volume 70 page 186. INDEX # 6587.

John MURPHY; pension awarded 23 Sep 1818; residence - Perth, Ontario, Canada; died in 1848. SOURCE: WO120 Volume 70 page 186. INDEX # 6588.

Edwd MORAN; pension awarded 23 Sep 1818; residence - Toronto, Ontario, Canada. SOURCE: WO120 Volume 70 page 186. INDEX # 6589.

Thos MURRAY; pension awarded 23 Sep 1818; residence - Kingston, Ontario, Canada; died 21 Jan 1856. SOURCE: WO120 Volume 70 page 186. INDEX # 6590.

Wm MULDOON; pension awarded 23 Sep 1818; residence - Bytown, Ontario, Canada; died 23 Aug 1849. SOURCE: WO120 Volume 70 page 186. INDEX # 6591.

Stew^t MOORHEAD; pension awarded 20 May 1829; residence - New South Wales, Australia; died in 1852. SOURCE: WO120 Volume 70 page 187. INDEX # 6592.

Jno ONEILL; pension awarded 23 Sep 1818; residence - Bytown, Ontario, Canada; died in 1847. SOURCE: WO120 Volume 70 page 187. INDEX # 6593.

Richd SHORT; pension awarded 23 Sep 1818; residence - Toronto, Ontario, Canada; died 23 Mar 1854. SOURCE: WO120 Volume 70 page 187. INDEX # 6594.

Jno WETHERS; pension awarded 23 Sep 1818; residence - Bytown, Ontario, Canada; died 18 May 1855. SOURCE: WO120 Volume 70 page 187. INDEX # 6595.

Hugh WILSON; pension awarded 23 Sep 1818; residence - Richmond, Ontario, Canada. SOURCE: WO120 Volume 70 page 187. INDEX # 6596.

Jno MCFARLANE; pension awarded 8 Jul 1835; residence - Perth; died 12 Jun 1848. SOURCE: WO120 Volume 70 page 187. INDEX # 6597.

Edwd MARCH; pension awarded 23 Sep 1818; residence - St. Jean, Quebec, Canada; died 11 Feb 1857. SOURCE: WO120 Volume 70 page 187. INDEX # 6598.

Henry BYRNE; pension awarded 23 Sep 1818; residence - Montreal, Quebec, Canada. SOURCE: WO120 Volume 70 page 187. INDEX # 6599.

Willm PENDER; pension awarded 23 Sep 1818; residence - Bytown, Ontario, Canada. SOURCE: WO120 Volume 70 page 187. INDEX # 6600.

John PHILIPS; pension awarded 23 Sep 1818; residence - Bytown, Ontario, Canada. SOURCE: WO120 Volume 70 page 187. INDEX # 6601.

Mart^n SMYTH; pension awarded 23 Sep 1818; residence - St. Jean, Quebec, Canada. SOURCE: WO120 Volume 70 page 187. INDEX # 6602.

John GIBSON; pension awarded 25 Sep 1818; residence - Richmond, Ontario, Canada. SOURCE: WO120 Volume 70 page 187. INDEX # 6603.

Thos MCGUIRE; pension awarded 25 Sep 1818; residence - Toronto, Ontario, Canada; died 24 May 1856. SOURCE: WO120 Volume 70 page 187. INDEX # 6604.

Robt MCGILL; pension awarded 15 Dec 1819; residence - Halifax, Nova Scotia, Canada. SOURCE: WO120 Volume 70 page 187. INDEX # 6605.

WO120 VOLUME 70

99th Regiment of Foot (continued)

Pat^k MURPHY; pension awarded 25 Sep 1818; residence - St. Jean, Quebec, Canada; died in Apr 1851. SOURCE: WO120 Volume 70 page 187. INDEX # 6606.

Willm SHEA; pension awarded 25 Sep 1818; residence - Richmond, Ontario, Canada; died 26 Feb 1859. SOURCE: WO120 Volume 70 page 187. INDEX # 6607.

Peter TANZEY; pension awarded 28 Oct 1818; residence - Montreal, Quebec, Canada. SOURCE: WO120 Volume 70 page 187. INDEX # 6608.

Willm NEWTON; pension awarded 23 Sep 1818; residence - Bytown, Ontario, Canada; died 29 May 1851. SOURCE: WO120 Volume 70 page 187. INDEX # 6609.

Mich^l CASSSADY; pension awarded 23 Sep 1818; residence - Bytown, Ontario, Canada. SOURCE: WO120 Volume 70 page 187. INDEX # 6610.

Bernard MCAULEY; pension awarded 28 Oct 1818; residence - New South Wales, Australia. SOURCE: WO120 Volume 70 page 187. INDEX # 6611.

Cormac KEELAGHER; pension awarded 23 Sep 1818; residence - Cornwall, Ontario, Canada; died in 1846. SOURCE: WO120 Volume 70 page 188. INDEX # 6612.

Chas KITT; pension awarded 7 Dec 1820; residence - Richmond, Ontario, Canada. SOURCE: WO120 Volume 70 page 188. INDEX # 6613.

Ja^s FALLON; pension awarded 23 Sep 1818; residence - Carillon, Quebec, Canada. SOURCE: WO120 Volume 70 page 188. INDEX # 6614.

Thos JONES; pension awarded 23 Sep 1818; residence - Bytown, Ontario, Canada; died 13 Apr 1855. SOURCE: WO120 Volume 70 page 188. INDEX # 6615.

Mich^l BRADY; pension awarded 23 Sep 1818; residence - Richmond, Ontario, Canada. SOURCE: WO120 Volume 70 page 188. INDEX # 6616.

Willm VAUGHAN; pension awarded 23 Sep 1818; residence - Bytown, Ontario, Canada; died 23 Dec 1859. SOURCE: WO120 Volume 70 page 188. INDEX # 6617.

Ja^s STANAGE; pension awarded 23 Sep 1818; residence - Bytown, Ontario, Canada; died 14 Sep 1853. SOURCE: WO120 Volume 70 page 188. INDEX # 6618.

Simon KERRISON; pension awarded 23 Sep 1818; residence - Bytown, Ontario, Canada. SOURCE: WO120 Volume 70 page 188. INDEX # 6619.

Nathl BROWNLEE; pension awarded 25 Sep 1818; residence - Bytown, Ontario, Canada. SOURCE: WO120 Volume 70 page 188. INDEX # 6620.

Robt COLE; pension awarded 23 Sep 1818; residence - Montreal, Quebec, Canada. SOURCE: WO120 Volume 70 page 188. INDEX # 6621.

Fra^s MCKENA; pension awarded 23 Sep 1818; residence - Bytown, Ontario, Canada; died in 1847. SOURCE: WO120 Volume 70 page 188. INDEX # 6622.

Jno HAZLETON; pension awarded 23 Sep 1818; residence - Perth, Ontario, Canada; died in 1845. SOURCE: WO120 Volume 70 page 188. INDEX # 6623.

Den^s CAMPBELL; pension awarded 10 Mar 1841; residence - Norfolk Island, Australia. SOURCE: WO120 Volume 70 page 188. INDEX # 6624.

John LEE; pension awarded 26 Aug 1845; residence - Sydney, New South Wales, Australia; died in Sep 1851. SOURCE: WO120 Volume 70 page 188. INDEX # 6625.

John MORRIS; pension awarded 25 Jun 1818; residence - Bytown, Ontario, Canada. SOURCE: WO120 Volume 70 page 188. INDEX # 6626.

Pat^k LEONARD; pension awarded 26 Aug 1845; residence - Sydney, New South Wales, Australia; died 31 Mar 1853. SOURCE: WO120 Volume 70 page 188. INDEX # 6627.

Chas WALTERS; pension awarded 26 Aug 1845; residence - Sydney, New South Wales, Australia; died 14 Jan 1877, New South Wales, Australia. SOURCE: WO120 Volume 70 page 188. INDEX # 6628.

Pat^k MCGOWEN; pension awarded 28 Jul 1815; residence - Montreal, Quebec, Canada; died 1 Oct 1847. SOURCE: WO120 Volume 70 page 188. INDEX # 6629.

Silv^r DEMPSEY; pension awarded 23 Sep 1818; residence - Bytown, Ontario, Canada; died in 1847. SOURCE: WO120 Volume 70 page 188. INDEX # 6630.

Ja^s ROSS; pension awarded 15 Jul 1840; residence - Packenham, Ontario, Canada. SOURCE: WO120 Volume 70 page 188. INDEX # 6631.

99th Regiment of Foot (continued)

Mich^l REYNOLDS; pension awarded 10 Jun 1846; residence - Roxburgh. SOURCE: WO120 Volume 70 page 189. INDEX # 6632.

Wm MILLINGTON; pension awarded 13 Oct 1846. SOURCE: WO120 Volume 70 page 189. INDEX # 6633.

Jno GLOVER; pension awarded 13 Oct 1846. SOURCE: WO120 Volume 70 page 189. INDEX # 6634.

Ja^s WINTERS; pension awarded 13 Oct 1846; residence - New South Wales, Australia; died in 1853. SOURCE: WO120 Volume 70 page 189. INDEX # 6635.

Jno TRACY; pension awarded 14 Sep 1847. SOURCE: WO120 Volume 70 page 189. INDEX # 6636.

Jno BURNS; pension awarded 14 Sep 1847. SOURCE: WO120 Volume 70 page 189. INDEX # 6637.

Wm DANE; pension awarded 14 Sep 1847. SOURCE: WO120 Volume 70 page 189. INDEX # 6638.

Thos JORDAN; pension awarded 14 Sep 1847. SOURCE: WO120 Volume 70 page 189. INDEX # 6639.

Ja^s KELLY; pension awarded 14 Sep 1847; died 16 Jul 1885, New Zealand. SOURCE: WO120 Volume 70 page 189. INDEX # 6640.

Thos LEE; pension awarded 14 Sep 1847. SOURCE: WO120 Volume 70 page 189. INDEX # 6641.

Hen^y MACDONALD; pension awarded 14 Sep 1847. SOURCE: WO120 Volume 70 page 189. INDEX # 6642.

And^w MCQUILLAN; pension awarded 14 Sep 1847. SOURCE: WO120 Volume 70 page 189. INDEX # 6543.

Thos MCNAUGHT; pension awarded 14 Sep 1847; residence - New South Wales, Australia; died in 1853. SOURCE: WO120 Volume 70 page 189. INDEX # 6644.

Ja^s SINCLAIR; pension awarded 14 Sep 1847. SOURCE: WO120 Volume 70 page 189. INDEX # 6645.

Wm SHEARMAN; pension awarded 14 Sep 1847. SOURCE: WO120 Volume 70 page 189. INDEX # 6646.

Thos STAFFORD; pension awarded 14 Sep 1847. SOURCE: WO120 Volume 70 page 189. INDEX # 6647.

Thos WADE; pension awarded 14 Sep 1847; died 11 Jun 1885, Victoria, Australia. SOURCE: WO120 Volume 70 page 189. INDEX # 6648.

Pat^k WARD; pension awarded 14 Sep 1847; died in Jun 1875. SOURCE: WO120 Volume 70 page 189. INDEX # 6649.

Ja^s WINTERS; pension awarded 14 Sep 1847; residence - Sydney, Australia. SOURCE: WO120 Volume 70 page 189. INDEX # 6650.

Peter BYERS; pension awarded 25 Jan 1848. SOURCE: WO120 Volume 70 page 189. INDEX # 6651.

Ja^s GIBSON; pension awarded 25 Jan 1848; died 26 May 1878, Sydney, Australia. SOURCE: WO120 Volume 70 page 190. INDEX # 6652.

And^w CARNACHONG; pension awarded 25 Jan 1848. SOURCE: WO120 Volume 70 page 190. INDEX # 6653.

Richd SEYMOUR; pension awarded 25 Jan 1848. SOURCE: WO120 Volume 70 page 190. INDEX # 6654.

Geo^e WADE; pension awarded 25 Jan 1848. SOURCE: WO120 Volume 70 page 190. INDEX # 6655.

Thos WARD; pension awarded 25 Jan 1848; died 15 Apr 1885, Sydney, Australia. SOURCE: WO120 Volume 70 page 190. INDEX # 6656.

Geo^e GRAHAM; pension awarded 14 Mar 1848. SOURCE: WO120 Volume 70 page 190. INDEX # 6657.

Abr^m TIGHE; pension awarded 14 Mar 1848. SOURCE: WO120 Volume 70 page 190. INDEX # 6658.

Alex^r MCCAFFRY; pension awarded 23 May 1848. SOURCE: WO120 Volume 70 page 190. INDEX # 6659.

Don^d MCKAY; pension awarded 6 Jun 1848. SOURCE: WO120 Volume 70 page 190. INDEX # 6660.

Ed^wd CADDAN; pension awarded 27 Jun 1848; died 11 Feb 1853. SOURCE: WO120 Volume 70 page 190. INDEX # 6661.

Chr^r ARMSTRONG; pension awarded 27 Jun 1848; died 12 Jan 1881, Sydney, Australia. SOURCE: WO120 Volume 70 page 190. INDEX # 6662.

Mich^l FLANAGAN; pension awarded 27 Jun 1848. SOURCE: WO120 Volume 70 page 190. INDEX # 6663.

Thos MCGOWAN; pension awarded 27 Jun 1848. SOURCE: WO120 Volume 70 page 190. INDEX # 6664.

Ja^s KERR; pension awarded 27 Jun 1848. SOURCE: WO120 Volume 70 page 190. INDEX # 6665.

Wm LOGAN; pension awarded 27 Jun 1848; died in Jun 1870. SOURCE: WO120 Volume 70 page 190. INDEX # 6666.

Ed^wd MCCARDILL; pension awarded 27 Jun 1848. SOURCE: WO120 Volume 70 page 190. INDEX # 6667.

Jno MCGRATH; pension awarded 27 Jun 1848. SOURCE: WO120 Volume 70 page 190. INDEX # 6668.

Ed^wd MCLOUGHLIN; pension awarded 27 Jun 1848. SOURCE: WO120 Volume 70 page 190. INDEX # 6669.

Jno RAE; pension awarded 26 Dec 1848. SOURCE: WO120 Volume 70 page 190. INDEX # 6670.

Ja^s ROBERTSON; pension awarded 26 Dec 1848. SOURCE: WO120 Volume 70 page 190. INDEX # 6671.

99th Regiment of Foot (continued)

Thos EDWARDS; pension awarded 10 Jul 1849. SOURCE: WO120 Volume 70 page 191. INDEX # 6672.
Edwd MANLEY; pension awarded 14 Aug 1849. SOURCE: WO120 Volume 70 page 191. INDEX # 6673.
Mich^l HORAN; pension awarded 14 Aug 1849. SOURCE: WO120 Volume 70 page 191. INDEX # 6674.
Thos ALLMAN; pension awarded 14 Aug 1849. SOURCE: WO120 Volume 70 page 191. INDEX # 6675.
Jos^h BOON; pension awarded 14 Aug 1849. SOURCE: WO120 Volume 70 page 191. INDEX # 6676.
Wm CASSIDY; pension awarded 14 Aug 1849. SOURCE: WO120 Volume 70 page 191. INDEX # 6677.
Thos DONNOLLY; pension awarded 14 Aug 1849; died 31 Jan 1872, Van Diemen's Land, Australia. SOURCE: WO120 Volume 70 page 191. INDEX # 6678.
Wm HOWARTH; pension awarded 14 Aug 1849. SOURCE: WO120 Volume 70 page 191. INDEX # 6679.
Ja^s MITCHELL; pension awarded 14 Aug 1849. SOURCE: WO120 Volume 70 page 191. INDEX # 6680.
Thos MORRELL; pension awarded 14 Aug 1849. SOURCE: WO120 Volume 70 page 191. INDEX # 6681.
Ja^s NORTON; pension awarded 14 Aug 1849; died 15 Aug 1881, Hobart Town, Australia. SOURCE: WO120 Volume 70 page 191. INDEX # 6682.
Stafford WALSH; pension awarded 23 Sep 1818; died 23 Jan 1856, Canada. SOURCE: WO120 Volume 70 page 191. INDEX # 6683.
Ja^s HILL; pension awarded 16 Jul 1850; died 26 Sep 1879, Sydney, New South Wales, Australia. SOURCE: WO120 Volume 70 page 191. INDEX # 6684.
Chas FALLICK; pension awarded 16 Jul 1850. SOURCE: WO120 Volume 70 page 191. INDEX # 6685.
Jno ASHWORTH; pension awarded 16 Jul 1850. SOURCE: WO120 Volume 70 page 191. INDEX # 6686.
And^w PHEGAN; pension awarded 16 Jul 1850. SOURCE: WO120 Volume 70 page 191. INDEX # 6687.
Ja^s SAVAGE; pension awarded 16 Jul 1850. SOURCE: WO120 Volume 70 page 191. INDEX # 6688.
Jos^h SHAW; pension awarded 16 Jul 1850; died 24 Jul 1860, Sydney, Australia. SOURCE: WO120 Volume 70 page 191. INDEX # 6689.
Saml TILLMAN; pension awarded 16 Jul 1850. SOURCE: WO120 Volume 70 page 191. INDEX # 6690.
Mich^l CLEARY; pension awarded 1 Jul 1851. SOURCE: WO120 Volume 70 page 191. INDEX # 6691.
Samuel WILSON; pension awarded 1 Jul 1851. SOURCE: WO120 Volume 70 page 191. INDEX # 6692.
Jno BYRON; pension awarded 1 Jul 1851; died 29 Jun 1881, Sydney, New South Wales, Australia. SOURCE: WO120 Volume 70 page 192. INDEX # 6693.
Wm BAYLEY; pension awarded 1 Jul 1851. SOURCE: WO120 Volume 70 page 192. INDEX # 6694.
Ja^s GABRIEL; pension awarded 1 Jul 1851; died 2 Nov 1885, New Zealand. SOURCE: WO120 Volume 70 page 192. INDEX # 6695.
Martin LONG; pension awarded 1 Jul 1851. SOURCE: WO120 Volume 70 page 192. INDEX # 6696.
Jno MCBRIDE; pension awarded 1 Jul 1851. SOURCE: WO120 Volume 70 page 192. INDEX # 6697.
Wm THOMPSON; pension awarded 1 Jul 1851. SOURCE: WO120 Volume 70 page 192. INDEX # 6698.
Jno HASTINGS; pension awarded 27 Jan 1852. SOURCE: WO120 Volume 70 page 192. INDEX # 6699.
Pat^k OKEEFE; pension awarded 13 Jul 1852; died 6 Dec 1879, Tasmania, Australia. SOURCE: WO120 Volume 70 page 192. INDEX # 6700.
Mich^l COLLINS; pension awarded 13 Jul 1852. SOURCE: WO120 Volume 70 page 192. INDEX # 6701.
Pat^k DONAGHUE; pension awarded 13 Jul 1852. SOURCE: WO120 Volume 70 page 192. INDEX # 6702.
W^m GUY; pension awarded 13 Jul 1852; died 17 Jun 1880, Tasmania, Australia. SOURCE: WO120 Volume 70 page 192. INDEX # 6703.
Martin HALLINAN; pension awarded 13 Jul 1852. SOURCE: WO120 Volume 70 page 192. INDEX # 6704.
Luke KENNY; pension awarded 13 Jul 1852; died 17 Apr 1883, Melbourne, Australia. SOURCE: WO120 Volume 70 page 192. INDEX # 6705.
Edwd LOTHIER; pension awarded 13 Jul 1852. SOURCE: WO120 Volume 70 page 192. INDEX # 6706.
Danl NEALON; pension awarded 13 Jul 1852. SOURCE: WO120 Volume 70 page 192. INDEX # 6707.
Peter PROCTOR; pension awarded 10 Aug 1852. SOURCE: WO120 Volume 70 page 192. INDEX # 6708.
Ja^s WOODS; pension awarded 14 Dec 1852. SOURCE: WO120 Volume 70 page 192. INDEX # 6709.
Tim^y CROWLEY; pension awarded 8 Feb 1853; died 5 Nov 1880, Melbourne, Australia. SOURCE: WO120 Volume 70 page 192. INDEX # 6710.
Ja^s FRASER; pension awarded 8 Mar 1853. SOURCE: WO120 Volume 70 page 192. INDEX # 6711.
Wm JAMES; pension awarded 8 Mar 1853. SOURCE: WO120 Volume 70 page 192. INDEX # 6712.
Dennis MEARA; pension awarded 8 Mar 1853. SOURCE: WO120 Volume 70 page 193. INDEX # 6713.

BRITISH ARMY PENSIONERS ABROAD

99th Regiment of Foot (continued)

Richd FITZGERALD; pension awarded 8 Mar 1853. SOURCE: WO120 Volume 70 page 193. INDEX # 6714.
Jno JOHNSON; pension awarded 8 Mar 1853. SOURCE: WO120 Volume 70 page 193. INDEX # 6715.
Chas DONNOLLY; pension awarded 9 Aug 1853. SOURCE: WO120 Volume 70 page 193. INDEX # 6716.
Thos FARR; pension awarded 9 Aug 1853. SOURCE: WO120 Volume 70 page 193. INDEX # 6717.
Austin THYNNE; pension awarded 9 Aug 1853; died 9 Jan 1881, Sydney, Australia. SOURCE: WO120 Volume 70 page 193. INDEX # 6718.
Ja^s GILLIES; pension awarded 9 Aug 1853. SOURCE: WO120 Volume 70 page 193. INDEX # 6719.
Robt AGNEW; pension awarded 9 Aug 1853; died 15 Jul 1872, Hobarttown, Australia. SOURCE: WO120 Volume 70 page 193. INDEX # 6720.
Geo^e ANDREW; pension awarded 9 Aug 1853. SOURCE: WO120 Volume 70 page 193. INDEX # 6721.
Reynolds COOKE; pension awarded 9 Aug 1853; died 10 Jul 1886, Tasmania, Australia. SOURCE: WO120 Volume 70 page 193. INDEX # 6722.
Pat^k KELLY; pension awarded 9 Aug 1853. SOURCE: WO120 Volume 70 page 193. INDEX # 6723.
Fra^s SMITH; pension awarded 9 Aug 1853. SOURCE: WO120 Volume 70 page 193. INDEX # 6724.
Jno CASSIDY; pension awarded 15 Jun 1854; died 17 Mar 1879, Tasmania, Australia. SOURCE: WO120 Volume 70 page 193. INDEX # 6725.
Ja^s HENTHORN; pension awarded 13 Jun 1854. SOURCE: WO120 Volume 70 page 193. INDEX # 6726.
Mich^l CORRIGAN; pension awarded 13 Jun 1854. SOURCE: WO120 Volume 70 page 193. INDEX # 6727.
Wm ROONEY; pension awarded 13 Jun 1854. SOURCE: WO120 Volume 70 page 193. INDEX # 6728.
Richd TAYLOR; pension awarded 13 Jun 1854. SOURCE: WO120 Volume 70 page 193. INDEX # 6729.
Wm HOUGHTON; pension awarded 25 Jul 1854. SOURCE: WO120 Volume 70 page 193. INDEX # 6730.
William CLEARY; pension awarded 8 May 1855. SOURCE: WO120 Volume 70 page 193. INDEX # 6731.
William MORRIS; pension awarded 8 May 1855; residence - New South Wales, Australia; died 11 Feb 1858. SOURCE: WO120 Volume 70 page 193. INDEX # 6732.
Patrick MCGENNISS; pension awarded 8 May 1855. SOURCE: WO120 Volume 70 page 194. INDEX # 6733.
Thomas MALRENNAN; pension awarded 8 May 1855. SOURCE: WO120 Volume 70 page 194. INDEX # 6734.
James DUNDAS; pension awarded 18 Sep 1855. SOURCE: WO120 Volume 70 page 194. INDEX # 6735.
Michael MOORE; pension awarded 18 Sep 1855. SOURCE: WO120 Volume 70 page 194. INDEX # 6736.
Patrick DUGGAN; pension awarded 12 Feb 1856. SOURCE: WO120 Volume 70 page 194. INDEX # 6737.
Thomas FORBES; pension awarded 12 Feb 1856. SOURCE: WO120 Volume 70 page 194. INDEX # 6738.
James HILL; pension awarded 12 Feb 1856. SOURCE: WO120 Volume 70 page 194. INDEX # 6739.

100th Regiment of Foot

Willm LEVISTON; pension awarded 27 Apr 1818; residence - Hobart Town, Australia. SOURCE: WO120 Volume 70 page 200. INDEX # 6740.
Dav^d HARBISON; pension awarded 7 Feb 1816; residence - Bytown, Ontario, Canada. SOURCE: WO120 Volume 70 page 200. INDEX # 6741.

101st Regiment of Foot

Richd MURPHY; pension awarded 5 Feb 1817; residence - Smithsfalls, Ontario, Canada. SOURCE: WO120 Volume 70 page 200. INDEX # 6742.
Robt CARSON; pension awarded 6 May 1820; residence - Bytown, Ontario, Canada. SOURCE: WO120 Volume 70 page 200. INDEX # 6743.
John LONG; pension awarded 7 Dec 1809; residence - Toronto, Ontario, Canada; died 20 Oct 1859. SOURCE: WO120 Volume 70 page 200. INDEX # 6744.

102nd Regiment of Foot

Jos^h EADES; pension awarded 11 Oct 1811. SOURCE: WO120 Volume 70 page 206. INDEX # 6745.

102nd Regiment of Foot (continued)

John DELL; pension awarded 3 Apr 1821; died in 1866. SOURCE: WO120 Volume 70 page 206. INDEX # 6746.

Geo^e WHITTLE; pension awarded 13 Aug 1811. SOURCE: WO120 Volume 70 page 206. INDEX # 6747.

Willm IKIN; pension awarded 25 Oct 1815. SOURCE: WO120 Volume 70 page 206. INDEX # 6748.

103rd Regiment of Foot

Ed^{wd} MAY; pension awarded 10 Dec 1817; residence - Quebec, Quebec, Canada; died in Feb 1848. SOURCE: WO120 Volume 70 page 208. INDEX # 6749.

Fra^s WILLOCK; pension awarded 9 May 1823; residence - Toronto, Ontario, Canada; died 10 Mar 1860. SOURCE: WO120 Volume 70 page 208. INDEX # 6750.

Jno MCCARTHY; pension awarded 29 Apr 1818; residence - Richmond, Ontario, Canada. SOURCE: WO120 Volume 70 page 208. INDEX # 6751.

Thos MCGINNIS; pension awarded 10 Dec 1817; residence - Wm Henry, Quebec, Canada. SOURCE: WO120 Volume 70 page 208. INDEX # 6752.

Chas MCMANUS; pension awarded 10 Dec 1817; residence - Kingston, Ontario, Canada. SOURCE: WO120 Volume 70 page 208. INDEX # 6753.

Saml NEEDHAM; pension awarded 28 Nov 1815; residence - Bytown, Ontario, Canada. SOURCE: WO120 Volume 70 page 208. INDEX # 6754.

Ja^s MCKINNON; pension awarded 30 May 1816; residence - Quebec, Quebec, Canada; died 30 Mar 1879, Montreal, Quebec, Canada. SOURCE: WO120 Volume 70 page 208. INDEX # 6755.

Dav^d WILSON; pension awarded 13 May 1819; residence - Toronto, Ontario, Canada. SOURCE: WO120 Volume 70 page 208. INDEX # 6756.

Willm WATSON; pension awarded 12 Sep 1821; residence - Perth; died 3 Sep 1857. SOURCE: WO120 Volume 70 page 208. INDEX # 6757.

Ja^s CARTER; pension awarded 10 Dec 1817; residence - Hobart Town, Australia. SOURCE: WO120 Volume 70 page 208. INDEX # 6758.

Pat^k MCMAHON; pension awarded 25 Jun 1818; residence - New South Wales, Australia. SOURCE: WO120 Volume 70 page 208. INDEX # 6759.

104th Regiment of Foot

Alexis LOMERY; pension awarded 13 Dec 1826; residence - Montreal, Quebec, Canada. SOURCE: WO120 Volume 70 page 210. INDEX # 6760.

Thos POMPHREY; pension awarded 11 Jul 1838; residence - Fredericton, New Brunswick, Canada. SOURCE: WO120 Volume 70 page 210. INDEX # 6761.

Jno CAMPBELL; pension awarded 5 Jun 1817; residence - Fredericton, New Brunswick, Canada; died 17 May 1850. SOURCE: WO120 Volume 70 page 210. INDEX # 6762.

Cato CLARKE; pension awarded 5 Jun 1817; residence - Fredericton, New Brunswick, Canada; died 29 Dec 1845. SOURCE: WO120 Volume 70 page 210. INDEX # 6763.

Moses HOLMES; pension awarded 21 Aug 1817; residence - Fredericton, New Brunswick, Canada; died 8 Jan 1880, Nova Scotia, Canada. SOURCE: WO120 Volume 70 page 210. INDEX # 6764.

Jno MCLAUCHLAN; pension awarded 5 Jun 1817; residence - Fredericton, New Brunswick, Canada; died 22 Apr 1852. SOURCE: WO120 Volume 70 page 210. INDEX # 6765.

Thos GEE; pension awarded 31 Oct 1827; residence - Fredericton, New Brunswick, Canada; died 4 Dec 1874. SOURCE: WO120 Volume 70 page 210. INDEX # 6766.

Alex^r MURCHISON; pension awarded 21 Aug 1817; residence - Fredericton, New Brunswick, Canada. SOURCE: WO120 Volume 70 page 210. INDEX # 6767.

Finnon MCDONELL; pension awarded 21 Aug 1817; residence - Cornwall, Ontario, Canada; died 10 Sep 1856. SOURCE: WO120 Volume 70 page 210. INDEX # 6768.

Jabesh SQUIRES; pension awarded 26 Jul 1820; residence - Fredericton, New Brunswick, Canada. SOURCE: WO120 Volume 70 page 210. INDEX # 6769.

BRITISH ARMY PENSIONERS ABROAD

104th Regiment of Foot (continued)

Geo^e BAIN; pension awarded 23 May 1821; residence - Fredericton, New Brunswick, Canada; died 5 Jun 1850. SOURCE: WO120 Volume 70 page 210. INDEX # 6770.

Ja^s FAULKNER; pension awarded 5 Jun 1817; residence - Halifax, Nova Scotia, Canada. SOURCE: WO120 Volume 70 page 210. INDEX # 6771.

Arch^d MCLEAN; pension awarded 21 Aug 1817; residence - Fredericton, New Brunswick, Canada; died 18 Jul 1852. SOURCE: WO120 Volume 70 page 210. INDEX # 6772.

Jno WOOD; pension awarded 21 Aug 1817; residence - Wm Henry, Quebec, Canada; died in 1846. SOURCE: WO120 Volume 70 page 210. INDEX # 6773.

Richd HARRIS; pension awarded 21 Aug 1817; residence - Toronto, Ontario, Canada; died 24 May 1863. SOURCE: WO120 Volume 70 page 210. INDEX # 6774.

Eber PORTER; pension awarded 31 Jul 1822; residence - Fredericton, New Brunswick, Canada. SOURCE: WO120 Volume 70 page 210. INDEX # 6775.

John MARLEY; pension awarded 12 May 1819; residence - Quebec, Quebec, Canada. SOURCE: WO120 Volume 70 page 210. INDEX # 6776.

Rifle Brigade

Richd DRISCOLL; pension awarded 4 Feb 1824; residence - Quebec, Quebec, Canada. SOURCE: WO120 Volume 70 page 212. INDEX # 6777.

Chas OLIVE; pension awarded 20 Nov 1824; residence - New South Wales, Australia. SOURCE: WO120 Volume 70 page 212. INDEX # 6778.

Thos WOOD; pension awarded 30 Dec 1818; residence - New South Wales, Australia; died 27 Apr 1855. SOURCE: WO120 Volume 70 page 212. INDEX # 6779.

Willm WOOD; pension awarded 23 Sep 1818; residence - New South Wales, Australia; died in 1854. SOURCE: WO120 Volume 70 page 212. INDEX # 6780.

George DOOMSDAY; pension awarded 29 Nov 1820; residence - Montreal, Quebec, Canada; died 23 Mar 1852. SOURCE: WO120 Volume 70 page 212. INDEX # 6781.

Saml COULSTON; pension awarded 14 Dec 1818; residence - New South Wales, Australia; died 27 Dec 1847. SOURCE: WO120 Volume 70 page 212. INDEX # 6782.

Willm WILSON; pension awarded 26 Nov 1817; residence - New South Wales, Australia; died in 1850. SOURCE: WO120 Volume 70 page 212. INDEX # 6783.

Willm CHATER; pension awarded 30 Dec 1815; residence - New South Wales, Australia. SOURCE: WO120 Volume 70 page 212. INDEX # 6784.

John MCKELLY; pension awarded 26 Jul 1829; residence - New South Wales, Australia. SOURCE: WO120 Volume 70 page 212. INDEX # 6785.

Richd KUNCHEON; pension awarded 8 Aug 1832; residence - Halifax, Nova Scotia, Canada. SOURCE: WO120 Volume 70 page 212. INDEX # 6786.

Willm TAYLOR; pension awarded 20 Jan 1819; residence - New South Wales, Australia; died in Sep 1851. SOURCE: WO120 Volume 70 page 212. INDEX # 6787.

Jno STEPHENSON; pension awarded 9 Aug 1816; residence - Toronto, Ontario, Canada. SOURCE: WO120 Volume 70 page 212. INDEX # 6788.

Geo^e HOPKINSS; pension awarded 14 Sep 1831; residence - Montreal, Quebec, Canada. SOURCE: WO120 Volume 70 page 212. INDEX # 6789.

John DALBY; pension awarded 11 May 1831; residence - Van Diemen's Land, Australia. SOURCE: WO120 Volume 70 page 212. INDEX # 6782.

Ja^s HARGRAVES; pension awarded 27 Aug 1844; residence - Halifax, Nova Scotia, Canada. SOURCE: WO120 Volume 70 page 212. INDEX # 6791.

Geo^e CHAPMAN; pension awarded 26 Aug 1845; residence - Halifax, Nova Scotia, Canada. SOURCE: WO120 Volume 70 page 212. INDEX # 6792.

Willm HARBOUR; pension awarded 20 Jun 1827; residence - Toronto, Ontario, Canada; died 5 Dec 1869, London, Ontario, Canada. SOURCE: WO120 Volume 70 page 212. INDEX # 6793.

WO120 VOLUME 70

Rifle Brigade (continued)

Ja^s DAVIES; pension awarded 13 Mar 1839; residence - Halifax, Nova Scotia, Canada; died 23 Dec 1878, London, Ontario, Canada. SOURCE: WO120 Volume 79 page 212. INDEX # 6794.

John SKEA; pension awarded 14 Nov 1843; residence - Cape of Good Hope, South Africa; died 3 Jul 1850. SOURCE: WO120 Volume 70 page 212. INDEX # 6795.

Thos FLINN; pension awarded 9 Dec 1845; residence - Halifax, Nova Scotia, Canada. SOURCE: WO120 Volume 70 page 212. INDEX # 6796.

Pat^k MCLOUGHLIN; pension awarded 27 Jun 1843; residence - Jamaica. SOURCE: WO120 Volume 70 page 213. INDEX # 6797.

Ja^s WINTERBOTTOM; pension awarded 16 Jun 1825; residence - New South Wales, Australia; died 25 Jun 1847. SOURCE: WO120 Volume 70 page 213. INDEX # 6798.

Willm RYAN; pension awarded 9 Dec 1845; residence - Halifax, Nova Scotia, Canada; died 11 May 1873, Halifax, Nova Scotia, Canada. SOURCE: WO120 Volume 70 page 213. INDEX # 6799.

Jno PARKINSON; pension awarded 25 Apr 1838; residence - Malta. SOURCE: WO120 Volume 70 page 213. INDEX # 6800.

Dav^d TAYLOR; pension awarded 27 Sep 1837; residence - Gibraltar. SOURCE: WO120 Volume 70 page 213. INDEX # 6801.

Thos EVANS; pension awarded 12 Aug 1845; residence - Corfu; died 17 Apr 1876, Gloucester. SOURCE: WO120 Volume 70 page 213. INDEX # 6802.

Mich^l OHARA; pension awarded 9 Dec 1845; residence - Prince Edward Island, Canada. SOURCE: WO120 Volume 70 page 213. INDEX # 6803.

Ja^s MITCHELL; pension awarded 6 Feb 1819; residence - New South Wales, Australia; died 3 Aug 1848. SOURCE: WO120 Volume 70 page 213. INDEX # 6804.

Jno TROTTER; pension awarded 28 Nov 1838; residence - Malta. SOURCE: WO120 Volume 70 page 213. INDEX # 6805.

Ja^s WILLIAMS; pension awarded 9 Dec 1845; residence - Halifax, Nova Scotia, Canada. SOURCE: WO120 Volume 70 page 213. INDEX # 6806.

Jno PASKETT; pension awarded 11 Jan 1837; residence - St. Johns. SOURCE: WO120 Volume 70 page 213. INDEX # 6807.

Jno HEAPE; pension awarded 14 Apr 1846; residence - Halifax, Nova Scotia, Canada; died 5 Apr 1879, Jersey. SOURCE: WO120 Volume 70 page 213. INDEX # 6808.

Jno MORAN; pension awarded 27 Oct 1846. SOURCE: WO120 Volume 70 page 213. INDEX # 6809.

Wm GRANT; pension awarded 8 Dec 1846; died 24 Oct 1871, Nova Scotia, Canada. SOURCE: WO120 Volume 70 page 213. INDEX # 6810.

Jno EGAN; pension awarded 12 Oct 1847. SOURCE: WO120 Volume 70 page 213. INDEX # 6811.

Wm DUNBAR; pension awarded 12 Oct 1847. SOURCE: WO120 Volume 70 page 213. INDEX # 6812.

Jno GRIGGLISTONE; pension awarded 12 Oct 1847; residence - Toronto, Ontario, Canada; died 25 Sep 1847. SOURCE: WO120 Volume 70 page 213. INDEX # 6813.

Wm BROWN; pension awarded 12 Oct 1847; died 16 Dec 1878, Hamilton, Ontario, Canada. SOURCE: WO120 Volume 70 page 213. INDEX # 6814.

Jno CONNOR; pension awarded 12 Oct 1847; died 14 Feb 1879, Cork. SOURCE: WO120 Volume 70 page 213. INDEX # 6815.

Pat^k DOLAN; pension awarded 12 Oct 1847. SOURCE: WO120 Volume 70 page 213. INDEX # 6816.

Alex^r DOYLE; pension awarded 12 Oct 1847. SOURCE: WO120 Volume 70 page 214. INDEX # 6817.

Ja^s KIERNAN; pension awarded 12 Oct 1847. SOURCE: WO120 Volume 70 page 214. INDEX # 6818.

Thos GITTINS; pension awarded 12 Oct 1847; died 7 Dec 1879. SOURCE: WO120 Volume 70 page 214. INDEX # 6819.

Edwd MCLOUGHLIN; pension awarded 12 Oct 1847; died 28 Jan 1879, New Brunswick, Canada. SOURCE: WO120 Volume 70 page 214. INDEX # 6820.

Thos MCINTYRE; pension awarded 12 Oct 1847. SOURCE: WO120 Volume 70 page 214. INDEX # 6821.

Ronald MCNICOLL; pension awarded 12 Oct 1847. SOURCE: WO120 Volume 70 page 214. INDEX # 6822.

Pat^k TINNERRY; pension awarded 6 Jun 1848. SOURCE: WO120 Volume 70 page 214. INDEX # 6823.

Rifle Brigade (continued)

Wm WEBB; pension awarded 6 Jun 1848. SOURCE: WO120 Volume 70 page 214. INDEX # 6824.

And^w WILLIAMSON; pension awarded 27 Jun 1848. SOURCE: WO120 Volume 70 page 214. INDEX # 6825.

Wm ROSS; pension awarded 24 Oct 1848; died 5 Aug 1884, Halifax, Nova Scotia, Canada. SOURCE: WO120 Volume 70 page 214. INDEX # 6827.

Wm BYRNE; pension awarded 24 Oct 1848. SOURCE: WO120 Volume 70 page 214. INDEX # 6827.

David BURTON; pension awarded 24 Oct 1848; residence - Halifax, Nova Scotia, Canada; died 5 Jan 1852. SOURCE: WO120 Volume 70 page 214. INDEX # 6828.

Ja^s DONNELLY; pension awarded 24 Oct 1848; died Hamilton, Ontario, Canada. SOURCE: WO120 Volume 70 page 214. INDEX # 6829.

Jno GALVIN; pension awarded 24 Oct 1848. SOURCE: WO120 Volume 70 page 214. INDEX # 6830.

Wm GARSIDE; pension awarded 24 Oct 1848; residence - London, Ontario, Canada; died 30 Apr 1855. SOURCE: WO120 Volume 70 page 214. INDEX # 6831.

Garrett HEGARTY; pension awarded 24 Oct 1848. SOURCE: WO120 Volume 70 page 214. INDEX # 6832.

Pat^k JENNINGS; pension awarded 24 Oct 1848. SOURCE: WO120 Volume 70 page 214. INDEX # 6833.

Jno JOHNSON; pension awarded 24 Oct 1848. SOURCE: WO120 Volume 70 page 214. INDEX # 6834.

And^w LINDSEY; pension awarded 24 Oct 1848. SOURCE: WO120 Volume 70 page 214. INDEX # 6835.

Jno LONG; pension awarded 24 Oct 1848; died London, Ontario, Canada. SOURCE: WO120 Volume 70 page 214. INDEX # 6836.

Jno REA; pension awarded 24 Oct 1848. SOURCE: WO120 Volume 70 page 215. INDEX # 6837.

Jno REYNOLDS; pension awarded 24 Oct 1848; residence - Toronto, Ontario, Canada; died 22 Aug 1856. SOURCE: WO120 Volume 70 page 215. INDEX # 6838.

And^w ROSS; pension awarded 24 Oct 1848. SOURCE: WO120 Volume 70 page 215. INDEX # 6839.

Ed^{md} WALSH; pension awarded 24 Oct 1848; died 29 Jan 1872, Nova Scotia, Canada. SOURCE: WO120 Volume 70 page 215. INDEX # 6840.

Jno DUNN; pension awarded 22 May 1849; residence - London, Ontario, Canada; died 22 Jul 1850. SOURCE: WO120 Volume 70 page 215. INDEX # 6841.

Wm MCPHERSON; pension awarded 23 Oct 1849; died 20 Sep 1874, Toronto, Ontario, Canada. SOURCE: WO120 Volume 70 page 215. INDEX # 6842.

Robt MUNRO; pension awarded 23 Oct 1849; died 20 Dec 1858. SOURCE: WO120 Volume 70 page 215. INDEX # 6843.

Robt STALKER; pension awarded 23 Oct 1849; residence - Hamilton, Ontario, Canada; died 17 Aug 1874. SOURCE: WO120 Volume 70 page 215. INDEX # 6844.

Hugh TULLY; pension awarded 23 Oct 1849. SOURCE: WO120 Volume 70 page 215. INDEX # 6845.

Jno DOWNEY; pension awarded 22 Jan 1850; died 4 Feb 1864, Cape of Good Hope, South Africa. SOURCE: WO120 Volume 70 page 215. INDEX # 6846.

John SMYTH; pension awarded 4 Oct 1816; died 4 Aug 1862, Toronto, Ontario, Canada. SOURCE: WO120 Volume 70 page 215. INDEX # 6847.

Jno BROWN; pension awarded 1 Oct 1850. SOURCE: WO120 Volume 70 page 215. INDEX # 6848.

Saml BRIERLY; pension awarded 1 Oct 1850. SOURCE: WO120 Volume 70 page 215. INDEX # 6849.

Bernard CALLAGHAN; pension awarded 1 Oct 1850. SOURCE: WO120 Volume 70 page 215. INDEX # 6850.

Geo^e CAMP; pension awarded 1 Oct 1850. SOURCE: WO120 Volume 70 page 215. INDEX # 6851.

Jno DAVIS; pension awarded 1 Oct 1850. SOURCE: WO120 Volume 70 page 215. INDEX # 6852.

Hen^y Chas JOHNSON; pension awarded 1 Oct 1850. SOURCE: WO120 Volume 70 page 215. INDEX # 6853.

Thos JOYCE; pension awarded 1 Oct 1850. SOURCE: WO120 Volume 70 page 215. INDEX # 6854.

Jno LEONARD; pension awarded 1 Oct 1850. SOURCE: WO120 Volume 70 page 215. INDEX # 6855.

Wm ALLCOCK; pension awarded 1 Oct 1850. SOURCE: WO120 Volume 70 page 215. INDEX # 6856.

Martin SCOTT; pension awarded 1 Oct 1850; died 22 Aug 1887, Toronto, Ontario, Canada. SOURCE: WO120 Volume 70 page 215. INDEX # 6857.

Pat^k MCINNEREY; pension awarded 5 Aug 1851. SOURCE: WO120 Volume 70 page 216. INDEX # 6858.

Pat^k GALLAGHER; pension awarded 5 Aug 1851; died 3 Dec 1886, Toronto, Ontario, Canada. SOURCE: WO120 Volume 70 page 216. INDEX # 6859.

Rifle Brigade

Jn⁰ CAMPBELL; pension awarded 5 Aug 1851; died 2 Oct 1880, London, Ontario, Canada. SOURCE: WO120 Volume 70 page 216. INDEX # 6860.

Danˡ MCCARTHY; pension awarded 5 Aug 1851. SOURCE: WO120 Volume 70 page 216. INDEX # 6861.

Wᵐ JUDD; pension awarded 22 Jun 1852. SOURCE: WO120 Volume 70 page 216. INDEX # 6862.

Wᵐ MILLAR; pension awarded 22 Jun 1852; died 14 Feb 1884, Toronto, Ontario, Canada. SOURCE: WO120 Volume 70 page 216. INDEX # 6863.

Wᵐ WILKINSON; pension awarded 22 Jun 1852. SOURCE: WO120 Volume 70 page 216. INDEX # 6864.

Jn⁰ IRVING; pension awarded 22 Jun 1852. SOURCE: WO120 Volume 70 page 216. INDEX # 6865.

Jn⁰ AHERN; pension awarded 22 Jun 1852. SOURCE: WO120 Volume 70 page 216. INDEX # 6866.

Wᵐ CRANKSHAW; pension awarded 22 Jun 1852; residence - Kingston, Ontario, Canada; died 8 Aug 1853. SOURCE: WO120 Volume 70 page 216. INDEX # 6867.

Danˡ LANG; pension awarded 22 Jun 1852. SOURCE: WO120 Volume 70 page 216. INDEX # 6868.

Joshˢ SOLLEY; pension awarded 22 Jun 1852. SOURCE: WO120 Volume 70 page 216. INDEX # 6869.

Samˡ WHITE; pension awarded 22 Jun 1852; died 13 Feb 1885, Toronto, Ontario, Canada. SOURCE: WO120 Volume 70 page 216. INDEX # 6870.

Robᵗ BURMAN; pension awarded 22 Jun 1852. SOURCE: WO120 Volume 70 page 216. INDEX # 6871.

Samˡ COOPER; pension awarded 22 Jun 1852. SOURCE: WO120 Volume 70 page 216. INDEX # 6872.

Edwᵈ FAIRBROTHER; pension awarded 22 Jun 1852; died 23 Jul 1871, Halifax, Nova Scotia, Canada. SOURCE: WO120 Volume 70 page 216. INDEX # 6873.

Malcolm MCCULLOCH; pension awarded 22 Jun 1852; died 27 Sep 1880, Toronto, Ontario, Canada. SOURCE: WO120 Volume 70 page 216. INDEX # 6874.

Patᵏ MITCHELL; pension awarded 22 Jun 1852; died 27 Jul 1884, Toronto, Ontario, Canada. SOURCE: WO120 Volume 70 page 216. INDEX # 6875.

Donᵈ MUSTARD; pension awarded 22 Jun 1852; died 8 Oct 1858. SOURCE: WO120 Volume 70 page 216. INDEX # 6876.

Chaˢ TERRY; pension awarded 22 Jun 1852; died 8 May 1860, Toronto, Ontario, Canada. SOURCE: WO120 Volume 70 page 216. INDEX # 6877.

Jaˢ TURNER; pension awarded 22 Jun 1852; residence - Toronto, Ontario, Canada; died 9 Aug 1854. SOURCE: WO120 Volume 70 page 217. INDEX # 6878.

Jaˢ SHEWBRIDGE; pension awarded 11 Jan 1853. SOURCE: WO120 Volume 70 page 217. INDEX # 6879.

Royal Garrison Battalion

Wᵐ MCMILLAN; pension awarded 16 Jul 1783; residence - Halifax, Nova Scotia, Canada. SOURCE: WO120 Volume 70 page 224. INDEX # 6880.

Wᵐ OVERY; pension awarded 17 May 1802; residence - London, Ontario, Canada; died 24 Aug 1847. SOURCE: WO120 Volume 70 page 224. INDEX # 6881.

1st Garrison Battalion

Patᵏ ROURKE; pension awarded 30 Jun 1813; residence - Toronto, Ontario, Canada; died 23 Oct 1862, Hamilton, Ontario, Canada. SOURCE: WO120 Volume 70 page 226. INDEX # 6882.

2nd Garrison Battalion

Jaˢ TROTTER; pension awarded 23 Oct 1816; residence - Hobart Town, Australia; died 2 Dec 1847. SOURCE: WO120 Volume 70 page 227. INDEX # 6883.

Michˡ BRENNAN; pension awarded 23 Oct 1816; residence - Toronto, Ontario, Canada; died 18 Jan 1848. SOURCE: WO120 Volume 70 page 227. INDEX # 6884.

Culloˡ MCDONALD; pension awarded 23 Oct 1816; residence - Penetanguishene, Ontario, Canada; died 11 Apr 1857. SOURCE: WO120 Volume 70 page 227. INDEX # 6885.

Arthʳ WOODS; pension awarded 20 Oct 1816; residence - Montreal, Quebec, Canada. SOURCE: WO120 Volume 70 page 227. INDEX # 6886.

BRITISH ARMY PENSIONERS ABROAD

2nd Garrison Battalion (continued)

Jos^h KIESER; pension awarded 28 Jul 1815; residence - Ostend, Belgium. SOURCE: WO120 Volume 70 page 227. INDEX # 6887.

3rd Garrison Battalion

Saml SALT; pension awarded 22 Oct 1816; residence - Toronto, Ontario, Canada; died 16 Jun 1854. SOURCE: WO120 Volume 70 page 229. INDEX # 6888.

Isaac MOYNES; pension awarded 26 Apr 1816; residence - Toronto, Ontario, Canada; died 21 Aug 1870, Toronto, Ontario, Canada. SOURCE: WO120 Volume 70 page 229. INDEX # 6889.

Ja^s BASKELL; pension awarded 22 Oct 1816; residence - Van Diemen's Land, Australia. SOURCE: WO120 Volume 70 page 229. INDEX # 6890.

Fra^s TONE; pension awarded 24 Apr 1816; residence - Niagara, Ontario, Canada; died 24 Sep 1869, Hamilton, Ontario, Canada. SOURCE: WO120 Volume 70 page 229. INDEX # 6891.

Ja^s FARLEY; pension awarded 7 Sep 1814; residence - Quebec, Quebec, Canada; died in 1847. SOURCE: WO120 Volume 70 page 229. INDEX # 6892.

Ja^s LODGEWICK; pension awarded 7 Jan 1817; residence - Toronto, Ontario, Canada; died 7 Feb 1875. SOURCE: WO120 Volume 70 page 229. INDEX # 6893.

Willm BARKER; pension awarded ; residence - London, Ontario, Canada. SOURCE: WO120 Volume 70 page 229. INDEX # 6894.

Willm TUTE; pension awarded 28 Nov 1815; residence - Montreal, Quebec, Canada. SOURCE: WO120 Volume 70 page 229. INDEX # 6895.

4th Garrison Battalion

Austin ALLEN; pension awarded 3 Apr 1811; residence - Fractown; died 7 Dec 1855. SOURCE: WO120 Volume 70 page 231. INDEX # 6896.

1st Garrison Company

Willm SUTHERLAND; pension awarded 19 Sep 1816; residence - London, Ontario, Canada; died 12 May 1873, London, Ontario, Canada. SOURCE: WO120 Volume 70 page 232. INDEX # 6897.

2nd Garrison Company

Jno PLUNKETT; pension awarded 4 Aug 1816; residence - Toronto, Ontario, Canada; died 1 Oct 1854. SOURCE: WO120 Volume 70 page 233. INDEX # 6898.

Don^d MCKAY; pension awarded 4 Oct 1816; residence - Halifax, Nova Scotia, Canada. SOURCE: WO120 Volume 70 page 233. INDEX # 6899.

3rd Garrison Company

Ja^s STEWART; pension awarded 19 Sep 1816; residence - Niagara, Ontario, Canada. SOURCE: WO120 Volume 70 page 235. INDEX # 6900.

Walter RICKEY; pension awarded 19 Sep 1816; residence - Smithsfalls, Ontario, Canada; died 5 Sep 1883, Armagh. SOURCE: WO120 Volume 70 page 235. INDEX # 6901.

Cape Garrison Companies

Jno WINKWORTH; pension awarded 25 Mar 1818; residence - Cape of Good Hope, South Africa. SOURCE: WO120 Volume 70 page 237. INDEX # 6902.

Willm SMITH; pension awarded 25 Nov 1818; residence - Cape of Good Hope, South Africa; died 22 Sep 1849. SOURCE: WO120 Volume 70 page 237. INDEX # 6903.

Cape Garrison Companies (continued)

Jn⁰ PRESTON; pension awarded 25 Nov 1818. SOURCE: WO120 Volume 70 page 237. INDEX # 6904.

Edwᵈ GRIFFITHS; pension awarded 7 Jan 1818; residence - Cape of Good Hope, South Africa; died 4 Jul 1845. SOURCE: WO120 Volume 70 page 237. INDEX # 6905.

Thoˢ PUGH; pension awarded 25 Nov 1818; residence - Cape of Good Hope, South Africa; died 25 Nov 1848. SOURCE: WO120 Volume 70 page 237. INDEX # 6906.

Edwᵈ ODONNELL; pension awarded 25 Nov 1818. SOURCE: WO120 Volume 70 page 237. INDEX # 6907.

West India Garrison Companies

Lake COSSAM; pension awarded 24 Oct 1821; residence - St. Vincent. SOURCE: WO120 Volume 70 page 240. INDEX # 6908.

Willᵐ REED; pension awarded 24 Oct 1821; residence - St. Vincent; died 9 Mar 1849. SOURCE: WO120 Volume 70 page 240. INDEX # 6909.

Staff Garrison Company

Henʸ DRENNAN; pension awarded 14 Sep 1847; residence - Auckland, Cape of Good Hope, South Africa; died in 1851. SOURCE: WO120 Volume 70 page 241. INDEX # 6910.

Garrison Staff

Wᵐ MCDONALD; pension awarded 22 Nov 1842; residence - Cape of Good Hope, South Africa; died 17 Jul 1853. SOURCE: WO120 Volume 70 page 242. INDEX # 6911.

Thoˢ RODGERS; pension awarded 12 Sep 1848. SOURCE: WO120 Volume 70 page 242. INDEX # 6912.

Wᵐ WALLACE; pension awarded 13 Jun 1854; died 2 Nov 1883, Cape of Good Hope, South Africa. SOURCE: WO120 Volume 70 page 242. INDEX # 6913.

Canadian Staff

Thoˢ BRADLEY; pension awarded 13 Apr 1852; died 3 Jan 1873, Hamilton, Ontario, Canada. SOURCE: WO120 Volume 70 page 243. INDEX # 6914.

1st Veterans Battalion

John FARRAH; pension awarded 27 Jun 1821; residence - London, Ontario, Canada. SOURCE: WO120 Volume 70 page 244. INDEX # 6915.

John DELANY; pension awarded 2 Jul 1816; residence - Toronto, Ontario, Canada; died 11 Dec 1864. SOURCE: WO120 Volume 70 page 244. INDEX # 6916.

Josʰ FOSTER; pension awarded 29 Jul 1814; residence - Halifax, Nova Scotia, Canada. SOURCE: WO120 Volume 70 page 244. INDEX # 6917.

Josʰ HALL; pension awarded 29 Jul 1814; residence - Halifax, Nova Scotia, Canada. SOURCE: WO120 Volume 70 page 244. INDEX # 6918.

Thoˢ ROXBY; pension awarded 29 Jul 1814; residence - Halifax, Nova Scotia, Canada. SOURCE: WO120 Volume 70 page 244. INDEX # 6919.

Samˡ COOPER; pension awarded 2 Jul 1816; residence - Toronto, Ontario, Canada; died in Apr 1846. SOURCE: WO120 Volume 70 page 244. INDEX # 6920.

Willᵐ WAGER; pension awarded 27 Jun 1821; residence - Sydney. SOURCE: WO120 Volume 70 page 244. INDEX # 6921.

2nd Veterans Battalion

Michˡ CROZIER; pension awarded 8 Sep 1830; residence - Fredericton, New Brunswick, Canada. SOURCE: WO120 Volume 70 page 247. INDEX # 6922.

2nd Veterans Battalion (continued)

Ja^s CROOK; pension awarded 7 Jun 1816; residence - Hobart Town, Australia; died 5 Jul 1845. SOURCE: WO120 Volume 70 page 247. INDEX # 6923.

Hugh FOULKES; pension awarded 25 Jan 1815; residence - South Australia, Australia. SOURCE: WO120 Volume 70 page 247. INDEX # 6924.

Thos WEBB; pension awarded 12 Sep 1821; residence - New South Wales, Australia. SOURCE: WO120 Volume 70 page 247. INDEX # 6925.

Jno BUTLER; pension awarded 30 May 1821; residence - London, Ontario, Canada. SOURCE: WO120 Volume 70 page 247. INDEX # 6926.

Ralph WALSH; pension awarded 6 Jun 1826; residence - Toronto, Ontario, Canada; died in Sep 1856, Toronto, Ontario, Canada. SOURCE: WO120 Volume 70 page 247. INDEX # 6927.

3rd Veterans Battalion

Richd BROWNING; pension awarded 16 Jun 1831; residence - New South Wales, Australia. SOURCE: WO120 Volume 70 page 249. INDEX # 6928.

Ja^s DEVILLE; pension awarded 19 Jul 1826; residence - New South Wales, Australia; died 15 Dec 1862, Melbourne, Australia. SOURCE: WO120 Volume 70 page 249. INDEX # 6929.

John MULVENEY; pension awarded 19 Jul 1826; residence - St. Johns. SOURCE: WO120 Volume 70 page 249. INDEX # 6930.

Don^d SUTHERLAND; pension awarded 19 Jul 1826; residence - London, Ontario, Canada; died 20 Apr 1854. SOURCE: WO120 Volume 70 page 249. INDEX # 6931.

Jno MCGILLEVRAY; pension awarded 31 Jul 1816; residence - Quebec, Quebec, Canada. SOURCE: WO120 Volume 70 page 249. INDEX # 6932.

Ja^s FARNEY; pension awarded 19 Jul 1816; residence - Penetanguishene, Ontario, Canada; died in Mar 1845. SOURCE: WO120 Volume 70 page 249. INDEX # 6933.

Kenn^h MCKENZIE; pension awarded 31 Jul 1816; residence - Toronto, Ontario, Canada; died 2 Feb 1850. SOURCE: WO120 Volume 70 page 249. INDEX # 6934.

John SMITH; pension awarded 31 May 1816; residence - Halifax, Nova Scotia, Canada. SOURCE: WO120 Volume 70 page 249. INDEX # 6935.

4th Veterans Battalion

Thos BACKHOUSE; pension awarded 5 Jun 1817; residence - Kingston, Ontario, Canada; died 25 Apr 1859. SOURCE: WO120 Volume 70 page 251. INDEX # 6936.

Jacques BURTON; pension awarded 5 Jun 1817; residence - Quebec, Quebec, Canada. SOURCE: WO120 Volume 70 page 251. INDEX # 6937.

Wm DANGERFIELD; pension awarded 5 Jun 1817; residence - Montreal, Quebec, Canada. SOURCE: WO120 Volume 70 page 251. INDEX # 6938.

Geo^e EDGLEY; pension awarded 5 Jun 1817; residence - Quebec, Quebec, Canada. SOURCE: WO120 Volume 70 page 251. INDEX # 6939.

Thos SMITH; pension awarded 5 Jun 1817; residence - Perth, Ontario, Canada. SOURCE: WO120 Volume 70 page 251. INDEX # 6940.

Richd MACE; pension awarded 5 Jun 1817; residence - Drum^d Ville, Quebec, Canada. SOURCE: WO120 Volume 70 page 251. INDEX # 6941.

Ja^s MITCHELL; pension awarded 5 Jun 1817; residence - Prescott, Ontario, Canada. SOURCE: WO120 Volume 70 page 251. INDEX # 6942.

Jno PEARSON; pension awarded 5 Jun 1817; residence - Drum^d Ville, Quebec, Canada. SOURCE: WO120 Volume 70 page 251. INDEX # 6943.

Jno PIERCE; pension awarded 5 Jun 1817; residence - Quebec, Quebec, Canada. SOURCE: WO120 Volume 70 page 251. INDEX # 6944.

Jno SMITH; pension awarded 5 Jun 1817; residence - Smithsfalls, Ontario, Canada. SOURCE: WO120 Volume 70 page 251. INDEX # 6945.

4th Veterans Battalion (continued)

Lewis SHIPMAN; pension awarded 5 Jun 1817; residence - Quebec, Quebec, Canada. SOURCE: WO120 Volume 70 page 251. INDEX # 6946.

Wm THORNTON; pension awarded 5 Jun 1817; residence - Kingston, Ontario, Canada; died 15 Apr 1858. SOURCE: WO120 Volume 70 page 251. INDEX # 6947.

Danl THOMPSON; pension awarded 27 Sep 1814; residence - Toronto, Ontario, Canada; died 25 Jun 1850. SOURCE: WO120 Volume 70 page 251. INDEX # 6948.

John COOTE; pension awarded 5 Jun 1817; residence - Quebec, Quebec, Canada. SOURCE: WO120 Volume 70 page 251. INDEX # 6949.

Richd BRANSTON; pension awarded 25 Jul 1821; residence - Niagara, Ontario, Canada. SOURCE: WO120 Volume 70 page 251. INDEX # 6950.

John BURTON; pension awarded 5 Jun 1817; residence - Bytown, Ontario, Canada. SOURCE: WO120 Volume 70 page 251. INDEX # 6951.

Ed^wd CONNOLLY; pension awarded 5 Jun 1817; residence - Wm Henry, Quebec, Canada; died 24 Aug 1857, Quebec, Quebec, Canada. SOURCE: WO120 Volume 70 page 251. INDEX # 6952.

Miles CONNORS; pension awarded 5 Jun 1817; residence - Montreal, Quebec, Canada; died in Apr 1850. SOURCE: WO120 Volume 70 page 251. INDEX # 6953.

Baker CASTLE; pension awarded 20 May 1817; residence - Bytown, Ontario, Canada; died in 1848. SOURCE: WO120 Volume 70 page 251. INDEX # 6954.

Ja^s FRAZER; pension awarded 5 Jun 1817; residence - Quebec, Quebec, Canada. SOURCE: WO120 Volume 70 page 251. INDEX # 6955.

Chr^r HILL; pension awarded 5 Jun 1817; residence - Montreal, Quebec, Canada. SOURCE: WO120 Volume 70 page 251. INDEX # 6956.

Jno HORSALL; pension awarded 5 Jun 1817; residence - Wm Henry, Quebec, Canada; died 18 Mar 1848. SOURCE: WO120 Volume 70 page 252. INDEX # 6957.

Saml MARMAN; pension awarded 5 Jun 1817; residence - Quebec, Quebec, Canada; died 11 Feb 1849. SOURCE: WO120 Volume 70 page 252. INDEX # 6958.

Fra^s POTTASK; pension awarded 21 Aug 1817; residence - Gibraltar; died 4 Sep 1848. SOURCE: WO120 Volume 70 page 252. INDEX # 6959.

Ja^s SMITHERMAN; pension awarded 5 Jun 1817; residence - Perth, Ontario, Canada; died 8 Apr 1850. SOURCE: WO120 Volume 70 page 252. INDEX # 6960.

Jno SUGHRAE; pension awarded 5 Jun 1817; residence - Kingston, Ontario, Canada; died in 1848. SOURCE: WO120 Volume 70 page 252. INDEX # 6961.

H^y SANDERSON; pension awarded 5 Jun 1817; residence - Niagara, Ontario, Canada; died in 1847. SOURCE: WO120 Volume 70 page 252. INDEX # 6962.

Wm WELLS; pension awarded 5 Jun 1817; residence - Toronto, Ontario, Canada; died in Jun 1848. SOURCE: WO120 Volume 70 page 252. INDEX # 6963.

Isaac WALTERS; pension awarded 5 Jun 1817; residence - Quebec, Quebec, Canada. SOURCE: WO120 Volume 70 page 252. INDEX # 6964.

Lyman WHITEHEAD; pension awarded 5 Jun 1817; residence - Fredericton, New Brunswick, Canada; died 24 Apr 1851. SOURCE: WO120 Volume 70 page 252. INDEX # 6965.

Willm CLIFFORD; pension awarded 5 Jun 1817; residence - Quebec, Quebec, Canada. SOURCE: WO120 Volume 70 page 252. INDEX # 6966.

Jno MCKERGEN; pension awarded 5 Jun 1817; residence - Quebec, Quebec, Canada. SOURCE: WO120 Volume 70 page 252. INDEX # 6967.

Wm SIMPSON; pension awarded 5 Jun 1817; residence - St. Johns; died 1 Jun 1847. SOURCE: WO120 Volume 70 page 252. INDEX # 6968.

Thos POWELL; pension awarded 4 Sep 1817; residence - Charlottetown, Prince Edward Island, Canada; died 28 Feb 1848. SOURCE: WO120 Volume 70 page 252. INDEX # 6969.

John RAY; pension awarded 5 Jun 1817; residence - Chambly, Quebec, Canada. SOURCE: WO120 Volume 70 page 252. INDEX # 6970.

Thos COOK; pension awarded 5 Jun 1817; residence - Kingston, Ontario, Canada; died in 1844. SOURCE: WO120 Volume 70 page 252. INDEX # 6971.

BRITISH ARMY PENSIONERS ABROAD

4th Veterans Battalion (continued)

Jos^h FARNELL; pension awarded 5 Jun 1817; residence - Perth, Ontario, Canada; died in 1848. SOURCE: WO120 Volume 70 page 252. INDEX # 6972.

Saml PROSSER; pension awarded 5 Jun 1817; residence - Wm Henry, Quebec, Canada; died 15 Mar 1857. SOURCE: WO120 Volume 70 page 252. INDEX # 6973.

Richd SLIGHT; pension awarded 5 Jun 1817; residence - Riviere du Lac. SOURCE: WO120 Volume 70 page 252. INDEX # 6974.

Jno VANDERDISKIN; pension awarded 5 Jun 1817; residence - Quebec, Quebec, Canada. SOURCE: WO120 Volume 70 page 252. INDEX # 6975.

John MAIR; pension awarded 5 Jun 1817; residence - Wm Henry, Quebec, Canada. SOURCE: WO120 Volume 70 page 253. INDEX # 6976.

Hugh HOGG; pension awarded 5 Jun 1817; residence - Quebec, Quebec, Canada. SOURCE: WO120 Volume 70 page 253. INDEX # 6977.

Richd HOLT; pension awarded 5 Jun 1817; residence - Quebec, Quebec, Canada. SOURCE: WO120 Volume 70 page 253. INDEX # 6978.

Danl YOUDS; pension awarded 5 Jun 1817; residence - Perth, Ontario, Canada; died 25 May 1854. SOURCE: WO120 Volume 70 page 253. INDEX # 6979.

Wm GOODENOUGH; pension awarded 5 Jun 1817; residence - Quebec, Quebec, Canada. SOURCE: WO120 Volume 70 page 253. INDEX # 6980.

Robt YOUNG; pension awarded 27 Sep 1814; residence - Quebec, Quebec, Canada. SOURCE: WO120 Volume 70 page 253. INDEX # 6981.

Fred^k MCKAY; pension awarded 5 Jun 1817; residence - Quebec, Quebec, Canada. SOURCE: WO120 Volume 70 page 253. INDEX # 6982.

John ALLEN; pension awarded 5 Jun 1817; residence - Montreal, Quebec, Canada; died 30 Sep 1847. SOURCE: WO120 Volume 70 page 253. INDEX # 6983.

Ja^s WATT; pension awarded 5 Jun 1817; residence - Quebec, Quebec, Canada. SOURCE: WO120 Volume 70 page 253. INDEX # 6984.

Ja^s CURRIE; pension awarded 5 Jun 1817; residence - Wm Henry, Quebec, Canada. SOURCE: WO120 Volume 70 page 253. INDEX # 6985.

Fra^s WADE; pension awarded 5 Jun 1817; residence - Quebec, Quebec, Canada. SOURCE: WO120 Volume 70 page 253. INDEX # 6986.

5th Veterans Battalion

Wm HERRON; pension awarded 3 May 1816; residence - Toronto, Ontario, Canada. SOURCE: WO120 Volume 70 page 256. INDEX # 6987.

Jno MCEVOY; pension awarded 26 Jul 1814; residence - Penetanguishene, Ontario, Canada; died 11 Dec 1858. SOURCE: WO120 Volume 70 page 256. INDEX # 6988.

Geo^e LAYMAN; pension awarded 26 Jul 1814; residence - Hobart Town, Australia; died in 1851. SOURCE: WO120 Volume 70 page 256. INDEX # 6989.

Arthur Anthony REITMAN; pension awarded 26 Jul 1814; residence - Berne, Switzerland; died 18 Apr 1847. SOURCE: WO120 Volume 70 page 256. INDEX # 6990.

6th Veterans Battalion

Don^d MCKENZIE; pension awarded 7 Sep 1814; residence - Halifax, Nova Scotia, Canada; died in 1844. SOURCE: WO120 Volume 70 page 258. INDEX # 6991.

Willm WILMORE; pension awarded 18 Apr 1821; residence - Prescott, Ontario, Canada; died 31 Mar 1877, Ottawa, Ontario, Canada. SOURCE: WO120 Volume 70 page 258. INDEX # 6992.

Thos CLARK; pension awarded 12 Jun 1816; residence - Toronto, Ontario, Canada. SOURCE: WO120 Volume 70 page 258. INDEX # 6993.

Geo^e TURNER; pension awarded 18 Apr 1821; residence - London, Ontario, Canada. SOURCE: WO120 Volume 70 page 258. INDEX # 6994.

6th Veterans Battalion (continued)

Neil ODONNELL; pension awarded 12 Jun 1816; residence - Toronto, Ontario, Canada; died 2 Apr 1847. SOURCE: WO120 Volume 70 page 258. INDEX # 6995.

Thos BOYD; pension awarded 12 Jun 1816; residence - New South Wales, Australia. SOURCE: WO120 Volume 70 page 258. INDEX # 6996.

Jno TURNER; pension awarded 12 Jun 1816; residence - Halifax, Nova Scotia, Canada; died in Mar 1857. SOURCE: WO120 Volume 70 page 258. INDEX # 6997.

Matt^w CALLAGHAN; pension awarded 13 Jun 1816; residence - Montreal, Quebec, Canada. SOURCE: WO120 Volume 70 page 258. INDEX # 6998.

Neil MCDONALD; pension awarded 7 Sep 1814; residence - Sydney. SOURCE: WO120 Volume 70 page 258. INDEX # 6999.

7th Veterans Battalion

Jno TURNER; pension awarded 7 Jun 1816; residence - London, Ontario, Canada; died 24 Nov 1846. SOURCE: WO120 Volume 79 page 260. INDEX # 7000.

Ant^y WISEMAN; pension awarded 24 Jan 1816; residence - Perth, Ontario, Canada. SOURCE: WO120 Volume 70 page 260. INDEX # 7001.

Fra^s MCCABE; pension awarded 7 Jun 1816; residence - Toronto, Ontario, Canada; died 9 Aug 1862, Toronto, Ontario, Canada. SOURCE: WO120 Volume 70 page 260. INDEX # 7002.

Gilbert WRIGHT; pension awarded 7 Jun 1816; residence - Sydney. SOURCE: WO120 Volume 70 page 260. INDEX # 7003.

Danl MUNROE; pension awarded 7 Jun 1816; residence - Halifax, Nova Scotia, Canada. SOURCE: WO120 Volume 70 page 260. INDEX # 7004.

Angus MCDONALD; pension awarded 7 Jun 1816; residence - Charlottetown, Prince Edward Island, Canada. SOURCE: WO120 Volume 70 page 260. INDEX # 7005.

Pat^k GRIFFIN; pension awarded 7 Jun 1816; residence - Montreal, Quebec, Canada. SOURCE: WO120 Volume 70 page 260. INDEX # 7006.

Jno HENDERSON; pension awarded 19 Jul 1816; residence - St. Johns. SOURCE: WO120 Volume 70 page 260. INDEX # 7007.

Felix BROWN; pension awarded 7 Jun 1816; residence - New South Wales, Australia. SOURCE: WO120 Volume 70 page 260. INDEX # 7008.

Alex^r KENNEDY; pension awarded 7 Jun 1816; residence - New South Wales, Australia. SOURCE: WO120 Volume 70 page 260. INDEX # 7009.

Willm DOWNER; pension awarded 7 Jun 1816; residence - Toronto, Ontario, Canada. SOURCE: WO120 Volume 70 page 260. INDEX # 7010.

Willm STILLMAN; pension awarded 13 Aug 1811; residence - Kingston, Ontario, Canada. SOURCE: WO120 Volume 70 page 260. INDEX # 7011.

8th Veterans Battalion

Fra^s ABLE; pension awarded 5 Aug 1814; residence - New South Wales, Australia; died in Mar 1852. SOURCE: WO120 Volume 70 page 263. INDEX # 7012.

Jno LAVINGSTON; pension awarded 2 Feb 1815; residence - Kingston, Ontario, Canada. SOURCE: WO120 Volume 70 page 263. INDEX # 7013.

9th Veterans Battalion

Jno BUCHANAN; pension awarded 5 Aug 1811; residence - Toronto, Ontario, Canada; died in 1847. SOURCE: WO120 Volume 70 page 266. INDEX # 7014.

Willm MILLER; pension awarded 7 Sep 1814; residence - Toronto, Ontario, Canada; died 30 Jun 1856, Toronto, Ontario, Canada. SOURCE: WO120 Volume 70 page 266. INDEX # 7015.

Willm MCDONALD; pension awarded 5 Aug 1814; residence - Toronto, Ontario, Canada. SOURCE: WO120 Volume 70 page 266. INDEX # 7016.

244 BRITISH ARMY PENSIONERS ABROAD

10th Veterans Battalion

Allen MCDONALD; pension awarded 21 May 1828. SOURCE: WO120 Volume 70 page 268. INDEX # 7017.

11th Veterans Battalion

Bern^d BOYD; pension awarded 13 Aug 1830; residence - Toronto, Ontario, Canada; died 15 Oct 1846. SOURCE: WO120 Volume 70 page 270. INDEX # 7018.

John CAMPBELL; pension awarded 10 Aug 1814; residence - Penetanguishene, Ontario, Canada. SOURCE: WO120 Volume 70 page 270. INDEX # 7019.

12th Veterans Battalion

Thos BUCKLEY; pension awarded 18 Jun 1814; residence - Toronto, Ontario, Canada; died 29 Apr 1864. SOURCE: WO120 Volume 70 page 272. INDEX # 7020.

Jno WILKINSON; pension awarded 20 Jan 1819; residence - Halifax, Nova Scotia, Canada; died 16 Jan 1859, Cork. SOURCE: WO120 Volume 70 page 272. INDEX # 7021.

Saml TWEEDY; pension awarded 25 Jun 1814; residence - Toronto, Ontario, Canada. SOURCE: WO120 Volume 70 page 272. INDEX # 7022.

John GREHAM; pension awarded 15 Jun 1814; residence - Toronto, Ontario, Canada; died 24 Apr 1857. SOURCE: WO120 Volume 70 page 272. INDEX # 7023.

Chas MALLON; pension awarded 25 Jun 1814; residence - Montreal, Quebec, Canada. SOURCE: WO120 Volume 70 page 272. INDEX # 7024.

Danl RYAN; pension awarded 25 Jun 1814; residence - London, Ontario, Canada. SOURCE: WO120 Volume 70 page 272. INDEX # 7025.

Ja^s CAMPBELL; pension awarded 25 Jun 1814; residence - Kingston, Ontario, Canada; died 7 Apr 1874, Toronto, Ontario, Canada. SOURCE: WO120 Volume 70 page 272. INDEX # 7026.

Jno LONGWORTH; pension awarded 15 Jun 1814; residence - Canada. SOURCE: WO120 Volume 70 page 272. INDEX # 7027.

13th Veterans Battalion

Willm DAKIN; pension awarded 25 Apr 1815; residence - Penetanguishene, Ontario, Canada; died 6 Jul 1852. SOURCE: WO120 Volume 70 page 274. INDEX # 7028.

Geuseppi CANDILLO; pension awarded 12 May 1815; residence - Palermo, Italy; died 20 Jan 1853. SOURCE: WO120 Volume 70 page 274. INDEX # 7029.

New South Wales Veterans Company

H^y JAMES; pension awarded 12 Nov 1834; residence - New South Wales, Australia. SOURCE: WO120 Volume 70 page 276. INDEX # 7030.

Thos MOORE; pension awarded 9 Jan 1823; residence - Melbourne, Australia; died in 1852. SOURCE: WO120 Volume 70 page 276. INDEX # 7031.

John GRILLS; pension awarded 14 Jul 1830; residence - New South Wales, Australia. SOURCE: WO120 Volume 70 page 276. INDEX # 7032.

Wm HEATH; pension awarded 14 Sep 1831; residence - New South Wales, Australia. SOURCE: WO120 Volume 70 page 276. INDEX # 7033.

Jno BROWN; pension awarded 10 Oct 1832; residence - Sydney, Australia. SOURCE: WO120 Volume 70 page 276. INDEX # 7034.

Jno BOOKER; pension awarded 10 Oct 1832; residence - New South Wales, Australia; died in Jun 1852. SOURCE: WO120 Volume 70 page 276. INDEX # 7035.

Thos MCCONNELL; pension awarded 8 Sep 1830; residence - New South Wales, Australia; died 29 May 1864. SOURCE: WO120 Volume 70 page 276. INDEX # 7036.

Benjn ABELL; pension awarded 14 Sep 1831; residence - New South Wales, Australia. SOURCE: WO120 Volume 70 page 276. INDEX # 7037.

New South Wales Veterans Company (continued)

Richd MORTIMER; pension awarded 13 Jun 1832. SOURCE: WO120 Volume 70 page 276. INDEX # 7038.

Pat^k HUMPHRYS; pension awarded 13 Jun 1832; residence - Sydney, Australia; died in 1846. SOURCE: WO120 Volume 70 page 276. INDEX # 7039.

Alex^r MONAGHAN; pension awarded 13 Jun 1832; residence - New South Wales, Australia. SOURCE: WO120 Volume 70 page 276. INDEX # 7040.

Willm PERKINS; pension awarded 14 Sep 1831; residence - New South Wales, Australia; died 21 Jun 1857. SOURCE: WO120 Volume 70 page 276. INDEX # 7041.

John HEFFERON; pension awarded 13 Jun 1832; residence - New South Wales, Australia; died in 1846. SOURCE: WO120 Volume 70 page 276. INDEX # 7042.

Geo^e CUPITT; pension awarded 13 Jun 1832; residence - New South Wales, Australia; died 13 Aug 1846. SOURCE: WO120 Volume 70 page 276. INDEX # 7043.

Wm Jos^h BAYLIS; pension awarded 13 Jun 1832; residence - New South Wales, Australia. SOURCE: WO120 Volume 70 page 276. INDEX # 7044.

Mich^l CARROLL; pension awarded 13 Jun 1832; residence - New South Wales, Australia. SOURCE: WO120 Volume 70 page 276. INDEX # 7045.

Richd SALTMARSH; pension awarded 13 Jun 1832; residence - New South Wales, Australia. SOURCE: WO120 Volume 70 page 276. INDEX # 7046.

Pat^k SMITH; pension awarded 13 Jun 1832; residence - Sydney, Australia. SOURCE: WO120 Volume 70 page 276. INDEX # 7047.

Thos ASBURY; pension awarded 13 Jun 1832; residence - New South Wales, Australia; died in Sep 1848. SOURCE: WO120 Volume 70 page 276. INDEX # 7048.

Jno HOARE; pension awarded 13 Jun 1832; residence - New South Wales, Australia. SOURCE: WO120 Volume 70 page 276. INDEX # 7049.

Thos HUMPHRIES; pension awarded 13 Jun 1832; residence - New South Wales, Australia. SOURCE: WO120 Volume 70 page 277. INDEX # 7050.

John GILZAN; pension awarded 10 Nov 1830; residence - New South Wales, Australia. SOURCE: WO120 Volume 70 page 277. INDEX # 7051.

Newfoundland Veterans Company

Willm SPIERS; pension awarded 9 Oct 1839; residence - Halifax, Nova Scotia, Canada. SOURCE: WO120 Volume 70 page 281. INDEX # 7052.

Jno VENABLES; pension awarded 9 Oct 1839; residence - Newfoundland, Canada. SOURCE: WO120 Volume 70 page 281. INDEX # 7053.

Mich^l CONNORS; pension awarded 5 Sep 1843; residence - Newfoundland, Canada. SOURCE: WO120 Volume 70 page 281. INDEX # 7054.

Jno CUSACK; pension awarded 8 Oct 1844; residence - Newfoundland, Canada; died 26 Feb 1874, Cavan. SOURCE: WO120 Volume 70 page 281. INDEX # 7055.

Ja^s ENGLAND; pension awarded 8 Oct 1844; residence - Newfoundland, Canada; died 1 Apr 1857. SOURCE: WO120 Volume 70 page 281. INDEX # 7056.

H^y NEEDHAM; pension awarded 8 Oct 1844; residence - Newfoundland, Canada. SOURCE: WO120 Volume 70 page 281. INDEX # 7057.

Edwd FITZPATRICK; pension awarded 14 Oct 1845; residence - Newfoundland, Canada; died 2 Aug 1875, Halifax, Nova Scotia, Canada. SOURCE: WO120 Volume 70 page 281. INDEX # 7058.

Murd^k MCCONNELL; pension awarded 14 Oct 1845; residence - Newfoundland, Canada. SOURCE: WO120 Volume 70 page 281. INDEX # 7059.

John KEEFE; pension awarded 14 Oct 1845; residence - Newfoundland, Canada. SOURCE: WO120 Volume 70 page 281. INDEX # 7060.

Jer^h CROWLEY; pension awarded 12 Sep 1838; residence - Newfoundland, Canada; died 27 Dec 1872, Halifax, Nova Scotia, Canada. SOURCE: WO120 Volume 70 page 281. INDEX # 7061.

Mich^l FAULKNER; pension awarded 9 Aug 1842; residence - Newfoundland, Canada; died 3 Nov 1875, London, Ontario, Canada. SOURCE: WO120 Volume 70 page 281. INDEX # 7062.

BRITISH ARMY PENSIONERS ABROAD

Newfoundland Veterans Company (continued)

H^y HAWKINGS; pension awarded 9 Oct 1839; residence - Newfoundland, Canada; died 21 Oct 1878, Halifax, Nova Scotia, Canada. SOURCE: WO120 Volume 70 page 281. INDEX # 7063.

Ch^r MCGUIRE; pension awarded 5 Sep 1843; residence - London, Ontario, Canada; died 26 Mar 1867. SOURCE: WO120 Volume 70 page 281. INDEX # 7064.

Saml KIDSON; pension awarded 23 Sep 1840; residence - Charlottetown, Prince Edward Island, Canada. SOURCE: WO120 Volume 70 page 281. INDEX # 7065.

Willm MARTIN; pension awarded 23 Sep 1840; residence - Newfoundland, Canada. SOURCE: WO120 Volume 70 page 281. INDEX # 7066.

Jno GAMBERG; pension awarded 23 Sep 1840; residence - Newfoundland, Canada. SOURCE: WO120 Volume 70 page 281. INDEX # 7067.

Wm FRANCIS; pension awarded 10 Oct 1828; residence - Newfoundland, Canada; died 25 Mar 1873, Halifax, Nova Scotia, Canada. SOURCE: WO120 Volume 70 page 281. INDEX # 7068.

Wm GUNN; pension awarded 13 Nov 1833; residence - Toronto, Ontario, Canada; died 8 Aug 1862, Hamilton, Ontario, Canada. SOURCE: WO120 Volume 70 page 281. INDEX # 7069.

Thos BENNETT; pension awarded 5 Sep 1843; residence - Charlottetown, Prince Edward Island, Canada. SOURCE: WO120 Volume 70 page 281. INDEX # 7070.

John JACKSON; pension awarded 10 Feb 1845; residence - Newfoundland, Canada; died 23 Feb 1874, Halifax, Nova Scotia, Canada. SOURCE: WO120 Volume 70 page 281. INDEX # 7071.

Willm STEWART; pension awarded 10 Oct 1846; residence - Newfoundland, Canada. SOURCE: WO120 Volume 70 page 282. INDEX # 7072.

Ant^y DEVANY; pension awarded 13 Oct 1846; residence - Newfoundland, Canada. SOURCE: WO120 Volume 70 page 282. INDEX # 7073.

Hugh MCGUINESS; pension awarded 13 Oct 1846; residence - Newfoundland, Canada; died 17 Nov 1881, Halifax, Nova Scotia, Canada. SOURCE: WO120 Volume 70 page 282. INDEX # 7074.

Thos RODGERS; pension awarded 13 Oct 1846; residence - Newfoundland, Canada; died 1 Nov 1847. SOURCE: WO120 Volume 70 page 282. INDEX # 7075.

Jno HALL; pension awarded 9 Aug 1842; residence - Charlottetown, Prince Edward Island, Canada. SOURCE: WO120 Volume 70 page 282. INDEX # 7076.

Mich^l COONERTY; pension awarded 28 Sep 1847. SOURCE: WO120 Volume 70 page 282. INDEX # 7077.

Thos WEEKS; pension awarded 28 Sep 1847. SOURCE: WO120 Volume 70 page 282. INDEX # 7078.

Robt HOWES; pension awarded 28 Sep 1847. SOURCE: WO120 Volume 70 page 282. INDEX # 7079.

Jno ODONNELL; pension awarded 28 Sep 1847. SOURCE: WO120 Volume 70 page 282. INDEX # 7080.

Mich^l COLLINS; pension awarded 28 Sep 1847; died 6 Jan 1880, Limerick. SOURCE: WO120 Volume 70 page 282. INDEX # 7081.

Owen CONNORS; pension awarded 28 Sep 1847. SOURCE: WO120 Volume 70 page 282. INDEX # 7082.

Mich^l FOLEY; pension awarded 28 Sep 1847. SOURCE: WO120 Volume 70 page 282. INDEX # 7083.

Hen^y GOLDSWORTHY; pension awarded 28 Sep 1847. SOURCE: WO120 Volume page . INDEX # 7084.

Mich^l LANTRY; pension awarded 28 Sep 1847. SOURCE: WO120 Volume 70 page 282. INDEX # 7085.

Thos MURRAY; pension awarded 28 Sep 1847. SOURCE: WO120 Volume 70 page 282. INDEX # 7086.

Danl OBRIEN; pension awarded 28 Sep 1847; died 8 Sep 1855, Roscommon. SOURCE: WO120 Volume 70 page 282. INDEX # 7087.

Jno PIERCE; pension awarded 28 Sep 1847. SOURCE: WO120 Volume 70 page 282. INDEX # 7088.

Robt REDDOCK; pension awarded 28 Sep 1847; died 5 Jan 1881, Chelsea Hosp^l, England. SOURCE: WO120 Volume 70 page 282. INDEX # 7089.

Mich^l SMITH; pension awarded 28 Sep 1847; died 11 Aug 1864, Newfoundland, Canada. SOURCE: WO120 Volume 70 page 282. INDEX # 7090.

Jos^h VENABLES; pension awarded 28 Sep 1847. SOURCE: WO120 Volume 70 page 282. INDEX # 7091.

Geo^e SLOANE; pension awarded 26 Oct 1847; residence - Toronto, Ontario, Canada; died 22 Aug 1853. SOURCE: WO120 Volume 70 page 283. INDEX # 7092.

Jno HARWOOD; pension awarded 26 Oct 1847. SOURCE: WO120 Volume 70 page 283. INDEX # 7093.

Newfoundland Veterans Company (continued)

Geo^e FAGAN; pension awarded 26 Oct 1847; residence - Toronto, Ontario, Canada; died 18 Oct 1856. SOURCE: WO120 Volume 70 page 283. INDEX # 7094.

Mich^l FITZPATRICK; pension awarded 26 Oct 1847; residence - Newfoundland, Canada; died 21 Dec 1856. SOURCE: WO120 Volume 70 page 283. INDEX # 7095.

Thos GRAHAM; pension awarded 26 Oct 1847. SOURCE: WO120 Volume 70 page 283. INDEX # 7096.

Geo^e JACKSON; pension awarded 26 Oct 1847. SOURCE: WO120 Volume 70 page 283. INDEX # 7097.

Martin LEYDON; pension awarded 26 Oct 1847. SOURCE: WO120 Volume 70 page 283. INDEX # 7098.

Alex^r MCARTHUR; pension awarded 26 Oct 1847. SOURCE: WO120 Volume 70 page 283. INDEX # 7099.

Wm MCINTYRE; pension awarded 26 Oct 1847; residence - Halifax, Nova Scotia, Canada; died 24 Mar 1876. SOURCE: WO120 Volume 70 page 283. INDEX # 7100.

Ja^s MCLELLAN; pension awarded 26 Oct 1847; died 24 Dec 1878, Halifax, Nova Scotia, Canada. SOURCE: WO120 Volume 70 page 283. INDEX # 7101.

Ja^s MCQUILLIAN; pension awarded 26 Oct 1847. SOURCE: WO120 Volume 70 page 283. INDEX # 7102.

Arthur OBRIEN; pension awarded 26 Oct 1847; residence - St. John's, Newfoundland, Canada; died 14 Nov 1854. SOURCE: WO120 Volume 70 page 283. INDEX # 7103.

Wm OMAND; pension awarded 26 Sep 1848. SOURCE: WO120 Volume 70 page 283. INDEX # 7104.

Fra^s CONNOLLY; pension awarded 26 Sep 1848. SOURCE: WO120 Volume 70 page 283. INDEX # 7105.

Thos EVANS; pension awarded 26 Sep 1848; residence - London, Ontario, Canada; died 23 May 1856. SOURCE: WO120 Volume 70 page 283. INDEX # 7106.

Jno FRISSELL; pension awarded 26 Sep 1848; residence - Toronto, Ontario, Canada; died 13 Oct 1854. SOURCE: WO120 Volume 70 page 283. INDEX # 7107.

Saml KELLY; pension awarded 26 Sep 1848; died 20 Aug 1874, Halifax, Nova Scotia, Canada. SOURCE: WO120 Volume 70 page 283. INDEX # 7108.

Ja^s MCAREAVEY; pension awarded 26 Sep 1848; residence - Toronto, Ontario, Canada; died 13 Nov 1853. SOURCE: WO120 Volume 70 page 283. INDEX # 7109.

Mich^l REDMOND; pension awarded 26 Sep 1848; died 25 Aug 1873, Toronto, Ontario, Canada. SOURCE: WO120 Volume 70 page 283. INDEX # 7110.

Ja^s SMITH; pension awarded 26 Sep 1848; died 30 Sep 1872, Nova Scotia, Canada. SOURCE: WO120 Volume 70 page 283. INDEX # 7111.

Ja^s CLANCY; pension awarded 26 Dec 1848. SOURCE: WO120 Volume 70 page 284. INDEX # 7112.

Matt^w WAUGH; pension awarded 23 Oct 1849; died 4 Jan 1884, Halifax, Nova Scotia, Canada. SOURCE: WO120 Volume 70 page 284. INDEX # 7113.

Pat^k DONOHOE; pension awarded 23 Oct 1849. SOURCE: WO120 Volume 70 page 284. INDEX # 7114.

Pat^k LIDDY; pension awarded 23 Oct 1849. SOURCE: WO120 Volume 70 page 284. INDEX # 7115.

Thos DALTON; pension awarded 23 Oct 1849; residence - Toronto, Ontario, Canada; died 20 Sep 1876. SOURCE: WO120 Volume 70 page 284. INDEX # 7116.

David EVANS; pension awarded 23 Oct 1849. SOURCE: WO120 Volume 70 page 284. INDEX # 7117.

Wm KING; pension awarded 23 Oct 1849. SOURCE: WO120 Volume 70 page 284. INDEX # 7118.

And^w HEAKE; pension awarded 22 Oct 1850. SOURCE: WO120 Volume 70 page 284. INDEX # 7119.

Wm CARR; pension awarded 22 Oct 1850; residence - London, Ontario, Canada. SOURCE: WO120 Volume 70 page 284. INDEX # 7120.

Pat^k DONILEY; pension awarded 22 Oct 1850. SOURCE: WO120 Volume 70 page 284. INDEX # 7121.

Jno MCORMACK; pension awarded 22 Oct 1850. SOURCE: WO120 Volume 70 page 284. INDEX # 7122.

Mich^l MONGAN; pension awarded 22 Oct 1850; died 20 Jan 1887, Nova Scotia, Canada. SOURCE: WO120 Volume 70 page 284. INDEX # 7123.

Fred^k MURPHY; pension awarded 22 Oct 1850. SOURCE: WO120 Volume 70 page 284. INDEX # 7124.

Chas MCDEVITT; pension awarded 22 Jul 1851. SOURCE: WO120 Volume 70 page 284. INDEX # 7125.

Chas CURRAN; pension awarded 14 Oct 1851; residence - Toronto, Ontario, Canada; died 26 Dec 1859. SOURCE: WO120 Volume 70 page 284. INDEX # 7126.

Matt^w WEISEY; pension awarded 14 Oct 1851; residence - Toronto, Ontario, Canada; died 4 Nov 1867. SOURCE: WO120 Volume 70 page 284. INDEX # 7127.

Ja^s MOORE; pension awarded 14 Oct 1851; residence - London, Ontario, Canada; died 4 Jan 1862. SOURCE: WO120 Volume 70 page 284. INDEX # 7128.

BRITISH ARMY PENSIONERS ABROAD

Newfoundland Veterans Company (continued)

Wm SHAW; pension awarded 14 Oct 1851. SOURCE: WO120 Volume 70 page 284. INDEX # 7129.

Thos IRWIN; pension awarded 14 Sep 1852; died 8 Feb 1872, Toronto, Ontario, Canada. SOURCE: WO120 Volume 70 page 284. INDEX # 7130.

Mich^l LEO; pension awarded 14 Sep 1852. SOURCE: WO120 Volume 70 page 284. INDEX # 7131.

Philip DORAN; pension awarded 14 Sep 1852. SOURCE: WO120 Volume 70 page 285. INDEX # 7132.

Wm WALSH; pension awarded 14 Sep 1852; died Prince Edward Island, Canada. SOURCE: WO120 Volume 70 page 285. INDEX # 7133.

Jno GARRETT; pension awarded 14 Sep 1852. SOURCE: WO120 Volume 70 page 285. INDEX # 7134.

Wm KENNY; pension awarded 14 Sep 1852; died 28 Apr 1879, Limerick. SOURCE: WO120 Volume 70 page 285. INDEX # 7135.

Jno WOOLLAM; pension awarded 14 Sep 1852; residence - Nova Scotia, Canada. SOURCE: WO120 Volume 70 page 285. INDEX # 7136.

Jno KAVANAGH; pension awarded 14 Sep 1852; died 21 Feb 1887, Nova Scotia, Canada. SOURCE: WO120 Volume 70 page 285. INDEX # 7137.

Mich^l TAYLOR; pension awarded 14 Dec 1852. SOURCE: WO120 Volume 70 page 285. INDEX # 7138.

Thos EGAN; pension awarded 27 Sep 1853; died 9 Jul 1861, London, Ontario, Canada. SOURCE: WO120 Volume 70 page 285. INDEX # 7139.

Thos BURNS; pension awarded 27 Sep 1853. SOURCE: WO120 Volume 70 page 285. INDEX # 7140.

Wm BAILEY; pension awarded 11 Oct 1853; residence - Newfoundland, Canada; died 31 Oct 1856. SOURCE: WO120 Volume 70 page 285. INDEX # 7141.

Ja^s GRAY; pension awarded 14 Nov 1854. SOURCE: WO120 Volume 70 page 285. INDEX # 7142.

Thos OCONNOR; pension awarded 9 Jan 1855. SOURCE: WO120 Volume 70 page 285. INDEX # 7143.

Arthur HAMILL; pension awarded 12 Jun 1855. SOURCE: WO120 Volume 70 page 285. INDEX # 7144.

Francis BRADLEY; pension awarded 12 Jun 1855. SOURCE: WO120 Volume 70 page 285. INDEX # 7145.

George GURLEY; pension awarded 12 Jun 1855. SOURCE: WO120 Volume 70 page 285. INDEX # 7146.

John LEARMOUTH; pension awarded 12 Jun 1855. SOURCE: WO120 Volume 70 page 285. INDEX # 7147.

John BUTCHER; pension awarded 12 Jun 1855. SOURCE: WO120 Volume 70 page 285. INDEX # 7148.

George PRICE; pension awarded 12 Jun 1855. SOURCE: WO120 Volume 70 page 285. INDEX # 7149.

David COOPER; pension awarded 12 Jun 1855. SOURCE: WO120 Volume 70 page 285. INDEX # 7150.

Patrick HENDRICK; pension awarded 12 Jun 1855. SOURCE: WO120 Volume 70 page 285. INDEX # 7151.

William OBRIEN; pension awarded 12 Jun 1855. SOURCE: WO120 Volume 70 page 286. INDEX # 7152.

Charles SLATE; pension awarded 12 Jun 1855. SOURCE: WO120 Volume 70 page 286. INDEX # 7153.

Michael BURKE; pension awarded 12 Jun 1855. SOURCE: WO120 Volume 70 page 286. INDEX # 7153.

Michael HICKEY; pension awarded 12 Jun 1855; residence - Toronto, Ontario, Canada; died 10 Mar 1865. SOURCE: WO120 Volume 70 page 286. INDEX # 7155.

John LEES; pension awarded 12 Jun 1855. SOURCE: WO120 Volume 70 page 286. INDEX # 7156.

Robert WALLS; pension awarded 12 Jun 1855. SOURCE: WO120 Volume 70 page 286. INDEX # 7157.

Patrick AHERN; pension awarded 12 Jun 1855. SOURCE: WO120 Volume 70 page 286. INDEX # 7158.

John BARBER; pension awarded 12 Jun 1855. SOURCE: WO120 Volume 70 page 286. INDEX # 7159.

John BRIDGES; pension awarded 12 Jun 1855. SOURCE: WO120 Volume 70 page 286. INDEX # 7160.

John CARROLL; pension awarded 12 Jun 1855. SOURCE: WO120 Volume 70 page 286. INDEX # 7161.

George CLARKE; pension awarded 12 Jun 1855. SOURCE: WO120 Volume 70 page 286. INDEX # 7162.

James CONQUEST; pension awarded 12 Jun 1855. SOURCE: WO120 Volume 70 page 286. INDEX # 7163.

Martin DEVANNY; pension awarded 12 Jun 1855. SOURCE: WO120 Volume 70 page 286. INDEX # 7164.

Patrick DORAN; pension awarded 12 Jun 1855. SOURCE: WO120 Volume 70 page 286. INDEX # 7165.

George DREW; pension awarded 12 Jun 1855. SOURCE: WO120 Volume 70 page 286. INDEX # 7166.

Jeremiah DUNN; pension awarded 12 Jun 1855. SOURCE: WO120 Volume 70 page 286. INDEX # 7057.

Francis FINNIGAN; pension awarded 12 Jun 1855. SOURCE: WO120 Volume 70 page 286. INDEX # 7168.

Thomas GORMAN; pension awarded 12 Jun 1855. SOURCE: WO120 Volume 70 page 286. INDEX # 7169.

Robert FLORENCE; pension awarded 12 Jun 1855. SOURCE: WO120 Volume 70 page 286. INDEX # 7170.

Joseph HALSEY; pension awarded 12 Jun 1855. SOURCE: WO120 Volume 70 page 286. INDEX # 7171.

Newfoundland Veterans Company (continued)

William HOOK; pension awarded 12 Jun 1855. SOURCE: WO120 Volume 70 page 287. INDEX # 7172.
David KELLY; pension awarded 12 Jun 1855; residence - Halifax, Nova Scotia, Canada; died 21 Dec 1878. SOURCE: WO120 Volume 70 page 287. INDEX # 7173.
Patrick MORIARTY; pension awarded 12 Jun 1855. SOURCE: WO120 Volume 70 page 287. INDEX # 7174.
Edmund POWER; pension awarded 12 Jun 1855; residence - Halifax, Nova Scotia, Canada; died 23 Feb 1857. SOURCE: WO120 Volume 70 page 287. INDEX # 7175.
Thomas PRINGLE; pension awarded 12 Jun 1855. SOURCE: WO120 Volume 70 page 287. INDEX # 7176.
John RYAN; pension awarded 12 Jun 1855. SOURCE: WO120 Volume 70 page 287. INDEX # 7177.
William SEWARD; pension awarded 12 Jun 1855. SOURCE: WO120 Volume 70 page 287. INDEX # 7178.
John SHANKSTER; pension awarded 12 Jun 1855. SOURCE: WO120 Volume 70 page 287. INDEX # 7179.
Henry WILLIAMS; pension awarded 12 Jun 1855. SOURCE: WO120 Volume 70 page 287. INDEX # 7180.
William HEWERCLINE; pension awarded 26 Aug 1856. SOURCE: WO120 Volume 70 page 287. INDEX # 7181.
Henry LOWE; pension awarded 26 Aug 1856. SOURCE: WO120 Volume 70 page 287. INDEX # 7182.
Thomas MCDONOUGH; pension awarded 15 Sep 1857. SOURCE: WO120 Volume 70 page 287. INDEX # 7183.
Robert OXLEY; pension awarded 15 Sep 1857. SOURCE: WO120 Volume 70 page 287. INDEX # 7184.
William MURRAY; pension awarded 15 Sep 1857. SOURCE: WO120 Volume 70 page 287. INDEX # 7185.

Royal Canadian Rifle Regiment

Geo^e PHILLIPS; pension awarded 9 Sep 1845; residence - Toronto, Ontario, Canada. SOURCE: WO120 Volume 70 page 290. INDEX # 7186.
Edwd OBRIEN; pension awarded 9 Sep 1845; residence - Toronto, Ontario, Canada; died 30 Jul 1884. SOURCE: WO120 Volume 70 page 290. INDEX # 7187.
Alex^r BRYSON; pension awarded 9 Sep 1845; residence - Toronto, Ontario, Canada. SOURCE: WO120 Volume 70 page 290. INDEX # 7188.
Ja^s HOLMES; pension awarded 26 Aug 1845; residence - Montreal, Quebec, Canada. SOURCE: WO120 Volume 70 page 290. INDEX # 7189.
Danl BRIAN; pension awarded 13 Jan 1846; residence - Toronto, Ontario, Canada; died 8 Feb 1851. SOURCE: WO120 Volume 70 page 290. INDEX # 7190.
Geo^e WEIGHTMAN; pension awarded 13 Jan 1846. SOURCE: WO120 Volume 70 page 290. INDEX # 7191.
Peter WILSON; pension awarded 22 Sep 1846. SOURCE: WO120 Volume 70 page 290. INDEX # 7192.
Wm JORDAN; pension awarded 22 Sep 1846. SOURCE: WO120 Volume 70 page 290. INDEX # 7193.
Geo^e MCCOMMIE; pension awarded 22 Sep 1846; died 17 Oct 1866, Hamilton, Ontario, Canada. SOURCE: WO120 Volume 70 page 290. INDEX # 7194.
Hugh NEESON; pension awarded 22 Sep 1846; residence - Toronto, Ontario, Canada; died in 1847. SOURCE: WO120 Volume 70 page 290. INDEX # 7195.
Ja^s UTTON; pension awarded 22 Sep 1846. SOURCE: WO120 Volume 70 page 290. INDEX # 7196.
Thos MALADY; pension awarded 22 Sep 1846. SOURCE: WO120 Volume 70 page 290. INDEX # 7197.
Ja^s MALONE; pension awarded 22 Sep 1846; died 26 Aug 1873, Cork. SOURCE: WO120 Volume 70 page 290. INDEX # 7198.
Uriah BROTHERS; pension awarded 22 Sep 1846. SOURCE: WO120 Volume 70 page 290. INDEX # 7199.
Ja^s LINEGAR; pension awarded 22 Sep 1846; residence - Toronto, Ontario, Canada; died 12 Dec 1871. SOURCE: WO120 Volume 70 page 290. INDEX # 7200.
Wm PEACHEY; pension awarded 22 Sep 1846. SOURCE: WO120 Volume 70 page 290. INDEX # 7201.
Ja^s AGNEW; pension awarded 22 Sep 1846. SOURCE: WO120 Volume 70 page 290. INDEX # 7202.
Peter CADWELL; pension awarded 22 Sep 1846; residence - London, Ontario, Canada; died 11 Mar 1847. SOURCE: WO120 Volume 70 page 290. INDEX # 7203.
Danl DALY; pension awarded 22 Sep 1846; residence - London, Ontario, Canada; died 24 Mar 1857. SOURCE: WO120 Volume 70 page 290. INDEX # 7204.

BRITISH ARMY PENSIONERS ABROAD

Royal Canadian Rifle Regiment (continued)

Edwd KENNEDY; pension awarded 22 Sep 1846; died 2 Apr 1874, London, Ontario, Canada. SOURCE: WO120 Volume 70 page 290. INDEX # 7205.

Jno LAVERY; pension awarded 22 Sep 1846. SOURCE: WO120 Volume 70 page 291. INDEX # 7206.

Jno ALBON; pension awarded 12 Oct 1847; residence - Niagara, Ontario, Canada; died 20 Dec 1849. SOURCE: WO120 Volume 70 page 291. INDEX # 7207.

Wm LAVELL; pension awarded 12 Oct 1847; residence - Quebec, Quebec, Canada; died 6 Jul 1849. SOURCE: WO120 Volume 70 page 291. INDEX # 7208.

Pat^k MADDEN; pension awarded 12 Oct 1847; residence - London, Ontario, Canada; died 10 Jan 1868. SOURCE: WO120 Volume 70 page 291. INDEX # 7209.

Jno GRAY; pension awarded 12 Oct 1847; residence - Toronto, Ontario, Canada; died 20 Jun 1854. SOURCE: WO120 Volume 70 page 291. INDEX # 7210.

Mich^l MCCABE; pension awarded 12 Oct 1847. SOURCE: WO120 Volume 70 page 291. INDEX # 7211.

Augustine BARRY; pension awarded 12 Oct 1847; residence - Niagara, Ontario, Canada; died 23 Sep 1850. SOURCE: WO120 Volume 70 page 291. INDEX # 7212.

Mark BROWN; pension awarded 12 Oct 1847. SOURCE: WO120 Volume 70 page 291. INDEX # 7213.

Mich^l BEATTY; pension awarded 12 Oct 1847; died 25 Oct 1872, Hamilton, Ontario, Canada. SOURCE: WO120 Volume 70 page 291. INDEX # 7214.

Saml BRATT; pension awarded 12 Oct 1847; died 22 Mar 1883, Toronto, Ontario, Canada. SOURCE: WO120 Volume 70 page 291. INDEX # 7215.

Robt COOGAN; pension awarded 12 Oct 1847. SOURCE: WO120 Volume 70 page 291. INDEX # 7216.

Jno DERMODY; pension awarded 12 Oct 1847; died 17 Feb 1882, Galway. SOURCE: WO120 Volume 70 page 291. INDEX # 7217.

Tho^a FARRELL; pension awarded 12 Oct 1847; residence - Kingston, Ontario, Canada; died 20 Mar 1855. SOURCE: WO120 Volume 70 page 291. INDEX # 7218.

Pat^k FARRELL; pension awarded 12 Oct 1847; residence - London, Ontario, Canada; died 9 Mar 1875. SOURCE: WO120 Volume 70 page 291. INDEX # 7219.

Pat^k FITZPATRICK; pension awarded 12 Oct 1847. SOURCE: WO120 Volume 70 page 291. INDEX # 7220.

Saml GILMORE; pension awarded 12 Oct 1847; residence - Toronto, Ontario, Canada; died 24 Aug 1866. SOURCE: WO120 Volume 70 page 291. INDEX # 7221.

Jno HALL; pension awarded 12 Oct 1847; residence - Niagara, Ontario, Canada; died 22 Feb 1854. SOURCE: WO120 Volume 70 page 291. INDEX # 7222.

Saml HARVEY; pension awarded 12 Oct 1847; residence - London, Ontario, Canada; died 22 Jun 1864. SOURCE: WO120 Volume 70 page 291. INDEX # 7223.

Hen^y HEWETT; pension awarded 12 Oct 1847. SOURCE: WO120 Volume 70 page 291. INDEX # 7224.

Jno HICKEN; pension awarded 12 Oct 1847; residence - Ontario, Canada; died 11 Jan 1853. SOURCE: WO120 Volume 70 page 291. INDEX # 7225.

David HUSTON; pension awarded 12 Oct 1847. SOURCE: WO120 Volume 70 page 292. INDEX # 7226.

Robert JONES; pension awarded 12 Oct 1847; residence - Niagara, Ontario, Canada; died 29 Oct 1847. SOURCE: WO120 Volume 70 page 292. INDEX # 7227.

Thos MCKEW; pension awarded 12 Oct 1847; residence - Canada; died 21 Jun 1849. SOURCE: WO120 Volume 70 page 292. INDEX # 7228.

Jos^h MCMAHON; pension awarded 12 Oct 1847. SOURCE: WO120 Volume 70 page 292. INDEX # 7229.

Jno MAHER; pension awarded 12 Oct 1847. SOURCE: WO120 Volume 70 page 292. INDEX # 7230.

David MILLER; pension awarded 12 Oct 1847; residence - Canada; died 1 Sep 1847. SOURCE: WO120 Volume 70 page 292. INDEX # 7231.

Wm MORRISON; pension awarded 12 Oct 1847; residence - Prescott, Ontario, Canada. SOURCE: WO120 Volume 70 page 292. INDEX # 7232.

Thos MORAN; pension awarded 12 Oct 1847; residence - Kingston, Ontario, Canada; died in 1852. SOURCE: WO120 Volume 70 page 292. INDEX # 7233.

Corn^s MULLIGAN; pension awarded 12 Oct 1847; died 28 Dec 1872, London, Ontario, Canada. SOURCE: WO120 Volume 70 page 292. INDEX # 7234.

Royal Canadian Rifle Regiment (continued)

Jn⁰ OLIVER; pension awarded 12 Oct 1847; residence - Hamilton, Ontario, Canada; died 24 Feb 1868. SOURCE: WO120 Volume 70 page 292. INDEX # 7235.
Jn⁰ PHILLIPS; pension awarded 12 Oct 1847. SOURCE: WO120 Volume 70 page 292. INDEX # 7236.
Robᵗ SEATON; pension awarded 12 Oct 1847; residence - Canada; died in Jun 1851. SOURCE: WO120 Volume 70 page 292. INDEX # 7237.
Mathʷ SHEPHERD; pension awarded 12 Oct 1847. SOURCE: WO120 Volume 70 page 292. INDEX # 7238.
Charles STEVENSON; pension awarded 12 Oct 1847; residence - Niagara, Ontario, Canada; died 13 Jul 1852. SOURCE: WO120 Volume 70 page 292. INDEX # 7239.
Wᵐ WRIGHT; pension awarded 12 Oct 1847; residence - Hamilton, Ontario, Canada; died 6 May 1865. SOURCE: WO120 Volume 70 page 292. INDEX # 7240.
Wᵐ ARCHER; pension awarded 22 Feb 1848; residence - London, Ontario, Canada; died 21 Aug 1863. SOURCE: WO120 Volume 70 page 292. INDEX # 7241.
Henʸ SEVERN; pension awarded 22 Feb 1848; residence - London, Ontario, Canada; died 2 Jan 1869. SOURCE: WO120 Volume 70 page 292. INDEX # 7242.
Fraˢ DRUMMOND; pension awarded 22 Feb 1848; residence - Amherstburg, Ontario, Canada; died in May 1848. SOURCE: WO120 Volume 70 page 292. INDEX # 7243.
Jaˢ MADILL; pension awarded 22 Feb 1848. SOURCE: WO120 Volume 70 page 292. INDEX # 7244.
Jn⁰ BROOKS; pension awarded 22 Feb 1848; residence - Amherstburg, Ontario, Canada; died 25 Aug 1855. SOURCE: WO120 Volume 70 page 292. INDEX # 7245.
Thoˢ BURKE; pension awarded 22 Feb 1848. SOURCE: WO120 Volume 70 page 293. INDEX # 7246.
Luke CLEGG; pension awarded 22 Feb 1848; residence - Niagara, Ontario, Canada; died 9 May 1855. SOURCE: WO120 Volume 70 page 293. INDEX # 7247.
Richᵈ COMB; pension awarded 22 Feb 1848; residence - Amherstburg, Ontario, Canada; died 18 Jan 1850. SOURCE: WO120 Volume 70 page 293. INDEX # 7248.
Jaˢ COLE; pension awarded 22 Feb 1848; residence - Amherstburg, Ontario, Canada; died 3 Jun 1848. SOURCE: WO120 Volume 70 page 293. INDEX # 7249.
Henʸ CUNNINGHAM; pension awarded 22 Feb 1848; residence - Niagara, Ontario, Canada; died 7 Jan 1848. SOURCE: WO120 Volume 70 page 293. INDEX # 7250.
Geoᵉ EDWARDS; pension awarded 22 Feb 1848. SOURCE: WO120 Volume 70 page 293. INDEX # 7251.
Johnston ELLIOTT; pension awarded 22 Feb 1848; residence - Bytown, Ontario, Canada; died in Dec 1857. SOURCE: WO120 Volume 70 page 293. INDEX # 7252.
Thoˢ FINN; pension awarded 22 Feb 1848; residence - Toronto, Ontario, Canada; died 1 Sep 1864. SOURCE: WO120 Volume 70 page 293. INDEX # 7253.
Jn⁰ GAY; pension awarded 22 Feb 1848; residence - Niagara, Ontario, Canada; died 27 Mar 1850. SOURCE: WO120 Volume 70 page 293. INDEX # 7254.
Wᵐ HINES; pension awarded 22 Feb 1848; died 12 Dec 1881, Canada. SOURCE: WO120 Volume 70 page 293. INDEX # 7255.
Jn⁰ KERROGHAN; pension awarded 22 Feb 1848. SOURCE: WO120 Volume 70 page 293. INDEX # 7256.
Jaˢ MCNAMARA; pension awarded 22 Feb 1848; died 12 Mar 1859, Niagara, Ontario, Canada. SOURCE: WO120 Volume 70 page 293. INDEX # 7257.
Wᵐ MILLS; pension awarded 22 Feb 1848; residence - Amherstburg, Ontario, Canada; died 17 Apr 1848. SOURCE: WO120 Volume 70 page 293. INDEX # 7258.
Thoˢ POWELL; pension awarded 22 Feb 1848. SOURCE: WO120 Volume 70 page 293. INDEX # 7259.
Geoᵉ SHAW; pension awarded 22 Feb 1848; residence - Hamilton, Ontario, Canada; died 19 Apr 1852. SOURCE: WO120 Volume 70 page 293. INDEX # 7260.
Martin SHEA; pension awarded 22 Feb 1848; residence - Toronto, Ontario, Canada. SOURCE: WO120 Volume 70 page 293. INDEX # 7261.
Robson Cruise GEORGE; pension awarded 14 Mar 1848; residence - Niagara, Ontario, Canada; died in 1848. SOURCE: WO120 Volume 70 page 293. INDEX # 7262.
Jn⁰ GREENACRE; pension awarded 14 Mar 1848; died 13 Apr 1877, London, Ontario, Canada. SOURCE: WO120 Volume 70 page 293. INDEX # 7263.
Samˡ FOURMIDGE; pension awarded 24 Oct 1848. SOURCE: WO120 Volume 70 page 293. INDEX # 7264.

BRITISH ARMY PENSIONERS ABROAD

Royal Canadian Rifle Regiment (continued)

Mich[l] MOYLAN; pension awarded 24 Oct 1848. SOURCE: WO120 Volume 70 page 293. INDEX # 7265.

Nich[s] RYAN; pension awarded 24 Oct 1848. SOURCE: WO120 Volume 70 page 294. INDEX # 7266.

W[m] CORBETT; pension awarded 24 Oct 1848. SOURCE: WO120 Volume 70 page 294. INDEX # 7267.

Hen[y] BRODER; pension awarded 24 Oct 1848; died 11 Mar 1876, Toronto, Ontario, Canada. SOURCE: WO120 Volume 70 page 294. INDEX # 7268.

Hugh MURPHY; pension awarded 24 Oct 1848. SOURCE: WO120 Volume 70 page 294. INDEX # 7269.

John OAKLEY; pension awarded 24 Oct 1848; residence - Niagara, Ontario, Canada; died 14 Mar 1855. SOURCE: WO120 Volume 70 page 294. INDEX # 7270.

Jn[o] ASH; pension awarded 24 Oct 1848; residence - Niagara, Ontario, Canada; died 10 Oct 1855. SOURCE: WO120 Volume 70 page 294. INDEX # 7271.

Hen[y] BUCKLEY; pension awarded 24 Oct 1848. SOURCE: WO120 Volume 70 page 294. INDEX # 7272.

Tho[s] CAMPBELL; pension awarded 24 Oct 1848; residence - Toronto, Ontario, Canada; died 16 Feb 1870. SOURCE: WO120 Volume 70 page 294. INDEX # 7273.

Tho[s] CARNEY; pension awarded 24 Oct 1848; died 4 Mar 1869, London, Ontario, Canada. SOURCE: WO120 Volume 70 page 294. INDEX # 7274.

Martin CORCORAN; pension awarded 24 Oct 1848; died 23 Apr 1862, Hamilton, Ontario, Canada. SOURCE: WO120 Volume 70 page 294. INDEX # 7275.

Solomon EVANS; pension awarded 24 Oct 1848; residence - Amherstburg, Ontario, Canada; died 27 Aug 1852. SOURCE: WO120 Volume 70 page 294. INDEX # 7276.

Jn[o] FIZZELL; pension awarded 24 Oct 1848; died 2 May 1853. SOURCE: WO120 Volume 70 page 294. INDEX # 7277.

Denis FOWLER; pension awarded 24 Oct 1848; died 15 Dec 1872, London, Ontario, Canada. SOURCE: WO120 Volume 70 page 294. INDEX # 7278.

Pat[k] HAYES; pension awarded 24 Oct 1848; residence - Amherstburg, Ontario, Canada. SOURCE: WO120 Volume 70 page 294. INDEX # 7279.

Jn[o] JOHNSTON; pension awarded 24 Oct 1848. SOURCE: WO120 Volume 70 page 294. INDEX # 7280.

Ja[s] KELLY; pension awarded 24 Oct 1848; residence - Kingston, Ontario, Canada; died in Dec 1855. SOURCE: WO120 Volume 70 page 294. INDEX # 7281.

Mich[l] LYNCH; pension awarded 24 Oct 1848; residence - Niagara, Ontario, Canada; died 3 Mar 1853. SOURCE: WO120 Volume 70 page 294. INDEX # 7282.

Jn[o] MCALLISTER; pension awarded 24 Oct 1848. SOURCE: WO120 Volume 70 page 294. INDEX # 7283.

Step[n] MORRISS; pension awarded 24 Oct 1848; residence - Amherstburg, Ontario, Canada; died 8 Apr 1852. SOURCE: WO120 Volume 70 page 294. INDEX # 7284.

Geo[e] NEWMAN; pension awarded 24 Oct 1848; residence - London, Ontario, Canada; died 19 Dec 1849. SOURCE: WO120 Volume 70 page 294. INDEX # 7285.

Ja[s] NOWLAN; pension awarded 24 Oct 1848. SOURCE: WO120 Volume 70 page 295. INDEX # 7286.

Rob[t] OBRIEN; pension awarded 24 Oct 1848; residence - Toronto, Ontario, Canada; died 9 Sep 1854. SOURCE: WO120 Volume 70 page 295. INDEX # 7287.

W[m] ROADS; pension awarded 24 Oct 1848; residence - Philipsburg, Ontario, Canada; died 20 Feb 1849. SOURCE: WO120 Volume 70 page 295. INDEX # 7288.

W[m] REDDY; pension awarded 24 Oct 1848; residence - Niagara, Ontario, Canada; died 16 Nov 1855. SOURCE: WO120 Volume 70 page 295. INDEX # 7289.

Tho[s] ROGERS; pension awarded 24 Oct 1848; residence - Ameliasburg, Ontario, Canada; died 19 Nov 1851. SOURCE: WO120 Volume 70 page 295. INDEX # 7290.

Peter SKIVINGTON; pension awarded 24 Oct 1848; residence - Bytown, Ontario, Canada; died 19 Mar 1850. SOURCE: WO120 Volume 70 page 295. INDEX # 7291.

Jos[h] WILSON; pension awarded 24 Oct 1848; residence - Toronto, Ontario, Canada; died 9 Aug 1858. SOURCE: WO120 Volume 70 page 295. INDEX # 7292.

W[m] WILSON; pension awarded 24 Oct 1848; died 22 Jul 1872, London, Ontario, Canada. SOURCE: WO120 Volume 70 page 295. INDEX # 7293.

Peter WOODS; pension awarded 24 Oct 1848. SOURCE: WO120 Volume 70 page 295. INDEX # 7294.

W[m] SMITH; pension awarded 23 Oct 1849; died 10 Apr 1862, London, Ontario, Canada. SOURCE: WO120 Volume 70 page 295. INDEX # 7295.

WO120 VOLUME 70

Royal Canadian Rifle Regiment (continued)

Wm RUMBLE; pension awarded 23 Oct 1849; died 24 Apr 1849, London, Ontario, Canada. SOURCE: WO120 Volume 70 page 295. INDEX # 7296.

Ja^s IMLAY; pension awarded 23 Oct 1849. SOURCE: WO120 Volume 70 page 295. INDEX # 7297.

Wm CLUTTERBUCK; pension awarded 23 Oct 1849. SOURCE: WO120 Volume 70 page 295. INDEX # 7298.

Farrell CONROY; pension awarded 23 Oct 1849; died 9 Aug 1875, London, Ontario, Canada. SOURCE: WO120 Volume 70 page 295. INDEX # 7299.

Tim^y CURLEY; pension awarded 23 Oct 1849; died 21 Mar 1867. SOURCE: WO120 Volume 70 page 295. INDEX # 7300.

Jno DWYER; pension awarded 23 Oct 1849. SOURCE: WO120 Volume 70 page 295. INDEX # 7301.

Jno JOLLEY; pension awarded 23 Oct 1849; residence - Toronto, Ontario, Canada; died 26 Nov 1850. SOURCE: WO120 Volume 70 page 295. INDEX # 7302.

Jno TURNBULL; pension awarded 23 Oct 1849; died 20 Feb 1873, Hamilton, Ontario, Canada. SOURCE: WO120 Volume 70 page 295. INDEX # 7303.

Jesse WAITE; pension awarded 23 Oct 1849. SOURCE: WO120 Volume 70 page 295. INDEX # 7304.

Alex^r FRASER; pension awarded 23 Oct 1849; residence - London, Ontario, Canada; died 15 Apr 1855. SOURCE: WO120 Volume 70 page 295. INDEX # 7305.

Mich^l GLASPOLE; pension awarded 23 Oct 1849; residence - London, Ontario, Canada; died 7 Jun 1865. SOURCE: WO120 Volume 70 page 296. INDEX # 7306.

Jno LITTLE; pension awarded 23 Oct 1849. SOURCE: WO120 Volume 70 page 296. INDEX # 7307.

Wm MCBEATH; pension awarded 23 Oct 1849; died 6 Dec 1863, Hamilton, Ontario, Canada. SOURCE: WO120 Volume 70 page 296. INDEX # 7308.

Jno NEALON; pension awarded 23 Oct 1849; residence - London, Ontario, Canada; died in Apr 1852. SOURCE: WO120 Volume 70 page 296. INDEX # 7309.

Robt ARMSTRONG; pension awarded 23 Oct 1849; residence - Niagara, Ontario, Canada; died 4 Apr 1854. SOURCE: WO120 Volume 70 page 296. INDEX # 7310.

W^m ASH; pension awarded 23 Oct 1849; residence - London, Ontario, Canada; died in Jul 1856. SOURCE: WO120 Volume 70 page 296. INDEX # 7311.

Wm BAND; pension awarded 23 Oct 1849; residence - Hamilton, Ontario, Canada; died 17 Feb 1871. SOURCE: WO120 Volume 70 page 296. INDEX # 7312.

Jno BALDRY; pension awarded 23 Oct 1849. SOURCE: WO120 Volume 70 page 296. INDEX # 7313.

Jno BARRETT; pension awarded 23 Oct 1849. SOURCE: WO120 Volume 70 page 296. INDEX # 7314.

Ed^{wd} BARRY; pension awarded 23 Oct 1849. SOURCE: WO120 Volume 70 page 296. INDEX # 7315.

Wm BRIEN; pension awarded 23 Oct 1849; residence - London, Ontario, Canada; died 25 Mar 1854. SOURCE: WO120 Volume 70 page 296. INDEX # 7316.

Robt BOAG; pension awarded 23 Oct 1849; residence - Toronto, Ontario, Canada; died 4 Sep 1850. SOURCE: WO120 Volume 70 page 296. INDEX # 7317.

Jno BOLTON; pension awarded 23 Oct 1849; residence - Amherstburg, Ontario, Canada; died 23 Jan 1855. SOURCE: WO120 Volume 70 page 296. INDEX # 7318.

Wm BOYTON; pension awarded 23 Oct 1849; residence - Colchester, Ontario, Canada; died 15 Dec 1851. SOURCE: WO120 Volume 70 page 296. INDEX # 7319.

Hugh BYRNE; pension awarded 23 Oct 1849; residence - Toronto, Ontario, Canada; died 9 Oct 1855. SOURCE: WO120 Volume 70 page 296. INDEX # 7320.

Pat^k CARTY; pension awarded 23 Oct 1849; died 11 Nov 1860, Toronto, Ontario, Canada. SOURCE: WO120 Volume 70 page 296. INDEX # 7321.

Thos CORDALL; pension awarded 23 Oct 1849. SOURCE: WO120 Volume 70 page 296. INDEX # 7322.

Jno DALEY; pension awarded 23 Oct 1849; died 3 Dec 1858. SOURCE: WO120 Volume 70 page 296. INDEX # 7323.

Maur^e DALTON; pension awarded 23 Oct 1849. SOURCE: WO120 Volume 70 page 296. INDEX # 7324.

Ja^s DRAPER; pension awarded 23 Oct 1849; died 22 May 1878, Galway. SOURCE: WO120 Volume 70 page 296. INDEX # 7325.

Jno DEARDON; pension awarded 23 Oct 1849; residence - Niagara, Ontario, Canada; died 16 Jul 1856. SOURCE: WO120 Volume 70 page 297. INDEX # 7326.

Royal Canadian Rifle Regiment (continued)

Mich^l DESMOND; pension awarded 23 Oct 1849; residence - Amherstburg, Ontario, Canada; died in 1849. SOURCE: WO120 Volume 70 page 297. INDEX # 7327.

Benjn DIVER; pension awarded 23 Oct 1849; died 19 Jan 1872, London, Ontario, Canada. SOURCE: WO120 Volume 70 page 297. INDEX # 7328.

Wm DONNELLAN; pension awarded 23 Oct 1849; residence - Hamilton, Ontario, Canada; died 17 Jan 1860. SOURCE: WO120 Volume 70 page 297. INDEX # 7329.

Martin FALLON; pension awarded 23 Oct 1849. SOURCE: WO120 Volume 70 page 297. INDEX # 7330.

Thos FEENEY; pension awarded 23 Oct 1849; residence - Kingston, Ontario, Canada; died 12 Feb 1855. SOURCE: WO120 Volume 70 page 297. INDEX # 7331.

Jno FOSTER; pension awarded 23 Oct 1849. SOURCE: WO120 Volume 70 page 297. INDEX # 7332.

Ja^s GEARNON; pension awarded 23 Oct 1849; residence - Hamilton, Ontario, Canada; died 31 Aug 1865. SOURCE: WO120 Volume 70 page 297. INDEX # 7333.

Mich^l GORMAN; pension awarded 23 Oct 1849. SOURCE: WO120 Volume 70 page 297. INDEX # 7334.

Edwd HALPIN; pension awarded 23 Oct 1849. SOURCE: WO120 Volume 70 page 297. INDEX # 7335.

Step^n HANNAGH; pension awarded 23 Oct 1849. SOURCE: WO120 Volume 70 page 297. INDEX # 7336.

Saml JOHNSTON; pension awarded 23 Oct 1849; residence - London, Ontario, Canada; died 26 Nov 1851. SOURCE: WO120 Volume 70 page 297. INDEX # 7337.

Mich^l KEEFE; pension awarded 23 Oct 1849; residence - Prescott, Ontario, Canada; died in 1853. SOURCE: WO120 Volume 70 page 297. INDEX # 7338.

Crawford KENNEDY; pension awarded 23 Oct 1849. SOURCE: WO120 Volume 70 page 297. INDEX # 7339.

Edm^d KENNEDY; pension awarded 23 Oct 1849. SOURCE: WO120 Volume 70 page 297. INDEX # 7340.

Sexton KEOUGH; pension awarded 23 Oct 1849. SOURCE: WO120 Volume 70 page 297. INDEX # 7341.

Pat^k KILLALLY; pension awarded 23 Oct 1849; residence - Niagara, Ontario, Canada; died 11 Aug 1854. SOURCE: WO120 Volume 70 page 297. INDEX # 7342.

Thos LANCASTER; pension awarded 23 Oct 1849; residence - Toronto, Ontario, Canada; died 30 Dec 1857. SOURCE: WO120 Volume 70 page 297. INDEX # 7343.

Ja^s LARRISY; pension awarded 23 Oct 1849; residence - London, Ontario, Canada; died 9 Apr 1876. SOURCE: WO120 Volume 70 page 297. INDEX # 7344.

David LLOYD; pension awarded 23 Oct 1849; residence - Windsor, Ontario, Canada; died 3 Apr 1850. SOURCE: WO120 Volume 70 page 297. INDEX # 7345.

Wm LOTHIAN; pension awarded 23 Oct 1849; died 28 Sep 1876, Hamilton, Ontario, Canada. SOURCE: WO120 Volume 70 page 298. INDEX # 7346.

Jno LOWE; pension awarded 23 Oct 1849. SOURCE: WO120 Volume 70 page 298. INDEX # 7347.

Bern^d MCBRYAN; pension awarded 23 Oct 1849. SOURCE: WO120 Volume 70 page 298. INDEX # 7348.

Jno MCCARTY; pension awarded 23 Oct 1849; residence - London, Ontario, Canada; died 28 Nov 1849. SOURCE: WO120 Volume 70 page 298. INDEX # 7349.

Martin MCCORMICK; pension awarded 23 Oct 1849. SOURCE: WO120 Volume 70 page 298. INDEX # 7350.

Jno MCDONALD; pension awarded 23 Oct 1849; residence - Drummondville, Quebec, Canada; died 20 Dec 1849. SOURCE: WO120 Volume 70 page 298. INDEX # 7351.

Ja^s MCGOLDRICK; pension awarded 23 Oct 1849; residence - Sorel, Quebec, Canada; died 1 Jan 1849. SOURCE: WO120 Volume 70 page 298. INDEX # 7352.

Geo^e MCKNIGHT; pension awarded 23 Oct 1849. SOURCE: WO120 Volume 70 page 298. INDEX # 7353.

Mich^l MANUEL; pension awarded 23 Oct 1849. SOURCE: WO120 Volume 70 page 298. INDEX # 7354.

Wm MASON; pension awarded 23 Oct 1849. SOURCE: WO120 Volume 70 page 298. INDEX # 7355.

Edwd MELVIN; pension awarded 23 Oct 1849; residence - Hamilton, Ontario, Canada; died 24 Jan 1863. SOURCE: WO120 Volume 70 page 298. INDEX # 7356.

Simon MOORE; pension awarded 23 Oct 1849. SOURCE: WO120 Volume 70 page 298. INDEX # 7357.

Wm MORLING; pension awarded 23 Oct 1849. SOURCE: WO120 Volume 70 page 298. INDEX # 7358.

Ja^s NELSON; pension awarded 23 Oct 1849; residence - Hamilton, Ontario, Canada; died 15 Apr 1863. SOURCE: WO120 Volume 70 page 298. INDEX # 7359.

Wm NUNN; pension awarded 23 Oct 1849. SOURCE: WO120 Volume 70 page 298. INDEX # 7360.

Royal Canadian Rifle Regiment (continued)

Clement PAINE; pension awarded 23 Oct 1849; residence - Niagara, Ontario, Canada; died 17 Nov 1850. SOURCE: WO120 Volume 70 page 298. INDEX # 7361.

Wm POLLARD; pension awarded 23 Oct 1849; residence - Montreal, Quebec, Canada; died 11 Nov 1865. SOURCE: WO120 Volume 70 page 298. INDEX # 7362.

Jno PORTER; pension awarded 23 Oct 1849. SOURCE: WO120 Volume 70 page 298. INDEX # 7363.

Ja^s POUGUE; pension awarded 23 Oct 1849; died 3 Jun 1883, Nova Scotia, Canada. SOURCE: WO120 Volume 70 page 298. INDEX # 7364.

Richd ROGERS; pension awarded 23 Oct 1849; residence - Toronto, Ontario, Canada; died 10 Oct 1862. SOURCE: WO120 Volume 70 page 298. INDEX # 7365.

Geo^e SANDON; pension awarded 23 Oct 1849. SOURCE: WO120 Volume 70 page 299. INDEX # 7366.

Chas SCOTT; pension awarded 23 Oct 1849; residence - Ottawa, Ontario, Canada; died 16 Feb 1855. SOURCE: WO120 Volume 70 page 299. INDEX # 7367.

Jno SHANAKEN; pension awarded 23 Oct 1849; residence - Amherstburg, Ontario, Canada; died 19 Nov 1854. SOURCE: WO120 Volume 70 page 299. INDEX # 7368.

Jno JOHNSTON; pension awarded 23 Oct 1849; residence - Amherstburg, Ontario, Canada; died 19 Nov 1854. SOURCE: WO120 Volume 70 page 299. INDEX # 7369.

Mich^l SHERIDAN; pension awarded 23 Oct 1849; residence - Toronto, Ontario, Canada; died 6 May 1863. SOURCE: WO120 Volume 70 page 299. INDEX # 7370.

Thos STEWART; pension awarded 23 Oct 1849; residence - Niagara, Ontario, Canada; died 14 Apr 1859. SOURCE: WO120 Volume 70 page 299. INDEX # 7371.

Edwd SWEENEY; pension awarded 23 Oct 1849. SOURCE: WO120 Volume 70 page 299. INDEX # 7372.

Ant^y VANDAM; pension awarded 23 Oct 1849; residence - Hamilton, Ontario, Canada; died 16 Nov 1860. SOURCE: WO120 Volume 70 page 299. INDEX # 7373.

Jno WERTY; pension awarded 23 Oct 1849; residence - Amherstburg, Ontario, Canada; died in 1849. SOURCE: WO120 Volume 70 page 299. INDEX # 7374.

Hen^y WILLIAMS; pension awarded 23 Oct 1849. SOURCE: WO120 Volume 70 page 299. INDEX # 7375.

Thos TOLMIE; pension awarded 1 Oct 1850; died 7 Sep 1886, Toronto, Ontario, Canada. SOURCE: WO120 Volume 70 page 299. INDEX # 7376.

Jno CLARKE; pension awarded 1 Oct 1850; died 20 Apr 1875, London, Ontario, Canada. SOURCE: WO120 Volume 70 page 299. INDEX # 7377.

Robt ELLIOTT; pension awarded 1 Oct 1850; residence - Chippawa, Ontario, Canada; died 20 Sep 1851. SOURCE: WO120 Volume 70 page 299. INDEX # 7378.

Jno WILSON; pension awarded 1 Oct 1850; died 2 Feb 1872, London, Ontario, Canada. SOURCE: WO120 Volume 70 page 299. INDEX # 7379.

Ge^o ALLEN; pension awarded 1 Oct 1850; died 27 Feb 1875, Hamilton, Ontario, Canada. SOURCE: WO120 Volume 70 page 299. INDEX # 7380.

Mark APPLEBY; pension awarded 1 Oct 1850; died 30 Jun 1881, Hamilton, Ontario, Canada. SOURCE: WO120 Volume 70 page 299. INDEX # 7381.

Wm ENGLAND; pension awarded 1 Oct 1850; residence - London, Ontario, Canada; died 2 Aug 1869. SOURCE: WO120 Volume 70 page 299. INDEX # 7382.

Mich^l FAHEY; pension awarded 1 Oct 1850. SOURCE: WO120 Volume 70 page 299. INDEX # 7383.

Seth HARLING; pension awarded 1 Oct 1850; died 9 Jul 1883, Bury St. Edmunds. SOURCE: WO120 Volume 70 page 299. INDEX # 7384.

Ja^s HOLLOWAY; pension awarded 1 Oct 1850; residence - Hamilton, Ontario, Canada; died 20 Oct 1867. SOURCE: WO120 Volume 70 page 299. INDEX # 7385.

Thos JOHNSON; pension awarded 1 Oct 1850. SOURCE: WO120 Volume 70 page 299. INDEX # 7386.

Robt LAWSON; pension awarded 1 Oct 1850. SOURCE: WO120 Volume 70 page 300. INDEX # 7387.

Jno MAGGS; pension awarded 1 Oct 1850; died 3 Aug 1884, Toronto, Ontario, Canada. SOURCE: WO120 Volume 70 page 300. INDEX # 7388.

David PICKEN; pension awarded 1 Oct 1850. SOURCE: WO120 Volume 70 page 300. INDEX # 7389.

Geo^e SMITH; pension awarded 1 Oct 1850. SOURCE: WO120 Volume 70 page 300. INDEX # 7390.

Jno WILSON; pension awarded 1 Oct 1850; died 22 Mar 1872, Toronto, Ontario, Canada. SOURCE: WO120 Volume 70 page 300. INDEX # 7391.

Royal Canadian Rifle Regiment (continued)

Ja^s ANDERSON; pension awarded 1 Oct 1850; residence - Toronto, Ontario, Canada; died 28 Jun 1858. SOURCE: WO120 Volume 70 page 300. INDEX # 7392.

Bernard BOYLE; pension awarded 1 Oct 1850; residence - Kingston, Ontario, Canada; died in 1854. SOURCE: WO120 Volume 70 page 300. INDEX # 7393.

Jno COOK; pension awarded 1 Oct 1850; died 23 Dec 1862, London, Ontario, Canada. SOURCE: WO120 Volume 70 page 300. INDEX # 7394.

Ja^s ELLIOTT; pension awarded 1 Oct 1850; died 10 Sep 1884, Toronto, Ontario, Canada. SOURCE: WO120 Volume 70 page 300. INDEX # 7395.

Jonah KING; pension awarded 1 Oct 1850. SOURCE: WO120 Volume 70 page 300. INDEX # 7396.

Mich^l MEIGHAN; pension awarded 1 Oct 1850; residence - Hamilton, Ontario, Canada; died 21 Mar 1871. SOURCE: WO120 Volume 70 page 300. INDEX # 7397.

Wm NEWMAN; pension awarded 1 Oct 1850. SOURCE: WO120 Volume 70 page 300. INDEX # 7398.

Jno PATTERSON; pension awarded 1 Oct 1850. SOURCE: WO120 Volume 70 page 300. INDEX # 7399.

Chas WISDOM; pension awarded 1 Oct 1850; residence - Toronto, Ontario, Canada; died 2 Jan 1865. SOURCE: WO120 Volume 70 page 300. INDEX # 7400.

Ja^s ADAMS; pension awarded 1 Oct 1850. SOURCE: WO120 Volume 70 page 300. INDEX # 7401.

Robt AILLES; pension awarded 1 Oct 1850; residence - Niagara, Ontario, Canada; died 12 Aug 1854. SOURCE: WO120 Volume 70 page 300. INDEX # 7402.

Walter AIRD; pension awarded 1 Oct 1850; residence - Roxburgh, Ontario, Canada; died 11 Sep 1852. SOURCE: WO120 Volume 70 page 300. INDEX # 7403.

Ja^s ANGUS; pension awarded 1 Oct 1850; residence - Kingston, Ontario, Canada; died 30 Apr 1854. SOURCE: WO120 Volume 70 page 300. INDEX # 7404.

Jno BRADY; pension awarded 1 Oct 1850; residence - Prescott, Ontario, Canada; died 2 Apr 1852. SOURCE: WO120 Volume 70 page 300. INDEX # 7405.

Jno BAKER; pension awarded 1 Oct 1850; died 25 Feb 1874, London, Ontario, Canada. SOURCE: WO120 Volume 70 page 300. INDEX # 7406.

Robin BRANNIGAN; pension awarded 1 Oct 1850; residence - Hamilton, Ontario, Canada; died 12 Apr 1869. SOURCE: WO120 Volume 70 page 301. INDEX # 7407.

Terence BRANNIGAN; pension awarded 1 Oct 1850; residence - Amherstburg, Ontario, Canada; died 19 Aug 1856. SOURCE: WO120 Volume 70 page 301. INDEX # 7408.

Peter BERGIN; pension awarded 1 Oct 1850; residence - Bytown, Ontario, Canada; died 23 Sep 1851. SOURCE: WO120 Volume 70 page 301. INDEX # 7409.

John BERGIN; pension awarded 1 Oct 1850; residence - Canada; died 30 Dec 1853. SOURCE: WO120 Volume 70 page 301. INDEX # 7410.

Mich^l BUCKLEY; pension awarded 1 Oct 1850; residence - London, Ontario, Canada; died 12 Jan 1868. SOURCE: WO120 Volume 70 page 301. INDEX # 7411.

Jno BUSH; pension awarded 1 Oct 1850. SOURCE: WO120 Volume 70 page 301. INDEX # 7412.

Ja^s BYRNE; pension awarded 1 Oct 1850; died 10 Nov 1876, Toronto, Ontario, Canada. SOURCE: WO120 Volume 70 page 301. INDEX # 7413.

Ja^s CANSHER; pension awarded 1 Oct 1850. SOURCE: WO120 Volume 70 page 301. INDEX # 7414.

Thos CHAPLIN; pension awarded 1 Oct 1850. SOURCE: WO120 Volume 70 page 301. INDEX # 7415.

Robt CLAYTON; pension awarded 1 Oct 1850; died 1 Mar 1859. SOURCE: WO120 Volume 70 page 301. INDEX # 7416.

Pat^k CALLAGHAN; pension awarded 1 Oct 1850. SOURCE: WO120 Volume 70 page 301. INDEX # 7417.

Wm CARLTON; pension awarded 1 Oct 1850; died 13 Jan 1872, London, Ontario, Canada. SOURCE: WO120 Volume 70 page 301. INDEX # 7418.

Jno CARROLL; pension awarded 1 Oct 1850; residence - Toronto, Ontario, Canada; died 5 Aug 1854. SOURCE: WO120 Volume 70 page 301. INDEX # 7419.

Thos CARSHORE; pension awarded 1 Oct 1850; residence - Toronto, Ontario, Canada; died 7 Apr 1866. SOURCE: WO120 Volume 70 page 301. INDEX # 7420.

Ja^s CASEY; pension awarded 1 Oct 1850. SOURCE: WO120 Volume 70 page 301. INDEX # 7421.

Chas CAVANAGH; pension awarded 1 Oct 1850. SOURCE: WO120 Volume 70 page 301. INDEX # 7422.

Royal Canadian Rifle Regiment (continued)

Reuben CRESWELL; pension awarded 1 Oct 1850; residence - London, Ontario, Canada; died 5 Jan 1864. SOURCE: WO120 Volume 70 page 301. INDEX # 7423.

Thos CLIFFORD; pension awarded 1 Oct 1850. SOURCE: WO120 Volume 70 page 301. INDEX # 7424.

Jno CHIVINS; pension awarded 1 Oct 1850; residence - London, Ontario, Canada; died 19 Mar 1875. SOURCE: WO120 Volume 70 page 301. INDEX # 7425.

Thos COLEMAN; pension awarded 1 Oct 1850; residence - Chambly, Quebec, Canada; died 21 Mar 1851. SOURCE: WO120 Volume 70 page 301. INDEX # 7426.

Jno COLEMAN; pension awarded 1 Oct 1850; residence - Toronto, Ontario, Canada; died 28 Nov 1871. SOURCE: WO120 Volume 70 page 302. INDEX # 7427.

Ja^s COLLINS; pension awarded 1 Oct 1850. SOURCE: WO120 Volume 70 page 302. INDEX # 7428.

Pat^k CONBOY; pension awarded 1 Oct 1850; residence - London, Ontario, Canada; died 4 Apr 1871. SOURCE: WO120 Volume 70 page 302. INDEX # 7429.

Pat^k CONNELL; pension awarded 1 Oct 1850; residence - Hamilton, Ontario, Canada; died 19 Oct 1852. SOURCE: WO120 Volume 70 page 302. INDEX # 7430.

Wm CONNELL; pension awarded 1 Oct 1850; residence - Toronto, Ontario, Canada; died 1 Jan 1864. SOURCE: WO120 Volume 70 page 302. INDEX # 7431.

Jno CONNELLY; pension awarded 1 Oct 1850; residence - Hamilton, Ontario, Canada. SOURCE: WO120 Volume 70 page 302. INDEX # 7432.

Peter CONROY; pension awarded 1 Oct 1850. SOURCE: WO120 Volume 70 page 302. INDEX # 7433.

Jno COWLEY; pension awarded 1 Oct 1850; residence - Kingston, Ontario, Canada; died 2 Aug 1857. SOURCE: WO120 Volume 70 page 302. INDEX # 7434.

Daniel CUDMORE; pension awarded 1 Oct 1850; died 6 May 1883, Toronto, Ontario, Canada. SOURCE: WO120 Volume 70 page 302. INDEX # 7435.

Ja^s DAVIS; pension awarded 1 Oct 1850. SOURCE: WO120 Volume 70 page 302. INDEX # 7436.

David DAVIDSON; pension awarded 1 Oct 1850; died 29 Jun 1886, Toronto, Ontario, Canada. SOURCE: WO120 Volume 70 page 302. INDEX # 7437.

Pat^k DELMORE; pension awarded 1 Oct 1850. SOURCE: WO120 Volume 70 page 302. INDEX # 7438.

Fra^s DONNELLY; pension awarded 1 Oct 1850. SOURCE: WO120 Volume 70 page 302. INDEX # 7439.

Thos DOWSER; pension awarded 1 Oct 1850. SOURCE: WO120 Volume 70 page 302. INDEX # 7440.

Geo^e DUNCAN; pension awarded 1 Oct 1850; died 1 May 1873, London, Ontario, Canada. SOURCE: WO120 Volume 70 page 302. INDEX # 7441.

Pat^k DURCAN; pension awarded 1 Oct 1850. SOURCE: WO120 Volume 70 page 302. INDEX # 7442.

Thos DUNLING; pension awarded 1 Oct 1850; died 7 Apr 1879, Toronto, Ontario, Canada. SOURCE: WO120 Volume 70 page 302. INDEX # 7443.

David DUKESBURY; pension awarded 1 Oct 1850; residence - Toronto, Ontario, Canada; died 19 Jul 1858. SOURCE: WO120 Volume 70 page 302. INDEX # 7444.

Jer^h DWYER; pension awarded 1 Oct 1850. SOURCE: WO120 Volume 70 page 302. INDEX # 7445.

Robt ELLINS; pension awarded 1 Oct 1850; residence - Hamilton, Ontario, Canada; died 31 May 1870. SOURCE: WO120 Volume 70 page 302. INDEX # 7446.

Alex^r FLACK; pension awarded 1 Oct 1850; residence - Bytown, Ontario, Canada; died 6 Jan 1854. SOURCE: WO120 Volume 70 page 303. INDEX # 7447.

Jno FIGG; pension awarded 1 Oct 1850; died 12 May 1867 London, Ontario, Canada. SOURCE: WO120 Volume 70 page 303. INDEX # 7448.

Saml FLETCHER; pension awarded 1 Oct 1850; residence - Toronto, Ontario, Canada; died 8 Feb 1855. SOURCE: WO120 Volume 70 page 303. INDEX # 7449.

Wm GARDEN; pension awarded 1 Oct 1850. SOURCE: WO120 Volume 70 page 303. INDEX # 7450.

Owen GARRIGAN; pension awarded 1 Oct 1850. SOURCE: WO120 Volume 70 page 303. INDEX # 7451.

Pat^k GRANTIN; pension awarded 1 Oct 1850. SOURCE: WO120 Volume 70 page 303. INDEX # 7452.

Gladwin GEALE; pension awarded 1 Oct 1850. SOURCE: WO120 Volume 70 page 303. INDEX # 7453.

Jno HARRISON; pension awarded 1 Oct 1850. SOURCE: WO120 Volume 70 page 303. INDEX # 7454.

Chas HEWER; pension awarded 1 Oct 1850; died 6 Feb 1856. SOURCE: WO120 Volume 70 page 303. INDEX # 7455.

Royal Canadian Rifle Regiment (continued)

Ja^s HILL; pension awarded 1 Oct 1850; residence - Toronto, Ontario, Canada; died 8 Dec 1877. SOURCE: WO120 Volume 70 page 303. INDEX # 7456.

Jno HOLMES; pension awarded 1 Oct 1850. SOURCE: WO120 Volume 70 page 303. INDEX # 7457.

Jno HOYLE; pension awarded 1 Oct 1850. SOURCE: WO120 Volume 70 page 303. INDEX # 7458.

Thos HULBERT; pension awarded 1 Oct 1850; residence - Toronto, Ontario, Canada; died 2 Dec 1861. SOURCE: WO120 Volume 70 page 303. INDEX # 7459.

Jno HURST; pension awarded 1 Oct 1850; died 4 Apr 1862, Toronto, Ontario, Canada. SOURCE: WO120 Volume 70 page 303. INDEX # 7460.

Chas JONES; pension awarded 1 Oct 1850. SOURCE: WO120 Volume 70 page 303. INDEX # 7461.

Hen^y LANGLEY; pension awarded 1 Oct 1850. SOURCE: WO120 Volume 70 page 303. INDEX # 7462.

Mich^l LAWLESS; pension awarded 1 Oct 1850. SOURCE: WO120 Volume 70 page 303. INDEX # 7463.

Ja^s LAWRENCE; pension awarded 1 Oct 1850. SOURCE: WO120 Volume 70 page 303. INDEX # 7464.

Thos LEONARD; pension awarded 1 Oct 1850; died 9 Mar 1883. SOURCE: WO120 Volume 70 page 303. INDEX # 7465.

And^w LIGHTBODY; pension awarded 1 Oct 1850; died 2 Mar 1859. SOURCE: WO120 Volume 70 page 303. INDEX # 7466.

Jno LIVERMORE; pension awarded 1 Oct 1850. SOURCE: WO120 Volume 70 page 304. INDEX # 7467.

Ja^s LOCKHART; pension awarded 1 Oct 1850; died 23 Jan 1884, Toronto, Ontario, Canada. SOURCE: WO120 Volume 70 page 304. INDEX # 7468.

Geo^e LOFTUS; pension awarded 1 Oct 1850. SOURCE: WO120 Volume 70 page 304. INDEX # 7469.

Wm LOGUE; pension awarded 1 Oct 1850. SOURCE: WO120 Volume 70 page 304. INDEX # 7470.

Jno LOWRY; pension awarded 1 Oct 1850; residence Prescott, Ontario, Canada; died 11 Apr 1852. SOURCE: WO120 Volume 70 page 304. INDEX # 7471.

Mich^l LYNCH; pension awarded 1 Oct 1850; residence - Toronto, Ontario, Canada; died 20 Jul 1854. SOURCE: WO120 Volume 70 page 304. INDEX # 7472.

Mich^l LYONS; pension awarded 1 Oct 1850; residence - Amherstburg, Ontario, Canada; died 15 Oct 1857. SOURCE: WO120 Volume 70 page 304. INDEX # 7473.

Jno MCCRAYE; pension awarded 1 Oct 1850; residence - Niagara, Ontario, Canada; died 26 Apr 1859. SOURCE: WO120 Volume 70 page 304. INDEX # 7474.

Chas MCDONNELL; pension awarded 1 Oct 1850. SOURCE: WO120 Volume 70 page 304. INDEX # 7475.

Ja^s MCDOWAL; pension awarded 1 Oct 1850. SOURCE: WO120 Volume 70 page 304. INDEX # 7476.

Jno MCDOWALL; pension awarded 1 Oct 1850; residence - Amherstburg, Ontario, Canada. SOURCE: WO120 Volume 70 page 304. INDEX # 7477.

Pat^k MCELLIGOT; pension awarded 1 Oct 1850; residence - London, Ontario, Canada; died 12 Oct 1868. SOURCE: WO120 Volume 70 page 304. INDEX # 7478.

Ja^s MCGUIRE; pension awarded 1 Oct 1850; residence - Toronto, Ontario, Canada; died 17 Apr 1866. SOURCE: WO120 Volume 70 page 304. INDEX # 7479.

Jno MCHUGH; pension awarded 1 Oct 1850. SOURCE: WO120 Volume 70 page 304. INDEX # 7480.

Don^d MCKAY; pension awarded 1 Oct 1850; residence - Toronto, Ontario, Canada; died 19 Jul 1853. SOURCE: WO120 Volume 70 page 304. INDEX # 7481.

Ja^s MCKEOWN; pension awarded 1 Oct 1850; died 19 Sep 1882, Halifax, Nova Scotia, Canada. SOURCE: WO120 Volume 70 page 304. INDEX # 7482.

Phillip MCKERNON; pension awarded 1 Oct 1850; residence - London, Ontario, Canada; died 23 Aug 1870. SOURCE: WO120 Volume 70 page 304. INDEX # 7483.

Jno MCLEAN; pension awarded 1 Oct 1850; died 10 Dec 1864, Glasgow. SOURCE: WO120 Volume 70 page 304. INDEX # 7484.

Wm METCALF; pension awarded 1 Oct 1850. SOURCE: WO120 Volume 70 page 304. INDEX # 7485.

Mich^l MOORE; pension awarded 1 Oct 1850. SOURCE: WO120 Volume 70 page 304. INDEX # 7486.

Matt^w MULLIGAN; pension awarded 1 Oct 1850; residence - Toronto, Ontario, Canada; died 9 Jan 1853. SOURCE: WO120 Volume 70 page 305. INDEX # 7487.

Jno MURRAY; pension awarded 1 Oct 1850. SOURCE: WO120 Volume 70 page 305. INDEX # 7488.

Geo^e NAGLE; pension awarded 1 Oct 1850; died 12 Jan 1867. SOURCE: WO120 Volume 70 page 305. INDEX # 7489.

Royal Canadian Rifle Regiment (continued)

Laur^e NEVILLE; pension awarded 1 Oct 1850; residence - Bytown, Ontario, Canada; died 20 Jul 1856. SOURCE: WO120 Volume 70 page 305. INDEX # 7490.

Jno NIXON; pension awarded 1 Oct 1850; residence - Kingston, Ontario, Canada; died in Apr 1852. SOURCE: WO120 Volume 70 page 305. INDEX # 7491.

Jno NIXON; pension awarded 1 Oct 1850; residence - Hamilton, Ontario, Canada; died 13 Oct 1876. SOURCE: WO120 Volume 70 page 305. INDEX # 7492.

Richd NORMAN; pension awarded 1 Oct 1850; residence - Niagara, Ontario, Canada; died 16 Apr 1853. SOURCE: WO120 Volume 70 page 305. INDEX # 7493.

Jno OCONNOR; pension awarded 1 Oct 1850; residence - Kingston, Ontario, Canada; died 4 Dec 1853. SOURCE: WO120 Volume 70 page 305. INDEX # 7494.

Tim^y OLEARY; pension awarded 1 Oct 1850. SOURCE: WO120 Volume 70 page 305. INDEX # 7495.

Gordon ONEILL; pension awarded 1 Oct 1850. SOURCE: WO120 Volume 70 page 305. INDEX # 7496.

Thos OWENS; pension awarded 1 Oct 1850; residence - Amherstburg, Ontario, Canada; died 20 Apr 1856. SOURCE: WO120 Volume 70 page 305. INDEX # 7497.

Wm PARKER; pension awarded 1 Oct 1850. SOURCE: WO120 Volume 70 page 305. INDEX # 7498.

Thos PEACOCK; pension awarded 1 Oct 1850; residence - Toronto, Ontario, Canada; died 18 May 1866. SOURCE: WO120 Volume 70 page 305. INDEX # 7499.

Wm PEAKE; pension awarded 1 Oct 1850; residence - Kingston, Ontario, Canada; died 27 Jan 1856. SOURCE: WO120 Volume 70 page 305. INDEX # 7500.

Robt PETER; pension awarded 1 Oct 1850. SOURCE: WO120 Volume 70 page 305. INDEX # 7501.

Ja^s POCOCK; pension awarded 1 Oct 1850; residence - Toronto, Ontario, Canada; died 25 Apr 1878. SOURCE: WO120 Volume 70 page 305. INDEX # 7502.

Jno PUGH; pension awarded 1 Oct 1850; died 29 May 1872, London, Ontario, Canada. SOURCE: WO120 Volume 70 page 305. INDEX # 7503.

Chas QUINN; pension awarded 1 Oct 1850. SOURCE: WO120 Volume 70 page 305. INDEX # 7504.

Hugh QUINN; pension awarded 1 Oct 1850. SOURCE: WO120 Volume 70 page 305. INDEX # 7505.

Mich^l READY; pension awarded 1 Oct 1850; residence - Amherstburg, Ontario, Canada; died 27 Apr 1852. SOURCE: WO120 Volume 70 page 305. INDEX # 7506.

Jno RENDELL; pension awarded 1 Oct 1850; died 2 Jul 1884, Toronto, Ontario, Canada. SOURCE: WO120 Volume 70 page 306. INDEX # 7507.

Wm RIDER; pension awarded 1 Oct 1850. SOURCE: WO120 Volume 70 page 306. INDEX # 7508.

Saml ROPER; pension awarded 1 Oct 1850. SOURCE: WO120 Volume 70 page 306. INDEX # 7509.

Geo^e RUTHERFORD; pension awarded 1 Oct 1850. SOURCE: WO120 Volume 70 page 306. INDEX # 7510.

Jno RYAN; pension awarded 1 Oct 1850; died 28 Oct 1863, London, Ontario, Canada. SOURCE: WO120 Volume 70 page 306. INDEX # 7511.

Thos SAMSON; pension awarded 1 Oct 1850. SOURCE: WO120 Volume 70 page 306. INDEX # 7512.

Wm SAUNDERS; pension awarded 1 Oct 1850; residence - Kingston, Ontario, Canada; died 9 Oct 1855. SOURCE: WO120 Volume 70 page 306. INDEX # 7513.

Fra^s SLAIN; pension awarded 1 Oct 1850; residence - Kingston, Ontario, Canada. SOURCE: WO120 Volume 70 page 306. INDEX # 7514.

Jno SHELTON; pension awarded 1 Oct 1850. SOURCE: WO120 Volume 70 page 306. INDEX # 7515.

Thos SPELLMAN; pension awarded 1 Oct 1850. SOURCE: WO120 Volume 70 page 306. INDEX # 7516.

Jno SMILLIE; pension awarded 1 Oct 1850; died 1 Oct 1872, Toronto, Ontario, Canada. SOURCE: WO120 Volume 70 page 306. INDEX # 7517.

Jno STOW; pension awarded 1 Oct 1850; died 27 Apr 1873, Toronto, Ontario, Canada. SOURCE: WO120 Volume 70 page 306. INDEX # 7518.

Ja^s SULLIVAN; pension awarded 1 Oct 1850. SOURCE: WO120 Volume 70 page 306. INDEX # 7519.

Jno SUTHERLAND; pension awarded 1 Oct 1850; residence - Toronto, Ontario, Canada; died 25 Jul 1854. SOURCE: WO120 Volume 70 page 306. INDEX # 7520.

Jno SUTTON; pension awarded 1 Oct 1850; died in Apr 1877, Leicester. SOURCE: WO120 Volume 70 page 306. INDEX # 7521.

BRITISH ARMY PENSIONERS ABROAD

Royal Canadian Rifle Regiment (continued)

Wm TAYLOR; pension awarded 1 Oct 1850; residence - Kingston, Ontario, Canada; died 24 Mar 1853. SOURCE: WO120 Volume 70 page 306. INDEX # 7522.

Jere^h TRACEY; pension awarded 1 Oct 1850; residence - Kingston, Ontario, Canada; died 5 Jul 1859. SOURCE: WO120 Volume 70 page 306. INDEX # 7523.

Wm TURNEY; pension awarded 1 Oct 1850; residence - Toronto, Ontario, Canada; died 24 Jul 1854. SOURCE: WO120 Volume 70 page 306. INDEX # 7524.

Hen^y VENNALION; pension awarded 1 Oct 1850. SOURCE: WO120 Volume 70 page 306. INDEX # 7525.

Jno WALSH; pension awarded 1 Oct 1850. SOURCE: WO120 Volume 70 page 306. INDEX # 7526.

Mich^l WATERS; pension awarded 1 Oct 1850; residence - Toronto, Ontario, Canada; died in 1854. SOURCE: WO120 Volume 70 page 307. INDEX # 7527.

Richd WILKINS; pension awarded 1 Oct 1850. SOURCE: WO120 Volume 70 page 307. INDEX # 7528.

Walter WINNING; pension awarded 1 Oct 1850; died 12 May 1874, London, Ontario, Canada. SOURCE: WO120 Volume 70 page 307. INDEX # 7529.

Hugh WISHART; pension awarded 1 Oct 1850. SOURCE: WO120 Volume 70 page 307. INDEX # 7530.

Ja^s WHOLOHAN; pension awarded 1 Oct 1850; died 13 Apr 1851. SOURCE: WO120 Volume 70 page 307. INDEX # 7531.

David WHITE; pension awarded 1 Oct 1850; residence - Bytown, Ontario, Canada; died in 1853. SOURCE: WO120 Volume 70 page 307. INDEX # 7532.

Fra^s BONNER; pension awarded 1 Oct 1850; died 27 Nov 1868, Exeter. SOURCE: WO120 Volume 70 page 307. INDEX # 7533.

Chas CHAPMAN; pension awarded 1 Oct 1850; residence - Kingston, Ontario, Canada; died 26 Aug 1853. SOURCE: WO120 Volume 70 page 307. INDEX # 7534.

Wm SATCHWELL; pension awarded 1 Oct 1850; residence - Bytown, Ontario, Canada; died 24 Jun 1857. SOURCE: WO120 Volume 70 page 307. INDEX # 7535.

Geo^e STEWART; pension awarded 1 Oct 1850; residence - Niagara, Ontario, Canada; died in 1854. SOURCE: WO120 Volume 70 page 307. INDEX # 7536.

Wm RUSSOM; pension awarded 1 Jul 1851. SOURCE: WO120 Volume 70 page 307. INDEX # 7537.

Jno MEEK; pension awarded 1 Jul 1851. SOURCE: WO120 Volume 70 page 307. INDEX # 7538.

Shadrack CRISP; pension awarded 1 Jul 1851; died 6 Sep 1880, Hamilton, Ontario, Canada. SOURCE: WO120 Volume 70 page 307. INDEX # 7539.

Jno WANDLESS; pension awarded 1 Jul 1851; residence - Toronto, Ontario, Canada; died 3 Oct 1867. SOURCE: WO120 Volume 70 page 307. INDEX # 7540.

John BOHAN; pension awarded 1 Jul 1851; residence - Hamilton, Ontario, Canada; died 9 Mar 1878. SOURCE: WO120 Volume 70 page 307. INDEX # 7541.

Mich^l CARROLL; pension awarded 1 Jul 1851; residence - London, Ontario, Canada; died 7 Jan 1868. SOURCE: WO120 Volume 70 page 307. INDEX # 7542.

Morgan FLAHERTY; pension awarded 1 Jul 1851. SOURCE: WO120 Volume 70 page 307. INDEX # 7543.

Jno GILL; pension awarded 1 Jul 1851; died 26 Jul 1883, Toronto, Ontario, Canada. SOURCE: WO120 Volume 70 page 307. INDEX # 7544.

Jno GOODWIN; pension awarded 1 Jul 1851. SOURCE: WO120 Volume 70 page 307. INDEX # 7545.

J. MCKENZIE; pension awarded 1 Jul 1851. SOURCE: WO120 Volume 70 page 307. INDEX # 7546.

Thos SHARP; pension awarded 1 Jul 1851; died 15 Apr 1866, London, Ontario, Canada. SOURCE: WO120 Volume 70 page 308. INDEX # 7547.

Thos Haar WATTS; pension awarded 1 Jul 1851. SOURCE: WO120 Volume 70 page 308. INDEX # 7548.

Wm AERES; pension awarded 1 Jul 1851. SOURCE: WO120 Volume 70 page 307. INDEX # 7549.

Wm AUSTIN; pension awarded 1 Jul 1851; residence - Amherstburg, Ontario, Canada; died 25 Sep 1851. SOURCE: WO120 Volume 70 page 308. INDEX # 7550.

Alex^r BLACK; pension awarded 1 Jul 1851; residence - London, Ontario, Canada; died 12 Jun 1876. SOURCE: WO120 Volume 70 page 308. INDEX # 7551.

Richd BRACKEN; pension awarded 1 Jul 1851. SOURCE: WO120 Volume 70 page 308. INDEX # 7552.

Jno BOOTH; pension awarded 1 Jul 1851; residence - London, Ontario, Canada; died 3 Mar 1877. SOURCE: WO120 Volume 70 page 308. INDEX # 7553.

WO120 VOLUME 70

Royal Canadian Rifle Regiment (continued)

Robt BOYTON; pension awarded 1 Jul 1851; died 12 May 1883. SOURCE: WO120 Volume 70 page 308. INDEX # 7554.

Corn^s BURNS; pension awarded 1 Jul 1851. SOURCE: WO120 Volume 70 page 308. INDEX # 7555.

Thos BUTTERWORTH; pension awarded 1 Jul 1851. SOURCE: WO120 Volume 70 page 308. INDEX # 7556.

Thos CALLAGHAN; pension awarded 1 Jul 1851; residence - Niagara, Ontario, Canada; died 22 May 1854. SOURCE: WO120 Volume 70 page 308. INDEX # 7557.

Geo^e CAMPBELL; pension awarded 1 Jul 1851; died 25 Jan 1879. SOURCE: WO120 Volume 70 page 308. INDEX # 7558.

Thos CODY; pension awarded 1 Jul 1851; residence - Niagara, Ontario, Canada; died 1 Jun 1854. SOURCE: WO120 Volume 70 page 308. INDEX # 7559.

Ja^s COWEN; pension awarded 1 Jul 1851; residence - Niagara, Ontario, Canada; died 11 Dec 1854. SOURCE: WO120 Volume 70 page 308. INDEX # 7560.

Jno DEVERALL; pension awarded 1 Jul 1851. SOURCE: WO120 Volume 70 page 308. INDEX # 7561.

Edwd DONNELLY; pension awarded 1 Jul 1851; residence - Kingston, Ontario, Canada; died in 1854. SOURCE: WO120 Volume 70 page 308. INDEX # 7562.

Richd EDWARDS; pension awarded 1 Jul 1851; residence - Windsor, Ontario, Canada; died 5 Apr 1852. SOURCE: WO120 Volume 70 page 308. INDEX # 7563.

Wm HACKER; pension awarded 1 Jul 1851. SOURCE: WO120 Volume 70 page 308. INDEX # 7564.

Thos HARRIS; pension awarded 1 Jul 1851. SOURCE: WO120 Volume 70 page 308. INDEX # 7565.

Robt HEREMAN; pension awarded 1 Jul 1851; residence - Amherstburg, Ontario, Canada. SOURCE: WO120 Volume 70 page 308. INDEX # 7566.

Hen^y HINDLE; pension awarded 1 Jul 1851; residence - Hamilton, Ontario, Canada; died 17 Feb 1875. SOURCE: WO120 Volume 70 page 309. INDEX # 7567.

Jno HUTTON; pension awarded 1 Jul 1851. SOURCE: WO120 Volume 70 page 309. INDEX # 7568.

Richd JONES; pension awarded 1 Jul 1851; died 11 Jan 1857, London, Ontario, Canada. SOURCE: WO120 Volume 70 page 309. INDEX # 7569.

Danl JONES; pension awarded 1 Jul 1851; residence - London, Ontario, Canada; died 9 Jan 1871. SOURCE: WO120 Volume 70 page 309. INDEX # 7570.

Peter KILRAIN; pension awarded 1 Jul 1851. SOURCE: WO120 Volume 70 page 309. INDEX # 7571.

Edwd LACAN; pension awarded 1 Jul 1851; died 12 Jul 1857, Penetanguishene, Ontario, Canada. SOURCE: WO120 Volume 70 page 309. INDEX # 7572.

Chas LEONARD; pension awarded 1 Jul 1851; died 29 Jan 1872, Toronto, Ontario, Canada. SOURCE: WO120 Volume 70 page 309. INDEX # 7573.

Jno LOVE; pension awarded 1 Jul 1851. SOURCE: WO120 Volume 70 page 309. INDEX # 7574.

Constantine MCCAFFERY; pension awarded 1 Jul 1851; residence - Niagara, Ontario, Canada; died in Jan 1852. SOURCE: WO120 Volume 70 page 309. INDEX # 7575.

Wm MCGOWAN; pension awarded 1 Jul 1851. SOURCE: WO120 Volume 70 page 309. INDEX # 7576.

Pat^k OBRIEN; pension awarded 1 Jul 1851; died 28 Feb 1874, Hamilton, Ontario, Canada. SOURCE: WO120 Volume 70 page 309. INDEX # 7577.

Jno OHALLORAN; pension awarded 1 Jul 1851. SOURCE: WO120 Volume 70 page 309. INDEX # 7578.

Ja^s PUCKSLEY; pension awarded 1 Jul 1851; died 31 Jan 1881, Warley. SOURCE: WO120 Volume 70 page 309. INDEX # 7579.

Wm ROBINSON; pension awarded 1 Jul 1851; died 23 Jun 1884, Toronto, Ontario, Canada. SOURCE: WO120 Volume 70 page 309. INDEX # 7580.

Jno ROWAN; pension awarded 1 Jul 1851. SOURCE: WO120 Volume 70 page 309. INDEX # 7581.

Thos TOMLINSON; pension awarded 1 Jul 1851; residence - London, Ontario, Canada; died 26 Feb 1863. SOURCE: WO120 Volume 70 page 309. INDEX # 7582.

Ja^s WHITEFORD; pension awarded 1 Jul 1851; residence - Hamilton, Ontario, Canada; died 3 Jul 1860. SOURCE: WO120 Volume 70 page 309. INDEX # 7583.

And^w COYLE; pension awarded 8 Jul 1851; residence - London, Ontario, Canada; died 25 Jun 1877. SOURCE: WO120 Volume 70 page 309. INDEX # 7584.

Jos^h RAYMOND; pension awarded 22 Jul 1851; residence - Toronto, Ontario, Canada; died 20 Sep 1878. SOURCE: WO120 Volume 70 page 309. INDEX # 7585.

BRITISH ARMY PENSIONERS ABROAD

Royal Canadian Rifle Regiment (continued)

Pat^k WELSH; pension awarded 22 Jul 1851; died 30 Jun 1876, Toronto, Ontario, Canada. SOURCE: WO120 Volume 70 page 309. INDEX # 7586.

Geo^e BOOTH; pension awarded 22 Jul 1851; died 10 Mar 1879, Toronto, Ontario, Canada. SOURCE: WO120 Volume 70 page 310. INDEX # 7587.

Ja^s RAWLING; pension awarded 22 Jul 1851; residence - Canada; died in 1852. SOURCE: WO120 Volume 70 page 310. INDEX # 7588.

Matt^w SHEERAN; pension awarded 22 Jul 1851. SOURCE: WO120 Volume 70 page 310. INDEX # 7589.

Luke WOODS; pension awarded 22 Jul 1851; residence - Toronto, Ontario, Canada; died 27 Jun 1877, Toronto, Ontario, Canada. SOURCE: WO120 Volume 70 page 310. INDEX # 7590.

Thos BAILEY; pension awarded 22 Jul 1851; died 13 Nov 1872, London, Ontario, Canada. SOURCE: WO120 Volume 70 page 310. INDEX # 7591.

Wm ESDON; pension awarded 22 Jul 1851. SOURCE: WO120 Volume 70 page 310. INDEX # 7592.

Jno HANDCOCK; pension awarded 22 Jul 1851. SOURCE: WO120 Volume 70 page 310. INDEX # 7593.

Ja^s JOHNSTON; pension awarded 5 Aug 1851. SOURCE: WO120 Volume 70 page 310. INDEX # 7594.

Benjn STANDER; pension awarded 5 Aug 1851. SOURCE: WO120 Volume 70 page 310. INDEX # 7595.

Robt STEWART; pension awarded 5 Aug 1851; died 26 Jan 1882, Bristol. SOURCE: WO120 Volume 70 page 310. INDEX # 7596.

Ja^s DOIG; pension awarded 5 Aug 1851; residence - Hamilton, Ontario, Canada; died 14 Oct 1871. SOURCE: WO120 Volume 70 page 310. INDEX # 7597.

David HEATON; pension awarded 5 Aug 1851. SOURCE: WO120 Volume 70 page 310. INDEX # 7598.

Geo^e ABBOTTS; pension awarded 5 Aug 1851. SOURCE: WO120 Volume 70 page 310. INDEX # 7599.

Ja^s ALLWRIGHT; pension awarded 5 Aug 1851. SOURCE: WO120 Volume 70 page 310. INDEX # 7600.

Jno BEAZLEY; pension awarded 5 Aug 1851; residence - Niagara, Ontario, Canada; died 17 Apr 1853. SOURCE: WO120 Volume 70 page 310. INDEX # 7601.

Chas BEST; pension awarded 5 Aug 1851. SOURCE: WO120 Volume 70 page 310. INDEX # 7602.

Thos BRENNAN; pension awarded 5 Aug 1851; died 2 Oct 1881, Hamilton, Ontario, Canada. SOURCE: WO120 Volume 70 page 310. INDEX # 7603.

Jno BUCKLEY; pension awarded 5 Aug 1851. SOURCE: WO120 Volume 70 page 310. INDEX # 7604.

Pat^k CROWE; pension awarded 5 Aug 1851; residence - Amherstburg, Ontario, Canada. SOURCE: WO120 Volume 70 page 310. INDEX # 7605.

Matt^w CUFF; pension awarded 5 Aug 1851; died 26 Jan 1884, Montreal, Quebec, Canada. SOURCE: WO120 Volume 70 page 310. INDEX # 7606.

Jno DAVIS; pension awarded 5 Aug 1851. SOURCE: WO120 Volume 70 page 311. INDEX # 7607.

Morris DESMOND; pension awarded 5 Aug 1851. SOURCE: WO120 Volume 70 page 311. INDEX # 7608.

Denis DELANEY; pension awarded 5 Aug 1851. SOURCE: WO120 Volume 70 page 311. INDEX # 7609.

Jno DORAN; pension awarded 5 Aug 1851. SOURCE: WO120 Volume 70 page 311. INDEX # 7610.

Wm ELLISON; pension awarded 5 Aug 1851; residence - Ottawa, Ontario, Canada; died 27 Aug 1854. SOURCE: WO120 Volume 70 page 311. INDEX # 7611.

Danl FARRELL; pension awarded 5 Aug 1851. SOURCE: WO120 Volume 70 page 311. INDEX # 7612.

Jno FISH; pension awarded 5 Aug 1851; died 18 Dec 1880, Ottawa, Ontario, Canada. SOURCE: WO120 Volume 70 page 311. INDEX # 7613.

Pat^k FITZGERALD; pension awarded 5 Aug 1851. SOURCE: WO120 Volume 70 page 311. INDEX # 7614.

Jno GILLERAN; pension awarded 5 Aug 1851. SOURCE: WO120 Volume 70 page 311. INDEX # 7615.

Robt GORDON; pension awarded 5 Aug 1851; residence - Niagara, Ontario, Canada; died 22 Jun 1856. SOURCE: WO120 Volume 70 page 311. INDEX # 7616.

Pat^k HIGGINS; pension awarded 5 Aug 1851. SOURCE: WO120 Volume 70 page 311. INDEX # 7617.

Jno HOBLEY; pension awarded 5 Aug 1851. SOURCE: WO120 Volume 70 page 311. INDEX # 7618.

Wm ISAACS; pension awarded 5 Aug 1851; residence - Kingston, Ontario, Canada; died 24 Nov 1853. SOURCE: WO120 Volume 70 page 311. INDEX # 7619.

Wm JENKINS; pension awarded 5 Aug 1851. SOURCE: WO120 Volume 70 page 311. INDEX # 7620.

Wm JOHNSTON; pension awarded 5 Aug 1851. SOURCE: WO120 Volume 70 page 311. INDEX # 7621.

Pat^k HANAHAN; pension awarded 5 Aug 1851. SOURCE: WO120 Volume 70 page 311. INDEX # 7622.

WO120 VOLUME 70

Royal Canadian Rifle Regiment (continued)

Thos KELLY; pension awarded 5 Aug 1851; residence - Hamilton, Ontario, Canada; died 18 Jun 1867. SOURCE: WO120 Volume 70 page 311. INDEX # 7623.
Jas LANE; pension awarded 5 Aug 1851. SOURCE: WO120 Volume 70 page 311. INDEX # 7624.
Jas LEE; pension awarded 5 Aug 1851; residence - Hamilton, Ontario, Canada; died 5 Dec 1868. SOURCE: WO120 Volume 70 page 311. INDEX # 7625.
Wm LONGLEY; pension awarded 5 Aug 1851; residence - Windsor, Ontario, Canada; died 19 Aug 1852. SOURCE: WO120 Volume 70 page 311. INDEX # 7626.
Jas MCCONAGHY; pension awarded 5 Aug 1851. SOURCE: WO120 Volume 70 page 312. INDEX # 7627.
Alexr MCDOOLE; pension awarded 5 Aug 1851. SOURCE: WO120 Volume 70 page 312. INDEX # 7628.
Patk MCGUIRE; pension awarded 5 Aug 1851; died 26 Jul 1880, Hamilton, Ontario, Canada. SOURCE: WO120 Volume 70 page 312. INDEX # 7629.
Jas MCGUIRE; pension awarded 5 Aug 1851; died 30 May 1877, Toronto, Ontario, Canada. SOURCE: WO120 Volume 70 page 312. INDEX # 7630.
Bernd MCGOWAN; pension awarded 5 Aug 1851; residence - Bytown, Ontario, Canada; died 26 May 1858. SOURCE: WO120 Volume 70 page 312. INDEX # 7631.
Wm MCGREGOR; pension awarded 5 Aug 1851. SOURCE: WO120 Volume 70 page 312. INDEX # 7632.
Roger MCSTRAVICK; pension awarded 5 Aug 1851. SOURCE: WO120 Volume 70 page 312. INDEX # 7633.
Jas MCNEELY; pension awarded 5 Aug 1851. SOURCE: WO120 Volume 70 page 312. INDEX # 7634.
Jas MALLYON; pension awarded 5 Aug 1851; residence - Niagara, Ontario, Canada; died 21 Nov 1856. SOURCE: WO120 Volume 70 page 312. INDEX # 7635.
Jas MERNA; pension awarded 5 Aug 1851. SOURCE: WO120 Volume 70 page 312. INDEX # 7636.
Benjn PARKINSON; pension awarded 5 Aug 1851. SOURCE: WO120 Volume 70 page 312. INDEX # 7637.
Jno Henson RIDDLE; pension awarded 5 Aug 1851. SOURCE: WO120 Volume 70 page 312. INDEX # 7638.
Wm RYAN; pension awarded 5 Aug 1851; residence - Amherstburg, Ontario, Canada; died 2 Oct 1851. SOURCE: WO120 Volume 70 page 312. INDEX # 7639.
Jno STEPHENS; pension awarded 5 Aug 1851; residence - Amherstburg, Ontario, Canada; died 26 Nov 1853. SOURCE: WO120 Volume 70 page 312. INDEX # 7640.
Saml STEWART; pension awarded 5 Aug 1851; residence - Amherstburg, Ontario, Canada; died 16 Sep 1855. SOURCE: WO120 Volume 70 page 312. INDEX # 7641.
Thos SHORT; pension awarded 5 Aug 1851. SOURCE: WO120 Volume 70 page 312. INDEX # 7642.
Wm VIGGERSTAFF; pension awarded 5 Aug 1851; residence - Amherstburg, Ontario, Canada; died 6 May 1856. SOURCE: WO120 Volume 70 page 312. INDEX # 7643.
Garret WELSH; pension awarded 5 Aug 1851; died 25 May 1874. SOURCE: WO120 Volume 70 page 312. INDEX # 7644.
Patk WISELEY; pension awarded 5 Aug 1851; residence - Bytown, Ontario, Canada. SOURCE: WO120 Volume 70 page 312. INDEX # 7645.
Wm WHITELY; pension awarded 5 Aug 1851; died 27 Apr 1859, London, Ontario, Canada. SOURCE: WO120 Volume 70 page 312. INDEX # 7646.
Jas BAILEY; pension awarded 12 Aug 1851. SOURCE: WO120 Volume 70 page 313. INDEX # 7647.
Jas COLLINS; pension awarded 12 Aug 1851. SOURCE: WO120 Volume 70 page 313. INDEX # 7648.
Jas DAINES; pension awarded 12 Aug 1851; died 14 Oct 1862, Hamilton, Ontario, Canada. SOURCE: WO120 Volume 70 page 313. INDEX # 7649.
Philip MCGINNIS; pension awarded 12 Aug 1851. SOURCE: WO120 Volume 70 page 313. INDEX # 7650.
Ezra SHELDRICK; pension awarded 12 Aug 1851. SOURCE: WO120 Volume 70 page 313. INDEX # 7651.
Thos CANTILLON; pension awarded 12 Aug 1851. SOURCE: WO120 Volume 70 page 313. INDEX # 7652.
Martin LYONS; pension awarded 12 Aug 1851. SOURCE: WO120 Volume 70 page 313. INDEX # 7653.
Saml MEPHAN; pension awarded 12 Aug 1851. SOURCE: WO120 Volume 70 page 313. INDEX # 7654.
Jno SPENCER; pension awarded 12 Aug 1851. SOURCE: WO120 Volume 70 page 313. INDEX # 7655.
Josh FLINT; pension awarded 12 Aug 1851; died 6 Feb 1883, Toronto, Ontario, Canada. SOURCE: WO120 Volume 70 page 313. INDEX # 7656.
Geoe HOWES; pension awarded 12 Aug 1851. SOURCE: WO120 Volume 70 page 313. INDEX # 7657.

BRITISH ARMY PENSIONERS ABROAD

Royal Canadian Rifle Regiment (continued)

Hen^y ADAMS; pension awarded 12 Aug 1851; died 30 Apr 1872, Toronto, Ontario, Canada. SOURCE: WO120 Volume 70 page 313. INDEX # 7658.

Wm ALLEN; pension awarded 12 Aug 1851; residence - Niagara, Ontario, Canada; died 4 Oct 1854. SOURCE: WO120 Volume 70 page 313. INDEX # 7659.

Richd ARMSTRONG; pension awarded 12 Aug 1851; residence - Kingston, Ontario, Canada; died 8 Sep 1852. SOURCE: WO120 Volume 70 page 313. INDEX # 7660.

Thos AUGHEY; pension awarded 12 Aug 1851; residence - London, Ontario, Canada; died 9 Mar 1853. SOURCE: WO120 Volume 70 page 313. INDEX # 7661.

Robt BLAKEMORE; pension awarded 12 Aug 1851. SOURCE: WO120 Volume 70 page 313. INDEX # 7662.

Wm BAKER; pension awarded 12 Aug 1851. SOURCE: WO120 Volume 70 page 313. INDEX # 7663.

Thos BLACK; pension awarded 12 Aug 1851; died 25 Oct 1873, Toronto, Ontario, Canada. SOURCE: WO120 Volume 70 page 313. INDEX # 7664.

Richd BLACK; pension awarded 12 Aug 1851; died 2 Nov 1874, Toronto, Ontario, Canada. SOURCE: WO120 Volume 70 page 313. INDEX # 7665.

Wm BRADY; pension awarded 12 Aug 1851; residence - Toronto, Ontario, Canada; died 4 Aug 1854. SOURCE: WO120 Volume 70 page 313. INDEX # 7666.

Jno BRADY; pension awarded 12 Aug 1851. SOURCE: WO120 Volume 70 page 314. INDEX # 7667.

Jno BROWNSETT; pension awarded 12 Aug 1851; residence - Montreal, Quebec; died 27 Sep 1858. SOURCE: WO120 Volume 70 page 314. INDEX # 7668.

Jno BURKE; pension awarded 12 Aug 1851; died 12 Mar 1877, London, Ontario, Canada. SOURCE: WO120 Volume 70 page 314. INDEX # 7669.

Jno CUSICK; pension awarded 12 Aug 1851. SOURCE: WO120 Volume 70 page 314. INDEX # 7670.

David COWHIG; pension awarded 12 Aug 1851; died 10 Oct 1878, Cork. SOURCE: WO120 Volume 70 page 314. INDEX # 7671.

Ber^d CARROLL; pension awarded 12 Aug 1851. SOURCE: WO120 Volume 70 page 314. INDEX # 7672.

Edwd CONNERS; pension awarded 12 Aug 1851; died 24 Apr 1859, Toronto, Ontario, Canada. SOURCE: WO120 Volume 70 page 314. INDEX # 7673.

Geo^e CROSS; pension awarded 12 Aug 1851; residence - Kingston, Ontario, Canada; died 10 Apr 1854. SOURCE: WO120 Volume 70 page 314. INDEX # 7674.

Jno CROWLEY; pension awarded 12 Aug 1851; residence - London, Ontario, Canada; died 7 Jul 1865. SOURCE: WO120 Volume 70 page 314. INDEX # 7675.

Tim^y DAY; pension awarded 12 Aug 1851. SOURCE: WO120 Volume 70 page 314. INDEX # 7676.

Ja^s DAVIDSON; pension awarded 12 Aug 1851. SOURCE: WO120 Volume 70 page 314. INDEX # 7677.

Mich^l DONOGHUE; pension awarded 12 Aug 1851. SOURCE: WO120 Volume 70 page 314. INDEX # 7678.

Wm EASSON; pension awarded 12 Aug 1851. SOURCE: WO120 Volume 70 page 314. INDEX # 7679.

Maurice ELLIS; pension awarded 12 Aug 1851; residence - Hamilton, Ontario, Canada; died 12 Oct 1869. SOURCE: WO120 Volume 70 page 314. INDEX # 7680.

Nich^s EGAN; pension awarded 12 Aug 1851. SOURCE: WO120 Volume 70 page 314. INDEX # 7681.

Saml ENIES; pension awarded 12 Aug 1851; residence - Prescott, Ontario, Canada; died 25 Dec 1852. SOURCE: WO120 Volume 70 page 314. INDEX # 7682.

Wm FINCH; pension awarded 12 Aug 1851; residence - Toronto, Ontario, Canada; died 22 Dec 1857. SOURCE: WO120 Volume 70 page 314. INDEX # 7683.

Hiram FITZGERALD; pension awarded 12 Aug 1851. SOURCE: WO120 Volume 70 page 314. INDEX # 7684.

Jno FOSTER; pension awarded 12 Aug 1851. SOURCE: WO120 Volume 70 page 314. INDEX # 7685.

Jno FRANCIS; pension awarded 12 Aug 1851. SOURCE: WO120 Volume 70 page 314. INDEX # 7686.

Jno GOW; pension awarded 12 Aug 1851; residence - Hamilton, Ontario, Canada; died 16 Nov 1864. SOURCE: WO120 Volume 70 page 315. INDEX # 7687.

Jos^h GAILEY; pension awarded 12 Aug 1851; residence - Toronto, Ontario, Canada; died 8 May 1871. SOURCE: WO120 Volume 70 page 315. INDEX # 7688.

Richd GOUDE; pension awarded 12 Aug 1851; died 6 Feb 1880, Toronto, Ontario, Canada. SOURCE: WO120 Volume 70 page 315. INDEX # 7689.

Martin HUGHES; pension awarded 12 Aug 1851. SOURCE: WO120 Volume 70 page 315. INDEX # 7690.

Royal Canadian Rifle Regiment (continued)

Wm HOWE; pension awarded 12 Aug 1851. SOURCE: WO120 Volume 70 page 315. INDEX # 7691.
Jno HICKSON; pension awarded 12 Aug 1851; died 6 Jun 1881, Toronto, Ontario, Canada. SOURCE: WO120 Volume 70 page 315. INDEX # 7692.
Jno HUFFA; pension awarded 12 Aug 1851. SOURCE: WO120 Volume 70 page 315. INDEX # 7693.
Mich^l KELLY; pension awarded 12 Aug 1851. SOURCE: WO120 Volume 70 page 315. INDEX # 7694.
Elias KELLY; pension awarded 12 Aug 1851; residence - Hamilton, Ontario, Canada; died 5 Aug 1866. SOURCE: WO120 Volume 70 page 315. INDEX # 7695.
Mich^l KENNY; pension awarded 12 Aug 1851. SOURCE: WO120 Volume 70 page 315. INDEX # 7696.
Alex^r MCLENNAN; pension awarded 12 Aug 1851; residence - Niagara, Ontario, Canada; died 16 Jan 1859. SOURCE: WO120 Volume 70 page 315. INDEX # 7697.
Thos LESHFORD; pension awarded 12 Aug 1851; residence - Kingston, Ontario, Canada; died 13 Mar 1858. SOURCE: WO120 Volume 70 page 315. INDEX # 7698.
Ja^s LORIMER; pension awarded 12 Aug 1851. SOURCE: WO120 Volume 70 page 315. INDEX # 7699.
Saml MCCOUBREY; pension awarded 12 Aug 1851; died 14 Aug 1856. SOURCE: WO120 Volume 70 page 315. INDEX # 7700.
Wm MARTIN; pension awarded 12 Aug 1851; residence - Toronto, Ontario, Canada. SOURCE: WO120 Volume 70 page 315. INDEX # 7701.
Jno MILLAR; pension awarded 12 Aug 1851. SOURCE: WO120 Volume 70 page 315. INDEX # 7702.
Thos MOONEY; pension awarded 12 Aug 1851. SOURCE: WO120 Volume 70 page 315. INDEX # 7703.
Jno MURDY; pension awarded 12 Aug 1851; residence - Niagara, Ontario, Canada; died 6 Apr 1855. SOURCE: WO120 Volume 70 page 315. INDEX # 7704.
Jno MURPHY; pension awarded 12 Aug 1851. SOURCE: WO120 Volume 70 page 315. INDEX # 7705.
Ja^s NICHOLDS; pension awarded 12 Aug 1851. SOURCE: WO120 Volume 70 page 315. INDEX # 7706.
Jno NASH; pension awarded 12 Aug 1851; died 10 Jan 1859, Toronto, Ontario, Canada. SOURCE: WO120 Volume 70 page 316. INDEX # 7707.
Alex^r REID; pension awarded 12 Aug 1851; residence - Montreal, Quebec, Canada; died 13 Mar 1854. SOURCE: WO120 Volume 70 page 316. INDEX # 7708.
Thos ROBERTS; pension awarded 12 Aug 1851. SOURCE: WO120 Volume 70 page 316. INDEX # 7709.
Ralph SIMPSON; pension awarded 12 Aug 1851. SOURCE: WO120 Volume 70 page 316. INDEX # 7710.
Geo^e SMITH; pension awarded 12 Aug 1851. SOURCE: WO120 Volume 70 page 316. INDEX # 7711.
Ja^s SHEENAN; pension awarded 12 Aug 1851; residence - Toronto, Ontario, Canada; died 25 Apr 1871. SOURCE: WO120 Volume 70 page 316. INDEX # 7712.
Wm SCOTT; pension awarded 12 Aug 1851. SOURCE: WO120 Volume 70 page 316. INDEX # 7713.
Geo^e STONE; pension awarded 12 Aug 1851. SOURCE: WO120 Volume 70 page 316. INDEX # 7714.
Thos TERRY; pension awarded 12 Aug 1851; died 1 Jan 1881, Toronto, Ontario, Canada. SOURCE: WO120 Volume 70 page 316. INDEX # 7715.
Danl TRAINOR; pension awarded 12 Aug 1851. SOURCE: WO120 Volume 70 page 316. INDEX # 7716.
Thos TAYLOR; pension awarded 12 Aug 1851; died 17 Nov 1881, Toronto, Ontario, Canada. SOURCE: WO120 Volume 70 page 316. INDEX # 7717.
Lee THOMPSON; pension awarded 12 Aug 1851; residence - Toronto, Ontario, Canada; died 12 Aug 1858. SOURCE: WO120 Volume 70 page 316. INDEX # 7718.
Mich^l TYBURN; pension awarded 12 Aug 1851. SOURCE: WO120 Volume 70 page 316. INDEX # 7719.
Ed^{wd} WALKER; pension awarded 12 Aug 1851; residence - Toronto, Ontario, Canada; died 7 Sep 1863. SOURCE: WO120 Volume 70 page 316. INDEX # 7720.
Robt WATERHOUSE; pension awarded 12 Aug 1851. SOURCE: WO120 Volume 70 page 316. INDEX # 7721.
Geo^e WETHERALL; pension awarded 12 Aug 1851. SOURCE: WO120 Volume 70 page 316. INDEX # 7722.
Danl WITTS; pension awarded 12 Aug 1851. SOURCE: WO120 Volume 70 page 316. INDEX # 7723.
Jno WOOD; pension awarded 12 Aug 1851. SOURCE: WO120 Volume 70 page 316. INDEX # 7724.
Ja^s WRIGHT; pension awarded 12 Aug 1851. SOURCE: WO120 Volume 70 page 316. INDEX # 7725.
Pat^k PHELAN; pension awarded 12 Jan 1852. SOURCE: WO120 Volume 70 page 317. INDEX # 7726.
Robt BOOTH; pension awarded 24 Feb 1852. SOURCE: WO120 Volume 70 page 317. INDEX # 7727.
Ja^s BUTLER; pension awarded 24 Feb 1852. SOURCE: WO120 Volume 70 page 317. INDEX # 7728.
Jos^h FIRTH; pension awarded 24 Feb 1852. SOURCE: WO120 Volume 70 page 317. INDEX # 7729.

BRITISH ARMY PENSIONERS ABROAD

Royal Canadian Rifle Regiment (continued)

Wm GUDGEON; pension awarded 24 Feb 1852; residence - London, Ontario, Canada; died 20 Nov 1871. SOURCE: WO120 Volume 70 page 317. INDEX # 7730.

Thos KELLY; pension awarded 24 Feb 1852. SOURCE: WO120 Volume 70 page 317. INDEX # 7731.

Wm LAVERTON; pension awarded 24 Feb 1852; residence - Toronto, Ontario, Canada; died 11 Aug 1853. SOURCE: WO120 Volume 70 page 317. INDEX # 7732.

Thos MCALAY; pension awarded 24 Feb 1852; residence - London, Ontario, Canada; died 24 Apr 1864. SOURCE: WO120 Volume 70 page 317. INDEX # 7733.

Saml MCLEOD; pension awarded 24 Feb 1852; died 23 Oct 1881, Toronto, Ontario, Canada. SOURCE: WO120 Volume 70 page 317. INDEX # 7734.

Saml MOORE; pension awarded 24 Feb 1852. SOURCE: WO120 Volume 70 page 317. INDEX # 7735.

Saml RILEY; pension awarded 24 Feb 1852; died 24 Jan 1859, London, Ontario, Canada. SOURCE: WO120 Volume 70 page 317. INDEX # 7736.

Geo^e SHAPCOTT; pension awarded 24 Feb 1852; died 10 Dec 1880, Hamilton, Ontario, Canada. SOURCE: WO120 Volume 70 page 317. INDEX # 7737.

Denis TIGHE; pension awarded 24 Feb 1852; residence - London, Ontario, Canada; died 12 Jan 1864. SOURCE: WO120 Volume 70 page 317. INDEX # 7738.

Ja^s MCGOWAN; pension awarded 13 Apr 1852; died 7 Oct 1883, Toronto, Ontario, Canada. SOURCE: WO120 Volume 70 page 317. INDEX # 7739.

Ja^s CONWAY; pension awarded 13 Apr 1852. SOURCE: WO120 Volume 70 page 317. INDEX # 7740.

Hen^y CONNOLLY; pension awarded 13 Apr 1852. SOURCE: WO120 Volume 70 page 317. INDEX # 7741.

Wm ELLIOTT; pension awarded 13 Apr 1852; died 26 Feb 1857. SOURCE: WO120 Volume 70 page 317. INDEX # 7742.

Jno FULTON; pension awarded 27 Apr 1852. SOURCE: WO120 Volume 70 page 317. INDEX # 7743.

Thos GEORGE; pension awarded 27 Apr 1852; died 21 Feb 1872, Hamilton, Ontario, Canada. SOURCE: WO120 Volume 70 page 317. INDEX # 7744.

Ch^r RIGG; pension awarded 27 Apr 1852; died 1 Nov 1872, London, Ontario, Canada. SOURCE: WO120 Volume 70 page 317. INDEX # 7745.

Alex^r YOUL; pension awarded 27 Apr 1852; died 9 May 1859, Toronto, Ontario, Canada. SOURCE: WO120 Volume 70 page 317. INDEX # 7746.

Robt SUTHERLAND; pension awarded 22 Jun 1852. SOURCE: WO120 Volume 70 page 318. INDEX # 7747.

Jno ROGERS; pension awarded 22 Jun 1852. SOURCE: WO120 Volume 70 page 318. INDEX # 7748.

Peter MARTIN; pension awarded 22 Jun 1852; died 22 Apr 1875, Cavan. SOURCE: WO120 Volume 70 page 318. INDEX # 7749.

Pat^k WARD; pension awarded 22 Jun 1852; died 25 May 1883, Toronto, Ontario, Canada. SOURCE: WO120 Volume 70 page 318. INDEX # 7750.

Ja^s WARD; pension awarded 22 Jun 1852; residence - Toronto, Ontario, Canada; died 18 Apr 1869. SOURCE: WO120 Volume 70 page 318. INDEX # 7751.

Chas ATKINSON; pension awarded 22 Jun 1852. SOURCE: WO120 Volume 70 page 318. INDEX # 7752.

Martin BANN; pension awarded 22 Jun 1852. SOURCE: WO120 Volume 70 page 318. INDEX # 7753.

Bernard BRADY; pension awarded 22 Jun 1852. SOURCE: WO120 Volume 70 page 318. INDEX # 7754.

Thos DAVIS; pension awarded 22 Jun 1852; residence - Toronto, Ontario, Canada; died 6 Apr 1868. SOURCE: WO120 Volume 70 page 318. INDEX # 7755.

Jno ELLIOTT; pension awarded 22 Jun 1852. SOURCE: WO120 Volume 70 page 318. INDEX # 7756.

Hen^y MCNALLY; pension awarded 22 Jun 1852. SOURCE: WO120 Volume 70 page 318. INDEX # 7757.

Peter MCGUIGAN; pension awarded 13 Jul 1852; residence - London, Ontario, Canada; died 8 Feb 1868. SOURCE: WO120 Volume 70 page 318. INDEX # 7758.

Martin COUGHLAN; pension awarded 27 Jul 1852; died 31 Aug 1886, Toronto, Ontario, Canada. SOURCE: WO120 Volume 70 page 318. INDEX # 7759.

Thos STEWART; pension awarded 22 Jun 1852. SOURCE: WO120 Volume 70 page 318. INDEX # 7760.

Robt DAVIS; pension awarded 22 Jun 1852. SOURCE: WO120 Volume 70 page 318. INDEX # 7761.

Jno ROGERS; pension awarded 27 Jul 1852; died 22 May 1880, Toronto, Ontario, Canada. SOURCE: WO120 Volume 70 page 318. INDEX # 7762.

Royal Canadian Rifle Regiment (continued)

Jas WILKINSON; pension awarded 27 Jul 1852; residence - Niagara, Ontario, Canada; died 17 Dec 1855. SOURCE: WO120 Volume 70 page 318. INDEX # 7763.

Geoe BOWYER; pension awarded 27 Jul 1852. SOURCE: WO120 Volume 70 page 318. INDEX # 7764.

Jas HEGGS; pension awarded 27 Jul 1852. SOURCE: WO120 Volume 70 page 318. INDEX # 7765.

David HILLHOUSE; pension awarded 27 Jul 1852. SOURCE: WO120 Volume 70 page 318. INDEX # 7766.

Wm SCOTT; pension awarded 27 Jul 1852. SOURCE: WO120 Volume 70 page 319. INDEX # 7767.

Jno HENDERSON; pension awarded 27 Jul 1852; residence - Toronto, Ontario, Canada; died 31 Mar 1855. SOURCE: WO120 Volume 70 page 319. INDEX # 7768.

Edmd DAVEY; pension awarded 27 Jul 1852; died 17 Aug 1881, Montreal, Quebec, Canada. SOURCE: WO120 Volume 70 page 319. INDEX # 7769.

Jas ALLMOND; pension awarded 27 Jul 1852. SOURCE: WO120 Volume 70 page 319. INDEX # 7770.

Robt BAKER; pension awarded 27 Jul 1852; residence - Hamilton, Ontario, Canada; died 15 Aug 1871. SOURCE: WO120 Volume 70 page 319. INDEX # 7771.

Heny BRAWNSTON; pension awarded 27 Jul 1852; residence - Toronto, Ontario, Canada; died 2 Feb 1872. SOURCE: WO120 Volume 70 page 319. INDEX # 7772.

Jno BRUCE; pension awarded 27 Jul 1852; residence - Amherstburg, Ontario, Canada; died 12 Jan 1855. SOURCE: WO120 Volume 70 page 319. INDEX # 7773.

Jno BURNHAM; pension awarded 27 Jul 1852. SOURCE: WO120 Volume 70 page 319. INDEX # 7774.

Wm CALGEY; pension awarded 27 Jul 1852. SOURCE: WO120 Volume 70 page 319. INDEX # 7775.

Jno CAMPBELL; pension awarded 27 Jul 1852; residence - Toronto, Ontario, Canada; died 3 Oct 1870. SOURCE: WO120 Volume 70 page 319. INDEX # 7776.

Michl CARROLL; pension awarded 27 Jul 1852; died 2 Dec 1879. SOURCE: WO120 Volume 70 page 319. INDEX # 7777.

Thos CLIFF; pension awarded 27 Jul 1852. SOURCE: WO120 Volume 70 page 319. INDEX # 7778.

Jas CLIFFEN; pension awarded 27 Jul 1852; residence - London, Ontario, Canada; died 27 Aug 1878. SOURCE: WO120 Volume 70 page 319. INDEX # 7779.

Jno CHOULERTON; pension awarded 27 Jul 1852. SOURCE: WO120 Volume 70 page 319. INDEX # 7780.

Geoe COCHRANE; pension awarded 27 Jul 1852. SOURCE: WO120 Volume 70 page 319. INDEX # 7781.

Jno COLLINS; pension awarded 27 Jul 1852. SOURCE: WO120 Volume 70 page 319. INDEX # 7782.

Jas CULLEN; pension awarded 27 Jul 1852. SOURCE: WO120 Volume 70 page 319. INDEX # 7783.

Jas DAVEY; pension awarded 27 Jul 1852; died 15 Jan 1873, Hamilton, Ontario, Canada. SOURCE: WO120 Volume 70 page 319. INDEX # 7784.

Jas DUNFORD; pension awarded 27 Jul 1852; died 20 Sep 1875, London, Ontario, Canada. SOURCE: WO120 Volume 70 page 319. INDEX # 7785.

Wm EGGS; pension awarded 27 Jul 1852; residence - London, Ontario, Canada; died 7 Aug 1870. SOURCE: WO120 Volume 70 page 319. INDEX # 7786.

Jno FRANCIS; pension awarded 27 Jul 1852; residence - Montreal, Quebec, Canada; died 15 Mar 1857. SOURCE: WO120 Volume 70 page 320. INDEX # 7787.

Geoe FIELD; pension awarded 27 Jul 1852. SOURCE: WO120 Volume 70 page 320. INDEX # 7788.

Denis GALLAGHER; pension awarded 27 Jul 1852. SOURCE: WO120 Volume 70 page 320. INDEX # 7789.

Thos GODWIN; pension awarded 27 Jul 1852; residence - Toronto, Ontario, Canada; died 14 May 1868. SOURCE: WO120 Volume 70 page 320. INDEX # 7790.

Jas GREER; pension awarded 27 Jul 1852. SOURCE: WO120 Volume 70 page 320. INDEX # 7791.

Jas GRIGSBY; pension awarded 27 Jul 1852. SOURCE: WO120 Volume 70 page 320. INDEX # 7792.

Jas HAMILTON; pension awarded 27 Jul 1852; died 30 Apr 1882, Toronto, Ontario, Canada. SOURCE: WO120 Volume 70 page 320. INDEX # 7793.

Saml HARRIS; pension awarded 27 Jul 1852; died 15 Dec 1873, Toronto, Ontario, Canada. SOURCE: WO120 Volume 70 page 320. INDEX # 7794.

Jno HAYWOOD; pension awarded 27 Jul 1852. SOURCE: WO120 Volume 70 page 320. INDEX # 7795.

Fras HOLMES; pension awarded 27 Jul 1852; residence - Toronto, Ontario, Canada; died 8 Aug 1854. SOURCE: WO120 Volume 70 page 320. INDEX # 7796.

Jas IRWIN; pension awarded 27 Jul 1852. SOURCE: WO120 Volume 70 page 320. INDEX # 7797.

Royal Canadian Rifle Regiment (continued)

Jn⁰ JOHNSTON; pension awarded 27 Jul 1852; residence - London, Ontario, Canada; died 5 Nov 1857. SOURCE: WO120 Volume 70 page 320. INDEX # 7798.

Randle JORDAN; pension awarded 27 Jul 1852; died 17 Apr 1884, Galway. SOURCE: WO120 Volume 70 page 320. INDEX # 7799.

Peter KENNY; pension awarded 27 Jul 1852; died 28 Mar 1870. SOURCE: WO120 Volume 70 page 320. INDEX # 7800.

Ja^s KILBOY; pension awarded 27 Jul 1852; died Galway. SOURCE: WO120 Volume 70 page 320. INDEX # 7801.

Jn⁰ KNAPTON; pension awarded 27 Jul 1852. SOURCE: WO120 Volume 70 page 320. INDEX # 7802.

Reuben LAWRENCE; pension awarded 27 Jul 1852. SOURCE: WO120 Volume 70 page 320. INDEX # 7803.

Jere^h LEHANE; pension awarded 27 Jul 1852; residence - Amherstburg, Ontario, Canada; died 26 Sep 1853. SOURCE: WO120 Volume 70 page 320. INDEX # 7804.

Thos MCLAUGHLIN; pension awarded 27 Jul 1852. SOURCE: WO120 Volume 70 page 320. INDEX # 7805.

Mich^l MACK; pension awarded 27 Jul 1852. SOURCE: WO120 Volume 70 page 320. INDEX # 7806.

Wm MABEY; pension awarded 27 Jul 1852. SOURCE: WO120 Volume 70 page 321. INDEX # 7807.

Dennis MINAGHAN; pension awarded 27 Jul 1852. SOURCE: WO120 Volume 70 page 321. INDEX # 7808.

Bernard MULDOON; pension awarded 27 Jul 1852; died 10 Apr 1881, Toronto, Ontario, Canada. SOURCE: WO120 Volume 70 page 321. INDEX # 7809.

Robt MULLIN; pension awarded 27 Jul 1852; died 25 May 1873, Toronto, Ontario, Canada. SOURCE: WO120 Volume 70 page 321. INDEX # 7810.

Peter NOWDEN; pension awarded 27 Jul 1852; died 2 Aug 1869, Toronto, Ontario, Canada. SOURCE: WO120 Volume 70 page 321. INDEX # 7811.

Pat^k ODOWD; pension awarded 27 Jul 1852. SOURCE: WO120 Volume 70 page 321. INDEX # 7812.

Davis POLLOCK; pension awarded 27 Jul 1852; died 17 Apr 1873, Glasgow. SOURCE: WO120 Volume 70 page 321. INDEX # 7813.

Ja^s PURCELL; pension awarded 27 Jul 1852. SOURCE: WO120 Volume 70 page 321. INDEX # 7814.

Robt QUINN; pension awarded 27 Jul 1852; died 8 Aug 1853. SOURCE: WO120 Volume 70 page 321. INDEX # 7815.

Robt RYAN; pension awarded 27 Jul 1852; residence - Hamilton, Ontario, Canada; died 9 Feb 1864. SOURCE: WO120 Volume 70 page 321. INDEX # 7816.

Pat^k SCANLON; pension awarded 27 Jul 1852; residence - Toronto, Ontario, Canada. SOURCE: WO120 Volume 70 page 321. INDEX # 7817.

Richd TANNER; pension awarded 27 Jul 1852. SOURCE: WO120 Volume 70 page 321. INDEX # 7818.

Mich^l TIERNEY; pension awarded 27 Jul 1852; residence - Montreal, Quebec, Canada; died 27 Jun 1858. SOURCE: WO120 Volume 70 page 321. INDEX # 7819.

Ja^s THOMPSON; pension awarded 27 Jul 1852. SOURCE: WO120 Volume 70 page 321. INDEX # 7820.

Saml THOMPSON; pension awarded 27 Jul 1852; residence - Hamilton, Ontario, Canada; died 6 Jul 1863. SOURCE: WO120 Volume 70 page 321. INDEX # 7821.

Thos TRAFFORD; pension awarded 27 Jul 1852. SOURCE: WO120 Volume 70 page 321. INDEX # 7822.

Richd VICK; pension awarded 27 Jul 1852. SOURCE: WO120 Volume 70 page 321. INDEX # 7823.

Thos WILKINSON; pension awarded 27 Jul 1852. SOURCE: WO120 Volume 70 page 321. INDEX # 7824.

Thos WOVENDON; pension awarded 27 Jul 1852; residence - Montreal, Quebec, Canada; died 7 Aug 1854. SOURCE: WO120 Volume 70 page 321. INDEX # 7825.

Wm WRIGHT; pension awarded 27 Jul 1852; died 23 Nov 1861, Hamilton, Ontario, Canada. SOURCE: WO120 Volume 70 page 321. INDEX # 7826.

Wm WOOD; pension awarded 24 Aug 1852. SOURCE: WO120 Volume 70 page 322. INDEX # 7827.

Jere^h MADDEN; pension awarded 28 Sep 1852. SOURCE: WO120 Volume 70 page 322. INDEX # 7828.

Peter CARROLL; pension awarded 23 Nov 1852; died 19 Mar 1872, Hamilton, Ontario, Canada. SOURCE: WO120 Volume 70 page 322. INDEX # 7829.

Jn⁰ SCOTT; pension awarded 23 Nov 1852; residence - Toronto, Ontario, Canada; died 15 Jul 1854. SOURCE: WO120 Volume 70 page 322. INDEX # 7830.

Jn⁰ SPOONER; pension awarded 23 Nov 1852; residence - Amherstburg, Ontario, Canada; died 27 Nov 1852. SOURCE: WO120 Volume 70 page 322. INDEX # 7831.

Royal Canadian Rifle Regiment (continued)

Thos GIBBINS; pension awarded 28 Dec 1852; residence - London, Ontario, Canada; died 27 Jun 1866. SOURCE: WO120 Volume 70 page 322. INDEX # 7832.

Geoe COOKE; pension awarded 25 Jan 1853. SOURCE: WO120 Volume 70 page 322. INDEX # 7833.

Wm DEATON; pension awarded 25 Jan 1853. SOURCE: WO120 Volume 70 page 322. INDEX # 7834.

Chas HUNT; pension awarded 25 Jan 1853; died 16 Dec 1881, Canada. SOURCE: WO120 Volume 70 page 322. INDEX # 7835.

Chas ROGERS; pension awarded 25 Jan 1853; died 17 May 1879, Toronto, Ontario, Canada. SOURCE: WO120 Volume 70 page 322. INDEX # 7836.

Jereh DRISCOLL; pension awarded 15 Feb 1853; died 4 Oct 1863, Hamilton, Ontario, Canada. SOURCE: WO120 Volume 70 page 322. INDEX # 7837.

Richd BURTON; pension awarded 15 Feb 1853; died 29 Sep 1861, Toronto, Ontario, Canada. SOURCE: WO120 Volume 70 page 322. INDEX # 7838.

Wm CUNNINGHAM; pension awarded 15 Feb 1853. SOURCE: WO120 Volume 70 page 322. INDEX # 7839.

Alexr KNOTT; pension awarded 15 Feb 1853. SOURCE: WO120 Volume 70 page 322. INDEX # 7840.

Patk MADDEN; pension awarded 15 Feb 1853. SOURCE: WO120 Volume 70 page 322. INDEX # 7841.

Silvanus SEDDON; pension awarded 15 Feb 1853; residence - Toronto, Ontario, Canada; died 1 Jan 1864. SOURCE: WO120 Volume 70 page 322. INDEX # 7842.

Josh BELL; pension awarded 12 Apr 1853. SOURCE: WO120 Volume 70 page 322. INDEX # 7843.

Berd RIELLY; pension awarded 12 Apr 1853. SOURCE: WO120 Volume 70 page 322. INDEX # 7844.

Patk DAWSON; pension awarded 12 Apr 1853. SOURCE: WO120 Volume 70 page 322. INDEX # 7845.

Edwd MCGUIRE; pension awarded 12 Apr 1853. SOURCE: WO120 Volume 70 page 322. INDEX # 7846.

Edwd ROONEY; pension awarded 12 Apr 1853; died 31 Jan 1872, Toronto, Ontario, Canada. SOURCE: WO120 Volume 70 page 323. INDEX # 7847.

Jas DEEHAN; pension awarded 10 May 1853; residence - Montreal, Quebec, Canada; died 21 Apr 1857. SOURCE: WO120 Volume 70 page 323. INDEX # 7848.

Robt BEVIN; pension awarded 10 May 1853; died 10 Feb 1882, Canada. SOURCE: WO120 Volume 70 page 323. INDEX # 7849.

Duncan CUMMING; pension awarded 10 May 1853. SOURCE: WO120 Volume 70 page 323. INDEX # 7850.

Patk JENNINGS; pension awarded 10 May 1853; residence - London, Ontario, Canada; died 29 Aug 1856. SOURCE: WO120 Volume 70 page 323. INDEX # 7851.

Jas MCKAY; pension awarded 10 May 1853; residence - Kingston, Ontario, Canada; died 10 Sep 1857. SOURCE: WO120 Volume 70 page 323. INDEX # 7852.

Roger SWEENEY; pension awarded 10 May 1853; residence - Hamilton, Ontario, Canada; died 15 Jan 1875. SOURCE: WO120 Volume 70 page 323. INDEX # 7853.

Wm BURKE; pension awarded 14 Jun 1853; residence - Toronto, Ontario, Canada; died 14 Mar 1877. SOURCE: WO120 Volume 70 page 323. INDEX # 7854.

Jno CAMPBELL; pension awarded 14 Jun 1853; died 9 May 1861, Toronto, Ontario, Canada. SOURCE: WO120 Volume 70 page 323. INDEX # 7855.

Fras CASHEN; pension awarded 14 Jun 1853. SOURCE: WO120 Volume 70 page 323. INDEX # 7856.

Jno MURDIE; pension awarded 14 Jun 1853. SOURCE: WO120 Volume 70 page 323. INDEX # 7857.

Wm MUSTARD; pension awarded 28 Jun 1853; died 1 Jan 1857, Niagara, Ontario, Canada. SOURCE: WO120 Volume 70 page 323. INDEX # 7858.

Robt PEPPER; pension awarded 28 Jun 1853; died 28 Jan 1872, Toronto, Ontario, Canada. SOURCE: WO120 Volume 70 page 323. INDEX # 7859.

Wm SMITH; pension awarded 28 Jun 1853. SOURCE: WO120 Volume 70 page 323. INDEX # 7860.

Wm BARRON; pension awarded 28 Jun 1853; died 1 Jul 1883, Nova Scotia. SOURCE: WO120 Volume 70 page 323. INDEX # 7861.

Jno BELL; pension awarded 28 Jun 1853. SOURCE: WO120 Volume 70 page 323. INDEX # 7862.

Michl BRIDE; pension awarded 28 Jun 1853; residence - Toronto, Ontario, Canada; died 1 Mar 1855. SOURCE: WO120 Volume 70 page 323. INDEX # 7863.

Jno CAFFERKEY; pension awarded 28 Jun 1853; residence - Hamilton, Ontario, Canada; died 1 Mar 1875. SOURCE: WO120 Volume 70 page 323. INDEX # 7864.

Geoe CHYNE; pension awarded 28 Jun 1853. SOURCE: WO120 Volume 70 page 323. INDEX # 7865.

Royal Canadian Rifle Regiment (continued)

Pat^k CONNOLLY; pension awarded 28 Jun 1853; died 8 Apr 1883, Kilmainham. SOURCE: WO120 Volume 70 page 323. INDEX # 7866.

Walter CROCKER; pension awarded 28 Jun 1853; died 18 Aug 1884, Halifax, Nova Scotia, Canada. SOURCE: WO120 Volume 70 page 324. INDEX # 7867.

Jno CUSICK; pension awarded 28 Jun 1853; died 3 Aug 1885, Cork. SOURCE: WO120 Volume 70 page 324. INDEX # 7868.

Darby GORMAN; pension awarded 28 Jun 1853. SOURCE: WO120 Volume 70 page 324. INDEX # 7869.

Wm HARDWICK; pension awarded 28 Jun 1853; died 12 Oct 1884, Toronto, Ontario, Canada. SOURCE: WO120 Volume 70 page 324. INDEX # 7870.

Absalom HUNT; pension awarded 28 Jun 1853; residence - Quebec, Canada; died 21 Jun 1854. SOURCE: WO120 Volume 70 page 324. INDEX # 7871.

Dan^lo JEFFREY; pension awarded 28 Jun 1853. SOURCE: WO120 Volume 70 page 324. INDEX # 7872.

Jno JENNINGS; pension awarded 28 Jun 1853. SOURCE: WO120 Volume 70 page 324. INDEX # 7873.

Wm JENNINGS; pension awarded 28 Jun 1853; residence - Hamilton, Ontario, Canada; died 30 Jan 1878. SOURCE: WO120 Volume 70 page 324. INDEX # 7874.

Jno LEWIS; pension awarded 28 Jun 1853; residence - Toronto, Ontario, Canada; died 1 Jul 1854. SOURCE: WO120 Volume 70 page 324. INDEX # 7875.

Danl MCPHAIL; pension awarded 28 Jun 1853; died 9 Oct 1859, Toronto, Ontario, Canada. SOURCE: WO120 Volume 70 page 324. INDEX # 7876.

Robt MANNERS; pension awarded 28 Jun 1853. SOURCE: WO120 Volume 70 page 324. INDEX # 7877.

Nathl PATTERSON; pension awarded 28 Jun 1853. SOURCE: WO120 Volume 70 page 324. INDEX # 7878.

Robt POCOCK; pension awarded 28 Jun 1853. SOURCE: WO120 Volume 70 page 324. INDEX # 7879.

Geo^e ROBERTSON; pension awarded 28 Jun 1853; residence - London, Ontario, Canada; died 20 Jul 1854. SOURCE: WO120 Volume 70 page 324. INDEX # 7880.

Jno SMITH; pension awarded 28 Jun 1853. SOURCE: WO120 Volume 70 page 324. INDEX # 7881.

Peter SMITH; pension awarded 28 Jun 1853. SOURCE: WO120 Volume 70 page 324. INDEX # 7582.

Wm TAYLOR; pension awarded 28 Jun 1853; died 9 Dec 1885, Toronto, Ontario, Canada. SOURCE: WO120 Volume 70 page 324. INDEX # 7883.

Jno THOM; pension awarded 28 Jun 1853; residence - Toronto, Ontario, Canada; died 27 Feb 1860. SOURCE: WO120 Volume 70 page 324. INDEX # 7884.

Thos UPTON; pension awarded 28 Jun 1853. SOURCE: WO120 Volume 70 page 324. INDEX # 7885.

Jos^h VINEY; pension awarded 28 Jun 1853. SOURCE: WO120 Volume 70 page 324. INDEX # 7886.

Fred^k BROWN; pension awarded 28 Jun 1853; residence - Hamilton, Ontario, Canada; died 17 Dec 1877. SOURCE: WO120 Volume 70 page 325. INDEX # 7887.

Jos^h LARKIN; pension awarded 28 Jun 1853. SOURCE: WO120 Volume 70 page 325. INDEX # 7888.

Ja^s COBB; pension awarded 28 Jun 1853. SOURCE: WO120 Volume 70 page 325. INDEX # 7889.

Peter KEEVIL; pension awarded 28 Jun 1853. SOURCE: WO120 Volume 70 page 325. INDEX # 7890.

Jno MURPHY; pension awarded 28 Jun 1853; residence - Bytown, Ontario, Canada; died 8 Jul 1854. SOURCE: WO120 Volume 70 page 325. INDEX # 7891.

Ja^s YOUNG; pension awarded 26 Jul 1853. SOURCE: WO120 Volume 70 page 325. INDEX # 7892.

Absalom JOHNSON; pension awarded 26 Jul 1853; died 12 Sep 1876, Toronto, Ontario, Canada. SOURCE: WO120 Volume 70 page 325. INDEX # 7893.

Ed^wd WHYMAN; pension awarded 26 Jul 1853; died 12 Oct 1883, Toronto, Ontario, Canada. SOURCE: WO120 Volume 70 page 325. INDEX # 7894.

Jno DUKE; pension awarded 26 Jul 1853. SOURCE: WO120 Volume 70 page 325. INDEX # 7895.

Robt STEVEN; pension awarded 13 Sep 1853. SOURCE: WO120 Volume 70 page 325. INDEX # 7896.

Mich^l TANSEY; pension awarded 13 Sep 1853. SOURCE: WO120 Volume 70 page 325. INDEX # 7897.

Robt PHIBBS; pension awarded 13 Sep 1853. SOURCE: WO120 Volume 70 page 325. INDEX # 7898.

Richd READING; pension awarded 11 Oct 1853; died 27 Sep 1861, Toronto, Ontario, Canada. SOURCE: WO120 Volume 70 page 325. INDEX # 7899.

Wm RYAN; pension awarded 11 Oct 1853. SOURCE: WO120 Volume 70 page 325. INDEX # 7900.

Robt BLACK; pension awarded 13 Dec 1853. SOURCE: WO120 Volume 70 page 325. INDEX # 7901.

Royal Canadian Rifle Regiment (continued)

Thos WATSON; pension awarded 28 Jun 1853; died 8 Feb 1859, Kingston, Ontario, Canada. SOURCE: WO120 Volume 70 page 325. INDEX # 7902.

Richd PHILLIPS; pension awarded 14 Feb 1854; died 20 Feb 1881, Toronto, Ontario, Canada. SOURCE: WO120 Volume 70 page 325. INDEX # 7903.

Jno FITZGERALD; pension awarded 14 Mar 1854. SOURCE: WO120 Volume 70 page 325. INDEX # 7904.

Wm MARSHALL; pension awarded 14 Mar 1854; residence - Niagara, Ontario, Canada; died 21 Aug 1854. SOURCE: WO120 Volume 70 page 325. INDEX # 7905.

Jno SUTHERLAND; pension awarded 11 Apr 1854. SOURCE: WO120 Volume 70 page 325. INDEX # 7906.

Edwd DAVIS; pension awarded 23 May 1854; residence - Niagara, Ontario, Canada; died 11 Jul 1857. SOURCE: WO120 Volume 70 page 326. INDEX # 7907.

Jno CAMPBELL; pension awarded 13 Jun 1854; died 24 Apr 1873, Omagh. SOURCE: WO120 Volume 70 page 326. INDEX # 7908.

Heny LETHERBY; pension awarded 13 Jun 1854; residence - Hamilton, Ontario, Canada; died 26 Jul 1863. SOURCE: WO120 Volume 70 page 326. INDEX # 7909.

Geoe GOUDIE; pension awarded 25 Jul 1854; residence - Bytown, Ontario, Canada; died 4 Sep 1855. SOURCE: WO120 Volume 70 page 326. INDEX # 7910.

Jno HOLLAND; pension awarded 25 Jul 1854; died 7 Oct 1862, Toronto, Ontario, Canada. SOURCE: WO120 Volume 70 page 326. INDEX # 7911.

Jno RAYNOR; pension awarded 25 Jul 1854; died 29 Jun 1868, Hamilton, Ontario, Canada. SOURCE: WO120 Volume 70 page 326. INDEX # 7912.

Geoe BOULTON; pension awarded 8 Aug 1854. SOURCE: WO120 Volume 70 page 326. INDEX # 7913.

Jno KIRBY; pension awarded 8 Aug 1854; died 7 Jan 1879, Hamilton, Ontario, Canada. SOURCE: WO120 Volume 70 page 326. INDEX # 7914.

Patk BURNS; pension awarded 8 Aug 1854. SOURCE: WO120 Volume 70 page 326. INDEX # 7915.

Mattw FLINN; pension awarded 8 Aug 1854; died 10 Jun 1877, Birr. SOURCE: WO120 Volume 70 page 326. INDEX # 7916.

Jno GURRIVIN; pension awarded 8 Aug 1854; died 17 Dec 1878, Hamilton, Ontario, Canada. SOURCE: WO120 Volume 70 page 326. INDEX # 7917.

Jno HAYES; pension awarded 8 Aug 1854; died 18 Aug 1884, Toronto, Ontario, Canada. SOURCE: WO120 Volume 70 page 326. INDEX # 7918.

Edwd REEVE; pension awarded 8 Aug 1854. SOURCE: WO120 Volume 70 page 326. INDEX # 7919.

Edwd SPENCER; pension awarded 8 Aug 1854. SOURCE: WO120 Volume 70 page 326. INDEX # 7920.

Geoe WHITHORN; pension awarded 8 Aug 1854; residence - Toronto, Ontario, Canada; died 10 Oct 1870. SOURCE: WO120 Volume 70 page 326. INDEX # 7921.

Jas MCGAIN; pension awarded 12 Sep 1854; died 7 May 1862, Toronto, Ontario, Canada. SOURCE: WO120 Volume 70 page 326. INDEX # 7922.

Douglas THORPE; pension awarded 12 Sep 1854; residence - London, Ontario, Canada; died 2 Feb 1869. SOURCE: WO120 Volume 70 page 326. INDEX # 7923.

Geoe LIDDLE; pension awarded 10 Oct 1854; residence - Hamilton, Ontario, Canada; died 29 Jul 1878. SOURCE: WO120 Volume 70 page 326. INDEX # 7924.

Wm LANGSHAW; pension awarded 14 Nov 1854. SOURCE: WO120 Volume 70 page 326. INDEX # 7925.

Jas MCEVOY; pension awarded 12 Dec 1854. SOURCE: WO120 Volume 70 page 326. INDEX # 7926.

Archd STEWART; pension awarded 9 Jan 1855. SOURCE: WO120 Volume 70 page 327. INDEX # 7927.

John TUNNACLIFFE; pension awarded 13 Feb 1855. SOURCE: WO120 Volume 70 page 327. INDEX # 7928.

Thomas BYRNE; pension awarded 8 May 1855. SOURCE: WO120 Volume 70 page 327. INDEX # 7929.

John DALTON; pension awarded 8 May 1855. SOURCE: WO120 Volume 70 page 327. INDEX # 7930.

John DAVIES; pension awarded 8 May 1855. SOURCE: WO120 Volume 70 page 327. INDEX # 7931.

James HAYES; pension awarded 8 May 1855. SOURCE: WO120 Volume 70 page 327. INDEX # 7932.

James MOORE; pension awarded 12 Jun 1855; residence - London, Ontario, Canada; died 12 Jun 1855. SOURCE: WO120 Volume 70 page 327. INDEX # 7933.

John SHAW; pension awarded 24 Jun 1855. SOURCE: WO120 Volume 70 page 327. INDEX # 7934.

William BROWN; pension awarded 24 Jun 1855. SOURCE: WO120 Volume 70 page 327. INDEX # 7935.

BRITISH ARMY PENSIONERS ABROAD

Royal Canadian Rifle Regiment (continued)

Charles SMITH; pension awarded 24 Jun 1855; died 7 Dec 1862, Toronto, Ontario, Canada. SOURCE: WO120 Volume 70 page 327. INDEX # 7936.

John HURST; pension awarded 13 Nov 1855. SOURCE: WO120 Volume 70 page 327. INDEX # 7937.

William WATSON; pension awarded 15 Jan 1856. SOURCE: WO120 Volume 70 page 327. INDEX # 7938.

Noble LEE; pension awarded 15 Jan 1856. SOURCE: WO120 Volume 70 page 327. INDEX # 7939.

James NORRIS; pension awarded 15 Jan 1856. SOURCE: WO120 Volume 70 page 327. INDEX # 7940.

Joseph MASTERS; pension awarded 11 Mar 1856. SOURCE: WO120 Volume 70 page 327. INDEX # 7941.

Isaac DYKE; pension awarded 25 Mar 1856. SOURCE: WO120 Volume 70 page 327. INDEX # 7942.

Richard HARRIMAN; pension awarded 25 Mar 1856. SOURCE: WO120 Volume 70 page 327. INDEX # 7943.

William SANDERSON; pension awarded 25 Mar 1856; residence - Toronto, Ontario, Canada; died 7 Sep 1866. SOURCE: WO120 Volume 70 page 327. INDEX # 7944.

James RICHARDSON; pension awarded 22 Apr 1856. SOURCE: WO120 Volume 70 page 327. INDEX # 7945.

Thomas ARNOTT; pension awarded 22 Apr 1856. SOURCE: WO120 Volume 70 page 327. INDEX # 7946.

William GLANCEY; pension awarded 22 Apr 1856. SOURCE: WO120 Volume 70 page 328. INDEX # 7947.

John GRAY; pension awarded 22 Apr 1856. SOURCE: WO120 Volume 70 page 328. INDEX # 7948.

James HARLERY; pension awarded 22 Apr 1856. SOURCE: WO120 Volume 70 page 328. INDEX # 7949.

John HOUSE; pension awarded 22 Apr 1856. SOURCE: WO120 Volume 70 page 328. INDEX # 7950.

Thomas JACOBS; pension awarded 22 Apr 1856. SOURCE: WO120 Volume 70 page 328. INDEX # 7951.

Jesse KEITLEY; pension awarded 22 Apr 1856. SOURCE: WO120 Volume 70 page 328. INDEX # 7952.

Robert NOBLES; pension awarded 22 Apr 1856. SOURCE: WO120 Volume 70 page 328. INDEX # 7953.

Thomas SMITH; pension awarded 22 Apr 1856. SOURCE: WO120 Volume 70 page 328. INDEX # 7954.

Oliver MASON; pension awarded 20 May 1856. SOURCE: WO120 Volume 70 page 328. INDEX # 7955.

William CALEW; pension awarded 20 May 1856. SOURCE: WO120 Volume 70 page 328. INDEX # 7956.

Robert SMITH; pension awarded 20 May 1856. SOURCE: WO120 Volume 70 page 328. INDEX # 7957.

John CLAY; pension awarded 24 Jun 1856. SOURCE: WO120 Volume 70 page 328. INDEX # 7958.

Hugh JACK; pension awarded 24 Jun 1856. SOURCE: WO120 Volume 70 page 328. INDEX # 7959.

Patrick KILEEN; pension awarded 15 Jul 1856. SOURCE: WO120 Volume 70 page 328. INDEX # 7960.

Edward KEMP; pension awarded 29 Jul 1856. SOURCE: WO120 Volume 70 page 328. INDEX # 7961.

Alexander WALKER; pension awarded 29 Jul 1856. SOURCE: WO120 Volume 70 page 328. INDEX # 7962.

Thomas DOUGLAS; pension awarded 29 Jul 1856. SOURCE: WO120 Volume 70 page 328. INDEX # 7963.

John AUSTIN; pension awarded 29 Jul 1856. SOURCE: WO120 Volume 70 page 328. INDEX # 7964.

John CARTER; pension awarded 29 Jul 1856. SOURCE: WO120 Volume 70 page 328. INDEX # 7965.

Timothy DALY; pension awarded 29 Jul 1856. SOURCE: WO120 Volume 70 page 328. INDEX # 7966.

William DAY; pension awarded 29 Jul 1856. SOURCE: WO120 Volume 70 page 329. INDEX # 7967.

Robert DUNLOP; pension awarded 29 Jul 1856. SOURCE: WO120 Volume 70 page 329. INDEX # 7968.

George EVANS; pension awarded 29 Jul 1856. SOURCE: WO120 Volume 70 page 329. INDEX # 7969.

William FORREST; pension awarded 29 Jul 1856. SOURCE: WO120 Volume 70 page 329. INDEX # 7970.

Patrick GIBBONS; pension awarded 29 Jul 1856. SOURCE: WO120 Volume 70 page 329. INDEX # 7971.

Thomas HOWS; pension awarded 29 Jul 1856. SOURCE: WO120 Volume 70 page 329. INDEX # 7972.

Robert KNIGHT; pension awarded 29 Jul 1856; died 3 Mar 1857, London, Ontario, Canada. SOURCE: WO120 Volume 70 page 329. INDEX # 7973.

Patrick MONAGHAN; pension awarded 29 Jul 1856; residence - Hamilton, Ontario, Canada; died 13 Aug 1863. SOURCE: WO120 Volume 70 page 329. INDEX # 7974.

William MITCHELL; pension awarded 29 Jul 1856. SOURCE: WO120 Volume 70 page 329. INDEX # 7975.

John OBYRNE; pension awarded 29 Jul 1856. SOURCE: WO120 Volume 70 page 329. INDEX # 7976.

Joseph PARKER; pension awarded 29 Jul 1856. SOURCE: WO120 Volume 70 page 329. INDEX # 7977.

William STREET; pension awarded 29 Jul 1856. SOURCE: WO120 Volume 70 page 329. INDEX # 7978.

Royal Canadian Rifle Regiment (continued)

James MURDAH; pension awarded 26 Aug 1856. SOURCE: WO120 Volume 70 page 329. INDEX # 7979.
James JONES; pension awarded 26 Aug 1856. SOURCE: WO120 Volume 70 page 329. INDEX # 7980.
James GRASSHAM; pension awarded 26 Aug 1856; residence - Toronto, Ontario, Canada; died 16 Aug 1857. SOURCE: WO120 Volume 70 page 329. INDEX # 7981.
James REILLY; pension awarded 26 Aug 1856. SOURCE: WO120 Volume 70 page 329. INDEX # 7982.
William JOHNSTON; pension awarded 1 Oct 1856; died 3 Oct 1879, Toronto, Ontario, Canada. SOURCE: WO120 Volume 70 page 329. INDEX # 7983.
Richard WRIGHT; pension awarded 21 Oct 1856. SOURCE: WO120 Volume 70 page 329. INDEX # 7984.
James WATSON; pension awarded 2 Dec 1856. SOURCE: WO120 Volume 70 page 329. INDEX # 7985.
William GRIEVE; pension awarded 2 Dec 1856. SOURCE: WO120 Volume 70 page 329. INDEX # 7986.
Hugh STOREY; pension awarded 2 Dec 1856. SOURCE: WO120 Volume 70 page 329. INDEX # 7987.
Joseph TROWLES; pension awarded 13 Jan 1857. SOURCE: WO120 Volume 70 page 330. INDEX # 7988.
John GUNN; pension awarded 13 Jan 1857. SOURCE: WO120 Volume 70 page 330. INDEX # 7989.
John HUNT; pension awarded 13 Jan 1857. SOURCE: WO120 Volume 70 page 330. INDEX # 7990.
George LEE; pension awarded 13 Jan 1857. SOURCE: WO120 Volume 70 page 330. INDEX # 7991.
William LUNN; pension awarded 13 Jan 1857. SOURCE: WO120 Volume 70 page 330. INDEX # 7992.
William HATCH; pension awarded 10 Feb 1857. SOURCE: WO120 Volume 70 page 330. INDEX # 7993.
Josiah HELSDEN; pension awarded 10 Feb 1857. SOURCE: WO120 Volume 70 page 330. INDEX # 7994.
Joseph FREEMAN; pension awarded 24 Mar 1857. SOURCE: WO120 Volume 70 page 330. INDEX # 7995.
Abraham COOK; pension awarded 5 May 1857. SOURCE: WO120 Volume 70 page 330. INDEX # 7996.
Joseph ARNELL; pension awarded 5 May 1857. SOURCE: WO120 Volume 70 page 330. INDEX # 7997.
John BUFTON; pension awarded 5 May 1857. SOURCE: WO120 Volume 70 page 330. INDEX # 7998.
Charles CARTER; pension awarded 5 May 1857. SOURCE: WO120 Volume 70 page 330. INDEX # 7999.
James CLARKE; pension awarded 5 May 1857. SOURCE: WO120 Volume 70 page 330. INDEX # 8000.
John DOUGLAS; pension awarded 5 May 1857. SOURCE: WO120 Volume 70 page 330. INDEX # 8001.
Charles FRENCH; pension awarded 5 May 1857. SOURCE: WO120 Volume 70 page 330. INDEX # 8002.
John NIDD; pension awarded 5 May 1857. SOURCE: WO120 Volume 70 page 330. INDEX # 8003.
John WATERS; pension awarded 5 May 1857. SOURCE: WO120 Volume 70 page 330. INDEX # 8004.
John KELLY; pension awarded 9 Jun 1857. SOURCE: WO120 Volume 70 page 330. INDEX # 8005.
Thomas OBRIAN; pension awarded 4 Aug 1857. SOURCE: WO120 Volume 70 page 330. INDEX # 8006.
Amos STEVENSON; pension awarded 4 Aug 1857. SOURCE: WO120 Volume 70 page 330. INDEX # 8007.
Florence SULLIVAN; pension awarded 11 Aug 1857. SOURCE: WO120 Volume 70 page 331. INDEX # 8008.
Thomas BOSTRIDGE; pension awarded 11 Aug 1857. SOURCE: WO120 Volume 70 page 331. INDEX # 8009.
John BULLEN; pension awarded 11 Aug 1857. SOURCE: WO120 Volume 70 page 331. INDEX # 8010.
George CLIFFORD; pension awarded 11 Aug 1857. SOURCE: WO120 Volume 70 page 331. INDEX # 8011.
Stephen CONNOR; pension awarded 11 Aug 1857. SOURCE: WO120 Volume 70 page 331. INDEX # 8012.
William DUKE; pension awarded 11 Aug 1857. SOURCE: WO120 Volume 70 page 331. INDEX # 8013.
Simon FRASER; pension awarded 11 Aug 1857. SOURCE: WO120 Volume 70 page 331. INDEX # 8014.
John GIBBS; pension awarded 11 Aug 1857. SOURCE: WO120 Volume 70 page 331. INDEX # 8015.
Charles GOODMAN; pension awarded 11 Aug 1857; died 28 Sep 1879, Toronto, Ontario, Canada. SOURCE: WO120 Volume 70 page 331. INDEX # 8016.
Robert GRINSTEAD; pension awarded 11 Aug 1857. SOURCE: WO120 Volume 70 page 331. INDEX # 8017.
Peter GUNN; pension awarded 11 Aug 1857. SOURCE: WO120 Volume 70 page 331. INDEX # 8018.
John HADLEY; pension awarded 11 Aug 1857. SOURCE: WO120 Volume 70 page 331. INDEX # 8019.
Henry KNOWLES; pension awarded 11 Aug 1857. SOURCE: WO120 Volume 70 page 331. INDEX # 8020.
Thomas LUCKHURST; pension awarded 11 Aug 1857. SOURCE: WO120 Volume 70 page 331. INDEX # 8021.
George MCARTHUR; pension awarded 11 Aug 1857. SOURCE: WO120 Volume 70 page 331. INDEX # 8022.

Royal Canadian Rifle Regiment (continued)

Thomas MEHERAN; pension awarded 11 Aug 1857. SOURCE: WO120 Volume 70 page 331. INDEX # 8023.
John MARA; pension awarded 11 Aug 1857. SOURCE: WO120 Volume 70 page 331. INDEX # 8024.
Martin RUBERY; pension awarded 11 Aug 1857. SOURCE: WO120 Volume 70 page 331. INDEX # 8025.
Richard SEATON; pension awarded 11 Aug 1857. SOURCE: WO120 Volume 70 page 331. INDEX # 8026.
William STEPHENS; pension awarded 11 Aug 1857. SOURCE: WO120 Volume 70 page 331. INDEX # 8027.
James TAYLOR; pension awarded 11 Aug 1857. SOURCE: WO120 Volume 70 page 332. INDEX # 8028.
Thomas THOMPSON; pension awarded 11 Aug 1857. SOURCE: WO120 Volume 70 page 332. INDEX # 8029.
William URQUHART; pension awarded 11 Aug 1857. SOURCE: WO120 Volume 70 page 332. INDEX # 8030.
Peter WHELAN; pension awarded 11 Aug 1857. SOURCE: WO120 Volume 70 page 332. INDEX # 8031.
Daniel MULLEN; pension awarded 1 Sep 1857. SOURCE: WO120 Volume 70 page 332. INDEX # 8032.

Cape Mounted Rifles

David KETTLES; pension awarded 8 May 1849. SOURCE: WO120 Volume 70 page 340. INDEX # 8033.
Bern^d MCCABE; pension awarded 8 May 1849. SOURCE: WO120 Volume 70 page 340. INDEX # 8034.
Robt BELL; pension awarded 10 Jul 1849. SOURCE: WO120 Volume 70 page 340. INDEX # 8035.
Thos LITTLE; pension awarded 10 Jul 1849. SOURCE: WO120 Volume 70 page 340. INDEX # 8036.
Ja^s DAWSON; pension awarded 28 Aug 1849. SOURCE: WO120 Volume 70 page 340. INDEX # 8037.
Wm NEWTH; pension awarded 23 Jul 1850. SOURCE: WO120 Volume 70 page 340. INDEX # 8038.
Wm SLATTERY; pension awarded 23 Jul 1850. SOURCE: WO120 Volume 70 page 340. INDEX # 8039.

Cape Infantry

John LORDON; pension awarded 23 May 1831; residence - Cape of Good Hope, South Africa. SOURCE: WO120 Volume 70 page 344. INDEX # 8040.
Jos^h LERCY; pension awarded 21 May 1828; residence - Cape of Good Hope, South Africa; died 19 Aug 1850. SOURCE: WO120 Volume 70 page 344. INDEX # 8041.

Canadian Volunteers

Willm KIDD; pension awarded 12 May 1841; residence - Huntingdon, Quebec, Canada. SOURCE: WO120 Volume 70 page 346. INDEX # 8042.
Willm DURHAM; pension awarded 12 May 1841; residence - St. Jean, Quebec, Canada. SOURCE: WO120 Volume 70 page 346. INDEX # 8043.
Matt^w LEICH; pension awarded 12 May 1841; residence - Montreal, Quebec, Canada. SOURCE: WO120 Volume 70 page 346. INDEX # 8044.
Hethington FOSTER; pension awarded 23 Jan 1841; residence - Toronto, Ontario, Canada. SOURCE: WO120 Volume 70 page 346. INDEX # 8045.
Robt MORRISON; pension awarded 12 May 1841; residence - St. Jean, Quebec, Canada. SOURCE: WO120 Volume 70 page 346. INDEX # 8046.
Philip ATKINS; pension awarded 12 May 1841; residence - Ontario, Canada. SOURCE: WO120 Volume 70 page 346. INDEX # 8047.

Military Laborers

Ja^s CORNER; pension awarded 10 Feb 1846; died 9 Aug 1846. SOURCE: WO120 Volume 70 page 348. INDEX # 8048.

Ceylon Rifle Regiment

H^y MILLER; pension awarded 12 Dec 1832; residence - Ceylon. SOURCE: WO120 Volume 70 page 349. INDEX # 8049.

Geo^e FOWLER; pension awarded 9 Jan 1832; residence - Ceylon. SOURCE: WO120 Volume 70 page 349. INDEX # 8050.

Ja^s CONNELLAN; pension awarded 13 Oct 1846; residence - Ceylon. SOURCE: WO120 Volume 70 page 349. INDEX # 8051.

Jno BRADLEY; pension awarded 22 Aug 1848; residence - Ceylon; died 28 Oct 1848. SOURCE: WO120 Volume 70 page 349. INDEX # 8052.

4th Ceylon Regiment

Ja^s WATTS; pension awarded 9 Aug 1816; residence - Bytown, Ontario, Canada. SOURCE: WO120 Volume 70 page 352. INDEX # 8053.

Ja^s BAIRD; pension awarded 2 Nov 1815; residence - Toronto, Ontario, Canada; died 6 Apr 1850. SOURCE: WO120 Volume 70 page 352. INDEX # 8054.

De Meuron's Regiment

Nich^s BOURGNON; pension awarded 27 Jan 1817; residence - St. Jean, Quebec, Canada; died 4 Feb 1845. SOURCE: WO120 Volume 70 page 354. INDEX # 8055.

Canadian Fencibles

Richd CUDNEY; pension awarded 27 Jan 1817; residence - Toronto, Ontario, Canada; died 9 Apr 1869, Hamilton, Ontario, Canada. SOURCE: WO120 Volume 70 page 355. INDEX # 8056.

John CLARKE; pension awarded 29 Sep 1819; residence - Perth, Ontario, Canada; died in 1847. SOURCE: WO120 Volume 70 page 355. INDEX # 8057.

Wm MATHEWSON; pension awarded 23 Nov 1825; residence - Perth, Ontario, Canada. SOURCE: WO120 Volume 70 page 355. INDEX # 8058.

Danl BUCHANAN; pension awarded 27 Jan 1817; residence - Perth, Ontario, Canada. SOURCE: WO120 Volume 70 page 355. INDEX # 8059.

Ja^s NESBITT; pension awarded 29 Jul 1818; residence - Toronto, Ontario, Canada; died 17 Sep 1847. SOURCE: WO120 Volume 70 page 355. INDEX # 8060.

Glengarry Fencibles

John SULLIVAN; pension awarded 24 Nov 1824; residence - Bytown, Ontario, Canada. SOURCE: WO120 Volume 70 page 358. INDEX # 8061.

Willm DUKES; pension awarded 14 Feb 1843; residence - Penetanguishene, Ontario, Canada; died 24 Apr 1848. SOURCE: WO120 Volume 70 page 258. INDEX # 8062.

Ja^s DOYLE; pension awarded 28 Jul 1845; residence - Kingston, Ontario, Canada; died 28 Sep 1861, Toronto, Ontario, Canada. SOURCE: WO120 Volume 70 page 358. INDEX # 8063.

Robt DEA; pension awarded 23 May 1821; residence - Kingston, Ontario, Canada. SOURCE: WO120 Volume 70 page 358. INDEX # 8064.

Lyman HUMERSTON; pension awarded 28 Jul 1815; residence - Kingston, Ontario, Canada. SOURCE: WO120 Volume 70 page 358. INDEX # 8065.

Thaddeus LEWIS; pension awarded 23 May 1821; residence - Kingston, Ontario, Canada; died 1 Jul 1866. SOURCE: WO120 Volume 70 page 358. INDEX # 8066.

Barney MCGUIRE; pension awarded 5 Jun 1817; residence - Toronto, Ontario, Canada. SOURCE: WO120 Volume 70 page 358. INDEX # 8067.

Jno MCDONALD; pension awarded 16 Jan 1800; residence - Montreal, Quebec, Canada. SOURCE: WO120 Volume 70 page 358. INDEX # 8068.

Glengarry Fencibles (continued)

And^w HUFFMAN; pension awarded 28 Jul 1815; residence - Quebec, Quebec, Canada. SOURCE: WO120 Volume 70 page 358. INDEX # 8069.

Donante FERRARO; pension awarded 28 Jul 1815; residence - Montreal, Quebec, Canada. SOURCE: WO120 Volume 70 page 358. INDEX # 8070.

Neal MCLEAN; pension awarded 28 Jul 1815; residence - Quebec, Quebec, Canada. SOURCE: WO120 Volume 70 page 358. INDEX # 8071.

Alex^r MATHESON; pension awarded 12 May 1819; residence - Smiths Falls, Ontario, Canada. SOURCE: WO120 Volume 70 page 358. INDEX # 8072.

David VONOOLKENBURG; pension awarded 10 Aug 1847; died 15 Jan 1877, Toronto, Ontario, Canada. SOURCE: WO120 Volume 70 page 358. INDEX # 8073.

James CUMMINGS; pension awarded 28 Jul 1815; residence - Toronto, Ontario, Canada. SOURCE: WO120 Volume 70 page 358. INDEX # 8074.

Gordon Fencibles

Robt MCKENZIE; pension awarded 6 May 1797; residence - Perth; died in 1846. SOURCE: WO120 Volume 70 page 359. INDEX # 8075.

Newfoundland Fencibles

Den^s BRYAN; pension awarded 30 Aug 1826; residence - Halifax, Nova Scotia, Canada. SOURCE: WO120 Volume 70 page 360. INDEX # 8076.

Willm DRISCOLL; pension awarded 5 Jul 1820; residence - Halifax, Nova Scotia, Canada. SOURCE: WO120 Volume 70 page 360. INDEX # 8077.

Willm DWYER; pension awarded 8 Aug 1838; residence - Halifax, Nova Scotia, Canada. SOURCE: WO120 Volume 70 page 360. INDEX # 8078.

John HUNT; pension awarded 5 Jul 1820; residence - Halifax, Nova Scotia, Canada. SOURCE: WO120 Volume 70 page 360. INDEX # 8079.

Willm HASLETT; pension awarded 5 Jul 1820; residence - Halifax, Nova Scotia, Canada. SOURCE: WO120 Volume 70 page 360. INDEX # 8080.

Richd HARRIS; pension awarded 5 Jul 1820; residence - Halifax, Nova Scotia, Canada. SOURCE: WO120 Volume 70 page 360. INDEX # 8081.

Thos HARLEY; pension awarded 25 Jun 1829; residence - Halifax, Nova Scotia, Canada. SOURCE: WO120 Volume 70 page 360. INDEX # 8082.

Richd LANE; pension awarded 5 Jul 1820; residence - Halifax, Nova Scotia, Canada. SOURCE: WO120 Volume 70 page 360. INDEX # 8083.

John MITCHELL; pension awarded 30 Jun 1825; residence - Halifax, Nova Scotia, Canada. SOURCE: WO120 Volume 70 page 360. INDEX # 8084.

Willm PROUT; pension awarded 5 Jul 1820; residence - Halifax, Nova Scotia, Canada. SOURCE: WO120 Volume 70 page 360. INDEX # 8085.

Pat^k RILEY; pension awarded 30 Jun 1825; residence - Halifax, Nova Scotia, Canada. SOURCE: WO120 Volume 70 page 360. INDEX # 8086.

Willm WILKINS; pension awarded 30 Jan 1828; residence - Halifax, Nova Scotia, Canada. SOURCE: WO120 Volume 70 page 360. INDEX # 8087.

Ja^s BUTLER; pension awarded 20 Mar 1822; residence - St. Johns; died 15 Dec 1848. SOURCE: WO120 Volume 70 page 360. INDEX # 8088.

John WHITNEY; pension awarded 12 Sep 1831; residence - St. Johns. SOURCE: WO120 Volume 70 page 360. INDEX # 8089.

Willm LUSH; pension awarded 5 Jul 1820; residence - Halifax, Nova Scotia, Canada. SOURCE: WO120 Volume 70 page 360. INDEX # 8090.

Jos^h LAROUX; pension awarded 13 Apr 1824; residence - Halifax, Nova Scotia, Canada. SOURCE: WO120 Volume 70 page 360. INDEX # 8091.

Newfoundland Fencibles (continued)

Eman^l MURDEN; pension awarded 28 Mar 1821; residence - Halifax, Nova Scotia, Canada. SOURCE: WO120 Volume 70 page 360. INDEX # 8092.

Chas MCGARAHAN; pension awarded 8 Feb 1814; residence - Montreal, Quebec, Canada; died 11 Jul 1848. SOURCE: WO120 Volume 70 page 360. INDEX # 8093.

Ed^wd POWER; pension awarded 7 Feb 1822; residence - Quebec, Quebec, Canada; died 22 Feb 1849. SOURCE: WO120 Volume 70 page 360. INDEX # 8094.

John SPARROW; pension awarded 16 Sep 1814; residence - Bytown, Ontario, Canada; died 31 Jan 1856. SOURCE: WO120 Volume 70 page 360. INDEX # 8095.

Henry EMBERLEY; pension awarded 19 Sep 1815; residence - Kingston, Ontario, Canada; died 12 Dec 1868, Toronto, Ontario, Canada. SOURCE: WO120 Volume 70 page 361. INDEX # 8096.

Ja^s BARNARD; pension awarded 30 Oct 1816; residence - Newfoundland, Canada; died 21 Oct 1851. SOURCE: WO120 Volume 70 page 361. INDEX # 8097.

John MAHONS; pension awarded 4 Feb 1820; residence - Toronto, Ontario, Canada. SOURCE: WO120 Volume 70 page 361. INDEX # 8098.

Nova Scotia Fencibles

Ja^s BROWN; pension awarded 28 Mar 1831; residence - Sydney, Nova Scotia, Canada; died 22 Jan 1870. SOURCE: WO120 Volume 70 page 363. INDEX # 8099.

Jno BUCHANON; pension awarded 23 Jul 1823; residence - Charlottetown, Prince Edward Island, Canada. SOURCE: WO120 Volume 70 page 363. INDEX # 8100.

Willm BRIDLE; pension awarded 30 Aug 1826; residence - Halifax, Nova Scotia, Canada. SOURCE: WO120 Volume 70 page 363. INDEX # 8101.

Moses BROWN; pension awarded 11 Oct 1826; residence - Halifax, Nova Scotia, Canada. SOURCE: WO120 Volume 70 page 363. INDEX # 8102.

Ja^s BROPHY; pension awarded 25 Sep 1822; residence - Halifax, Nova Scotia, Canada. SOURCE: WO120 Volume 70 page 363. INDEX # 8103.

Jno COREY; pension awarded 25 Sep 1822; residence - Halifax, Nova Scotia, Canada; died 17 Oct 1846. SOURCE: WO120 Volume 70 page 363. INDEX # 8104.

Willm CORBIN; pension awarded 30 Jun 1825; residence - Halifax, Nova Scotia, Canada. SOURCE: WO120 Volume 70 page 363. INDEX # 8105.

Reynolds CUMMINS; pension awarded 31 Oct 1827; residence - Sydney, Nova Scotia, Canada. SOURCE: WO120 Volume 70 page 363. INDEX # 8106.

Pat^k DRISCOLL; pension awarded 25 Sep 1822; residence - Halifax, Nova Scotia, Canada; died 2 Apr 1858. SOURCE: WO120 Volume 70 page 363. INDEX # 8107.

Geo^e ELLIOTT; pension awarded 23 Jul 1823; residence - Halifax, Nova Scotia, Canada. SOURCE: WO120 Volume 70 page 363. INDEX # 8108.

Jos^h GATES; pension awarded 25 Sep 1822; residence - Halifax, Nova Scotia, Canada. SOURCE: WO120 Volume 70 page 363. INDEX # 8109.

Thos GUEST; pension awarded 1 Feb 1826; residence - Halifax, Nova Scotia, Canada. SOURCE: WO120 Volume 70 page 363. INDEX # 8110.

Ja^s GIFFORD; pension awarded 11 Oct 1826; residence - Halifax, Nova Scotia, Canada; died 1 Feb 1852. SOURCE: WO120 Volume 70 page 363. INDEX # 8111.

John GRAY; pension awarded 8 Aug 1827; residence - Halifax, Nova Scotia, Canada. SOURCE: WO120 Volume 70 page 363. INDEX # 8112.

John JONES; pension awarded 13 Dec 1826; residence - Halifax, Nova Scotia, Canada; died 5 Apr 1850. SOURCE: WO120 Volume 70 page 363. INDEX # 8113.

Jacob LOUNDER; pension awarded 23 Jul 1823; residence - Halifax, Nova Scotia, Canada. SOURCE: WO120 Volume 70 page 363. INDEX # 8114.

Willm LORRAMORE; pension awarded 7 Mar 1827. SOURCE: WO120 Volume 70 page 363. INDEX # 8115.

John LITCHEN; pension awarded 8 Aug 1827; residence - Halifax, Nova Scotia, Canada. SOURCE: WO120 Volume 70 page 363. INDEX # 8116

Nova Scotia Fencibles (continued)

John MURPHY; pension awarded 25 Sep 1822; residence - Charlottetown, Prince Edward Island, Canada; died 15 Nov 1852. SOURCE: WO120 Volume 70 page 363. INDEX # 8117.

Peter MORAN; pension awarded 25 Sep 1822; residence - Halifax, Nova Scotia, Canada. SOURCE: WO120 Volume 70 page 363. INDEX # 8118.

Jno MARLINSON; pension awarded 21 Jan 1824; residence - Halifax, Nova Scotia, Canada. SOURCE: WO120 Volume 70 page 364. INDEX # 8119.

Jno MCNEIL; pension awarded 23 Jul 1823; residence - Charlottetown, Prince Edward Island, Canada. SOURCE: WO120 Volume 70 page 364. INDEX # 8120.

Don^d MCINNES; pension awarded 15 Mar 1826; residence - Halifax, Nova Scotia, Canada. SOURCE: WO120 Volume 70 page 364. INDEX # 8121.

Wm PARSONS; pension awarded 7 Mar 1827; residence - Halifax, Nova Scotia, Canada. SOURCE: WO120 Volume 70 page 364. INDEX # 8122.

Moses PIFFY; pension awarded 9 Dec 1827; residence - Halifax, Nova Scotia, Canada; died 30 Sep 1856. SOURCE: WO120 Volume 70 page 364. INDEX # 8123.

Lawr^e SOURWINE; pension awarded 12 May 1824; residence - Sydney, Nova Scotia, Canada; died 2 Apr 1849. SOURCE: WO120 Volume 70 page 364. INDEX # 8124.

Ja^s SECAUR; pension awarded 13 Dec 1826; residence - Halifax, Nova Scotia, Canada. SOURCE: WO120 Volume 70 page 364. INDEX # 8125.

Chr^r VINER; pension awarded 9 Jun 1830; residence - Halifax, Nova Scotia, Canada. SOURCE: WO120 Volume 70 page 364. INDEX # 8126.

John LEWIS; pension awarded 20 Mar 1822; residence - Charlottetown, Prince Edward Island, Canada. SOURCE: WO120 Volume 70 page 364. INDEX # 8127.

John KARNEY; pension awarded 25 Sep 1822; residence - Halifax, Nova Scotia, Canada. SOURCE: WO120 Volume 70 page 364. INDEX # 8128.

Thos PENDEGAST; pension awarded 1 May 1822; residence - Halifax, Nova Scotia, Canada; died in 1847. SOURCE: WO120 Volume 70 page 364. INDEX # 8129.

Jno N. REESE; pension awarded 25 Sep 1822; residence - Halifax, Nova Scotia, Canada. SOURCE: WO120 Volume 70 page 364. INDEX # 8130.

Jno ONEILL; pension awarded 25 Sep 1822; residence - Halifax, Nova Scotia, Canada; died in Sep 1856. SOURCE: WO120 Volume 70 page 364. INDEX # 8131.

Jno HIGGS; pension awarded 12 Sep 1821; residence - Halifax, Nova Scotia, Canada. SOURCE: WO120 Volume 70 page 364. INDEX # 8132.

Ja^s NORRIS; pension awarded 1 May 1822; residence - Halifax, Nova Scotia, Canada; died in 1853. SOURCE: WO120 Volume 70 page 364. INDEX # 8133.

Willm NORRIS; pension awarded 25 Sep 1822; residence - Halifax, Nova Scotia, Canada. SOURCE: WO120 Volume 70 page 364. INDEX # 8135.

Thos STACEY; pension awarded 29 Oct 1828; residence - Halifax, Nova Scotia, Canada; died in Apr 1851. SOURCE: WO120 Volume 70 page 364. INDEX # 8135.

Peter SAVAGE; pension awarded 30 Oct 1816; residence - Halifax, Nova Scotia, Canada; died 26 Aug 1845. SOURCE: WO120 Volume 70 page 364. INDEX # 8136.

Robt PATTERSON; pension awarded 25 Sep 1822; residence - Halifax, Nova Scotia, Canada. SOURCE: WO120 Volume 70 page 364. INDEX # 8137.

St. Helena Regiment

Mall^w CARTER; pension awarded 13 Jan 1852; died 16 Sep 1881, St. Helena. SOURCE: WO120 Volume 70 page 366. INDEX # 8138.

Royal Africa Corps

Joseph HALL; pension awarded 11 Nov 1817; residence - Sierra Leone, Africa. SOURCE: WO120 Volume 70 page 367. INDEX # 8139.

Foreign British Legion

Lawr^e DANNIAN; pension awarded 5 Aug 1799; residence - Gibraltar; died 14 Mar 1854. SOURCE: WO120 Volume 70 page 368. INDEX # 8140.

Independent Company

John DRAIN; pension awarded 7 Feb 1803; residence - Toronto, Ontario, Canada; died in 1846. SOURCE: WO120 Volume 70 page 369. INDEX # 8141.

New York Regiment

Jno HELMER; pension awarded 9 Aug 1842; residence - Cornwall, Ontario, Canada; died 1 May 1849. SOURCE: WO120 Volume 70 page 370. INDEX # 8142.

King's German Legion

Justus SCHREIBER; pension awarded 19 Jul 1816; residence - Kingston, Ontario, Canada; died 25 Feb 1855. SOURCE: WO120 Volume 70 page 370. INDEX # 8143.

Chr^r HARTJE; pension awarded - date missing. SOURCE: WO120 Volume 70 page 370. INDEX # 8144.

Staff Corps

Ja^s CLIMO; pension awarded 11 Nov 1829; residence - Carillon, Quebec, Canada. SOURCE: WO120 Volume 70 page 371. INDEX # 8145.

Willm KING; pension awarded 11 Apr 1832; residence - Bytown, Ontario, Canada. SOURCE: WO120 Volume 70 page 371. INDEX # 8146.

John SCOTT; pension awarded 11 Apr 1832; residence - Bytown, Ontario, Canada; died 13 Nov 1853. SOURCE: WO120 Volume 70 page 371. INDEX # 8147.

Ja^s MURRAY; pension awarded 14 Nov 1832; residence - Montreal, Quebec, Canada; died 28 Sep 1853. SOURCE: WO120 Volume 70 page 371. INDEX # 8148.

Geo^e R. THOMAS; pension awarded 9 Feb 1831; residence - Ceylon. SOURCE: WO120 Volume 70 page 371. INDEX # 8149.

Edm^d WILLIAMS; pension awarded 11 Apr 1832; residence - Toronto, Ontario, Canada; died 14 Apr 1853. SOURCE: WO120 Volume 70 page 371. INDEX # 8150.

Don^d CORMICK; pension awarded 8 Aug 1832; residence - Mauritius; died 15 Jun 1854. SOURCE: WO120 Volume 70 page 371. INDEX # 8151.

Jno KEATLEY; pension awarded 14 Nov 1832; residence - Carillon, Quebec, Canada. SOURCE: WO120 Volume 70 page 371. INDEX # 8152.

Thos TAYLOR; pension awarded 14 Nov 1832; residence - Carillon, Quebec, Canada; died 29 Oct 1876, Ottawa, Ontario, Canada. SOURCE: WO120 Volume 70 page 371. INDEX # 8153.

Richd BIRD; pension awarded 10 Aug 1831; residence - Carillon, Quebec, Canada; died in May 1847. SOURCE: WO120 Volume 70 page 371. INDEX # 8154.

Jno HORNBY; pension awarded 11 Apr 1832; residence - Quebec, Quebec, Canada. SOURCE: WO120 Volume 70 page 371. INDEX # 8155.

Jos^h TANNER; pension awarded 20 Jul 1825; residence - Toronto, Ontario, Canada. SOURCE: WO120 Volume 70 page 371. INDEX # 8156.

Jno HILLIARD; pension awarded 14 Nov 1832; residence - Carillon, Quebec, Canada; died London, Ontario, Canada. SOURCE: WO120 Volume 70 page 371. INDEX # 8157.

Dav^d REEVES; pension awarded 11 Apr 1832; residence - Montreal, Quebec, Canada. SOURCE: WO120 Volume 70 page 371. INDEX # 8158.

Ja^s MOUNTSTEPHEN; pension awarded 10 Aug 1831; residence - Montreal, Quebec, Canada. SOURCE: WO120 Volume 70 page 371. INDEX # 8159.

1st West India Regiment

Benjn PINTO; pension awarded 2 Jun 1825; residence - Barbadoes, West Indies. SOURCE: WO120 Volume 70 page 373. INDEX # 8160.

Jno BLACK; pension awarded 14 Oct 1821; residence - St. Lucia, West Indies; died 29 Jun 1872. SOURCE: WO120 Volume 70 page 373. INDEX # 8161.

Wm STEWART; pension awarded 9 May 1848; died 26 Oct 1864, Jamaica, West Indies. SOURCE: WO120 Volume 70 page 373. INDEX # 8162.

2nd West India Regiment

Saml PETERS; pension awarded 28 Jul 1841; residence - Jamaica, West Indies; died 16 Nov 1864. SOURCE: WO120 Volume 70 page 375. INDEX # 8163.

John NIXON; pension awarded 7 Mar 1827; residence - Bahamas, West Indies. SOURCE: WO120 Volume 70 page 375. INDEX # 8164.

Colin BLYTH; pension awarded 27 Feb 1839; residence - Jamaica, West Indies. SOURCE: WO120 Volume 70 page 375. INDEX # 8165.

Willm PERKINS; pension awarded 13 Apr 1836; residence - Bahamas, West Indies. SOURCE: WO120 Volume 70 page 375. INDEX # 8166.

3rd West India Regiment

Jacob VOGEL; pension awarded 20 Nov 1839; residence - St. Lucia, West Indies; died 6 Aug 1879, Barbadoes, West Indies. SOURCE: WO120 Volume 70 page 377. INDEX # 8167.

Benjn BUTTERWORTH; pension awarded 8 May 1849. SOURCE: WO120 Volume 70 page 377. INDEX # 8168.

Wm MITCHELL; pension awarded 13 Dec 1853; residence - Sierra Leone, Africa; died 10 Dec 1853. SOURCE: WO120 Volume 70 page 377. INDEX # 8169.

Herbert MENDS; pension awarded 24 Oct 1843; residence - Trinidad, West Indies. SOURCE: WO120 Volume 70 page 377. INDEX # 8170.

4th West India Regiment

Fred^k HEYLIGER; pension awarded 30 Sep 1822; residence - Trinidad, West Indies; died 1 Aug 1848. SOURCE: WO120 Volume 70 page 379. INDEX # 8171.

Jos^h CORBISHLEY; pension awarded 25 Sep 1817; residence - London; died 3 Jun 1848. SOURCE: WO120 Volume 70 page 379. INDEX # 8172.

Victor COLE; pension awarded 15 Mar 1826; residence - Dominica, West Indies; died 4 Oct 1855. SOURCE: WO120 Volume 70 page 379. INDEX # 8173.

6th West India Regiment

Jno MANUEL; pension awarded 26 Oct 1821; residence - Trinidad, West Indies. SOURCE: WO120 Volume 70 page 381. INDEX # 8174.

Philip BOATERS; pension awarded 22 Dec 1824; residence - Grenada, West Indies; died 14 Aug 1856. SOURCE: WO120 Volume 70 page 381. INDEX # 8175.

John LOWE; pension awarded 24 Oct 1821; residence - St. Vincent, West Indies; died 21 Aug 1845. SOURCE: WO120 Volume 70 page 381. INDEX # 8176.

7th West India Regiment

Isaac PETER; pension awarded 21 Aug 1817; residence - Sierra Leone, Africa. SOURCE: WO120 Volume 70 page 383. INDEX # 8177.

John TIMOTHY; pension awarded 21 Aug 1817; residence - Sierra Leone, Africa; died 11 Mar 1853. SOURCE: WO120 Volume 70 page 383. INDEX # 8178.

Yeomanry

Hill WILSON; pension awarded 25 Jun 1806; residence - Cornwall, Ontario, Canada; died 30 Jul 1850. SOURCE: WO120 Volume 70 page 384. INDEX # 8179.
Ja^s SAUNDERS; pension awarded 28 Feb 1821; residence - Richmond, Ontario, Canada. SOURCE: WO120 Volume 70 page 383. INDEX # 8180.
John GREENLY; pension awarded 20 Jan 1819; residence - Perth, Ontario, Canada; died 15 Sep 1854. SOURCE: WO120 Volume 70 page 384. INDEX # 8181.

York Chasseurs

Thos LEONARD; pension awarded 24 Oct 1821; residence - Perth, Ontario, Canada. SOURCE: WO120 Volume 70 page 386. INDEX # 8182.

Militia

Thos POTH; pension awarded 16 Apr 1808; residence - Belleville, Ontario, Canada; died 17 Jan 1850. SOURCE: WO120 Volume 70 page 388. INDEX # 8183.
Willm BROWNE; pension awarded 29 May 1811; residence - Wm Henry, Quebec, Canada. SOURCE: WO120 Volume 70 page 388. INDEX # 8184.
Jos^h FRY; pension awarded 30 Sep 1812; residence - Toronto, Ontario, Canada. SOURCE: WO120 Volume 70 page 388. INDEX # 8185.
Luke SCOTT; pension awarded 9 Jan 1823; residence - Toronto, Ontario, Canada. SOURCE: WO120 Volume 70 page 388. INDEX # 8186.
Jos^h HUNTER; pension awarded 25 Jun 1829; residence - St. Johns; died in Jul 1846. SOURCE: WO120 Volume 70 page 388. INDEX # 8187.
Dav^d TAYLOR; pension awarded 17 Jun 1829; residence - New South Wales, Australia. SOURCE: WO120 Volume 70 page 388. INDEX # 8188.
Const^l MAGUIRE; pension awarded 15 Jul 1829; residence - St. Johns. SOURCE: WO120 Volume 70 page 388. INDEX # 8189.
John LEITH; pension awarded 25 Jun 1829; residence - Quebec, Quebec, Canada. SOURCE: WO120 Volume 70 page 388. INDEX # 8190.
Jos^h CHARTERS; pension awarded 16 Sep 1829; residence - Montreal, Quebec, Canada. SOURCE: WO120 Volume 70 page 388. INDEX # 8191.
Ja^s GLENNY; pension awarded 25 Jun 1829; residence - London, Ontario, Canada. SOURCE: WO120 Volume 70 page 388. INDEX # 8192.
Richd ANDERSON; pension awarded 17 Jun 1829; residence - Toronto, Ontario, Canada. SOURCE: WO120 Volume 70 page 388. INDEX # 8193.
John CRAIG; pension awarded 17 Jun 1829; residence - Toronto, Ontario, Canada. SOURCE: WO120 Volume 70 page 388. INDEX # 8194.
Mich^l WHITE; pension awarded 11 Nov 1835; residence - Fredericton, New Brunswick, Canada. SOURCE: WO120 Volume 70 page 388. INDEX # 8195.
And^w ROSS; pension awarded 11 Nov 1835; residence - Port Macquarie, Australia. SOURCE: WO120 Volume 70 page 388. INDEX # 8196.
Robt MILLS; pension awarded 25 25 Jun 1829; residence - D^d Ville, Quebec, Canada. SOURCE: WO120 Volume 70 page 388. INDEX # 8197.
Pat^k SMITH; pension awarded 20 Oct 1835; residence - Sydney. SOURCE: WO120 Volume 70 page 388. INDEX # 8198.
Willm REED; pension awarded 25 Jun 1829; residence - South Australia, Australia. SOURCE: WO120 Volume 70 page 388. INDEX # 8199.
Martin FOYLE; pension awarded 17 Jun 1829; residence - Montreal, Quebec, Canada. SOURCE: WO120 Volume 70 page 388. INDEX # 8200.
Robt MCKONE; pension awarded 25 Jun 1829; residence - Bytown, Ontario, Canada; died 16 Apr 1846. SOURCE: WO120 Volume 70 page 388. INDEX # 8201.

Militia (continued)

And^w GIVENS; pension awarded 19 Jun 1822; residence - Perth, Ontario, Canada; died 25 Dec 1857. SOURCE: WO120 Volume 70 page 388. INDEX # 8202.

Wm WILSON; pension awarded 12 May 1819; residence - St. Johns. SOURCE: WO120 Volume 70 page 389. INDEX # 8203.

Jno MCNICKLE; pension awarded 17 Jan 1799; residence - Prescott, Ontario, Canada; died in 1848. SOURCE: WO120 Volume 70 page 389. INDEX # 8204.

Jno WALSH; pension awarded 22 Dec 1824; residence - Toronto, Ontario, Canada; died 23 Nov 1866. SOURCE: WO120 Volume 70 page 389. INDEX # 8205.

Willm KEYS; pension awarded 24 Apr 1816; residence - Toronto, Ontario, Canada; died in 1850. SOURCE: WO120 Volume 70 page 389. INDEX # 8206.

Ja^s ROGERS; pension awarded 26 Oct 1814; residence - Toronto, Ontario, Canada; died 31 Oct 1846. SOURCE: WO120 Volume 70 page 389. INDEX # 8207.

John WHYTE; pension awarded 21 Jan 1831; residence - Montreal, Quebec, Canada. SOURCE: WO120 Volume 70 page 389. INDEX # 8208.

Willm DOLMAGE; pension awarded 9 Jan 1833; residence - Toronto, Ontario, Canada; died 24 Feb 1854. SOURCE: WO120 Volume 70 page 389. INDEX # 8209.

Robt CAMPBELL; pension awarded 20 Jan 1819; died 7 Sep 1853. SOURCE: WO120 Volume 70 page 389. INDEX # 8210.

Mich^l CONNOR; pension awarded 20 Jan 1819; residence - Perth, Ontario, Canada; died in 1849. SOURCE: WO120 Volume 70 page 389. INDEX # 8211.

Hugh JAMES; pension awarded 30 Nov 1814; residence - Niagara, Ontario, Canada. SOURCE: WO120 Volume 70 page 389. INDEX # 8212.

Hugh MILLER; pension awarded 27 Mar 1816; residence - Chambly, Quebec, Canada. SOURCE: WO120 Volume 70 page 389. INDEX # 8213.

Robt BOLES; pension awarded 18 Aug 1823; residence - Halifax, Nova Scotia, Canada; died in Aug 1853. SOURCE: WO120 Volume 70 page 389. INDEX # 8214.

Jno NORTHWOOD; pension awarded 30 Nov 1814; residence - Amherstburg, Ontario, Canada. SOURCE: WO120 Volume 70 page 389. INDEX # 8215.

Jer^h MCCROHAN; pension awarded 20 Oct 1836; residence - New South Wales, Australia. SOURCE: WO120 Volume 70 page 389. INDEX # 8216.

Ed^{wd} WARD; pension awarded 27 May 1829; residence - Quebec, Quebec, Canada. SOURCE: WO120 Volume 70 page 389. INDEX # 8217.

John BURGESS; pension awarded 25 Oct 1835; residence - Toronto, Ontario, Canada. SOURCE: WO120 Volume 70 page 389. INDEX # 8218.

Thos WELDON; pension awarded 31 Aug 1814; residence - Toronto, Ontario, Canada. SOURCE: WO120 Volume 70 page 389. INDEX # 8219.

Ja^s MILLS; pension awarded 19 Jun 1822; residence - Bytown, Ontario, Canada. SOURCE: WO120 Volume 70 page 389. INDEX # 8220.

H^y DONOUGHUE; pension awarded 7 Jun 1823; residence - Montreal, Quebec, Canada. SOURCE: WO120 Volume 70 page 389. INDEX # 8221.

J. KENWARD; pension awarded 12 May 1816; residence - London, Ontario, Canada. SOURCE: WO120 Volume 70 page 389. INDEX # 8222.

Willm SCOLES; pension awarded 1 Mar 1823; residence - Montreal, Quebec, Canada. SOURCE: WO120 Volume 70 page 390. INDEX # 8223.

Thos FORSYTHE; pension awarded 17 Jun 1831; residence - Toronto, Ontario, Canada. SOURCE: WO120 Volume 70 page 390. INDEX # 8224.

Ja^s MCCLELLAND; pension awarded 26 Feb 1817; residence - Quebec, Quebec, Canada. SOURCE: WO120 Volume 70 page 390. INDEX # 8225.

And^w STEVENSON; pension awarded 20 Oct 1835; residence - Toronto, Ontario, Canada; died 24 Nov 1854. SOURCE: WO120 Volume 70 page 390. INDEX # 8226.

Tim^y CAHALANE; pension awarded 26 Oct 1814; residence - Saint John, New Brunswick, Canada; died 18 Jun 1878, Saint John, New Brunswick , Canada. SOURCE: WO120 Volume 70 page 390. INDEX # 8227.

Militia (continued)

Chas SCOTT; pension awarded 11 Nov 1835; residence - Toronto, Ontario, Canada. SOURCE: WO120 Volume 70 page 390. INDEX # 8228.

Robt EDWARDS; pension awarded 9 Dec 1835; residence - Toronto, Ontario, Canada; died in 1853. SOURCE: WO120 Volume 70 page 390. INDEX # 8229.

Arch^d LYONS; pension awarded 20 Oct 1835; residence - Montreal, Quebec, Canada. SOURCE: WO120 Volume 70 page 390. INDEX # 8230.

Fra^s STEWART; pension awarded 20 Oct 1835; residence - Toronto, Ontario, Canada. SOURCE: WO120 Volume 70 page 390. INDEX # 8231.

Ja^s FALLON; pension awarded 11 Nov 1835; residence - London, Ontario, Canada; died 29 Jul 1865. SOURCE: WO120 Volume 70 page 390. INDEX # 8232.

Thos HARRIS; pension awarded 17 Jun 1829; residence - Quebec, Quebec, Canada; died 6 May 1855. SOURCE: WO120 Volume 70 page 390. INDEX # 8233.

Saml ROBINSON; pension awarded 11 Nov 1835; residence - London, Ontario, Canada; died 28 Nov 1861. SOURCE: WO120 Volume 70 page 390. INDEX # 8234.

Peter GARDINER; pension awarded 17 Jun 1829; residence - London, Ontario, Canada; died 16 Jul 1872, London, Ontario, Canada. SOURCE: WO120 Volume 70 page 390. INDEX # 8235.

Ja^s HORNE; pension awarded 26 Feb 1817; residence - Niagara, Ontario, Canada; died 2 May 1857. SOURCE: WO120 Volume 70 page 390. INDEX # 8236.

And^w WEAL; pension awarded 21 Jun 1826; residence - Toronto, Ontario, Canada; died 2 Jul 1846. SOURCE: WO120 Volume 70 page 390. INDEX # 8237.

Geo^e DAVIS; pension awarded 11 Nov 1835; residence - Quebec, Quebec, Canada; died 28 Jan 1857, Toronto, Ontario, Canada. SOURCE: WO120 Volume 70 page 390. INDEX # 8238.

Hugh SMITH; pension awarded 28 Apr 1813; residence - Penetanguishene, Ontario, Canada. SOURCE: WO120 Volume 70 page 390. INDEX # 8239.

Arch^d MCGREGOR; pension awarded ; residence - Quebec, Quebec, Canada. SOURCE: WO120 Volume 70 page 390. INDEX # 8240.

Mich^l TULLEY; pension awarded 11 Nov 1835; residence - Sydney; died 23 Jun 1849. SOURCE: WO120 Volume 70 page 390. INDEX # 8241.

Arch^d MCGREGOR; pension awarded 3 Sep 1823; residence - Quebec, Quebec, Canada. SOURCE: WO120 Volume 70 page 390. INDEX # 8242.

Mat^w DOBSON; pension awarded 9 Jan 1823; residence - Toronto, Ontario, Canada; died 29 Jul 1860. SOURCE: WO120 Volume 70 page 391. INDEX # 8243.

Staff Corps - Ordnance

Ja^s MONTEITH; pension awarded 14 Nov 1838; residence - South Australia, Australia. SOURCE: WO120 Volume 70 page 400. INDEX # 8244.

Thos HORGAN; pension awarded 8 Jan 1834; residence - Halifax, Nova Scotia, Canada. SOURCE: WO120 Volume 70 page 400. INDEX # 8245.

Willm BINDER; pension awarded 25 Apr 1835; residence - Jamaica, West Indies. SOURCE: WO120 Volume 70 page 400. INDEX # 8246.

John NORTHE; pension awarded 14 Mar 1838; residence - New South Wales, Australia; died 7 Jan 1875, Auckland, New Zealand. SOURCE: WO120 Volume 70 page 400. INDEX # 8247.

Jno WILLIAMS; pension awarded 8 Jan 1834; residence - Halifax, Nova Scotia, Canada. SOURCE: WO120 Volume 70 page 400. INDEX # 8248.

Geo^e SAXBY; pension awarded 25 Apr 1838; residence - New South Wales, Australia. SOURCE: WO120 Volume 70 page 400. INDEX # 8249.

Ja^s BARR; pension awarded 1 Dec 1832; residence - Charlottetown, Prince Edward Island, Canada. SOURCE: WO120 Volume 70 page 400. INDEX # 8250.

Royal Horse Artillery

Jn⁰ ATKINSON; pension awarded 8 Jan 1834; residence - London, Ontario, Canada. SOURCE: WO120 Volume 70 page 406. INDEX # 8251.

Ja⁵ ALDRIDGE; pension awarded 3 Feb 1821; residence - Hamilton, Ontario, Canada; died 26 Jan 1868. SOURCE: WO120 Volume 70 page 406. INDEX # 8252.

Tho⁵ DUDLOW; pension awarded 30 May 1820; residence - Montreal, Quebec, Canada. SOURCE: WO120 Volume 70 page 406. INDEX # 8253.

Ja⁵ MCKENZIE; pension awarded 1 Apr 1815; residence - Toronto, Ontario, Canada; died 9 Jun 1869. SOURCE: WO120 Volume 70 page 406. INDEX # 8254.

Jn⁰ GOODAL; pension awarded 1 Sep 1818; residence - Toronto, Ontario, Canada; died in 1852. SOURCE: WO120 Volume 70 page 406. INDEX # 8255.

Matt^w ALEXANDER; pension awarded 1 Apr 1819; residence - Toronto, Ontario, Canada; died 13 Sep 1866. SOURCE: WO120 Volume 70 page 406. INDEX # 8256.

Jos^h LOVE; pension awarded 1 Apr 1816; residence - Prescott, Ontario, Canada; died 29 Jun 1858. SOURCE: WO120 Volume 70 page 406. INDEX # 8257.

Tho⁵ NESBITT; pension awarded 1 Nov 1825; residence - Jamaica, West Indies; died 16 Apr 1877, Jamaica, West Indies. SOURCE: WO120 Volume 70 page 406. INDEX # 8258.

Willm BUGG; pension awarded 1 Aug 1821; residence - Buenos Aires, Argentina. SOURCE: WO120 Volume 70 page 406. INDEX # 8259.

Dun^n MCIVER; pension awarded 10 Jun 1822; residence - Bytown, Ontario, Canada. SOURCE: WO120 Volume 70 page 406. INDEX # 8260.

Geo^e FITZGERALD; pension awarded ; residence - South Australia, Australia; died 1 Jan 1863. SOURCE: WO120 Volume 70 page 406. INDEX # 8261.

1st Battalion of Artillery

Cha⁵ STEWART; pension awarded 12 Jan 1842; residence - Quebec, Quebec, Canada. SOURCE: WO120 Volume 70 page 414. INDEX # 8262.

Ja⁵ BARCLAY; pension awarded 13 Jan 1841; residence - Toronto, Ontario, Canada; died in Sep 1852. SOURCE: WO120 Volume 70 page 414. INDEX # 8263.

Alex^r JOHNSON; pension awarded 10 Jan 1838; residence - London, Ontario, Canada; died 21 Nov 1869. SOURCE: WO120 Volume 70 page 414. INDEX # 8264.

Geo^e WANLESS; pension awarded 1 Oct 1839; residence - Montreal, Quebec, Canada; died 6 May 1882. SOURCE: WO120 Volume 70 page 414. INDEX # 8257.

John WATT; pension awarded 12 Jul 1842; residence - Toronto, Ontario, Canada; died 30 Nov 1853. SOURCE: WO120 Volume 70 page 414. INDEX # 8266.

Jos^h TODD; pension awarded 10 Jan 1843; residence - Halifax, Nova Scotia, Canada. SOURCE: WO120 Volume 70 page 414. INDEX # 8267.

Willm GOLDSMITH; pension awarded 11 Jul 1843; residence - Kingston, Ontario, Canada; died 12 Sep 1869, Toronto, Ontario, Canada. SOURCE: WO120 Volume 70 page 414. INDEX # 8268.

Fra⁵ NICOLL; pension awarded 9 Apr 1844; residence - Toronto, Ontario, Canada; died 26 Jan 1873, Toronto, Ontario, Canada. SOURCE: WO120 Volume 70 page 414. INDEX # 8269.

Willm SCOTT; pension awarded 10 Jan 1843; residence - Halifax, Nova Scotia, Canada. SOURCE: WO120 Volume 70 page 414. INDEX # 8270.

Sampson BRIDGEWOOD; pension awarded 8 Jul 1835; residence - New South Wales, Australia. SOURCE: WO120 Volume 70 page 414. INDEX # 8271.

Ed^wd SHANN; pension awarded 8 Apr 1835; residence - Halifax, Nova Scotia, Canada. SOURCE: WO120 Volume 70 page 414. INDEX # 8272.

And^w WHITE; pension awarded 1 Jul 1834; residence - St. Johns. SOURCE: WO120 Volume 70 page 414. INDEX # 8273.

Geo^e PATTEN; pension awarded 11 Apr 1838; residence - Montreal, Quebec, Canada; died 6 Jul 1846. SOURCE: WO120 Volume 70 page 414. INDEX # 8274.

1st Battalion of Artillery (continued)

Ja^s RIDDELL; pension awarded 13 Oct 1846; residence - Halifax, Nova Scotia, Canada. SOURCE: WO120 Volume 70 page 414. INDEX # 8275.

Geo^e GURNETT; pension awarded 12 Jan 1847; residence - Van Diemen's Land, Australia; died 5 Dec 1884, Melbourne, Australia. SOURCE: WO120 Volume 70 page 414. INDEX # 8276.

Robt BURGESS; pension awarded 12 Jan 1847; residence - Van Diemen's Land, Australia; died in 1867, Hobarton, Australia. SOURCE: WO120 Volume 70 page 414. INDEX # 8277.

Thos HEULT; pension awarded 1 Apr 1833; residence - Halifax, Nova Scotia, Canada. SOURCE: WO120 Volume 70 page 414. INDEX # 8278.

Willm WILSON; pension awarded 1 Jan 1833; residence - Halifax, Nova Scotia, Canada. SOURCE: WO120 Volume 70 page 414. INDEX # 8279.

Peter DOWLING; pension awarded 1 Apr 1833; residence - Halifax, Nova Scotia, Canada. SOURCE: WO120 Volume 70 page 414. INDEX # 8280.

Ja^s AMBROSE; pension awarded 1 Jul 1833; residence - Adelaide; died 18 Sep 1858. SOURCE: WO120 Volume 70 page 414. INDEX # 8281.

Ja^s CRAWFORD; pension awarded 1 Jul 1833; residence - Charlottetown, Prince Edward Island, Canada. SOURCE: WO120 Volume 70 page 415. INDEX # 8282.

Willm SHIELDS; pension awarded 1 Apr 1833; residence - Halifax, Nova Scotia, Canada. SOURCE: WO120 Volume 70 page 415. INDEX # 8283.

Don^d MCINTOSH; pension awarded 1 Apr 1832; residence - Bytown, Ontario, Canada. SOURCE: WO120 Volume 70 page 415. INDEX # 8284.

Dav^d J. THOMPSON; pension awarded 1 Apr 1832; residence - Charlottetown, Prince Edward Island, Canada. SOURCE: WO120 Volume 70 page 415. INDEX # 8285.

Ja^s IRONS; pension awarded 1 Jan 1832; residence - Halifax, Nova Scotia, Canada. SOURCE: WO120 Volume 70 page 415. INDEX # 8286.

Robt HENRY; pension awarded 30 Jan 1824; residence - Montreal, Quebec, Canada. SOURCE: WO120 Volume 70 page 415. INDEX # 8287.

Dav^d ARMSTRONG; pension awarded 1 May 1817; residence - Huntingdon, Quebec, Canada. SOURCE: WO120 Volume 70 page 415. INDEX # 8288.

Jno JAMIESON; pension awarded 1 Sep 1816; residence - St. Johns. SOURCE: WO120 Volume 70 page 415. INDEX # 8289.

Willm LITTLE; pension awarded 1 Jul 1817; residence - Smiths Falls, Ontario, Canada; died 3 Jun 1858, Edinburgh. SOURCE: WO120 Volume 70 page 415. INDEX # 8290.

Ja^s GRAHAM; pension awarded 1 Jan 1815; residence - Perth, Ontario, Canada. SOURCE: WO120 Volume 70 page 415. INDEX # 8291.

Jno MCINTOSH; pension awarded 1 Sep 1825; residence - Halifax, Nova Scotia, Canada. SOURCE: WO120 Volume 70 page 415. INDEX # 8292.

Jno SPEAKMAN; pension awarded 18 Mar 1827; residence - Halifax, Nova Scotia, Canada. SOURCE: WO120 Volume 70 page 415. INDEX # 8293.

Jno OATES; pension awarded 9 Oct 1828; residence - Gibraltar; died 13 Feb 1852. SOURCE: WO120 Volume 70 page 415. INDEX # 8294.

Peter A. WRIGHT; pension awarded 1 Aug 1820; residence - Niagara, Ontario, Canada; died 27 Mar 1868, Hamilton, Ontario, Canada. SOURCE: WO120 Volume 70 page 415. INDEX # 8295.

Willm BOOTH; pension awarded 1 Apr 1827; residence - Quebec, Quebec, Canada. SOURCE: WO120 Volume 70 page 415. INDEX # 8296.

Willm DAVIS; pension awarded 1 Jul 1827; residence - Halifax, Nova Scotia, Canada. SOURCE: WO120 Volume 70 page 415. INDEX # 8297.

Moses ABBOTT; pension awarded 1 Oct 1814; residence - Wm Henry, Quebec, Canada. SOURCE: WO120 Volume 70 page 415. INDEX # 8298.

Robt BROWN; pension awarded 1 Jan 1826; residence - Barbadoes, West Indies. SOURCE: WO120 Volume 70 page 415. INDEX # 8299.

Ja^s ADAIR; pension awarded 1 Sep 1818; residence - Toronto, Ontario, Canada; died 12 May 1857. SOURCE: WO120 Volume 70 page 415. INDEX # 8300.

1st Battalion of Artillery (continued)

John FORBES; pension awarded 1 May 1813; residence - Halifax, Nova Scotia, Canada; died 15 Jan 1852. SOURCE: WO120 Volume 70 page 415. INDEX # 8301.

Thos MURPHY; pension awarded 1 Apr 1815; residence - Toronto, Ontario, Canada; died 21 Jul 1859. SOURCE: WO120 Volume 70 page 416. INDEX # 8302.

Davd LOGGIE; pension awarded 1 Nov 1827; residence - Quebec, Quebec, Canada. SOURCE: WO120 Volume 70 page 416. INDEX # 8303.

Willm FRASER; pension awarded 1 Jul 1816; residence - Penetanguishene, Ontario, Canada; died 20 Apr 1865, Hamilton, Ontario, Canada. SOURCE: WO120 Volume 70 page 416. INDEX # 8304.

Jehu Jno UNSWORTH; pension awarded 1 Oct 1817; residence - New South Wales, Australia; died 12 May 1851. SOURCE: WO120 Volume 70 page 416. INDEX # 8305.

Alexr ANDERSON; pension awarded ; residence - Montreal, Quebec, Canada; died 12 Apr 1858, Edinburgh. SOURCE: WO120 Volume 70 page 416. INDEX # 8306.

Jas RIDDELL; pension awarded 13 Oct 1846. SOURCE: WO120 Volume 70 page 416. INDEX # 8307.

Jas BLANEY; pension awarded 13 Jul 1847; residence - Montreal, Quebec, Canada; died 1 Nov 1880. SOURCE: WO120 Volume 70 page 416. INDEX # 8308.

Jas MOUNT; pension awarded 23 Nov 1847; died 18 Feb 1873, Halifax, Nova Scotia, Canada. SOURCE: WO120 Volume 70 page 416. INDEX # 8309.

Jas KIRK; pension awarded 23 Nov 1847. SOURCE: WO120 Volume 70 page 416. INDEX # 8310.

Jno MCCABE; pension awarded 23 Nov 1847; residence - London, Ontario, Canada; died 13 Dec 1863. SOURCE: WO120 Volume 70 page 416. INDEX # 8311.

Jno MCNULTY; pension awarded 23 Nov 1847. SOURCE: WO120 Volume 70 page 416. INDEX # 8312.

Jas EDWARDS; pension awarded 23 Nov 1847; died Boston, United States of America. SOURCE: WO120 Volume 70 page 416. INDEX # 8313.

Audley MCALLISTOR; pension awarded 23 Nov 1847; died 26 Dec 1872, Halifax, Nova Scotia, Canada. SOURCE: WO120 Volume 70 page 416. INDEX # 8314.

Wm BOWIE; pension awarded 23 Nov 1847. SOURCE: WO120 Volume 70 page 416. INDEX # 8315.

Wm TAYLOR; pension awarded 11 Apr 1848. SOURCE: WO120 Volume 70 page 416. INDEX # 8316.

Chrr HARTLEY; pension awarded 12 Sep 1848. SOURCE: WO120 Volume 70 page 416. INDEX # 8317.

Chas MCKEE; pension awarded 12 Sep 1848; died 6 Dec 1856. SOURCE: WO120 Volume 70 page 416. INDEX # 8318.

Wm DARLING; pension awarded 24 Jul 1849. SOURCE: WO120 Volume 70 page 416. INDEX # 8319.

Jno MEDCALF; pension awarded 9 Oct 1849. SOURCE: WO120 Volume 70 page 416. INDEX # 8320.

Jas WEIR; pension awarded 22 Dec 1849; died 2 Jun 1884, Sydney. SOURCE: WO120 Volume 70 page 416. INDEX # 8321.

Geoe TAIT; pension awarded 13 Aug 1850. SOURCE: WO120 Volume 70 page 417. INDEX # 8322.

Jas WILSON; pension awarded 13 Aug 1850. SOURCE: WO120 Volume 70 page 417. INDEX # 8323.

Jno GILMORE; pension awarded 8 Oct 1850; residence - Halifax, Nova Scotia, Canada; died 17 May 1857. SOURCE: WO120 Volume 70 page 417. INDEX # 8324.

Jas SAGE; pension awarded 25 Feb 1851; died 28 May 1882, Nova Scotia, Canada. SOURCE: WO120 Volume 70 page 417. INDEX # 8325.

Jas STUDD; pension awarded 8 Apr 1851. SOURCE: WO120 Volume 70 page 417. INDEX # 8326.

Danl ALLEN; pension awarded 8 Jul 1851. SOURCE: WO120 Volume 70 page 417. INDEX # 8327.

Wm Thos DRIVER; pension awarded 8 Jul 1851; died 26 Feb 1879, Toronto, Ontario, Canada. SOURCE: WO120 Volume 70 page 417. INDEX # 8328.

Robert THOMPSON; pension awarded 12 Jun 1855. SOURCE: WO120 Volume 70 page 417. INDEX # 8329.

2nd Battalion of Artillery

Geoe WATSON; pension awarded 18 Oct 1842; residence - Toronto, Ontario, Canada. SOURCE: WO120 Volume 70 page 426. INDEX # 8330.

Thos SMITH; pension awarded 11 Jan 1837; residence - Montreal, Quebec, Canada; died 9 Sep 1882, Armagh. SOURCE: WO120 Volume 70 page 426. INDEX # 8331.

WO120 VOLUME 70

2nd Battalion of Artillery (continued)

Jn⁰ MUSTARD; pension awarded 14 Oct 1845; residence - Montreal, Quebec, Canada; died in 1848. SOURCE: WO120 Volume 70 page 426. INDEX # 8332.

Robt PURVES; pension awarded 14 Oct 1845; residence - Montreal, Quebec, Canada; died 14 Jan 1864, London, Ontario, Canada. SOURCE: WO120 Volume 70 page 426. INDEX # 8333.

Willm WELSH; pension awarded 14 Oct 1845; residence - Montreal, Quebec, Canada; died in 1846. SOURCE: WO120 Volume 70 page 426. INDEX # 8334.

Geo^e HENNARD; pension awarded 14 Jul 1841; residence - Montreal, Quebec, Canada. SOURCE: WO120 Volume 70 page 426. INDEX # 8335.

Thos SMITH; pension awarded 13 Jan 1841; residence - Trinidad, West Indies. SOURCE: WO120 Volume 70 page 426. INDEX # 8336.

Robt REID; pension awarded 8 Mar 1837; residence - Ionian Isles. SOURCE: WO120 Volume 70 page 426. INDEX # 8337.

Willm THOMPSON; pension awarded 13 Jan 1841; residence - Ceylon. SOURCE: WO120 Volume 70 page 426. INDEX # 8338.

Ja^s MACHRAY; pension awarded 5 Sep 1843; residence - Kingston, Ontario, Canada; died 22 Feb 1859, Ontario, Canada. SOURCE: WO120 Volume 70 page 426. INDEX # 8339.

Willm BROWN; pension awarded 9 Dec 1840; residence - Gibraltar; died 22 Apr 1857. SOURCE: WO120 Volume 70 page 426. INDEX # 8340.

Robt WILLIAMSON; pension awarded 14 Oct 1845; residence - Montreal, Quebec, Canada. SOURCE: WO120 Volume 70 page 446. INDEX # 8341.

Hal^l KERR; pension awarded 8 Jul 1835; residence - Hobart Town, Australia. SOURCE: WO120 Volume 70 page 426. INDEX # 8342.

Ja^s ATTWOOD; pension awarded 13 Apr 1836; residence - London, Ontario, Canada; died 8 Dec 1848. SOURCE: WO120 Volume 70 page 426. INDEX # 8343.

Saml BOYD; pension awarded 11 Oct 1837; residence - Hobart Town, Australia; died 2 Nov 1877, Portsmouth. SOURCE: WO120 Volume 70 page 426. INDEX # 8344.

Ja^s FORSYTHE; pension awarded 27 Jan 1846; residence - Canada. SOURCE: WO120 Volume 70 page 426. INDEX # 8345.

Jn⁰ WATSON; pension awarded 13 Oct 1846; residence - Toronto, Ontario, Canada. SOURCE: WO120 Volume 70 page 426. INDEX # 8346.

Mich^l HANLON; pension awarded 12 Jan 1847; residence - Van Diemen's Land, Australia. SOURCE: WO120 Volume 70 page 426. INDEX # 8347.

Gavin FINLAYSON; pension awarded 12 Jan 1847; residence - Van Diemen's Land, Australia. SOURCE: WO120 Volume 70 page 426. INDEX # 8348.

Ja^s HALLIDAY; pension awarded 12 Jan 1847; residence - Montreal, Quebec, Canada. SOURCE: WO120 Volume 70 page 426. INDEX # 8349.

Wm CORRINS; pension awarded 1 Jul 1832; residence - Toronto, Ontario, Canada; died 10 Feb 1855. SOURCE: WO120 Volume 70 page 427. INDEX # 8350.

Neil DOUGHERTY; pension awarded 1 May 1818; residence - Cape of Good Hope, South Africa; died 9 Jul 1859. SOURCE: WO120 Volume 70 page 427. INDEX # 8351.

Alex^r YOUNIE; pension awarded 1 Nov 1818; residence - Montreal, Quebec, Canada. SOURCE: WO120 Volume 70 page 427. INDEX # 8352.

Jn⁰ CORMACK; pension awarded 1 Aug 1810; residence - Halifax, Nova Scotia, Canada. SOURCE: WO120 Volume 70 page 427. INDEX # 8353.

Willm HOOD; pension awarded 31 May 1818; residence - Sydney. SOURCE: WO120 Volume 70 page 427. INDEX # 8354.

Willm HORNER; pension awarded 1 Oct 1809; residence - Halifax, Nova Scotia, Canada; died in May 1847. SOURCE: WO120 Volume 70 page 427. INDEX # 8355.

Peter DOYLE; pension awarded 1 Aug 1816; residence - New Zealand; died 1 Jun 1851. SOURCE: WO120 Volume 70 page 427. INDEX # 8356.

John LAMB; pension awarded 1 Jun 1809; residence - New Zealand. SOURCE: WO120 Volume 70 page 427. INDEX # 8357.

2nd Battalion of Artillery (continued)

Geo^e FLEET; pension awarded 1 May 1818; residence - New Zealand. SOURCE: WO120 Volume 70 page 427. INDEX # 8358.

Geo^e DONALDSON; pension awarded ; residence - Bytown, Ontario, Canada; died in 1848. SOURCE: WO120 Volume 70 page 427. INDEX # 8359.

Robt GEDDIS; pension awarded 1 Sep 1814; residence - London, Ontario, Canada; died 7 Aug 1847. SOURCE: WO120 Volume 70 page 427. INDEX # 8360.

Jno DOUGHERTY; pension awarded 1 Nov 1828; residence - Three Rivers, Quebec, Canada; died 20 Aug 1868, Toronto, Ontario, Canada. SOURCE: WO120 Volume 70 page 427. INDEX # 8361.

Geo^e SMITH; pension awarded 7 Aug 1828; residence - Halifax, Nova Scotia, Canada. SOURCE: WO120 Volume 70 page 427. INDEX # 8362.

Ja^s WILSON; pension awarded ; residence - St. Johns; died 11 Aug 1850. SOURCE: WO120 Volume 70 page 427. INDEX # 8363.

Thos JOHNSON; pension awarded 1 Aug 1810; residence - Halifax, Nova Scotia, Canada; died in 1846. SOURCE: WO120 Volume 70 page 427. INDEX # 8364.

Jos^h COCKBURN; pension awarded 1 Jan 1813; residence - Penetanguishene, Ontario, Canada. SOURCE: WO120 Volume 70 page 427. INDEX # 8365.

Ja^s HAGGARTY; pension awarded 1 Jul 1827; residence - Gibraltar. SOURCE: WO120 Volume 70 page 427. INDEX # 8366.

Robt MILES; pension awarded 1 Dec 1826; residence - Gibraltar. SOURCE: WO120 Volume 70 page 427. INDEX # 8367.

Willm DAVIDSON; pension awarded 1 Nov 1828; residence - Newfoundland, Canada; died 6 Sep 1880, Halifax, Nova Scotia, Canada. SOURCE: WO120 Volume 70 page 427. INDEX # 8368.

Dav^d PIGGOTT; pension awarded 1 Jul 1818; residence - Charlottetown, Prince Edward Island, Canada. SOURCE: WO120 Volume 70 page 428. INDEX # 8369.

Jno LINDSAY; pension awarded 1 Nov 1825; residence - Malta. SOURCE: WO120 Volume 70 page 428. INDEX # 8370.

Jno MCROBIE; pension awarded 1 Apr 1830; residence - Montreal, Quebec, Canada; died 8 Jun 1853. SOURCE: WO120 Volume 70 page 428. INDEX # 8371.

Ja^s ANDERSON; pension awarded 1 Mar 1836; residence - Newfoundland, Canada; died 7 Feb 1852. SOURCE: WO120 Volume 70 page 428. INDEX # 8372.

Dav^d HAY; pension awarded 1 Jan 1821; residence - Halifax, Nova Scotia, Canada. SOURCE: WO120 Volume 70 page 428. INDEX # 8373.

Geo^e HAMILTON; pension awarded 1 May 1816; residence - Halifax, Nova Scotia, Canada; died 24 Jan 1847. SOURCE: WO120 Volume 70 page 428. INDEX # 8374.

John MOORE; pension awarded 4 Nov 1825; residence - Montreal, Quebec, Canada; died 2 Oct 1846. SOURCE: WO120 Volume 70 page 428. INDEX # 8375.

Jno BREMNER; pension awarded 23 Nov 1847; residence - London, Ontario, Canada; died 21 Jul 1852. SOURCE: WO120 Volume 70 page 428. INDEX # 8376.

Ja^s CRAWFORD; pension awarded 23 Nov 1847; residence - London, Ontario, Canada; died 10 Jan 1879. SOURCE: WO120 Volume 70 page 428. INDEX # 8377.

Hen^y HOWARD; pension awarded 23 Nov 1847; died 5 Dec 1874, London, Ontario, Canada. SOURCE: WO120 Volume 70 page 428. INDEX # 8378.

Jno JOHNSTON; pension awarded 23 Nov 1847; residence - London, Ontario, Canada; died 11 Feb 1852. SOURCE: WO120 Volume 70 page 428. INDEX # 8379.

Alex^r MCLEAN; pension awarded 23 Nov 1847; died 30 May 1872, London, Ontario, Canada. SOURCE: WO120 Volume 70 page 428. INDEX # 8380.

Wm YOUNG; pension awarded 23 Nov 1847. SOURCE: WO120 Volume 70 page 428. INDEX # 8381.

Robt COLQUHOUN; pension awarded 11 Jan 1848; residence - Montreal, Quebec, Canada; died 18 Aug 1877. SOURCE: WO120 Volume 70 page 428. INDEX # 8382.

Jno BARTLAY; pension awarded 10 Oct 1848. SOURCE: WO120 Volume 70 page 428. INDEX # 8383.

Paul KEENAN; pension awarded 10 Oct 1848. SOURCE: WO120 Volume 70 page 428. INDEX # 8384.

Chas Hen^y CRAIG; pension awarded 25 May 1852. SOURCE: WO120 Volume 70 page 428. INDEX # 8385.

2nd Battalion of Artillery (continued)

Hugh CUMMING; pension awarded 12 Jul 1853. SOURCE: WO120 Volume 70 page 428. INDEX # 8386.
Ja^s BURTON; pension awarded 12 Jul 1853. SOURCE: WO120 Volume 70 page 428. INDEX # 8387.
And^w COWIE; pension awarded 12 Jul 1853. SOURCE: WO120 Volume 70 page 428. INDEX # 8388.
Ja^s MADDISON; pension awarded 23 Aug 1853. SOURCE: WO120 Volume 70 page 429. INDEX # 8389.
Ja^s DUFFEY; pension awarded 13 Jun 1854. SOURCE: WO120 Volume 70 page 429. INDEX # 8390.
Matt^w WALLACE; pension awarded 11 Jul 1854; died 17 Jan 1884, Omagh. SOURCE: WO120 Volume 70 page 429. INDEX # 8391.
Wm SCOTT; pension awarded 11 Jul 1854; died 28 Oct 1880, Toronto, Ontario, Canada. SOURCE: WO120 Volume 70 page 429. INDEX # 8392.

3rd Battalion of Artillery

Ja^s ULDRITT; pension awarded 12 Mar 1844; residence - Quebec, Quebec, Canada; died 23 Jun 1868, London, Ontario, Canada. SOURCE: WO120 Volume 70 page 438. INDEX # 8393.
Jno MCLEAN; pension awarded 9 Oct 1839; residence - Kingston, Ontario, Canada; died 24 Mar 1858. SOURCE: WO120 Volume 70 page 438. INDEX # 8394.
Thos SMITH; pension awarded 9 Oct 1839; residence - Kingston, Ontario, Canada; died 3 Mar 1875, Toronto, Ontario, Canada. SOURCE: WO120 Volume 70 page 438. INDEX # 8395.
Thos COULSTON; pension awarded 12 Jan 1842; residence - Kingston, Ontario, Canada; died 19 Jun 1876, New York. SOURCE: WO120 Volume 70 page 438. INDEX # 8396.
Willm CHEETHAM; pension awarded 13 Jul 1836; residence - Belleville, Ontario, Canada; died 9 Jan 1854. SOURCE: WO120 Volume 70 page 438. INDEX # 8397.
Peter COLLINS; pension awarded 10 Jan 1838; residence - Kingston, Ontario, Canada. SOURCE: WO120 Volume 70 page 438. INDEX # 8398.
Willm NELSON; pension awarded 10 Oct 1837; residence - Toronto, Ontario, Canada; died 25 Jun 1875, Toronto, Ontario, Canada. SOURCE: WO120 Volume 70 page 438. INDEX # 8399.
Ja^s THORN; pension awarded 13 Jan 1836; residence - Newfoundland, Canada. SOURCE: WO120 Volume 70 page 438. INDEX # 8400.
Willm CHESTER; pension awarded 10 Jan 1838; residence - Kingston, Ontario, Canada; died in 1847. SOURCE: WO120 Volume 70 page 438. INDEX # 8401.
Willm WHAREN; pension awarded 10 Jan 1843; residence - Toronto, Ontario, Canada; died 30 May 1887, Toronto, Ontario, Canada. SOURCE: WO120 Volume 70 page 438. INDEX # 8402.
Ja^s FARELL; pension awarded ; residence - Montreal, Quebec, Canada; died 7 Sep 1851. SOURCE: WO120 Volume 70 page 438. INDEX # 8403.
Gregory GREEN; pension awarded 27 Jan 1846; residence - Ceylon. SOURCE: WO120 Volume 70 page 438. INDEX # 8404.
John HURST; pension awarded 1 Jul 1833; residence - Kingston, Ontario, Canada. SOURCE: WO120 Volume 70 page 438. INDEX # 8405.
Pat^k SAVAGE; pension awarded 7 Oct 1827; residence - Halifax, Nova Scotia, Canada. SOURCE: WO120 Volume 70 page 438. INDEX # 8406.
Ralph SIMPSON; pension awarded 1 Jul 1817; residence - Toronto, Ontario, Canada; died 10 Jan 1864, London, Ontario, Canada. SOURCE: WO120 Volume 70 page 438. INDEX # 8407.
John JEFFRY; pension awarded 10 Aug 1814; residence - London, Ontario, Canada; died 30 Mar 1863, Ontario, Canada. SOURCE: WO120 Volume 70 page 438. INDEX # 8408.
Thos WALKER; pension awarded 1 May 1818; residence - Montreal, Quebec, Canada; died 23 Jan 1849. SOURCE: WO120 Volume 70 page 438. INDEX # 8409.
Thos MCKEWEN; pension awarded 1 Oct 1829; residence - Ceylon. SOURCE: WO120 Volume 70 page 438. INDEX # 8410.
Thos MCKEON; pension awarded 1 Oct 1829; residence - Ceylon. SOURCE: WO120 Volume 70 page 438. INDEX # 8411.
Matt^w BARCLAY; pension awarded 31 Dec 1811; residence - Toronto, Ontario, Canada; died 20 Dec 1867. SOURCE: WO120 Volume 70 page 439. INDEX # 8412.

3rd Battalion of Artillery (continued)

Robt RITCHIE; pension awarded 1 Jun 1828; residence - Bytown, Ontario, Canada; died 22 Apr 1872, Toronto, Ontario, Canada. SOURCE: WO120 Volume 70 page 439. INDEX # 8413.

Robt CRAIG; pension awarded 1 Jun 1829; residence - Ceylon; died in Feb 1846. SOURCE: WO120 Volume 70 page 439. INDEX # 8414.

Ja^s MCKELVEY; pension awarded 27 Mar 1816; residence - Quebec, Quebec, Canada. SOURCE: WO120 Volume 70 page 439. INDEX # 8415.

Epaphras DENNY; pension awarded 23 Nov 1847. SOURCE: WO120 Volume 70 page 439. INDEX # 8416.

Tim^y MACARTHY; pension awarded 23 Nov 1847. SOURCE: WO120 Volume 70 page 439. INDEX # 8417.

Chas MCCAFFERY; pension awarded 23 Nov 1847; died 15 Dec 1878, Toronto, Ontario, Canada. SOURCE: WO120 Volume 70 page 439. INDEX # 8418.

Eben^r STOREY; pension awarded 11 Jan 1848; died 14 Aug 1884. SOURCE: WO120 Volume 70 page 439. INDEX # 8419.

Jno ALEXANDER; pension awarded 12 Sep 1848; died 30 Jun 1872, Glasgow. SOURCE: WO120 Volume 70 page 439. INDEX # 8420.

Hugh CUNNINGHAM; pension awarded 12 Sep 1848; residence - Toronto, Ontario, Canada; died 17 Apr 1869. SOURCE: WO120 Volume 70 page 439. INDEX # 8421.

Robt FULLER; pension awarded 12 Sep 1848; residence - London, Ontario, Canada. SOURCE: WO120 Volume 70 page 439. INDEX # 8422.

Geo^e SUGDEN; pension awarded 13 May 1851; residence - Newfoundland, Canada; died in 1854. SOURCE: WO120 Volume 70 page 439. INDEX # 8423.

4th Battalion of Artillery

Wm RAMSBOTTOM; pension awarded 13 Jan 1842; residence - Perth, Ontario, Canada. SOURCE: WO120 Volume 70 page 448. INDEX # 8424.

Jno HALLUM; pension awarded 13 Jan 1836; residence - Montreal, Quebec, Canada. SOURCE: WO120 Volume 70 page 448. INDEX # 8425.

Ja^s ANDERSON; pension awarded 26 Nov 1844; residence - Cape of Good Hope, South Africa. SOURCE: WO120 Volume 70 page 448. INDEX # 8426.

Edwd MCGURK; pension awarded 8 Jan 1834; residence - Kingston, Ontario, Canada; died 30 Mar 1863, Toronto, Ontario, Canada. SOURCE: WO120 Volume 70 page 448. INDEX # 8427.

Wm LIPSEY; pension awarded 12 Jul 1837; residence - Quebec, Quebec, Canada. SOURCE: WO120 Volume 70 page 448. INDEX # 8428.

Richd GREGGETT; pension awarded 14 Oct 1835; residence - Charlottetown, Prince Edward Island, Canada. SOURCE: WO120 Volume 70 page 448. INDEX # 8429.

Ja^s CAMERON; pension awarded 8 Apr 1835; residence - Halifax, Nova Scotia, Canada. SOURCE: WO120 Volume 70 page 448. INDEX # 8430.

Hugh MALLEN; pension awarded 14 Oct 1835; residence - Quebec, Quebec, Canada; died 13 Oct 1852. SOURCE: WO120 Volume 70 page 448. INDEX # 8431.

Fra^s DOYLE; pension awarded 8 Jan 1834; residence - Quebec, Quebec, Canada. SOURCE: WO120 Volume 70 page 448. INDEX # 8432.

Willm CLARK; pension awarded 10 Jan 1843; residence - Quebec, Quebec, Canada. SOURCE: WO120 Volume 70 page 448. INDEX # 8433.

Willm SWINDON; pension awarded 14 Oct 1835; residence - Halifax, Nova Scotia, Canada. SOURCE: WO120 Volume 70 page 448. INDEX # 8434.

Ja^s GALLAGHER; pension awarded 14 Oct 1835; residence - Halifax, Nova Scotia, Canada. SOURCE: WO120 Volume 70 page 448. INDEX # 8435.

Arch^d MCCOULL; pension awarded 11 Oct 1837; residence - Halifax, Nova Scotia, Canada; died 16 Apr 1850. SOURCE: WO120 Volume 70 page 448. INDEX # 8436.

John DAVIS; pension awarded 14 Oct 1835. SOURCE: WO120 Volume 70 page 448. INDEX # 8437.

Willm PICKLES; pension awarded 14 Oct 1835; residence - Halifax, Nova Scotia, Canada. SOURCE: WO120 Volume 70 page 448. INDEX # 8438.

4th Battalion of Artillery (continued)

Willm ROBINSON; pension awarded 10 Oct 1838; residence - Halifax, Nova Scotia, Canada. SOURCE: WO120 Volume 70 page 448. INDEX # 8439.

Thos TELFER; pension awarded 10 Oct 1838; died in 1853. SOURCE: WO120 Volume 70 page 448. INDEX # 8440.

Ja^s SHAND; pension awarded 8 Apr 1838; residence - Halifax, Nova Scotia, Canada; died 6 May 1874, Stirling. SOURCE: WO120 Volume 70 page 448. INDEX # 8441.

Ja^s DENOON; pension awarded 13 Oct 1841; residence - Three Rivers, Quebec, Canada. SOURCE: WO120 Volume 70 page 448. INDEX # 8442.

Thos BREMNER; pension awarded 13 Jul 1836; residence - Malta; died 18 Nov 1849. SOURCE: WO120 Volume 70 page 449. INDEX # 8443.

Ja^s DODD; pension awarded 14 Nov 1838; residence - Montreal, Quebec, Canada; died 25 Sep 1858. SOURCE: WO120 Volume 70 page 449. INDEX # 8444.

Willm HOWE; pension awarded 11 Oct 1837; residence - Halifax, Nova Scotia, Canada. SOURCE: WO120 Volume 70 page 449. INDEX # 8445.

Robt BOAK; pension awarded 9 Sep 1839; residence - Halifax, Nova Scotia, Canada. SOURCE: WO120 Volume 70 page 449. INDEX # 8446.

Danl NICKER; pension awarded 11 Oct 1837; residence - Malta; died 16 Jul 1884, Yarmouth. SOURCE: WO120 Volume 70 page 449. INDEX # 8447.

John CALLIER; pension awarded 2 Oct 1836; residence - Charlottetown, Prince Edward Island, Canada. SOURCE: WO120 Volume 70 page 449. INDEX # 8448.

John LANCASTER; pension awarded 26 May 1846; residence - Cape of Good Hope, South Africa. SOURCE: WO120 Volume 70 page 449. INDEX # 8449.

Dav^d PORTER; pension awarded 27 Jan 1846; residence - Cape of Good Hope, South Africa. SOURCE: WO120 Volume 70 page 449. INDEX # 8450.

Mark WILSON; pension awarded 13 Apr 1847; residence - Barbadoes, West Indies; died 8 Apr 1857. SOURCE: WO120 Volume 70 page 449. INDEX # 8451.

Geo^e PENNOCK; pension awarded 11 Jul 1838; residence - Cape of Good Hope, South Africa; died 10 Nov 1864. SOURCE: WO120 Volume 70 page 449. INDEX # 8452.

Jere^h HIRST; pension awarded 1 Apr 1832; residence - Toronto, Ontario, Canada. SOURCE: WO120 Volume 70 page 449. INDEX # 8453.

John JOHNSTON; pension awarded 1 Jan 1832; residence - Bytown, Ontario, Canada; died 22 Jul 1855. SOURCE: WO120 Volume 70 page 449. INDEX # 8454.

Alex^r MITCHELL; pension awarded 1 Oct 1832; residence - Kingston, Ontario, Canada. SOURCE: WO120 Volume 70 page 449. INDEX # 8455.

Robt GUNN; pension awarded 18 Nov 1821; residence - St. Johns; died 16 Oct 1852. SOURCE: WO120 Volume 70 page 449. INDEX # 8456.

Ja^s WALLACE; pension awarded 30 Nov 1819; residence - Niagara, Ontario, Canada; died 5 Dec 1847. SOURCE: WO120 Volume 70 page 449. INDEX # 8457.

Jno CARTWRIGHT; pension awarded 9 May 1821; residence - Quebec, Quebec, Canada. SOURCE: WO120 Volume 70 page 449. INDEX # 8458.

Alex^r MCDONALD; pension awarded 23 Feb 1821. SOURCE: WO120 Volume 70 page 449. INDEX # 8459.

Jno ANDERSON; pension awarded 19 May 1826; residence - Prescott, Ontario, Canada; died in 1848. SOURCE: WO120 Volume 70 page 449. INDEX # 8460.

Willm CHALMERS; pension awarded 8 Nov 1821; residence - Prescott, Ontario, Canada. SOURCE: WO120 Volume 70 page 449. INDEX # 8461.

John GREEN; pension awarded 29 Oct 1820; residence - Smiths Falls, Ontario, Canada. SOURCE: WO120 Volume 70 page 450. INDEX # 8462.

John WILSON; pension awarded 1 Mar 1821; residence - Perth, Ontario, Canada. SOURCE: WO120 Volume 70 page 450. INDEX # 8463.

Robt ROBERTSON; pension awarded 1 Aug 1825; residence - St. Johns. SOURCE: WO120 Volume 70 page 450. INDEX # 8464.

Jno DAWSON; pension awarded 10 Dec 1815; residence - Toronto, Ontario, Canada; died 4 Jan 1858. SOURCE: WO120 Volume 70 page 450. INDEX # 8465.

4th Battalion of Artillery (continued)

Ja^s WARD; pension awarded 1 Apr 1810; residence - Toronto, Ontario, Canada. SOURCE: WO120 Volume 70 page 450. INDEX # 8466.

Jno CROSSLEY; pension awarded 1 Apr 1816; residence - St. Johns. SOURCE: WO120 Volume 70 page 450. INDEX # 8467.

Ja^s DORAN; pension awarded 1 Jan 1815; residence - Bytown, Ontario, Canada; died 16 May 1861, Bytown, Ontario, Canada. SOURCE: WO120 Volume 70 page 450. INDEX # 8468.

Ja^s LANG; pension awarded 10 Aug 1814; residence - Quebec, Quebec, Canada. SOURCE: WO120 Volume 70 page 450. INDEX # 8469.

John WATTS; pension awarded 2 May 1822; residence - Chambly, Quebec, Canada. SOURCE: WO120 Volume 70 page 450. INDEX # 8470.

Thos MORRIS; pension awarded 10 Mar 1829; residence - Toronto, Ontario, Canada; died 1 Oct 1852. SOURCE: WO120 Volume 70 page 450. INDEX # 8471.

Hy RAMMAGE; pension awarded 1 Jan 1815; residence - Toronto, Ontario, Canada; died 28 Sep 1867, London, Ontario, Canada. SOURCE: WO120 Volume 70 page 450. INDEX # 8472.

Ja^s REACH; pension awarded 1 Nov 1814; residence - St. Johns. SOURCE: WO120 Volume 70 page 450. INDEX # 8473.

Thos HENDERSON; pension awarded 1 Jan 1830; residence - Kingston, Ontario, Canada; died 21 Mar 1860. SOURCE: WO120 Volume 70 page 450. INDEX # 8474.

Jno GOWDY; pension awarded 1 Oct 1829; residence - Belleville, Ontario, Canada; died 12 Jul 1852. SOURCE: WO120 Volume 70 page 450. INDEX # 8475.

Hy DEAS; pension awarded 20 Aug 1815; residence - St. Johns; died 31 Mar 1845. SOURCE: WO120 Volume 70 page 450. INDEX # 8476.

Willm NEEDHAM; pension awarded 1 May 1815; residence - Montreal, Quebec, Canada; died 10 Apr 1848. SOURCE: WO120 Volume 70 page 450. INDEX # 8477.

Alex^r LOUTHOOD; pension awarded 1 Jun 1825; residence - Quebec, Quebec, Canada; died 30 Oct 1853. SOURCE: WO120 Volume 70 page 450. INDEX # 8478.

Don^d GRANT; pension awarded 1 May 1816; residence - Quebec, Quebec, Canada; died 4 Aug 1849. SOURCE: WO120 Volume 70 page 450. INDEX # 8479.

Chas VAN KOUNE; pension awarded 3 May 1812; residence - Niagara, Ontario, Canada; died 15 Jan 1847. SOURCE: WO120 Volume 70 page 450. INDEX # 8480.

Jno DALLAS; pension awarded 6 Jun 1848. SOURCE: WO120 Volume 70 page 449. INDEX # 8481.

Danl LAMONT; pension awarded 8 Aug 1848; residence - Halifax, Nova Scotia, Canada; died 2 Oct 1877. SOURCE: WO120 Volume 70 page 451. INDEX # 8482.

Ja^s PHILLIPS; pension awarded 11 Oct 1853. SOURCE: WO120 Volume 70 page 451. INDEX # 8483.

Thos PATTERSON; pension awarded 11 Oct 1853. SOURCE: WO120 Volume 70 page 451. INDEX # 8484.

Jno HOWARD; pension awarded 11 Jul 1854; residence - Toronto, Ontario, Canada; died 22 Oct 1867. SOURCE: WO120 Volume 70 page 451. INDEX # 8485.

Matt CULHANE; pension awarded 11 Jul 1854; died 27 Feb 1875, Toronto, Ontario, Canada. SOURCE: WO120 Volume 70 page 451. INDEX # 8486.

Jno MOLONY; pension awarded 11 Jul 1854; residence - Toronto, Ontario, Canada; died 13 Jul 1864. SOURCE: WO120 Volume 70 page 451. INDEX # 8487.

Wm ROBINSON; pension awarded 10 Oct 1854; residence - Toronto, Ontario, Canada; died 9 Sep 1867. SOURCE: WO120 Volume 70 page 451. INDEX # 8488.

5th Battalion of Artillery

Saml MITCHELL; pension awarded 11 Jul 1843; residence - London, Ontario, Canada; died 20 Jan 1862. SOURCE: WO120 Volume 70 page 460. INDEX # 8489.

Smith ALLEN; pension awarded 8 Apr 1835; residence - Montreal, Quebec, Canada. SOURCE: WO120 Volume 70 page 460. INDEX # 8490.

Phalim MCCORMICK; pension awarded 14 Oct 1835; residence - Halifax, Nova Scotia, Canada; died 20 Mar 1852. SOURCE: WO120 Volume 70 page 460. INDEX # 8491.

5th Battalion of Artillery (continued)

Robt MURRAY; pension awarded 10 Oct 1838; residence - Halifax, Nova Scotia, Canada. SOURCE: WO120 Volume 70 page 460. INDEX # 8492.

Thos STANFIELD; pension awarded 8 Jul 1835; residence - Toronto, Ontario, Canada; died 27 Feb 1861. SOURCE: WO120 Volume 70 page 460. INDEX # 8493.

Jno MCINTIRE; pension awarded 8 Apr 1835; residence - Montreal, Quebec, Canada. SOURCE: WO120 Volume 70 page 460. INDEX # 8494.

Saml VOLANS; pension awarded 12 Oct 1836; residence - Halifax, Nova Scotia, Canada; died 1 Oct 1850. SOURCE: WO120 Volume 70 page 460. INDEX # 8495.

Geo^e WEST; pension awarded 14 Oct 1835; residence - Halifax, Nova Scotia, Canada. SOURCE: WO120 Volume 70 page 460. INDEX # 8496.

Jos^h RICHARDSON; pension awarded 12 Oct 1836; residence - Kingston, Ontario, Canada; died 20 Apr 1879, Toronto, Ontario, Canada. SOURCE: WO120 Volume 70 page 460. INDEX # 8497.

Ralph KING; pension awarded 16 Jul 1843; residence - Kingston, Ontario, Canada. SOURCE: WO120 Volume 70 page 460. INDEX # 8498.

Willm WESTON; pension awarded 16 Jul 1843; residence - London, Ontario, Canada; died 29 May 1891. SOURCE: WO120 Volume 70 page 460. INDEX # 8499.

Willm GRAHAM; pension awarded 16 Jul 1843; residence - Malta. SOURCE: WO120 Volume 70 page 460. INDEX # 8500.

Ja^s PILSON; pension awarded 9 Jul 1844; residence - Bytown, Ontario, Canada. SOURCE: WO120 Volume 70 page 460. INDEX # 8501.

Jno CARSTAIRS; pension awarded 18 Oct 1842; residence - Malta; died 27 Jun 1853. SOURCE: WO120 Volume 70 page 460. INDEX # 8502.

Ja^s ROBERTSON; pension awarded 10 Jan 1843; residence - Toronto, Ontario, Canada; died 21 Mar 1867. SOURCE: WO120 Volume 70 page 460. INDEX # 8503.

Robt GRIGG; pension awarded 12 Jul 1837; residence - New South Wales, Australia. SOURCE: WO120 Volume 70 page 460. INDEX # 8504.

Ja^s GASCOIGNE; pension awarded 14 Oct 1840; residence - Quebec, Quebec, Canada. SOURCE: WO120 Volume 70 page 460. INDEX # 8505.

John WARREN; pension awarded 16 Jul 1841; residence - Chambly, Quebec, Canada. SOURCE: WO120 Volume 70 page 460. INDEX # 8506.

Thos WOOLLEY; pension awarded 11 Jul 1838; residence - Wm Henry, Quebec, Canada. SOURCE: WO120 Volume 70 page 460. INDEX # 8507.

Willm ROBBS; pension awarded 11 Jul 1838; residence - Kingston, Ontario, Canada; died 10 Feb 1857, Kingston, Ontario, Canada. SOURCE: WO120 Volume 70 page 460. INDEX # 8508.

Ja^s SMITH; pension awarded 13 Jan 1846; residence - Gibraltar; died 11 Mar 1851. SOURCE: WO120 Volume 70 page 461. INDEX # 8509.

Willm MANLEY; pension awarded 12 Jan 1847; residence - Cape of Good Hope, South Africa. SOURCE: WO120 Volume 70 page 461. INDEX # 8510.

Willm MORRISON; pension awarded 12 Jan 1847; residence - Van Diemen's Land, Australia. SOURCE: WO120 Volume 70 page 461. INDEX # 8511.

John LAIRD; pension awarded 1 Apr 1832; residence - Quebec, Quebec, Canada. SOURCE: WO120 Volume 70 page 461. INDEX # 8512.

John MCNAUGHT; pension awarded 1 Jan 1833; residence - New Brunswick, Canada. SOURCE: WO120 Volume 70 page 461. INDEX # 8513.

Thos ANDERSON; pension awarded 1 Jun 1817; residence - Halifax, Nova Scotia, Canada. SOURCE: WO120 Volume 70 page 461. INDEX # 8514.

Willm CLOUGHLY; pension awarded 6 Feb 1819; residence - Toronto, Ontario, Canada. SOURCE: WO120 Volume 70 page 461. INDEX # 8515.

Dun^n MACKENZIE; pension awarded 30 Dec 1827; residence - London, Ontario, Canada; died 2 Aug 1875, London, Ontario, Canada. SOURCE: WO120 Volume 70 page 461. INDEX # 8516.

Walter BURNS; pension awarded 7 Mar 1827; residence - Perth, Ontario, Canada; died 27 Sep 1857. SOURCE: WO120 Volume 70 page 461. INDEX # 8517.

5th Battalion of Artillery (continued)

Ja^s HENRY; pension awarded 22 Nov 1820; residence - Charlottetown, Prince Edward Island, Canada. SOURCE: WO120 Volume 70 page 461. INDEX # 8518.

Ja^s LECKIE; pension awarded 1 Mar 1824; residence - Kingston, Ontario, Canada; died 27 Jan 1871, Toronto, Ontario, Canada. SOURCE: WO120 Volume 70 page 461. INDEX # 8519.

Willm WALKER; pension awarded 1 Nov 1818; residence - Kingston, Ontario, Canada; died 17 Aug 1864, Toronto, Ontario, Canada. SOURCE: WO120 Volume 70 page 461. INDEX # 8520.

Jno RICHARDSON; pension awarded 1 May 1823; residence - London, Ontario, Canada; died in 1849. SOURCE: WO120 Volume 70 page 461. INDEX # 8521.

Chas GALLAGHER; pension awarded 1 Jan 1830; residence - Halifax, Nova Scotia, Canada. SOURCE: WO120 Volume 70 page 461. INDEX # 8522.

John BARNETT; pension awarded 30 Jan 1831; residence - Halifax, Nova Scotia, Canada. SOURCE: WO120 Volume 70 page 461. INDEX # 8523.

Robt CUMMINGS; pension awarded 1 Aug 1817; residence - Halifax, Nova Scotia, Canada. SOURCE: WO120 Volume 70 page 461. INDEX # 8524.

Ja^s TODD; pension awarded 30 Nov 1823; residence - Halifax, Nova Scotia, Canada; died in 1846. SOURCE: WO120 Volume 70 page 461. INDEX # 8525.

John HARTLEY; pension awarded 1 Nov 1818; residence - Toronto, Ontario, Canada; died 1 Dec 1864. SOURCE: WO120 Volume 70 page 461. INDEX # 8526.

Tim^y RIVETT; pension awarded 27 Oct 1825; residence - Halifax, Nova Scotia, Canada; died 17 May 1853. SOURCE: WO120 Volume 70 page 462. INDEX # 8527.

Willm WATSON; pension awarded 30 Nov 1830; residence - Cape of Good Hope, South Africa. SOURCE: WO120 Volume 70 page 462. INDEX # 8528.

Robt GIBSON; pension awarded 1 Nov 1825; residence - Toronto, Ontario, Canada; died 1 May 1855. SOURCE: WO120 Volume 70 page 462. INDEX # 8529.

Thos ECCLES; pension awarded 25 Aug 1817; residence - Cape of Good Hope, South Africa; died 16 Aug 1853. SOURCE: WO120 Volume 70 page 462. INDEX # 8530.

Thos YORKE; pension awarded 1 Oct 1816; residence - Saint John, New Brunswick, Canada. SOURCE: WO120 Volume 70 page 462. INDEX # 8531.

Ja^s ROBERTS; pension awarded 1 Jan 1813; residence - Toronto, Ontario, Canada; died 13 Jan 1863. SOURCE: WO120 Volume 70 page 462. INDEX # 8532.

Robt WHALLEY; pension awarded 1 Jan 1823; residence - Quebec, Quebec, Canada. SOURCE: WO120 Volume 70 page 462. INDEX # 8533.

Henry MORGAN; pension awarded 1 Aug 1816; residence - Halifax, Nova Scotia, Canada. SOURCE: WO120 Volume 70 page 462. INDEX # 8534.

Willm PORTMORE; pension awarded 1 Aug 1816; residence - St. Johns; died 12 Sep 1853. SOURCE: WO120 Volume 70 page 462. INDEX # 8535.

Willm HOUIE; pension awarded 1 Jan 1823; residence - Quebec, Quebec, Canada. SOURCE: WO120 Volume 70 page 462. INDEX # 8536.

Jno HEDDERWICK; pension awarded 1 Jul 1821; residence - Montreal, Quebec, Canada. SOURCE: WO120 Volume 70 page 462. INDEX # 8537.

Robt FENTON; pension awarded ; residence - St. Johns; died 17 Aug 1851. SOURCE: WO120 Volume 70 page 462. INDEX # 8538.

Thos JACKSON; pension awarded 1 Jan 1823; residence - Buenos Aires, Argentina; died in 1849. SOURCE: WO120 Volume 70 page 462. INDEX # 8547.

John ROSS; pension awarded 1 Jan 1823; residence - Cape of Good Hope, South Africa. SOURCE: WO120 Volume 70 page 462. INDEX # 8540.

Hen^y KENYON; pension awarded 23 Nov 1847. SOURCE: WO120 Volume 70 page 462. INDEX # 8541.

Wm STUBBS; pension awarded 23 Nov 1847; residence - Toronto, Ontario, Canada; died 3 Sep 1855. SOURCE: WO120 Volume 70 page 462. INDEX # 8542.

Saml POPE; pension awarded 11 Jul 1848; died 3 Feb 1879, Montreal, Quebec, Canada. SOURCE: WO120 Volume 70 page 462. INDEX # 8543.

Geo^e DIXON; pension awarded 12 Sep 1848; residence - Quebec, Quebec, Canada; died 14 Jun 1852. SOURCE: WO120 Volume 70 page 462. INDEX # 8544.

WO120 VOLUME 70

5th Battalion of Artillery (continued)

Jn⁰ HAMILTON; pension awarded 12 Sep 1848; died 9 Jan 1881, Toronto, Ontario, Canada. SOURCE: WO120 Volume 70 page 462. INDEX # 8545.

Edw⁴ SMART; pension awarded 9 Jul 1850; died 24 Mar 1873, London, Ontario, Canada. SOURCE: WO120 Volume 70 page 462. INDEX # 8546.

Rob⁺ MCLAUGHLIN; pension awarded 13 Dec 1853. SOURCE: WO120 Volume 70 page 463. INDEX # 8547.

Jn⁰ FLANAGAN; pension awarded 11 Jul 1854. SOURCE: WO120 Volume 70 page 463. INDEX # 8548.

Ja⁵ DOUGALL; pension awarded 14 Nov 1854. SOURCE: WO120 Volume 70 page 463. INDEX # 8549.

Rob⁺ NOWLAN; pension awarded 14 Nov 1854; died 20 Feb 1882, Nova Scotia, Canada. SOURCE: WO120 Volume 70 page 463. INDEX # 8550.

6th Battalion of Artillery

Tho⁵ WEBB; pension awarded 11 Oct 1837; residence - Kingston, Ontario, Canada. SOURCE: WO120 Volume 70 page 472. INDEX # 8551.

Ralph CLEWES; pension awarded 11 Jul 1843; residence - Quebec, Quebec, Canada; died in Aug 1847. SOURCE: WO120 Volume 70 page 472. INDEX # 8552.

Edw⁴ PATTON; pension awarded 14 Oct 1835; residence - Quebec, Quebec, Canada. SOURCE: WO120 Volume 70 page 472. INDEX # 8553.

John HURST; pension awarded 14 Oct 1835; residence - St. Johns; died 17 Nov 1855. SOURCE: WO120 Volume 70 page 472. INDEX # 8554.

Edw⁴ GRESHON; pension awarded 23 Sep 1845; residence - Malta. SOURCE: WO120 Volume 70 page 472. INDEX # 8555.

John FORBES; pension awarded 11 Jul 1843; residence - Carillon, Quebec, Canada. SOURCE: WO120 Volume 70 page 472. INDEX # 8556.

John WATT; pension awarded 10 Oct 1843; residence - Quebec, Quebec, Canada; died 30 Sep 1878, London, Ontario, Canada. SOURCE: WO120 Volume 70 page 472. INDEX # 8557.

John NAIRN; pension awarded 12 Mar 1844; residence - Toronto, Ontario, Canada; died 23 Aug 1852. SOURCE: WO120 Volume 70 page 472. INDEX # 8558.

George RYDER; pension awarded 13 Oct 1846; died 2 Aug 1881, Nova Scotia, Canada. SOURCE: WO120 Volume 70 page 472. INDEX # 8559.

Ja⁵ WILSON; pension awarded 12 Jan 1847; residence - Bermuda, West Indies; died 30 Sep 1880, Bermuda, West Indies. SOURCE: WO120 Volume 70 page 472. INDEX # 8560.

Alex⁻ WALKER; pension awarded 10 Jan 1838; residence - New Zealand. SOURCE: WO120 Volume 70 page 472. INDEX # 8561.

John MUNRO; pension awarded 1 Jan 1833; residence - Halifax, Nova Scotia, Canada. SOURCE: WO120 Volume 70 page 472. INDEX # 8562.

Willm BELL; pension awarded 1 Apr 1831; residence - Bytown, Ontario, Canada. SOURCE: WO120 Volume 70 page 472. INDEX # 8563.

Saml NEWTON; pension awarded 1 Apr 1831; residence - Bytown, Ontario, Canada. SOURCE: WO120 Volume 70 page 472. INDEX # 8564.

Dav⁴ WYLIE; pension awarded 1 Jun 1818; residence - Halifax, Nova Scotia, Canada. SOURCE: WO120 Volume 70 page 472. INDEX # 8565.

Jos^h PLASTON; pension awarded 1 Nov 1822; residence - Hobart Town, Australia. SOURCE: WO120 Volume 70 page 472. INDEX # 8566.

Jn⁰ DAVIE; pension awarded 1 May 1821; residence - Halifax, Nova Scotia, Canada; died in 1846. SOURCE: WO120 Volume 70 page 472. INDEX # 8567.

Dav⁴ MCCARDLE; pension awarded 1 Jan 1818; residence - London, Ontario, Canada; died 2 Feb 1864. SOURCE: WO120 Volume 70 page 472. INDEX # 8568.

Willm ANDERSON; pension awarded 1 Sep 1825; residence - Halifax, Nova Scotia, Canada. SOURCE: WO120 Volume 70 page 473. INDEX # 8569.

Ja⁵ WOOD; pension awarded 1 May 1826; residence - Toronto, Ontario, Canada; died 24 Feb 1865, London, Ontario, Canada. SOURCE: WO120 Volume 70 page 473. INDEX # 8570.

BRITISH ARMY PENSIONERS ABROAD

6th Battalion of Artillery (continued)

Geo^e MILLER; pension awarded 1 May 1822; residence - Malta; died 18 Dec 1855. SOURCE: WO120 Volume 70 page 473. INDEX # 8571.

Willm LITTLE; pension awarded 1 Nov 1825; residence - Halifax, Nova Scotia, Canada. SOURCE: WO120 Volume 70 page 473. INDEX # 8572.

Alex^r HAY; pension awarded 1 Apr 1826; residence - Halifax, Nova Scotia, Canada; died 12 Feb 1845. SOURCE: WO120 Volume 70 page 473. INDEX # 8573.

Willm FAIRBURN; pension awarded 1 Nov 1825; residence - Fredericton, New Brunswick, Canada; died 18 Jun 1846. SOURCE: WO120 Volume 70 page 473. INDEX # 8574.

David MOFFITT; pension awarded 13 Jul 1847. SOURCE: WO120 Volume 70 page 473. INDEX # 8575.

Chas NEWINGTON; pension awarded 13 Jul 1847. SOURCE: WO120 Volume 70 page 473. INDEX # 8576.

Mich^l CLINTON; pension awarded 13 Nov 1847. SOURCE: WO120 Volume 70 page 473. INDEX # 8577.

Ed^{wd} INGHAM; pension awarded 12 Sep 1848. SOURCE: WO120 Volume 70 page 473. INDEX # 8578.

Dav^d YOUNG; pension awarded 10 Oct 1848. SOURCE: WO120 Volume 70 page 473. INDEX # 8579.

Isaac PLUNKETT; pension awarded 9 Jan 1849; died 11 Mar 1881, W. London. SOURCE: WO120 Volume 70 page 473. INDEX # 8580.

Geo^e GUNNING; pension awarded 9 Oct 1849; died in Sep 1883, Halifax, Nova Scotia, Canada. SOURCE: WO120 Volume 70 page 473. INDEX # 8581.

William RUSSELL; pension awarded 24 Jul 1855. SOURCE: WO120 Volume 70 page 473. INDEX # 8582.

7th Battalion of Artillery

John MORRIS; pension awarded 30 Jan 1823; residence - Montreal, Quebec, Canada. SOURCE: WO120 Volume 70 page 482. INDEX # 8583.

Willm HODGKINSON; pension awarded 26 Feb 1835; residence - Penetanguishene, Ontario, Canada; died 31 Jan 1873, Hamilton, Ontario, Canada. SOURCE: WO120 Volume 70 page 482. INDEX # 8584.

Thos KENNEDY; pension awarded 11 Oct 1843; residence - Newfoundland, Canada; died 7 Oct 1850. SOURCE: WO120 Volume 70 page 482. INDEX # 8585.

Geo^e PHILLIPS; pension awarded 14 Jan 1845. SOURCE: WO120 Volume 70 page 482. INDEX # 8586.

Willm GRIMSTEAD; pension awarded 11 Oct 1837; residence - Newfoundland, Canada. SOURCE: WO120 Volume 70 page 482. INDEX # 8587.

Jno HUGHSTON; pension awarded 14 Jan 1845; residence - Newfoundland, Canada; died 4 Jul 1848. SOURCE: WO120 Volume 70 page 482. INDEX # 8588.

Jno DEVLIN; pension awarded 9 Jul 1844; residence - Halifax, Nova Scotia, Canada. SOURCE: WO120 Volume 70 page 482. INDEX # 8589.

Henry HANNA; pension awarded 1 Jan 1837; residence - Bytown, Ontario, Canada. SOURCE: WO120 Volume 70 page 482. INDEX # 8590.

Pat^k BURKE; pension awarded 13 Jan 1841; residence - Newfoundland, Canada; died 24 Oct 1881, Halifax, Nova Scotia, Canada. SOURCE: WO120 Volume 70 page 482. INDEX # 8591.

John HILLUM; pension awarded 30 Dec 1824; residence - South Australia, Australia. SOURCE: WO120 Volume 70 page 482. INDEX # 8592.

Ja^s GILLESPIE; pension awarded 1 May 1816; residence - Cornwall, Ontario, Canada; died 31 Mar 1850. SOURCE: WO120 Volume 70 page 482. INDEX # 8593.

Thos SMITH; pension awarded 1 Jun 1819; residence - Prescott, Ontario, Canada; died in Nov 1847. SOURCE: WO120 Volume 70 page 482. INDEX # 8594.

Ja^s BRISLAND; pension awarded 1 Sep 1816; residence - St. Johns. SOURCE: WO120 Volume 70 page 482. INDEX # 8595.

Hugh TORNEY; pension awarded 1 Jul 1816; residence - Montreal, Quebec, Canada; died 12 Mar 1863, London, Ontario, Canada. SOURCE: WO120 Volume 70 page 482. INDEX # 8596.

Ja^s WALSH; pension awarded 1 Jun 1802; residence - Quebec, Quebec, Canada. SOURCE: WO120 Volume 70 page 482. INDEX # 8597.

7th Battalion of Artillery (continued)

Hen^y ELLIOTT; pension awarded 1 Jul 1816; residence - Kingston, Ontario, Canada; died 18 Jan 1857. SOURCE: WO120 Volume 70 page 482. INDEX # 8598.

And^w RITCHIE; pension awarded 22 Jul 1816; residence - New South Wales, Australia. SOURCE: WO120 Volume 70 page 482. INDEX # 8599.

Ja^s WATSON; pension awarded 20 Apr 1809; residence - London, Ontario, Canada; died 16 Jul 1863. SOURCE: WO120 Volume 70 page 482. INDEX # 8600.

John SMITH; pension awarded 1 Mar 1822; residence - New South Wales, Australia. SOURCE: WO120 Volume 70 page 483. INDEX # 8601.

John COAPLAND; pension awarded 1 Sep 1824; residence - St. Johns. SOURCE: WO120 Volume 70 page 483. INDEX # 8602.

Willm QUINN; pension awarded 1 Jun 1819; residence - Fredericton, New Brunswick, Canada; died 22 Mar 1855. SOURCE: WO120 Volume 70 page 483. INDEX # 8603.

Richd CULLEN; pension awarded 17 Oct 1826; residence - Perth, Ontario, Canada. SOURCE: WO120 Volume 70 page 483. INDEX # 8604.

Saml BAILEY; pension awarded 1 Jan 1824; residence - Perth, Ontario, Canada; died in 1851. SOURCE: WO120 Volume 70 page 483. INDEX # 8605.

Felix CAMPBELL; pension awarded 1 Aug 1810; residence - Kingston, Ontario, Canada; died 25 Jun 1847. SOURCE: WO120 Volume 70 page 483. INDEX # 8606.

Thos DOUGHERTY; pension awarded 1 Jan 1824; residence - Perth, Ontario, Canada; died 21 Jan 1855. SOURCE: WO120 Volume 70 page 483. INDEX # 8607.

John KING; pension awarded 15 Dec 1826; residence - Perth, Ontario, Canada. SOURCE: WO120 Volume 70 page 483. INDEX # 8608.

Ja^s MCFADDEN; pension awarded 1 Nov 1816; residence - Prescott, Ontario, Canada; died 9 Jan 1858. SOURCE: WO120 Volume 70 page 483. INDEX # 8609.

Alex^r STEWART; pension awarded 1 Jan 1818; residence - Toronto, Ontario, Canada; died 22 Apr 1861, Armagh. SOURCE: WO120 Volume 70 page 483. INDEX # 8610.

Robt HERBERTSON; pension awarded 1 Dec 1817; residence - Belleville, Ontario, Canada. SOURCE: WO120 Volume 70 page 483. INDEX # 8611.

John SAYERS; pension awarded 1 Nov 1825; residence - Lunce; died 20 Aug 1849. SOURCE: WO120 Volume 70 page 483. INDEX # 8612.

Richd KEATING; pension awarded 1 May 1826; residence - Montreal, Quebec, Canada; died 27 Dec 1855. SOURCE: WO120 Volume 70 page 483. INDEX # 8613.

John CAREY; pension awarded 1 Dec 1827; residence - Toronto, Ontario, Canada. SOURCE: WO120 Volume 70 page 483. INDEX # 8614.

Geo^e HOWIE; pension awarded 1 Dec 1826; residence - Gibraltar. SOURCE: WO120 Volume 70 page 483. INDEX # 8615.

Baptist YOUNG; pension awarded 1 Oct 1816; residence - Quebec, Quebec, Canada. SOURCE: WO120 Volume 70 page 483. INDEX # 8616.

Jno MANEALY; pension awarded 1 Jan 1816; residence - Niagara, Ontario, Canada; died 4 Apr 1860. SOURCE: WO120 Volume 70 page 483. INDEX # 8617.

Ja^s HISCOCK; pension awarded 1 Jan 1830; residence - Grenada, West Indies. SOURCE: WO120 Volume 70 page 483. INDEX # 8618.

And^w BOYLE; pension awarded 1 Dec 1827; residence - Toronto, Ontario, Canada; died 3 Jan 1861. SOURCE: WO120 Volume 70 page 483. INDEX # 8619.

Henry PATTON; pension awarded 14 Jul 1816; residence - Quebec, Quebec, Canada; died in 1848. SOURCE: WO120 Volume 70 page 483. INDEX # 8620.

Danl LIVINGSTON; pension awarded 1 Nov 1824; residence - St. Johns; died 17 Jul 1845. SOURCE: WO120 Volume 70 page 484. INDEX # 8621.

Thos PORTER; pension awarded 1 Aug 1825; residence - Toronto, Ontario, Canada; died 6 Apr 1855. SOURCE: WO120 Volume 70 page 484. INDEX # 8622.

Phi^p CASEMENT; pension awarded 1 Jun 1819; residence - Toronto, Ontario, Canada; died 13 Apr 1847. SOURCE: WO120 Volume 70 page 484. INDEX # 8623.

BRITISH ARMY PENSIONERS ABROAD

7th Battalion of Artillery (continued)

Edwd PRENTICE; pension awarded 1 May 1819; residence - Montreal, Quebec, Canada. SOURCE: WO120 Volume 70 page 484. INDEX # 8624.

Thos THOMPSON; pension awarded 4 Apr 1816; residence - Penetanguishene, Ontario, Canada; died 20 Jan 1855. SOURCE: WO120 Volume 70 page 484. INDEX # 8625.

John MACLEAN; pension awarded 1 Jan 1816; residence - Kingston, Ontario, Canada. SOURCE: WO120 Volume 70 page 484. INDEX # 8626.

John CHRISTIE; pension awarded 10 Aug 1814; residence - Cape of Good Hope, South Africa. SOURCE: WO120 Volume 70 page 484. INDEX # 8627.

John SAYERS; pension awarded 1 Nov 1825; residence - Lunce. SOURCE: WO120 Volume 70 page 484. INDEX # 8628.

Richd CAREY; pension awarded 14 Oct 1845; residence - Montreal, Quebec, Canada; died in 1852. SOURCE: WO120 Volume 70 page 484. INDEX # 8629.

Jos^h IRWIN; pension awarded 14 Oct 1840; residence - Hobart Town, Australia. SOURCE: WO120 Volume 70 page 484. INDEX # 8630.

Fra^s SHORT; pension awarded 16 Jan 1845; residence - Cape of Good Hope, South Africa. SOURCE: WO120 Volume 70 page 484. INDEX # 8631.

Jno SIMPSON; pension awarded 14 Jan 1835; residence - Norfolk Island, Australia; died 30 Nov 1847. SOURCE: WO120 Volume 70 page 484. INDEX # 8632.

Edwd UTTING; pension awarded 8 Oct 1834; residence - Kingston, Ontario, Canada; died 8 Aug 1872, Toronto, Ontario, Canada. SOURCE: WO120 Volume 70 page 484. INDEX # 8633.

Robt MCLEAN; pension awarded 12 Oct 1836; residence - Hobart Town, Australia. SOURCE: WO120 Volume 70 page 484. INDEX # 8634.

Richd STEWART; pension awarded 11 Aug 1846; residence - Prince Edward Island, Canada; died 16 Dec 1876, Toronto, Ontario, Canada. SOURCE: WO120 Volume 70 page 484. INDEX # 8635.

Abr^m PEARSON; pension awarded 12 Jan 1847; residence - Montreal, Quebec, Canada. SOURCE: WO120 Volume 70 page 484. INDEX # 8636.

Saml FARR; pension awarded 23 Nov 1847; died 25 Feb 1878, London, Ontario, Canada. SOURCE: WO120 Volume 70 page 484. INDEX # 8637.

Jno LETTIMORE; pension awarded 23 Nov 1847; residence - Hamilton, Ontario, Canada; died 18 Jun 1866. SOURCE: WO120 Volume 70 page 484. INDEX # 8638.

Jno MCGARRY; pension awarded 23 Nov 1847. SOURCE: WO120 Volume 70 page 484. INDEX # 8639.

Robt STURGEON; pension awarded 23 Nov 1847. SOURCE: WO120 Volume 70 page 485. INDEX # 8640.

Thos WALLACE; pension awarded 23 Nov 1847. SOURCE: WO120 Volume 70 page 485. INDEX # 8641.

Ja^s PATTISON; pension awarded 11 Jan 1848; residence - Northumb^d; died 6 Mar 1852. SOURCE: WO120 Volume 70 page 485. INDEX # 8642.

Jno WILLSON; pension awarded 27 Jun 1848. SOURCE: WO120 Volume 70 page 485. INDEX # 8643.

Wm AULD; pension awarded 27 Jun 1848. SOURCE: WO120 Volume 70 page 485. INDEX # 8644.

Wm HOWARTH; pension awarded 27 Jun 1848. SOURCE: WO120 Volume 70 page 485. INDEX # 8645.

Geo^e NEWSOME; pension awarded 12 Sep 1848. SOURCE: WO120 Volume 70 page 485. INDEX # 8646.

Nathl HAGAN; pension awarded 12 Sep 1848. SOURCE: WO120 Volume 70 page 485. INDEX # 8647.

Ja^s MCMULLEN; pension awarded 12 Sep 1848. SOURCE: WO120 Volume 70 page 485. INDEX # 8648.

Hen^y MCCLEAVE; pension awarded 10 Jul 1849. SOURCE: WO120 Volume 70 page 485. INDEX # 8649.

Ja^s JOHNSTON; pension awarded 10 Jul 1849; died 3 Dec 1872, Toronto, Ontario, Canada. SOURCE: WO120 Volume 70 page 485. INDEX # 8650.

Wm FAIRBROTHER; pension awarded 10 Jul 1849. SOURCE: WO120 Volume 70 page 485. INDEX # 8651.

Jno WHARIN; pension awarded 24 Jul 1849. SOURCE: WO120 Volume 70 page 485. INDEX # 8652.

Hen^y START; pension awarded 9 Jul 1850. SOURCE: WO120 Volume 70 page 485. INDEX # 8653.

Robt LINDSAY; pension awarded 13 Aug 1850; died 19 Aug 1874, Cape Town, South Africa. SOURCE: WO120 Volume 70 page 485. INDEX # 8654.

Ja^s HOOK; pension awarded 14 Oct 1851. SOURCE: WO120 Volume 70 page 485. INDEX # 8655.

Wm DORAN; pension awarded 13 Jul 1852. SOURCE: WO120 Volume 70 page 485. INDEX # 8656.

Geo^e STEWART; pension awarded 10 Jan 1854. SOURCE: WO120 Volume 70 page 485. INDEX # 8657.

WO120 VOLUME 70

8th Battalion of Artillery

Ja^s MCCARTNEY; pension awarded 13 Apr 1842; residence - Bermuda, West Indies; died 2 Jul 1863, Toronto, Ontario, Canada. SOURCE: WO120 Volume 70 page 494. INDEX # 8658.

Alex^r MCKAY; pension awarded 9 Jan 1844; residence - Jamaica, West Indies. SOURCE: WO120 Volume 70 page 494. INDEX # 8659.

John CHAPMAN; pension awarded 14 Apr 1841; residence - Cape of Good Hope, South Africa; died 28 Sep 1851. SOURCE: WO120 Volume 70 page 494. INDEX # 8660.

Thos PAISLEY; pension awarded 8 Jul 1845; residence - Nova Scotia, Canada; died 7 Oct 1881, Nova Scotia, Canada. SOURCE: WO120 Volume 70 page 494. INDEX # 8661.

Thos SOUTHWORTH; pension awarded 12 Jan 1842; residence - Bermuda, West Indies. SOURCE: WO120 Volume 70 page 494. INDEX # 8662.

Chas GRANT; pension awarded 11 Apr 1843; residence - Halifax, Nova Scotia, Canada. SOURCE: WO120 Volume 70 page 494. INDEX # 8663.

Adam KILLOCK; pension awarded 8 Jul 1835; residence - Ionian Isles; died 3 Mar 1847. SOURCE: WO120 Volume 70 page 494. INDEX # 8664.

Willm CORNWALL; pension awarded in 1846; residence - New Brunswick, Canada. SOURCE: WO120 Volume 70 page 494. INDEX # 8665.

John EDWARD; pension awarded 13 Oct 1846; residence - Fredericton, New Brunswick, Canada. SOURCE: WO120 Volume 70 page 494. INDEX # 8666.

Thos HUME; pension awarded 12 Jan 1847; residence - Van Diemen's Land, Australia. SOURCE: WO120 Volume 70 page 494. INDEX # 8667.

John MCARTHUR; pension awarded 12 Jan 1847; residence - Van Diemen's Land, Australia. SOURCE: WO120 Volume 70 page 494. INDEX # 8668.

John YATES; pension awarded 12 Jan 1847; residence - Van Diemen's Land, Australia. SOURCE: WO120 Volume 70 page 494. INDEX # 8669.

Edwd FAIR; pension awarded 1 Jan 1833; residence - Montreal, Quebec, Canada. SOURCE: WO120 Volume 70 page 494. INDEX # 8670.

John BOWE; pension awarded 17 Dec 1819; residence - Gibraltar; died 23 Mar 1850. SOURCE: WO120 Volume 70 page 494. INDEX # 8671.

Eph^r MILLER; pension awarded 30 Dec 1818; residence - Toronto, Ontario, Canada; died 4 Oct 1847. SOURCE: WO120 Volume 70 page 494. INDEX # 8672.

John BALDWIN; pension awarded 25 Nov 1816; residence - Toronto, Ontario, Canada. SOURCE: WO120 Volume 70 page 494. INDEX # 8673.

Ja^s BLACK; pension awarded 1 Feb 1819; residence - Huntingdon, Quebec, Canada; died 16 Jun 1855. SOURCE: WO120 Volume 70 page 494. INDEX # 8674.

Jno HANNAH; pension awarded 1 Jan 1823; residence - Fredericton, New Brunswick, Canada. SOURCE: WO120 Volume 70 page 494. INDEX # 8675.

Willm MCNAUGHT; pension awarded 1 Mar 1819; residence - Real del Monti, Mexico. SOURCE: WO120 Volume 70 page 494. INDEX # 8676.

John SYKES; pension awarded 1 Mar 1819; residence - Kingston, Ontario, Canada. SOURCE: WO120 Volume 70 page 495. INDEX # 8677.

Dav^d BROOKS; pension awarded 1 Jun 1816; residence - Toronto, Ontario, Canada; died 17 Dec 1864, London, Ontario, Canada. SOURCE: WO120 Volume 70 page 495. INDEX # 8678.

Thos PLUNKETT; pension awarded 1 Jan 1823; residence - New South Wales, Australia. SOURCE: WO120 Volume 70 page 495. INDEX # 8679.

John HILLIS; pension awarded 1 Jun 1822; residence - New South Wales, Australia; died 30 Jul 1849. SOURCE: WO120 Volume 70 page 495. INDEX # 8680.

Geo^e BAYCROFT; pension awarded 28 Sep 1828; residence - Toronto, Ontario, Canada; died 1 Oct 1858. SOURCE: WO120 Volume 70 page 495. INDEX # 8681.

Mart^n MCLAUGHLAN; pension awarded 31 Jan 1819; residence - Hobart Town, Australia. SOURCE: WO120 Volume 70 page 495. INDEX # 8682.

Ja^s MCCONNELL; pension awarded 1 May 1818; residence - St. Johns; died in May 1844. SOURCE: WO120 Volume 70 page 495. INDEX # 8683.

8th Battalion of Artillery (continued)

Thos VARNER; pension awarded 1 Jul 1818; residence - Gibraltar; died 9 Apr 1847. SOURCE: WO120 Volume 70 page 495. INDEX # 8684.

John LANCASTER; pension awarded 1 Dec 1827; residence - Toronto, Ontario, Canada; died 22 Mar 1862. SOURCE: WO120 Volume 70 page 495. INDEX # 8685.

Jno CRASTY; pension awarded 10 Oct 1848; residence - London, Ontario, Canada; died 27 Feb 1856. SOURCE: WO120 Volume 70 page 495. INDEX # 8686.

Alexr BURTON; pension awarded 8 Jan 1850. SOURCE: WO120 Volume 70 page 495. INDEX # 8687.

James TASKER; pension awarded 12 Jun 1855. SOURCE: WO120 Volume 70 page 495. INDEX # 8688.

9th Battalion of Artillery

Josiah BOOTH; pension awarded 12 Jul 1842; residence - Gibraltar; died 9 Feb 1857. SOURCE: WO120 Volume 70 page 504. INDEX # 8689.

John STEWART; pension awarded 16 Jul 1841; residence - Gibraltar; died 27 Aug 1882, Dublin. SOURCE: WO120 Volume 70 page 504. INDEX # 8690.

Robt LEMON; pension awarded 1 Jul 1834; residence - Charlottetown, Prince Edward Island, Canada. SOURCE: WO120 Volume 70 page 504. INDEX # 8691.

Jas COULSTON; pension awarded 13 Jan 1841; residence - Malta; died 4 Oct 1855. SOURCE: WO120 Volume 70 page 504. INDEX # 8692.

Willm WEIR; pension awarded 8 Jan 1840; residence - Gibraltar; died 15 Feb 1851. SOURCE: WO120 Volume 70 page 495. INDEX # 8693.

Alexr THOM; pension awarded 11 Apr 1843; residence - Gibraltar; died 0 Oct 1878, Montreal, Quebec, Canada. SOURCE: WO120 Volume 70 page 504. INDEX # 8694.

Josh DICKSON; pension awarded 8 Jul 1840; residence - Gibraltar. SOURCE: WO120 Volume 70 page 504. INDEX # 8695.

Thos LEE; pension awarded 13 Oct 1841; residence - Cape of Good Hope, South Africa; died 12 Sep 1871, Woolwich. SOURCE: WO120 Volume 70 page 504. INDEX # 8696.

Willm MARTIN; pension awarded 13 Jan 1836; residence - Kingston, Ontario, Canada; died 12 Jun 1868, Toronto, Ontario, Canada. SOURCE: WO120 Volume 70 page 504. INDEX # 8697.

Willm PAUL; pension awarded 1 Jan 1827; residence - Kingston, Ontario, Canada; died 29 Jul 1849. SOURCE: WO120 Volume 70 page 504. INDEX # 8698.

Jas GORMLEY; pension awarded 3 Feb 1832; residence - Halifax, Nova Scotia, Canada. SOURCE: WO120 Volume 70 page 504. INDEX # 8699.

Willm MASSEY; pension awarded 1 Aug 1822; residence - Kingston, Ontario, Canada; died 22 Sep 1863, Toronto, Ontario, Canada. SOURCE: WO120 Volume 70 page 504. INDEX # 8700.

Saml GASTON; pension awarded 17 Oct 1823; residence - Halifax, Nova Scotia, Canada. SOURCE: WO120 Volume 70 page 504. INDEX # 8701.

Job BAVEN; pension awarded 1 Nov 1826; residence - Charlottetown, Prince Edward Island, Canada. SOURCE: WO120 Volume 70 page 504. INDEX # 8702.

Patk LOVATT; pension awarded 1 Jul 1816; residence - Toronto, Ontario, Canada; died 2 Jan 1850. SOURCE: WO120 Volume 70 page 504. INDEX # 8703.

John NICOLL; pension awarded 1 Jun 1827; residence - Charlottetown, Prince Edward Island, Canada. SOURCE: WO120 Volume 70 page 504. INDEX # 8704.

Geoe MCELHINEY; pension awarded 1 Feb 1819; residence - Saint John, New Brunswick, Canada. SOURCE: WO120 Volume 70 page 504. INDEX # 8705.

John MORGAN; pension awarded 1 Mar 1824; residence - Toronto, Ontario, Canada; died 30 May 1863. SOURCE: WO120 Volume 70 page 504. INDEX # 8706.

Robt MOORE; pension awarded 1 Jan 1826; residence - Toronto, Ontario, Canada; died 17 Jul 1845. SOURCE: WO120 Volume 70 page 504. INDEX # 8707.

Jas COUSINS; pension awarded 1 Nov 1826; residence - Amherstburg, Ontario, Canada; died 15 Feb 1871, London, Ontario, Canada. SOURCE: WO120 Volume 70 page 505. INDEX # 8708.

9th Battalion of Artillery (continued)

Willm CRANSTON; pension awarded 1 Jul 1826; residence - Charlottetown, Prince Edward Island, Canada. SOURCE: WO120 Volume 70 page 505. INDEX # 8709.

Jos^h JONES; pension awarded 1 Jan 1830; residence - Halifax, Nova Scotia, Canada; died 15 Jan 1872, Nova Scotia, Canada. SOURCE: WO120 Volume 70 page 505. INDEX # 8710.

And^w SMITH; pension awarded 1 Aug 1819; residence - Ostend, Belgium; died in 1848. SOURCE: WO120 Volume 70 page 505. INDEX # 8711.

Danl RATTLE; pension awarded 9 Jul 1850; died 21 Aug 1874, London, Ontario, Canada. SOURCE: WO120 Volume 70 page 505. INDEX # 8712.

Ja^s DAVIS; pension awarded 8 Jul 1851; died 1 Mar 1886, Toronto, Ontario, Canada. SOURCE: WO120 Volume 70 page 505. INDEX # 8713.

Wm Henry COURTIER; pension awarded 28 Jun 1853. SOURCE: WO120 Volume 70 page 505. INDEX # 8714.

Jos^h KILPATRICK; pension awarded 23 Aug 1853; died 5 Sep 1883. SOURCE: WO120 Volume 70 page 505. INDEX # 8715.

Nich^s FARR; pension awarded 22 Nov 1853; died 26 Jun 1826. SOURCE: WO120 Volume 70 page 505. INDEX # 8716.

Wm BASS; pension awarded 11 Apr 1854. SOURCE: WO120 Volume 70 page 505. INDEX # 8717.

10th Battalion of Artillery

Hugh WILSON; pension awarded 1 Jan 1833; residence - St. Johns. SOURCE: WO120 Volume 70 page 514. INDEX # 8718.

Richd HAIRBOTTLE; pension awarded 1 Nov 1814; residence - Cape of Good Hope, South Africa; died 13 Jul 1856. SOURCE: WO120 Volume 70 page 514. INDEX # 8719.

Wm TERRENCE; pension awarded 1 Jan 1813; residence - Prescott, Ontario, Canada; died 15 Oct 1852. SOURCE: WO120 Volume 70 page 514. INDEX # 8720.

Thos Bill PIPER; pension awarded 1 Jul 1813; residence - Cape of Good Hope, South Africa; died 25 Sep 1854. SOURCE: WO120 Volume 70 page 514. INDEX # 8721.

Richd BOND; pension awarded 1 Mar 1832; residence - Toronto, Ontario, Canada; died 4 Jul 1853. SOURCE: WO120 Volume 70 page 514. INDEX # 8722.

Thos FOX; pension awarded 30 Oct 1818; residence - Amherstburg, Ontario, Canada; died 20 Feb 1862, Toronto, Ontario, Canada. SOURCE: WO120 Volume 70 page 514. INDEX # 8723.

Ja^s DALGLEISH; pension awarded 31 Jul 1817; residence - Cape of Good Hope, South Africa. SOURCE: WO120 Volume 70 page 514. INDEX # 8724.

And^w POGUE; pension awarded 12 Jan 1847; died 24 May 1885, Tasmania, Australia. SOURCE: WO120 Volume 70 page 514. INDEX # 8725.

Peter GRAHAM; pension awarded 14 Oct 1851. SOURCE: WO120 Volume 70 page 514. INDEX # 8726.

Jno WILSON; pension awarded 14 Oct 1851. SOURCE: WO120 Volume 70 page 514. INDEX # 8727.

Jno ROBBS; pension awarded 27 Apr 1852; residence - Kingston, Ontario, Canada; died 15 Jul 1854. SOURCE: WO120 Volume 70 page 514. INDEX # 8728.

David FOSTER; pension awarded 13 Jul 1852. SOURCE: WO120 Volume 70 page 514. INDEX # 8729.

Wm FERGUSON; pension awarded 13 Jul 1852; residence - Toronto, Ontario, Canada; died 7 Jun 1858. SOURCE: WO120 Volume 70 page 514. INDEX # 8730.

Ja^s ELSDON; pension awarded 13 Dec 1853. SOURCE: WO120 Volume 70 page 514. INDEX # 8731.

Chas PIERCEY; pension awarded 13 Dec 1853. SOURCE: WO120 Volume 70 page 514. INDEX # 8732.

Jno TIERNEY; pension awarded 10 Oct 1854. SOURCE: WO120 Volume 70 page 514. INDEX # 8733.

Richd KENNEDY; pension awarded 10 Oct 1854. SOURCE: WO120 Volume 70 page 514. INDEX # 8735.

Arthur HOUSTON; pension awarded 1 Oct 1855. SOURCE: WO120 Volume 70 page 514. INDEX # 8735.

Hugh BOGLE; pension awarded 23 Oct 1855. SOURCE: WO120 Volume 70 page 514. INDEX # 8736.

John CHAPMAN; pension awarded 23 Oct 1855. SOURCE: WO120 Volume 70 page 514. INDEX # 8737.

Richard CURTIS; pension awarded 23 Oct 1855. SOURCE: WO120 Volume 70 page 515. INDEX # 8738.

Thomas HARDY; pension awarded 23 Oct 1855. SOURCE: WO120 Volume 70 page 515. INDEX # 8739.

Thomas LYNCH; pension awarded 23 Oct 1855. SOURCE: WO120 Volume 70 page 515. INDEX # 8740.

BRITISH ARMY PENSIONERS ABROAD

10th Battalion of Artillery (continued)

Matthew MCDONNELL; pension awarded 23 Oct 1855. SOURCE: WO120 Volume 70 page 515. INDEX # 8741.

Robert MULLEN; pension awarded 23 Oct 1855. SOURCE: WO120 Volume 70 page 515. INDEX # 8742.

John ORR; pension awarded 23 Oct 1855. SOURCE: WO120 Volume 70 page 515. INDEX # 8743.

John ROSS; pension awarded 23 Oct 1855. SOURCE: WO120 Volume 70 page 515. INDEX # 8744.

Sappers and Miners

Willm BRANDER; pension awarded 13 Jan 1841; residence - New South Wales, Australia; died 31 Jan 1881, Inverness. SOURCE: WO120 Volume 70 page 522. INDEX # 8745.

Richd PASCOE; pension awarded 9 Apr 1834; residence - London, Ontario, Canada; died 5 Mar 1877, London, Ontario, Canada. SOURCE: WO120 Volume 70 page 522. INDEX # 8746.

Ja^s THOMPSON; pension awarded 9 Apr 1834; residence - London, Ontario, Canada. SOURCE: WO120 Volume 70 page 522. INDEX # 8747.

Jno MCKENZIE; pension awarded 9 Apr 1834; residence - Toronto, Ontario, Canada; died 25 Jun 1846. SOURCE: WO120 Volume 70 page 522. INDEX # 8748.

Simon OBRIEN; pension awarded 8 Oct 1834; residence - Kingston, Ontario, Canada. SOURCE: WO120 Volume 70 page 522. INDEX # 8749.

Jos^h WATTS; pension awarded 25 May 1843; residence - Cape of Good Hope, South Africa; died 9 Nov 1857, Cape of Good Hope, South Africa. SOURCE: WO120 Volume 70 page 522. INDEX # 8750.

Jos^h CAVE; pension awarded 26 Jan 1843; residence - St. Johns. SOURCE: WO120 Volume 70 page 522. INDEX # 8751.

Peter HOOD; pension awarded 9 May 1843; residence - Halifax, Nova Scotia, Canada. SOURCE: WO120 Volume 70 page 522. INDEX # 8752.

Ja^s FRASER; pension awarded 9 Apr 1834; residence - Montreal, Quebec, Canada. SOURCE: WO120 Volume 70 page 522. INDEX # 8753.

Neil MULLAN; pension awarded 9 Apr 1834; residence - Kingston, Ontario, Canada; died 11 Feb 1860, Toronto, Ontario, Canada. SOURCE: WO120 Volume 70 page 522. INDEX # 8754.

John ROGERS; pension awarded 9 Apr 1834; residence - Bytown, Ontario, Canada; died 11 May 1856. SOURCE: WO120 Volume 70 page 522. INDEX # 8755.

Ja^s BOWICK; pension awarded 9 Apr 1834; residence - Quebec, Quebec, Canada. SOURCE: WO120 Volume 70 page 522. INDEX # 8756.

Willm MCINTOSH; pension awarded 8 Oct 1834; residence - Cape of Good Hope, South Africa. SOURCE: WO120 Volume 70 page 522. INDEX # 8757.

And^w MOORE; pension awarded 8 Jul 1835; residence - Hobart Town, Australia. SOURCE: WO120 Volume 70 page 522. INDEX # 8758.

Willm BELL; pension awarded 24 Jan 1843; residence - Montreal, Quebec, Canada; died 20 May 1876, Toronto, Ontario, Canada. SOURCE: WO120 Volume 70 page 522. INDEX # 8759.

Ja^s EAGAN; pension awarded 9 Apr 1834; residence - London, Ontario, Canada. SOURCE: WO120 Volume 70 page 522. INDEX # 8760.

Robt BOOTH; pension awarded 8 Oct 1834; residence - Penetanguishene, Ontario, Canada. SOURCE: WO120 Volume 70 page 522. INDEX # 8761.

Ja^s ROBERTSON; pension awarded 9 Jul 1844; residence - St. Johns. SOURCE: WO120 Volume 70 page 522. INDEX # 8762.

Jno FRASER; pension awarded 8 Aug 1843; residence - Bermuda, West Indies. SOURCE: WO120 Volume 70 page 522. INDEX # 8763.

Chas WALKEM; pension awarded 25 Feb 1845; residence - Quebec, Quebec, Canada. SOURCE: WO120 Volume 70 page 522. INDEX # 8764.

Willm GILES; pension awarded 28 May 1845; residence - Gibraltar; died 13 May 1856. SOURCE: WO120 Volume 70 page 523. INDEX # 8765.

John CATT; pension awarded 16 Jan 1835; residence - Gibraltar; died 12 Aug 1864. SOURCE: WO120 Volume 70 page 523. INDEX # 8766.

Sappers and Miners (continued)

Jos^h DAVIS; pension awarded 11 Jul 1843; residence - Bermuda, West Indies. SOURCE: WO120 Volume 70 page 523. INDEX # 8767.

Thos KELLY; pension awarded 9 May 1843; residence - Halifax, Nova Scotia, Canada. SOURCE: WO120 Volume 70 page 523. INDEX # 8768.

Benjn FISHER; pension awarded 25 Apr 1843; residence - Gibraltar; died 22 Nov 1854. SOURCE: WO120 Volume 70 page 523. INDEX # 8769.

Ja^s MILLER; pension awarded 27 Apr 1842; residence - Cape of Good Hope, South Africa. SOURCE: WO120 Volume 70 page 523. INDEX # 8770.

Mich^l FINERAN; pension awarded 8 Oct 1834; residence - Cape of Good Hope, South Africa; died 2 Dec 1848. SOURCE: WO120 Volume 70 page 523. INDEX # 8771.

Jno MCLAREN; pension awarded 10 Jan 1838; residence - South Australia, Australia; died 8 Mar 1877. SOURCE: WO120 Volume 70 page 523. INDEX # 8772.

Jno HEMMING; pension awarded 28 Jan 1845; residence - Cape of Good Hope, South Africa. SOURCE: WO120 Volume 70 page 523. INDEX # 8773.

Alex^r SMITH; pension awarded 9 Oct 1839; residence - Hobart Town, Australia; died 9 Jan 1884, Tasmania, Australia. SOURCE: WO120 Volume 70 page 523. INDEX # 8774.

Robt H. MOULTON; pension awarded 1 Nov 1842; residence - South Australia, Australia. SOURCE: WO120 Volume 70 page 523. INDEX # 8775.

John MOORE; pension awarded 10 Jan 1843; residence - Bytown, Ontario, Canada; died 15 Aug 1869, Toronto, Ontario, Canada. SOURCE: WO120 Volume 70 page 523. INDEX # 8776.

Barth^w CLINTON; pension awarded 9 Jul 1834; residence - Gibraltar; died 29 Jan 1857, Woolwich. SOURCE: WO120 Volume 70 page 523. INDEX # 8777.

Willm CHALMERS; pension awarded 9 Jul 1844; residence - Smiths Falls, Ontario, Canada; died in 1849. SOURCE: WO120 Volume 70 page 523. INDEX # 8778.

Lewis LEWIS; pension awarded 9 Jul 1834; residence - Quebec, Quebec, Canada. SOURCE: WO120 Volume 70 page 523. INDEX # 8779.

John JOHNSTON; pension awarded 8 Oct 1834; residence - Smiths Falls, Ontario, Canada. SOURCE: WO120 Volume 70 page 523. INDEX # 8780.

Dav^d PATTERSON; pension awarded 9 Apr 1834; residence - London, Ontario, Canada; died in Feb 1847. SOURCE: WO120 Volume 70 page 523. INDEX # 8781.

Dav^d MCGILL; pension awarded 1 Jul 1834; residence - Cape of Good Hope, South Africa. SOURCE: WO120 Volume 70 page 523. INDEX # 8782.

John SHEAN; pension awarded 13 Jul 1842; residence - Halifax, Nova Scotia, Canada; died 13 Dec 1878, Halifax, Nova Scotia, Canada. SOURCE: WO120 Volume 70 page 523. INDEX # 8783.

Jos^h DAVIE; pension awarded 12 Oct 1836; residence - Hobart Town, Australia. SOURCE: WO120 Volume 70 page 523. INDEX # 8784.

Alex^r DUFF; pension awarded 16 Apr 1841; residence - Mauritius; died in 1847. SOURCE: WO120 Volume 70 page 524. INDEX # 8785.

Thos JONES; pension awarded 1 Jan 1832; residence - Bytown, Ontario, Canada. SOURCE: WO120 Volume 70 page 524. INDEX # 8786.

Ja^s HOOD; pension awarded 1 Oct 1832; residence - Gibraltar; died 14 Jun 1848. SOURCE: WO120 Volume 70 page 524. INDEX # 8787.

John COLES; pension awarded 10 Nov 1842; residence - South Australia, Australia. SOURCE: WO120 Volume 70 page 524. INDEX # 8788.

John RICKARD; pension awarded 26 Dec 1831; residence - Penetanguishene, Ontario, Canada. SOURCE: WO120 Volume 70 page 524. INDEX # 8789.

Thos JENKINS; pension awarded 1 Jul 1832; residence - Smiths Falls, Ontario, Canada; died in 1847. SOURCE: WO120 Volume 70 page 524. INDEX # 8790.

Willm ADDISON; pension awarded 1 Jan 1832; residence - Bytown, Ontario, Canada. SOURCE: WO120 Volume 70 page 524. INDEX # 8791.

Jos^h COOMBS; pension awarded 1 Mar 1832; residence - Bytown, Ontario, Canada; died 19 May 1856. SOURCE: WO120 Volume 70 page 524. INDEX # 8792.

1856. SOURCE: WO120 Volume 70 page 524. INDEX # 8792.

Sappers and Miners (continued)

Ja^s DUNLAP; pension awarded 30 May 1827; residence - Bytown, Ontario, Canada. SOURCE: WO120 Volume 70 page 524. INDEX # 8793.

Danl LYNCH; pension awarded 30 May 1827; residence - Bytown, Ontario, Canada. SOURCE: WO120 Volume 70 page 524. INDEX # 8794.

Ja^s MCROARY; pension awarded 30 Nov 1828; residence - Quebec, Quebec, Canada. SOURCE: WO120 Volume 70 page 524. INDEX # 8795.

Step^n WOOD; pension awarded 29 Sep 1820; residence - Kingston, Ontario, Canada. SOURCE: WO120 Volume 70 page 524. INDEX # 8796.

Thos MURPHY; pension awarded 3 Sep 1826; residence - Perth, Ontario, Canada; died 24 Aug 1853. SOURCE: WO120 Volume 70 page 524. INDEX # 8797.

Richd FRELOGGAN; pension awarded 30 Apr 1823; residence - Newfoundland, Canada; died 20 Oct 1871, Nova Scotia, Canada. SOURCE: WO120 Volume 70 page 524. INDEX # 8798.

Jno MCGUIGAN; pension awarded 7 Apr 1827; residence - Bytown, Ontario, Canada. SOURCE: WO120 Volume 70 page 524. INDEX # 8799.

Jno DUNNAGE; pension awarded 17 Jun 1827; residence - New South Wales, Australia. SOURCE: WO120 Volume 70 page 524. INDEX # 8800.

Richd LOBB; pension awarded 1 Oct 1810; residence - Kingston, Ontario, Canada; died 19 Aug 1848. SOURCE: WO120 Volume 70 page 524. INDEX # 8801.

Danl RUDDOCK; pension awarded 8 Mar 1819; residence - Richmond, Ontario, Canada. SOURCE: WO120 Volume 70 page 524. INDEX # 8802.

Leon^d ROBERTSON; pension awarded 10 Jan 1819; residence - Quebec, Quebec, Canada. SOURCE: WO120 Volume 70 page 525. INDEX # 8803.

Jacob OUDERKIRK; pension awarded 1 Jan 1818; residence - Halifax, Nova Scotia, Canada. SOURCE: WO120 Volume 70 page 525. INDEX # 8804.

Dav^d GRIFFITHS; pension awarded 1 May 1818; residence - Hobart Town, Australia. SOURCE: WO120 Volume 70 page 525. INDEX # 8805.

Robt BEATTIE; pension awarded 1 Apr 1818; residence - Montreal, Quebec, Canada. SOURCE: WO120 Volume 70 page 525. INDEX # 8806.

Willm SULLIVAN; pension awarded 1 Oct 1821; residence - New South Wales, Australia. SOURCE: WO120 Volume 70 page 525. INDEX # 8807.

And^w HUNTER; pension awarded 1 Oct 1829; residence - Montreal, Quebec, Canada. SOURCE: WO120 Volume 70 page 525. INDEX # 8808.

Ja^s NUGENT; pension awarded 1 Sep 1824; residence - Bytown, Ontario, Canada. SOURCE: WO120 Volume 70 page 525. INDEX # 8809.

John WARD; pension awarded 1 Oct 1823; residence - Montreal, Quebec, Canada. SOURCE: WO120 Volume 70 page 525. INDEX # 8810.

Ja^s BARRY; pension awarded 1 Apr 1817; residence - Quebec, Quebec, Canada. SOURCE: WO120 Volume 70 page 525. INDEX # 8811.

Ja^s KIDNEY; pension awarded 24 Jan 1817; residence - Perth, Ontario, Canada; died 6 Jul 1849. SOURCE: WO120 Volume 70 page 525. INDEX # 8812.

Ja^s ANDREWS; pension awarded 1 Oct 1821; residence - Wm Henry, Quebec, Canada; died 10 Jan 1882, Montreal, Quebec, Canada. SOURCE: WO120 Volume 70 page 525. INDEX # 8813.

John CARROL; pension awarded 1 Nov 1826; residence - Gibraltar. SOURCE: WO120 Volume 70 page 525. INDEX # 8814.

John BLACKIE; pension awarded 1 Mar 1824; residence - Adelaide. SOURCE: WO120 Volume 70 page 525. INDEX # 8815.

Willm MENDELL; pension awarded 1 Nov 1825; residence - Prescott, Ontario, Canada. SOURCE: WO120 Volume 70 page 525. INDEX # 8816.

Ja^s DAVIES; pension awarded 13 Jun 1817; residence - Halifax, Nova Scotia, Canada; died in Dec 1862, Nova Scotia, Canada. SOURCE: WO120 Volume 70 page 525. INDEX # 8817.

And^w TAYLOR; pension awarded 1 Jan 1816; residence - Halifax, Nova Scotia, Canada; died 19 Jan 1846. SOURCE: WO120 Volume 70 page 525. INDEX # 8818.

Sappers and Miners (continued)

Willm CLAY; pension awarded 1 Nov 1819; residence - Gibraltar. SOURCE: WO120 Volume 70 page 525. INDEX # 8819.

Chas MOLONY; pension awarded 1 Jun 1819; residence - Lorient, France. SOURCE: WO120 Volume 70 page 525. INDEX # 8820.

Ja^s MULLIGAN; pension awarded 28 Jul 1846; residence - Toronto, Ontario, Canada. SOURCE: WO120 Volume 70 page 525. INDEX # 8821.

Thos DUMBLE; pension awarded 28 Jul 1846; residence - Cobourg, Ontario, Canada; died 16 Mar 1883, Toronto, Ontario, Canada. SOURCE: WO120 Volume 70 page 525. INDEX # 8822.

Don^d BREMNER; pension awarded 26 May 1846. SOURCE: WO120 Volume 70 page 526. INDEX # 8823.

Walter TREVENER; pension awarded 24 Nov 1846; died 9 Jan 1880, Falmouth. SOURCE: WO120 Volume 70 page 526. INDEX # 8824.

Ardy BROOKE; pension awarded 12 Jan 1847. SOURCE: WO120 Volume 70 page 526. INDEX # 8825.

Wm MADEN; pension awarded 12 Jan 1847. SOURCE: WO120 Volume 70 page 526. INDEX # 8826.

Ja^s MATHIESON; pension awarded 12 Jan 1847. SOURCE: WO120 Volume 70 page 526. INDEX # 8827.

Geo^e SHEPHERD; pension awarded 13 Apr 1847. SOURCE: WO120 Volume 70 page 526. INDEX # 8828.

Wm COLWELL; pension awarded 8 Jun 1847. SOURCE: WO120 Volume 70 page 526. INDEX # 8829.

Jno CONRAN; pension awarded 8 Jun 1847. SOURCE: WO120 Volume 70 page 526. INDEX # 8830.

Wm BARNS; pension awarded 24 Aug 1847. SOURCE: WO120 Volume 70 page 526. INDEX # 8831.

Philip LEWIS; pension awarded 24 Aug 1847. SOURCE: WO120 Volume 70 page 526. INDEX # 8832.

Jno REID; pension awarded 24 Aug 1847. SOURCE: WO120 Volume 70 page 526. INDEX # 8833.

Thos CRUMLEY; pension awarded 27 Jun 1848. SOURCE: WO120 Volume 70 page 526. INDEX # 8834.

Thos RAMAGE; pension awarded 27 Jun 1848. SOURCE: WO120 Volume 70 page 526. INDEX # 8835.

Moses PEARSON; pension awarded 11 Jul 1848; died 29 Dec 1880, Adelaide. SOURCE: WO120 Volume 70 page 526. INDEX # 8836.

Wm MELASS; pension awarded 22 Aug 1848. SOURCE: WO120 Volume 70 page 526. INDEX # 8837.

Pat^k HERRALD; pension awarded 12 Sep 1848. SOURCE: WO120 Volume 70 page 526. INDEX # 8838.

Jno MCKILLOP; pension awarded 14 Nov 1848; died 27 Oct 1883, Guildford. SOURCE: WO120 Volume 70 page 526. INDEX # 8839.

Jno DICKSON; pension awarded 27 Feb 1849. SOURCE: WO120 Volume 70 page 526. INDEX # 8840.

Wm SMITH; pension awarded 27 Feb 1849. SOURCE: WO120 Volume 70 page 526. INDEX # 8841.

Edwin S. WALES; pension awarded 27 Feb 1849. SOURCE: WO120 Volume 70 page 526. INDEX # 8842.

Ja^s BYRONS; pension awarded 27 Feb 1849; died 18 Jan 1855. SOURCE: WO120 Volume 70 page 527. INDEX # 8843.

Ja^s GARDNER; pension awarded 22 May 1849; residence - Cape of Good Hope, South Africa; died in 1849. SOURCE: WO120 Volume 70 page 527. INDEX # 8844.

Jno BEATTIE; pension awarded 22 May 1849. SOURCE: WO120 Volume 70 page 527. INDEX # 8845.

Wm HILLMAN; pension awarded 22 May 1849. SOURCE: WO120 Volume 70 page 527. INDEX # 8846.

Alex^r IRVINE; pension awarded 22 May 1849. SOURCE: WO120 Volume 70 page 527. INDEX # 8847.

David MOORE; pension awarded 22 May 1849. SOURCE: WO120 Volume 70 page 527. INDEX # 8848.

Jno WRIGHT; pension awarded 22 May 1849. SOURCE: WO120 Volume 70 page 527. INDEX # 8849.

Jno WILLIAMS; pension awarded 22 May 1849. SOURCE: WO120 Volume 70 page 527. INDEX # 8850.

Robt IRWIN; pension awarded 26 Mar 1850; residence - Hong Kong; died 24 Aug 1850. SOURCE: WO120 Volume 70 page 527. INDEX # 8851.

Hugh ANDREW; pension awarded 25 Jun 1850. SOURCE: WO120 Volume 70 page 527. INDEX # 8852.

Ja^s CUMMING; pension awarded 25 May 1852. SOURCE: WO120 Volume 70 page 527. INDEX # 8853.

Geo^e WHARRAM; pension awarded 25 May 1852. SOURCE: WO120 Volume 70 page 527. INDEX # 8854.

Hugh MCINTYRE; pension awarded 22 Jun 1852. SOURCE: WO120 Volume 70 page 527. INDEX # 8855.

Jno SHAW; pension awarded 26 Jul 1853. SOURCE: WO120 Volume 70 page 527. INDEX # 8856.

Thos BARRABLE; pension awarded 26 Jul 1853; died 12 Dec 1883, Cape of Good Hope, South Africa. SOURCE: WO120 Volume 70 page 527. INDEX # 8857.

Ed^wd BAILEY; pension awarded 23 Aug 1853. SOURCE: WO120 Volume 70 page 527. INDEX # 8858.

Alex^r SPALDING; pension awarded 27 Sep 1853. SOURCE: WO120 Volume 70 page 527. INDEX # 8859.

Sappers and Miners (continued)

Robt BARLOW; pension awarded 11 Apr 1854. SOURCE: WO120 Volume 70 page 527. INDEX # 8861.
Jno HOPKINS; pension awarded 11 Apr 1854. SOURCE: WO120 Volume 70 page 527. INDEX # 8862.
Hugh MUNRO; pension awarded 11 Apr 1854; died 27 Nov 1872, Malta. SOURCE: WO120 Volume 70 page 528. INDEX # 8863.
Ja^s WOOD; pension awarded 11 Apr 1854; died 12 Dec 1879, Luas. SOURCE: WO120 Volume 70 page 528. INDEX # 8864.
Ja^s COLLOCOTT; pension awarded 13 Jun 1854; died 13 Feb 1873, Cape of Good Hope, South Africa. SOURCE: WO120 Volume 70 page 528. INDEX # 8865.
Robt GARDINER; pension awarded 13 Jun 1854. SOURCE: WO120 Volume 70 page 528. INDEX # 8866.
Chr^r DART; pension awarded 13 Feb 1855. SOURCE: WO120 Volume 70 page 528. INDEX # 8867.
Jos^h CRUMP; pension awarded 13 Feb 1855. SOURCE: WO120 Volume 70 page 528. INDEX # 8868.
Hen^y BURNS; pension awarded 27 Feb 1855. SOURCE: WO120 Volume 70 page 528. INDEX # 8869.
John SPENCER; pension awarded 14 Aug 1855. SOURCE: WO120 Volume 70 page 528. INDEX # 8870.
Joseph MOORE; pension awarded 14 Aug 1855. SOURCE: WO120 Volume 70 page 528. INDEX # 8871.

Royal Engineers

James ROBERTSON; pension awarded 30 Jun 1857. SOURCE: WO120 Volume 70 page 528. INDEX # 8872.
James MEALEY; pension awarded 30 Jun 1857. SOURCE: WO120 Volume 70 page 528. INDEX # 8873.
William COLLINS; pension awarded 18 Aug 1857. SOURCE: WO120 Volume 70 page 528. INDEX # 8874.
Peter PEIRCE; pension awarded 18 Aug 1857. SOURCE: WO120 Volume 70 page 528. INDEX # 8875.
William BEER; pension awarded 18 Aug 1857. SOURCE: WO120 Volume 70 page 528. INDEX # 8876.
Richard WAUGH; pension awarded 18 Aug 1857. SOURCE: WO120 Volume 70 page 528. INDEX # 8877.

Artillery Drivers

Moses SCOTT; pension awarded 10 Mar 1818; residence - Halifax, Nova Scotia, Canada. SOURCE: WO120 Volume 70 page 534. INDEX # 8878.
Ja^s WEBB; pension awarded 21 Mar 1824; residence - Chambly, Quebec, Canada. SOURCE: WO120 Volume 70 page 534. INDEX # 8879.
Ja^s GRANT; pension awarded 19 Mar 1825; residence - Richmond, Ontario, Canada. SOURCE: WO120 Volume 70 page 534. INDEX # 8880.
Dav^d CRAIG; pension awarded 1 May 1816; residence - Quebec, Quebec, Canada. SOURCE: WO120 Volume 70 page 534. INDEX # 8881.
Wm Thomas HICKS; pension awarded 30 Jan 1821; residence - Bytown, Ontario, Canada. SOURCE: WO120 Volume 70 page 534. INDEX # 8882.
John NUTTALL; pension awarded 4 Feb 1824; residence - Kingston, Ontario, Canada; died 9 Aug 1858. SOURCE: WO120 Volume 70 page 534. INDEX # 8883.
Ja^s GARVIN; pension awarded 30 Aug 1821; residence - Perth, Ontario, Canada. SOURCE: WO120 Volume 70 page 534. INDEX # 8884.
Willm MOORE; pension awarded 8 Apr 1820; residence - Perth, Ontario, Canada; died 21 Mar 1851. SOURCE: WO120 Volume 70 page 534. INDEX # 8885.
Saml RICH; pension awarded 17 May 1822; residence - Toronto, Ontario, Canada; died 19 May 1846. SOURCE: WO120 Volume 70 page 534. INDEX # 8886.
Henry AIRTH; pension awarded 10 Apr 1816; residence - Bytown, Ontario, Canada. SOURCE: WO120 Volume 70 page 534. INDEX # 8887.
John MORRIS; pension awarded 31 Jan 1828; residence - Toronto, Ontario, Canada; died 6 Jul 1868, London, Ontario, Canada. SOURCE: WO120 Volume 70 page 534. INDEX # 8888.
Jos^h PEARSON; pension awarded 9 Feb 1820; residence - St. Johns. SOURCE: WO120 Volume 70 page 534. INDEX # 8889.
Dav^d ASKIN; pension awarded 1 Nov 1814; residence - Montreal, Quebec, Canada. SOURCE: WO120 Volume 70 page 534. INDEX # 8890.

Artillery Drivers (continued)

Dennis MARTIN; pension awarded 10 Aug 1814; residence - Montreal, Quebec, Canada. SOURCE: WO120 Volume 70 page 534. INDEX # 8891.

Rob[t] MAYBLE; pension awarded 1 Jan 1807; residence - Montreal, Quebec, Canada; died 22 Feb 1848. SOURCE: WO120 Volume 70 page 534. INDEX # 8892.

Harris HALL; pension awarded 1 Dec 1818; residence - Belleville, Ontario, Canada. SOURCE: WO120 Volume 70 page 534. INDEX # 8893.

John TAYLOR; pension awarded 26 Mar 1825; residence - Halifax, Nova Scotia, Canada; died 31 Mar 1853. SOURCE: WO120 Volume 70 page 534. INDEX # 8894.

Moses KERR; pension awarded 1 Jul 1816; residence - New South Wales, Australia. SOURCE: WO120 Volume 70 page 534. INDEX # 8895.

Edw[d] BREAKEN; pension awarded 22 Nov 1818; residence - Toronto, Ontario, Canada. SOURCE: WO120 Volume 70 page 534. INDEX # 8896.

Will[m] HOWARTH; pension awarded ; residence - New South Wales, Australia. SOURCE: WO120 Volume 70 page 534. INDEX # 8897.

Benj[n] CURRAN; pension awarded 1 Dec 1818; residence - Montreal, Quebec, Canada. SOURCE: WO120 Volume 70 page 535. INDEX # 8898.

Owen GRAY; pension awarded 1 Jul 1816; residence - Quebec, Quebec, Canada. SOURCE: WO120 Volume 70 page 535. INDEX # 8899.

Mich[l] NAUGHTON; pension awarded 1 Oct 1829; residence - London, Ontario, Canada. SOURCE: WO120 Volume 70 page 535. INDEX # 8900.

Will[m] HARVEY; pension awarded 1 Jul 1809; residence - Kingston, Ontario, Canada; died 22 Jul 1867, Toronto, Ontario, Canada. SOURCE: WO120 Volume 70 page 535. INDEX # 8901.

Will[m] MENERY; pension awarded 19 Mar 1825; residence - Toronto, Ontario, Canada; died 21 Mar 1858. SOURCE: WO120 Volume 70 page 535. INDEX # 8902.

John GLEESON; pension awarded 1 Sep 1819; residence - Smiths Falls, Ontario, Canada; died 16 Oct 1849. SOURCE: WO120 Volume 70 page 535. INDEX # 8903.

John HARDY; pension awarded 1 Jun 1816; residence - Penetanguishene, Ontario, Canada; died 11 Jun 1859. SOURCE: WO120 Volume 70 page 535. INDEX # 8904.

Dav[d] KINNIBURGH; pension awarded 30 Jun 1823; residence - Cape of Good Hope, South Africa. SOURCE: WO120 Volume 70 page 535. INDEX # 8905.

Farrel HANNOPHY; pension awarded 20 Feb 1816; residence - Bytown, Ontario, Canada; died in 1848. SOURCE: WO120 Volume 70 page 535. INDEX # 8906.

Will[m] GREENWAY; pension awarded 1 Feb 1819; residence - Amherstburg, Ontario, Canada; died 31 Mar 1866, London, Ontario, Canada. SOURCE: WO120 Volume 70 page 535. INDEX # 8907.

Tho[s] RUSSELL; pension awarded 1 Nov 1814; residence - Halifax, Nova Scotia, Canada; died in Sep 1851. SOURCE: WO120 Volume 70 page 535. INDEX # 8908.

Fra[s] Loftus OBREE; pension awarded 20 Aug 1815; residence - Halifax, Nova Scotia, Canada; died 3 Aug 1847. SOURCE: WO120 Volume 70 page 535. INDEX # 8909.

Will[m] ATHORNE; pension awarded 1 May 1817; residence - New South Wales, Australia. SOURCE: WO120 Volume 70 page 535. INDEX # 8910.

Rob[t] MULHOLLAND; pension awarded 1 Nov 1814; residence - Montreal, Quebec, Canada; died in Nov 1856. SOURCE: WO120 Volume 70 page 535. INDEX # 8911.

John CORNER; pension awarded 1 Feb 1819; residence - Amherstburg, Ontario, Canada; died 28 Sep 1848. SOURCE: WO120 Volume 70 page 535. INDEX # 8912.

Geo[e] KENNEDY; pension awarded 1 Nov 1816; residence - Kingston, Ontario, Canada. SOURCE: WO120 Volume 70 page 535. INDEX # 8913.

Dav[d] BREEN; pension awarded 1 Jan 1833; residence - Fredericton, New Brunswick, Canada. SOURCE: WO120 Volume 70 page 535. INDEX # 8914.

Rob[t] JACKSON; pension awarded ; residence - Montreal, Quebec, Canada; died 1 May 1877. SOURCE: WO120 Volume 70 page 535. INDEX # 8915.

Invalid Detachment

Chas NIMENS; pension awarded 13 Apr 1842; residence - Toronto, Ontario, Canada; died 24 May 1874. SOURCE: WO120 Volume 70 page 544. INDEX # 8916.

Alex^r MCGREGOR; pension awarded 10 Oct 1838; residence - Toronto, Ontario, Canada. SOURCE: WO120 Volume 70 page 544. INDEX # 8917.

Thos SANDERSON; pension awarded 8 Jul 1845; residence - Toronto, Ontario, Canada; died 18 Jun 1876, Toronto, Ontario, Canada. SOURCE: WO120 Volume 70 page 544. INDEX # 8918.

Jno MAGARITY; pension awarded 11 Jul 1848; died 3 Apr 1878, Malta. SOURCE: WO120 Volume page 544. INDEX # 8919.

Invalid Battalion

Chas JACKSON; pension awarded 10 Aug 1814; residence - Montreal, Quebec, Canada; died 7 Jan 1855, Toronto, Ontario, Canada. SOURCE: WO120 Volume 70 page 552. INDEX # 8920.

John BROWN; pension awarded 1 Dec 1818; residence - Quebec, Quebec, Canada. SOURCE: WO120 Volume 70 page 552. INDEX # 8921.

H^y LAWRENCE; pension awarded 1 Dec 1818; residence - Toronto, Ontario, Canada; died 23 Oct 1863, Hamilton, Ontario, Canada. SOURCE: WO120 Volume 70 page 552. INDEX # 8922.

Willm MURRAY; pension awarded 1 Dec 1825; residence - London, Ontario, Canada; died 27 Oct 1857. SOURCE: WO120 Volume 70 page 552. INDEX # 8923.

Moses YARNELD; pension awarded 1 Dec 1818; residence - Chambly, Quebec, Canada. SOURCE: WO120 Volume 70 page 552. INDEX # 8924.

John DOGHERTY; pension awarded 1 Sep 1818; residence - Toronto, Ontario, Canada. SOURCE: WO120 Volume 70 page 552. INDEX # 8925.

Willm JURY; pension awarded 1 Jan 1812; residence - London, Ontario, Canada; died 10 Jun 1865. SOURCE: WO120 Volume 70 page 552. INDEX # 8926.

Peter BLAIR; pension awarded 1 Dec 1818; residence - New York. SOURCE: WO120 Volume 70 page 552. INDEX # 8927.

Ordnance Barrack Company

Thos HILL; pension awarded 1 Oct 1832; residence - Mauritius. SOURCE: WO120 Volume 70 page 560. INDEX # 8928.

Riding House Establishment

Willm GORDON; pension awarded 1 Mar 1824; residence - Toronto, Ontario, Canada; died 23 Dec 1855. SOURCE: WO120 Volume 70 page 562. INDEX # 8929.

Ja^s CRAIG; pension awarded 1 Jun 1822; residence - London, Ontario, Canada; died in Feb 1848. SOURCE: WO120 Volume 70 page 562. INDEX # 8930.

Ordnance Military Artificers

Willm WAGSTAFF; pension awarded 1 May 1810; residence - Halifax, Nova Scotia, Canada. SOURCE: WO120 Volume 70 page 568. INDEX # 8931.

John GIBBS; pension awarded 2 Mar 1807; residence - Halifax, Nova Scotia, Canada; died 9 Apr 1856. SOURCE: WO120 Volume 70 page 568. INDEX # 8932.

Ordnance Military Laborers

John MANCINI; pension awarded 1 Feb 1828; residence - Barbadoes, West Indies. SOURCE: WO120 Volume 70 page 574. INDEX # 8933.

Foreign Artillery

Carlo VEISS; pension awarded 1 Dec 1816; residence - Jamaica, West Indies. SOURCE: WO120 Volume 70 page 584. INDEX # 8934.

END OF VOLUME 70

PLACES OF RESIDENCE

British veterans lived in many places throughout the world. Most of the places will be known to the reader, but some may be hard to find because of name changes or changes in spelling. The following list may be of some help - distances are approximate and are only a very rough guide to locate places of residence mentioned in the text.

Adelaide - capital of the state of South Australia, Australia; also township in Middlesex County, near London, Ontario, Canada
Agra - 100 miles, 160 km., south of New Delhi, India
Ahmednuggar, Ahmadnagar - 100 miles, 160 km., east of Bombay, India
Allahabad - 300 miles, 500 km., southeast of New Delhi, India
Ambala - 100 miles, 160 km., north of Delhi, India
Ameliasburg - township and hamlet on the Bay of Quinte in Prince Edward County, 40 miles, 65 km., west of Kingston, Ontario, Canada
Amherstburg - 20 miles, 35 km., south of Windsor, Ontario, Canada
Antigua - island 300 miles, 500 km., east of Puerto Rico
Auckland - on the North Island of New Zealand; also unlocated place in Cape of Good Hope, South Africa
Bahamas - islands 100 miles, 160 km., off the east coast of Florida, U. S. A.
Bangalore - in southern India, 200 miles, 300 km., west of Madras
Baranagar - on the northern edge of Calcutta, India
Barbados, Barbadoes - islands 500 miles, 800 km., southeast of Puerto Rico
Bellary - 300 miles, 480 km., southeast of Bombay, India
Belleville - 40 miles, 65 km., west of Kingston, Ontario, Canada
Bengal - region in India and Bangdalesh north of Calcutta, India
Berbice - district in the northern part of Guyana, South America
Bermuda - islands 600 miles, 950 km., east of North Carolina, U. S. A.
Berne, Bern - capital of Switzerland
Bombay - city on the west coast of India
Buenos Aires - capital of Argentina, South America
Bytown - now called Ottawa, capital of Canada
Calais - port city in France on the Strait of Dover
Calcutta - city in northeast India
Camp Deesa - see Deesa
Camp Meerut - see Meerut
Camp Poonah - see Poona
Campbellton - at the west end of Chaleur Bay in New Brunswick, Canada
Cannanore - 600 miles, 1000 km., south of Bombay on the west coast of India
Cape, Cape of Good Hope - town and province at southern tip of Africa
Cape Town, Capetown - at southwest tip of Cape of Good Hope, South Africa
Carillon, Carrillon - 35 miles, 55 km., west of Montreal, Quebec, Canada
Cawnpore, Kanpur - 600 miles, 1000 km., northwest of Calcutta, India
Ceylon - now Sri Lanka, island southeast of India
Chambly - 10 miles, 15 km., east of Montreal, Quebec, Canada
Charlottetown - capital of Prince Edward Island, Canada
Chinsurah - northwest of Calcutta, India
Chippawa - south of Niagara Falls, Ontario, Canada
Chusan - island 90 miles, 150 km., south of Shanghai, China
Cobourg - 75 miles, 120 km., east of Toronto, Ontario, Canada
Colchester - 20 miles, 35 km., south of Windsor, Ontario, Canada
Colombo - capital of Ceylon, now Sri Lanka
Constantinople - now Istanbul, Turkey

PLACES OF RESIDENCE

Corfu - now Kerkyra, island off the northwest coast of Greece
Cork - on the south shore of Ireland
Cornwall - 60 miles, 100 km., southeast of Ottawa, Ontario, Canada
Coteau du Lac - 30 miles, 50 km., southwest of Montreal, Quebec, Canada
D^d, D^n, Drummond Ville, Drummondville - 50 miles, 80 km., northeast of Montreal, Quebec, Canada
Deesa - 350 miles, 600 km., east of Karachi, India
Demarara, Demerara - east of Georgetown, Guyana, South America
Dinapore, Dinajpur - 225 miles, 350 km., north of Calcutta, India
Dominica - island 350 miles, 550 km., south east of Puerto Rico
Easthope - township in Perth County west of Stratford, Ontario, Canada
Exeter - 30 miles, 50 km., northwest of London, Ontario, Canada
Fermoy - 20 miles, 35 km., northeast of Cork, Ireland
Ferozepore - 200 miles, 350 km., northwest of Delhi, India
Fort Beauport - 200 miles, 350 km., northeast of Port Elizabeth, South Africa
Fort Erie - 20 miles, 35 km., south of Niagara Falls, Ontario, Canada
Fort Garry - an early name for Winnipeg, capital of Manitoba, Canada
Fort St. George - in the vicinity of Madras, India
Fort William - in the vicinity of Calcutta, India
Fractown - possibly a misspelling of Franktown
Franktown - hamlet in Lanark County near Smiths Falls, Ontario, Canada
Fredericton - capital of New Brunswick, Canada
Gambia - country adjacent to Senegal on the west coast of Africa
Geelong - 60 miles, 100 km., southwest of Melbourne, Australia
Gibraltar - at the western entrance to the Mediterranean Sea
Gore - possibly Gore District in the vicinity of Hamilton, Ontario, Canada
Grahams Town, Grahamstown - 60 miles, 100 km., northeast of Port Elizabeth, South Africa
Grenada - 450 miles, 750 km., south east of Puerto Rico
Halifax - capital of Nova Scotia, Canada
Hamburgh - possibly Hamburg on the north shore of Germany
Hamilton - 40 miles, 65 km., southwest of Toronto, Ontario, Canada
Hobart Town, Hobarton, Hobart - on south shore of Tasmania, Australia
Honduras - country in Central America
Hong Kong - on the south shore of China below Kwangchow (Canton)
Huntingdon - 40 miles, 65 km., southwest of Montreal, Quebec, Canada
Ionian Isles - Greek islands in the Ionian Sea west of Greece
Jamaica - island 80 miles, 130 km., south of Cuba in the Caribbean Sea
Jullundar, Jullundur - 200 miles, 320 km., northwest of Delhi, India
Kandy - in Ceylon, now Sri Lanka
Kingston - 100 miles, 160 km., southwest of Ottawa, Ontario, Canada
Kirkee, Kirkie - on the northern edge of Poona, Pune
Kurnool - 400 miles, 650 km., southeast of Bombay, India
Kussowlie, Kasauli - 160 miles, 260 km., north of Delhi near Chandigarh
Lahore - in Pakistan, 250 miles, 400 km., northwest of Delhi, India
Landour - 140 miles, 225 km., north of Delhi near Dehra Dun
Launceston - on the north shore of Tasmania, Australia
Leicester - 35 miles, 60 km., northeast of Birmingham, England
Limerick - on the west coast of Ireland
London - 100 miles, 160 km., southwest of Toronto, Ontario, Canada
Lorient - 275 miles, 450 km., southwest of Paris, France
Lunce - cannot locate this place; the entry for # 8612 indicates it may be in South America
Madras - on southeast coast of India 250 miles, 400 km., north of Sri Lanka

Malta - island 60 miles, 100 km., south of Sicily
Mauritius - island 450 miles, 700 km., east of Madagascar, Africa
Meerut - 100 miles, 160 km., north of Delhi, India
Melbourne - city on southeast coast of Australia
Montreal - at juncture of Ottawa and St. Lawrence Rivers in Quebec, Canada
Niagara - now Niagara-on-the-Lake, 15 miles, 25 km., north of Niagara Falls, Ontario, Canada
New Brunswick - eastern province of Canada on the Gulf of St. Lawrence
Newfoundland - island and easternmost province of Canada
New South Wales - state in southeast part of Australia
New Zealand - islands and country 1200 miles, 1900 km., east of Australia
New London - now London, Ontario, Canada
New York - city and state in northern part of the United States of America
Niagara - now Niagara-on-the-Lake, 30 miles, 50km., south of Toronto, Ontario, Canada
Norfolk Island - 500 miles, 800 km., northwest of New Zealand
Northumberland - possibly county 100 miles, 160 km., west of Kingston, Ontario, Canada
Nova Scotia - province of Canada east of New Brunswick
Ontario - province of Canada west of the Ottawa River
Ostend - now Oostende, on the west coast of Belgium
Ottawa - capital of Canada
Packenham, Pakenham - 30 miles, 50 km., west of Ottawa, Ontario, Canada
Paisley - west of Glasgow, Scotland; also place 100 miles, 160 km., northwest of Toronto, Ontario, Canada
Palermo - on the northwest corner of the island of Sicily, Italy
Paris - capital of France
Parramatta - northwest of Sydney, Australia
Penetanguishene - on Georgian Bay, 80 miles, 130 km., north of Toronto, Ontario, Canada
Perth - 40 miles, 65 km., southwest of Ottawa, Ontario, Canada; also city on the southwest coast of Australia
Philipsburg - possibly place in Waterloo County 12 miles, 18 km., west of Kitchener, Ontario, Canada
Picton - on Bay of Quinte 35 miles, 55 km., southwest of Kingston, Ontario, Canada
Poona - 50 miles, 80 km., southeast of Bombay, India
Poonamalee - on the western edge of Madras, India
Port Louis - on northwest coast of island of Mauritius
Port Macquarie - 200 miles north of Sydney, Australia
Port Philip - southwest of Melbourne, Australia
Prescot, Prescott - 50 miles, 80 km., south of Ottawa, Ontario, Canada
Prince Edward Island - island and province of Canada in the Gulf of St. Lawrence
Quebec - capital of province of Quebec, which is on the east side of the Ottawa River in Canada
Richmond - 20 miles, 35 km., south of Ottawa, Ontario, Canada
Rio de Janeiro - capital of Brazil
Riviere du Lac - possibly misspelling of Rivière du Loup, 100 miles, 160 km., northwest of Quebec, Quebec
Rome - capital of Italy
Rotterdam - on southwest coast of the Netherlands

Roxburgh, Roxborough - township in Stormont County, 20 miles, 35 km., north of Cornwall, Ontario, Canada
South Australia - state on the south coast of Australia
Saint John - capital of New Brunswick, Canada
Saint Johns, St. Johns - as capital of Newfoundland, it is spelled St. John's; as capital of New Brunswick, it is spelled Saint John; as place 25 miles, 40 km., southeast of Montreal, Quebec, Canada, it is now called St. Jean. Most of the places which are not specifically identified with a province are likely St. Jean, Quebec, Canada
Secunderabad - 300 miles, 480 km., northwest of Madras, India
Sierra Leone - country on the west coast of Africa
Simla - 150 miles, 240 km., north of Delhi, India
Smithsfalls, Smiths Falls - 30 miles, 50 km., south of Ottawa, Ontario, Canada
Sorel - 40 miles, 65 km., northeast of Montreal, Quebec, Canada
St. Andrews - 50 miles, 80 km., west of Saint John, New Brunswick, Canada
St. Helen's Isle - in Montreal, Quebec, Canada
St. Helena - 100 miles, 160 km., north of Cape Town, South Africa
St. John's - capital of Newfoundland, Canada
St. Kitts - 225 miles, 350 km., east of Puerto Rico
St. Lucia - island 400 miles, 650 km., southeast of Puerto Rico
St. Vincent - island 450 miles, 700 km., southeast of Puerto Rico
Sukkur - 500 miles, 800 km., west of Delhi, India
Sydney - capital of New South Wales on east coast of Australia; also place on Cape Breton in Nova Scotia, Canada
Talbot - Talbot Settlement in southwestern Ontario on Lake Erie, south of London, Ontario, Canada
Three Rivers - now Trois Rivières, 90 miles, 145 km., northeast of Montreal, Quebec, Canada
Toronto - capital of Ontario, Canada
Trinidad - island off the northeast coast of Venezuela, South America
Umballa - see Ambala
V. D. Land, Van D. Land, Van Diemen's Land - now Tasmania, island and state of Australia, southeast of the mainland
Wm Henry, William Henry - now called Sorel
W^t London, West London - likely part of London, England
Western Australia - state on the west side of Australia
Windsor - at the west end of Lake Erie, 200 miles, 320 km., southwest of Toronto, Ontario, Canada
Woolford - possibly Wolford Township, Grenville County, 50 miles, 80 km., south of Ottawa, Ontario, Canada
Worcestor - possibly Worcester 100 miles, 160 km., northwest of London, England; also place 60 miles, 100 km., east of Capetown, South Africa

LIST OF MILITARY UNITS

MILITARY UNITS	PAGES	MILITARY UNITS	PAGES
1st Battalion of Artillery	284-286	8th Veterans Battalion	243
1st Garrison Battalion	237	9th Battalion of Artillery	300-301
1st Garrison Company	238	9th Regiment of Dragoons	92-93
1st Regiment of Dragoon Guards	87-88	9th Regiment of Foot	11, 114-115
1st Regiment of Dragoons	90	10th Battalion of Artillery	301-302
1st Regiment of Foot	7-9, 105-107	10th Regiment of Dragoons	93
1st Regiment of Foot Guards	102-103	10th Regiment of Foot	11, 115-116
1st Regiment of Life Guards	87	10th Veterans Battalion	83, 244
1st Royal Garrison Battalion	84	11th Regiment of Dragoons	2-3, 93-94
1st Veterans Battalion	239	11th Regiment of Foot	11, 116-118, 195-197
1st West India Regiment	280	11th Veterans Battalion	244
2nd Battalion of Artillery	286-289	12th Regiment of Dragoons	94
2nd Garrison Battalion	237-238	12th Regiment of Foot	11, 118-119
2nd Garrison Company	238	12th Veterans Battalion	84, 244
2nd Regiment of Dragoon Guards	1, 88	13th Regiment of Dragoons	3-4, 94-96
2nd Regiment of Dragoons	1, 90	13th Regiment of Foot	11-12, 119-120
2nd Regiment of Foot	107-108	13th Veterans Battalion	244
2nd Regiment of Foot Guards	104	14th Regiment of Dragoons	96-97
2nd Regiment of Life Guards	87	14th Regiment of Foot	12, 120-121
2nd Veterans Battalion	239-240	15th Regiment of Dragoons	4, 97-98
2nd West India Regiment	280	15th Regiment of Foot	12-13, 121
3rd Battalion of Artillery	289-290	16th Regiment of Dragoons	4, 98-99
3rd Garrison Battalion	238	16th Regiment of Foot	13, 121-123
3rd Garrison Company	238	17th Regiment of Dragoons	4, 99
3rd Regiment of Dragoon Guards	1, 88	17th Regiment of Foot	13-14, 123-124
3rd Regiment of Dragoons	1, 90-91	18th Regiment of Dragoons	4, 99
3rd Regiment of Foot	9, 108-109	18th Regiment of Foot	14, 124-125
3rd Regiment of Foot Guards	104	19th Regiment of Dragoons	5, 99
3rd Veterans Battalion	240	19th Regiment of Foot	14-15, 125-126
3rd West India Regiment	280	20th Regiment of Dragoons	5
4th Battalion of Artillery	290-292	20th Regiment of Foot	15, 126-128
4th Ceylon Regiment	275	21st Regiment of Dragoons	5, 100
4th Garrison Battalion	238	21st Regiment of Foot	16, 128-129
4th Regiment of Dragoon Guards	1, 88	22nd Regiment of Dragoons	5, 100
4th Regiment of Dragoons	1, 91	22nd Regiment of Foot	16, 129-130
4th Regiment of Foot	9-10, 109-111	23rd Regiment of Dragoons	6, 100
4th Veterans Battalion	80-83, 240-242	23rd Regiment of Foot	16-17, 130-133
4th West India Regiment	280	24th Regiment of Dragoons	6, 100
5th Battalion of Artillery	292-295	24th Regiment of Foot	17, 133
5th Regiment of Dragoon Guards	88-89	25th Regiment of Dragoons	6-7, 100
5th Regiment of Dragoons	1, 91	25th Regiment of Foot	17, 133-135
5th Regiment of Foot	10, 111-112	26th Regiment of Foot	17, 135
5th Veterans Battalion	242	27th Regiment of Foot	18, 135-137
6th Battalion of Artillery	295-296		
6th Regiment of Dragoon Guards	1, 89		
6th Regiment of Dragoons	91		
6th Regiment of Foot	10, 112-113		
6th Veterans Battalion	83, 242-243		
6th West India Regiment	280		
7th Battalion of Artillery	296-298		
7th Regiment of Dragoon Guards	1, 89		
7th Regiment of Dragoons	92		
7th Regiment of Foot	10, 113		
7th Veterans Battalion	83, 243		
7th West India Regiment	280		
8th Battalion of Artillery	299-300		
8th Regiment of Dragoons	1-2, 92	28th Regiment of Foot	18, 137-139
8th Regiment of Foot	10-11, 113-114		

LIST OF MILITARY UNITS 315

MILITARY UNITS	PAGES	MILITARY UNITS	PAGES
29th Regiment of Foot	18, 139-140	67th Regiment of Foot	41, 185
30th Regiment of Foot	19-21, 140-141	68th Regiment of Foot	41, 185-186
31st Regiment of Foot	85, 141-143	69th Regiment of Foot	42-45, 186, 188
32nd Regiment of Foot	21, 143-144	70th Regiment of Foot	45, 188
33rd Regiment of Foot	144-145	71st Regiment of Foot	45-46, 188-190
34th Regiment of Foot	21-23, 145-146	72nd Regiment of Foot	46-48, 191-192
35th Regiment of Foot	23, 146	73rd Regiment of Foot	48, 192-194
36th Regiment of Foot	23, 146	74th Regiment of Foot	49, 194-195
37th Regiment of Foot	23-24, 146-147	75th Regiment of Foot	49, 195
38th Regiment of Foot	24, 147-148	76th Regiment of Foot	49, 198
39th Regiment of Foot	24-25, 148-150	77th Regiment of Foot	49, 198-199
40th Regiment of Foot	25, 150-151	78th Regiment of Foot	49, 200
41st Regiment of Foot	25-26, 151-153	79th Regiment of Foot	49-50, 200-202
42nd Regiment of Foot	26, 153-154	80th Regiment of Foot	50, 202-204
43rd Regiment of Foot	27, 154-155	81st Regiment of Foot	50, 204-205
44th Regiment of Foot	27, 155-156	82nd Regiment of Foot	50-51, 205-207
45th Regiment of Foot	27, 156-157	83rd Regiment of Foot	51-52, 207-208
46th Regiment of Foot	27-28, 157-158	84th Regiment of Foot	52-53, 208-209
47th Regiment of Foot	28, 158-159	85th Regiment of Foot	209-210
48th Regiment of Foot	28-29, 159-160	86th Regiment of Foot	53-54, 210
49th Regiment of Foot	29-31, 160-161	87th Regiment of Foot	54-55, 210-211
50th Regiment of Foot	31, 161-163	88th Regiment of Foot	55, 211-212
51st Regiment of Foot	31, 163-165	89th Regiment of Foot	55-57, 212-214
52nd Regiment of Foot	31-32, 165-166	90th Regiment of Foot	57, 214
53rd Regiment of Foot	32-33, 166-167	91st Regiment of Foot	57, 1214-216
54th Regiment of Foot	33-34, 167-168	92nd Regiment of Foot	217
55th Regiment of Foot	34, 168-171	93rd Regiment of Foot	57, 217-218
56th Regiment of Foot	34-35, 171-172	94th Regiment of Foot	57, 218-219
57th Regiment of Foot	35-36, 172-174	95th Regiment of Foot	219-220
58th Regiment of Foot	36, 174-177	96th Regiment of Foot	57, 220-222
59th Regiment of Foot	36-37, 177-178	97th Regiment of Foot	57-58, 222-223
60th Regiment of Foot	37-39, 178-179	98th Regiment of Foot	58-63, 223-226
61st Regiment of Foot	39, 180	99th Regiment of Foot	63-67, 86, 226-232
62nd Regiment of Foot	39, 180	100th Regiment of Foot	232
63rd Regiment of Foot	40, 180-181	101st Regiment of Foot	232
64th Regiment of Foot	40, 181-182	102nd Regiment of Foot	67, 232-233
65th Regiment of Foot	40, 182-183	103rd Regiment of Foot	67, 233
66th Regiment of Foot	40-41, 183-185	104th Regiment of Foot	67-69, 233-234
		Artillery Drivers	306-307
		Cambrian Rangers	75
		Canadian Fencibles	275
		Canadian Staff	239
		Canadian Volunteers	274
		Cape Cavalry	70, 100-101

LIST OF MILITARY UNITS

MILITARY UNITS	PAGES
Cape Garrison Company	71-72, 238-239
Cape Infantry	71, 274
Cape Mounted Rifles	101-102, 197, 274
Ceylon Regiment	74-75
Ceylon Rifle Regiment	275
De Meuron's Regiment	275
De Watteville's Regiment	75
Duke of Brunswick's Corps	75
Fencibles	76-80
Foreign Artillery	309
Foreign British Legion	279
Foreign Veterans Battalion	80
Garrison Staff	239
Glengarry Fencibles	275-276
Glengarry Light Infantry	75
Gordon Fencibles	276
Independent Company	279
Invalid Battalion	308
Invalid Detachment	308
King's German Legion	279
King's German Legion Hussars	84
King's German Legion Infantry	84-85
Military Laborers	75, 274
Militia	84, 281-283
New South Wales Veterans	76, 85-86
New South Wales Veterans Company	244-245
New York Regiment	279
Newfoundland Fencibles	276-277
Newfoundland Veterans Company	245-249
Nova Scotia Fencibles	277-278
Ordnance Barrack Company	308
Ordnance Military Artificers	308
Ordnance Military Laborers	308
Provisional Cavalry	100
Riding House Establishment	308
Rifle Brigade	69, 234-237
Royal African Corps	73-74, 278
Royal Canadian Rifle Regiment	249-274
Royal Engineers	306
Royal Garrison Battalion	237
Royal Garrison Company	70
Royal Horse Artillery	284
Royal Horse Guards	87
Royal Regiment of Malta	75
Royal York Rangers	75
Sappers and Miners	302-306
Staff Corps	74, 279
Staff Corps - Ordnance	283
Staff Garrison Company	239
St. Helena Regiment	278
Wagon Train	102
West India Garrison Companies	239
West India Regiments	72-73
Yeomanry	76, 281
York Chasseurs	74

NOTES ON THE SOURCES

Two British institutions awarded pensions to army veterans on the basis of disabilities or long service: the Royal Hospital, Kilmainham in Dublin and the Royal Hospital, Chelsea in London. Pensioners who lived in these hospitals were called in-pensioners; those who lived outside them were known as out-pensioners. Records of admission to Kilmainham are separate from those in Chelsea but in 1822 Chelsea became responsible for paying surviving out-pensioners from Kilmainham. Thus all out-pensioners living in 1822 and later years should be found in Chelsea records.

Registers of Chelsea out-pensioners are arranged in regimental sequence in W.O. 120 in 70 volumes. This book is based on volumes 35, 69 and 70, which list those out-pensioners who resided outside Britain when they initially drew their pensions. The original records are in the Public Record Office in Kew, England but are readily available for examination on microfilm at various locations throughout the world. In Canada, the National Archives of Canada has a complete set of the microfilms for researchers and also makes another set available for interlibrary loan. The Family History Library in Salt Lake City, Utah has a set and makes films available to researchers elsewhere through its network of Family History Centers.

Volume 35 mainly covers the period 1817-1838. A few entries fall outside this range - # 14 in 1772 and # 2639 in 1899. This volume provides much detail about the soldier, including age and rank when he was admitted to pension and the amount of pension, place of birth, years of service in various ranks including time in India and the West Indies, medical condition when discharged, and trade or occupation. A remarks column often indicates where he resided. In some cases a brief physical description gives his height, colour of hair, eyes and complexion.

Volumes 69 and 70 are quite different and cover the period 1795-1857. Volume 70 is a continuation of volume 69 and is in the same format. Some of the names in these volumes duplicate those in volume 35; for example John Gee of the 89th Regiment of Foot appears in volume 35 as # 1644 and in volume 70 as # 6132. The information in volumes 69 and 70 includes the amount of pension and date of admission, place of residence, and columns headed from 1845 to 1854 for changes in the pension rate and other events such as death in those years. Additional notes are frequently inserted - for example # 6836 was convicted of murder in London, Ontario, Canada.

See pages 318-319 for illustrations of the column headings for volumes 35 and for both volumes 69 and 70.

The reference numbers of the Chelsea Regimental Pension Registers available in Ottawa and Salt Lake City are as follows:

National Archives of Canada MG 13, W.O. 120 microfilm B-5705 for volume 35, microfilms B-5713 and B-5714 for volume 69, and microfilm B-5714 for volume 70.

Family History Library microfilm 854,664 for volume 35, 852,021 for volume 69, and microfilm 852,022 for volume 70.

Royal Hospital, Chelsea Pension Registers Volume 35 - left side of page 276 [WO120/35]. Crown copyright, used with permission of the Public Record Office, Kew, England

Royal Hospital, Chelsea Pension Registers Volume 69 - left side of page 79 [WO120/69]. Crown copyright, used with permission of the Public Record Office, Kew, England.

NOTES ON THE SOURCES

Royal Hospital, Chelsea Pension Registers Volume 35 - right side of page 276 [W.O. 120/35]. Crown copyright, used with permission of the Public Record Office, Kew, England

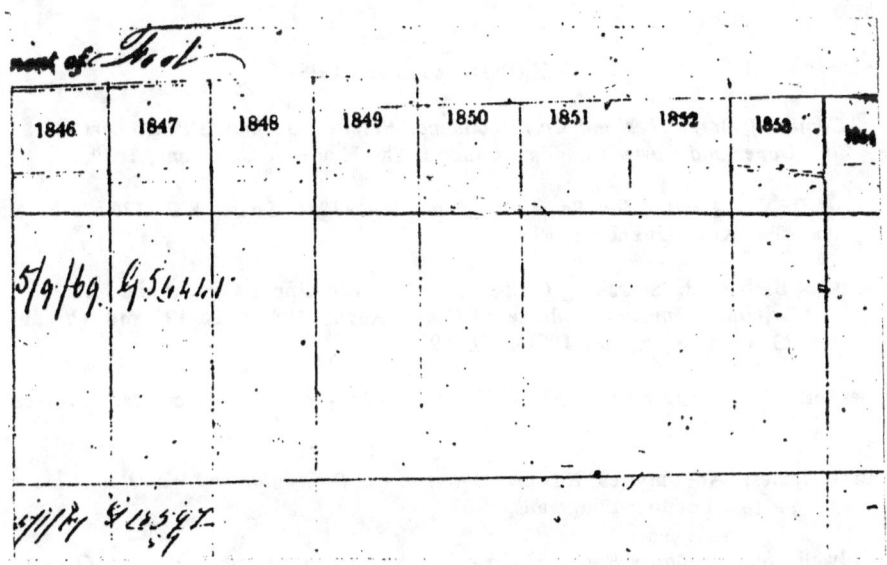

Royal Hospital, Chelsea Pension Registers Volume 69 - right side of page 79 [W.O. 120/69]. Crown copyright, used with permission of the Public Record Office, Kew, England.

BIBLIOGRAPHY

PRIMARY SOURCES

Public Record Office W.O. 120 Volume 35, Royal Hospital, Chelsea Pension Registers - out-pensioners receiving their pensions in the colonies 1772-1899.

Public Record Office W.O. 120 Volume 69, Royal Hospital, Chelsea Pension Registers - out-pensioners receiving their pensions in the colonies 1795-1857.

Public Record Office W.O. 120 Volume 70, Royal Hospital, Chelsea Pension Registers - out-pensioners receiving their pensions in the colonies 1783-1857.

National Archives of Canada MG 13 W.O. 28: Headquarters Records, 1775-1856.

National Archives of Canada RG 1, L1 Quebec, Lower Canada, Upper Canada, Canada Land Books, 1787-1867.

National Archives of Canada RG1, L3 L Lower Canada Land Petitions.

National Archives of Canada RG1, L3 Upper Canada Land Petitions, 1790-1867.

SECONDARY SOURCES

- *Copies of Despatches and Correspondence Relative to Chelsea Pensioners in Upper and Lower Canada.* London: The House of Commons, 1839

- *INDEX - Chelsea Out Pensioners From 1806-1836: Source WO 120/20-33 at Kew.* Kew: Unknown, 1990.

Aitken, Barbara B. "Searching Chelsea Pensioners in Upper Canada and Great Britain." *Families* (Volume 23 No. 3, August 1984): 114-127 and (Volume 23 No. 4, November 1984): 178-197.

Beckett, J. D. *Pensioners Index - W.O. 120/23/24 & 25.* Manchester: Project Coordinator, n.d.

Brett-James, Anthony, ed. *Edward Costello: the Peninsular and Waterloo Campaigns.* London: Longmans, 1967.

Colwell, Stella. *Family Roots: Discovering the Past in the Public Record Office.* London: Weidenfeld and Nicolson, 1991.

Cooper, R. K. "Notes on the British Corps and Regiments that Served in Australia and New Zealand 1788-1870." *The South Australian Genealogist* (Volume 14 No. 2, April 1987): 7-14.

BIBLIOGRAPHY

Cox, Jane and Timothy Padfield. *Tracing Your Ancestors in the Public Record Office.* London: Her Majesty's Stationery Office, 1983.

Creed, Catherine M. "Soldier Pensioners." *Niagara Historical Society Transactions* (No. 18, 1909): 19-28.

Dean, C. G. T. *The Royal Hospital, Chelsea.* London: Hutchinson & Co., 1950.

Dubé, Timothy. *The Unknown Soldier: Documenting the Military Forces of Canada, 1665 to the Present.* Ottawa: National Archives of Canada, 1991.

- *Tommy Atkins, We Never Knew Ye: Documenting the British Soldier in Canada, 1759-1871.* Ottawa: National Archives of Canada, 1992.

- *The Enrolled Pensioner Scheme in Canada West, 1851-1858, With Specific Reference to the Plan at Amherstburg.* Master's thesis, Faculty of Graduate Studies, University of Windsor, 1982.

Fowler, Simon. *Army Records for Family Historians.* London: Public Record Office, 1992.

Gleig, G. R. *Chelsea Hospital and Its Traditions.* London: Richard Bentley, 1839.

Hamilton-Edwards, Gerald. *In Search of Army Ancestry.* London: Phillimore & Co., 1977.

Hutt, George. *Papers Illustrative of the Origin and Early History of the Royal Hospital at Chelsea.* London: Her Majesty's Stationery Office, 1872.

Johnson, J. K. "The Chelsea Pensioners in Upper Canada." *Ontario History* (Volume 53 No. 4 December 1961): 273-289.

Kitzmiller, John M. *In Search of the "Forlorn Hope": A Comprehensive Guide to Locating British Regiments and Their Records (1640-WW I).* Salt Lake City, Utah: Manuscript Publishing Foundation, 1988.

Mather, F. C. "Army Pensioners and the Maintenance of Civil Order in Early Nineteenth-Century England." *Journal of the Society for Army Historical Research* (volume 36 1958): 110-124.

Oliver, Rosemary M. "War Office District Pension Returns, 1842-62." *Genealogists' Magazine* (Volume 21 No. 6, June 1984): 196-199.

Porter, A. N., ed. *Atlas of British Overseas Expansion.* London: Routledge, 1991.

Raudzens, George K. "A Successful Military Settlement: Earl Grey's Enrolled Pensioners of 1846 in Canada." *The Canadian Historical Review* (Volume LII No. 4, December 1971): 389-403.

Stacey, C. P. *Canada and the British Army, 1846-1871.* Toronto: University of Toronto Press, 1963.

Taylor, Neville C. *Sources for Anglo-Indian Genealogy in the Library of the Society of Genealogists.* London: Society of Genealogists, n.d

Thornton, Edward. *A Gazetteer of the Territories Under the Government or the East India Company and of the Native States on the Continent of India.* London: Wm. H. Allen & Co., 1854.

Tulloch, J. D. G. *Report on the Inspection of Pensioners in the North American Provinces.* London: Foreign Office, 1850.

Watts, Christopher T. and Michael J. "In Search of a Soldier Ancestor." *Genealogists' Magazine* (Volume 19 No. 4, December 1977): 125-128.

White, Arthur S., comp. *A Bibliography of Regimental Histories of the British Army.* London: The Society of Army Historical Research, 1965.

Whitfield, Carol M. *Tommy Atkins: The British Soldier in Canada, 1759-1870.* Ottawa: Environment Canada, 1981.

INDEX

ABBOTT: Edwd, 3298; Jos^h, 4754; Moses, 8298; W^m, 922, 5286
ABBOTTS: Geo^e, 7599
ABDAAM: Riquett, 2177
ABEL: Jno, 1547
ABELL: Benjn, 2268, 7037; Jno, 2137
ABLE: Fra^s, 7012
ABREY: James, 4413
ACHESON: Alex^r, 510
ACKLEY: Willm, 218
ACRES: Robt, 2850
ACRET: Ja^s, 3386
ACTON: Jno, 4051
ADAIR: Geo^e, 4978; Ja^s, 8300; Jno, 2491
ADAMS: Dav^d, 5679; Hen^y, 6439, 7658; Ja^s, 7401; John, 1797, 4515; Mich^l, 3862; Robt, 1315, 5462
ADAMSON: Jno, 2250, 2293
ADCOCK: Thos, 591
ADDISON: Willm, 8791
ADIE: Willm, 2919
AERES: W^m, 7549
AGNEW: Ja^s, 7202; John, 6413; Luke, 1050; Robt, 6720
AHERN: Jno, 6866; Patrick, 7158
AILLES: Robt, 7402
AIRD: Walter, 7403
AIRTH: Henry, 8887
AITKEN: Robt, 4253
AKHURST: W^m, 710; Willm, 4345
ALBON: Jno, 7207
ALCORN: Saml, 4800
ALDERTON: Chas, 1645, 6137
ALDRIDGE: Ja^s, 8252
ALEXANDER: Alex^r, 5576; Jno, 8420; John Edward, 5747; Matt^w, 8256; Samuel, 3991
ALFRED: Mich^l, 3198
ALGATE: Geo^o, 272
ALLAIRE: Jean Baptiste, 2011
ALLAN: Patrick, 4533; Thos, 1338
ALLCOCK: W^m, 6856
ALLEN: Austin, 6896; Danl, 8327; Edwd, 757; Geo^o, 7380; Hugh, 5247; Ja^s, 6392; Jno, 131, 1032, 2527, 4134; John, 2760, 3247, 6983; Jos^h, 5227; Smith, 8490; Thos, 2091; W^m, 4002, 7659; Willm, 3449, 5449
ALLISON: Jno, 6394
ALLMAN: Thos, 6675
ALLMOND: Ja^s, 7770
ALLSOP: Jno, 5285
ALLTIMES: Valentine, 4371
ALLWRIGHT: Ja^s, 7600
ALSOP: W^m, 5412; Willm, 1279
ALSTON: Ja^s, 6245

AMBROSE: Ja^s, 8281
AMERY: Jos^h, 550
ANDERSON: Alex^r, 3976, 8306; Ja^s, 2854, 7392, 8372, 8426; Jno, 1889, 3601, 4953, 6267, 8460; Rich^d, 8193; Robt, 2274; Thos, 8514; W^m, 307; Willm, 1682, 2786, 8569
ANDERTON: Ja^s, 1185, 5319
ANDRAOS: Chas, 5895
ANDREW: Geo^e, 6721; Hugh, 8852
ANDREWS: Ja^s, 8813; Jno, 5897; Robt, 28; W^m, 3318
ANEAN: W^m, 625
ANEAR: W^m, 4216
ANGEL: Robt, 4466
ANGUS: Ja^s, 7404; Peter, 3237
ANSON: Chr^r, 6188
ANTINGHAM: W^m, 5242; Willm, 1166
ANTOINE: Pierre, 2175
APPLEBY: Mark, 7381
APPLEGATE: John, 4463
APPLETON: Rich^d, 3667
ARAM: Geo^o, 1163
ARCHBOLD: Ja^s, 85
ARCHER: W^m, 7241
AREM: W^m, 5676
ARGENT: Chas, 299, 3408
ARKIS: Ja^s, 2576
ARMITAGE: John, 4911
ARMSTRONG: And^w, 4008; Chr^r, 6662; Dav^d, 8288; Erwin, 3005, 6054; Geo^o, 1010, 2891; Geo^e, 4322; Jno, 5212; John, 5046; Rich^d, 7660; Robt, 7310
ARNE: Jno, 1562
ARNELL: Joseph, 7997
ARNOLD: Hen^y, 1914; Robert, 5716
ARNOTT: Thomas, 7946
ART: John, 1799
ARTER: Jno, 992
ARTHURS: Jno, 5431
ASBURY: Thos, 2275, 7048
ASH: Jno, 7271; W^m, 7311
ASHBOURNE: W^m, 1431
ASHBURNE: W^m, 5794
ASHBY: Jno, 2457
ASHCROFT: Jno, 25
ASHENDEN: W^m, 5583
ASHER: Jno, 4361
ASHFIELD: Saml, 2917
ASHMAN: George, 4535
ASHTON: Jno, 3887; Lot, 5773; Thos, 828
ASHURST: Ja^s, 1541
ASHWORTH: Jno, 6686
ASKEW: Geo^e, 5735
ASKIN: Dav^d, 8890
ASKINS: Peter, 531, 4113
ASPINALL: Jno, 3894
ATHERSTON: Jno, 6144
ATHORNE: Willm, 8910

ATKINS: Chas, 3949; Philip, 8047; Thos, 1720, 5774, 6469
ATKINSON: Adam, 1528; Chas, 7752; Jno, 8251; Thos, 4750, 5775
ATTWOOD: Ja^s, 8343
AUCHIE: Jno, 3829
AUGHEY: Thos, 7661
AULD: W^m, 8644
AURELL: Christ^n, 2041
AUSTIN: John, 7964; Jos^h, 1850, 6562; Rich^d, 1730, 6470; W^m, 7550; Willm, 1723
AVERS: Geo^o, 752
AVERY: Jos^h, 2035
AXEN: Ja^s, 98
AYLMER: Hen^y, 2492
AYRES: Willm, 1684
BACKHANS: Hen^y, 2657
BACKHOUSE: Thos, 2545, 6936
BACON: John, 4838; William, 4531
BADDOW: Geo^o, 2174
BADGER: Jno, 2936; W^d, 1836
BAGGERLEY: Robt, 3101
BAGWILL: Jno, 5645
BAHT: Chas, 2658
BAILEY: Edwd, 8858; Ephriam, 4105; Fra^s, 4016; Geo^o, 1219; Ja^s, 2247, 7647; John, 3215; Robt, 687; Saml, 8605; Thos, 3597, 7591; W^m, 7141; Willm, 1239, 5417
BAILLIE: Geo^e, 4502
BAIN: David, 2798; Geo^o, 2020; Geo^e, 6770
BAIRD: Dav^d, 2463; Ja^s, 8054; Saml, 1592, 6090; W^m, 1467
BAKER: Ja^s, 2319; Jno, 7406; Robt, 1281, 7771; Saml, 759, 4451; Samuel, 4601; W^m, 2969, 7663
BALDRY: Jno, 7313
BALDWIN: John, 8673; Nich^s, 3782; W^m, 58; Willm, 2880, 5873
BALES: Thos, 6474
BALF: Mich^l, 6146
BALL: Jos^h, 966; Saml, 792, 4930
BALLCOTT: Ja^s, 4338
BALMER: Jno, 5303
BANCE: Mic^l, 72
BANCROFT: Saml, 2417
BAND: W^m, 7312
BANKS: Chas, 4627; Jno, 460; Jos^h, 5346; Willm, 1600, 1633
BANN: Martin, 7753
BANNAN: Ja^s, 2538
BANNERMAN: John, 5811
BANNISTER: Barth^w, 3491
BANNON: Ja^s, 3; Jno, 3955, 5373; Pat^k, 1774

BARBER: Chas, 1192, 5323; John, 2759, 7159; Jos^h, 3002; Thos, 1085
BARCLAY: Ja^s, 8263; Jno, 1800; Matt^w, 8412
BARDEN: Mich^l, 6147
BARKER: Isaiah, 5680; Thos, 136; W^m, 45, 2887; Willm, 6894
BARLOW: Robt, 8861
BARNARD: Ja^s, 8097; Job, 445
BARNCLIFFE: Jno, 688
BARNES: Mark, 6062; Saml, 4933; Thos, 1551
BARNETT: Abs^m, 3973; John, 8523; Jos^h, 4736; W^m, 5907, 6417
BARNFIELD: Jos^h, 2227
BARNS: Edwd, 4184; W^m, 3422, 8831
BARR: Ja^s, 8250
BARRABLE: Thos, 8857
BARRELL: Nathl, 3071
BARRETT: Hen^y, 3283; Jno, 7314; Mich^l, 4397
BARRON: W^m, 7861
BARROW: Willm, 2258
BARROWCLOUGH: Jonas, 125
BARRY: Augustine, 7212; Edwd, 205, 7315; Ja^s, 4854, 8811; Mich^l, 1187, 5320, 6015; Robt Jno, 3228; Thos, 1779
BARRYMAN: Ja^s, 1214, 5384
BARTHOLOMEW: W^m, 254, 3250
BARTLAY: Jno, 8383
BARTLETT: Isaac, 2388, 2443; Willm, 967
BARTLEY: Ja^s, 4471
BARTON: Alex^r, 2273; Ja^s, 4949; Saml, 5985
BASKELL: Ja^s, 6890
BASLEY: Thos, 4700
BASLLIQUE: Larva, 2888
BASS: W^m, 8717
BASTLIQUE: Law^e, 31
BASTOW: Willm, 219
BATES: Benjn, 5037; John, 3411; Joseph, 3625; Thos, 1758; W^m, 5497
BATTISON: Jno, 1254
BATTY: Willm, 1080
BAVEN: Job, 8702
BAVINGTON: Jno, 4878
BAXTER: John, 5577; Pat^k, 1609; Rich^d, 413; Saml, 2772; Thos, 4842
BAY: Benjn, 4120
BAYCROFT: Geo^e, 8681
BAYLEY: W^m, 6694
BAYLIS: Thos, 5012; Wm Jos^h, 2276, 7044
BAYLISS: Fred^k, 3930
BAYNES: Thomas, 5690
BEAGHAN: Jno, 3546
BEALE: W^m, 97; Willm, 2915
BEARD: William, 6084
BEASLEY: Ja^s, 6395
BEATTIE: Dav^d, 5512; Jno, 3189, 8845; Robt, 8806

BEATTY: George, 5151; Mich^l, 7214
BEAUMONT: H^y, 3040
BEAZLEY: Jno, 7601
BEBBINGTON: Matt^w, 3115
BECK: Ja^s, 1028
BECKER: Fred^k, 1118
BEDDING: Ja^s, 968
BEDMORE: Jno, 158
BEDWELL: W^m, 2085
BEECHAMS: Anth^y, 2626
BEECHING: Step^n, 3259
BEER: William, 8876
BEESLEY: Jos^h, 3847
BEESTON: Jos^h, 2551
BEGG: Robt, 1447
BEHL: Christ^n, 2097
BEIRNE: Ja^s, 6367
BELFOUR: Riquett, 2176
BELL: Abr^m, 3608; And^w, 1362; Ge^o, 1679; Ja^s, 4680; Jno, 16, 397, 725, 4476, 5021, 7862; John, 6138; Jos^h, 553, 7843; Robt, 3062, 5396, 8035; Thos, 4258; Willm, 8563, 8759
BELLAMY: Thos, 1097
BELLENGER: John, 5140
BELSHAW: Thos, 728
BENDALL: Jno, 2228
BENNARD: W^m, 5298
BENNETT: Chas, 4713; Ge^o, 1169; Geo^e, 5267; Isaac, 5692; James, 3360; Jno, 33; Jos^h, 6344; Rich^d, 4247; Thos, 7070; W^m, 3184; Willm, 186, 3406
BENSON: Ja^s, 3154
BENTHAM: George, 3643
BENTLEY: Thos, 3354
BENTON: Ja^s, 2277
BERGIN: John, 7410; Peter, 7409; Thos, 3409
BERNARD: John, 3433
BERRICREE: Jno, 5063
BERRY: Ja^s, 5912; Thos, 376; Zach^h, 250
BERTH: Jos^h, 1866
BESSENT: Willm, 542
BEST: Chas, 7602; Geo^e, 4918
BESTT: Thos, 2127
BESTWICK: Thos, 4742
BESWICK: Ja^s, 340
BETTISON: Robert, 5209
BETTS: Hen^y, 3255
BEVIN: Robt, 7849
BIBBEY: Thos, 544
BICKNELL: Jno, 5969
BIERY: Peter, 1464, 5915
BIGGS: Ge^o, 1621; Geo^e, 6131
BIGNELL: Jno, 2455
BILBY: Jos^h, 3596
BILLETT: Benjn, 3246; Thos, 4053
BILSON: Jos^h, 3522
BINDER: Willm, 8246
BINGHAM: Peter, 616
BIRCH: Geo^e, 6142; Jon^n, 848
BIRCHAM: Ja^s, 2800

BIRD: Jos^h, 441; Rich^d, 2214, 8154; Robt, 539; Thos, 3678; W^m, 3568
BIRMINGHAM: James, 6171; Mar^n, 3828
BIRNEY: Geo^e, 4109
BIRT: Jno, 2282
BISHOP: Jno, 6247; Jos^h, 1615, 6128; Robt, 882
BISSET: W^m, 5207
BISSLAND: Alex^r, 5508
BLACK: Alex^r, 5846, 7551; And^w, 551; Fred^k, 6451; Ja^s, 2735, 5240, 8674; Jno, 2191, 3153, 8161; Rich^d, 7665; Robt, 7901; Thos, 7664; W^m, 5509; Willm, 5533
BLACKBURN: W^m, 446, 3841
BLACKEY: Jno, 157
BLACKGROVES: Thos, 1260
BLACKIE: John, 8815
BLACKLAWS: David, 6327
BLACKMAN: W^m, 4990
BLACKSHAW: Rich^d, 2135
BLADES: H^y, 5413; Hen^y, 1238
BLAIR: Mich^l, 1142; Peter, 8927; Robt, 2320
BLAKE: Benjn, 144, 1069; William, 5717
BLAKEMORE: Robt, 7662
BLAKENEY: Chas W^m, 6520
BLAKES: Ja^s, 4432
BLAKEY: Major, 5268
BLANEY: Arth^r, 1205; Ja^s, 8308
BLAVIN: W^m, 3469
BLIZARD: Willm, 824
BLOCKSOME: W^m, 5681
BLOMLY: Iain, 4781
BLORE: Jos^h, 5278
BLOW: John, 3575
BLOWES: Ja^s, 4137
BLUNDEN: Benjn, 3709
BLYTH: Colin, 8165
BOAG: Robt, 7317
BOAK: Robt, 8446
BOARDMAN: Jno, 829, 4658
BOATERS: Phil^p, 2192; Philip, 8175
BODELL: Thos, 2929
BODY: Thos, 4646
BOERMELL: Alex^r, 4004
BOGIE: And^w, 6228
BOGLE: Hugh, 8736
BOHAN: John, 7541
BOLAND: Den^s, 5241; Willm, 2096
BOLES: Robt, 8214
BOLGER: Mich^l, 5197
BOLONGE: Reed, 2178
BOLT: Ambrose, 2814
BOLTE: Hen^y, 1110
BOLTON: Jno, 702, 7318; Thos, 2278
BOND: Pat^k, 3099; Rich^d, 8722
BONE: Jno, 3429; W^m, 3284
BONFIELD: Pat^k, 5078
BONN: Widelius, 5929; Windilius, 1461
BONNER: Fra^s, 7533

INDEX 325

BONNINGTON: Edwd, 1549
BOOKER: Jno, 2710, 7035
BOON: Jos^h, 6676
BOOTH: Geo^e, 7587; Hen^y, 1257; Jno, 5554, 7553; Josiah, 8689; Robt, 7727, 8761; Willm, 1276, 5408, 8296
BOOTY: Philip, 2185
BORDINI: Jos^h, 2255
BOREBANK: W^m, 6027
BOREHAM: Chas, 3291
BORLAND: Hugh, 1208
BORSDALE: Jno, 946; John, 4808
BORTHICK: W^m, 2294
BOSSOM: Ja^s, 919, 4825
BOSTRIDGE: Thomas, 8009
BOSWARD: Thos, 5435
BOTTERILL: Edwd, 341; Edw^s, 3592
BOTTS: Hen^y, 923; Henry, 4821
BOUCHER: Edwd, 468
BOUCHIE: Jos^h, 2015
BOULTON: Geo^e, 7913
BOURGNON: Nich^s, 8055
BOURKE: Edward, 3644
BOURNE: Jos^h, 695, 4317
BOURNES: Jno, 5940
BOURNS: Lewis, 2370
BOWDEN: Ja^s, 3425
BOWE: John, 8671
BOWERS: Benjn, 5456; Isaac, 552
BOWICK: Ja^s, 8756
BOWIE: Alex^r, 5884; Allison, 3146; Jno, 5847; W^m, 8315; Willm, 1228, 1316
BOWLES: Jer^h, 5274; Thos, 2101
BOWMAN: Thos, 6251
BOWYER: Geo^e, 7764
BOXALL: Arth^r, 315; Ge^o, 2842
BOXER: W^m, 2577
BOYD: Bern^d, 7018; Errol, 2405; Ja^s, 5924; Jno, 885; John, 4702; Robt, 5611; Saml, 8344; Thos, 6996; W^m, 3155; Willm, 1275, 5420
BOYLE: And^w, 8619; Bernard, 3492, 7393; Chas, 4026; Edwd, 4562; J., 3068; Jno, 1715, 6472; Mic^l, 904; Mich^l, 4724; Thos, 2727
BOYS: Jno, 290, 3385
BOYTON: Robt, 7554; W^m, 7319
BRABY: W^m, 5494
BRACKEN: Rich^d, 7552
BRACKENBURY: Ja^s, 1579; Jno, 1510
BRACKENING: Ja^s, 2279
BRACKIN: Jno, 5397
BRADBURY: Jno, 1011, 2263; Thos, 226, 3180
BRADLEY: Francis, 7145; Jno, 8052; Thos, 6914

BRADY: Bernard, 7754; Ja^s, 5077; Jno, 1960, 7405, 7667; John, 2862, 5919, 6532; Mic^l, 1933; Mich^l, 4517, 6616; Thos, 1625; W^m, 7666
BRAHANY: Pat^k, 5304
BRAILEY: Ja^s, 1282
BRAILSFORD: John, 2997
BRAITHWAITE: Ge^o, 863
BRAND: Thos, 5966
BRANDER: Willm, 8745
BRANDON: Thos, 4683
BRANNAN: Den^s, 1262, 5416
BRANNIGAN: Robin, 7407; Terence, 7408
BRANNON: Thomas, 4591
BRANSTON: Rich^d, 6950
BRATT: John, 5043; Saml, 7215
BRAWN: Ja^s, 1280
BRAWNSTON: Hen^y, 7772
BRAY: Jno, 3292; Samuel, 3626
BRAZIER: Saml, 2454
BREADING: Jno R., 5767
BREADON: Ge^o, 787
BREAKEN: Edwd, 8896
BREARLEY: Willm, 1273
BREEN: Dav^d, 8914
BREEZE: John, 4300
BREMNER: Don^d, 8823; Jno, 1383, 8376; Thos, 8443
BRENAN: John, 5027
BRENEY: Thos, 187
BRENNAM: Thos, 3600
BRENNAN: Aug^s, 5158; Daniel, 6033; Ja^s, 1237; Jer^h, 6448; John, 3361; Mich^l, 6884; Pat^k, 3716; Thos, 7603
BRENNEN: Peter, 681
BRERETON: Thos, 6102
BRERTON: Hen^y, 7724
BRESINGTON: Thos, 5663
BRETT: Thos, 3941
BREWER: Jno, 4791
BRIAN: Danl, 7190; Ja^s, 2474; Jno, 3717
BRIDE: Law^e, 2967; Mich^l, 7863
BRIDGE: Jno, 5986
BRIDGES: John, 7160
BRIDGEWOOD: Sampson, 8271
BRIDLE: W^m, 2414; Willm, 8101
BRIEN: Owen, 4711; Pat^k, 5348; W^m, 1913, 7316
BRIERLY: Saml, 6849
BRIGHAM: Robert, 2962
BRIGHT: W^m, 4054
BRIMMER: Jno, 1437; Saml, 1489
BRINDLEY: Ja^s, 5997; Joseph, 3533
BRISLAND: Ja^s, 8595
BRISTER: Henry, 5358
BRITTIAN: Ja^s, 1507
BRITTON: Ge^o, 134; Geo^e, 3032
BROADHEAD: W^m, 41; Willm, 2873
BROADHURST: Jno, 211

BROCK: Ja^s, 655; James, 4270
BRODER: Hen^y, 7268
BRODIE: Paul, 5556; Tim^y, 404
BROGAN: Jno, 2235; Pat^k, 1497
BROMELL: Corn^s, 5619
BROMNLEY: Thos, 5338
BROOK: Alex^r, 6306; Chas, 6106
BROOKE: Ardy, 8825; Willm, 284, 3367
BROOKES: Matt^w, 4382
BROOKS: Dav^d, 8678; Ge^o, 747; Geo^e, 4443; Geo^e Hen^y, 5709; Jno, 7245; Jos^h, 3102, 5347; Thos, 419, 3058
BROPHEY: Ja^s, 2362
BROPHY: Danl, 3580; Ja^s, 8103; Mich^l, 686
BROTHERHOOD: Willm, 2744
BROTHERS: Uriah, 7199
BROW: Thos, 101; W^m, 6114
BROWN: Danl, 1689; Felix, 7008; Fra^s, 1374; Fred^k, 7887; Frederick, 4529; H^y, 6019; Hugh, 111, 3006; Hutley, 2874; Ja^s, 1358, 1550, 2325, 3876, 4906, 5424, 8099; Jno, 337, 425, 1417, 1807, 2280, 2709, 3590, 3759, 4510, 5294, 6475, 6848, 7034; John, 2112, 3047, 4206, 8921; Mark, 7213; Moses, 2418, 8102; Pat^k, 5101; Peter, 47; Rich^d, 5609; Robt, 8299; Sol^n, 4894; Thos, 545, 555, 1029, 2406; W^m, 400, 554, 996, 6814; Willm, 3079, 4862, 8340; William, 3627, 5597, 7935
BROWNE: Jos^h, 4052; Robt, 5393; Saml, 4350; Samuel, 4387; Thos, 4453; Willm, 8184
BROWNING: Rich^d, 6928; Saml, 1153
BROWNLEE: Nathl, 1955, 6620
BROWNSETT: Jno, 7668
BRUCE: Edwd Brown, 3504; Jno, 7773
BRUCKSHAW: Jos^h, 1006
BRUNDLE: W^m, 6389
BRUNT: Thos, 3199
BRYAN: David, 3481; Den^s, 2410, 8076; Jno, 995, 6028; John, 4867; Pat^k, 5952; Sylvester, 3877; Willm, 6360
BRYANT: Ja^s, 2303; Jer^h, 5575
BRYCE: Ja^s, 5275
BRYEN: Willm, 4392
BRYSON: Alex^r, 7188
BUCHANAN: Danl, 8059; Jno, 2382, 2543, 7014; Peter, 3835
BUCHANNAN: Ja^s, 1354
BUCHANON: Jno, 8101

INDEX

BUCHS: Jos^h, 1098
BUCKLEY: Bern^d, 1301; Chas, 4923; Hen^y, 7272; Hugh, 3219; Jno, 7604; Jos^h, 3412; Mich^l, 7411; Peter, 1650; Thos, 7020; W^m, 5045
BUDD: Danl, 6316
BUFTON: John, 7998
BUGG: Willm, 8259
BUGGLE: Jno, 1170
BULCHOR: Rich^d, 6177
BULL: Robt, 1181
BULLEN: John, 8010
BULLIVANT: Jno, 895, 4732
BULLOCK: Ja^s, 2281; Robt, 6403; Willm, 5454
BURDETT: Jer^h, 5297
BURFIELD: Saml, 5381
BURFORD: Benjn, 2140
BURGES: Jno, 1490
BURGESS: Jno, 4508; John, 8218; Jos^h, 1253; Robt, 954, 4843, 8277; Thos, 2493
BURIDGE: Dav^d, 2056
BURK: Jno, 1639
BURKE: Jno, 161, 540, 1699, 1759, 1888, 2720, 6252, 6471, 7669; John, 3043, 3097; Mich^l, 5761; Michael, 7153; Miles, 1638, 6136; Pat^k, 6053, 8591; Thos, 2353, 7246; W^m, 1835, 4084, 7854
BURKETT: Ja^s, 3613
BURMAN: Robt, 6871
BURN: Godfrey, 5433
BURNES: Jno, 5941
BURNET: W^m, 1882
BURNETT: Robt, 6204
BURNHAM: Jno, 7774
BURNIE: Jno, 5153
BURNIP: Ja^s, 4540
BURNS: Corn^s, 7555; Fra^s, 5287; Hen^y, 8869; Ja^s, 5903; Jno, 6637; Pat^k, 7915; Thos, 2553, 5206, 7140; W^m, 438, 3834, 4196, 6437; Walter, 8517; Willm, 4745
BURRARD: Rich^d, 1480
BURROUGHS: Walter, 2973
BURROWS: Geo^e, 5271; Jno, 4718; John, 2924, 6086; Trevor, 1548; W^m, 1428
BURTON: Alex^r, 8687; David, 6828; Ja^s, 8387; Jacques, 2566, 6937; Jno, 2494; John, 6951; Rich^d, 7838; Thos, 374, 3605
BUSH: Ja^s, 5664; Jno, 7412; Willm, 3851
BUSHMAN: Danl, 5168; Fred^k, 1103
BUSSEY: Robt, 210, 3185
BUSTARD: W^m, 4055
BUTCHER: Jno, 711, 1407, 5154; John, 7148
BUTLER: Ja^s, 1846, 2342, 3238, 6563, 7728, 8088; Jno, 1725, 6473, 6926; Patrick, 4416; Percival,

BUTLER (continued) 2810; Thomas, 6032
BUTLIN: Willm, 74
BUTTERBY: Benjn, 3119
BUTTERWORTH: Benjn, 8168; Ja^s, 3470; Thos, 7556
BUTTS: Ja^s, 4335
BUTWELL: W^m, 3535
BUXEY: Edwd, 3734
BYERS: Jno, 2366, 4573; Peter, 6651
BYRNE: Edwd, 498; Hen^y, 1920; Henry, 6599; Hugh, 7320; Ja^s, 7413; Jno, 291, 5157, 6216; John, 6068; Lawr^e, 4344; Mich^l, 3684; Simon, 5961; Thomas, 7929; W^m, 5108, 6827; Willm, 8
BYRNES: Ja^s, 2828
BYRON: Jno, 6693; Thos, 3718; Val^e, 4221
BYRONS: Ja^s, 8843
BYWAY: Thos, 260
CADDAN: Edwd, 6661
CADWELL: Peter, 7203
CAFFERKEY: Jno, 7864
CAFFRAY: John, 6557
CAFFREY: Jno, 4624
CAFFRY: Jno, 5131
CAHALANE: Tim^y, 8227
CAHILL: Ja^s, 978; Jno, 4372; Jos^h, 4404; Martin, 3072; Mich^l, 1502, 5908
CAIN: Ja^s, 5617
CAIRNS: Jno, 4919
CAITIN: Thos, 6194
CALDWELL: Thos, 5190
CALEW: William, 7956
CALGEY: W^m, 7775
CALLAGAHN: Mich^l, 5769
CALLAGHAN: Bernard, 6850; Danl, 343, 3598; Den^s, 831; Hen^y, 6255; Jno, 1813, 1947, 3181, 3478, 6535; John, 224; Matt^w, 1951, 6998; Mich^l, 4005, 4370; Murtaugh, 6456; Pat^k, 7417; Thos, 7557; Timothy, 3687
CALLIER: John, 8448
CAMERON: Alex^r, 2006; Ang^s, 2292; Angus, 2249; Danl, 5482; Dug^l, 5820; Ja^s, 8430; Jno, 5514
CAMP: Geo^e, 6851
CAMPBELL: Arch^d, 6358; Den^s, 6624; Felix, 8606; Fra^s, 303, 3458; Geo^e, 3080, 5776, 7558; Ja^s, 127, 3224, 4023, 7026; Jno, 188, 504, 796, 2043, 6276, 6762, 6860, 7776, 7855, 7908; John, 7019; Mich^l, 3262; Pat^k, 6566; Patt, 1868; Peter, 1451, 5814; Robt, 2647, 8210; Robert, 3359, 4651; Thos, 1435, 3818, 7273; Thomas, 5721; W^m, 6253
CAMPHOR: Carolus, 386
CANDILLO: Geuseppi, 7029; Guiseppe, 2952

CANNELL: John, 6056
CANNON: James, 3688; Jere^h, 730; Pat^k, 673, 4288; Thos, 2124, 3854; W^m, 402
CANSHER: Ja^s, 7414
CANTILLON: Thos, 7652
CANTRELL: W^m, 4539
CARDELL: Pat^k, 1934, 6534
CAREY: Edwd, 6030; John, 8614; Mich^l, 6393; Rich^d, 8629
CARLAND: Ja^s, 5050
CARLEY: Jon^n, 3972
CARLING: Isaac, 2733
CARLISLE: And^w, 5943; Ja^s, 5944
CARLOS: Hen^y, 138
CARLTON: W^m, 7418
CARLY: Ja^s, 4675
CARMACK: Don^d, 2223
CARMICHAEL: Hugh, 2446; Ja^s, 1183
CARNACHONG: And^w, 6653
CARNEY: Jno, 6248; Thos, 7274
CARR: Geo^e, 4433; Jos^h, 1552, 4913, 6078; Mich^l, 193; Pat^k, 4616; W^m, 4315, 6430, 7120
CARRICK: Willm, 1182
CARROL: John, 8814
CARROLL: Art^r, 3726; Ber^d, 7672; Bern^d, 342, 3595; Danl, 3960; Ja^s, 2921, 2961, 5596; Jno, 2283, 7419; John, 7161; Mich^l, 2708, 7045, 7542, 7777; Pat^k, 1614; Peter, 7829; Rich^d, 1300; W^m, 1893, 3493; William, 6034
CARSHORE: Thos, 7420
CARSON: John, 5279; Mich^l, 4644; Robt, 6743; Saml, 5592; Simon, 4200
CARSTAIRS: Jno, 8502
CARTER: Charles, 7999; Ja^s, 813, 4973, 5230, 6758; Jno, 6376; John, 4899, 7965; Mall^w, 8138; Mark, 314; W^m, 556; Willm, 4407
CARTHORN: Willm, 541
CARTTEDGE: Jno, 1250
CARTWRIGHT: Ge^o, 2484; Jno, 8458; Quintin, 1529
CARTY: Chas, 5295; Corn^s, 3888; Ja^s, 858; Jno, 3961; Luke, 3878; Pat^k, 7321
CASEMENT: Phi^p, 8623
CASEY: Ja^s, 7421; Jeremiah, 5138; Jno, 4639; John, 5565
CASHEN: Fra^s, 7856
CASSADY: Jno, 471; John, 3858; Mic^l, 1978
CASSELS: Jno, 6217
CASSIDY: Jno, 6725; Mich^l, 5646; W^m, 6677
CASSSADY: Mich^l, 6610
CASTER: Edwd, 2057
CASTLE: Baker, 6954

INDEX 327

CASTLES: Jn⁰, 380
CATELLA: Josʰ, 5777
CATOR: Josʰ, 776
CATT: John, 8766
CAVALAN: Mattʷ, 634
CAVANAGH: Chaˢ, 7422; Jn⁰, 5109; Michˡ, 4993; Peter, 1819
CAVANAUGH: Peter, 6537
CAVE: Jaˢ, 1794; Josʰ, 8751
CAVERS: Jaˢ, 3143
CAVERT: Samˡ, 253
CAVEY: Thoˢ, 261
CAWLEY: John, 6103
CEACY: John, 5564
CHADWICK: Ge⁰, 1487
CHALMERS: Willᵐ, 8461, 8778
CHAMBERS: Josʰ, 4717; Michˡ, 4340; Patᵏ, 2661; Wᵐ, 5848
CHAMPLEY: Jn⁰, 354
CHANDLER: Jn⁰, 1067, 3518
CHAPLIN: Thoˢ, 7415
CHAPMAN: Abrᵐ, 4075; Chaˢ, 7534; Ge⁰ᵉ, 6792; Henʸ, 309; John, 8660, 8737; Josʰ, 48, 2766, 2878; Richᵈ, 1886; Samˡ, 864; Thoˢ, 964, 4343; Wᵐ, 3003; William, 5625
CHARLES: Jn⁰, 2172
CHARLTON: Wᵐ, 1671, 2284; Willᵐ, 1664
CHARRIOTTE: Fraˢ, 2479
CHARTERS: Josʰ, 8191
CHATER: Willᵐ, 6784
CHATTEN: Ge⁰, 411; Ge⁰ᵉ, 3758
CHATWIN: Samˡ, 2567
CHECK: Jn⁰, 1082
CHEEK: Wᵐ, 3271
CHEETHAM: Willᵐ, 8397
CHERRINGTON: John, 75, 2909
CHERRY: Jn⁰, 3907; Patᵏ, 4859; Wᵐ, 597
CHESTER: Samˡ, 3279; Willᵐ, 8401
CHESTNUT: Isaac, 5757
CHILDS: Richᵈ, 5665
CHILVERS: Jn⁰, 2141
CHIPP: Thoˢ, 2002
CHISHOLME: John, 5476
CHISLETE: Thoˢ Day, 3225
CHISLETT: Jn⁰, 369, 3666
CHITTOCK: Samˡ, 5753
CHITTY: Caleb, 3078
CHIVINS: Jn⁰, 7425
CHOULERTON: Jn⁰, 7780
CHRISTIAN: Jn⁰, 1553; Michˡ, 665
CHRISTIE: Andʷ, 5011; Claudius, 5436; John, 8627; Wᵐ, 854
CHRISTOPHER: Thoˢ, 3889
CHURCH: Jn⁰, 648; Samˡ, 3139
CHYNE: Ge⁰ᵉ, 7865
CLAIR: Jaˢ, 4474
CLAMP: Edwᵈ, 3254
CLANCY: Jaˢ, 7112; Michˡ, 4229, 4231
CLAPHAM: Mathew, 2989

CLARIN: Fraˢ, 3760
CLARK: Andʷ, 1008; Jn⁰, 3299; Josʰ, 4602; Robᵗ, 4259; Thoˢ, 6993; Wᵐ, 2645, 3984, 5551, 5849; Willᵐ, 1466, 8433
CLARKE: Cat0, 6763; Cato, 2044; Chaˢ, 1038, 3444, 4985, 6020; Fraˢ, 3216; George, 7162; HY, 4424; Henʸ, 726; James, 8000; Jn⁰, 2285, 2302, 7377; Job, 2796; John, 8057; Josʰ, 91, 2940, 6374; Lawrᵉ, 4984; Mattʷ, 1323, 5466; Michˡ, 3520; Robᵗ, 5264; Robert, 4592; Wᵐ, 454, 1336, 2816, 6223; Willᵐ, 4511, 5473
CLAY: John, 7958; Samˡ, 4107; Willᵐ, 8819
CLAYTON: Robᵗ, 7416
CLEARY: Michˡ, 6691; Thoˢ, 4817; Willᵐ, 6095; William, 6731
CLEGG: Luke, 7247
CLEMENT: Jn⁰, 5850
CLEMENTS: Gustˢ, 5467; Gustavus, 1324; Jn⁰, 2245
CLENDENING: Andʷ, 3300
CLEVES: Thoˢ, 2413
CLEWES: Ralph, 8552
CLIFF: Thoˢ, 7778
CLIFFEN: Jaˢ, 7779
CLIFFORD: George, 8011; John, 3837, 4705; Thoˢ, 7424; Wᵐ, 2529; Willᵐ, 6966
CLIMO: Jaˢ, 8145
CLINTON: Barthʷ, 8777; Michˡ, 8577
CLORAN: Thoˢ, 2432
CLOSE: Jn⁰, 690; Willᵐ, 2838
CLOUGHLY: Willᵐ, 8515
CLOUT: Benjⁿ, 5088; Josʰ, 5066
CLOVER: Wᵐ, 3844; Willᵐ, 442
CLUER: Jn⁰, 779
CLUFF: Jn⁰, 1012
CLUNEY: Alfred, 3081
CLUTTERBUCK: Wᵐ, 7298
COAKES: Samˡ, 2859
COALMAN: Thoˢ, 3301
COAPLAND: John, 8602
COATES: Josʰ, 257
COBB: Jaˢ, 7889
COCHRAN: Jaˢ, 2401
COCHRANE: Ge⁰ᵉ, 7781; Henʸ, 3082; Jn⁰, 5493; Joseph, 3645; Septimus, 3646
COCKBURN: Josʰ, 8365
COCUS: John, 5561
CODD: Fraˢ, 1697
CODE: Patᵏ, 6024
CODY: Thoˢ, 7559
COFFEE: Michˡ, 4617
COFFELL: Patᵏ, 925; Tarrell, 924
COFFEY: Jn⁰, 1817, 6536; Willᵐ, 1035

COGLEY: Patᵏ, 2404
COHRS: Henʸ, 2650
COLBERT: Davᵈ, 5480
COLBOURNE: Willᵐ, 1463
COLCOMB: Thoˢ, 2629
COLE: Jaˢ, 7249; John, 2934; Lionel, 126; Robᵗ, 1959, 6621; Thoˢ, 2990; Thomas, 3537; Victor, 2196, 8173
COLEMAN: Andʷ, 1465, 5935; George, 3278; Jn⁰, 7427; Job, 256; Mark, 5878; Thoˢ, 7426; Timʸ, 1698; Wᵐ, 602, 3285; Willᵐ, 4154
COLERICK: Samˡ, 4217
COLES: John, 8788
COLLESHAW: Thoˢ, 1225
COLLINS: Cornˢ, 1660; Isaac, 4194; Jaˢ, 724, 3699, 7428, 7648; Jn⁰, 220, 246, 249, 3183, 5545, 6023, 7782; Mattʷ, 3020; Michˡ, 1686, 3176, 6701, 7081; Patᵏ, 6075; Peter, 8398; Thoˢ, 865; William, 8874
COLLIS: Josʰ, 5253
COLLOCOTT: Jaˢ, 8865
COLOLOUGH: Robᵗ, 2822
COLQUHOUN: Dugald, 5851; Jn⁰, 1537, 6018; Robᵗ, 8382
COLVIN: Willᵐ, 2794
COLWELL: Wᵐ, 8829
COMB: Richᵈ, 7248
COMBS: Jn⁰, 1317
COMMINS: Redmond, 3647
COMPTON: Jn⁰, 1499
CONALLY: Michˡ, 769, 786
CONBOY: Patᵏ, 7429
CONLAN: Michˡ, 3302; Patᵏ, 2541
CONLIN: Joseph, 6039
CONLON: Jaˢ, 798, 4560
CONNALLY: Jaˢ, 4948
CONNELL: Danˡ, 5363; Jn⁰, 3761; Patᵏ, 1760, 6477, 7430; Wᵐ, 3463, 7431
CONNELLAN: Jaˢ, 8051
CONNELLY: Jn⁰, 4915, 7432; Philip, 3912
CONNERS: Edwᵈ, 7673
CONNETT: Leon, 2173
CONNING: Jn⁰, 5778
CONNOLLY: Danˡ, 5917; Edʷ, 3578; Edwᵈ, 2497, 6952; Fraˢ, 7105; Ge⁰ᵉ, 5837; Henʸ, 7741; Martin, 4009; Patᵏ, 5058, 7866; Thomas, 3640
CONNOR: Jaˢ, 1917; Jn⁰, 6815; Mauᵉ, 1923; Michˡ, 2646, 8211; Stephen, 8012; Wᵐ, 296, 3895
CONNORS: Edwᵈ, 1743; Michˡ, 7054; Miles, 2565, 6953; Owen, 7082
CONQUEST: James, 7163
CONRAN: Jn⁰, 8830
CONRE: Arthur, 3919
CONREY: Josʰ, 4774

CONROY: Farrell, 7299; Jn⁰, 3727; John, 5920; Michˡ, 5971; Patᵏ, 6569; Peter, 7433; Wᵐ, 1826
CONSADINE: Jaˢ, 3896
CONTADES: Jn⁰, 965
CONWAY: Jaˢ, 6362, 7740; Jn⁰, 3920; Martin, 3494; Patᵏ, 3865
COOGAN: Jn⁰, 5185; Robᵗ, 7216
COOGHRAN: Samˡ, 4461
COOK: Abraham, 7996; Angus, 5486; Chaˢ, 332, 3565; Jn⁰, 310, 2625, 7394; John, 4101; Phelan, 4318; Stepⁿ, 557, 4139; Thoˢ, 1343, 2495, 6971; Willᵐ, 4400
COOKE: Geoᵉ, 7833; Jonⁿ, 1070; Reynolds, 6722; Thoˢ, 2337, 4914; Willᵐ, 666
COOKLEY: Patᵏ, 6071
COOKSON: Fraˢ, 3891
COOMBES: Samˡ, 1595, 1628
COOMBS: Joshʰ, 8792
COOMES: Willᵐ, 2421
COONERTY: Michˡ, 7077
COONEY: Benjⁿ, 3169; Patᵏ, 2378
COOPER: Chaˢ, 1596, 1629, 6126; David, 7150; Edward, 6031; Jaˢ, 1206, 5371; Jn⁰, 5584; Robᵗ, 2286, 4524; Samˡ, 6872, 6920; Silas, 4464; Thoˢ, 850, 4665; Willᵐ, 1493, 6006
COOTE: Jn⁰, 2480; John, 6949
COPELAND: Jaˢ, 3694; Robᵗ, 5995
CORBETT: Jaˢ, 3371; John, 2896; Wᵐ, 7267
CORBIE: Jn⁰ F., 1134
CORBIN: Willᵐ, 2399, 8105
CORBISHLEY: Joshʰ, 8172
CORCORAN: Laughlin, 1669; Martin, 7275; Stepⁿ, 3217
CORCORCAN: Loughⁿ, 6416
CORDALL: Thoˢ, 7322
CORDINGLY: Thoˢ, 4325
COREY: Jn⁰, 2354, 8104; Wᵐ, 2991
CORMAC: Ewᵈ, 5067
CORMACK: Jn⁰, 8353
CORMICK: Donᵈ, 8151; Thoˢ, 5682
CORNEALSON: Jn⁰, 3599
CORNER: Jaˢ, 8048; Jn⁰, 3704; John, 8912
CORNES: Chaˢ, 6254
CORNWALL: Willᵐ, 1580, 8665
CORNWELL: Wᵐ, 1511
CORNYN: Murtagh, 1457
CORRIGAN: Michˡ, 2781, 6727; Thoˢ, 4685
CORRINS: Wᵐ, 8350
COSGROVE: Edwᵈ, 1780, 1818; Fraˢ, 1756, 6476; Thoˢ, 6118
COSSAM: Lake, 6908; Sake, 2179

COSSER: Richᵈ, 5065
COSTELLO: Jn⁰, 1190, 5322; Thoˢ, 6185, 6521
COSTIGAN: Thomas, 5691
COTE: Peter, 2034
COTHAM: Richᵈ, 962
COTT: Michˡ, 1681
COTTER: Jn⁰, 2200
COUGHLAN: Danˡ, 4615; Fraˢ, 6364; Jn⁰, 4197; Martin, 7759; Thoˢ, 2496
COUGHLIN: Danˡ, 1851, 6568
COULBOURNE: Wᵐ, 5937
COULSTON: Jaˢ, 8692; Samˡ, 6782; Thoˢ, 8396
COURNAN: Jn⁰, 6355
COURSER: Thoˢ, 3570
COURT: Benjⁿ, 777
COURTIER: Wᵐ Henry, 8714
COURTNEY: Danˡ, 375; Jaˢ, 4046; James, 5598; John, 5694; Thoˢ, 5181
COUSINS: Jaˢ, 8708; Jn⁰, 5187; Spalter, 34; Spatter, 2879
COUTS: Willᵐ, 1598, 1631
COUTTS: Lewis, 6211
COVE: Davᵈ, 266; Jonⁿ, 620
COVELL: Jn⁰, 3735
COWELL: Geᵒ, 1648
COWEN: Jaˢ, 7560
COWHIG: David, 7671
COWIE: Andʷ, 8388
COWLEY: Jn⁰, 7434
COWLLTHORPE: Jaˢ, 5727
COWTHORP: Jaˢ, 1426
COX: Fraˢ, 1942; Jn⁰, 122, 1782; John, 3031, 6478; Michˡ, 1852, 6565; Patᵏ, 1847, 1869, 6564; Thoˢ, 1845; Wᵐ, 3297, 4040
COXHEAD: Chaˢ, 293
COYLE: Andʷ, 7584; Jn⁰, 6440; Michˡ, 1897; Owen, 1783; Patᵏ, 5087
COZENS: Jn⁰, 3962
CRABB: Jn⁰, 4095
CRADOCK: Joshʰ, 4606
CRAGEN: Jn⁰, 1908
CRAIG: Chaˢ Henʸ, 8385; Davᵈ, 8881; Hugh, 367; Jaˢ, 8930; John, 8194; Robᵗ, 8414
CRAMPTON: Peter, 963
CRANE: Samˡ, 3230; Thoˢ, 420
CRANKSHAW: Wᵐ, 6867
CRANSTON: Jaˢ, 4861; Willᵐ, 8709
CRASTY: Jn⁰, 8686
CRAWFORD: Andʷ, 5376; Chaˢ, 5166; Fredᵏ, 3719; Geᵒ, 3691; Jaˢ, 8282, 8377; Jn⁰, 4274; Robᵗ, 3161; Wᵐ, 3202, 5330
CRAY: Jaˢ, 3793
CREAKE: Jn⁰, 1240
CREANE: Jn⁰, 3303
CREED: Henʸ, 5763
CREEVEY: Jn⁰, 1961
CREIGHTON: Jn⁰, 5231; Samuel, 3357
CRERAR: Alexʳ, 6193

CRESWELL: Reuben, 7423
CRICK: Isiah, 830
CRIMMINS: Thoˢ, 653
CRIPPEN: Richᵈ, 2920
CRISP: Shadrack, 7539
CRITCH: Jn⁰, 2365
CRITCHLEY: Willᵐ, 4663
CROCKER: Walter, 7867
CROFT: Wᵐ, 2481
CROFTS: Thoˢ, 1613
CROKER: Jn⁰ Wallis, 140; Samˡ, 5647
CROMMER: Wᵐ, 1957
CRONE: Thoˢ, 3226
CRONEN: Owen, 2077
CRONIN: Jn⁰, 3791
CROOK: Jaˢ, 6923
CROSHAW: Matʷ, 5648
CROSLAND: Robᵗ, 1283
CROSS: Geoᵉ, 7674; Samˡ, 1210; Thoˢ, 57
CROSSLAND: Edwᵈ, 4255
CROSSLEY: Jn⁰, 8467
CROW: John Jonah, 4420
CROWE: Martin, 4179; Patᵏ, 7605; Samˡ, 87, 2935; Thoˢ, 558, 4142
CROWLEY: Jerʰ, 2451, 7061; Jn⁰, 7675; Timʸ, 4074, 6710
CROWLY: John, 4239
CROZIER: Jn⁰, 1894, John, 6567; Michˡ, 6922; Thoˢ, 1678
CRUMLEY: Thoˢ, 8834
CRUMMY: Jn⁰, 5089
CRUMP: Joshʰ, 8868
CRYAN: Thoˢ, 3748
CUDDY: Martin, 5909
CUDMORE: Daniel, 7435
CUDNEY: Richᵈ, 8056
CUFF: Mattʷ, 7606
CULBERT: Robᵗ, 6162
CULHANE: Matt, 8486
CULLEN: Jaˢ, 7783; Jn⁰, 658, 1331; John, 5470; Mattʷ, 2318; Michˡ, 3393; Richᵈ, 8604
CULLINGFORD: John, 3137
CULLY: Samˡ, 3454
CUMMING: Duncan, 7850; Hugh, 8386; Jaˢ, 8853; Thoˢ, 2081, 2211
CUMMINGS: James, 8074; Jn⁰, 322, 2668; Lawᵉ, 832, 852; Lawrᵉ, 4649; Robᵗ, 8524; Thoˢ, 1787; Wᵐ, 6237
CUMMINS: Geoᵉ, 5349; Jn⁰, 2027; Renoldi, 2435; Reynolds, 8106
CUNNINGHAM: Geᵒ, 921; Henʸ, 7250; Hugh, 8421; Jaˢ, 1063, 4782; Jn⁰, 189; Patᵏ, 3001; Robᵗ, 3794; Wᵐ, 1922, 6533, 7839
CUNNINGTON: John, 2950
CUPITT: Geᵒ, 2669; Geoᵉ, 7043
CURLEY: Timʸ, 7300
CURRAN: Andʷ, 4822; Benjⁿ, 8898; Chaˢ, 7126; Jn⁰,

INDEX

CURRAN (continued) 2662, 3239, 4191; Laurence, 3210; Mich^l, 1637
CURRELL: Saml, 1673
CURREN: Henry, 4041; Pat^k, 926
CURRIE: Ja^s, 2462, 6985; Laughlin, 5398; Thos, 1491
CURRY: Hen^y, 6431; Ja^s, 3543; Lewis, 2670; Pat^k, 6122; Saml, 3506; Thos, 3188
CURTIS: Chas, 955; Jno, 3736; Richard, 8738; Thos, 3277, 4383
CUSACK: Jno, 7055; Pat^k, 4991
CUSHLEY: W^m, 3083
CUSICK: Jno, 7670, 7868; Philip, 2498
CUSSLEY: Ben^{jn}, 2671
CUTHBERTSON: Ge^o, 6
CUTTS: Ja^s, 2557
DAHENNY: William, 3648
DAILEY: Jer^h, 2058; Thos, 3555; Willm, 3017
DAINES: Ja^s, 7649
DAKIN: Willm, 7028
DALBY: John, 6782
DALEY: Jno, 7323; John, 6051; Mich^l, 4019; Robt, 2301; Willm, 3451
DALGLEISH: Ja^s, 8724
DALL: Jno, 2531
DALLAS: David, 5544; Jno, 8481
DALLING: W^m, 4903
DALMAGE: Jacob, 3045
DALTON: Dav^d, 1284; Jno, 3471; John, 3338, 7930; Maur^c, 7324; Thos, 7116; W^m, 49
DALY: Andrew, 3423; Bern^d, 2575; Danl, 7204; Timothy, 7966; W^m, 1831, 3698, 4940
DALZIEL: Jno, 5799
DAMARUM: W^m, 1013, 4922
DAMERUM: Ja^s, 4954
DANE: W^m, 6638
DANGERFIELD: W^m, 2477, 6938
DANIELS: Ja^s, 5028
DANNIAN: Lawr^e, 8140
DANTON: Thos, 997
DANVERS: Ja^s, 1386
DANZIE: Willm, 3384
DARBY: Alex^r, 633; Edwd, 2719; Ja^s, 2858
DARCEY: Ja^s, 6120
DARCY: Edwd, 6396
DARGAN: Pat^k, 1716
DARGIE: Willm, 289
DARGIN: Peter, 2672
DARLING: Ja^s, 5880; W^m, 8319
DARON: Michael, 3619
DARRAGH: Ja^s, 5983
DART: Chr^r, 8867
DATES: Chr^r, 1026
DAVENNY: Thos, 4373

DAVEY: Edm^d, 7769; Ja^s, 7784
DAVIDSON: Alex^r, 1318, 5463; And^w, 1512, 1581, 5999; David, 7437; Ja^s, 7677; James, 5695; Jno, 68; W^m, 344; Willm, 8368
DAVIE: Archibald, 3638; Jno, 8567; Jos^h, 8784
DAVIES: Hen^y, 807; Ja^s, 6794, 8817; John, 7931; Thos, 3084
DAVIS: Arthur, 6112; Chas, 2004; Dav^d, 1554; Edwd, 7907; Edwin, 6070; Ge^o, 1513, 1582; Geo^e, 6000, 8238; H^y, 3936; Ja^s, 7436, 8713; Jno, 4642, 6852, 7607; John, 5948, 8437; Jos^h, 2983, 4267, 8767; Robt, 881, 7761; Thos, 3963, 7755; W^m, 3551; Willm, 8297
DAVY: Melchizideck, 2393
DAWE: Fra^s, 2298
DAWES: Jos^h, 5666; Rich^d, 3260; Thos, 3795
DAWSON: Ja^s, 3064, 8037; Jno, 2711, 8465; Mich^l, 1748, 6482; Pat^k, 7845; W^m, 1160; Willm, 5237
DAY: Edwd, 3811; Edwd Thos, 4294; Jno, 1220; Tim^y, 7676; Willm, 2102; William, 7967
DEA: Edm^d, 2327; Robt, 2330, 8064
DEACON: Thos, 493; W^m, 4931
DEADY: Martin, 4073
DEAKERS: Lambert, 3732
DEALY: Jno, 6148
DEAN: Ge^o, 100; Ja^s, 3921; Jno, 974
DEANE: Thos, 277
DEARDON: Jno, 7326
DEAS: H^y, 8476
DEASE: Dav^d, 2158
DEATON: W^m, 7834
DEDOMINICO: Fra^s, 417
DEE: Ja^s, 3593; Thos, 4369
DEEGAN: Ja^s, 2804; Jno, 5732
DEEHAN: Ja^s, 7848
DEER: Hen^y, 424
DEGOOD: Peter, 190
DEIGAN: Ja^s, 1
DELAHUNT: Den^s, 1804
DELAHYDE: Jno, 659
DELANEY: Denis, 7609
DELANY: John, 6916; Thos, 866
DELASERAS: Val^e, 5165; Valen^e, 1140
DELL: John, 6746
DELLICOTE: W^m, 920
DELMORE: Pat^k, 7438
DEMPSEY: Jno, 927; John, 2113, 3052; Silv^r, 6630; Sylvest^r, 1838
DENEHY: John, 2980
DENISON: Jno, 1984
DENN: John, 5877

DENNIS: Ja^s, 1357, 5515; Jos^h, 3093; Robt, 1373
DENNISON: Geo^e, 4287
DENNY: Epaphras, 8416
DENOON: Ja^s, 8442
DENSMORE: Jno, 5404
DENTON: Willm, 2741
DERMODY: Jno, 7217
DERNING: Alex^r, 1195
DESCARROUR: Charles, 2025
DESCHAMPS: Louis, 2416
DESMOND: Jno, 5299; Mich^l, 7327; Morris, 7608
DEVANNEY: Arth^r, 4908
DEVANNY: Martin, 7164
DEVANY: Ant^y, 7073
DEVATT: Ja^s, 5120
DEVENPORT: Jno, 1251
DEVERALL: Jno, 7561
DEVERELL: W^m, 3275
DEVEREUX: Pat^k, 4977
DEVILLE: Ja^s, 6929
DEVIN: Ja^s, 1985, 6538
DEVINE: Jno, 5392; Keron, 1416
DEVLIN: Ja^s, 4036; Jno, 8589
DEWETT: Zeph^r, 4439; Zephaniah, 742
DICKENSON: Willm, 4866
DICKER: Ja^s, 989, 4856
DICKINS: Chas, 84; Charles, 2948
DICKINSON: Ja^s, 1503; Oliver, 1555
DICKSON: Jno, 8840; Jos^h, 8695
DIDDLESTON: Ja^s, 1339
DIGBY: Saml, 3931
DIGNEY: Jno, 6191
DIKOW: Chas, 2262
DILLEN: Pat^k, 6465
DILLON: Fred^k, 859, 4670; Jno, 5736; Luke, 1875, 6570; Mich^l, 2996; Pat^k, 1695, 6441, 6479; Thos, 2568
DINAHAN: Rich^d, 6077
DINAN: Peter, 1949
DINEEN: Geo^e, 3476
DINGWALL: Alex^r, 1396, 5527
DINNIN: Mich^l, 5107
DINNON: Jno, 5852
DIVER: Ben^{jn}, 7328
DIXON: Chas, 5770; Geo^e, 8544; Hen^y, 112; Jno, 1911; Thos, 3011
DOBBIE: Robt, 5118
DOBBIN: Patrick, 3616
DOBSON: Chas, 2499; Dav^d, 2764; Jno, 5614; Mat^w, 8243
DODD: Ja^s, 8444; Willm, 2870
DODDS: Geo^e, 5103
DOGHERTY: Edwd, 1930; Ja^s, 2729; John, 8925; Mich^l, 4072
DOHERTY: Patrick, 5742
DOIG: Ja^s, 7597
DOLAN: Pat^k, 6816
DOLMAGE: Willm, 8209
DOMINICO: Fra^s D., 3752

DONAGHOE: Den^s, 1870; Jno, 294; John, 3398, 6134
DONAGHUE: Ja^s, 3611; Pat^k, 6702
DONAHOE: Malachi, 3871; Mar^n, 3544
DONAHUE: Ja^s, 6356
DONALDSON: Geo^e, 8359; Ja^s, 1623, 5683, 6135; Jno, 6176; Robt, 494
DONELEY: Ja^s, 3113
DONELLY: Hugh, 4028
DONILEY: Pat^k, 7121
DONNELL: Chas, 6233
DONNELLAN: Pat^k, 1714, 6481; W^m, 7329
DONNELLY: Edwd, 1977, 7562; Fra^s, 7439; Ja^s, 4284, 6829; Jno, 1486, 3174; Lawrence, 4848
DONNOLLY: Chas, 6716; Thos, 6678
DONOGHOE: Jno, 1640
DONOGHUE: Mich^l, 7678
DONOHOE: Chas, 4056; Pat^k, 7114
DONOHUE: Barth^w, 983
DONOUGHEY: Thos, 4957
DONOUGHUE: Hy, 8221
DONOVAN: Danl, 2376; Jno, 3218; Mich^l, 6443; Peter, 6442
DOOGAN: Danl, 5804
DOOLAN: Ja^s, 980; Law^e, 4082
DOOLE: Saml, 5288
DOOLITTLE: Jno, 4347
DOOMSDAY: George, 6781
DORAN: Ja^s, 5434, 8468; Jno, 7610; Patrick, 7165; Philip, 7132; Thos, 208, 4125; W^m, 8656
DORCEY: Jno, 1059
DOREY: Anthony, 4240
DORNHOFFER: Philip, 65, 2910
DORRIS: Ja^s, 1821, 6539
DOUBLE: Jno, 4130
DOUGALL: Ja^s, 8549
DOUGHANEY: Mich^l, 3496
DOUGHERTY: Ja^s, 535, 2569, 4114; Jno, 8361; Neil, 8351; Thos, 8607
DOUGLAS: John, 8001; Thomas, 7963; W^m, 3434
DOVE: John, 3085
DOWD: Mich^l, 4826
DOWDELL: Pat^k, 3069
DOWDEN: Ja^s, 2449
DOWELL: Robt, 2592; Willm, 147
DOWIE: Dav^d, 5530
DOWLAN: Pat^k, 2500
DOWLING: Peter, 8280; Philip, 5620; Thos, 6163
DOWNER: Willm, 7010
DOWNEY: Jno, 6846; Mich^l, 1617
DOWNHAM: Jno, 2789
DOWNIE: Geo^e, 4260; Pat^k, 6321
DOWNING: Jno, 3762
DOWNS: W^m, 3276

DOWSER: Thos, 7440
DOYLE: Alex^r, 3879, 6817; Anth^y, 1217; Denis, 4575; Fra^s, 8432; Hen^y, 414, 3756; Hugh, 2663; Ja^s, 3964, 6386, 8063; Jno, 3755; Mich^l, 3495; Owen, 1924; Pat^k, 4779; Peter, 8356
DRABY: Willm, 421
DRACUP: Isaac, 1530
DRAIN: John, 8141
DRAKE: Fra^s, 4759; Henry, 2848
DRAPER: Ja^s, 7325
DRENNAN: Hen^y, 6910
DREW: Danl, 1033; George, 7166; Jno, 4890
DRING: Simon, 5232
DRISCOLL: Jer^h, 5386; Jere^h, 7837; Pat^k, 2358, 8107; Rich^d, 6777; W^m, 2317; Willm, 8077
DRIVER: Wm Thos, 8328
DRUMMOND: Fra^s, 7243
DUAN: Pat^k, 3474
DUDLOW: Thos, 8253
DUFF: Alex^r, 8785; Chas, 6055; Ja^s, 1364, 5524
DUFFEY: Ja^s, 8390; Pat^k, 3511
DUFFIE. Mich^l, 191
DUFFY: Bern^d, 1827; Chas, 1180; Ja^s, 214, 3177; Jno, 2269; John, 4707; Pat^k, 251, 3251
DUGARD: Thos, 1539
DUGGAN: Pat^k, 490, 3946; Patrick, 6737
DUHRKOP: Christoph, 2653
DUKE: Jno, 7895; William, 8013
DUKES: Edwd, 2142; Willm, 8062
DUKESBURY: David, 7444
DULLARD: Pat^k, 4237
DUMBLE: Thos, 8822
DUMMIGAN: Willm, 833
DUMPLER: Fred^k, 2059
DUNBAR: Jno, 1939, 2485; W^m, 6812
DUNCAN: And^w, 1411, 5606; Geo^e, 7441; Jno, 181
DUNDAS: James, 6735
DUNFORD: Ja^s, 7785
DUNLAP: Ja^s, 8793
DUNLING: Thos, 7443
DUNLOP: Robt, 4354; Robert, 7968
DUNN: And^w, 415; Hugh, 2104; James, 3628; Jeremiah, 7057; Jno, 1752, 5102, 5341, 6841; John, 6141, 6483; Luke, 4299; Pat^k, 4057, 4080
DUNNAGE: Jno, 8800
DUNNE: William, 6038
DUNT: Saml, 372
DUPREE: Chas, 559
DURAN: Jno, 698
DURANT: Robt, 3018; W^m, 107
DURCAN: Pat^k, 7442

DURHAM: Danl, 496; Willm, 8043
DUTTON: Thos, 590
DWYER: Jer^h, 7445; Jno, 7301; John, 6080; Matt^w, 6480; Mich^l, 3783; Thos, 4891; W^m, 2450; Willm, 8078
DYE: Robt, 355, 3676
DYER: Ge^o, 1051; George, 5000; Matt^w, 1696; Mich^l, 4405, 6350
DYKE: Isaac, 7942
DYKES: Ja^s, 5141
DYSON: Jos^h, 4207
EADES: Jos^h, 6745
EADEY: Robt, 680, 4301
EAGAN: Ja^s, 3235, 8760; W^m, 3720
EALEY: And^w, 2984
EAMES: Thos, 4932
EARDLEY: Mau^e, 1184; Maur^e, 5335
EARLE: Chas, 40, 2876
EARLY: Pat^k, 6353
EASSON: W^m, 7679
EASTON: Thos, 368, 4273; W^m, 5073
EATON: John, 5626; Rich^d, 92
ECCLES: Thos, 8530
ECHLIN: Ch^r, 3258; Thos, 3669
EDGE: Ge^o, 1837; Geo^e, 6011
EDGERTON: Saml, 5899
EDGLEY: Ge^o, 2561; Geo^e, 6939
EDMED: Willm, 2821
EDMONDS: Rich^d, 3567
EDMUNDS: Eph^m, 792
EDNEY: John, 5567
EDWARD: John, 8666
EDWARDS: Edwd, 3339; Evan, 378; Geo^e, 7251; Ja^s, 4175, 8313; Jno, 1221; Rich^d, 7563; Robt, 8229; Thos, 5513, 6672; W^m, 2966, 3475
EGAN: And^w, 1969; Jno, 6811; Nich^s, 7681; Thos, 7139
EGGS: Benjn, 3134; W^m, 7786
EGLESTON: Thos, 1224
EGLETON: George, 5748
EGLINTON: Jno, 1285
EKINS: W^m, 3697
ELDRED: Alfred, 3978
ELDRIDGE: Jos^h, 2673
ELLINS: Robt, 7446
ELLIOTT: And^w, 5960; Ge^o, 2379; Geo^e, 8108; Hen^y, 8598; Ja^s, 5613, 7395; Jno, 3304, 3710, 7756; John, 2746, 4593, 4766; Johnston, 7252; Robt, 7378; Simon, 4355; Thos, 1844, 4898; W^m, 2958, 6457, 7742; Willm, 1702
ELLIS: Chas, 3468, 4176; Hen^y, 3485; Ja^s, 3712, 4384; John, 5801; Maurice,

ELLIS (continued) 7680
ELLISON: W^m, 7611
ELPHICK: Walter, 3123
ELSDON: Ja^s, 8731
EMBERLEY: Henry, 8096
EMBLER: Jno, 1263
EMERSON: Ge^o, 878; Step^n, 6406
EMERY: Willm, 1546
EMMERSON: Ge^o, 4676
EMMETT: Benjn, 216, 3178; Ja^s, 5029
EMMINGS: Ja^s, 5226
EMSLEY: Jos^h, 4472
EMSWELL: John, 4757
ENDSOR: Jno, 1241
ENGLAND: Hen^y, 6407; Ja^s, 7056; W^m, 7382
ENGLISH: Thos, 5192
ENIES: Saml, 7682
ENNIS: Laughlin, 4809; Mich^l, 5284
ENOCK: Willm, 1269
ENOS: John, 5409
ENRIGHT: Matt^w, 981; Pat^k, 4328
ESDON: W^m, 7592
EVANS: And^w, 2578; Chas, 76; David, 7117; Enoch, 4519; Evan, 3906; Ge^o, 1027; George, 7969; Ja^s, 712; Rich^d, 3249; Saml, 5879; Solomon, 7276; Thos, 825, 2911, 4648, 6802, 7106; W^m, 2061; Willm, 6061
EVERETT: W^m, 913
EWENS: Chas, 912, 4748
EYRES: Thos, 3190
EZIAS: Ab^m, 2052
FAGAN: Ge^o, 7094
FAHEY: Jno, 5079; Mich^l, 7383
FAHY: Nich^s, 4628
FAIR: Edwd, 6256, 8670; Jno, 6322; John, 4632
FAIRBROTHER: Edwd, 6873; W^m, 8651
FAIRBURN: Willm, 8574
FAIRHURST: W^m, 239
FALANT: Derik, 5191; Dirk, 1137
FALCONER: Alex^r, 6198
FALIHE: John, 6558
FALING: Jno, 2010
FALKNER: Ja^s, 2037
FALLICK: Chas, 6685
FALLON: Ja^s, 1839, 6614, 8232; Jno, 2633; Martin, 7330; Thos, 5926
FANNING: Rich^d, 6408
FANNON: W^m, 6458; Willm, 1701
FARELL: Ja^s, 8403
FARELLY: Hugh, 4686
FARLARDE: Lewis, 5182
FARLEY: Ja^s, 6892; James, 4594; Pat^k, 6013; Willm, 4693
FARMER: Ge^o, 42; Rich^d, 1286; Thos, 5755
FARMSLEY: Matt^w, 2229

FARNELL: Jos^h, 2544, 6972
FARNEY: Ja^s, 6933
FARR: Hen^y, 3373; Nich^s, 8716; Saml, 8637; Thos, 6717
FARRAH: John, 6915; Saml, 5972
FARRALL: Edwd, 1944
FARRELL: Danl, 7612; Ja^s, 1834, 6571; Jno, 1478; Pat^k, 4337, 7219; Peter, 1975; Terence, 3381; Thos, 6377, 7218
FARROW: Jno, 6444
FAULKNER: Ja^s, 6337, 6771; Jno, 3305; Mich^l, 7062
FAWL: Bryan, 3526
FAY: Thos, 5159
FEAGAN: Jno, 4619
FEARIS: Ja^s, 4327
FEARMAN: Rich^d, 4827; Saml, 5030
FEATHERSTONE: Robt, 2115
FEE: Willm, 162
FEEHAN: John, 5479
FEELEY: John, 4188
FEENEY: Connor, 4481; Denis, 5656; Martin, 3487; Pat^k, 3521; Thos, 7331
FEENY: Mich^l, 4058, 5361
FEHRENSEN: Ernest, 2655
FELLOWS: Fra^s, 1901
FENN: W^m, 2110
FENTON: Robt, 8538; Willm, 969
FENWICK: Jno, 1376
FERDINAND: Jno, 231
FERGUSON: Hugh, 5440; Ja^s, 1398, 2971, 3223; Jno, 4077, 6145; Thos, 50, 1342, 2884; W^m, 1468, 5457, 8730; Willm, 5949, 6292
FERNANDO: Domingo, 2184
FERNE: Robt, 2143
FERNEY: Francis, 4595
FERRARA: Bicente, 2193
FERRARO: Donante, 8070
FEST: W^m, 5198
FIDDES: W^m, 2831
FIELD: Ge^o, 7788; Hen^y, 753; Mich^l, 5074
FIELDING: Ja^s, 4087; Jno, 741, 4426; Thos, 3461
FIELDS: Jno, 1287
FIGG: Jno, 7448
FILLACKY: Mich^l, 5199
FILLIS: Ja^s, 5307
FINAN: Ja^s, 1925
FINCH: W^m, 7683
FINDLEY: Mich^l, 2570
FINEGAN: Pat^k, 1710
FINERAN: Mich^l, 8771
FINHERTY: Jno, 2501
FINIGAN: Ja^s, 3796; Math^w, 304
FINLAYSON: Gavin, 8348; Jno, 5756
FINLEY: Robt, 3147
FINN: Jno, 951; Martin, 6359; Thos, 7253
FINNEGAN: Pat^k, 6514
FINNESS: Court, 3344

FINNIGAN: Francis, 7168; W^m, 5152; Willm, 1086
FIRTH: Jos^h, 7729
FISH: Jno, 7613
FISHER: Benjn, 8769; Danl, 2593; Fred^k, 640; Ja^s, 603, 4161; Jno, 4034, 4578; Marshall, 2945; Willm, 1087; Ziba, 3127
FISON: Jno, 1379
FITCHET: Dav^d, 1399
FITCHETT: Dav^d, 5534
FITZGERALD: Bern^d, 3086; Garrett, 1833, 6065, 6540; Ge^o, 8261; Hiram, 7684; Jno, 6429, 7904; Maur^e, 6273; Pat^k, 7614; Rich^d, 6714; Thos, 3737
FITZMAURICE: Danl, 2207
FITZPATRICK: Barney, 1808; Bern^d, 3306, 5038; Danl, 3524; Edwd, 7058; Hugh, 285, 1854, 6572; Ja^s, 4687; Jno, 1576; Mich^l, 4333, 7095; Pat^k, 3349, 7220; Philip, 180
FITZSIMMONS: Ja^s, 4060; Robt, 2861
FITZSIMONDS: Owen, 1641
FIZETT: Mich^l, 4330
FIZZALL: Tobias, 3859
FIZZELL: Jno, 7277
FLACK: Alex^r, 7447
FLAHERTY: Jno, 1073; Morgan, 7543; Pat^k, 3922
FLANAGAN: Jno, 1709, 8548; Mich^l, 6663
FLANDERS: Pat^k, 5090
FLANERY: Pat^k, 1950
FLANNIGAN: Jno, 1853
FLATTERY: Pat^k, 2976
FLECK: Willm, 4297
FLEET: Ge^o, 8358; Thos, 3142
FLEMING: Ge^o, 1995; H^y, 5391; Hen^y, 2021
FLEMMING: Edmond, 5091; Hen^y, 2062
FLETCHER: Rich^d, 2918; Saml, 7449; Thos, 1425, 3566, 5726; W^m, 560, 4147
FLINN: Matt^w, 7916; Thos, 6796
FLINT: Jos^h, 7656; Willm, 538
FLOOD: W^m, 5023
FLORENCE: Robert, 7170
FLOREY: Willm, 5889
FLYN: Mich^l, 727
FLYNN: Edmund, 2386; John, 43; Math^w, 4059; Peter, 4597; Step^n, 4833; Thos, 3869
FLYNNE: Ja^s, 4362
FOLEY: Danl, 6354; Fra^s, 5382; Jno, 1201, 1377, 2408; John, 5521; Mich^l, 7083; Thos, 5595
FOLLENUS: John, 5581
FOODY: William, 3620
FOOT: Jno, 3293
FORBES: Jno, 6278; John, 8301, 8556; Thomas, 6738;

FORBES (continued)
W^m, 2206
FORD: Fra^s, 4884; Ja^s, 345, 3609; Jos^h, 4765; Mich^l, 664, 4278, 6385; Pat^k, 4947
FORDER: Rich^d, 443
FOREHAM: Jeremiah, 3424
FORREST: R^d H^y, 3700; William, 7970
FORSTER: Hen^y, 4100; Jno, 5896; Robt, 2953
FORSYTH: Adam, 1932, 6574
FORSYTHE: Ja^s, 8345; Thos, 8224
FOSTER: Benjn, 3437; David, 8729; Hethington, 8045; Isaac, 945, 4807; Ja^s, 2830; Jno, 7, 5543, 7332, 7685; Jos^h, 6917; Robt, 46, 2886
FOULKES: Hugh, 6924
FOULSTONE: Thos, 1015, 4936
FOURMIDGE: Saml, 7264
FOWLER: Denis, 7278; Ge^o, 2243; Ge^e, 8050; John, 3686; Nathl, 821, 4662; Thos, 282
FOWLES: Edwd, 242
FOX: Chas, 2170; Jno, 897; Luke, 2777; Martin, 3480; Pat^k, 1504; Thos, 8723; W^m, 4427
FOXCROFT: Ge^o, 1395
FOY: Pat^k, 1919, 6573
FOYAR: Walter, 3157
FOYLE: Martin, 8200
FRANCIS: Jno, 1242, 5411, 7686, 7787; Robt, 5987; W^m, 4010, 7068
FRANKLAND: Ge^o, 2594
FRANKLIN: Jno, 598; Rich^d, 1556
FRANSHAM: Thos, 5293
FRASER: Alex^r, 3166, 3175, 4321, 7305; Fotheringham, 5636; Hugh, 2118; Ja^s, 2458, 6274, 6711, 8753; Jno, 883, 3152, 4672, 8763; Robt, 1402, 5532; Simon, 8014; Thos, 5795; W^m, 2119; Willm, 8304
FRAYER: W^m, 2559
FRAZER: Alex^r, 699; Ja^s, 391, 6955; Saml, 4753
FREDERICK: Antoine, 1102
FREEMAN: Jno, 4111; Jos^h, 5020; Joseph, 7995
FREER: Robt, 3486
FRELOGGAN: Rich^d, 8798
FRENCH: Charles, 8002; Peter, 4688; Thos, 3807
FREND: Jno, 3850
FRIANDO: Jos^h, 2186
FRIEND: W^m, 2114
FRISSELL: Jno, 7107
FRITH: Robt, 2839
FROMOW: George, 3374
FROOD: Mich^l, 2305
FROST: W^m, 6149
FRUISH: And^w, 3322
FRY: H^y, 5337; Jos^h, 8185; W^m, 3321

FRYER: Willm, 389
FUDGE: Azariah, 3377
FULLAM: Peter, 515
FULLAN: Peter, 512
FULLER: Jno, 4430; Robt, 1014, 8422; Willm, 3421
FULTON: Ja^s, 5252; Jno, 7743
FURLONG: James, 3993, 5633
FURMAGE: Ja^s, 4955
GABBETT: John, 4760
GABRIEL: Ja^s, 6695
GADD: Willm, 3420
GAFFNEY: Bern^d, 4242
GAHAGAN: Mich^l, 1199
GAILEY: Jos^h, 7688
GAINER: Thos, 561
GAIR: Jno, 6307
GALARDI: Ant^y, 1113
GALARIDI: Ant^y, 5170
GALES: Robt, 1843, 6575
GALLAGHER: Chas, 8522; Denis, 7789; Ferigle, 5110; Fran^s, 6330; George, 5134; Hugh, 3087; Ja^s, 5111, 8435; Jno, 887, 3577; Neil, 1325; Pat^k, 6859; Roger, 4761; Thos, 3701
GALLANT: Robt, 1498
GALLERY: Thos, 3076
GALTON: Reuben, 2347
GALVIN: Ja^s, 3234; Jno, 6830; John, 6261; W^m, 1018
GAMBERG: Jno, 7067
GAMBLE: Robt, 5260
GAMBLES: Ja^s, 4353
GAME: Ant^y, 814
GAMMAGE: Willm, 64
GANDY: Jno, 1471; Rich^d, 760, 4470
GANNON: Jno, 780
GANT: Ge^o, 1161; Ge^e, 5238
GARDEN: W^m, 7450
GARDINER: Jno, 4505; Peter, 8235; Robt, 8866
GARDNER: And^w, 3108; Dav^d, 2537; Ja^s, 3378, 8844; Jno, 4035; Walter, 953
GARFORTH: Ja^s, 3116
GARLAND: Willm, 5962
GARNER: Chas, 3979
GARNETT: Willm, 2778
GARRALL: Ge^o, 2209
GARRETT: Jno, 7134
GARRETY: Ja^s, 2844
GARRIGAN: Owen, 7451
GARSIDE: W^m, 6831
GARVEY: Corn^s, 1693; Ja^s, 96, 2926; Pat^k, 2126
GARVIN: Hugh, 915; Ja^s, 8884
GASCOIGNE: Ja^s, 8505
GASCOYNE: Thos, 229
GAST: Antoni, 1531
GASTON: Saml, 8701
GATES: Ja^s, 4236; Jos^h, 2360, 8109; Saml, 2542
GAVIN: Jno, 6129; John, 1616
GAWKE: Ja^s, 317

GAY: Jno, 7254; W^m, 3863
GAYER: Fred^k, 1105
GAYNOR: Pat^k, 5024
GAZEY: Jno, 697
GEALE: Gladwin, 7453
GEAR: Jesse, 5003
GEARNON: Ja^s, 7333
GEBHARDT: Willm, 1119
GEDDIS: Robt, 8360
GEE: H^y, 4814; John, 1644, 6132; Thos, 2022, 6766
GEELHOET: Emman^l, 1111
GEERIN: Mich^l, 6323
GELLOW: Ja^s, 2384
GENTLEMAN: Jno, 5766
GEORGE: Jno, 495; Peter, 2523; Robson Cruise, 7262; Thos, 7744; Willm, 394; William, 5270
GERBER: Carl, 1148
GEURONE: Bern^d, 2046
GIBBINS: Jno, 5213; Thos, 7832
GIBBONS: Ja^s, 1052; Pat^k, 1197; Patrick, 7971; Rich^d, 3880
GIBBS: Hen^y, 1268; Henry, 5430; John, 8015, 8932; Pat^k, 3482
GIBLON: Pat^k, 1363
GIBNEY: Bartholomew, 3649
GIBSON: Ja^s, 6652; Jno, 1881; John, 6603; Robt, 8529; Saml, 2674; W^m, 5113, 5526
GIBZAN: John, 2267
GIFFORD: Ja^s, 2420, 8111
GILES: Edwd, 5654; Willm, 8765
GILL: Jno, 7544; Thos, 2099; Thomas, 5599
GILLAWAY: Mich^l, 2528
GILLERAN: Jno, 7615
GILLESPIE: Den^s, 903, 4728; Edwd, 301; Ja^s, 8593
GILLETT: Jno, 1068
GILLEY: John, 2739
GILLIES: Ja^s, 6719
GILLIGAN: Hugh, 905, 4725; Ja^s, 5289; John, 3629
GILLIS: Ja^s, 5405; Peter, 143
GILLON: Alex^r, 532; Jno, 1954
GILMAR: Saml, 4889
GILMORE: Andrew, 5749; Ge^e, 6432; Hugh, 5593; Jno, 6328, 8324; Saml, 7221
GILMOUR: Jno, 3179
GILROY: Pat^k, 656
GILSON: Ja^s, 604, 4140
GILSTAIN: Arth^r, 889
GILZAN: John, 7051
GINN: Jno, 1477
GIRLING: Ge^e, 5660; Jno, 3319
GIRMAN: Ja^s, 5017
GITTINGS: Tim^y, 592, 4160
GITTINS: Thos, 6819
GIVENS: And^w, 2641, 8202
GLANCEY: William, 7947
GLASPOLE: Mich^l, 7306

INDEX 333

GLASS: Robt, 2832
GLAVEY: Peter, 3362
GLEESON: John, 8903
GLEN: Ja^s, 5825
GLENN: Matt^w, 5443
GLENNY: Ja^s, 8192
GLINN: Ja^s, 4629
GLOVER: Jno, 6634; W^m, 1319, 5464
GOBLE: Geo^e, 4292
GODBY: Robt, 192
GODFRAY: Edwd, 3695
GODFREY: Thos, 1040, 4983; W^m, 3587; Willm, 5367
GODIE: Jos^h, 1127
GODWIN: Thos, 7790
GOFF: Thos, 2595
GOING: John, 4556
GOLDING: Giles, 2675; Pat^k, 4314; Richard, 4536
GOLDRICK: Terc^e, 2558
GOLDSMITH: Chas, 5491; Ge^o, 1053; Willm, 8268
GOLDSWORTHY: Hen^y, 7084
GOLLEDGE: Thos, 2677
GOMMO: Peter, 2045
GOODAL: Jno, 8255
GOODALL: Ja^s, 5092
GOODE: Tim^y, 3426
GOODENOUGH: W^m, 2588, 6980
GOODEY: Ja^s, 5350
GOODFELLOW: Robt, 3864
GOODGER: Benjn, 1871
GOODING: Jno, 51; John, 2877
GOODLAND: Ja^s, 2218
GOODMAN: Charles, 8016; Rich^d, 693; W^m, 2257
GOODWIN: Arthur, 4647; Jno, 7545; Luke, 1350; Willm, 4860
GORDAN: John, 5340
GORDON: Hen^y, 9; Hugh, 1409; Pat^k, 2639; Robt, 7616; St^n, 6289; Thos, 2843; Willm, 8929
GORMAN: Connor, 3874; Darby, 7869; Hugh, 6257; Ja^s, 4811; Jno, 2546, 6213; Mich^l, 7334; Pat^k, 3227, 5125; Thomas, 7169
GORMLEY: Hugh, 1842; Ja^s, 8699
GORMONLY: Tim^y, 4436
GOSLING: Ja^s, 4623
GOSS: John, 5336
GOTT: Jno, 2000
GOUCH: Ja^s, 2596
GOUDE: Rich^d, 7689
GOUDIE: Geo^e, 7910
GOULD: Jno, 473; John, 4419
GOULDING: Jno, 663
GOW: Jno, 7687
GOWDY: Jno, 8475
GRACE: Jno, 2502
GRADY: Denis, 4363
GRAHAM: Dav^d, 855; Geo^e, 6093, 6657; Hen^y, 5649; Ja^s, 8291; Jno, 6433; Jos^h, 3131; Peter, 8726; Robt, 622, 1189, 4204; Thos, 7096; W^m, 2064,

GRAHAM (continued) 5853, 6164; Willm, 8500
GRANGE: Edmond, 6227
GRANGER: W^m, 2023
GRANNARY: Philip, 6200
GRANT: Chas, 8663; Dav^d, 1962, 6576; David, 6294; Don^d, 8479; Ja^s, 8880; Jno, 1378, 1443, 3417; John, 5540, 5810; W^m, 501, 6226, 6810
GRANTIN: Pat^k, 7452
GRASSHAM: James, 7981
GRAVES: Ja^s, 638, 3497; Phi^p, 1878
GRAY: Arch^d, 6197; Geo^e, 5292; Ja^s, 4276, 7142; Jno, 2415, 2431, 7210; John, 7948, 8112; Owen, 8899; Simon, 2459; Thos, 1252; W^m, 4499
GREADY: Jno, 6143
GREEN: Danl, 154; Edwd, 1088; Gregory, 8404; Harrison, 5290; Ja^s, 1557; Jno, 1494, 3581, 6375; John, 3536, 3822, 6040, 8462; Mich^l, 5300; W^m, 1047, 3103, 3135; Wilby, 278; Willm, 4996
GREENACRE: Jno, 7263
GREENE: Ja^s, 4465
GREENFIELD: Ja^s, 1223
GREENLY: Jno, 2288; John, 8181
GREENSMITH: Fra^s, 2139
GREENWALZ: Chas, 5149
GREENWAY: Willm, 8907
GREENWOOD: Jos^h, 2618; Robt, 2905
GREER: Ja^s, 7791
GREGGETT: Rich^d, 8429
GREGORY: Jno, 4385; Jos^h, 1031
GREHAM: John, 7023
GRENNIER: Willm, 2144
GRENWALTZ: Chas, 1079
GRESHON: Edwd, 8555
GRIBBON: Neil, 433, 3827
GRICE: Jno, 5650
GRIEF: Henry, 4880
GRIERSON: John, 5563
GRIEVE: Jno, 6300; William, 7986
GRIFFEN: Willm, 149
GRIFFIN: Ja^s, 2954; Mich^l, 2676; Pat^k, 7006; W^m, 2296; Willm, 4768
GRIFFITH: Edwd, 4574
GRIFFITHS: Dav^d, 8805; Edwd, 2087, 6905; Elea, 82; Jos^h, 113, 3012; Rich^d, 735; W^m, 5104
GRIGG: Robt, 8504
GRIGGLISTONE: Jno, 6813
GRIGSBY: Ja^s, 7792
GRILLS: John, 7032
GRIMES: Edwd, 2871; James, 6009; Willm, 956, 1700, 6484
GRIMLEY: Rich^d, 3348
GRIMSTEAD: Willm, 8587
GRIMSTON: John, 4974

GRINDLEY: Thos, 2841
GRINSTEAD: Robert, 8017
GRIPTON: Robt, 2753
GROOM: John, 4929
GROVES: W^m, 4326; Willm, 696
GRUBB: Chas, 5266; W^m, 4981; Willm, 1037
GRUBERT: Art^r, 6512
GUART: Ja^s, 329
GUDGEON: W^m, 7730
GUEST: Edwd, 3848; Jno, 328, 1071, 1231; John, 4612; Thos, 2403, 8110
GUILE: Thos, 682, 4302
GULLIVER: Jno, 3388
GUMMER: George, 5632
GUNN: Alex^r, 5481; Angus, 2014; Don^d, 2128, 6280; Ja^s Mich^l, 4374; Jno, 1391; John, 3056, 5793, 7989; Marcus, 4815; Peter, 8018; Robt, 8456; Ter^e, 4721; Thos, 899; W^m, 7069
GUNNING: Geo^e, 8581; Thos, 1046
GURK: Chas de, 2865
GURLEY: George, 7146
GURNETT: Geo^e, 8276
GURNEY: W^m, 5031
GURREN: Mich^l, 4061
GURRIVIN: Jno, 7917
GUTTERIDGE: Ja^s, 3813
GUTTERSON: Robt, 2912
GUY: John, 2985; W^m, 6703; Wm Edwd, 4976
HACK: Jno, 1474; John, 5957; W^m, 3610
HACKER: W^m, 7564
HADDICK: Jno, 2678
HADDIEAN: Jno, 6212
HADE: Willm, 3256
HADLEY: John, 8019
HAGAN: Edwd, 2938; Nathl, 8647
HAGGAN: Owen, 398
HAGGARTY: Ja^s, 8366
HAGUE: Matt^w, 928
HAINES: Geo^e, 3163
HAINSWORTH: Fra^s, 2264; Ja^s, 3351
HAIRBOTTLE: Rich^d, 8719
HALES: Edwd, 4549; Jno, 206; John, 3187
HALFPENNY: Chas, 3165
HALKETT: Thos, 639, 4283
HALL: Chas, 6445; Ge^o, 165; Geo^e, 3042; Harris, 8893; Ja^s, 5236; Jno, 618, 1041, 2637, 3460, 7076, 7222; John, 2748, 4201, 5740; Jos^h, 2204, 6918; Joseph, 8139; Robt, 3016; Thos, 59, 184, 2900, 3897; W^m, 3980, 3990, 5331; Willm, 182, 1558, 3035
HALLAGHAN: Jno, 3489
HALLANAN: Danl, 1691
HALLIBURN: Edwd, 3280
HALLIDAY: Ja^s, 8349; Thos, 3109

HALLIGAN: Fra^s, 3559
HALLINAN: Martin, 6704
HALLS: Jno, 3579; Jos^h, 4394
HALLUM: Jno, 8425
HALPIN: Edwd, 7335
HALSEY: Joseph, 7171
HALY: Thos, 2368
HAMER: Robt, 4550
HAMILL: Arthur, 7144; Pat^k, 4520
HAMILTON: Angus, 1438, 5813; Ge^o, 856; Ge^e, 3455, 8374; Hugh, 1196, 5365; Ja^s, 1381, 4552, 5779, 5807, 5910, 7793; Jno, 5993, 8545; Pat^k, 5992; Robt, 635, 4280; W^m, 2986, 6021; Wm Gunn, 5845; Willm, 817
HAMMILL: Ge^o, 5194; Ja^s, 5308
HAMMOND: Jno, 3427, 6401
HAMON: And^w, 3323
HAMPE: Fred^k, 223
HAMPTON: Edwd Jno, 6378
HAMSON: W^m, 4375
HANAHAN: Pat^k, 7622
HANAN: John, 2895
HANDCOCK: Jno, 7593; Robt, 3923, 4183
HANDIBO: Jno, 3324
HANDLON: Hugh, 3983
HANDS: Chas, 3325; Edwd, 5068
HANKINS: Thos, 669
HANLEY: Mich^l, 6091
HANLON: Bryan, 4618; Mark, 3824; Mich^l, 8347; Sack, 5552
HANNA: Geo^e, 3733; Henry, 8590
HANNAGH: Step^n, 7336
HANNAH: Jno, 3838, 8675
HANNAN: Anth^y, 1680
HANNEY: Jno, 3908
HANNOPHY: Farrel, 8906
HANRAHAN: Fra^s, 4092; Pat^k, 6370
HANRAN: Fra^s, 4093
HANSON: George, 3621
HANTON: W^m, 1403; Willm, 5541
HANWAY: Hugh, 5984
HARAGAN: Thos, 1891, 6579
HARBISON: Dav^d, 6741; W^m, 6047
HARBOUR: Willm, 6793
HARDIMAN: Jno, 3817
HARDING: Jos^h, 562, 4148
HARDMAN: Abel, 5900
HARDWATER: Willm, 1492
HARDWICK: W^m, 7870
HARDY: Benjn, 1532; Jno, 5882; John, 8904; Jos^h, 5970; Moses, 2992; Robt, 2620; Saml, 2086; Thomas, 8739; Willm, 2241
HARE: John, 4818
HARES: Benjn, 667
HARFIGH: Edwd, 894, 4679
HARGRAVES: Ja^s, 6791
HARGROVE: Jno, 2038

HARKIN: Robt, 1898
HARKINS: Jno, 1968, 5459
HARLERY: James, 7949
HARLEY: Thos, 2445, 2897, 8082
HARLING: Hen^y, 1174; Seth, 7384
HARMAN: Jno, 2422
HARPER: Alexander, 5743; Ephram, 2892; James, 6041
HARRAD: William, 5139
HARRAGE: Ja^s, 1514, 1583
HARRIMAN: Richard, 7943
HARRINGTON: Corn^s, 1856, 3483, 6577; Dennis, 83; Edwd, 2679; Pat^k, 3477; Thos, 3512
HARRIS: Chas, 3407; Ge^o, 1785; Ge^e, 5281, 6460; George, 5715; Ja^s, 911, 1043; Jno, 1408, 2145, 6380; John, 5568; Rich^d, 2065, 2312, 6774, 8081; Saml, 7794; Thos, 2680, 3341, 7565, 8233; W^m, 4454
HARRISON: Ge^o, 163, 1538; James, 593; Jno, 164, 7454; Jos^h, 624; Rich^d, 3510; Robt, 3702
HARROLD: Thos, 906, 4723
HART: Edwd, 2664, 4185; Malachi, 3749; Thos, 1521; W^m, 4233, 5898
HARTE: Christian, 2453; Thos, 1204
HARTJE: Chr^r, 8144
HARTLETT: Edwd, 318
HARTLEY: Chr^r, 8317; Jabez, 1259; Jno, 3527; John, 8526; Roland, 3707; Rowland, 390
HARTNELL: Mich^l, 5075
HARTNETT: John, 3994
HARVEY: Geo^e, 4950; Hugh, 1326; Jos^h, 744, 4444; Moses, 1560; Saml, 7223; W^m, 6446; Willm, 8901
HARWOOD: Jno, 7093
HASELTINE: Jos^h Nelson, 3560
HASKETT: W^m, 1855
HASKINS: Robt, 383, 3706
HASLEM: Peter, 2749
HASLETT: George, 5327; W^m, 2311; Willm, 8080
HASPLINK: Hen^y, 5193
HASTINGS: Jno, 6699
HASTY: Ja^s, 3693
HATCH: W^m, 4836; William, 7993
HAUGHTON: Jno, 5013; W^m, 6345
HAUGHY: Saml, 5069
HAVERTY: John, 4744
HAWKE: Rich^d, 3334
HAWKES: Jno, 1072
HAWKINGS: H^y, 7063
HAWKINS: Jos^h, 4088; Mich^l, 525, 4076; Robt, 1306
HAWKSWORTH: Jno, 2815
HAWTHORNE: Jno, 1729

HAY: Alex^r, 8573; Dav^d, 8373; Ja^s, 5981; Willm, 1372
HAYES: James, 7932; Jno, 2133, 7918; Pat^k, 7279; Patrick, 4588; Rich^d, 2867; Thos, 1608
HAYFIELD: Adam, 2806
HAYLOCK: Thos, 4942
HAYNES: Jos^h, 2051
HAYS: Moses, 5255
HAYSTEAD: Jno, 4391
HAYWOOD: Jno, 1802, 6517, 7795; Job, 2925; W^m, 851
HAZELL: W^m, 5988
HAZELTON: Jno, 1884
HAZLETON: Jno, 6623
HEADY: Robt, 546
HEAKE: And^w, 7119
HEALEY: Jno, 2624; Mich^l, 2784; Thos, 2613
HEALY: Edwd, 2820; Jno, 3232; Mich^l, 5326; Pat^k, 5352, 5388
HEANY: Nich^s, 5360; Pat^k, 2977
HEAPE: Jno, 6808
HEAPHY: Willm, 6421
HEARD: Benjn, 121
HEARN: W^m, 3582
HEATH: Jos^h, 5503; W^m, 2270, 6123, 7030
HEATLEY: Saml, 4144; Thos, 8860
HEATON: David, 7598
HEATTEY: Saml, 563
HEAZLEY: Jos^h, 2503
HEDDERWICK: Jno, 8537
HEFFERAN: Pat^k, 3721
HEFFERNON: Jno, 1089
HEFFERON: Jno, 2681; John, 7042
HEGARTY: Garrett, 6832
HEGGS: Ja^s, 7765
HEIGHLAND: W^m, 5946
HEIGUE: Robt, 651
HEINECKE: Hen^y, 1133
HELFERICK: Jno, 679
HELFRICK: Jno, 4303
HELMER: Jno, 8142
HELSDEN: Josiah, 7994
HELY: Pat^k, 3513
HEMMING: Jno, 8773
HEMPHILL: John, 6139
HENBERGH: John, 4613
HENDERSON: Dunc^n, 2047; Gavin, 4951; Ge^o, 1445; Geo^e, 5830, 5838, 6299; Ja^s, 3445; Jno, 513, 516, 4014, 4488, 7007, 7768; Jos^h, 232; Thos, 8474
HENDRICK: Mich^l, 1895, 6580; Patrick, 7151; W^m, 605
HENDRICKSON: And^w, 1145, 5175
HENEGAN: Luke, 2147
HENKELL: Willm, 222
HENLEY: Isaac, 1222; Wm Jos^h, 5594
HENNARD: Geo^e, 8335

INDEX 335

HENNESSEY: Ja^s, 5901; Jno, 1742, 4735
HENNESSY: Barth^w, 3764; Jno, 896, 6485
HENRION: Fra^s, 5186
HENRY: Hugh, 1883, 6578; Ja^s, 2534, 8518; Patrick, 4411; Robt, 2504, 8287; Valent^e, 731; Willm, 6279
HENSHALL: Jno, 907, 4727
HENTHORN: Ja^s, 6726
HENTICOTT: Ja^s, 2402
HEPWOOD: John, 2899
HERBERTSON: Robt, 8611
HERDSMAN: Rich^d, 2756
HEREMAN: Robt, 7566
HERLEY: Nicholas, 6170
HERLIHY: Jno, 2721
HERRALD: Pat^k, 8838
HERRING: Jno, 4509
HERRITAGE: W^m, 4737
HERRON: Saml, 3333; W^m, 6987
HERTMAN: Ja^s, 3816
HERVEY: Robt, 312
HESLER: Jno Hen^y, 2146
HESSE: Conrad, 1146; Fred^k, 1116
HETT: James, 3622
HEULT: Thos, 8278
HEUSE: Jno, 5667
HEWER: Chas, 7455
HEWERCLINE: William, 7181
HEWETT: Hen^y, 7224; Joseph, 4530
HEWINGS: Jno, 1246
HEWITT: Jos^h, 5651
HEWS: W^m, 5684
HEWSON: Willm, 274, 3345
HEYLIGER: Fred^k, 2191, 8171
HEYLOTT: Jno, 114; John, 3010
HIBBERD: Jno, 3307
HIBBS: Robt, 2341
HICKEN: Jno, 7225
HICKESSEY: Thos, 4733
HICKEY: Ja^s, 4710; Michael, 7155; W^m, 3778
HICKIE: Jno, 2202
HICKLIN: W^m, 3206
HICKS: Ge^o, 2505; Robt, 2849; Wm Thomas, 8882
HICKSON: Jno, 7692
HIGGINS: Carbro, 929, 4802; Fra^s, 4219, 5351; James, 4598; John, 3026, 3881; Mich^l, 6165; Pat^k, 7617; W^m, 2031
HIGGINSON: Rich^d, 452
HIGGS: Ja^s, 4921; Jno, 2334, 8132
HIGH: Benjn, 52, 2882; Jno, 3956
HIGHFIELD: Thos, 654, 4275
HILL: And^w, 1863; Chr^r, 6956; Christ^r, 2506; Edwd, 4548; Ja^s, 6684, 7456; James, 6739; Jno, 4982, 6363; Jos^h, 2089, 3046; Thos, 195, 4778, 8928
HILLAN: Edwd, 6067

HILLHOUSE: David, 7766
HILLIARD: Jno, 2226, 8157; W^m, 2552
HILLIER: Jno, 2369
HILLIS: John, 8680
HILLMAN: W^m, 8846
HILLS: Jos^h, 2117
HILLUM: John, 8592
HILTON: Beld, 4868; Jno, 834, 1370; Saml, 845
HINCHLIFF: William, 4587
HINDLE: Hen^y, 7567; Step^n, 403
HINDS: Edwd, 3150; Ja^s, 4849
HINDSON: Jno, 4261
HINE: Jno, 320
HINES: John, 4762; W^m, 7255
HINSELL: Ja^s, 137
HIRD: Edwd H., 4521
HIRST: Jere^h, 8453
HISCOCK: Ja^s, 8618
HISCOTT: Rich^d, 5728
HISLOP: Alexander, 3630
HOARE: Jno, 2682, 7049
HOBBS: Willm, 352
HOBLEY: Jno, 7618; Saml, 450
HOCKADAY: Thos, 4310
HODDER: Chas, 3243
HODGE: W^m, 3509
HODGES: Jos^h, 4907
HODGKINSON: Willm, 8584
HOGAN: Danl, 14; David, 5301; Jno, 5214; Mich^l, 1744
HOGDEN: Robt, 227
HOGG: Hugh, 2532, 6977; Jno, 3924; Robt, 2840
HOLBURN: Edwd, 2765
HOLDING: Ja^s, 3352; Rich^d, 1261, 5415; Richd Harvey, 3308; Robt, 1271; Willm, 1533
HOLDSWORTH: Jos^h, 4604
HOLGATE: Jos^h, 4579 Jno, 7911; Pat^k, 194; W^m, 448, 2597
HOLLIDAY: Jno, 957; W^m, 4135
HOLLIS: Thos, 5428
HOLLIWELL: Thos, 6014
HOLLOWAY: Ja^s, 7385; Saml, 2845
HOLLOWELL: W^m, 3773
HOLMAN: Ja^s, 3037
HOLMES: Benjn, 183; Fra^s, 1248, 7796; Francis, 6172; Ja^s, 7189; Jno, 3473, 3745, 5657, 7457; Moses, 2054, 6764; Pat^k, 1788, 6459; Phi^p, 1801; Thos, 1737
HOLSBY: Jno, 4863
HOLT: Chas, 4783; Rich^d, 2586, 6978; Step^n, 4747
HOLTON: Ja^s, 4694
HOLTZAPPEL: Jno, 1132; John, 1150
HOMER: Thos, 1606, 1712
HOOD: Ja^s, 8787; Peter, 8752; Richard, 5718; Willm, 8354

HOOK: Ja^s, 2590, 8655; William, 7172
HOOPER: John, 73, 2903
HOPEWELL: And^w, 930, 4803
HOPKINS: Barth^w, 6409; Jer^h, 2060; Jno, 8862
HOPKINSON: Jon^n, 4245; Thos, 4938
HOPKINSS: Ge^oe, 6789
HOPLEY: W^m, 3507
HOPWOOD: Thos, 3014, 3965
HORAN: John, 2907; Mich^l, 6674
HORGAN: Thos, 8245
HORN: Thos, 4571
HORNBY: Geoffrey, 5500; Jno, 2216, 8155; Mich^l, 6412; W^m, 5387
HORNE: Ja^s, 8236
HORNER: Alex^r, 1753, 6486; Willm, 8355
HORNIBROOK: Augustus, 1057
HORSALL: Jno, 2581, 6957
HORSHAM: Abr^m, 5250
HORTON: Jno, 849; Thos, 4946
HOSEA: John, 5150
HOSIE: And^w, 1390, 5538
HOSSACK: Don^d, 4486
HOSSOP: Edwd, 6025
HOSTLER: W^m, 5839
HOUGHTON: W^m, 6730
HOUIE: Willm, 8536
HOUSE: John, 7950
HOUSIGO: Jno, 6410
HOUSTON: Arthur, 8735; Robt, 6246
HOWARD: Edwin, 3584; Hen^y, 8378; Jno, 8485; Jos^h, 4967
HOWARTH: Thos, 3898; W^m, 6679, 8645; Willm, 8897
HOWE: John, 3041; Jos^h, 4695; W^m, 7691; Willm, 8445
HOWELL: H^y, 3128; Jno, 1054, 5001; Thomas, 3631
HOWERTH: W^m, 338
HOWES: Ge^oe, 7657; Robt, 7079
HOWIE: Ge^oe, 8615; Peter, 6195
HOWLING: John, 4885
HOWS: Thomas, 7972
HOWSON: Fra^s, 159
HOYLE: Henry, 5574; Jno, 7458
HUBBARD: Hen^y, 6339; Jno, 1289
HUCKSTEPP: Chas, 2824
HUDSON: Ja^s, 1747; Richard, 5745
HUEY: Jno, 1413, 5610
HUFF: Jno, 2478
HUFFA: Jno, 7693
HUFFMAN: And^w, 8069
HUFFTON: Rich^d, 1527
HUGGARD: Willm, 3614
HUGHES: Bern^d, 1832, 1986, 6541; Hen^y, 1356, 3808, 5309; Ja^s, 1366, 2383; Jno, 196, 2683, 3203, 5504; John, 2750; Martin,

INDEX

HUGHES (continued) 526, 4078, 7690; Pat^k, 5607, 5780; Thos, 627, 4021, 4177, 4211; W^m, 1867, 4751
HUGHSTON: Jno, 8588
HULBERT: Thos, 7459
HULL: Chas, 2224; Ja^s, 3839; Thos, 1523
HULME: Ja^s, 1781, 4241
HUME: Thos, 8667
HUMERSTON: Lyman, 8065
HUMM: Danl, 3612
HUMPHREY: Thos, 2684
HUMPHRIES: And^w, 1559; Robt, 1719; Thos, 7050
HUMPHRYS: Pat^k, 2685, 7039
HUNT: Absalom, 7871; Benjn, 4308; Chas, 713, 4346, 7835; Geo^e, 4828; Ja^s, 3440; Jno, 2306, 3205; John, 7990, 8079; Jos^h, 4311; Robt, 5385
HUNTER: And^w, 8808; Dav^d, 3410; Geo^o, 2598; Jos^h, 8187; Peter, 1340; Thos, 1307; Willm, 1375
HURCHINS: Jno, 1058
HURD: Edwd, 430, 3757
HURDLEY: Willm, 809
HURLEY: Ja^s, 4897; Jer^h, 217, 5305; Jno, 2232; Tim^y, 5918
HURST: Edwd, 1534, 6017; Jno, 7460; John, 7937, 8405, 8554; Jos^h, 2053; Thos, 1255; Willm, 880
HUSBAND: Thos, 1025
HUSSEY: Robt, 1249
HUSTON: David, 7226; Ja^s, 4067
HUTCHESON: Jno, 2622
HUTCHINS: Robt, 4507
HUTCHINSON: Chas, 3525; Hugh, 1761, 6487
HUTTON: Jno, 7568; Peter, 6304; Willm, 4442
HYLAND: Geo, 1522
HYNDES: Edwd, 674
IBBETSON: Thos, 3104
IKIN: Willm, 6748
IMBRIE: Alex^r, 497
IMLAY: Ja^s, 7297
IMPETT: Jno, 4440
INCE: Sylvester, 630
INGHAM: Edwd, 8578; Isaac, 3957
INGRAM: And^w, 6180; Jno, 1365; Thos, 5887; Thomas, 6262
INSELL: Saml, 3849
INSKIP: James, 4599
INVERNESS: Thos, 1429, 5790
IRONS: Ja^s, 8286
IRVEN: And^w, 1367
IRVINE: Alex^r, 8847; Rich^d, 4577
IRVING: Jno, 6865
IRVINS: Martin, 3326
IRWIN: Arch^d, 4871; H^y, 5923; Ja^s, 1175, 7797; Jno, 1007; Jos^h, 8630; Rich^d, 4098; Robt, 1274;

IRWIN (continued) 8851; Thos, 21, 4712, 5939, 7130; W^m, 258, 3265; Willm, 1751
ISAAC: Ja^s, 2428
ISAACS: Isaac, 5707; W^m, 7619
IVES: Jno, 6258
IZZARD: Ja^s, 3943
JACK: Hugh, 7959
JACKSON: Abr^m, 6333; Chas, 8920; Fra^s, 1876; Geo, 2869; Geo^e, 7097; Hen^y, 77; Ja^s, 1526; Jno, 2846; John, 5701, 7071; Jos^h, 3110; Robt, 8915; Step^n, 4262; Thos, 8547; W^m, 799, 5256; Willm, 846, 4563
JACOB: Raphael, 4567
JACOBS: Robt, 5202; Thomas, 7951
JACQUES: Thos, 3138
JAMES: H^y, 7030; Hen^y, 2714; Henry, 4180; Hugh, 2642, 8212; Jos^h, 4342; Math^w, 3413; W^m, 6712
JAMESON: Pat^k, 4117; Thos, 5189
JAMIESON: And^w, 6229; Jno, 8289
JANKOWITZ: Wortzech, 1113
JARDINE: W^m, 6530
JARVIS: Ja^s, 2180; W^m, 5586
JASCOITZ: Jacob, 5178
JEFFERYS: John, 5049
JEFFREY: Dan^{lo}, 7872
JEFFREYS: Jno, 120
JEFFRY: John, 8408
JENKINS: Alex^r, 3416; Ja^s, 3414; Thos, 8790; W^m, 4199, 7620
JENNERY: Zach^a, 860
JENNINGS: Jno, 7873; Pat^k, 6833, 7851; Redm^d, 4323; W^m, 7874
JEPSON: John, 1472; Willm, 4664
JERUTTA: And^w, 357
JESSMAN: John, 4498
JESSOP: John, 5403
JOBE: Ja^s, 1646
JOHN: Dav^d, 808, 4610
JOHNSON: Absalom, 7893; Alex^r, 8264; Benjn, 90, 2944; Chas, 6189; Edwd, 970, 1495; Ephr^m, 1290, 5425; Geo^e, 3098; Hen^y Chas, 6853; Ja^s, 2972; Jno, 6715, 6834; John, 2100; Rich^d, 2932; Simon, 4798; Thos, 2799, 7386, 8364
JOHNSTON: Dav^d, 998; Geo^e, 3685; Ja^s, 7594, 8650; Jno, 505, 2166, 4013, 7280, 7369, 7798, 8379; John, 8454, 8780; Saml, 3432, 7337; Thos, 3242; W^m, 7621; Willm, 5370; William, 7983
JOHNSTONE: And^w, 5114

JOICE: Austin, 1207
JOLLEY: Jno, 7302
JOLLY: Hen^y, 932
JONES: Ant^y, 2198; Chas, 7461; Danl, 130, 1462, 5932, 7570; Edwd, 1806, 6518; Ge^o, 2614; George, 5702; Hen^y, 3088; Ja^s, 99, 1515, 1584, 2936; James, 7980; Jno, 660, 862, 987, 1516, 1585, 1605, 2424, 2660, 5998; John, 8113; Jos^h, 2465, 8710; Justinian, 4698; Noah, 4006; Rees, 4514; Rich^d, 2473, 3552, 7569; Robert, 7227; Saml, 384; Silvenus, 2248; Thos, 166, 931, 1247, 1848, 2187, 2615, 6615, 8786; Thomas, 3641; W^m, 2348, 5339, 5675, 5902; W^m H^y, 4668; Willm, 61, 1561
JORDAN: Jno, 3607; Randle, 7799; Thos, 6639; W^m, 511, 7193
JOSEPH: Jno, 1258, 5407; John, 3823
JOYCE: Jno, 1114; Pat^k, 1674, 5686; Thos, 381, 6854
JOYER: Pat^k, 5685
JUDD: W^m, 6862
JUDGE: Chas, 1948
JUNIPER: William, 4412
JUNKIN: Dean, 1814, 1994, 6542
JURE: Nich^s, 2507
JURY: Willm, 8926
JUSTIN: Hen^y, 5051
KAIN: Hugh, 6361; Jno, 1304
KARNEY: Jno, 2352; John, 8128
KAVANAGH: Edwd, 1308; Jno, 3809, 7137
KAY: John, 1798
KAYE: Zacchens, 1524
KEAN: Jos^h, 3987
KEANE: Maurice, 6318; Peter, 4399; Thos, 811
KEARNEY: Jno, 5911; Pat^k, 1704, 1966, 5634, 6489; W^m, 3532
KEARNS: Barth^w, 1603; Jno, 3805; Mich^l, 6467; Robt, 132
KEATHLEY: Nathl, 644
KEATING: John, 4085; Rich^d, 8613
KEATINGE: Maur^e, 2923
KEATLEY: Jno, 2230, 8152
KEEFE: John, 6099, 7060; Mich^l, 7338; W^m, 437
KEEFFE: Edm^d, 487
KEEGAN: Miles, 678, 4307
KEELAGHER: Cormac, 1900, 6612
KEELER: Robt, 2889
KEELEY: Den^s, 5395; Jno, 5257
KEELING: Bern^d, 867; W^m, 3459
KEELY: Dennis, 1211

KEENAN: Const^e, 3240; Jno, 5054; Paul, 8384
KEEVERS: W^m, 365, 3672
KEEVES: Jno, 35
KEEVIL: Peter, 7890
KEILLY: Ja^s, 1991
KEITLEY: Jesse, 7952
KELCHER: Jno, 6026
KELK: Edwd, 4801
KELLER: Peter, 2033
KELLY: And^w, 4816; Bern^d, 2464; Brien, 1562; Bry^n, 1479; Darby, 5696; David, 7173; Edwd, 4032, 4780; Elias, 7695; Fra^s, 506, 4024, 6150; Geo^e, 4572; Ja^s, 1649, 3200, 6105, 6425, 6640, 7281; James, 6454; Jno, 1509, 1578, 1762, 4635; Jno Bern^d, 2564; John, 3650, 6005, 8005; Mich^l, 7694; Owen, 4062; Pat^k, 1763, 5914, 6723; Robt, 1722; Saml, 7108; Thos, 387, 629, 1327, 1711, 4927, 6063, 6490, 7623, 7731, 8768; Willm, 1042, 4767
KEMBLE: W^m, 2321
KEMP: Edward, 7961; Simon, 745
KENDALL: Jno, 606, 4141
KENDRICK: W^m, 453
KENNEBY: W^m, 4965
KENNEDY: Alex^r, 7009; Benjn, 2067; Crawford, 7339; Edm^d, 7340; Edwd, 7205; Geo^e, 8913; Gilb^t, 2599; Hen^y, 6022; Ja^s, 521, 5093, 6182; Jno, 528, 1312; John, 4079; Michael, 4532; Pat^k, 1912, 6526; Peter, 1016, 4969; Rich^d, 8735; Thos, 868, 8585
KENNEY: Jos^h, 4126
KENNY: Ja^s, 3723, 3769; Jno, 645, 5055; Luke, 6705; Mich^l, 5781, 7696; Pat^k, 3602; Peter, 7800; Step^n, 4106; W^m, 7135
KENT: Abr^m, 358; Thos, 637, 4282
KENWARD: J., 8222
KENWORTHY: Jno, 4187
KENYON: Edwd, 456; Hen^y, 8541; Zach^h, 275, 3346
KENZIE: Jos^h, 1022
KEOUGH: Jno, 523, 4096; Sexton, 7341
KERNAN: Mich^l, 5273
KERR: Edw^s, 4296; Hall, 8342; Ja^s, 6665; Jno, 565; Jos^h, 1653; Moses, 8895; Robt, 1830, 6581
KERRISH: Denis, 4482
KERRISK: Denis, 754
KERRISON: Simon, 1971, 6619
KERROGHAN: Jno, 7256
KERSHAW: W^m, 5655
KETTLE: Mich^l, 5133; Thos, 5400
KETTLES: David, 3060, 8033

KEY: John, 2797; W^m, 2725
KEYES: Jno, 3750
KEYS: Jno, 410; Willm, 8206
KIDD: Willm, 8042
KIDNEY: Ja^s, 8812
KIDSON: Saml, 7065
KIERNAN: Ja^s, 6818; Jno, 1610; W^m, 4319
KIESER: Jos^h, 6887
KIFFORD: Thos, 2762
KILBOY: Ja^s, 7801
KILBY: Ja^s, 2215
KILEEN: Den^s, 1666; Patrick, 7960
KILFOYLE: Mich^l, 3370
KILGOUR: Peter, 5642
KILLALLY: Pat^k, 7342
KILLEEN: Den^s, 6420
KILLMAIN: Willm, 2946
KILLOCK: Adam, 8664
KILPATRICK: Jos^h, 8715
KILRAIN: Peter, 7571
KILROY: Thos, 3327
KILTY: Jno, 1943
KILWORTH: Jno, 3958
KIMMETT: Ja^s, 4063
KIMPSON: Jno, 3294
KING: Dav^d, 4769; Ja^s, 1019; Jno, 649, 3328; John, 8608; Jonah, 7396; Jos^h, 1264, 5342, 5421; Matt^w, 1194; Mich^l, 3464; Ralph, 8498; Robt, 6312; Thos, 3925, 5406, 6340; W^m, 812, 2217, 3670, 7118; Willm, 8146
KINGSBY: Ja^s, 3369
KINGSLEY: John, 6522
KINNIBURGH: Dav^d, 8905
KINSLEY: Pat^k, 3589
KIRBY: Jno, 7914; Robt, 1191, 5333, 6519; Thos, 237, 4293
KIRK: Affleck, 4238; Ja^s, 18, 8310; John, 4963; Pat^k, 1563; W^m, 564
KIRKE: Clay, 4356
KIRKLAND: Wm Henry, 4600
KIRKWOOD: Alex^r, 1368
KIRWIN: Jno, 348
KITSON: Jno, 2583
KITT: Chas, 1811, 6613
KNABB: Hen^y, 167
KNAPTON: Jno, 7802; Thos, 3913
KNIGHT: George, 3557; Ja^s, 462; Jno, 3852; John, 3067; Robert, 7973; Thos, 636; W^m, 2148; Willm, 6187
KNIGHTON: Thos, 3722
KNOTT: Alex^r, 7840; Fra^s, 3132
KNOWLES: Henry, 8020
KNOX: Robt, 1687, 6488
KOESTER: Ge^o, 1108
KOTCHEL: Ja^s, 427
KOUGH: Pat^k, 518
KRIBS: Matt^w, 1126
KUNCHEON: Rich^d, 6786
KUPPERSCH: Leon^d, 1129
KUTSBY: Benjn, 1288

KYLE: Ja^s, 3830; Thos, 5505; Walter, 5705
LACAN: Edwd, 7572
LACE: Fra^s, 5345; Pat^k, 5328
LACK: Geo^e, 6081
LACKEY: John, 4020
LAING: Ja^s, 5816; Robt, 3023, 5854
LAIRD: John, 8512
LALLY: Ja^s, 6415
LAMB: Jno, 2469; John, 8357; Willm, 139
LAMBERT: Ja^s, 608; Jno, 1152; Rich^d, 13, 2855; Willm, 4937
LAMBKIN: Jos^h, 5032
LAMONT: Danl, 8482
LAMPOORT: Thos, 444
LAMPORT: Thos, 3843
LANCASTER: John, 8449, 8685; Thos, 7343
LAND: Jno, 259; John, 3266
LANDERS: Edwd, 2783; Rich^d, 5938, 6050; Timothy, 3651
LANDS: W^m, 3057; Willm, 5448
LANE: Ja^s, 1746, 7624; Rich^d, 2313, 2619, 8083; W^m, 3490
LANG: Alex^r, 2835; Danl, 6868; Ge^o, 1611; Geo^e, 6140; Henry, 5261; Ja^s, 8469; Nathl, 2055
LANGFORD: Jno, 933; John, 5251
LANGHAM: Chas, 2001
LANGLEY: Hen^y, 7462; Willm, 66
LANGSHAW: W^m, 7925
LANTRY: Mich^l, 7085
LAPHAM: Jno, 6449
LAPOINTE: Alexis, 5183
LAPRAIK: Ja^s, 6411
LARBY: Ja^s, 428
LARKE: Robt, 2803
LARKIN: Danl, 3926; Jno, 1694; John, 119; Jos^h, 7888; Thos, 1622
LARMER: Dav^d, 3446
LARMONDEAU: Jos^h, 2018
LARNER: John, 5394
LARNEY: Thos, 4045
LAROUX: Jos^h, 2389, 8091
LARRISY: Ja^s, 7344
LASKIE: W^m, 5833
LATHAM: John, 4493
LATIMER: George, 3397
LAUGHLIN: And^w, 761, 4459
LAVELL: W^m, 3465, 7208
LAVERTON: W^m, 7732
LAVERY: Chas, 4512; Henry, 5343; Jno, 7206; John, 4920
LAVINGSTON: Jno, 7013
LAWLER: Thos, 1721
LAWLESS: John, 869; Mich^l, 7463
LAWRENCE: Edwd, 1164, 5244; H^y, 8922; Ja^s, 7464; Jno, 607, 790; Reuben, 7803; W^m, 4958

LAWSON: Geo, 822; Hy, 4873; Heny, 1000; Robt, 7387; Wm, 2827
LAYMAN: Geoe, 6989
LAYTON: Jno, 1483; John, 5996
LEADER: Jno, 1095
LEAHENY: Patk, 5203
LEAR: Willm, 78
LEARMOUTH: John, 7147
LEARY: Denis, 3498; Jas, 4181; Josh, 2300; Thos, 1829
LEBRE: Josh, 1120, 5161
LECKIE: Alexander, 5211; Jas, 8519
LEE: Anthy, 1176; Benjn, 2956; Corns, 1805; Cornelius, 1792; George, 7991; Henry, 6035; Jas, 2090, 7625; Jno, 1824, 2686, 3387; John, 4869, 6545, 6625; Noble, 7939; Peter, 6270; Richd, 5248; Robt, 1987, 6544; Thos, 6641, 8696; Willm, 4987
LEECH: John, 3034; Richd, 108, 3007; Thos, 4232
LEES: Jas, 1369; John, 7156; Mark, 6371
LEESON: Thos, 3899
LEGGATT: Thos, 2847
LEHANE: Jereh, 7804
LEIB: Heny, 221
LEICH: Mattw, 8044
LEIGHTON: Alexr, 5842
LEITH: John, 8190
LELAND: Thos, 1786, 6492
LEMERY: Alexis, 2017
LEMMING: Jno, 2344
LEMON: Robt, 8691
LENAGHAN: Edwd, 4829
LENNAN: Geoe, 4489
LENNON: Heny, 1482; Jas, 1931, 6543; Jno, 1789, 6368; Peter, 4018
LEO: Michl, 7131
LEOMAN: Jno, 934
LEONARD: Chas, 7573; Jas, 6381; Jno, 6855; John, 5719; Patk, 6627; Thos, 2236, 2981, 7465, 8182
LERCY: Josh, 8041
LESHFORD: Thos, 7698
LESLIE: Geo, 1330; Geoe, 5483; John, 5815; Saml, 2857
LETHERBY: Heny, 7909
LETT: Josh, 4810; Thos, 2868
LETTIMORE: Jno, 8638
LEUBE: Chas, 2162
LEVEY: Josh, 2129
LEVICK: John, 2863
LEVINS: Thos, 3192
LEVINSTONE: Jas, 5519
LEVISTON: Robt, 4706; Saml, 3674; Willm, 6740
LEWIE: John, 3248
LEWIS: Benjn, 5280; Davd, 3860; Geo, 1517, 1586; Jno, 2343, 7875; John, 8127; Lewis, 8779; Mattw,

LEWIS (continued) 1459, 5933; Patk, 2556; Philip, 8832; Thaddeus, 2329, 8066
LEYDON: Martin, 7098
LIDDLE: Geoe, 7924
LIDDY: Patk, 7115
LIEBERT: Anty, 1661
LIEDER: Augs, 1130
LIGHT: Wm, 2307
LIGHTBODY: Andw, 7466
LILLEY: Jno, 2547
LILLY: Josh, 2149
LILLYWHITE: John, 2988
LINCE: Jas, 3867
LINDEM: Fredk, 2656
LINDENBERG: Saml, 3725
LINDSAY: Chas, 5973; Jno, 8370; Robt, 1360, 8654
LINDSEY: Andw, 6835; Saml, 5115
LINEGAR: Jas, 7200
LINFIELD: Edwd, 2812
LINGARD: Jno, 5142
LINSTER: John, 3935
LINTON: Jas, 4892; Jno, 2635
LINUS: Bernd, 5438
LIPPETT: Gibeon, 778
LIPSEY: Wm, 8428
LITCHEN: Jno, 2433; John, 8116
LITTLE: George, 5603; Jno, 4846, 7307; John, 5600; Moses, 5605; Richd, 3221; Thos, 3063, 5485, 8036; Willm, 8290, 8572
LITTLER: Thos, 1485
LITTLEWORTH: Jas, 5953
LIVERMORE: Jno, 7467
LIVEWRIGHT: Archd, 6202
LIVINGSTON: Danl, 8621; Dugald, 5855
LIVINGSTONE: Hy, 4022; Jno, 2068
LLOYD: David, 7345; Richard, 3652; Thos, 973; Wm, 749
LOANE: Jas, 233
LOBB: Richd, 8801
LOCHEAD: Jno, 5782
LOCKERBIE: Willm, 4496
LOCKETT: Jno, 359, 3499
LOCKHART: Jas, 7468
LODGE: Thos, 2890
LODGEWICK: Jas, 6893
LOFTUS: Geoe, 7469
LOGAN: Hugh, 6287; Wm, 6666
LOGGIE: Davd, 8303
LOGUE: Wm, 7470
LOMBER: Jacob, 988
LOMERY: Alexis, 6760
LONERGAN: Michl, 1764; Wm, 1733; Willm, 1765, 6494; William, 6495
LONG: Geoe, 5783; Jas, 1690, 6491; Jno, 6836; John, 6744; Martin, 6696; Saml, 2094; William, 4198
LONGFORD: Richd, 2687
LONGLEY: Wm, 7626
LONGWORTH: Jno, 7027
LONSOR: Philp, 2040
LORD: Benjn, 3290

LORDON: Jno, 2123; John, 8040
LORIMER: Jas, 7699
LORRAMER: Willm, 2441
LORRAMORE: Willm, 8115
LOTHIAN: Wm, 7346
LOTHIER: Edwd, 6706
LOUGH: Wm, 3988
LOUGHLAN: Hugh, 1227
LOUGHLIN: Henry, 5750; Jno, 268; Martin, 3529
LOUGHREY: Cormick, 3966
LOUNDER: Jacob, 2380, 8114
LOUTHOOD: Alexr, 8478
LOVATT: Patk, 8703
LOVE: Jas, 4215, 4224; Jno, 7574; Josh, 8257; Peter, 4214
LOVEDAY: Wm, 2121
LOVELL: Jas, 5016
LOVETT: Jas, 3441; John, 5329
LOW: Andw, 3820
LOWDON: Andw, 4657
LOWE: Heny, 5669; Henry, 7182; Jno, 2167, 7347; John, 8176; Willm, 476
LOWMAN: Thos, 935
LOWNAN: Richd, 999
LOWREY: John, 5559
LOWRIE: Jno, 6209; John, 2754; Robt, 646; Thos, 6190; Timy, 5085
LOWRY: Davd, 2834; Jno, 7471; John, 4637; Robt, 1776, 6496
LUCAS: Chas, 4696; Heny, 5200; Isaac, 1501; Wm, 2103; Willm, 15, 3094
LUCKHURST: Thomas, 8021
LUDLOW: Thos, 3550
LUMSDEN: Jacob, 1453
LUNN: Willm, 958; William, 7992
LUNNEY: Danl, 4796
LUSCUTT: Wm, 93; Willm, 2904
LUSH: Wm, 2310; Willm, 8090
LYALL: Jno, 5353
LYLE: Jno, 5668
LYNCH: Danl, 8794; Heny, 5282; Jas, 5615; Michl, 7282, 7472; Thomas, 8740
LYON: Gordon, 746, 4479
LYONS: Archd, 8230; Jas, 1766, 6493; Jno, 5687; Martin, 7653; Michl, 7473
LYTH: Michl, 689
LYTTLE: Patk, 1612
MABEY: Wm, 7807
MCAFEE: Jno, 3229
MCALAY: Thos, 7733
MCALEER: Jas, 1967
MCALEES: Patk, 1965
MCALINDAN: Danl, 3797
MCALISTER: Chas, 1822
MCALLISTER: Chas, 1983; Jno, 7283; Wm, 5832
MCALLISTOR: Audley, 8314
MCALPINE: Jas, 3207
MCARDLE: James, 3561
MCAREAVEY: Jas, 7109

INDEX 339

MCARTHUR: Alex^r, 5536, 7099; George, 8022; Jno, 3985; John, 8668
MACARTHY: Tim^y, 8417
MCARTIE: Denis, 4378
MCASHEE: Danl, 4850
MCAULAY: Jno, 736
MCAULEY: Bernard, 6611; Jno, 4441; Peter, 363, 3664
MCBEATH: Jno, 6286; W^m, 7308
MCBETH: Temple, 5276
MCBRIDE: Bern^d, 1937, 6546; Jno, 6697
MCBRIEN: Jno, 4132
MCBRYAN: Bern^d, 7348
MCCABE: Alex^r, 1941, 6582; Bern^d, 3061, 4048, 8034; Fra^s, 7002; Jno, 5623, 8311; Mich^l, 7211
MCCAFFERY: Chas, 8418; Constantine, 7575
MCCAFFREY: Jno, 3376
MCCAFFRY: Alex^r, 6659; Jno, 3900; Philip, 3264; Thos, 806, 4603
MCCALL: Dav^d, 6074; Jno, 3448
MCCAMBLY: Danl, 1226
MCCAMMON: Thos, 230
MCCANDLISH: Ge^o, 1440
MCCANN: Ja^s, 5499, 5950; Jno, 102
MCCANNA: Ja^s, 1717
MCCARDILL: Edwd, 6667
MCCARDLE: Dav^d, 8568
MCCARNEY: Jno, 1157, 5223
MCCARROLL: Mich^l, 4290
MCCARTEN: Pat^k, 3472
MCCARTER: Alex^r, 5537; Wyms, 2600
MCCARTHY: And^w, 3562; Danl, 3774, 6861; Den^s, 1745; Florence, 886; Jno, 1777, 4230, 6007, 6462, 6751; Maurice, 3024; Pat^k, 2511; Thos, 4228
MCCARTNEY: Ja^s, 8658
MCCARTY: Jno, 7349
MCCASLIN: Alex^r, 1974, 6547
MCCLEAN: Jno, 4208; W^m, 626, 4205
MCCLEAVE: Hen^y, 8649
MCCLELLAND: Arch^d, 1446; Dav^d, 4608; Ja^s, 8225
MCCLEMMENS: Saml, 416
MCCLIEVE: Hugh, 295
MCCLURE: Fran^s, 6121; Ja^s, 4042
MCCLUSKY: Jno, 1291; Mich^l, 2959
MCCOLLEN: Jno, 6346
MCCOMMIE: Geo^e, 7194
MCCONAGHY: Ja^s, 7627
MCCONKEY: John, 3549
MCCONNELL: Ja^s, 8683; Jno, 3705; Murd^k, 7059; Thos, 7036
MCCONNOLLY: Bern^d, 6497
MCCONOCHIE: Step^n, 6239
MCCONOLLY: Bern^d, 1767
MCCONWELL: Thos, 2266

MCCOOEY: Edwd, 4576
MCCOPPEN: Geo^e, 4069
MCCORD: Thos, 2252
MCCORLEY: Peter, 3245
MCCORMACK: Ge^o, 1840
MCCORMICK: Edwd, 4720; Jno, 1619; Martin, 7350; Pat^k, 2107, 3049; Phalim, 8491
MCCOUBREY: Saml, 7700
MCCOULL: And^w, 1404, 5520; Arch^d, 8436
MCCOURT: Ja^s, 4341
MCCOY: Ja^s, 3810; Jno, 4813; Willm, 4037
MCCRACKEN: Thos, 2914; W^m, 3211
MCCRACKIN: Jos^h, 6083
MCCRAW: Finlay, 5458
MCCRAYE: Jno, 7474
MCCREADIE: W^m, 1450, 5824
MCCRETE: Den^s, 1731; Jos^h, 884
MCCROCKIN: Ter^e, 4213
MCCROHAN: Jer^h, 8216
MCCROHON: Jno, 263
MCCRUM: Hugh, 5306
MCCULLEN: Pat^k, 5205
MCCULLOCH: Malcolm, 6874
MCCULLOUGH: Willm, 3453
MCCURDY: Danl, 2261
MCDANIEL: Danl, 2340
MCDAVID: John, 4756
MCDERMOTT: And^w, 3158; Jno, 1964; John, 6583; Joseph, 4526; Pat^k, 4071; Peter, 6347; Ter^e, 3954
MCDEVITT: Chas, 7125
MCDONAGH: Pat^k, 1907
MACDONALD: Alex^r, 2121; Colin, 1448; Hen^y, 6642; Jno, 271, 1432
MCDONALD: Alex^r, 548, 2939, 6175, 8459; Allan, 1652, 2548; Allen, 300, 2632, 7017; Angus, 5835, 6290, 7005; Arch^d, 723; Bern^d, 2690; Colin, 5831; Cullo, 6885; Don^d, 3125, 5216; Edwd, 5546; Fra^s, 418, 2490; Ge^o, 827, 1188; Geo^e, 5321; Hugh, 2049; Ja^s, 1400, 4797, 5516; Jno, 466, 1203, 2013, 2426, 2439, 3156, 3442, 3845, 6214, 7351, 8068; Neil, 6999; Pat^k, 3514; Robert, 5714; Ron^d, 4487; Thos, 1768, 6498; W^m, 2071, 6365, 6911; Willm, 7016
MCDONAUGH: Jno, 60
MCDONELL: Finnon, 2069, 6768; Hen^y, 1981
MCDONNELL: Bern^d, 5094; Chas, 7475; Hen^y, 6560; Matthew, 8741; Mich^l, 1577
MCDONOUGH: Pat^k, 3775; Thos, 5283; Thomas, 7183
MCDOOLE: Alex^r, 7628
MCDOWAL: Ja^s, 7476

MCDOWALL: Fra^s, 4124; Jno, 7477; Thos, 4210
MACE: Rich^d, 2508, 6941; W^m, 1003; Willm, 4870
MCELHINEY: Geo^e, 8705
MCELLIGOT: Pat^k, 7478
MCELROY: Hen^y, 676
MCENANY: Dav^d, 4030
MCEVOY: Ant^y, 4775; Ja^s, 5930, 7926; Jno, 6988
MCFADDEN: Ja^s, 8609; Jno, 4824; Robt, 6113; W^m, 6548
MCFARLAN: Ja^s, 3814
MCFARLANE: Arthur, 4264; Ja^s, 936; Jno, 6597; Walter, 3689; Watt, 2030
MCGAIN: Ja^s, 7922
MCGARAHAN: Chas, 8093
MCGARR: Ja^s, 4064
MCGARRY: Ja^s, 1873, 1899; Jno, 8639; Mich^l, 4893
MCGEE: Alex^r, 2860, 4634; Hen^y, 3772; Pat^k, 3952; Thos, 234
MCGENNISS: Patrick, 6733
MCGHEE: Jno, 4172
MCGILL: Dav^d, 8782; Robt, 1810, 6605
MCGILLEVRAY: Jno, 6932
MCGILLICUDDY: Jno, 5070
MCGILLIVRAY: Ja^s, 5787
MCGILVREY: Robt, 1433
MCGINLEY: Jno, 5117
MCGINN: Bern^d, 4666; Leslie, 4546
MCGINNESS: Ja^s, 4234
MCGINNIS: Danl, 5076; Jno, 720; Philip, 7650; Thos, 6752
MCGITTRIE: Mich^l, 5764
MCGIVENEY: Alex^r, 4537
MCGIVERN: Hugh, 4847
MCGLADE: Peter, 4785
MCGLINN: Dav^d, 4799; Saml, 3172
MCGLYNN: Thos, 4541
MCGOFF: Thos, 5215
MCGOLDRICK: Ja^s, 7352
MCGOREY: Danl, 715; Ja^s, 1980
MCGOVERN: Peter, 5080
MCGOWAN: Alex^r, 3989; Bern^d, 7631; Dav^d, 3394; Ja^s, 7739; Jno, 1337, 4272, 6151; John, 3261; Thos, 1757, 3556, 6664; W^m, 7576
MCGOWEN: Pat^k, 6629
MCGRATH: Fran^s, 5856; Jno, 5053, 6668; John, 4421; Mich^l, 5217; Roger, 6082
MACGREGOR: Don^d, 244
MCGREGOR: Alex^r, 8917; Arch^d, 8240, 8242; Gregor, 3488; W^m, 7632
MCGRORY: W^m, 2723
MCGUIGAN: Jno, 8799; Peter, 7758
MCGUINESS: Hugh, 7074
MCGUINNESS: Jno, 5925

MCGUIRE: Barney, 2437, 8067; Ch^r, 7064; Danl, 4630; Edwd, 7846; Hen^y, 347; Ja^s, 6450, 7479, 7630; Jno, 1896; John, 6584; Pat^k, 4559, 7629; Thos, 703, 2726, 6604
MACGUIRE: Thos, 4667
MCGURK: Edwd, 8427; Pat^k, 6166
MCGURRAN: Chas, 6127
MCGWYNN: Edwd, 2430
MACHESTNEY: John, 6100
MACHRAY: Ja^s, 8339
MCHUGH: Jno, 7480
MCILGREW: Pat^k, 2512
MCILHEANEY: Ja^s, 5116
MCILREA: Ja^s, 5857
MCILROY: Jonathan, 6173
MCINNEREY: Pat^k, 6858
MCINNES: Don^d, 8121; Duncan, 5872; Jno, 5829
MCINNIS: Alex^r, 5004; Don^d, 2407
MCINTIRE: Jno, 8494
MCINTOSH: Don^d, 8284; Jno, 6272, 8292; W^m, 2078; Willm, 8757
MACINTYRE: Don^d, 1655
MCINTYRE: Edwd, 4250; Hugh, 8855; Ja^s, 1320; Jno, 6203, 6271; Mal^m, 1384; Thos, 6821; W^m, 7100
MCIVER: Don^d, 1419; Dun^n, 8260; Evander, 5798
MCJAMMESON: Jno, 5891
MCJANETT: Robt, 3500
MACK: Math^w, 360; Mich^l, 7806
MCKASEY: And^w, 3746
MCKAY: Alex^r, 8659; Chas, 5806; Danl, 1335, 5472; Don^d, 5638, 6235, 6660, 6899, 7481; Fred^k, 2580, 6982, Ge^o, 1434, George, 3617; Ja^s, 6291, 7852; Jno, 4500, 5616; John, 5751; Murd^k, 5788; Robt, 6277; Trevor, 1993, 6585; W^m, 5796, 5858, 6285
MACKAY: Ge^o, 1393, 5525; Wm A., 436, 3831; Willm, 6295
MCKECHNIE: Hugh, 5836; Robt, 5496
MCKEE: Chas, 8318; Dav^d, 5272; Jno, 5145; Thos, 491, 662, 3944; W^m, 6089
MCKEGG: Edwd, 62
MCKELLAR: Doug^l, 2691
MCKELLY: John, 6785
MCKELVEY: Ja^s, 8415
MCKENA: Fra^s, 1972, 6622
MCKENLEY: Jno, 53
MCKENNA: And^w, 3918; Edwd, 5105; Ja^s, 1973
MACKENZIE: Dun^n, 8516
MCKENZIE: Alex^r, 5555, 5859; Arch^d, 6243; Don^d, 773, 4503, 6991; J., 7546; Ja^s, 8254; Jno, 1349, 1439, 5517, 5827, 8748;

MCKENZIE (continued) Kenn^h, 6934; Robt, 5622, 8075; W^m, 5800; Willm, 4793
MCKEON: Jno, 1890, 4523; Thos, 8411
MCKEOWN: Bern^d, 5640; Ja^s, 7482
MCKERGEN: Jno, 6967
MCKERGOW: Jno, 2468
MCKERNON: Jno, 5263; Phillip, 7483
MCKEW: Thos, 7228
MCKEWEN: Thos, 8410
MACKILL: Ja^s, 1935
MCKILLOP: Jno, 8839
MCKINLEY: John, 2885
MCKINNON: Alex^r, 155
MACKINNON: Ang^s, 270
MCKINNON: Don^d, 6201, 6263; Ja^s, 6755; Jno, 1441
MCKIVER: Danl, 5432
MCKIZER: Thos, 2631
MCKNIGHT: Geo^e, 7353
MCKONE: Robt, 8201
MCLACHLAN: Angus, 6404
MCLARE: Ja^s, 642
MCLAREN: Dav^d, 4504; Jno, 1353, 5784, 8772
MCLARNEY: Pat^k, 4212
MCLAUCHLAN: Jno, 2048, 6765; Jos^h, 5044
MCLAUCHLIN: And^w, 3343
MCLAUGHLAN: Arch^d, 1075; Ja^s, 1156; Mart^n, 8682
MCLAUGHLIN: Ch^r, 70; Hugh, 1996, 4123, 6586; Luke, 3882; Mich^l, 3396; Robt, 8547; Thos, 7805
MCLAUGHTIN: Willm, 2634
MCLEAN: Alex^r, 8380; And^w, 459; Arch^d, 2070, 6772; Chas, 1328, 5468; Don^d, 5580
MACLEAN: Fra^s, 694
MCLEAN: Hugh, 5553; Ja^s, 4083; Jno, 7484, 8394
MACLEAN: John, 8626
MCLEAN: Neal, 8071; Robt, 2771, 8634; W^m, 1321, 4309
MCLELLAN: Ja^s, 7101
MCLENNAN: Alex^r, 7697
MCLEOD: Aug^s, 3833; Don^d, 768, 4483, 5809; Ja^s, 5817; Saml, 7734; Thos, 2539; W^m, 6268
MCLERNON: Geo^e, 3692
MCLOUGHLIN: Edwd, 6669, 6820; Hen^y, 2130; Jno, 5502; Mic^l, 1963; Mich^l, 3792; Pat^k, 2665, 4190, 6797; William, 5135
MCLOUGAN: Ja^s, 5224
MCMAHON: Fra^s, 5126; Fra^s Hugh, 6524; Jno, 3763, 5121; Jos^h, 7229; Mich^l, 6357; Pat^k, 6352, 6759; Patrick, 5136; Thos, 6059
MCMAKIN: Thos, 984
MCMANUS: Chas, 6753; Pat^k, 3967, 5033; Thos, 4025

MCMASTER: Hugh, 5477; Ja^s, 4012
MCMILLAN: W^m, 6880
MCMULLEN: Ja^s, 3450, 8648; Robt, 4633; Thos, 3779; W^m, 517, 3780
MCMULLIN: Jno, 4089
MCNAB: James, 3405
MCNALLY: Hen^y, 7757; Ja^s, 684
MCNAMARA: Den^s, 1857; Ja^s, 7257; Jno, 5302; Matt^w, 5378; Mich^l, 5042
MCNAUGHT: John, 8513; Thos, 6644; Willm, 8676
MCNAUGHTON: Ge^o, 1420
MCNEELY: Ja^s, 7634
MCNEIL: And^w, 6264; Jno, 2381, 8120
MCNERNEY: Thos, 3873
MCNESPY: Pat^k, 5184
MCNICKLE: Jno, 8204
MCNICOL: Allan, 5557
MCNICOLL: Ronald, 6822
MCNIEL: Jno, 1392
MCNIFFE: Jno, 22, 2853
MCNULTY: Jno, 8312
MCORMACK: Jno, 7122
MCPHAIL: Danl, 7876
MCPHATERS: Ja^s, 1449, 5826
MCPHERSON: Dav^d, 6205; Don^d, 770, 771, 4484; Dun^c, 1361; Dun^n, 4497; Ewen, 4485; Hugh, 1412; Paul, 351; Peter, 6266; W^m, 6842
MCPHIE: Angus, 5771
MCQUADE: Edwd, 3937
MCQUAY: Jno, 17
MCQUEEN: Thos, 5840
MCQUILLAN: Alex^r, 2628; And^w, 6543; Willm, 4348
MCQUILLEN: And^w, 3089
MCQUILLIAN: Ja^s, 7102
MCQUILLIN: Call, 783
MCQUINN: Felix, 1992
MCRAE: Danl, 5488
MACRAE: Jno, 1049
MCRAE: Jno, 1654
MCREA: Thos, 71
MCROARY: Ja^s, 8795
MCROBIE: Jno, 8371
MCSENNESON: Ja^s, 1455
MCSTRAVICK: Roger, 7633
MCSWEENEY: Danl, 4614
MCTAVISH: Robt, 6207
MCTERNON: H^y, 4734
MCVEIGH: Jno, 2210; Pat^k, 4835
MCVEY: Robt, 5974
MADDEN: Jere^h, 7828; Jno, 3170; Lawr^c, 5402; Pat^k, 3603, 7209, 7841; Thos, 5754
MADDISON: Ja^s, 8389
MADDOCK: Thos, 94
MADEN: W^m, 8826
MADILL: Ja^s, 7244
MAGARITY: Jno, 8919
MAGEE: Bern^d, 370
MAGGS: Jno, 7388
MAGILL: Jno, 2790

INDEX 341

MAGUIRE: Const^l, 8189; Pat^k, 3022
MAHER: Danl, 3909; Edwd, 4746; Jno, 7230; Mich^l, 5061; Peter, 5359; Philip, 4777; Thos, 4641
MAHON: Nich^s, 2510; Thos, 755, 4478
MAHONEY: Edwd, 2350; Fred^k, 1741, 6501; Matthew, 3623
MAHONS: John, 8098
MAHORTER: Thos, 740
MAIN: Peter, 3090
MAIR: Jno, 2509; John, 6976
MAISEY: William, 5630
MAITLAND: Wm Aug^s, 465
MAJOR: George, 4527
MALADY: Thos, 7197
MALCOLM: Geo^e, 6161
MALKIN: Rich^d, 595
MALLEN: Hugh, 8431
MALLON: Chas, 7024; Hugh, 1936; Mich^l, 4090; Thos, 3021
MALLYON: Ja^s, 7635
MALONE: Edwd, 5262; Ja^s, 7198; Martin, 4131; Thos, 4376; W^m, 1672; Willm, 1665
MALONEY: Ja^s, 3940; Peter, 4626; Thos, 1708, 6499
MALRENNAN: Thomas, 6734
MALTON: Jno, 2722
MANCINI: Jno, 2256; John, 8933
MANDRILL: Hen^y, 169
MANEALY: Jno, 8617
MANLEY: Edwd, 6673; Willm, 8510
MANN: Jno, 1341
MANNERS: Robt, 7877
MANNING: Edwd, 1879; W^m, 705; Willm, 5876
MANNION: Pat^k, 1784
MANNON: Martin, 6196
MANSELL: Simeon, 3335; Simon, 267
MANSER: Burket, 4999
MANSFIELD: Willm, 1389
MANUEL: Edwd, 2390; Jno, 2164, 8174; Mich^l, 7354
MAPISH: W^m, 568
MAPLE: Thos, 5034
MARA: John, 8024; Thos, 6133
MARBERTON: Ja^s, 714
MARCH: Edwd, 1902, 6598; Willm, 870, 4677
MARCHAM: Henry, 4887; W^m, 4886
MARIE: Jno, 2171
MARJORAM: David, 6324
MARKEY: Ja^s, 439
MARKHAM: Jno, 4406
MARKOE: John, 2960
MARKOSKY: Jos^h, 2150
MARKS: Willm, 1371, 5523
MARLAND: Ja^s, 835
MARLBOROUGH: Jno, 4912
MARLEY: Jno, 2024; John, 6776
MARLINSON: Jno, 8119

MARMAN: Saml, 2555, 6958
MARRS: Peter, 283
MARSDEN: William, 3356
MARSH: Edwd, 990; Geo^e, 6372; Jno, 4368
MARSHALL: Ja^s, 5688; Jno, 4543, 5975; Jos^h, 661, 4281; Saml, 6302; W^m, 599, 7905
MARTELL: Jno, 3927
MARTIN: Ant^y, 1430; Dennis, 8891; Em^l, 3268; Eman^l, 265; Ja^s, 455, 2315, 4336; Jno, 1469, 5354; John, 4654; Peter, 3144, 7749; Robt, 1001, 4864; Ter^e, 5913; Thos, 4110; Thomas, 3538; W^m, 3715, 4097, 5733, 6152, 7701; Willm, 7066, 8697
MARTINSON: Jno, 2385
MARTZIAN: Ignace, 1143, 5167
MASDEN: Isaac, 4837
MASELAS: Fred^k, 2623
MASH: W^m, 3320
MASKALL: W^m, 4390
MASKELL: Francis, 3363; Jno, 600; John, 4165
MASLIN: Jno, 4568
MASON: Chas, 5758; Isaac, 3977; Ja^s, 5945; Oliver, 7955; Thos, 3105; W^m, 7355
MASSEY: Jos^h, 3309; Willm, 8700
MASTERS: John, 3653; Joseph, 7941
MATHER: Row^d, 2734; Thos, 4377
MATHERS: Thos, 4102
MATHESON: Alex^r, 2297, 8072; W^m, 2400
MATHEWS: John, 3632; W^m, 2093, 4455; Willm, 1564
MATHEWSON: W^m, 8058
MATHIAS: John, 5928
MATHIESON: Ja^s, 8827
MATHISON: Geo^e, 5447
MATTHEWS: Chas, 2793; Danl, 2883; John, 5579; Willm, 4513
MATTHIAS: Fred^k, 1125
MATTOX: Willm, 641
MAURICE: Paul, 481, 3942
MAXWELL: Jno, 321, 1828; Mich^l, 6096; W^m, 5762
MAY: Edwd, 6749
MAYBLE: Robt, 8892
MAYES: W^m, 2111; Willm, 3051
MAYO: Fra^s, 758, 4446; Willm, 6002
MEAD: Jacob, 2156
MEADOWS: Thos, 537, 4116
MEAGHER: Dennis, 1332; Pat^k, 2785
MEAKIN: Thos, 566, 4157
MEALEY: James, 8873; Malachy, 774; Mich^l, 2438
MEANEY: Edwd, 2387, 2434
MEARA: Dennis, 6713; Jno, 1726; Pat^k, 1727; Willm, 1724

MEARE: Edw^w, 2836
MEASURES: Jno, 570
MECKLY: Geo^e, 3842
MEDCALF: Jno, 8320
MEDLEY: Jos^h, 245
MEE: Jno, 5310; Robt, 3974
MEEHAN: Fra^s, 4445; Pat^k, 4103
MEEK: Jno, 7538
MEEKLEY: Ge^o, 470
MEESSON: Alex^r, 2833
MEGGISON: Jos^h, 1454
MEHERAN: Thomas, 8023
MEIGHAN: Fran^s, 3812; Mich^l, 7397
MELANO: Peter, 1141
MELASS: W^m, 8837
MELERICK: Ja^s, 5143
MELVIN: Edwd, 7356
MENCE: Ge^o, 743
MENDELL: Willm, 8816
MENDS: Chas, 2955; Herbert, 8170
MENERY: Willm, 8902
MENSFORTH: Jno, 4772
MENTZ: Jno, 2579
MEPHAM: Edw^{dn}, 652
MEPHAN: Saml, 7654
MERCER: W^m, 4669
MERCES: John, 5474
MEREDITH: W^m, 2549
MERNA: Ja^s, 7636
MERRETT: Jno, 6153; Thos, 6382
MERRYMAN: Ge^o, 1410
METCALF: W^m, 7485
MEYER: Hen^y, 2649
MIDDENDORF: Leon^d, 3342
MIDDLETON: Geo^e, 5006; Jno, 5127
MIERS: Thos, 5498
MILES: Chas, 4872; Ja^s, 3905; Mich^l, 5390; Robt, 8367
MILLANE: Jer^h, 4379
MILLAR: Jno, 7702; W^m, 6863
MILLARD: Jno, 1544
MILLER: Chas, 918, 5860; David, 7231; Edwd, 3724; Eph^r, 8672; Geo^e, 8571; H^y, 8049; Hen^y, 2242; Hugh, 8213; Ja^s, 4516, 5641, 8770; John, 5177; Jos^h, 3091; Robt, 6208; W^m, 621, 1405, 4203; Willm, 86, 2928, 5542, 7015
MILLETT: Thos, 569
MILLINGTON: Thos, 1266; W^m, 6633
MILLS: Abr^m, 3713; Abra^m, 373; Dav^d, 1418, 5644; Ja^s, 2638, 8220; Robt, 8197; Thos, 4386; W^m, 2550, 7258
MILNE: Alex^r, 3576; Ja^s, 6230
MILTON: Jno, 732
MIMMS: Isaac, 1162
MINAGHAN: Dennis, 7808
MINCHIN: Chas, 1542
MINEHAN: Pat^k, 6109

INDEX

MINES: Rich^d, 145
MINGAY: Ja^s, 3136
MINNY: Saml, 572, 4152
MINSON: David Edwd, 3310
MINTON: Pat^k, 1470, 5956
MINTY: Ja^s, 2338
MIRK: Ja^s, 1351
MIST: Vincent, 5624
MITCHELL: Alex^r, 8455; Ja^s, 2601, 6680, 6804, 6942; Jno, 4, 2396, 5239; John, 8084; Nathl, 4605; Pat^k, 6875; Saml, 5265, 8489; W^m, 2811, 5861, 8169; William, 7975
MITCHELMORE: W^m, 567
MOFFAT: Abr^m, 5862
MOFFATT: Pat^k, 3574; Saml, 2791; W^m, 6244
MOFFITT: David, 8575
MOHAN: Pat^k, 1685
MOLES: Willm, 4313
MOLESWORTH: Willm, 734
MOLINARY: Guisippe, 5171
MOLLOY: Danl, 5566; Edwd, 20; Martin, 3728
MOLONEY: Dennis, 5048
MOLONY: Chas, 8820; Jno, 8487
MOLQNEANY: Saml, 5936
MOLYNEUX. Saml, 1456
MONAGHAN: Alex^r, 2688, 7040; Jno, 489, 3939; Patrick, 7974
MONAHAN: Jno, 5612
MONDIDAN: John, 596
MONGAN: Mich^l, 7123
MONK: Jos^h, 447; Robt, 594, 4146
MONRO: Hector, 2189
MONTEITH: Ja^s, 2234, 8244
MONTFORD: Thos, 6423
MONTGOMERY: Jno, 1039
MOONEY: Ja^s, 5451; Robt, 3914; Thos, 2780, 4133, 7703
MOORCROFT: Christmas, 3655; Thomas, 3654
MOORE: And^w, 5, 2787, 8758; Benjⁿ, 3505; Chas, 3286; David, 8848; Fargus, 5179; Fergus, 1101; Ja^s, 871, 5495, 7128; James, 7933; Jno, 197, 1056, 1198; John, 3364, 4924, 8375, 8776; Jonⁿ, 2326; Jos^h, 1083; Joseph, 8871; Law^c, 872; Lawr^c, 4671; Lewis, 5892; Mich^l, 7486; Michael, 6736; Phil^p, 650; Robt, 2016, 6107, 8707; Saml, 5959, 7735; Simon, 7357; Thos, 2712, 7031; W^m, 1979; Willm, 2823, 8885
MOORHEAD: Ge^o, 152; Stew^t, 6592; William, 6042
MOPSEY: Jno, 308
MORAN: Edwd, 1892, 6589; Ja^s, 1597, 1630; Jno, 890, 2082, 6809; Patrick, 6010; Peter, 1790, 2357, 6500, 8118; Robt, 1359,

MORAN (continued) 5522; Roger, 5585; Thos, 7233
MORE: W^m, 5863
MOREHEAD: Willm, 3452
MORGAN: Fra^s, 1872, 6587; Hen^y, 1154; Henry, 8534; Jno, 520; John, 8706; Jos^h, 4364; Moses, 1624; Pat^k, 6073, 6529; Robt, 3121; Stepⁿ, 3311
MORIARTY: Patrick, 7174
MORLEY: Jos^h, 3738
MORLING: W^m, 7358
MORRELL: Thos, 6681
MORRIS: Danl, 971; Edwd, 6072; Ja^s, 1401, 5535; Jno, 1658, 1809; John, 6626, 8583, 8888; Thos, 8471; W^m, 36; Wm Lowther, 3539; William, 6732
MORRISON: Don^d, 412, 3744, 5786; Fra^s, 5558; Ja^s, 4027; Jno, 4542; John, 5562; Law^e, 3462; Mich^l, 6349; Robt, 8046; W^m, 994, 3030, 4879, 7232; Willm, 8511
MORRISS: Stepⁿ, 7284
MORROU: Fra^s, 1090
MORROW: Fra^s, 875
MORTIMER: Rich^d, 2689, 7038
MORTON: Jno, 5128
MOSES: John, 4127
MOSLEY: Willm, 4729
MOSS: Ge^o, 3253; Jonathan, 2219; Robt, 1002, 4876; W^m, 2640
MOTHERSOLE: W^m, 3530
MOTLEY: Jno, 1091
MOTT: Rich^d, 1345; Willm, 5570
MOTTRAM: Saml, 4784
MOULDER: Ja^s, 571; John, 5802
MOULTON: Robt H., 8775
MOUNT: Ja^s, 8309
MOUNTAIN: Matt^w, 733; Rich^d, 168; Willm, 509
MOUNTSTEPHEN: Ja^s, 8159
MOUNTSTEPHENS: Ja^s, 2213
MOWLAN: W^m, 5060
MOYLAN: Mich^l, 7265
MOYNES: Isaac, 6889
MUIR: Ja^s, 2978; Jno, 4257
MULCAHY: Jno, 2562; Pat^k, 4227
MULDOON: Bernard, 7809; W^m, 1906, 6591
MULHOLLAND: Ja^s, 6549; Robt, 8911
MULLAMY: Ja^s, 5324
MULLAN: Neil, 8754
MULLEN: Daniel, 8032; Jno, 1688; Mic^l, 1940; Peter, 2475; Robert, 8742; Stewart, 2084
MULLERS: Pat^k, 1508
MULLIGAN: Corn^s, 7234; Ja^s, 8821; John, 5698; Matt^w, 7487; Philip, 5670

MULLIN: Pat^k, 5129; Robt, 7810
MULLONY: Thomas, 3618
MULLOWNEY: Jno, 3479
MULLOWNY: Peter, 3435
MULROGUE: Hugh, 1313
MULVENEY: John, 6930
MULVEY: Loughlin, 3875; Martin, 3204; Pat^k C., 5332
MUNRO: And^w, 6265; Hugh, 8863; Ja^s, 5805; John, 8562; Peter, 857; Robt, 6843
MUNROE: Danl, 7004
MUNROTT: James, 4852
MURCH: W^m, 6527
MURCHESON: Alex^r, 2072
MURCHISON: Alex^r, 6767
MURDAH: James, 7979
MURDEN: Eman^l, 2324, 8092
MURDIE: Jno, 7857
MURDOCH: David, 5697
MURDOCK: Alex^r W^m, 5507; Edwd, 4653; Robt, 2943; Willm, 1302
MURDY: Jno, 7704
MURKELL: Charles, 5723
MURNANE: John, 6094
MURPHY: Alex^r, 339, 3591; Corn^s, 4845; Denis, 5081; Edm^d, 3729; Francis, 4589; Fred^k, 7124; Ge^o, 6379; Hugh, 7269; Ja^s, 4086, 6428; Jno, 1874, 1916, 2412, 2616, 3571, 7705, 7891; John, 2364, 5627, 6588, 8117; Mich^l, 2731, 2805; Pat^k, 1728, 1905, 1998, 2602, 3379, 3798, 4169, 4625, 4758, 6461, 6606; Patrick, 4528; Patt, 1865; Peter, 23; Rich^d, 6742; Saml, 6045; Silvester, 529; Thos, 150, 8302, 8797; W^m, 1915; Willm, 3191
MURRAY: Bern^d, 4209; Don^d, 6284; Francis, 3656; Ja^s, 2225, 6348, 8148; Jno, 3910, 7488; John, 4730, 5604, 5823; Mich^l, 5442; Neil, 5144; Rich^d, 103, 3009; Robt, 543, 2466, 8492; Thos, 1903, 6590, 7086; Willm, 2747, 8923; William, 7185
MURRELL: Chas, 1545, 3281
MURRY: Lawrence, 5269
MUSGROVE: Rich^d, 407
MUSTARD: Don^d, 6876; Jno, 8332; W^m, 7858
MUTLOW: Mark, 4434
MYERS: Elias, 1171; Samuel, 3542
NAGLE: Ge^o, 7489
NAIRN: John, 8558
NANGLE: Matt^w, 6004
NASH: Ja^s, 2237; Jno, 7707
NAUGHTON: Ja^s, 5132; Mich^l, 8900
NAYLOR: Willm, 1525

NEAL: Cornelius, 5741; Pat^k, 3861
NEALIS: Mich^l, 4039
NEALON: Danl, 6707; Jno, 7309
NEAVES: Edwd, 1565, 6076; Thos, 3272
NEEDHAM: Hy, 7057; Saml, 6754; Willm, 8477
NEESON: Hugh, 7195
NEGUS: W^m, 3968
NEIL: Thos, 767
NEILL: Thos, 530
NELIS: Mich^l, 5071
NELSON: Alex^r, 4118; Ja^s, 7359; Jos^h, 2482; Willm, 8399
NESBETT: Ja^s, 2291
NESBITT: Ja^s, 8060; Jno, 5059; Thos, 8258; W^m, 1988
NETHERCOTT: Ja^s, 3563
NETTING: Thos, 4900
NETTLES: Jno, 729, 4425
NETTLETON: Jno, 2792
NEUBLE: Ja^s, 671
NEUT: Willm, 135
NEVILLE: Laur^e, 7490
NEWALL: Thos, 4773
NEWBOLD: Jno, 1277, 5422
NEWBOLT: Geo, 1055; Geo^e, 5002
NEWELL: Jno, 1200
NEWINGTON: Chas, 8576
NEWMAN: Edwd, 5677; Geo^e, 6523, 7285; Hen^y, 6231; John, 6036; Thos, 1034; W^m, 2295, 4263, 7398
NEWSOME: Geo^e, 8646
NEWSTEAD: Nathl, 6402
NEWTH: W^m, 3065, 8038
NEWTON: Ja^s, 1292; Rich^d, 4645; Saml, 8564; W^m, 1910; Willm, 6609
NEYLAND: Peter, 3547
NIBLETT: Phil^p, 323
NIBLICK: Bern^d, 1020, 4979
NICHOL: Willm, 292
NICHOLDS: Ja^s, 7706
NICHOLL: Thos, 3274
NICHOLS: Ab^m, 2718; Abr^m, 6551; Benjn, 451; Robt, 316
NICHOLSON: Geo^e, 6066; Willm, 2745
NICKER: Danl, 8447
NICKLE: W^m, 1444, 5808
NICOLL: Fra^s, 8269; John, 8704
NIDD: John, 8003
NIELL: John, 4410
NIMENS: Chas, 8916
NIXON: Jno, 2197, 7491, 7492; John, 3164, 8164; Willm, 4349
NOAH: Thos, 717, 4396
NOAKES: Ja^s, 5052
NOBLE: Armour, 6317; Ja^s, 2584
NOBLES: Robert, 7953
NOCTON: Pat^k, 1738
NOICE: Thomas, 3661

NOLAN: Chas, 6426; Laurence, 3639
NOONAN: Den^s, 722
NOONE: Pat^k, 937
NORDBECK: Peter, 1100, 5169
NORMAN: Jos^h, 2, 2761; Pat^k, 6436; Rich^d, 7493
NORRIS: Ja^s, 2349, 8133; James, 7940; Jno, 2486; John, 4752; W^m, 2356; Willm, 8135
NORTH: Hen^y, 959
NORTHE: John, 8247
NORTHWOOD: Jno, 8215
NORTON: Ja^s, 6682; Jno, 982; Mic^l, 1647; Mich^l, 6130; Thos, 4771
NOWDEN: Peter, 7811
NOWLAN: Ja^s, 7286; Pat^k, 3466, 5062; Robt, 8550; W^m, 4128
NUGENT: Ja^s, 8809; Jno, 1775; John, 6466; Thos, 1796
NUNAN: Jere^h, 6250
NUNN: James, 4534; W^m, 7360
NUNNICK: Thomas, 2743
NURTON: Corn^s, 478
NUTTALL: John, 8883; Rich^d, 3679
OAKES: Ja^s, 37; Thos, 748
OAKLEY: John, 7270
OAKMAN: Jno, 800
OATES: Jno, 8294
OBREE: Fra^s Loftus, 8909
OBRIAN: Thomas, 8006
OBRIEN: Arthur, 7103; Ch^r, 3415; Corn^s, 6419; Cornelias, 1670; Danl, 7087; Dav^d, 2092; Den^s, 5921; Edwd, 7187; Harding, 5571; Ja^s, 382, 1740, 6503; Jno, 1734; Mich^l, 4631, 4851; Thos, 1718, 6334, 7577; Philip, 5095; Robt, 7287; Simon, 8749; Terence, 2088; Thos, 2807; Tim^y, 2767, 5219; William, 7152
OBRINE: Jno, 1703
OBRYAN: Ja^s, 5389; Pat^k, 5453
OBYRNE: John, 7976
OCONNELL: Cornelius, 6037
OCONNOR: Garrett, 5706; Jno, 5362, 5674, 7494; Thos, 7143
ODAM: Ja^s, 5489
ODDY: Jno, 2367
ODELL: Edward, 4417
ODONALD: Hugh, 2692
ODONNELL: Edwd, 2134, 6907; Hugh, 6210; Jno, 5368, 7080; Neil, 6995; Patrick Healy, 5744
ODOWD: Pat^k, 7812
OGDEN: Thos, 3380
OHAGAN: Ja^s, 3027
OHALLORAN: Jno, 7578
OHARA: Jno, 2460, 2715; Mic^l, 1938; Mich^l, 6550, 6803; Robt, 3173; Willm, 4033

OHARE: Philip, 6183
OKEEFE: Danl, 118; Pat^k, 6700
OLEARY: Tim^y, 7495
OLIVE: Chas, 6778
OLIVER: Geo, 240; Hen^y, 2322; Jno, 7235; Lewis, 153
OMALLEY: Peter, 5344
OMAND: W^m, 7104
ONEAL: Alex^r, 3853; Mich^l, 3784; W^m, 938, 6502; Willm, 1692
ONEIL: Felix, 5713; Jno, 4091, 4830; Pat^k, 2328; Thos, 2299
ONEILL: Danl, 4395; Gordon, 7496; Ja^s, 892, 1990; Jno, 1858, 2351, 6593, 8131; Pat^k, 5934; Robt, 4917
ONEY: Ja^s, 1167
ONIS: W^m, 4966
OPENSHAW: Ja^s, 3295
ORCHARD: Jno, 4975
OREILLY: Francis, 5704
ORIORDAN: Robt, 5976
ORMSBY: Ja^s, 4820; Robt, 1626; Saml, 1230
ORR: John, 8743; Thos, 5864
OSBORNE: Jos^h, 2837; Saml, 2809; Willm, 1812
OSBOURNE: Jessie, 4701
OSBURNE: W^m, 2272
OSHEA: Jno, 6434; Mich^l, 5547
OSTEN: Bern^d, 2132
OTTY: John, 44
OUDERKIRK: Jacob, 8804
OVERBECK: Willm, 2246
OVERY: W^m, 6881
OWENS: Alex^r, 1385; David, 4741; Hugh, 2693; Jno, 4108, 4431, 4851; Thos, 7497; W^m, 1956; Willm, 1815
OXBOROUGH: W^m, 4043; Willm, 507
OXLEY: Robert, 7184
PACK: Saml, 683
PADDLE: Mich^l, 3148
PAGE: Thos, 802, 4561; W^m, 5258; Willm, 4295
PAGET: Thos, 692
PAIN: Jno, 801; John, 4564
PAINE: Clement, 7361
PAISLEY: Thos, 8661
PALLISTER: Jno, 1535
PALMER: Geo^e, 5760; Jno, 461, 2694, 4456, 5296; Nich^s, 3959; Robt, 502; Thos, 1536
PANCUTT: Jno, 985
PANTON: Ja^s, 4490
PANTONY: Robt, 574, 4145
PAPPIN: Estepham, 709
PARHAM: W^m, 3312
PARKER: Frederick, 3995; Henry, 3657; Jno, 2456; Jos^h, 3117; Joseph, 7977; Martin, 3996; W^m, 5671, 7498; Willm, 2751
PARKINGTON: Thos, 80, 2902

INDEX

PARKINSON: Benjn, 7637; David, 2795; Jno, 6800; Jon^n, 1004
PARNELL: John, 2758
PARR: Jno, 908; Thos, 1481, 6003
PARROTT: Jno, 349; Willm, 6313
PARSONS: Thos, 2083; W^m, 2442, 8122
PARTRIDGE: John, 2949
PASCOE: Rich^d, 8746
PASKETT: Jno, 6807
PATON: Willm, 5487
PATTEN: Geo^e, 8274
PATTERSON: Alex^r, 1442; Chas, 297; Dav^d, 8781; Ja^s, 6181; Jno, 7399; Nathl, 7878; Peter, 2332; Robt, 2361, 6154, 8137; Thos, 1567, 8484; W^m, 1859
PATTISON: Ja^s, 8642
PATTON: Edwd, 8553; Henry, 8620; Jno, 269; Pat^k, 3168; Thos, 379
PAUL: Willm, 8698
PAULMAN: Lewis, 2654
PAULSON: W^m, 1424; WW^m, 5731
PAVEY: Robt, 3313
PAWSON: Edwd, 469
PAYLOR: Jno, 483, 3938
PAYNE: H^y, 2829; Ja^s, 2265; Saml, 2540; Willm, 3368
PEACH: Hen^y, 3583
PEACHELL: Willm, 1566
PEACHEY: W^m, 7201
PEACOCK: Thos, 7499
PEADON: Alex^r, 1017, 4928
PEAKE: W^m, 7500
PEANE: Pat^k, 4770
PEARCE: Isaac, 2906; Ja^s, 1601, 1634; Thos, 6373
PEARNS: Jno, 5875
PEARSON: Abr^m, 8636; Ja^s, 914, 5955; Jno, 486, 2524, 6943; Jos^h, 8889; Moses, 8836
PEASLEY: Dav^d, 5922
PEAT: W^m, 5834
PEDDIE: Dav^d, 3428
PEGG: Ja^s, 3662
PEGGS: Peter, 5254
PEIRCE: Peter, 8875
PENCHEON: Jno, 939
PENDEGAST: Thos, 2346, 8129
PENDER: W^m, 1945; Willm, 6600
PENGILLEY: W^m, 4925
PENNELL: Willm, 129
PENNOCK: Geo^e, 8452
PENSON: Jos^h, 2373
PENTLETON: Jno, 4050
PEORGE: Caroley, 405
PEPPER: Robt, 7859; W^m, 575; Willm, 4153
PEPWORTH: William, 5628
PERCIVAL: Geo^e W., 6044
PERCY: Ja^s, 1663
PERKINS: Ja^s, 4457; W^m, 2271; Willm, 2203, 7041;

PERKINS (continued) 8166
PERRIER: Ge^o, 2363, 2398
PERRINS: Jno, 4475
PERRY: Chas, 2513; James, 5631; Jno, 69; Thos, 1540; Willm, 2201
PERRYMAN: Jno, 3263
PETER: Hen^y, 1107; Isaac, 2160, 8177; Robt, 7501
PETERS: Jno, 2181, 2526; Saml, 8163; W^m, 4569; Willm, 4298
PETTICK: Edwd, 5146
PETTIGREW: Ja^s, 4477
PETTINARI: Jasper, 2259
PETTIT: Thos, 4518
PETTRICK: Edwd, 5147
PEYTON: Fra^s, 1299
PHAIR: Jno, 2165
PHEGAN: And^w, 6687
PHELAN: Jno, 4622; Mich^l, 6160; Pat^k, 7726
PHIBBS: Robt, 7898
PHILIPS: Jno, 2716; John, 6601
PHILLIPS: Geo^e, 7186, 8586; George, 3997; Ja^s, 8483; Jno, 3443, 3883, 6029, 7236; Jos^h, 364, 3665, 4992; Nich^s, 2168; Rich^d, 3975, 7903, W^m, 4857; W^m Jno, 5311; Willm, 225, 6101
PHILPOT: Thos, 1816, 1927
PICKEN: David, 7389
PICKETT: Rich^d, 5501
PICKLES: Willm, 8438
PICKSTOCK: W^m, 2695
PIDGEON: Peter, 5621
PIERCE: Jno, 2603, 6944, 7088
PIERCEY: Chas, 8732
PIERRE: Fra^s, 2182
PIFFY: Moses, 8123
PIGG: Jno, 88; John, 2927; Robt, 1394
PIGGOTT: Dav^d, 8369
PIKE: W^m, 6111; Willm, 12
PILKINGTON: Mich^l, 6046; Rich^d, 3355
PILLING: Jos^h, 836
PILMER: Valentine, 3624
PILSON: Ja^s, 8501
PINCKNEY: Abr^m, 5383; Abra^m, 1209
PINDAR: Edwd, 6159; Hiram, 4681; Willm, 1243
PINER: Jos^h, 700, 4320
PINK: W^m, 3803
PINKNEY: Thos, 4555
PINTO: Benjn, 2194, 8160
PIPER: Ja^s, 6186; Thos Bill, 8721
PIPPY: Moses, 2447
PITCHELLO: Silv^r, 38, 2881
PITCHER: Step^n, 4994
PITHERS: Willm, 810, 4607
PITMAN: Thos, 212
PITT: Geo^e, 3075; John, 975, 4839
PITTMAN: Edwd, 215
PLASTON: Jos^h, 8566

PLATT: Ge^o, 823
PLAYFORD: Thos, 2742
PLEVINS: Thos, 815
PLOWRIGHT: Saml, 326, 3572
PLUMB: Isaac, 5195
PLUNKETT: Art^r, 5539; Arth^r, 1380; Isaac, 8580; Jno, 6898; Peter, 861, 4678; Thos, 8679
POCOCK: Ja^s, 7502; Robt, 7879
POGUE: And^w, 8723
POHL: Otto Fr^k Edwd, 5710
POINT: Chas, 1215
POLLACK: Jos^h, 2169
POLLARD: Danl, 2696; Ge^o, 276; Geo^e, 6405; Ja^s, 426; W^m, 7362
POLLEY: Abra^m, 4380
POLLIS: Thos, 820
POLLOCK: Davis, 7813; Ja^s, 4643; John, 3073
POLSON: Danl, 791
POMPHREY: Thos, 2080, 6761
POOLE: Jno, 5064; John, 4881
POPE: Saml, 8543; Thos, 5399; Willm, 170, 3044
PORCH: Ja^s, 3969
PORTER: Danl, 2585; Dav^d, 8450; Eber, 2009, 6775; Jno, 7363; John, 3819; Thos, 4351, 8622; Thomas, 4388; Willm, 876, 5401
PORTMORE: Willm, 8535
POSPIESCHEL: Jos^h, 1121
POSSNER: Jacob, 2427
POTH: Thos, 8183
POTTAGE: Chas, 335
POTTASH: Fra^s, 2621
POTTASK: Fra^s, 6959
POTTER: Ja^s, 1232, 4989; Jno, 408; Jno Robt, 5967
POTTS: Ge^o, 794; George, 4551; H^y, 4905
POUGUE: Ja^s, 7364
POULTNEY: Charles, 3358; Uriah, 4522
POUND: Ja^s, 6049
POVER: Robt, 643
POWEL: Thos, 2470
POWELL: Charles, 2941; Ge^o, 1005; George, 4874; John, 6559; Thos, 6969, 7259
POWER: Edmund, 7175; Edwd, 2339, 8094; Jno, 1769, 6167; William, 6043
PRAST: Fred^k, 1099
PRATT: Geo^e, 6332
PRENDAVILLE: Thos, 4786
PRENTICE: Edwd, 8624; Willm, 1234
PRESTON: Ge^o, 2309; Hen^y, 573, 2336; Jno, 2151, 6904; Jon^n, 3785; Willm, 3055
PRETTIG: Peter, 5162
PRICE: Ge^o, 2105; George, 7149; Ja^s, 171, 1841, 2582, 2697; John, 2933; Robt, 2098; W^m, 4935, 5904; Wm H., 1793

INDEX   345

PRIESTLEY: Edwin, 4435
PRINGLE: Thomas, 7176
PRITCHARD: Ja^s, 1636; Jno, 6314
PROBART: Thos W^m, 1044
PROBERT: Evan, 2931
PROCTOR: Peter, 6708; Saml, 3096
PROSSER: Ja^s, 393; Jno, 262; Saml, 2515, 6973
PROUDLOVE: Ja^s, 5894
PROUT: W^m, 2314; Willm, 8085
PROVAN: Arch^d, 5478
PUCKSLEY: Ja^s, 7579
PUGH: Jno, 7503; Thos, 2152, 6906
PUNG: H^y, 4986; Hen^y, 1036
PURCELL: Ja^s, 7814; Jos^h, 115; Pat^k, 11, 2826
PURDON: Jno, 4841
PURDY: Thos, 5608
PURVES: Robt, 8333
PYKE: Ge^o, 500
QUADE: Thos, 1735
QUAIL: Robt, 5951
QUAILS: Robt, 5455
QUARTERMAN: Ja^s, 431, 3754
QUIGLEY: Mich^l, 3436
QUILLER: W^m, 940
QUILLINAN: Mich^l, 5659
QUILTY: Danl, 6455; Jno, 1770; John, 6504; Thos, 1733
QUIN: Ja^s, 4017; Philip, 3836; Robt, 1849
QUINLAN: W^m, 3870
QUINLISH: John, 5635
QUINN: Bern^d, 1293; Chas, 7504; Chr^r, 2763; Daniel, 3534; Hugh, 7505; Matt^w, 6218; Pat^k, 1982, 6552; Robt, 7815; Thos, 3806; Willm, 4011, 8603
QUINNELL: Ja^s, 4174
QUINTON: Jeremiah, 5259
QUIRK: Willm, 1736
RACEY: Thos, 104, 3008
RAE: Jno, 6670; W^m, 5865
RAINEY: Ja^s, 2999
RAITING: Jno, 527
RAKEN: John, 3054
RALPH: Hen^y, 3296
RAMAGE: Thos, 8835
RAMM: Danl, 2153
RAMMAGE: H^y, 8472
RAMPLIN: Ja^s, 5977
RAMSBOTTOM: W^m, 8424
RAMSOM: Robt, 785
RANDALL: W^m, 3141
RANKIN: Ge^o, 2698; Jno, 3786
RANSCH: Jno, 1128, 5174
RANSOM: Abr^m, 3671
RAPSEY: Ja^s, 3929
RASH: Jos^h, 3329
RASTON: Jno, 1305
RATCHFORD: Peter, 950
RATH: Thos, 1928, 6554
RATTLE: Danl, 8712
RATTRAY: Ja^s, 6179
RAWLING: Ja^s, 7588
RAWSON: Jno, 366, 3680

RAY: Jno, 2516; John, 6970
RAYMOND: Jno, 172; Jos^h, 7585
RAYNER: Thos, 319
RAYNOR: Jno, 7912
REA: Jno, 6837
REACH: Ja^s, 8473
READ: Ja^s, 3776
READE: Mich^l, 704
READING: Rich^d, 7899
READY: Jno, 5082; Mich^l, 7506; Thomas, 3658
REALE: Ja^s, 29
REARDON: Danl, 1575; Jere^h, 5662
REASALL: Edwd, 2050
REASE: Dav^d, 388
REDDING: Jno, 5725
REDDLE: James, 3659
REDDOCK: Robt, 7089
REDDY: W^m, 7289
REDFORD: W^m, 2998
REDMOND: Lawrence, 5106; Mich^l, 6427, 7110
REDROBE: Rich^d, 79
REED: Benjn, 247, 3244; Chas, 2163; Henry, 5372; Isaac, 128; Ja^s, 141, 4638; Thos, 4202, 4831; W^m, 2183, 3314; Willm, 6909, 8199
REEKS: Thos, 4220
REESE: Jno N., 2359, 8130; John, 718
REEVE: Edwd, 7919
REEVES: Dav^d, 2220, 8158
REGAN: Jno, 524, 3447, 3799, 4099
REGAZZO: Gaitino, 3743
REGUA: Hen^y, 2652
REID: Alex^r, 7708; Caleb, 1771; Jno, 8833; Jos^h, 5768; Robt, 8337; Thos, 1885
REILEY: John, 3347
REILLEY: Bern^d, 4832
REILLY: Corn^s, 3730; Ja^s, 4195; James, 7982; Jno, 1303, 4715; John, 2982; Mich^l, 3519; Tim^y, 6311
REILY: Pat^k, 1918, 6553
REITMAN: Arthur Anthony, 6990
REITTER: Jacob, 1109
RENDELL: Jno, 7507
RENNIE: Fran^s, 5587; Jno, 6238
RENSHAW: Jon^n, 762, 4467
REVEREND: Jos^h, 1138
REVILL: Chas, 4352; Charles, 4389
REYNOLDS: Chas, 685, 4065, 4305; Ge^o, 6079; George, 6516; Ja^s, 2913; Jno, 1045, 6838; Mich^l, 6632; Peter, 3399; Robt, 311; Thos, 706, 4883, 4888; Willm, 2109; Willm, 972, 3050, 6468
RHODES: Saml, 2199; W^m, 5057
RICE: Jno, 2304, 2423; John, 3124; Peter, 3633

RICH: Saml, 8886
RICHARDS: Ge^o, 1295; Ge^o^{e}, 5426; Rich^d, 2287, 2290
RICHARDSBY: Chas, 1518, 1587, 6001
RICHARDSON: Ge^o^{e}, 4223; Ja^s, 3074; James, 7945; Jno, 8521; John, 5578; Jos^h, 8497; W^m, 577, 4964
RICHENBERG: Jos^h, 716, 4403
RICHES: Benjn, 628, 4277
RICHFORD: Thos, 6505
RICHMOND: Ge^o^{e}, 3111
RICKABY: Ge^o^{e}, 4398
RICKARD: John, 8789
RICKERT: Jno, 1124
RICKETTS: Mich^l, 2026
RICKEY: Walter, 6901
RIDDELL: Ja^s, 8275, 8307
RIDDETT: Ja^s Cooper, 4409
RIDDLE: Adam, 952, 4840; Jno, 5652; Jno Henson, 7638
RIDER: W^m, 7508
RIDGEWAY: Ja^s, 3982; Jno, 5208
RIDLER: Jno, 3901
RIELLY: Ber^d, 7844; Const^e, 5317; Jno, 5096; John, 4166; Peter, 3800
RIGG: Ch^r, 7745
RILEY: John, 5963; Jos^h, 3681; Pat^k, 2397, 6097, 8086; Saml, 7736
RINGWOOD: Ge^o^{e}, 6397
RIORDEN: Ja^s, 3932
RITCHIE: And^w, 8599; Robt, 8413
RIVETT: Isaac, 3663; Tim^y, 8527
ROACH: Jno, 3787
ROADS: W^m, 7288
ROAN: Pat^k, 3855
ROARKE: And^w, 2864
ROBBS: Jno, 8728; Willm, 8508
ROBERTS: Chas, 4178; Ja^s, 8532; Jno, 2699; John, 2930, 6064; Rich^d, 173, 2604; Robt, 3028; Thos, 2161, 5014, 7709; W^m, 5931
ROBERTSON: Alex^r, 5792; Danl, 3951; Don^d, 1347; Ge^o^{e}, 7880; Ja^s, 6671, 8503, 8762; James, 8872; Jno, 213, 1081, 1382, 5866; Leon^d, 8803; Peter, 492; Robt, 8464
ROBINSON: Ch^n, 1989; Ja^s, 2073, 5916; James, 1795; Jno, 361, 707, 5572, 6168; John James, 5452; Mich^l, 3788; Saml, 4910, 8234; Thos, 1265; W^m, 1333, 5471, 7580, 8488; Willm, 241, 781, 3395, 8439
ROBSON: W^m, 3029
ROCHE: Ja^s, 5083; Jno, 5785; Pat^k, 6452; Thos, 877

ROCHFORD: Thos, 1705
ROCK: Jas, 6387; Jno, 2042; Michl, 2659, 4168; Patk, 5357
ROCKFORD: Heny, 4066
RODERICK: Ambre, 2801
RODGERS: Jno, 243; John, 3196; Patk, 4580; Peter, 6155; Saml, 110, 3013; Thos, 6912, 7075
RODWELL: Thos, 4243
ROGERS: Chas, 7836; Jas, 609, 8207; Jno, 619, 7748, 7762; John, 81, 8755; Richd, 7365; Robt, 4988; Saml, 4244; Thos, 7290; Wm, 5982
ROLLINGS: Wm, 5730
ROLLINS: Jno, 4834
ROLSTON: Jas, 4332
ROMNEY: Wm, 3586
ROOKE: Richd, 1909; Saml, 3140
ROONEY: Edwd, 7847; Hy, 2894; Wm, 6728
ROPER: Saml, 7509
ROSE: Alexr, 6222; Alexr Jas, 10, 2825; Christoph, 2651; Fras, 4926; Heny, 3515; Jno, 5550; John, 2965; Willm, 5938
ROSENDALL: Jno, 1094
ROSIA: Elisha, 1256
ROSID: Elisha, 5410
ROSS: Adam, 133; Alexr, 772, 4494, 4501, 5035; Andw, 1352, 6839, 8196; Davd, 6269; Geoe, 5047, 6283; Hector, 5828; Hugh, 2852; Jas, 1475, 6303, 6309, 6631; Jno, 5867, 6232; John, 8540, 8744; Robt, 5954, 6293; Thos, 1421; Wm, 6827; Willm, 4495, 5643, 5791
ROSSBOROUGH: Thos, 5639
ROSSE: Jno, 19
ROTHWELL: Wm, 4566
ROUNDTREE: Thos, 4689
ROURKE: Barths, 3765; Michl, 623; Patk, 2648, 6882
ROUTE: Jas, 4182
ROWAN: Jas, 4462; Jno, 7581; Willm, 3167
ROWDEN: Thos, 2700
ROWE: Hugh, 2605; Patk, 6259; Wm, 576
ROWLAND: Benjn, 795; Jno, 185; Wm, 3233
ROXBY: Thos, 6919
ROYCROFT: Geoe, 3467
ROYLE: Richd, 160
RUBERY: Martin, 8025
RUBY: Isaac, 477
RUDD: Davd, 2108; David, 3048
RUDDOCK: Danl, 8802
RUDDY: Saml, 3585; Thos, 6057
RUDGE: Josh, 1294, 5418
RUFF: Chas, 2521
RUMBLE: Wm, 7296

RUNCHY: Thos, 1820
RUNDOCK: Edwin, 3668
RUSK: Benjn, 3766
RUSSELL: Chas, 67; Chrr, 2740; Clemt, 1348; Davd, 5218; Jas, 1334; Patk, 2233; Robt, 5868; Thos, 8908; William, 8582
RUSSOM: Wm, 7537
RUTH: Patk, 1750, 6507
RUTHERFORD: Adam, 2779; Allan, 5044; Geoe, 7510
RUTTER: Wm, 3092
RYAN: Danl, 7025; Edwd, 916, 2606, 4749; Jas, 395, 1772, 1825, 6561; James, 4414; Jeremiah, 2970; Jno, 1749, 1877, 3866, 6351, 7511; John, 6506, 7177; Martin, 6422; Michl, 3884; Nichs, 7266; Patk, 675, 2773, 4304, 4365, 4980, 5366, 6224; Robt, 7816; Simon, 4709; Thos, 4289; Wm, 5007, 7639, 7900; Willm, 6799; William, 4418
RYDER: George, 8559; Patk, 3731
RYE: Fras, 3531; Jno, 27, 1021; John, 2872
RYLEY: Thos, 818
RYRNES: Dens, 3677
SAGE: Jas, 8325; Thos, 4998
SAGEMAN: Willm, 4794
SALAMONE: Antonio, 2251
SALISBURY: Jerh, 3558; Wm, 464
SALMON: Geoe, 2968
SALT: Saml, 6888
SALTER: Jno, 3545; Richd, 893, 4682
SALTMARSH: Richd, 2701, 7046
SALTRY: Jno, 3753; Keans, 1414
SAMSON: Thos, 7512
SAMUEL: Jno, 2131
SAMWAYS: John, 2979
SANDERSON: Hy, 6962; Heny, 2563; Thos, 4962, 8918; William, 7944
SANDON: Geoe, 7366
SANDY: Jas, 5890
SANKEY: Jas, 3418
SANSVIE: Willm, 1078
SATCHWELL: Wm, 7535
SAUNDERS: George, 3634; Jas, 2289, 8180; Jereh, 1642; Robt, 5588; Saml, 721; Stepn, 5653; Thos, 4003; Wm, 3209, 4186, 7513; William, 3635
SAUNDERSON: Thos, 2775
SAVAGE: Jas, 6688; James, 3365; Jno, 2591, 5084, 5729; Patk, 8406; Peter, 8136; Thomas, 5739
SAVEALL: Jesse, 4596
SAXBY: Geoe, 8249
SAXTON: Willm, 2471
SAYERS: John, 8612, 8628

SAYWELL: Geoe, 5041
SCALES: Geo, 54; Thos, 5072
SCALLEY: Chr, 4081
SCALLION: Patk, 1668
SCALLON: Patk, 6418
SCALTON: Patk, 1667
SCAMMELL: Heny, 5672
SCANLAN: Thos, 2987
SCANLON: Laure, 3885; Patk, 7817
SCARA: Jno, 1739
SCARROW: Jno, 3801
SCHALECK: Ignatius, 1096, 5172
SCHMIDT: Gotlieb, 1144, 5160
SCHOCH: Jas, 4882
SCHOFIELD: Jas, 2154
SCHOP: Adam, 1136, 5164
SCHOUTEN: Peter, 1106, 5176
SCHREIBER: Justus, 8143
SCHUTTLESKOPF: Phip, 5173
SCHWALLER: Jno, 1093
SCHWEITZER: Chas, 5163
SCISCO: Paolo, 286, 3375
SCOFIELD: Wm, 2254
SCOLES: Willm, 8223
SCOLTOR: Edwd, 4855
SCONCE: Fras, 2253
SCOTT: Carey, 474; Chas, 336, 7367, 8228; Fras, 3287; Jas, 804, 4015; Jno, 750, 2221, 2667, 7830; John, 8147; Josh, 4000, 5888; Luke, 8186; Martin, 6857; Moses, 8878; Robt, 174; Thos, 2489, 5843; Thomas, 3636; Wm, 7713, 7767, 8392; Wm Pittman, 3315; Willm, 8270
SCOWAN: Nathan, 5990
SCRAGG: Geoe, 3222
SCROGUE: Jas, 5812
SCULLEN: Denis, 5122
SEADON: George, 4660
SEARGEANT: Wm, 5989
SEARS: Thos, 853
SEATON: Richard, 8026; Robt, 7237
SECAUR: Jas, 2425, 8125
SEDDON: Giles, 610, 4158; Silvanus, 7842
SEELER: David, 6156
SEGAR: Wm, 4428; Willm, 737
SELF: Robt, 2106
SELLARS: Jno, 392; John, 3708
SELLORS: Geo, 5124
SEMPLE: Hugh, 1976
SERGEANT: Benjn, 5759
SERRANT: Jno, 2195
SEVERN: Heny, 7242
SEWARD: William, 7178
SEWELL: Mattw, 580, 4151
SEXTON: Dens, 1473; Jno, 874; Wm, 5291
SEYMOUR: Jas, 4726; Richd, 6654
SHADBOLT: Josh, 4189
SHALLOW: Luck, 6117
SHANAHAN: Jno, 5589

SHANAKEN: Jn⁰, 7368
SHAND: Jaˢ, 8441
SHANDLY: Jn⁰, 4449
SHANKSTER: John, 7179
SHANLEY: Wᵐ, 3902
SHANN: Edwᵈ, 8272
SHANNAGHAN: Jaˢ, 5885
SHANNAN: Matʷ, 3201
SHANNON: Bernᵈ, 4070; Jn⁰, 4251; Michˡ, 5364; Robᵗ, 4381
SHAPCOTT: Geoᵉ, 7737
SHARP: Hʸ, 3129; John, 5475; Thoˢ, 7547
SHARPLEY: Arthur, 1999
SHAW: Edwᵈ, 4582; Geoᵉ, 7260; Jn⁰, 457, 514, 8856; John, 7934; Josʰ, 432, 6689; Peter, 2240; Richᵈ, 691, 4316; Thoˢ, 763, 764; Wᵐ, 7129
SHEA: Denˢ, 4699; Jn⁰, 6008; Martin, 7261; Michˡ, 2308; Timʸ, 5978; Wᵐ, 1864; Willᵐ, 6607
SHEAL: Jn⁰, 5097
SHEAN: John, 8783
SHEARMAN: Wᵐ, 6646
SHEEHAN: Martin, 4248
SHEENAN: Jaˢ, 7712
SHEERAN: Jaˢ, 6390; Mattʷ, 7589
SHEERIN: Jaˢ, 941, 4804
SHELDON: Benjⁿ, 993
SHELDRICK: Ezra, 7651
SHELLY: Timʸ, 888
SHELTON: Jn⁰, 109, 7515
SHEMINSKIE: Thoˢ, 2066
SHEPHERD: Geoᵉ, 8828; Mathʷ, 7238
SHEPPARD: Benjⁿ, 5130
SHERIDAN: Jaˢ, 1880; Michˡ, 7370
SHERLAND: Thoˢ, 2702
SHERLOCK: Robᵗ, 533
SHEWBRIDGE: Jaˢ, 6879
SHIBLY: Jn⁰, 6342
SHIELD: Chʳ, 4193
SHIELDS: Patᵏ, 1953; Willᵐ, 8283
SHIELS: Patᵏ, 4755
SHILLINGTON: Thoˢ, 4631
SHIPMAN: Lewis, 6946
SHIPP: John, 3038
SHIRE: Benjⁿ, 3220
SHOLES: Jn⁰, 2375
SHORT: Fraˢ, 8631; Richᵈ, 1862, 6594; Thoˢ, 7642; Wᵐ, 672; Willᵐ, 5529
SHUFFLEBOTTOM: Thoˢ, 2608
SHUTTELKOLF: Philᵖ, 1115
SIBBALD: Ge⁰, 2208
SIDDONS: John, 3120
SILK: Michˡ, 4136
SILLERS: Malcolm, 6242
SILVESTER: Jn⁰, 647
SIMMONDS: Hʸ, 4776; Jaˢ, 4764; Jn⁰, 4902; Philip, 5225; Thoˢ, 117
SIMMONS: James, 5724
SIMONSKY: Albert, 1139
SIMPSON: Edwᵈ, 3714; Jaˢ, 142, 156, 1422, 1921, 3036; James, 3934; Jn⁰, 3270, 3986, 8632; Josʰ, 891; Lenox, 4438; Ralph, 7710, 8407; Thoˢ, 2768; Wᵐ, 2517, 6968
SINCLAIR: Jaˢ, 4468, 6645; Neil, 6199
SINDON: Wᵐ, 5018
SINGLETON: Thoˢ, 3400
SINNOTT: Dennis, 4739
SIZE: Sepko, 3186; Sipko, 199
SIZELAND: Jaˢ, 5039
SKEA: John, 6795
SKEARNEY: Lawᵉ, 847
SKELLETT: John, 4469
SKERRER: Wᵐ, 3703
SKINE: Jaˢ, 1159, 5249
SKIPPON: Thoˢ, 2898
SKITT: Willᵐ, 288, 3383
SKIVINGTON: Peter, 7291
SKUSE: Jn⁰, 2609
SKYE: Thomas, 485
SLAIN: Fraˢ, 7514
SLANE: John, 5233
SLATE: Charles, 7153; Jn⁰, 198
SLATER: Edwᵈ, 1929; Josʰ, 5560; Wᵐ, 3573; Willᵐ, 324
SLATTERY: Jn⁰, 4690; Mattʷ, 6157; Thoˢ, 1778, 6509; Wᵐ, 3066, 8039
SLIGHT: Richᵈ, 2536, 6974
SLOAN: John, 1618
SLOANE: Geoᵉ, 7092
SMALL: Wᵐ, 4171
SMART: Edwᵈ, 8546; George, 4716; Josʰ, 235
SMILLIE: Jn⁰, 7517
SMITH: Alexʳ, 1388, 5119, 5518, 8774; Andʷ, 8711; Bernᵈ, 3236; Chʳ, 3353; Chaˢ, 279, 6178; Charles, 7936; Danˡ, 4997; Davᵈ, 334, 2514, 3594; Edwᵈ, 313; Fraˢ, 6724; Geoᵉ, 5886, 6069, 7390, 7711, 8362; George, 4544, 5601; Goliah, 6329; Hugh, 8239; Isiah, 3739; Jaˢ, 960, 2440, 4049, 4895, 5325, 6119, 7111, 8509; James, 1186, 5703; Jn⁰, 617, 1062, 1355, 1591, 1602, 1635, 2607, 2703, 3430, 3606, 3832, 4138, 5123, 5712, 6945, 7881; Job, 601, 4164; John, 2752, 3112, 4312, 5528, 5893, 6092, 6935, 8601; Josʰ, 4581; Michˡ, 95, 7090; Nichˢ, 508, 4044; Noah, 5025; Patᵏ, 2704, 7047, 8198; Peter, 7582; Richᵈ, 2032; Robᵗ, 3767; Robert, 3403, 7957; Samˡ, 1158, 5246; Stephen, 6399; Thoˢ, 39, 116, 331, 788, 2587, 3004, 3389, 4358, 4547, 6391, 6940, 8331, 8336, 8395, 8594; Thomas, 7954; Wᵐ, 578, 611, 615, 2155, 2630, 4256, 4506, 7295, 7860, 8841; Willᵐ, 917, 1296, 1599, 1632, 2782, 3553, 4159, 4823, 6903; William, 5699
SMITHERMAN: Jaˢ, 2518, 6960
SMITHERS: James, 6085
SMYTH: Davᵈ, 6124; John, 6847; Martⁿ, 1860, 6602; Traver, 4068
SNAPE: Josʰ, 6016
SNELL: Henʸ, 2705
SNELLING: Henry, 4268; James, 4269
SNEYD: Samˡ, 3501
SNOBER: Chaˢ, 612
SNODGRASS: Jaˢ, 6215
SOLLEY: Josʰ, 6869
SONTAG: Josʰ, 1117
SOOLEY: Solomon, 2260
SOURWINE: Lawrᵉ, 2391, 8124
SOUTHWORTH: Thoˢ, 8662
SPAIN: Jn⁰, 4331
SPALDING: Alexʳ, 8859
SPARROW: John, 8095
SPEAKMAN: Jn⁰, 8293
SPEAR: Willᵐ, 1406
SPEARMAN: Andʷ, 1823, 6556
SPECKMAN: Thoˢ, 2610
SPEIGHT: Richᵈ, 5979
SPEIN: John Hʸ, 3162
SPELLICY: Michˡ, 3872
SPELLMAN: Thoˢ, 7516
SPENCELY: Thoˢ, 4401
SPENCER: Edmᵈ, 5312; Edwᵈ, 7920; Jaˢ, 6369; Jn⁰, 1270, 7655; John, 5429, 8870
SPERLING: Jn⁰, 1122
SPICER: Thoˢ, 2736
SPIERS: Willᵐ, 7052
SPILLARD: Jaˢ, 6398
SPINK: Robert, 4590
SPITTALE: Jaˢ, 909
SPITTALS: Jaˢ, 4714
SPOONER: Jn⁰, 1267, 5419, 7831
SPRENT: Jn⁰, 5678
SPROUL: Noble, 5818
SPROWLES: John, 6515
SPURRILL: John, 4225
SPYRON: Isaac, 6234
SQUIERS: Jabish, 2028
SQUIRES: Jabesh, 6769
STACEY: Thoˢ, 8135
STACK: Thoˢ, 298
STACY: Thoˢ, 2444, 2713
STAFFORD: Geoᵉ, 3252; Jaˢ, 4941, 5100; Thoˢ, 6647; Willᵐ, 6184
STALKER: Jn⁰, 5869; Robᵗ, 6844
STANAGE: Jaˢ, 1946, 6618
STANDER: Benjⁿ, 7595
STANDLEY: Jacob, 3846
STANELAND: Jaˢ, 5734
STANFIELD: Thoˢ, 8493
STANKO: Ge⁰, 1104
STANLEY: Hʸ, 5243; Henʸ, 1168; Samˡ, 1074

INDEX

STANTON: Pat^k, 3696; W^m, 3856
STAPLETON: Jno, 3330
STARS: Robt, 4112
START: Hen^y, 8653
STATEHAM: Jos^h, 1590
STAUNTON: Geo^e, 5380
STEDMAN: Mich^l, 2643
STEED: Hen^y, 5693
STEEL: Jno, 3282, 5506; Thos, 837, 4659
STEELLS: Anth^y, 2732
STEEN: George, 305
STEIN: Jno, 1172
STENGELL: Ge^o, 2377
STENNET: Jos^h, 579
STENSION: FRancis, 3660
STEP: Danl, 5573
STEPHENS: George, 5720; Jno, 7640; W^m, 2611; William, 8027
STEPHENSON: Jno, 6788; Thos, 4473
STEVEN: Robt, 7896
STEVENS: Robt, 396; Willm, 1569
STEVENSON: Amos, 8007; And^w, 8226; Charles, 7239; Rich^d, 3528; Thos, 3160; W^m, 6241
STEWART: Adam, 1503; Ale^{xr}, 8610; Alexander, 4586; Arch^d, 6125, 7927; Chas, 287, 3391, 5235, 8262; Ed^{wd}, 6319; Fra^s, 2355, 8231; Geo^e, 7536, 8657; Horatio, 4285; Ja^s, 6900; Jno, 6305; John, 977, 8690; Martin, 5708; Rich^d, 5201, 8635; Robt, 838, 7596; Saml, 1178, 7641; Thos, 7371, 7760; W^m, 8162; Willm, 7072
STILLMAN: Willm, 7011
STIRLEY: Thos, 4812
STODDART: Robt, 1754, 6508
STOLE: Fred^k, 201
STONE: Chas, 3402; Geo^e, 7714; Ja^s, 1677, 6453; Rich^d, 4934; Willm, 146
STONELEY: Randle, 2818
STOREY: Eben^r, 8419; Hugh, 7987; Jno, 4339
STOVEN: Jno, 3431
STOW: Jno, 7518
STRACHAN: Ja^s, 2573, 2706
STRAIN: Ja^s, 5737
STRATTON: David, 4254
STREET: William, 7978
STRETTON: Thos, 3673
STRINGER: Rich^d, 3372
STRIPMAN: Lewis, 2525
STRONG: Jon^n, 175
STRUDGEON: Thos, 5377
STUART: John, 4492; Robt, 6435
STUBBINS: Thos, 4877
STUBBS: W^m, 8542; Willm, 4554
STUCK: Jos^h, 1165
STUDD: Ja^s, 8326
STURGEON: Robt, 8640

STURROCK: W^m, 1452; Willm, 5821
SUCKLING: Isaac, 4007
SUGDEN: Geo^e, 8423; Jos^h, 976; Willm, 4558
SUGHRAE: Jno, 2530, 6961
SULLIVAN: Danl, 4674, 5994; Florence, 8008; Fra^s, 4904; Ja^s, 4909, 7519; Jer^h, 4819; Jeremiah, 3683; Jno, 1676, 2372, 2394, 3741, 3768, 3886; John, 4557, 8061; Matt^w, 1568; Matthew, 5746; Mich^l, 5549, 6528; Pat^k, 5086, 6115; Patrick, 5137; Thos, 1500; W^m, 6048; Willm, 4366, 8807
SUMMERS: Ge^o, 1543
SUMPTER: Willm, 4545
SUNNEVILLE: Ant^y, 5188
SUNSMAN: Jno, 4447
SUTCLIFFE: W^m, 4265
SUTHERLAND: Adam, 6281; Alex^r, 1436, 5511, 6298; Don^d, 6931; Ja^s, 440, 5789, 5819, 6301; Jno, 1077, 1557, 4038, 6282, 7520, 7906; Mal^m, 1656; Malc^m, 6275; Robt, 3821, 6288, 7747; W^m, 3241; Willm, 252, 6897
SUTHERWOOD: Willm, 1024
SUTTON: Chas, 3130; Jno, 7521; Jos^h, 2738, 4367
SWAINFIELD: Ja^s, 2345
SWAN: Chas J., 2813
SWANN: Ja^s, 3331
SWASBROOK: Lewis, 4959
SWATMAN: George, 3540
SWEENEY: Danl, 4673; Ed^{wd}, 7372; Jno, 5379; Mich^l, 4306; Roger, 7853; W^m, 3740
SWEET: Jno, 632
SWEETMAN: Mic^l, 371
SWIFT: Thos, 4787
SWIM: Jos^h, 2012
SWINDLES: Thos, 89
SWINDON: Willm, 8434
SWITZER: James, 3637
SYKES: Ja^s, 350, 3604; Jno, 1970, 6555; John, 8677
SYMES: Jno, 4553
SYMS: Jno, 4235
TABBERRAH: Jno, 3903
TACKLE: Robt, 5318
TAIT: Geo^e, 8322; W^m, 4968
TALBOT: Rich^d, 1229
TANNEHILL: Jno, 6192
TANNER: Jos^h, 8156; Rich^d, 7818
TANSEY: Mich^l, 7897
TANZEY: Peter, 6608
TAPLEY: Ja^s, 5009
TAPLIN: Jno, 362
TASKER: James, 8688; Jno, 942; Rich^d, 3332
TATTLER: Fra^s, 4583
TAYETTE: Peter, 2063
TAYLOR: And^w, 8818; Benjamin, 5752; Dav^d,

TAYLOR (continued) 6801, 8188; Ge^o, 1755; Geo^e, 6510; Hen^y Arth^r, 2975; Ja^s, 480, 519, 1460, 2802, 2951; James, 8028; Jno, 947, 5355, 5905, 6169; John, 8894; Jos^h, 961, 1202, 4609, 4944, 5369; Mich^l, 7138; Rich^d, 6729; Robt, 4738; Thos, 816, 2231, 4640, 5883, 7717, 8153; W^m, 1346, 4460, 6326, 7522, 7883, 8316; Willm, 6787
TEAHAN: Danl, 6158
TEALE: W^m, 901; Willm, 4719
TEEVAN: Thos, 910, 4708
TELFER: Jno, 5870; Thos, 8440
TEMPLETON: David, 6308; Jno, 6108
TERCE: Rich^d, 5947
TERNAN: Willm, 839
TERRENCE: W^m, 8720
TERRY: Chas, 6877; Thos, 7715
TETLOW: Peter, 4252
THAILE: Matt^w, 2076
THAIN: Geo^e, 5234
THATCHER: Jno, 2079
THEAKSTON: John, 2993
THIPTHORPE: W^m, 3289
THISTLEWAITE: Thos, 5015
THOM: Alex^r, 8694; Jno, 7884
THOMAS: Dav^d, 3273; David, 5673; Ed^{wd}, 5927; Ge^o, 991; Ge^o Reuben, 2212; Geo^e R., 8149; Jer^h, 5148; Jno, 1235, 5414; Saml, 2095; W^m, 3516
THOMPSON: Alex^r, 209, 3502, 6087; Charles, 5314; Danl, 6948; Dav^d, 238, 3149; Dav^d J., 8285; Hen^y, 6320; Ja^s, 677, 5229, 7820, 8747; Jno, 30, 124, 202, 1458, 3114, 3390, 4246, 4995; Jos^h, 6325; Laughlan, 536, 4115; Lee, 7718; Peter, 377; Rich^d, 63, 1643, 2901, 6116; Robt, 5569; Robert, 8329; Saml, 7821; Thos, 581, 1236, 1397, 4047, 4155, 6438, 8625; Thomas, 8029; W^m, 6698; Willm, 8338
THOMS: Willm, 1311
THOMSON: Thos, 6296
THORN: Ja^s, 8400
THORNBURY: Ed^{wd}, 1887
THORNHILL: Ja^s, 333
THORNLEY: Robt, 409
THORNTON: W^m, 2519, 6947
THOROGOOD: Ja^s, 1213, 5375; Jno, 330
THORP: Willm, 1496
THORPE: Douglas, 7923; Fra^s, 434; Fran^s, 3825
THORTON: Fra^s, 2116
THRUSSELL: Jos^h, 4956

INDEX

THURMAN: Jn⁰, 4621
THYNNE: Austin, 6718
TIEFENBACH: Christⁿ, 1135
TIERNAY: Bryan, 3212
TIERNEY: Edwᵈ, 4029; Jaˢ, 826; Jn⁰, 8733; Michˡ, 7819
TIGHE: Abrᵐ, 6658; Denis, 7738
TILL: Jn⁰, 2157
TILLEY: Ge⁰, 2707
TILLIARD: Jaˢ, 4691
TILLMAN: Herman, 1216; Samˡ, 6690
TILLY: Wᵐ, 4104
TIMMINS: Wᵐ, 6424
TIMOTHY: Jn⁰, 2159; John, 8178
TINCLAIR: Gasper, 2409
TINDALL: Robᵗ, 3970
TINNERRY: Patᵏ, 6823
TIPPING: Jonⁿ, 5019
TIPSON: Andʷ, 123
TODD: Jaˢ, 613, 4162, 8525; Joshʰ, 8267; Thomas, 3541
TODMAN: Samˡ, 306
TOFTS: Bishop, 840, 4650
TOLMIE: Thoˢ, 7376
TOLSON: Antʸ, 2075
TOMASSON: Hugh, 32
TOMBLIN: Benjⁿ, 401, 3711
TOMLIN: Jaˢ, 5036
TOMLINSON: Thoˢ, 7582
TONE: Fraˢ, 6891
TOOHEY: Antʸ, 3159
TOOLE: Alexʳ, 3523; Edwᵈ, 1803, 6463; Fraˢ, 2395; Henʸ, 3213; Jaˢ, 5099; James, 2963; Jn⁰, 5450
TOOMEY: Michˡ, 5022
TOPPING: Robᵗ, 3340
TORNEY: Hugh, 8596; Simon, 784
TORPY: Dennis, 3439
TORR: Robᵗ, 2125
TORRING: Jaˢ, 148
TOTTON: Richᵈ, 2535
TOWELL: Jaˢ, 5881
TOWERS: Samuel, 5602; Wᵐ, 738
TOWNSEND: Ge⁰, 4943; Jaˢ, 4192; Wᵐ, 3953
TRACEY: Fraˢ, 1707; Jerehʰ, 7523; Patᵏ, 151; Wᵐ, 482
TRACY: Jaˢ, 3890; Jn⁰, 6636; Peter, 6220
TRAFFORD: Thoˢ, 7822
TRAINOR: Danˡ, 7716; Patᵏ, 5098
TRANTER: Wᵐ, 3893
TRAVERS: Jn⁰, 26
TRAYNER: Peter, 4661
TRAYNOR: Patᵏ, 4360
TREACY: Thoˢ B., 2755; Timʸ, 3588
TREADWELL: Chaˢ, 4458
TREGEAR: Thoˢ, 5204
TREVENER: Walter, 8824
TRIBE: Danˡ, 6236
TRINDER: Joshʰ, 6383
TROTT: Robᵗ, 1570
TROTTER: Jaˢ, 6883; Jn⁰, 6805; Thoˢ, 2003

TROUP: Alexʳ, 4122
TROWBRIDGE: Ge⁰, 2331; Willᵐ, 1488
TROWLES: Joseph, 7988
TROY: Patᵏ, 200; Thomas, 4853
TRUEMAN: Stepⁿ, 228; Stephⁿ, 3171
TUAFE: Richᵈ, 6058
TUBB: Jaˢ, 325
TUCKER: Jn⁰, 765, 4452; Robᵗ, 4939
TUGNETT: Ge⁰, 255; Ge⁰ᵉ, 3269
TULLEY: Michˡ, 8241
TULLY: Hugh, 6845; Patᵏ, 1952
TUNNACLIFFE: John, 7928
TURBETT: Peter, 4636
TURLEY: Wᵐ, 3033
TURNBULL: Jn⁰, 7303; Thoˢ, 488, 3947
TURNER: Alexʳ, 463; Arthʳ, 176; Chaˢ, 1064; Danˡ, 4359; Edwᵈ, 4743; Ge⁰ᵉ, 3106, 4655, 6994; George, 3257; Henʸ, 6335; Jaˢ, 6878; Jn⁰, 2627, 6997, 7000; Joshʰ, 353, 3675, 3892; Mathew, 5222; Paul, 5965; Philᵖ, 203; Thoˢ, 1009, 4960
TURNEY: Jaˢ, 3815; Wᵐ, 7524
TUTE: Willᵐ, 6895
TWEEDALE: Jn⁰, 1084, 5156
TWEEDY: Samˡ, 7022
TWIGG: Wᵐ, 2472
TWYE: Micˡ, 1519, 1588
TWYFORD: Jn⁰, 5968
TWYMAN: Wᵐ, 2974
TYDD: Wᵐ, 4704
TYGHE: Jaˢ, 3438
TYLER: Thoˢ, 3337
TYNAN: Andrew, 5316
TYBURN: Michˡ, 7719
ULDRITT: Jaˢ, 8393
UNDERWOOD: Jesse, 3771
UNION: Jaˢ, 3457
UNSWORTH: Jehu Jn⁰, 8305
UNWIN: Thoˢ, 346
UPTON: Thoˢ, 7885
URCH: Benjⁿ, 5582
URCY: Fraˢ, 631
URE: Jaˢ, 5460
URQUHART: Jn⁰, 6297; William, 8030
URSON: Jn⁰, 1244
USHER: Hʸ, 4844; Thoˢ, 582
UTTING: Edwᵈ, 8633
UTTON: Jaˢ, 7196; Smith, 6330
VALE: Thoˢ, 4222
VALLENSNE: Thoˢ, 5277
VALLESNO: Thoˢ, 1173
VAN KOUNE: Chaˢ, 8480
VAN WILSON: Antʸ, 1066
VANANTWERPEN: Peter, 1123
VANANTWIRPEN: Peter, 5180
VANDAM: Antʸ, 7373
VANDERDISKIN: Jn⁰, 2533, 6975
VANDERMEY: Jn⁰, 1131

VANZANT: Jaˢ, 3917
VARNER: Thoˢ, 8684
VARNEY: Joshʰ, 6174
VAUGHAN: Anthʸ, 1297; Michˡ, 5618; Wᵐ, 1904; Willᵐ, 6617
VEISS: Carlo, 8934
VEIT: Chaˢ, 1423
VEITCH: Thoˢ, 4329
VENABLES: Jn⁰, 7053; Joshʰ, 7091
VENN: Jaˢ, 5492
VENNALION: Henʸ, 7525
VERNON: Christⁿ, 1193; Joshʰ, 2205
VERTILLS: Joshʰ, 805
VERTUE: Robᵗ, 2776
VETTERS: Jn⁰, 1179
VICARS: Jn⁰ Henʸ, 5590
VICENTE: Francesco, 1415
VICK: Richᵈ, 7823
VICKERS: Jn⁰, 583, 4149
VICTORY: Jaˢ, 3751
VIET: Fredᵏ, 1427, 5722
VIGGERSTAFF: Wᵐ, 7643
VINCENT: Henry, 3025; Isaac, 3151; Robᵗ, 1958; Wᵐ, 4429
VINER: Chⁿ, 2448; Chrʳ, 8126
VINEY: Joshʰ, 7886; Willᵐ, 302
VINT: Benjⁿ, 4491
VOGEL: Jacob, 8167
VOLANS: Samˡ, 8495
VONOOLKENBURG: David, 8073
WABBY: Jaˢ, 4525
WADE: Fraˢ, 2461, 6986; Ge⁰ᵉ, 6655; Thoˢ, 6648
WADSWORTH: David, 3000; Joshʰ, 4249; Thoˢ, 3122
WAGER: Thoˢ, 1151; Willᵐ, 6921
WAGSTAFF: John, 2893; Joshʰ, 1520, 1589; Willᵐ, 8931
WAINSBOROUGH: Wᵐ, 2957
WAINWRIGHT: Wᵐ, 4970
WAITE: Jesse, 7304; Roger, 1076
WAKEFIELD: Jaˢ, 756, 4480
WALDRON: Edwᵈ, 5964
WALE: William, 6414
WALES: Alexʳ, 4684; Edwin S., 8842; Matʷ, 3826; Mattʷ, 435
WALFORD: Jn⁰, 3948
WALKEM: Chaˢ, 8764
WALKER: Alexʳ, 8561; Alexander, 7962; Edwᵈ, 6249, 7720; Ephraim, 3404; Fraˢ, 1773; Fredᵏ, 6513; Ge⁰, 55, 2866; Jaˢ, 4167, 6219; Jn⁰, 6341; John, 3100, 6206; Thoˢ, 8409; Wᵐ, 902, 4731; Willᵐ, 8520
WALL: Jaˢ, 2851; Joshʰ, 2019; Willᵐ, 1233
WALLACE: Jaˢ, 8457; Mattʷ, 8391; Thoˢ, 1060, 8641; Wᵐ, 6913
WALLIS: Jn⁰, 5803

WALLS: Robert, 7157; Simon, 775
WALSH: And^w, 3195; Edm^d, 6840; Edward, 4415; Ja^s, 499, 3382, 8597; Jno, 1791, 2374, 2728, 4620, 7526, 8205; John, 6464; Jos^h, 3508; Lewis, 5661; Mar^n, 4692; Martin, 4408; Mich^l, 2429, 6110; Pat^k, 2411, 4173; Peter, 3197, 3336; Ralph, 6927; Richard, 4422; Stafford, 1997, 6683; Thos, 1675; W^m, 3118, 7133
WALTERS: Chas, 6628; Isaac, 2612, 6964; John, 4611; Thos, 5056; Willm, 4286
WALTON: Thos, 1061
WANDLESS: Jno, 7540
WANLESS: Geo^o, 8257
WARD: Abr^m, 2916; Chas, 24; Dan^d, 3316; Edwd, 8217; Geo, 475, 2522; Ja^s, 2120, 7751, 8466; Jno, 1177, 3802; John, 8810; Jos^h, 4538; Pat^k, 6649, 7750; Peter, 898; Philip, 5356; Robert, 3366; Saml, 280; Thos, 6656; W^m, 3317; Willm, 1278, 5423
WARDE: Willm, 5374
WARDLOW: Ja^s, 3804
WARDROPE: Rich^d, 5461
WARHAM: Thos, 4334
WARMINGHAM: W^m, 4858
WARN: Ibodnagh, 4763
WARNE: Thos, 1309, 5444
WARNER: Geo, 1620; Saml, 327, 3564
WARREN: Geo^e, 5221; John, 8506; Thos, 1310, 5445; Willm, 1594, 1627, 5437
WARRINGTON: W^m, 2520
WASHINGTON: Matt^w, 766, 4450
WATCHORN: W^m, 3742
WATERHOUSE: Robt, 7721
WATERS: Dav^d, 2937; Jno, 5906; John, 3642, 8004; Mich^l, 7527; Nich^s, 5689; Peter, 6338
WATERSTONE: Jno, 2730
WATSON: Edwd, 3392; Fra^s, 5026; Ge^o, 986; Geo^e, 8330; Hen^y, 4031; Ja^s, 8600; James, 7985; Jno, 6315, 6336, 8346; Rich^d, 6525; Saml, 5196; Thos, 2922, 3133, 7902; W^m, 2371, 4448, 4792; Willm, 2007, 2942, 3690, 6757, 8528; William, 7938
WATT: Ja^s, 2467, 6984; Jno, 484, 1387, 5772; John, 3145, 3945, 8266; 8557; Robt, 943, 4805; Willm, 4119
WATTS: Ja^s, 8053; John, 8470; Jos^h, 4218, 8750; Thos Haar, 7548; W^m, 3981

WAUD: Thos, 2571
WAUGH: Ja^s, 6310; Matt^w, 7113; Richard, 8877
WAYNE: Rich^d, 4865
WAYSON: Robt, 5548
WEAL: And^w, 8237
WEATHERALL: Jos^h, 2572
WEBB: Isaac, 449; Ja^s, 8869; Thos, 6925, 8551; Thomas, 3998; W^m, 6824
WEBSTER: Chas, 949; William, 5629
WEEKS: Jos^h, 4393; Thos, 7078
WEIGHT: Joseph, 5315
WEIGHTMAN: Geo^e, 7191
WEIR: Ja^s, 8321; Willm, 8693
WEISEY: Matt^w, 7127
WELDING: Matt^w, 5637
WELDON: Thos, 8219
WELLER: Charles, 5210
WELLINGS: Willm, 1571
WELLS: Ge^o, 2244; Geo^e, 4901; Ja^s, 3288; Jno, 5765; Jos^h, 586; Peter, 2554, 5490; Rich^d, 4961; Thos, 585, 1218, 3554, 4156; W^m, 2589, 6963
WELSH: Garret, 7644; Pat^k, 7586; Thos, 1344, 5439; Willm, 8334
WELTON: Jno, 3615
WENNER: Willm, 3857
WENNIGSEN: Hen^y, 2452
WERTY: Jno, 7374
WESLEY: W^m, 472
WEST: Ben^{jn}, 841, 4656; Chas Edwd, 3781; Ge^o, 719; Geo^e, 8496; Ja^s, 2039, 2717, 2817; John, 3747; Step^n, 5245; W^m, 4291
WESTCOMBE: Geo^e, 6331
WESTERMAN: Jno, 2136
WESTFORD: Jno, 2188
WESTMAN: Jesse, 5005
WESTON: Jno, 751; John, 4423; Willm, 8499
WESTWOOD: Moses, 547
WETHERALL: Geo^e, 7722; Thos, 5738
WETHERS: Jno, 1861, 6595
WHAIT: Saml, 3770
WHALAN: Chas, 819
WHALLEY: Robt, 8533
WHAREN: Willm, 8402
WHARIN: Jno, 8652
WHARRAM: Geo^e, 8854
WHARTON: Jno, 3419
WHEAT: Jos^h, 1212
WHEATON: David, 4971
WHEELER: Rich^d, 2788; Thos, 5822; Willm D., 5531
WHELAN: Lawrence, 3789; Pat^k, 522, 4094; Peter, 8031; Simon, 3911
WHELON: Jno, 1314
WHITAKER: Jno, 873; Robt, 4584; Step^n, 4896
WHITBREAD: Philip, 4916

WHITE: And^w, 4266, 8273; David, 7532; Edwd, 248; Geo^e, 3915; Hugh, 3456; Jno, 1706, 3777, 6447, 6531; John, 1659, 2947, 3214, 4585; Jonas, 2323; Mich^l, 5441, 5942, 8195; Peter, 979, 4952; Rich^d, 1573; Saml, 6870; Simon, 588, 4143; W^m, 589, 3790
WHITEFORD: Ja^s, 7583
WHITEHEAD: Ja^s, 1048, 5010; Lyman, 2617, 6965; Thos, 273; Tim^y, 2666
WHITELAW: Alex^r, 3208
WHITELY: W^m, 7646
WHITEMAN: Jno, 2774
WHITENKNACT: Jno, 2029
WHITHORN: Geo^e, 7921
WHITMILL: Thos, 3517
WHITMORE: Jno, 467
WHITNEY: Jno, 2335; John, 8089
WHITT: Saml, 4945
WHITTAKER: Jno, 2819
WHITTEL: Thos, 843
WHITTLE: Geo^e, 6747
WHITTY: Jno, 458, 3840
WHOLOHAN: Ja^s, 7531
WHYMAN: Edwd, 7894
WHYTE: John, 8208
WICKHAM: Ben^{jn}, 4402
WICKSON: Ja^s, 2994
WIGGINS: Jno, 207; John, 3950
WIGMORE: Willm, 6343
WILCOX: Jno, 708; John, 4357; Solo^n, 2419
WILD: Jon^n, 2856
WILDE: H^y, 6012
WILEY: Willm, 1683, 6511
WILGOS: Thos, 2808
WILKINS: Danl, 5871; Rich^d, 56, 2875, 7528; Thos, 178, 1298, 5427; W^m, 2436; Willm, 8087
WILKINSON: Arth^r, 5991; Cinnamon, 4652; Ja^s, 7763; Jno, 503, 2636, 2737, 7021; Thos, 3916, 7824; W^m, 6864
WILKS: Step^n, 4972
WILL: Robt, 1604
WILLEY: Ja^s, 3182
WILLIAMS: Edm^d, 2222, 8150; Edwd, 264, 2238, 3267; Hen^y, 7375; Henry, 7180; Ja^s, 6806; Jno, 1245, 2239, 3904, 4788, 8248, 8850; Morgan, 2483; Rich^d, 1651; Thos, 587, 3928, 4150, 5874; W^m, 670, 4271, 5228; Willm, 385; William, 5700
WILLIAMSON: And^w, 6825; Ja^s, 3231; Jno, 1572; Robt, 8341; Silas, 4703
WILLINGDALE: Jno, 5658
WILLIS: Geo^e, 5313; Jno, 5155; Rich^d, 4001
WILLMORE: Alex^r, 3070
WILLOCK: Fra^s, 2008, 6750
WILLOX: Ja^s, 236

INDEX 351

WILLSON: Jn⁰, 8643
WILMORE: Willᵐ, 6992
WILMOT: Willᵐ, 1607, 1713
WILSON: Andʷ Todd, 3077; Archᵈ, 4129; Chaˢ, 1149; Davᵈ, 2005, 6756; Geoᵉ, 5220; Hʸ, 3019; Hill, 8179; Hugh, 1926, 6596, 8718; Jaˢ, 4121, 4437, 8323, 8363, 8560; Jn⁰, 3484, 7379, 7391, 8727; John, 5797, 6060, 8463; Joshʰ, 7292; Lawˢ, 2964; Mark, 8451; Martin, 842; Peter, 7192; Samuel, 6692; Theophˢ, 1155; Wᵐ, 1322, 2316, 2644, 5465, 7293, 8203; Willᵐ, 657, 4279, 6783, 8279
WILSONCROFT: Joshʰ, 739
WILTON: Joshʰ, 668
WILTSHAN: Jn⁰, 422
WILTSHIRE: James, 3992
WINCKWORTH: Wᵐ, 4170
WINDEL: Neheʰ, 177
WINDSOR: Jn⁰, 584
WINDUS: Jn⁰, 6384
WINGFIELD: Robᵗ, 5510
WINKWORTH: Jn⁰, 2138, 6902
WINN: Jn⁰, 5040; Michˡ, 3682
WINNING: Walter, 7529
WINRICE: Peter, 2574
WINSLOW: Joshʰ, 2560
WINTER: Gabriel, 3868; Robᵗ, 4226; Thoˢ, 5980; Willᵐ, 2757
WINTERBOTTOM: Jaˢ, 6798
WINTERS: Danˡ, 2770; Jaˢ, 6635, 6650
WISDOM: Chaˢ, 7400

WISE: Hugh, 3193
WISEBY: Edwᵈ, 1092
WISELEY: Patᵏ, 7645
WISEMAN: Antʸ, 7001
WISHART: Hugh, 7530; Robᵗ, 3569
WISTAFF: Jn⁰, 2476
WITTS: Danˡ, 7723
WIXLEY: Edwᵈ, 399
WOOD: Aaron, 797; Carney, 4806; Carny, 944; Jaˢ, 844, 5008, 8570, 8864; Jn⁰, 2074, 6773, 7724; Joshʰ, 3350; Joshua, 4790; Stepⁿ, 8796; Thoˢ, 6779; Wᵐ, 7827; Willᵐ, 6780
WOODHALL: Henʸ, 281
WOODLAND: Hʸ, 3053
WOODS: Andʷ, 6366; Arthʳ, 6886; Davᵈ, 1030; Hʸ, 2908; Henʸ, 6388; Jaˢ, 789, 6240, 6709; Jn⁰, 614; Joshʰ, 105; Luke, 7590; Michˡ, 5334; Patᵏ, 4795; Peter, 7294; Thoˢ, 1023; Wᵐ, 3107
WOODWARD: Chaˢ, 429; Jn⁰, 3194; Thomas, 3999
WOOLDRIDGE: Wᵐ, 900; Willᵐ, 4722
WOOLGER: Geoᵉ, 3971
WOOLLAM: Jn⁰, 7136
WOOLLEY: Thoˢ, 8507
WORSLEY: Robᵗ, 3503; Willᵐ, 948
WOVENDON: Thoˢ, 7825
WRAY: Jn⁰, 5446
WREN: Samˡ, 3933
WRIGHT: Abrᵐ, 4163; Abraᵐ, 549; Benjⁿ, 4697; Geᵒ, 1476; Gilbert, 7003; Hʸ,

WRIGHT (continued)
6098; Henʸ, 1593; Jaˢ, 406, 1506, 6260, 7725; Jn⁰, 2333, 8849; Joshʰ, 701, 3059; Nibb, 5469; Noble, 1329; Peter A., 8295; Richard, 7984; Robᵗ, 3126; Thoˢ, 1484, 3039, 4570; Wᵐ, 803, 2392, 6221, 7240, 7826; Willᵐ, 179, 1272, 4565, 4875
WYATT: Jn⁰, 4740
WYBLE: Richᵈ, 204
WYE: Willᵐ, 1065
WYLIE: Davᵈ, 8565; John, 6052
WYNCH: Jaˢ, 782
WYNN: Robᵗ, 2995
WYNNE: Samˡ, 4789
WYRE: Patᵏ, 3548
WYSE: Geᵒ, 534
YARNELD: Moses, 8924
YATES: John, 8669
YEATES: Patᵏ, 6225
YORK: Jaˢ, 5484; Jn⁰, 479
YORKE: Thoˢ, 8531
YOUDS: Danˡ, 2487, 6979
YOUL: Alexʳ, 7746
YOUNG: Baptist, 8616; Davᵈ, 423, 8579; Jaˢ, 3095, 6104, 7892; Jn⁰, 106, 5591; John, 3015; Robᵗ, 6400, 6981; Thoˢ, 3401; Wᵐ, 8381; Willᵐ, 1574, 4324
YOUNIE: Alexʳ, 8352
YUILLE: Wᵐ, 5841
ZAMPHIRE: Peter, 879
ZIEDMAN: Adam, 5711
ZRESSENBACH: Joshʰ, 1147

www.ingramcontent.com/pod-product-compliance
Lightning Source LLC
Chambersburg PA
CBHW071148300426
44113CB00009B/1128